# SYMBOLS

## RELIEF

| METRES | | FEET |
|---|---|---|
| 6000 | | 19686 |
| 5000 | | 16409 |
| 4000 | | 13124 |
| 3000 | | 9843 |
| 2000 | | 6562 |
| 1000 | | 3281 |
| 500 | | 1640 |
| 200 | | 656 |
| SEA | | LEVEL |
| 200 | | 656 |
| 2000 | | 6562 |
| 4000 | | 13124 |
| 6000 | | 19686 |

Additional bathymetric contour layers are shown at scales greater than 1:2m. These are labelled on an individual basis.

213 △ Summit
*height in metres*

## BOUNDARIES

| | |
|---|---|
| ·-·-· | International |
| ·+·+· | International disputed |
| ····· | Ceasefire line |
| ------ | Main administrative (U.K.) |
| —— | Main administrative |
| – – | Main administrative through water |

## COMMUNICATIONS

| | |
|---|---|
| ═══ | Motorway |
| ⋯⋯ | Motorway tunnel |

Motorways are classified separately at scales greater than 1:5 million. At smaller scales motorways are classified with main roads.

| | |
|---|---|
| —— | Main road |
| – – – | Main road under construction |
| ·········· | Main road tunnel |
| —— | Other road |
| – – – | Other road under construction |
| ·········· | Other road tunnel |
| ·········· | Track |
| ▬▬▬ | Main railway |
| ▬ ▬ ▬ | Main railway under construction |
| ▪▪▪▪▪ | Main railway tunnel |
| —— | Other railway |
| – – – | Other railway under construction |
| ▪▪▪▪▪ | Other railway tunnel |
| ⊕ | Main airport |
| ✈ | Other airport |

## PHYSICAL FEATURES

| | |
|---|---|
| ⬭ | Freshwater lake |
| ⬭ | Seasonal freshwater lake |
| ⬭ | Saltwater lake *or* Lagoon |
| ⬭ | Seasonal saltwater lake |
| ⬭ | Dry salt lake *or* Salt pan |
| ▨ | Marsh |
| —— | River |
| —•— | Waterfall |
| —⊦— | Dam or Barrage |
| - - - | Seasonal river *or* Wadi |
| —— | Canal |
| ·········· | Flood dyke |
| —— | Reef |
| ▲ | Volcano |
| ▭ | Lava field |
| ▭ | Sandy desert |
| ▭ | Rocky desert |
| ˅ | Oasis |
| ·········· | Escarpment |
| ≍ 923 | Mountain pass *height in metres* |
| ⬭ | Ice cap or Glacier |

## OTHER FEATURES

| | |
|---|---|
| - - - - | National park |
| ·········· | Reserve |
| ∿∿∿ | Ancient wall |
| ∴ | Historic or Tourist site |

## STYLES OF LETTERING

| | | | | |
|---|---|---|---|---|
| Country name | **ZAIRE** | Island | *Gran Canaria* | |
| | **BARBADOS** | Lake | *LAKE ERIE* | |
| Main administrative name | PORTO | Mountain | *ANDES* | |
| Area name | *ARTOIS* | River | *Zambeze* | |

## SETTLEMENTS

| POPULATION | NATIONAL CAPITAL | ADMINISTRATIVE CAPITAL | CITY OR TOWN |
|---|---|---|---|
| Over 5 million | ▣ **Beijing** | ◉ **Tianjin** | ◉ **New York** |
| 1 to 5 million | ▣ **Seoul** | ◉ **Lagos** | ◉ **Barranquilla** |
| 500000 to 1 million | ▣ **Bangui** | ◉ **Douala** | ◉ **Memphis** |
| 100000 to 500000 | ▢ Wellington | ◌ Mansa | ○ Mara |
| 50000 to 100000 | ▢ Port of Spain | ◌ Lubango | ○ Arecibo |
| 10000 to 50000 | ▫ Malabo | ◦ Chinhoyi | ◦ El Tigre |
| Less than 10000 | ▫ Roseau | ◦ Áti | ◦ Soledad |
| ▭ Urban area | | | |

© Collins

# READER'S DIGEST
## BARTHOLOMEW

# ILLUSTRATED ATLAS OF THE WORLD

## THIRD REVISED EDITION

Reader's Digest

**The Reader's Digest Association, Inc.**
**Pleasantville, New York • Montreal**
**Cape Town • Sydney**

# ILLUSTRATED ATLAS OF THE WORLD

# CONTENTS

**SYMBOLS**
*Endpapers*

## THE WORLD

COUNTRIES *4-5*
PHYSICAL FEATURES *6-7*
ENVIRONMENT *8-9*
CLIMATE *10-11*
ATLANTIC OCEAN 1:58M *12*
INDIAN OCEAN 1:58M *13*
PACIFIC OCEAN 1:58M *14-15*

## NORTH AMERICA

COUNTRIES : POPULATION
*16-17*
RELIEF : CLIMATE
*18-19*

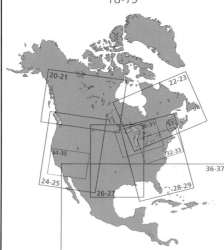

Western CANADA
1:7M *20-21*
Eastern CANADA
1:7M *22-23*
Western USA
1:7M *24-25*
Central USA
1:7M *26-27*
Eastern USA
1:7M *28-29*
THE GREAT LAKES
1:3.5M *30-31*
Northeastern USA
1:3.5M *32-33*
Southwestern USA 1:3.5M
(inset) HAWAII 1:6M *34-35*
CENTRAL AMERICA
and the CARIBBEAN
1:14M *36-37*

## SOUTH AMERICA

COUNTRIES : POPULATION
*38-39*
RELIEF : CLIMATE
*40-41*

Northern SOUTH AMERICA
1:15M *42-43*
Southern SOUTH AMERICA
1:15M *44*
VENEZUELA and
COLOMBIA
1:7.5M *45*
Southeastern BRAZIL
1:7.5M *46*
URUGUAY, Central CHILE
and Central ARGENTINA
1:7.5M *47*

First published by Bartholomew 1987
Third Revised Edition 1997

Copyright ©HarperCollinsPublishers

Collins
*An Imprint of HarperCollinsPublishers*
77-85 Fulham Palace Road
London W6 8JB

Printed in Italy

ISBN 0 89577 937 4

Photo credits:
Pages 16-19: Tony Stone Images
All other photos: Pictor International - London

KH 9233 Imp 001

# EUROPE

**COUNTRIES : POPULATION**
*48-51*

**RELIEF : CLIMATE**
*52-53*

**SCANDINAVIA
and the BALTIC STATES**
1:5M  *54-55*

**BRITISH ISLES**  1:5M  *56*

**SCOTLAND**  1:2M  *57*

**ENGLAND and WALES**
1:2M  *58-59*

**IRELAND**  1:2M  *60*

**BELGIUM and
NETHERLANDS**
1:2M  *61*

**North Central EUROPE**
1:5M  *62-63*

**FRANCE**  1:5M  *64*

**SPAIN and PORTUGAL**  1:5M  *65*

**ITALY and the BALKANS**
1:5M  *66-67*

**Western RUSSIA,
BELARUS and UKRAINE**
1:7M  *68-69*

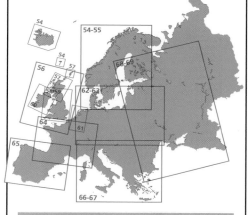

# ASIA

**COUNTRIES : POPULATION**
*70-73*

**RELIEF : CLIMATE**
*74-75*

**RUSSIAN FEDERATION**
1:21M  *76-77*

**Southwestern ASIA
and the MIDDLE EAST**
1:12.5M  *78-79*

**Eastern MEDITERRANEAN**
1:5M  *80-81*

**Southern ASIA**  1:14M  *82-83*

**Northern INDIA, Eastern PAKISTAN
and BANGLADESH**  1:7M  *84-85*

**CHINA**  1:15M  *86-87*

**Central CHINA**  1:7.5M  *88-89*

**JAPAN**  1:4M  *90-91*

**SOUTHEAST ASIA**  1:15M  *92-93*

**PHILIPPINES**  1:7M  *94*

**THAILAND, CAMBODIA and
Peninsular MALAYSIA**  1:7.5M  *95*

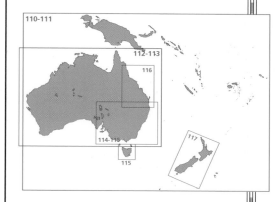

# AFRICA

**COUNTRIES : POPULATION**
*96-97*

**RELIEF : CLIMATE**
*98-99*

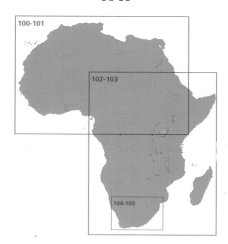

**Northern AFRICA** 1:16M  *100-101*

**Central and Southern AFRICA**
1:16M  *102-103*

**REPUBLIC OF SOUTH AFRICA**
1:5M  *104-105*

# OCEANIA

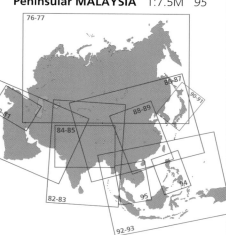

**COUNTRIES : POPULATION**
*106-107*

**RELIEF : CLIMATE**
*108-109*

**AUSTRALIA and
Southwestern PACIFIC**
1:20M  *110-111*

**AUSTRALIA**
1:12M  *112-113*

**Southeastern AUSTRALIA**
1:5M  *114-115*

**Northeastern AUSTRALIA**
1:5M  *116*

**NEW ZEALAND**  1:5M  *117*

# POLAR

**THE ARCTIC**  1:32M  *118*

**ANTARCTICA**  1:32M  *119*

**ABBREVIATIONS
and GLOSSARY**  *120*

**INDEX**  *121-184*

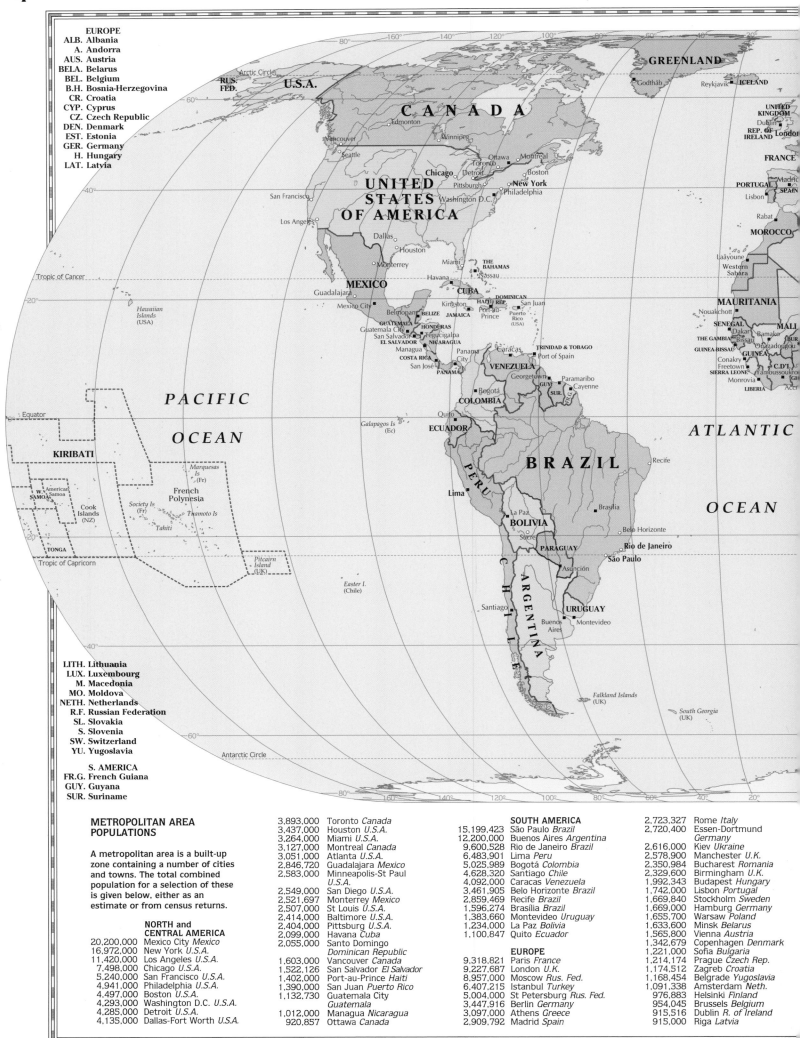

**4**

EUROPE
ALB. Albania
A. Andorra
AUS. Austria
BELA. Belarus
BEL. Belgium
B.H. Bosnia-Herzegovina
CR. Croatia
CYP. Cyprus
CZ. Czech Republic
DEN. Denmark
EST. Estonia
GER. Germany
H. Hungary
LAT. Latvia

LITH. Lithuania
LUX. Luxembourg
M. Macedonia
MO. Moldova
NETH. Netherlands
R.F. Russian Federation
SL. Slovakia
S. Slovenia
SW. Switzerland
YU. Yugoslavia

S. AMERICA
FR.G. French Guiana
GUY. Guyana
SUR. Suriname

Eckert IV Projection

## METROPOLITAN AREA POPULATIONS

A metropolitan area is a built-up zone containing a number of cities and towns. The total combined population for a selection of these is given below, either as an estimate or from census returns.

### NORTH and CENTRAL AMERICA

| | |
|---|---|
| 20,200,000 | Mexico City *Mexico* |
| 16,972,000 | New York *U.S.A.* |
| 11,420,000 | Los Angeles *U.S.A.* |
| 7,498,000 | Chicago *U.S.A.* |
| 5,240,000 | San Francisco *U.S.A.* |
| 4,941,000 | Philadelphia *U.S.A.* |
| 4,497,000 | Boston *U.S.A.* |
| 4,293,000 | Washington D.C. *U.S.A.* |
| 4,285,000 | Detroit *U.S.A.* |
| 4,135,000 | Dallas-Fort Worth *U.S.A.* |
| 3,893,000 | Toronto *Canada* |
| 3,437,000 | Houston *U.S.A.* |
| 3,264,000 | Miami *U.S.A.* |
| 3,127,000 | Montreal *Canada* |
| 3,051,000 | Atlanta *U.S.A.* |
| 2,846,720 | Guadalajara *Mexico* |
| 2,583,000 | Minneapolis-St Paul *U.S.A.* |
| 2,549,000 | San Diego *U.S.A.* |
| 2,521,697 | Monterrey *Mexico* |
| 2,507,000 | St Louis *U.S.A.* |
| 2,414,000 | Baltimore *U.S.A.* |
| 2,404,000 | Pittsburg *U.S.A.* |
| 2,099,000 | Havana *Cuba* |
| 2,055,000 | Santo Domingo *Dominican Republic* |
| 1,603,000 | Vancouver *Canada* |
| 1,522,126 | San Salvador *El Salvador* |
| 1,402,000 | Port-au-Prince *Haiti* |
| 1,390,000 | San Juan *Puerto Rico* |
| 1,132,730 | Guatemala City *Guatemala* |
| 1,012,000 | Managua *Nicaragua* |
| 920,857 | Ottawa *Canada* |

### SOUTH AMERICA

| | |
|---|---|
| 15,199,423 | São Paulo *Brazil* |
| 12,200,000 | Buenos Aires *Argentina* |
| 9,600,528 | Rio de Janeiro *Brazil* |
| 6,483,901 | Lima *Peru* |
| 5,025,989 | Bogotá *Colombia* |
| 4,628,320 | Santiago *Chile* |
| 4,092,000 | Caracas *Venezuela* |
| 3,461,905 | Belo Horizonte *Brazil* |
| 2,859,469 | Recife *Brazil* |
| 1,596,274 | Brasília *Brazil* |
| 1,383,660 | Montevideo *Uruguay* |
| 1,234,000 | La Paz *Bolivia* |
| 1,100,847 | Quito *Ecuador* |

### EUROPE

| | |
|---|---|
| 9,318,821 | Paris *France* |
| 9,227,687 | London *U.K.* |
| 8,957,000 | Moscow *Rus. Fed.* |
| 6,407,215 | Istanbul *Turkey* |
| 5,004,000 | St Petersburg *Rus. Fed.* |
| 3,447,916 | Berlin *Germany* |
| 3,097,000 | Athens *Greece* |
| 2,909,792 | Madrid *Spain* |
| 2,723,327 | Rome *Italy* |
| 2,720,400 | Essen-Dortmund *Germany* |
| 2,616,000 | Kiev *Ukraine* |
| 2,578,900 | Manchester *U.K.* |
| 2,350,984 | Bucharest *Romania* |
| 2,329,600 | Birmingham *U.K.* |
| 1,992,343 | Budapest *Hungary* |
| 1,742,000 | Lisbon *Portugal* |
| 1,669,840 | Stockholm *Sweden* |
| 1,669,000 | Hamburg *Germany* |
| 1,655,700 | Warsaw *Poland* |
| 1,633,600 | Minsk *Belarus* |
| 1,565,800 | Vienna *Austria* |
| 1,342,679 | Copenhagen *Denmark* |
| 1,221,000 | Sofia *Bulgaria* |
| 1,214,174 | Prague *Czech Rep.* |
| 1,174,512 | Zagreb *Croatia* |
| 1,168,454 | Belgrade *Yugoslavia* |
| 1,091,338 | Amsterdam *Neth.* |
| 976,883 | Helsinki *Finland* |
| 954,045 | Brussels *Belgium* |
| 915,516 | Dublin *R. of Ireland* |
| 915,000 | Riga *Latvia* |

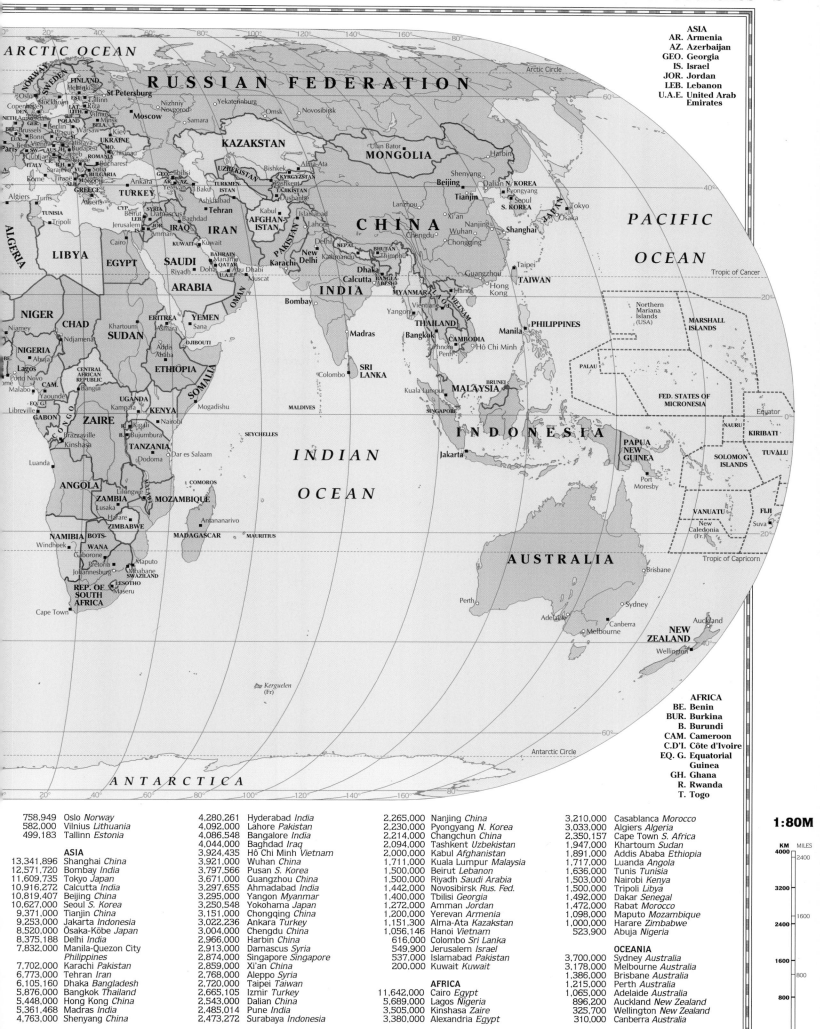

ASIA
AR. Armenia
AZ. Azerbaijan
GEO. Georgia
IS. Israel
JOR. Jordan
LEB. Lebanon
U.A.E. United Arab
Emirates

AFRICA
BE. Benin
BUR. Burkina
B. Burundi
CAM. Cameroon
C.D'I. Côte d'Ivoire
EQ. G. Equatorial
Guinea
GH. Ghana
R. Rwanda
T. Togo

**1:80M**

| | | |
|---|---|---|
| 758,949 | Oslo *Norway* | |
| 582,000 | Vilnius *Lithuania* | |
| 499,183 | Tallinn *Estonia* | |
| | **ASIA** | |
| 13,341,896 | Shanghai *China* | |
| 12,571,720 | Bombay *India* | |
| 11,609,735 | Tokyo *Japan* | |
| 10,916,272 | Calcutta *India* | |
| 10,819,407 | Beijing *China* | |
| 10,627,000 | Seoul *S. Korea* | |
| 9,371,000 | Tianjin *China* | |
| 9,253,000 | Jakarta *Indonesia* | |
| 8,520,000 | Ōsaka-Kōbe *Japan* | |
| 8,375,188 | Delhi *India* | |
| 7,832,000 | Manila-Quezon City *Philippines* | |
| 7,702,000 | Karachi *Pakistan* | |
| 6,773,000 | Tehran *Iran* | |
| 6,105,160 | Dhaka *Bangladesh* | |
| 5,876,000 | Bangkok *Thailand* | |
| 5,448,000 | Hong Kong *China* | |
| 5,361,468 | Madras *India* | |
| 4,763,000 | Shenyang *China* | |

| | | |
|---|---|---|
| 4,280,261 | Hyderabad *India* | |
| 4,092,000 | Lahore *Pakistan* | |
| 4,086,548 | Bangalore *India* | |
| 4,044,000 | Baghdad *Iraq* | |
| 3,924,435 | Hô Chi Minh *Vietnam* | |
| 3,921,000 | Wuhan *China* | |
| 3,797,566 | Pusan *S. Korea* | |
| 3,671,000 | Guangzhou *China* | |
| 3,297,655 | Ahmadabad *India* | |
| 3,295,000 | Yangon *Myanmar* | |
| 3,250,548 | Yokohama *Japan* | |
| 3,151,000 | Chongqing *China* | |
| 3,022,236 | Ankara *Turkey* | |
| 3,004,000 | Chengdu *China* | |
| 2,966,000 | Harbin *China* | |
| 2,913,000 | Damascus *Syria* | |
| 2,874,000 | Singapore *Singapore* | |
| 2,859,000 | Xi'an *China* | |
| 2,768,000 | Aleppo *Syria* | |
| 2,720,000 | Taipei *Taiwan* | |
| 2,665,105 | Izmir *Turkey* | |
| 2,543,000 | Dalian *China* | |
| 2,485,014 | Pune *India* | |
| 2,473,272 | Surabaya *Indonesia* | |

| | | |
|---|---|---|
| 2,265,000 | Nanjing *China* | |
| 2,230,000 | Pyongyang *N. Korea* | |
| 2,214,000 | Changchun *China* | |
| 2,094,000 | Tashkent *Uzbekistan* | |
| 2,000,000 | Kabul *Afghanistan* | |
| 1,711,000 | Kuala Lumpur *Malaysia* | |
| 1,500,000 | Beirut *Lebanon* | |
| 1,500,000 | Riyadh *Saudi Arabia* | |
| 1,442,000 | Novosibirsk *Rus. Fed.* | |
| 1,400,000 | Tbilisi *Georgia* | |
| 1,272,000 | Amman *Jordan* | |
| 1,200,000 | Yerevan *Armenia* | |
| 1,151,300 | Alma-Ata *Kazakstan* | |
| 1,056,146 | Hanoi *Vietnam* | |
| 616,000 | Colombo *Sri Lanka* | |
| 549,900 | Jerusalem *Israel* | |
| 537,000 | Islamabad *Pakistan* | |
| 200,000 | Kuwait *Kuwait* | |
| | **AFRICA** | |
| 11,642,000 | Cairo *Egypt* | |
| 5,689,000 | Lagos *Nigeria* | |
| 3,505,000 | Kinshasa *Zaire* | |
| 3,380,000 | Alexandria *Egypt* | |

| | | |
|---|---|---|
| 3,210,000 | Casablanca *Morocco* | |
| 3,033,000 | Algiers *Algeria* | |
| 2,350,157 | Cape Town *S. Africa* | |
| 1,947,000 | Khartoum *Sudan* | |
| 1,891,000 | Addis Ababa *Ethiopia* | |
| 1,717,000 | Luanda *Angola* | |
| 1,636,000 | Tunis *Tunisia* | |
| 1,503,000 | Tripoli *Libya* | |
| 1,500,000 | Tripoli *Libya* | |
| 1,492,000 | Dakar *Senegal* | |
| 1,472,000 | Rabat *Morocco* | |
| 1,098,000 | Maputo *Mozambique* | |
| 1,000,000 | Harare *Zimbabwe* | |
| 523,900 | Abuja *Nigeria* | |
| | **OCEANIA** | |
| 3,700,000 | Sydney *Australia* | |
| 3,178,000 | Melbourne *Australia* | |
| 1,386,000 | Brisbane *Australia* | |
| 1,215,000 | Perth *Australia* | |
| 1,065,000 | Adelaide *Australia* | |
| 896,200 | Auckland *New Zealand* | |
| 325,700 | Wellington *New Zealand* | |
| 310,000 | Canberra *Australia* | |

KM  MILES
4000  2400
3200
2400  1600
1600  800
800
0  0

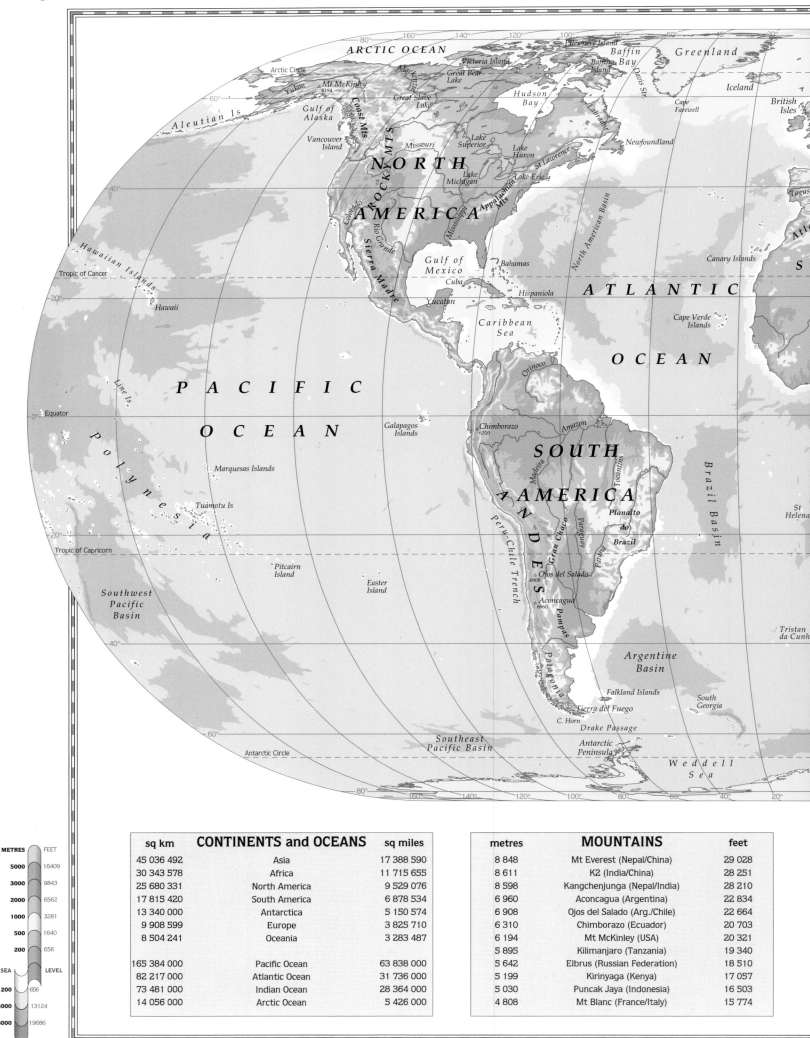

| METRES | FEET |
|---|---|
| 5000 | 16409 |
| 3000 | 9843 |
| 2000 | 6562 |
| 1000 | 3281 |
| 500 | 1640 |
| 200 | 656 |
| SEA | LEVEL |
| 200 | 656 |
| 4000 | 13124 |
| 6000 | 19686 |

| sq km | **CONTINENTS and OCEANS** | sq miles |
|---|---|---|
| 45 036 492 | Asia | 17 388 590 |
| 30 343 578 | Africa | 11 715 655 |
| 25 680 331 | North America | 9 529 076 |
| 17 815 420 | South America | 6 878 534 |
| 13 340 000 | Antarctica | 5 150 574 |
| 9 908 599 | Europe | 3 825 710 |
| 8 504 241 | Oceania | 3 283 487 |
| 165 384 000 | Pacific Ocean | 63 838 000 |
| 82 217 000 | Atlantic Ocean | 31 736 000 |
| 73 481 000 | Indian Ocean | 28 364 000 |
| 14 056 000 | Arctic Ocean | 5 426 000 |

| metres | **MOUNTAINS** | feet |
|---|---|---|
| 8 848 | Mt Everest (Nepal/China) | 29 028 |
| 8 611 | K2 (India/China) | 28 251 |
| 8 598 | Kangchenjunga (Nepal/India) | 28 210 |
| 6 960 | Aconcagua (Argentina) | 22 834 |
| 6 908 | Ojos del Salado (Arg./Chile) | 22 664 |
| 6 310 | Chimborazo (Ecuador) | 20 703 |
| 6 194 | Mt McKinley (USA) | 20 321 |
| 5 895 | Kilimanjaro (Tanzania) | 19 340 |
| 5 642 | Elbrus (Russian Federation) | 18 510 |
| 5 199 | Kirinyaga (Kenya) | 17 057 |
| 5 030 | Puncak Jaya (Indonesia) | 16 503 |
| 4 808 | Mt Blanc (France/Italy) | 15 774 |

Eckert IV Projection

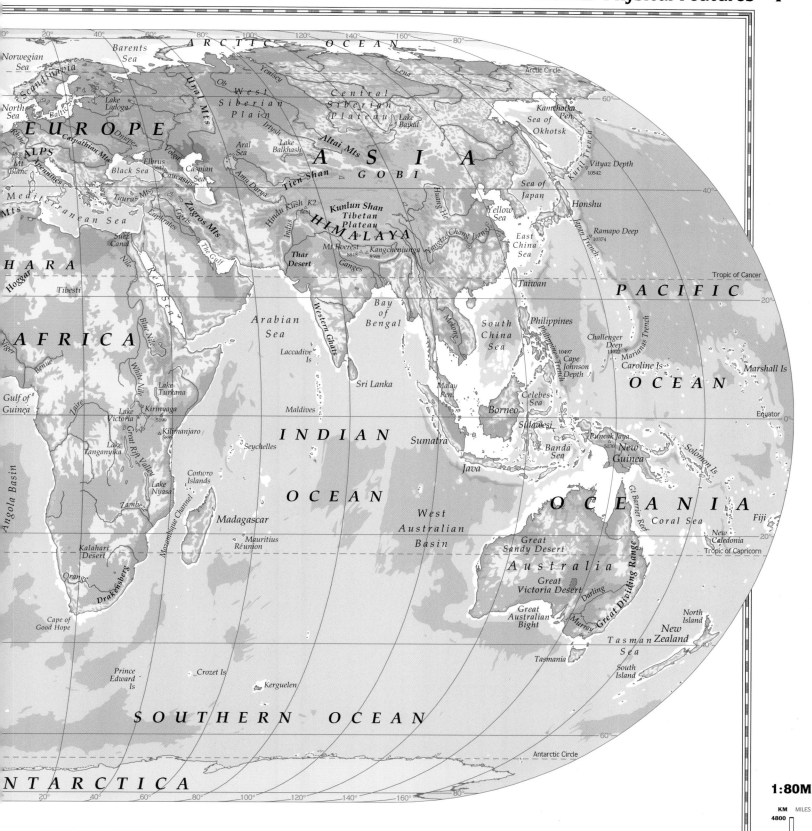

1:80M

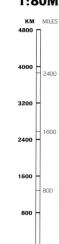

| KM | MILES |
|---|---|
| 4800 | |
| 4000 | 2400 |
| 3200 | |
| | 1600 |
| 2400 | |
| 1600 | 800 |
| 800 | |
| 0 | 0 |

| sq km | LAKES | sq miles |
|---|---|---|
| 371 000 | Caspian Sea (Asia) | 143 205 |
| 83 270 | Lake Superior (N. America) | 32 140 |
| 68 800 | Lake Victoria (Africa) | 26 560 |
| 60 700 | Lake Huron (N. America) | 23 430 |
| 58 020 | Lake Michigan (N. America) | 22 395 |
| 33 640 | Aral Sea (Asia) | 12 985 |
| 32 900 | Lake Tanganyika (Africa) | 12 700 |
| 31 790 | Great Bear Lake (N. America) | 12 270 |
| 30 500 | Lake Baikal (Asia) | 11 775 |
| 28 440 | Great Slave Lake (N. America) | 10 980 |
| 25 680 | Lake Erie (N. America) | 9 915 |
| 22 490 | Lake Nyasa (Africa) | 8 680 |

| kilometres | RIVERS | miles |
|---|---|---|
| 6 695 | Nile (Africa) | 4 160 |
| 6 516 | Amazon (S. America) | 4 048 |
| 6 380 | Yangtze (Chang Jiang) (Asia) | 3 964 |
| 6 020 | Mississippi-Missouri (N. America) | 3 740 |
| 5 570 | Ob-Irtysh (Asia) | 3 461 |
| 5 464 | Huang He (Asia) | 3 395 |
| 4 667 | Zaire (Africa) | 2 900 |
| 4 425 | Mekong (Asia) | 2 749 |
| 4 416 | Amur (Asia) | 2 744 |
| 4 400 | Lena (Asia) | 2 734 |
| 4 250 | Mackenzie (N. America) | 2 640 |
| 4 090 | Yenisey (Asia) | 2 541 |

© Collins

## ICE CAP

Areas of permanent ice cap around the north and south poles. The intense cold, dry weather and the ice cover render these regions almost lifeless. In Antarctica, tiny patches of land free of ice have a cover of mosses and lichens which provide shelter for some insects and mites.

## TUNDRA and MOUNTAIN

Sub-arctic areas or mountain tops which are usually frozen. Tundra vegetation is characterized by mosses, lichens, rushes, grasses and flowering herbs; animals include the arctic fox and reindeer. Mountain vegetation is also characterized by mosses and lichens, and by low growing birch and willow.

## TAIGA (NORTHERN FOREST)

Found only in the high latitudes of the northern hemisphere where winters are long and very cold, and summers are short. The characteristic vegetation is coniferous trees, including spruce and fir; animals include beavers, squirrels and deer.

## MIXED and DECIDUOUS FOREST

Typical of both temperate mid-latitude regions and of eastern subtropical regions. The vegetation is a mixture of broadleaf and coniferous trees, including oak, beech and maple. Humankind has had a major impact on these regions, and in many areas little natural vegetation remains.

## MEDITERRANEAN SCRUB

Long, hot, dry summers and short, warm, wet winters characterize these areas. A variety of herbaceous plants grow beneath shrub thickets with pine, oak and gorse.

## GRASSLAND

Areas of long grasslands (prairies) and short grasslands (steppe) in both the northern and southern hemispheres. These grasslands have hot summers, cold winters and moderate rainfall.

Arctic Circle

60°

40°

20°

Tropic of Cancer

Equator 0°

20°

Tropic of Capricorn

40°

60°

Antarctic Circle

160° 140° 120° 100° 80° 60°

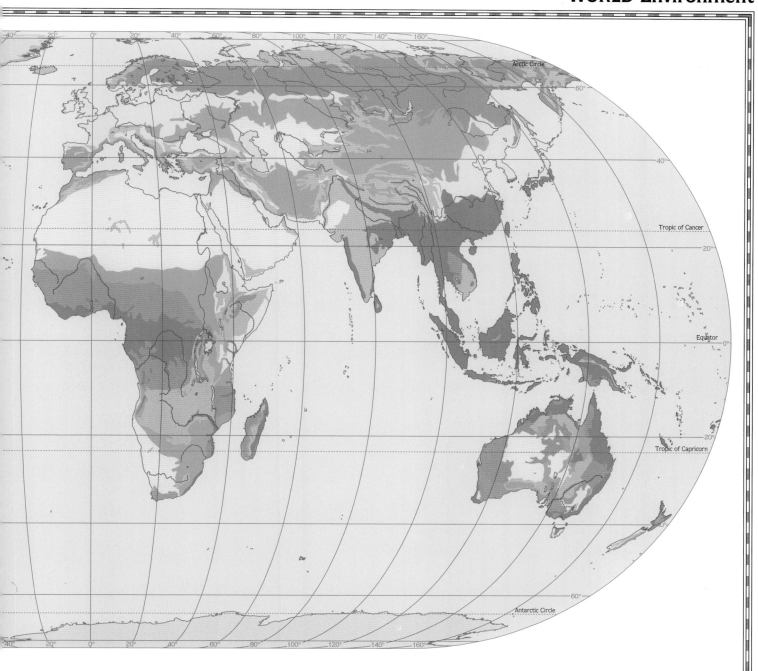

**1:100M**

**SAVANNA**
Tropical grasslands with a short rainy season; areas of grassland are interspersed with thorn bushes and deciduous trees such as acacia and eucalyptus.

**RAINFOREST**
Dense evergreen forests found in areas of high rainfall and continuous high temperatures. Up to three tree layers grow above a variable shrub layer: high trees, the tree canopy and the open canopy.

**DRY TROPICAL FOREST and SCRUB**
Low to medium size semi-deciduous trees and thorny scrub with thick bark and long roots characterize the forest areas; in the scrub areas the trees are replaced by shrubs, bushes and succulents.

**DESERT**
Little vegetation grows in the very hot, dry climate of desert areas. The few shrubs, grasses and cacti have adapted by storing water when it is available.

**10**

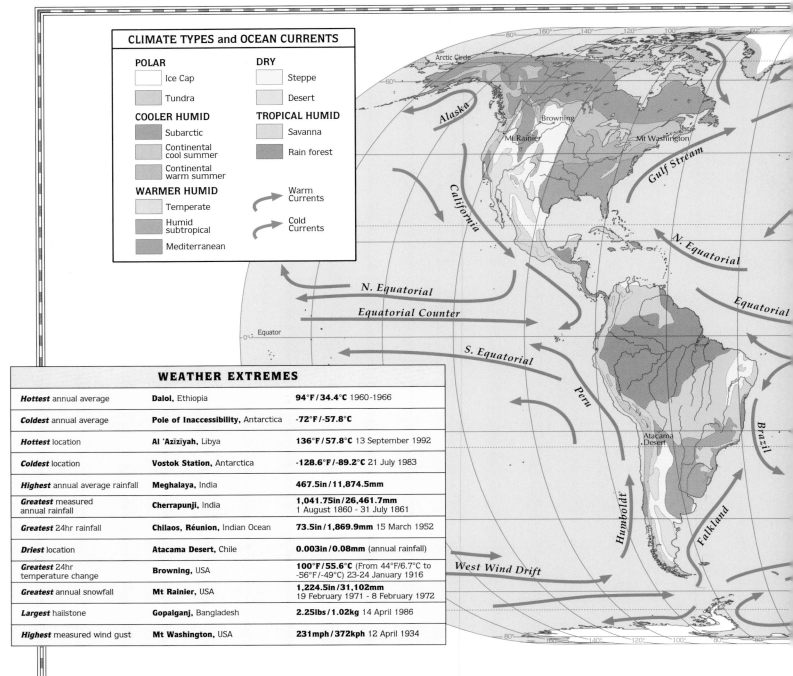

## CLIMATE TYPES and OCEAN CURRENTS

**POLAR**
- ☐ Ice Cap
- ☐ Tundra

**COOLER HUMID**
- ☐ Subarctic
- ☐ Continental cool summer
- ☐ Continental warm summer

**WARMER HUMID**
- ☐ Temperate
- ☐ Humid subtropical
- ☐ Mediterranean

**DRY**
- ☐ Steppe
- ☐ Desert

**TROPICAL HUMID**
- ☐ Savanna
- ☐ Rain forest

- ⟶ Warm Currents
- ⟶ Cold Currents

### WEATHER EXTREMES

| | | |
|---|---|---|
| ***Hottest*** annual average | **Dalol**, Ethiopia | **94°F / 34.4°C** 1960-1966 |
| ***Coldest*** annual average | **Pole of Inaccessibility**, Antarctica | **-72°F / -57.8°C** |
| ***Hottest*** location | **Al 'Azīzīyah**, Libya | **136°F / 57.8°C** 13 September 1992 |
| ***Coldest*** location | **Vostok Station**, Antarctica | **-128.6°F / -89.2°C** 21 July 1983 |
| ***Highest*** annual average rainfall | **Meghalaya**, India | **467.5in / 11,874.5mm** |
| ***Greatest*** measured annual rainfall | **Cherrapunji**, India | **1,041.75in / 26,461.7mm** 1 August 1860 - 31 July 1861 |
| ***Greatest*** 24hr rainfall | **Chilaos, Réunion**, Indian Ocean | **73.5in / 1,869.9mm** 15 March 1952 |
| ***Driest*** location | **Atacama Desert**, Chile | **0.003in / 0.08mm** (annual rainfall) |
| ***Greatest*** 24hr temperature change | **Browning**, USA | **100°F / 55.6°C** (From 44°F/6.7°C to -56°F/-49°C) 23-24 January 1916 |
| ***Greatest*** annual snowfall | **Mt Rainier**, USA | **1,224.5in / 31,102mm** 19 February 1971 - 8 February 1972 |
| ***Largest*** hailstone | **Gopalganj**, Bangladesh | **2.25lbs / 1.02kg** 14 April 1986 |
| ***Highest*** measured wind gust | **Mt Washington**, USA | **231mph / 372kph** 12 April 1934 |

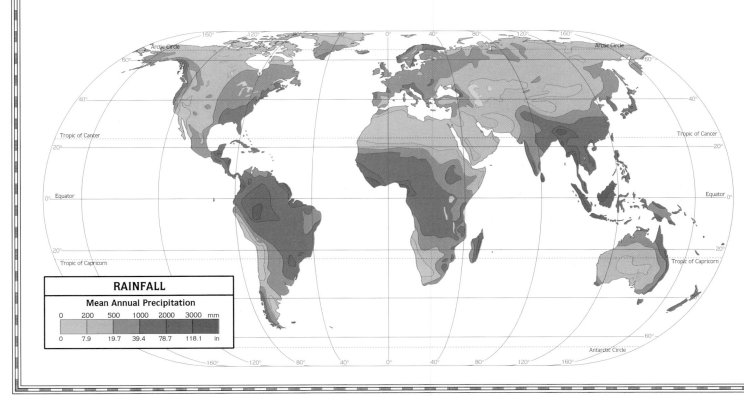

### RAINFALL

**Mean Annual Precipitation**

| 0 | 200 | 500 | 1000 | 2000 | 3000 | mm |
|---|---|---|---|---|---|---|
| 0 | 7.9 | 19.7 | 39.4 | 78.7 | 118.1 | in |

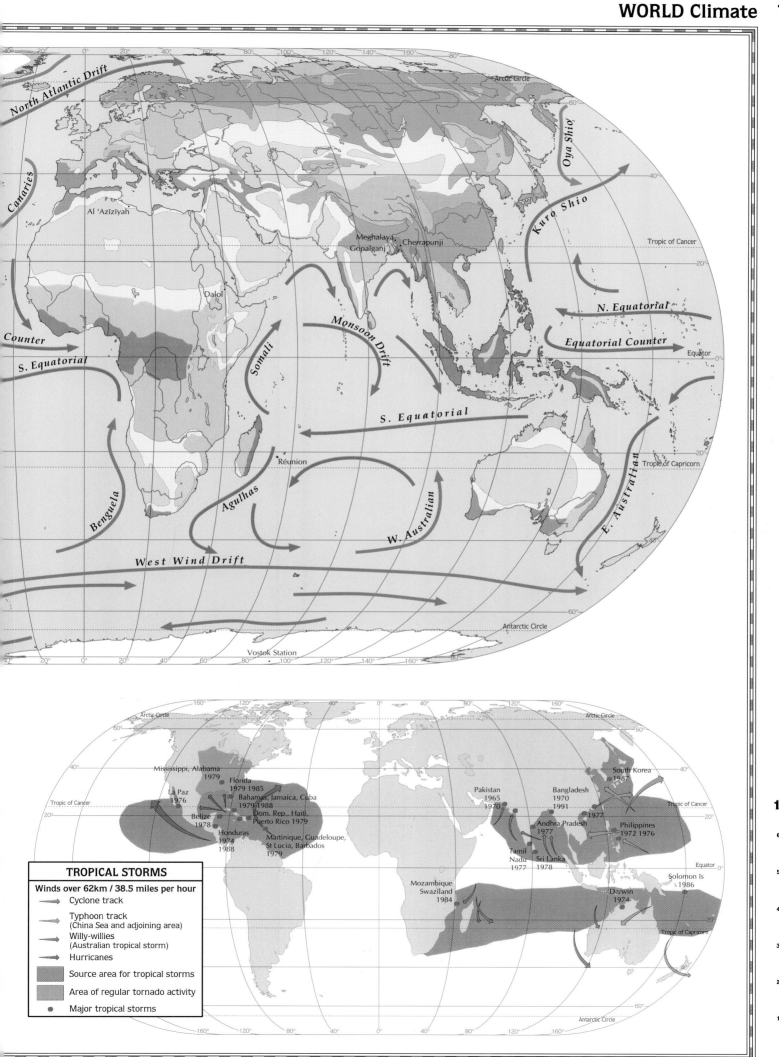

North Atlantic Drift

Canaries

Counter

S. Equatorial

Benguela

West Wind Drift

Agulhas

Somali

Monsoon Drift

S. Equatorial

W. Australian

E. Australian

Equatorial Counter

N. Equatorial

Kuro Shio

Oya Shio

Al 'Azīzīyah

Dalol

Meghalaya
Gopalganj • Cherrapunji

Réunion

Vostok Station

Arctic Circle

Tropic of Cancer

Equator

Tropic of Capricorn

Antarctic Circle

**TROPICAL STORMS**

Winds over 62km / 38.5 miles per hour

→ Cyclone track

→ Typhoon track
(China Sea and adjoining area)

→ Willy-willies
(Australian tropical storm)

→ Hurricanes

Source area for tropical storms

Area of regular tornado activity

• Major tropical storms

Mississippi, Alabama
1979

La Paz
1976

Florida
1979 1985

Bahamas, Jamaica, Cuba
1979 1988

Belize
1978

Dom. Rep., Haiti,
Puerto Rico 1979

Honduras
1974
1988

Martinique, Guadeloupe,
St Lucia, Barbados
1979

Pakistan
1965
1970

Andhra Pradesh
1977

Tamil
Nadu
1977

Sri Lanka
1978

Mozambique
Swaziland
1984

Bangladesh
1970
1991

South Korea
1987

Philippines
1972 1976

Solomon Is
1986

Darwin
1974

Arctic Circle

Tropic of Cancer

Equator

Tropic of Capricorn

Antarctic Circle

**1:100M**

KM    MILES
6000

5000    3000

4000    2000

3000

2000    1000

1000

0    0

© Collins

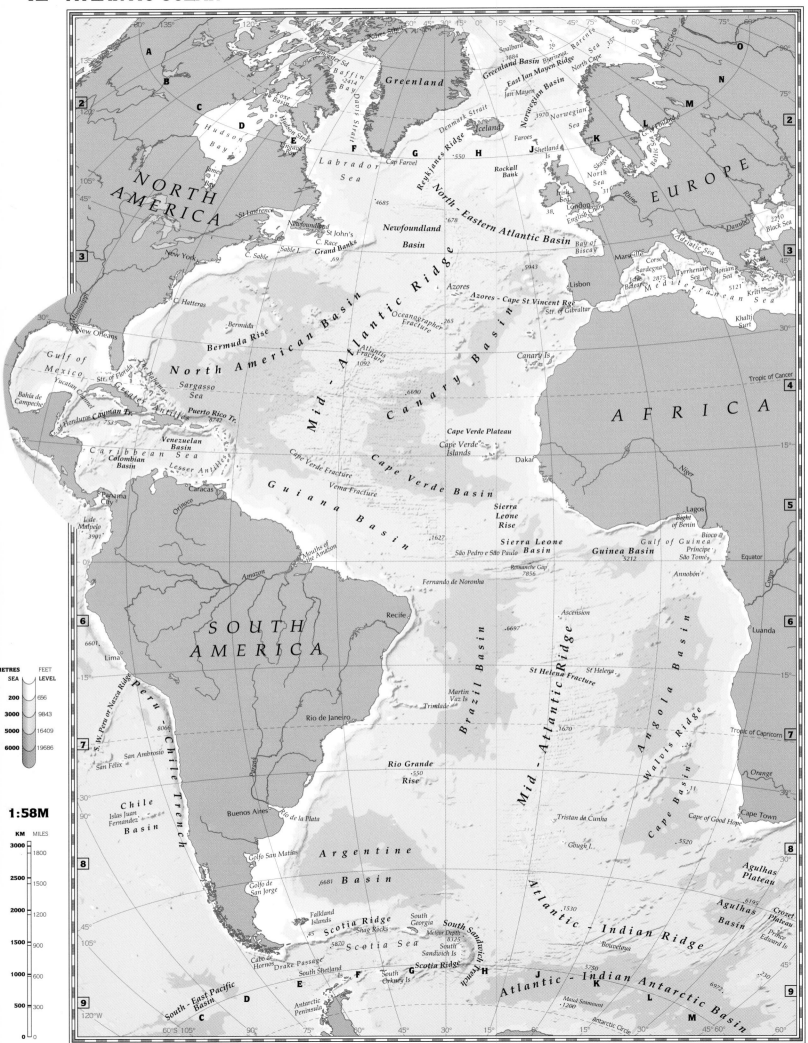

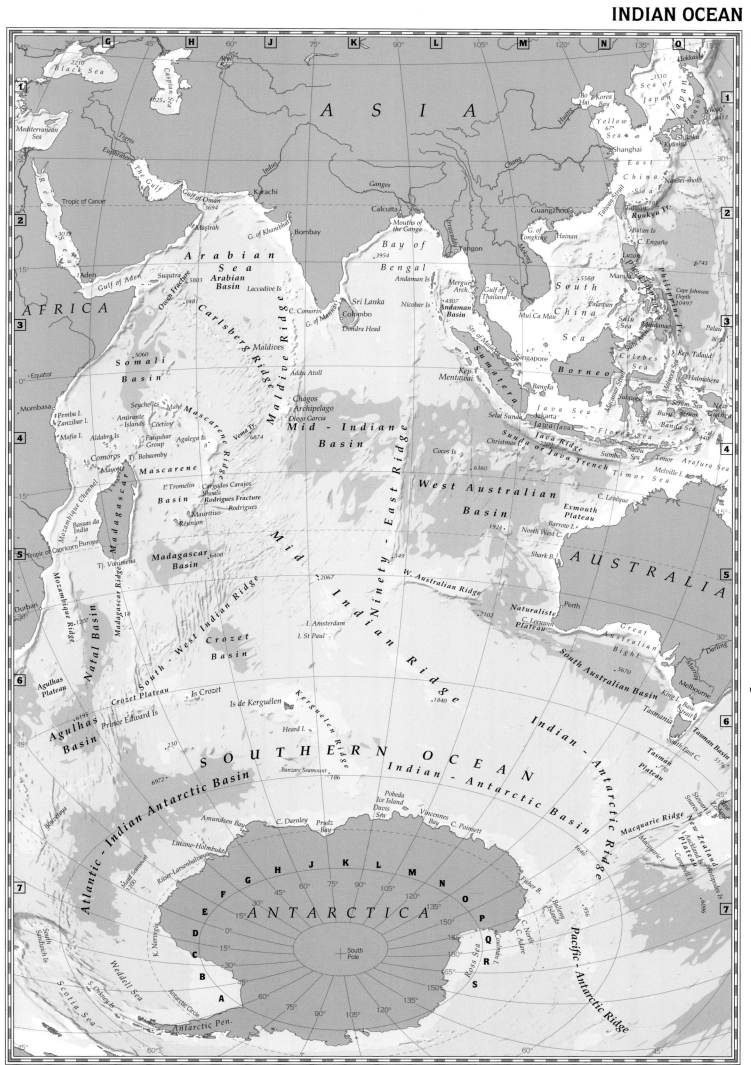

ASIA

Black Sea
Caspian Sea
Mediterranean Sea
Tigris
Euphrates
The Gulf
Red Sea
Tropic of Cancer
Gulf of Oman
Karachi
Indus
Ganges
Calcutta
Mouths of the Ganga
Bay of Bengal
Guangzhou
Hainan
G. of Tongking
Shanghai
East China Sea
Sea of Japan
Hokkaido
Korea Bay
Bo Hai
Yellow Sea
Tokyo
Honshu
Shikoku
Kyushu
Nansei-shoto
Taiwan
Ryukyu Is.
Batan Is.
C. Engaño
Manila
Luzon
Philippine Is.
Cape Johnson Depth
Palau

AFRICA

Aden
Gulf of Aden
Suqutra
Owen Fracture
Arabian Sea
Arabian Basin
Laccadive Is
G. of Khambhat
Bombay
C. Comorin
G. of Mannar
Sri Lanka
Colombo
Dondra Head
Maldives
Maldive Ridge
Carlsberg Ridge
Somali Basin
Mombasa
Equator
Pemba I.
Zanzibar I.
Mafia I.
Seychelles
Mahé
Amirante Islands
Coëtivy
Aldabra Is
Farquhar Group
Agalega Is
Comoros
Mayotte
Mascarene Ridge
Mascarene Basin
Tj. Bobaomby
Madagascar
Bassas da India
Europa
Tromelin
Cargados Carajos Shoals
Rodrigues Fracture
Rodrigues
Mauritius
Réunion
Chagos Archipelago
Diego Garcia
Addu Atoll
Mid-Indian Basin
Andaman Is
Nicobar Is
Mergui Arch.
Andaman Basin
Gulf of Thailand
Mui Ca Mau
Yangon
Irrawaddy
Mekong
Chang
Str. of Malacca
Singapore
Sumatera
Kep. Mentawai
Java Ridge
Sunda or Java Trench
Cocos Is
West Australian Basin
South China Sea
Palawan
Sulu Sea
Mindanao
Celebes Sea
Borneo
Kep. Talaud
Halmahera
Molucca Sea
Buru
Seram Sea
Seram
Banda Sea
Jakarta
Jawa (Java)
Selat Sunda
Christmas I.
Java Sea
Flores Sea
Sumba
Sulawesi
Makassar Strait
Bangka
Sawu Sea
Timor Sea
Timor
Arafura Sea
Melville I.
C. Lévêque
Exmouth Plateau
Barrow I.
North West C.
Shark B.

AUSTRALIA

Mid-Indian Ridge
Ninety-East Ridge
West Australian Ridge
W. Australian Ridge
Madagascar Basin
Tj. Vohimena
Durban
Mozambique Channel
Mozambique Ridge
Natal Basin
South-West Indian Ridge
Crozet Basin
I. Amsterdam
I. St Paul
Naturaliste Plateau
C. Leeuwin
Perth
Great Australian Bight
South Australian Basin
Darling
Murray
Melbourne
King I.
Bass Strait
Tasmania
Tasman Basin
South East C.
Agulhas Plateau
Agulhas Basin
Prince Edward Is
Is Crozet
Crozet Plateau
Is de Kerguélen
Kerguelen Ridge
Heard I.
Indian-Antarctic Ridge
Indian-Antarctic Basin
Tasman Plateau
Macquarie Ridge

SOUTHERN OCEAN

Atlantic-Indian Antarctic Basin
Banzare Seamount
Indian-Antarctic Basin
Bouvetøya
Maud Seamount
South Sandwich Is
South Orkney Is
Scotia Sea
Weddell Sea
Antarctic Circle
Antarctic Pen.

Amundsen Bay
C. Darnley
Prydz Bay
Davis Sea
Vincennes Bay
C. Poinsett
Pobeda Ice Island
Lützow-Holmbukta
Rüser-Larsenhalvøya

ANTARCTICA

South Pole

Fisher B.
Balleny Islands
C. North
C. Adare
Coulman I.
Ross Sea
Stewart I.
Snares Is
New Zealand
Antipodes Is
Auckland Plateau
Campbell I.
Macquarie I.
Pacific-Antarctic Ridge

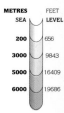

METRES / FEET
SEA LEVEL

| METRES | FEET |
|---|---|
| 200 | 656 |
| 3000 | 9843 |
| 5000 | 16409 |
| 6000 | 19686 |

1:58M

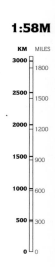

KM / MILES

3000 / 1800
2500 / 1500
2000 / 1200
1500 / 900
1000 / 600
500 / 300
0 / 0

Lambert Azimuthal Equal Area Projection

© Collins

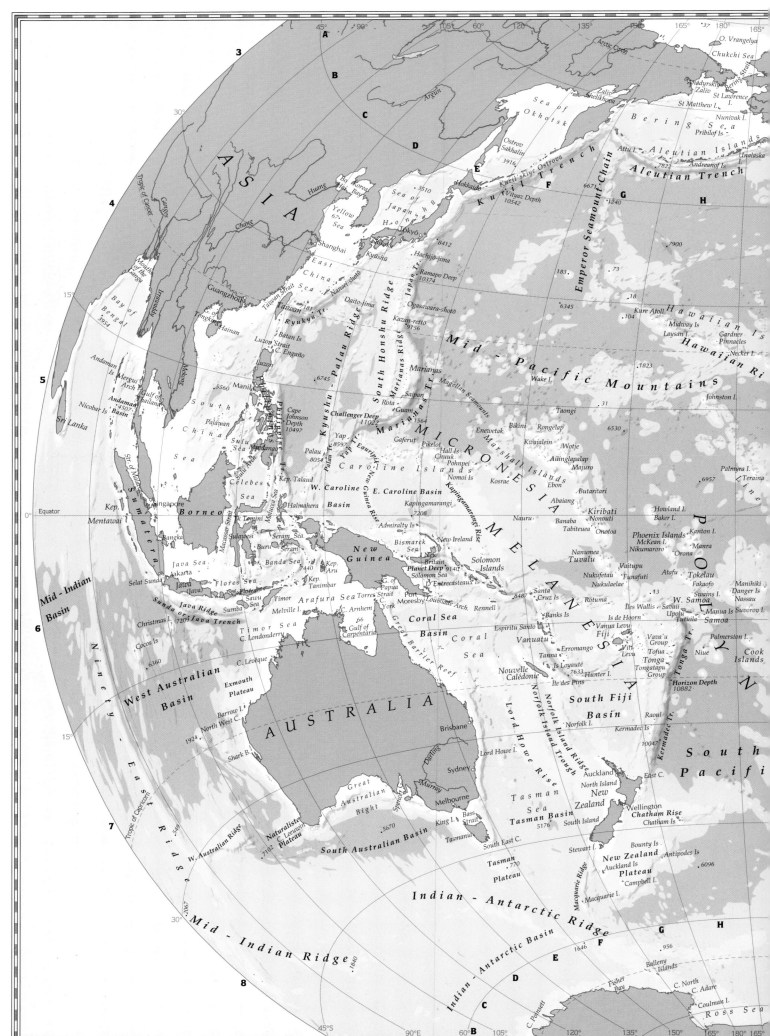

**3**
**4**
**5**
**6**
**7**
**8**

O. Vrangelya
Chukchi Sea
Arctic Circle
Mys Dezhneva
Zaliv Lavrentiya
St Lawrence I.
Bering Strait
Zaliv Shelikhova
Ostrov Sakhalin
Sea of Okhotsk
Bering Sea
Pribilof Is
Nunivak I.
St Matthew I.
Attu I.
Andreanof Is
Unalaska
Aleutian Islands
Aleutian Trench
Kuril'skiye Ostrova
Hokkaido
Kuril Tr.
Vityaz Depth 10542
Kuril Trench
Emperor Seamount Chain
.6671
.7822
.1240
**F**
**G**
**H**

A S I A
Tropic of Cancer
Huang
Korea
Bo Hai
Yellow Sea
Sea of Japan
Honshu
Tōkyō
Shikoku
Kyūshū
Shanghai
Guangzhou
Chang
Ganges
Mouths of the Ganges
Irrawaddy
Bay of Bengal
3954
Mergui Arch.
Andaman Is
Nicobar Is
Sri Lanka
Andaman Basin
4507
Gulf of Thailand
Kep.
Mentawai
Singapore
Sumatra
Str. of Malacca
Bangka
Selat Sunda
Jakarta
Jawa (Java)
Java Sea
Christmas I.
Cocos Is
.6360
Mid - Indian Basin
West Australian Basin
Ninety
East Ridge

.3510
Hokkaidō
.3916
8412
Hachijō-jima
Ramapo Deep 10374
Japan Tr.
Ogasawara-shotō
Nansei-shotō
Daito-jima
East China Sea
Taiwan Strait
Taiwan
.181
Tongking
Hainan
S o u t h
C h i n a
S e a
Palawan
Manila
.5560
Philippine
Cape Johnson Depth 10497
Mindanao
Sulu Sea
Celebes Sea
Kep. Talaud
Halmahera
Molucca Sea
Sulawesi
Macassar Strait
Buru
Seram
Seram Sea
Banda Sea
Kep. Aru
Kep. Tanimbar
7440
Flores Sea
Flores
Sawu Sea
Sumba
Timor
Java Trench
7209
Sunda or Java Trench
Melville I.
C. Londonderry
Timor Sea
Arafura Sea
C. Arnhem
Gulf of Carpentaria
Great Barrier Reef
C. York
Torres Strait
G. of Papua
Port Moresby
.66

Ryukyu Tr.
Kyushu - Palau Ridge
South Honshu Ridge
Marianas Ridge
Kazan-rettō 9756
Marianas
Saipan
Rota
Guam
Marianas Tr.
Challenger Deep 11022
.6745
Yap Tr.
Yap .8597
Palau Ridge
Palau 8054
Hall Is
Gaferut
Pikelot
Chuuk
Caroline Islands
W. Caroline Basin
E. Caroline Basin
New Guinea Rise
Kapingamarangi Rise
New Guinea
Bismarck Sea
New Britain
New Ireland
Admiralty Is
Solomon Sea
Solomon Islands
Planet Deep 9140
D'Entrecasteaux Is
Louisiade Arch.
Rennell
.8487
Coral Sea Basin
Coral Sea
AUSTRALIA

Mid - Pacific Mountains
Magellan Seamounts
Wake I.
Taongi
.31
Enewetak
Bikini
Rongelap
Marshall Islands
Kwajalein
Ailinglapalap
Wotje
Majuro
Ebon
Butaritari
Kosrae
Nomoi Is
Pohnpei
Kapingamarangi
7208
Nauru
Banaba
Tabiteuea
Onotoa
MICRONESIA
MELANESIA
.6530
.6345
.18
.1823
.104
Kure Atoll
Midway Is
Laysan I.
Gardner Pinnacles
Necker I.
Hawaiian Is
Hawaiian Ri
Johnston I.
.7900
.73
183.
Abaiang
Kiribati
Howland I.
Baker I.
Phoenix Islands
McKean I.
Nikumaroro
Orona
Manra
Nanumea
Tuvalu
Nanumanga
Nukufetau
Funafuti
Atafu
Nukulaelae
.13
Rotuma
Santa Cruz Is
Banks Is
Espiritu Santo
Vanuatu
Erromango
Tanna
Îles Loyauté
Nouvelle Calédonie
Île des Pins
Hunter I.
7633
Norfolk Island Ridge
Norfolk I.
.10047
South Fiji Basin
Lord Howe Rise
Fiji
Vanua Levu
Viti Levu
Tofua
Tonga
Tongatapu Group
Vava'u Group
Niue
Horizon Depth 10882
Tonga Tr.
Kermadec Tr.
Kermadec Is
Raoul I.
POLYNESIA
Palmyra I.
.6957
Teraina
Line
Kanton I.
Samoa
Savai'i
Upolu
Tutuila
Manua Is
W. Samoa
Îles Wallis
Is de Hoorn
Fakaofo
Tokelau
Swains I.
Suvorov I.
Nassau
Manihiki
Danger Is
Palmerston I.
Cook Islands
.6096
Auckland
East C.
North Island
New Zealand
Wellington
Chatham Rise
Chatham Is
South Island
Stewart I.
Bounty Is
Antipodes Is
New Zealand Plateau
Auckland Is
Campbell I.
Macquarie Ridge
Macquarie I.
Indian - Antarctic Ridge
.1646
.956
Balleny Islands
Fisher Bay
C. North
C. Adare
Coulman I.
Ross Sea
C. Poinsett
Indian - Antarctic Basin
.1840
Mid - Indian Ridge
.2002

Equator
0°
15°
30°
45°N
Tropic of Cancer
Tropic of Capricorn
Borneo
Seram
G. of Tomini
Timor
Sunda Ridge
Java Ridge
W. Australian Ridge
Naturaliste Plateau
7102
C. Leeuwin
South Australian Basin
.5670
Great Australian Bight
Spencer G.
King I.
Bass Strait
Tasmania
South East C.
Tasman
Tasman Basin 5176
Tasman Plateau
.770
Murray
Darling
Sydney
Melbourne
Brisbane
Exmouth Plateau
Barrow I.
North West C.
.1924
Shark B.
C. Léveque
South
Pacifi
South Pacifi
Lord Howe I.
New Caledonia
Tasman Sea

METRES
SEA LEVEL
200
3000
5000
6000

FEET
656
9843
16409
19686

Lambert Azimuthal Equal Area Projection

45°S
30°
15°
0°
15°
30°E
45°
60°
75°
90°
105°
120°
135°
150°
165°
180°
165°

**A**
**B**
**C**
**D**
**E**
**F**
**G**
**H**

Pt Barrow
Gulf of Alaska
Kodiak I.
Alexander Archipelago
Queen Charlotte Islands
Vancouver Island
Vancouver
Columbia
MacKenzie

Hudson Bay
Missouri
Mississippi
Rio Grande
Colorado

NORTH AMERICA

New York
C. Hatteras
Bermuda
Bermuda Rise

Newfoundland
C. Sable I.
C. Sable

North American Basin
North American Basin
Mid - Atlantic Ridge

Mendocino Seascarp
2733
C. Mendocino
San Francisco
Los Angeles
Golfo de California
Guadalupe

Erben Tablemount
412
Murray Seascarp
6217
Molokai Fracture Zone

New Orleans
Gulf of Mexico
Bahía de Campeche
Yucatán Channel
Str. of Florida
The Bahamas
Greater Antilles
Puerto Rico Tr.
8742

lands
Kauai
Oahu Maui
Hawaii
dge
7022
Clarion Fracture Zone
I. Clarión
Is Revillagigedo
I. Socorro
East Pacific Rise

G. de Tehuantepec
Tehuantepec Ridge
Middle America Trench
6662
Cayman Tr.
G. of Honduras
7535

Venezuelan Basin
Colombian Basin
Caribbean Sea
Lesser Antilles
Caracas
Orinoco
Guiana Basin

Clipperton Fracture Zone
Clipperton I.
.20
.10

Tabuaeran
Kiritimati
Jarvis I.
Islands
Malden I.
Starbuck I.
Tongareva
Caroline I.
Nuku Hiva
Is Marquises
Hiva Oa
Flint I.

I. de Coco
Cocos Ridge
I. de Malpelo
3901.
Panama City
Galapagos Is
(Islas Galápagos)
Carnegie Ridge
G. de Guayaquil

SOUTH AMERICA

Mouths of the Amazon
Amazon

Is du Roi Georges
Iles de Désappointement
Fenua Ura
Raiatea
Tahiti
Is de la Société
Anaa
Raroia
Hao
Hérêhérétúé
Is Tuamotu
Hervey Is
Rarotonga
Iles Maria
Iles Duc de Gloucester
Mangaia
Tubuai
Mururoa
Is Gambier
Groupe Actéon
Is Tubuai
Raivavae
Rapa

4385.
1929.
East Pacific Ridge

Peru Basin
6601
5470
Lima

Peru - Chile Trench
S.W. Peru or Nazca Ridge

Henderson I.
Ducie I.
Pitcairn I.
.1344
Easter Island Fracture Zone
Easter I.
I. Sala y Gómez
571
San Félix
San Ambrosio
8066

E S I A
West
c Basin
5420

Challenger Fracture Zone
Is Juan Fernández
Robinson Crusoe
.2743
Chile Basin

Rio de Janeiro

Santiago
Paraná
Buenos Aires
Río de la Plata

Pacific - Antarctic Ridge
Eltanin Fracture Zone
5230.

Golfo San Matías
Golfo San Jorge
Argentine Basin

South - East Pacific Basin
Cabo de Hornos
Drake Passage
Scotia Ridge
Scotia Sea
5870
Amundsen Sea
Peter I Øy
Antarctic Circle
Falkland Islands
6681

1:58M

KM MILES
3000 — 1800
2500 — 1500
2000 — 1200
1500 — 900
1000 — 600
500 — 300
0 — 0

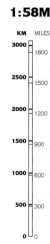

**U.S.A.**

St Lawrence I.
Bering Str.
Kotzebue Sd.
Nome
Point Hope
Barrow
Aleutian Islands
Alaska Pen.
Bristol Bay
Kodiak I.
Gulf of Alaska
Kenai
Valdez
Anchorage
Mt McKinley
Fairbanks
Tanacross
Dawson
Yukon
**A L A S K A**
**Y U K O N**
**T E R R I T O R Y**
Whitehorse
Mt Logan

Alexander Archipelago
Juneau
Prince Rupert
Queen Charlotte Islands
**BRITISH**
**COLUMBIA**
Peace
Fraser
Kamloops
**Vancouver**
Vancouver Island
Victoria
**Seattle**
**WASHINGTON**
**Portland**
Olympia
Salem
**OREGON**
Columbia
Eureka
Snake
**IDAHO**
Boise
**Sacramento**
Reno
Carson City
**San Francisco**
Fresno
**CALIFORNIA**
Las Vegas
**NEVADA**
Salt Lake City
Great Salt L.
**UTAH**
**Los Angeles**
**San Diego**
Mexicali
**ARIZONA**
Santa Fe
**Phoenix**
Tucson
Albuquerque
**NEW MEXICO**
Colorado
Guadalupe (Mex.)
Gulf of California
Revillagigedo Is. (Mex.)
Hermosillo
Ciudad Juarez
**El Paso**
Rio Grande
Chihuahua
Nuevo Laredo
Culiacan
Saltillo
**Monterrey**

Inuvik
Mackenzie
**N O R T H W E S T   T E R R I T O R I E S**
Great Bear Lake
Port Simpson
Liard
Yellowknife
Great Slave Lake
Fort Simpson
Uranium City
Lake Athabasca
Dubawnt L.
**A L B E R T A**
Grande Prairie
Edmonton
**SASKATCHEWAN**
La Ronge
Calgary
Medicine Hat
Saskatoon
The Pas
Lake Winnipeg
Regina
**MANITOBA**
Churchill
Nelson
**Winnipeg**
Chesterfield Inlet

**C A N A D A**

Queen Elizabeth Islands
Parry Islands
Melville Island
Banks Island
Victoria Island
Prince of Wales
Cambridge Bay
Bathurst Inlet
Somerset Island
King William I.
Queen Maud Gulf
Gulf of Boothia
Boothia Pen.
Devon Island
Bylot I.
Pond Inlet
Baffin Island
Foxe Basin
Southampton I.
Foxe Channel
Ivujivik
Hall Beach
Prince Charles I.
Cumberland Sd.
Clyde River
Dundas

**Greenland**
**(Denmark)**
King Frederik VIII Land
Scoresbysund
Scoresby
Christian X Land
King Christian IX Land
King Frederik VI Coast
Angmagssalik
Godthåb
Frederikshåb
C. Farewell

Davis Strait
Baffin Bay

**H u d s o n   B a y**
Churchill
James Bay
Belcher Is.
Ivujivik
Inukjuak
Ungava Bay
Kuujjuaq
**N E W F O U N D L A N D**
**LABRADOR**
Schefferville
Goose Bay
Caniapiscau Res.
Hudson Strait

**O N T A R I O**
L. Nipigon
Thunder Bay
Lake Superior
Duluth
Sudbury
Rouyn
Chicoutimi
**Québec**
Sept-Iles
Anticosti I.
St Lawrence
Corner Brook
**Q U É B E C**
Gander
Newfoundland
St John's
C. Race
St Pierre & Miquelon (Fr.)
Cabot Str.
Str. of Belle Isle

**MONTANA**
Helena
**WYOMING**
Yellowstone
Billings
**NORTH DAKOTA**
Bismarck
**SOUTH DAKOTA**
Pierre
Casper
Cheyenne
**NEBRASKA**
**Denver**
Colorado Springs
**COLORADO**
Colorado
Arkansas
**KANSAS**
Topeka
**Kansas City**
Lincoln
**Omaha**
**MINNESOTA**
St Paul
**Minneapolis**
**WISCONSIN**
Madison
**IOWA**
Des Moines
**ILLINOIS**
Springfield
**Chicago**
**Milwaukee**
**MICHIGAN**
Lansing
Lake Michigan
L. Huron
**Detroit**
**Toronto**
Ottawa
**Montréal**
L. Ontario
Albany
**NEW YORK**
Montpelier
N.H.
Concord
**Boston**
MASS.
Providence
R.I.
Hartford
CT.
**New York**
**Philadelphia**
N.J.
Trenton
PENNS.
**Pittsburgh**
Harrisburg
Dover
DEL.
MD.
Annapolis
**Washington D.C.**
Richmond
W.V.
Charleston
Frankfort
**Cincinnati**
OHIO
**Columbus**
**Indianapolis**
INDIANA
St Louis
**MISSOURI**
Jefferson City
Erie
L. Erie
**Cleveland**
Maine
Augusta
Portland
Halifax
**NOVA SCOTIA**
Sable I.
C. Sable
**NEW BRUNSWICK**
P.E.I.
St John
Fredericton
Charlottetown

Missouri
Red
**OKLAHOMA**
Oklahoma City
**ARKANSAS**
Little Rock
**TENNESSEE**
Nashville
**KENTUCKY**
**VIRGINIA**
**Ft Worth**
**Dallas**
**TEXAS**
Austin
**San Antonio**
**Houston**
Baton Rouge
**LOUISIANA**
**New Orleans**
Mississippi
MISS.
Jackson
**Birmingham**
ALABAMA
**Atlanta**
GEORGIA
Montgomery
Tallahassee
**FLORIDA**
Jacksonville
**Tampa**
**Miami**
Str. of Florida
Charlotte
Columbia
S. CAROLINA
N. CAROLINA
Raleigh
C. Hatteras
Charleston
Bermuda (U.K.)

**UNITED STATES OF AMERICA**

**ATLANTIC**
**OCEAN**

**M E X I C O**
Ciudad Victoria
**Guadalajara**
León
Querétaro
**Mexico City**
**Puebla**
Veracruz
Campeche
Bahía de Campeche
Yucatán
Acapulco
G. of Tehuantepec

**G U L F   O F**
**M E X I C O**

Nassau
**THE BAHAMAS**
**Havana**
Camagüey
**CUBA**
Santiago de Cuba
Cayman Is. (U.K.)
Turks & Caicos Is. (U.K.)
Greater Antilles
**HAITI**
Port-au-Prince
**DOMINICAN REP.**
Santo Domingo
**JAMAICA**
Kingston
Virgin Is.
San Juan
Puerto Rico (U.S.A.)
Virgin Is. (U.K.)
Anguilla
**ANTIGUA & BARBUDA**
**ST KITTS NEVIS**
Guadeloupe (Fr.)
Montserrat (U.K.)
**DOMINICA**
Martinique (Fr.)
**ST LUCIA**
**ST VINCENT & THE GRENADINES**
**BARBADOS**
**GRENADA**
Lesser Antilles
**TRINIDAD & TOBAGO**

**PACIFIC**
**OCEAN**

**BELIZE**
Belmopan
Puerto Barrios
**GUATEMALA**
**Guatemala City**
**HONDURAS**
Tegucigalpa
**San Salvador**
**EL SALVADOR**
**NICARAGUA**
Managua
L. Nicaragua
**COSTA RICA**
Puntarenas
Limón
San José
Colón
**PANAMA**
Panama City
G. of Darien

**C A R I B B E A N**
**S E A**
Aruba (Neth.)
Neth. Antilles (Neth.)

**Caracas**
Port of Spain
Orinoco
**VENEZUELA**
**COLOMBIA**
Bogotá
Georgetown
**GUYANA**

**CONTINENTAL FACTS**
TOTAL POPULATION
**450,755,240**
LARGEST COUNTRY POPULATION
**U.S.A. 263,034,000**
LARGEST COUNTRY AREA
**CANADA**
**9,970,610 sq km 3,849,653 sq miles**
LARGEST CITY POPULATION
**MEXICO CITY, Mexico 20,200,000**

**New York.** Covering an area of 777 sq km, the city is made up of five boroughs, of which only one, the Bronx, is on the mainland.

 **CANADA**
FEDERATION
Area: 9,970,610 sq km (3,849,653 sq mls)
Population: 29,606,000
Capital: Ottawa
Language: English, French, Amerindian Languages
Religion: R.Catholic, Protestant, Greek Orthodox
Currency: Dollar

 **UNITED STATES OF AMERICA** (USA)
REPUBLIC
Area: 9,372,610 sq km (3,618,785 sq mls)
Population: 263,034,000
Capital: Washington
Language: English, Spanish, Amerindian Languages
Religion: Protestant, R.Catholic, Muslim, Jewish
Currency: Dollar

 **MEXICO**
REPUBLIC
Area: 1,972,545 sq km (761,604 sq mls)
Population: 90,487,000
Capital: Mexico City
Language: Spanish, Amerindian Languages
Religion: R.Catholic, Protestant
Currency: Peso

**THE BAHAMAS**
MONARCHY
Area: 13,939 sq km (5,382 sq mls)
Population: 278,000
Capital: Nassau
Language: English, Creole, French Creole
Religion: Protestant, R.Catholic
Currency: Dollar

**CUBA**
REPUBLIC
Area: 110,860 sq km (42,803 sq mls)
Population: 11,041,000
Capital: Havana
Language: Spanish
Religion: R.Catholic, Protestant
Currency: Peso

**JAMAICA**
MONARCHY
Area: 10,991 sq km (4,244 sq mls)
Population: 2,530,000
Capital: Kingston
Language: English, Creole
Religion: Protestant, R.Catholic, Rastafarian
Currency: Dollar

 **GUATEMALA**
REPUBLIC
Area: 108,890 sq km (42,043 sq mls)
Population: 10,621,000
Capital: Guatemala City
Language: Spanish, Mayan Languages
Religion: R.Catholic, Protestant
Currency: Quetzal

 **BELIZE**
MONARCHY
Area: 22,965 sq km (8,867 sq mls)
Population: 217,000
Capital: Belmopan
Language: English, Creole, Spanish, Mayan
Religion: R.Catholic, Protestant, Hindu
Currency: Dollar

 **EL SALVADOR**
REPUBLIC
Area: 21,041 sq km (8,124 sq mls)
Population: 5,768,000
Capital: San Salvador
Language: Spanish
Religion: R.Catholic, Protestant
Currency: Cólon

 **DOMINICAN REPUBLIC**
REPUBLIC
Area: 48,442 sq km (18,704 sq mls)
Population: 7,915,000
Capital: Santo Domingo
Language: Spanish, French Creole
Religion: R.Catholic, Protestant
Currency: Peso

 **HAITI**
REPUBLIC
Area: 27,750 sq km (10,714 sq mls)
Population: 7,180,000
Capital: Port-au-Prince
Language: French, French Creole
Religion: R.Catholic, Protestant, Voodoo
Currency: Gourde

**HONDURAS**
REPUBLIC
Area: 112,088 sq km (43,277 sq mls)
Population: 5,953,000
Capital: Tegucigalpa
Language: Spanish, Amerindian Languages
Religion: R.C., Protestant
Currency: Lempira

**NICARAGUA**
REPUBLIC
Area: 130,000 sq km (50,193 sq mls)
Population: 4,539,000
Capital: Managua
Language: Spanish, Amerindian Languages
Religion: R.Catholic, Protestant
Currency: Córdoba

**COSTA RICA**
REPUBLIC
Area: 51,100 sq km (19,730 sq mls)
Population: 3,333,000
Capital: San José
Language: Spanish
Religion: R.Catholic, Protestant
Currency: Cólon

**PANAMA**
REPUBLIC
Area: 77,082 sq km (29,762 sq mls)
Population: 2,631,000
Capital: Panama City
Language: Spanish, English Creole
Religion: R.Catholic, Protestant, Sunni Muslim, Baha'i
Currency: Balboa

**ANTIGUA AND BARBUDA**
MONARCHY
Area: 442 sq km (171 sq mls)
Population: 66,000
Capital: St John's
Language: English, Creole
Religion: Protestant, R.Catholic
Currency: E.Carib.Dollar

**Sayil, Yucatan, Mexico.** Mayan palace of about 85 rooms built between 6thC and 9thC AD.

## POPULATION

 **DOMINICA**
REPUBLIC
Area: 750 sq km (290 sq mls)
Population: 71,000
Capital: Roseau
Language: English, French Creole
Religion: R.Catholic, Protestant
Currency: E.Carib.Dollar, Pound Sterling, French Franc

 **BARBADOS**
MONARCHY
Area: 430 sq km (166 sq mls)
Population: 264,000
Capital: Bridgetown
Language: English, Creole (Bajan)
Religion: Protestant, R.Catholic
Currency: Dollar

 **ST KITTS-NEVIS**
MONARCHY
Area: 261 sq km (101 sq mls)
Population: 42,000
Capital: Basseterre
Language: English, Creole
Religion: Protestant, R.Catholic
Currency: E.Carib.Dollar

**ST VINCENT AND THE GRENADINES**
MONARCHY
Area: 389 sq km (150 sq mls)
Population: 111,000
Capital: Kingstown
Language: English, Creole
Religion: Protestant, R.Catholic
Currency: E.Carib.Dollar

**TRINIDAD AND TOBAGO**
REPUBLIC
Area: 5,130 sq km (1,981 sq mls)
Population: 1,306,000
Capital: Port of Spain
Language: English, Creole, Hindi
Religion: R.Catholic, Hindu, Protestant, Muslem
Currency: Dollar

**GRENADA**
MONARCHY
Area: 378 sq km (146 sq mls)
Population: 92,000
Capital: St George's
Language: English, Creole
Religion: R.Catholic, Protestant
Currency: E.Carib.Dollar

**POPULATION**
Inhabitants
per sq km / per sq ml
over 200 / over 500
100-200 / 250-500
40-100 / 100-250
10-40 / 25-100
2-10 / 5-25
0-2 / 0-5
uninhabited

**CITIES**
- Over 5 million population
• 2.5 - 5 million population

Paramaribo
Cayenne
SURINAME FRENCH GUIANA

© Collins

**St Lawrence I.**
Nunivak I.
Nunivak I.
Nome
Seward Pen.
Norton Sound
**Brooks Range**
Pt Barrow
**B e a u f o r t**
**S e a**
Porcupine

Queen Elizabeth Islands
Prince Patrick Island
Borden I.
Axel Heiberg Island
Ellef Ringnes I.
Amund Ringnes I.

King Frederik VIII Land
Frederik VIII Land
King Christian X Land
King Oscar Fj.
Scoresby Sd

**G r e e n l a n d**

Mt McKinley
**A l a s k a  R a n g e**
Tanana I.
Alaska Pen.
Kodiak I.
**G u l f**
**o f**
**A l a s k a**
Mt Logan
Yukon
**Mackenzie Mts**
**Selwyn Mts**
Mackenzie
Great Bear

Banks I.
Parry Islands
Melville I.
Devon I.

Somerset I.
Prince of Wales I.
Bylot I.
**B a f f i n**
**B a y**
Disko
Home B.

Christian IX Land
King Frederik VI Coast
C. Farewell

Alexander Archipelago
Dixon Entrance
Queen Charlotte Islands
Hecate Str.
**C o a s t  M o u n t a i n s**
Mt Logan
Cassiar Mts
Liard
Caribou Mts
Peace

**V i c t o r i a**
**I s l a n d**
Great Slave
Dubawnt L.

Boothia Pen.
G. of Boothia
King William I.
Melville Peninsula
Prince Charles I.
**B a f f i n  I s l a n d**
Foxe Basin
Nettilling L.
Cumberland Pen.
Cumberland Sd
Foucher B.

**D a v i s  S t r a i t**

**L a b r a d o r**
**S e a**

Vancouver Island
Blanco
**C a s c a d e  R a**
**C o a s t  R a n g e**
Columbia
Fraser
**R O C K Y  M O U N T A I N S**
F. D. Roosevelt L.
Fort Peck Res.
Bitterfoot Ra
L. Sakakawea

Lake Athabasca
Wollaston L.
Reindeer L.
Southern Indian L.
Churchill
Nelson
Severn

Southampton I.
Coats I.
Mansel I.
**H u d s o n**
**B a y**
Belcher Is
James Bay

Ungava Bay
Hudson Strait
C. Chidley

**L a b r a d o r**
Caniapiscau Res.
Smallwood Res.
L. Bienville
La Grande Res.

**S i e r r a  N e v a d a**
Snake
Great Basin
Great Salt L.
Yellowstone
L. Oahe
Missouri
Arkansas

L. Winnipegosis
Lake Winnipeg
L. Sakakawea
L. Winnipeg
Lake of the Woods
L. Nipigon
Lake Superior
L. Michigan
Huron

St Lawrence
Anticosti I.
Str. of Belle Isle
Gulf of St Lawrence
Cabot Str.
**Newfoundland**
C. Race
St Pierre & Miquelon
Cape Breton I.
Sable I.

**C o l o r a d o**
**P l a t e a u**
Grand Canyon
Colorado
Llano Estacado
Red
Ozark Plateau
Ohio
Mississippi
**A p p a l a c h i a n  M t s**
Allegheny Mts
Chesapeake B.
C. Hatteras
C. Fear
L. Erie
L. Ontario
Long I.
Massachusetts Bay
C. Sable
C. Cod

I. Socorro
Baja California
**G u l f  o f  C a l i f o r n i a**
Rio Grande
**S i e r r a  M a d r e  O c c i d e n t a l**
**S i e r r a  M a d r e  O r i e n t a l**
Edwards Plateau

Bermuda

**A T L A N T I C**
**O C E A N**

C. Canaveral
Gd Bahama
Gt Abaco
Str. of Florida
Andros
Acklins I.
Turks & Caicos Is
Gt Inagua

**G U L F  O F**
**M E X I C O**
Bahía de Campeche
Yucatán
Yucatán Channel
Cayman Is
**G r e a t e r  A n t i l l e s**
**C u b a**
**H i s p a n i o l a**
Puerto Rico
Anguilla
Virgin Is
Guadeloupe
Dominica
Martinique
St Lucia

S.a Madre del Sur
**P A C I F I C**
**O C E A N**
G. of Honduras
Jamaica
**C A R I B B E A N**
**S E A**
Aruba
Neth. Antilles
**L e s s e r  A n t i l l e s**
L. Nicarâgua
Pen. de Nicoya
G. of Darien
Orinoco
Trinidad

---

**CONTINENTAL FACTS**
TOTAL AREA
**25,680,331 sq km   9,529,076 sq miles**
HIGHEST PEAK, MT McKINLEY
**6,194 m   20,321 ft**
LARGEST LAKE, SUPERIOR
**83,270 sq km   32,140 sq miles**
LONGEST RIVER, MISSISSIPPI-MISSOURI
**6,020 km   3,740 miles**

**Guatemala.** Deforestation as a result of pressure for land to sustain families and their crops.

**Mt McKinley, Alaska.** The highest peak in North America can generate its own weather system due to its comparative height and isolation.

## CLIMATE

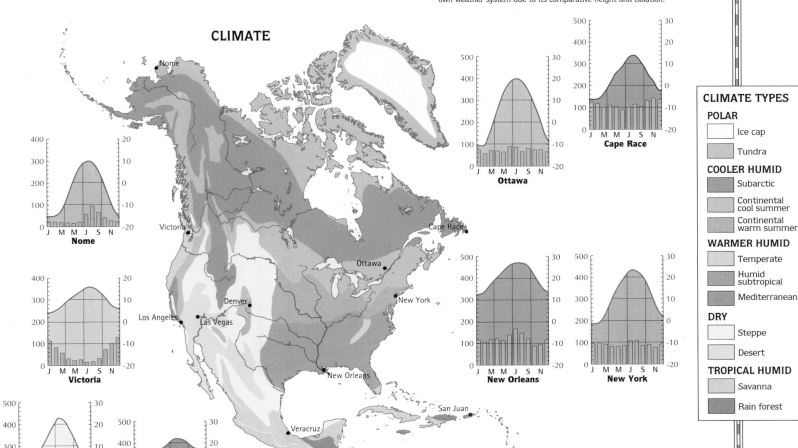

**Ottawa**

**Cape Race**

**Nome**

**Victoria**

**New Orleans**

**New York**

**Denver**

**Los Angeles**

**Las Vegas**

**San Juan**

### CLIMATE TYPES

**POLAR**
- Ice cap
- Tundra

**COOLER HUMID**
- Subarctic
- Continental cool summer
- Continental warm summer

**WARMER HUMID**
- Temperate
- Humid subtropical
- Mediterranean

**DRY**
- Steppe
- Desert

**TROPICAL HUMID**
- Savanna
- Rain forest

Rain mm

Temp °C

average monthly temperature

colour refers to climate type shown on map

average monthly rainfall

**Veracruz**

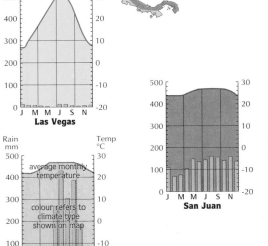

**St Lucia.** Stunning scenery and a tropical climate have helped make the Caribbean a popular holiday destination.

**Bryce Canyon, Utah.** Weathered sandstone formations in canyons up to 300m deep.

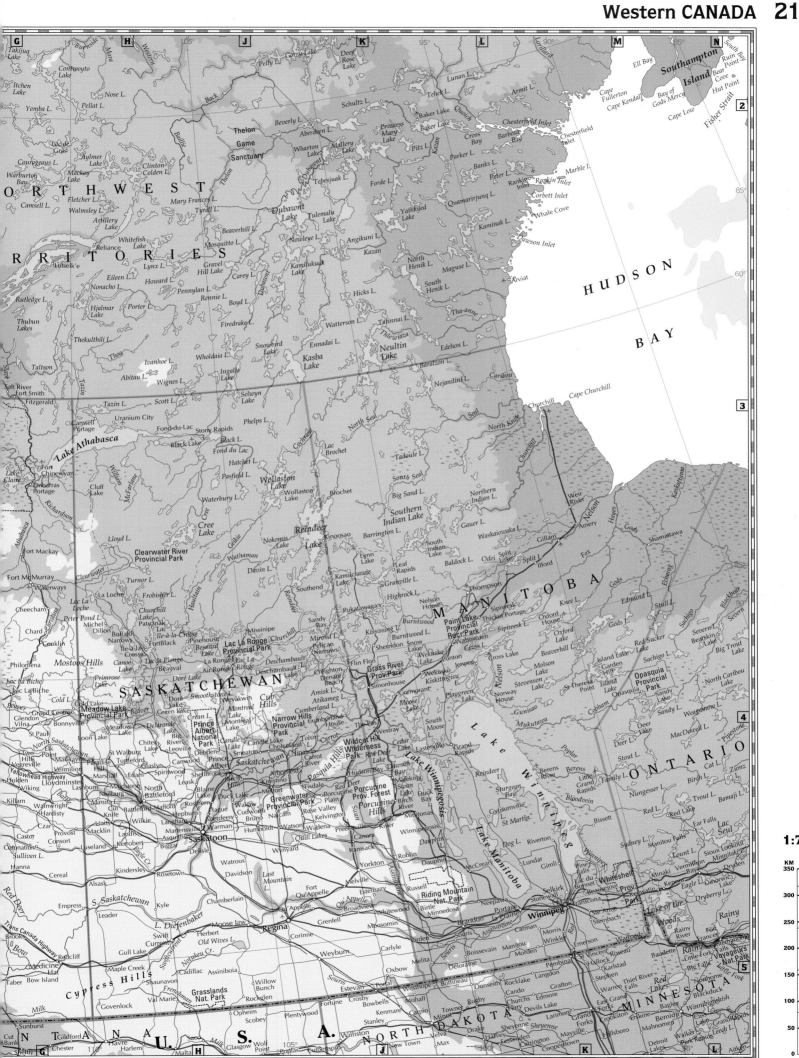

**NORTHWEST TERRITORIES**

Takijua Lake
Burnside
Contwoyto Lake
Itchen Lake
Yamba L.
Nose L.
Pellat L.
Marra
Western
Pelly Lake
Garry Lake
Deep Rose Lake
Southampton Island
Ell Bay
Bear Point
Ruin Point
Hut Point
Lac de Gras
Courageous L.
Mackay Lake
Aylmer Lake
Clinton Colden L.
Back
Baillie
Thelon
Game Sanctuary
Beverly L.
Aberdeen L.
Schultz L.
Tehek L.
Lunan L.
Armit L.
Bay of Gods Mercy
Cape Fullerton
Cape Kendall
Cape Low
Fisher Strait

Warburton Bay
Camsell L.
Fletcher L.
Walmsley L.
Artillery Lake
Whitefish Lake
Reliance
Mary Frances L.
Tyrrll L.
Dubawnt Lake
Wharton Lake
Mallery Lake
Princess Mary Lake
Baker Lake
Quoich
Baker Lake
Cross Bay
Barbour Bay
Chesterfield Inlet
Chesterfield

Rutledge L.
Thubun Lakes
Taltson
Hjalmar Lake
Porter L.
Firedrake L.
Thekulthili L.
Thoa
Ivanhoe L.
Wignes L.
Abitau L.
Ingalls Lake
Selwyn Lake
Kasba Lake
Neultin Lake
Baralzon L.
Caribou
Nejanilini L.
Cape Churchill

**HUDSON BAY**

Lake Athabasca
Uranium City
Camsell Portage
Fond-du-Lac
Stony Rapids
Black Lake
Fond du Lac
Hatchet L.
Wollaston Lake
Brochet
South Seal
Big Sand L.
Northern Indian L.
Churchill
Weir River
Nelson

**SASKATCHEWAN**

**MANITOBA**

Fort McMurray
Clearwater River Provincial Park
Reindeer Lake
Lac La Ronge Provincial Park
Lake Winnipeg
Lake Manitoba
Lake Winnipegosis

Saskatoon
Regina
Prince Albert
Winnipeg

**ONTARIO**

**U.S.A.**

**NORTH DAKOTA**
**MINNESOTA**

© Collins

1:7M

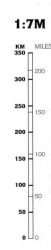

KM 350 / MILES
300
250
200
150
100
50
0

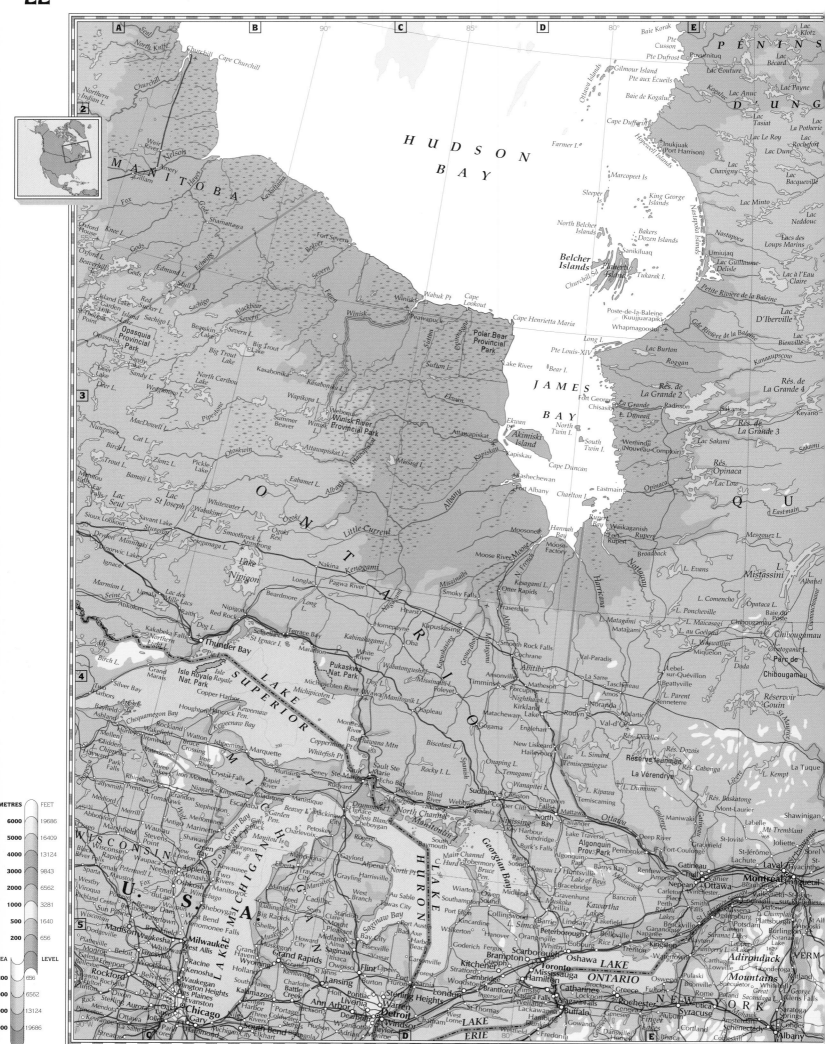

HUDSON BAY

JAMES BAY

MANITOBA

ONTARIO

QUÉBEC

PÉNINSULE D'UNGAVA

WISCONSIN

U.S.A.

NEW YORK

LAKE SUPERIOR

LAKE MICHIGAN

LAKE HURON

LAKE ERIE

LAKE ONTARIO

Georgian Bay

METRES    FEET
6000      19686
5000      16409
4000      13124
3000      9843
2000      6562
1000      3281
500       1640
200       656
SEA       LEVEL
200       656
2000      6562
4000      13124
6000      19686

Transverse Mercator Projection

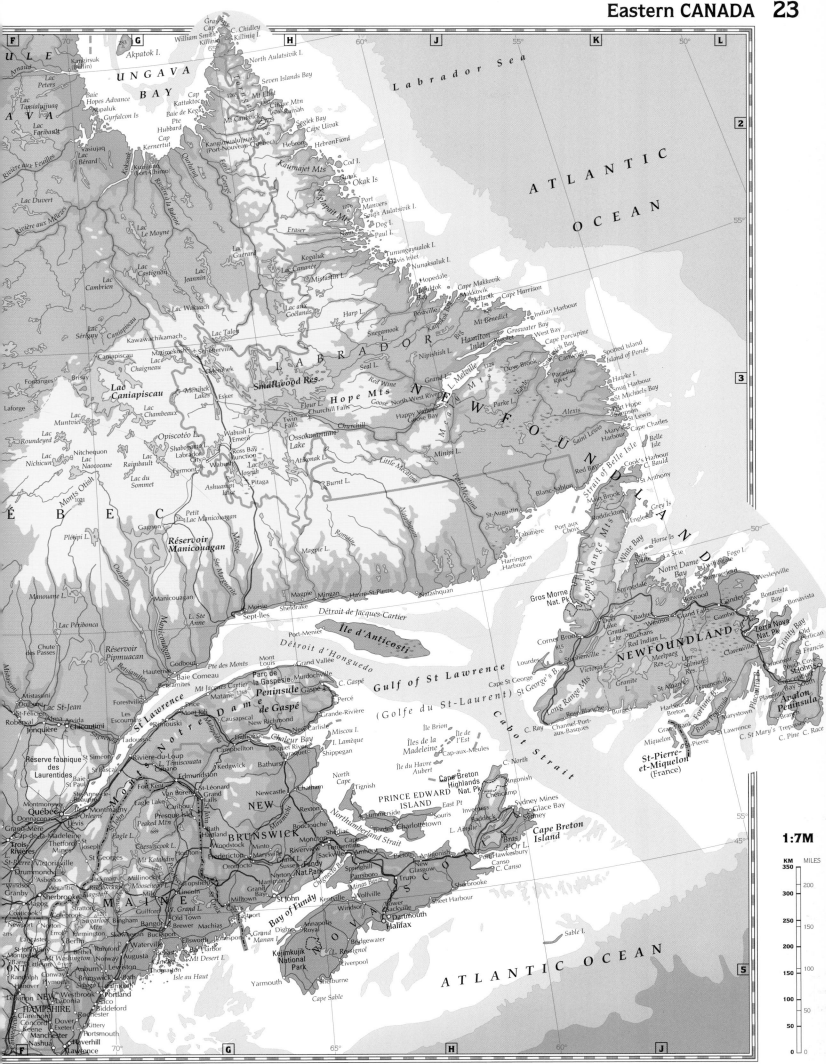

Lambert Conformal Conic Projection

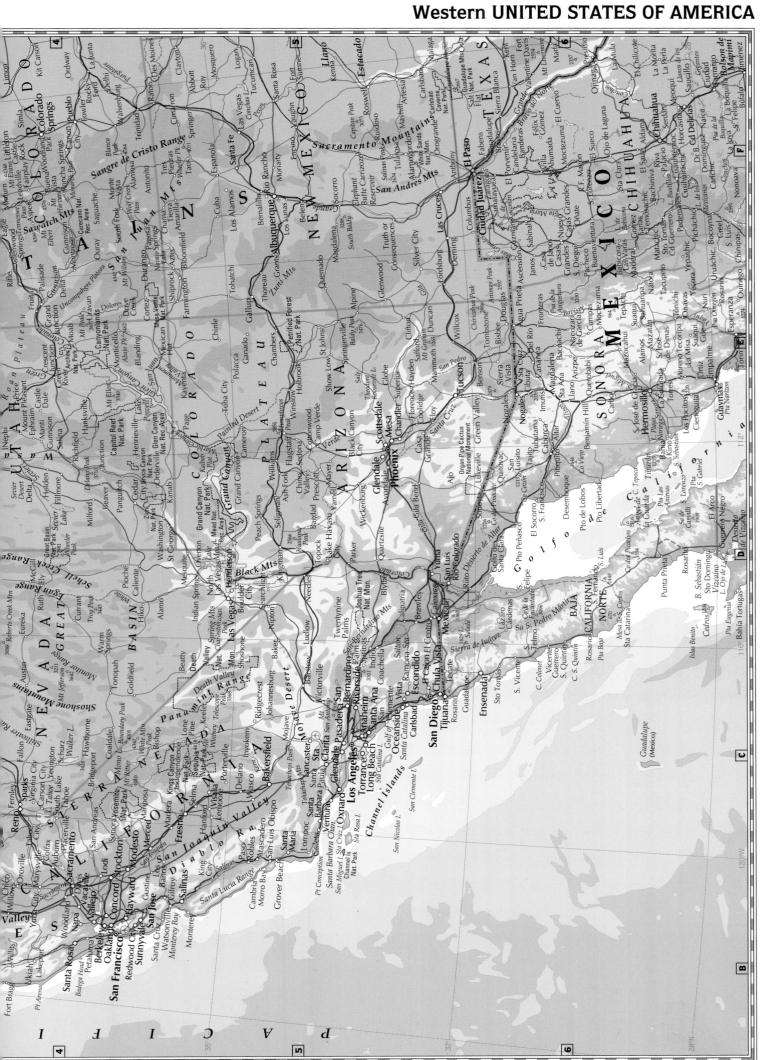

1:7M

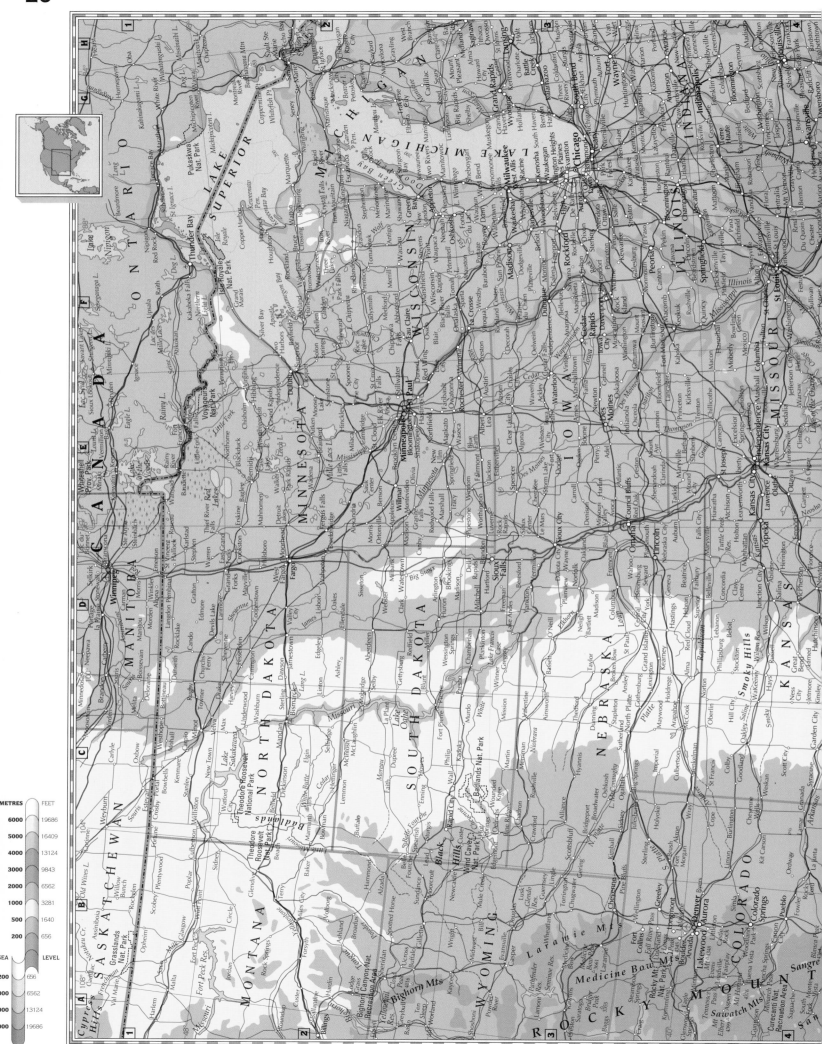

Lambert Conformal Conic Projection

1:7M

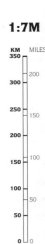

© Collins

1:7M

| KM | MILES |
|---|---|
| 350 | |
| 300 | 200 |
| 250 | 150 |
| 200 | |
| 150 | 100 |
| 100 | |
| 50 | 50 |
| 0 | 0 |

© Collins

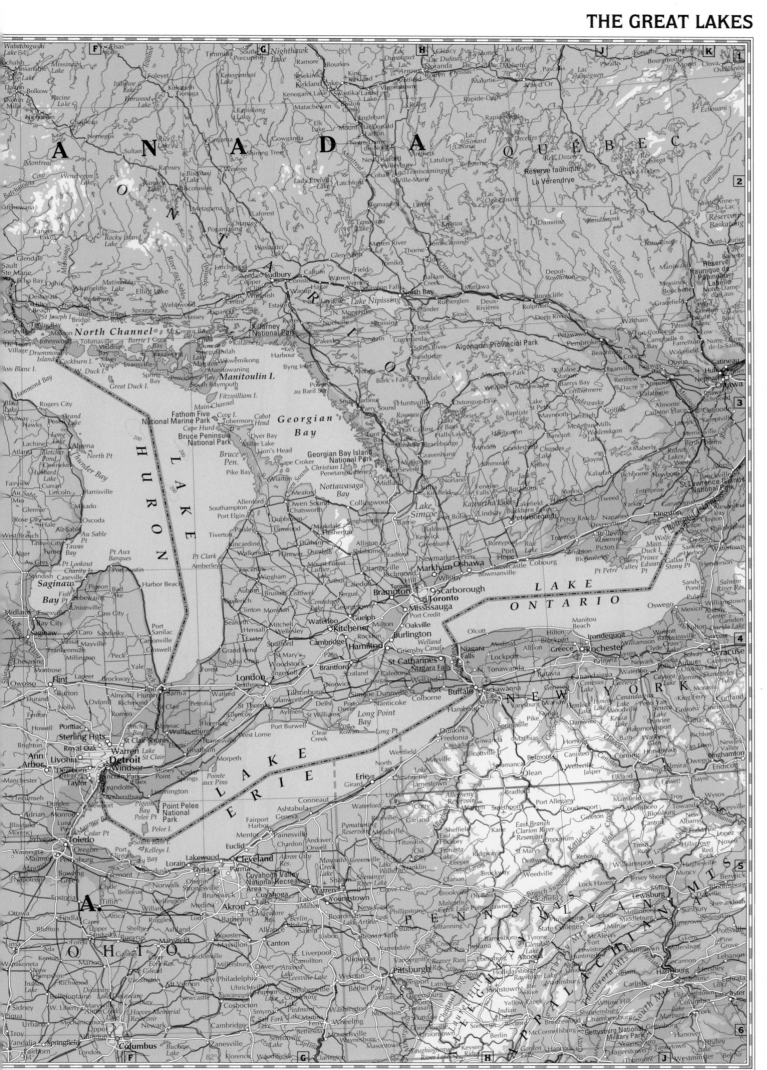

1:3.5M

© Collins

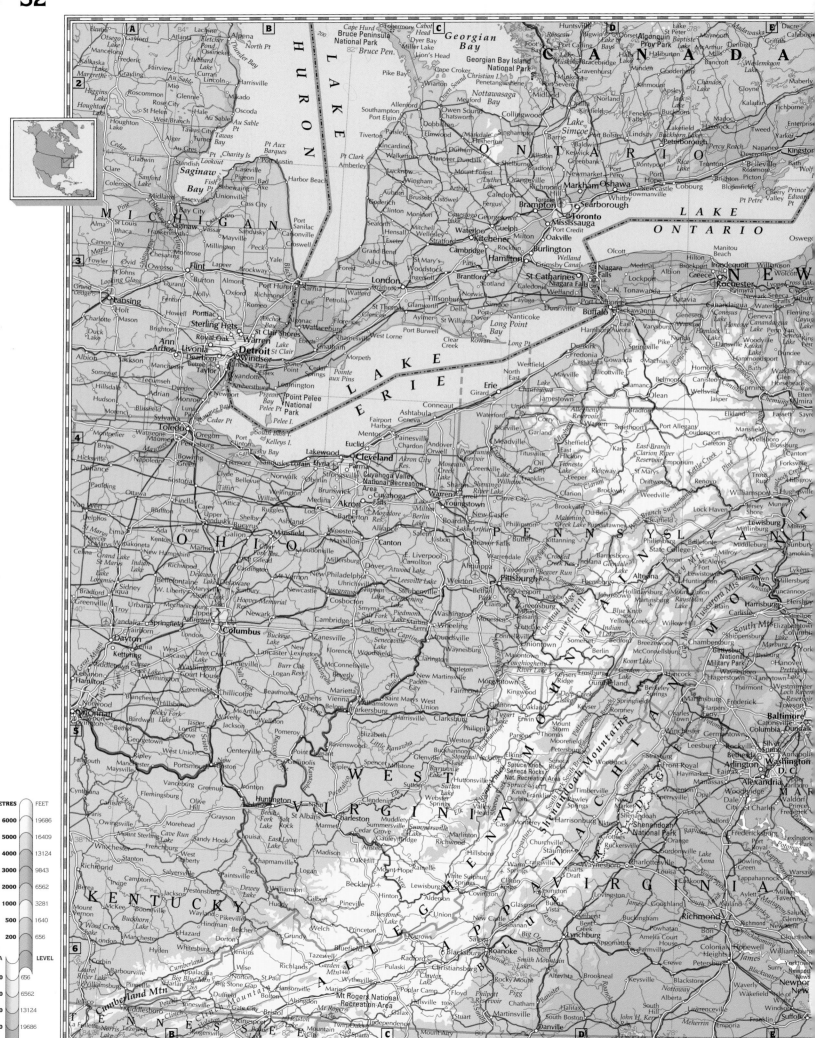

1:3.5M

continuation at the same scale

© Collins

Lambert Conformal Conic Projection

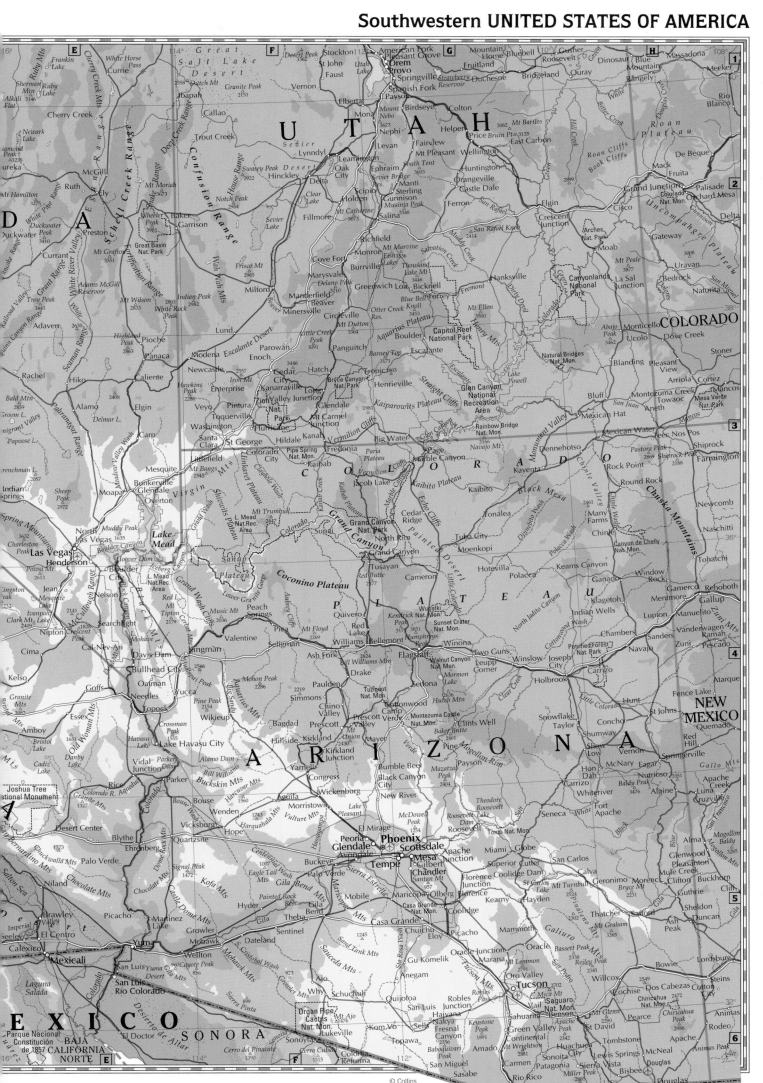

1:3.5M

Lambert Azimuthal Equal Area Projection

ATLANTIC OCEAN

BERMUDA (U.K.) Hamilton

NORTH CAROLINA

SOUTH CAROLINA

GEORGIA

THE BAHAMAS

Grand Bahama
Little Abaco
Great Abaco
Freeport
Eleuthera
Berry Is
Nassau
Andros
San Salvador (Watling)
Cat Island
Rum Cay
Long Island
Great Exuma
Crooked Island
Acklins Island
Mayaguana

Tropic of Cancer

TURKS AND CAICOS ISLANDS (U.K.)

Caicos Is
Cockburn Town
Turks Is

HISPANIOLA

LEEWARD ISLANDS

Anegada (U.K.)
ANGUILLA (U.K.)
VIRGIN IS (U.K.)
Saint Martin (Fr.)
St Maarten (Neth.)
VIRGIN IS (U.S.A.)
St Barthélemy (Fr.)
ANTIGUA AND BARBUDA
St John's
ST KITTS-NEVIS
MONTSERRAT (U.K.)
GUADELOUPE (Fr.)
Marie Galante
Roseau
DOMINICA
MARTINIQUE (Fr.)
Fort-de-France
Castries
ST LUCIA
ST VINCENT & THE GRENADINES
Kingstown
Bridgetown
BARBADOS
GRENADA
St George's
TRINIDAD AND TOBAGO
Scarborough
Port of Spain
WINDWARD ISLANDS

CUBA
Havana (Habana)
Matanzas
Pinar del Río
Cienfuegos
Santa Clara
Sancti Spíritus
Ciego de Ávila
Camagüey
Holguín
Bayamo
Santiago de Cuba
Guantánamo

GREATER ANTILLES

CAYMAN ISLANDS (U.K.)
Grand Cayman
Little Cayman
Cayman Brac

JAMAICA
Montego Bay
Kingston
Spanish Town
Mandeville

HAITI
Port-au-Prince
Gonaïves
Cap-Haïtien
Jérémie
Les Cayes
Jacmel

DOMINICAN REPUBLIC
Santiago
Santo Domingo
La Romana
Barahona

PUERTO RICO (U.S.A.)
San Juan
Ponce
Mayagüez
Aguadilla

CARIBBEAN SEA

LESSER ANTILLES

NETHERLANDS ANTILLES
ARUBA (Neth.)
Curaçao
Bonaire
Willemstad

VENEZUELA
Caracas
Maracaibo
Valencia
Barquisimeto
Barcelona
Maturín
Ciudad Bolívar
Ciudad Guayana

COLOMBIA
Barranquilla
Cartagena
Medellín
Bogotá
Cali
Manizales
Pereira

PANAMA
Panamá
Colón
David

COSTA RICA
San José

NICARAGUA
Managua

HONDURAS

1:14M

KM 700
600
500
400
300
200
100
0

MILES
400
300
200
100
0

© Collins

**CONTINENTAL FACTS**
TOTAL POPULATION
**314,932,206**
LARGEST COUNTRY POPULATION
**BRAZIL 155,822,000**
LARGEST COUNTRY AREA
**BRAZIL**
**8,511,965 sq km 3,286,470 sq miles**
LARGEST CITY POPULATION
**SÃO PAULO, Brazil 15,199,423**

*CARIBBEAN SEA*

**VENEZUELA**
REPUBLIC
Area: 912,050 sq km
(352,144 sq mls)
Population: 21,644,000
Capital: Caracas
Language: Spanish,
Amerindian Languages
Religion: R.Catholic, Protestant
Currency: Bolívar

**GUYANA**
REPUBLIC
Area: 214,969 sq km
(83,000 sq mls)
Population: 835,000
Capital: Georgetown
Language: English, Creole, Hindi,
Amerindian Language
Religion: Protestant, Hindu,
R.Catholic, Sunni
Muslim
Currency: Dollar

*ATLANTIC*

*OCEAN*

*Aruba*
*(Neth.)*
*Netherlands*
*Antilles*
*Curaçao*
*Lesser Antilles*
**TRINIDAD &**
**TOBAGO**
Port of Spain

Barranquilla
Cartagena
Maracaibo
Valencia
Caracas
Cumaná
Barquisimeto
Montería
Ciudad Guayana

**VENEZUELA**

Georgetown
Paramaribo
Cayenne
**FRENCH**
**GUIANA**
**SURINAME**

Medellín
Manizales
**Bogotá**
Buenaventura
**Cali**
Boa Vista

**COLOMBIA**
Florencia
*Orinoco*

*Orinoco*
*Negro*

*Amazon*
*Delta*

*Galapagos Islands*
*(Ecuador)*

Quito
Portoviejo
**ECUADOR**
**Guayaquil**
Cuenca
Iquitos
*Marañón*
*Amazon*

*Amazon*
**Manaus**
Itaituba
Altamira
**Belém**
São Luís
Parnaíba
Bacabal
Codó
**Fortaleza**
Teresina
Maraba
Imperatriz

Piura
Chiclayo
Trujillo
Pucallpa

*Purus*

**B   R   A   Z   I   L**

Araguaína

*São Francisco*

**Salvador**

*PACIFIC*
Callao
**Lima**

**PERU**
Pôrto Velho
Rio Branco
Ariquemes

*OCEAN*
Ica
Ayacucho

Trinidad
Cáceres
Cuiabá
**Brasília**
Espinosa
Goiânia
Teófilo
Otôni

Juliaca
*Lake Titicaca*
Arequipa
**La Paz**
Cochabamba
Santa Cruz
**BOLIVIA**
Sucre
*Izozog*
*Marshes*
Uberaba
**Belo Horizonte**
Vitória

Arica
Potosí
Campo Grande
Nova
Iguaçu
Campos

Iquique
Tarija
Douardos
Aracatuba
**Campinas**
**Rio de Janeiro**

Calama
Antofagasta
San Salvador
de Jujuy
**PARAGUAY**
**São Paulo**
Sto André

*Islas de los*
*Desventurados*
*(Chile)*
San Pedro
Asunción
Foz do Iguaçu
**Curitiba**

San Miguel
de Tucumán
Florianopolis

Catamarca
Corrientes
Posadas

*Juan Fernandez*
*Islands*
*(Chile)*
La Serena
**Córdoba**
Santa Fé
Santa Maria
Uruguaiana
**Porto**
**Alegre**

*Aconcagua*
San Juan
*A.6960*
Mendoza
Paraná
Tacuarembó
Rio Grande
Valparaíso
Rosario
**URUGUAY**
**Santiago**

Talca
**Buenos Aires**
La Plata
**Montevideo**
Rocha

Concepción
Santa Rosa

Temuco
Bahía Blanca
Neuquén
Mar del Plata

**COLOMBIA**
REPUBLIC
Area: 1,141,748 sq km
(440,831 sq mls)
Population: 35,099,000
Capital: Bogotá
Language: Spanish, Amerindian
Languages
Religion: R.Catholic, Protestant
Currency: Peso

**ECUADOR**
REPUBLIC
Area: 272,045 sq km
(105,037 sq mls)
Population: 11,460,000
Capital: Quito
Language: Spanish, Quechua,
Amerindian Languages
Religion: R.Catholic, Protestant
Currency: Sucre

**PERU**
REPUBLIC
Area: 1,285,216 sq km
(496,225 sq mls)
Population: 23,560,000
Capital: Lima
Language: Spanish, Quechua, Aymara
Religion: R.Catholic, Protestant
Currency: Sol

**BOLIVIA**
REPUBLIC
Area: 1,098,581 sq km
(424,164 sq mls)
Population: 7,414,000
Capital: La Paz
Language: Spanish, Quechua, Aymara
Religion: R. Catholic, Protestant,
Baha'i
Currency: Boliviano

**CHILE**
REPUBLIC
Area: 756,945 sq km
(292,258 sq mls)
Population: 14,210,000
Capital: Santiago
Language: Spanish,
Amerindian Languages
Religion: R. Catholic, Protestant
Currency: Peso

*Atacama Desert*

**C   H   I   L   E**

**A   R   G   E   N   T   I   N   A**

*P   A   T   A   G   O   N   I   A*

Viedma
Puerto Montt
*Isla de*
*Chiloé*
Esquel
Rawson

*Archipiélago de*
*los Chonos*
Comodoro
Rivadavia
Deseado
*Pta Medanosa*

Cochrane
*Falkland Islands*
*(UK)*
Puerto Natales
Río Gallegos
Stanley
*Strait of*
*Magellan*
Punta Arenas
*Tierra del*
*Fuego*
Ushuaia
*Cape Horn*

*South Georgia (UK)*

**PARAGUAY**
REPUBLIC
Area: 406,752 sq km
(157,048 sq mls)
Population: 4,828,000
Capital: Asunción
Language: Spanish, Guaraní
Religion: R.Catholic, Protestant
Currency: Guaraní

**ARGENTINA**
REPUBLIC
Area: 2,766,889 sq km
(1,068,302 sq mls)
Population: 34,768,000
Capital: Buenos Aires
Language: Spanish, Italian,
Amerindian Languages
Religion: R.Catholic, Protestant,
Jewish
Currency: Peso

**URUGUAY**
REPUBLIC
Area: 176,215 sq km
(68,037 sq mls)
Population: 3,186,000
Capital: Montevideo
Language: Spanish
Religion: R.Catholic, Protestant,
Jewish
Currency: Peso

**Peru.** Local Uros Indians make fishing boats by collecting and tying together the reeds found around Lake Titicaca.

Natal

João Pessoa

**Recife**

Maceió

Aracaju

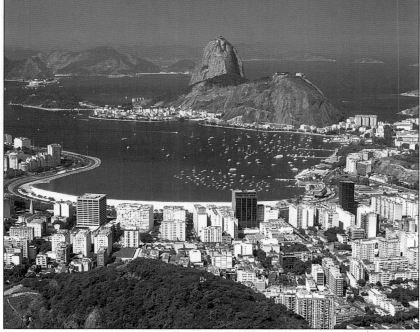

**Rio de Janeiro.** Sugar Loaf Mountain stands at the entrance to the harbour in one of Brazil's major ports.

 **SURINAME**

REPUBLIC

Area: 163,820 sq km
(63,251 sq mls)
Population: 423,000
Capital: Paramaribo
Language: Dutch, Surinamese,
English, Hindi, Javanese
Religion: Hindu, R.Catholic,
Protestant, Sunni
Muslim
Currency: Guilder

 **FRENCH GUIANA**

FRENCH TERRITORY

Area: 90,000 sq km
(34,749 sq mls)
Population: 147,000
Capital: Cayenne
Language: French, French Creole
Religion: R.Catholic, Protestant
Currency: French Franc

 **BRAZIL**

REPUBLIC

Area: 8,511,965 sq km
(3,286,470 sq mls)
Population: 155,822,000
Capital: Brasília
Language: Portuguese, German,
Japanese, Italian,
Amerindian Languages
Religion: R. Catholic, Spiritist,
Protestant
Currency: Real

# POPULATION

Caracas

Bogotá

Recife

Lima

Belo Horizonte

Rio de Janeiro

São Paulo

Pôrto Alegre

Santiago

Buenos Aires

| POPULATION | |
|---|---|
| Inhabitants | |
| per sq km | per sq ml |
| over 200 | over 500 |
| 100-200 | 250-500 |
| 40-100 | 100-250 |
| 10-40 | 25-100 |
| 2-10 | 5-25 |
| 0-2 | 0-5 |
| uninhabited | |

**CITIES**

■ Over 5 million
population

● 2.5 - 5 million
population

**La Parva, Chile.** A resort in the Andes near Santiago where skiing is possible to over 3600m.

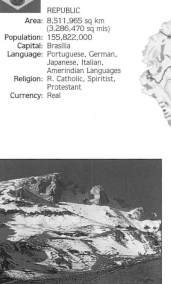

CARIBBEAN SEA

ATLANTIC OCEAN

L. Nicaragua

Gallinas Pt
Aruba
Netherlands Antilles
Curaçao
Lesser Antilles
Margarita

Trinidad

G. of Darien

L. Maracaibo

Orinoco

Orinoco Delta

Waini Point

Cordillera Occidental

Cordillera Central

Cordillera Oriental

Llanos

Meta

Guaviare

Pointe Isère

Cabo Orange

Cotopaxi
5896

Chimborazo
6310

Caquetá

Putumayo

Iapurá

Negro

Branco

Balbina Resr.

Amazon Delta

I. de Marajó

Amazon

Tocantins

Parnaíba

A
N
D
E
S

Cordillera Central

Huascarán
6768

Ucayali

Amazon

Purus

Juruá

Madeira

Tapajós

Iriri

Xingu

Tucuruí Resr.

Tocantins

Selvas

Beni

Guaporé

Jiparaná

Teles Pires

Juruena

Arinos

Araguaia

São Francisco

Cordillera Oriental

Lake Titicaca

Lago de San Luis

Yungas

San Miguel

Planalto do Mato Grosso

Planalto do Brasil

Cordillera Occidental

Altiplano

L. Poopó

Cordillera Central

Izozog Marshes

Paraguay

Paranaíba

Grande

Velhas

PACIFIC OCEAN

Cabo de São Tomé

C. Frio

Pta Tetas

Atacama Desert

Gran Chaco

Pilcomayo

Teuco

Paraná

Paranapanema

Iguaçu Falls

ATLANTIC OCEAN

Islas de los Desventurados
(Chile)

Pta Ballena

Pta Morro

Salado

Uruguay

Juan Fernandez Islands
(Chile)

Salinas Grandes

Desaguadero

Sierras de Córdoba

Paraná

Aconcagua
6960

Pampas

Lagoa dos Patos

Lagoa Mirim

Rio de la Plata

Colorado

Bahía Blanca

Negro

Golfo San Matías

Península Valdés

Isla de Chiloé

Archipiélago de los Chonos

Golfo de Penas

Golfo de San Jorge

Pta Medanosa

P
A
T
A
G
O
N
I
A

L. San Martín

Argentina

Strait of Magellan

Tierra del Fuego

I. de los Estados

Cape Horn

**Falkland Islands**
West Falkland
East Falkland

---

**Iguaçu Falls.** These spectacular waterfalls on the border of Brazil and Argentina plunge between 60 and 80 m.

**Jaguar.** Found in Amazonia and the Gran Chaco, these big cats vary from the colour of the one in the photograph to plain black or white coats.

---

**CONTINENTAL FACTS**
TOTAL AREA
17,815,420 sq km   6,878,534 sq miles
HIGHEST PEAK, ACONCAGUA
6,960 m   22,834 ft
LARGEST LAKE, TITICACA
8,340 sq km   3,220 sq miles
LONGEST RIVER, AMAZON
6,516 km   4,048 miles

# CLIMATE

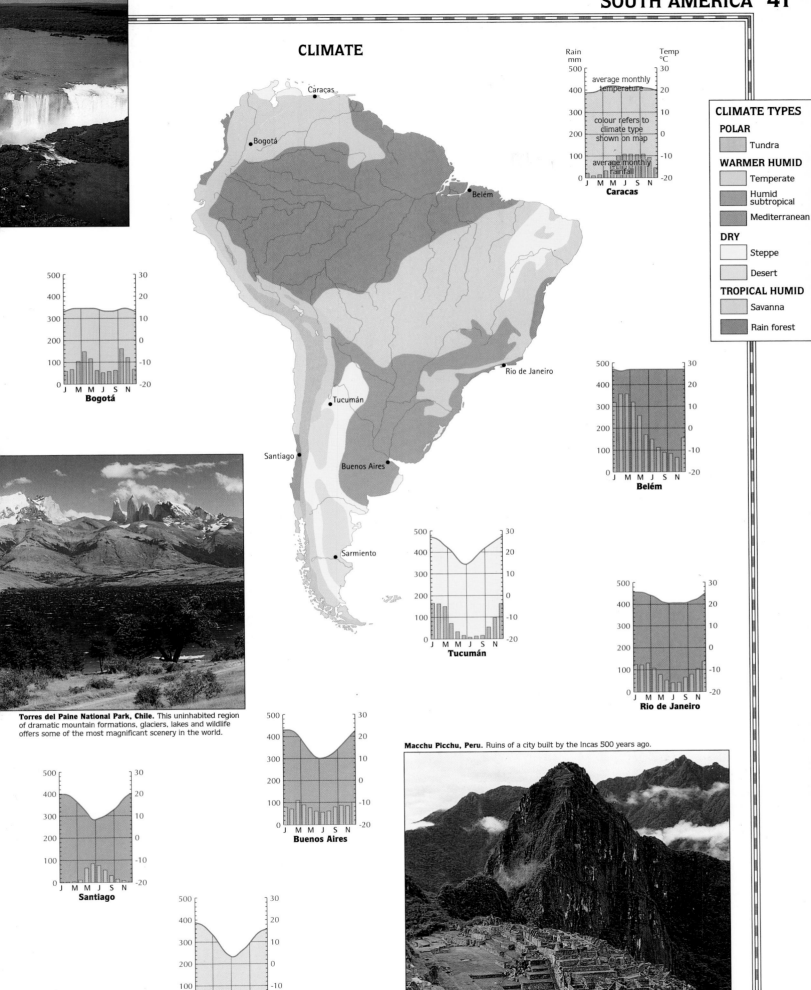

Rain mm / Temp °C

**Caracas**
- average monthly temperature
- colour refers to climate type shown on map
- average monthly rainfall

## CLIMATE TYPES

**POLAR**
- Tundra

**WARMER HUMID**
- Temperate
- Humid subtropical
- Mediterranean

**DRY**
- Steppe
- Desert

**TROPICAL HUMID**
- Savanna
- Rain forest

**Bogotá**

**Belém**

**Tucumán**

**Rio de Janeiro**

**Buenos Aires**

**Santiago**

**Sarmiento**

**Torres del Paine National Park, Chile.** This uninhabited region of dramatic mountain formations, glaciers, lakes and wildlife offers some of the most magnificant scenery in the world.

**Macchu Picchu, Peru.** Ruins of a city built by the Incas 500 years ago.

© Collins

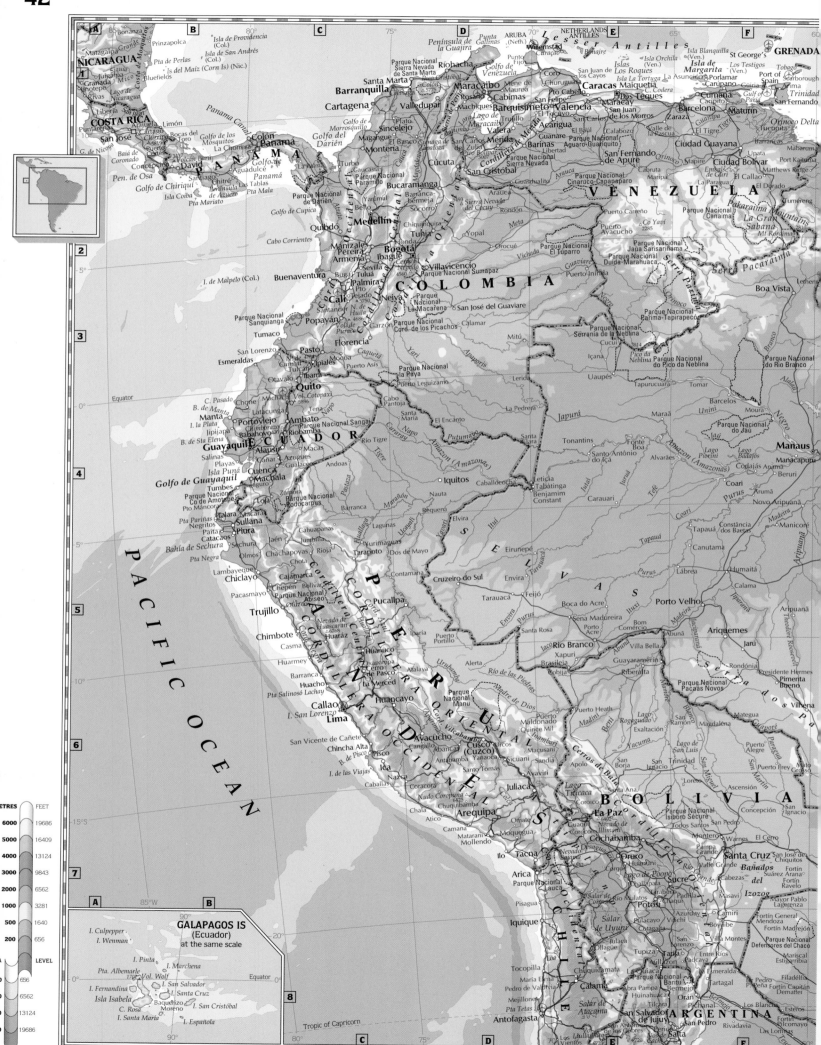

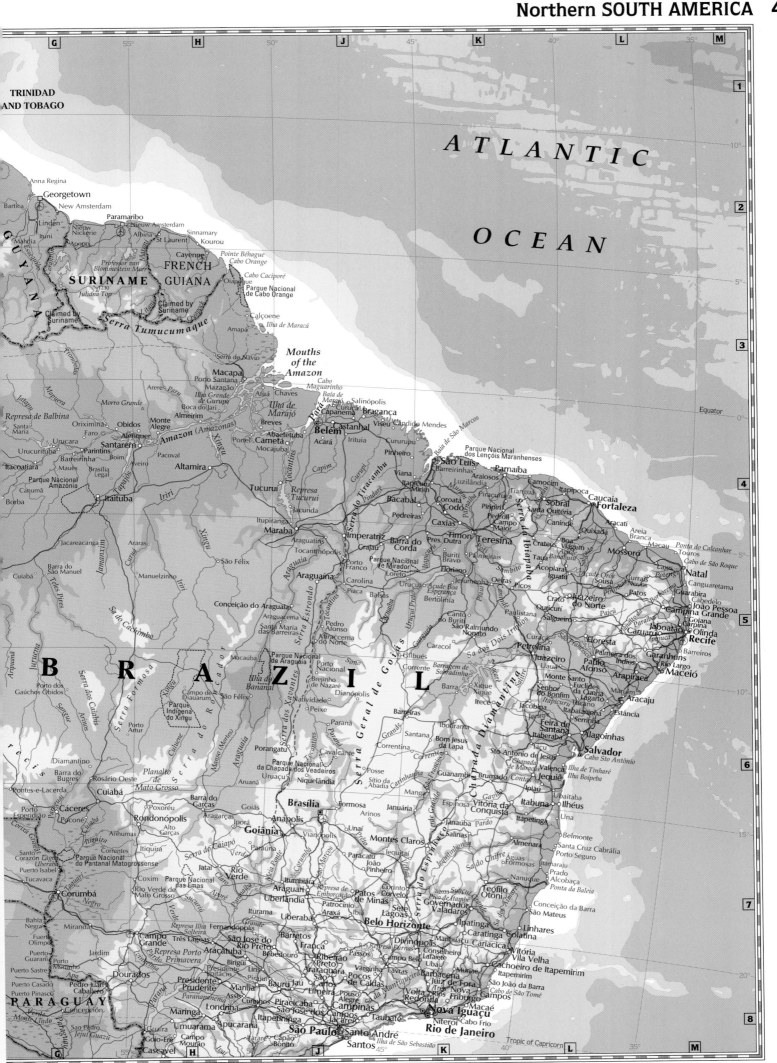

ATLANTIC

OCEAN

**TRINIDAD
AND TOBAGO**

TRINIDAD AND TOBAGO

Anna Regina
Bartica
Georgetown
New Amsterdam
Linden
Ituni
Nieuw
Nickerie
Paramaribo
Nieuw Amsterdam
Albina
St Laurent
Sinnamary
Kourou
Mahdia
**GUYANA**
**SURINAME**
Cayenne
**FRENCH
GUIANA**
Professor van
Blommestein Meer
Juliana Top
Claimed by
Suriname
Pointe Béhague
Cabo Orange
Oiapoque
Parque Nacional
de Cabo Orange
Claimed by
Suriname
Serra Tumucumaque
Calçoene
Ilha de Maracá

Mouths
of the
Amazon

Serra do Navio
Macapá
Porto Santana
Mazagão
Cabo
Maguarinho
Baía de
Marajó
Salinópolis
Arere
Paru
Ilha Grande
de Gurupá
Afuá
Chaves
Curuçá
Bragança
Morro Grande
Breves
Abaetetuba
Capanema
Viseu
Cândido Mendes
Boca do Jari
Almeirim
Portel
Cametá
Acará
Irituia
Pinheiro
Cururupu
Parque Nacional
dos Lençóis Maranhenses
Oriximiná
Óbidos
Monte
Alegre
**Belém**
Castanhal
Baía de São Marcos
Santa
Maria
Alenquer
Santarém
Boim
Aveiro
Pacoval
**São Luís**
Viana
Barreirinhas
Parnaíba
Camocim
Urucará
Parintins
Barreirinha
Brasília
Legal
Altamira
Itapecuru
Mirim
Araioses
Luzilândia
Piracuruca
Tianguá
Itapipoca
Caucaia
**Fortaleza**
Itacoatiara
Maués
Bacabal
Coroatá
Codó
Pinpiri
Campo
Maior
Sobral
Santa Quitéria
Canindé
Aracati
Parque Nacional
Amazônia
Canumã
Borba
Itaituba
Tapajós
Iriri
Tucuruí
Represa
Tucuruí
Jacundá
Itupiranga
Pedreiras
Caxias
Timon
Teresina
Pres.
Dutra
Buriti
Bravo
Oeiras
Picos
Crateús
Boa
Viagem
Taua
Açude Orós
Iguatu
Acopiara
Quixadá
Quixeramobim
Mossoró
Areia
Branca
Macau
Ponta do Calcanhar
**Maraba**
Imperatriz
Barra do
Corda
Floriano
Canto
do Buriti
São
Raimundo
Nonato
Paulistana
Salgueiro
Serra da Ibiapaba
Crato
**Juazeiro
do Norte**
Patos
Currais
Novos
Cabo de São Roque
**Natal**
Guarabira
Tocantinópolis
Grajaú
Porto
Franco
Carolina
Loreto
Balsas
Bertolínia
Canto do
Buriti
Paulistana
Curral
Novos
Campina
Grande
**João Pessoa**
Cabedelo
**Araguaína**
Piaca
Conceição do Araguaia
Araguacema
Santa Maria
das Barreiras
Pedro
Afonso
Miracema
do Norte
Caracol
São
Raimundo
Nonato
Serra do
Boqueirão
Paraíba
Gojana
Olinda
Jaboatão
Carpina
Caruaru
**Recife**
Conceição do Araguaia
Macaúba
Parque Nacional
de Araguaia
Porto
Nacional
Brejinho
de Nazaré
Dianópolis
Barragem de
Sobradinho
Barra
Xique
Xique
Irecê
Petrolina
**Juazeiro**
Floresta
Palmeira
dos
Índios
Garanhuns
Barreiros
Rio Largo
**Maceió**
Natividade
Peixe
São Félix
Paranã
Santana
Barreiras
Ibotirama
Bom Jesus
da Lapa
Sto Antônio
de Jesus
Chapada
de Maraís
Euclides
da Cunha
Ribeira
Santo
Monte Santo
Senhor
do Bonfim
Jacobina
Itiúba
Serrinha
Tucano
Paulo
Afonso
Arapiraca
**Aracaju**
Estância
Porangatu
Cavalcante
Posse
Correntina
Corrente
Guanambi
Brumado
Contas
Valença
Jequié
Ilha de Tinharé
Ilha Boipeba
**BRAZIL**
Niquelândia
Sítio do
Abadia
Manga
Ipiaú
Itabuna
Ubaitaba
**Ilhéus**
Aruanã
Planalto
de Mato Grosso
Barra do
Garças
Goiás
Iporá
Formosa
Januária
Espinosa
Vitória da
Conquista
Una
Itapetinga
Poxoréu
Rondonópolis
**Brasília**
Anápolis
Unaí
Montes Claros
Salinas
Almenara
Belmonte
Santa Cruz Cabrália
Porto Seguro
**Goiânia**
Vianópolis
Paracatu
Jequitaí
Pardo
Itamaraju
Prado
Alcobaça
Nanuque
Itumbiara
João
Pinheiro
Saldo Chifre
Águas
Formosas
Conceição da Barra
São Mateus
Jataí
Rio
Verde
Rio Verde de
Mato Grosso
Caiapó
Paraúna
Patos
de Minas
Corinto
Curvelo
Teófilo
Otoni
Governador
Valadares
Ponta da Baleia
Três Lagoas
Campo
Grande
Fernandópolis
Uberlândia
Araxá
Ibiá
Sete
Lagoas
Ipatinga
Manhuaçu
Caratinga
Colatina
Linhares
Araçatuba
**Belo Horizonte**
Cariacica
Vitória
Vila Velha
Três Lagoas
Barretos
França
Campo Belo
Lafaiete
Muriaé
Cachoeiro de Itapemirim
São José do
Rio Preto
Bebedouro
Ribeirão
Preto
Passos
Divinópolis
Barbacena
Juiz de Fora
São João da Barra
Campos
**PARAGUAY**
Dourados
Presidente
Prudente
Marília
Bauru
Jaú
Araraquara
São
Carlos
Poços
de Caldas
Varginha
Lavras
Volta
Redonda
Nova
Friburgo
Cabo Frio
Macaé
Ilha de São Sebastião
Umuarama
Campo
Mourão
Maringá
Londrina
Apucarana
Itapetininga
Piracicaba
Limeira
Campinas
**Campinas**
Taubaté
Pouso
Alegre
Jacareí
**Nova Iguaçu**
**Rio de Janeiro**
Niterói
Cascavel
Goio-Erê
**São Paulo**
Santo
André
Santos
Tropic of Capricorn

**1:15M**

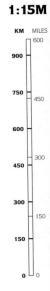

© Collins

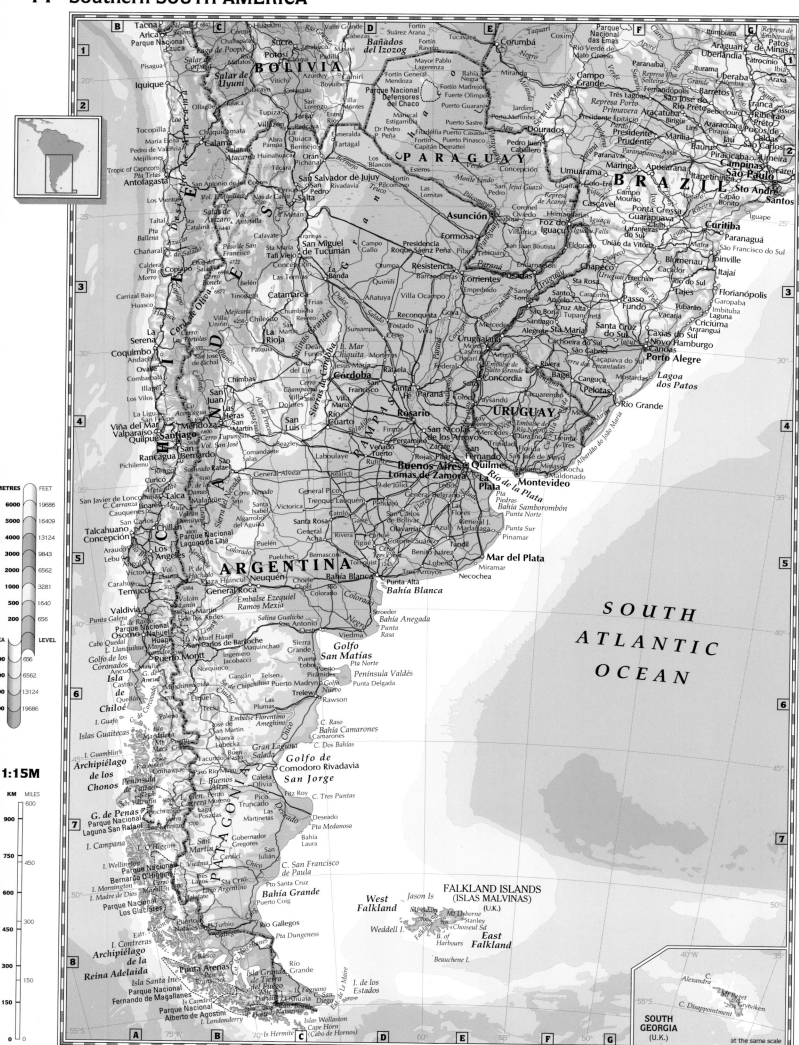

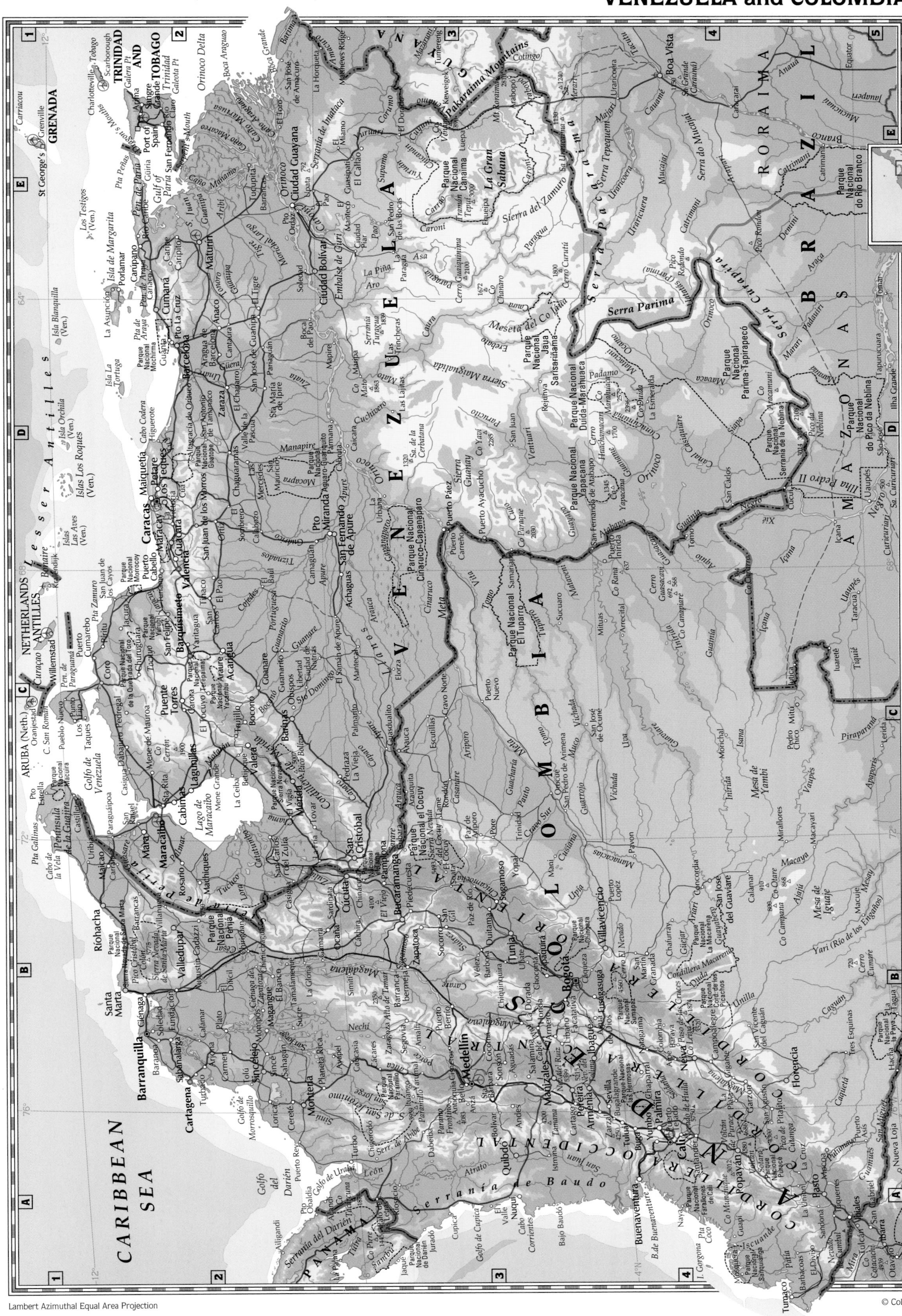

GRENADA

TRINIDAD AND TOBAGO

NETHERLANDS ANTILLES

ARUBA (Neth.)

CARIBBEAN SEA

Lesser Antilles

VENEZUELA

COLOMBIA

BRAZIL

RORAIMA

AMAZONAS

PANAMA

GUYANA

La Gran Sabana

Serra Parima

Orinoco Delta

Gulf of Venezuela

Lago de Maracaibo

Golfo de Venezuela

Caracas · Maracay · Valencia · Barquisimeto · Maracaibo · Ciudad Bolívar · Cumaná · Barcelona · Maturín · Bogotá · Medellín · Cali · Cúcuta · Bucaramanga · Villavicencio

CORDILLERA OCCIDENTAL · CORDILLERA CENTRAL · CORDILLERA ORIENTAL

Santa Marta · Barranquilla · Cartagena · Riohacha

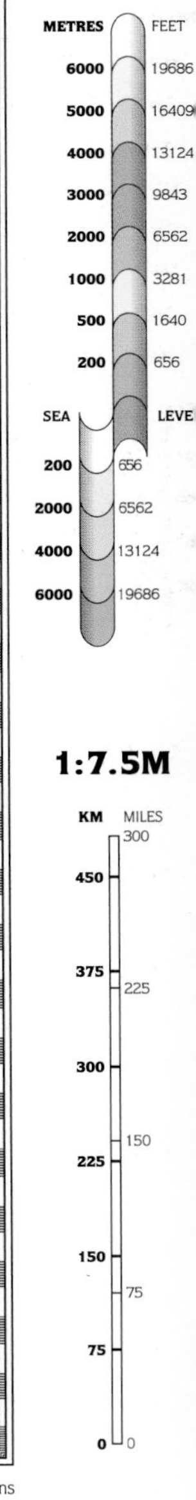

METRES / FEET

6000 — 19686
5000 — 16409
4000 — 13124
3000 — 9843
2000 — 6562
1000 — 3281
500 — 1640
200 — 656
SEA LEVEL
200 — 656
2000 — 6562
4000 — 13124
6000 — 19686

1:7.5M

KM / MILES
450 — 300
375 — 225
300 — 150
225 — 150
150 — 75
75
0 — 0

Lambert Azimuthal Equal Area Projection

© Collins

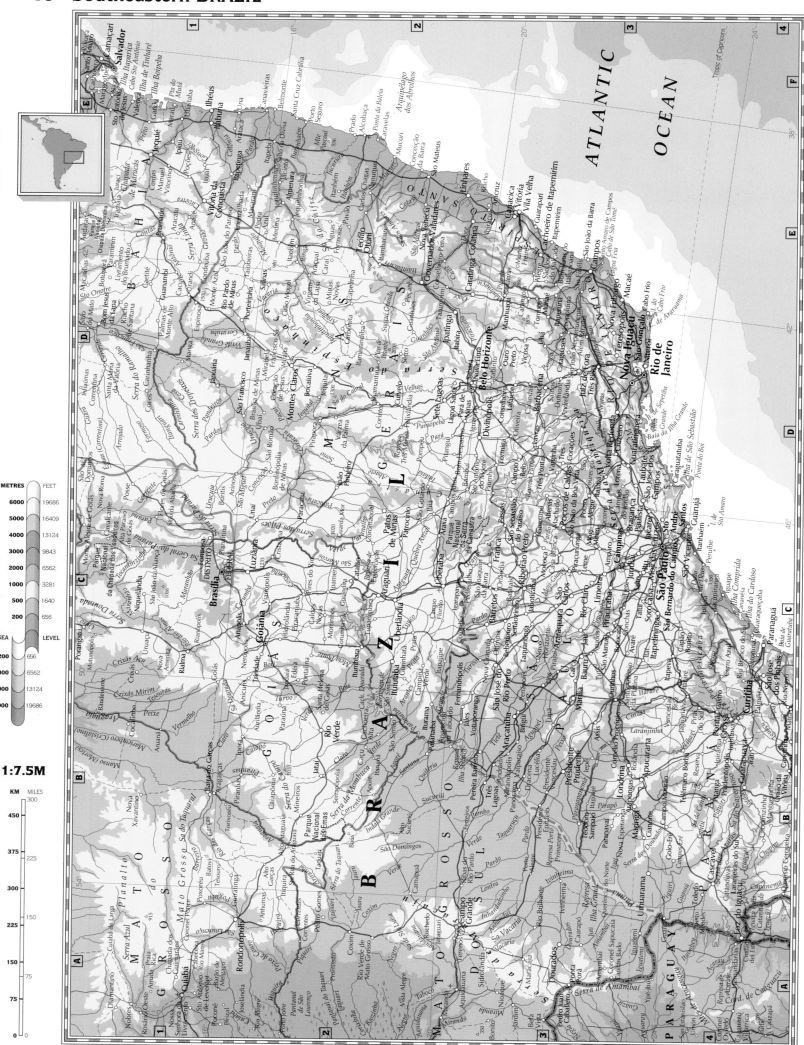

1:7.5M

Lambert Azimuthal Equal Area Projection

© Collins

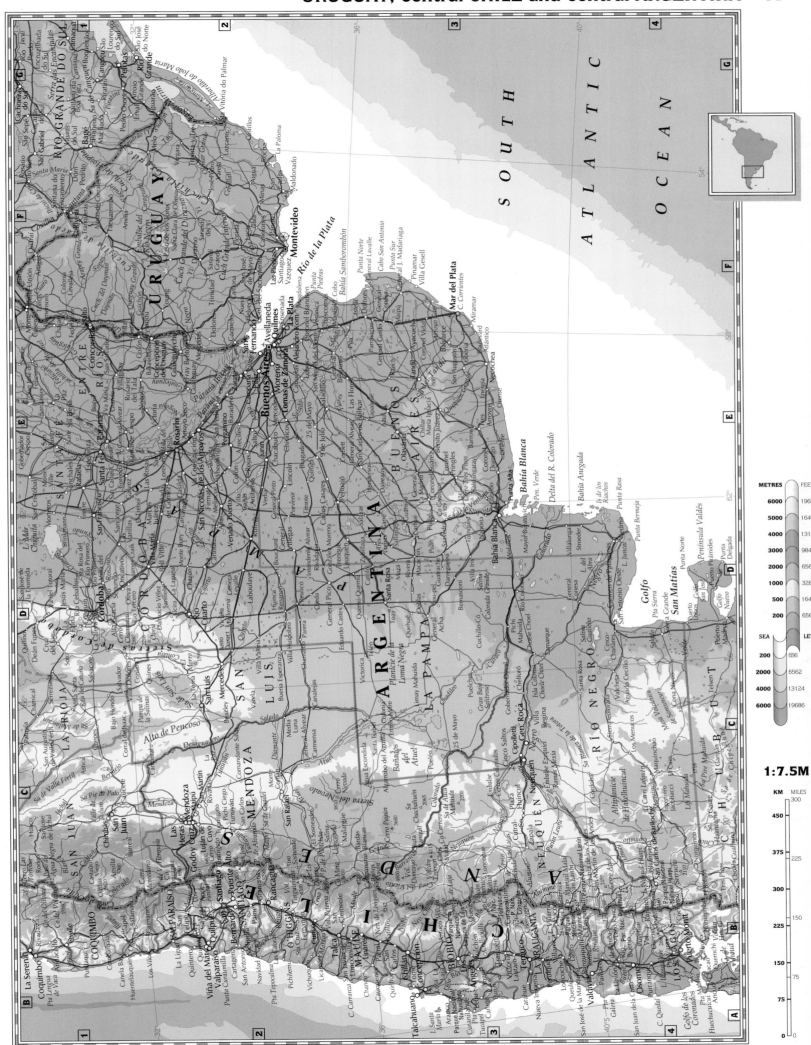

Lambert Azimuthal Equal Area Projection

© Collins

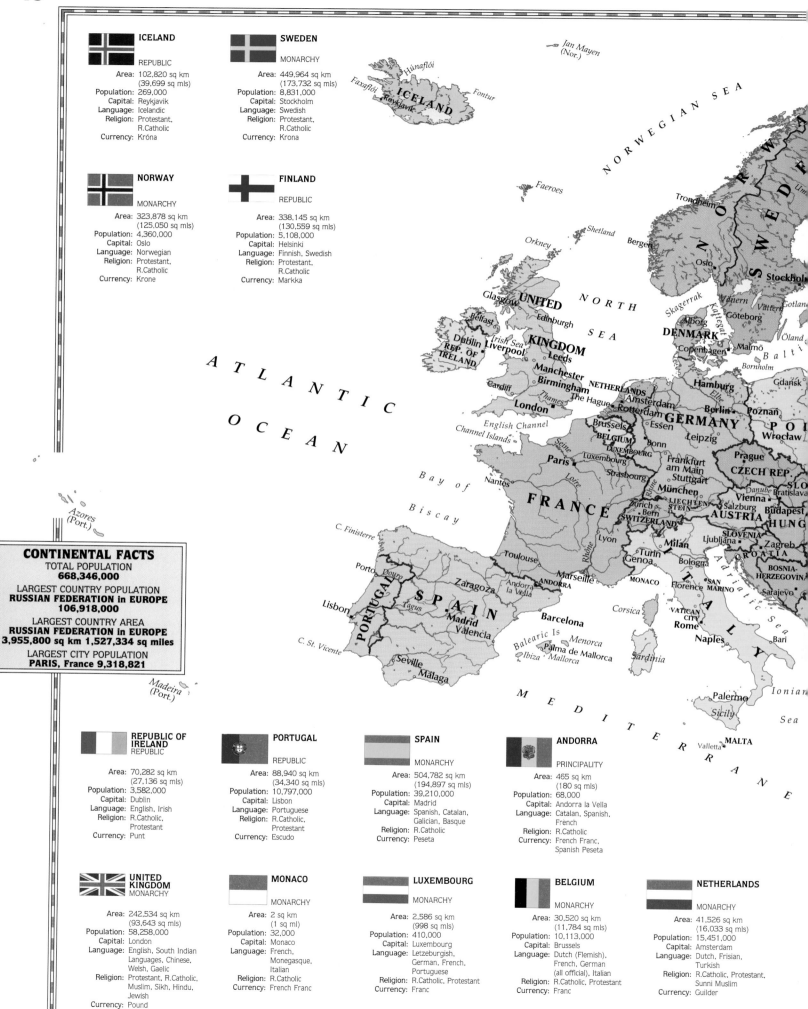

### ICELAND
REPUBLIC
Area: 102,820 sq km
(39,699 sq mls)
Population: 269,000
Capital: Reykjavik
Language: Icelandic
Religion: Protestant,
R.Catholic
Currency: Króna

### SWEDEN
MONARCHY
Area: 449,964 sq km
(173,732 sq mls)
Population: 8,831,000
Capital: Stockholm
Language: Swedish
Religion: Protestant,
R.Catholic
Currency: Krona

### NORWAY
MONARCHY
Area: 323,878 sq km
(125,050 sq mls)
Population: 4,360,000
Capital: Oslo
Language: Norwegian
Religion: Protestant,
R.Catholic
Currency: Krone

### FINLAND
REPUBLIC
Area: 338,145 sq km
(130,559 sq mls)
Population: 5,108,000
Capital: Helsinki
Language: Finnish, Swedish
Religion: Protestant,
R.Catholic
Currency: Markka

### CONTINENTAL FACTS
TOTAL POPULATION
**668,346,000**
LARGEST COUNTRY POPULATION
**RUSSIAN FEDERATION in EUROPE
106,918,000**
LARGEST COUNTRY AREA
**RUSSIAN FEDERATION in EUROPE
3,955,800 sq km 1,527,334 sq miles**
LARGEST CITY POPULATION
**PARIS, France 9,318,821**

### REPUBLIC OF IRELAND
REPUBLIC
Area: 70,282 sq km
(27,136 sq mls)
Population: 3,582,000
Capital: Dublin
Language: English, Irish
Religion: R.Catholic,
Protestant
Currency: Punt

### PORTUGAL
REPUBLIC
Area: 88,940 sq km
(34,340 sq mls)
Population: 10,797,000
Capital: Lisbon
Language: Portuguese
Religion: R.Catholic,
Protestant
Currency: Escudo

### SPAIN
MONARCHY
Area: 504,782 sq km
(194,897 sq mls)
Population: 39,210,000
Capital: Madrid
Language: Spanish, Catalan,
Galician, Basque
Religion: R.Catholic
Currency: Peseta

### ANDORRA
PRINCIPALITY
Area: 465 sq km
(180 sq mls)
Population: 68,000
Capital: Andorra la Vella
Language: Catalan, Spanish,
French
Religion: R.Catholic
Currency: French Franc,
Spanish Peseta

### UNITED KINGDOM
MONARCHY
Area: 242,534 sq km
(93,643 sq mls)
Population: 58,258,000
Capital: London
Language: English, South Indian
Languages, Chinese,
Welsh, Gaelic
Religion: Protestant, R.Catholic,
Muslim, Sikh, Hindu,
Jewish
Currency: Pound

### MONACO
MONARCHY
Area: 2 sq km
(1 sq ml)
Population: 32,000
Capital: Monaco
Language: French,
Monegasque,
Italian
Religion: R.Catholic
Currency: French Franc

### LUXEMBOURG
MONARCHY
Area: 2,586 sq km
(998 sq mls)
Population: 410,000
Capital: Luxembourg
Language: Letzeburgish,
French, German,
Portuguese
Religion: R.Catholic, Protestant
Currency: Franc

### BELGIUM
MONARCHY
Area: 30,520 sq km
(11,784 sq mls)
Population: 10,113,000
Capital: Brussels
Language: Dutch (Flemish),
French, German
(all official), Italian
Religion: R.Catholic, Protestant
Currency: Franc

### NETHERLANDS
MONARCHY
Area: 41,526 sq km
(16,033 sq mls)
Population: 15,451,000
Capital: Amsterdam
Language: Dutch, Frisian,
Turkish
Religion: R.Catholic, Protestant,
Sunni Muslim
Currency: Guilder

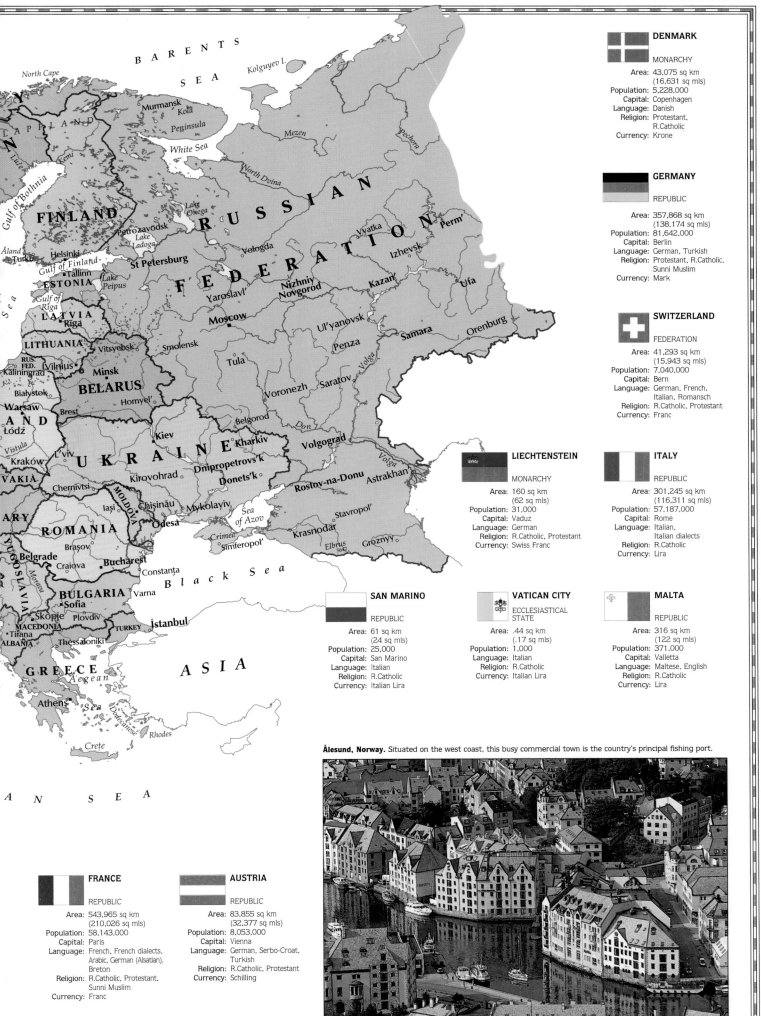

BARENTS
SEA

North Cape
Kolguyev I.

Murmansk
Kola
Peninsula
Mezen
Pechora

LAPPLAND
White Sea
North Dvina

Luleå
Kemi

Gulf of Bothnia

FINLAND
Petrozavodsk
Lake
Onega
RUSSIAN
Vologda
Vyatka
Perm'

Åland
Turku
Helsinki
Gulf of Finland
St Petersburg
Lake
Ladoga
FEDERATION
Nizhniy
Novgorod
Kazan'
Izhevsk
Ufa

Tallinn
ESTONIA
Lake
Peipus
Yaroslavl'
Sea

Gulf of
Riga
LATVIA
Riga
Moscow
Ul'yanovsk
Samara
Orenburg

LITHUANIA
Vitsyebsk
Smolensk
Penza

RUS.
FED.
Vilnius
Tula
Voronezh
Saratov
Volga

Kaliningrad
Minsk
BELARUS
Homyel'
Don
Volgograd

Białystok
Belgorod

WARSAW
Brest
Kiev
Astrakhan

AND
Łódź
Kharkiv
Volga

Vistula
L'viv
UKRAINE
Dnipropetrovs'k
Rostov-na-Donu

Kraków
Kirovohrad
Donets'k

VAKIA
Chernivtsi
MOLDOVA
Iaşi
Chişinău
Mykolayiv
Sea
of Azov
Stavropol'
Krasnodar
Groznyy

ARY
ROMANIA
Odesa
Crimea
Simferopol'
Elbrus
5642

YUGOSLAVIA
Braşov
Bucharest
Constanţa

Belgrade
Craiova

Black Sea

Morava
BULGARIA
Varna

Skopje
Sofia
Plovdiv
TURKEY
İstanbul

MACEDONIA
Tirana
Thessaloniki

ALBANIA
ASIA

GREECE
Aegean

Athens
Sea

Dodecanese
Rhodes

AN    S    E    A

Crete

## DENMARK
MONARCHY
Area: 43,075 sq km
(16,631 sq mls)
Population: 5,228,000
Capital: Copenhagen
Language: Danish
Religion: Protestant,
R.Catholic
Currency: Krone

## GERMANY
REPUBLIC
Area: 357,868 sq km
(138,174 sq mls)
Population: 81,642,000
Capital: Berlin
Language: German, Turkish
Religion: Protestant, R.Catholic,
Sunni Muslim
Currency: Mark

## SWITZERLAND
FEDERATION
Area: 41,293 sq km
(15,943 sq mls)
Population: 7,040,000
Capital: Bern
Language: German, French,
Italian, Romansch
Religion: R.Catholic, Protestant
Currency: Franc

## LIECHTENSTEIN
MONARCHY
Area: 160 sq km
(62 sq mls)
Population: 31,000
Capital: Vaduz
Language: German
Religion: R.Catholic, Protestant
Currency: Swiss Franc

## ITALY
REPUBLIC
Area: 301,245 sq km
(116,311 sq mls)
Population: 57,187,000
Capital: Rome
Language: Italian,
Italian dialects
Religion: R.Catholic
Currency: Lira

## SAN MARINO
REPUBLIC
Area: 61 sq km
(24 sq mls)
Population: 25,000
Capital: San Marino
Language: Italian
Religion: R.Catholic
Currency: Italian Lira

## VATICAN CITY
ECCLESIASTICAL
STATE
Area: .44 sq km
(.17 sq mls)
Population: 1,000
Language: Italian
Religion: R.Catholic
Currency: Italian Lira

## MALTA
REPUBLIC
Area: 316 sq km
(122 sq mls)
Population: 371,000
Capital: Valletta
Language: Maltese, English
Religion: R.Catholic
Currency: Lira

**Ålesund, Norway.** Situated on the west coast, this busy commercial town is the country's principal fishing port.

## FRANCE
REPUBLIC
Area: 543,965 sq km
(210,026 sq mls)
Population: 58,143,000
Capital: Paris
Language: French, French dialects,
Arabic, German (Alsatian),
Breton
Religion: R.Catholic, Protestant,
Sunni Muslim
Currency: Franc

## AUSTRIA
REPUBLIC
Area: 83,855 sq km
(32,377 sq mls)
Population: 8,053,000
Capital: Vienna
Language: German, Serbo-Croat,
Turkish
Religion: R.Catholic, Protestant
Currency: Schilling

© Collins

**Budapest, Hungary.** The picturesque old part of the city (Buda) shown in the photograph is separated from the administrative and commercial centre (Pest) by the River Danube.

### POLAND
REPUBLIC
Area: 312,683 sq km
(120,728 sq mls)
Population: 38,588,000
Capital: Warsaw
Language: Polish, German
Religion: R.Catholic,
Polish Orthodox
Currency: Złoty

### SLOVAKIA
REPUBLIC
Area: 49,035 sq km
(18,933 sq mls)
Population: 5,364,000
Capital: Bratislava
Language: Slovak, Hungarian,
Czech
Religion: R.Catholic, Protestant,
Orthodox
Currency: Koruna

### SLOVENIA
REPUBLIC
Area: 20,251 sq km
(7,819 sq mls)
Population: 1,984,000
Capital: Ljubljana
Language: Slovene, Serbo-Croat
Religion: R.Catholic, Protestant
Currency: Tólar

### CROATIA
REPUBLIC
Area: 56,538 sq km
(21,829 sq mls)
Population: 4,495,000
Capital: Zagreb
Language: Serbo-Croat
Religion: R.Catholic, Orthodox,
Sunni Muslim
Currency: Kuna

### BOSNIA-
HERZEGOVINA
REPUBLIC
Area: 51,130 sq km
(19,741 sq mls)
Population: 4,484,000
Capital: Sarajevo
Language: Serbo-Croat
Religion: Sunni Muslim,
Serbian Orthodox,
R.Catholic, Protestant
Currency: Dinar

### YUGOSLAVIA
REPUBLIC
Area: 102,173 sq km
(39,449 sq mls)
Population: 10,544,000
Capital: Belgrade
Language: Serbo-Croat,
Albanian, Hungarian
Religion: Serbian Orthodox,
Montenegrin Orthodox,
Sunni Muslim
Currency: Dinar

### MACEDONIA
(F.Y.R.O.M.)
REPUBLIC
Area: 25,713 sq km
(9,928 sq mls)
Population: 2,163,000
Capital: Skopje
Language: Macedonian, Albanian,
Serbo-Croat, Turkish,
Romany
Religion: Macedonian Orthodox,
Sunni Muslim,
R.Catholic
Currency: Denar

### GREECE
REPUBLIC
Area: 131,957 sq km
(50,949 sq mls)
Population: 10,458,000
Capital: Athens
Language: Greek, Macedonian
Religion: Greek Orthodox,
Sunni Muslim
Currency: Drachma

### BULGARIA
REPUBLIC
Area: 110,994 sq km
(42,855 sq mls)
Population: 8,402,000
Capital: Sofia
Language: Bulgarian, Turkish,
Romany, Macedonian
Religion: Bulgarian Othodox,
Sunni Muslim
Currency: Lev

### ROMANIA
REPUBLIC
Area: 237,500 sq km
(91,699 sq mls)
Population: 22,680,000
Capital: Bucharest
Language: Romanian,
Hungarian
Religion: Romanian Orthodox,
R.Catholic, Protestant
Currency: Leu

### MOLDOVA
REPUBLIC
Area: 33,700 sq km
(13,012 sq mls)
Population: 4,432,000
Capital: Chişinău
Language: Romanian, Russian,
Ukrainian, Gagauz
Religion: Moldovan Orthodox,
Russian Orthodox
Currency: Leu

### CZECH
REPUBLIC
REPUBLIC
Area: 78,864 sq km
(30,450 sq mls)
Population: 10,331,000
Capital: Prague
Language: Czech, Moravian,
Slovak
Religion: R.Catholic, Protestant
Currency: Koruna

### UKRAINE
REPUBLIC
Area: 603,700 sq km
(233,090 sq mls)
Population: 51,639,000
Capital: Kiev
Language: Ukrainian, Russian,
Regional Languages
Religion: Ukrainian Orthodox,
R.Catholic
Currency: Karbovanets

### HUNGARY
REPUBLIC
Area: 93,030 sq km
(35,919 sq mls)
Population: 10,225,000
Capital: Budapest
Language: Hungarian, Romany,
German, Slovak
Religion: R.Catholic, Protestant
Currency: Forint

### LITHUANIA
REPUBLIC
Area: 65,200 sq km
(25,174 sq mls)
Population: 3,715,000
Capital: Vilnius
Language: Lithuanian, Russian,
Polish
Religion: R.Catholic, Protestant,
Russian Orthodox
Currency: Litas

### BELARUS
REPUBLIC
Area: 207,600 sq km
(80,155 sq mls)
Population: 10,141,000
Capital: Minsk
Language: Belorussian,
Russian, Ukrainian
Religion: Belorussian Orthodox,
R.Catholic
Currency: Rouble

### ALBANIA
REPUBLIC
Area: 28,748 sq km
(11,100 sq mls)
Population: 3,645,000
Capital: Tirana
Language: Albanian (Gheg, Tosk
dialects), Greek
Religion: Sunni Muslim, Greek
Orthodox, R.Catholic
Currency: Lek

### ESTONIA
REPUBLIC
Area: 45,200 sq km
(17,452 sq mls)
Population: 1,530,000
Capital: Tallinn
Language: Estonian, Russian
Religion: Protestant,
Russian Orthodox
Currency: Kroon

**Ronda, Spain.** The town is precariously situated on a rocky shelf which falls on three sides to a depth of 120m.

# POPULATION

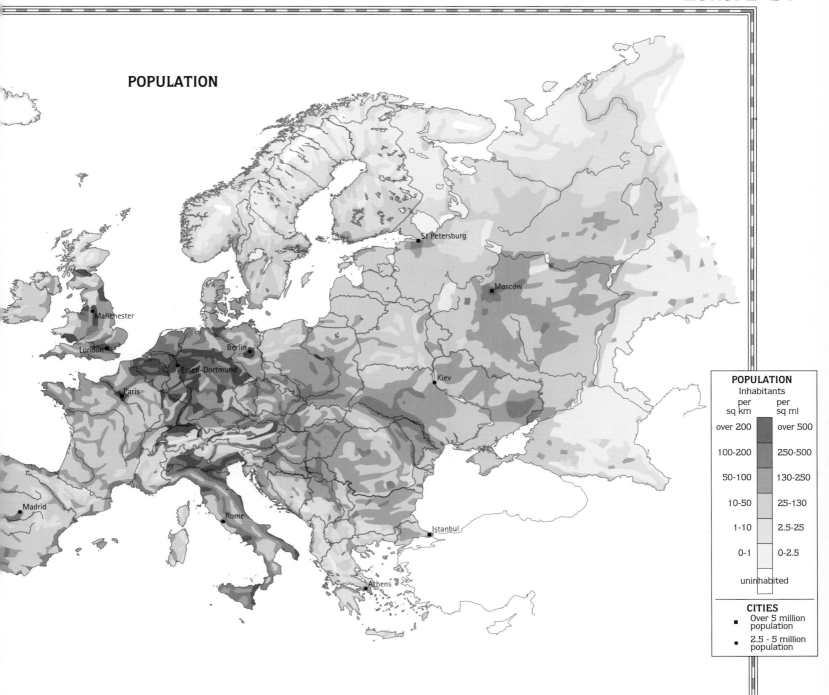

| POPULATION | |
|---|---|
| Inhabitants | |
| per sq km | per sq ml |
| over 200 | over 500 |
| 100-200 | 250-500 |
| 50-100 | 130-250 |
| 10-50 | 25-130 |
| 1-10 | 2.5-25 |
| 0-1 | 0-2.5 |
| uninhabited | |

### CITIES
- ■ Over 5 million population
- ● 2.5 - 5 million population

**Grindelwald, Switzerland.** A resort popular with skiers and climbers, as it is spread across an expanse of Alpine meadows and is near many majestic peaks and glaciers.

### LATVIA
REPUBLIC

Area: 63,700 sq km
(24,595 sq mls)
Population: 2,515,000
Capital: Riga
Language: Latvian, Russian
Religion: Protestant, R.Catholic,
Russian Orthodox
Currency: Lat

### RUSSIAN FEDERATION

| | REPUBLIC | in Europe |
|---|---|---|
| Area: | 17,075,400 sq km | 3,955,800 sq km |
| | (6,592,849 sq mls) | (1,527,334 sq mls) |
| Population: | 148,141,000 | 106,918,000 |
| Capital: | Moscow | |
| Language: | Russian, Tatar, Ukrainian, Local Languages | |
| Religion: | Russian Orthodox, Sunni Muslim, Other Christian, Jewish | |
| Currency: | Rouble | |

© Collins

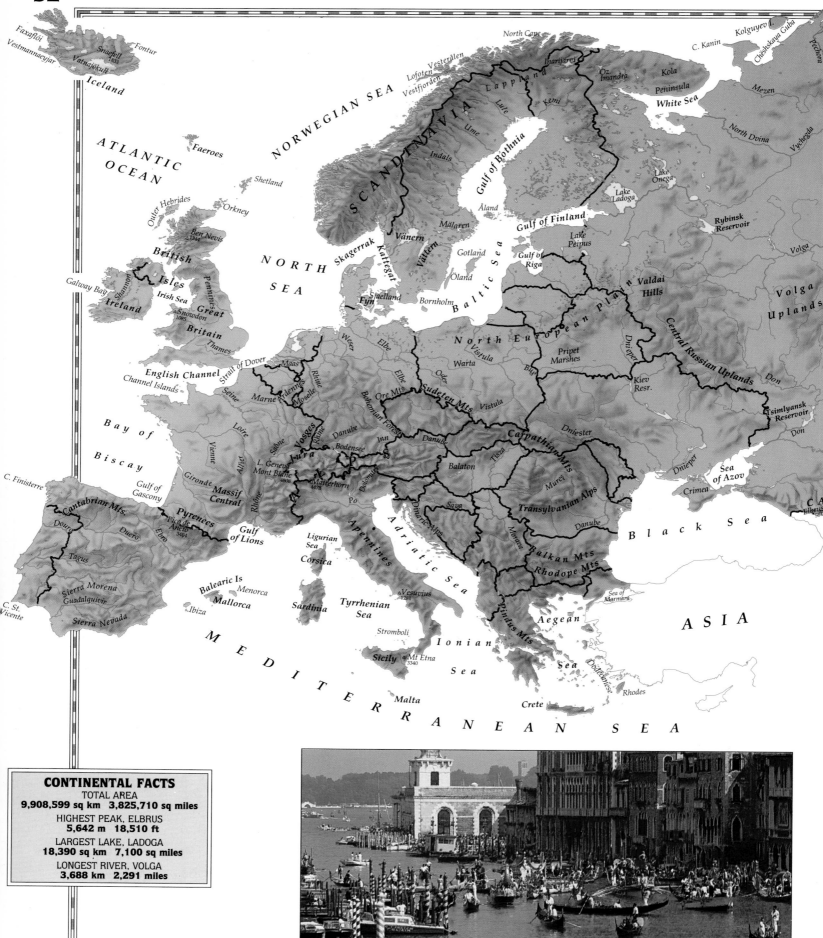

Faxaflói
Vestmannaeyjar
Snaefell
1833
Vatnajökull
Fontur
Iceland

ATLANTIC
OCEAN

NORWEGIAN SEA

North Cape

C. Kanin
Kolguyev I.
Chëshskaya Guba
Pechora

Lofoten Vesterålen
Vestfjorden
Inarijärvi

Oz.
Imandra
Kola
Peninsula

Mezen

North Dvina

Vychegda

Faeroes

Lapland

SCANDINAVIA

Lule
Kemi

Ume

Indals

Gulf of Bothnia

White Sea

Lake
Onega

Shetland

Åland

Lake
Ladoga

Rybinsk
Reservoir

NORTH

Outer Hebrides
Orkney

Ben Nevis
1344

British

Isles

Skagerrak
Kattegat

Vänern

Mälaren

Vättern

Gulf of Finland

Lake
Peipus

Valdai
Hills

Volga

SEA

Gotland

Baltic Sea

Gulf of
Riga

Volga
Uplands

Galway Bay
Shannon

Ireland

Irish Sea

Pennines

Great

Snowdon
1085

Britain

Thames

Fyn
Sjaelland

Öland

Bornholm

North European Plain

Vistula

Warta

Pripet
Marshes

Dnieper

Central Russian Uplands

Kiev
Resr.

Don

English Channel

Channel Islands

Strait of Dover

Seine

Maas

Ardennes

Rhine

Weser

Elbe

Elbe

Oder

Ore Mts

Bohemian Forest

Sudeten Mts

Vistula

Dniester

Tsimlyansk
Reservoir

Bay of

Biscay

C. Finisterre

Marne
Moselle

Loire

Vosges

Jura

Vienne
Allier

Danube

Rhine

Bodensee

Inn

Danube

Danube

Balaton

Tisza

Carpathian Mts

Mures

Don

Dnieper

Sea
of Azov

L. Geneva
Mont Blanc
4808

Matterhorn
4478

Dolomites

Po

Sava

Dinaric Alps

Transylvanian Alps

Crimea

CA
Elbrus
5642

Gironde

Massif
Central

Rhône

Gulf of
Gascony

Cantabrian Mts.

Pyrenees

Douro

Duero

Ebro

Pico de
Aneto
3404

Gulf
of Lions

Ligurian
Sea

Apennines

Adriatic Sea

Morava

Danube

Balkan Mts

Rhodope Mts

Black Sea

Tagus

Sierra Morena
Guadalquivir

C. St.
Vicente

Sierra Nevada

Balearic Is

Ibiza

Mallorca

Menorca

Corsica

Sardinia

Tyrrhenian
Sea

Vesuvius
1281

Stromboli

Ionian

Pindus Mts

Aegean

Sea

ASIA

Sea of
Marmara

Sicily

Mt Etna
3340

Sea

Dodecanese

Rhodes

Malta

Crete

MEDITERRANEAN SEA

<table>
<tr><td colspan="2">CONTINENTAL FACTS</td></tr>
<tr><td colspan="2">TOTAL AREA</td></tr>
<tr><td>9,908,599 sq km</td><td>3,825,710 sq miles</td></tr>
<tr><td colspan="2">HIGHEST PEAK, ELBRUS</td></tr>
<tr><td>5,642 m</td><td>18,510 ft</td></tr>
<tr><td colspan="2">LARGEST LAKE, LADOGA</td></tr>
<tr><td>18,390 sq km</td><td>7,100 sq miles</td></tr>
<tr><td colspan="2">LONGEST RIVER, VOLGA</td></tr>
<tr><td>3,688 km</td><td>2,291 miles</td></tr>
</table>

**Venice, Italy.** Boats are the primary mode of transport as the town is built on 118 islands and traversed by over 100 canals.

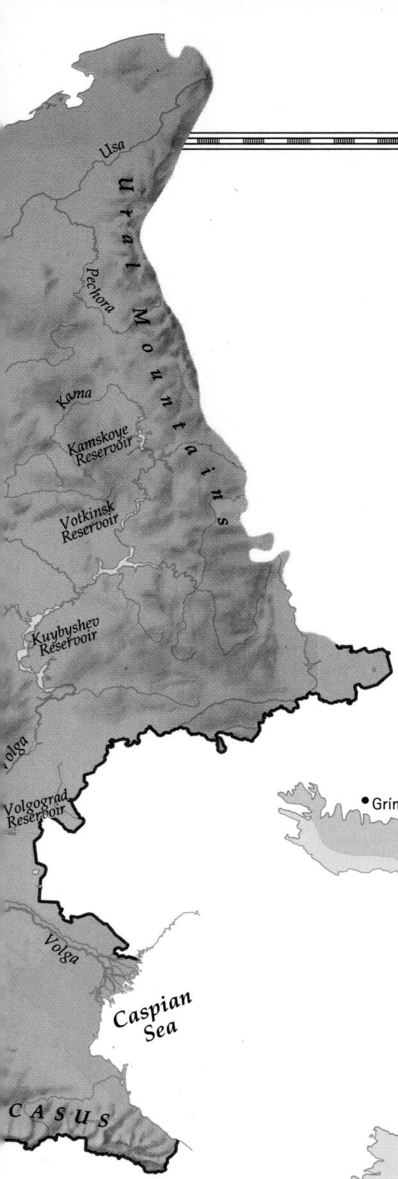

**Strokkur Geyser, Iceland.** This hot spring erupts every 3 minutes, throwing steam clouds up to 20m high.

## CLIMATE

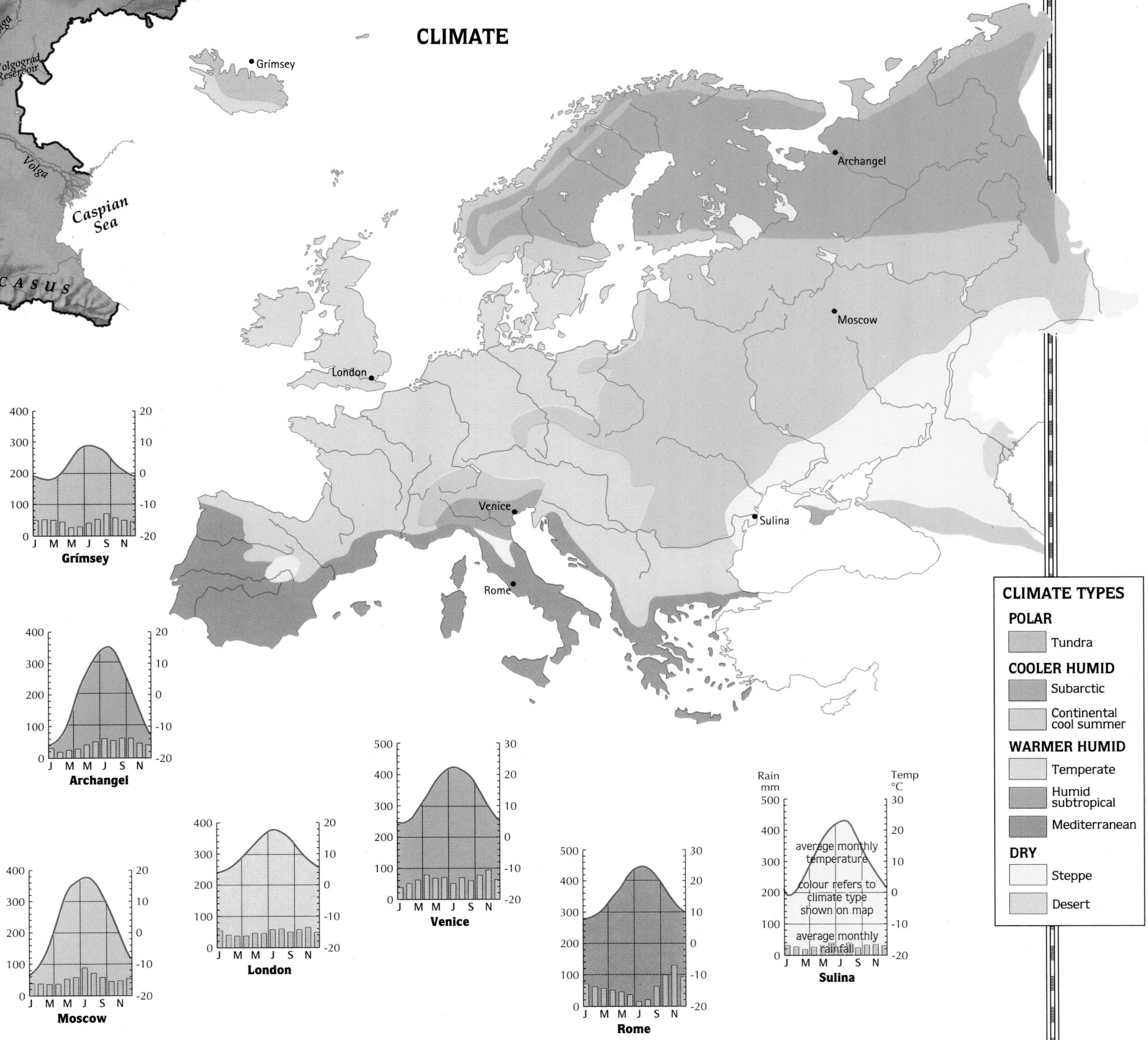

Usa
Pechora
Ural Mountains
Kama
Kamskoye Reservoir
Votkinsk Reservoir
Kuybyshev Reservoir
Volga
Volgograd Reservoir
Volga
Caspian Sea
CASUS

Grímsey

Archangel

Moscow

London

Venice

Sulina

Rome

**Grímsey**

**Archangel**

**London**

**Venice**

**Moscow**

**Rome**

Rain mm
Temp °C
average monthly temperature
colour refers to climate type shown on map
average monthly rainfall

**Sulina**

### CLIMATE TYPES

**POLAR**
- Tundra

**COOLER HUMID**
- Subarctic
- Continental cool summer

**WARMER HUMID**
- Temperate
- Humid subtropical
- Mediterranean

**DRY**
- Steppe
- Desert

© Collins

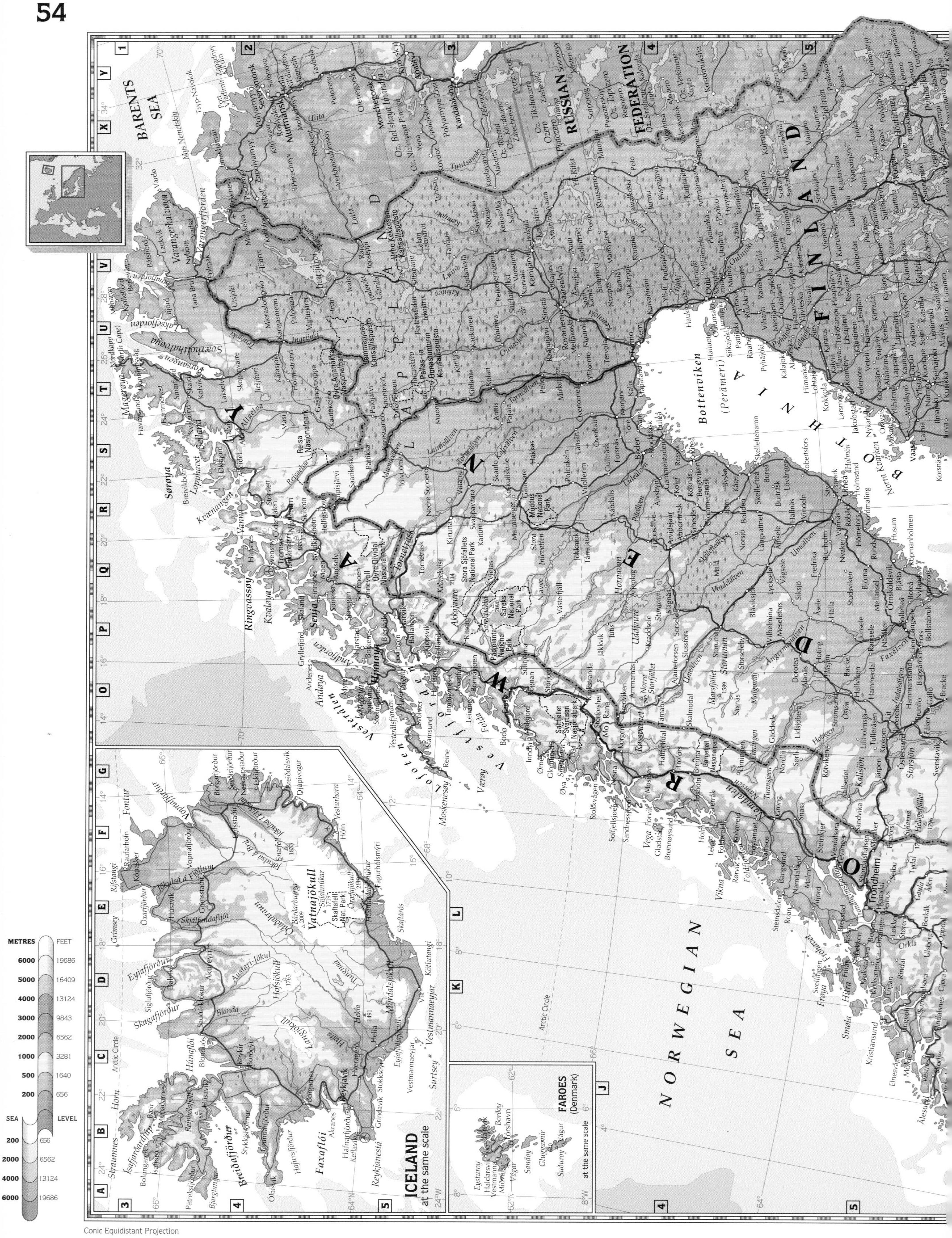

BARENTS SEA

RUSSIAN FEDERATION

FINLAND

LAPLAND

Bottenviken (Perämeri)

NORWEGIAN SEA

Vesterålen

Lofoten

Trondheim

Bodø

Narvik

Tromsø

Kiruna

Oulu

Murmansk

Arctic Circle

**METRES** — **FEET**

| METRES | FEET |
|---|---|
| 6000 | 19686 |
| 5000 | 16409 |
| 4000 | 13124 |
| 3000 | 9843 |
| 2000 | 6562 |
| 1000 | 3281 |
| 500 | 1640 |
| 200 | 656 |
| SEA | LEVEL |
| 200 | 656 |
| 2000 | 6562 |
| 4000 | 13124 |
| 6000 | 19686 |

**ICELAND**
at the same scale

Vatnajökull

Reykjavík

Faxaflói

Arctic Circle

**FAROES**
(Denmark)
at the same scale

Tórshavn

Conic Equidistant Projection

1:5M

| KM | MILES |
|----|-------|
| 250 | 150 |
| 200 | |
| 150 | 100 |
| 100 | |
| | 50 |
| 50 | |
| 0 | 0 |

1:5M

Conic Equidistant Projection

© Collins

ATLANTIC
OCEAN

NORTH
SEA

SCOTLAND

GRAMPIAN MOUNTAINS

SOUTHERN UPLANDS

NORTHERN
IRELAND

ENGLAND

SHETLAND
at the same scale

1:2M

Conic Equidistant Projection

© Collins

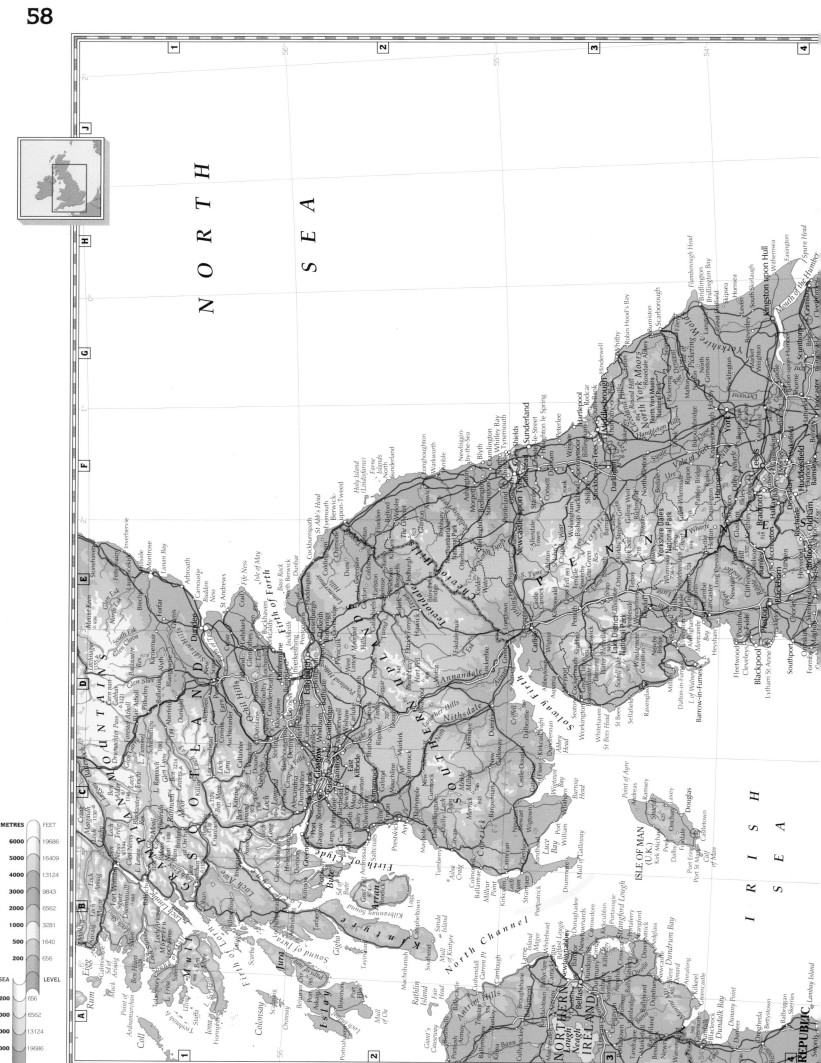

Conic Equidistant Projection

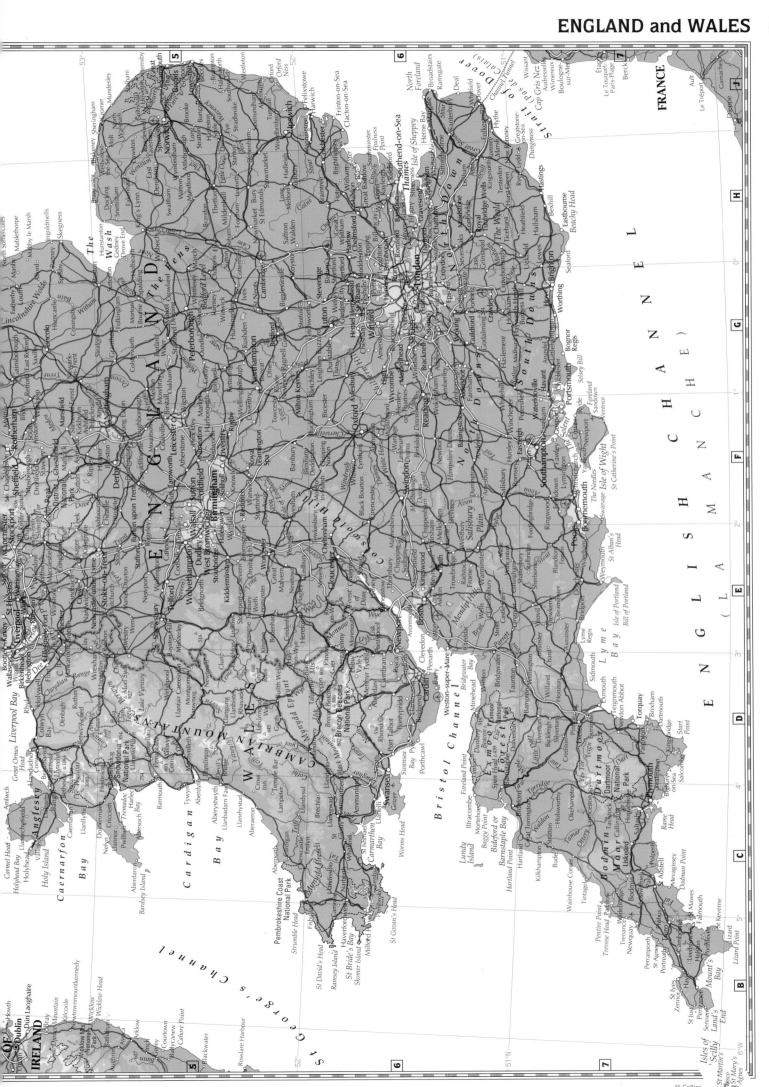

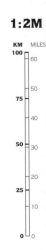

**1:2M**

KM MILES
100
75
60
50
50
40
25
30
20
0 10
0

FRANCE

IRELAND

© Collins

ATLANTIC
OCEAN

SCOTLAND

NORTHERN
IRELAND

REPUBLIC
OF
IRELAND

IRISH
SEA

1:2M

Conic Equidistant Projection

© Collins

Conic Equidistant Projection

© Collins

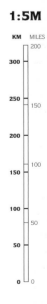

**1:5M**

KM MILES
300 — 200
250 — 150
200 — 100
150
100 — 50
50
0 — 0

© Collins

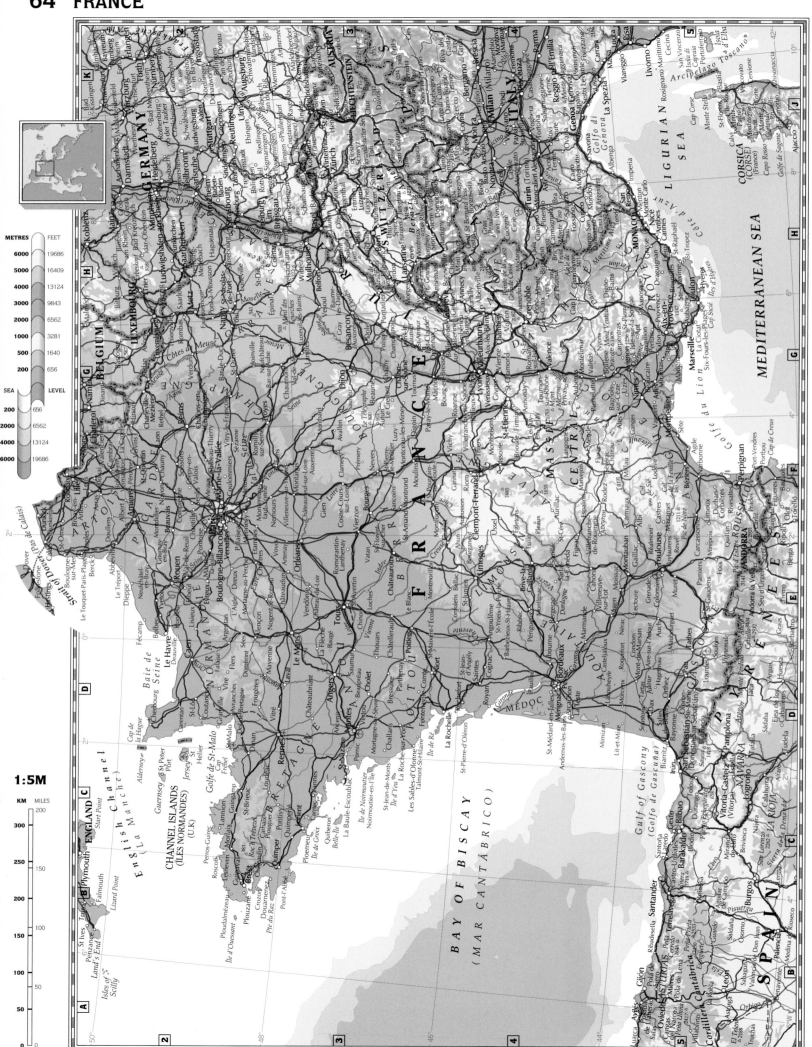

1:5M

Conic Equidistant Projection

© Collins

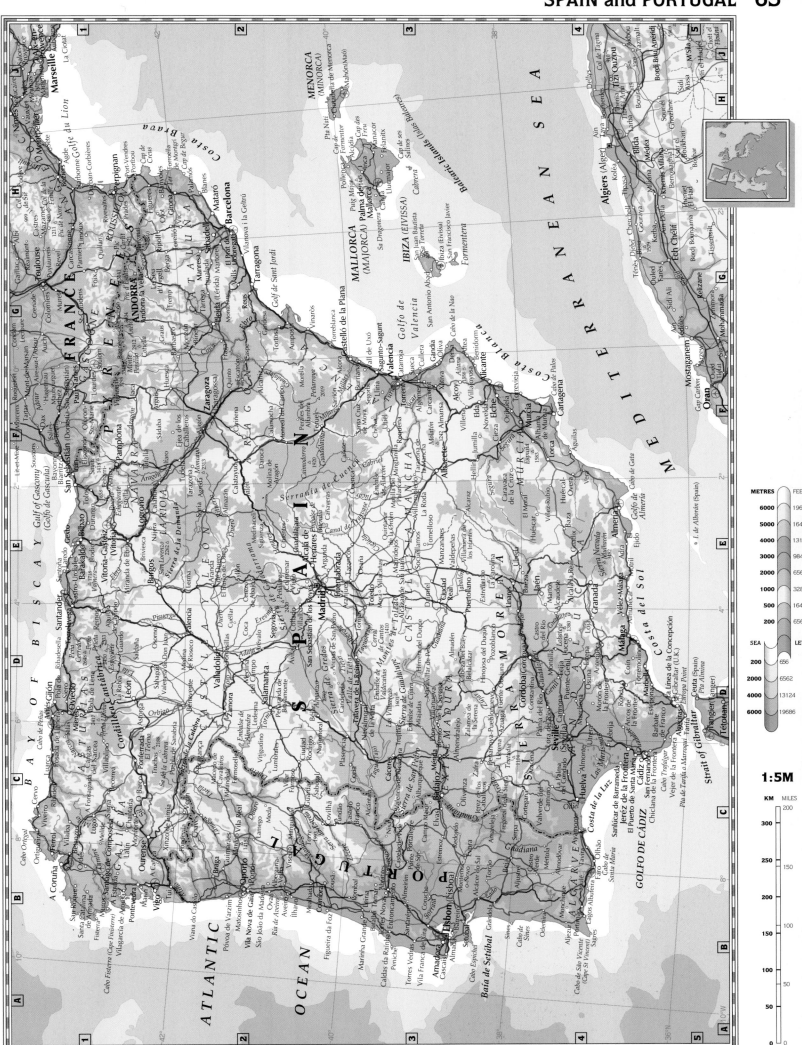

Conic Equidistant Projection

**1:5M**

KM | MILES

Transverse Mercator Projection

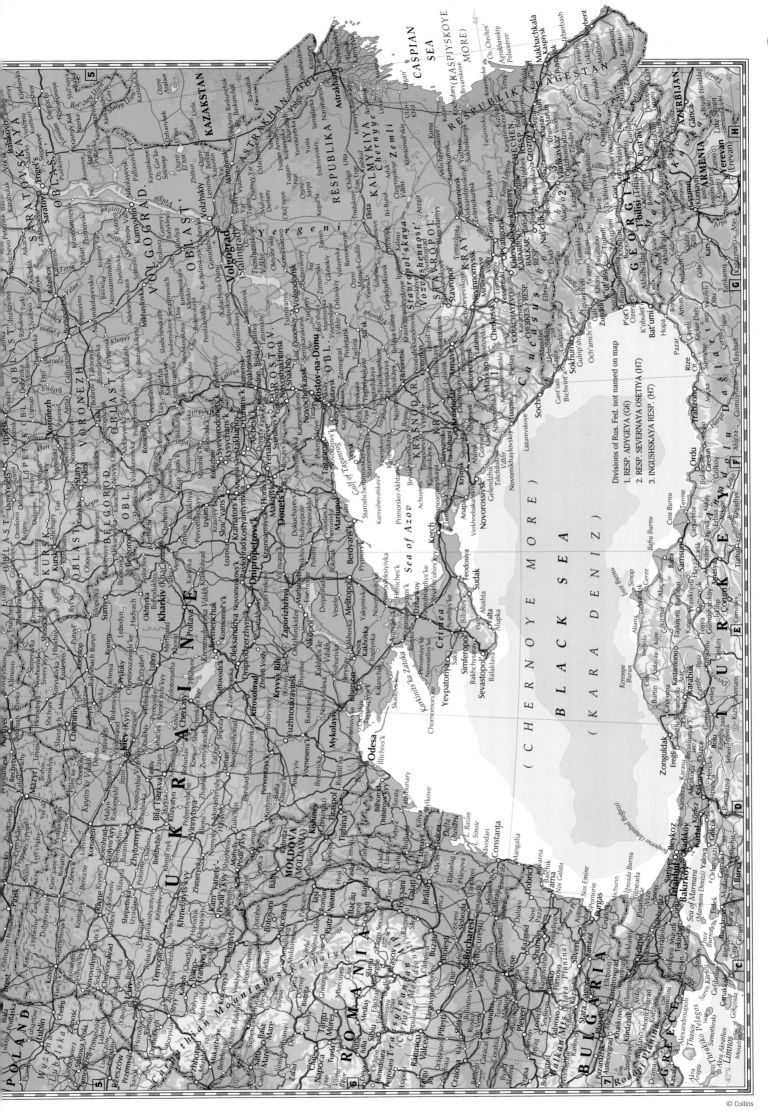

1:7M

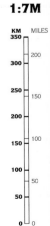

KM    MILES
350
         200
300
250      150
200
150      100
100
         50
50
0      0

© Collins

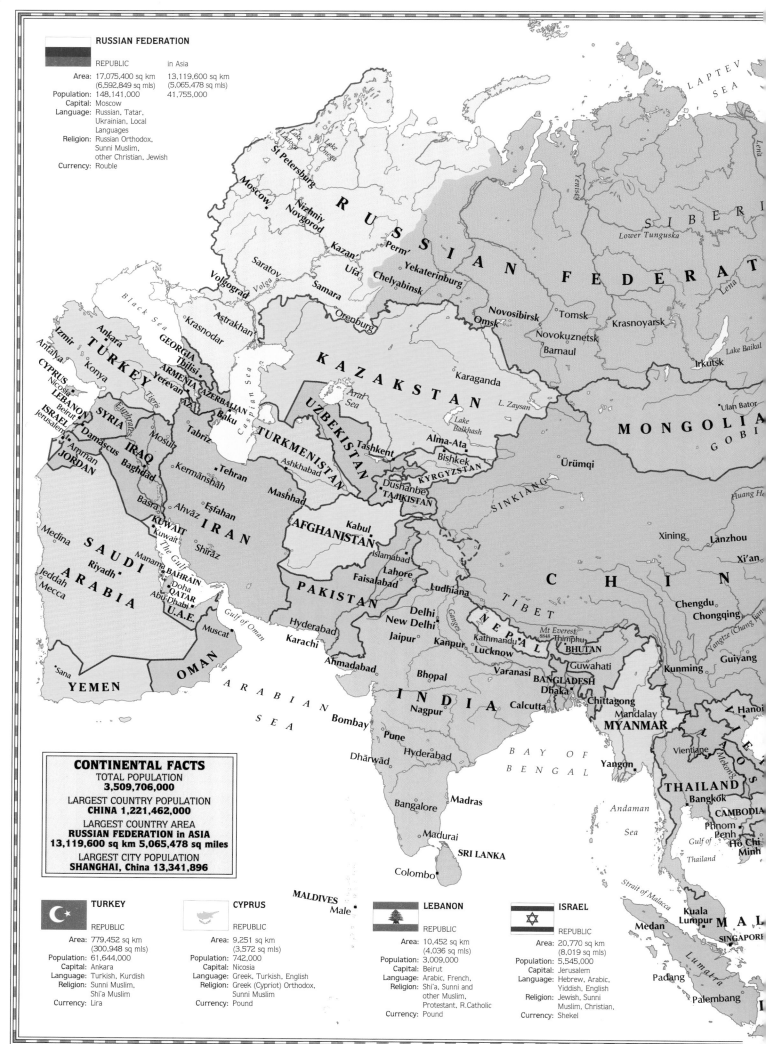

**RUSSIAN FEDERATION**

REPUBLIC   in Asia

Area: 17,075,400 sq km     13,119,600 sq km
(6,592,849 sq mls)    (5,065,478 sq mls)
Population: 148,141,000     41,755,000
Capital: Moscow
Language: Russian, Tatar,
Ukrainian, Local
Languages
Religion: Russian Orthodox,
Sunni Muslim,
other Christian, Jewish
Currency: Rouble

**CONTINENTAL FACTS**

TOTAL POPULATION
**3,509,706,000**

LARGEST COUNTRY POPULATION
**CHINA 1,221,462,000**

LARGEST COUNTRY AREA
**RUSSIAN FEDERATION in Asia**
**13,119,600 sq km 5,065,478 sq miles**

LARGEST CITY POPULATION
**SHANGHAI, China 13,341,896**

**TURKEY**

REPUBLIC

Area: 779,452 sq km
(300,948 sq mls)
Population: 61,644,000
Capital: Ankara
Language: Turkish, Kurdish
Religion: Sunni Muslim,
Shi'a Muslim
Currency: Lira

**CYPRUS**

REPUBLIC

Area: 9,251 sq km
(3,572 sq mls)
Population: 742,000
Capital: Nicosia
Language: Greek, Turkish, English
Religion: Greek (Cypriot) Orthodox,
Sunni Muslim
Currency: Pound

**LEBANON**

REPUBLIC

Area: 10,452 sq km
(4,036 sq mls)
Population: 3,009,000
Capital: Beirut
Language: Arabic, French,
Religion: Shi'a, Sunni and
other Muslim,
Protestant, R.Catholic
Currency: Pound

**ISRAEL**

REPUBLIC

Area: 20,770 sq km
(8,019 sq mls)
Population: 5,545,000
Capital: Jerusalem
Language: Hebrew, Arabic,
Yiddish, English
Religion: Jewish, Sunni
Muslim, Christian,
Currency: Shekel

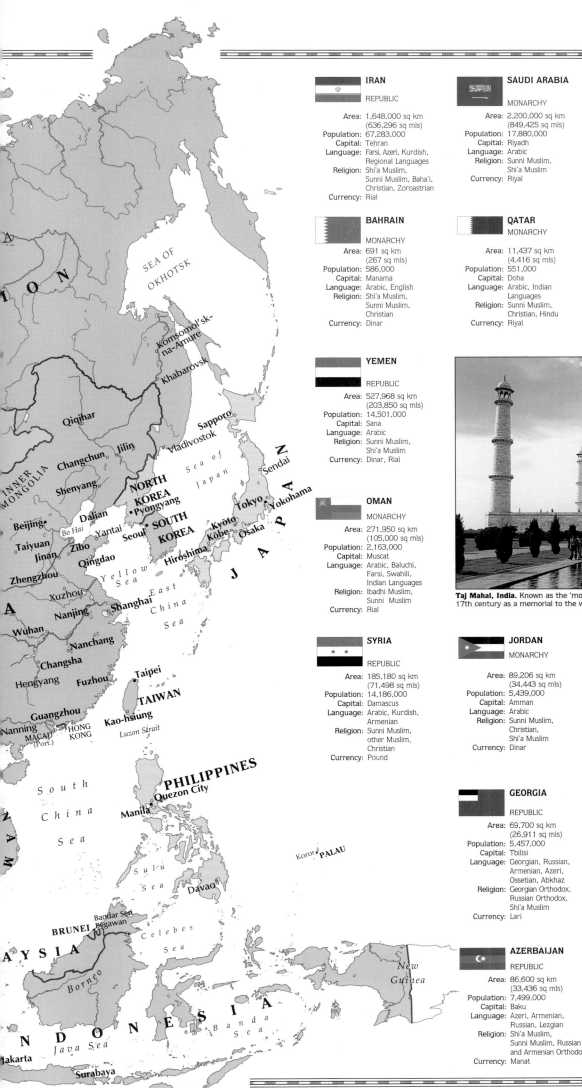

### IRAN
REPUBLIC

Area: 1,648,000 sq km
(636,296 sq mls)
Population: 67,283,000
Capital: Tehran
Language: Farsi, Azeri, Kurdish,
Regional Languages
Religion: Shi'a Muslim,
Sunni Muslim, Baha'i,
Christian, Zoroastrian
Currency: Rial

### SAUDI ARABIA
MONARCHY

Area: 2,200,000 sq km
(849,425 sq mls)
Population: 17,880,000
Capital: Riyadh
Language: Arabic
Religion: Sunni Muslim,
Shi'a Muslim
Currency: Riyal

### KUWAIT
MONARCHY

Area: 17,818 sq km
(6,880 sq mls)
Population: 1,691,000
Capital: Kuwait
Language: Arabic
Religion: Sunni, Shi'a and
other Muslim,
Christian, Hindu
Currency: Dinar

### BAHRAIN
MONARCHY

Area: 691 sq km
(267 sq mls)
Population: 586,000
Capital: Manama
Language: Arabic, English
Religion: Shi'a Muslim,
Sunni Muslim,
Christian
Currency: Dinar

### QATAR
MONARCHY

Area: 11,437 sq km
(4,416 sq mls)
Population: 551,000
Capital: Doha
Language: Arabic, Indian
Languages
Religion: Sunni Muslim,
Christian, Hindu
Currency: Riyal

### UNITED ARAB EMIRATES
FEDERATION

Area: 77,700 sq km
(30,000 sq mls)
Population: 2,314,000
Capital: Abu Dhabi
Language: Arabic (official),
English, Hindi,
Urdu, Farsi
Religion: Sunni Muslim,
Shi'a Muslim,
Christian
Currency: Dirham

### YEMEN
REPUBLIC

Area: 527,968 sq km
(203,850 sq mls)
Population: 14,501,000
Capital: Sana
Language: Arabic
Religion: Sunni Muslim,
Shi'a Muslim
Currency: Dinar, Rial

### OMAN
MONARCHY

Area: 271,950 sq km
(105,000 sq mls)
Population: 2,163,000
Capital: Muscat
Language: Arabic, Baluchi,
Farsi, Swahili,
Indian Languages
Religion: Ibadhi Muslim,
Sunni Muslim
Currency: Rial

**Taj Mahal, India.** Known as the 'monument to love' this tomb of white marble was built in the mid 17th century as a memorial to the wife of the Emperor Shah Jahan.

### SYRIA
REPUBLIC

Area: 185,180 sq km
(71,498 mls)
Population: 14,186,000
Capital: Damascus
Language: Arabic, Kurdish,
Armenian
Religion: Sunni Muslim,
other Muslim,
Christian
Currency: Pound

### JORDAN
MONARCHY

Area: 89,206 sq km
(34,443 sq mls)
Population: 5,439,000
Capital: Amman
Language: Arabic
Religion: Sunni Muslim,
Christian,
Shi'a Muslim
Currency: Dinar

### IRAQ
REPUBLIC

Area: 438,317 sq km
(169,235 sq mls)
Population: 20,449,000
Capital: Baghdad
Language: Arabic, Kurdish,
Turkmen
Religion: Shi'a Muslim,
Sunni Muslim,
R.Catholic
Currency: Dinar

### GEORGIA
REPUBLIC

Area: 69,700 sq km
(26,911 sq mls)
Population: 5,457,000
Capital: Tbilisi
Language: Georgian, Russian,
Armenian, Azeri,
Ossetian, Abkhaz
Religion: Georgian Orthodox,
Russian Orthodox,
Shi'a Muslim
Currency: Lari

### ARMENIA
REPUBLIC

Area: 29,800 sq km
(11,506 sq mls)
Population: 3,599,000
Capital: Yerevan
Language: Armenian, Azeri,
Russian
Religion: Armenian Othodox,
R.Catholic,
Shi'a Muslim
Currency: Dram

### AZERBAIJAN
REPUBLIC

Area: 86,600 sq km
(33,436 sq mls)
Population: 7,499,000
Capital: Baku
Language: Azeri, Armenian,
Russian, Lezgian
Religion: Shi'a Muslim,
Sunni Muslim, Russian
and Armenian Orthodox
Currency: Manat

### TURKMENISTAN
REPUBLIC

Area: 488,100 sq km
(188,456 sq mls)
Population: 4,099,000
Capital: Ashkhabad
Language: Turkmen, Russian
Religion: Sunni Muslim
Currency: Manat

© Collins

**KAZAKSTAN**

REPUBLIC

Area: 2,717,300 sq km
(1,049,155 sq mls)
Population: 16,590,000
Capital: Alma-Ata
Language: Kazakh, Russian,
German, Ukrainian,
Uzbek, Tatar
Religion: Sunni Muslim, Russian
Orthodox, Protestant
Currency: Tanga

 **UZBEKISTAN**

REPUBLIC

Area: 447,400 sq km
(172,742 sq mls)
Population: 22,843,000
Capital: Tashkent
Language: Uzbek, Russian,
Tajik, Kazakh
Religion: Sunni Muslim
Russian Orthodox
Currency: Som

 **KYRGYZSTAN**

REPUBLIC

Area: 198,500 sq km
(76,641 sq mls)
Population: 4,668,000
Capital: Bishkek
Language: Kirghiz, Russian,
Uzbek
Religion: Sunni Muslim,
Russian Orthodox
Currency: Som

 **TAJIKISTAN**

REPUBLIC

Area: 143,100 sq km
(55,251 sq mls)
Population: 5,836,000
Capital: Dushanbe
Language: Tajik, Uzbek,
Russian
Religion: Sunni Muslim
Currency: Rouble

**AFGHANISTAN**

REPUBLIC

Area: 652,225 sq km
(251,825 sq mls)
Population: 20,141,000
Capital: Kabul
Language: Dari, Pushtu,
Uzbek, Turkmen
Religion: Sunni Muslim,
Shi'a Muslim
Currency: Afghani

**PAKISTAN**

REPUBLIC

Area: 803,940 sq km
(310,403 sq mls)
Population: 129,808,000
Capital: Islamabad
Language: Urdu (official),
Punjabi, Sindhi,
Pushtu, English
Religion: Sunni Muslim,
Shi'a Muslim,
Christian, Hindu
Currency: Rupee

**Great Wall of China.** Stretching 3460 km, this is the longest wall in the world and dates from the 3rdC BC.

 **MYANMAR**

REPUBLIC

Area: 676,577 sq km
(261,228 sq mls)
Population: 46,527,000
Capital: Yangon
Language: Burmese, Shan,
Karen, Local Languages
Religion: Buddhist, Sunni Muslim,
Protestant, R.Catholic
Currency: Kyat

**Japan.** The speedy 'Bullet train' travels past Mount Fuji, a volcano which last erupted in 1707.

 **INDIA**

REPUBLIC

Area: 3,287,263 sq km
(1,269,219 sq mls)
Population: 935,744,000
Capital: New Delhi
Language: Hindi, English (official),
Many Regional Languages
Religion: Hindu, Sunni Muslim,
Sikh, Christian,
Buddhist, Jain
Currency: Rupee

**SRI LANKA**

REPUBLIC

Area: 65,610 sq km
(25,332 sq mls)
Population: 18,354,000
Capital: Colombo
Language: Sinhalese, Tamil,
English
Religion: Buddhist, Hindu,
Sunni Muslim,
R. Catholic
Currency: Rupee

**MALDIVES**

REPUBLIC

Area: 298 sq km
(115 sq mls)
Population: 254,000
Capital: Male
Language: Divehi (Maldivian)
Religion: Sunni Muslim
Currency: Rufiyaa

 **NEPAL**

MONARCHY

Area: 147,181 sq km
(56,827 sq mls)
Population: 21,918,000
Capital: Kathmandu
Language: Nepali, Maithili,
Bhojpuri, English,
Many Local Languages
Religion: Hindu, Buddhist,
Sunni Muslim
Currency: Rupee

 **BHUTAN**

MONARCHY

Area: 46,620 sq km
(18,000 sq mls)
Population: 1,638,000
Capital: Thimphu
Language: Dzongkha, Nepali
Assamese, English
Religion: Buddhist, Hindu
Currency: Ngultrum,
Indian Rupee

 **BANGLADESH**

REPUBLIC

Area: 143,998 sq km
(55,598 sq mls)
Population: 120,433,000
Capital: Dhaka
Language: Bengali, Bihari,
Hindi, English,
Local Languages
Religion: Sunni Muslim, Hindu,
Buddhist, Christian
Currency: Taka

**PHILIPPINES**

REPUBLIC

Area: 300,000 sq km
(115,831 sq mls)
Population: 70,267,000
Capital: Manila
Language: English, Filipino
(Tagalog), Cebuano
Religion: R.Catholic, Aglipayan,
Sunni Muslim,
Protestant
Currency: Peso

**POPULATION**
Inhabitants

| per sq km | per sq ml |
|---|---|
| over 200 | over 500 |
| 100-200 | 250-500 |
| 40-100 | 100-250 |
| 10-40 | 25-100 |
| 2-10 | 5-25 |
| 0-2 | 0-5 |
| uninhabited | |

**CITIES**
■ Over 5 million
population
● 2.5 - 5 million
population

St. Petersburg
Moscow
Izmir
Ankara
Aleppo
Damascus
Baghdad    Tehran
Lahore
Delhi
Karachi
Ahmadabad    Dhak
Bombay    Calcutta
Hyderabad
Bangalore    Madras

## THAILAND

MONARCHY
Area: 513,115 sq km
(198,115 sq mls)
Population: 59,401,000
Capital: Bangkok
Language: Thai, Lao, Chinese,
Malay,
Mon-Khmer Languages
Religion: Buddhist,
Sunni Muslim
Currency: Baht

## LAOS
REPUBLIC
Area: 236,800 sq km
(91,429 sq mls)
Population: 4,882,000
Capital: Vientiane
Language: Lao, Local Languages
Religion: Buddhist,
Trad. Beliefs,
R.Catholic,
Sunni Muslim
Currency: Kip

## CAMBODIA

MONARCHY
Area: 181,000 sq km
(69,884 sq mls)
Population: 9,836,000
Capital: Phnom Penh
Language: Khmer,
Vietnamese
Religion: Buddhist, R.Catholic,
Sunni Muslim
Currency: Riel

## VIETNAM
REPUBLIC
Area: 329,565 sq km
(127,246 sq mls)
Population: 74,545,000
Capital: Hanoi
Language: Vietnamese, Thai,
Khmer, Chinese, Many
Local Languages
Religion: Buddhist, Taoist,
R.Catholic, Cao Dai
Currency: Dong

## CHINA

REPUBLIC
Area: 9,560,900 sq km
(3,691,484 sq mls)
Population: 1,221,462,000
Capital: Beijing
Language: Chinese (Mandarin
official), Many
Regional Languages
Religion: Confucian, Taoist, Buddhist,
Sunni Muslim, R.Catholic
Currency: Yuan

## MONGOLIA

REPUBLIC
Area: 1,565,000 sq km
(604,250 sq mls)
Population: 2,410,000
Capital: Ulan Bator
Language: Khalka (Mongolian),
Kazakh, Local Languages
Religion: Buddhist, Sunni Muslim,
Trad. Beliefs
Currency: Tugrik

## NORTH KOREA

REPUBLIC
Area: 120,538 sq km
(46,540 sq mls)
Population: 23,917,000
Capital: Pyongyang
Language: Korean
Religion: Trad. Beliefs,
Chondoist, Buddhist,
Confucian, Taoist
Currency: Won

## SOUTH KOREA
REPUBLIC
Area: 99,274 sq km
(38,330 sq mls)
Population: 44,851,000
Capital: Seoul
Language: Korean
Religion: Buddhist, Protestant,
R.Catholic, Confucian,
Trad. Beliefs
Currency: Won

## POPULATION

Harbin

Shenyang

Tokyo
Beijing Dalian Seoul Yokohama
Tianjin Pusan Osaka-Kōbe

Xi'an

Chengdu Wuhan
Chongqing Shanghai

Taipei

Guangzhou

Yangon

Bangkok

Hô Chi Minh

Manila–Quezon City

Singapore

Jakarta

## JAPAN
MONARCHY
Area: 377,727 sq km
(145,841 sq mls)
Population: 125,197,000
Capital: Tokyo
Language: Japanese
Religion: Shintoist, Buddhist,
Christian
Currency: Yen

## TAIWAN
REPUBLIC
Area: 36,179 sq km
(13,969 sq mls)
Population: 21,211,000
Capital: Taipei
Language: Chinese (Mandarin
official, Fukien,
Hakka), Local Languages
Religion: Buddhist, Taoist,
Confucian, Christian
Currency: Dollar

**Hong Kong.** A traditional Chinese sailing ship, known as a junk, sails in the spectacular harbour.

## MACAU

PORTUGUESE
TERRITORY
Area: 17 sq km
(7 sq mls)
Population: 418,000
Capital: Macau
Language: Cantonese,
Portuguese
Religion: Buddhist,
R.Catholic,
Protestant
Currency: Pataca

## PALAU

REPUBLIC
Area: 497 sq km
(192 sq mls)
Population: 17,000
Capital: Koror
Language: Palauan, English
Religion: R.Catholic, Protestant,
Trad. Beliefs
Currency: US Dollar

## MALAYSIA

FEDERATION
Area: 332,665 sq km
(128,442 sq mls)
Population: 20,140,000
Capital: Kuala Lumpur
Language: Malay, English,
Chinese, Tamil,
Local Languages
Religion: Sunni Muslim,
Buddhist, Hindu,
Christian, Trad. Beliefs
Currency: Dollar (Ringgit)

## SINGAPORE

REPUBLIC
Area: 639 sq km
(247 sq mls)
Population: 2,987,000
Capital: Singapore
Language: Chinese, English,
Malay, Tamil
Religion: Buddhist, Taoist,
Sunni Muslim,
Christian, Hindu
Currency: Dollar

## BRUNEI

MONARCHY
Area: 5,765 sq km
(2,226 sq mls)
Population: 285,000
Capital: Bandar Seri Begawan
Language: Malay, English,
Chinese
Religion: Sunni Muslim,
Buddhist, Christian
Currency: Dollar (Ringgit)

## INDONESIA

REPUBLIC
Area: 1,919,445 sq km
(741,102 sq mls)
Population: 194,564,000
Capital: Jakarta
Language: Indonesian (official),
Many Local Languages
Religion: Sunni Muslim, Protestant,
R.Catholic, Hindu,
Buddhist
Currency: Rupiah

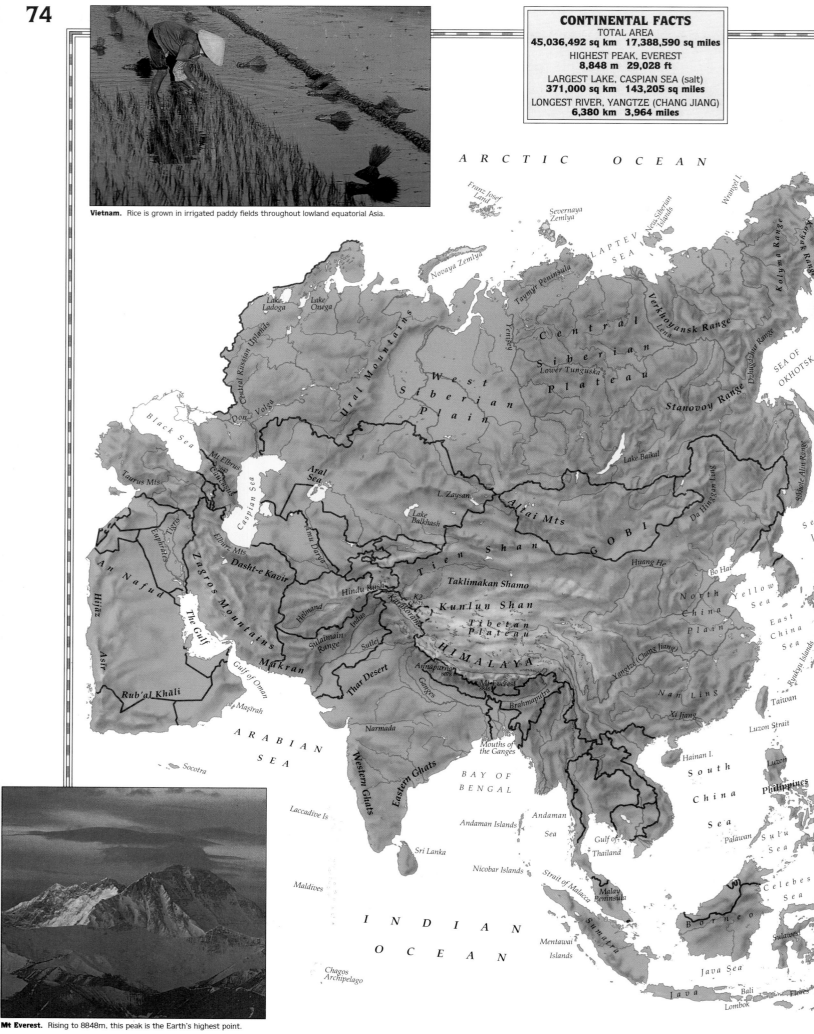

**Vietnam.** Rice is grown in irrigated paddy fields throughout lowland equatorial Asia.

**CONTINENTAL FACTS**
TOTAL AREA
**45,036,492 sq km   17,388,590 sq miles**
HIGHEST PEAK, EVEREST
**8,848 m   29,028 ft**
LARGEST LAKE, CASPIAN SEA (salt)
**371,000 sq km   143,205 sq miles**
LONGEST RIVER, YANGTZE (CHANG JIANG)
**6,380 km   3,964 miles**

ARCTIC OCEAN

Franz Josef Land

Severnaya Zemlya

Novaya Zemlya

New Siberian Islands

Wrangel I.

LAPTEV SEA

Taymyr Peninsula

Kolyma Range

Anadyr Range

SEA OF OKHOTSK

Lake Ladoga

Lake Onega

Central Russian Uplands

Ural Mountains

West Siberian Plain

Yenisey

Central Siberian Plateau

Lower Tunguska

Lena

Verkhoyansk Range

Dzhugdzhur Range

Stanovoy Range

Sikhote Alin Range

Don

Volga

Black Sea

Mt Elbrus

Caucasus

Taurus Mts

Caspian Sea

Aral Sea

Amu Darya

L. Zaysan

Lake Balkhash

Lake Baikal

Altai Mts

GOBI

Da Hinggan Ling

Tien Shan

Taklimakan Shamo

Huang He

Bo Hai

Yellow Sea

North China Plain

East China Sea

Ryukyu Islands

Euphrates

Tigris

Zagros Mountains

Elburz Mts.

Dasht-e Kavir

Hindu Kush

Karakoram

K2

Kunlun Shan

Tibetan Plateau

HIMALAYA

Yangtze (Chang Jiang)

Nan Ling

Xi Jiang

Taiwan

Luzon Strait

An Nafud

Hijāz

Asīr

The Gulf

Helmand

Sulaiman Range

Indus

Sutlej

Annapurna

Mt Everest

Brahmaputra

Ganges

Makran

Thar Desert

Gulf of Oman

Maṣīrah

Narmada

Mouths of the Ganges

Luzon

Hainan I.

South China Sea

Philippines

Rub' al Khāli

ARABIAN SEA

Socotra

Western Ghats

Eastern Ghats

BAY OF BENGAL

Andaman Islands

Andaman Sea

Sulu Sea

Palawan

Laccadive Is

Sri Lanka

Nicobar Islands

Gulf of Thailand

Celebes Sea

Maldives

Strait of Malacca

Malay Peninsula

Borneo

Sulawesi

INDIAN OCEAN

Chagos Archipelago

Mentawai Islands

Sumatra

Java Sea

Java

Bali

Lombok

Flores

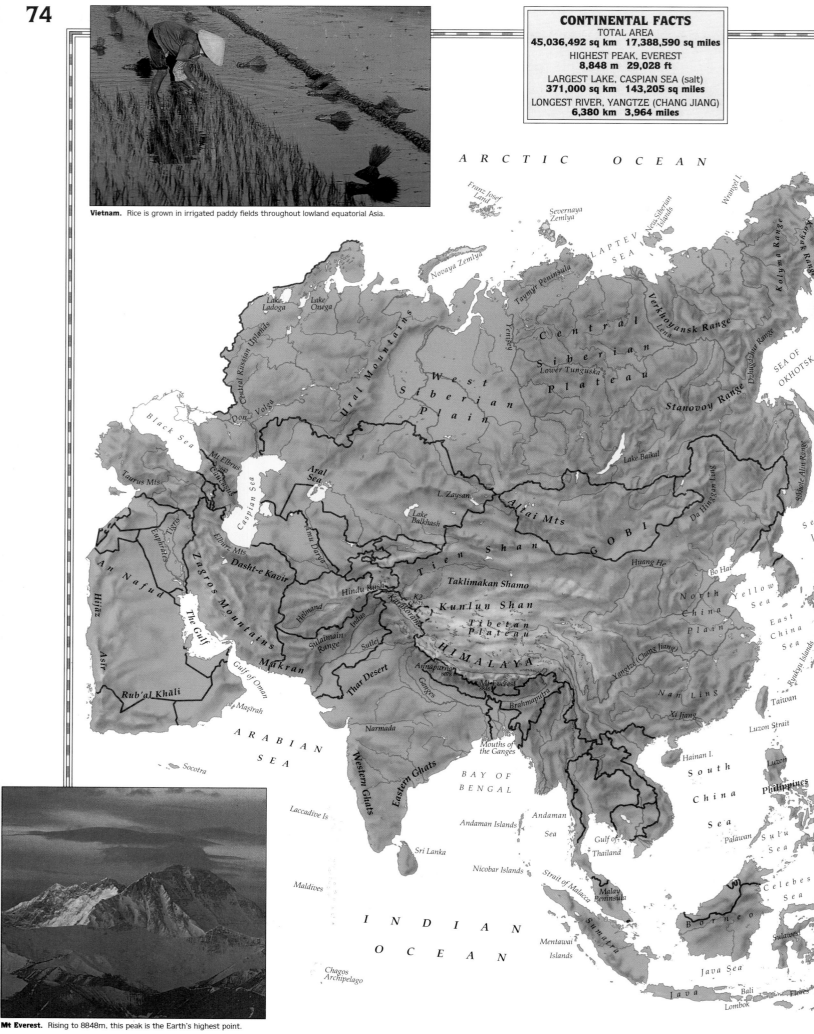

**Mt Everest.** Rising to 8848m, this peak is the Earth's highest point.

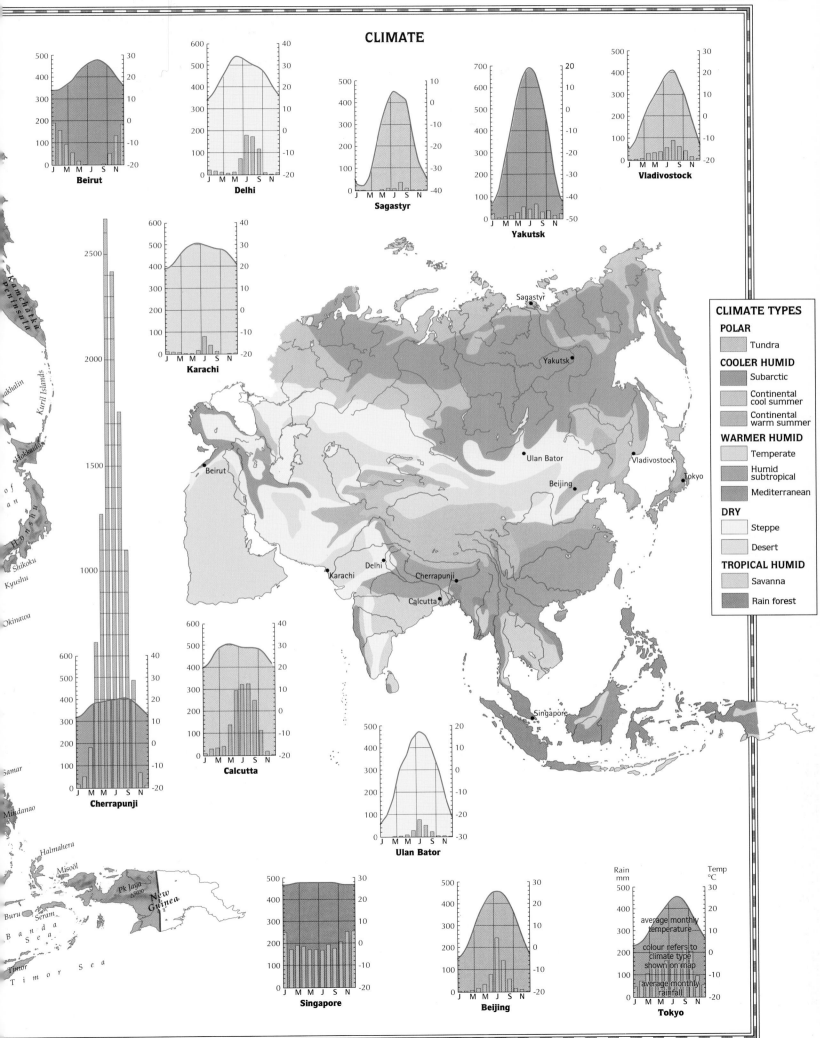

## CLIMATE

**CLIMATE TYPES**

**POLAR**
- Tundra

**COOLER HUMID**
- Subarctic
- Continental cool summer
- Continental warm summer

**WARMER HUMID**
- Temperate
- Humid subtropical
- Mediterranean

**DRY**
- Steppe
- Desert

**TROPICAL HUMID**
- Savanna
- Rain forest

© Collins

Conic Equidistant Projection

1:21M

KM    MILES
1000  600
800   450
600   300
400   150
200
0     0

© Collins

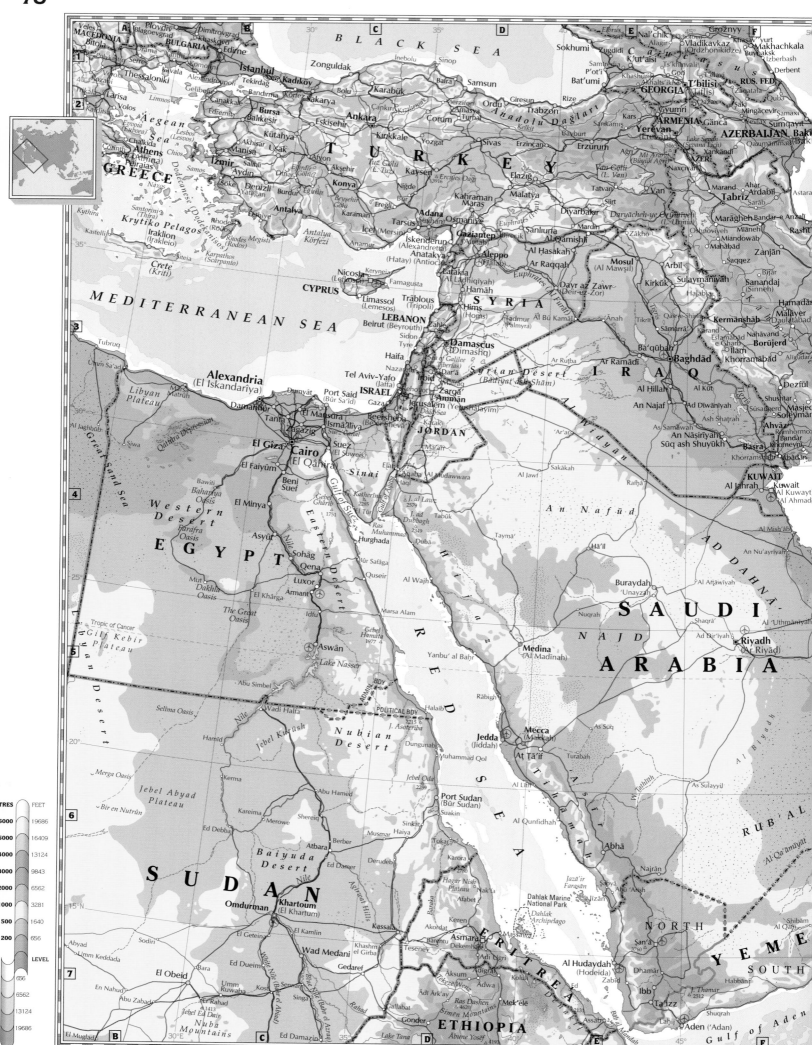

Albers Equal Area Conic Projection

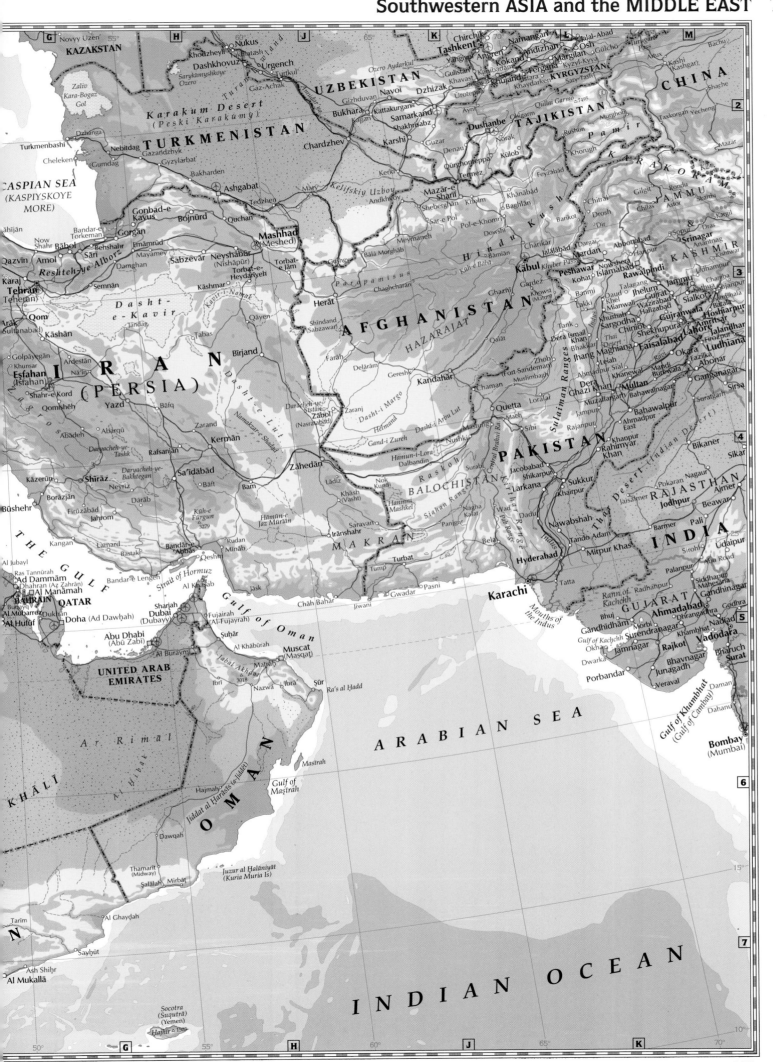

Conic Equidistant Projection

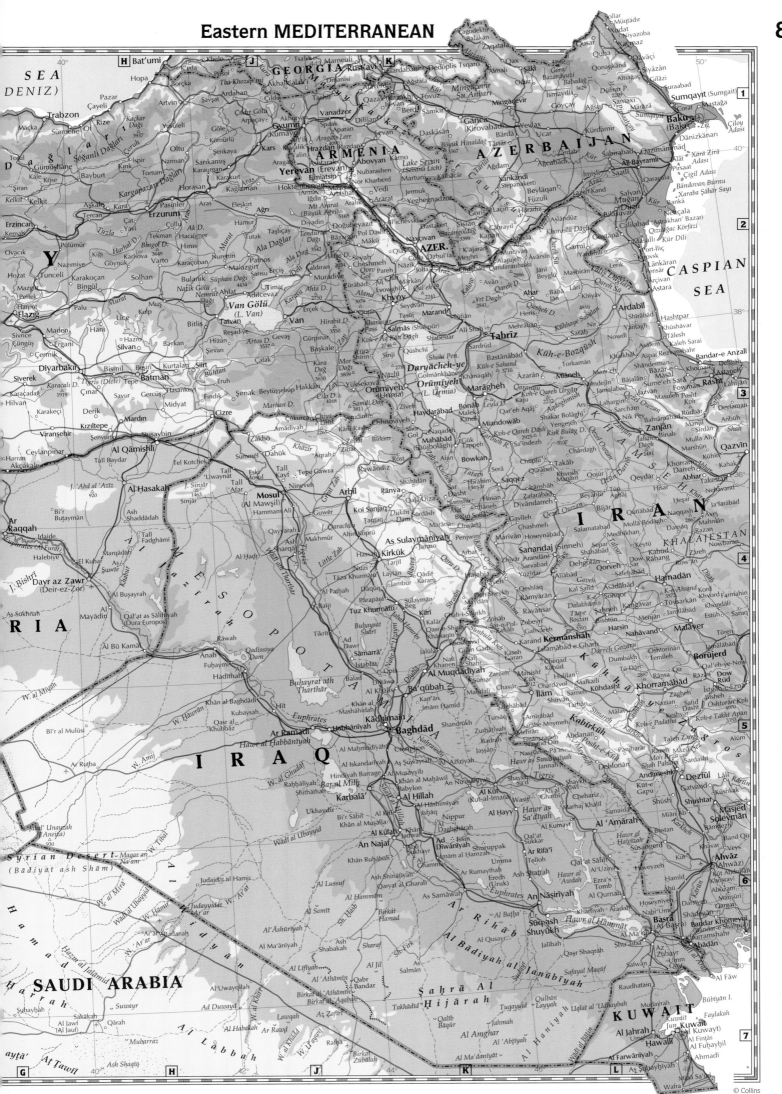

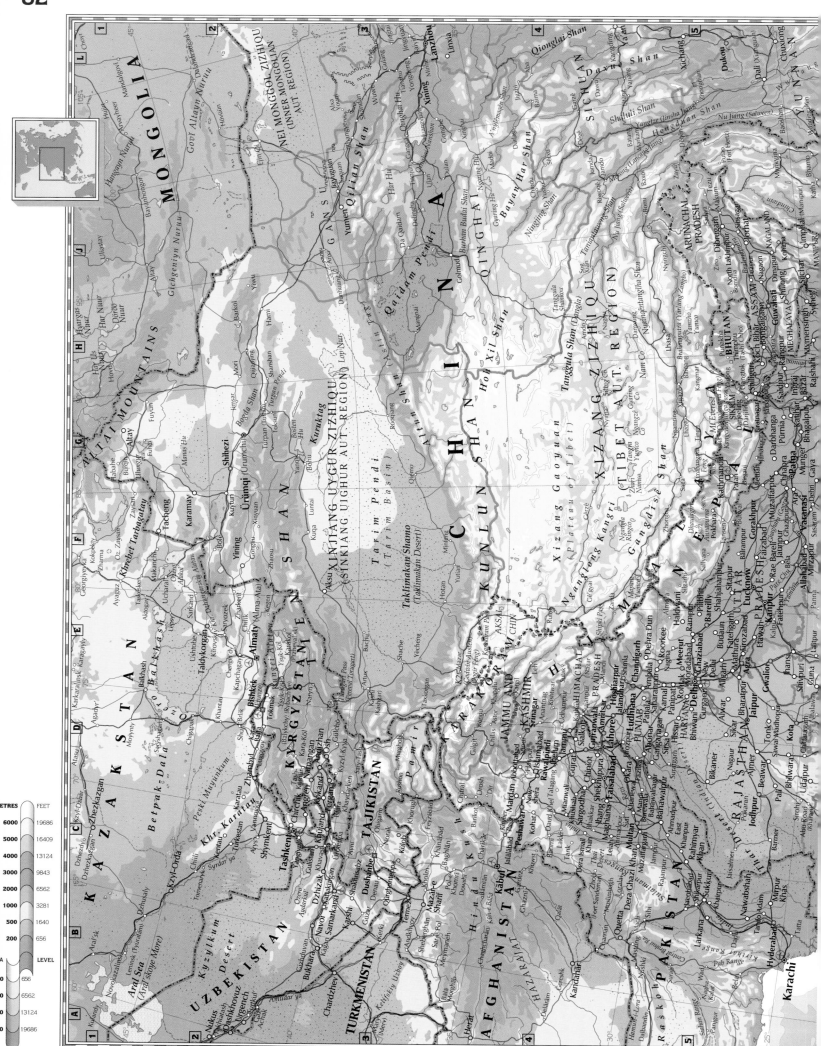

METRES / FEET

| METRES | FEET |
|---|---|
| 6000 | 19686 |
| 5000 | 16409 |
| 4000 | 13124 |
| 3000 | 9843 |
| 2000 | 6562 |
| 1000 | 3281 |
| 500 | 1640 |
| 200 | 656 |
| SEA | LEVEL |
| 200 | 656 |
| 000 | 6562 |
| 000 | 13124 |
| 000 | 19686 |

Transverse Mercator Projection

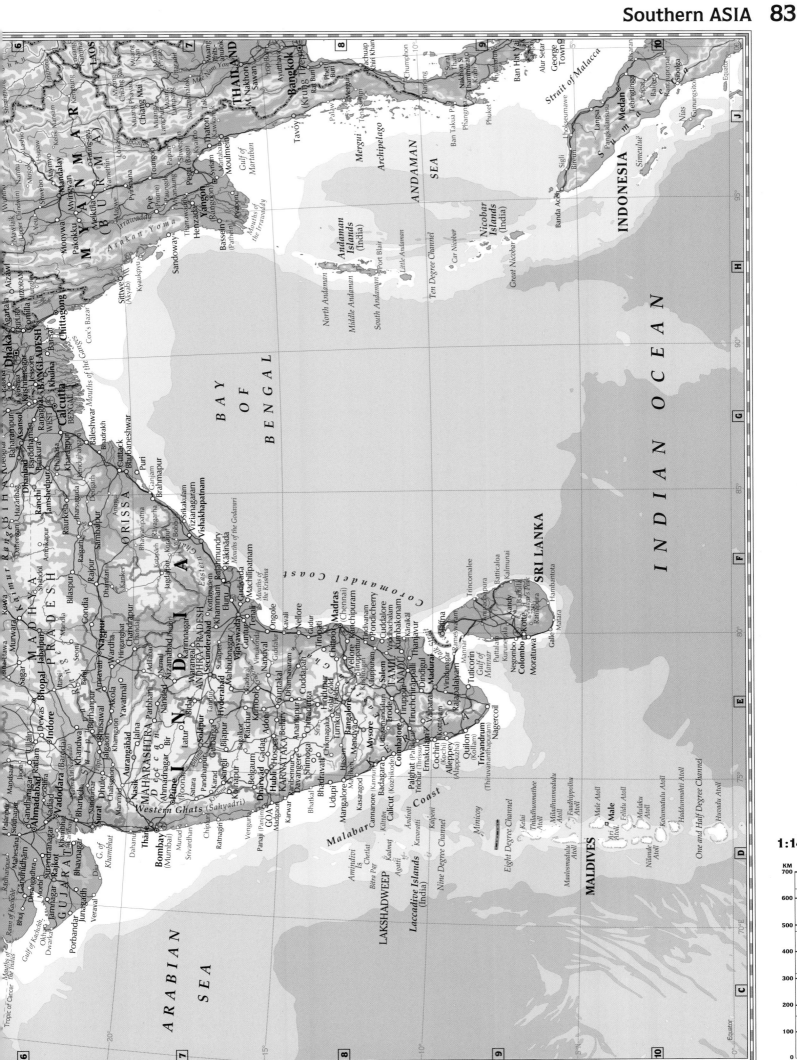

ARABIAN SEA

INDIAN OCEAN

BAY OF BENGAL

ANDAMAN SEA

Strait of Malacca

INDIA

SRI LANKA

MALDIVES

INDONESIA

THAILAND

MYANMAR (BURMA)

BANGLADESH

LAOS

1:14M

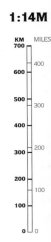

KM 700
600
500
400
300
200
100
0

MILES
400
300
200
100
0

© Collins

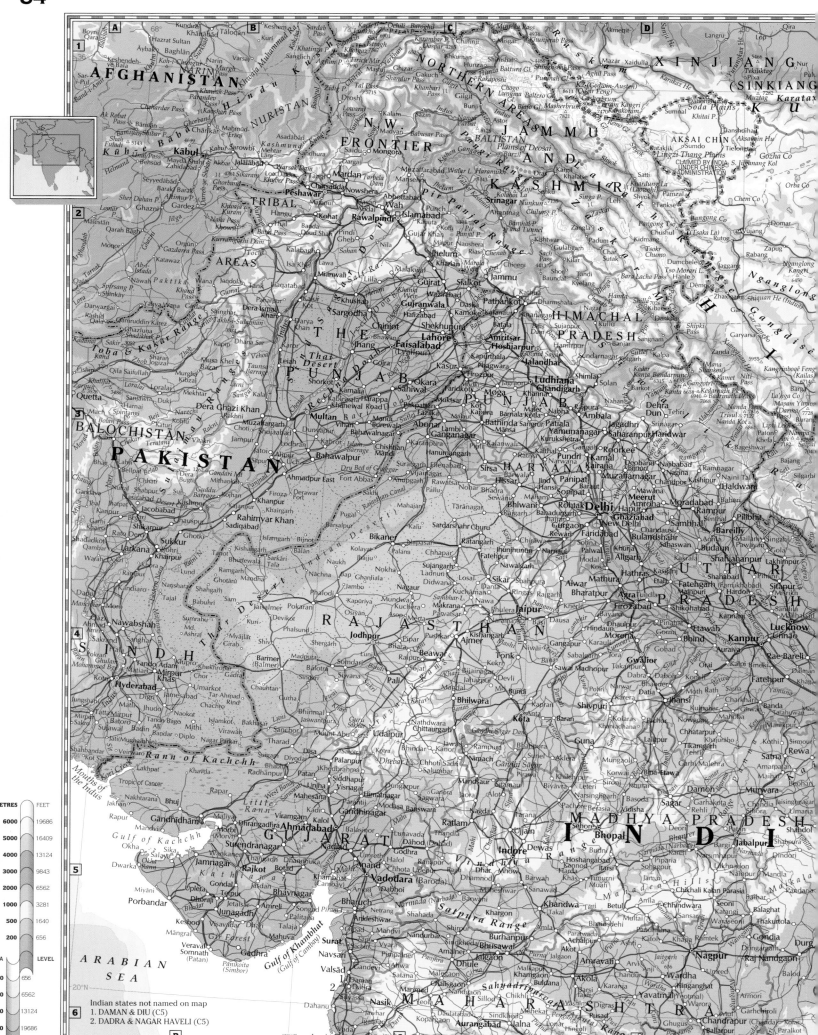

METRES | FEET
6000 | 19686
5000 | 16409
4000 | 13124
3000 | 9843
2000 | 6562
1000 | 3281
500 | 1640
200 | 656

SEA | LEVEL

200 | 656
2000 | 6562
4000 | 13124
6000 | 19686

Indian states not named on map
1. DAMAN & DIU (C5)
2. DADRA & NAGAR HAVELI (C5)

Conic Equidistant Projection

© Collins

Albers Equal Area Conic Projection

1:15M

| KM | MILES |
|---|---|
| | 600 |
| 900 | |
| | 450 |
| 750 | |
| | 300 |
| 600 | |
| | 150 |
| 450 | |
| 300 | |
| | 0 |

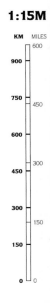

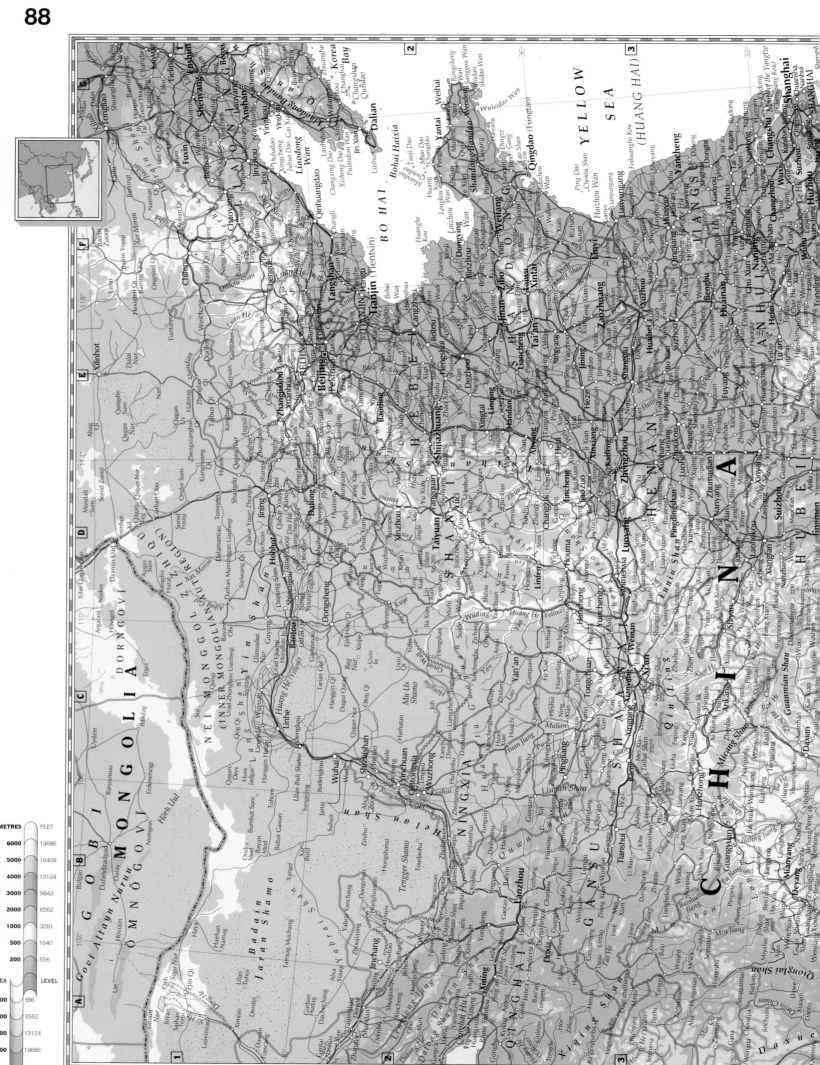

METRES | FEET
6000 | 19686
5000 | 16409
4000 | 13124
3000 | 9843
2000 | 6562
1000 | 3281
500 | 1640
200 | 656

SEA | LEVEL
200 | 656
2000 | 6562
4000 | 13124
6000 | 19686

Conic Equidistant Projection

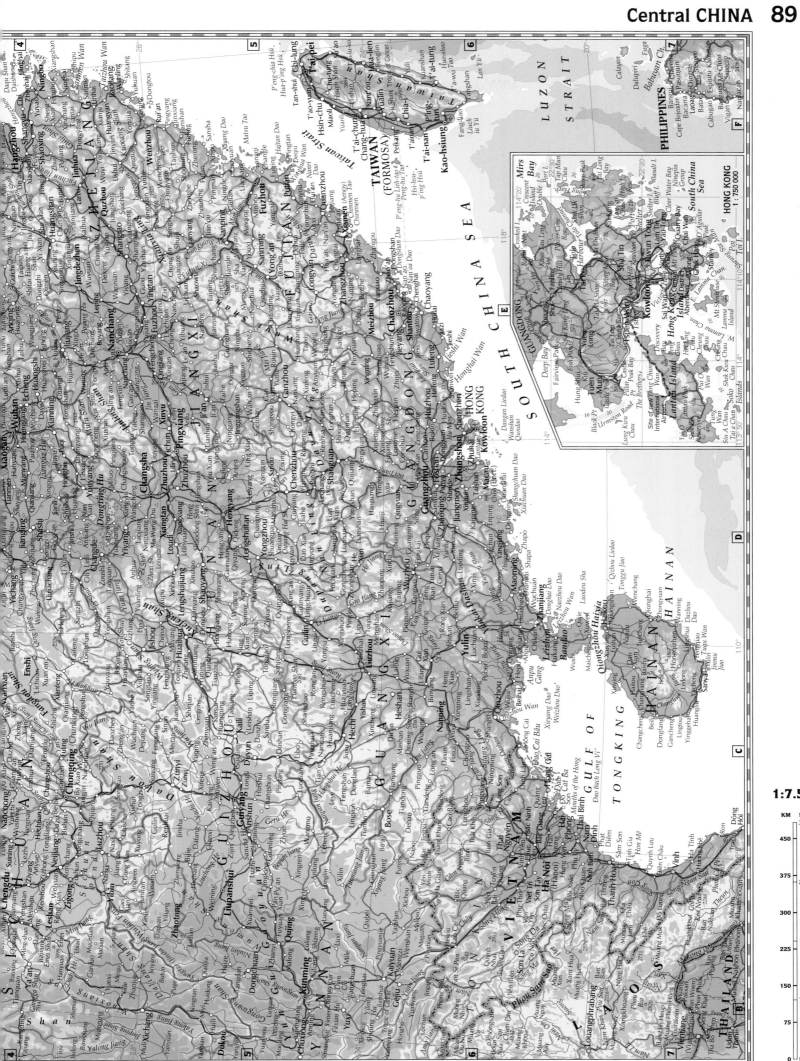

1:7.5M

© Collins

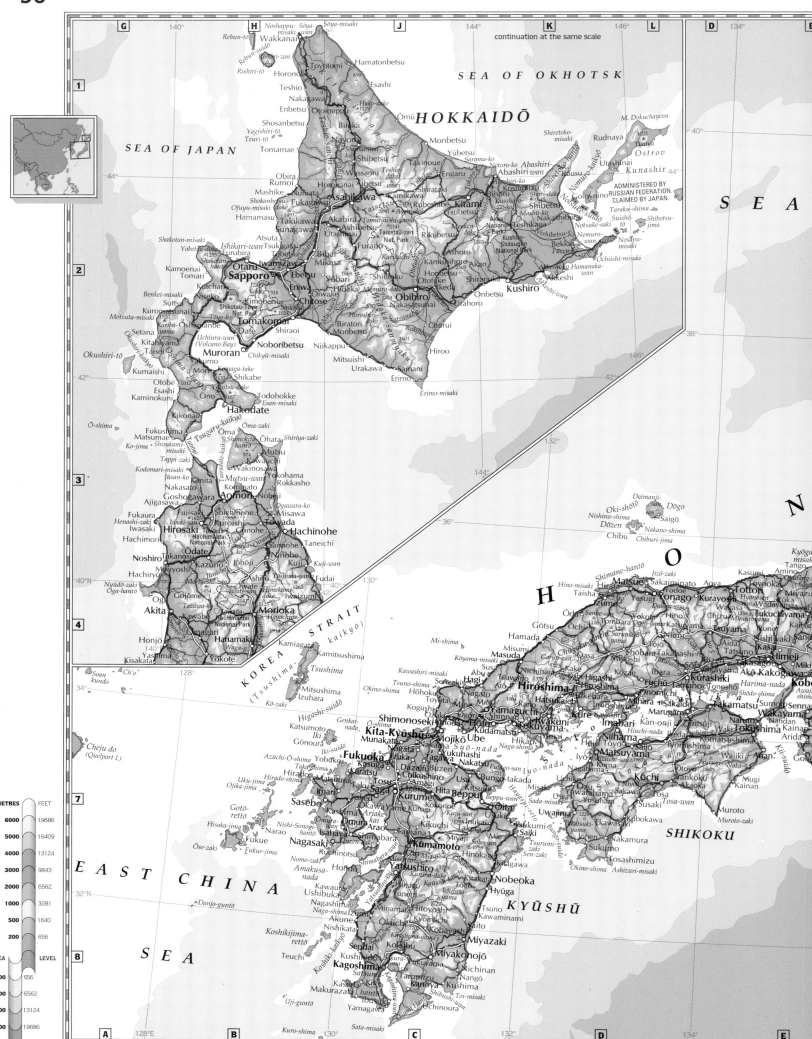

Conic Equidistant Projection

OF JAPAN

Ū

S H

S

PACIFIC OCEAN

Kashima-
nada

Sendai wan

1:4M

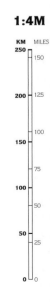

KM MILES
250 — 150

200 — 125

— 100

150 — 75

100 — 50

50 — 25

0 — 0

© Collins

PACIFIC

OCEAN

PHILIPPINE

SEA

NORTHERN

MARIANA

ISLANDS

(U.S.A.)

PHILIPPINES

FEDERATED STATES

OF MICRONESIA

PALAU
(BELAU)

Celebes
Sea

Molucca
Sea

Sulu Sea

Moro
Gulf

Davao
Gulf

Sulu
Archipelago

Makassar Strait

Sulawesi
(Celebes)

Teluk
Bone

Flores Sea

Banda Sea

Seram Sea (Ceram Sea)

Maluku Sea

Arafura
Sea

IRIAN

JAYA

PAPUA

NEW

GUINEA

AUSTRALIA

© Collins

1:15M

| KM | MILES |
|---|---|
| | 600 |
| 900 | |
| | 450 |
| 750 | |
| 600 | 300 |
| 450 | |
| | 150 |
| 300 | |
| 150 | |
| 0 | 0 |

Tropic of Cancer

Equator

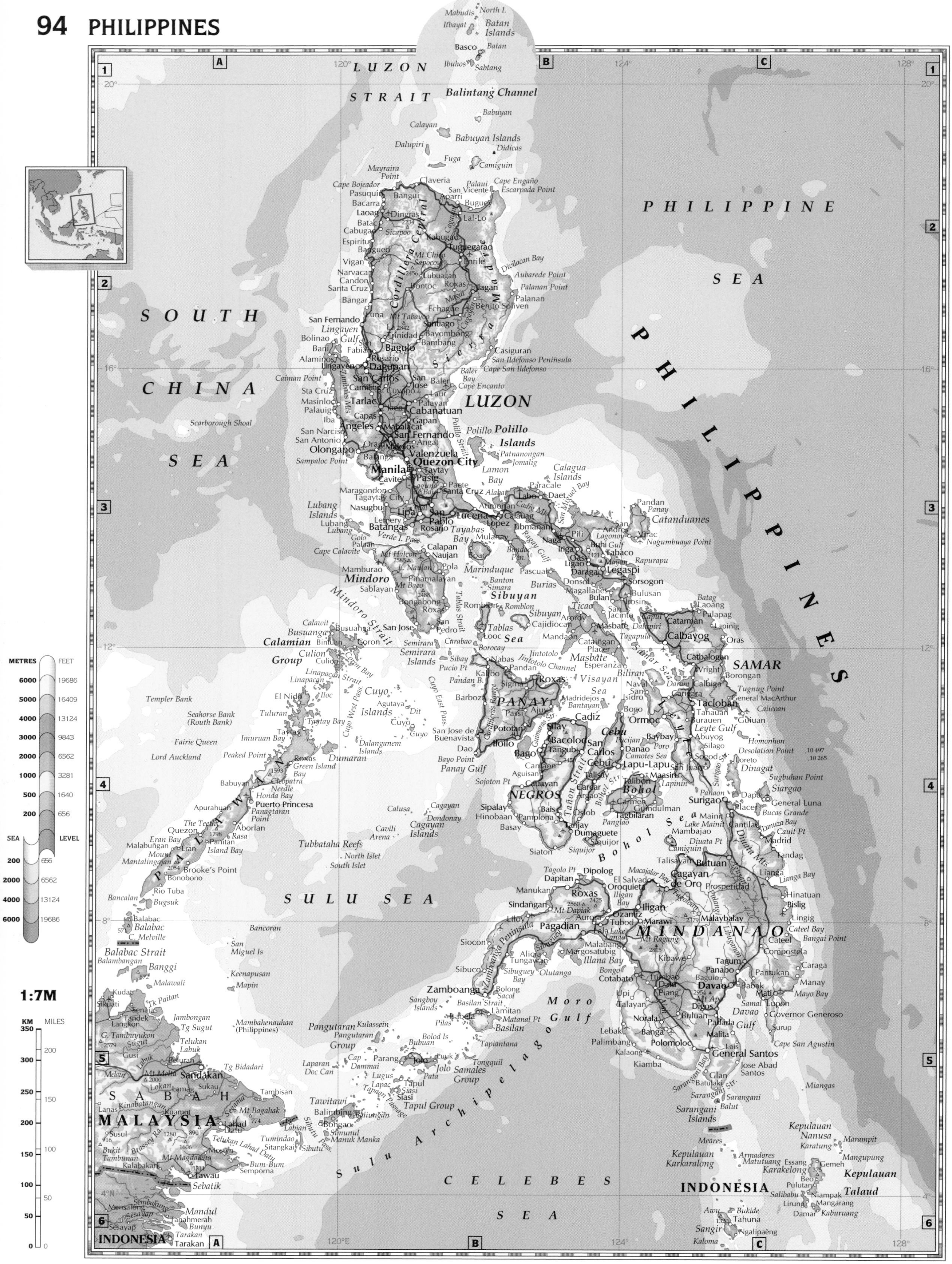

LUZON STRAIT

Balintang Channel

North I.
Mabudis
Itbayat · Batan
Islands
Basco · Batan
Ibuhos · Sabtang

PHILIPPINE

SEA

SOUTH

CHINA

SEA

Calayan
Babuyan
Babuyan Islands
Dalupiri
Fuga · Camiguin

Mayraira
Point
Cape Bojeador · Claveria · Palaui
Pasuquin · San Vicente · Cape Engaño
Bacarra · Aparri · Buguey · Escarpada Point
Laoag · Dingras · Lal-Lo
Batac · Sicapoo · Tuguegarao
Cabugao · Mt Chico · Ilagan
Espiritu · Enrile
Bangued · Divilacan Bay
Vigan · Lubuagan · Aubarede Point
Narvacan · Bontoc · Palanan Point
Candon · Echague · Palanan
Santa Cruz · Santiago
Bangar · Bayombong · Casiguran
San Fernando · Bambang · San Ildefonso Peninsula
Bolinao · Trinidad · San Ildefonso
Bani · Fabia · Baguio · Cape San Ildefonso
Alaminos · Rosario · LUZON
Lingayen · Dagupan · Baler
Caiman Point · San Carlos · Baler Bay
Sta Cruz · Camiling · San Jose · Cape Encanto
Masinloc · Tarlac · Palayan
Palauig · Capas · Cabanatuan
Iba · Angeles · Gapan
San Narciso · Mabalacat · Polillo
San Antonio · San Fernando · Polillo Islands
Olongapo · Angat · Patnanongan
Balanga · Valenzuela · Jomalig
Sampaloc Point · Malolos · Lamon
Manila · Quezon City · Calagua Islands
Cavite · Pasig · Taytay
Maragondon · Santa Cruz · Paracale
Tagaytay City · Paete · Panay
Nasugbu · Alabat · Daet
Lubang · San · Lucena · Lagonoy · Virac
Islands · Pablo · Lopez · Catanduanes
Lubang · Lipa · Gumaca · Naga · Pili
Batangas · Lemery · Tayabas · Iriga
Lubang · Rosario · Bay · Mulanay · Bulan Gulf
Golo · Verde I. Passe · Bondoc · Oas · Tabaco
Cape Calavite · Calapan · Boac · Ligao · Moyon · Rapurapu
Mamburao · Naujan · Daraga · Legaspi
Mt Halcon · Pola · Pascual · Donsol · Sorsogon
Mindoro · Marinduque · Magallanes · Bulusan
Sablayan · Mt Baco · Banton · Bulan
Pinamalayan · Simara · Burias · Batag
San Jose · Romblon · Romblon · Laoang · Palapag
Calawit · Sibuyan · Ticao · Catarman · Oras
Busuanga · Roxas · Masbate · Calbayog
Calamian · Binluit · Coron · Tablas · Cajidiocan · Aroroy · Catbalogan · SAMAR
Group · Culion · Semirara · Sea · Jintotolo Channel · Placer · Borongan
Culion · Islands · Looc · Esperanza · Wright · Tugnug Point
Linapacan · Cataingan · Calbiga · General MacArthur
Linapacan Strait · Sibay · Nabas · Masbate · Naval · Tacloban · Calicoan
El Nido · Cuyo West Pass · Pucio Pt · Kalibo · Isidro · Catbalogan · Burauen · Guiuan
Tuluran · Islands · Pandan · Biliran · Daram · Baybay · Leyte Gulf · Homonhon
Taytay · Cuyo · Roxas · Ajuy · Ormoc · Abuyog · Desolation Point
Imuruan Bay · Cuyo · Barboza · Madridejos · Silago · 10 497 · 10 265
Roxas · Agutaya · Dit · PANAY · Bantayan · Sogod · Dinagat
Peaked Point · Dumaran · San Jose de Buenavista · Cadiz · San · Baybay · Siargao
Babuyan · Dalanganem Islands · Dao · Iloilo · Cebu · Danao · General Luna
Cleopatra · Islands · Bayo Point · Tanguib · Camotes Sea · Surigao
Needle · Green Island · Bago · Talisay · Lapu-Lapu · Dapa
Puerto Princesa · Cavili · Cagayan · Sipalay · Carcar · Maasin · Bucas Grande
Panagtaran · Arena · Islands · Hinobaan · Pamplona · Argao · Cauit Pt
Point · Calusa · NEGROS · Oslob · Carmen · Madrid
Aborlan · Dondonay · Basay · Dumaguete · Camiguin · Butuan · Lianga
Eran Bay · Cagayan · Siaton · Siquijor · Mambajao · Lianga Bay
Quezon · Islands · Bohol Sea · Diuata Mts
The Teeth · Tubbataha Reefs · Tagolo Pt · Talisayan · Tandag
Eran · North Islet · Dipolog · Mainit · Cantilan
Malabungan · South Islet · Dapitan · El Salvador · Compostela
Mount · Manukan · Oroquieta · Cagayan de Oro · Bislig
Mantalingajan · Sindangan · Ozamiz · Prosperidad · Hinatuan
Rasa · Iligan · Bislig
Bugsuk · Liloy · Aurora · Mt Ragang · Malaybalay · Cateel Bay
Brooke's Point · Tubod · Marawi · Malaybalay · Bangai Point
Rio Tuba · MINDANAO · Caraga
Bancalan · Zamboanga Peninsula · Pagadian · La Sala Lake · Kibawe · Compostela
Balabac · Siocon · Margosatubig · Panabo · Pantukan
C. Melville · Cotabato · Tagum · Panabo
Balabac Strait · San Miguel Is · Alicia · Illana Bay · Babak
Balambangan · Banggi · Siay · Tungawan · Upi · Davao · Samal
Zamboanga · Sibuguey · Talayan · Norala · Baguio · Lupon
Malawali · Bay · Cotabato · Digos · Mayo Bay
Kudat · Jambongan · Tg Sugut · Mambahenauhan · Pangutaran · Basilan · Lebak · Banga · Governor Generoso
Tandek · Pilas · Malita · Davao
Telukan · (Philippines) · Pangutaran Group · Bolod Is · Malita · Surup
Sandakan · Siasi · Palimbang · Cape San Agustin
Zamboanga · Jolo · Polomoloc
Kalabakan · Lapac · Jolo · Tongquil · Pata · Samales · Kiamba · General Santos
Tawitawi · Siasi · Group · Jose Abad Santos
Balimbing · Bilungan · Tawau · Sarangani Bay · Glan · Miangas
MALAYSIA · SABAH · Bongao · Sibutu · Sarangani Islands · Balut · Sangir · Kepulauan

PHILIPPINES

SOUTH CHINA SEA

SULU SEA

CELEBES SEA

SULU ARCHIPELAGO

Moro Gulf

Cordillera Central

Sierra Madre

Zambales Mts

Visayan Sea

Sibuyan Sea

Tablas Strait

Samar Sea

Leyte

Panay Gulf

Bohol

Mindoro Strait

Cuyo East Pass

Tañon Strait

INDONESIA

INDONESIA

Kepulauan Talaud

Kepulauan Nanusa

METRES / FEET
6000 / 19686
5000 / 16409
4000 / 13124
3000 / 9843
2000 / 6562
1000 / 3281
500 / 1640
200 / 656
SEA / LEVEL
200 / 656
2000 / 6562
4000 / 13124
6000 / 19686

1:7M

KM / MILES
350
300 / 200
250 / 150
200
150 / 100
100
50
0 / 0

Mercator Projection

© Collins

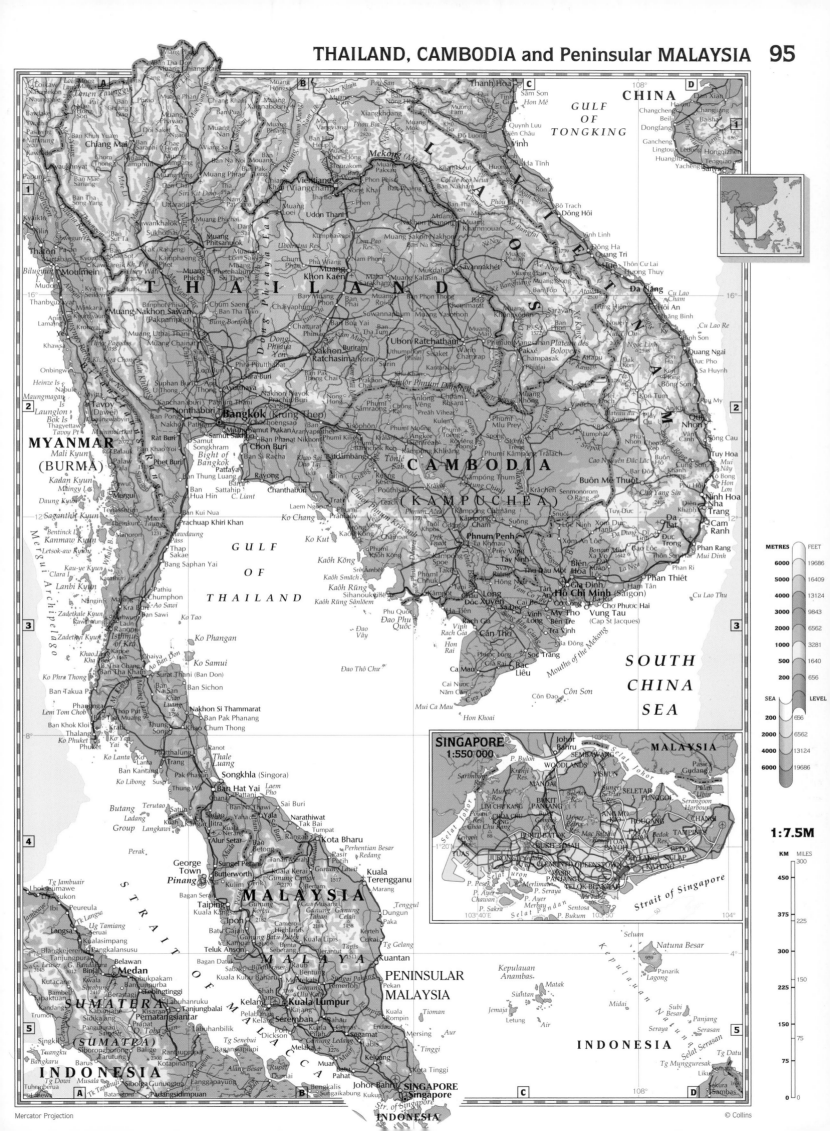

MYANMAR (BURMA)

THAILAND

LAOS

VIETNAM

CAMBODIA (KAMPUCHEA)

GULF OF THAILAND

SOUTH CHINA SEA

MALAYSIA

PENINSULAR MALAYSIA

SUMATERA (SUMATRA)

INDONESIA

STRAIT OF MALACCA

SINGAPORE
1:550 000

SINGAPORE
Singapore

| METRES | FEET |
|--------|------|
| 6000 | 19686 |
| 5000 | 16404 |
| 4000 | 13124 |
| 3000 | 9843 |
| 2000 | 6562 |
| 1000 | 3281 |
| 500 | 1640 |
| 200 | 656 |
| SEA | LEVEL |
| 200 | 656 |
| 2000 | 6562 |
| 4000 | 13124 |
| 6000 | 19686 |

1:7.5M

| KM | MILES |
|----|-------|
| | 300 |
| 450 | 225 |
| 375 | |
| 300 | 150 |
| 225 | |
| 150 | 75 |
| 75 | |
| 0 | 0 |

Mercator Projection

© Collins

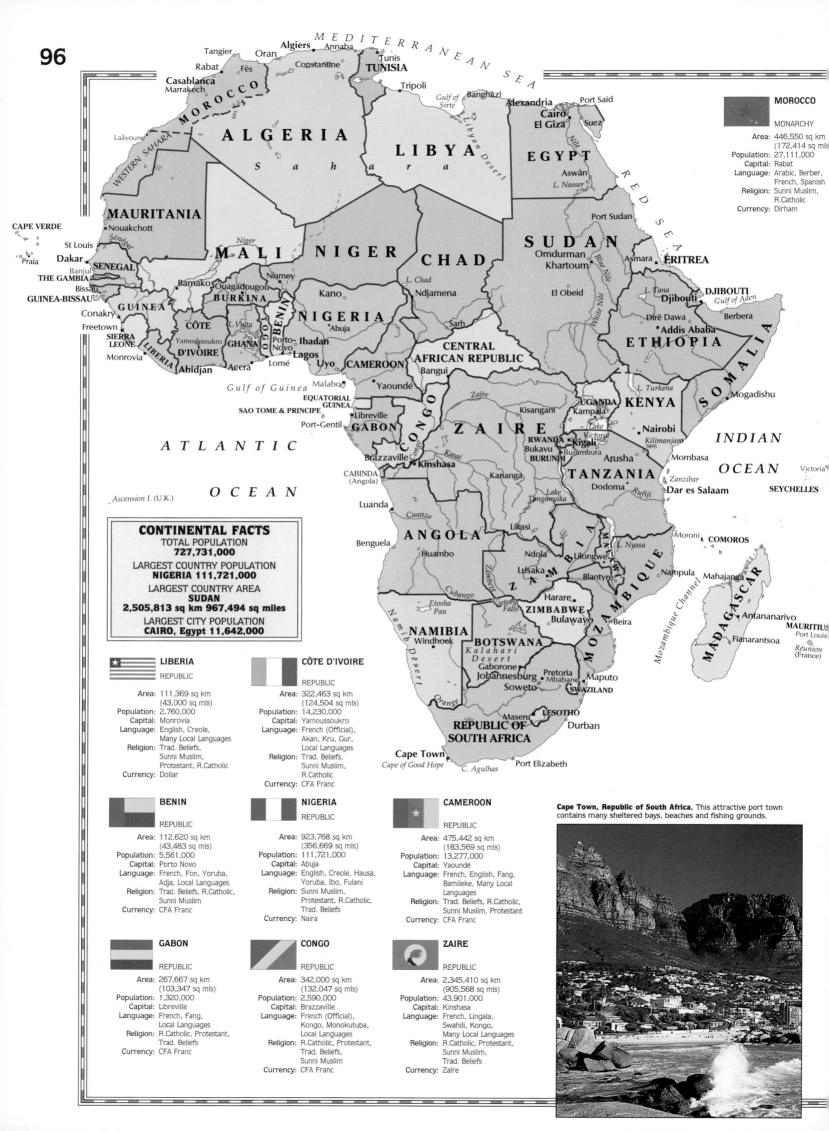

MEDITERRANEAN SEA

Tangier · Oran · Algiers · Annaba
Rabat · Fès · Constantine · Tunis · **TUNISIA**
**Casablanca**
Marrakech · Tripoli
**MOROCCO** · Gulf of Sirte · Banghāzī · Port Said
**WESTERN SAHARA** · **Alexandria**
Laâyoune · **ALGERIA** · **LIBYA** · **EGYPT** · Cairo · El Gîza · Suez

Sahara · L. Nasser · Aswân

**MAURITANIA**
Nouakchott · Sénégal · Niger · Libyan Desert · Port Sudan
**CAPE VERDE**
St Louis · **MALI** · **NIGER** · **CHAD** · **SUDAN**
Praia · Dakar · **SENEGAL** · Bamako · Ouagadougou · Niamey · Omdurman · Khartoum · Asmara · **ERITREA**
**THE GAMBIA** · Banjul · **BURKINA** · Kano · L. Chad · Ndjamena · El Obeid · L. Tana · **DJIBOUTI**
Bissau · **GUINEA-BISSAU** · **BENIN** · **NIGERIA** · Djibouti · Gulf of Aden
Conakry · **GUINEA** · **TOGO** · Abuja · Sarh · Dirē Dawa · Berbera
Freetown · **CÔTE** · L. Volta · Ibadan · **CENTRAL** · **Addis Ababa**
**SIERRA** · **D'IVOIRE** · **GHANA** · Porto- · Lagos · **AFRICAN REPUBLIC** · **ETHIOPIA**
**LEONE** · Yamoussoukro · Novo · Bangui · **SOMALIA**
Monrovia · **LIBERIA** · Accra · Lomé · Uyo · **CAMEROON**
Abidjan · Gulf of Guinea · Malabo · Yaoundé · L. Turkana
**EQUATORIAL** · **CONGO** · **UGANDA** · **KENYA** · Mogadishu
**GUINEA** · Kisangani · Kampala · **Nairobi**
**SAO TOME & PRINCIPE** · Libreville · **ZAIRE** · Lake Victoria · Kilimanjaro 5895
Port-Gentil · **GABON** · **RWANDA** · Arusha · Mombasa
**ATLANTIC** · Brazzaville · Bukavu · Kigali · **TANZANIA** · Zanzibar
Kinshasa · **BURUNDI** · Bujumbura · Dodoma · **Dar es Salaam** · **SEYCHELLES**
CABINDA (Angola) · Kananga · Lake Tanganyika · Rufiji · **INDIAN**
**OCEAN** · Luanda · Kasai · **OCEAN** · Victoria
Ascension I. (U.K.) · Cuanza · Likasi · Moroni · **COMOROS**
**ANGOLA** · Ndola · Lilongwe · Nampula · Mahajanga
Benguela · Huambo · Lusaka · Blantyre · **MOZAMBIQUE** · **MADAGASCAR** · Antananarivo
**ZAMBIA** · Harare · Beira · **MAURITIUS**
Cubango · Zambezi · **ZIMBABWE** · Port Louis
Etosha Pan · Victoria Falls · Bulawayo · Réunion (France)
Namib Desert · **NAMIBIA** · Windhoek · **BOTSWANA** · Kalahari Desert · Mozambique Channel · Fianarantsoa
Gaborone · Pretoria · Maputo
Johannesburg · Mbabane · **SWAZILAND**
Soweto · Maseru · **LESOTHO** · Durban
Orange · **REPUBLIC OF** · **SOUTH AFRICA**
Cape Town · Cape of Good Hope · C. Agulhas · Port Elizabeth

---

## CONTINENTAL FACTS
TOTAL POPULATION
**727,731,000**
LARGEST COUNTRY POPULATION
**NIGERIA 111,721,000**
LARGEST COUNTRY AREA
**SUDAN**
**2,505,813 sq km 967,494 sq miles**
LARGEST CITY POPULATION
**CAIRO, Egypt 11,642,000**

---

**MOROCCO**
MONARCHY
Area: 446,550 sq km (172,414 sq mls)
Population: 27,111,000
Capital: Rabat
Language: Arabic, Berber, French, Spanish
Religion: Sunni Muslim, R.Catholic
Currency: Dirham

**LIBERIA**
REPUBLIC
Area: 111,369 sq km (43,000 sq mls)
Population: 2,760,000
Capital: Monrovia
Language: English, Creole, Many Local Languages
Religion: Trad. Beliefs, Sunni Muslim, Protestant, R.Catholic
Currency: Dollar

**CÔTE D'IVOIRE**
REPUBLIC
Area: 322,463 sq km (124,504 sq mls)
Population: 14,230,000
Capital: Yamoussoukro
Language: French (Official), Akan, Kru, Gur, Local Languages
Religion: Trad. Beliefs, Sunni Muslim, R.Catholic
Currency: CFA Franc

**BENIN**
REPUBLIC
Area: 112,620 sq km (43,483 sq mls)
Population: 5,561,000
Capital: Porto Novo
Language: French, Fon, Yoruba, Adja, Local Languages
Religion: Trad. Beliefs, R.Catholic, Sunni Muslim
Currency: CFA Franc

**NIGERIA**
REPUBLIC
Area: 923,768 sq km (356,669 sq mls)
Population: 111,721,000
Capital: Abuja
Language: English, Creole, Hausa, Yoruba, Ibo, Fulani
Religion: Sunni Muslim, Protestant, R.Catholic, Trad. Beliefs
Currency: Naira

**CAMEROON**
REPUBLIC
Area: 475,442 sq km (183,569 sq mls)
Population: 13,277,000
Capital: Yaoundé
Language: French, English, Fang, Bamileke, Many Local Languages
Religion: Trad. Beliefs, R.Catholic, Sunni Muslim, Protestant
Currency: CFA Franc

**GABON**
REPUBLIC
Area: 267,667 sq km (103,347 sq mls)
Population: 1,320,000
Capital: Libreville
Language: French, Fang, Local Languages
Religion: R.Catholic, Protestant, Trad. Beliefs
Currency: CFA Franc

**CONGO**
REPUBLIC
Area: 342,000 sq km (132,047 sq mls)
Population: 2,590,000
Capital: Brazzaville
Language: French (Official), Kongo, Monokutuba, Local Languages
Religion: R.Catholic, Protestant, Trad. Beliefs, Sunni Muslim
Currency: CFA Franc

**ZAIRE**
REPUBLIC
Area: 2,345,410 sq km (905,568 sq mls)
Population: 43,901,000
Capital: Kinshasa
Language: French, Lingala, Swahili, Kongo, Many Local Languages
Religion: R.Catholic, Protestant, Sunni Muslim, Trad. Beliefs
Currency: Zaire

**Cape Town, Republic of South Africa.** This attractive port town contains many sheltered bays, beaches and fishing grounds.

### ALGERIA
REPUBLIC

Area: 2,381,741 sq km
(919,595 sq mls)
Population: 28,548,000
Capital: Algiers
Language: Arabic, French, Berber
Religion: Sunni Muslim,
R.Catholic
Currency: Dinar

### TUNISIA
REPUBLIC

Area: 164,150 sq km
(63,379 sq mls)
Population: 8,896,000
Capital: Tunis
Language: Arabic, French
Religion: Sunni Muslim
Currency: Dinar

### LIBYA
REPUBLIC

Area: 1,759,540 sq km
(679,362 sq mls)
Population: 5,407,000
Capital: Tripoli
Language: Arabic, Berber
Religion: Sunni Muslim,
R.Catholic
Currency: Dinar

### EGYPT
REPUBLIC

Area: 1,000,250 sq km
(386,199 sq mls)
Population: 59,226,000
Capital: Cairo
Language: Arabic, French
Religion: Sunni Muslim,
Coptic Christian
Currency: Pound

### MAURITANIA
REPUBLIC

Area: 1,030,700 sq km
(397,955 sq mls)
Population: 2,284,000
Capital: Nouakchott
Language: Arabic, French,
Local Languages
Religion: Sunni Muslim
Currency: Ouguiya

### MALI
REPUBLIC

Area: 1,240,140 sq km
(478,821 sq mls)
Population: 10,795,000
Capital: Bamako
Language: French, Bambara,
Many Local Languages
Religion: Sunni Muslim,
Trad. Beliefs,
R.Catholic
Currency: CFA Franc

### BURKINA
REPUBLIC

Area: 274,200 sq km
(105,869 sq mls)
Population: 10,200,000
Capital: Ouagadougou
Language: French, More (Mossi),
Fulani, Local Languages
Religion: Trad. Beliefs,
Sunni Muslim,
R.Catholic
Currency: CFA Franc

### NIGER
REPUBLIC

Area: 1,267,000 sq km
(489,191 sq mls)
Population: 9,151,000
Capital: Niamey
Language: French (Official),
Hausa, Fulani,
Local Languages
Religion: Sunni Muslim,
Trad. Beliefs
Currency: CFA Franc

### CHAD
REPUBLIC

Area: 1,284,000 sq km
(495,755 sq mls)
Population: 6,361,000
Capital: Ndjamena
Language: Arabic, French,
Many Local
Languages
Religion: Sunni Muslim,
Trad. Beliefs,
R.Catholic
Currency: CFA Franc

### SUDAN
REPUBLIC

Area: 2,505,813 sq km
(967,494 sq mls)
Population: 28,098,000
Capital: Khartoum
Language: Arabic, Dinka, Nubian,
Beja, Nuer,
Local Languages
Religion: Sunni Muslim, Trad.
Beliefs, R.Catholic,
Protestant
Currency: Dinar

### ERITREA
REPUBLIC

Area: 117,400 sq km
(45,328 sq mls)
Population: 3,531,000
Capital: Asmara
Language: Tigrinya, Arabic,
Tigre, English
Religion: Sunni Muslim,
Coptic Christian
Currency: Ethiopian Birr

### ETHIOPIA
REPUBLIC

Area: 1,133,880 sq km
(437,794 sq mls)
Population: 56,677,000
Capital: Addis Ababa
Language: Amharic, Oromo,
Local Languages
Religion: Ethiopian Orthodox,
Sunni Muslim,
Trad. Beliefs
Currency: Birr

### DJIBOUTI
REPUBLIC

Area: 23,200 sq km
(8,958 sq mls)
Population: 577,000
Capital: Djibouti
Language: Somali, French,
Arabic, Issa, Afar
Religion: Sunni Muslim,
R.Catholic
Currency: Franc

**Harare.** Following Zimbabwe's independence in 1980 this city became the focus for the population and the economy.

### SENEGAL
REPUBLIC

Area: 196,720 sq km
(75,954 sq mls)
Population: 8,347,000
Capital: Dakar
Language: French (Official),
Wolof, Fulani,
Local Languages
Religion: Sunni Muslim,
R.Catholic,
Trad. Beliefs
Currency: CFA Franc

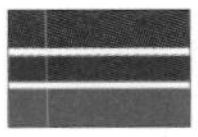

### THE GAMBIA
REPUBLIC

Area: 11,295 sq km
(4,361 sq mls)
Population: 1,118,000
Capital: Banjul
Language: English (Official),
Malinke, Fulani,
Wolof
Religion: Sunni Muslim,
Protestant
Currency: Dalasi

### GUINEA-BISSAU
REPUBLIC

Area: 36,125 sq km
(13,948 sq mls)
Population: 1,073,000
Capital: Bissau
Language: Portuguese,
Portuguese Creole,
Local Languages
Religion: Trad. Beliefs,
Sunni Muslim,
R.Catholic
Currency: Peso

### GUINEA
REPUBLIC

Area: 245,857 sq km
(94,926 sq mls)
Population: 6,700,000
Capital: Conakry
Language: French, Fulani,
Malinke, Local
Languages
Religion: Sunni Muslim,
Trad. Beliefs,
R.Catholic
Currency: Franc

### SIERRA LEONE
REPUBLIC

Area: 71,740 sq km
(27,699 sq mls)
Population: 4,509,000
Capital: Freetown
Language: English, Creole,
Mende, Temne,
Local Languages
Religion: Trad. Beliefs,
Sunni Muslim,
Protestant, R.Catholic
Currency: Leone

### GHANA
REPUBLIC

Area: 238,537 sq km
(92,100 sq mls)
Population: 17,453,000
Capital: Accra
Language: English (Official),
Hausa, Akan,
Local Languages
Religion: Protestant, R.Catholic,
Sunni Muslim,
Trad. Beliefs
Currency: Cedi

### TOGO
REPUBLIC

Area: 56,785 sq km
(21,925 sq mls)
Population: 4,138,000
Capital: Lomé
Language: French, Ewe, Kabre,
Many Local Languages
Religion: Trad. Beliefs,
R.Catholic,
Sunni Muslim,
Protestant
Currency: CFA Franc

## POPULATION

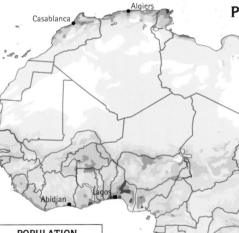

### CENTRAL AFRICAN REPUBLIC
REPUBLIC

Area: 622,436 sq km
(240,324 sq mls)
Population: 3,315,000
Capital: Bangui
Language: French, Sango, Banda,
Baya, Local Languages
Religion: Protestant, R.Catholic,
Trad. Beliefs,
Sunni Muslim
Currency: CFA Franc

### EQUATORIAL GUINEA
REPUBLIC

Area: 28,051 sq km
(10,831 sq mls)
Population: 400,000
Capital: Malabo
Language: Spanish, Fang
Religion: R.Catholic,
Trad. Beliefs
Currency: CFA Franc

### UGANDA
REPUBLIC

Area: 241,038 sq km
(93,065 sq mls)
Population: 19,848,000
Capital: Kampala
Language: English, Swahili
(Official), Luganda,
Many Local Languages
Religion: R.Catholic, Protestant,
Sunni Muslim,
Trad. Beliefs
Currency: Shilling

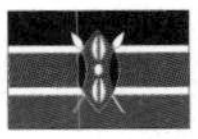

### KENYA
REPUBLIC

Area: 582,646 sq km
(224,961 sq mls)
Population: 30,522,000
Capital: Nairobi
Language: Swahili (Official),
English, Many
Local Languages
Religion: R.Catholic,
Protestant,
Trad. Beliefs
Currency: Shilling

**POPULATION**
Inhabitants

| per sq km | per sq ml |
| --- | --- |
| over 200 | over 500 |
| 100-200 | 250-500 |
| 40-100 | 100-250 |
| 10-40 | 25-100 |
| 2-10 | 5-25 |
| 0-2 | 0-5 |
| uninhabited | |

Algiers
Casablanca
Alexandria
Cairo
El Gîza
Abidjan
Lagos
Kinshasa
Johannesburg
Cape Town

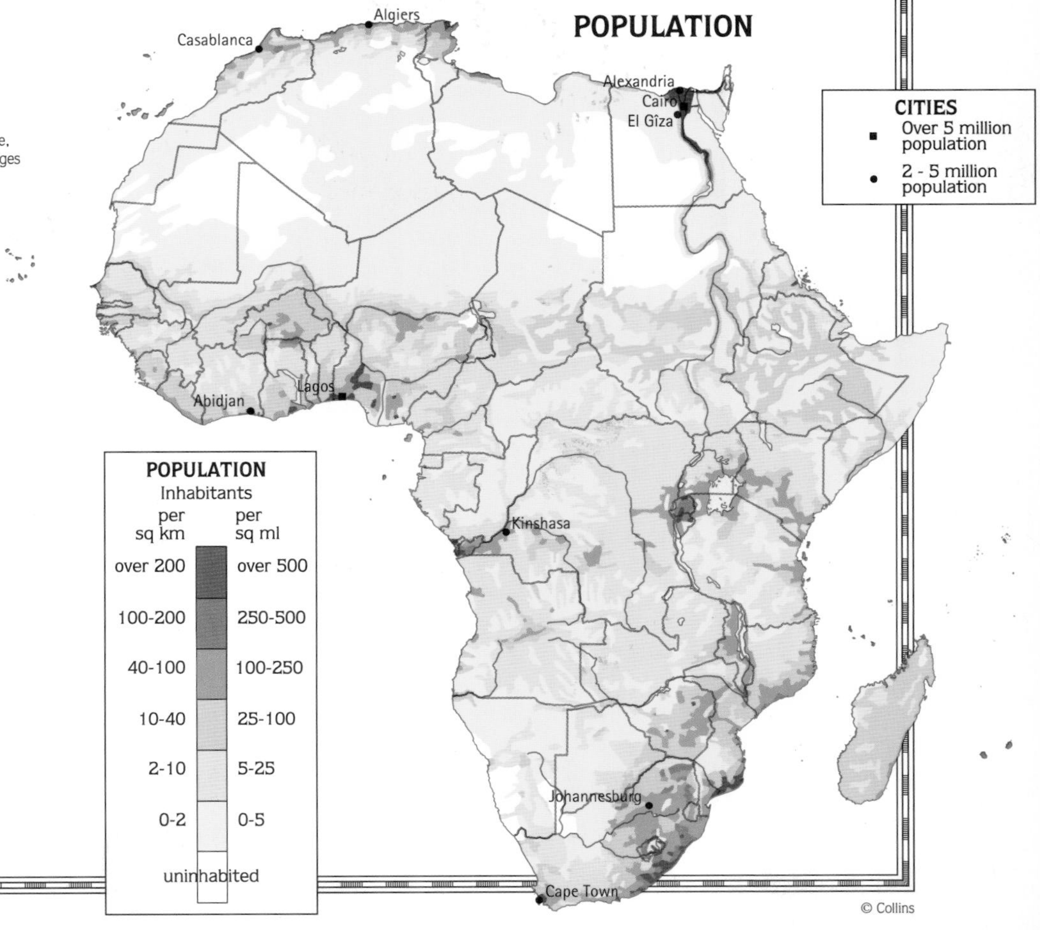

© Collins

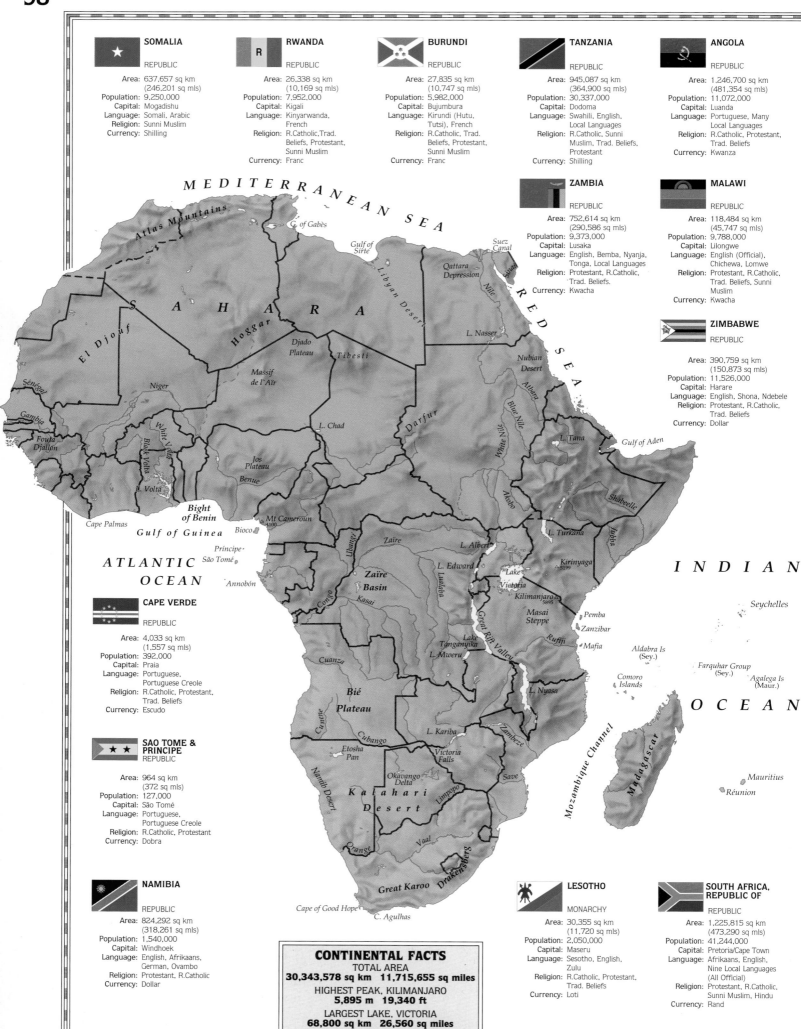

### SOMALIA
REPUBLIC

Area: 637,657 sq km
(246,201 sq mls)
Population: 9,250,000
Capital: Mogadishu
Language: Somali, Arabic
Religion: Sunni Muslim
Currency: Shilling

### RWANDA
REPUBLIC

Area: 26,338 sq km
(10,169 sq mls)
Population: 7,952,000
Capital: Kigali
Language: Kinyarwanda,
French
Religion: R.Catholic,Trad.
Beliefs, Protestant,
Sunni Muslim
Currency: Franc

### BURUNDI
REPUBLIC

Area: 27,835 sq km
(10,747 sq mls)
Population: 5,982,000
Capital: Bujumbura
Language: Kirundi (Hutu,
Tutsi), French
Religion: R.Catholic, Trad.
Beliefs, Protestant,
Sunni Muslim
Currency: Franc

### TANZANIA
REPUBLIC

Area: 945,087 sq km
(364,900 sq mls)
Population: 30,337,000
Capital: Dodoma
Language: Swahili, English,
Local Languages
Religion: R.Catholic, Sunni
Muslim, Trad. Beliefs,
Protestant
Currency: Shilling

### ANGOLA
REPUBLIC

Area: 1,246,700 sq km
(481,354 sq mls)
Population: 11,072,000
Capital: Luanda
Language: Portuguese, Many
Local Languages
Religion: R.Catholic, Protestant,
Trad. Beliefs
Currency: Kwanza

### ZAMBIA
REPUBLIC

Area: 752,614 sq km
(290,586 sq mls)
Population: 9,373,000
Capital: Lusaka
Language: English, Bemba, Nyanja,
Tonga, Local Languages
Religion: Protestant, R.Catholic,
Trad. Beliefs.
Currency: Kwacha

### MALAWI
REPUBLIC

Area: 118,484 sq km
(45,747 sq mls)
Population: 9,788,000
Capital: Lilongwe
Language: English (Official),
Chichewa, Lomwe
Religion: Protestant, R.Catholic,
Trad. Beliefs, Sunni
Muslim
Currency: Kwacha

### ZIMBABWE
REPUBLIC

Area: 390,759 sq km
(150,873 sq mls)
Population: 11,526,000
Capital: Harare
Language: English, Shona, Ndebele
Religion: Protestant, R.Catholic,
Trad. Beliefs
Currency: Dollar

### CAPE VERDE
REPUBLIC

Area: 4,033 sq km
(1,557 sq mls)
Population: 392,000
Capital: Praia
Language: Portuguese,
Portuguese Creole
Religion: R.Catholic, Protestant,
Trad. Beliefs
Currency: Escudo

### SAO TOME &
### PRINCIPE
REPUBLIC

Area: 964 sq km
(372 sq mls)
Population: 127,000
Capital: São Tomé
Language: Portuguese,
Portuguese Creole
Religion: R.Catholic, Protestant
Currency: Dobra

### NAMIBIA
REPUBLIC

Area: 824,292 sq km
(318,261 sq mls)
Population: 1,540,000
Capital: Windhoek
Language: English, Afrikaans,
German, Ovambo
Religion: Protestant, R.Catholic
Currency: Dollar

### LESOTHO
MONARCHY

Area: 30,355 sq km
(11,720 sq mls)
Population: 2,050,000
Capital: Maseru
Language: Sesotho, English,
Zulu
Religion: R.Catholic, Protestant,
Trad. Beliefs
Currency: Loti

### SOUTH AFRICA,
### REPUBLIC OF
REPUBLIC

Area: 1,225,815 sq km
(473,290 sq mls)
Population: 41,244,000
Capital: Pretoria/Cape Town
Language: Afrikaans, English,
Nine Local Languages
(All Official)
Religion: Protestant, R.Catholic,
Sunni Muslim, Hindu
Currency: Rand

### CONTINENTAL FACTS
TOTAL AREA
**30,343,578 sq km   11,715,655 sq miles**
HIGHEST PEAK, KILIMANJARO
**5,895 m   19,340 ft**
LARGEST LAKE, VICTORIA
**68,800 sq km   26,560 sq miles**
LONGEST RIVER, NILE
**6,695 km   4,160 miles**

## COMOROS

REPUBLIC

Area: 1,862 sq km
(719 sq mls)
Population: 653,000
Capital: Moroni
Language: Comorian, French,
Arabic
Religion: Sunni Muslim,
R.Catholic
Currency: Franc

## SEYCHELLES

REPUBLIC

Area: 455 sq km
(176 sq mls)
Population: 75,000
Capital: Victoria
Language: Seychellois (Seselwa,
French Creole),
English
Religion: R.Catholic, Protestant
Currency: Rupee

## MAURITIUS

REPUBLIC

Area: 2,040 sq km
(788 sq mls)
Population: 1,122,000
Capital: Port Louis
Language: English, French Creole,
Hindi, Indian Languages
Religion: Hindu, R.Catholic,
Sunni Muslim,
Protestant
Currency: Rupee

## MADAGASCAR

REPUBLIC

Area: 587,041 sq km
(226,658 sq mls)
Population: 14,763,000
Capital: Antananarivo
Language: Malagasy, French
Religion: Trad. Beliefs,
R.Catholic, Protestant,
Sunni Muslim,
Currency: Franc

## MOZAMBIQUE

REPUBLIC

Area: 799,380 sq km
(308,642 sq mls)
Population: 17,423,000
Capital: Maputo
Language: Portuguese, Makua,
Tsonga, Local Languages
Religion: Trad. Beliefs,
R.Catholic,
Sunni Muslim
Currency: Metical

## BOTSWANA

REPUBLIC

Area: 581,370 sq km
(224,468 sq mls)
Population: 1,456,000
Capital: Gaborone
Language: English, Setswana,
Shona, Local Languages
Religion: Trad. Beliefs,
Protestant, R.Catholic
Currency: Pula

## SWAZILAND

MONARCHY

Area: 17,364 sq km
(6,704 sq mls)
Population: 908,000
Capital: Mbabane
Language: Swazi (Siswati),
English
Religion: Protestant, R.Catholic,
Trad. Beliefs
Currency: Emalangeni

# CLIMATE

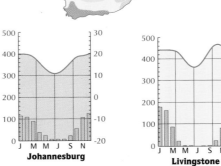

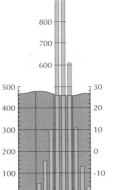

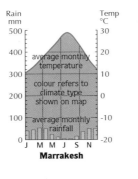

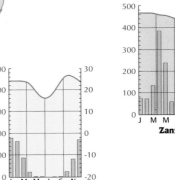

**Aswân**

**Marrakesh**

average monthly
temperature

colour refers to
climate type
shown on map

average monthly
rainfall

**Freetown**

**Johannesburg**

**Livingstone**

**Zanzibar**

## CLIMATE TYPES
### WARMER HUMID

| | Temperate |
| | Mediterranean |

### DRY

| | Steppe |
| | Desert |

### TROPICAL HUMID

| | Savanna |
| | Rain forest |

**Botswana.** Elephants are one of the many types of native wildlife to be found in the Chobe National Park.

**River Nile, Egypt.** 96% of Egypt's population live in the Nile Delta and a 20km wide strip along the river.

© Collins

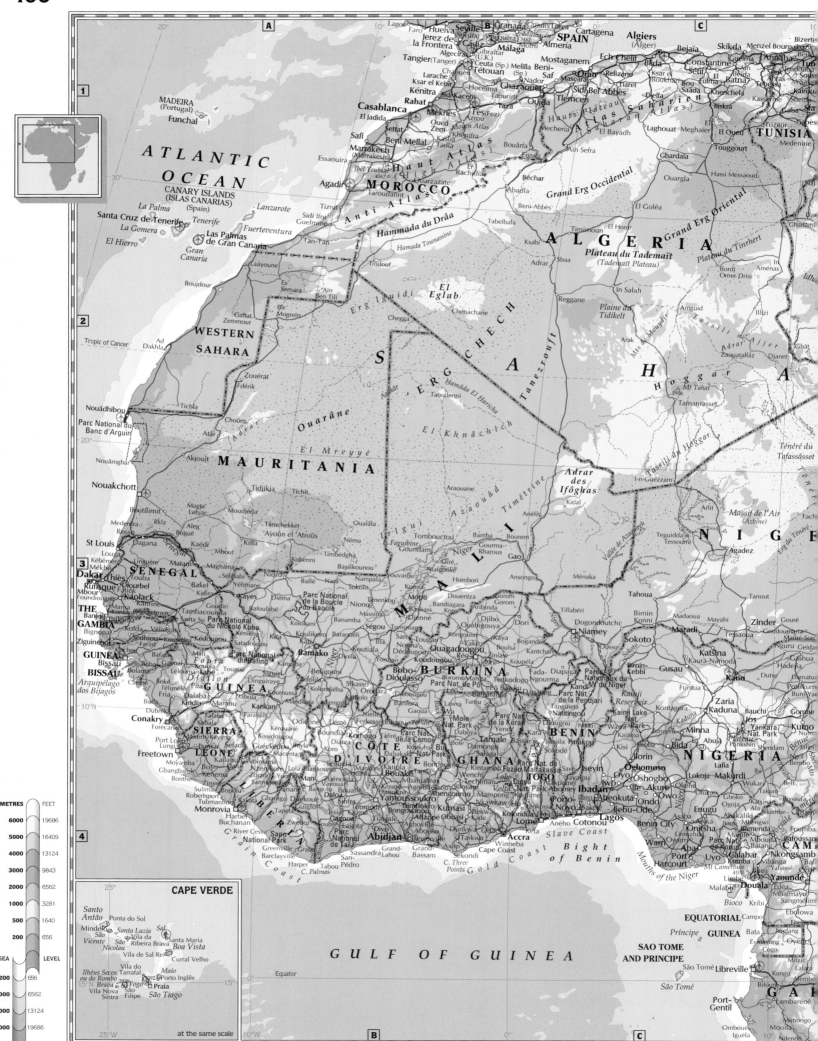

Lambert Azimuthal Equal Area Projection

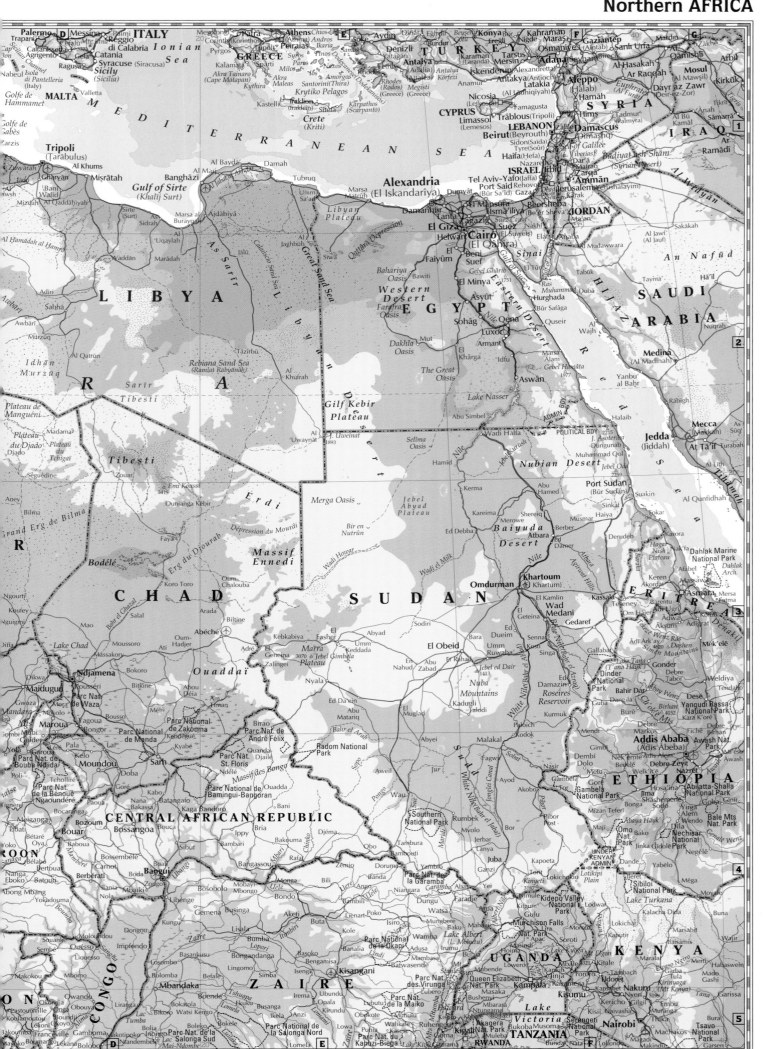

1:16M

KM    MILES
1000
            600
800
            500
600
            400
400
            300
            200
200
            100
0         0

© Collins

Lambert Azimuthal Equal Area Projection

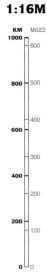

1:16M

| KM | MILES |
|----|-------|
| 1000 | 600 |
| 800 | 500 |
| | 400 |
| 600 | 300 |
| 400 | 200 |
| 200 | 100 |
| 0 | 0 |

© Collins

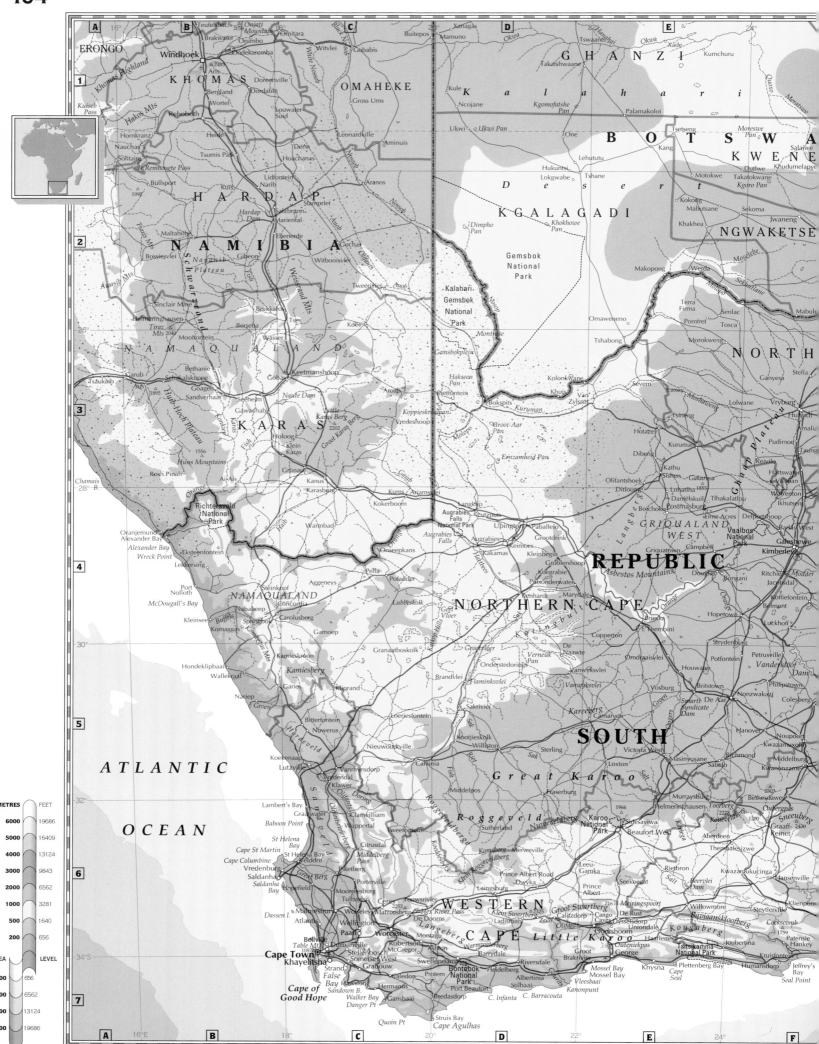

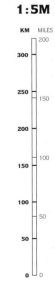

1:5M

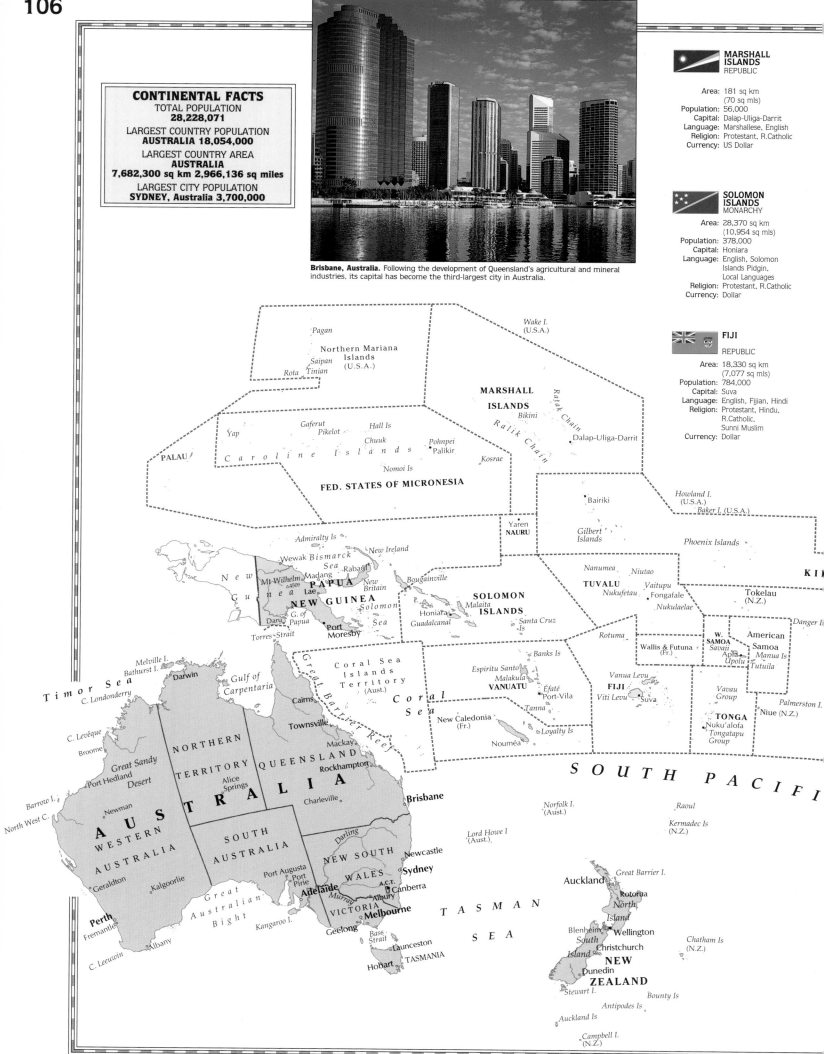

**CONTINENTAL FACTS**
TOTAL POPULATION
**28,228,071**
LARGEST COUNTRY POPULATION
**AUSTRALIA 18,054,000**
LARGEST COUNTRY AREA
**AUSTRALIA**
**7,682,300 sq km  2,966,136 sq miles**
LARGEST CITY POPULATION
**SYDNEY, Australia 3,700,000**

**Brisbane, Australia.** Following the development of Queensland's agricultural and mineral industries, its capital has become the third-largest city in Australia.

**MARSHALL ISLANDS**
REPUBLIC

Area: 181 sq km
(70 sq mls)
Population: 56,000
Capital: Dalap-Uliga-Darrit
Language: Marshallese, English
Religion: Protestant, R.Catholic
Currency: US Dollar

**SOLOMON ISLANDS**
MONARCHY

Area: 28,370 sq km
(10,954 sq mls)
Population: 378,000
Capital: Honiara
Language: English, Solomon
Islands Pidgin,
Local Languages
Religion: Protestant, R.Catholic
Currency: Dollar

**FIJI**
REPUBLIC

Area: 18,330 sq km
(7,077 sq mls)
Population: 784,000
Capital: Suva
Language: English, Fijian, Hindi
Religion: Protestant, Hindu,
R.Catholic,
Sunni Muslim
Currency: Dollar

### FED. STATES OF MICRONESIA
REPUBLIC

Area: 701 sq km
(271 sq mls)
Population: 105,000
Capital: Palikir
Language: English, Trukese,
Pohnpeian,
Local Languages
Religion: Protestant, R.Catholic
Currency: US Dollar

### PAPUA NEW GUINEA
MONARCHY

Area: 462,840 sq km
(178,704 sq mls)
Population: 4,074,000
Capital: Port Moresby
Language: English,
Tok Pisin (Pidgin),
Local Languages
Religion: Protestant, R.Catholic,
Trad. Beliefs
Currency: Kina

### NAURU
REPUBLIC

Area: 21 sq km
(8 sq mls)
Population: 11,000
Capital: Yaren
Language: Nauruan, Gilbertese,
English
Religion: Protestant, R.Catholic
Currency: Australian Dollar

### KIRIBATI
REPUBLIC

Area: 717 sq km
(277 sq mls)
Population: 79,000
Capital: Bairiki
Language: I-Kiribati (Gilbertese),
English
Religion: R.Catholic, Protestant,
Baha'i, Mormon
Currency: Australian Dollar

### TONGA
MONARCHY

Area: 748 sq km
(289 sq mls)
Population: 98,000
Capital: Nuku'alofa
Language: Tongan, English
Religion: Protestant, R.Catholic,
Mormon
Currency: Pa'anga

### TUVALU
MONARCHY

Area: 25 sq km
(10 sq mls)
Population: 10,000
Capital: Fongafale
Language: Tuvaluan,
English (official)
Religion: Protestant
Currency: Dollar

### VANUATU
REPUBLIC

Area: 12,190 sq km
(4,707 sq mls)
Population: 169,000
Capital: Port-Vila
Language: English, Bislama
(English Creole),
French (all official)
Religion: Protestant, R.Catholic,
Trad. Beliefs
Currency: Vatu

### WESTERN SAMOA
MONARCHY

Area: 2,831 sq km
(1,093 sq mls)
Population: 171,000
Capital: Apia
Language: Samoan, English
Religion: Protestant, R.Catholic,
Sunni Muslim
Currency: Tala

## POPULATION

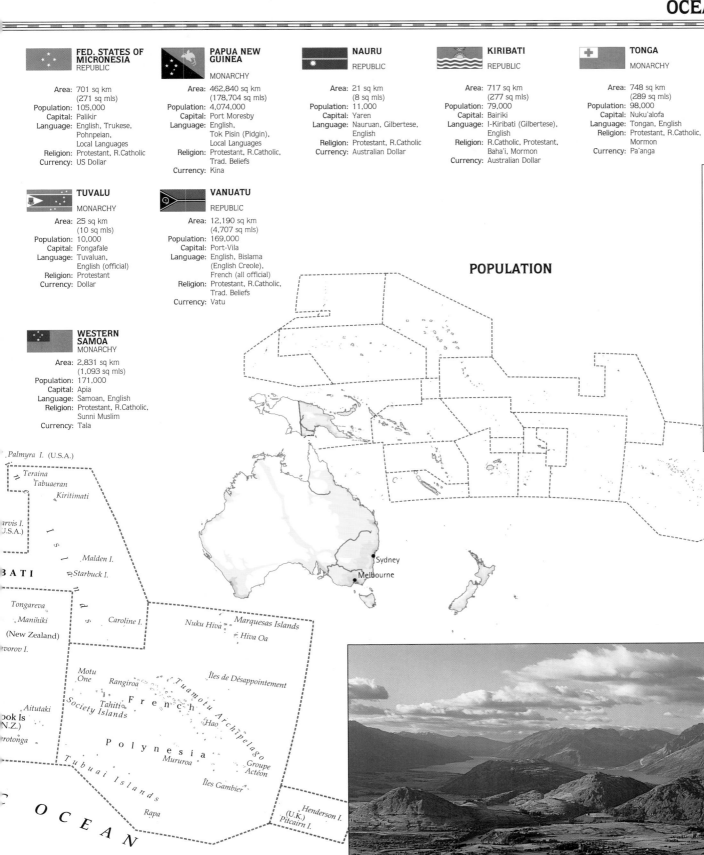

### POPULATION
Inhabitants

| per sq km | per sq ml |
|---|---|
| over 200 | over 500 |
| 100-200 | 250-500 |
| 40-100 | 100-250 |
| 10-40 | 25-100 |
| 2-10 | 5-25 |
| 0-2 | 0-5 |
| uninhabited | |

### CITIES
■ Over 5 million population
● 2.5 - 5 million population

### AUSTRALIA
FEDERATION

Area: 7,682,300 sq km
(2,966,136 sq mls)
Population: 18,054,000
Capital: Canberra
Language: English, Italian,
Greek, Aboriginal
Languages
Religion: Protestant, R.Catholic,
Orthodox, Aboriginal
Currency: Dollar

### NEW ZEALAND
MONARCHY

Area: 270,534 sq km
(104,454 sq mls)
Population: 3,542,000
Capital: Wellington
Language: English, Maori
Religion: Protestant, R.Catholic
Currency: Dollar

**New Zealand.** The mountainous South Island is fringed by extensive plains where cereals are grown and huge flocks of sheep are grazed.

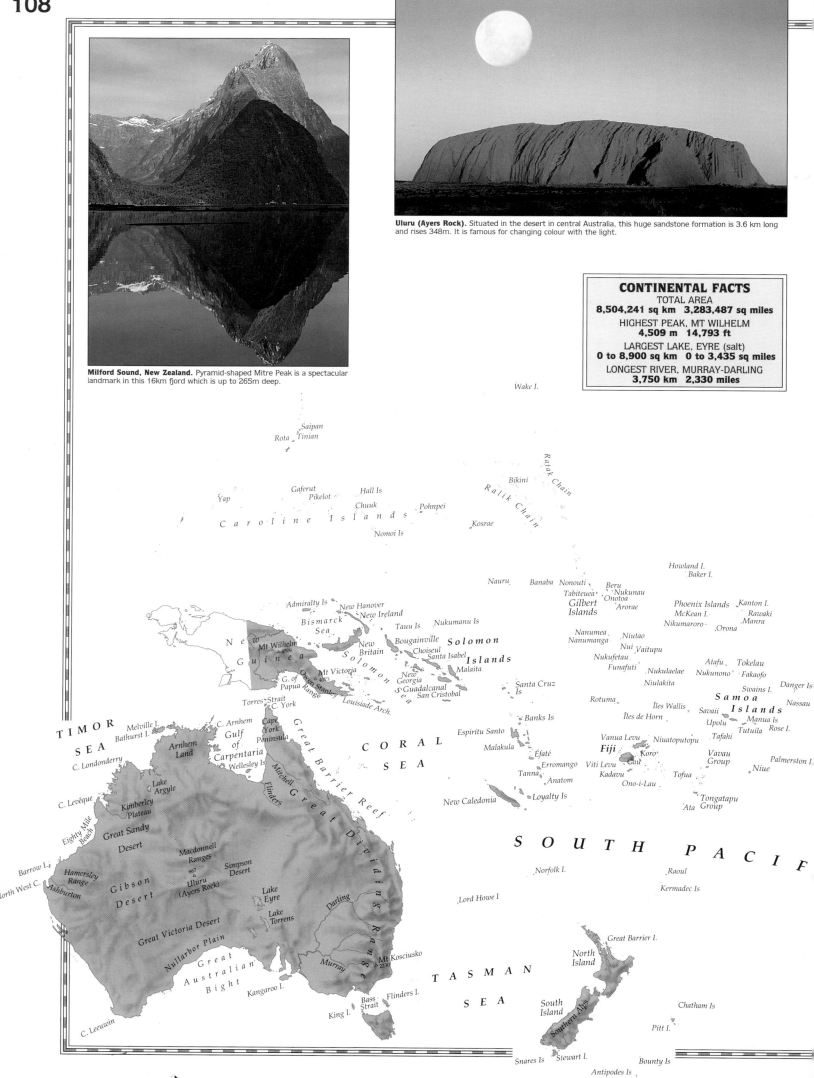

**Uluru (Ayers Rock).** Situated in the desert in central Australia, this huge sandstone formation is 3.6 km long and rises 348m. It is famous for changing colour with the light.

**Milford Sound, New Zealand.** Pyramid-shaped Mitre Peak is a spectacular landmark in this 16km fjord which is up to 265m deep.

## CONTINENTAL FACTS
**TOTAL AREA**
8,504,241 sq km   3,283,487 sq miles
**HIGHEST PEAK, MT WILHELM**
4,509 m   14,793 ft
**LARGEST LAKE, EYRE (salt)**
0 to 8,900 sq km   0 to 3,435 sq miles
**LONGEST RIVER, MURRAY-DARLING**
3,750 km   2,330 miles

Wake I.

Saipan
Rota  Tinian

Ratak Chain

Bikini
Gaferut    Hall Is
Pikelot
Yap                Chuuk       Pohnpei        Ralik Chain
C a r o l i n e   I s l a n d s
Nomoi Is                    Kosrae

Howland I.
Baker I.

Nauru    Banaba  Nonouti    Beru
Tabiteuea  Nukunau
Onotoa        Phoenix Islands    Kanton I.
Gilbert    Arorae         McKean I.      Rawaki
Admiralty Is   New Hanover    Islands                Nikumaroro    Manra
Bismarck   New Ireland                         Nikumaroro-  .Orona
Sea      Tauu Is  Nukumanu Is            Nanumea    Niutao
N e w        Bougainville  S o l o m o n          Nanumanga  Vaitupu
Mt Wilhelm  Britain  Choiseul Santa Isabel  Islands       Nui
G u i n e a  4509  New       Malaita                 Nukufetau          Atafu   Tokelau
Mt Victoria  Georgia  Guadalcanal                Funafuti  Nukulaelae  Nukunono  Fakaofo
G. of  4073  Owen Stanley  San Cristobal       Niulakita              Swains I.  Danger Is
Papua  Range              Santa Cruz                 Rotuma    Îles Wallis       S a m o a  Nassau
Torres Strait      Louisiade Arch.       Is                            Savaii  I s l a n d s
C. York                                   Îles de Horn    Upolu  Manua is
T I M O R  Melville I.    C. Arnhem  Cape        Banks Is              Vanua Levu  Niuatoputapu  Tafahi  Tutuila  Rose I.
Bathurst I.  Gulf  York  Great       Espiritu Santo             Niuatoputopu
S E A          Arnhem  of  Peninsula  Barrier       Malakula  C O R A L  Vanua Levu  Fiji   Koro        Vavau
C. Londonderry  Land  Carpentaria           Éfaté   S E A   Viti Levu  Gau        Group
Wellesley Is                  Erromango  Tanna  Kadavu        Niue
C. Lévêque      Lake          Mitchell  Anatom      Ono-i-Lau  Tofua      Palmerston I.
Kimberley  Argyle   Flinders  G r e a t   D i v i d i n g   New Caledonia  Loyalty Is            Tongatapu
Plateau                                      Ata  Group
Eighty Mile  Great Sandy       Macdonnell              S O U T H   P A C I F
Beach  Desert      Ranges  Simpson             Norfolk I.       Raoul
Hamersley          867  Desert
Barrow I.  Range  Gibson  Uluru            Lake             Kermadec Is
North West C.  Ashburton  Desert  (Ayers Rock)  Eyre   Lord Howe I
C. Leeuwin                  Lake     Darling                          Great Barrier I.
Great Victoria Desert  Torrens                               North
Nullarbor Plain                  Mt Kosciusko        Island
G r e a t        Murray  2230   T A S M A N
A u s t r a l i a n   Kangaroo I.  Bass        S E A            South    Chatham Is
B i g h t      Flinders I.  Strait                    Island   Southern Alps
King I.                                              Pitt I.
Snares Is  Stewart I.        Bounty Is
Antipodes I.

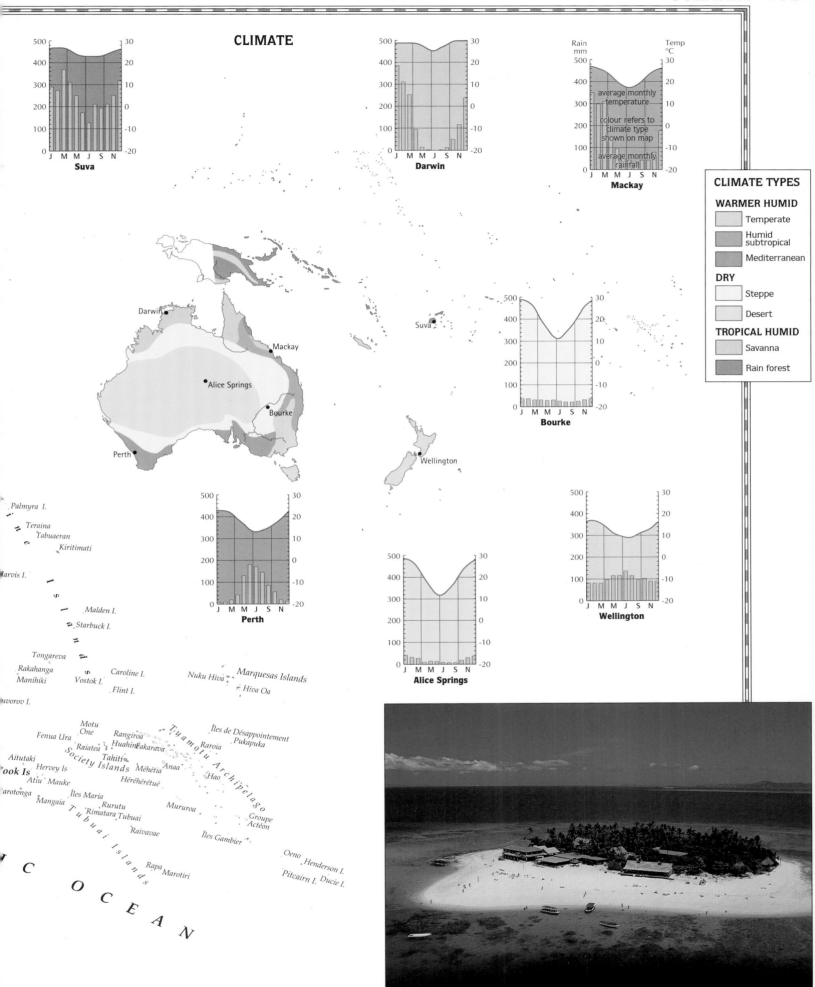

## CLIMATE

**Suva**

**Darwin**

Rain mm / Temp °C

average monthly temperature

colour refers to climate type shown on map

average monthly rainfall

**Mackay**

**CLIMATE TYPES**

**WARMER HUMID**

- Temperate
- Humid subtropical
- Mediterranean

**DRY**

- Steppe
- Desert

**TROPICAL HUMID**

- Savanna
- Rain forest

**Bourke**

**Perth**

**Alice Springs**

**Wellington**

Darwin
Mackay
Suva
Alice Springs
Bourke
Perth
Wellington

Palmyra I.
Teraina
Tabuaeran
Kiritimati
Jarvis I.
Line Islands
Malden I.
Starbuck I.
Tongareva
Rakahanga
Manihiki
Vostok I.
Caroline I.
Flint I.
Suvorov I.
Nuku Hiva
Marquesas Islands
Hiva Oa

Motu One
Fenua Ura
Rangiroa
Raiatea
Huahine
Fakarava
Aitutaki
Hervey Is
Tahiti
Society Islands
Méhétia
Anaa
Hao
Cook Is
Atiu
Mauke
Héréhérétué
Rarotonga
Íles Maria
Mangaia
Rurutu
Rimatara
Tubuai
Mururoa
Groupe
Actéon
Raivavae
Íles Gambier
Rapa
Marotiri
Oeno
Henderson I.
Pitcairn I.
Ducie I.

Tuamotu Archipelago
Íles de Désappointement
Raroia
Pukapuka

Tubuai Islands

PACIFIC OCEAN

**Beachcomber Island, Fiji.** Tourists are attracted to the sandy beach and beautiful coral reef which surrounds the island.

© Collins

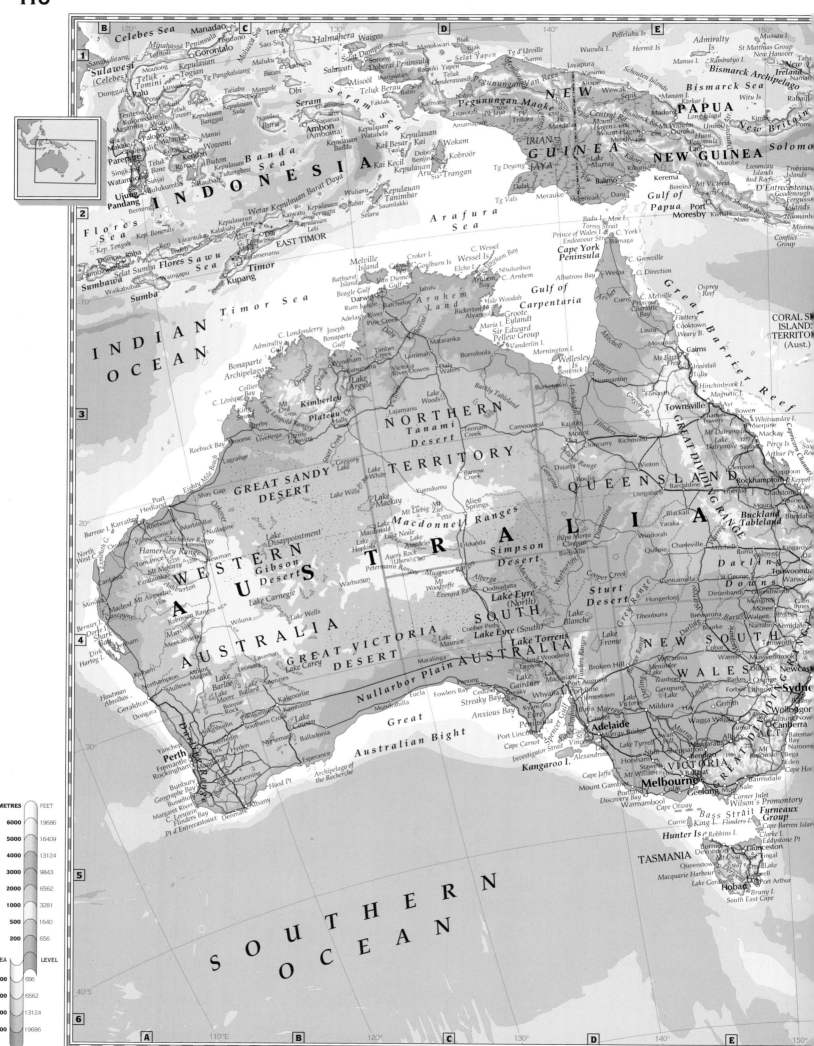

METRES FEET
6000  19686
5000  16409
4000  13124
3000  9843
2000  6562
1000  3281
500   1640
200   656
SEA   LEVEL
200   656
2000  6562
4000  13124
6000  19686

Lambert Azimuthal Equal Area Projection

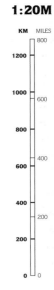

**1:20M**

KM · MILES

800

1200 · 600

1000

800 · 400

600

400 · 200

200

0 · 0

© Collins

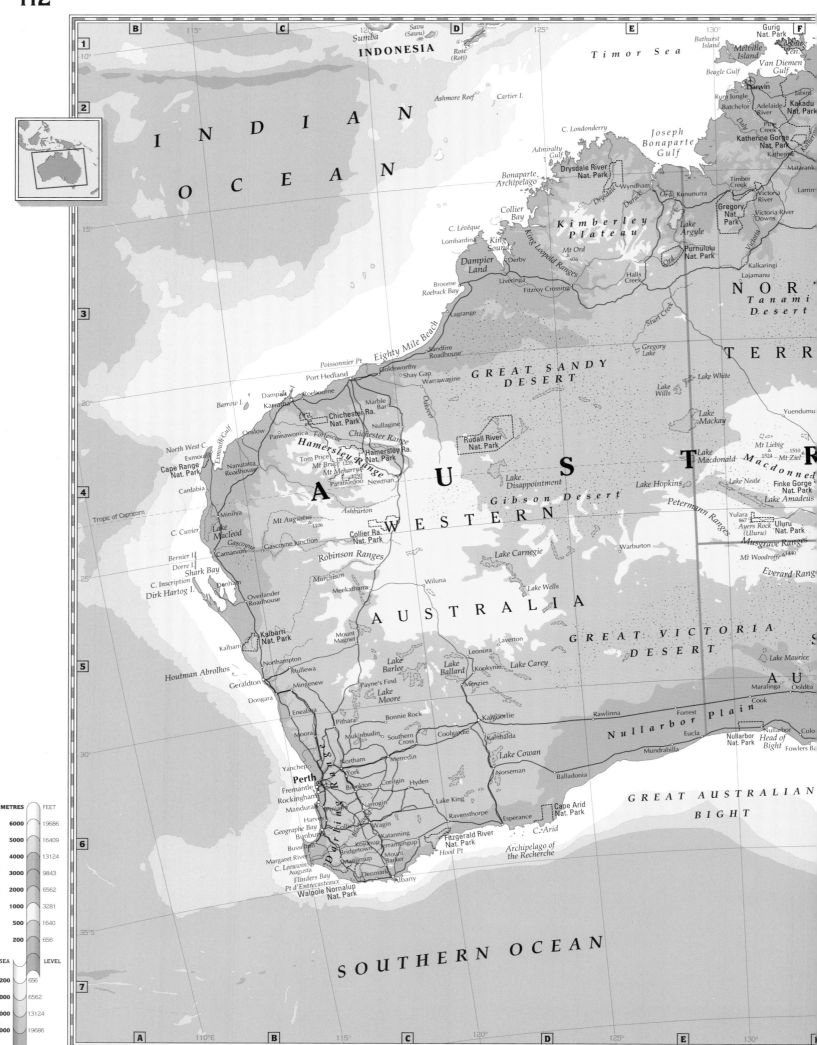

Lambert Azimuthal Equal Area Projection

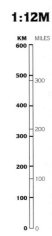

**1:12M**

KM   MILES
600
500          300
400
300          200
200
100          100
0            0

© Collins

Lambert Azimuthal Equal Area Projection

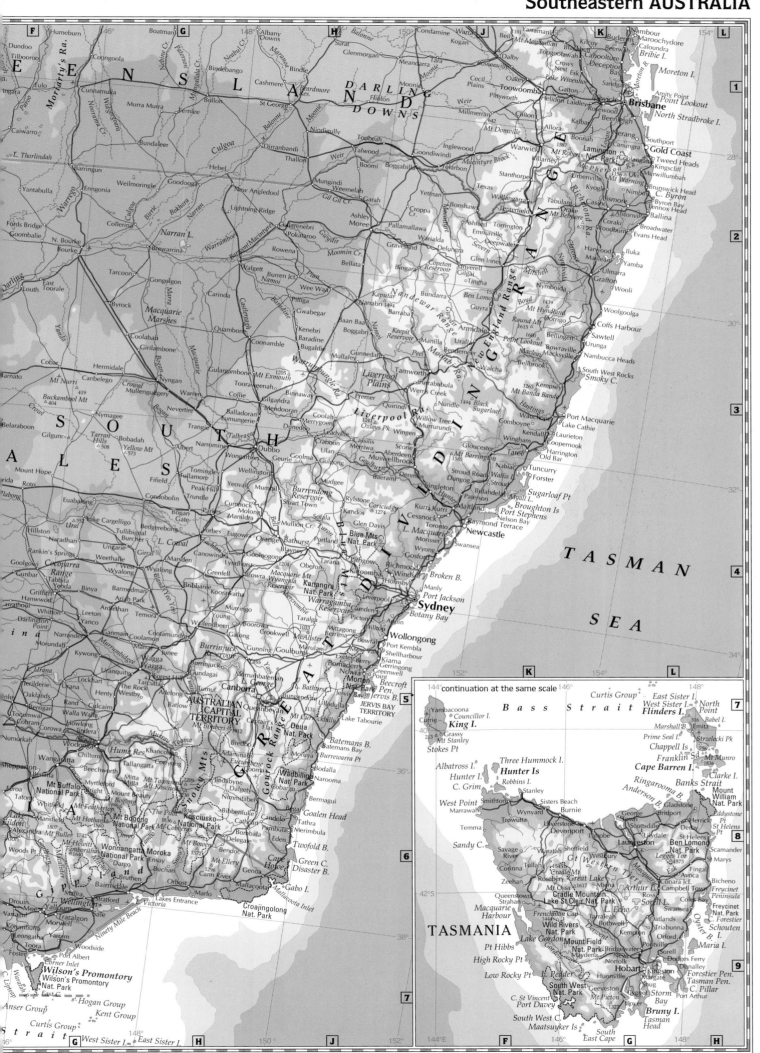

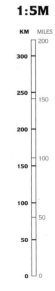

1:5M

KM  MILES
300 — 200

250 — 150

200 —

150 — 100

100 —

50

0 — 0

© Collins

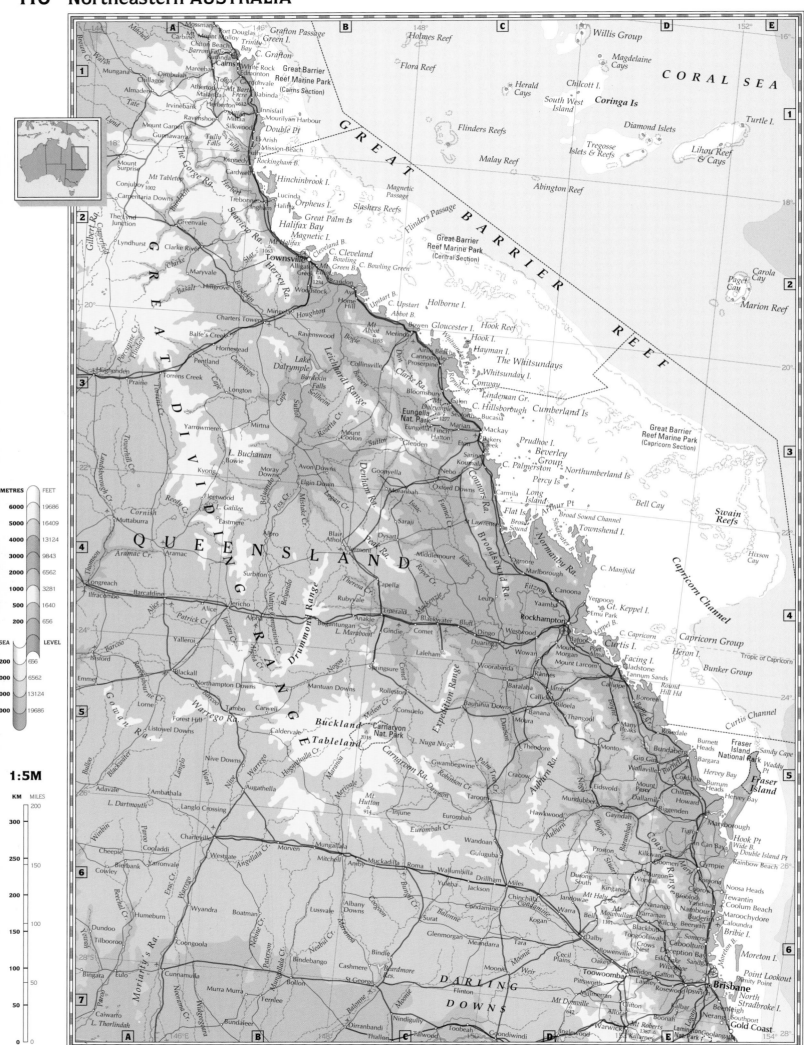

METRES / FEET

| METRES | FEET |
|---|---|
| 6000 | 19686 |
| 5000 | 16409 |
| 4000 | 13124 |
| 3000 | 9843 |
| 2000 | 6562 |
| 1000 | 3281 |
| 500 | 1640 |
| 200 | 656 |
| SEA | LEVEL |
| 200 | 656 |
| 2000 | 6562 |
| 4000 | 13124 |
| 6000 | 19686 |

1:5M

| KM | MILES |
|---|---|
| 300 | 200 |
| 250 | 150 |
| 200 | 100 |
| 150 | 50 |
| 100 | |
| 50 | |
| 0 | 0 |

Lambert Azimuthal Equal Area Projection

© Collins

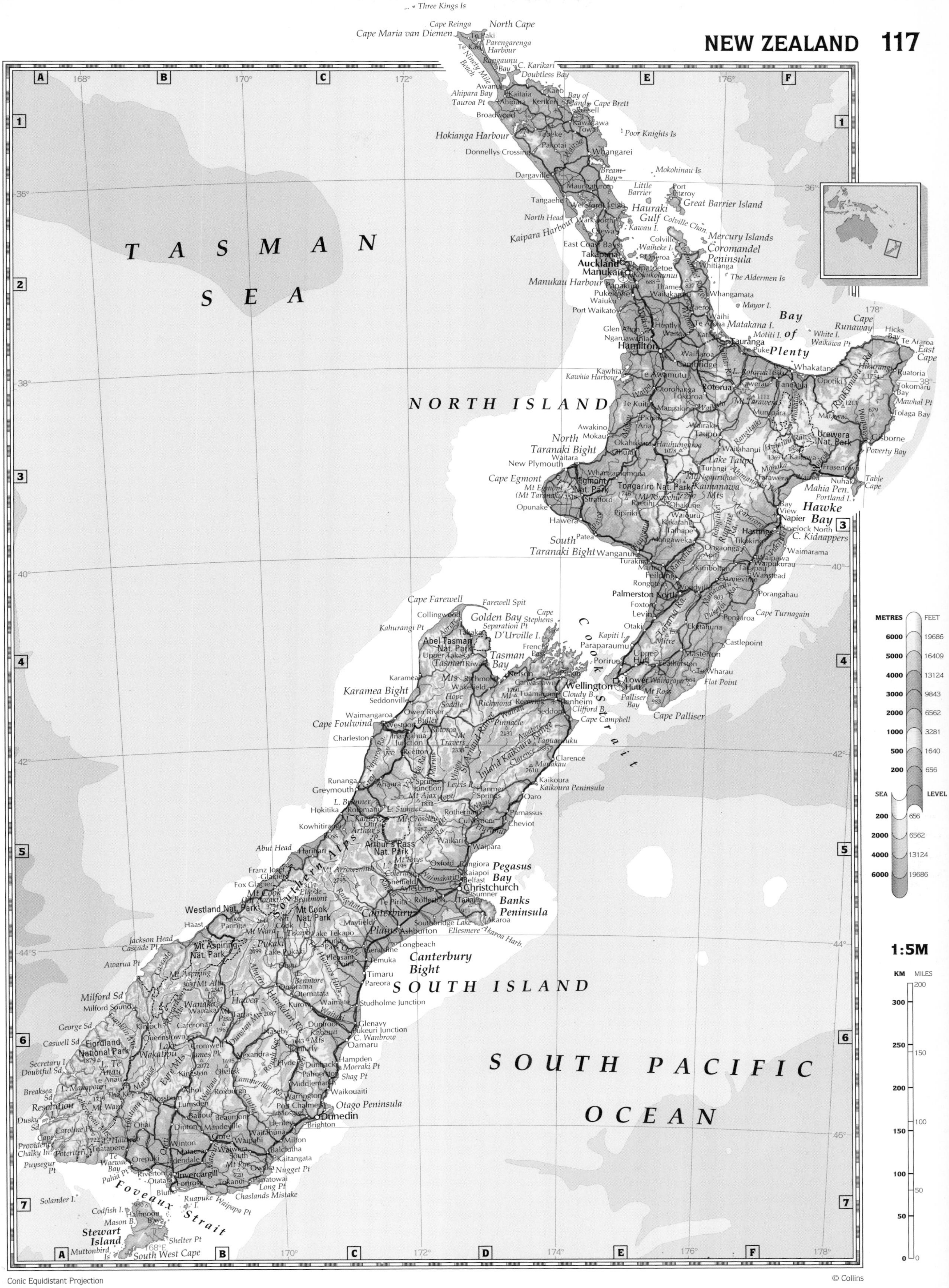

Three Kings Is

Cape Reinga   North Cape
Cape Maria van Diemen
Te Paki
Parengarenga Harbour
C. Karikari
Doubtless Bay
Rangaunu Bay
Ahipara Bay   Kaitaia   Kerikeri   Cape Brett
Tauroa Pt   Ahipara   Bay of Islands   Russell
Broadwood   Kawakawa
Poor Knights Is
Hokianga Harbour   Tabeke
Pakotai
Donnellys Crossing   Whangarei
Dargaville   Maungaturoto   Mokohinau Is
Tangaehe   Little Barrier   Port Fitzroy
North Head   Warkworth   Great Barrier Island
Kaipara Harbour   Orewa   Colville Chan.
Kawau I.   Coromandel Peninsula
East Coast Bay   Waiheke I.   Whitianga
Takapuna   Mercury Islands
**Auckland**   The Aldermen Is
Manukau   Koukohunui   Whangamata
Manukau Harbour   Papakura   Mayor I.
Pukekohe   Waihi   Bay of Plenty
Waiuku   Te Aroha   Matakana I.   Cape Runaway
Port Waikato   Tauranga   White I.   Hicks Bay
Glen Afton   Huntly   Te Araroa   East Cape
Ngaruawahia   Cambridge   Ruatoria
**Hamilton**   Rotorua   Tokomaru Bay
Kawhia   Te Awamutu   Mt Tarawera   Mawhai Pt
Kawhia Harbour   Otorohanga   Tolaga Bay
Te Kuiti   Tokoroa   Opotiki   Urewera Nat. Park

**NORTH ISLAND**

North Taranaki Bight   Awakino   Mokau   Aria
New Plymouth   Waitara   Okahukura   Hauhungaroa
Cape Egmont   Egmont   Lake Taupo   Gisborne
Mt Egmont   Nat. Park   Tongariro Nat. Park   Kaimanawa Mts   Poverty Bay
(Mt Taranaki)   Stratford   Turangi   Table Cape
Opunake   Ngauruhoe   Mahia Pen.
Hawera   Raetihi   Ohakune   Portland I.
South   Patea   Waiouru   Hawke Bay
Taranaki Bight   Wanganui   Napier   Hastings
Turakina   Havelock North
Marton   C. Kidnappers
Feilding   Waipukurau   Waimarama
Rongotea   Dannevirke
**Palmerston North**   Woodville
Foxton   Porangahau
Levin   Cape Turnagain
Otaki   Eketahuna
Kapiti I.   Castlepoint
Paraparaumu   Masterton
Porirua   Upper Hutt   Flat Point

Cape Farewell   Farewell Spit
Collingwood   Cape Stephens
Kahurangi Pt   Takaka   Separation Pt
Abel Tasman   D'Urville I.
Nat. Park   French Pass
Upper Takaka   Nelson   Picton   Kapiti I.
Karamea   Richmond   Blenheim
Karamea Bight   Wakefield   Cloudy Bay
Seddonville   Hope Saddle   Renwick   Clifford B.
Waimangaroa   Owen River   Seddon   Cape Campbell
Cape Foulwind   Westport   Buller   Ward   Cape Palliser
Charleston   Inangahua Junction   L. Rotoiti
Reefton   Mt Travers
Runanga   Murchison   Kaikoura
Greymouth   Springs Junction   Kaikoura Peninsula
Ahaura   Lewis P.   Hanmer Springs   Oaro
Hokitika   L. Brunner   L. Sumner   Rotherham
Kowhitirangi   Hope   Culverden   Parnassus
Ross   Otira   Arthur's Pass   Cheviot
Arthur's Pass Nat. Park   Waikari
Abut Head   Harihari   Oxford   Rangiora   Waipara
Franz Josef Glacier   Mt Hutt   Pegasus Bay
Fox Glacier   Belfast   Rolleston
Mt Cook   Sheffield   **Christchurch**
Westland Nat. Park   Darfield   Sumner
Haast   Mt Cook Nat. Park   Te Pirita   Banks Peninsula
Jackson Head   Southern Alps   Mayfield   Akaroa
Cascade Pt   Ashburton   Lake Ellesmere
Awarua Pt   Mt Ward   Tekapo   Southbridge
Mt Aspiring   Lake Tekapo   Geraldine
Mt Aspiring   Nat. Park   Temuka   Canterbury Bight
Milford Sd   Pukaki   Timaru
Milford Sound   Lake Pukaki   Pareora
George Sd   Bennore   Studholme Junction

**SOUTH ISLAND**

Caswell Sd   Cromwell   Waimate
Fiordland National Park   Alexandra   Glenavy
Secretary I.   Lake Wakatipu   Kurow   Duntroon
Doubtful Sd   Queenstown   Kakanui   C. Wanbrow
Te Anau   Cardrona   Oamaru
Breaksea Sd   L. Te Anau   Hyde   Moeraki Pt
Resolution   Mossburn   Dunback   Shag Pt
Dusky Sd   Lumsden   Middlemarch   Waikouaiti
Providence   Ohai   Roxburgh   Otago Peninsula
Chalky In.   Winton   Port Chalmers
Puysegur Pt   Gore   **Dunedin**
Riverton   Invercargill   Mataura   Brighton
Solander I.   Otatara   Mosgiel
Bluff   Balclutha   Nugget Pt
Foveaux Strait   Kaitangata
Codfish I.   Halfmoon Bay   Waipapa Pt
Mason B.   Ruapuke I.   Long Pt
**Stewart Island**   Chaslands Mistake
Muttonbird I.   South West Cape   Shelter Pt

**TASMAN SEA**

**NORTH ISLAND**

**SOUTH ISLAND**

**SOUTH PACIFIC OCEAN**

Cook Strait

| METRES | FEET |
|---|---|
| 6000 | 19686 |
| 5000 | 16409 |
| 4000 | 13124 |
| 3000 | 9843 |
| 2000 | 6562 |
| 1000 | 3281 |
| 500 | 1640 |
| 200 | 656 |
| SEA | LEVEL |
| 200 | 656 |
| 2000 | 6562 |
| 4000 | 13124 |
| 6000 | 19686 |

1:5M

| KM | MILES |
|---|---|
| | 200 |
| 300 | 150 |
| 250 | |
| 200 | 100 |
| 150 | |
| | 50 |
| 100 | |
| 50 | |
| 0 | 0 |

Conic Equidistant Projection

© Collins

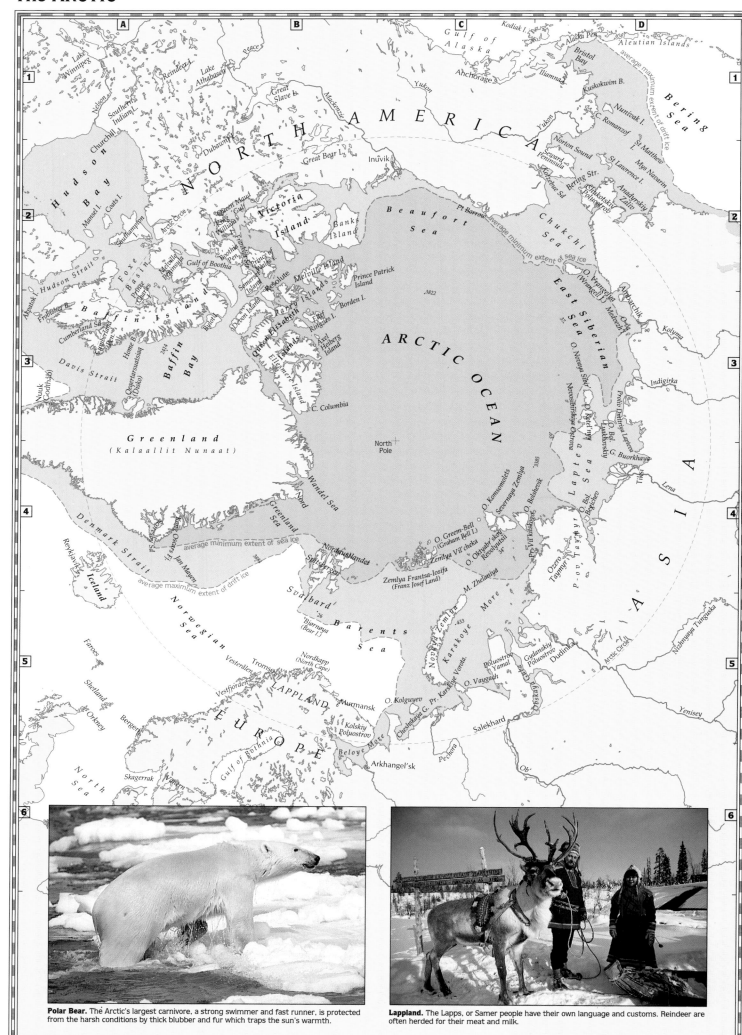

**Polar Bear.** The Arctic's largest carnivore, a strong swimmer and fast runner, is protected from the harsh conditions by thick blubber and fur which traps the sun's warmth.

**Lappland.** The Lapps, or Samer people have their own language and customs. Reindeer are often herded for their meat and milk.

**1:32M**

| KM | MILES |
| --- | --- |
| 1200 | 800 |
| 1000 | 600 |
| 800 | |
| 600 | 400 |
| 400 | |
| 200 | 200 |
| 0 | 0 |

Polar Stereographic Projection

© Collins

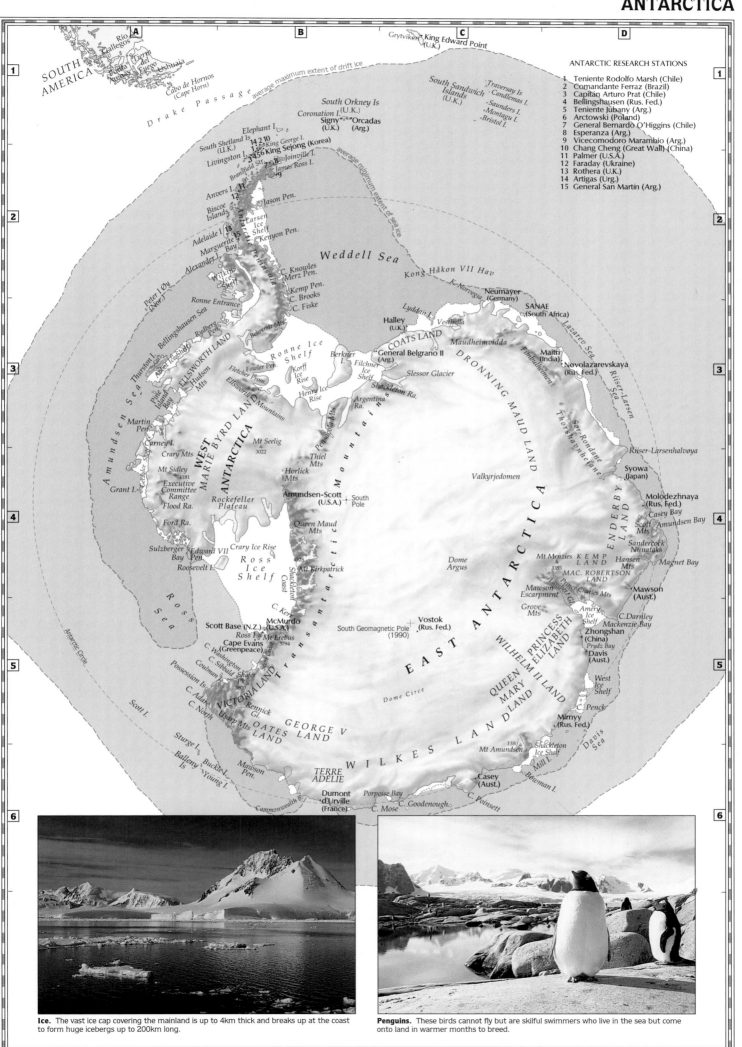

SOUTH AMERICA

Río Gallegos
Punta Arenas · Tierra del Fuego · Ushuaia
Cabo de Hornos (Cape Horn)

Drake Passage
average maximum extent of drift ice

Grytviken · King Edward Point (U.K.)

Traversay Is
South Sandwich Islands (U.K.) · Candlemas I.
· Saunders I.
· Montagu I.
· Bristol I.

South Orkney Is
Coronation I. (U.K.)
Signy (U.K.) · Orcadas (Arg.)

### ANTARCTIC RESEARCH STATIONS

1 Teniente Rodolfo Marsh (Chile)
2 Comandante Ferraz (Brazil)
3 Capitán Arturo Prat (Chile)
4 Bellingshausen (Rus. Fed.)
5 Teniente Jubany (Arg.)
6 Arctowski (Poland)
7 General Bernardo O'Higgins (Chile)
8 Esperanza (Arg.)
9 Vicecomodoro Marambio (Arg.)
10 Chang Cheng (Great Wall) (China)
11 Palmer (U.S.A.)
12 Faraday (Ukraine)
13 Rothera (U.K.)
14 Artigas (Urg.)
15 General San Martín (Arg.)

Elephant I.
South Shetland Is (U.K.) · 14 2 10
King George I.
Livingston · 3 5 6 King Sejong (Korea)
Bransfield Str. · 8 Joinville I.
James Ross I.
Anvers I. 11 · 9
12
Biscoe Islands
Jason Pen.
Adelaide I. 13
Marguerite 15 · Larsen Ice Shelf
Bay
Alexander I. · Kenyon Pen.

average maximum extent of sea ice

Weddell Sea

Kong Håkon VII Hav
K. Norvegia

South Sandwich Islands

Peter I Øy (Nor.)
Wilkins Ice Shelf
Ronne Entrance
C. Knowles
Merz Pen.
Kemp Pen.
C. Brooks
C. Fiske

Lyddan I. · Vestfjella
Halley (U.K.)
COATS LAND
Neumayer (Germany)
SANAE (South Africa)
Maudheimvidda
Maitri (India)
Novolazarevskaya (Rus. Fed.)

Belgrano Ice Shelf
Bellingshausen Sea
Rudberg Pen.
ELLSWORTH LAND
Hudson Mts
Behrendt Mts
Ronne Ice Shelf
Berkner I.
General Belgrano II (Arg.)
Filchner Ice Shelf
Slessor Glacier
DRONNING MAUD LAND
Finnbukhelmen
Lazarev Sea
Riiser-Larsen Sea

Amundsen Sea
Thurston I.
Abbot Ice Shelf
Fletcher Prom.
Fowler Pen.
Korff Ice Rise
Shackleton Ra.
Henry Ice Rise
Argentina Ra.
Sør-Rondane
Thorshavnheiane
Riiser-Larsenhalvøya

Martin Pen.
Carney I.
Phil. Island
Thiel Mts
Ellsworth Mountains
1897
Pensacola Mts
Valkyrjedomen
Syowa (Japan)
ENDERBY LAND

Crary Mts
Mt Seelig 3022
WEST ANTARCTICA
MARIE BYRD LAND
Horlick Mts
Molodezhnaya (Rus. Fed.)
Casey Bay
Scott Mts · Amundsen Bay

Mt Sidley 4181
Executive Committee Range
Flood Ra.
Rockefeller Plateau
Amundsen-Scott (U.S.A.) · South Pole
Sandercock Nunataks
Magnet Bay

Grant I.
Ford Ra.
Mt Menzies KEMP LAND
Hansen Mts
MAC. ROBERTSON LAND

Sulzberger Bay
Edward VII Pen.
Crary Ice Rise
Queen Maud Mts
Dome Argus
Mawson Escarpment
Prince Charles Mts
Mawson (Aust.)

Roosevelt I.
Ross Ice Shelf
Mt Kirkpatrick
Grove Mts
Amery Ice Shelf
C. Darnley
Mackenzie Bay

Shackleton Coast
Vostok (Rus. Fed.)
EAST ANTARCTICA
PRINCESS ELIZABETH LAND
Zhongshan (China)
Prydz Bay
Davis (Aust.)

Ross Sea
C. Kerr
South Geomagnetic Pole (1990)
QUEEN MARY LAND
WILHELM II LAND
West Ice Shelf

Antarctic Circle
Scott Base (N.Z.)
McMurdo (U.S.A.)
Ross I. · Mt Erebus 3794
Cape Evans (Greenpeace)
Dome Circe
C. Penck
Mirnyy (Rus. Fed.)
Davis Sea

Scott I.
C. Washington
C. Sibbald
Coulman I.
VICTORIA LAND
Transantarctic Mountains
Mt Amundsen 1380
Shackleton Ice Shelf
Bowman I.

Possession Is.
C. Adare
C. North
Rennick Gl.
Usarp Mts
GEORGE V LAND
OATES LAND
WILKES LAND
Casey (Aust.)
C. Poinsett

Sturge I.
Buckle I.
Balleny Is
Young I.
Matson Pen.
TERRE ADÉLIE
Dumont d'Urville (France)
Porpoise Bay
Commonwealth B.
C. Mose · C. Goodenough

**Ice.** The vast ice cap covering the mainland is up to 4km thick and breaks up at the coast to form huge icebergs up to 200km long.

**Penguins.** These birds cannot fly but are skilful swimmers who live in the sea but come onto land in warmer months to breed.

**1:32M**

KM  MILES
800
1200
1000
600
800
600
400
400
200
200
0  0

© Collins

THE INDEX includes the names on the maps in the ATLAS. The names are generally indexed to the largest scale map on which they appear, and can be located using the grid reference letters and numbers around the map frame. Names on insets have a symbol: □, followed by the inset number.

Abbreviations used to describe features in the index and on the maps are explained below.

## ABBREVIATIONS AND GLOSSARY

A. Alp Alpen Alpi *alp*
Alt *upper*
A.C.T. Australian Capital Territory
Afgh. Afghanistan
Afr. Africa African
Aig. Aiguille *peak*
AK Alaska
AL Alabama
Alg. Algeria
Alta Alberta
Appno Appennino *mountains*
AR Arkansas
Arch. Archipelago
Arg. Argentina
Arr. Arrecife *reef*
Austr. Australia
AZ Arizona
Azer. Azerbaijan

B. Bad *spa*
Ban *village*
Bay
Bangla. Bangladesh
B.C. British Columbia
Bg Berg *mountain*
Bge. Barragem *reservoir*
Bgt Bight Bugt *bay*
Bj Burj *hills*
Bol. Bolivia
Bos.-Herz. Bosnia Herzegovina
Br. Burun Burnu *point, cape*
Bt Bukit *bay*
Bü. Büyük *big*
Bulg. Bulgaria

C. Cape
Col *high pass*
Ç. Çay *river*
CA California
Cabo Cabeço *summit*
Can. Canada
Canal Canale *canal, channel*
Cañon Canyon *canyon*
C.A.R. Central African Republic
Cat. Cataract
Catena *mountains*
Cd Ciudad *town city*
Ch. Chaung *stream*
Chott *salt lake, marsh*
Chan. Channel
Che Chaîne *mountain chain*
Cma Cima *summit*
Cno Corno *peak*
Co Cerro *hill, peak*
CO Colorado
Col. Colombia
Cord. Cordillera *mountain chain*
Cr. Creek
CT Connecticut
Cuch. Cuchilla *chain of mountains*
Czo Cozzo *mountain*

D. Da *big, river*
Dag Dagh Dağı *mountain*
Dağları *mountains*
-d. -dake *peak*
DE Delaware
Dj. Djebel *mountain*
Dom. Rep. Dominican Republic

Eil. Eiland *island*
Eilanden *islands*
Emb. Embalse *reservoir*
Equat. Equatorial
Escarp. Escarpment
Est. Estuary
Eth. Ethiopia
Etg Etang *lake, lagoon*

F. Firth
Fin. Finland

Fj. Fjell *mountain*
Fjord Fjördur *fjord*
Fl. Fleuve *river*
FL Florida

G. Gebel *mountain*
Göl Gölö Göl *lake*
G. Golfe Golfo Gulf *gulf, bay*
Góra *mountain*
Gunung *mountain*
-g. -gawa *river*
GA Georgia
Gd Grand *big*
Gde Grande *big*
Geb. Gebergte *mountainrange*
Gebirge *mountains*
Gl. Glacier
Ger. Germany
Gr. Graben *trench, ditch*
Gross Grosse
Grande *big*
Grp Group
Gt Great Groot Groote *big*
Gy Góry Gory *mountains*

H. Hawr *lake*
Hill
Hoch *high*
Hora *mountain*
Hory *mountains*
Halv. Halvøy *peninsula*
Harb. Harbour
Hd Head
Hg. Hegység *mountains*
Hgts Heights
HI Hawaii
Ht Haut *high*
Hte Haute *high*

I. Île Ilha Insel Isla
Island Isle *island, isle*
Isola Isole *island*
IA Iowa
ID Idaho
IL Illinois
IN Indiana
Indon. Indonesia
Is Islas Îles Ilhas
Islands Isles
*islands, isles*
Isr. Israel
Isth. Isthmus

J. Jabal Jebel *mountain*
Jibāl *mountains*
Jrvi Jaure Jezero
Jezioro *lake*
Jökull *glacier*

K. Kaap Kap Kapp *cape*
Kaikyō *strait*
Kato Káto *lower*
Kiang *river or stream*
Ko *island, lake, inlet*
Koh Kūh Kūhha *island*
Kolpos *gulf*
Kopf *hill*
Kuala *estuary*
Kyst *coast*
Küçük *small*
Kan. Kanal Kanaal *canal*
Kazak. Kazakstan
Kep. Kepulauan *archipelago, islands*
Kg Kampong *village*
Khr. Khrebet *mountain range*
Kl. Klein Kleine *small*
Kör. Körfez Körfezi *bay, gulf*
KS Kansas
KY Kentucky
Kyrg. Kyrgyzstan

L. Lac Lago Lake
Liqen Loch Lough *lake, loch*
Lam *stream*

LA Louisiana
Lag. Lagoon Laguna
Lagôa *lagoon*
Lith. Lithuania
Lux. Luxembourg

M. Mae *river*
Me *great, chief, mother*
Meer *lake, sea*
Muang *kingdom, province, town*
Muong *town*
Mys *cape*
Maloye *small*
MA Massachusetts
Mad. Madagascar
Man. Manitoba
Maur. Mauritania
MD Maryland
ME Maine
Mex. Mexico
Mf Massif *mountains, upland*
Mgna Montagna *mountain*
Mgne Montagne *mountain*
Mgnes Montagnes *mountains*
MI Michigan
MN Minnesota
MO Missouri
Mon. Monasterio Monastery *monastery*
Monument *monument*
Moz. Mozambique
MS Mississippi
Mt Mont Mount *mountain*
Mt. Mountain
MT Montana
Mte Monte *mountain*
Mtes Montes *mountains*
Mti Monti Munţi *mountains*
Mtii Munţii *mountains*
Mth Mouth
Mths Mouths
Mtn Mountain
Mts Monts Mountains

N. Nam *south(ern), river*
Neu Ny *new*
Nevado *peak*
Nudo *mountain*
Noord Nord Nörre
Nørre *north*
Nos *spit, point*
Nac. Nacional *national*
Nat. National
N.B. New Brunswick
NC North Carolina
ND North Dakota
NE Nebraska
Neth. Netherlands
Nfld Newfoundland
NH New Hampshire
Nic. Nicaragua
Nizh. Nizhneye Nizhniy
Nizhnyaya *lower*
Nizm. Nizmennost' *lowland*
NJ New Jersey
NM New Mexico
N.O. Noord Oost Nord Ost *northeast*
Nov. Novyy Novaya
Noviye
Novoye *new*
N.S. Nova Scotia
N.S.W. New South Wales
N.T. Northern Territory
NV Nevada
Nva Nueva *new*
N.W.T. Northwest Territories
NY New York
N.Z. New Zealand

O. Oost Ost *east*
Ostrov *island*
Ø Østre *east*
Ob. Ober *upper, higher*
Oc. Ocean
Ode Oude *old*
Ogl. Oglat *well*
OH Ohio
OK Oklahoma
Ont. Ontario
Or. Óri Óros Ori *mountains*
Oros *mountain*
OR Oregon
Orm. Ormos *bay*
O-va Ostrova *islands*
Ot Olet *mountain*

Öv. Över Övre *upper*
Oz. Ozero *lake*
Ozera *lakes*

P. Pass
Pic Pico Piz *peak, summit*
Pou *mountain*
Pulau *island*
PA Pennsylvania
Pak. Pakistan
Para. Paraguay
Pass. Passage
Peg. Pegunungan *mountain range*
P.E.I. Prince Edward Island
Pen. Peninsula Penisola *peninsula*
Per. Pereval *pass*
Phil. Philippines
Phn. Phnom *hill, mountain*
Pgio Poggio *hill*
Pl. Planina Planinski *mountain(s)*
Pla Playa *beach*
Plat. Plateau
Plosk. Ploskogor'ye *plateau*
P.N.G. Papua New Guinea
Pno Pantano *reservoir, swamp*
Pol. Poland
Por. Porog *rapids*
Port. Portugal
P-ov Poluostrov *peninsula*
P.P. Pulau-pulau *islands*
Pr. Proliv *strait*
Przylądek *cape*
Presq. Presqu'île *peninsula*
Prom. Promontory
Prov. Province Provincial
Psa Presa *dam*
Pso Passo *dam*
Pt Point
Pont *bridge*
Petit *small*
Pta Ponta Punta *cape, point*
Puerta *narrow pass*
Pte Pointe *cape, point*
Ponte Puente *bridge*
Pto Porto Puerto *harbour, port*
Pzo Pizzo *mountain peak, mountain*

Qld. Queensland
Que. Quebec

R. Reshteh *mountain range*
Rūd *river*
Ra. Range
Rca Rocca *rock, fortress*
Reg. Region
Rep. Republic
Res. Reserve
Reservoir
Resp. Respublika *republic*
Rf Reef
Rge Ridge
RI Rhode Island
Riba Ribeira *coast, bottom of the river valley*
Rte Route
Rus. Fed. Russian Federation

S. Salar Salina *salt pan*
San São *saint*
See *lake*
Seto *strait, channel*
Sjö *lake*
Sör Süd Sud Syd *south*
sur *on*
Sa Serra Sierra *mountain range*
S.A. South Australia
Sab. Sabkhat *salt flat*
Sask. Saskatchewan
S. Arabia Saudi Arabia
SC South Carolina
Sc. Scoglio *rock, reef*
Sd Sound Sund *sound*
SD South Dakota
Seb. Sebjet Sebkhat Sebkra *salt flat*
Serr. Serranía *mountain range*
Sev. Severnaya Severnyy *north(ern)*
Sh. Shā'ib *watercourse*
Shaṭṭ *river (-mouth)*
Shima *island*
Shankou *pass*

Si Sidi *lord, master*
Sing. Singapore
Sk. Shuiku *reservoir*
Skt Sankt *saint*
Smt Seamount
Snra Senhora *Mrs, lady*
Snro Senhoro *Mr, gentleman*
Sp. Spain Spanish
Spitze *peak*
Sr Sönder Sonder *southern*
Sr. Sredniy Srednyaya *middle*
St Saint Sint
Staryy *old*
St. Stor Store *big*
Stung *river*
Sta Santa *saint*
Ste Sainte *saint*
Store *big*
Sto Santo *saint*
Str. Strait Stretta *strait*
Sv. Sväty Sveti *holy, saint*
Switz. Switzerland

T. Tal *valley*
Tall Tell *hill*
Tepe Tepesi *hill, peak*
Tajik. Tajikistan
Tan. Tanzania
Tas. Tasmania
Terr. Territory
Tg Tanjung Tanjong *cape, point*
Thai. Thailand
Tk Teluk *bay*
Tmt Tablemount
TN Tennessee
Tr. Trench Trough
Tre Torre *tower, fortress*
Tte Teniente *lieutenant*
Turk. Turkmenistan
TX Texas

U.A.E. United Arab Emirates
Ug Ujung *point, cape*
U.K. United Kingdom
Ukr. Ukraine
Unt. Unter *lower*
Upr Upper
Uru. Uruguay
U.S.A. United States of America
UT Utah
Uzbek. Uzbekistan

V. Val Valle Valley *valley*
Väster Vest Vester *west(ern)*
Vatn *lake*
Ville *town*
Va Vila *small town*
VA Virginia
Venez. Venezuela
Vic. Victoria
Vol. Volcán Volcan
Volcano *volcano*
Vdkhr. Vodokhranilishche *reservoir*
Vdskh. Vodoskhovshche
Vodaskhovishcha *reservoir*
Vel. Velikiy Velikaya
Velikiye *big*
Verkh. Verkhniy Verkhneye
Verkhne *upper*
Verkhnyaya *upper*
Vost. Vostochnyy *eastern*
Vozv. Vozvyshennost' *hills, upland*
VT Vermont

W. Wadi *watercourse*
Wald *forest*
Wan *bay*
Water *water*
WA Washington
W.A. Western Australia
Wr Wester
WV West Virginia
WY Wyoming

-y -yama *mountain*
Yt. Ytre Ytter Ytri *outer*
Yugo. Yugoslavia
Yuzh. Yuzhnaya Yuzhno
Yuzhnyy *southern*

Zal. Zaliv *bay*
Zap. Zapadnyy Zapadnaya
Zapadno Zapadnoye *western*
Zem. Zemlya *land*

# A

62 C5 Aachen Ger.
62 E6 Aalen Ger.
61 C2 Aalsmeer Neth.
61 C4 Aalst Belgium
61 C4 Aarschot Belgium
88 A3 Aba China
100 C4 Aba Nigeria
102 D3 Aba Zaire
81 M6 Ābādān Iran
79 G3 Ābādeh Iran
100 B1 Abadla Alg.
46 D2 Abaeté r. Brazil
43 J4 Abaetetuba Brazil
88 E1 Abag Qi China
25 E4 Abajo Pk summit U.S.A.
100 C4 Abakaliki Nigeria
86 F1 Abakan Rus. Fed.
86 E1 Abakanskiy Khrebet mts Rus. Fed.
69 E7 Abana Turkey
42 D6 Abancay Peru
79 G3 Abarqū Iran
90 K1 Abashiri Japan
90 K2 Abashiri-gawa r. Japan
90 K2 Abashiri-ko l. Japan
90 K1 Abashiri-wan b. Japan
110 E3 Abau P.N.G.
102 D3 Ābaya Hāyk' l. Eth.
Ābay Wenz r. see Blue Nile
86 F1 Abaza Rus. Fed.
66 C4 Abbasanta Sardinia Italy
61 A5 Abbaye de Chaalis France
61 D5 Abbaye d'Orval Belgium
30 C2 Abbaye, Pt U.S.A.
102 E2 Abbe, L. l. Eth.
64 E1 Abbeville France
27 E6 Abbeville LA U.S.A.
29 D5 Abbeville SC U.S.A.
60 B5 Abbeyfeale Rep. of Ireland
57 E6 Abbey Head hd U.K.
60 D5 Abbeyleix Rep. of Ireland
58 D3 Abbeytown U.K.
54 Q4 Abborrträsk Sweden
116 B2 Abbot B. b. Ant.
119 A3 Abbot Ice Shelf ice feature Ant.
116 B3 Abbot, Mt mt Austr.
20 E5 Abbotsford Can.
30 B3 Abbotsford U.S.A.
25 F4 Abbott U.S.A.
84 C2 Abbottabad Pak.
81 H3 'Abd al 'Azīz, J. h. Syria
81 L5 Abdanan Iran
101 E3 Abéché Chad
117 D4 Abel Tasman National Park nat. park N.Z.
100 B4 Abengourou Côte d'Ivoire
55 L9 Åbenrå Denmark
100 C4 Abeokuta Nigeria
59 C5 Aberaeron U.K.
57 F3 Aberchirder U.K.
115 H5 Abercrombie r. Austr.
59 D6 Aberdare U.K.
59 C5 Aberdaron U.K.
115 J4 Aberdeen Austr.
21 H4 Aberdeen Can.
89 □ Aberdeen Hong Kong China
104 F6 Aberdeen S. Africa
57 F3 Aberdeen U.K.
33 E5 Aberdeen MD U.S.A.
27 F5 Aberdeen MS U.S.A.
26 D2 Aberdeen SD U.S.A.
24 B2 Aberdeen WA U.S.A.
21 J2 Aberdeen Lake l. Can.
59 C5 Aberdyfi U.K.
57 E4 Aberfeldy U.K.
58 F4 Aberford U.K.
57 D4 Aberfoyle U.K.
59 D6 Abergavenny U.K.
27 C5 Abernathy U.S.A.
59 C5 Aberporth U.K.
59 C5 Abersoch U.K.
59 C5 Aberystwyth U.K.
78 E6 Abhā S. Arabia
81 M3 Abhar Iran
81 M4 Abhar r. Iran
Abiad, Bahr el r. see White Nile
45 A2 Abibe, Serranía de mts Col.
100 B4 Abidjan Côte d'Ivoire
84 B2 Ab-i-Istada l. Afgh.
102 D3 Abijatta-Shalla National Park nat. park Eth.
91 H6 Abiko Japan
26 D4 Abilene KS U.S.A.
27 D5 Abilene TX U.S.A.
59 F6 Abingdon U.K.
30 B5 Abingdon IL U.S.A.
32 C6 Abingdon VA U.S.A.
116 C2 Abington Reef rf Coral Sea Is Terr.
69 H6 Abinsk Rus. Fed.
42 C5 Abiseo, Parque Nacional nat. park Peru
21 H2 Abitau Lake l. Can.
22 D4 Abitibi r. Can.
22 E4 Abitibi, Lake l. Can.
100 B4 Aboisso Côte d'Ivoire
100 C4 Abomey Benin
101 D4 Abong Mbang Cameroon
94 A4 Aborlan Phil.
101 D3 Abou Déia Chad
81 K1 Abovyan Armenia
59 F6 Aboyne U.K.
47 D4 Abra, L. del l. Arg.

65 B3 Abrantes Port.
44 C2 Abra Pampa Arg.
46 E2 Abrolhos, Arquipélago dos is Brazil
24 E2 Absaroka Range mts U.S.A.
90 C6 Abu Japan
78 E6 Abū 'Arīsh S. Arabia
79 G5 Abu Dhabi U.A.E.
101 F3 Abu Hamed Sudan
100 C4 Abuja Nigeria
91 H5 Abukuma-gawa r. Japan
91 H5 Abukuma-kochi plat. Japan
101 E3 Abu Matariq Sudan
42 E6 Abunã r. Bol.
42 E5 Abunã Brazil
80 C6 Abu Qīr, Khalīg b. Egypt
82 D6 Abu Road India
78 C5 Abu Simbel Egypt
81 K6 Abū Şukhayr Iraq
117 C5 Abut Head hd N.Z.
94 C4 Abuyog Phil.
101 E3 Abu Zabad Sudan
Abū Zabī see Abu Dhabi
81 M6 Abūzam Iran
101 E3 Abyad Sudan
101 E4 Abyei Sudan
33 J2 Acadia Nat. Park nat. park U.S.A.
36 D4 Acambaro Mex.
45 A2 Acandí Col.
65 B1 A Cañiza Spain
36 C4 Acaponeta Mex.
36 E5 Acapulco Mex.
43 J4 Acará Brazil
43 K4 Acaraú r. Brazil
46 A4 Acaray r. Para.
44 E3 Acaray, Represa de resr Para.
45 E2 Acarigua Venez.
36 F5 Acayucán Mex.
100 B4 Accra Ghana
58 E4 Accrington U.K.
45 C3 Achaguas Venez.
84 D5 Achalpur India
77 T3 Achayvayam Rus. Fed.
60 B4 Achill Rep. of Ireland
60 A4 Achill Island i. Rep. of Ireland
57 D2 Achiltibuie U.K.
76 L4 Achinsk Rus. Fed.
57 C3 Achnasheen U.K.
57 C3 A'Chralaig mt U.K.
69 F6 Achuyevo Rus. Fed.
80 B3 Acigöl l. Turkey
80 B3 Acıpayam Turkey
66 F6 Acireale Sicily Italy
26 E3 Ackley U.S.A.
37 K4 Acklins Island i. Bahamas
59 J5 Acle U.K.
47 J5 Aconcagua r. Chile
43 L5 Acopiara Brazil
65 B1 A Coruña Spain
66 C2 Acqui Terme Italy
114 A4 Acraman, L. salt flat Austr.
80 E5 Acre Israel
66 G5 Acri Italy
62 J7 Ács Hungary
109 Actéon, Groupe atolls Fr. Polynesia Pac. Oc.
32 A4 Ada OH U.S.A.
27 D5 Ada OK U.S.A.
65 D2 Adaja r. Spain
115 H6 Adaminaby Austr.
44 E8 Adam, Mt h. Falkland Is
33 G3 Adams MA U.S.A.
30 C4 Adams WV U.S.A.
20 F4 Adams L. l. Can.
35 E2 Adams McGill Reservoir resr U.S.A.
24 B2 Adams, Mt mt. U.S.A.
20 C3 Adams, Mt. mt. U.S.A.
83 E9 Adam's Peak mt Sri Lanka
34 B2 Adams Peak mt. U.S.A.
'Adan see Aden
80 C5 Adana Turkey
60 C5 Adare Rep. of Ireland
119 A5 Adare, C. c. Ant.
116 A5 Adavale Austr.
35 E2 Adaven U.S.A.
78 F5 Ad Dahnā' des. S. Arabia
100 A2 Ad Dakhla Western Sahara
79 G4 Ad Dammām S. Arabia
81 J4 Ad Dawr Iraq
78 F5 Ad Dir'īyah S. Arabia
102 D3 Addis Ababa Eth.
Ad Dawhah see Doha
33 K2 Addison U.S.A.
81 K6 Ad Dīwānīyah Iraq
59 G6 Addlestone U.K.
13 J4 Addu Atoll atoll Maldives
81 J6 Ad Duwayd w. S. Arabia
29 D6 Adel GA U.S.A.
26 E3 Adel IA U.S.A.
114 C5 Adelaide Austr.
105 G6 Adelaide S. Africa
29 E7 Adelaide Bahamas
119 B2 Adelaide I i. Ant.
112 F2 Adelaide River Austr.
34 D4 Adelanto U.S.A.
115 H5 Adelong Austr.
78 E7 Aden Yemen
102 E2 Aden, Gulf of g. Somalia/Yemen
93 J7 Adi i. Indon.
102 D2 Ādī Ārk'ay Eth.
102 D2 Ādīgrat Eth.
84 D6 Adilabad India
81 J2 Adilcevaz Turkey
24 B3 Adin U.S.A.

101 D2 Adīrī Libya
33 F2 Adirondack Mountains mts U.S.A.
Ādīs Ābeba see Addis Ababa
102 D3 Ādīs Alem Eth.
102 D2 Adi Ugri Eritrea
80 G3 Adıyaman Turkey
63 N7 Adjud Romania
23 J3 Adlavik Islands is Can.
112 E2 Admiralty Gulf b. Austr.
20 C3 Admiralty Island i. U.S.A.
20 C3 Admiralty Island Nat. Monument res. U.S.A.
110 E2 Admiralty Islands is P.N.G.
119 A5 Admiralty Mts mts Ant.
83 E7 Adoni India
64 D5 Adour r. France
65 E4 Adra Spain
66 F6 Adrano Sicily Italy
100 C4 Adrar mts Alg.
100 B2 Adrar Alg.
100 C3 Adrar des Ifôghas reg. Mali
101 D3 Adré Chad
31 E5 Adrian MI U.S.A.
27 C5 Adrian TX U.S.A.
52 Adriatic Sea sea Europe
102 C3 Adusa Zaire
102 D2 Ādwa Eth.
77 P3 Adycha r. Rus. Fed.
69 F6 Adygeya, Respublika div. Rus. Fed.
69 F6 Adygeysk Rus. Fed.
69 H6 Adyk Rus. Fed.
100 B4 Adzopé Côte d'Ivoire
52 Aegean Sea sea Greece/Turkey
65 B1 A Estrada Spain
102 D2 Afabet Eritrea
81 K3 Afan Iran
70 Afghanistan country Asia
54 M5 Afjord Norway
102 E3 Afmadow Somalia
65 C1 A Fonsagrada Spain
80 F3 'Afrīn r. Syria/Turkey
80 F2 Afşin Turkey
61 D2 Afsluitdijk barrage Neth.
24 E3 Afton U.S.A.
43 H4 Afuá Brazil
80 E5 'Afula Israel
80 C4 Afyon Turkey
100 C3 Agadez Niger
100 B1 Agadir Morocco
82 D4 Agadyr' Kazak.
93 L4 Agana Guam Pac. Oc.
85 G5 Agartala India
84 C6 Agashi India
67 M6 Agathonisi i. Greece
83 D8 Agatti i. India
100 B4 Agboville Côte d'Ivoire
81 L1 Ağcabädi Azer.
81 L2 Ağdam Azer.
64 F5 Agde France
64 E4 Agen France
91 G5 Ageo Japan
104 C4 Aggeneys S. Africa
61 F4 Agger r. Ger.
84 D1 Aghil Pass pass China
60 C3 Aghla Mountain h. Rep. of Ireland
67 L2 Agia Vervara Greece
80 C2 Ağın Turkey
67 K6 Agios Dimitrios Greece
67 L5 Agios Efstratios i. Greece
67 M5 Agios Fokas, Akra pt Greece
67 K5 Agios Konstantinos Greece
67 L7 Agios Nikolaos Greece
67 K4 Agiou Orous, Kolpos b. Greece
101 F3 Agirwat Hills h. Sudan
105 F3 Agisanang S. Africa
100 B4 Agnibilékrou Côte d'Ivoire
67 L2 Agnita Romania
88 D2 Agong China
84 D4 Agra India
69 H7 Agrakhanskiy Poluostrov pen. Rus. Fed.
84 B1 Agram Pass pass Pak.
81 F2 Agreda Spain
81 J2 Ağrı Turkey
67 K7 Agria Gramvousa i. Greece
66 F6 Agrigento Sicily Italy
93 L3 Agrihan i. N. Mariana Is
67 J5 Agrinio Greece
47 B3 Agrio r. Arg.
66 F4 Agropoli Italy
81 M1 Ağsu Azer.
45 B3 Aguadas Col.
45 B3 Agua de Dios Col.
37 L5 Aguadilla Puerto Rico
37 H7 Aguadulce Panama
36 D4 Aguanaval r. Mex.
47 C1 Agua Negra, Paso del pass Arg./Chile
46 B3 Aguapeí r. Brazil
36 C2 Agua Prieta Mex.
46 A3 Aguaray Guazú r. Para.
45 D2 Aguaro-Guariquito, Parque Nacional nat. park Venez.
36 D4 Aguascalientes Mex.
46 D3 Águas Formosas Brazil
46 D2 Agudos Brazil
65 D1 Aguilar de Campóo Spain

65 F4 Águilas Spain
94 B4 Aguisan Phil.
13 F7 Agulhas Basin sea feature Indian Ocean
104 D7 Agulhas, Cape c. S. Africa
46 D3 Agulhas Negras mt Brazil
13 F6 Agulhas Plateau sea feature Indian Ocean
92 Agung, G. volc. Indon.
94 C4 Agusan r. Phil.
94 B4 Agutaya Phil.
81 L2 Ahar Iran
117 C5 Ahaura N.Z.
61 F2 Ahaus Ger.
117 F3 Ahimanawa Ra. mts N.Z.
81 J2 Ahlat Turkey
84 C5 Ahmadabad India
83 D7 Ahmadnagar India
84 B3 Ahmadpur East Pak.
79 L3 Ahmadpur Sial Pak.
81 J2 Ahta D. mt Turkey
54 T5 Ähtäri Fin.
55 U7 Ahtme Estonia
81 M6 Ahū Iran
64 F3 Ahun France
117 B6 Ahuriri r. N.Z.
81 M6 Ahvāz Iran
84 C5 Ahwa India
Ahwāz see Ahvāz
104 B3 Ai-Ais Namibia
88 D1 Aibag Gol r. China
90 J2 Aibetsu Japan
91 F6 Aichi Japan
90 E6 Aioi Japan
34 □1 Aiea U.S.A.
80 E4 Aigialousa Cyprus
67 K6 Aigina i. Greece
67 K5 Aigio Greece
64 H4 Aigle de Chambeyron mt France
47 F2 Aiguá Uru.
87 N1 Aihui China
91 K4 Aikawa Japan
29 D5 Aiken U.S.A.
45 A2 Ailigandi Panama
31 G4 Ailsa Craig Can.
57 C4 Ailsa Craig i. U.K.
46 E2 Aimorés, Sa dos h. Brazil
100 C1 Aïn Beïda Alg.
100 B2 'Aïn Ben Tili Maur.
65 H4 Aïn Defla Alg.
65 H5 Aïn el Hadjel Alg.
100 B1 Aïn Sefra Alg.
23 H4 Ainslie, Lake l. Can.
26 D3 Ainsworth U.S.A.
Aintab see Gaziantep
65 H4 Aïn Taya Alg.
65 G5 Aïn Tédélès Alg.
45 B4 Aipe Col.
95 C5 Air i. Indon.
20 G4 Airdrie Can.
57 E5 Airdrie U.K.
64 D5 Aire-sur-l'Adour France
88 D1 Airgin Sum China
116 C3 Airlie Beach Austr.
100 C3 Aïr, Massif de l' mts Niger
21 H3 Air Ronge Can.
44 B7 Aisén, Pto Chile
88 F2 Ai Shan h. China
20 B2 Aishihik Can.
20 B2 Aishihik Lake l. Can.
64 G2 Aisne r. France
47 M8 Aitana mt Spain
26 E2 Aitkin U.S.A.
109 Aitutaki i. Cook Islands Pac. Oc.
63 L7 Aiud Romania
64 G5 Aix-en-Provence France
64 G4 Aix-les-Bains France
20 D3 Aiyansh Can.
85 H5 Aizawl India
55 T8 Aizkraukle Latvia
55 R8 Aizpute Latvia
91 G5 Aizutakada Japan
91 G5 Aizu-wakamatsu Japan
66 C2 Ajaccio Corsica France
45 B4 Ajajú r. Col.
Ajanta h. see Sahyadriparvat Range
54 O4 Ajaureforsen Sweden
117 D5 Ajax, Mt mt. N.Z.
101 E1 Ajdābiyā Libya
a-Jiddet gravel area see Jiddat al Harāsīs
90 H3 Ajigasawa Japan
80 E5 'Ajlūn Jordan
84 C4 Ajmer India
35 F5 Ajo U.S.A.
35 F5 Ajo, Mt mt. U.S.A.
94 B4 Ajuy Phil.
90 J2 Akabira Japan
91 G5 Akadomari Japan
91 G4 Aka-gawa r. Japan
102 D4 Akagera National Park nat. park Rwanda
90 K2 Akan Japan
90 K2 Akan National Park nat. park Japan
80 D4 Akanthou Cyprus
90 D7 Akaoka Japan
117 D5 Akaroa N.Z.
117 D5 Akaroa Har in. N.Z.
85 H4 Akas reg. India
84 B2 Akbar Afgh.
84 B2 Akbarpur India
76 G4 Akbulak Rus. Fed.
80 F2 Akçadağ Turkey
80 F2 Akçakale Turkey
80 C1 Akçakoca Turkey

81 J3 Akçali D. mt Turkey
80 C3 Ak D. mt Turkey
81 H2 Ak D. mts Turkey
80 E2 Akdağmadeni Turkey
55 Q7 Åkersberga Sweden
61 C2 Akersloot Neth.
79 H5 Akhdar, Jabal mts Oman
81 J1 Akhalk'alak'i Georgia
69 G7 Akhalts'ikhe Georgia
85 G5 Akhaura Bangl.
79 H5 Akhdar, Jabal mts Oman
80 A2 Akhisar Turkey
80 F3 Akhtarīn Syria
69 H5 Akhtubinsk Rus. Fed.
81 J1 Akhuryan Armenia
90 D7 Aki Japan
22 D3 Akimiski Island i. Can.
80 E3 Akıncı Burun pt Turkey
80 G1 Akıncılar Turkey
91 H4 Akita Japan
91 H4 Akita Japan
100 A3 Akjoujt Maur.
54 P3 Akkajaure l. Sweden
80 C1 Akkaya Turkey
90 K2 Akkeshi Japan
90 K2 Akkeshi-ko l. Japan
90 K2 Akkeshi-wan b. Japan
'Akko see Acre
80 F1 Akkuş Turkey
84 D4 Aklera India
55 R8 Akmenrags pt Latvia
76 J4 Akmola Kazak.
101 E4 Akobo Sudan
102 D2 Akordat Eritrea
80 D3 Akören Turkey
84 D5 Akot India
23 G1 Akpatok Island i. Can.
54 B4 Akranes Iceland
69 G7 Akrathos, Akra pt Greece
55 J7 Åkrehamne Norway
84 A2 Ak Robat Pass pass Afgh.
24 G3 Akron CO U.S.A.
32 C4 Akron OH U.S.A.
32 C4 Akron City Reservoir resr U.S.A.
84 D2 Aksai Chin terr. China/India
80 E2 Aksaray Turkey
80 C2 Akseki Turkey
76 H5 Akshiganak Kazak.
82 F2 Aksu China
80 C3 Aksu r. Turkey
102 D2 Aksum Eth.
85 F1 Aktag mt China
81 K2 Aktas D. mt Turkey
76 G5 Aktau Kazak.
82 E1 Aktogay Kazak.
63 O4 Aktsyabrski Belarus
76 H4 Aktyubinsk Kazak.
90 C7 Akune Japan
100 C4 Akure Nigeria
54 D4 Akureyri Iceland
85 G1 Akxokesay China
Akyab see Sittwe
80 C3 Akziyaret Turkey
54 L6 Äl Norway
29 C5 Alabama div. U.S.A.
29 C5 Alabama r. U.S.A.
29 C5 Alabaster U.S.A.
94 B3 Alabat i. Phil.
81 K7 Al 'Abţīyah w. Iraq
80 E1 Alaca Turkey
80 F2 Alacahan Turkey
80 E2 Alaçam Turkey
80 B2 Alaçam Dağları mts Turkey
81 J2 Ala Dag mt Turkey
81 J2 Ala Dağlar mts Turkey
81 J2 Ala Dağlar mts Turkey
69 H7 Alagir Rus. Fed.
43 L6 Alagoinhas Brazil
65 F2 Alagón Spain
94 B3 Alah r. Phil.
54 S5 Alahärmä Fin.
81 L7 Al Ahmadī Kuwait
54 T5 Alajärvi Fin.
81 L2 Alajujeh Iran
37 H6 Alajuela Costa Rica
84 D3 Alaknanda r. India
82 F1 Alakol', Ozero salt l. Kazak.
54 W3 Alakurtti Rus. Fed.
81 L4 Alalāū r. Brazil
81 J3 Al 'Amādīyah Iraq
93 L6 Alamagan i. N. Mariana Is
81 L6 Al 'Amārah Iraq
85 H3 Alamdo China
81 K7 Al Amghar waterhole Iraq
94 A2 Alaminos Phil.
35 E3 Alamo U.S.A.
35 E3 Alamo Dam dam U.S.A.
25 F5 Alamogordo U.S.A.
27 D6 Alamo Heights U.S.A.
25 F4 Alamos Sonora Mex.
25 F4 Alamosa U.S.A.
54 O4 Åland is Fin.
55 Q6 Åland is Fin.
81 K2 Aland r. Iran
95 E1 Alang Besar i. Indon.
30 D5 Alanson U.S.A.
80 D3 Alanya Turkey
80 D3 Alaplı Turkey
80 C1 Alaplı Turkey

Alappuzha see Alleppey
65 E3 Alarcón, Embalse de resr Spain
78 F4 Al Arṭāwīyah S. Arabia
80 B2 Alaşehir Turkey
81 J6 Al 'Āshūrīyah w. Iraq
16 Alaska div. U.S.A.
18 Alaska, Gulf of g. U.S.A.
20 E3 Alaska Highway Can./U.S.A.
18 Alaska Peninsula pen. U.S.A.
18 Alaska Range mts U.S.A.
81 M2 Ālāt Azer.
81 J6 Al 'Athāmīn h. Iraq
68 H4 Alatyr' r. Rus. Fed.
68 H4 Alatyr' Rus. Fed.
42 C4 Alausí Ecuador
81 K1 Alaverdi Armenia
54 T4 Alavieska Fin.
54 S5 Alavus Fin.
114 D5 Alawoona Austr.
81 L1 Alazani r. Azer./Georgia
81 K5 Al 'Azīzīyah Iraq
66 C2 Alba Italy
80 F3 Al Bāb Syria
65 F3 Albacete Spain
114 D5 Albacutya, L. l. Austr.
81 K6 Al Bādiyah al Janūbīyah h. Iraq
67 K1 Alba Iulia Romania
22 C3 Albanel, L. l. Can.
49 Albania country Europe
112 C7 Albany Austr.
22 C3 Albany r. Can.
29 C6 Albany GA U.S.A.
30 E5 Albany IN U.S.A.
28 C4 Albany KY U.S.A.
33 G3 Albany NY U.S.A.
24 B2 Albany OR U.S.A.
115 H1 Albany Downs Austr.
47 G2 Albardão do João Maria coastal area Brazil
Al Başrah see Basra
81 K6 Al Baţha' marsh Iraq
81 L6 Al Bāţin, Wādī watercourse Asia
113 H2 Albatross Bay b. Austr.
115 F8 Albatross I. i. Austr.
101 E1 Al Baydā' Libya
42 □ Albemarle, Pta pt Galapagos Is Ecuador
29 E5 Albemarle Sd chan. U.S.A.
66 C2 Albenga Italy
65 D3 Alberche r. Spain
113 F5 Alberga watercourse Austr.
65 B2 Albergaria-a-Velha Port.
115 G4 Albert France
64 E4 Albert France
20 F4 Albert div. Can.
32 E6 Alberta, Mt mt. Can.
20 F4 Alberta, Mt mt. Can.
104 D7 Albertinia S. Africa
61 D4 Albert Kanaal canal Belgium
114 C5 Albert, Lake l. Austr.
102 D3 Albert, Lake l. Uganda/Zaire
26 E3 Albert Lea U.S.A.
101 F4 Albert Nile r. Sudan/Uganda
44 B8 Alberto de Agostini, Parque Nacional nat. park Chile
105 H3 Alberton S. Africa
64 H4 Albertville France
64 F5 Albi France
43 H2 Albina Suriname
34 A2 Albion CA U.S.A.
33 J2 Albion ME U.S.A.
30 E4 Albion MI U.S.A.
32 D3 Albion NY U.S.A.
65 E3 Alborán, Isla de i. Spain
55 L8 Ålborg Denmark
55 M8 Ålborg Bugt b. Denmark
20 F4 Albreda Can.
116 B4 Albro Austr.
65 B4 Albufeira Port.
81 H4 Al Bū Kamāl Syria
25 F5 Albuquerque U.S.A.
79 H5 Al Buraymī Oman
65 C3 Alburquerque Spain
115 G6 Albury Austr.
81 H4 Al Buşayrah Syria
80 G7 Al Buşayţā' plain S. Arabia
65 B3 Alcácer do Sal Port.
65 E2 Alcalá de Henares Spain
65 E4 Alcalá la Real Spain
66 E6 Alcamo Sicily Italy
65 F2 Alcañiz Spain
65 D3 Alcántara Spain
65 E4 Alcaraz Spain
65 D4 Alcaudete Spain
65 E3 Alcázar de San Juan Spain
69 F5 Alchevs'k Ukr.
46 D2 Alcobaça Brazil
65 F2 Alcora Spain
65 E3 Alcorta Arg.
65 E4 Alcoy Spain
103 E4 Aldabra Islands is Seychelles
81 K5 Ad Daghghārah Iraq
77 O4 Aldan Rus. Fed.
77 P3 Aldan r. Rus. Fed.
59 J5 Aldeburgh U.K.
117 F2 Aldermen Is, The is N.Z.
56 E7 Alderney i. U.K.
34 B4 Alder Peak summit U.S.A.

59 G6 Aldershot U.K.
32 C6 Alderson U.S.A.
58 D3 Aldingham U.K.
59 F5 Aldridge U.K.
30 B5 Aledo U.S.A.
100 A3 Aleg Maur.
46 E3 Alegre Brazil
44 E3 Alegrete Brazil
47 E2 Alejandro Korn Arg.
68 E2 Alekhovshchina Rus. Fed.
68 F3 Aleksandrov Rus. Fed.
69 J5 Aleksandrov Gay Rus. Fed.
69 H6 Aleksandrovskoye Rus. Fed.
87 Q1 Aleksandrovsk-Sakhalinskiy Rus. Fed.
76 J4 Alekseyevka Kazak.
69 F5 Alekseyevka Rus. Fed.
69 F5 Alekseyevka Rus. Fed.
69 G5 Alekseyevskaya Rus. Fed.
68 F4 Aleksin Rus. Fed.
67 J3 Aleksinac Yugo.
36 E5 Alemán, Presa, M. *resr* Mex.
102 B4 Alèmbé Gabon
80 E1 Alembeyli Turkey
46 D3 Além Paraíba Brazil
54 M5 Ålen Norway
64 E2 Alençon France
43 H4 Alenquer Brazil
34 □2 Alenuihaha Channel *chan.* U.S.A.
80 F3 Aleppo Syria
42 D6 Alerta Peru
20 D4 Alert Bay Can.
64 G4 Alès France
63 L7 Aleşd Romania
66 C2 Alessandria Italy
54 K5 Ålesund Norway
16 Aleutian Islands *is* U.S.A.
15 G2 Aleutian Trench *sea feature* Pac. Oc.
77 R4 Alevina, Mys *c.* Rus. Fed.
Alevişik *see* Samandağı
33 K2 Alexander U.S.A.
20 B3 Alexander Archipelago *is* U.S.A.
104 B4 Alexander Bay *b.* Namibia/S. Africa
104 B4 Alexander Bay S. Africa
29 C5 Alexander City U.S.A.
119 A2 Alexander I. *i.* Ant.
115 F6 Alexandra Austr.
117 B6 Alexandra N.Z.
44 □ Alexandra, C. *c.* S. Georgia Atlantic Ocean
67 K4 Alexandreia Greece
Alexandretta *see* İskenderun
33 F2 Alexandria Can.
78 B3 Alexandria Egypt
67 L3 Alexandria Romania
105 G6 Alexandria S. Africa
57 D5 Alexandria U.K.
30 E5 Alexandria *IN* U.S.A.
27 E6 Alexandria *LA* U.S.A.
26 E2 Alexandria *MN* U.S.A.
32 E5 Alexandria *VA* U.S.A.
33 F2 Alexandria Bay U.S.A.
114 C5 Alexandrina, L. *l.* Austr.
67 L4 Alexandroupoli Greece
23 J3 Alexis *r.* Can.
30 B5 Alexis U.S.A.
20 E4 Alexis Creek Can.
86 D1 Aleysk Rus. Fed.
65 F1 Alfaro Spain
81 L7 Al Farwānīyah Kuwait
81 J4 Al Fatḥah Iraq
81 M7 Al Fāw Iraq
46 D3 Alfenas Brazil
81 M7 Al Fințās Kuwait
63 K7 Alföld *plain* Hungary
59 H4 Alford U.K.
33 F2 Alfred Can.
33 H3 Alfred U.S.A.
81 M7 Al Fuḥayḥīl Kuwait
Al-Fujayrah *see* Fujairah
Al Furāt *r. see* Euphrates
55 J7 Algård Norway
47 C3 Algarrobo del Aguilla Arg.
65 B4 Algarve *reg.* Port.
68 G4 Algasovo Rus. Fed.
65 D4 Algeciras Spain
65 F3 Algemesí Spain
Alger *see* Algiers
31 E3 Alger U.S.A.
96 Algeria *country* Africa
81 K6 Al Ghammas Iraq
79 G6 Al Ghayḍah Yemen
66 C4 Alghero *Sardinia* Italy
100 C1 Algiers Alg.
105 F6 Algoa Bay *b.* S. Africa
30 D3 Algoma U.S.A.
26 E3 Algona U.S.A.
31 F4 Algonac U.S.A.
31 H3 Algonquin Park Can.
31 H3 Algonquin Provincial Park *res.* Can.
81 J7 Al Habakah *w.* S. Arabia
81 J4 Al Hadīthah Iraq
81 J4 Al Ḥaḍr Iraq
80 F4 Al Ḥaffah Syria
81 G6 Al Hamad *reg.* Jordan/S. Arabia
101 D2 Al Ḥamādah al Ḥamrā' *plat.* Libya
65 F4 Alhama de Murcia Spain
81 J6 Al Hammām *w.* Iraq
81 K7 Al Haniyah *escarpment* Iraq
81 G6 Al Ḥarrah *reg.* S. Arabia
81 H3 Al Ḥasakah Syria
81 K5 Al Hāshimīyah Iraq
81 L5 Al Ḥayy Iraq
79 G6 Al Ḥibāk S. Arabia
81 K5 Al Ḥillah Iraq
100 B1 Al Hoceima Morocco
78 E7 Al Hudaydah Yemen
79 F4 Al Hufūf S. Arabia
81 L4 'Alīābād Iran
67 M5 Aliağa Turkey
67 K4 Aliakmonas *r.* Greece
81 L5 'Alī al Gharbī Iraq
84 B4 Ali Bandar Pak.
81 M2 Äli Bayramlı Azer.
65 F3 Alicante Spain
116 A4 Alice *watercourse* Austr.
116 A4 Alice Austr.
105 G6 Alice S. Africa
27 D7 Alice U.S.A.
20 D3 Alice Arm Can.
113 F4 Alice Springs Austr.
29 E7 Alice Town Bahamas
94 B5 Alicia Phil.
84 D4 Aligarh India
80 F1 Alīgūdarz Iran
102 B4 Alima *r.* Congo
55 N8 Alingsås Sweden
80 B2 Aliova *r.* Turkey
84 B3 Alipur Pak.
85 G4 Alipur Duar India
32 C4 Aliquippa U.S.A.
102 E2 Ali Sabieh Djibouti
80 F6 'Al 'Īsāwīyah S. Arabia
81 K2 Alī Shah Iran
81 K5 Al Iskandarīyah Iraq
25 E6 Alisos *r.* Mex.
67 L5 Aliveri Greece
105 G5 Aliwal North S. Africa
20 G4 Alix Can.
101 E1 Al Jabal al Akhḍar *mts* Libya
101 E2 Al Jaghbūb Libya
81 L7 Al Jahrah Kuwait
78 D4 Al Jawf S. Arabia
101 D1 Al Jawsh Libya
81 G3 Al Jazīrah *reg.* Iraq/Syria
65 B4 Aljezur Port.
81 J6 Al Jil *w.* Iraq
80 E6 Al Jīzah Jordan
79 F4 Al Jubayl S. Arabia
65 B4 Aljustrel Port.
79 H5 Al Khābūrah Oman
81 K5 Al Khālis Iraq
79 H4 Al Khaṣab Oman
101 E2 Al Khufrah Libya
101 D1 Al Khums Libya
81 K5 Al Kifl Iraq
61 C2 Alkmaar Neth.
81 K5 Al Kūfah Iraq
81 L5 Al Kumayt Iraq
81 K5 Al Kūt Iraq
Al Kuwayt *see* Kuwait
81 H7 Al Labbah *plain* S. Arabia
Al Lādhiqīyah *see* Latakia
33 J1 Allagash *ME* U.S.A.
33 J1 Allagash *r. ME* U.S.A.
33 J1 Allagash Lake *l.* U.S.A.
85 E4 Allahabad India
80 F5 Al Lajā *lava* Syria
77 P3 Allakh-Yun' Rus. Fed.
105 G3 Allanridge S. Africa
105 H1 Alldays S. Africa
30 E4 Allegan U.S.A.
32 D4 Allegheny *r.* U.S.A.
32 C6 Allegheny Mountains *mts* U.S.A.
32 D4 Allegheny Reservoir *resr* U.S.A.
29 D5 Allendale U.S.A.
58 E3 Allendale Town U.K.
31 G3 Allenford Can.
60 C3 Allen, Lough *l.* Rep. of Ireland
33 F4 Allentown U.S.A.
83 E9 Alleppey India
62 D4 Aller *r.* Ger.
26 C3 Alliance *NE* U.S.A.
32 C4 Alliance *OH* U.S.A.
81 J6 Al Līfīyah *w.* Iraq
116 B2 Alligator Creek Austr.
55 O9 Allinge-Sandvig Denmark
31 H3 Alliston Can.
78 E5 Al Līth S. Arabia
57 E4 Alloa U.K.
115 K2 Allora Austr.
81 J6 Al Lussuf *w.* Iraq
23 F4 Alma Can.
30 E4 Alma *MI* U.S.A.
26 D3 Alma *NE* U.S.A.
35 H5 Alma *NM* U.S.A.
81 J6 Al Ma'ānīyah Iraq
Alma-Ata *see* Almaty
65 B3 Almada Port.
81 K7 Al Ma'danīyāt *w.* Iraq
116 A1 Almaden Austr.
65 D3 Almadén Spain
Al Madīnah *see* Medina
81 K5 Al Maḥmūdiyah Iraq
81 L1 Almalı Azer.
79 G4 Al Manāmah Bahrain
34 B1 Almanor, Lake *l.* U.S.A.
65 F3 Almansa Spain
65 D2 Almanzor *mt* Spain
81 L6 Al Ma'qil Iraq
101 E1 Al Marj Libya
46 C1 Almas, Rio das *r.* Brazil
82 E2 Almaty Kazak.
Al Mawṣil *see* Mosul
81 H4 Al Mayādīn Syria
65 E2 Almazán Spain
77 N3 Almaznyy Rus. Fed.
43 H4 Almeirim Brazil
65 B3 Almeirim Port.
61 E2 Almelo Neth.
46 E2 Almenara Brazil
65 C2 Almendra, Embalse de *resr* Spain
65 C3 Almendralejo Spain
61 D2 Almere Neth.
65 E4 Almería Spain
65 E4 Almería, Golfo de *b.* Spain
76 G4 Al'met'yevsk Rus. Fed.
55 O8 Älmhult Sweden
65 D5 Almina, Pta *pt* Morocco
78 F4 Al Mish'āb S. Arabia
80 F5 Al Mismīyah Syria
65 B4 Almodôvar Port.
31 F4 Almont U.S.A.
31 J3 Almonte Can.
65 C4 Almonte Spain
82 E5 Almora India
79 F4 Al Mubarrez S. Arabia
80 E7 Al Mudawwara Jordan
79 F7 Al Mukallā Yemen
65 E4 Almuñécar Spain
81 K5 Al Muqdādīyah Iraq
80 F1 Almus Turkey
81 K5 Al Musayyib Iraq
67 L7 Almyrou, Ormos *b.* Greece
34 □1 Alna Haina U.S.A.
58 F2 Alnwick U.K.
85 H5 Alon Myanmar
85 H3 Along India
67 K5 Alonnisos *i.* Greece
93 G8 Alor *i.* Indon.
93 G8 Alor, Kepulauan *is* Indon.
Alost *see* Aalst
84 C5 Alot India
113 K2 Alotau P.N.G.
54 W4 Alozero Rus. Fed.
34 C4 Alpaugh U.S.A.
31 F3 Alpena U.S.A.
116 B4 Alpha Austr.
116 B4 Alpha Cr. *r.* Austr.
66 D1 Alpi Dolomitiche *mts* Italy
35 H5 Alpine *AZ* U.S.A.
27 C6 Alpine *TX* U.S.A.
24 E3 Alpine *WY* U.S.A.
52 Alps *mts* Europe
78 F6 Al Qa'āmīyāt *reg.* S. Arabia
101 D1 Al Qaddāḥīyah Libya
80 F4 Al Qadmūs Syria
81 H3 Al Qāmishlī Syria
80 F4 Al Qaryatayn Syria
78 F6 Al Qaṭn Yemen
101 D2 Al Qaṭrūn Libya
80 E5 Al Qunayṭirah Syria
78 E6 Al Qunfidhah S. Arabia
81 L6 Al Qurnah Iraq
81 K6 Al Qusayr Iraq
80 F5 Al Quṭayfah Syria
64 H2 Alsace *reg.* France
59 E4 Alsager U.K.
81 J6 Al Samīt *w.* Iraq
21 H4 Alsask Can.
58 E3 Alston U.K.
115 K2 Alstonville Austr.
55 R8 Alsunga Latvia
54 S2 Alta Norway
54 S2 Altaelva *r.* Norway
47 D1 Alta Gracia Arg.
45 D2 Altagracia de Orituco Venez.
74 Altai Mountains *mts* China/Mongolia
29 D6 Altamaha *r.* U.S.A.
43 H4 Altamira Brazil
117 B6 Alta, Mt *mt.* N.Z.
66 G4 Altamura Italy
46 C1 Alta Paraiso de Goiás Brazil
32 D6 Altavista U.S.A.
82 G1 Altay China
86 G2 Altay Mongolia
65 F3 Altea Spain
54 S1 Alteidet Norway
85 H1 Altenqoke China
81 M1 Altıağaç Azer.
84 B2 Altimur Pass *pass* Afgh.
81 K4 Altin Köprü Iraq
67 M5 Altınoluk Turkey
80 C2 Altıntaş Turkey
42 E7 Altiplano *plain* Bol.
62 E6 Altmühl *r.* Ger.
46 B2 Alto Araguaia Brazil
47 C2 Alto de Pencoso *h.* Arg.
45 B3 Alto de Tamar *mt* Col.
46 B2 Alto Garças Brazil
103 D5 Alto Molócuè Moz.
28 B4 Alton *IL* U.S.A.
27 F4 Alton *MO* U.S.A.
33 H3 Alton *NH* U.S.A.
26 D1 Altona Can.
32 D4 Altoona U.S.A.
46 B2 Alto Sucuriú Brazil
62 F6 Altötting Ger.
59 E4 Altrincham U.K.
82 G3 Altun Shan *mts* China
24 B3 Alturas U.S.A.
27 D5 Altus U.S.A.
80 G1 Alucra Turkey
55 U8 Alūksne Latvia
81 M5 Alūm Iran
32 B4 Alum Creek Lake *l.* U.S.A.
47 B3 Aluminé *r.* Arg.
47 B3 Aluminé, L. *l.* Arg.
69 E6 Alupka Ukr.
101 D1 Al 'Uqaylah Libya
92 C5 Alur Setar Malaysia
69 E6 Alushta Ukr.
81 K4 'Alut Iran
78 F4 Al 'Uthmānīyah S. Arabia
101 E2 Al 'Uwaynāt Libya
81 J6 Al 'Uwayqīlah S. Arabia
81 L6 Al 'Uzayr Iraq
27 D4 Alva U.S.A.
47 C2 Alvarado, P. de *pass* Chile
42 F4 Alvarães Brazil
55 M5 Ålvdal Norway
55 O6 Älvdalen Sweden
55 O8 Ålvesta Sweden
55 K6 Ålvik Norway
27 E6 Alvin U.S.A.
54 R4 Älvsbyn Sweden
78 D4 Al Wajh S. Arabia
84 D4 Alwar India
81 H5 Al Widyān *plat.* Iraq/S. Arabia
88 A2 Alxa Youqi China
88 B2 Alxa Zuoqi China
113 G2 Alyangula Austr.
57 E4 Alyth U.K.
55 T9 Alytus Lith.
24 F2 Alzada U.S.A.
45 E3 Amacuro *r.* Guyana/Venez.
112 F4 Amadeus, Lake *salt flat* Austr.
35 G6 Amado U.S.A.
65 B3 Amadora Port.
90 C7 Amagi Japan
90 C7 Amakusa-Kami-shima *i.* Japan
90 B7 Amakusa-nada *b.* Japan
90 C7 Amakusa-Shimo-shima *i.* Japan
55 N7 Åmal Sweden
87 L1 Amalat *r.* Rus. Fed.
45 B3 Amalfi Col.
104 F3 Amalia S. Africa
67 J6 Amaliada Greece
84 C5 Amalner India
93 K7 Amamapare Indon.
46 A3 Amambaí Brazil
46 A3 Amambaí *r.* Brazil
46 A3 Amambaí, Serra de *h.* Brazil/Para.
87 N6 Amami-guntō *is* Japan
87 N6 Amami-Ōshima *i.* Japan
76 H4 Amangel'dy Kazak.
66 G5 Amantea Italy
105 J5 Amanzimtoti S. Africa
43 H3 Amapá Brazil
65 C3 Amareleja Port.
34 D3 Amargosa Desert *des.* U.S.A.
34 D3 Amargosa Range *mts* U.S.A.
34 D3 Amargosa Valley U.S.A.
27 C5 Amarillo U.S.A.
66 F3 Amaro, Monte *mt* Italy
84 E4 Amarpatan India
80 E1 Amasya Turkey
43 H3 Amazon *r.* S. America
45 D4 Amazonas *div.* Brazil
Amazonas *r. see* Amazon
43 G4 Amazônia, Parque Nacional *nat. park* Brazil
43 J3 Amazon, Mouths of the *est.* Brazil
84 C6 Ambad India
84 D3 Ambala India
103 E6 Ambalavao Madag.
103 E5 Ambanja Madag.
77 S3 Ambarchik Rus. Fed.
116 A5 Ambathala Austr.
42 C4 Ambato Ecuador
103 E5 Ambato Boeny Madag.
103 E6 Ambato Finandrahana Madag.
103 E5 Ambatolampy Madag.
103 E5 Ambatomainty Madag.
103 E5 Ambatondrazaka Madag.
62 E6 Amberg Ger.
36 G5 Ambergris Cay *i.* Belize
64 G4 Ambérieu-en-Bugey France
31 G3 Amberley Can.
85 E5 Ambikapur India
103 E5 Ambilobe Madag.
115 G5 Ambition, Mt *mt.* Can.
58 F2 Amble U.K.
58 E3 Ambleside U.K.
61 D4 Amblève *r.* Belgium
61 D4 Amblève, Vallée de l' *v.* Belgium
103 E6 Amboasary Madag.
103 E6 Ambohidratrimo Madag.
103 E6 Ambohimahasoa Madag.
Amboina *see* Ambon
93 H7 Ambon *i.* Indon.
93 H7 Ambon Indon.
103 E6 Ambositra Madag.
103 E6 Ambovombe Madag.
35 E4 Amboy *CA* U.S.A.
30 C5 Amboy *IL* U.S.A.
33 F3 Amboy Center U.S.A.
103 B4 Ambriz Angola
111 G3 Ambrym *i.* Vanuatu
92 □ Ambunten Indon.
116 C6 Amby Austr.
85 G2 Amdo China
61 D1 Ameland *i.* Neth.
32 E6 Amelia Court House U.S.A.
33 G4 Amenia U.S.A.
24 D3 American Falls U.S.A.
24 D3 American Falls Res. *resr* U.S.A.
35 G1 American Fork U.S.A.
106 American Samoa *terr.* Pacific Ocean
29 C5 Americus U.S.A.
61 D2 Amersfoort Neth.
105 H3 Amersfoort S. Africa
59 G6 Amersham U.K.
21 L3 Amery Can.
119 D5 Amery Ice Shelf *ice feature* Ant.
26 E3 Ames U.S.A.
59 F6 Amesbury U.K.
33 H3 Amesbury U.S.A.
85 E4 Amethi India
67 K5 Amfissa Greece
77 P3 Amga Rus. Fed.
87 P2 Amgu Rus. Fed.
100 C2 Amguid Alg.
77 P4 Amgun' *r.* Rus. Fed.
23 H4 Amherst Can.
33 G3 Amherst *MA* U.S.A.
33 J2 Amherst *ME* U.S.A.
32 D6 Amherst *VA* U.S.A.
31 F4 Amherstburg Can.
66 D3 Amiata, Monte *mt* Italy
64 F2 Amiens France
81 H5 Amij, Wādī *watercourse* Iraq
83 D8 Amindivi Islands *is* India
90 E6 Amino Japan
104 C1 Aminuis Namibia
81 L5 Amīrābād Iran
21 J4 Amisk L. *l.* Can.
36 D3 Amistad, Represa de *resr* Mex./U.S.A.
27 C6 Amistad Res. *resr* Mex./U.S.A.
115 K1 Amity Point Austr.
84 D5 Amla *Madhya Pradesh* India
84 D5 Amla *Madhya Pradesh* India
55 L7 Åmli Norway
59 C4 Amlwch U.K.
80 E6 'Ammān Jordan
59 D6 Ammanford U.K.
54 V4 Ämmänsaari Fin.
54 P4 Ammarnäs Sweden
62 E7 Ammersee *l.* Ger.
Ammochostos *see* Famagusta
84 C5 Amod India
89 B6 Amo Jiang *r.* China
79 G2 Amol Iran
67 L6 Amorgos *i.* Greece
22 E4 Amos Can.
Amoy *see* Xiamen
46 C3 Amparo Brazil
62 E6 Amper *r.* Ger.
65 G2 Amposta Spain
84 D5 Amravati India
84 B5 Amreli India
84 B4 Amri Pak.
80 E4 'Amrit Syria
84 C3 Amritsar India
84 D3 Amroha India
54 Q4 Åmsele Sweden
61 C2 Amstelveen Neth.
61 C2 Amsterdam Neth.
105 J3 Amsterdam S. Africa
33 F3 Amsterdam U.S.A.
13 K6 Amsterdam, Île *i.* Indian Ocean
62 G6 Amstetten Austria
101 E3 Am Timan Chad
79 J1 Amudar'ya *r.* Turkm./Uzbek.
18 Amund Ringnes I. *i.* Can.
119 D4 Amundsen Bay *b.* Ant.
119 C5 Amundsen, Mt *mt.* Ant.
119 B4 Amundsen-Scott *U.S.A. Base* Ant.
119 A3 Amundsen Sea *sea* Ant.
92 F7 Amuntai Indon.
87 P1 Amur *r.* China/Rus. Fed.
87 P1 Amursk Rus. Fed.
69 F6 Amvrosiyivka Ukr.
30 E1 Amyot Can.
85 H6 An Myanmar
109 Anaa *i. Fr. Polynesia* Pac. Oc.
93 G7 Anabanua Indon.
77 N2 Anabar *r.* Rus. Fed.
77 N2 Anabarskiy Zaliv *b.* Rus. Fed.
114 D4 Ana Branch *r.* Austr.
34 C4 Anacapa Is *is* U.S.A.
45 D2 Anaco Venez.
24 D2 Anaconda U.S.A.
24 B1 Anacortes U.S.A.
27 D5 Anadarko U.S.A.
80 F1 Anadolu Dağları *mts* Turkey
77 T3 Anadyr' *r.* Rus. Fed.
77 U3 Anadyrskiy Zaliv *b.* Rus. Fed.
67 L6 Anafi *i.* Greece
46 E1 Anagé Brazil
81 H4 'Ānah Iraq
34 D5 Anaheim U.S.A.
20 D4 Anahim Lake Can.
27 C7 Anahuac Mex.
116 B4 Anakie Austr.
103 E5 Analalava Madag.
42 F4 Anamã Brazil
92 D6 Anambas, Kepulauan *is* Indon.
30 B4 Anamosa U.S.A.
80 D3 Anamur Turkey
80 D3 Anamur Burnu *pt* Turkey
90 E7 Anan Japan
84 C5 Anand India
85 F5 Anandapur India
85 F5 Anandpur *r.* India
83 E8 Anantapur India
84 C2 Anantnag Jammu and Kashmir
69 D6 Anan'yiv Ukr.
69 F6 Anapa Rus. Fed.
46 C2 Anápolis Brazil
93 L3 Anatahan *i.* N. Mariana Is
80 D2 Anatolia *reg.* Turkey
111 G4 Anatom *i.* Vanuatu
44 D3 Añatuya Arg.
45 E4 Anauá *r.* Brazil
81 M3 Anbūh Iran
64 D3 Ancenis France
16 Anchorage U.S.A.
31 F4 Anchor Bay *b.* U.S.A.
66 E3 Ancona Italy
44 B6 Ancud Chile
47 B4 Ancud, Golfo de *g.* Chile
47 B1 Andacollo Chile
85 F5 Andal India
54 K5 Åndalsnes Norway
65 D4 Andalucía *div.* Spain
27 G6 Andalusia U.S.A.
83 H8 Andaman and Nicobar Islands *div.* India
13 L3 Andaman Basin *sea feature* Indian Ocean
83 H8 Andaman Islands *is* Andaman and Nicobar Is
92 B4 Andaman Sea *sea* Asia
114 B3 Andamooka Austr.
103 E5 Andapa Madag.
46 E1 Andaraí Brazil
54 P2 Andenes Norway
61 D4 Andenne Belgium
61 C4 Anderlecht Belgium
64 D4 Andernos-les-Bains France
30 E5 Anderson *IN* U.S.A.
27 E4 Anderson *MO* U.S.A.
29 D5 Anderson *SC* U.S.A.
115 G8 Anderson B. *b.* Austr.
40 Andes *mts* S. America
26 D3 Andes, Lake *l.* U.S.A.
54 P2 Andfjorden *chan.* Norway
83 E7 Andhra Pradesh *div.* India
103 E5 Andilamena Madag.
103 E5 Andilanatoby Madag.
81 M5 Andīmeshk Iran
80 F3 Andırın Turkey
69 H7 Andiyskoye Koysu *r.* Rus. Fed.
79 L1 Andizhan Uzbek.
79 K2 Andkhvoy Afgh.
103 E5 Andoany Madag.
42 C4 Andoas Peru
87 N4 Andong S. Korea
48 Andorra *country* Europe
65 G1 Andorra la Vella Andorra
59 F6 Andover U.K.
33 H2 Andover *ME* U.S.A.
32 C4 Andover *OH* U.S.A.
54 O2 Andøya *i.* Norway
46 B3 Andradina Brazil
68 E3 Andreapol' Rus. Fed.
58 C3 Andreas U.K.
102 C3 André Félix, Parc National de *nat. park* C.A.R.
46 D3 Andrelândia Brazil
27 C5 Andrews U.S.A.
66 G4 Andria Italy
103 E6 Androka Madag.
67 L6 Andros *i.* Greece
29 E7 Andros *i.* Bahamas
33 H2 Androscoggin *r.* U.S.A.
29 E7 Andros Town Bahamas
83 D8 Āndrott *i.* India
69 D5 Andrushivka Ukr.
54 Q2 Andselv Norway
65 D3 Andújar Spain
103 B5 Andulo Angola
100 C3 Anéfis Mali
37 M5 Anegada *i.* Virgin Is
47 D4 Anegada, Bahía *b.* Arg.
35 F5 Anegam U.S.A.
100 C4 Aného Togo
'Aneiza, Jabal *h. see* 'Unayzah, Jabal
35 H3 Aneth U.S.A.
65 G1 Aneto *mt* Spain
101 D3 Aney Niger
89 E5 Anfu China
103 E5 Angadoka, Lohatanjona *hd* Madag.
86 H1 Angara *r.* Rus. Fed.
86 H1 Angarsk Rus. Fed.
94 B3 Angat Phil.
55 O5 Ånge Sweden
36 B3 Angel de la Guarda *i.* Mex.
94 B3 Angeles Phil.
55 N8 Ängelholm Sweden
116 B6 Angellala Cr. *r.* Austr.
36 E5 Angel, Pto Mex.
34 B2 Angels Camp U.S.A.
54 P4 Ångermanälven *r.* Sweden
64 D3 Angers France
21 K2 Angikuni Lake *l.* Can.
95 B2 Angkor Cambodia
59 C4 Anglesey *i.* U.K.
27 E6 Angleton U.S.A.
31 H2 Angliers Can.
95 □ Ang Mo Kio Sing.
102 C3 Ango Zaire
103 D5 Angoche Moz.
47 B3 Angol Chile
96 Angola *country* Africa
30 E5 Angola U.S.A.
12 K7 Angola Basin *sea feature* Atlantic Ocean
36 F5 Angostura, Presa de la *resr* Mex.
64 E4 Angoulême France
79 L1 Angren Uzbek.
95 B2 Ang Thong Thai.
37 M5 Anguilla *terr.* Caribbean
88 E1 Anguli Nur *l.* China
88 E2 Anguo China

46 A3 Anhanduí r. Brazil
55 M8 Anholt i. Denmark
89 D4 Anhua China
88 E3 Anhui div. China
46 A2 Anhumas Brazil
46 C2 Anicuns Brazil
68 G3 Anikovo Rus. Fed.
35 H6 Animas U.S.A.
35 H6 Animas Peak summit U.S.A.
95 A2 Anin Myanmar
87 Q2 Aniva, Mys c. Rus. Fed.
87 Q2 Aniva, Zaliv b. Rus. Fed.
111 G3 Aniwa i. Vanuatu
61 B5 Anizy-le-Château France
55 U6 Anjalankoski Fin.
89 F4 Anji China
84 D5 Anji India
91 F6 Anjō Japan
64 D3 Anjou reg. France
103 E5 Anjouan i. Comoros
103 E5 Anjozorobe Madag.
87 N4 Anjŭ N. Korea
103 E6 Ankaboa, Tanjona pt Madag.
88 C3 Ankang China
80 D2 Ankara Turkey
103 E6 Ankazoabo Madag.
103 E5 Ankazobe Madag.
95 D2 An Khê Vietnam
84 C5 Ankleshwar India
61 D5 Anlier, Forêt d' forest Belgium
89 B5 Anlong China
95 C2 Ânlong Vêng Cambodia
88 D4 Anlu China
69 G5 Anna Rus. Fed.
100 C1 Annaba Alg.
80 F4 An Nabk Syria
78 E4 An Nafūd des. S. Arabia
58 A3 Annahilt N. Ireland U.K.
81 K6 An Najaf Iraq
91 G5 Annaka Japan
32 E5 Anna, Lake l. U.S.A.
60 D3 Annalee r. Rep. of Ireland
60 F3 Annalong U.K.
57 E6 Annan Scot. U.K.
57 E6 Annan r. U.K.
57 E5 Annandale v. U.K.
32 E5 Annapolis U.S.A.
23 G5 Annapolis Royal Can.
85 E3 Annapurna mt Nepal
31 F4 Ann Arbor U.S.A.
43 G2 Anna Regina Guyana
81 L6 An Nāṣirīyah Iraq
33 H3 Ann, Cape hd U.S.A.
64 H4 Annecy France
64 H3 Annemasse France
20 C4 Annette I. i. U.S.A.
89 B5 Anning China
29 C5 Anniston U.S.A.
12 K6 Annobón i. Equatorial Guinea
64 G4 Annonay France
78 F4 An Nu'ayrīyah S. Arabia
81 K5 An Nu'mānīyah Iraq
26 E2 Anoka U.S.A.
103 E5 Anorontany, Tanjona hd Madag.
67 L7 Ano Viannos Greece
89 D6 Anpu China
89 C6 Anpu Gang b. China
89 E4 Anqing China
88 F2 Anqiu China
89 D5 Anren China
88 C2 Ansai China
80 F4 Ansariye, J. el mts Syria
115 G7 Anser Group is Austr.
88 G1 Anshan China
89 B5 Anshun China
47 C1 Ansilta mt Arg.
47 F1 Ansina Uru.
26 D3 Ansley U.S.A.
27 D5 Anson U.S.A.
100 C3 Ansongo Mali
22 D4 Ansonville Can.
32 C5 Ansted U.S.A.
84 D4 Anta India
42 D6 Antabamba Peru
80 F3 Antakya Turkey
103 F5 Antalaha Madag.
80 C3 Antalya Turkey
80 C3 Antalya Körfezi g. Turkey
103 E5 Antananarivo Madag.
119 B2 Antarctic Peninsula pen. Ant.
57 C3 An Teallach mt U.K.
34 D2 Antelope Range mts U.S.A.
65 D4 Antequera Spain
25 F5 Anthony U.S.A.
100 B2 Anti Atlas mts Morocco
64 H5 Antibes France
23 H4 Anticosti, Île d' i. Can.
30 C3 Antigo U.S.A.
23 H4 Antigonish Can.
37 M5 Antigua i. Antigua
36 F6 Antigua Guatemala
16 Antigua and Barbuda country Caribbean Sea
36 E4 Antiguo-Morelos Mex.
67 K7 Antikythira i. Greece
67 K7 Antikythiro, Steno chan. Greece
Anti Lebanon mts see Sharqi, Jebel esh
Antioch see Antakya
34 B3 Antioch CA U.S.A.
30 C4 Antioch IL U.S.A.
45 B3 Antioquia Col.
67 L5 Antipsara i. Greece
27 E5 Antlers U.S.A.
44 B2 Antofagasta Chile
44 C3 Antofalla, Vol. volc. Arg.
46 C4 Antonina Brazil
46 E1 Antônio r. Brazil
34 B3 Antonio r. U.S.A.
25 F4 Antonito U.S.A.
60 E3 Antrim U.K.
60 E2 Antrim Hills h. U.K.
103 E5 Antsalova Madag.
103 E5 Antsirabe Madag.
103 E5 Antsirañana Madag.
103 E5 Antsohihy Madag.
54 S3 Anttis Sweden
55 U6 Anttola Fin.
47 B3 Antuco Chile
47 B3 Antuco, Volcán volc. Chile
61 C3 Antwerp Belgium
33 F2 Antwerp U.S.A.
Antwerpen see Antwerp
22 E2 Anuc, Lac l. Can.
85 F5 Anugul India
84 C3 Anupgarh India
83 F9 Anuradhapura Sri Lanka
Anvers see Antwerp
119 B2 Anvers I. i. Ant.
89 F5 Anxi Fujian China
82 J2 Anxi Gansu China
88 B4 An Xian China
89 D4 Anxiang China
88 E2 Anxin China
114 A4 Anxious Bay b. Austr.
88 E2 Anyang China
67 L6 Anydro i. Greece
82 J4 A'nyêmaqên Shan mts China
89 E4 Anyi China
89 E5 Anyuan China
89 B4 Anyue China
77 S3 Anyuysk Rus. Fed.
45 B3 Anzá Col.
88 D2 Anze China
76 K4 Anzhero-Sudzhensk Rus. Fed.
102 C4 Anzi Zaire
66 E4 Anzio Italy
111 G3 Aoba i. Vanuatu
95 A3 Ao Ban Don b. Thai.
88 F1 Aohan Qi China
90 H3 Aomori Japan
90 H3 Aomori Japan
84 D3 Aonla India
Aoraki, Mt mt. see Cook, Mt
117 D4 Aorere r. N.Z.
95 A3 Ao Sawi b. Thai.
66 B2 Aosta Italy
100 B2 Aoukâr reg. Mali/Maur.
90 E6 Aoya Japan
43 G8 Apa r. Brazil
102 D3 Apac Uganda
35 H6 Apache U.S.A.
35 H5 Apache Creek U.S.A.
35 G5 Apache Junction U.S.A.
35 G6 Apache Peak summit U.S.A.
29 C6 Apalachee Bay b. U.S.A.
29 C6 Apalachicola U.S.A.
45 C5 Apaporis r. Col.
81 K1 Aparan Armenia
46 B3 Aparecida do Tabuado Brazil
94 B2 Aparri Phil.
54 X3 Apatity Rus. Fed.
36 D5 Apatzingán Mex.
55 U8 Ape Latvia
61 D2 Apeldoorn Neth.
84 E3 Api mt Nepal
111 J3 Apia Western Samoa
117 E3 Apiti N.Z.
43 G2 Apoera Suriname
114 E7 Apollo Bay Austr.
42 E6 Apolo Bol.
94 C5 Apo, Mt volc. Phil.
29 D6 Apopka, L. l. U.S.A.
46 B2 Aporé r. Brazil
46 B2 Aporé Brazil
28 B2 Apostle Islands is U.S.A.
30 B2 Apostle Islands National Lakeshore res. U.S.A.
80 E4 Apostolos Andreas, Cape c. Cyprus
32 B6 Appalachia U.S.A.
18 Appalachian Mountains mts U.S.A.
66 E3 Appennino Abruzzese mts Italy
66 D2 Appennino Tosco-Emiliano mts Italy
66 E3 Appennino Umbro-Marchigiano mts Italy
115 J5 Appin Austr.
57 C3 Applecross U.K.
26 D2 Appleton MN U.S.A.
30 C3 Appleton WV U.S.A.
34 D4 Apple Valley U.S.A.
32 D6 Appomattox U.S.A.
66 E4 Aprilia Italy
69 F6 Apsheronsk Rus. Fed.
114 D6 Apsley Austr.
31 H3 Apsley Can.
64 G5 Apt France
46 B3 Apucarana Brazil
94 A4 Apurahuan Phil.
45 D3 Apure r. Venez.
42 D6 Apurímac r. Peru
80 E7 'Aqaba Jordan
78 C4 Aqaba, Gulf of g. Asia
81 K2 Aq Chai r. Iran
81 L3 Aqdoghmish r. Iran
81 K3 Āq Kān Dāgh, Kūh-e mt Iran
86 E4 Aqqikkol Hu salt l. China
81 J3 'Aqrah Iraq
35 F4 Aquarius Mts mts U.S.A.
35 G3 Aquarius Plateau plat. U.S.A.
66 G4 Aquaviva delle Fonti Italy
46 A3 Aquidauana Brazil
46 A3 Aquidauana r. Brazil
45 D4 Aquio r. Col.
64 D4 Aquitaine reg. France
85 F4 Ara India
29 C5 Arab U.S.A.
101 E4 Arab, Bahr el watercourse Sudan
13 J3 Arabian Basin sea feature Indian Ocean
74 Arabian Sea sea Indian Ocean
45 E3 Arabopó r. Venez.
45 E3 Arabopó Venez.
80 D1 Araç Turkey
45 E4 Araça r. Brazil
43 L6 Aracaju Brazil
45 D4 Aracamuni, Co summit Venez.
46 A4 Aracanguy, Mtes de h. Para.
43 L4 Aracati Brazil
46 E1 Aracatu Brazil
46 B3 Araçatuba Brazil
65 C4 Aracena Spain
46 E2 Aracruz Brazil
46 D2 Araçuaí Brazil
46 D2 Araçuaí r. Brazil
67 J1 Arad Romania
101 E3 Arada Chad
81 L6 Aradah Iraq
110 D2 Arafura Sea sea Austr./Indon.
46 B1 Aragarças Brazil
81 J1 Aragats Armenia
81 K1 Aragats Lerr mt Armenia
91 G5 Ara-gawa r. Japan
65 F2 Aragón div. Spain
65 F1 Aragón r. Spain
43 J5 Araguacema Brazil
45 D2 Aragua de Barcelona Venez.
43 J5 Araguaia r. Brazil
43 H6 Araguaia, Parque Nacional de nat. park Brazil
43 J5 Araguaína Brazil
46 C2 Araguari r. Minas Gerais Brazil
46 C2 Araguari Brazil
43 J5 Araguatins Brazil
69 H7 Aragvi r. Georgia
91 G5 Arai Japan
43 K4 Araiosos Brazil
100 C2 Arak Alg.
79 F3 Arāk Iran
83 H6 Arakan Yoma mts Myanmar
81 K2 Aralık Turkey
82 B1 Aral Sea salt l. Kazak./Uzbek.
82 B1 Aral'sk Kazak.
Aral'skoye More salt l. see Aral Sea
116 A4 Aramac Austr.
116 A4 Aramac Cr. watercourse Austr.
93 L8 Aramia r. P.N.G.
84 D6 Aran r. India
65 E2 Aranda de Duero Spain
81 L4 Arandān Iran
67 J2 Aranđelovac Yugo.
60 C3 Aran Island i. Rep. of Ireland
60 B4 Aran Islands is Rep. of Ireland
65 E2 Aranjuez Spain
103 B6 Aranos Namibia
27 D7 Aransas Pass U.S.A.
46 B2 Arantes r. Brazil
111 H1 Aranuka i. Gilbert Is
90 C7 Arao Japan
100 B3 Araouane Mali
26 D3 Arapahoe U.S.A.
45 E4 Arapari r. Brazil
47 F1 Arapey Grande r. Uru.
43 L5 Arapiraca Brazil
67 L4 Arapis, Akra pt Greece
80 G2 Arapkir Turkey
46 B3 Arapongas Brazil
85 F4 A Rapti Doon r. Nepal
81 H6 'Ar'ar S. Arabia
44 G3 Araranguá Brazil
46 C3 Araraquara Brazil
43 H5 Araras Brazil
46 B4 Araras, Serra das mts Brazil
81 K2 Ararat Armenia
114 E6 Ararat Austr.
81 K2 Ararat, Mt mt Turkey
85 F4 Araria India
46 D3 Araruama, Lago de lag. Brazil
81 J6 'Ar'ar, W. watercourse Iraq/S. Arabia
81 J1 Aras r. Turkey
81 J2 Aras Turkey
46 E1 Arataca Brazil
45 C3 Arauca Col.
45 C3 Arauca r. Venez.
47 B3 Arauco Chile
45 C3 Arauquita Col.
45 C2 Araure Venez.
84 C4 Aravalli Range mts India
55 T7 Aravete Estonia
111 F2 Arawa P.N.G.
46 C2 Araxá Brazil
45 D2 Araya, Pen. de pen. Venez.
45 D2 Araya, Pta de pt Venez.
80 C2 Arayıt Dağı mt Turkey
81 M2 Araz r. Asia
81 K4 Arbat Iraq
68 J3 Arbazh Rus. Fed.
81 K3 Arbīl Iraq
55 O7 Arboga Sweden
21 J4 Arborfield Can.
57 F4 Arbroath U.K.
34 A2 Arbuckle U.S.A.
79 J4 Arbu Lut, Dasht-e des. Afgh.
64 D4 Arcachon France
29 D7 Arcadia U.S.A.
24 A3 Arcata U.S.A.
34 D2 Arc Dome summit U.S.A.
68 G1 Archangel Rus. Fed.
113 H2 Archer r. Austr.
113 H2 Archer Bend National Park nat. park Austr.
35 H2 Arches Nat. Park nat. park U.S.A.
81 M2 Ärçivan Azer.
114 A2 Arckaringa watercourse Austr.
24 D3 Arco U.S.A.
65 D4 Arcos de la Frontera Spain
118 C3 Arctic Ocean ocean
119 B2 Arctowski Poland Base Ant.
81 M2 Ardabīl Iran
81 J1 Ardahan Turkey
55 K6 Årdalstangen Norway
60 C3 Ardara Rep. of Ireland
67 L4 Ardas r. Bulg.
68 H4 Ardatov Mordov. Rus. Fed.
68 G4 Ardatov Nizheg. Rus. Fed.
31 G3 Ardbeg Can.
60 E4 Ardee Rep. of Ireland
114 B4 Arden, Mount h. Austr.
61 C5 Ardenne, Plateau de l' plat. Belgium
61 C5 Ardennes, Canal des canal France
79 G3 Ardestān Iran
60 F3 Ardglass U.K.
65 C3 Ardila r. Port.
115 G5 Ardlethan Austr.
27 D5 Ardmore U.S.A.
57 B4 Ardnamurchan, Point of pt U.K.
57 C4 Ardrishaig U.K.
114 B5 Ardrossan Austr.
57 D5 Ardrossan U.K.
57 C3 Ardvasar U.K.
47 E2 Areco r. Arg.
43 L4 Areia Branca Brazil
61 E4 Aremberg h. Ger.
94 B4 Arena rf Phil.
34 A2 Arena, Pt pt U.S.A.
65 D2 Arenas de San Pedro Spain
55 L7 Arendal Norway
59 D5 Arenig Fawr h. U.K.
67 K6 Areopoli Greece
42 D7 Arequipa Peru
43 H4 Arere Brazil
65 D2 Arévalo Spain
66 D3 Arezzo Italy
80 G6 'Arfajah w. S. Arabia
88 D1 Argalant Mongolia
65 E2 Arganda Spain
94 B4 Argao Phil.
66 D2 Argenta Italy
64 D2 Argentan France
66 D3 Argentario, Monte h. Italy
66 B2 Argentera, Cima dell' mt Italy
38 Argentina country S. America
119 B3 Argentina Ra. mts Ant.
12 F8 Argentine Basin sea feature Atlantic Ocean
44 B8 Argentino, Lago l. Arg.
67 L2 Argeș r. Romania
84 A3 Arghandab r. Afgh.
80 C2 Argıthanı Turkey
67 K6 Argolikos Kolpos b. Greece
67 K6 Argos Greece
67 J5 Argostoli Greece
65 F1 Arguís Spain
87 M1 Argun' r. China/Rus. Fed.
69 H7 Argun Rus. Fed.
119 C4 Argus Dome ice feature Ant.
34 D4 Argus Range mts U.S.A.
30 C4 Argyle U.S.A.
112 E3 Argyle, Lake l. Austr.
57 C4 Argyll reg. U.K.
87 M3 Ar Horqin Qi China
55 M8 Århus Denmark
117 E3 Aria N.Z.
115 G5 Ariah Park Austr.
90 C7 Ariake-kai b. Japan
103 B6 Ariamsvlei Namibia
66 F4 Ariano Irpino Italy
45 B4 Ariari r. Col.
47 D2 Arias Arg.
83 D10 Ari Atoll atoll Maldives
45 E2 Aribí r. Venez.
100 B3 Aribinda Burkina
44 B1 Arica Chile
90 E6 Arida Japan
112 D6 Arid, C. c. Austr.
57 C4 Arienas, Loch l. U.K.
80 F4 Arīḥā Syria
24 G4 Arikaree r. U.S.A.
45 E2 Arima Trinidad and Tobago
46 C1 Arinos Brazil
43 G6 Arinos r. Brazil
45 C3 Ariporo r. Col.
42 F5 Aripuanã Brazil
42 F5 Ariquemes Brazil
46 B2 Ariranhá r. Brazil
104 B1 Aris Namibia
57 C4 Arisaig U.K.
57 C4 Arisaig, Sound of chan. U.K.
20 D4 Aristazabal I. i. Can.
35 G4 Arizona div. U.S.A.
54 P3 Arjeplog Sweden
45 B2 Arjona Col.
92 □ Arjuna, G. volc. Indon.
69 G5 Arkadak Rus. Fed.
27 E5 Arkadelphia U.S.A.
57 C4 Arkaig, Loch l. U.K.
76 H4 Arkalyk Kazak.
27 E5 Arkansas div. U.S.A.
27 F5 Arkansas r. U.S.A.
27 D4 Arkansas City U.S.A.
85 G1 Arkatag Shan mts China
Arkhangel'sk see Archangel
68 G2 Arkhangel'skaya Oblast' div. Rus. Fed.
68 F4 Arkhangel'skoye Rus. Fed.
60 E5 Arklow Rep. of Ireland
67 M6 Arkoi i. Greece
62 F3 Arkona, Kap hd Ger.
76 K2 Arkticheskogo Instituta, Ostrova is Rus. Fed.
33 F3 Arkville U.S.A.
64 G5 Arles France
105 G4 Arlington S. Africa
24 B2 Arlington OR U.S.A.
26 D2 Arlington SD U.S.A.
32 E5 Arlington VA U.S.A.
30 D4 Arlington Heights U.S.A.
100 C3 Arlit Niger
61 D5 Arlon Belgium
94 C5 Armadores i. Indon.
60 E3 Armagh U.K.
78 C4 Armant Egypt
69 G6 Armavir Rus. Fed.
70 Armenia country Asia
45 B3 Armenia Col.
61 A4 Armentières France
45 B3 Armero Col.
115 J3 Armidale Austr.
21 L2 Armit Lake l. Can.
84 E5 Armori India
20 B3 Armour, Mt mt. Can./U.S.A.
60 E2 Armoy U.K.
20 F4 Armstrong B.C. Can.
22 C3 Armstrong Ont. Can.
69 E6 Armyans'k Ukr.
80 D4 Arnaoutis, Cape c. Cyprus
23 F1 Arnaud r. Can.
55 M6 Årnes Norway
27 D4 Arnett U.S.A.
61 D3 Arnhem Neth.
113 G2 Arnhem Bay b. Austr.
113 G2 Arnhem, C. c. Austr.
113 F2 Arnhem Land reg. Austr.
66 D3 Arno r. Italy
114 B4 Arno Bay Austr.
59 F4 Arnold U.K.
30 D2 Arnold U.S.A.
31 H1 Arnoux, Lac l. Can.
31 J3 Arnprior Can.
62 D5 Arnsberg Ger.
31 H3 Arnstein Can.
31 H1 Arntfield Can.
45 E3 Aro r. Venez.
103 B6 Aroab Namibia
66 C2 Arona Italy
33 K1 Aroostook Can.
33 J1 Aroostook r. Can./U.S.A.
111 H2 Arorae i. Kiribati
94 B3 Aroroy Phil.
81 J1 Arpaçay Turkey
81 J5 Ar Ramādī Iraq
80 E7 Ar Ramlah Jordan
57 C5 Arran i. U.K.
81 G4 Ar Raqqah Syria
64 F1 Arras France
80 F4 Ar Rastan Syria
81 J7 Ar Rawḍ w. S. Arabia
45 C4 Arrecifal Col.
47 E2 Arrecifes Arg.
36 F5 Arriaga Mex.
47 E2 Arribeños Arg.
81 L6 Ar Rifā'ī Iraq
81 K6 Ar Rihāb salt flat Iraq
79 G5 Ar Rimāl reg. S. Arabia
35 H3 Arriola U.S.A.
Ar Riyāḍ see Riyadh
57 D4 Arrochar U.K.
47 G2 Arroio Grande Brazil
46 D1 Arrojado r. Brazil
30 B1 Arrow Lake l. Can.
60 C3 Arrow, Lough l. Rep. of Ireland
24 D3 Arrowrock Res. resr U.S.A.
117 C5 Arrowsmith, Mt mt. N.Z.
47 F3 Arroyo Grande r. Arg.
34 B4 Arroyo Grande U.S.A.
47 E2 Arroyo Seco Arg.
46 A1 Arruda Brazil
81 K6 Ar Rumaythah Iraq
80 G4 Ar Ruṣāfah Syria
81 H5 Ar Ruṭba Iraq
55 L8 Års Denmark
81 L3 Ars Iran
68 J3 Arsk Rus. Fed.
80 E3 Arslanköy Turkey
67 J5 Arta Greece
81 K2 Artashat Armenia
69 F5 Artemivs'k Ukr.
64 E2 Artenay France
25 F5 Artesia U.S.A.
31 G4 Arthur Can.
115 G8 Arthur L. l. Austr.
114 B3 Arthur, Lake salt flat Austr.
32 C4 Arthur, Lake l. U.S.A.
116 D4 Arthur Pt pt Austr.
117 C5 Arthur's Pass pass N.Z.
117 C5 Arthur's Pass National Park nat. park N.Z.
29 F7 Arthur's Town Bahamas
119 B1 Artigas Uruguay Base Ant.
47 F1 Artigas Uru.
81 J1 Art'ik Armenia
21 H2 Artillery Lake l. Can.
105 G2 Artisia Botswana
64 F1 Artois reg. France
61 A4 Artois, Collines d' h. France
81 J2 Artos D. mt Turkey
80 F1 Artova Turkey
69 D6 Artsyz Ukr.
82 E3 Artux China
81 H1 Artvin Turkey
102 D3 Arua Uganda
46 B1 Aruanã Brazil
37 L6 Aruba terr. Caribbean
93 J8 Aru, Kepulauan is Indon.
42 F4 Arumã Brazil
85 F4 Arun r. Nepal
85 H3 Arunachal Pradesh div. India
59 G7 Arundel U.K.
102 D4 Arusha Tanz.
26 B4 Arvada U.S.A.
60 D4 Arvagh Rep. of Ireland
86 H2 Arvayheer Mongolia
84 D5 Arvi India
21 L2 Arviat Can.
23 F4 Arvida Can.
54 Q4 Arvidsjaur Sweden
55 N7 Arvika Sweden
34 C4 Arvin U.S.A.
77 O2 Ary Rus. Fed.
82 C2 Arys' Kazak.
68 G4 Arzamas Rus. Fed.
65 F5 Arzew Alg.
69 H6 Arzgir Rus. Fed.
45 E3 Asa r. Venez.
100 C4 Asaba Nigeria
84 B2 Asadābād Afgh.
81 M4 Asadābād Iran
80 G3 Asad, Buḥayrat al resr Syria
95 A5 Asahan r. Indon.
91 H6 Asahi Japan
91 G4 Asahi-dake mt. Japan
90 J2 Asahi-dake volc. Japan
90 D6 Asahi-gawa r. Japan
90 J2 Asahikawa Japan
91 G6 Asaka Japan
81 M3 Asālem Iran
91 G5 Asama-yama volc. Japan
85 F5 Asansol India
23 F4 Asbestos Can.
104 E4 Asbestos Mountains mts S. Africa
33 F4 Asbury Park U.S.A.
66 F4 Ascea Italy
42 F7 Ascensión Bol.
36 G5 Ascensión, B. de la b. Mex.
96 Ascension Island island Atlantic Ocean
62 D6 Aschaffenburg Ger.
61 F3 Ascheberg Ger.
66 E3 Ascoli Piceno Italy
55 O8 Åseda Sweden
54 P4 Åsele Sweden
59 E6 Ashbourne U.K.
112 C4 Ashburton watercourse W.A. Austr.
117 C5 Ashburton N.Z.
30 D1 Ashburton Bay b. Can.
20 E4 Ashcroft Can.
80 E6 Ashdod Israel
27 E5 Ashdown U.S.A.
29 E5 Asheboro U.S.A.
29 D5 Asheville U.S.A.
115 J2 Ashford Austr.
59 H6 Ashford U.K.
35 F4 Ash Fork U.S.A.
79 H2 Ashgabat Turkm.
90 J2 Ashibetsu Japan
91 G5 Ashikaga Japan
58 F2 Ashington U.K.
91 H3 Ashiro Japan
68 J3 Ashit r. Rus. Fed.
90 D7 Ashizuri-misaki pt Japan
27 D4 Ashland KS U.S.A.
32 B5 Ashland KY U.S.A.
33 J1 Ashland ME U.S.A.
24 F2 Ashland MT U.S.A.
33 H3 Ashland NH U.S.A.
32 B4 Ashland OH U.S.A.
24 B3 Ashland OR U.S.A.
32 E6 Ashland VA U.S.A.
30 B2 Ashland WV U.S.A.
115 H2 Ashley Austr.
26 D2 Ashley U.S.A.
112 D2 Ashmore Reef rf Ashmore and Cartier Is
68 C4 Ashmyany Belarus
90 J2 Ashoro Japan
35 H5 Ash Peak U.S.A.
80 E6 Ashqelon Israel
84 B4 Ashraf, Md. Pak.
81 J6 Ash Shabakah Iraq
81 H3 Ash Shaddādah Syria
81 H7 Ash Shaqīq w. S. Arabia
81 J4 Ash Sharqāṭ Iraq
81 L6 Ash Shaṭrah Iraq
79 F7 Ash Shiḥr Yemen
81 K6 Ash Shināfīyah Iraq

32 C4 Ashtabula U.S.A.
81 K1 Ashtarak Armenia
84 D5 Ashti India
104 D6 Ashton S. Africa
24 E2 Ashton U.S.A.
58 E4 Ashton-under-Lyne U.K.
29 C5 Ashville U.S.A.
85 F6 Āsika India
80 E3 'Āşī, Nahr al r. Asia
66 C4 Asinara, Golfo dell' b. Sardinia Italy
76 K4 Asino Rus. Fed.
68 D4 Asipovichy Belarus
78 E5 'Asīr reg. S. Arabia
81 H2 Aşkale Turkey
55 M7 Asker Norway
55 O7 Askersund Sweden
55 M7 Askim Norway
86 F1 Askiz Rus. Fed.
81 L2 Aşlāndüz Iran
102 D2 Åsmara Eritrea
55 O8 Åsnen l. Sweden
67 L3 Asneovgrad Bulg.
84 C4 Asop India
90 B6 Asō-wan b. Japan
81 M3 Aspar Iran
58 D3 Aspatria U.K.
25 F4 Aspen U.S.A.
27 C5 Aspermont U.S.A.
117 B6 Aspiring, Mt mt. N.Z.
21 H4 Asquith Can.
80 F4 As Sa'an Syria
102 E2 Assab Eritrea
80 F3 As Safīrah Syria
81 K6 As Salmān Iraq
85 H4 Assam div. India
85 G4 As Samāwah Iraq
80 F5 Aş Şanamayn Syria
101 E2 As Sarīr reg. Libya
33 F5 Assateague I. i. U.S.A.
33 F6 Assateague Island National Seashore res. U.S.A.
61 E1 Assen Neth.
61 D4 Assesse Belgium
85 F5 Assia Hills h. India
101 E3 As Sidrah Libya
21 H5 Assiniboia Can.
21 K5 Assiniboine r. Can.
20 F4 Assiniboine, Mt mt. Can.
46 B3 Assis Brazil
66 E3 Assisi Italy
81 L7 Aş Şubayḩīyah Kuwait
81 G4 As Şukhnah Syria
81 K4 As Sulaymānīyah Iraq
78 F5 As Sulayyil S. Arabia
78 E5 As Sūq S. Arabia
81 H4 Aş Şuwār Syria
80 F5 Aş Şuwaydā' Syria
81 K5 Aş Şuwayrah Iraq
57 C2 Assynt, Loch l. U.K.
67 M4 Astakida i. Greece
81 M3 Astaneh Iran
81 M2 Astara Azer.
66 C2 Asti Italy
34 A2 Asti U.S.A.
47 C1 Astica Arg.
Astin Tag mts see Altun Shan
84 C2 Astor Jammu and Kashmir
84 C2 Astor r. Pak.
65 C1 Astorga Spain
24 B2 Astoria U.S.A.
55 N8 Åstorp Sweden
69 J6 Astrakhan' Rus. Fed.
Astrakhan' Bazar see Cälilabad
69 H6 Astrakhanskaya Oblast' div. Rus. Fed.
68 C4 Astravyets Belarus
65 C1 Asturias div. Spain
67 M6 Astypalaia i. Greece
93 L3 Asuncion i. N. Mariana Is
44 C2 Asunción Para.
78 C5 Aswân Egypt
78 C4 Asyût Egypt
111 J4 Ata i. Tonga
45 D4 Atabapo r. Col./Venez.
44 C2 Atacama, Desierto de des. Chile
111 J2 Atafu i. Tokelau
100 C4 Atakpamé Togo
67 K5 Atalanti Greece
42 D6 Atalaya Peru
91 G6 Atami Japan
100 A2 Atâr Maur.
95 A1 Ataran r. Myanmar
35 H4 Atarque U.S.A.
34 B4 Atascadero U.S.A.
82 D1 Atasu Kazak.
93 H8 Atauro i. Indon.
101 F3 Atbara r. Sudan
101 F3 Atbara Sudan
76 H4 Atbasar Kazak.
27 F6 Atchafalaya Bay b. U.S.A.
26 E4 Atchison U.S.A.
66 E3 Aterno r. Italy
66 F3 Atessa Italy
61 B4 Ath Belgium
20 F4 Athabasca Can.
21 G3 Athabasca, Lake l. Can.
60 E4 Athboy Rep. of Ireland
60 E4 Athenry Rep. of Ireland
31 K3 Athens Can.
67 K6 Athens Greece
29 C5 Athens AL U.S.A.
29 D5 Athens GA U.S.A.
32 B5 Athens OH U.S.A.
29 C5 Athens TN U.S.A.
27 E5 Athens TX U.S.A.
59 F5 Atherstone U.K.
116 A1 Atherton Austr.
Athina see Athens

60 C4 Athleague Rep. of Ireland
60 D4 Athlone Rep. of Ireland
117 B6 Athol N.Z.
33 G3 Athol U.S.A.
57 E4 Atholl, Forest of reg. U.K.
67 L4 Athos mt Greece
81 J4 Ath Tharthār, Wādī r. Iraq
60 E5 Athy Rep. of Ireland
101 D3 Ati Chad
42 D7 Atico Peru
21 J4 Atikameg L. l. Can.
22 B4 Atikokan Can.
23 H3 Atikonak L. l. Can.
94 B3 Atimonan Phil.
109 Atiu i. Cook Is. Pac. Oc.
77 R3 Atka Rus. Fed.
69 H5 Atkarsk Rus. Fed.
29 C5 Atlanta GA U.S.A.
30 C5 Atlanta IL U.S.A.
31 E3 Atlanta MI U.S.A.
80 D2 Atlantı Turkey
26 E3 Atlantic U.S.A.
33 F5 Atlantic City U.S.A.
13 D7 Atlantic-Indian Antarctic Basin sea feature Atlantic Ocean
12 J9 Atlantic-Indian Ridge sea feature Indian Ocean
104 C6 Atlantis S. Africa
12 G3 Atlantis Fracture sea feature Atlantic Ocean
100 C1 Atlas Saharien mts Alg.
20 C3 Atlin Can.
20 C3 Atlin Lake l. Can.
20 C3 Atlin Prov. Park Can.
80 E5 'Atlit Israel
27 G6 Atmore U.S.A.
90 C6 Atō Japan
27 D5 Atoka U.S.A.
95 C1 Atouat mt Laos
85 A4 Atra r. India
45 A3 Atrato r. Col.
33 F5 Atsion U.S.A.
91 G6 Atsugi Japan
91 G4 Atsumi Japan
90 H2 Atsuta Japan
78 E5 Aţ Ţā'if S. Arabia
29 C5 Attalla U.S.A.
95 C2 Attapu Laos
67 M6 Attavyros mt Greece
22 B3 Attawapiskat Can.
22 D3 Attawapiskat Can.
22 C3 Attawapiskat r. Can.
81 G7 Aţ Ţawīl mts S. Arabia
62 F7 Attersee l. Austria
30 D5 Attica IN U.S.A.
32 B4 Attica OH U.S.A.
33 H3 Attleboro U.S.A.
59 J5 Attleborough U.K.
80 F7 Aţ Ţubayq h. S. Arabia
14 G2 Attu Island i. U.S.A.
57 B2 a' Tuath, Loch b. U.K.
47 C2 Atuel r. Arg.
55 O7 Åtvidaberg Sweden
32 C4 Atwood Lake l. U.S.A.
76 G5 Atyrau Kazak.
64 G5 Aubagne France
94 B2 Aubarede Point pt Phil.
64 G4 Aubenas France
35 F4 Aubrey Cliffs cliff U.S.A.
114 C5 Auburn Austr.
116 D5 Auburn r. Austr.
31 G4 Auburn Can.
29 C5 Auburn AL U.S.A.
34 C4 Auburn CA U.S.A.
30 E5 Auburn IN U.S.A.
33 H2 Auburn ME U.S.A.
26 E3 Auburn NE U.S.A.
32 E3 Auburn NY U.S.A.
24 B2 Auburn WA U.S.A.
116 D5 Auburn Ra. h. Austr.
64 E3 Auch France
57 E4 Auchterarder U.K.
117 E2 Auckland N.Z.
111 G7 Auckland Islands is N.Z.
33 H2 Audet Can.
59 J7 Audresselles France
116 B5 Augathella Austr.
60 D3 Augher U.K.
60 E3 Aughnacloy U.K.
60 E5 Aughrim Rep. of Ireland
104 D4 Augrabies S. Africa
104 D4 Augrabies Falls waterfall S. Africa
104 D4 Augrabies Falls National Park nat. park S. Africa
31 F3 Au Gres U.S.A.
62 E6 Augsburg Ger.
112 C6 Augusta Austr.
66 F6 Augusta Sicily Italy
29 D5 Augusta GA U.S.A.
27 D4 Augusta KS U.S.A.
33 J2 Augusta ME U.S.A.
30 B3 Augusta WV U.S.A.
45 B2 Augustin Cadazzi Col.
112 C4 Augustus, Mt mt Austr.
61 B4 Aulnoye-Aymeries France
103 B6 Auob r. Namibia
23 G2 Aupaluk Can.
95 G2 Aur i. Malaysia
55 S6 Aura Fin.
84 A3 Auraiya India
84 C6 Aurangābād India
62 C4 Aurich Ger.
46 B2 Aurilândia Brazil
64 F4 Aurillac France
24 B5 Aurora CO U.S.A.

30 C5 Aurora IL U.S.A.
33 J2 Aurora ME U.S.A.
27 E4 Aurora MO U.S.A.
113 H2 Aurukun Austr.
103 B6 Aus Namibia
33 G2 Ausable r. U.S.A.
31 E3 Au Sable r. U.S.A.
31 F3 Au Sable r. U.S.A.
33 G2 Ausable Forks U.S.A.
30 D2 Au Sable Pt pt MI U.S.A.
31 E3 Au Sable Pt pt MI U.S.A.
57 F1 Auskerry i. U.K.
54 D4 Austari-Jökulsá r. Iceland
26 E3 Austin MN U.S.A.
34 D2 Austin NV U.S.A.
27 D6 Austin TX U.S.A.
106 Australia country Australasia
115 H5 Australian Capital Territory div. Austr.
48 Austria country Europe
54 O2 Austvågøy i. Norway
54 U3 Autti Fin.
64 G3 Autun France
64 F4 Auvergne reg. France
64 F3 Auxerre France
64 G3 Auxonne France
33 H4 Ava r. U.S.A.
64 F3 Avallon France
34 C5 Avalon U.S.A.
23 K4 Avalon Peninsula pen. Can.
81 L2 Avān Iran
80 E2 Avanos Turkey
46 C3 Avaré Brazil
81 L2 Āvārsīn Iran
34 D4 Avawatz Mts mts U.S.A.
43 G4 Aveiro Brazil
65 B2 Aveiro Port.
65 B2 Aveiro, Ria de est. Port.
81 M4 Avej Iran
47 E2 Avellaneda Arg.
66 F4 Avellino Italy
34 B3 Avenal U.S.A.
114 F6 Avenel Austr.
66 F4 Aversa Italy
61 B4 Avesnes-sur-Helpe France
55 P6 Avesta Sweden
64 F4 Aveyron r. France
66 E3 Avezzano Italy
57 E3 Aviemore U.K.
66 F4 Avigliano Italy
64 G5 Avignon France
65 D2 Ávila Spain
65 D1 Avilés Spain
68 H2 Avnyugskiy Rus. Fed.
115 G8 Avoca Tas. Austr.
114 E6 Avoca r. Vic. Austr.
114 E6 Avoca Vic. Austr.
60 E5 Avoca Rep. of Ireland
26 E3 Avoca U.S.A.
66 F6 Avola Sicily Italy
59 F5 Avon r. Eng. U.K.
59 F7 Avon r. Eng. U.K.
30 B5 Avon U.S.A.
35 F4 Avondale U.S.A.
116 B3 Avon Downs Austr.
59 E6 Avonmouth U.K.
29 D7 Avon Park U.S.A.
64 D2 Avranches France
61 A5 Avre r. France
111 G2 Avuavu Solomon Is
90 E6 Awaji-shima i. Japan
117 E3 Awakino N.Z.
117 D1 Awanui N.Z.
117 B6 Awarua Pt pt N.Z.
102 E2 Awash r. Eth.
102 E3 Āwash Eth.
91 G4 Awa-shima i. Japan
102 D3 Awash National Park nat. park Eth.
104 C4 Awasib Mts mts Namibia
117 D4 Awatere r. N.Z.
101 D2 Awbārī Libya
60 C5 Awbeg r. Rep. of Ireland
81 L6 'Awdah, Hawr al l. Iraq
102 E3 Aw Dheegle Somalia
101 E4 Aweil Sudan
57 C4 Awe, Loch l. U.K.
100 C4 Awka Nigeria
94 C6 Awu volc. Indon.
114 F6 Axedale Austr.
18 Axel Heiberg Island i. Can.
100 B4 Axim Ghana
59 E7 Axminster U.K.
91 E6 Ayabe Japan
47 E3 Ayacucho Arg.
42 D6 Ayacucho Peru
82 F1 Ayaguz Kazak.
86 E4 Ayakkum Hu salt l. China
65 C4 Ayamonte Spain
77 P4 Ayan Rus. Fed.
69 F5 Ayancık Turkey
45 B2 Ayapel Col.
80 D1 Ayaş Turkey
42 D6 Ayaviri Peru
84 B1 Āybak Afgh.
69 F5 Aydar r. Ukr.
79 K3 Aydarkul', Ozero l. Uzbek.
80 A3 Aydın Turkey
80 A2 Aydın Dağları mts Turkey
95 □ Ayer Chawan, P. i. Sing.
95 □ Ayer Merbau, P. i. Sing.
112 F5 Ayers Rock h. Austr.
77 N3 Aykhal Rus. Fed.
68 J2 Aykino Rus. Fed.
117 D5 Aylesbury N.Z.
59 G6 Aylesbury U.K.
32 E6 Aylett U.S.A.

65 E2 Ayllón Spain
31 G4 Aylmer Can.
21 G4 Aylmer Lake l. Can.
79 K2 Ayní Tajik.
80 G3 'Ayn 'Īsá Syria
101 F4 Ayod Sudan
77 S3 Ayon, O. i. Rus. Fed.
100 B3 'Ayoûn el 'Atroûs Maur.
116 B2 Ayr Austr.
57 D5 Ayr U.K.
57 D5 Ayr r. U.K.
80 D3 Ayrancı Turkey
58 C3 Ayre, Point of pt Isle of Man
67 M3 Aytos Bulg.
95 B2 Ayutthaya Thai.
67 M5 Ayvalı Turkey
80 F2 Ayvalı Turkey
67 M5 Ayvalık Turkey
85 E4 Azamgarh India
100 B3 Azaouâd reg. Mali
100 C3 Azaouagh, Vallée de watercourse Mali/Niger
81 L3 'Āzarān Iran
Azbine mts see Aïr, Massif de l'
80 D1 Azdavay Turkey
70 Azerbaijan country Asia
31 G2 Azilda Can.
33 H2 Aziscohos Lake l. U.S.A.
54 C4 Azogues Ecuador
76 F3 Azopol'ye Rus. Fed.
48 Azores territory Europe
12 H3 Azores - Cape St Vincent Ridge sea feature Atlantic Ocean
69 F6 Azov Rus. Fed.
69 F6 Azov, Sea of sea Rus. Fed./Ukr.
100 B1 Azrou Morocco
25 F4 Aztec U.S.A.
65 D3 Azuaga Spain
44 B3 Azucar r. Chile
90 B7 Azūchi-Ō-shima i. Japan
37 H7 Azuero, Península de pen. Panama
47 E3 Azul Arg.
47 B4 Azul, Cerro mt Arg.
42 C6 Azul, Cordillera mts Peru
44 A1 Azul, Serra h. Brazil
42 F8 Azurduy Bol.
66 B6 Azzaba Alg.
80 F5 Az Zabadānī Syria
81 J6 Az Zafīrī reg. Iraq
Az Zahrān see Dhahran
81 L6 Az Zubayr Iraq

# B

80 E5 Ba'abda Lebanon
80 F4 Ba'albek Lebanon
115 H3 Baan Baa Austr.
102 E3 Baardheere Somalia
67 M5 Baba Burnu pt Turkey
81 M1 Babadağ mt Azer.
67 N2 Babadag Romania
69 C7 Babaeski Turkey
42 C4 Babahoyo Ecuador
85 E3 Babai r. Nepal
88 B1 Babai Gaxun China
81 L2 Bābā Jān r. Iran
94 C5 Babak Phil.
84 B2 Bābā, Kūh-e mts Afgh.
78 E7 Bāb al Mandab str. Africa/Asia
93 H8 Babar i. Indon.
93 H8 Babar, Kepulauan is Indon.
102 D4 Babati Tanz.
68 E3 Babayevo Rus. Fed.
69 H7 Babayurt Rus. Fed.
30 B2 Babbitt U.S.A.
115 H7 Babel I. i. Austr.
116 A1 Babinda Austr.
20 D4 Babine Lake l. Can.
93 J7 Babo Indon.
79 G2 Bābol Iran
104 C6 Baboon Point pt S. Africa
35 G6 Baboquivari Peak summit U.S.A.
102 B3 Baboua C.A.R.
67 J4 Babruysk Belarus
84 D4 Babuhri India
84 C2 Babusar Pass pass Pak.
86 J1 Babushkin Rus. Fed.
94 B2 Babuyan i. Phil.
94 A4 Babuyan Phil.
89 F7 Babuyan Channel chan. Phil.
94 B2 Babuyan Islands is Phil.
81 K5 Babylon Iraq
43 K4 Bacabal Brazil
80 C1 Bacakliyayla T. mt Turkey
93 H7 Bacan i. Indon.
94 B2 Bacarra Phil.
67 N2 Bacău Romania
95 C6 Băc Giang Vietnam
25 C6 Bachiniva Mex.
82 E3 Bachu China
67 J1 Back r. Can.
67 J4 Bačka Palanka Yugo.
20 D2 Backbone Ranges mts Can.
54 P5 Backe Sweden
114 B5 Backstairs Pass. chan. Austr.

57 E4 Backwater Reservoir resr U.K.
89 B6 Bac Lac Vietnam
95 C3 Bac Liêu Vietnam
89 C6 Băc Ninh Vietnam
94 B4 Bacolod Phil.
94 B3 Baco, Mt mt Phil.
89 B6 Băc Quang Vietnam
22 F2 Bacqueville, Lac l. Can.
83 E8 Badagara India
88 A1 Badain Jaran Shamo des. China
42 F4 Badajós, Lago l. Brazil
65 C3 Badajoz Spain
81 H6 Badanah S. Arabia
85 H4 Badarpur India
31 F4 Bad Axe U.S.A.
23 H4 Baddeck Can.
80 C3 Bademli Geçidi pass Turkey
62 H6 Baden Austria
62 D7 Baden Switz.
62 D6 Baden-Baden Ger.
57 D4 Badenoch reg. U.K.
23 J4 Badger Can.
62 D5 Bad Hersfeld Ger.
62 F7 Bad Hofgastein Austria
66 D2 Badia Polesine Italy
84 B4 Badin Pak.
62 F7 Bad Ischl Austria
Bādiyat ash Shām des. see Syrian Desert
62 D6 Bad Kissingen Ger.
62 C6 Bad Kreuznach Ger.
26 C2 Badlands reg. U.S.A.
26 C3 Badlands Nat. Park nat. park U.S.A.
62 D6 Bad Mergentheim Ger.
61 F4 Bad Neuenahr-Ahrweiler Ger.
88 D4 Badong China
95 C3 Ba Đông Vietnam
62 E5 Bad Salzungen Ger.
62 E4 Bad Schwartau Ger.
62 E4 Bad Segeberg Ger.
113 H2 Bad I. i. Austr.
83 F9 Badulla Sri Lanka
54 B3 Bær Iceland
115 J4 Baerami Austr.
65 E4 Baeza Spain
100 D4 Bafang Cameroon
100 A3 Bafatá Guinea-Bissau
79 H2 Bāfq Iran
80 E1 Bafra Turkey
69 F7 Bafra Burnu pt Turkey
79 H4 Bāft Iran
102 C3 Bafwasende Zaire
85 F4 Bagaha India
94 A5 Bagahak, Mt h. Malaysia
83 E7 Bagalkot India
102 D4 Bagamoyo Tanz.
92 C6 Bagan Datuk Malaysia
95 B4 Bagan Serai Malaysia
95 B5 Bagansiapiapi Indon.
35 F4 Bagdad U.S.A.
81 K5 Baghdād Iraq
84 B3 Baghlān Afgh.
26 E2 Baggs U.S.A.
85 E3 Baglung Nepal
65 G1 Bagnères-de-Luchon France
64 G4 Bagnols-sur-Cèze France
85 F4 Bagnuiti r. Nepal
88 C2 Bag Nur l. China
Bago see Pegu
94 B4 Bago Phil.
63 K3 Bagrationovsk Rus. Fed.
94 C5 Baguio Phil.
94 B2 Bagulo Phil.
84 D3 Bahadurgarh India
16 Bahamas, The country Caribbean Sea
85 E4 Baharampur India
78 B4 Bahariya Oasis oasis Egypt
92 C3 Bahau Malaysia
84 C3 Bahawalnagar Pak.
84 B3 Bahawalpur Pak.
80 F3 Bahçe Turkey
88 C4 Ba He r. China
84 D5 Baheri India
102 D4 Bahi Tanz.
46 E1 Bahia div. Brazil
47 D3 Bahía Blanca Arg.
36 G5 Bahía, Islas de la is Honduras
44 C7 Bahía Laura Arg.
44 C4 Bahía Negra Para.
102 D2 Bahir Dar Eth.
85 H4 Bahraich India
70 Bahrain country Asia
81 M3 Bahrāmābād Iran
Bahr el Azraq r. see Blue Nile
63 L7 Baia Mare Romania
87 M2 Baicheng China

23 G4 Baie Comeau Can.
22 F3 Baie du Poste Can.
23 G4 Baie Saint Paul Can.
23 J4 Baie Verte Can.
88 E2 Baigou r. China
84 E5 Baihar India
83 H3 Baihe Jilin China
88 D3 Baihe Shaanxi China
81 J4 Baiji Iraq
Baikal, Lake l. see Baykal, Ozero
67 K2 Băilești Romania
67 K2 Băileștilor, Câmpia plain Romania
61 A4 Bailleul France
21 H2 Baillie r. Can.
60 E4 Baillieborough Rep. of Ireland
88 B3 Bailong Jiang r. China
82 K4 Baima China
59 G4 Bain r. U.K.
82 E3 Bainang China
29 C6 Bainbridge GA U.S.A.
33 F3 Bainbridge NY U.S.A.
85 G3 Baingoin China
85 E2 Bairab Co l. China
85 H4 Bairagnia India
106 Bairiki Kiribati
88 F1 Bairin Youqi China
88 F1 Bairin Zuoqi China
115 G6 Bairnsdale Austr.
80 F6 Bā'ir, Wādī watercourse Jordan
94 B4 Bais Phil.
89 C7 Baisha Hainan China
89 B3 Baisha Jiangxi China
88 C4 Baisha Sichuan China
87 N3 Baishan China
88 B3 Baishui Jiang r. China
89 B7 Bai Thương Vietnam
88 F1 Baitle r. China
88 F1 Baixingt China
88 F1 Baiyin China
101 F3 Baiyuda Desert des. Sudan
67 H1 Baja Hungary
36 A2 Baja California pen. Mex.
81 M3 Bājalān Iran
85 G5 Baj Baj India
45 D1 Bajo Baudó Col.
47 D1 Bajo Hondo Arg.
116 D4 Bajool Austr.
100 A3 Bakel Senegal
34 C4 Baker CA U.S.A.
24 E2 Baker MT U.S.A.
35 E2 Baker NV U.S.A.
24 C2 Baker OR U.S.A.
35 G4 Baker Butte summit U.S.A.
20 C3 Baker I. i. U.S.A.
111 J1 Baker Island i. Pac. Oc.
21 K2 Baker Lake Can.
21 K2 Baker Lake l. Can.
24 B1 Baker, Mt volc. U.S.A.
116 E3 Bakers Creek Austr.
22 E2 Bakers Dozen Islands is Can.
34 C4 Bakersfield U.S.A.
95 C3 Bã Kêv Cambodia
79 H2 Bakharden Turkm.
84 B4 Bakhasar India
69 E6 Bakhchysaray Ukr.
69 E5 Bakhmach Ukr.
79 G3 Bakhtegan, Daryācheh-ye salt pan Iran
Baki see Baku
80 B1 Bakırköy Turkey
102 D3 Bako Eth.
102 A3 Bakouma C.A.R.
102 B4 Bakoumba Gabon
69 G7 Baksan Rus. Fed.
81 M1 Baku Azer.
102 D3 Baku Zaire
80 D2 Balâ Turkey
59 D5 Bala U.K.
94 A5 Balabac Phil.
94 A5 Balabac i. Phil.
94 A5 Balabac Strait str. Malaysia/Phil.
42 E6 Bala, Cerros de mts Bol.
81 K4 Balad Iraq
84 E5 Balaghat India
81 L1 Balakän Azer.
69 H5 Balakhna Rus. Fed.
114 C5 Balaklava Austr.
69 E6 Balaklava Ukr.
69 F5 Balakliya Ukr.
94 A5 Balambangan i. Malaysia
79 J2 Bālā Morghāb Afgh.
84 E4 Bālān India
69 H5 Balanda r. Rus. Fed.
94 B3 Balanga Phil.
81 L3 Balāngīr India
69 G5 Balashov Rus. Fed.
85 G4 Balasinor India
62 H7 Balaton l. Hungary
62 H7 Balatonboglár Hungary
62 H7 Balatonfüred Hungary
43 J5 Balbina, Represa de resr Brazil
60 E4 Balbriggan Rep. of Ireland
114 C3 Balcanoona Austr.
47 E4 Balcarce Arg.
67 N3 Balchik Bulg.
117 B7 Balclutha N.Z.
27 D5 Bald Knob U.S.A.
35 E3 Bald Mtn mt. U.S.A.
21 K3 Baldock Lake l. Can.
31 H3 Baldwin Can.

29 D6 **Baldwin** *FL* U.S.A.
30 E4 **Baldwin** *MI* U.S.A.
30 A3 **Baldwin** *WV* U.S.A.
33 H3 **Baldwinsville** U.S.A.
35 H5 **Baldy Peak** *mt.* U.S.A.
**Baleares, Islas** *is see*
**Balearic Islands**
65 H3 **Balearic Islands** *is* Spain
46 E2 **Baleia, Ponta da** *pt* Brazil
23 G2 **Baleine, Rivière à la** *r.*
Can.
102 D3 **Bale Mts National Park**
*nat. park* Eth.
94 B3 **Baler** Phil.
94 B3 **Baler Bay** *b.* Phil.
85 F5 **Bāleshwar** India
55 K6 **Balestrand** Norway
116 A3 **Balfe's Creek** Austr.
117 B6 **Balfour** N.Z.
92 □ **Bali** *i.* Indon.
92 □ **Bali** *div.* Indon.
92 B6 **Balige** Indon.
85 E5 **Baliguda** India
88 F1 **Balihan** China
80 A2 **Balıkesir** Turkey
92 F7 **Balikpapan** Indon.
94 A5 **Balimbing** Phil.
110 E2 **Balimo** P.N.G.
62 D6 **Balingen** Ger.
94 B2 **Balintang Channel** *chan.*
Phil.
57 E3 **Balintore** U.K.
92 F8 **Bali Sea** *g.* Indon.
94 B5 **Baliungan** *i.* Phil.
52 **Balkan Mountains** *mts*
Bulg./Yugo.
84 A1 **Balkhab** *r.* Afgh.
82 D1 **Balkhash** Kazak.
82 D1 **Balkhash, Ozero** *l.* Kazak.
57 C4 **Ballachulish** U.K.
112 D6 **Balladonia** Austr.
115 H3 **Balladoran** Austr.
60 C4 **Ballaghaderreen** Rep. of
Ireland
114 F6 **Ballan** Austr.
54 P2 **Ballangen** Norway
24 E2 **Ballantine** U.S.A.
57 D5 **Ballantrae** U.K.
114 E6 **Ballarat** Austr.
112 D5 **Ballard, L.** *salt flat* Austr.
84 D4 **Ballarpur** India
57 E3 **Ballater** U.K.
100 B3 **Ballé** Mali
44 B3 **Ballena, Pta** *pt* Chile
119 A6 **Balleny Is** *is* Ant.
85 F4 **Ballia** India
115 K2 **Ballina** Austr.
60 B3 **Ballina** Rep. of Ireland
60 C3 **Ballinafad** Rep. of Ireland
60 D4 **Ballinalack** Rep. of Ireland
60 D3 **Ballinamore**
Rep. of Ireland
60 C4 **Ballinasloe** Rep. of Ireland
60 C4 **Ballindine** Rep. of Ireland
27 D6 **Ballinger** U.S.A.
57 E4 **Ballinluig** U.K.
60 B4 **Ballinrobe** Rep. of Ireland
33 G3 **Ballston Spa** U.S.A.
60 E3 **Ballybay** Rep. of Ireland
60 A6 **Ballybrack** Rep. of Ireland
60 B5 **Ballybunnion**
Rep. of Ireland
60 E5 **Ballycanew**
Rep. of Ireland
60 B3 **Ballycastle** Rep. of Ireland
60 E2 **Ballycastle** U.K.
60 F3 **Ballyclare** U.K.
60 A4 **Ballyconneely Bay** *b.*
Rep. of Ireland
60 D3 **Ballyconnell**
Rep. of Ireland
60 C4 **Ballygar** Rep. of Ireland
60 D3 **Ballygawley** U.K.
60 D2 **Ballygorman**
Rep. of Ireland
60 C4 **Ballyhaunis**
Rep. of Ireland
60 B5 **Ballyheige**
Rep. of Ireland
60 C5 **Ballyhoura Mts** *h.*
Rep. of Ireland
60 D2 **Ballykelly** U.K.
60 D5 **Ballylynan** Rep. of Ireland
60 D5 **Ballymacmague**
Rep. of Ireland
60 D4 **Ballymahon**
Rep. of Ireland
60 E3 **Ballymena** U.K.
60 E2 **Ballymoney** U.K.
60 C3 **Ballymote** Rep. of Ireland
60 F3 **Ballynahinch** U.K.
60 E5 **Ballyshannon**
Rep. of Ireland
60 E5 **Ballyteige Bay** *b.*
Rep. of Ireland
60 B4 **Ballyvaughan**
Rep. of Ireland
56 C3 **Ballyvoy** U.K.
60 E3 **Ballyward** U.K.
57 A3 **Balmartin** U.K.
**Balmer** *see* **Barmer**
114 D6 **Balmoral** Austr.
27 C6 **Balmorhea** U.S.A.
84 A3 **Balochistān** *reg.* Pak.
84 E5 **Balod** India
85 E5 **Baloda Bazar** India
115 H2 **Balonne** *r. Qld.* Austr.
84 C4 **Balotra** India
85 E4 **Balrampur** India
114 E5 **Balranald** Austr.
67 L2 **Balş** Romania
31 H2 **Balsam Creek** Can.
43 J5 **Balsas** Brazil
69 D6 **Balta** Ukr.

68 J3 **Baltasi** Rus. Fed.
57 □ **Baltasound** U.K.
84 D2 **Baltero Gl.** *gl.* Pak.
69 C6 **Bălţi** Moldova
52 **Baltic Sea** *g.* Europe
80 C6 **Baltîm** Egypt
105 H1 **Baltimore** S. Africa
32 E5 **Baltimore** U.S.A.
60 E5 **Baltinglass** Rep. of Ireland
84 C2 **Baltistan** *reg.*
Jammu and Kashmir
63 J3 **Baltiysk** Rus. Fed.
85 G4 **Balurghat** India
94 C5 **Balut** *i.* Phil.
55 U8 **Balvi** Latvia
67 M5 **Balya** Turkey
**Balykchy** *see* **Ysyk-Köl**
79 H4 **Bam** Iran
89 C5 **Bama** China
113 H2 **Bamaga** Austr.
22 B3 **Bamaji L.** *l.* Can.
100 B3 **Bamako** Mali
100 B3 **Bamba** Mali
94 B3 **Bambang** Phil.
102 C3 **Bambari** C.A.R.
95 A5 **Bambel** Indon.
62 E6 **Bamberg** Ger.
29 D5 **Bamberg** U.S.A.
102 C3 **Bambili** Zaire
105 G5 **Bamboesberg** *mts*
S. Africa
102 C3 **Bambouti** C.A.R.
46 D3 **Bambuí** Brazil
81 M6 **Bāmdezh** Iran
100 D4 **Bamenda** Cameroon
84 A2 **Bāmiān** Afgh.
88 G1 **Bamiancheng** China
102 C3 **Bamingui-Bangoran,**
**Parc National de**
*nat. park* C.A.R.
84 B2 **Bamiyan** Afgh.
59 D7 **Bampton** U.K.
111 G2 **Banaba** *i.* Kiribati
43 L5 **Banabuiu, Açude** *resr*
Brazil
47 C3 **Bañados del Atuel**
*marsh* Arg.
42 F7 **Bañados del Izozog**
*swamp* Bol.
60 D4 **Banagher** Rep. of Ireland
102 C3 **Banalia** Zaire
105 K1 **Banamana, Lagoa** *l.* Moz.
100 B3 **Banamba** Mali
116 D5 **Banana** Austr.
43 H6 **Bananal, Ilha do** *i.* Brazil
85 F6 **Bānapur** India
95 B2 **Ban Aranyaprathet** Thai.
84 D4 **Banas** *r.* India
80 B2 **Banaz** Turkey
95 B1 **Ban Ban** Laos
85 H3 **Banbar** China
95 B4 **Ban Betong** Thai.
60 E3 **Banbridge** U.K.
95 B2 **Ban Bua Yai** Thai.
59 F5 **Banbury** U.K.
94 A4 **Bancalan** *i.* Phil.
114 D3 **Bancannia, Lake** *salt flat*
Austr.
57 F3 **Banchory** U.K.
36 G5 **Banco Chinchorro** *is*
Mex.
94 A5 **Bancoran** *i.* Phil.
31 J3 **Bancroft** Can.
84 E4 **Banda** India
102 C3 **Banda** Zaire
92 B5 **Banda Aceh** Indon.
115 K3 **Banda Banda, Mt** *mt*
Austr.
84 B2 **Banda Daud Shah** Pak.
95 A5 **Bandahara, G.** *mt* Indon.
91 H5 **Bandai-Asahi National**
**Park** *nat. park* Japan
93 H7 **Banda, Kepulauan** *is*
Indon.
85 H5 **Bandarban** Bangl.
79 H4 **Bandar-e 'Abbās** Iran
81 M3 **Bandar-e Anzalī** Iran
79 G4 **Bandar-e Lengeh** Iran
**Bandar-e Shāhpūr** *see*
**Bandar Khomeynī**
79 G2 **Bandar-e Torkeman** Iran
81 M6 **Bandar Khomeynī** Iran
92 F5 **Bandar Labuan** Malaysia
84 D3 **Bandarpunch** *mt* India
92 E6 **Bandar Seri Begawan**
Brunei
93 H8 **Banda Sea** *sea* Indon.
46 B1 **Bandeirante** Brazil
46 E3 **Bandeiras, Pico de** *mt*
Brazil
105 H1 **Bandelierkop** S. Africa
36 C4 **Banderas, Bahía de** *b.*
Mex.
84 C4 **Bandi** *r. Rajasthan* India
84 C4 **Bandi** *r. Rajasthan* India
84 E6 **Bandia** *r.* India
100 B3 **Bandiagara** Mali
84 A1 **Band-i-Amir** *r.* Afgh.
80 A1 **Bandırma** Turkey
60 C6 **Bandon** Rep. of Ireland
60 C6 **Bandon** *r.* Rep. of Ireland
**Ban Don** *see* **Surat Thani**
81 M2 **Bāndovan Burnu** *pt* Azer.
81 M6 **Band Qīr** Iran
102 B4 **Bandundu** Zaire
92 □ **Bandung** Indon.
81 K4 **Bāneh** Iran
37 J4 **Banes** Cuba
20 F4 **Banff** Can.
57 F3 **Banff** U.K.

20 F4 **Banff National Park**
*nat. park* Can.
100 B3 **Banfora** Burkina
94 C5 **Banga** Phil.
102 C4 **Banga** Zaire
94 C5 **Bangai Point** *pt* Phil.
83 E8 **Bangalore** India
84 D4 **Banganga** *r.* India
85 G5 **Bangaon** India
94 B2 **Bangar** Phil.
102 C3 **Bangassou** C.A.R.
85 E2 **Bangdag Co** *salt l.* China
95 C1 **Bangfai, Xée** *r.* Laos
93 G7 **Banggai** Indon.
93 G7 **Banggai, Kepulauan** *is*
Indon.
93 F5 **Banggi** *i.* Malaysia
101 E1 **Banghāzī** Libya
95 C1 **Banghiang, Xé** *r.* Laos
92 □ **Bangil** Indon.
92 D7 **Bangka** *i.* Indon.
92 □ **Bangkalan** Indon.
95 A5 **Bangkaru** *i.* Indon.
92 C7 **Bangko** Indon.
85 G3 **Bangkog Co** *salt l.* China
95 B2 **Bangkok** Thai.
95 B2 **Bangkok, Bight of** *b.*
Thai.
70 **Bangladesh** *country* Asia
100 B4 **Bangolo** Côte d'Ivoire
84 D2 **Bangong Co** *l.* China
60 F3 **Bangor** *N. Ireland* U.K.
59 C4 **Bangor** *Wales* U.K.
33 J2 **Bangor** *ME* U.S.A.
30 D4 **Bangor** *MI* U.S.A.
33 F4 **Bangor** *PA* U.S.A.
60 B3 **Bangor Erris**
Rep. of Ireland
95 B2 **Bang Saphan Yai** Thai.
35 F3 **Bangs, Mt** *mt* U.S.A.
54 M4 **Bangsund** Norway
94 B2 **Bangued** Phil.
102 B3 **Bangui** C.A.R.
94 B2 **Bangui** Phil.
95 A5 **Bangunpurba** Indon.
103 C5 **Bangweulu, Lake** *l.*
Zambia
95 B4 **Ban Hat Yai** Thai.
103 D6 **Banhine, Parque**
**Nacional de** *nat. park*
Moz.
95 B1 **Ban Hin Heup** Laos
95 A2 **Ban Hua Hin** Thai.
102 C3 **Bani** C.A.R.
94 A2 **Bani** Phil.
102 B3 **Bania** C.A.R.
84 C2 **Banihal Pass and Tunnel**
*pass* Jammu and Kashmir
32 C6 **Banister** *r.* U.S.A.
101 D1 **Banī Walīd** Libya
80 E4 **Bāniyās** Syria
80 E5 **Bāniyās** Syria
66 G2 **Banja Luka** Bos.-Herz.
84 D3 **Banjar** India
92 E7 **Banjarmasin** Indon.
100 A3 **Banjul** The Gambia
81 M2 **Banka** Azer.
85 E4 **Banka** India
113 F3 **Banka Banka** Austr.
95 A4 **Ban Kantang** Thai.
100 B3 **Bankass** Mali
95 B2 **Ban Khao Yoi** Thai.
95 C1 **Ban Khemmarat** Thai.
95 A3 **Ban Khok Kloi** Thai.
95 A1 **Ban Khun Yuam** Thai.
85 F5 **Bankis** India
18 **Banks I.** *i.* Can.
111 G3 **Banks Islands** *is* Vanuatu
24 C2 **Banks I.** U.S.A.
21 L2 **Banks Lake** *l.* Can.
117 D6 **Banks Peninsula** *pen.*
N.Z.
115 H8 **Banks Strait** *chan.* Austr.
95 B1 **Ban Kui Nua** Thai.
85 F5 **Bankura** India
95 A1 **Ban Mae Sariang** Thai.
95 A1 **Ban Mae Sot** Thai.
79 L3 **Banmi** Pak.
95 B1 **Ban Mouang** Laos
95 B2 **Ban Muang Phon** Thai.
60 E5 **Bann** *r.* Rep. of Ireland
60 E3 **Bann** *r.* U.K.
95 C1 **Na Na Kae** Thai.
95 C1 **Ban Nakham** Laos
95 B1 **Ban Na Noi** Thai.
95 A3 **Ban Na San** Thai.
95 B4 **Ban Na Thawi** Thai.
30 C5 **Banner** U.S.A.
29 E7 **Bannerman Town**
Bahamas
34 D5 **Banning** U.S.A.
47 B3 **Baños Maule** Chile
95 B1 **Ban Pak-Leng** Laos
95 B3 **Ban Pak Phanang** Thai.
95 B2 **Ban Pak Thong Chai** Thai.
95 C1 **Ban Phaeng** Thai.
95 B1 **Ban Phai** Thai.
95 B2 **Ban Phanat Nikhom** Thai.
95 C2 **Ban Phon** Laos
95 B1 **Ban Phon Thong** Thai.
95 A2 **Banphot Phisai** Thai.
95 A2 **Ban Pong** Thai.
95 B1 **Ban Pua** Thai.
95 A1 **Ban Saraphi** Thai.
95 B1 **Ban Sattahip** Thai.
95 A3 **Ban Sawi** Thai.
85 E4 **Bansi** India
95 A3 **Ban Sichon** Thai.
95 B2 **Ban Si Racha** Thai.
63 J6 **Banská Bystrica** Slovakia
95 A1 **Ban Sut Ta** Thai.
84 C5 **Banswara** India
95 A3 **Ban Takua Pa** Thai.
94 B4 **Bantayan** *i.* Phil.

60 C5 **Banteer** Rep. of Ireland
95 A3 **Ban Tha Chang** Thai.
95 A1 **Ban Tha Don** Thai.
95 A3 **Ban Thai Muang** Thai.
95 A1 **Ban Tha Kham** Thai.
95 A1 **Ban Tha Song Yang** Thai.
95 B2 **Ban Tha Tako** Thai.
95 B2 **Ban Tha Tum** Thai.
95 C1 **Ban Tha Uthen** Thai.
94 B3 **Banton** *i.* Phil.
95 B1 **Ban Thung Luang** Thai.
60 C6 **Bantry** Rep. of Ireland
60 B6 **Bantry Bay** *b.*
Rep. of Ireland
92 □ **Bantul** Indon.
95 B1 **Ban Woen** Laos
100 D4 **Banyo** Cameroon
65 H1 **Banyoles** Spain
92 □ **Banyuwangi** Indon.
13 J7 **Banzare Seamount**
*sea feature* Indian Ocean
88 B3 **Bao'an** China
88 E2 **Baoding** China
88 D3 **Baofeng** China
89 C4 **Baoji** China
88 D4 **Baojing** China
88 D4 **Baokang** China
95 C3 **Bao Lôc** Vietnam
82 J5 **Baoshan** China
88 D1 **Baotou** China
89 C4 **Baoxing** China
88 F3 **Baoying** China
84 D4 **Bap** India
61 A4 **Bapaume** France
31 H3 **Baptiste Lake** *l.* Can.
85 H2 **Baqêm** China
85 H2 **Baqên** China
81 K5 **Ba'qūbah** Iraq
42 □ **Baquerizo Moreno**
*Galapagos Is* Ecuador
67 H3 **Bar** Yugo.
101 F3 **Bara** Sudan
102 E3 **Baraawe** Somalia
85 F4 **Barabar Hills** *h.* India
30 C4 **Baraboo** U.S.A.
30 C4 **Baraboo** U.S.A.
37 K4 **Baracoa** Cuba
47 E2 **Baradero** Arg.
115 H3 **Baradine** Austr.
115 H3 **Baradine** *r.* Austr.
30 C2 **Baraga** U.S.A.
85 E3 **Baragarh** India
37 K5 **Barahona** Dom. Rep.
84 D2 **Barail Range** *mts* India
85 H4 **Barak** *r.* India
102 D2 **Baraka** *watercourse*
Eritrea/Sudan
65 E1 **Barakaldo** Spain
84 B2 **Barakī Barak** Afgh.
85 F5 **Bārākot** India
116 C5 **Baralaba** Austr.
84 D2 **Bara Lacha Pass** *pass*
Jammu and Kashmir
81 J5 **Baŗ al Milḥ** *l.* Iraq
21 K3 **Baralzon Lake** *l.* Can.
116 D5 **Barambah** *r.* Austr.
84 D4 **Baran** India
84 B4 **Baran** *r.* Pak.
68 D4 **Baranavichy** Belarus
77 S3 **Baranikha** Rus. Fed.
69 C5 **Baranivka** Ukr.
45 B2 **Baranoa** Col.
20 B3 **Baranof Island** *i.* U.S.A.
46 C4 **Barão de Melgaço** Brazil
100 B3 **Baraoueli** Mali
61 D4 **Baraque de Fraiture** *h.*
Belgium
93 H8 **Barat Daya, Kepulauan**
*is* Indon.
114 C4 **Baratta** Austr.
84 D3 **Baraut** India
45 B4 **Barbacena** Brazil
46 D3 **Barbacena** Brazil
45 A4 **Barbacoas** Col.
16 **Barbados** *country*
Caribbean Sea
65 G1 **Barbastro** Spain
65 D4 **Barbate de Franco** Spain
34 □1 **Barbers Pt** *pt* U.S.A.
105 J2 **Barberton** S. Africa
32 C4 **Barberton** U.S.A.
64 D4 **Barbezieux-St-Hilaire**
France
45 B3 **Barbosa** Col.
21 L2 **Barbour Bay** *b.* Can.
32 B6 **Barbourville** U.S.A.
94 B4 **Barboza** Phil.
37 M5 **Barbuda** *i.* Antigua
116 A4 **Barcaldine** Austr.
65 H2 **Barcelona** Spain
45 D2 **Barcelona** Venez.
42 F4 **Barcelos** Brazil
100 B4 **Barclayville** Liberia
116 A4 **Barcoo** *watercourse*
Austr.
66 G2 **Barcs** Hungary
81 L1 **Bärdä** Azer.
54 L1 **Bárðarbunga** *mt* Iceland
47 C2 **Bardas Blancas** Arg.
85 H3 **Barddhamān** India
63 K6 **Bardejov** Slovakia
95 C2 **Bar Dôn** Vietnam
59 C2 **Bardsey Island** *i.* U.K.
28 C4 **Bardstown** U.S.A.
32 B5 **Bardwell** U.S.A.
84 D3 **Bareilly** India
76 D2 **Barentsøya** *i.* Svalbard
76 F2 **Barents Sea** *sea*
Arctic Ocean
102 D2 **Barentu** Eritrea
84 E3 **Barga** China
116 E5 **Bargara** Austr.

84 D5 **Bargi** India
57 D5 **Bargrennan** U.K.
85 G5 **Barguna** Bangl.
86 E6 **Bari** India
33 J2 **Bar Harbor** U.S.A.
66 G4 **Bari** Italy
95 C3 **Ba Ria** Vietnam
84 C3 **Bari Doab** *lowland* Pak.
79 L2 **Barikot** Nepal
85 E3 **Barikot** Nepal
45 E2 **Barima** *r.* Venez.
45 C2 **Barinas** Venez.
85 G5 **Barisal** Bangl.
92 C7 **Barisan, Pegunungan** *mts*
Indon.
92 E7 **Barito** *r.* Indon.
42 F8 **Baritu, Parque Nacional**
*nat. park* Arg.
88 B4 **Barkam** China
55 U8 **Barkava** Latvia
20 C4 **Barkerville** Can.
28 C4 **Barkley, L.** *l.* U.S.A.
20 D5 **Barkley Sd** *in.* Can.
105 G5 **Barkly East** S. Africa
82 H2 **Barkol** China
84 D3 **Barkot** India
63 N7 **Bârlad** Romania
64 G2 **Bar-le-Duc** France
112 C5 **Barlee, L.** *salt flat* Austr.
66 G4 **Barletta** Italy
115 G4 **Barmedman** Austr.
84 B4 **Barmer** India
114 D5 **Barmera** Austr.
59 C5 **Barmouth** U.K.
84 C3 **Barnala** India
58 F3 **Barnard Castle** U.K.
115 F3 **Barnato** Austr.
76 K4 **Barnaul** Rus. Fed.
33 F5 **Barnegat** U.S.A.
33 F5 **Barnegat Bay** *b.* U.S.A.
32 D4 **Barnesboro** U.S.A.
35 G3 **Barney Top** *mt.* U.S.A.
27 C6 **Barnhart** U.S.A.
58 F4 **Barnsley** U.K.
59 C6 **Barnstaple** U.K.
**Barnstaple Bay** *b. see*
**Bideford Bay**
29 D5 **Barnwell** U.S.A.
**Baroda** *see* **Vadodara**
84 C1 **Baroghil Pass** *pass* Afgh.
85 H4 **Barpathar** India
85 G4 **Barpeta** India
30 D3 **Barques, Pt Aux** *pt*
*MI* U.S.A.
31 F3 **Barques, Pt Aux** *pt*
*MI* U.S.A.
45 C2 **Barquisimeto** Venez.
43 K6 **Barra** Brazil
57 A4 **Barra** *i.* U.K.
115 J3 **Barra** Austr.
104 D7 **Barracouta, Cape** *hd*
S. Africa
43 G6 **Barra do Bugres** Brazil
43 J5 **Barra do Corda** Brazil
46 B1 **Barra do Garças** Brazil
43 G2 **Barra do São Manuel**
Brazil
42 C6 **Barranca** *Lima* Peru
42 C4 **Barranca** *Loreto* Peru
45 B3 **Barranca-bermeja** Col.
47 C3 **Barrancas** *r.*
*Mendoza/Neuquén* Arg.
45 B2 **Barrancas** Col.
45 C2 **Barrancas** Venez.
44 E3 **Barranqueras** Arg.
45 B2 **Barranquilla** Col.
57 A3 **Barra, Sound of** *chan.*
U.K.
33 G2 **Barre** U.S.A.
47 C1 **Barreal** Arg.
43 K6 **Barreiras** Brazil
43 G4 **Barreirinha** Brazil
43 K4 **Barreirinhas** Brazil
46 B1 **Barreiro** *r.* Brazil
65 B3 **Barreiro** Port.
43 L5 **Barreiros** Brazil
46 C3 **Barretos** Brazil
20 G4 **Barrhead** Can.
31 H3 **Barrie** Can.
31 F3 **Barrie I** *i.* Can.
20 E4 **Barrière** Can.
114 D3 **Barrier Range** *h.* Austr.
21 J3 **Barrington Lake** *l.* Can.
115 J4 **Barrington, Mt** *mt* Austr.
115 F2 **Barringun** Austr.
30 B3 **Barron** U.S.A.
116 A1 **Barron Falls** *waterfall*
Austr.
27 C7 **Barroterán** Mex.
47 E2 **Barrow** *r.* Rep. of Ireland
60 E5 **Barrow** *r.* Rep. of Ireland
16 **Barrow** U.S.A.
113 F4 **Barrow Creek** Austr.
112 C4 **Barrow I.** *i.* Austr.
58 D3 **Barrow-in-Furness** U.K.
59 D6 **Barry** U.K.
104 D6 **Barrydale** S. Africa
31 J3 **Barrys Bay** Can.
84 C3 **Barsalpur** India
84 D3 **Barsi** India
34 D4 **Barstow** U.S.A.
64 G2 **Bar-sur-Aube** France
62 F3 **Barth** Ger.
43 G2 **Bartica** Guyana
80 D1 **Bartın** Turkey
116 A1 **Bartle Frere, Mt** *mt*
Austr.
35 G2 **Bartles, Mt** *mt.* U.S.A.
26 D3 **Bartlett** *NE* U.S.A.

33 H2 **Bartlett** *NH* U.S.A.
20 F2 **Bartlett Lake** *l.* Can.
33 G2 **Barton** U.S.A.
58 G4 **Barton-upon-Humber**
U.K.
63 K3 **Bartoszyce** Pol.
95 B5 **Barumun** *r.* Indon.
92 □ **Barung** *i.* Indon.
45 A5 **Barus** Indon.
88 B1 **Baruunsuu** Mongolia
87 K2 **Baruun Urt** Mongolia
37 H7 **Barú, Volcán** *volc.*
Panama
84 D5 **Barwah** India
84 C3 **Barwala** India
84 C5 **Barwani** India
115 H2 **Barwon** *r.* Austr.
68 D4 **Barysaw** Belarus
68 H4 **Barysh** *r.* Rus. Fed.
68 H4 **Barysh** Rus. Fed.
116 A2 **Basalt** *r.* Austr.
34 C3 **Basalt** U.S.A.
89 □ **Basalt I.** *i.* Hong Kong
China
102 B3 **Basankusu** Zaire
67 N2 **Basarabi** Romania
47 E2 **Basavilbaso** Arg.
94 B4 **Basay** Phil.
94 B1 **Basco** Phil.
62 C7 **Basel** Switz.
30 B1 **Basswood Lake** *l.* U.S.A.
20 G4 **Bashaw** Can.
105 H6 **Bashee** *r.* S. Africa
84 B2 **Bashgul** *r.* Afgh.
68 G4 **Bashmakovo** Rus. Fed.
69 D6 **Bashtanka** Ukr.
84 D3 **Basi** India
85 F5 **Basia** India
94 B5 **Basilan** *i.* Phil.
94 B5 **Basilan Strait** *chan.* Phil.
59 H6 **Basildon** U.K.
24 E2 **Basin** U.S.A.
59 F6 **Basingstoke** U.K.
81 K4 **Bāsīra** *r.* Iraq
85 G5 **Basirhat** India
33 K2 **Baskahegan Lake** *l.*
U.S.A.
81 K2 **Başkale** Turkey
31 K2 **Baskatong, Réservoir**
*resr* Can.
69 H5 **Baskunchak, Ozero** *l.*
Rus. Fed.
**Basle** *see* **Basel**
84 D5 **Basoda** India
102 C3 **Basoko** Zaire
81 L6 **Basra** Iraq
66 D2 **Bassano del Grappa** Italy
100 B3 **Bassar** Togo
103 D6 **Bassas da India** *i.*
Indian Ocean
83 H7 **Bassein** Myanmar
58 D3 **Bassenthwaite Lake** *l.*
U.K.
100 A3 **Basse Santa Su** The
Gambia
37 M5 **Basse Terre** Guadeloupe
37 M5 **Basseterre** St Kitts-Nevis
26 D3 **Bassett** U.S.A.
35 G5 **Bassett Peak** *summit*
U.S.A.
33 J2 **Bass Harbor** U.S.A.
100 B3 **Bassikounou** Maur.
100 C4 **Bassila** Benin
57 F4 **Bass Rock** *i.* U.K.
110 E5 **Bass Strait** *str.* Austr.
55 N8 **Båstad** Sweden
79 G4 **Bastak** Iran
81 L3 **Bastānābād** Iran
85 E3 **Basti** India
66 C3 **Bastia** *Corsica* France
61 D4 **Bastogne** Belgium
27 F5 **Bastrop** *LA* U.S.A.
27 D6 **Bastrop** *TX* U.S.A.
100 C4 **Bata** Equatorial Guinea
37 H4 **Batabanó, Golfo de** *b.*
Cuba
94 B2 **Batac** Phil.
94 B2 **Batag** *i.* Phil.
77 P3 **Batagay** Rus. Fed.
84 B2 **Batai Pass** *pass* Pak.
84 C3 **Batala** India
65 B3 **Batalha** Port.
95 C5 **Batam** *i.* Indon.
77 N3 **Batamay** Rus. Fed.
94 B1 **Batan** *i.* Phil.
82 J4 **Batang** China
102 B3 **Batangafo** C.A.R.
94 B3 **Batangas** Phil.
95 A5 **Batangtoru** Indon.
94 B1 **Batan Islands** *is* Phil.
46 C3 **Batatais** Brazil
**Batavia** *see* **Jakarta**
30 C5 **Batavia** *IL* U.S.A.
32 D3 **Batavia** *NY* U.S.A.
69 F6 **Bataysk** Rus. Fed.
31 H2 **Batchawana** *r.* Can.
30 E2 **Batchawana Bay** Can.
22 A2 **Batchawana Mtn** *h.* Can.
112 F2 **Batchelor** Austr.
31 E2 **Batchewana** Can.
95 C3 **Bătdâmbâng** Cambodia
115 J5 **Batemans B.** *b.* Austr.
115 J5 **Batemans Bay** Austr.
27 F5 **Batesville** *AR* U.S.A.
27 F5 **Batesville** *MS* U.S.A.
68 D4 **Batetskiy** Rus. Fed.
23 G4 **Bath** *N.B.* Can.
31 J3 **Bath** *Ont.* Can.
59 E6 **Bath** U.K.
33 J3 **Bath** *ME* U.S.A.
32 E3 **Bath** *NY* U.S.A.
57 E5 **Bathgate** U.K.
84 D3 **Bathinda** India
115 H4 **Bathurst** Austr.

23 G4 Bathurst Can.
105 G6 Bathurst S. Africa
16 Bathurst Inlet Can.
112 F2 Bathurst Island i. Austr.
115 H5 Bathurst, L. i. Austr.
58 F4 Batley U.K.
115 H5 Batlow Austr.
81 H3 Batman Turkey
100 C1 Batna Alg.
27 F6 Baton Rouge U.S.A.
101 D4 Batouri Cameroon
46 B1 Batovi Brazil
80 E4 Batroûn Lebanon
54 V1 Båtsfjord Norway
83 F9 Batticaloa Sri Lanka
66 F4 Battipaglia Italy
21 G4 Battle r. Can.
30 E4 Battle Creek U.S.A.
21 H4 Battleford Can.
24 C3 Battle Mountain U.S.A.
84 C1 Battura Glacier gl.
   Jammu and Kashmir
95 B4 Batu Gajah Malaysia
94 C5 Batulaki Phil.
81 H1 Bat'umi Georgia
92 C6 Batu Pahat Malaysia
92 B7 Batu, Pulau Pulau is
   Indon.
95 B4 Batu Puteh, Gunung mt
   Malaysia
93 G8 Baubau Indon.
100 C3 Bauchi Nigeria
26 E1 Baudette U.S.A.
45 A3 Baudo, Serranía de mts
   Col.
64 D3 Baugé France
116 C5 Bauhinia Downs Austr.
23 K3 Bauld, C. hd Can.
64 H3 Baume-les-Dames France
84 C2 Baundal India
46 C3 Bauru Brazil
46 B2 Baús Brazil
55 T8 Bauska Latvia
62 G5 Bautzen Ger.
104 E6 Baviaanskloofberg mts
   S. Africa
59 J5 Bawdeswell U.K.
92 Bawean i. Indon.
78 B4 Bawiti Egypt
100 B3 Bawku Ghana
95 A1 Bawlake Myanmar
89 A4 Bawolung China
88 B3 Baxi China
88 E2 Ba Xian Hebei China
89 C4 Ba Xian Sichuan China
29 D6 Baxley U.S.A.
82 J4 Baxoi China
37 J4 Bayamo Cuba
84 D4 Bayana India
82 J4 Bayan Har Shan mts
   China
86 H2 Bayanhongor Mongolia
88 B3 Bayan Mod China
88 C1 Bayan Obo China
94 C4 Baybay Phil.
81 H1 Bayburt Turkey
31 F4 Bay City MI U.S.A.
27 D6 Bay City TX U.S.A.
76 H3 Baydaratskaya Guba b.
   Rus. Fed.
102 E3 Baydhabo Somalia
62 F6 Bayerischer Wald mts
   Ger.
30 B2 Bayfield U.S.A.
67 M5 Bayındır Turkey
80 F6 Bāyir Jordan
87 J1 Baykal, Ozero l. Rus. Fed.
86 H1 Baykal'sk Rus. Fed.
86 J1 Baykal'sky Khr. mts
   Rus. Fed.
81 H2 Baykan Turkey
94 B3 Bay, Laguna de lag. Phil.
76 G4 Baymak Rus. Fed.
94 B2 Bayombong Phil.
64 D5 Bayonne France
94 B4 Bayo Point pt Phil.
67 M5 Bayramiç Turkey
62 E6 Bayreuth Ger.
27 F6 Bay St Louis U.S.A.
33 G4 Bay Shore U.S.A.
59 E5 Bayston Hill U.K.
27 E6 Baytown U.S.A.
117 F3 Bay View N.Z.
65 E4 Baza Spain
81 L1 Bazardyuzi, Gora mt
   Azer./Rus. Fed.
81 M3 Bāzār-e Māsāl Iran
81 K2 Bāzārgān Iran
69 H4 Bazarnyy Karabulak
   Rus. Fed.
103 D6 Bazaruto, Ilha do i. Moz.
88 C4 Bazhong China
95 C3 Be r. Vietnam
26 C3 Beach U.S.A.
31 J3 Beachburg Can.
33 F5 Beach Haven U.S.A.
114 D6 Beachport Austr.
33 F5 Beachwood U.S.A.
59 H7 Beachy Head hd U.K.
33 G4 Beacon U.S.A.
105 G6 Beacon Bay S. Africa
89 Beacon Hill h.
   Hong Kong China
59 G6 Beaconsfield U.K.
44 C8 Beagle, Canal chan. Arg.
112 F2 Beagle Gulf g. Austr.
103 E5 Bealanana Madag.
59 E7 Beaminster U.K.
24 E3 Bear r. U.S.A.
21 N2 Bear Cove b. Can.
22 C4 Beardmore Can.
115 H1 Beardmore Res. resr
   Austr.
30 B5 Beardstown U.S.A.

22 D3 Bear Island i. Can.
76 C2 Bear Island i. Svalbard
24 E3 Bear L. l. U.S.A.
20 D3 Bear Lake Can.
84 D4 Bearma r. India
57 A4 Bearnaraigh i. U.K.
24 E1 Bear Paw Mtn mt. U.S.A.
22 B3 Bearskin Lake Can.
34 B2 Bear Valley U.S.A.
84 C3 Beas r. India
84 C3 Beas Dam dam India
37 K5 Beata, Cabo c. Dom. Rep.
37 K5 Beata, I. i. Dom. Rep.
26 D3 Beatrice U.S.A.
20 E3 Beatton r. Can.
20 E3 Beatton River Can.
34 D3 Beatty U.S.A.
22 E4 Beattyville Can.
64 G5 Beaucaire France
44 E8 Beauchene I. i.
   Falkland Is
113 K5 Beaudesert Austr.
114 E6 Beaufort Austr.
29 D5 Beaufort U.S.A.
18 Beaufort Sea sea
   Can./U.S.A.
104 E6 Beaufort West S. Africa
22 F4 Beauharnois Can.
57 D3 Beauly U.K.
57 D3 Beauly Firth est. U.K.
59 C4 Beaumaris U.K.
61 C4 Beaumont Belgium
117 B6 Beaumont N.Z.
27 F6 Beaumont MS U.S.A.
32 B5 Beaumont OH U.S.A.
27 E6 Beaumont TX U.S.A.
64 G3 Beaune France
64 D3 Beaupréau France
61 C4 Beauraing Belgium
21 K4 Beausejour Can.
64 F2 Beauvais France
21 H3 Beauval Can.
20 D2 Beaver r. B.C./Y.T. Can.
22 C2 Beaver r. Ont. Can.
35 F2 Beaver r. U.S.A.
35 F2 Beaver r. U.S.A.
20 A2 Beaver Creek Can.
28 C4 Beaver Dam KY U.S.A.
30 C4 Beaver Dam WV U.S.A.
32 C4 Beaver Falls U.S.A.
24 D2 Beaverhead Mts mts
   U.S.A.
21 K4 Beaverhill L. l. Man. Can.
21 J2 Beaverhill L. l.
   N.W.T. Can.
30 E3 Beaver Island i. U.S.A.
27 E4 Beaver L. resr U.S.A.
20 F3 Beaverlodge Can.
32 D4 Beaver Run Reservoir
   resr U.S.A.
84 E4 Beawar India
47 C2 Beazley Arg.
46 C3 Bebedouro Brazil
59 D4 Bebington U.K.
22 F1 Bécard, Lac l. Can.
59 J5 Beccles U.K.
67 J2 Bečej Yugo.
65 C1 Becerreá Spain
100 B1 Béchar Alg.
32 C6 Beckley U.S.A.
58 F3 Bedale U.K.
33 J2 Beddington U.S.A.
102 D3 Bedelē Eth.
33 G2 Bedford Can.
105 J4 Bedford S. Africa
59 G5 Bedford U.K.
28 C4 Bedford IN U.S.A.
33 H3 Bedford MA U.S.A.
32 D4 Bedford PA U.S.A.
32 D6 Bedford VA U.S.A.
59 G5 Bedford Level lowland
   U.K.
115 G4 Bedgerebong Austr.
58 F2 Bedlington U.K.
95 Bedok Sing.
95 Bedok Res. resr Sing.
35 H2 Bedrock U.S.A.
59 F5 Bedworth U.K.
116 A6 Beechal Cr. watercourse
   Austr.
32 B5 Beech Fork Lake l. U.S.A.
30 C2 Beechwood U.S.A.
115 G6 Beechworth Austr.
115 J5 Beecroft Pen. pen. Austr.
115 K1 Beenleigh Austr.
60 A5 Beenoskee h.
   Rep. of Ireland
80 E6 Beersheba Israel
   Be'ér Sheva' see
   Beersheba
104 E6 Beervlai Dam dam
   S. Africa
115 K1 Beerwah Austr.
27 D6 Beeville U.S.A.
102 C3 Befale Zaire
103 E5 Befandriana Avaratra
   Madag.
115 H6 Bega Austr.
84 B3 Begari r. Pak.
79 K1 Begovat Uzbek.
65 H2 Begur, Cap de pt Spain
85 F4 Begusarai India
43 H3 Béhague, Pointe pt
   Fr. Guiana
20 C3 Behm Canal in. U.S.A.
119 B3 Behrendt Mts mts Ant.
79 G2 Behshahr Iran
84 A2 Behsūd Afgh.
87 N2 Bei'an China
89 C4 Beibei China
88 B3 Beichuan China
89 C6 Beihai China
89 D6 Bei Jiang r. China
88 E1 Beijing China

88 E2 Beijing div. China
89 C7 Beili China
89 D6 Beiliu China
57 C5 Beinn an Oir h. U.K.
57 D3 Beinn Dearg mt U.K.
88 F1 Beipiao China
103 D5 Beira Moz.
88 E3 Beiru r. China
80 E5 Beirut Lebanon
103 C6 Beitbridge Zimbabwe
57 D5 Beith U.K.
63 L7 Beiuş Romania
88 F1 Beizhen China
65 C3 Beja Port.
100 C1 Béja Tunisia
100 C1 Bejaïa Alg.
65 D2 Béjar Spain
84 B3 Beji r. Pak.
92 Bekasi Indon.
63 K7 Békés Hungary
63 K7 Békéscsaba Hungary
103 E6 Bekily Madag.
90 K2 Bekkai Japan
100 B4 Bekwai Ghana
85 E4 Bela India
79 K4 Bela Pak.
84 B3 Belab r. Pak.
105 H2 Bela-Bela S. Africa
101 D4 Bélabo Cameroon
67 J2 Bela Crkva Yugo.
33 L7 Bel Air U.S.A.
65 D3 Belalcázar Spain
115 F4 Belaraboon Austr.
49 Belarus country Europe
   Belau country see Palau
46 A3 Bela Vista Brazil
103 D6 Bela Vista Moz.
95 A5 Belawan Indon.
77 T3 Belaya r. Rus. Fed.
69 G6 Belaya Glina Rus. Fed.
69 G5 Belaya Kalitva Rus. Fed.
68 J3 Belaya Kholunitsa
   Rus. Fed.
63 J5 Bełchatów Pol.
32 B6 Belcher U.S.A.
80 F2 Belcik Turkey
60 D3 Belcoo U.K.
31 J1 Belcourt Can.
34 B1 Belden U.S.A.
102 E3 Beledweyne Somalia
43 J4 Belém Brazil
44 C3 Belén Arg.
80 F3 Belen Turkey
25 F5 Belen U.S.A.
111 G3 Belep, Îles is
   New Caledonia
68 F4 Belev Rus. Fed.
117 D5 Belfast N.Z.
105 J2 Belfast S. Africa
60 F3 Belfast U.K.
33 J2 Belfast U.K.
60 F3 Belfast Lough in. U.K.
26 C2 Belfield U.S.A.
58 F2 Belford U.K.
64 H3 Belfort France
83 D7 Belgaum India
48 Belgium country Europe
69 F5 Belgorod Rus. Fed.
69 F5 Belgorodskaya Oblast'
   div. Rus. Fed.
24 E2 Belgrade U.S.A.
67 J2 Belgrade Yugo.
100 D4 Beli Nigeria
66 E6 Belice r. Sicily Italy
68 C4 Belinskiy Rus. Fed.
92 D7 Belinyu Indon.
92 D7 Belitung i. Indon.
36 G5 Belize Belize
16 Belize country
   Central America
77 P2 Bel'kovskiy, O. i.
   Rus. Fed.
115 H4 Bell r. Austr.
115 J1 Bell Austr.
20 D4 Bella Bella Can.
64 E3 Bellac France
20 D4 Bella Coola Can.
27 E6 Bellaire U.S.A.
83 E7 Bellary India
115 H2 Bellata Austr.
47 F1 Bella Unión Uru.
115 G5 Bellbrook Austr.
116 D3 Bell Cay rf Austr.
32 B4 Bellefontaine U.S.A.
32 E4 Bellefonte U.S.A.
26 C2 Belle Fourche U.S.A.
26 C2 Belle Fourche r. U.S.A.
64 G3 Bellegarde-sur-Valserine
   France
29 D7 Belle Glade U.S.A.
64 C3 Belle-Île i. France
23 K3 Belle Isle i. Can.
23 J3 Belle Isle, Strait of str.
   Can.
35 G4 Bellemont U.S.A.
30 A5 Belle Plaine U.S.A.
31 H4 Belleterre Can.
31 J3 Belleville Can.
26 D4 Belleville U.S.A.
30 B4 Bellevue IA U.S.A.
24 D3 Bellevue ID U.S.A.
32 B4 Bellevue OH U.S.A.
24 B2 Bellevue WA U.S.A.
   Bellin see Kangirsuk
115 K3 Bellingen Austr.
58 E2 Bellingham U.K.
24 B1 Bellingham U.S.A.
119 B2 Bellingshausen Rus. Fed.
   Base Ant.
119 A3 Bellingshausen Sea sea
   Ant.
62 D7 Bellinzona Switz.
45 B3 Bello Col.
33 G3 Bellows Falls U.S.A.

84 B3 Bellpat Pak.
33 F5 Belltown U.S.A.
66 E1 Belluno Italy
47 D2 Bell Ville Arg.
104 C6 Bellville S. Africa
57 Belmont U.K.
32 D3 Belmont U.S.A.
46 E1 Belmonte Brazil
36 G5 Belmopan Belize
115 K2 Belmore, Mt h. Austr.
60 B3 Belmullet Rep. of Ireland
33 G2 Beloeil Can.
87 N1 Belogorsk Rus. Fed.
103 E6 Beloha Madag.
46 D2 Belo Horizonte Brazil
26 D4 Beloit KS U.S.A.
30 C4 Beloit WI U.S.A.
68 E1 Belomorsk Rus. Fed.
69 F6 Belorechensk Rus. Fed.
80 F3 Belören Turkey
76 G4 Beloretsk Rus. Fed.
   Belorussia country see
   Belarus
103 E5 Belo Tsiribihina Madag.
68 F1 Beloye, Ozero l. Rus. Fed.
   Beloye More g. see
   White Sea
68 F2 Beloye, Ozero l. Rus. Fed.
68 F2 Belozersk Rus. Fed.
32 C5 Belpre U.S.A.
24 C7 Belt U.S.A.
114 C3 Beltana Austr.
114 B2 Belt B. salt flat Austr.
34 D3 Belted Range mts U.S.A.
27 D6 Belton U.S.A.
94 A5 Beluran Malaysia
30 C4 Belvidere U.S.A.
116 B4 Belyando r. Austr.
68 H3 Belyshevo Rus. Fed.
68 E4 Belyy Rus. Fed.
76 J2 Belyy, O. i. Rus. Fed.
30 C6 Bement U.S.A.
26 E2 Bemidji U.S.A.
102 C4 Bena Dibele Zaire
57 D4 Ben Alder mt U.K.
115 F6 Benalla Austr.
66 D6 Ben Arous Tunisia
65 D1 Benavente Spain
57 E3 Ben Avon mt U.K.
60 B4 Benbaun h.
   Rep. of Ireland
57 A3 Benbecula i. U.K.
60 C3 Benbulben h.
   Rep. of Ireland
60 B4 Benburb U.K.
57 C4 Ben Cruachan mt U.K.
24 B2 Bend U.S.A.
105 G5 Bendearg mt S. Africa
115 J3 Bendemeer Austr.
102 E3 Bender-Bayla Somalia
114 F6 Bendigo Austr.
115 H6 Bendoc Austr.
103 D5 Bene Moz.
33 J2 Benedicta U.S.A.
23 J3 Benedict, Mount h. Can.
62 G6 Benešov Czech Rep.
66 F4 Benevento Italy
88 F3 Beng r. China
74 Bengal, Bay of sea Asia
102 C3 Bengamisa Zaire
88 E3 Bengbu China
95 B5 Bengkalis Indon.
92 C7 Bengkulu Indon.
55 N7 Bengtsfors Sweden
103 B5 Benguela Angola
80 C6 Benha Egypt
57 B4 Ben Hiant h. U.K.
57 D2 Ben Hope mt U.K.
42 E6 Beni r. Bol.
102 C3 Beni Zaire
100 B1 Beni-Abbès Alg.
65 F3 Benidorm Spain
100 B1 Beni Mellal Morocco
96 Benin country Africa
100 C4 Benin, Bight of g. Africa
100 C4 Benin City Nigeria
100 B1 Beni-Saf Alg.
78 C4 Beni Suef Egypt
47 E3 Benito Juárez Arg.
94 B2 Benito Soliven Phil.
42 E4 Benjamim Constant
   Brazil
36 B2 Benjamín Hill Mex.
93 J8 Benjina Indon.
90 H2 Benkei-misaki pt Japan
26 C3 Benkelman U.S.A.
57 D2 Ben Klibreck h. U.K.
57 D4 Ben Lawers mt U.K.
115 J3 Ben Lomond mt Austr.
57 D4 Ben Lomond mt U.K.
115 G8 Ben Lomond Nat. Park
   nat. park Austr.
57 D2 Ben Loyal h. U.K.
57 E3 Ben Macdui mt U.K.
57 B4 Ben More mt Scot. U.K.
57 D4 Ben More mt U.K.
57 D2 Ben More Assynt mt U.K.
117 C6 Benmore, L. l. N.Z.
77 Q2 Bennetta, O. i. Rus. Fed.
57 C4 Ben Nevis mt U.K.
33 G3 Bennington U.S.A.
105 H3 Benoni S. Africa
101 D4 Bénoué, Parc National
   de la nat. park
   Cameroon
35 G4 Benson AZ U.S.A.
26 E2 Benson MN U.S.A.
95 B4 Benta Seberang Malaysia
32 D6 Bent Creek U.S.A.
93 G8 Benteng Indon.
113 G3 Bentinck I. i. Austr.

95 A3 Bentinck I. i. Myanmar
58 F4 Bentley U.K.
33 K2 Benton Can.
27 E5 Benton AR U.S.A.
34 C3 Benton CA U.S.A.
28 B4 Benton IL U.S.A.
30 D4 Benton Harbor U.S.A.
95 C3 Bên Tre Vietnam
95 B5 Bentung Malaysia
100 C4 Benue r. Nigeria
57 D4 Ben Vorlich mt U.K.
60 B4 Benwee h. Rep. of Ireland
60 B3 Benwee Head hd
   Rep. of Ireland
57 D3 Ben Wyvis mt U.K.
88 G1 Benxi China
94 C5 Beo Indon.
85 G5 Beohari India
100 B4 Béoumi Côte d'Ivoire
89 C3 Bepian Jiang r. China
90 C7 Beppu Japan
90 C7 Beppu-wan b. Japan
111 H3 Beqa i. Fiji
84 C4 Berach r. India
23 G2 Bérard, Lac l. Can.
84 D5 Berasia India
95 A5 Berastagi Indon.
67 H4 Berat Albania
93 J7 Berau, Teluk b. Indon.
101 F3 Berber Sudan
102 E2 Berbera Somalia
102 B3 Berbérati C.A.R.
64 E1 Berck France
81 K1 Berd Armenia
77 O3 Berdigestyakh Rus. Fed.
69 F6 Berdyans'k Ukr.
69 D5 Berdychiv Ukr.
32 A6 Berea U.S.A.
69 B5 Berehove Ukr.
110 E2 Bereina P.N.G.
21 K4 Berens r. Can.
21 K4 Berens River Can.
26 D3 Beresford Can.
69 C5 Berezhany Ukr.
69 C6 Berezivka Ukr.
69 C5 Berezne Ukr.
68 G2 Bereznik Rus. Fed.
76 H3 Berezovo Rus. Fed.
61 D4 Berg Neth.
65 G1 Berga Spain
67 M5 Bergama Turkey
66 C2 Bergamo Italy
55 P6 Bergby Sweden
62 F3 Bergen Ger.
55 J6 Bergen Norway
61 C3 Bergen op Zoom Neth.
64 E4 Bergerac France
62 C5 Bergheim Ger.
61 F4 Bergisch Gladbach Ger.
104 B1 Bergland Namibia
30 C2 Bergland U.S.A.
55 P6 Bergsjö Sweden
54 R4 Bergviken Sweden
61 E1 Bergumermeer l. Neth.
105 H4 Bergville S. Africa
77 S4 Beringa, O. i. Rus. Fed.
61 D3 Beringen Belgium
77 T3 Beringovskiy Rus. Fed.
77 T4 Bering Sea sea Pac. Oc.
77 V3 Bering Strait str.
   Rus. Fed./U.S.A.
54 M5 Berkåk Norway
61 E2 Berkel r. Neth.
34 A3 Berkeley U.S.A.
32 D5 Berkeley Springs U.S.A.
61 D2 Berkhout Neth.
119 B2 Berkner I. i. Ant.
67 K3 Berkovitsa Bulg.
59 F6 Berkshire Downs h. U.K.
54 V1 Berlevåg Norway
62 F4 Berlin Ger.
33 F5 Berlin MD U.S.A.
33 H2 Berlin NH U.S.A.
32 D5 Berlin PA U.S.A.
30 C4 Berlin WI U.S.A.
32 C4 Berlin Lake l. U.S.A.
115 J6 Bermagui Austr.
47 D2 Bermeja, Pta pt Arg.
47 C3 Bermejo r. San Juan Arg.
44 D2 Bermejo r.
   Chaco/Formosa Arg./Bol.
42 F8 Bermejo Bol.
37 M2 Bermuda terr.
   Atlantic Ocean
12 E3 Bermuda i.
   Atlantic Ocean
12 E3 Bermuda Rise sea
   feature Atlantic Ocean
62 C7 Bern Switz.
25 F5 Bernalillo U.S.A.
44 A7 Bernardo O'Higgins,
   Parque Nacional
   nat. park Chile
47 D3 Bernasconi Arg.
30 E5 Berne U.S.A.
62 C7 Berner Alpen mts Switz.
57 A3 Berneray i. U.K.
112 B4 Bernier I. i. Austr.
62 E7 Bernina Pass pass Switz.
61 F5 Bernkastel-Kues Ger.
103 E6 Beroroha Madag.
62 G6 Beroun Czech Rep.
62 G6 Berounka r. Czech Rep.
114 D5 Berri Austr.
115 F5 Berriedale U.K.
115 F5 Berrigan Austr.
115 J5 Berrima Austr.
65 H4 Berrouaghia Alg.
115 J5 Berry Austr.
64 F3 Berry reg. France
34 A2 Berryessa, Lake l. U.S.A.
29 E7 Berry Islands is
   Bahamas

104 B3 Berseba Namibia
69 D5 Bershad' Ukr.
95 B4 Bertam Malaysia
43 K5 Bertolinía Brazil
101 D4 Bertoua Cameroon
60 B4 Bertraghboy Bay b.
   Rep. of Ireland
111 H2 Beru i. Kiribati
42 F4 Beruri Brazil
114 F7 Berwick U.S.A.
33 E4 Berwick U.S.A.
58 E2 Berwick-upon-Tweed
   U.K.
20 F3 Berwyn Can.
59 D4 Berwyn h. U.K.
69 E6 Beryslav Ukr.
103 E5 Besalampy Madag.
64 H3 Besançon France
81 H3 Beşiri Turkey
69 H7 Beslan Rus. Fed.
21 H3 Besnard Lake l. Can.
80 F3 Besni Turkey
60 E3 Bessbrook U.K.
29 C5 Bessemer AL U.S.A.
30 C2 Bessemer MI U.S.A.
103 E6 Betanty Madag.
65 B1 Betanzos Spain
101 D4 Bétaré Oya Cameroon
105 H3 Bethal S. Africa
104 B3 Bethanie Namibia
26 E3 Bethany MO U.S.A.
27 D5 Bethany OK U.S.A.
33 H2 Bethel ME U.S.A.
30 A6 Bethel MO U.S.A.
32 A5 Bethel OH U.S.A.
32 D4 Bethel Park U.S.A.
59 C4 Bethesda U.K.
32 E5 Bethesda MD U.S.A.
32 C5 Bethesda OH U.S.A.
104 F5 Bethesdaweg S. Africa
105 H4 Bethlehem S. Africa
33 F4 Bethlehem U.S.A.
80 E6 Bethlehem West Bank
105 F5 Bethulie S. Africa
61 A4 Béthune France
45 C2 Betijoque Venez.
103 E6 Betioky Madag.
82 C1 Betpak-Dala plain Kazak.
103 E6 Betroka Madag.
80 E5 Bet She'an Israel
23 G4 Betsiamites Can.
23 G4 Betsiamites r. Can.
103 E5 Betsiboka r. Madag.
30 D3 Betsie, Pt pt U.S.A.
30 E2 Betsy Lake l. U.S.A.
30 B5 Bettendorf U.S.A.
85 F4 Bettiah India
57 D2 Bettyhill U.K.
60 E4 Bettystown
   Rep. of Ireland
84 D5 Betul India
61 D3 Betuwe reg. Neth.
84 D4 Betwa r. India
59 D4 Betws-y-coed U.K.
114 E5 Beulah Austr.
30 D3 Beulah U.S.A.
59 H6 Beult r. U.K.
58 F4 Beverley U.K.
116 C3 Beverley Group is Austr.
33 H3 Beverly MA U.S.A.
32 C5 Beverly OH U.S.A.
34 C4 Beverly Hills U.S.A.
21 J2 Beverly Lake l. Can.
61 C2 Beverwijk Neth.
59 H7 Bexhill U.K.
81 L4 Beyänlü Iran
80 B2 Bey Dağları mts Turkey
80 B1 Beykoz Turkey
100 B4 Beyla Guinea
81 L2 Beyläqan Azer.
80 C1 Beypazarı Turkey
80 F2 Beypınarı Turkey
   Beyrouth see Beirut
80 B2 Beyşehir Turkey
80 C3 Beyşehir Gölü l. Turkey
69 F6 Beysug r. Rus. Fed.
81 J3 Beytüşşebap Turkey
68 J3 Bezbozhnik Rus. Fed.
68 F3 Bezhanitsy Rus. Fed.
68 F3 Bezhetsk Rus. Fed.
64 F5 Béziers France
85 E4 Bhabhar India
85 E4 Bhabua India
85 F4 Bhadgaon Nepal
84 C3 Bhadohi India
84 C3 Bhadra India
85 F5 Bhadrakh India
83 D8 Bhadravati India
84 A3 Bhag Pak.
84 D2 Bhaga r. India
85 G4 Bhagalpur India
85 G5 Bhainsdehi India
79 L3 Bhakkar Pak.
86 J6 Bhamo Myanmar
84 D4 Bhander India
85 F6 Bhanjanagar India
84 D5 Bhanrer Range h. India
84 B4 Bharatpur India
85 H4 Bhareli r. India
84 C4 Bhatapara India
83 D8 Bhatkal India
84 C5 Bhatpara India
84 C5 Bhawana Pak.
84 C5 Bhavnagar India
85 E4 Bhawanipatna India
105 J3 Bhekuzulu S. Africa
85 E3 Bheri r. Nepal
84 C4 Bhilwara India

83 E7 Bhima r. India
84 D4 Bhind India
84 C4 Bhindar India
85 E4 Bhinga India
84 C4 Bhinmal India
84 D3 Bhiwani India
85 F4 Bhojpur Nepal
105 H5 Bhongweni S. Africa
84 D5 Bhopal India
85 F5 Bhuban India
85 F5 Bhubaneshwar India
84 B5 Bhuj India
84 C4 Bhusawal India
70 Bhutan country Asia
84 B4 Bhuttewala India
84 C2 Biafo Gl. gl. Pak.
93 K7 Biak i. Indon.
93 K7 Biak Indon.
63 L4 Biała Podlaska Pol.
62 G4 Białogard Pol.
63 L4 Białystok Pol.
100 B4 Biankouma Côte d'Ivoire
64 D5 Biarritz France
62 D7 Biasca Switz.
90 H2 Bibai Japan
103 B5 Bibala Angola
115 H6 Bibbenluke Austr.
66 D3 Bibbiena Italy
62 D6 Biberach an der Riß Ger.
85 G4 Bibiyana r. Bangl.
80 C2 Biçer Turkey
59 F6 Bicester U.K.
21 G4 Biche, Lac La l. Can.
115 H8 Bicheno Austr.
69 G7 Bichvint'a Georgia
113 G2 Bickerton I. i. Austr.
59 D7 Bickleigh U.K.
35 G2 Bicknell U.S.A.
103 B5 Bicuari, Parque Nacional do nat. park Angola
100 C4 Bida Nigeria
94 A5 Bidadari, Tg pt Malaysia
83 E7 Bidar India
33 H3 Biddeford U.S.A.
57 C4 Bidean Nam Bian mt U.K.
59 C6 Bideford U.K.
59 C6 Bideford Bay b. U.K.
63 L4 Biebrza r. Pol.
62 C7 Biel Switz.
62 H5 Bielawa Pol.
62 D4 Bielefeld Ger.
66 C2 Biella Italy
63 J6 Bielsko-Biała Pol.
63 K3 Bielsk Podlaski Pol.
95 C3 Biên Hoa Vietnam
Bienne see Biel
22 F2 Bienville, Lac l. Can.
98 Bié Plateau Angola
116 A6 Bierbank Austr.
61 C3 Biesbosch, Nationaal Park de nat. park Neth.
105 F4 Biesiesvlei S. Africa
61 D5 Bièvre Belgium
102 B4 Bifoun Gabon
90 J1 Bifuka Japan
23 J3 Big r. Can.
34 A2 Big r. U.S.A.
69 C7 Biga Turkey
80 B2 Bigadiç Turkey
67 M5 Biga Yarımadası pen. Turkey
30 D2 Big Bay U.S.A.
30 D3 Big Bay de Noc b. U.S.A.
34 D4 Big Bear Lake U.S.A.
24 E2 Big Belt Mts mts U.S.A.
105 J3 Big Bend Swaziland
27 C6 Big Bend Nat. Park nat. park U.S.A.
27 F5 Big Black r. U.S.A.
59 D7 Bigbury-on-Sea U.K.
29 D7 Big Cypress Nat. Preserve res. U.S.A.
30 C3 Big Eau Pleine Reservoir resr U.S.A.
21 L5 Big Falls U.S.A.
21 H4 Biggar Can.
57 E5 Biggar U.K.
116 E5 Biggenden Austr.
20 B3 Bigger, Mt mt. Can.
59 G5 Biggleswade U.K.
24 D2 Big Hole r. U.S.A.
24 F2 Bighorn r. U.S.A.
24 E2 Bighorn Canyon Nat. Recreation Area res. U.S.A.
24 F2 Bighorn Mountains mts U.S.A.
29 F7 Bight, The Bahamas
20 F2 Big Island i. Can.
33 K2 Big Lake l. U.S.A.
100 A3 Bignona Senegal
32 D6 Big Otter r. U.S.A.
30 C3 Big Pine U.S.A.
30 E4 Big Rapids U.S.A.
30 C3 Big Rib r. U.S.A.
21 H4 Big River Can.
30 D3 Big Sable Pt pt U.S.A.
20 C2 Big Salmon r. Can.
21 K3 Big Sand Lake l. Can.
35 H4 Big Sandy r. U.S.A.
26 D2 Big Sioux r. U.S.A.
34 D2 Big Smokey Valley v. U.S.A.
27 C5 Big Spring U.S.A.
26 C3 Big Springs U.S.A.
32 B6 Big Stone Gap U.S.A.
34 B3 Big Sur U.S.A.
24 E2 Big Timber U.S.A.
22 C3 Big Trout Lake Can.
22 C3 Big Trout Lake l. Can.
35 G3 Big Water U.S.A.
31 H3 Bigwin Can.
66 H2 Bihać Bos.-Herz.
85 F4 Bihar div. India

85 F4 Bihar Sharif India
90 K2 Bihoro Japan
63 L7 Bihor, Vârful mt Romania
100 A3 Bijagós, Arquipélago dos is Guinea-Bissau
84 C4 Bijainagar India
83 E7 Bijapur India
81 L4 Bijār Iran
67 H2 Bijeljina Bos.-Herz.
67 H3 Bijelo Polje Yugo.
89 B5 Bijie China
85 G4 Bijni India
84 D3 Bijnor India
84 B3 Bijnot Pak.
84 C3 Bikaner India
87 O2 Bikin Rus. Fed.
87 O2 Bikin r. Rus. Fed.
108 Bikini i. Marshall Islands
102 B4 Bikoro Zaire
88 B3 Bikou China
84 C4 Bilara India
85 E5 Bilaspur India
81 M2 Biläsuvar Azer.
69 D5 Bila Tserkva Ukr.
95 A2 Bilauktaung Range mts Myanmar/Thai.
65 E1 Bilbao Spain
80 C6 Bilbeis Egypt
67 H3 Bileća Bos.-Herz.
80 B1 Bilecik Turkey
63 L5 Biłgoraj Pol.
102 D4 Bilharamulo Tanz.
69 D6 Bilhorod-Dnistrovs'kyy Ukr.
102 C3 Bili Zaire
77 S3 Bilibino Rus. Fed.
95 A1 Bilin Myanmar
94 C4 Biliran i. Phil.
24 F3 Bill U.S.A.
59 H6 Billericay U.K.
58 F3 Billingham U.K.
24 F2 Billings U.S.A.
59 E7 Bill of Portland hd U.K.
35 F4 Bill Williams r. U.S.A.
35 F4 Bill Williams Mtn mt. U.S.A.
101 D3 Bilma Niger
116 D5 Biloela Austr.
69 E6 Bilohir's'k Ukr.
63 N5 Bilohir"ya Ukr.
69 F5 Biloluts'k Ukr.
69 E5 Bilopillya Ukr.
69 F5 Bilovods'k Ukr.
29 B6 Biloxi U.S.A.
113 G5 Bilpa Morea Claypan salt flat Austr.
57 E5 Bilston U.K.
101 E3 Biltine Chad
95 A1 Bilugyun I. i. Myanmar
68 J4 Bilyarsk Rus. Fed.
69 D6 Bilyayivka Ukr.
115 H5 Bimberi, Mt mt Austr.
29 E7 Bimini Is is Bahamas
81 M3 Binab Iran
84 D4 Bina-Etawa India
93 H7 Binaija, G. mt Indon.
80 F2 Binboğa Daği mt Turkey
115 G1 Bindebango Austr.
84 E4 Bindki India
115 H1 Bindle Austr.
103 B4 Bindu Zaire
103 D5 Bindura Zimbabwe
65 G2 Binefar Spain
115 J2 Bingara N.S.W. Austr.
115 F2 Bingara Qld. Austr.
88 B2 Bingcaowan China
62 C6 Bingen am Rhein Ger.
100 B4 Bingerville Côte d'Ivoire
33 J2 Bingham U.S.A.
33 E3 Binghamton U.S.A.
81 J2 Bingöl Turkey
81 H2 Bingöl D. mt Turkey
89 C6 Binh Gia Vietnam
95 D2 Binh Sơn Vietnam
84 H4 Bini India
85 E5 Binika India
95 A5 Binjai Indon.
115 H3 Binnaway Austr.
95 □ Bintan i. Indon.
94 B3 Bintuan Phil.
92 C7 Bintuhan Indon.
92 E6 Bintulu Malaysia
88 D3 Bin Xian China
115 G5 Binya Austr.
89 C6 Binyang China
88 F2 Binzhou China
47 B3 Bío Bío r. Chile
47 B3 Biobío div. Chile
100 C4 Bioco i. Equatorial Guinea
66 F3 Biograd na Moru Croatia
66 G3 Biokovo mts Croatia
83 E7 Bir India
81 H5 Bi'r al Mulūsi Iraq
68 F2 Birandozero Rus. Fed.
102 C2 Birao C.A.R.
85 F4 Biratnagar Nepal
90 J2 Biratori Japan
81 K5 Bi'r Buṭaymān Syria
20 G3 Birch r. Can.
21 H4 Birch Hills Can.
114 E5 Birchip Austr.
20 F4 Birch Island Can.
22 B3 Birch L. l. Can.
30 D2 Birch Lake l. U.S.A.
20 G3 Birch Mountains h. Can.
21 J4 Birch River Can.
35 G2 Birdseye U.S.A.
113 G5 Birdsville Austr.
80 F3 Birecik Turkey
101 E3 Bir en Nutrûn w. Sudan
92 B5 Bireun Indon.
82 F5 Birganj Nepal
102 D2 Birhan mt Eth.
46 B3 Birigüi Brazil

79 H3 Bīrjand Iran
81 J6 Birkat al 'Aqabah w. Iraq
81 J6 Birkat al 'Athāmīn w. Iraq
81 K6 Birkát Hamad w. Iraq
81 J7 Birkat Zubālah waterhole S. Arabia
59 D4 Birkenhead U.K.
80 C7 Birket Qârûn l. Egypt
81 K3 Bīrkim Iraq
66 F7 Birkirkara Malta
59 F5 Birmingham U.K.
29 C5 Birmingham U.S.A.
100 A2 Bîr Mogreïn Maur.
80 B6 Bîr Nâḥid oasis Egypt
100 C3 Birnin-Kebbi Nigeria
100 D3 Birnin Konni Niger
87 O2 Birobidzhan Rus. Fed.
60 D4 Birr Rep. of Ireland
115 G2 Birrie r. Austr.
81 J5 Bi'r Sâbil Iraq
57 F1 Birsay U.K.
59 F5 Birstall U.K.
80 E7 Bîr Tâba Egypt
21 J4 Birtle Can.
85 H3 Biru China
55 T8 Biržai Lith.
35 H6 Bisbee U.S.A.
52 Biscay, Bay of sea France/Spain
29 D7 Biscayne Nat. Park nat. park U.S.A.
62 F7 Bischofshofen Austria
119 B2 Biscoe Islands is Ant.
31 E2 Biscotasi Lake l. Can.
31 F2 Biscotasing Can.
89 C4 Bishan China
81 M5 Bīsheh Iran
87 M1 Bishui China
100 C1 Biskra Alg.
94 C4 Bislig Phil.
26 C2 Bismarck U.S.A.
34 C3 Bishop U.S.A.
58 F3 Bishop Auckland U.K.
59 H6 Bishop's Stortford U.K.
81 G4 Bishrī, Jabal h. Syria
82 D2 Bishkek Kyrgyzstan
85 F5 Bishnupur India
105 G6 Bisho S. Africa
110 E2 Bismarck Archipelago is P.N.G.
110 E2 Bismarck Range mts P.N.G.
110 E2 Bismarck Sea sea P.N.G.
81 H3 Bismil Turkey
55 L6 Bismo Norway
81 L4 Bīsotūn Iran
54 P5 Bispgården Sweden
65 G4 Bissa, Djebel mt Alg.
100 A3 Bissau Guinea-Bissau
100 B4 Bissaula Nigeria
21 K4 Bissett Can.
20 F3 Bistcho Lake l. Can.
63 N7 Bistrița r. Romania
63 M7 Bistrița Romania
62 C6 Bitburg Ger.
61 F5 Bitche France
101 D3 Bitkine Chad
81 J2 Bitlis Turkey
67 J4 Bitola Macedonia
66 G4 Bitonto Italy
83 D8 Bitra Par rf India
35 H2 Bitter Creek r. U.S.A.
104 C5 Bitterfontein S. Africa
80 D6 Bitter Lakes lakes Egypt
24 D2 Bitterroot Range mts U.S.A.
69 G5 Bityug r. Rus. Fed.
101 D3 Biu Nigeria
88 D3 Biyang China
84 D5 Biyāvra India
102 E2 Bīye K'obē Eth.
86 E1 Biysk Rus. Fed.
105 H5 Bizana S. Africa
90 E6 Bizen Japan
100 C1 Bizerte Tunisia
54 A4 Bjargtangar hd Iceland
54 Q5 Bjästa Sweden
66 F2 Bjelovar Croatia
54 P2 Bjerkvik Norway
55 L8 Bjerringbro Denmark
55 P6 Björklinge Sweden
55 L5 Bjorli Norway
54 Q5 Björna Sweden
Bjørnøya i. see Bear Island
54 Q5 Bjurholm Sweden
100 B3 Bla Mali
57 B3 Bla Bheinn mt U.K.
27 F5 Black r. AR U.S.A.
35 H5 Black r. AZ U.S.A.
31 F4 Black r. MI U.S.A.
30 B3 Black r. WV U.S.A.
116 A5 Blackall Austr.
30 C1 Black Bay b. U.S.A.
22 B3 Blackbear r. Can.
59 F6 Black Bourton U.K.
58 E4 Blackburn U.K.
115 K1 Blackbutt Austr.
34 A2 Black Butte summit U.S.A.
34 A2 Black Butte L. l. U.S.A.
35 E4 Black Canyon U.S.A.
35 F4 Black Canyon City U.S.A.
26 E2 Blackduck U.S.A.
20 G4 Blackfalds Can.
24 D2 Black Foot r. U.S.A.
25 E4 Black Hills reg. U.S.A.
57 D3 Black Isle i. U.K.
21 H3 Black Lake Can.
21 H3 Black Lake l. Can.
31 E3 Black Lake l. U.S.A.

35 G3 Black Mesa plat. U.S.A.
59 D6 Black Mountain h. U.K.
34 D4 Black Mt mt. U.S.A.
59 D6 Black Mts h. U.S.A.
35 E4 Black Mts mts AZ U.S.A.
104 C1 Black Nossob watercourse Namibia
89 □ Black Point pt Hong Kong China
58 D4 Blackpool U.K.
30 B3 Black River Falls U.S.A.
58 A4 Blackrock Rep. of Ireland
24 C3 Black Rock Desert des. U.S.A.
32 C6 Blacksburg U.S.A.
52 Black Sea sea Asia/Europe
60 A3 Blacksod Bay b. Rep. of Ireland
60 E5 Blackstairs Mountain h. Rep. of Ireland
60 E5 Blackstairs Mountains h. Rep. of Ireland
32 E6 Blackstone U.S.A.
115 J3 Black Sugarloaf mt Austr.
100 B4 Black Volta r. Africa
116 A5 Blackwater watercourse Austr.
116 C4 Blackwater r. Austr.
60 D5 Blackwater r. Rep. of Ireland
60 E5 Blackwater r. Rep. of Ireland
60 E4 Blackwater r. Rep. of Ireland
60 E3 Blackwater r. Rep. of Ireland/U.K.
59 H6 Blackwater r. U.K.
32 C6 Blackwater Lake l. Can.
20 E2 Blackwater Lake l. Can.
57 D4 Blackwater Reservoir resr U.K.
27 D4 Blackwell U.S.A.
112 C6 Blackwood r. Austr.
69 G6 Blagodarnyy Rus. Fed.
67 K3 Blagoevgrad Bulg.
87 N1 Blagoveshchensk Rus. Fed.
32 E4 Blain U.S.A.
24 B1 Blaine U.S.A.
21 J2 Blaine Lake Can.
26 D3 Blair NE U.S.A.
30 B3 Blair WV U.S.A.
116 B4 Blair Athol Austr.
57 E4 Blair Atholl U.K.
57 E4 Blairgowrie U.K.
29 C6 Blakely U.S.A.
59 J5 Blakeney U.K.
30 C1 Blake Pt pt U.S.A.
47 C3 Blanca, Bahía b. Arg.
47 C3 Blanca de la Totora, Sa h. Arg.
25 F4 Blanca Peak summit U.S.A.
114 C2 Blanche, L. salt flat Austr.
32 D4 Blanchester U.S.A.
114 C5 Blanchetown Austr.
64 H4 Blanc, Mont mt France/Italy
47 C1 Blanco r. Arg.
42 F2 Blanco r. Bol.
24 A3 Blanco, C. c. U.S.A.
23 J3 Blanc-Sablon Can.
115 G2 Bland r. Austr.
54 C4 Blanda r. Iceland
59 E7 Blandford Forum U.K.
35 H3 Blanding U.S.A.
65 H2 Blanes Spain
30 E2 Blaney Park U.S.A.
95 A5 Blangkejeren Indon.
61 B3 Blankenberge Belgium
61 E4 Blankenheim Ger.
45 D2 Blanquilla, Isla i. Venez.
62 H6 Blansko Czech Rep.
103 D5 Blantyre Malawi
60 D5 Blarney Rep. of Ireland
54 Q4 Blåviksjön Sweden
115 H4 Blayney Austr.
117 D4 Blenheim N.Z.
60 E4 Blessington Lakes lakes Rep. of Ireland
59 G5 Bletchley U.K.
61 F5 Blies r. Ger.
111 H3 Bligh Water b. Fiji
31 F2 Blind River Can.
114 C3 Blinman Austr.
24 D3 Bliss U.S.A.
31 F5 Blissfield U.S.A.
33 H4 Block I. i. U.S.A.
33 H4 Block Island Sound chan. U.S.A.
105 G3 Bloemfontein S. Africa
105 F3 Bloemhof S. Africa
105 F3 Bloemhof Dam dam S. Africa
54 C4 Blönduós Iceland
33 E5 Bloodsworth I. i. U.S.A.
21 K4 Bloodvein r. Can.
60 C2 Bloody Foreland pt Rep. of Ireland
31 J4 Bloomfield Can.
30 A5 Bloomfield IA U.S.A.
30 B3 Bloomfield IN U.S.A.
25 E4 Bloomfield NM U.S.A.
30 C5 Bloomington IL U.S.A.
30 D5 Bloomington IN U.S.A.
26 E2 Bloomington MN U.S.A.
33 E4 Bloomsburg U.S.A.
116 C3 Bloomsbury Austr.
92 □ Blora Indon.

32 E4 Blossburg U.S.A.
105 H1 Blouberg S. Africa
59 F5 Bloxham U.K.
35 H5 Blue r. U.S.A.
35 G1 Bluebell U.S.A.
35 G2 Blue Bell Knoll summit U.S.A.
26 E3 Blue Earth U.S.A.
32 C6 Bluefield U.S.A.
37 H6 Bluefields Nic.
33 J2 Blue Hill U.S.A.
31 H5 Blue Knob h. U.S.A.
85 H5 Blue Mountain mt India
35 H1 Blue Mountain U.S.A.
33 F3 Blue Mountain Lake U.S.A.
105 G4 Blue Mountain Pass pass Lesotho
115 J4 Blue Mountains mts N.S.W. Austr.
24 C2 Blue Mountains mts U.S.A.
115 J4 Blue Mountains Nat. Park nat. park Austr.
78 C7 Blue Nile r. Eth./Sudan
29 C5 Blue Ridge U.S.A.
32 D6 Blue Ridge mts U.S.A.
20 F4 Blue River Can.
34 D2 Blue Springs U.S.A.
60 C3 Blue Stack mt Rep. of Ireland
60 C3 Blue Stack Mts h. Rep. of Ireland
32 C6 Bluestone Lake l. U.S.A.
116 C4 Bluff Austr.
117 B7 Bluff N.Z.
35 H3 Bluff U.S.A.
89 □ Bluff I. i. Hong Kong China
29 E7 Bluff, The Bahamas
30 E5 Bluffton IN U.S.A.
32 B4 Bluffton OH U.S.A.
44 G3 Blumenau Brazil
26 C2 Blunt U.S.A.
24 B3 Bly U.S.A.
114 C4 Blyth Austr.
58 F2 Blyth Eng. U.K.
59 F4 Blyth Eng. U.K.
35 E5 Blythe U.S.A.
27 F5 Blytheville U.S.A.
55 L7 Bø Norway
100 A4 Bo Sierra Leone
94 B3 Boac Phil.
43 K5 Boa Esperança, Açude resr Brazil
88 D3 Bo'ai Henan China
89 C6 Bo'ai Yunnan China
102 B3 Boali C.A.R.
105 K3 Boane Moz.
32 C4 Boardman U.S.A.
105 F1 Boatlaname Botswana
115 G1 Boatman Austr.
43 L5 Boa Viagem Brazil
45 A4 Boa Vista Brazil
100 □ Boa Vista i. Cape Verde
115 G4 Boadah Austr.
89 D6 Bobai China
103 E5 Bobaomby, Tanjona c. Madag.
83 F7 Bobbili India
100 B3 Bobo-Dioulasso Burkina
103 C6 Bobonong Botswana
69 G5 Bobrov Rus. Fed.
69 D5 Bobrovytsya Ukr.
69 E5 Bobrynets' Ukr.
103 E6 Boby mt Madag.
45 E2 Boca Araguao est. Venez.
45 D2 Boca do Pao Venez.
42 E2 Boca do Acre Brazil
43 H4 Boca do Jari Brazil
45 E2 Boca Grande est. Venez.
46 D2 Bocaiúva Brazil
45 C2 Bocaranga C.A.R.
102 B3 Bocaranga C.A.R.
29 D7 Boca Raton U.S.A.
37 H7 Bocas del Toro Panama
63 K6 Bochnia Pol.
62 C5 Bocholt Ger.
62 C5 Bochum Ger.
105 H1 Bochum S. Africa
45 C2 Boconó Venez.
102 B3 Boda C.A.R.
115 J6 Bodalla Austr.
77 N4 Bodaybo Rus. Fed.
27 E5 Bodcau Lake l. U.S.A.
57 G3 Boddam U.K.
34 A2 Bodega Head hd U.S.A.
101 D3 Bodélé reg. Chad
54 R4 Boden Sweden
59 E5 Bodenham Austr.
Bodensee l. see Constance, Lake
59 C7 Bodmin U.K.
59 C7 Bodmin Moor reg. U.K.
54 O3 Bodø Norway
67 M6 Bodrum Turkey
61 C5 Boechout Belgium
102 C4 Boende Zaire
100 A3 Boffa Guinea
85 H3 Boga India
27 F6 Bogalusa U.S.A.
115 G3 Bogan r. Austr.
100 B3 Bogandé Burkina
115 G4 Bogan Gate Austr.
116 B4 Bogantungan Austr.
68 J3 Bogatye Saby Rus. Fed.
80 E2 Bogazlıyan Turkey
85 F3 Bogcang Zangbo r. China
82 B2 Bogda Shan mts China
115 J2 Boggabilla Austr.
115 J3 Boggabri Austr.
60 B5 Boggeragh Mts h. Rep. of Ireland
65 H5 Boghar Alg.

116 B3 Bogie r. Austr.
59 G7 Bognor Regis U.K.
94 C4 Bogo Phil.
60 D4 Bog of Allen reg. Rep. of Ireland
68 G2 Bogolyubovo Rus. Fed.
115 G6 Bogong, Mt mt Austr.
92 □ Bogor Indon.
68 G3 Bogorodsk Rus. Fed.
68 J3 Bogorodskoye Rus. Fed.
45 B3 Bogotá Col.
85 G4 Bogra Bangl.
88 F2 Bo Hai g. China
88 D2 Bohai Haixia chan. China
64 F2 Bohain-en-Vermandois France
88 E2 Bohai Wan b. China
52 Bohemian Forest mts Czech Rep/Ger.
105 H4 Bohlokong S. Africa
62 F6 Böhmer Wald mts Ger.
69 E5 Bohodukhiv Ukr.
94 C4 Bohol i. Phil.
94 C4 Bohol Sea sea Phil.
94 B4 Bohol Str. chan. Phil.
82 B3 Bohu China
33 J2 Boiceville U.S.A.
104 E4 Boichoko S. Africa
105 G3 Boikhutso S. Africa
43 G4 Boim Brazil
85 H5 Boinu r. Myanmar
46 E1 Boipeba, Ilha i. Brazil
46 E1 Boi, Ponta do pt Brazil
46 C2 Bois r. Brazil
31 E3 Bois Blanc I. i. U.S.A.
61 C4 Bois de Chimay woodland Belgium
24 C3 Boise U.S.A.
27 C4 Boise City U.S.A.
21 J5 Boissevain Can.
105 H3 Boitumelong S. Africa
94 B2 Bojeador, Cape c. Phil.
79 H2 Bojnūrd Iran
92 □ Bojonegoro Indon.
85 G1 Bokadaban Feng mt China
85 H4 Bokajan India
85 F5 Bokaro India
102 B3 Bokatola Zaire
100 A3 Boké Guinea
102 C4 Bokele Zaire
115 G2 Bokhara r. Austr.
55 J7 Boknafjorden chan. Norway
101 D3 Bokoro Chad
69 G5 Bokovskaya Rus. Fed.
68 E3 Boksitogorsk Rus. Fed.
103 C6 Bokspits Botswana
102 C4 Bolaiti Zaire
100 A3 Bolama Guinea-Bissau
84 A3 Bolan r. Pak.
84 A3 Bolan Pass pass Pak.
64 F2 Bolbec France
82 F2 Bole China
100 B4 Bole Ghana
102 B4 Boleko Zaire
100 B3 Bolgatanga Ghana
69 D6 Bolhrad Ukr.
102 B4 Bolia Zaire
54 R4 Boliden Sweden
94 A2 Bolinao Phil.
67 L2 Bolintin-Vale Romania
45 A3 Bolívar Col.
42 C5 Bolívar Peru
27 F4 Bolívar MO U.S.A.
29 B5 Bolívar TN U.S.A.
38 Bolivia country S. America
80 E3 Bolkar Dağları mts Turkey
68 F4 Bolkhov Rus. Fed.
31 H1 Bolkow Can.
64 G4 Bollène France
55 P6 Bollnäs Sweden
115 G2 Bollon Austr.
54 P5 Bollstabruk Sweden
55 N8 Bolmen l. Sweden
69 H7 Bolnisi Georgia
102 B4 Bolobo Zaire
94 B5 Bolod Islands is Phil.
66 D2 Bologna Italy
63 F2 Bologovo Rus. Fed.
68 E3 Bologoye Rus. Fed.
105 H4 Bolokanang S. Africa
102 B3 Bolomba Zaire
94 B5 Bolong Phil.
76 K4 Bolotnoye Rus. Fed.
95 C2 Bolovens, Plateau des plat. Laos
85 F5 Bolpur India
66 D3 Bolsena, Lago di l. Italy
63 K3 Bol'shakovo Rus. Fed.
54 X3 Bol'shaya Imandra, Oz. l. Rus. Fed.
69 G6 Bol'shaya Martinovka Rus. Fed.
77 M2 Bol'shevik, O. i. Rus. Fed.
68 H2 Bol'shiye Chirki Rus. Fed.
77 S3 Bol'shoy Aluy r. Rus. Fed.
Bol'shoy Kavkaz mts see Caucasus
69 J5 Bol'shoy Uzen' r.
36 D3 Bolson de Mapimí des. Mex.
58 E4 Bolton U.K.
32 B6 Bolton U.S.A.
80 C1 Bolu Turkey
54 X3 Bolungarvík Iceland
89 E6 Boluo China

80 C2 Bolvadin Turkey
66 D1 Bolzano Italy
102 B4 Boma Zaire
115 J5 Bomaderry Austr.
115 H6 Bombala Austr.
83 D7 Bombay India
93 J7 Bomberai Peninsula *pen.* Indon.
42 E5 Bom Comércio Brazil
46 D2 Bom Despacho Brazil
85 H4 Bomdila India
85 H3 Bomi China
46 D1 Bom Jesus da Lapa Brazil
46 E3 Bom Jesus do Itabapoana Brazil
55 J7 Bømlo *i.* Norway
81 L3 Bonāb Iran
32 E6 Bon Air U.S.A.
37 L6 Bonaire *i.* Neth. Ant.
37 H6 Bonanza Nic.
112 D2 Bonaparte Archipelago *is* Austr.
57 D3 Bonar Bridge U.K.
23 K4 Bonavista Can.
23 K4 Bonavista Bay *b.* Can.
114 A3 Bon Bon Austr.
101 D1 Bon, Cap *c.* Tunisia
57 F5 Bonchester Bridge U.K.
102 C3 Bondo Zaire
94 B3 Bondoc Peninsula *pen.* Phil.
100 B4 Bondoukou Côte d'Ivoire
92 □ Bondowoso Indon.
30 A3 Bone Lake *l.* U.S.A.
93 G8 Bonerate, Kepulauan *is* Indon.
57 E4 Bo'ness U.K.
44 C3 Bonete, Cerro *mt* Arg.
93 G7 Bone, Teluk *b.* Indon.
46 D2 Bonfinópolis de Minas Brazil
102 D3 Bonga Eth.
94 B3 Bongabong Phil.
85 G4 Bongaigaon India
102 C3 Bongandanga Zaire
104 E4 Bongani S. Africa
94 A5 Bongao Phil.
85 G3 Bong Co *l.* China
94 C5 Bongo *i.* Phil.
103 E5 Bongolava *mts* Madag.
102 C3 Bongo, Massif des *mts* C.A.R.
101 D3 Bongor Chad
100 B4 Bongouanou Côte d'Ivoire
95 D2 Bông Sơn Vietnam
61 C3 Bonheiden Belgium
66 C4 Bonifacio *Corsica* France
66 C4 Bonifacio, Strait of *str.* France/Italy
46 A3 Bonito Brazil
62 C5 Bonn Ger.
54 O3 Bonnåsjøen Norway
24 C1 Bonners Ferry U.S.A.
64 H3 Bonneville France
114 D6 Bonney, L. *l.* Austr.
112 C6 Bonnie Rock Austr.
57 E5 Bonnyrigg U.K.
21 G4 Bonnyville Can.
94 A4 Bonobono Phil.
90 C8 Bōno-misaki *pt* Japan
95 C3 Bonom Mhai *mt* Vietnam
66 C4 Bonorva *Sardinia* Italy
115 J2 Bonshaw Austr.
104 D7 Bontebok National Park *nat. park* S. Africa
100 A4 Bonthe Sierra Leone
94 B2 Bontoc Phil.
93 F8 Bontosunggu Indon.
105 F6 Bontrug S. Africa
105 G1 Bonwapitse Botswana
35 H2 Book Cliffs *cliff* U.S.A.
114 E4 Boolaboolka L. *l.* Austr.
114 C4 Booleroo Centre Austr.
60 D5 Booley Hills *h.* Rep. of Ireland
114 F4 Booligal Austr.
115 H2 Boomi Austr.
115 K1 Boonah Austr.
26 E3 Boone *IA* U.S.A.
29 D4 Boone *NC* U.S.A.
32 B6 Boone Lake *l.* U.S.A.
32 B6 Booneville *KY* U.S.A.
27 F5 Booneville *MS* U.S.A.
34 A2 Boonville *CA* U.S.A.
28 C4 Boonville *IN* U.S.A.
26 E4 Boonville *MO* U.S.A.
33 F3 Boonville *NY* U.S.A.
114 F5 Booroorban Austr.
115 H5 Boorowa Austr.
114 E6 Boort Austr.
102 E2 Boosaaso Somalia
33 J3 Boothbay Harbor U.S.A.
18 Boothia, Gulf of *gulf* Can.
18 Boothia Peninsula *pen.* Can.
59 E4 Bootle U.K.
100 A4 Bopolu Liberia
61 F4 Boppard Ger.
47 G1 Boqueirão Brazil
101 F4 Bor Sudan
80 E3 Bor Turkey
67 K2 Bor Yugo.
24 D2 Borah Peak *summit* U.S.A.
55 N8 Borås Sweden
79 G4 Borāzjān Iran
43 G4 Borba Brazil
43 L5 Borborema, Planalto da *plat.* Brazil
81 H1 Borçka Turkey
80 B3 Bor D. *mt* Turkey
114 B5 Borda, C. *pt* Austr.
64 D4 Bordeaux France
23 H4 Borden *P.E.I.* Can.
18 Borden I. *i.* Can.
114 D6 Bordertown Austr.
54 C4 Borðeyri Iceland
65 J4 Bordj Bou Arréridj Alg.
65 G5 Bordj Bounaama Alg.
100 C2 Bordj Omer Driss Alg.
54 □ Borðoy *i.* Faroe Is
57 A3 Boreray *i.* U.K.
54 G4 Borgarfjörður Iceland
54 C4 Borgarnes Iceland
54 N4 Børgefjell Nasjonalpark *nat. park* Norway
27 C5 Borger U.S.A.
55 P8 Borgholm Sweden
66 B2 Borgo San Dalmazzo Italy
66 D3 Borgo San Lorenzo Italy
66 C2 Borgosesia Italy
61 B4 Borinage *reg.* Belgium
69 G5 Borisoglebsk Rus. Fed.
69 F5 Borisovka Rus. Fed.
68 F3 Borisovo-Sudskoye Rus. Fed.
69 G7 Borjomi Georgia
61 E3 Borken Ger.
54 P2 Borkenes Norway
61 E1 Borkum Ger.
61 E1 Borkum *i.* Ger.
55 O6 Borlänge Sweden
80 B2 Borlu Turkey
61 D1 Borndiep *chan.* Neth.
92 E6 Borneo *i.* Asia
55 O9 Bornholm *i.* Denmark
67 M5 Bornova Turkey
94 B4 Borocay *i.* Phil.
76 K3 Borodino Rus. Fed.
55 V6 Borodinskoye Rus. Fed.
69 D5 Borodyanka Ukr.
77 P3 Borogontsy Rus. Fed.
68 F3 Borok Rus. Fed.
100 B3 Boromo Burkina
94 C4 Borongan Phil.
116 D5 Bororen Austr.
58 F3 Boroughbridge U.K.
68 E3 Borovichi Rus. Fed.
68 J3 Borovoy *Kirovsk.* Rus. Fed.
68 K2 Borovoy *Komi* Rus. Fed.
68 E1 Borovoy *Korel.* Rus. Fed.
60 C5 Borrisokane Rep. of Ireland
113 G3 Borroloola Austr.
54 M5 Børsa Norway
63 M7 Borşa Romania
69 C5 Borshchiv Ukr.
87 K1 Borshchovochnyy Khrebet *mts* Rus. Fed.
81 M5 Borūjerd Iran
57 B3 Borve U.K.
69 B5 Boryslav Ukr.
69 D5 Boryspil' Ukr.
69 E5 Borzna Ukr.
87 L1 Borzya Rus. Fed.
66 G2 Bosanska Dubica Bos.-Herz.
66 G2 Bosanska Gradiška Bos.-Herz.
66 G2 Bosanska Krupa Bos.-Herz.
66 G2 Bosanski Novi Bos.-Herz.
66 G2 Bosansko Grahovo Bos.-Herz.
30 B4 Boscobel U.S.A.
89 C6 Bose China
105 F4 Boshof S. Africa
48 Bosnia-Herzegovina *country* Europe
102 B3 Bosobolo Zaire
91 H6 Bōsō-hantō *pen.* Japan
80 B1 Bosporus *str.* Turkey
102 B3 Bossangoa C.A.R.
102 B3 Bossembélé C.A.R.
27 E5 Bossier City U.S.A.
104 B2 Bossiesvlei Namibia
85 F1 Bostan China
81 L6 Bostan Iran
82 G2 Bosten Hu *l.* China
59 G5 Boston U.K.
33 H3 Boston U.S.A.
114 A5 Boston B. *b.* Austr.
31 H1 Boston Creek Can.
33 H3 Boston-Logan International *airport* U.S.A.
27 E5 Boston Mts *mts* U.S.A.
58 F4 Boston Spa U.K.
30 D5 Boswell U.S.A.
84 B5 Botad India
115 J4 Botany Bay *b.* Austr.
54 P5 Boteå Sweden
67 L3 Botev *mt* Bulg.
67 K3 Botevgrad Bulg.
105 G3 Bothaville S. Africa
52 Bothnia, Gulf of *g.* Fin./Sweden
115 G9 Bothwell Austr.
69 H5 Botkul', Ozero *l.* Kazak./Rus. Fed.
63 N7 Botoșani Romania
88 E2 Botou China
95 C1 Bô Trach Vietnam
105 G4 Botshabelo S. Africa
96 Botswana *country* Africa
66 G5 Botte Donato, Monte *mt* Italy
54 S4 Bottenviken *g.* Fin./Sweden
58 G4 Bottesford U.K.
26 C1 Bottineau U.S.A.
62 C5 Bottrop Ger.
46 C3 Botucatu Brazil
46 D1 Botuporã Brazil
23 K4 Botwood Can.
100 B4 Bouaflé Côte d'Ivoire
100 B4 Bouaké Côte d'Ivoire
102 B3 Bouar C.A.R.
100 B1 Bouârfa Morocco
101 D4 Bouba Ndjida, Parc National de *nat. park* Cameroon
102 B3 Bouca C.A.R.
47 D2 Bouchard, H. Arg.
33 G2 Boucherville Can.
31 K2 Bouchette Can.
100 B3 Boucle du Baoulé, Parc National de la *nat. park* Mali
23 H4 Bouctouche Can.
111 F2 Bougainville Island *i.* P.N.G.
100 B3 Bougouni Mali
61 D5 Bouillon Belgium
65 H4 Bouira Alg.
100 A2 Boujdour Western Sahara
24 F3 Boulder *CO* U.S.A.
24 D2 Boulder *MT* U.S.A.
35 G3 Boulder *UT* U.S.A.
35 E5 Boulder Canyon U.S.A.
35 E4 Boulder City U.S.A.
34 D5 Boulevard U.S.A.
47 E3 Boulevard Atlántico Arg.
113 G4 Boulia Austr.
64 F2 Boulogne-Billancourt France
64 E1 Boulogne-sur-Mer France
100 B3 Boulsa Burkina
102 B4 Boumango Gabon
101 D4 Boumba *r.* Cameroon
65 H4 Boumerdes Alg.
100 B4 Bouna Côte d'Ivoire
33 H2 Boundary Mountains *mts* U.S.A.
34 C3 Boundary Peak *summit* U.S.A.
100 B4 Boundiali Côte d'Ivoire
102 B4 Boundji Congo
95 D1 Boung *r.* Vietnam
89 A6 Boun Nua Laos
24 E3 Bountiful U.S.A.
111 H6 Bounty Islands *is* N.Z.
100 B3 Bourem Mali
64 E4 Bourganeuf France
64 G3 Bourg-en-Bresse France
64 F3 Bourges France
22 F4 Bourget Can.
31 K1 Bourgmont Can.
64 G3 Bourgogne *reg.* France
115 F3 Bourke Austr.
31 G1 Bourkes Can.
59 G5 Bourne U.K.
59 F7 Bournemouth U.K.
61 F2 Bourtanger Moor *reg.* Ger.
100 C1 Bou Saâda Alg.
66 C6 Bou Salem Tunisia
35 E5 Bouse U.S.A.
35 E5 Bouse Wash *r.* U.S.A.
101 D3 Bousso Chad
100 A3 Boutilimit Maur.
12 K9 Bouvetøya *i.* Atlantic Ocean
61 E5 Bouzonville France
47 E1 Bovril Arg.
21 G4 Bow *r.* Can.
26 C1 Bowbells U.S.A.
116 C3 Bowen Austr.
116 B3 Bowen *r.* Austr.
30 B5 Bowen U.S.A.
115 H6 Bowen, Mt *mt* Austr.
115 J1 Bowenville Austr.
116 A3 Bowie Austr.
35 H5 Bowie *AZ* U.S.A.
27 D5 Bowie *TX* U.S.A.
21 G5 Bow Island Can.
81 L3 Bowkan Iran
32 C4 Bowling Green *KY* U.S.A.
26 F4 Bowling Green *MO* U.S.A.
32 B4 Bowling Green *OH* U.S.A.
32 E5 Bowling Green *VA* U.S.A.
116 B2 Bowling Green B. *b.* Austr.
116 B2 Bowling Green, C. *pt* Austr.
26 C2 Bowman U.S.A.
119 C6 Bowman I. *i.* Ant.
24 E4 Bowman, Mt *mt.* Can.
31 H4 Bowmanville Can.
57 B5 Bowmore U.K.
115 J5 Bowral Austr.
115 K3 Bowraville Austr.
20 E4 Bowron *r.* Can.
20 E4 Bowron Lake Provincial Park *res.* Can.
88 E3 Bo Xian China
88 F2 Boxing China
61 D3 Boxtel Neth.
80 E1 Boyabat Turkey
89 E4 Boyang China
115 K3 Boyd *r.* Austr.
21 J2 Boyd Lake *l.* Can.
20 G4 Boyle Can.
60 C4 Boyle Rep. of Ireland
116 D5 Boyne *r.* *Qld.* Austr.
116 D5 Boyne *r.* *Qld.* Austr.
60 E4 Boyne *r.* Rep. of Ireland
84 A1 Boyni Qara Afgh.
29 D7 Boynton Beach U.S.A.
23 E3 Boysen Res. *resr* U.S.A.
42 F8 Boyuibe Bol.
81 K1 Böyük Hinaldağ *mt.* Azer.
67 M5 Bozcaada *i.* Turkey
67 M5 Bozdağ *mt.* Turkey
80 A2 Boz Dağları *mts* Turkey
80 B3 Bozdoğan Turkey
59 G5 Bozeat U.K.
24 E2 Bozeman U.S.A.
80 D3 Bozkır Turkey
102 B3 Bozoum C.A.R.
80 G3 Bozova Turkey
81 L3 Bozqūsh, Kūh-e *mts* Iran
80 C2 Bozüyük Turkey
66 B2 Bra Italy
66 G3 Brač *i.* Croatia
57 B3 Bracadale U.K.
57 B3 Bracadale, Loch *b.* U.K.
66 E3 Bracciano, Lago di *l.* Italy
31 H3 Bracebridge Can.
54 O5 Bracke Sweden
59 G6 Bracknell U.K.
66 G4 Bradano *r.* Italy
29 D7 Bradenton U.S.A.
31 H3 Bradford Can.
58 F4 Bradford U.K.
32 A4 Bradford *OH* U.S.A.
32 D4 Bradford *PA* U.S.A.
33 G3 Bradford *VT* U.S.A.
27 D6 Brady U.S.A.
20 B3 Brady Gl. *gl.* U.S.A.
57 □ Brae U.K.
114 C4 Braemar Austr.
57 E3 Braemar U.K.
65 B2 Braga Port.
47 E2 Bragado Arg.
43 J4 Bragança Brazil
65 C2 Bragança Port.
46 C3 Bragança Paulista Brazil
69 D5 Brahin Belarus
85 G5 Brahmanbaria Bangl.
85 F5 Brahmani *r.* India
83 F7 Brahmapur India
85 G4 Brahmaputra *r.* Asia
67 M2 Brăila Romania
26 E2 Brainerd U.S.A.
59 H6 Braintree U.K.
105 H1 Brak *r.* S. Africa
103 B6 Brakwater Namibia
20 E4 Bralorne Can.
55 L9 Bramming Denmark
55 P5 Brämön *i.* Sweden
31 H4 Brampton Can.
58 E3 Brampton *Eng.* U.K.
59 J5 Brampton *Eng.* U.K.
59 H5 Brancaster U.K.
23 K4 Branch Can.
45 E4 Branco *r.* Brazil
55 M6 Brandbu Norway
55 L9 Brande Denmark
62 F4 Brandenburg Ger.
105 G4 Brandfort S. Africa
116 B2 Brandon Austr.
21 K5 Brandon Can.
59 H5 Brandon U.K.
26 D3 Brandon *SD* U.S.A.
33 G3 Brandon *VT* U.S.A.
60 A5 Brandon Head *hd* Rep. of Ireland
60 E5 Brandon Hill *h.* Rep. of Ireland
60 A5 Brandon Mountain *mt.* Rep. of Ireland
104 D5 Brandvlei S. Africa
29 D6 Branford U.S.A.
63 J3 Braniewo Pol.
119 B2 Bransfield Str. *str.* Ant.
31 G4 Brantford Can.
114 D6 Branxholme Austr.
23 H4 Bras d'Or L. *l.* Can.
42 E6 Brasileia Brazil
46 C1 Brasília Brazil
46 D2 Brasília de Minas Brazil
43 G4 Brasília Legal Brazil
40 Brasil, Planalto do *plat.* Brazil
63 N3 Braslaw Belarus
67 L2 Brașov Romania
94 A5 Brassey Range *mts* Malaysia
33 J2 Brassua Lake *l.* U.S.A.
62 H6 Bratislava Slovakia
77 M4 Bratsk Rus. Fed.
33 G3 Brattleboro U.S.A.
62 F6 Braunau am Inn Austria
62 E4 Braunschweig Ger.
100 □ Brava *i.* Cape Verde
55 P7 Bråviken *in.* Sweden
36 E3 Bravo del Norte, Río *r.* Mex./U.S.A.
35 E5 Brawley U.S.A.
60 E4 Bray Rep. of Ireland
20 F4 Brazeau Can.
20 F4 Brazeau *r.* Can.
38 Brazil *country* S. America
12 H7 Brazil Basin *sea feature* Atlantic Ocean
27 D5 Brazos *r.* U.S.A.
102 B4 Brazzaville Congo
67 H2 Brčko Bos.-Herz.
117 A6 Breaksea Sd *in.* N.Z.
117 E1 Bream Bay *b.* N.Z.
117 E1 Bream Head *hd* N.Z.
92 □ Brebes Indon.
59 C6 Brechfa U.K.
57 F4 Brechin U.K.
61 C3 Brecht Belgium
26 D2 Breckenridge *MN* U.S.A.
27 D5 Breckenridge *TX* U.S.A.
62 H6 Břeclav Czech Rep.
59 D6 Brecon U.K.
59 D6 Brecon Beacons *h.* U.K.
59 D6 Brecon Beacons National Park U.K.
61 C3 Breda Neth.
104 D7 Bredasdorp S. Africa
115 H5 Bredbo Austr.
54 O3 Bredviken Norway
32 D5 Breezewood U.S.A.
62 D7 Bregenz Austria
54 B4 Breiðafjörður *b.* Iceland
54 F4 Breiðdalsvík Iceland
62 C6 Breisach am Rhein Ger.
54 S1 Breivikbotn Norway
43 J6 Brejinho de Nazaré Brazil
54 L5 Brekstad Norway
62 D4 Bremen Ger.
29 C5 Bremen *GA* U.S.A.
30 D5 Bremen *IN* U.S.A.
62 D4 Bremerhaven Ger.
24 B2 Bremerton U.S.A.
27 D6 Brenham U.S.A.
54 N4 Brenna Norway
62 E7 Brenner Pass *pass* Austria/Italy
31 H2 Brent Can.
66 D2 Brenta *r.* Italy
59 H6 Brentwood U.K.
34 B3 Brentwood *CA* U.S.A.
33 G4 Brentwood *NY* U.S.A.
66 D2 Brescia Italy
66 D1 Bressanone Italy
57 □ Bressay *i.* U.K.
64 D3 Bressuire France
69 B4 Brest Belarus
64 B2 Brest France
64 C2 Bretagne *reg.* France
27 F6 Breton Sound *b.* U.S.A.
117 E1 Brett, Cape *c.* N.Z.
59 E4 Bretton U.K.
29 D5 Brevard U.S.A.
43 H4 Breves Brazil
30 E2 Brevort U.S.A.
115 G2 Brewarrina Austr.
33 J2 Brewer U.S.A.
24 C1 Brewster U.S.A.
27 G6 Brewton U.S.A.
105 H3 Breyten S. Africa
Brezhnev *see* Naberezhnyye Chelny
63 J6 Brezno Slovakia
66 G2 Brezovo Polje *h.* Croatia
102 C3 Bria C.A.R.
64 H4 Briançon France
115 G5 Bribbaree Austr.
115 K1 Bribie I. *i.* Austr.
69 C5 Briceni Moldova
64 H4 Bric Froid *mt.* France/Italy
60 C5 Bride *r.* Rep. of Ireland
35 G1 Bridgeland U.S.A.
59 D6 Bridgend U.K.
57 D4 Bridge of Orchy U.K.
34 C2 Bridgeport *CA* U.S.A.
33 G4 Bridgeport *CT* U.S.A.
26 C3 Bridgeport *NE* U.S.A.
24 E2 Bridger U.S.A.
24 F3 Bridger Peak *summit* U.S.A.
33 F5 Bridgeton U.S.A.
112 C6 Bridgetown Austr.
37 N6 Bridgetown Barbados
115 G9 Bridgewater Austr.
23 H5 Bridgewater Can.
33 K1 Bridgewater U.S.A.
114 D7 Bridgewater, C. *hd* Austr.
59 E5 Bridgnorth U.K.
33 H2 Bridgton U.S.A.
59 D6 Bridgwater U.K.
59 D6 Bridgwater Bay *b.* U.K.
58 G3 Bridlington U.K.
58 G3 Bridlington Bay *b.* U.K.
115 G8 Bridport Austr.
59 E7 Bridport U.K.
62 C7 Brig Switz.
58 G4 Brigg U.K.
24 D3 Brigham City U.S.A.
115 G6 Bright Austr.
59 J6 Brightlingsea U.K.
31 J3 Brighton Can.
117 C6 Brighton N.Z.
59 G7 Brighton U.K.
31 F4 Brighton U.S.A.
64 H5 Brignoles France
100 A3 Brikama The Gambia
66 G4 Brindisi Italy
47 D1 Brinkmann Arg.
114 C4 Brinkworth Austr.
23 H4 Brion, Île *i.* Can.
64 F4 Brioude France
23 F3 Brisay Can.
115 K1 Brisbane Austr.
33 K1 Bristol Can.
59 E6 Bristol U.K.
33 G4 Bristol *CT* U.S.A.
33 F4 Bristol *PA* U.S.A.
32 B6 Bristol *TN* U.S.A.
16 Bristol Bay U.S.A.
59 C6 Bristol Channel *est.* U.K.
119 C1 Bristol I. *i.* *S. Sandwich Is* Atlantic Ocean
35 E4 Bristol Lake *l.* U.S.A.
20 D3 British Columbia *div.* Can.
105 G2 Brits S. Africa
104 E5 Britstown S. Africa
64 E4 Brive-la-Gaillarde France
65 E1 Briviesca Spain
59 D7 Brixham U.K.
82 D2 Brlik Kazak.
62 H6 Brno Czech Rep.
29 D5 Broad *r.* U.S.A.
33 F3 Broadalbin U.S.A.
22 E3 Broadback *r.* Can.
114 F6 Broadford Austr.
60 C5 Broadford Rep. of Ireland
57 C3 Broadford U.K.
57 E5 Broad Law *h.* U.K.
116 C4 Broad Sound *chan.* Austr.
116 D4 Broad Sound Channel *chan.* Austr.
116 C4 Broadsound Ra. *h.* Austr.
59 J6 Broadstairs U.K.
24 F2 Broadus U.S.A.
21 J4 Broadview Can.
115 K2 Broadwater Austr.
26 C3 Broadwater U.S.A.
117 D1 Broadwood N.Z.
55 S8 Brocēni Latvia
21 J3 Brochet Can.
21 J3 Brochet, Lac *l.* Can.
32 E3 Brockport U.S.A.
33 H3 Brockton U.S.A.
31 K3 Brockville Can.
31 F4 Brockway *MI* U.S.A.
32 D4 Brockway *PA* U.S.A.
30 C4 Brodhead U.S.A.
57 C5 Brodick U.K.
63 J4 Brodnica Pol.
69 C5 Brody Ukr.
27 E4 Broken Arrow U.S.A.
115 J4 Broken B. *b.* Austr.
26 D3 Broken Bow *NE* U.S.A.
27 E5 Broken Bow *OK* U.S.A.
114 D3 Broken Hill Austr.
59 G6 Bromley U.K.
59 E5 Bromsgrove U.K.
55 L8 Brønderslev Denmark
105 H2 Bronkhorstspruit S. Africa
54 N4 Brønnøysund Norway
30 E5 Bronson U.S.A.
59 J5 Brooke U.K.
94 A4 Brooke's Point Phil.
30 C4 Brookfield U.S.A.
27 F6 Brookhaven U.S.A.
24 A3 Brookings *OR* U.S.A.
26 D2 Brookings *SD* U.S.A.
33 H3 Brookline U.S.A.
30 A5 Brooklyn *IA* U.S.A.
30 B5 Brooklyn *IL* U.S.A.
26 E2 Brooklyn Center U.S.A.
32 D6 Brookneal U.S.A.
21 G4 Brooks Can.
34 A2 Brooks *CA* U.S.A.
33 J2 Brooks *ME* U.S.A.
119 B3 Brooks, C. *c.* Ant.
18 Brooks Range *mts* U.S.A.
29 D6 Brooksville U.S.A.
112 C6 Brookton Austr.
32 D4 Brookville U.S.A.
116 E6 Brooloo Austr.
112 D3 Broome Austr.
57 C3 Broom, Loch *in.* U.K.
57 E2 Brora U.K.
55 O9 Brösarp Sweden
60 D4 Brosna *r.* Rep. of Ireland
33 F3 Brothers U.S.A.
89 □ Brothers, The *is* *Hong Kong* China
58 E3 Brough U.K.
57 E1 Brough Head *hd* U.K.
60 E3 Broughshane U.K.
114 C4 Broughton *r.* Austr.
115 K4 Broughton Is *is* Austr.
63 P5 Brovary Ukr.
55 L8 Brovst Denmark
116 A1 Brown Cr. *r.* Austr.
27 C5 Brownfield U.S.A.
24 D1 Browning U.S.A.
114 C4 Brown, Mt *mt.* Austr.
30 D6 Brownsburg U.S.A.
33 F5 Browns Mills U.S.A.
29 B5 Brownsville *TN* U.S.A.
27 D7 Brownsville *TX* U.S.A.
33 J2 Brownville U.S.A.
33 J2 Brownville Junction U.S.A.
27 D6 Brownwood U.S.A.
63 O4 Brozha Belarus
64 F1 Bruay-en-Artois France
30 C2 Bruce Crossing U.S.A.
112 C4 Bruce, Mt *mt.* Austr.
24 D4 Bruce Pen. *pen.* Can.
31 G3 Bruce Peninsula National Park *nat. park* Can.
62 G7 Bruck an der Mur Austria
59 E6 Brue *r.* U.K.
61 B3 Bruges Belgium
Brugge *see* Bruges
35 G2 Bruin Pt *summit* U.S.A.
85 J3 Bruint India
104 C2 Brukkaros Namibia
30 B2 Brule U.S.A.
46 E1 Brumado Brazil
55 M6 Brumunddal Norway
24 D3 Bruneau U.S.A.
24 D3 Bruneau *r.* U.S.A.
71 □ Brunei *country* Asia
54 O5 Brunflo Sweden
66 D1 Brunico Italy
117 C5 Brunner, L. *l.* N.Z.
21 H4 Bruno Can.
62 D4 Brunsbüttel Ger.
29 D6 Brunswick *GA* U.S.A.
33 J3 Brunswick *ME* U.S.A.
32 C4 Brunswick *OH* U.S.A.
115 K2 Brunswick Head Austr.
44 B8 Brunswick, Península de *pen.* Chile
62 H6 Bruntál Czech Rep.
105 J4 Bruntville S. Africa
115 G9 Bruny I. *i.* Austr.
24 G3 Brush U.S.A.
61 C4 Brussels Belgium
31 G4 Brussels Can.
30 D3 Brussels U.S.A.
63 O5 Brusyliv Ukr.
115 G6 Bruthen Austr.
Bruxelles *see* Brussels
32 A4 Bryan *OH* U.S.A.
27 D6 Bryan *TX* U.S.A.
114 C4 Bryan, Mt *h.* Austr.
68 E4 Bryansk Rus. Fed.
68 E4 Bryanskaya Oblast' *div.* Rus. Fed.
69 H6 Bryanskoye Rus. Fed.
35 F3 Bryce Canyon Nat. Park *nat. park* U.S.A.
35 H5 Bryce Mt *mt.* U.S.A.
55 J7 Bryne Norway
69 F6 Bryukhovetskaya Rus. Fed.

62 H5 Brzeg Pol.
111 F2 Buala Solomon Is
100 A3 Buba Guinea-Bissau
81 M7 Būbiyān I. i. Kuwait
94 B5 Buboan i. Phil.
80 C3 Bucak Turkey
45 B3 Bucaramanga Col.
94 C4 Bucas Grande i. Phil.
116 C3 Bucasia Austr.
115 H6 Buchan Austr.
100 A4 Buchanan Liberia
30 D5 Buchanan MI U.S.A.
32 D6 Buchanan VA U.S.A.
116 A3 Buchanan, L. salt flat Austr.
27 D6 Buchanan, L. l. U.S.A.
23 J4 Buchans Can.
67 M2 Bucharest Romania
34 B4 Buchon, Point pt U.S.A.
63 M7 Bucin, Pasul pass Romania
115 F3 Buckambool Mt h. Austr.
35 F5 Buckeye U.S.A.
32 B5 Buckeye Lake l. U.S.A.
32 C5 Buckhannon r. U.S.A.
32 C5 Buckhannon U.S.A.
57 E4 Buckhaven U.K.
31 H3 Buckhorn Can.
35 H5 Buckhorn U.S.A.
31 H3 Buckhorn Lake l. Can.
32 B6 Buckhorn Lake l. U.S.A.
57 F3 Buckie U.K.
31 K3 Buckingham Can.
59 G5 Buckingham U.K.
32 D6 Buckingham U.S.A.
113 G2 Buckingham Bay b. Austr.
116 B5 Buckland Tableland reg. Austr.
114 B4 Buckleboo Austr.
119 A6 Buckle I. i. Ant.
35 F4 Buckskin Mts mts U.S.A.
34 B2 Bucks Mt mt. U.S.A.
33 J2 Bucksport U.S.A.
Bucureşti see Bucharest
32 B4 Bucyrus U.S.A.
63 P4 Buda-Kashalyova Belarus
63 J7 Budapest Hungary
84 D3 Budaun India
114 F3 Budda Austr.
57 F4 Buddon Ness pt U.K.
66 C4 Buddusò Sardinia Italy
59 C7 Bude U.K.
27 F6 Bude U.S.A.
69 H6 Budennovsk Rus. Fed.
115 K1 Buderim Austr.
84 D5 Budni India
68 E3 Budogoshch' Rus. Fed.
85 H2 Budongquan China
66 C4 Budoni Sardinia Italy
100 C4 Buea Cameroon
34 B4 Buellton U.S.A.
47 D2 Buena Esperanza Arg.
45 A4 Buenaventura Col.
36 C3 Buenaventura Mex.
45 A4 Buenaventure, B. de b. Col.
25 F4 Buena Vista CO U.S.A.
32 D6 Buena Vista VA U.S.A.
65 E2 Buendia, Embalse de resr Spain
47 B4 Bueno r. Chile
47 E3 Buenos Aires div. Arg.
47 E2 Buenos Aires Arg.
44 B7 Buenos Aires, L. l. Arg./Chile
44 C7 Buen Pasto Arg.
20 G3 Buffalo r. Can.
32 D3 Buffalo NY U.S.A.
27 D4 Buffalo OK U.S.A.
26 C2 Buffalo SD U.S.A.
27 D6 Buffalo TX U.S.A.
30 B3 Buffalo WV U.S.A.
24 F2 Buffalo WY U.S.A.
30 B3 Buffalo r. U.S.A.
20 F3 Buffalo Head Hills h. Can.
20 F2 Buffalo Lake l. Can.
115 G6 Buffalo, Mt mt Austr.
21 H3 Buffalo Narrows Can.
104 B4 Buffels watercourse S. Africa
105 G1 Buffels Drift S. Africa
29 D5 Buford U.S.A.
67 L2 Buftea Romania
63 K4 Bug r. Pol.
45 A4 Buga Col.
45 A3 Bugalagrande Col.
115 H3 Bugaldie Austr.
92 □ Bugel, Tanjung pt Indon.
66 G2 Bugojno Bos.-Herz.
94 A4 Bugsuk i. Phil.
94 B2 Buguey Phil.
81 J5 Buḥayrat ath Tharthār l. Iraq
81 K4 Buḥayrat Shārī l. Iraq
103 D5 Buhera Zimbabwe
94 B3 Buhi Phil.
24 D3 Buhl ID U.S.A.
30 A2 Buhl MN U.S.A.
81 J3 Bühtan r. Turkey
63 N7 Buhuşi Romania
59 D5 Builth Wells U.K.
100 B4 Bui National Park nat. park Ghana
68 J4 Buinsk Rus. Fed.
81 L4 Bu'in Soflā Iran
87 L2 Buir Nur l. Mongolia
103 B6 Buitepos Namibia
67 J3 Bujanovac Yugo.
102 C4 Bujumbura Burundi
87 L1 Bukachacha Rus. Fed.
117 F2 Buka I. i. P.N.G.
102 C4 Bukavu Zaire
79 J2 Bukhara Uzbek.
94 C6 Bukide i. Indon.
95 □ Bukit Batok Sing.
95 B5 Bukit Fraser Malaysia
95 □ Bukit Panjang Sing.
95 □ Bukit Timah Sing.
92 C7 Bukittinggi Indon.
102 D4 Bukoba Tanz.
95 □ Bukum, P. i. Sing.
93 J7 Bula Indon.
68 J4 Bula r. Rus. Fed.
62 D7 Bülach Switz.
115 K4 Bulahdelal Austr.
94 B3 Bulan Phil.
80 G1 Bulancak Turkey
84 D3 Bulandshahr India
81 J2 Bulanık Turkey
103 C6 Bulawayo Zimbabwe
80 F3 Bulbul Syria
80 B2 Buldan Turkey
84 D5 Buldana India
105 J2 Bulembu Swaziland
86 H2 Bulgan Hövsgöl Mongolia
88 B1 Bulgan Ömnögovĭ Mongolia
49 Bulgaria country Europe
114 E1 Bullawarra, Lake salt flat Austr.
114 D3 Bullea, Lake salt flat Austr.
117 D4 Buller r. N.Z.
115 G6 Buller, Mt mt Austr.
35 E4 Bullhead City U.S.A.
34 D4 Bullion Mts mts U.S.A.
114 E2 Bulloo watercourse Austr.
114 E2 Bulloo Downs Austr.
114 E2 Bulloo L. salt flat Austr.
104 B2 Büllsport Namibia
95 □ Buloh, P. i. Sing.
114 E5 Buloke, Lake l. Austr.
105 G4 Bultfontein S. Africa
94 C5 Buluan Phil.
93 G8 Bulukumba Indon.
77 O2 Bulun Rus. Fed.
102 B4 Bulungu Bandundu Zaire
102 C4 Bulungu Kasai-Occidental Zaire
94 C3 Bulusan Phil.
102 C3 Bumba Zaire
88 B1 Bumbat Sum China
35 F4 Bumble Bee U.S.A.
94 A5 Bum-Bum i. Malaysia
102 D3 Buna Kenya
102 B4 Buna Zaire
102 D4 Bunazi Tanz.
60 C2 Bunbeg Rep. of Ireland
112 C6 Bunbury Austr.
60 E5 Bunclody Rep. of Ireland
60 D2 Buncrana Rep. of Ireland
102 D4 Bunda Tanz.
116 E5 Bundaberg Austr.
115 G2 Bundaleer Austr.
115 J3 Bundarra Austr.
84 C4 Bundi India
60 C3 Bundoran Rep. of Ireland
85 F5 Bundu India
59 J5 Bungay U.K.
95 B2 Bung Boraphet l. Thai.
115 H5 Bungendore Austr.
116 C6 Bungil Cr. r. Austr.
Bungle Bungle National Park nat. park see Purnululu National Park
90 D7 Bungo-suidō chan. Japan
90 C7 Bungo-takada Japan
102 D3 Bunia Zaire
102 C4 Bunianga Zaire
114 E6 Buninyong Austr.
100 D3 Buni-Yadi Nigeria
84 C2 Bunji Jammu and Kashmir
116 E4 Bunker Group atolls Austr.
35 E3 Bunkerville U.S.A.
27 E6 Bunkie U.S.A.
29 D6 Bunnell U.S.A.
80 E2 Bünyan Turkey
94 A6 Bunyu i. Indon.
95 D2 Buôn Hô Vietnam
95 D2 Buôn Mê Thuôt Vietnam
77 P2 Buorkhaya, Guba b. Rus. Fed.
79 F4 Buqayq S. Arabia
102 D4 Bura Kenya
84 E3 Burang China
46 E2 Buranhaém r. Brazil
102 E3 Burao Somalia
94 C4 Burauen Phil.
78 E4 Buraydah S. Arabia
34 C4 Burbank U.S.A.
115 G4 Burcher Austr.
116 A3 Burdekin r. Qld. Austr.
116 B3 Burdekin Falls waterfall Austr.
80 C3 Burdur Turkey
102 D2 Burē Eth.
59 J5 Bure r. U.K.
54 R4 Bureå Sweden
87 O1 Bureinskiy Khrebet mts Rus. Fed.
80 D6 Būr Fu'ad Egypt
67 M3 Burgas Bulg.
29 E5 Burgaw U.S.A.
23 J4 Burgeo Can.
105 G5 Burgersdorp S. Africa
105 J2 Burgersfort S. Africa
59 G7 Burgess Hill U.K.
62 F6 Burghausen Ger.
57 E3 Burghead U.K.
61 B3 Burgh-Haamstede Neth.
66 F6 Burgio, Serra di h. Sicily Italy
65 E1 Burgos Spain
55 Q8 Burgsvik Sweden
82 J3 Burhan Budai Shan mts China
67 M5 Burhaniye Turkey
84 D5 Burhanpur India
85 E5 Burhar-Dhanpuri India
85 F4 Burhi Gandak r. India
94 B3 Burias i. Phil.
85 H4 Buri Dihing r. India
85 E4 Buri Gandak r. Nepal
23 J4 Burin Peninsula pen. Can.
95 B2 Buriram Thai.
43 K5 Buriti Bravo Brazil
46 C1 Buritis Brazil
117 C6 Burke Pass N.Z.
113 G3 Burketown Austr.
96 Burkina country Africa
31 H3 Burk's Falls Can.
24 D3 Burley U.S.A.
31 H4 Burlington Can.
26 C4 Burlington CO U.S.A.
30 B5 Burlington IA U.S.A.
30 D5 Burlington IN U.S.A.
33 J2 Burlington ME U.S.A.
33 G2 Burlington VT U.S.A.
30 C4 Burlington WV U.S.A.
Burma country see Myanmar
27 D6 Burnet U.S.A.
116 E5 Burnett r. Austr.
116 E5 Burnett Heads Austr.
24 B3 Burney U.S.A.
33 J2 Burnham U.S.A.
115 F8 Burnie Austr.
58 G3 Burniston U.K.
58 E4 Burnley U.K.
24 C3 Burns U.S.A.
21 H1 Burnside r. Can.
32 C5 Burnsville Lake l. U.S.A.
29 F7 Burnt Ground Bahamas
57 E4 Burntisland U.K.
23 H3 Burnt Lake l. Can.
21 K3 Burntwood r. Can.
21 J3 Burnt Wood Lake l. Can.
114 E5 Buronga Austr.
82 G1 Burqin China
80 G5 Burqu' Jordan
114 C4 Burra Austr.
57 □ Burravoe U.K.
57 F2 Burray i. U.K.
67 J4 Burrel Albania
115 H4 Burrendong Reservoir resr Austr.
115 H3 Burren Jct. Austr.
115 J5 Burrewarra Pt pt Austr.
65 F3 Burriana Spain
115 H5 Burrinjuck Austr.
115 H5 Burrinjuck Reservoir resr Austr.
32 B5 Burr Oak Reservoir resr U.S.A.
36 D3 Burro, Serranías del mts Mex.
57 D6 Burrow Head hd U.K.
116 E5 Burrum Heads Austr.
35 G2 Burrville U.S.A.
80 B1 Bursa Turkey
78 C4 Bûr Safâga Egypt
Bûr Sa'îd see Port Said
Būr Sudan see Port Sudan
114 D4 Burta Austr.
30 E3 Burt Lake l. U.S.A.
31 F4 Burton U.S.A.
22 E3 Burton, Lac l. Can.
60 C3 Burtonport Rep. of Ireland
59 F5 Burton upon Trent U.K.
54 R4 Burträsk Sweden
33 K1 Burtts Corner Can.
114 E4 Burtundy Austr.
93 H7 Buru i. Indon.
80 C6 Burullus, Bahra el lag. Egypt
102 C4 Bururi Burundi
20 B2 Burwash Landing Can.
57 F2 Burwick U.K.
69 E5 Buryn' Ukr.
59 H5 Bury St Edmunds U.K.
84 C2 Burzil Pass pass Jammu and Kashmir
102 C4 Busanga Zaire
60 E2 Bush r. U.K.
79 G4 Būshehr Iran
85 E2 Bushêngcaka China
102 D4 Bushenyi Uganda
60 E2 Bushmills U.K.
30 B5 Bushnell U.S.A.
102 C3 Businga Zaire
95 □ Busing, P. i. Sing.
80 F5 Buşrá ash Shām Syria
112 C6 Busselton Austr.
61 D2 Bussum Neth.
27 C7 Bustamante Mex.
66 C2 Busto Arsizio Italy
94 A3 Busuanga Phil.
94 A3 Busuanga i. Phil.
102 C3 Buta Zaire
95 A4 Butang Group is Thai.
47 C3 Buta Ranquil Arg.
102 C4 Butare Rwanda
114 B4 Bute Austr.
57 C5 Bute i. U.K.
20 D4 Butedale Can.
20 D4 Bute In. in. Can.
57 C5 Bute, Sound of chan. U.K.
105 H4 Butha Buthe Lesotho
30 E5 Butler IN U.S.A.
32 D4 Butler PA U.S.A.
60 D3 Butlers Bridge Rep. of Ireland
93 G7 Buton i. Indon.
24 D2 Butte U.S.A.
34 B1 Butte Meadows U.S.A.
92 C5 Butterworth Malaysia
105 H6 Butterworth S. Africa
60 C5 Buttevant Rep. of Ireland
20 D5 Buttle L. l. Can.
57 B2 Butt of Lewis hd U.K.
34 C4 Buttonwillow U.S.A.
94 C4 Butuan Phil.
89 B5 Butuo China
69 G5 Buturlinovka Rus. Fed.
85 E4 Butwal Nepal
102 E3 Buulobarde Somalia
102 E4 Buur Gaabo Somalia
102 E3 Buurhabaka Somalia
85 F4 Buxar India
59 F4 Buxton U.K.
68 G3 Buy Rus. Fed.
30 A1 Buyck U.S.A.
69 H7 Buynaksk Rus. Fed.
Büyük Ağri mt see Ararat, Mt
80 A3 Büyükmenderes r. Turkey
88 G1 Buyun Shan mt China
67 M2 Buzău Romania
90 C7 Buzen Japan
103 D5 Búzi Moz.
69 G5 Buzuluk r. Rus. Fed.
76 G4 Buzuluk Rus. Fed.
33 H4 Buzzards Bay b. U.S.A.
113 K2 Bwagaoia P.N.G.
85 G4 Byakar Bhutan
67 L3 Byala Bulg.
67 K3 Byala Slatina Bulg.
63 O4 Byalynichy Belarus
68 D4 Byarezina r. Belarus
68 C4 Byaroza Belarus
80 E4 Byblos Lebanon
62 J4 Bydgoszcz Pol.
68 D4 Byerazino Belarus
24 F4 Byers U.S.A.
63 O3 Byeshankovichy Belarus
55 K7 Bygland Norway
68 D4 Bykhaw Belarus
55 K7 Bykle Norway
18 Bylot I. i. Can.
31 G3 Byng Inlet Can.
55 K6 Byrkjelo Norway
115 G3 Byrock Austr.
30 C4 Byron IL U.S.A.
33 H2 Byron ME U.S.A.
115 K2 Byron Bay Austr.
115 K2 Byron, C. hd Austr.
77 M2 Byrranga, Gory mts Rus. Fed.
54 R4 Byske Sweden
77 P3 Bytantay r. Rus. Fed.
63 J5 Bytom Pol.
62 H3 Bytów Pol.

# C

44 E3 Caacupé Para.
46 A4 Caagazú, Cordillera de h. Para.
46 A4 Caaguazú Para.
46 A3 Caarapó Brazil
46 A4 Caazapá Para.
42 C6 Caballas Peru
42 D4 Caballococha Peru
94 B3 Cabanatuan Phil.
23 G4 Cabano Can.
102 E2 Cabdul Qaadir Somalia
46 A1 Cabeceira Rio Manso Brazil
43 M5 Cabedelo Brazil
65 D3 Cabeza del Buey Spain
42 F7 Cabezas Bol.
47 E3 Cabildo Arg.
45 C2 Cabimas Venez.
102 B4 Cabinda div. Angola
102 B4 Cabinda Angola
24 C1 Cabinet Mts mts U.S.A.
45 B3 Cable Way pass Col.
46 D3 Cabo Frio Brazil
46 E3 Cabo Frio, Ilha do i. Brazil
22 E4 Cabonga, Réservoir resr Can.
27 E4 Cabool U.S.A.
115 K1 Caboolture Austr.
43 H3 Cabo Orange, Parque Nacional de nat. park Brazil
42 C4 Cabo Pantoja Peru
36 B2 Caborca Mex.
31 G3 Cabot Head pt Can.
23 J4 Cabot Strait str. Can.
46 D2 Cabral, Serra do mts Brazil
81 L2 Cäbrayıl Azer.
65 H3 Cabrera i. Spain
65 C1 Cabrera, Sierra de la mts Spain
65 F3 Cabriel r. Spain
45 D3 Cabruta Venez.
94 B2 Cabugao Phil.
44 F3 Caçador Brazil
67 J3 Čačak Yugo.
47 G1 Caçapava do Sul Brazil
32 D5 Cacapon r. U.S.A.
45 B3 Cácares Col.
66 C4 Caccia, Capo pt Sardinia Italy
43 G7 Cáceres Brazil
65 C3 Cáceres Spain
24 D3 Cache Peak summit U.S.A.
100 A3 Cacheu Guinea-Bissau
44 C3 Cachi r. Arg.
43 H5 Cachimbo, Serra do h. Brazil
45 B3 Cáchira Col.
46 E1 Cachoeira Brazil
46 B2 Cachoeira Alta Brazil
47 G1 Cachoeira do Sul Brazil
46 E3 Cachoeiro de Itapemirim Brazil
100 A3 Cacine Guinea-Bissau
43 H3 Caciporé, Cabo pt Brazil
103 B5 Cacolo Angola
102 B4 Cacongo Angola
34 D3 Cactus Range mts U.S.A.
46 B2 Caçu Brazil
46 D1 Caculé Brazil
63 J6 Čadca Slovakia
114 A2 Cadibarrawirracanna, L. salt flat Austr.
94 B3 Cadig Mountains mts Phil.
31 H1 Cadillac Que. Can.
21 H5 Cadillac Sask. Can.
30 E3 Cadillac U.S.A.
94 B4 Cadiz Phil.
65 C4 Cádiz Spain
65 C4 Cádiz, Golfo de g. Spain
35 E4 Cadiz Lake l. U.S.A.
64 D2 Caen France
59 C4 Caernarfon U.K.
59 C4 Caernarfon Bay b. U.K.
59 D6 Caerphilly U.K.
32 B5 Caesar Creek Lake l. U.S.A.
80 E5 Caesarea Israel
46 D1 Caetité Brazil
44 C3 Cafayate Arg.
94 B4 Cagayan i. Phil.
94 B2 Cagayan r. Phil.
94 C4 Cagayan de Oro Phil.
94 B4 Cagayan Islands is Phil.
66 E3 Cagli Italy
66 C5 Cagliari Sardinia Italy
66 C5 Cagliari, Golfo di b. Sardinia Italy
45 B4 Caguán r. Col.
60 B6 Caha h. Rep. of Ireland
29 C5 Cahaba r. U.S.A.
60 B6 Caha Mts h. Rep. of Ireland
60 A6 Cahermore Rep. of Ireland
60 D5 Cahir Rep. of Ireland
60 A6 Cahirciveen Rep. of Ireland
103 D5 Cahora Bassa, Lago de resr Moz.
60 E5 Cahore Point pt Rep. of Ireland
64 E4 Cahors France
42 C5 Cahuapanas Peru
69 D6 Cahul Moldova
103 D5 Caia Moz.
43 G6 Caiabis, Serra dos h. Brazil
103 C5 Caianda Angola
46 B2 Caiapó r. Brazil
46 B2 Caiapônia Brazil
46 B2 Caiapó, Serra do mts Brazil
37 J4 Caibarién Cuba
95 C3 Cai Be Vietnam
45 D3 Caicara Venez.
37 K4 Caicos Is is Turks and Caicos Is
47 B1 Caimanes Chile
94 A3 Caiman Point pt Phil.
65 F2 Caimodorro mt. Spain
95 C3 Cai Nước Vietnam
57 E3 Cairn Gorm mt. U.K.
57 E3 Cairngorm Mountains mts U.K.
57 C6 Cairnryan U.K.
116 A1 Cairns Austr.
57 E3 Cairn Toul mt. U.K.
78 C4 Cairo Egypt
29 C6 Cairo U.S.A.
66 C2 Cairo Montenotte Italy
103 B5 Caiundo Angola
115 F2 Caiwarro Austr.
42 C5 Cajamarca Peru
94 B3 Cajidiocan Phil.
66 G1 Čakovec Croatia
80 B2 Çal Turkey
105 G5 Cala S. Africa
100 C4 Calabar Nigeria
31 J3 Calabogie Can.
45 D2 Calabozo Venez.
67 K3 Calafat Romania
44 B8 Calafate Arg.
94 B3 Calagua Islands is Phil.
65 F1 Calahorra Spain
103 B5 Calai Angola
64 E1 Calais France
33 K2 Calais U.S.A.
42 F5 Calama Brazil
44 C2 Calama Chile
45 B2 Calamar Bolívar Col.
45 B4 Calamar Guaviare Col.
94 A4 Calamian Group is Phil.
65 F2 Calamocha Spain
103 B4 Calandula Angola
101 E2 Calanscio Sand Sea des. Libya
94 B3 Calapan Phil.
67 M2 Călăraşi Romania
65 F2 Calatayud Spain
94 B3 Calauag Phil.
94 B3 Calavite, Cape pt Phil.
94 A3 Calawit i. Phil.
94 B2 Calayan i. Phil.
94 C3 Calbayog Phil.
94 C4 Calbiga Phil.
47 B4 Calbuco Chile
43 L5 Calcanhar, Ponta do pt Brazil
27 E6 Calcasieu L. l. U.S.A.
43 H3 Calçoene Brazil
85 G5 Calcutta India
65 B3 Caldas da Rainha Port.
46 C2 Caldas Novas Brazil
44 B3 Caldera Chile
116 B5 Caldervale Austr.
81 J2 Çaldıran Turkey
24 C3 Caldwell U.S.A.
32 D3 Caledon Can.
105 G5 Caledon r. Lesotho/S. Africa
104 C7 Caledon S. Africa
31 H4 Caledonia Can.
30 B4 Caledonia U.S.A.
116 C3 Calen Austr.
44 C7 Caleta Olivia Arg.
35 E5 Calexico U.S.A.
58 C3 Calf of Man i. U.K.
20 G4 Calgary Can.
29 C5 Calhoun U.S.A.
45 A4 Cali Col.
94 C4 Calicoan i. Phil.
83 E8 Calicut India
34 C4 Caliente CA U.S.A.
35 E3 Caliente NV U.S.A.
34 B3 California div. U.S.A.
34 B3 California Aqueduct canal U.S.A.
36 B2 California, Golfo de g. Mex.
34 C4 California Hot Springs U.S.A.
81 M2 Cälilabad Azer.
25 D5 Calipatria U.S.A.
34 A2 Calistoga U.S.A.
104 D6 Calitzdorp S. Africa
114 D2 Callabonna, L. salt flat Austr.
34 D2 Callaghan, Mt mt. U.S.A.
29 D6 Callahan U.S.A.
60 D5 Callan Rep. of Ireland
31 H2 Callander Can.
57 D4 Callander U.K.
42 C6 Callao Peru
35 F2 Callao U.S.A.
33 F4 Callicoon U.S.A.
116 D5 Callide Austr.
59 C7 Callington U.K.
116 D5 Calliope Austr.
31 G2 Callum Can.
20 G4 Calmar Can.
30 B4 Calmar U.S.A.
35 E4 Cal-Nev-Ari U.S.A.
29 D7 Caloosahatchee r. U.S.A.
115 K1 Caloundra Austr.
34 B2 Calpine U.S.A.
66 F6 Caltanissetta Sicily Italy
30 C2 Calumet U.S.A.
103 B5 Calunga Angola
103 B5 Caluquembe Angola
94 B4 Calusa i. Phil.
102 F2 Caluula Somalia
35 G5 Calva U.S.A.
113 G3 Calvert Hills Austr.
20 D4 Calvert I. i. Can.
66 C3 Calvi Corsica France
65 H3 Calvià Spain
104 C5 Calvinia S. Africa
66 F4 Calvo, Monte mt. Italy
59 H5 Cam r. U.K.
46 E1 Camaçari Brazil
34 B2 Camache Reservoir resr U.S.A.
103 B5 Camacuio Angola
103 B5 Camacupa Angola
45 D2 Camaguán Venez.
37 J4 Camagüey Cuba
37 J4 Camagüey, Arch. de is Cuba
95 B4 Camah, Gunung mt. Malaysia
Çamalan see Gülek
42 D7 Camana Peru
103 C5 Camanongue Angola
46 B2 Camapuã Brazil
47 G1 Camaquã r. Brazil
47 G1 Camaquã Brazil
80 E3 Çamardı Turkey
36 E3 Camargo Mex.
44 C6 Camarones Arg.
44 C6 Camarones, Bahía b. Arg.
24 B2 Camas U.S.A.
95 C3 Ca Mau Vietnam
Cambay see Khambhat
Cambay, Gulf of g. see Khambhat, Gulf of
59 G6 Camberley U.K.
70 Cambodia country Asia
59 B7 Camborne U.K.
64 F1 Cambrai France
34 B4 Cambria U.S.A.
59 D5 Cambrian Mountains reg. U.K.
31 G4 Cambridge Can.
117 E2 Cambridge N.Z.
59 H5 Cambridge U.K.
30 B5 Cambridge IL U.S.A.
33 H3 Cambridge MA U.S.A.
33 E5 Cambridge MD U.S.A.
26 E2 Cambridge MN U.S.A.
33 G3 Cambridge NY U.S.A.
32 C4 Cambridge OH U.S.A.
16 Cambridge Bay Can.
23 G2 Cambrien, Lac l. Can.
115 J5 Camden Austr.
29 C5 Camden AL U.S.A.
27 E5 Camden AR U.S.A.
33 J2 Camden ME U.S.A.
33 F5 Camden NJ U.S.A.
33 F3 Camden NY U.S.A.
29 D5 Camden SC U.S.A.
44 B8 Camden, Isla i. Chile
103 C5 Cameia, Parque Nacional da nat. park Angola

35 G4 Cameron AZ U.S.A.
27 E6 Cameron LA U.S.A.
26 E4 Cameron MO U.S.A.
27 D6 Cameron TX U.S.A.
30 B3 Cameron WV U.S.A.
95 B4 Cameron Highlands Malaysia
20 F3 Cameron Hills h. Can.
34 B2 Cameron Park U.S.A.
96 Cameroon country Africa
100 C4 Cameroun, Mt mt Cameroon
43 J4 Cametá Brazil
94 B2 Camiguin i. Phil.
94 C4 Camiguin i. Phil.
94 B3 Camiling Phil.
29 C6 Camilla U.S.A.
42 F8 Camiri Bol.
43 K4 Camocim Brazil
113 G3 Camooweal Austr.
94 C4 Camotes Sea g. Phil.
47 E2 Campana Arg.
45 B4 Campana, Co h. Col.
44 A7 Campana, I. i. Chile
47 B2 Campanario mt Arg./Chile
20 D4 Campania I. i. Can.
116 B3 Campaspe r. Austr.
104 E4 Campbell S. Africa
117 E4 Campbell, Cape c. N.Z.
20 D4 Campbell River Can.
31 J3 Campbells Bay Can.
28 C4 Campbellsville U.S.A.
23 G4 Campbellton Can.
115 G8 Campbell Town Austr.
57 C5 Campbeltown U.K.
36 F5 Campeche Mex.
36 F5 Campeche, Bahía de g. Mex.
114 E7 Camperdown Austr.
67 L2 Câmpina Romania
43 L5 Campina Grande Brazil
46 C3 Campinas Brazil
46 C2 Campina Verde Brazil
100 C4 Campo Cameroon
45 B4 Campoalegre Col.
66 F4 Campobasso Italy
46 D3 Campo Belo Brazil
43 H6 Campo de Diauarum Brazil
46 C2 Campo Florido Brazil
44 D3 Campo Gallo Arg.
46 A3 Campo Grande Brazil
43 K4 Campo Maior Brazil
65 C3 Campo Maior Port.
46 B4 Campo Mourão Brazil
46 E3 Campos Brazil
46 C2 Campos Altos Brazil
46 D3 Campos do Jordão Brazil
46 B4 Campos Erê reg. Brazil
57 D4 Campsie Fells h. U.K.
32 B6 Campton KY U.S.A.
33 H3 Campton NH U.S.A.
67 L2 Câmpulung Romania
63 M7 Câmpulung Moldovenesc Romania
35 G4 Camp Verde U.S.A.
95 D3 Cam Ranh Vietnam
20 G4 Camrose Can.
59 B6 Camrose U.K.
21 G2 Camsell Lake l. Can.
21 H3 Camsell Portage Can.
69 C7 Çan Turkey
33 G3 Canaan U.S.A.
16 Canada country North America
47 E2 Cañada de Gómez Arg.
33 H2 Canada Falls Lake l. U.S.A.
27 C5 Canadian r. U.S.A.
45 E3 Canaima, Parque Nacional nat. park Venez.
33 F3 Canajoharie U.S.A.
69 C7 Çanakkale Turkey
Çanakkale Boğazı str. see Dardanelles
47 C2 Canalejas Arg.
32 E3 Canandaigua U.S.A.
32 E3 Canandaigua Lake l. U.S.A.
36 B2 Cananea Mex.
23 H2 Cananée, Lac l. Can.
46 C4 Cananéia Brazil
45 C4 Canapiare, Co h. Col.
42 C4 Cañar Ecuador
Canarias, Islas is see Canary Islands
12 G4 Canary Basin sea feature Atlantic Ocean
100 A1 Canary Islands is Atlantic Ocean
33 F3 Canastota U.S.A.
46 C2 Canastra, Serra da mts Brazil
29 D6 Canaveral, Cape c. U.S.A.
65 E2 Cañaveras Spain
46 E1 Canavieiras Brazil
115 G3 Canbelego Austr.
115 H5 Canberra A.C.T. Austr.
24 B3 Canby CA U.S.A.
26 D2 Canby MN U.S.A.
36 G4 Cancún Mex.
25 F6 Candelaria Chihuahua Mex.
65 D2 Candeleda Spain
115 H6 Candelo Austr.
43 J4 Cândido Mendes Brazil
80 D1 Çandır Turkey
21 H4 Candle Lake Can.
21 H4 Candle Lake l. Can.
119 C1 Candlemas I. i. S. Sandwich Is Atlantic Ocean
33 G4 Candlewood, Lake l. U.S.A.
26 D1 Cando U.S.A.
94 B2 Candon Phil.
47 B1 Canela Baja Chile
47 F2 Canelones Uru.
47 B3 Cañete Chile
65 F2 Cañete Spain
42 D6 Cangallo Peru
103 B5 Cangamba Angola
65 C1 Cangas del Narcea Spain
104 E6 Cango Caves caves S. Africa
43 L5 Canguaretama Brazil
47 G1 Canguçu Brazil
47 G1 Canguçu, Sa do h. Brazil
89 D6 Cangwu China
88 E2 Cangzhou China
23 G2 Caniapiscau r. Can.
23 G3 Caniapiscau Can.
23 G3 Caniapiscau, Rés. resr Can.
66 E6 Canicattì Sicily Italy
20 E4 Canim Lake l. Can.
20 E4 Canim Lake Can.
43 L4 Canindé Brazil
43 K5 Canindé r. Brazil
57 C2 Canisp h. U.K.
32 E3 Canisteo r. U.S.A.
32 E3 Canisteo U.S.A.
80 D1 Çankırı Turkey
94 B4 Canlaon Phil.
20 F4 Canmore Can.
57 B3 Canna i. U.K.
83 E8 Cannanore India
64 H5 Cannes France
59 E5 Cannock U.K.
116 C3 Cannonvale Austr.
115 H6 Cann River Austr.
45 E2 Caño Araguao r. Venez.
44 F3 Canôas Brazil
21 H3 Canoe L. l. Can.
46 B4 Canoinhas Brazil
45 E2 Caño Macareo r. Venez.
45 E2 Caño Manamo r. Venez.
45 E2 Caño Mariusa r. Venez.
25 F4 Canon City U.S.A.
116 D4 Canoona Austr.
114 D4 Canopus Austr.
21 J4 Canora Can.
115 H4 Canowindra Austr.
23 H4 Canso, C. hd Can.
65 D1 Cantábrica, Cordillera mts Spain
Cantábrico, Mar sea see Biscay, Bay of
47 C2 Cantantal Arg.
45 D2 Cantaura Venez.
33 K2 Canterbury Can.
59 J6 Canterbury U.K.
117 C6 Canterbury Bight b. N.Z.
117 C5 Canterbury Plains plain N.Z.
95 C3 Cân Thơ Vietnam
94 C4 Cantilan Phil.
43 K5 Canto do Buriti Brazil
Canton see Guangzhou
30 B5 Canton IL U.S.A.
33 H2 Canton ME U.S.A.
30 B5 Canton MO U.S.A.
27 F5 Canton MS U.S.A.
33 F2 Canton NY U.S.A.
32 C4 Canton OH U.S.A.
32 E4 Canton PA U.S.A.
46 B4 Cantu r. Brazil
46 B4 Cantu, Serra do h. Brazil
47 E2 Cañuelas Arg.
43 G4 Canumã Brazil
115 K2 Canungra Austr.
42 F5 Canutama Brazil
117 D4 Canvastown N.Z.
59 H6 Canvey Island U.K.
27 C5 Canyon U.S.A.
24 C2 Canyon City U.S.A.
35 H3 Canyon de Chelly National Monument res. U.S.A.
24 D2 Canyon Ferry L. l. U.S.A.
35 H2 Canyonlands National Park nat. park U.S.A.
20 D2 Canyon Ranges mts Can.
24 B3 Canyonville U.S.A.
89 C6 Cao Bằng Vietnam
95 D2 Cao Nguyên Đắc Lắc plat. Vietnam
88 E3 Cao Xian China
94 B5 Cap i. Phil.
45 D3 Capanaparo r. Venez.
43 J4 Capanema Brazil
46 B4 Capanema r. Brazil
46 C4 Capão Bonito Brazil
45 C3 Caparo r. Venez.
45 C4 Caparro, Co h. Brazil
94 B3 Capas Phil.
23 H4 Cap-aux-Meules Can.
23 F4 Cap-de-la-Madeleine Can.
116 B3 Cape r. Austr.
112 D6 Cape Arid National Park nat. park Austr.
115 H8 Cape Barren Island i. Austr.
12 K8 Cape Basin sea feature Atlantic Ocean
23 H4 Cape Breton Highlands Nat. Pk nat. park Can.
23 H4 Cape Breton Island i. Can.
23 J3 Cape Charles Can.
33 E6 Cape Charles U.S.A.
100 B4 Cape Coast Ghana
33 H4 Cape Cod Bay b. U.S.A.
33 J4 Cape Cod National Seashore res. U.S.A.
29 D7 Cape Coral U.S.A.
31 G3 Cape Croker Can.
119 B5 Cape Evans Antarctic Base Ant.
18 Cape Farewell c. Greenland
29 E5 Cape Fear r. U.S.A.
27 F4 Cape Girardeau U.S.A.
14 D5 Cape Johnson Depth depth Pac. Oc.
46 D2 Capelinha Brazil
116 C4 Capella Austr.
33 F5 Cape May U.S.A.
33 F5 Cape May Court House U.S.A.
33 F5 Cape May Pt pt U.S.A.
103 B4 Capenda-Camulemba Angola
112 B4 Cape Range National Park nat. park Austr.
23 J4 Cape St George Can.
23 H4 Cape Tormentine Can.
104 C6 Cape Town S. Africa
96 Cape Verde country Africa
12 G5 Cape Verde Basin sea feature Atlantic Ocean
12 F5 Cape Verde Fracture sea feature Atlantic Ocean
12 H4 Cape Verde Plateau sea feature Atlantic Ocean
33 E2 Cape Vincent U.S.A.
113 H2 Cape York Peninsula pen. Austr.
37 K5 Cap-Haïtien Haiti
43 J4 Capim r. Brazil
119 B2 Capitán Arturo Prat Chile Base Ant.
46 A3 Capitán Bado Para.
25 F5 Capitan Peak mt. U.S.A.
35 G2 Capitol Reef National Park nat. park U.S.A.
66 G3 Čapljina Bos.-Herz.
66 F5 Capo d'Orlando Sicily Italy
60 D5 Cappoquin Rep. of Ireland
66 C3 Capraia, Isola di i. Italy
116 D4 Capricorn, C. pt Austr.
116 D4 Capricorn Channel chan. Austr.
116 E4 Capricorn Group atolls Austr.
66 F4 Capri, Isola di i. Italy
103 C5 Caprivi Strip reg. Namibia
Cap St Jacques see Vung Tau
34 □2 Captain Cook U.S.A.
115 H5 Captain's Flat Austr.
32 C5 Captina r. U.S.A.
94 C3 Capul i. Phil.
42 E4 Caquetá r. Col.
45 B3 Cáqueza Col.
94 B3 Carabao i. Phil.
67 L2 Caracal Romania
45 E4 Caracarai Brazil
45 D2 Caracas Venez.
43 K5 Caracol Brazil
94 C5 Caraga Phil.
47 F2 Caraguatá r. Uru.
46 D3 Caraguatatuba Brazil
47 B3 Carahue Chile
46 E2 Caraí Brazil
46 D3 Carandaí Brazil
46 D3 Carangola Brazil
67 K2 Caransebeș Romania
114 B4 Carappee Hill h. Austr.
23 H4 Caraquet Can.
45 B3 Carare r. Col.
37 H5 Caratasca, Laguna lag. Honduras
46 D2 Caratinga Brazil
42 E4 Carauari Brazil
Carauná mt see Grande, Serra
65 F3 Caravaca de la Cruz Spain
46 E2 Caravelas Brazil
44 F3 Carazinho Brazil
26 D1 Carberry Can.
66 C5 Carbonara, Capo pt Sardinia Italy
28 B4 Carbondale IL U.S.A.
33 F4 Carbondale PA U.S.A.
23 K4 Carbonear Can.
66 C5 Carbonia Sardinia Italy
46 D2 Carbonita Brazil
65 F3 Carcaixent Spain
94 B4 Carcar Phil.
47 E2 Carcarañá r. Arg.
64 F5 Carcassonne France
20 C2 Carcross Can.
112 B4 Cardabia Austr.
36 E4 Cárdenas Mex.
114 E2 Cardenyabba watercourse Austr.
44 B7 Cardiel, L. l. Arg.
59 D6 Cardiff U.K.
59 C5 Cardigan U.K.
59 C5 Cardigan Bay b. U.K.
33 F2 Cardinal Can.
32 B4 Cardington U.S.A.
47 F2 Cardona Uru.
46 C4 Cardoso, Ilha do i. Brazil
117 B6 Cardrona N.Z.
20 G5 Cardston Can.
116 B2 Cardwell Austr.
63 L7 Carei Romania
64 D2 Carentan France
32 B4 Carey U.S.A.
112 D5 Carey, L. salt flat Austr.
21 J2 Carey Lake l. Can.
13 J5 Cargados Carajos is Mauritius
64 C2 Carhaix-Plouguer France
47 D3 Carhué Arg.
46 E3 Cariacica Brazil
45 E2 Cariaco Venez.
18 Caribbean Sea sea Atlantic Ocean
20 E4 Cariboo Mts mts Can.
21 K3 Caribou r. Man. Can.
20 D2 Caribou r. N.W.T. Can.
33 K1 Caribou U.S.A.
20 E2 Caribou I. i. Can.
20 F3 Caribou Mountains mts Can.
94 C4 Carigara Phil.
61 D5 Carignan France
115 G3 Carinda Austr.
65 F2 Cariñena Spain
46 D1 Carinhanha Brazil
46 D1 Carinhanha r. Brazil
45 E2 Caripe Venez.
45 E2 Caripito Venez.
60 D3 Cark Mountain h. Rep. of Ireland
31 J3 Carleton Place Can.
105 G3 Carletonville S. Africa
24 C3 Carlin U.S.A.
60 E3 Carlingford Lough in. Rep. of Ireland/U.K.
58 E3 Carlisle U.K.
32 A5 Carlisle KY U.S.A.
32 E4 Carlisle PA U.S.A.
64 E5 Carlit, Pic mt France
47 E2 Carlos Casares Arg.
46 E2 Carlos Chagas Brazil
60 E5 Carlow Rep. of Ireland
57 B2 Carloway U.K.
34 D5 Carlsbad CA U.S.A.
25 F5 Carlsbad NM U.S.A.
27 C6 Carlsbad TX U.S.A.
25 F5 Carlsbad Caverns Nat. Park nat. park U.S.A.
13 J3 Carlsberg Ridge sea feature Indian Ocean
57 E5 Carluke U.K.
21 J5 Carlyle Can.
20 B2 Carmacks Can.
66 B2 Carmagnola Italy
21 K5 Carman Can.
59 C6 Carmarthen U.K.
59 C6 Carmarthen Bay b. U.K.
64 F4 Carmaux France
33 J2 Carmel U.S.A.
59 C4 Carmel Head hd U.K.
47 E2 Carmelo Uru.
45 B2 Carmen Col.
36 B3 Carmen i. Mex.
94 C4 Carmen Phil.
35 G6 Carmen U.S.A.
47 D4 Carmen de Patagones Arg.
47 C2 Carmensa Arg.
28 B4 Carmi U.S.A.
32 B2 Carmichael U.S.A.
116 C3 Carmila Austr.
65 D4 Carmona Spain
64 C3 Carnac France
112 B4 Carnarvon Austr.
104 E5 Carnarvon S. Africa
116 C5 Carnarvon Nat. Park nat. park Austr.
116 C5 Carnarvon Ra. mts Austr.
60 D2 Carndonagh Rep. of Ireland
59 D4 Carnedd Llywelyn mt. U.K.
112 D5 Carnegie, L. salt flat Austr.
15 O6 Carnegie Ridge sea feature Pac. Oc.
57 C3 Carn Eighe mt U.K.
30 D3 Carney U.S.A.
119 A3 Carney I. i. Ant.
58 E3 Carnforth U.K.
92 A5 Car Nicobar i. Andaman and Nicobar Is
60 F3 Carnlough U.K.
57 E4 Carn nan Gabhar mt U.K.
102 B3 Carnot C.A.R.
114 A5 Carnot, C. hd Austr.
57 F4 Carnoustie U.K.
60 E5 Carnsore Point pt Rep. of Ireland
57 E5 Carnwath U.K.
21 H4 Carnwood Can.
31 F4 Caro U.S.A.
116 E2 Carola Cay rf Coral Sea Is Terr.
29 D7 Carol City U.S.A.
43 J5 Carolina Brazil
105 J3 Carolina S. Africa
109 Caroline Island i. Kiribati
108 Caroline Islands is. Pac. Oc.
117 A6 Caroline Pk summit N.Z.
104 B4 Carolusberg S. Africa
45 E2 Caroní r. Venez.
45 C2 Carora Venez.
35 E3 Carp U.S.A.
52 Carpathian Mountains mts Romania/Ukr.
Carpații Meridionali mts see Transylvanian Alps
116 A2 Carpentaria Downs Austr.
113 G2 Carpentaria, Gulf of g. Austr.
64 G4 Carpentras France
66 D2 Carpi Italy
43 L5 Carpina Brazil
34 C4 Carpinteria U.S.A.
21 J5 Carpio U.S.A.
20 E4 Carp Lake Prov. Park res. Can.
33 H2 Carrabassett Valley U.S.A.
29 C6 Carrabelle U.S.A.
45 B2 Carraipía Col.
60 B4 Carra, Lough l. Rep. of Ireland
60 B6 Carran h. Rep. of Ireland
60 B6 Carrantuohill mt Rep. of Ireland
47 B2 Carranza, C. pt Chile
36 D3 Carranza, Presa V. l. Mex.
45 E3 Carrao r. Venez.
66 D2 Carrara Italy
115 F5 Carrathool Austr.
47 C3 Carrero, Co mt Arg.
45 E1 Carriacou i. Grenada
57 D5 Carrick reg. U.K.
60 F3 Carrickfergus U.K.
60 E4 Carrickmacross Rep. of Ireland
60 C4 Carrick-on-Shannon Rep. of Ireland
60 D5 Carrick-on-Suir Rep. of Ireland
114 C4 Carrieton Austr.
60 D4 Carrigallen Rep. of Ireland
60 C6 Carrigtwohill Rep. of Ireland
47 C4 Carri Lafquén, L. l. Arg.
26 D2 Carrington U.S.A.
44 B3 Carrizal Bajo Chile
35 H4 Carrizo AZ U.S.A.
35 G4 Carrizo AZ U.S.A.
34 D5 Carrizo Cr. r. U.S.A.
27 D6 Carrizo Springs U.S.A.
25 F5 Carrizozo U.S.A.
26 E3 Carroll U.S.A.
29 C5 Carrollton GA U.S.A.
28 C4 Carrollton KY U.S.A.
26 E4 Carrollton MO U.S.A.
32 C4 Carrollton OH U.S.A.
21 J4 Carrot r. Can.
21 J4 Carrot River Can.
58 B3 Carrowdore N. Ireland U.K.
60 B3 Carrowmore Lake l. Rep. of Ireland
33 F2 Carry Falls Reservoir resr U.S.A.
80 F1 Çarşamba Turkey
30 E4 Carson City MI U.S.A.
34 C2 Carson City NV U.S.A.
34 C2 Carson Lake l. U.S.A.
34 C2 Carson Sink l. U.S.A.
31 F4 Carsonville U.S.A.
47 B2 Cartagena Chile
45 B2 Cartagena Col.
65 F4 Cartagena Spain
45 B3 Cartago Col.
37 H7 Cartago Costa Rica
29 C5 Cartersville U.S.A.
30 B5 Carthage IL U.S.A.
27 E4 Carthage MO U.S.A.
33 F2 Carthage NY U.S.A.
27 E5 Carthage TX U.S.A.
31 G2 Cartier Can.
112 D2 Cartier Island i. Ashmore and Cartier Is
58 E3 Cartmel U.K.
23 J3 Cartwright Can.
43 L5 Caruaru Brazil
45 E2 Carúpano Venez.
34 D2 Carvers U.S.A.
61 A4 Carvin France
116 B5 Carwell Austr.
29 E5 Cary U.S.A.
114 E2 Caryapundy Swamp swamp Austr.
100 B1 Casablanca Morocco
46 C3 Casa Branca Brazil
25 E6 Casa de Janos Mex.
35 G5 Casa Grande U.S.A.
35 G5 Casa Grande National Monument res. U.S.A.
66 C2 Casale Monferrato Italy
66 D2 Casalmaggiore Italy
45 C3 Casanare r. Col.
67 H4 Casarano Italy
117 B6 Cascade r. N.Z.
30 B4 Cascade IA U.S.A.
24 C2 Cascade ID U.S.A.
24 E2 Cascade MT U.S.A.
117 B6 Cascade Pt pt N.Z.
24 B3 Cascade Range mts U.S.A.
24 D2 Cascade Res. resr U.S.A.
65 B3 Cascais Port.
46 B4 Cascavel Brazil
33 J3 Casco Bay b. U.S.A.
66 F4 Caserta Italy
31 F4 Caseville U.S.A.
119 C6 Casey Australia Base Ant.
119 D4 Casey Bay b. Ant.
60 D5 Cashel Rep. of Ireland
115 H1 Cashmere Austr.
30 B4 Cashton U.S.A.
45 C2 Casigua Falcón Venez.
45 B2 Casigua Zulia Venez.
94 B2 Casiguran Phil.
47 E2 Casilda Arg.
115 K2 Casino Austr.
45 D4 Casiquiare, Canal r. Venez.
42 C5 Casma Peru
30 E4 Casnovia U.S.A.
34 A2 Caspar U.S.A.
65 F2 Caspe Spain
24 F3 Casper U.S.A.
Caspian Lowland lowland see Prikaspiyskaya Nizmennost'
74 Caspian Sea sea Asia/Europe
32 D5 Cass U.S.A.
31 F4 Cass r. U.S.A.
32 D3 Cassadaga U.S.A.
103 C5 Cassai Angola
31 F4 Cass City U.S.A.
33 F2 Casselman Can.
20 D3 Cassiar Can.
20 C3 Cassiar Mountains mts Can.
115 H4 Cassilis Austr.
66 E4 Cassino Italy
26 E2 Cass Lake U.S.A.
43 J4 Castanhal Brazil
47 C1 Castaño r. Arg.
27 C7 Castaños Mex.
47 C1 Castaño Viejo Arg.
66 D2 Castelfranco Veneto Italy
64 E4 Casteljaloux France
66 F4 Castellammare di Stabia Italy
47 F3 Castelli Arg.
65 F3 Castelló de la Plana Spain
65 C3 Castelo Branco Port.
65 C3 Castelo de Vide Port.
66 C4 Castelsardo Sardinia Italy
66 E6 Casteltermini Sicily Italy
66 E6 Castelvetrano Sicily Italy
114 D6 Casterton Austr.
23 G2 Castignon, Lac l. Can.
65 E3 Castilla - La Mancha div. Spain
65 D2 Castilla y León div. Spain
45 C2 Castilletes Col.
47 G2 Castillos Uru.
60 B4 Castlebar Rep. of Ireland
57 A4 Castlebay U.K.
60 E4 Castlebellingham Rep. of Ireland
60 E3 Castleblayney Rep. of Ireland
60 E5 Castlebridge Rep. of Ireland
58 E3 Castle Carrock U.K.
59 E6 Castle Cary U.K.
35 G2 Castle Dale U.S.A.
60 D3 Castlederg U.K.
60 E5 Castledermot Rep. of Ireland
35 E5 Castle Dome Mts mts U.S.A.
59 F5 Castle Donnington U.K.
57 E6 Castle Douglas U.K.
58 F4 Castleford U.K.
20 F5 Castlegar Can.
60 A5 Castlegregory Rep. of Ireland
60 B5 Castleisland Rep. of Ireland
114 F6 Castlemaine Austr.
60 B5 Castlemaine Rep. of Ireland
60 C6 Castlemartyr Rep. of Ireland
34 B4 Castle Mt mt. U.S.A.
89 □ Castle Peak h. Hong Kong China
89 □ Castle Peak Bay b. Hong Kong China
117 F4 Castlepoint N.Z.
60 D4 Castlepollard Rep. of Ireland
60 C4 Castlerea Rep. of Ireland
115 H3 Castlereagh r. Austr.
25 F4 Castle Rock U.S.A.
30 B4 Castle Rock Lake l. U.S.A.
58 C3 Castletown Isle of Man
60 D5 Castletown Rep. of Ireland
21 G4 Castor Can.
64 F5 Castres France
61 C2 Castricum Neth.
37 M6 Castries St Lucia
46 C4 Castro Brazil
44 B6 Castro Chile
65 D4 Castro del Río Spain
65 E1 Castro-Urdiales Spain
65 B4 Castro Verde Port.
66 G5 Castrovillari Italy
34 B3 Castroville U.S.A.
117 A6 Caswell Sd in. N.Z.
81 H2 Çat Turkey
42 B5 Catacaos Peru
46 D3 Cataguases Brazil
27 E6 Catahoula L. l. U.S.A.
94 B3 Cataiñgan Phil.
81 J3 Çatak Turkey
46 C2 Catalão Brazil
65 G2 Cataluña div. Spain
44 C3 Catamarca Arg.
94 C3 Catanduanes i. Phil.
46 B4 Catanduvas Brazil
66 F6 Catania Sicily Italy
66 G5 Catanzaro Italy
27 D6 Catarina U.S.A.
94 C3 Catarman Phil.
65 F3 Catarroja Spain
114 A5 Catastrophe, C. hd Austr.
45 C2 Catatumbo r. Venez.
94 C4 Catbalogan Phil.
29 E7 Cat Cays is Bahamas
94 C5 Cateel Phil.
94 C5 Cateel Bay b. Phil.
105 K3 Catembe Moz.
115 H6 Cathcart Austr.
105 G6 Cathcart S. Africa
105 H4 Cathedral Peak mt S. Africa
60 A6 Catherdaniel Rep. of Ireland
35 F2 Catherine, Mt mt. U.S.A.
47 B3 Catillo Chile

29 E7 Cat Island i. Bahamas
22 B3 Cat L. l. Can.
36 G4 Catoche, C. c. Mex.
32 E5 Catonsville U.S.A.
47 D3 Catriló Arg.
45 E4 Catrimani r. Brazil
45 E4 Catrimani Brazil
33 G3 Catskill U.S.A.
33 F4 Catskill Mts mts U.S.A.
61 A4 Cats, Mont des h. France
105 K3 Catuane Moz.
45 E4 Cauamé r. Brazil
94 B4 Cauayan Phil.
23 H2 Caubvick, Mount mt. Can.
45 B3 Cauca r. Col.
43 L4 Caucaia Brazil
45 B3 Caucasia Col.
52 Caucasus mts Asia/Europe
47 C1 Caucete Arg.
33 J1 Caucomgomoc Lake l. U.S.A.
61 B4 Caudry France
94 C4 Cauit Point pt Phil.
47 B2 Cauquenes Chile
45 D3 Caura r. Venez.
23 G4 Causapscal Can.
64 G5 Cavaillon France
46 C1 Cavalcante Brazil
60 D4 Cavan Rep. of Ireland
27 F4 Cave City U.S.A.
46 E1 Caveira r. Brazil
114 E6 Cavendish Austr.
46 B4 Cavernoso, Serra do mts Brazil
32 B5 Cave Run Lake l. U.S.A.
94 B4 Cavili rf Phil.
94 B3 Cavite Phil.
57 E3 Cawdor U.K.
114 D4 Cawndilla Lake l. Austr.
59 J5 Cawston U.K.
43 K4 Caxias Brazil
44 F3 Caxias do Sul Brazil
103 B4 Caxito Angola
80 C2 Çay Turkey
29 D5 Cayce U.S.A.
80 D1 Çaycuma Turkey
81 H1 Çayeli Turkey
43 H3 Cayenne Fr. Guiana
80 E3 Çayhan Turkey
80 C1 Çayırhan Turkey
37 J5 Cayman Brac i. Cayman Is
37 H5 Cayman Islands terr. Caribbean
102 E3 Caynabo Somalia
31 H4 Cayuga Can.
32 E3 Cayuga Lake l. U.S.A.
33 F3 Cazenovia U.S.A.
103 C5 Cazombo Angola
47 F2 Cebollatí r. Uru.
94 B4 Cebu Phil.
94 B4 Cebu i. Phil.
30 C3 Cecil U.S.A.
115 J1 Cecil Plains Austr.
66 D3 Cecina Italy
30 A4 Cedar r. IA U.S.A.
26 C2 Cedar r. ND U.S.A.
30 D4 Cedarburg U.S.A.
35 F3 Cedar City U.S.A.
27 D5 Cedar Creek Res. resr U.S.A.
30 A4 Cedar Falls U.S.A.
30 D4 Cedar Grove WV U.S.A.
32 C5 Cedar Grove WV U.S.A.
33 F6 Cedar I. i. U.S.A.
21 J4 Cedar L. l. Can.
30 D5 Cedar Lake l. U.S.A.
32 B4 Cedar Pt pt U.S.A.
30 B5 Cedar Rapids U.S.A.
35 G3 Cedar Ridge U.S.A.
33 F5 Cedar Run U.S.A.
31 F4 Cedar Springs Can.
30 E4 Cedar Springs U.S.A.
29 C5 Cedartown U.S.A.
105 H5 Cedarville S. Africa
30 E3 Cedarville U.S.A.
36 A3 Cedros i. Mex.
113 F6 Ceduna Austr.
102 E3 Ceeldheere Somalia
102 E2 Ceerigaabo Somalia
66 F5 Cefalù Sicily Italy
63 J7 Cegléd Hungary
89 B5 Ceheng China
80 E1 Çekerek Turkey
95 B4 Celah, Gunung mt Malaysia
36 D4 Celaya Mex.
60 E4 Celbridge Rep. of Ireland
Celebes i. see Sulawesi
93 G6 Celebes Sea sea Indon./Phil.
32 A4 Celina U.S.A.
66 F1 Celje Slovenia
62 E4 Celle Ger.
56 C6 Celtic Sea sea Rep. of Ireland/U.K.
80 E1 Cemilbey Turkey
80 G2 Çemişgezek Turkey
93 K7 Cenderawasih, Teluk b. Indon.
89 C5 Cengong China
35 F5 Centennial Wash r. U.S.A.
27 E6 Center U.S.A.
33 G4 Centereach U.S.A.
29 C5 Center Point U.S.A.
32 B5 Centerville U.S.A.
105 G1 Central div. Botswana
96 Central African Republic country Africa
79 K4 Central Brahui Ra. mts Pak.
30 B4 Central City IA U.S.A.
26 D3 Central City NE U.S.A.
45 A4 Central, Cordillera mts Col.
42 C5 Central, Cordillera mts Peru
94 B2 Central, Cordillera mts Phil.
89 Central District Hong Kong China
28 B4 Centralia IL U.S.A.
24 B2 Centralia WA U.S.A.
30 A2 Central Lakes U.S.A.
24 B3 Central Point U.S.A.
110 E2 Central Ra. mts P.N.G.
52 Central Russian Uplands plat. Europe
29 C5 Centreville U.S.A.
89 D6 Cenxi China
Cephalonia i. see Kefallonia
Ceram i. see Seram
Ceram Sea g. see Seram Sea
45 D3 Cerbatana, Sa de la mt Venez.
35 E4 Cerbat Mts mts U.S.A.
21 G4 Cereal Can.
44 D3 Ceres Arg.
104 C6 Ceres S. Africa
45 B2 Cereté Col.
65 E2 Cerezo de Abajo Spain
66 F4 Cerignola Italy
80 D2 Çerikli Turkey
80 D1 Çerkeş Turkey
80 G3 Çermelik r. Syria
81 G2 Çermik Turkey
67 N2 Cernavodă Romania
36 C4 Cerralvo i. Mex.
67 H4 Cërrik Albania
36 D4 Cerritos Mex.
46 C4 Cerro Azul Brazil
42 B4 Cerro de Amotape, Parque Nacional nat. park Peru
42 C6 Cerro de Pasco Peru
45 D3 Cerro Jáua, Meseta del plat. Venez.
45 C2 Cerrón, Co mt. Venez.
47 C3 Cerros Colorados, Embalse resr Arg.
66 F4 Cervati, Monte mt. Italy
66 C3 Cervione Corsica France
65 C1 Cervo Spain
45 B2 César r. Col.
66 E2 Cesena Italy
55 T8 Cēsis Latvia
62 G6 České Budějovice Czech Rep.
62 G6 Český Krumlov Czech Rep.
62 F6 Český Les mts Czech Rep./Ger.
67 M5 Çeşme Turkey
115 J4 Cessnock Austr.
67 H3 Cetinje Yugo.
66 F5 Cetraro Italy
65 D5 Ceuta Spain
64 F4 Cévennes mts France
80 E3 Ceyhan r. Turkey
80 E3 Ceyhan Turkey
81 H3 Ceylanpınar Turkey
47 E2 Chacabuco Arg.
47 B4 Chacao Chile
47 C3 Chachahuén, Sa mt. Arg.
42 C5 Chachapoyas Peru
68 D4 Chachersk Belarus
95 B2 Chachoengsao Thai.
84 B4 Chachro Pak.
20 C4 Chacon, C. c. U.S.A.
96 Chad country Africa
86 H2 Chadaasan Mongolia
86 F1 Chadan Rus. Fed.
105 G1 Chadibe Botswana
47 C3 Chadileo r. Arg.
101 D3 Chad, Lake l. Africa
26 C3 Chadron U.S.A.
95 A1 Chae Hom Thai.
45 B4 Chafurray Col.
85 F2 Chagdo Kangri reg. China
79 K3 Chaghcharān Afgh.
64 G3 Chagny France
13 J4 Chagos Archipelago is British Indian Ocean Terr.
68 J4 Chagra r. Rus. Fed.
45 D2 Chaguaramas Venez.
85 G3 Cha'gyüngoinba China
79 J4 Chāh Bahār Iran
81 K4 Chah-i-Shurkh Iraq
85 F5 Chāībāsa India
23 G3 Chaigneau, Lac l. Can.
95 B2 Chai Si r. Thai.
89 Chai Wan Hong Kong China
95 A3 Chaiya Thai.
95 B2 Chaiyaphum Thai.
47 F1 Chajarí Arg.
84 B3 Chakar r. Pak.
85 H5 Chakaria Bangl.
85 E4 Chakia India
42 D7 Chala Peru
36 G6 Chalatenango El Salvador
23 G4 Chaleur Bay in. Can.
89 D5 Chaling China
84 C5 Chalisgaon India
67 K5 Chalkida Greece
117 A7 Chalky Inlet in. N.Z.
64 D3 Challans France
42 E7 Challapata Bol.
15 M8 Challenger Fracture Zone sea feature Pac. Oc.
24 D2 Challis U.S.A.
64 G2 Châlons-en-Champagne France
64 G3 Chalon-sur-Saône France
62 F6 Cham Ger.
25 F4 Chama U.S.A.
45 C2 Chama r. Venez.
103 D5 Chama Zambia
47 D2 Chamaico Arg.
104 A3 Chamais Bay b. Namibia
79 K3 Chaman Pak.
79 M3 Chamba India
84 D4 Chambal r. India
23 G3 Chambeaux, Lac l. Can.
21 H4 Chamberlain Can.
26 D3 Chamberlain U.S.A.
33 J1 Chamberlain Lake l. U.S.A.
35 H4 Chambers U.S.A.
32 E5 Chambersburg U.S.A.
64 G4 Chambéry France
103 D5 Chambeshi Zambia
66 C7 Chambi, Jebel mt. Tunisia
64 G4 Chamechaude mt. France
47 C1 Chamical Arg.
85 F4 Chamlang mt. Nepal
95 B3 Châmnar Cambodia
22 F4 Chamouchouane r. Can.
85 E5 Champa India
20 B2 Champagne Can.
64 G2 Champagne reg. France
105 H4 Champagne Castle mt. S. Africa
64 G3 Champagnole France
30 C5 Champaign U.S.A.
47 D1 Champaqui, Cerro mt. Arg.
95 C2 Champasak Laos
85 H5 Champhai India
30 D2 Champion U.S.A.
33 G2 Champlain U.S.A.
33 G2 Champlain, L. l. Can./U.S.A.
36 F5 Champotón Mex.
68 H4 Chamzinka Rus. Fed.
95 B4 Chana Thai.
44 B3 Chañaral Chile
45 E3 Chanaro, Co mt. Venez.
47 B2 Chanco Chile
Chanda see Chandrapur
85 E5 Chandarpur India
84 D3 Chandausi India
27 F6 Chandeleur Islands is U.S.A.
84 E5 Chandia India
84 D3 Chandigarh India
35 G5 Chandler U.S.A.
31 J3 Chandos Lake l. Can.
85 G5 Chandpur Bangl.
84 D3 Chandpur India
85 H5 Chandraghona Bangl.
84 D6 Chandrapur India
84 D5 Chandur India
103 D6 Changane r. Moz.
103 D5 Changara Moz.
87 N3 Changbai China
89 C7 Changcheng China
119 B1 Chang Cheng (Great Wall) China Base Ant.
87 N3 Changchun China
88 F2 Changdao China
89 D4 Changde China
88 E3 Changfeng China
88 G2 Changhai China
89 F5 Chang-hua Taiwan
95 D1 Changhua Jiang r. China
95 Changi Sing.
95 Changi airport Sing.
89 C7 Changjiang China
Chang Jiang r. see Yangtze
Changjiang Kou est. see Yangtze, Mouth of the
89 F5 Changle China
88 F2 Changli China
89 D5 Changning China
88 E1 Changping China
89 D4 Changsha China
89 F4 Changshan China
88 G2 Changshan Qundao is China
89 C4 Changshou China
89 D4 Changshoujie China
88 F4 Changshu China
89 C5 Changshun China
89 E5 Changtai China
89 E5 Changting China
88 G1 Changtu China
88 C3 Changwu China
88 F2 Changxing Dao i. China
89 D4 Changyang China
88 F2 Changyi China
88 E3 Changyuan China
88 D2 Changzhi China
88 F4 Changzhou China
67 L7 Chania Greece
88 B3 Chankou China
56 E7 Channel Islands is English Channel
34 C5 Channel Islands is U.S.A.
34 B5 Channel Is Nat. Park nat. park U.S.A.
23 J4 Channel-Port-aux-Basques Can.
59 J6 Channel Tunnel tunnel France/U.K.
30 C2 Channing U.S.A.
65 C1 Chantada Spain
95 B2 Chanthaburi Thai.
64 F2 Chantilly France
27 E4 Chanute U.S.A.
76 J4 Chany, Ozero salt l. Rus. Fed.
88 E2 Chaobai Xinhe r. China
88 E4 Chao Hu l. China
95 B2 Chao Phraya r. Thai.
100 B1 Chaouèn Morocco
85 H2 Chaowula Shan mts China
88 E4 Chao Xian China
89 E6 Chaoyang Guangdong China
88 F1 Chaoyang Liaoning China
89 E6 Chaozhou China
46 E1 Chapada Diamantina, Parque Nacional nat. park Brazil
46 A1 Chapada dos Guimarães Brazil
46 C1 Chapada dos Veadeiros, Parque Nacional da nat. park Brazil
36 D4 Chapala, L. de l. Mex.
45 B4 Chaparral Col.
76 G4 Chapayev Kazak.
68 J4 Chapayevsk Rus. Fed.
44 F3 Chapecó Brazil
44 F3 Chapecó r. Brazil
59 F4 Chapel-en-le-Frith U.K.
29 E5 Chapel Hill U.S.A.
59 F4 Chapeltown U.K.
30 D5 Chapin, Lake l. U.S.A.
31 F2 Chapleau Can.
68 F4 Chaplygin Rus. Fed.
69 E6 Chaplynka Ukr.
32 B6 Chapmanville U.S.A.
115 G8 Chappell Is is Austr.
42 E7 Chaqui Bol.
84 D2 Char Jammu and Kashmir
85 H3 Char Chu r. China
21 G3 Chard Can.
59 E7 Chard U.K.
81 L3 Chārdagh Iran
81 L5 Chardāvol Iran
32 C4 Chardon U.S.A.
79 J2 Chardzhev Turkm.
64 E3 Charente r. France
79 K2 Chārīkār Afgh.
26 E3 Chariton r. U.S.A.
31 F3 Charity Is i. U.S.A.
76 G3 Charkayuvom Rus. Fed.
84 D4 Charkhari India
61 C4 Charleroi Belgium
30 A4 Charles City U.S.A.
27 E6 Charles, Lake U.S.A.
117 C4 Charleston N.Z.
28 B4 Charleston IL U.S.A.
33 J2 Charleston ME U.S.A.
27 F4 Charleston MO U.S.A.
29 E5 Charleston SC U.S.A.
32 C5 Charleston WV U.S.A.
35 E3 Charleston Peak summit U.S.A.
60 C4 Charlestown Rep. of Ireland
33 G3 Charlestown NH U.S.A.
33 H4 Charlestown RI U.S.A.
32 E5 Charles Town U.S.A.
116 B6 Charleville Austr.
64 G2 Charleville-Mézières France
30 E3 Charlevoix U.S.A.
20 E3 Charlie Lake Can.
30 E4 Charlotte MI U.S.A.
29 D5 Charlotte NC U.S.A.
29 D7 Charlotte Harbor b. U.S.A.
32 D5 Charlottesville U.S.A.
23 H4 Charlottetown P.E.I. Can.
45 E2 Charlotteville Trinidad and Tobago
114 E6 Charlton Austr.
22 E3 Charlton I. i. Can.
68 F2 Charozero Rus. Fed.
84 B2 Charsadda Pak.
116 B3 Charters Towers Austr.
64 E2 Chartres France
47 E2 Chascomús Arg.
20 F4 Chase Can.
81 L4 Chashmeh Iran
68 D4 Chashniki Belarus
117 B7 Chaslands Mistake c. N.Z.
64 D3 Châteaubriant France
64 E3 Château-du-Loir France
64 E2 Châteaudun France
33 F2 Chateaugay U.S.A.
33 G2 Châteauguay Can.
64 B2 Châteaulin France
64 F3 Châteauneuf-sur-Loire France
64 E3 Châteauroux France
64 F2 Château-Thierry France
61 C4 Châtelet Belgium
64 E3 Châtellerault France
30 A4 Chatfield U.S.A.
23 G4 Chatham N.B. Can.
31 F4 Chatham Ont. Can.
59 H6 Chatham U.K.
33 H4 Chatham MA U.S.A.
33 G3 Chatham NY U.S.A.
32 D6 Chatham VA U.S.A.
111 J6 Chatham Islands is N.Z.
20 C4 Chatham Sd chan. Can.
20 C3 Chatham Strait chan. U.S.A.
85 F4 Chatra India
31 G3 Chatsworth Can.
30 C5 Chatsworth U.S.A.
29 C5 Chattanooga U.S.A.
59 H5 Chatteris U.K.
95 B2 Chatturat Thai.
95 C3 Châu Đôc Vietnam
84 B4 Chauhtan India
85 H5 Chauk Myanmar
84 E4 Chauka r. India
64 G2 Chaumont France
95 A2 Chaungwabyin Myanmar
77 S3 Chaunskaya Guba b. Rus. Fed.
64 F2 Chauny France
85 F4 Chauparan India
32 D3 Chautauqua, Lake l. U.S.A.
81 L5 Chavār Iran
43 J4 Chaves Brazil
65 C2 Chaves Port.
22 E2 Chavigny, Lac l. Can.
68 D4 Chavusy Belarus
84 A3 Chawal r. Pak.
89 B6 Chây r. Vietnam
Chäyul see Qayü
47 D2 Chazón Arg.
33 G2 Chazy U.S.A.
59 F5 Cheadle U.K.
32 D5 Cheat r. U.S.A.
62 F5 Cheb Czech Rep.
66 D7 Chebba Tunisia
68 H3 Cheboksary Rus. Fed.
30 E3 Cheboygan U.S.A.
69 H7 Chechen', Ostrov i. Rus. Fed.
69 H7 Chechenskaya Respublika div. Rus. Fed.
27 E5 Checotah U.S.A.
59 E6 Cheddar U.K.
21 G3 Cheecham Can.
116 A6 Cheepie Austr.
77 V3 Chefornak Alaska
105 K1 Chefu Moz.
100 B2 Chegga Maur.
103 D5 Chegutu Zimbabwe
24 B2 Chehalis U.S.A.
84 B2 Chehardar Pass pass Afgh.
81 L5 Chehariz Iraq
90 A7 Cheju Do i. S. Korea
87 N5 Cheju-haehyŏp chan. S. Korea
68 F4 Chekhov Rus. Fed.
24 B2 Chelan, L. l. U.S.A.
79 G2 Cheleken Turkm.
47 C3 Chelforó Arg.
65 G4 Chélif r. Alg.
76 G5 Chelkar Kazak.
63 L5 Chełm Pol.
59 H6 Chelmer r. U.K.
63 J4 Chełmno Pol.
59 H6 Chelmsford U.K.
33 H3 Chelmsford U.S.A.
59 E6 Cheltenham U.K.
65 F3 Chelva Spain
76 H4 Chelyabinsk Rus. Fed.
103 D5 Chemba Moz.
84 D2 Chem Co l. China
62 F5 Chemnitz Ger.
32 E3 Chemung r. U.S.A.
84 B3 Chenab r. Pak.
100 B2 Chenachane Alg.
33 F3 Chenango r. U.S.A.
24 C2 Cheney U.S.A.
27 D4 Cheney Res. resr U.S.A.
88 E2 Cheng'an China
89 D5 Chengbu China
88 E1 Chengde China
89 B4 Chengdu China
82 E2 Chengel'dy Kazak.
88 E3 Chenggu China
89 E6 Chenghai China
88 C4 Chengkou China
92 E3 Chengmai China
88 F3 Cheniu Shan i. China
Chennai see Madras
30 C5 Chenoa U.S.A.
89 D5 Chenxi China
89 D5 Chenzhou China
95 D2 Cheo Reo Vietnam
42 C5 Chepén Peru
47 C1 Chepes Arg.
59 E6 Chepstow U.K.
68 J3 Cheptsa r. Rus. Fed.
81 L5 Cheqad Kabūd Iran
30 B2 Chequamegon Bay b. U.S.A.
64 F3 Cher r. France
29 E5 Cheraw U.S.A.
64 D2 Cherbourg France
65 H4 Cherchell Alg.
64 J4 Cherdakly Rus. Fed.
86 H1 Cheremkhovo Rus. Fed.
68 F3 Cherepovets Rus. Fed.
68 H2 Cherevkovo Rus. Fed.
66 B7 Chéria Alg.
69 E5 Cherkasy Ukr.
69 G6 Cherkessk Rus. Fed.
103 C5 Chermenze Angola
76 K2 Chernaya Rus. Fed.
68 J3 Chernaya Kholunitsa Rus. Fed.
69 D5 Chernihiv Ukr.
69 F6 Cherninivka Ukr.
69 C5 Chernivtsi Ukr.
86 F1 Chernogorsk Rus. Fed.
68 H3 Chernovskoye Rus. Fed.
69 D5 Chernyakhiv Ukr.
63 K3 Chernyakhovsk Rus. Fed.
69 F5 Chernyanka Rus. Fed.
87 L1 Chernyshevsk Rus. Fed.
77 N3 Chernyshevskiy Rus. Fed.
69 H6 Chernyye Zemli reg. Rus. Fed.
69 H5 Chernyy Yar Rus. Fed.
26 E3 Cherokee IA U.S.A.
27 D4 Cherokee OK U.S.A.
27 E4 Cherokees, Lake o' the l. U.S.A.
29 E7 Cherokee Sound Bahamas
47 B3 Cherquenco Chile
85 G4 Cherrapunji India
35 E2 Cherry Creek U.S.A.
35 E1 Cherry Creek Mts mts U.S.A.
33 K2 Cherryfield U.S.A.
111 G3 Cherry Island i. Solomon Is
31 J4 Cherry Valley Can.
33 F3 Cherry Valley U.S.A.
77 Q3 Cherskogo, Khrebet mts Rus. Fed.
69 G5 Chertkovo Rus. Fed.
68 J2 Cherva Rus. Fed.
67 L3 Cherven Bryag Bulg.
69 C5 Chervonohrad Ukr.
69 E5 Chervonozavods'ke Ukr.
68 D4 Chervyen' Belarus
59 F6 Cherwell r. U.K.
68 D4 Cherykaw Belarus
31 E4 Chesaning U.S.A.
33 E6 Chesapeake U.S.A.
33 E5 Chesapeake Bay b. U.S.A.
59 G6 Chesham U.K.
33 G3 Cheshire U.S.A.
59 E4 Cheshire Plain lowland U.K.
76 F3 Cheshskaya Guba b. Rus. Fed.
59 G6 Cheshunt U.K.
59 E4 Chester U.K.
34 B1 Chester CA U.S.A.
28 B4 Chester IL U.S.A.
24 E1 Chester MT U.S.A.
33 F5 Chester PA U.S.A.
29 D5 Chester SC U.S.A.
33 E5 Chester r. U.S.A.
59 F4 Chesterfield U.K.
111 F3 Chesterfield, Îles is New Caledonia
21 L2 Chesterfield Inlet Can.
21 L2 Chesterfield Inlet in. Can.
58 F3 Chester-le-Street U.K.
33 E5 Chestertown MD U.S.A.
33 G3 Chestertown NY U.S.A.
33 F2 Chesterville Can.
32 D4 Chestnut Ridge ridge U.S.A.
33 J1 Chesuncook U.S.A.
33 J1 Chesuncook Lake l. U.S.A.
66 B6 Chetaïbi Alg.
23 H4 Chéticamp Can.
83 D8 Chetlat i. India
36 G5 Chetumal Mex.
20 E3 Chetwynd Can.
89 Cheung Chau i. Hong Kong China
89 Cheung Chau Hong Kong China
117 D5 Cheviot N.Z.
58 E2 Cheviot Hills h. U.K.
58 E2 Cheviot, The h. U.K.
24 C1 Chewelah U.S.A.
27 D5 Cheyenne OK U.S.A.
24 F3 Cheyenne WY U.S.A.
26 C3 Cheyenne r. U.S.A.
26 C4 Cheyenne Wells U.S.A.
20 E4 Chezacut Can.
84 C4 Chhapar India
85 F4 Chhapra India
84 D4 Chhatarpur India
84 B3 Chhatr Pak.
84 D5 Chhindwara India
84 C5 Chhota Udepur India
84 C4 Chhoti Sadri India
85 G4 Chhukha Bhutan
89 F6 Chia-i Taiwan
95 B1 Chiang Kham Thai.
95 B1 Chiang Khan Thai.
95 A1 Chiang Mai Thai.
66 C2 Chiari Italy
91 H6 Chiba Japan
91 H6 Chiba Japan
103 B5 Chibia Angola
103 D6 Chiboma Moz.
22 F4 Chibougamau Can.
22 F4 Chibougamau L. l. Can.
22 F4 Chibougamau, Parc de res. Can.
90 D5 Chibu Japan
90 D6 Chiburi-jima i. Japan
91 F5 Chibu-Sangaku Nat. Park nat. park Japan
105 K2 Chibuto Moz.
85 G2 Chibuzhang Hu l. China
30 D5 Chicago IL U.S.A.
30 D5 Chicago Heights U.S.A.
30 C5 Chicago Ship Canal canal U.S.A.
45 B3 Chicamocha r. Col.
45 E3 Chicanán r. Venez.
20 B3 Chichagof U.S.A.
20 B3 Chichagof Island i. U.S.A.
88 E1 Chicheng China
59 G7 Chichester U.K.
112 C4 Chichester Range mts Austr.
112 C4 Chichester Range National Park nat. park W.A. Austr.
91 G6 Chichibu Japan
91 G6 Chichibu-Tama National Park nat. park Japan
32 E6 Chickahominy r. U.S.A.
29 C5 Chickamauga L. l. U.S.A.
27 D5 Chickasha U.S.A.
65 C4 Chiclana de la Frontera Spain
42 C5 Chiclayo Peru
44 C6 Chico r. Chubut Arg.
47 B4 Chico r. Chubut/Río Negro Arg.
44 C7 Chico r. Santa Cruz Arg.
34 B2 Chico U.S.A.

105 L2 **Chicomo** Moz.
33 G3 **Chicopee** U.S.A.
94 B2 **Chico Sapocoy, Mt** *mt* Phil.
23 F4 **Chicoutimi** Can.
105 J1 **Chicualacuala** Moz.
105 L2 **Chidenguele** Moz.
23 H1 **Chidley, C.** *c.* Can.
105 L2 **Chiducuane** Moz.
29 D6 **Chiefland** U.S.A.
62 F7 **Chiemsee** *l.* Ger.
61 D5 **Chiers** *r.* France
66 F3 **Chieti** Italy
88 F1 **Chifeng** China
46 E2 **Chifre, Serra do** *mts* Brazil
82 D1 **Chiganak** Kazak.
23 G4 **Chignecto B.** *b.* Can.
45 A3 **Chigorodó** Col.
103 D6 **Chigubo** Moz.
85 G3 **Chigu Co** *l.* China
36 C3 **Chihuahua** Mex.
82 C2 **Chiili** Kazak.
89 D6 **Chikan** China
68 D3 **Chikhachevo** Rus. Fed.
84 D5 **Chikhali Kalan Parasia** India
84 D5 **Chikhli** India
83 E8 **Chikmagalur** India
91 G5 **Chikuma-gawa** *r.* Japan
91 G6 **Chikura** Japan
90 C7 **Chikushino** Japan
90 H2 **Chikyū-misaki** *pt* Japan
20 E4 **Chilanko Forks** Can.
82 D3 **Chilas** Jammu and Kashmir
34 B2 **Chilcoot** U.S.A.
20 E4 **Chilcotin** *r.* Can.
116 D1 **Chilcott I.** *i.* Coral Sea Is Terr.
116 E5 **Childers** Austr.
27 C5 **Childress** U.S.A.
38 □ **Chile** *country* S. America
15 O8 **Chile Basin** *sea feature* Pac. Oc.
44 C3 **Chilecito** Arg.
69 H6 **Chilgir** Rus. Fed.
30 C5 **Chilicothe** U.S.A.
82 E2 **Chilik** Kazak.
85 F6 **Chilika Lake** *l.* India
103 C5 **Chililabombwe** Zambia
20 E4 **Chilko** *r.* Can.
20 E4 **Chilko L.** *l.* Can.
116 A1 **Chillagoe** Austr.
47 B3 **Chillán** Chile
47 B3 **Chillán, Nevado** *mts* Chile
47 E3 **Chillar** Arg.
26 E4 **Chillicothe** *MO* U.S.A.
32 B5 **Chillicothe** *OH* U.S.A.
84 C1 **Chillinji** Pak.
20 E5 **Chilliwack** Can.
44 B6 **Chiloé, Isla de** *i.* Chile
24 B3 **Chiloquin** U.S.A.
36 E5 **Chilpancingo** Mex.
115 G6 **Chiltern** Austr.
59 G6 **Chiltern Hills** *h.* U.K.
30 C3 **Chilton** U.S.A.
89 F5 **Chi-lung** Taiwan
84 D2 **Chilung Pass** *pass* India
103 D4 **Chimala** Tanz.
61 C4 **Chimay** Belgium
47 C1 **Chimbas** Arg.
42 C4 **Chimborazo** *mt.* Ecuador
42 C5 **Chimbote** Peru
45 B2 **Chimichaguá** Col.
**Chimkent** *see* **Shymkent**
103 D5 **Chimoio** Moz.
70 **China** *country* Asia
45 B3 **Chinácota** Col.
34 D4 **China Lake** *l. CA* U.S.A.
33 J2 **China Lake** *l. ME* U.S.A.
36 G6 **Chinandega** Nic.
34 C5 **China Pt** *pt* U.S.A.
42 C6 **Chincha Alta** Peru
20 F3 **Chinchaga** *r.* Can.
116 D6 **Chinchilla** Austr.
33 F6 **Chincoteague B.** *b.* U.S.A.
103 D5 **Chinde** Moz.
82 J4 **Chindu** China
82 J6 **Chindwin** *r.* Myanmar
84 C2 **Chineni** Jammu and Kashmir
45 B3 **Chingaza, Parque Nacional** *nat. park* Col.
103 C5 **Chingola** Zambia
103 B5 **Chinguar** Angola
103 D5 **Chinhoyi** Zimbabwe
84 C3 **Chiniot** Pak.
87 N4 **Chinju** S. Korea
102 C3 **Chinko** *r.* C.A.R.
35 H3 **Chinle** U.S.A.
35 H3 **Chinle Valley** *v.* U.S.A.
35 H3 **Chinle Wash** *r.* U.S.A.
89 F5 **Chinmen** Taiwan
89 F5 **Chinmen Tao** *i.* Taiwan
91 G6 **Chino** Japan
64 E3 **Chinon** France
35 F4 **Chino Valley** U.S.A.
103 D5 **Chinsali** Zambia
66 E2 **Chioggia** Italy
67 L5 **Chios** *i.* Greece
67 M5 **Chios** Greece
103 D5 **Chipata** Zambia
47 C4 **Chipchihua, Sa de** *mts* Arg.
103 B5 **Chipindo** Angola
103 D6 **Chipinge** Zimbabwe
83 D7 **Chiplun** India
59 E6 **Chippenham** U.K.
30 B3 **Chippewa** *r.* U.S.A.
30 B3 **Chippewa Falls** U.S.A.
30 B3 **Chippewa, Lake** *l.* U.S.A.
59 F6 **Chipping Norton** U.K.
59 E6 **Chipping Sodbury** U.K.
33 K2 **Chiputneticook Lakes** *lakes* U.S.A.
36 G6 **Chiquimula** Guatemala
45 B3 **Chiquinquira** Col.
69 G5 **Chir** *r.* Rus. Fed.
84 C3 **Chirāwa** India
79 K1 **Chirchik** Uzbek.
103 D6 **Chiredzi** Zimbabwe
35 H5 **Chiricahua National Monument** *res.* U.S.A.
35 H6 **Chiricahua Peak** *summit* U.S.A.
45 B2 **Chiriguaná** Col.
37 H7 **Chiriquí, Golfo de** *b.* Panama
59 D5 **Chirk** U.K.
57 F5 **Chirnside** U.K.
67 L3 **Chirpan** Bulg.
37 H7 **Chirripo** *mt* Costa Rica
103 C5 **Chirundu** Zambia
22 E3 **Chisasibi** Can.
30 A2 **Chisholm** U.S.A.
84 C3 **Chishtian Mandi** Pak.
89 B4 **Chishur** China
**Chişinău** *see* **Kishinev**
63 K7 **Chişineu-Criş** Romania
68 J4 **Chistopol'** Rus. Fed.
87 K1 **Chita** Rus. Fed.
103 B5 **Chitado** Angola
103 D5 **Chitambo** Zambia
102 C4 **Chitato** Angola
21 H4 **Chitek Lake** Can.
103 B5 **Chitembo** Angola
103 D4 **Chitipa** Malawi
103 C5 **Chitokoloki** Zambia
90 H2 **Chitose** Japan
83 E8 **Chitradurga** India
84 B2 **Chitral** *r.* Pak.
79 L2 **Chitral** Pak.
37 H7 **Chitré** Panama
85 G5 **Chittagong** Bangl.
85 F5 **Chittaranjan** India
84 C4 **Chittaurgarh** India
83 E8 **Chittoor** India
103 D5 **Chitungulu** Zambia
103 D5 **Chitungwiza** Zimbabwe
103 C5 **Chiume** Angola
103 D5 **Chivhu** Zimbabwe
47 E2 **Chivilcoy** Arg.
89 D6 **Chixi** China
81 J3 **Chiya-e Linik** *h.* Iraq
90 E6 **Chizu** Japan
68 G3 **Chkalovsk** Rus. Fed.
95 □ **Choa Chu Kang** *h.* Sing.
95 □ **Choa Chu Kang** Sing.
95 C2 **Chŏâm Khsant** Cambodia
47 B1 **Choapa** *r.* Chile
103 C5 **Chobe National Park** *nat. park* Botswana
35 E5 **Chocolate Mts** *mts* U.S.A.
45 B3 **Chocontá** Col.
47 D3 **Choele Choel** Arg.
84 C2 **Chogo Lungma Gl.** *gl.* Pak.
69 H6 **Chograyskoye Vdkhr.** *resr* Rus. Fed.
21 J4 **Choiceland** Can.
111 F2 **Choiseul** *i.* Solomon Is
44 E8 **Choiseul Sound** *chan.* Falkland Is
62 H4 **Chojnice** Pol.
91 H4 **Chōkai-san** *volc.* Japan
27 D6 **Choke Canyon L.** *l.* U.S.A.
102 D2 **Ch'ok'ē Mts** *mts* Eth.
85 F3 **Choksum** China
77 Q2 **Chokurdakh** Rus. Fed.
103 D6 **Chókwé** Moz.
64 D3 **Cholet** France
47 B4 **Cholila** Arg.
36 G6 **Choluteca** Honduras
103 C5 **Choma** Zambia
85 G4 **Chomo Lhari** *mt.* Bhutan
95 A1 **Chom Thong** Thai.
62 F5 **Chomutov** Czech Rep.
77 M3 **Chona** *r.* Rus. Fed.
95 B2 **Chon Buri** Thai.
42 B4 **Chone** Ecuador
89 F5 **Chong'an** China
87 N3 **Ch'ŏngjin** N. Korea
87 N4 **Chŏngju** N. Korea
95 B2 **Chông Kal** Cambodia
89 C4 **Chongqing** China
89 E5 **Chongren** China
105 K2 **Chonguene** Moz.
103 C5 **Chongwe** Zambia
89 D4 **Chongyang** China
89 F5 **Chongyang Xi** *r.* China
89 E5 **Chongyi** China
89 C6 **Chongzuo** China
87 N5 **Chŏnju** S. Korea
85 F3 **Cho Oyu** *mt.* China
95 C3 **Chơ Phước Hai** Vietnam
46 B4 **Chopim** *r.* Brazil
46 B4 **Chopimzinho** Brazil
33 F5 **Choptank** *r.* U.S.A.
84 B4 **Chor** Pak.
58 E4 **Chorley** U.K.
69 D5 **Chornobyl'** Ukr.
69 E6 **Chornomors'ke** Ukr.
69 C5 **Chortkiv** Ukr.
91 H6 **Chōshi** Japan
47 B3 **Chos Malal** Arg.
62 G4 **Choszczno** Pol.
42 C5 **Chota** Peru
24 D2 **Choteau** U.S.A.
84 B3 **Choti** Pak.
100 A2 **Choûm** Maur.
34 B3 **Chowchilla** U.S.A.
20 F4 **Chown, Mt** *mt.* Can.
87 K2 **Choybalsan** Mongolia
86 J2 **Choyr** Mongolia
62 H6 **Chřiby** *h.* Czech Rep.
30 D6 **Chrisman** U.S.A.
105 J3 **Chrissiesmeer** S. Africa
117 D5 **Christchurch** N.Z.
59 F7 **Christchurch** U.K.
105 F3 **Christiana** S. Africa
31 G3 **Christian I.** *i.* Can.
32 C6 **Christiansburg** U.S.A.
20 C3 **Christian Sound** *chan.* U.S.A.
21 G3 **Christina** *r.* Can.
111 G6 **Christina, Mt** *mt* N.Z.
13 L4 **Christmas Island** *i.* Indian Ocean
62 G6 **Chrudim** Czech Rep.
67 L7 **Chrysi** *i.* Greece
76 H5 **Chu** *r.* Kazak.
85 G5 **Chuadanga** Bangl.
105 K2 **Chuali, L.** *l.* Moz.
88 F4 **Chuansha** China
24 D3 **Chubbuck** U.S.A.
44 C6 **Chubut** *r.* Arg.
47 C4 **Chubut** *div.* Arg.
35 E5 **Chuckwalla Mts** *mts* U.S.A.
69 D5 **Chudniv** Ukr.
68 D3 **Chudovo** Rus. Fed.
**Chudskoye Ozero** *l. see* **Peipus, Lake**
90 D6 **Chūgoku-sanchi** *mts* Japan
24 F3 **Chugwater** U.S.A.
69 E5 **Chuhuyiv** Ukr.
35 G5 **Chuichu** U.S.A.
87 P1 **Chukchagirskoye, Ozero** *l.* Rus. Fed.
77 V3 **Chukchi Sea** *sea* Rus. Fed./U.S.A.
68 G3 **Chukhloma** Rus. Fed.
77 U3 **Chukotskiy Poluostrov** *pen.* Rus. Fed.
68 H1 **Chulasa** Rus. Fed.
34 D5 **Chula Vista** U.S.A.
76 K4 **Chulym** Rus. Fed.
85 G4 **Chumbi** China
44 C3 **Chumbicha** Arg.
77 P4 **Chumikan** Rus. Fed.
95 B1 **Chum Phae** Thai.
95 A3 **Chumphon** Thai.
95 B2 **Chum Saeng** Thai.
77 L4 **Chuna** *r.* Rus. Fed.
89 F4 **Chun'an** China
87 N4 **Ch'unch'ŏn** S. Korea
**Chungking** *see* **Chongqing**
84 B2 **Chungur, Koh-i-** *mt* Afgh.
85 F3 **Chunit Tso** *salt l.* China
77 M3 **Chunya** *r.* Rus. Fed.
95 C3 **Chuŏr Phnum Dâmrei** *mts* Cambodia
95 C2 **Chuŏr Phnum Dângrêk** *mts* Cambodia/Thai.
95 B2 **Chuor Phnum Krâvanh** *mts* Cambodia
88 A4 **Chuosijia** China
81 L3 **Chūplū** Iran
42 D7 **Chuquibamba** Peru
44 C2 **Chuquicamata** Chile
62 D7 **Chur** Switz.
77 P3 **Churapcha** Rus. Fed.
21 K3 **Churchill** *r. Man./Sask.* Can.
23 H3 **Churchill** *r. Nfld* Can.
21 L3 **Churchill** Can.
21 L3 **Churchill, Cape** *c.* Can.
23 H3 **Churchill Falls** Can.
21 H3 **Churchill Lake** *l.* Can.
20 D3 **Churchill Peak** *summit* Can.
22 E2 **Churchill Sound** *chan.* Can.
26 D1 **Churchs Ferry** U.S.A.
32 D5 **Churchville** U.S.A.
85 F4 **Churia Ghati Hills** *mts* Nepal
68 H3 **Churov** Rus. Fed.
84 C3 **Churu** India
45 C2 **Churuguara** Venez.
90 J2 **Chūrui** Japan
84 D2 **Chushul** Jammu and Kashmir
35 H3 **Chuska Mountains** *mts* U.S.A.
23 F4 **Chute-des-Passes** Can.
31 J2 **Chute-Rouge** Can.
31 K2 **Chute-St-Philippe** Can.
89 F5 **Chu-tung** Taiwan
108 **Chuuk** *i.* Micronesia
68 H4 **Chuvashskaya Respublika** *div.* Rus. Fed.
88 F3 **Chu Xian** China
89 E5 **Chuxiong** China
95 D2 **Chư Yang Sin** *mt.* Vietnam
81 K4 **Chwārtā** Iraq
69 D6 **Ciadâr-Lunga** Moldova
92 □ **Ciamis** Indon.
92 □ **Cianjur** Indon.
46 B3 **Cianorte** Brazil
25 E6 **Cibuta** Mex.
66 F2 **Čićarija** *mts* Croatia
80 E2 **Çiçekdağı** Turkey
92 □ **Cidaun** Indon.
69 E7 **Cide** Turkey
63 K4 **Ciechanów** Pol.
37 J4 **Ciego de Avila** Cuba
45 B2 **Ciénaga** Col.
45 B2 **Ciénaga de Zapatoza** *l.* Col.
27 C7 **Ciénega de Flores** Mex.
25 E6 **Cieneguita** Mex.
37 H4 **Cienfuegos** Cuba
65 F3 **Cieza** Spain
65 E2 **Cifuentes** Spain
81 M2 **Çigil Adası** *i.* Azer.
65 E3 **Cigüela** *r.* Spain
80 D2 **Cihanbeyli** Turkey
65 D3 **Cijara, Embalse de** *resr* Spain
92 □ **Cikalong** Indon.
92 □ **Cilacap** Indon.
81 J1 **Çıldır** Turkey
81 J1 **Çıldır Gölü** *l.* Turkey
89 D4 **Cili** China
81 K3 **Cilo D.** *mt* Turkey
81 N1 **Çiloy Adası** *i.* Azer.
35 E4 **Cima** U.S.A.
92 □ **Cimahi** Indon.
27 D4 **Cimarron** *r.* U.S.A.
25 F4 **Cimarron** U.S.A.
69 D6 **Cimişlia** Moldova
66 D2 **Cimone, Monte** *mt* Italy
81 H3 **Çınar** Turkey
45 C3 **Cinaruco** *r.* Venez.
45 D3 **Cinaruco-Capanaparo, Parque Nacional** *nat. park* Venez.
65 G2 **Cinca** *r.* Spain
32 A5 **Cincinnati** U.S.A.
33 F3 **Cincinnatus** U.S.A.
47 D4 **Cinco Chañares** Arg.
47 C3 **Cinco Saltos** Arg.
59 E6 **Cinderford** U.K.
80 B3 **Çine** Turkey
61 D4 **Ciney** Belgium
64 J5 **Cinto, Monte** *mt.* France
46 B3 **Cinzas** *r.* Brazil
47 C3 **Cipolletti** Arg.
24 F2 **Circle** U.S.A.
32 B5 **Circleville** *OH* U.S.A.
35 F2 **Circleville** *UT* U.S.A.
92 □ **Cirebon** Indon.
59 F6 **Cirencester** U.K.
66 B2 **Ciriè** Italy
66 G5 **Cirò Marina** Italy
23 H2 **Cirque Mtn** *mt.* Can.
30 C6 **Cisco** *IL* U.S.A.
27 D5 **Cisco** *TX* U.S.A.
35 H2 **Cisco** *UT* U.S.A.
45 B3 **Cisneros** Col.
36 E5 **Citlaltépetl, Vol.** *volc.* Mex.
66 G3 **Čitluk** Bos.-Herz.
104 C6 **Citrusdal** S. Africa
66 E3 **Città di Castello** Italy
67 L2 **Ciucaș, Vârful** *mt.* Romania
36 D3 **Ciudad Acuña** Mex.
36 D5 **Ciudad Altamirano** Mex.
45 E3 **Ciudad Bolívar** Venez.
36 C3 **Ciudad Camargo** Mex.
36 F5 **Ciudad del Carmen** Mex.
46 A4 **Ciudad del Este** Para.
36 C3 **Ciudad Delicias** Mex.
45 C2 **Ciudad de Nutrias** Venez.
36 E4 **Ciudad de Valles** Mex.
45 E2 **Ciudad Guayana** Venez.
36 D5 **Ciudad Guzmán** Mex.
36 E5 **Ciudad Ixtepec** Mex.
36 C2 **Ciudad Juárez** Mex.
36 E4 **Ciudad Mante** Mex.
36 C3 **Ciudad Obregón** Mex.
45 E3 **Ciudad Piar** Venez.
65 E3 **Ciudad Real** Spain
65 C2 **Ciudad Rodrigo** Spain
36 E4 **Ciudad Victoria** Mex.
65 H2 **Ciutadella de Menorca** Spain
80 F1 **Cıva Burnu** *pt* Turkey
80 B2 **Civan Dağ** *mt.* Turkey
66 E1 **Cividale del Friuli** Italy
66 E3 **Civita Castellana** Italy
66 E3 **Civitanova Marche** Italy
66 D3 **Civitavecchia** Italy
80 B2 **Çivril** Turkey
89 F4 **Cixi** China
88 E2 **Ci Xian** China
81 J3 **Cizre** Turkey
59 J6 **Clacton-on-Sea** U.K.
60 D3 **Clady** U.K.
21 G3 **Claire, Lake** *l.* Can.
24 B3 **Clair Engle L.** *resr* U.S.A.
32 D4 **Clairton** U.S.A.
64 F3 **Clamecy** France
34 D2 **Clan Alpine Mts** *mts* U.S.A.
60 E4 **Clane** Rep. of Ireland
29 C5 **Clanton** U.S.A.
104 C6 **Clanwilliam** S. Africa
60 D4 **Clara** Rep. of Ireland
95 A3 **Clara I.** *i.* Myanmar
114 E4 **Clare** *N.S.W.* Austr.
114 C4 **Clare** *S.A.* Austr.
60 C4 **Clare** *r.* Rep. of Ireland
30 E4 **Clare** U.S.A.
60 C5 **Clarecastle** Rep. of Ireland
60 A4 **Clare Island** *i.* Rep. of Ireland
33 G3 **Claremont** U.S.A.
27 E4 **Claremore** U.S.A.
60 C4 **Claremorris** Rep. of Ireland
115 K2 **Clarence** *r.* Austr.
117 D5 **Clarence** N.Z.
20 C3 **Clarence Str.** *chan.* U.S.A.
29 F7 **Clarence Town** Bahamas
27 C5 **Clarendon** U.S.A.
23 K4 **Clarenville** Can.
20 G5 **Claresholm** Can.
26 E3 **Clarinda** U.S.A.
32 C5 **Clarington** U.S.A.
32 D4 **Clarion** *r.* U.S.A.
32 D4 **Clarion** U.S.A.
15 L4 **Clarion Fracture Zone** *sea feature* Pac. Oc.
26 D2 **Clark** U.S.A.
116 A2 **Clarke** *r.* Austr.
105 H5 **Clarkebury** S. Africa
115 H8 **Clarke I.** *i.* Austr.
116 C3 **Clarke Range** *mts* Austr.
116 A2 **Clarke River** Austr.
29 D5 **Clark Hill Res.** *resr* U.S.A.
35 E4 **Clark Mt** *mt.* U.S.A.
31 G3 **Clark, Pt** *pt* Can.
32 C5 **Clarksburg** U.S.A.
27 F5 **Clarksdale** U.S.A.
33 F4 **Clarks Summit** U.S.A.
24 C2 **Clarkston** U.S.A.
27 E5 **Clarksville** *AR* U.S.A.
30 A4 **Clarksville** *IA* U.S.A.
29 C4 **Clarksville** *TN* U.S.A.
46 B2 **Claro** *r. Goiás* Brazil
46 B1 **Claro** *r. Goiás* Brazil
60 D5 **Clashmore** Rep. of Ireland
60 D3 **Claudy** U.K.
94 B2 **Claveria** Phil.
33 G2 **Clayburg** U.S.A.
26 D4 **Clay Center** U.S.A.
35 F3 **Clayhole Wash** *r.* U.S.A.
29 D5 **Clayton** *GA* U.S.A.
25 G4 **Clayton** *NM* U.S.A.
33 E2 **Clayton** *NY* U.S.A.
33 J1 **Clayton Lake** U.S.A.
32 C6 **Claytor Lake** *l.* U.S.A.
60 B6 **Clear, Cape** *c.* Rep. of Ireland
31 G4 **Clear Creek** Can.
35 G4 **Clear Creek** *r.* U.S.A.
32 D4 **Clearfield** *PA* U.S.A.
24 E3 **Clearfield** *UT* U.S.A.
32 B4 **Clear Fork Reservoir** *resr* U.S.A.
20 F3 **Clear Hills** *mts* Can.
34 A2 **Clear Lake** *l. CA* U.S.A.
26 E3 **Clear Lake** *IA* U.S.A.
35 F2 **Clear Lake** *l. UT* U.S.A.
30 A3 **Clear Lake** *WV* U.S.A.
24 B3 **Clear L. Res.** *resr* U.S.A.
20 F4 **Clearwater** *r. Alta.* Can.
21 H3 **Clearwater** *r. Sask.* Can.
29 D7 **Clearwater** U.S.A.
89 □ **Clear Water Bay** *b.* *Hong Kong* China
24 D2 **Clearwater Mountains** *mts* U.S.A.
21 H3 **Clearwater River Provincial Park** *res.* Can.
27 D5 **Cleburne** U.S.A.
24 B2 **Cle Elum** U.S.A.
58 G4 **Cleethorpes** U.K.
95 □ **Clementi** Sing.
32 C5 **Clendenin** U.S.A.
32 C4 **Clendening Lake** *l.* U.S.A.
94 A4 **Cleopatra Needle** *mt.* Phil.
31 H1 **Cléricy** Can.
116 B4 **Clermont** Austr.
61 A5 **Clermont** France
29 D6 **Clermont** U.S.A.
64 F4 **Clermont-Ferrand** France
61 E4 **Clervaux** Lux.
66 D1 **Cles** Italy
114 B4 **Cleve** Austr.
59 E6 **Clevedon** U.K.
27 F5 **Cleveland** *MS* U.S.A.
32 C4 **Cleveland** *OH* U.S.A.
29 C5 **Cleveland** *TN* U.S.A.
116 B2 **Cleveland, B.** *b.* Austr.
116 B2 **Cleveland, C.** *hd* Austr.
30 D2 **Cleveland Cliffs Basin** *l.* U.S.A.
58 F3 **Cleveland Hills** *h.* U.K.
20 G5 **Cleveland, Mt** *mt.* U.S.A.
60 B4 **Clew Bay** *b.* Rep. of Ireland
29 D7 **Clewiston** U.S.A.
60 A4 **Clifden** Rep. of Ireland
35 H5 **Cliff** U.S.A.
60 C3 **Cliffoney** Rep. of Ireland
117 E4 **Clifford Bay** *b.* N.Z.
115 J1 **Clifton** Austr.
35 H5 **Clifton** U.S.A.
116 A1 **Clifton Beach** Austr.
32 D6 **Clifton Forge** U.S.A.
32 B6 **Clinch** *r.* U.S.A.
32 B6 **Clinch Mountain** *mts* U.S.A.
20 E4 **Clinton** *B.C.* Can.
31 G4 **Clinton** *Ont.* Can.
33 G4 **Clinton** *CT* U.S.A.
30 B5 **Clinton** *IA* U.S.A.
30 C5 **Clinton** *IL* U.S.A.
33 H3 **Clinton** *MA* U.S.A.
33 J2 **Clinton** *ME* U.S.A.
26 E4 **Clinton** *MO* U.S.A.
27 F5 **Clinton** *MS* U.S.A.
29 E5 **Clinton** *NC* U.S.A.
27 D5 **Clinton** *OK* U.S.A.
21 H2 **Clinton-Colden Lake** *l.* Can.
30 C5 **Clinton Lake** *l.* U.S.A.
30 C3 **Clintonville** U.S.A.
35 G4 **Clints Well** U.S.A.
15 L5 **Clipperton Fracture Zone** *sea feature* Pac. Oc.
15 M5 **Clipperton I.** *i.* Pac. Oc.
36 C6 **Clipperton Island** *terr.* Pac. Oc.
57 B3 **Clisham** *h.* U.K.
58 E4 **Clitheroe** U.K.
105 G4 **Clocolan** S. Africa
60 D4 **Cloghan** Rep. of Ireland
60 C6 **Clonakilty** Rep. of Ireland
60 C6 **Clonakilty Bay** *b.* Rep. of Ireland
60 C4 **Clonbern** Rep. of Ireland
113 H4 **Cloncurry** Austr.
60 D3 **Clones** Rep. of Ireland
60 D5 **Clonmel** Rep. of Ireland
60 D4 **Clonygowan** Rep. of Ireland
60 B5 **Cloonbannin** Rep. of Ireland
60 D4 **Clooneagh** Rep. of Ireland
30 A2 **Cloquet** U.S.A.
24 F2 **Cloud Peak** *summit* U.S.A.
117 E4 **Cloudy Bay** *b.* N.Z.
89 □ **Cloudy Hill** *h. Hong Kong* China
31 K1 **Clova** Can.
34 A2 **Cloverdale** U.S.A.
27 C5 **Clovis** U.S.A.
31 J3 **Cloyne** Can.
57 C3 **Cluanie, Loch** *l.* U.K.
21 H3 **Cluff Lake** Can.
63 L7 **Cluj-Napoca** Romania
59 D5 **Clun** U.K.
114 E6 **Clunes** Austr.
113 G4 **Cluny** Austr.
64 H3 **Cluses** France
59 D4 **Clwydian Range** *h.* U.K.
20 G4 **Clyde** Can.
57 D5 **Clyde** *r.* U.K.
32 E3 **Clyde** *NY* U.S.A.
32 B4 **Clyde** *OH* U.S.A.
57 D5 **Clydebank** U.K.
57 D5 **Clyde, Firth of** *est.* U.K.
25 C5 **Coachella** U.S.A.
47 B2 **Co Aconcagua** *mt* Arg.
20 D2 **Coal** *r.* Can.
30 C5 **Coal City** U.S.A.
34 D3 **Coaldale** U.S.A.
27 D5 **Coalgate** U.S.A.
34 B3 **Coalinga** U.S.A.
20 D3 **Coal River** Can.
59 F5 **Coalville** U.K.
42 F4 **Coari** Brazil
42 F5 **Coari** *r.* Brazil
29 C6 **Coastal Plain** *plain* U.S.A.
20 D4 **Coast Mountains** *mts* Can.
116 E5 **Coast Ra.** *h.* Austr.
24 B2 **Coast Range** *mts* U.S.A.
34 B3 **Coast Ranges** *mts* U.S.A.
57 E5 **Coatbridge** U.K.
33 F5 **Coatesville** U.S.A.
23 F4 **Coaticook** Can.
18 **Coats I.** *i.* Can.
119 C3 **Coats Land** *coastal area* Ant.
36 F5 **Coatzacoalcos** Mex.
31 H2 **Cobalt** Can.
36 F5 **Cobán** Guatemala
115 F3 **Cobar** Austr.
115 H6 **Cobargo** Austr.
115 H6 **Cobberas, Mt** *mt.* Austr.
114 E7 **Cobden** Austr.
31 J3 **Cobden** Can.
60 C6 **Cóbh** Rep. of Ireland
21 K4 **Cobham** *r.* Can.
42 E6 **Cobija** Bol.
33 F3 **Cobleskill** U.S.A.
31 H4 **Cobourg** Can.
112 F2 **Cobourg Peninsula** *pen.* Austr.
115 F5 **Cobram** Austr.
62 E5 **Coburg** Ger.
65 D2 **Coca** Spain
46 B1 **Cocalinho** Brazil
42 E7 **Cochabamba** Bol.
47 B4 **Cochamó** Chile
61 F4 **Cochem** Ger.
83 E9 **Cochin** India
35 H5 **Cochise** U.S.A.
20 G4 **Cochrane** *Alta.* Can.
22 D4 **Cochrane** *Ont.* Can.
21 J3 **Cochrane** *r.* Can.
44 B7 **Cochrane** Chile
114 D4 **Cockburn** Austr.
31 F3 **Cockburn I.** *i.* Can.
57 F5 **Cockburnspath** U.K.
29 F7 **Cockburn Town** Bahamas
37 K4 **Cockburn Town** Turks and Caicos Is
58 D3 **Cockermouth** U.K.
104 F6 **Cockscomb** *summit* S. Africa
37 H6 **Coco** *r.* Honduras/Nic.
36 G7 **Coco, Isla de** *i.* Col.
35 F4 **Coconino Plateau** *plat.* U.S.A.
115 G4 **Cocoparra Range** *h.* Austr.
45 A4 **Coco, Pta** *pt* Col.
45 B3 **Cocorná** Col.
46 D1 **Cocos** Brazil
13 L4 **Cocos Is** *is* Indian Ocean
15 O5 **Cocos Ridge** *sea feature* Pac. Oc.
45 B3 **Cocuy, Parque Nacional el** *nat. park* Col.
45 B3 **Cocuy, Sierra Nevada del** *mt* Col.
42 F4 **Codajás** Brazil
33 H4 **Cod, Cape** *c.* U.S.A.
45 D2 **Codera, C.** *pt* Venez.
117 A7 **Codfish I.** *i.* N.Z.
66 E2 **Codigoro** Italy
23 H2 **Cod Island** *i.* Can.
67 L2 **Codlea** Romania
43 K4 **Codó** Brazil
59 E5 **Codsall** U.K.
60 A6 **Cod's Head** *hd* Rep. of Ireland
24 E2 **Cody** U.S.A.
113 H2 **Coen** Austr.
13 H4 **Coëtivy Island** *i.* Seychelles
24 C2 **Coeur d'Alene** U.S.A.
24 C2 **Coeur d'Alene L.** *l.* U.S.A.
105 H5 **Coffee Bay** S. Africa

27 E4 Coffeyville U.S.A.
114 A5 Coffin B. b. Austr.
114 A5 Coffin Bay Austr.
115 K3 Coffs Harbour Austr.
105 G6 Cofimvaba S. Africa
30 B4 Coggon U.S.A.
64 D4 Cognac France
100 C4 Cogo Equatorial Guinea
32 E3 Cohocton r. U.S.A.
33 G3 Cohoes U.S.A.
114 F5 Cohuna Austr.
37 H7 Coiba, Isla i. Panama
44 C8 Coig r. Arg.
44 B7 Coihaique Chile
83 E8 Coimbatore India
65 B2 Coimbra Port.
65 D4 Coín Spain
42 E7 Coipasa, Salar de salt flat Bol.
45 C2 Cojedes r. Venez.
24 E3 Cokeville U.S.A.
114 E7 Colac Austr.
46 E2 Colatina Brazil
26 C4 Colby U.S.A.
42 D7 Colca r. Peru
59 H6 Colchester U.K.
30 B5 Colchester U.S.A.
57 F5 Coldingham U.K.
21 G4 Cold L. l. Can.
21 G4 Cold Lake Can.
57 F5 Coldstream U.K.
27 D4 Coldwater KS U.S.A.
30 E5 Coldwater MI U.S.A.
30 D1 Coldwell Can.
33 H2 Colebrook U.S.A.
30 E4 Coleman MI U.S.A.
27 D6 Coleman TX U.S.A.
105 H4 Colenso S. Africa
114 D6 Coleraine Austr.
60 E2 Coleraine U.K.
117 C5 Coleridge, L. l. N.Z.
115 H9 Coles Bay Austr.
104 F5 Colesberg S. Africa
34 B2 Colfax CA U.S.A.
24 C2 Colfax WA U.S.A.
57 Colgrave Sound chan. U.K.
105 G3 Coligny S. Africa
36 D5 Colima Mex.
57 B4 Coll i. U.K.
65 E2 Collado Villalba Spain
115 H2 Collarenebri Austr.
29 C5 College Park U.S.A.
27 D6 College Station U.S.A.
115 G2 Collerina Austr.
115 H3 Collie N.S.W. Austr.
112 C6 Collie W.A. Austr.
112 D3 Collier Bay b. Austr.
112 C4 Collier Range National Park nat. park W.A. Austr.
31 G3 Collingwood Can.
117 D4 Collingwood N.Z.
27 F6 Collins U.S.A.
116 B3 Collinsville Austr.
28 B4 Collinsville U.S.A.
47 B3 Collipulli Chile
60 C3 Collooney Rep. of Ireland
64 H2 Colmar France
65 E2 Colmenar Viejo Spain
57 D5 Colmonell U.K.
59 H6 Colne r. U.K.
115 J4 Colo r. Austr.
62 C5 Cologne Ger.
30 C3 Coloma U.S.A.
46 C3 Colômbia Brazil
38 Colombia country S. America
83 E9 Colombo Sri Lanka
64 E5 Colomiers France
47 E2 Colón Buenos Aires Arg.
47 E2 Colón Entre Ríos Arg.
37 H4 Colón Cuba
37 J7 Colón Panama
112 F6 Colona Austr.
25 C6 Colonet, C. c. Mex.
46 E1 Colônia r. Brazil
47 D3 Colonia Choele Choel, Isla i. Arg.
47 F2 Colonia del Sacramento Uru.
47 C3 Colonia Emilio Mitre Arg.
47 F1 Colonia Lavalleja Uru.
32 E6 Colonial Heights U.S.A.
35 F6 Colonia Reforma Mex.
66 G5 Colonna, Capo pt Italy
57 B4 Colonsay i. U.K.
47 D3 Colorada Grande, Salina l. Arg.
47 D3 Colorado r. La Pampa/Río Negro Arg.
47 C1 Colorado r. San Juan Arg.
35 E5 Colorado r. Mex./U.S.A.
27 D6 Colorado r. U.S.A.
25 F4 Colorado div. U.S.A.
35 F3 Colorado City AZ U.S.A.
27 C5 Colorado City TX U.S.A.
47 D3 Colorado, Delta del Río delta Arg.
34 D5 Colorado Desert des. U.S.A.
35 H2 Colorado National Monument res. U.S.A.
35 G3 Colorado Plateau plat. U.S.A.
35 E4 Colorado River Aqueduct canal U.S.A.
25 F4 Colorado Springs U.S.A.
59 G5 Colsterworth U.K.
59 J5 Coltishall U.K.
34 D4 Colton CA U.S.A.
33 F2 Colton NY U.S.A.
35 G2 Colton UT U.S.A.
24 B2 Columbia r. Can./U.S.A.
32 E5 Columbia MD U.S.A.
26 E4 Columbia MO U.S.A.
27 F6 Columbia MS U.S.A.
32 E4 Columbia PA U.S.A.
29 D5 Columbia SC U.S.A.
29 C5 Columbia TN U.S.A.
30 E5 Columbia City U.S.A.
32 E5 Columbia, District of div. U.S.A.
33 K2 Columbia Falls ME U.S.A.
24 D1 Columbia Falls MT U.S.A.
20 F4 Columbia Mountains mts Can.
20 F4 Columbia, Mt mt. Can.
24 C2 Columbia Plateau plat. U.S.A.
104 B6 Columbine, Cape pt S. Africa
29 C5 Columbus GA U.S.A.
28 C4 Columbus IN U.S.A.
27 F5 Columbus MS U.S.A.
24 E2 Columbus MT U.S.A.
26 D3 Columbus NE U.S.A.
25 F6 Columbus NM U.S.A.
32 B5 Columbus OH U.S.A.
27 D6 Columbus TX U.S.A.
30 C4 Columbus WV U.S.A.
30 B5 Columbus Jct U.S.A.
29 F7 Columbus Pt pt Bahamas
34 D2 Columbus Salt Marsh salt marsh U.S.A.
34 A2 Colusa U.S.A.
117 E2 Colville N.Z.
24 C1 Colville U.S.A.
117 E2 Colville Channel chan. N.Z.
59 D4 Colwyn Bay U.K.
66 E2 Comacchio Italy
66 E2 Comacchio, Valli di lag. Italy
85 G3 Comai China
47 B4 Comallo r. Arg.
27 D6 Comanche U.S.A.
119 B1 Comandante Ferraz Brazil Base Ant.
47 C2 Comandante Salas Arg.
63 N7 Comănești Romania
47 B1 Combarbalá Chile
60 F3 Comber U.K.
31 J3 Combermere Can.
85 H6 Combermere Bay b. Myanmar
105 K1 Combomune Moz.
115 K3 Comboyne Austr.
22 E3 Comencho, L. l. Can.
60 D5 Comeragh Mountains h. Rep. of Ireland
116 C5 Comet r. Austr.
116 C4 Comet Austr.
27 D6 Comfort U.S.A.
85 G5 Comilla Bangl.
66 C4 Comino, Capo pt Sardinia Italy
36 F5 Comitán de Domínguez Mex.
33 G4 Commack U.S.A.
31 H3 Commanda Can.
119 B6 Commonwealth B. b. Ant.
66 C2 Como Italy
85 G3 Como Chamling l. China
44 C7 Comodoro Rivadavia Arg.
100 B4 Comoé, Parc National de la nat. park Côte d'Ivoire
66 C2 Como, Lago di l. Italy
96 Comoros country Africa
64 F2 Compiègne France
36 D4 Compostela Mex.
94 C5 Compostela Phil.
46 C4 Comprida, Ilha i. Brazil
30 C5 Compton U.S.A.
69 D6 Comrat Moldova
57 E4 Comrie U.K.
27 C6 Comstock U.S.A.
85 H4 Cona China
100 A4 Conakry Guinea
47 C4 Cona Niyeo Arg.
115 G8 Conara Jct. Austr.
46 D2 Conceição r. Brazil
46 E2 Conceição da Barra Brazil
43 J5 Conceição do Araguaia Brazil
44 C3 Concepción Arg.
42 F7 Concepción Bol.
47 B3 Concepción Chile
37 H7 Concepción Panama
44 E2 Concepción Para.
47 E2 Concepción del Uruguay Arg.
23 K4 Conception Bay South Can.
29 F7 Conception I. i. Bahamas
34 B4 Conception, Pt pt U.S.A.
46 C3 Conchas Brazil
25 F5 Conchas L. l. U.S.A.
35 H4 Concho U.S.A.
36 D3 Conchos r. Chihuahua Mex.
36 E4 Conchos r. Tamaulipas Mex.
34 A3 Concord CA U.S.A.
29 D5 Concord NC U.S.A.
33 H3 Concord NH U.S.A.
47 F1 Concordia Arg.
45 B4 Concordia Col.
104 B4 Concordia S. Africa
26 D4 Concordia U.S.A.
116 D6 Condamine r. Austr.
115 J1 Condamine Austr.
95 C3 Côn Đao Vietnam
46 E1 Condeúba Brazil
115 G4 Condobolin Austr.
64 E5 Condom France
24 B2 Condon U.S.A.
61 D4 Condroz reg. Belgium
29 C6 Conecuh r. U.S.A.
66 E2 Conegliano Italy
32 D4 Conemaugh r. U.S.A.
31 G4 Conestogo Lake l. Can.
32 E3 Conesus Lake l. U.S.A.
Coney I. i. see Serangoon, P.
33 G4 Coney I. i. U.S.A.
110 F3 Conflict Group is P.N.G.
64 E3 Confolens France
35 F2 Confusion Range mts U.S.A.
89 D6 Conghua China
89 C5 Congjiang China
59 E4 Congleton U.K.
96 Congo country Africa
102 B4 Congo r. Congo/Zaire
35 F4 Congress U.S.A.
47 B3 Conguillo, Parque Nac. nat. park Chile
59 G4 Coningsby U.K.
22 D4 Coniston Can.
58 D3 Coniston U.K.
116 A2 Conjuboy Austr.
21 G3 Conklin Can.
47 D2 Conlara r. Arg.
47 D2 Conlara Arg.
32 C4 Conneaut U.S.A.
33 G4 Connecticut div. U.S.A.
28 F3 Connecticut r. U.S.A.
32 D4 Connellsville U.S.A.
60 B4 Connemara reg. Rep. of Ireland
60 B4 Connemara Nat. Park nat. park Rep. of Ireland
33 J1 Conners Can.
28 C4 Connersville U.S.A.
60 B3 Conn, Lough l. Rep. of Ireland
116 C3 Connors Ra. h. Austr.
114 F4 Conoble Austr.
89 B6 Co Nôi Vietnam
33 E5 Conowingo U.S.A.
24 E1 Conrad U.S.A.
27 E6 Conroe U.S.A.
46 D3 Conselheiro Lafaiete Brazil
46 E2 Conselheiro Pena Brazil
58 F3 Consett U.K.
95 C3 Côn Sơn i. Vietnam
21 G4 Consort Can.
62 D7 Constance, Lake l. Ger./Switz.
42 F5 Constância dos Baetas Brazil
67 N2 Constanța Romania
65 D4 Constantina Spain
100 C1 Constantine Alg.
30 E5 Constantine U.S.A.
35 E6 Constitución de 1857, Parque Nacional nat. park Mex.
116 C5 Consuelo Austr.
24 D3 Contact U.S.A.
42 C5 Contamana Peru
46 E1 Contas r. Brazil
35 G6 Continental U.S.A.
33 H3 Contoocook r. U.S.A.
44 B8 Contreras, I. i. Chile
21 G1 Contwoyto Lake l. Can.
27 E5 Conway AR U.S.A.
33 H3 Conway NH U.S.A.
29 E5 Conway SC U.S.A.
116 C3 Conway, C. pt Austr.
114 A2 Conway, L. salt flat Austr.
111 H4 Conway Reef rf Fiji
59 D4 Conwy U.K.
59 D4 Conwy r. U.K.
113 F5 Coober Pedy Austr.
116 C6 Coogoon r. Austr.
112 F6 Cook Austr.
30 A2 Cook U.S.A.
20 D4 Cook, C. c. Can.
29 C4 Cookeville U.S.A.
105 F6 Cookhouse S. Africa
109 Cook Islands is Pac. Oc.
117 C5 Cook, Mt mt. N.Z.
33 F3 Cooksburg U.S.A.
23 J3 Cook's Harbour Can.
60 E3 Cookstown U.K.
117 E4 Cook Strait str. N.Z.
113 G3 Cooktown Austr.
115 J3 Coolabah Austr.
116 A6 Cooladdi Austr.
115 H3 Coolah Austr.
115 G5 Coolamon Austr.
115 K2 Coolangatta Austr.
112 D6 Coolgardie Austr.
35 G5 Coolidge U.S.A.
35 G5 Coolidge Dam U.S.A.
116 E6 Coolum Beach Austr.
115 H6 Cooma Austr.
60 A6 Coomacarrea h. Rep. of Ireland
114 D4 Coombah Austr.
113 J6 Coonabarabran Austr.
114 C5 Coonalpyn Austr.
115 H3 Coonamble Austr.
114 D6 Coonawarra Austr.
114 A3 Coondambo Austr.
115 F1 Coongoola Austr.
114 C2 Cooper Creek watercourse Austr.
115 K3 Coopernook Austr.
33 J2 Coopers Mills U.S.A.
29 E7 Coopers Town Bahamas
26 D2 Cooperstown ND U.S.A.
33 F3 Cooperstown NY U.S.A.
114 C5 Coorong, The in. Austr.
116 E6 Cooroy Austr.
24 A3 Coos Bay U.S.A.
115 H5 Cootamundra Austr.
60 D3 Cootehill Rep. of Ireland
47 B3 Copahue, Volcán mt Chile
24 G4 Cope U.S.A.
55 N9 Copenhagen Denmark
115 J2 Copeton Reservoir resr Austr.
44 B3 Copiapo Chile
44 B3 Copiapo r. Chile
114 C3 Copley Austr.
66 D2 Copparo Italy
31 G2 Copper Cliff Can.
116 A2 Copperfield r. Austr.
30 D2 Copper Harbor U.S.A.
30 E2 Coppermine Pt pt Can.
104 E4 Copperton S. Africa
85 F3 Coqên China
47 B1 Coquimbo Chile
47 B1 Coquimbo div. Chile
67 L3 Corabia Romania
46 D2 Coração de Jesus Brazil
Coracesium see Alanya
42 D7 Coracora Peru
115 K2 Coraki Austr.
29 D7 Coral Gables U.S.A.
111 F3 Coral Sea sea Coral Sea Is Terr.
14 E6 Coral Sea Basin sea feature Pac. Oc.
106 Coral Sea Islands Territory terr. Pac. Oc.
30 B5 Coralville Reservoir resr U.S.A.
114 E7 Corangamite, L. l. Austr.
43 G3 Corantijn r. Suriname
81 M1 Corat Azer.
47 E2 Corbett Arg.
21 L2 Corbett Inlet in. Can.
61 A5 Corbie France
32 A6 Corbin U.S.A.
59 G5 Corby U.K.
34 C3 Corcoran U.S.A.
44 B6 Corcovado, G. de b. Chile
116 E5 Cordalba Austr.
29 D6 Cordele U.S.A.
45 B4 Cordillera de los Picachos, Parque Nacional nat. park Col.
94 B4 Cordilleras Range mts Phil.
47 D1 Córdoba Arg.
47 D2 Córdoba div. Arg.
47 C4 Córdoba Arg.
36 D3 Córdoba Durango Mex.
36 E5 Córdoba Vera Cruz Mex.
65 D4 Córdoba Spain
47 D2 Córdoba, Sierras de mts Arg.
Cordova see Córdoba
20 C4 Cordova Bay b. U.S.A.
33 K2 Corea U.S.A.
67 H5 Corfu i. Greece
65 C3 Coria Spain
115 J4 Coricudgy mt Austr.
66 G5 Corigliano Calabro Italy
116 D1 Coringa Is is Coral Sea Is Terr.
115 F8 Corinna Austr.
33 J2 Corinna U.S.A.
21 J4 Corinne Can.
27 F5 Corinth MS U.S.A.
33 G3 Corinth NY U.S.A.
46 D2 Corinto Brazil
43 G7 Corixa Grande r. Bol./Brazil
46 A2 Corixinha r. Brazil
60 C6 Cork Rep. of Ireland
66 E6 Corleone Sicily Italy
80 A1 Çorlu Turkey
21 J4 Cormorant Can.
105 H3 Cornelia S. Africa
46 B3 Cornélio Procópio Brazil
30 B3 Cornell U.S.A.
23 J4 Corner Brook Can.
115 G7 Corner Inlet b. Austr.
61 C5 Cornillet, Mont h. France
34 A2 Corning CA U.S.A.
32 E3 Corning NY U.S.A.
116 A4 Cornish watercourse Austr.
Corn Islands is see Maíz, Islas del
66 E3 Corno, Monte mt Italy
22 F4 Cornwall Can.
114 B5 Corny Pt pt Austr.
45 C2 Coro Venez.
43 K4 Coroatá Brazil
42 E7 Corocoro Bol.
60 B5 Corofin Rep. of Ireland
42 E7 Coroico Bol.
46 C2 Coromandel Brazil
83 F8 Coromandel Coast coastal area India
117 E2 Coromandel Peninsula pen. N.Z.
117 E2 Coromandel Range h. N.Z.
94 B3 Coron Phil.
114 D3 Corona Austr.
34 D5 Corona U.S.A.
34 D5 Coronado U.S.A.
37 H7 Coronado, Baiá de b. Costa Rica
47 B4 Coronados, Golfo de los b. Chile
21 G4 Coronation Can.
119 B1 Coronation I. i. S. Orkney Is Atlantic Ocean
20 C3 Coronation Island i. U.S.A.
94 B4 Coron Bay b. Phil.
47 E1 Coronda Arg.
47 E2 Coronel Brandsen Arg.
47 E3 Coronel Dorrego Arg.
44 E3 Coronel Oviedo Para.
46 A1 Coronel Ponce Brazil
47 E3 Coronel Pringles Arg.
46 A3 Coronel Sapucaia Brazil
47 E3 Coronel Suárez Arg.
47 F3 Coronel Vidal Arg.
67 J4 Çorovodë Albania
115 G5 Corowa Austr.
27 D7 Corpus Christi U.S.A.
27 D6 Corpus Christi, L. l. U.S.A.
42 E7 Corque Bol.
65 D3 Corral de Cantos mt Spain
47 C1 Corral de Isaac Arg.
46 D1 Corrente r. Bahia Brazil
46 B2 Corrente r. Goiás Brazil
46 C1 Corrente r. Brazil
43 J6 Corrente Brazil
46 A2 Correntes Brazil
46 A2 Correntes r. Brazil
46 D1 Correntina Brazil
Correntina r. see Éguas
60 B4 Corrib, Lough l. Rep. of Ireland
44 E3 Corrientes Arg.
44 E4 Corrientes r. Arg.
47 F3 Corrientes, C. hd Arg.
36 C4 Corrientes, C. c. Mex.
45 A3 Corrientes, Cabo hd Col.
27 E6 Corrigan U.S.A.
112 C6 Corrigin Austr.
59 D5 Corris U.K.
32 D4 Corry U.S.A.
115 G6 Corryong Austr.
Corse i. see Corsica
66 C3 Corse, Cap hd Corsica France
59 E6 Corsham U.K.
64 J5 Corsica i. France
27 D5 Corsicana U.S.A.
66 C3 Corte Corsica France
65 C4 Cortegana Spain
35 H3 Cortez U.S.A.
34 D1 Cortez Mts mts U.S.A.
66 E1 Cortina d'Ampezzo Italy
33 E3 Cortland U.S.A.
59 J5 Corton U.K.
66 D3 Cortona Italy
65 B3 Coruche Port.
81 H1 Çoruh r. Turkey
80 E1 Çorum Turkey
46 C2 Corumbá r. Brazil
43 G7 Corumbá Brazil
46 C2 Corumbaíba Brazil
45 E3 Corumo r. Venez.
24 B2 Corvallis U.S.A.
59 D5 Corwen U.K.
66 G5 Cosenza Italy
32 C4 Coshocton U.S.A.
64 F3 Cosne-Cours-sur-Loire France
47 D1 Cosquín Arg.
65 F3 Costa Blanca coastal area Spain
65 H2 Costa Brava coastal area France/Spain
65 C4 Costa de la Luz coastal area Spain
65 D4 Costa del Sol coastal area Spain
37 H6 Costa de Mosquitos coastal area Nic.
16 Costa Rica country Central America
36 C4 Costa Rica Mex.
67 L2 Costești Romania
33 J2 Costigan U.S.A.
94 C5 Cotabato Phil.
45 A4 Cotacachi, Co mt Ecuador
42 E8 Cotagaita Bol.
46 E2 Cotaxé r. Brazil
64 H5 Côte d'Azur coastal area France
96 Côte d'Ivoire country Africa
20 C3 Cote, Mt mt. U.S.A.
64 G2 Côtes de Meuse ridge France
59 D5 Cothi r. U.K.
65 G1 Cotiella mt Spain
45 E3 Cotingo r. Brazil
100 C4 Cotonou Benin
42 C4 Cotopaxi, Volcán volc. Ecuador
59 E6 Cotswold Hills h. U.K.
24 B3 Cottage Grove U.S.A.
62 G5 Cottbus Ger.
59 H5 Cottenham U.K.
35 H5 Cotton City U.S.A.
35 F4 Cottonwood U.S.A.
35 G4 Cottonwood Wash r. U.S.A.
27 D6 Cotulla U.S.A.
32 D4 Coudersport U.S.A.
114 B6 Couëdic, C. de c. Austr.
64 F2 Coulommiers France
31 J2 Coulonge r. Can.
34 B3 Coulterville U.S.A.
24 C2 Council U.S.A.
26 E3 Council Bluffs U.S.A.
114 F7 Councillor Island i. Austr.
21 G2 Courageous Lake l. Can.
55 R9 Courland Lagoon lag. Lith./Rus. Fed.
20 E5 Courtenay Can.
60 C6 Courtmacsherry Rep. of Ireland
60 E5 Courtown Rep. of Ireland
Courtrai see Kortrijk
27 E5 Coushatta U.S.A.
64 D2 Coutances France
22 E2 Couture, Lac l. Can.
61 C4 Couvin Belgium
35 F2 Cove Fort U.S.A.
31 G3 Cove I. i. Can.
32 E5 Cove Mts h. U.S.A.
59 F5 Coventry U.K.
33 E5 Cove Point U.S.A.
65 C2 Covilhã Port.
29 D5 Covington GA U.S.A.
30 D5 Covington IN U.S.A.
32 A5 Covington KY U.S.A.
29 B5 Covington TN U.S.A.
32 D6 Covington VA U.S.A.
31 F2 Cow r. Can.
115 G4 Cowal, L. l. Austr.
112 D6 Cowan, L. salt flat Austr.
33 G2 Cowansville Can.
57 E4 Cowdenbeath U.K.
114 B4 Cowell Austr.
114 F7 Cowes Austr.
59 F7 Cowes U.K.
58 E3 Cow Green Reservoir resr U.K.
116 A6 Cowley Austr.
32 D5 Cowpasture r. U.S.A.
115 H4 Cowra Austr.
46 D1 Coxá r. Brazil
47 F1 Coxilha de Santana h. Brazil/Uru.
46 A2 Coxim r. Brazil
46 A2 Coxim Brazil
33 G3 Coxsackie U.S.A.
85 H5 Cox's Bazar Bangl.
34 D4 Coyote Lake l. U.S.A.
35 E5 Coyote Peak summit AZ U.S.A.
34 C3 Coyote Peak summit CA U.S.A.
85 F2 Cozhê China
67 L2 Cozia, Vârful mt Romania
25 D6 Cozón, Co mt. Mex.
36 G4 Cozumel Mex.
36 G4 Cozumel, I. de i. Mex.
115 H4 Craboon Austr.
116 D5 Cracow Austr.
115 G8 Cradle Mountain Lake St Clair Nat. Park nat. park Austr.
115 G8 Cradle Mt mt Austr.
114 C3 Cradock Austr.
105 F6 Cradock S. Africa
57 C3 Craig U.K.
20 C3 Craig AK U.S.A.
24 F3 Craig CO U.S.A.
60 E3 Craigavon U.K.
114 F6 Craigieburn Austr.
32 D5 Craigsville U.S.A.
57 F4 Crail U.K.
62 E6 Crailsheim Ger.
67 K2 Craiova Romania
58 F2 Cramlington U.K.
33 F2 Cranberry L. l. U.S.A.
33 F2 Cranberry Lake U.S.A.
114 F7 Cranbourne Austr.
20 F5 Cranbrook Can.
30 C3 Crandon U.S.A.
24 C3 Crane OR U.S.A.
27 C6 Crane TX U.S.A.
30 A1 Crane Lake U.S.A.
33 H4 Cranston U.S.A.
119 B4 Crary Ice Rise ice feature Ant.
119 A4 Crary Mts mts Ant.
24 B3 Crater L. l. U.S.A.
24 B3 Crater Lake Nat. Pk nat. park U.S.A.
24 D3 Craters of the Moon Nat. Mon. res. U.S.A.
43 K5 Crateús Brazil
43 L5 Crato Brazil
45 C3 Cravo Norte Col.
45 C3 Cravo Sur r. Col.
26 C3 Crawford U.S.A.
30 D5 Crawfordsville U.S.A.
29 C6 Crawfordville U.S.A.
59 G6 Crawley U.K.
24 E2 Crazy Mts mts U.S.A.
57 D4 Creag Meagaidh mt U.K.
21 H4 Crean L. l. Can.
59 E5 Credenhill U.K.
59 D7 Crediton U.K.
21 H3 Cree r. Can.
21 H3 Cree Lake l. Can.
21 J4 Creighton Can.
61 A5 Creil France
66 D2 Cremona Italy
64 F2 Crépy-en-Valois France
66 F2 Cres i. Croatia
24 A3 Crescent City U.S.A.
89 Crescent I. i. Hong Kong China
35 H2 Crescent Junction U.S.A.
34 B1 Crescent Mills U.S.A.
35 E4 Crescent Peak summit U.S.A.
30 A4 Cresco U.S.A.
47 E2 Crespo Arg.
114 E7 Cressy Austr.
20 F5 Creston Can.
26 E3 Creston IA U.S.A.
24 F3 Creston WY U.S.A.
29 C6 Crestview U.S.A.
33 F5 Crestwood Village U.S.A.
114 E6 Creswick Austr.
67 L7 Crete i. Greece
65 H1 Creus, Cap de pt Spain
64 E3 Creuse r. France
59 E4 Crewe U.K.
32 D6 Crewe U.S.A.
59 E7 Crewkerne U.K.

57 D4 Crianlarich U.K.
59 C5 Criccieth U.K.
44 G3 Criciúma Brazil
57 E4 Crieff U.K.
57 E6 Criffell h. U.K.
66 F2 Crikvenica Croatia
69 E6 Crimea pen. Ukr.
57 G3 Crimond U.K.
33 F6 Crisfield U.S.A.
46 C2 Cristalina Brazil
Cristalino r. see Mariembero
45 B2 Cristóbal Colón, Pico mt. Col.
46 C1 Crixás Brazil
46 C1 Crixás Açu r. Brazil
46 B1 Crixás Mirim r. Brazil
Crna Gora div. see Montenegro
66 F2 Črnomelj Slovenia
60 B4 Croagh Patrick h. Rep. of Ireland
115 H6 Croajingolong Nat. Park nat. park Austr.
48 Croatia country Europe
27 E6 Crockett U.S.A.
33 F3 Croghan U.S.A.
110 D3 Croker I. i. Austr.
57 D3 Cromarty U.K.
57 D3 Cromarty Firth est. U.K.
57 E3 Cromdale, Hills of h. U.K.
59 J5 Cromer U.K.
117 B6 Cromwell N.Z.
58 F3 Crook U.K.
32 D4 Crooked Creek Reservoir resr U.S.A.
89 Crooked I. i. Hong Kong China
37 K4 Crooked I. Passage chan. Bahamas
37 K4 Crooked Island i. Bahamas
30 B1 Crooked Lake l. Can./U.S.A.
26 D2 Crookston U.S.A.
115 H5 Crookwell Austr.
60 C5 Croom Rep. of Ireland
115 J2 Croppa Creek Austr.
58 D4 Crosby U.K.
21 J5 Crosby U.S.A.
21 L2 Crosby Bay b. Can.
29 D6 Cross City U.S.A.
33 K1 Cross Creek Can.
27 E5 Crossett U.S.A.
58 E3 Cross Fell h. U.K.
60 F3 Crossgar U.K.
60 C6 Crosshaven Rep. of Ireland
59 C5 Cross Inn U.K.
21 K4 Cross Lake l. Can.
21 K4 Cross Lake Can.
32 E3 Cross Lake l. U.S.A.
60 E3 Crossmaglen U.K.
35 E4 Crossman Peak summit U.S.A.
20 B3 Cross Sound chan. U.S.A.
30 A4 Cross Village U.S.A.
29 C5 Crossville U.S.A.
31 F4 Croswell U.S.A.
66 G5 Crotone Italy
59 H6 Crouch r. U.K.
115 G3 Crowal watercourse Austr.
59 H6 Crowborough U.K.
115 F4 Crowl watercourse Austr.
59 G5 Crowland U.K.
27 E6 Crowley U.S.A.
34 C3 Crowley, Lake l. U.S.A.
30 D5 Crown Point IN U.S.A.
33 G3 Crown Point NY U.S.A.
115 K1 Crows Nest Austr.
20 G5 Crowsnest Pass Can.
113 H3 Croydon Austr.
59 G6 Croydon U.K.
13 H6 Crozet Basin sea feature Indian Ocean
13 H7 Crozet, Îles is Indian Ocean
13 G6 Crozet Plateau sea feature Indian Ocean
64 B2 Crozon France
57 G3 Cruden Bay U.K.
60 E3 Crumlin U.K.
60 C5 Crusheen Rep. of Ireland
44 F3 Cruz Alta Brazil
37 J5 Cruz, Cabo c. Cuba
47 D1 Cruz del Eje Arg.
46 D3 Cruzeiro Brazil
42 D5 Cruzeiro do Sul Brazil
35 H5 Cruzville U.S.A.
20 E3 Crysdale, Mt mt. Can.
114 C4 Crystal Brook Austr.
27 D6 Crystal City U.S.A.
30 C2 Crystal Falls U.S.A.
30 C4 Crystal Lake U.S.A.
63 K7 Csongrád Hungary
81 K5 Ctesiphon Iraq
45 D2 Cúa Venez.
95 C3 Cửa Lon r. Vietnam
103 C5 Cuando r. Angola/Zambia
103 B5 Cuangar Angola
102 B4 Cuango r. Angola/Zaire
103 B4 Cuanza r. Angola
45 D3 Cuao r. Venez.
47 F1 Cuaró r. Uru.
47 D2 Cuarto r. Arg.
36 C3 Cuauhtémoc Mex.
16 Cuba country Caribbean Sea
30 B4 Cuba IL U.S.A.
25 F4 Cuba NM U.S.A.
35 H2 Cubabi, Cerro summit Mex.
103 B5 Cubal Angola

103 B5 Cubango r. Angola/Namibia
45 B3 Cubara Col.
21 J4 Cub Hills h. Can.
80 D1 Çubuk Turkey
47 F1 Cuchilla Grande Inferior h. Uru.
47 D3 Cuchillo-Có Arg.
45 D3 Cuchivero r. Venez.
32 E6 Cuckoo U.S.A.
45 D4 Cucuí Brazil
45 B3 Cúcuta Col.
83 E8 Cuddalore India
83 E8 Cuddapah India
21 H4 Cudworth Can.
65 D2 Cuéllar Spain
103 B5 Cuemba Angola
42 C4 Cuenca Ecuador
65 E2 Cuenca Spain
65 E2 Cuenca, Serranía de mts Spain
36 E5 Cuernavaca Mex.
27 D6 Cuero U.S.A.
34 B4 Cuesta Pass pass U.S.A.
67 K2 Cugir Romania
43 G5 Cuiabá Amazonas Brazil
46 A1 Cuiabá Mato Grosso Brazil
46 A2 Cuiabá r. Brazil
46 A1 Cuiabá de Larga Brazil
57 B3 Cuillin Hills mts U.K.
57 B3 Cuillin Sound chan. U.K.
103 B4 Cuilo Angola
46 E2 Cuité r. Brazil
103 B5 Cuito r. Angola
103 B5 Cuito Cuanavale Angola
95 A4 Cukai Malaysia
81 J3 Çukurca Turkey
95 D2 Cu Lao Cham i. Vietnam
95 D2 Cu Lao Re i. Vietnam
95 D3 Cu Lao Thu i. Vietnam
24 F1 Culbertson MT U.S.A.
26 C3 Culbertson NE U.S.A.
115 G5 Culcairn Austr.
65 C2 Culebra, Sierra de la mts Spain
81 K2 Culfa Azer.
115 G2 Culgoa r. Austr.
36 C4 Culiacán Mex.
94 A4 Culion Phil.
94 A4 Culion i. Phil.
57 F3 Culkein U.K.
113 H2 Cullen Pt pt Austr.
65 F3 Cullera Spain
57 F2 Cullen U.K.
29 C5 Cullman U.S.A.
81 H2 Çullu Turkey
60 E3 Cullybackey U.K.
57 C2 Cul Mor h. U.K.
32 D5 Culpeper U.S.A.
42 Culpepper, Isla i. Galapagos Is Ecuador
43 H6 Culuene r. Brazil
117 D5 Culverden N.Z.
57 D5 Culzean Bay b. U.K.
45 D2 Cumaná Venez.
45 B4 Cumare, Cerro h. Col.
45 A4 Cumbal, Nevado de mt. Col.
32 D5 Cumberland MD U.S.A.
30 A4 Cumberland WV U.S.A.
28 C4 Cumberland r. U.S.A.
21 J4 Cumberland House Can.
116 C3 Cumberland Is is Austr.
21 J4 Cumberland Lake l. Can.
32 B6 Cumberland Mtn mts U.S.A.
18 Cumberland Peninsula pen. Can.
28 C4 Cumberland Plateau plat. U.S.A.
30 C2 Cumberland Pt pt U.S.A.
18 Cumberland Sound sound Can.
57 E5 Cumbernauld U.K.
34 A2 Cummings U.S.A.
114 A5 Cummins Austr.
115 H4 Cumnock Austr.
57 D5 Cumnock U.K.
80 D3 Çumra Turkey
60 D3 Cuncagh h. Rep. of Ireland/U.K.
103 B5 Cunene r. Angola
66 B2 Cuneo Italy
114 A4 Cungena Austr.
95 D2 Cung Son Vietnam
81 G2 Çüngüş Turkey
115 F2 Cunnamulla Austr.
57 Cunningsburgh U.K.
45 C4 Cunucunuma r. Venez.
66 B2 Cuorgnè Italy
57 E4 Cupar U.K.
45 A3 Cupica Col.
45 A3 Cupica, Golfo de b. Col.
43 L5 Curaçá Brazil
37 L6 Curaçao i. Neth. Ant.
47 B3 Curacautín Chile
47 D3 Curacó r. Arg.
45 D4 Curanilahue Chile
45 D4 Curapira, Serra mts Brazil/Venez.
42 C4 Curaray r. Ecuador
47 B2 Curaumilla, Punta pt Chile
114 B3 Curdlawidny Lagoon salt flat Austr.
25 F4 Curecanti Nat. Rec. Area res. U.S.A.
47 B2 Curicó Chile
45 D5 Curicuriari, Sa. h. Brazil
45 D5 Curicuriari r. Brazil
46 C4 Curitiba Brazil
114 C3 Curnamona Austr.

115 J3 Currabubula Austr.
43 L5 Currais Novos Brazil
100 Curral Velho Cape Verde
31 F3 Curran U.S.A.
60 A6 Currane, Lough l. Rep. of Ireland
35 E2 Currant U.S.A.
114 F3 Curranyalpa Austr.
113 H5 Currawilla Austr.
29 E7 Current Bahamas
115 E7 Currie Tas. Austr.
35 E1 Currie U.S.A.
115 J5 Currockbilly, Mt mt. Austr.
116 E5 Curtis Channel chan. Austr.
115 G7 Curtis Group is Austr.
116 D4 Curtis I. i. Qld. Austr.
43 H5 Curuá r. Brazil
43 J4 Curuçá Brazil
92 C7 Curup Indon.
43 K4 Cururupu Brazil
45 E3 Curutú, Cerro mt. Venez.
46 D2 Curvelo Brazil
42 D6 Cuzco Peru
60 E2 Cushendall U.K.
60 E2 Cushendun U.K.
27 D4 Cushing U.S.A.
45 C3 Cusiana r. Col.
29 C5 Cusseta U.S.A.
30 A1 Cusson U.S.A.
22 E1 Cusson, Pte pt Can.
24 C3 Custer MT U.S.A.
26 C3 Custer SD U.S.A.
45 A4 Cutanga, Pico de mt Col.
24 D1 Cut Bank U.S.A.
29 C6 Cuthbert U.S.A.
21 H4 Cut Knife Can.
33 K2 Cutler U.S.A.
29 D7 Cutler Ridge U.S.A.
47 C3 Cutral-Có Arg.
85 F5 Cuttack India
35 G5 Cutter U.S.A.
112 B4 Cuvier, C. hd Austr.
62 D4 Cuxhaven Ger.
32 C4 Cuxhaven U.S.A.
32 C4 Cuyahoga Falls U.S.A.
32 C4 Cuyahoga Valley National Recreation Area res. U.S.A.
34 C4 Cuyama U.S.A.
94 B3 Cuyapo Phil.
94 B4 Cuyo i. Phil.
94 B4 Cuyo Phil.
94 B4 Cuyo East Pass. chan. Phil.
94 B4 Cuyo Islands is Phil.
94 B4 Cuyo West Pass. chan. Phil.
45 E3 Cuyuni r. Guyana
Cuzco see Cusco
59 D6 Cwmbran U.K.
102 C4 Cyangugu Rwanda
67 L6 Cyclades is Greece
115 G9 Cygnet Austr.
32 A5 Cynthiana U.S.A.
21 G5 Cypress Hills mts Can.
71 Cyprus country Asia
21 G4 Czar Can.
48 Czech Republic country Europe
62 H4 Czersk Pol.
63 J5 Częstochowa Pol.

# D

87 M2 Da'an China
80 F6 Dab'a Jordan
45 C2 Dabajuro Venez.
100 B4 Dabakala Côte d'Ivoire
88 A2 Daban Shan mts China
88 B3 Daba Shan mts China
45 A3 Dabeiba Col.
84 C5 Dabhoi India
88 E4 Dabie Shan mts China
84 D4 Daboh India
100 A3 Dabola Guinea
100 B4 Daboya Ghana
84 D4 Dabra India
63 J5 Dąbrowa Górnicza Pol.
89 E5 Dabu China
Dacca see Dhaka
62 E6 Dachau Ger.
88 A2 Dachechang China
31 J3 Dacre Can.
80 D1 Daday Turkey
29 D6 Dade City U.S.A.
84 C5 Dadra India
84 C5 Dadra and Nagar Haveli div. India
84 A4 Dadu Pak.
89 B4 Dadu He r. China
95 C3 Đa Dung r. Vietnam
94 B3 Daet Phil.
89 B5 Dafang China
89 B7 Dafeng China
85 H4 Dafla Hills mts India
100 A3 Dagana Senegal
88 B3 Dagcanglhamo China
69 H7 Dagestan, Respublika div. Rus. Fed.
88 F2 Dagu r. China
91 H7 Dagu Indon.
89 D'Aguilar Peak h. Hong Kong China
94 B3 Dagupan Phil.
85 H1 Dagur China
85 G3 Dagzê China
85 F3 Dagzê Co salt l. China
84 C6 Dahanu India

88 D1 Dahei r. China
87 M3 Da Hinggan Ling mts China
102 E2 Dahlak Archipelago is Eritrea
102 E2 Dahlak Marine National Park nat. park Eritrea
66 C7 Dahmani Tunisia
84 C5 Dāhod India
84 D2 Dahongliutan China/Jammu and Kashmir
81 J3 Dahūk Iraq
88 D1 Dai Hai l. China
57 D1 Dailly U.K.
90 D5 Daimanji-san h. Japan
65 E3 Daimiel Spain
91 F6 Dainichiga-take volc. Japan
91 F6 Daiō Japan
91 F6 Daiō-zaki pt Japan
47 E3 Daireaux Arg.
30 A2 Dairyland U.S.A.
90 D6 Daisen volc. Japan
89 G4 Daishan China
89 F5 Daiyun Shan mts China
113 F4 Dajarra Austr.
88 A4 Dajin Chuan r. China
88 B2 Dajing China
85 H1 Da Juh China
100 A3 Dakar Senegal
85 G5 Dakhin Shahbaz-pur i. i. Bangl.
78 B4 Dakhla Oasis oasis Egypt
95 C4 Dak Kon Vietnam
68 D4 Dakol'ka r. Belarus
26 D3 Dakota City U.S.A.
67 J3 Đakovica Yugo.
67 H2 Đakovo Croatia
103 C5 Dala Angola
88 D1 Dalad Qi China
88 E1 Dalai Nur l. China
88 D1 Dalamamiao China
80 B3 Dalaman Turkey
80 B3 Dalaman r. Turkey
86 H3 Dalandzadgad Mongolia
94 B4 Dalanganem Islands is Phil.
106 Dalap-Uliga-Darrit Marshall Islands
95 D3 Da Lat Vietnam
88 B1 Dalay Mongolia
79 J4 Dalbandin Pak.
57 E6 Dalbeattie U.K.
115 J1 Dalby Austr.
58 C3 Dalby U.K.
55 J6 Dale Hordaland Norway
55 J6 Dale Sogn og Fjordane Norway
32 E5 Dale City U.S.A.
27 G4 Dale Hollow Lake l. U.S.A.
85 H6 Dalet Myanmar
85 H5 Daletme Myanmar
55 O6 Dalfors Sweden
115 H6 Dalgety Austr.
27 C4 Dalhart U.S.A.
23 G4 Dalhousie Can.
88 D3 Dali Shaanxi China
82 K5 Dali Yunnan China
88 F2 Dalian China
89 B4 Daliang Shan mts China
88 G1 Dalin China
88 F1 Daling r. China
57 E5 Dalkeith U.K.
85 F4 Dālkola India
116 E5 Dallarnil Austr.
33 F4 Dallas PA U.S.A.
27 D5 Dallas TX U.S.A.
30 B5 Dallas City U.S.A.
24 B2 Dalles, The U.S.A.
20 C4 Dall I. i. U.S.A.
47 D2 Dalmacio Vélez Sarsfield Arg.
84 A4 Dalman India
66 G3 Dalmatia reg. Croatia
57 D5 Dalmellington U.K.
100 B4 Daloa Côte d'Ivoire
89 C5 Dalou Shan mts China
57 D5 Dalry U.K.
57 D5 Dalrymple U.K.
116 B3 Dalrymple, L. l. Austr.
116 C3 Dalrymple, Mt mt. Austr.
85 F4 Daltenganj India
31 E1 Dalton U.S.A.
105 J4 Dalton S. Africa
29 C5 Dalton GA U.S.A.
33 G3 Dalton MA U.S.A.
58 D3 Dalton-in-Furness U.K.
31 E1 Dalton Mills U.S.A.
60 C5 Dalua r. Rep. of Ireland
94 B3 Dalupiri i. Phil.
94 C3 Dalupiri i. Phil.
84 D1 Dalvík Iceland
112 F4 Daly r. Austr.
34 A3 Daly City U.S.A.
113 F3 Daly Waters Austr.
84 C5 Daman India
84 C5 Daman and Diu div. India
78 C4 Damanhûr Egypt
88 M4 Damaqun Shan mts China
93 H8 Damar i. Indon.
94 C6 Damar Indon.
80 F5 Damascus Syria
47 B2 Damas, P. de las pass Arg./Chile
100 D3 Damaturu Nigeria
79 G2 Damghan Iran
88 D2 Daming China
89 D4 Daming Shan mt China
85 H2 Damjong China

94 B5 Dammai i. Phil.
84 D5 Damoh India
100 B4 Damongo Ghana
112 C4 Dampier Austr.
112 D3 Dampier Land reg. Austr.
110 E2 Dampier Strait chan. P.N.G.
93 J7 Dampir, Selat chan. Indon.
Damqoq Kanbab r. see Maquan He
85 H2 Dam Qu r. China
85 H3 Damroh India
82 H4 Damxung China
100 B4 Danané Côte d'Ivoire
95 D1 Đa Năng Vietnam
94 C4 Danao Phil.
88 A4 Danba China
33 G4 Danbury CT U.S.A.
33 H3 Danbury NH U.S.A.
33 G3 Danby U.S.A.
35 E4 Danby Lake l. U.S.A.
88 E3 Dancheng China
102 D3 Dande Eth.
114 F6 Dandenong Austr.
87 M3 Dandong China
59 E4 Dane r. U.K.
85 G3 Dangbe La pass China
88 B3 Dangchang China
108 Danger Islands is Cook Islands Pac. Oc.
104 C7 Danger Pt pt S. Africa
102 D2 Dangila Eth.
Dangla mts see Tanggula Shan
88 G3 Danggên China
36 G5 Dangriga Belize
88 E3 Dangshan China
88 E3 Dangtu China
88 D2 Dangyang China
24 D3 Daniel U.S.A.
104 E4 Daniëlskuil S. Africa
85 G3 Danilov Rus. Fed.
69 H5 Danilovka Rus. Fed.
68 G3 Danilovskaya Vozvyshennost' reg. Rus. Fed.
88 D2 Daning China
81 M1 Dänizkänarı Azer.
88 D3 Danjiangkou Sk. resr China
90 B7 Danjo-guntō is Japan
84 D2 Dankhar India
68 F4 Dankov Rus. Fed.
36 G6 Danlí Honduras
33 G2 Dannemora U.S.A.
117 F4 Dannevirke N.Z.
105 J4 Dannhauser S. Africa
95 B1 Dan Sai Thai.
32 E3 Dansville U.S.A.
84 C4 Danta India
67 M3 Danube r. Europe
30 D5 Danville IL U.S.A.
30 D6 Danville IN U.S.A.
28 C4 Danville KY U.S.A.
31 J5 Danville PA U.S.A.
32 D6 Danville VA U.S.A.
89 C7 Dan Xian China
88 F2 Danyang China
89 C5 Danzhai China
94 B4 Dao Phil.
89 C6 Đao Bach Long Vi i. Vietnam
89 C6 Đao Cai Bâu i. Vietnam
89 C6 Đao Cat Ba i. Vietnam
95 B3 Đao Phu Quôc i. Vietnam
95 B3 Đao Thô Chu i. Vietnam
100 B4 Daoukro Côte d'Ivoire
95 B4 Đao Vây i. Vietnam
89 D5 Dao Xian China
89 C5 Daozhen China
94 C4 Dapa Phil.
100 B4 Dapaong Togo
85 J4 Daphabum mt India
94 B4 Dapiak, Mt mt Phil.
94 B4 Dapitan Phil.
82 J3 Da Qaidam China
87 N2 Daqing China
88 D1 Daqing Shan mts China
81 K4 Dāqūq Iraq
89 C4 Daqu Shan i. China
80 F5 Dar'ā Syria
79 G3 Dārāb Iran
94 B3 Daraga Phil.
63 O4 Darahanava Belarus
100 D1 Daraj Libya
94 C4 Daram i. Phil.
87 K1 Darasun Rus. Fed.
85 F4 Darbhanga India
34 C2 Dardanelle U.S.A.
27 E5 Dardanelle, Lake l. U.S.A.
80 M4 Dardanelles str. Turkey
80 D2 Darende Turkey
102 D4 Dar es Salaam Tanz.
66 D2 Darfo Boario Terme Italy
84 B2 Dargai Pak.
117 D1 Dargaville N.Z.
115 G6 Dargo Austr.
86 J2 Darhan Mongolia
88 D1 Darhan Muminggan Lianheqi China
29 D6 Darien U.S.A.
45 A2 Darién, Golfo del g. Col.
37 J7 Darién, Parque Nacional de nat. park Panama
45 A2 Darién, Serranía del mts Panama
85 G4 Dārjiling India
114 B4 Darke Peak Austr.
82 J4 Darlag China

114 E4 Darling r. Austr.
115 H1 Darling Downs reg. Austr.
112 C6 Darling Range h. Austr.
58 F3 Darlington U.K.
30 E4 Darlington U.S.A.
115 G5 Darlington Point Austr.
62 H3 Darłowo Pol.
84 E3 Darma Pass pass China/India
62 D6 Darmstadt Ger.
84 C5 Darna r. India
101 E1 Darnah Libya
105 J4 Darnall S. Africa
114 E4 Darnick Austr.
119 D5 Darnley, C. c. Ant.
65 F2 Daroca Spain
68 G3 Darovka Rus. Fed.
68 H3 Darovskoy Rus. Fed.
47 D3 Darregueira Arg.
81 L4 Darreh Gozaru r. Iran
84 B2 Darreh-ye Shekārī r. Afgh.
81 M6 Darsīyeh Iran
59 J7 Dart r. U.K.
59 H6 Dartford U.K.
114 E6 Dartmoor Austr.
59 C7 Dartmoor reg. U.K.
59 D7 Dartmoor National Park U.K.
23 H5 Dartmouth Can.
59 D7 Dartmouth U.K.
116 A6 Dartmouth, L. salt flat Austr.
58 F4 Darton U.K.
60 C3 Darty Mts h. Rep. of Ireland
110 E2 Daru P.N.G.
100 A4 Daru Sierra Leone
85 G3 Darum Tso l. China
66 G2 Daruvar Croatia
84 A3 Darwazgai Afgh.
58 E4 Darwen U.K.
112 F2 Darwin Austr.
44 C8 Darwin, Mte mt Chile
84 A3 Darya Khan Pak.
88 D4 Dashennongjia mt China
79 H1 Dashkhovuz Turkm.
88 C2 Dashuikeng China
88 C2 Dashuitou China
84 C2 Daska Pak.
81 L1 Daşkäsän Azer.
84 C1 Daspar mt Pak.
104 C6 Dassen Island i. S. Africa
81 L2 Dastakert Armenia
67 M6 Datça Turkey
90 H2 Date Japan
35 H5 Dateland U.S.A.
84 D4 Datia India
89 E5 Datian China
88 A2 Datong Qinghai China
88 D1 Datong Shanxi China
88 B2 Datong He r. China
88 A2 Datong Shan mts China
94 C5 Datu Piang Phil.
95 D5 Datu, Tanjung c. Indon./Malaysia
79 L3 Daud Khel Pak.
68 C3 Daugava r. Belarus/Latvia
55 U9 Daugavpils Latvia
84 C6 Daulatabad India
61 E4 Daun Ger.
95 A2 Daung Kyun i. Myanmar
21 J4 Dauphin Can.
64 G4 Dauphiné reg. France
27 F6 Dauphin I. i. U.S.A.
21 K4 Dauphin L. l. Can.
84 D4 Dausa India
57 E3 Davel S. Africa
81 M1 Däväçi Azer.
83 E8 Davangere India
94 C5 Davao Phil.
94 C5 Davao Gulf b. Phil.
105 H3 Davel S. Africa
34 A3 Davenport CA U.S.A.
30 B5 Davenport IA U.S.A.
59 F5 Daventry U.K.
105 H3 Daveyton S. Africa
37 H7 David Panama
21 H4 Davidson Can.
21 J3 Davin Lake l. Can.
119 D5 Davis Australia Base Ant.
34 B2 Davis U.S.A.
35 E4 Davis Dam U.S.A.
23 H2 Davis Inlet Can.
119 D5 Davis Sea sea Ant.
18 Davis Strait strait Can./Green.
62 D7 Davos Switz.
88 A1 Dawan China
85 F3 Dawaxung China
88 B4 Dawe China
Dawei see Tavoy
88 E3 Dawen r. China
85 A1 Dawna Range mts Myanmar/Thai.
79 G6 Dawqah Oman
116 C5 Dawson r. Qld. Austr.
29 C6 Dawson GA U.S.A.
26 D2 Dawson ND U.S.A.
21 J4 Dawson Bay b. Can.
20 B2 Dawson Creek Can.
21 L2 Dawson Inlet in. Can.
20 B2 Dawson Range mts Can.
88 E4 Dawu Hubei China
82 K4 Dawu Sichuan China
64 D5 Dax France
88 E3 Daxian China
88 C6 Daxin China
89 C6 Daxing China
89 A4 Daxue Shan mts China
85 H4 Daying r. India
89 D6 Dayao Shan mts China
89 E4 Daye China

89 B4 Dayi China
114 F6 Daylesford Austr.
34 D3 Daylight Pass pass U.S.A.
47 F1 Daymán r. Uru.
47 F1 Daymán, Cuchilla del h. Uru.
89 D4 Dayong China
81 H4 Dayr az Zawr Syria
32 A5 Dayton OH U.S.A.
29 C5 Dayton TN U.S.A.
24 C2 Dayton WA U.S.A.
29 D6 Daytona Beach U.S.A.
89 E5 Dayu China
89 D5 Dayu Ling mts China
88 F3 Da Yunhe r. China
24 C2 Dayville U.S.A.
90 C7 Dazaifu Japan
89 D7 Dazhai Dao i. China
89 C4 Dazhu China
89 B4 Dazu China
104 F5 De Aar S. Africa
30 D2 Dead r. U.S.A.
29 F7 Deadman's Cay Bahamas
35 E4 Dead Mts mts U.S.A.
33 H2 Dead River r. U.S.A.
80 E6 Dead Sea salt l. Asia
59 J6 Deal U.K.
105 F4 Dealesville S. Africa
20 D4 Dean r. Can.
89 E4 De'an China
59 E6 Dean, Forest of forest U.K.
47 D1 Deán Funes Arg.
31 F4 Dearborn U.S.A.
20 D3 Dease r. Can.
20 C3 Dease Lake Can.
34 D3 Death Valley v. U.S.A.
34 D3 Death Valley Junction U.S.A.
34 D3 Death Valley National Monument res. U.S.A.
64 E2 Deauville France
92 E6 Debak Malaysia
89 C6 Debao China
67 J4 Debar Macedonia
21 H4 Debden Can.
59 J5 Debenham U.K.
35 H2 De Beque U.S.A.
33 J2 Deblois U.S.A.
102 D3 Debre Birhan Eth.
63 K7 Debrecen Hungary
102 D2 Debre Markos Eth.
102 D2 Debre Tabor Eth.
102 D3 Debre Zeyit Eth.
29 C5 Decatur AL U.S.A.
29 C5 Decatur GA U.S.A.
30 C6 Decatur IN U.S.A.
30 E5 Decatur IN U.S.A.
30 E4 Decatur MI U.S.A.
83 E7 Deccan plat. India
31 H2 Decelles, Réservoir resr Can.
115 K1 Deception Bay Austr.
62 G5 Děčín Czech Rep.
30 B4 Decorah U.S.A.
59 F6 Deddington U.K.
46 C4 Dedo de Deus mt Brazil
104 C6 De Doorns S. Africa
81 L1 Dedoplis Tsqaro Georgia
100 B3 Dédougou Burkina
68 D3 Dedovichi Rus. Fed.
103 D5 Dedza Malawi
59 D4 Dee r. England/Wales U.K.
57 F3 Dee r. Scot. U.K.
59 E4 Dee r. Wales U.K.
60 C5 Deel r. Rep. of Ireland
60 D3 Deele r. Rep. of Ireland
89 ☐ Deep Bay b. Hong Kong China
32 D5 Deep Creek Lake l. U.S.A.
35 F2 Deep Creek Range mts U.S.A.
31 J2 Deep River Can.
33 G4 Deep River U.S.A.
21 K1 Deep Rose Lake l. Can.
34 D3 Deep Springs U.S.A.
115 J2 Deepwater Austr.
32 B5 Deer Creek Lake l. U.S.A.
33 K2 Deer I. i. Can.
33 J2 Deer I. i. U.S.A.
33 J2 Deer Isle U.S.A.
22 B3 Deer L. l. Can.
23 J4 Deer Lake Nfld Can.
22 B3 Deer Lake Ont. Can.
24 D2 Deer Lodge U.S.A.
44 D2 Defensores del Chaco, Parque Nacional nat. park Para.
32 A4 Defiance U.S.A.
29 C6 De Funiak Springs U.S.A.
82 J4 Dêgê China
102 D3 Degeh Bur Eth.
85 G3 Dêgên China
62 F6 Deggendorf Ger.
84 C3 Degh r. Pak.
81 N3 Dehgâh Iran
81 L4 Dehgolân Iran
81 L5 Dehlonân Iran
84 D3 Dehra Dun India
85 F4 Dehri India
81 K4 Deh Sheykh Iran
89 F5 Dehua China
87 N3 Dehui China
61 H4 Deinze Belgium
80 E5 Deir el Qamer Lebanon
Deir-ez-Zor see Dayr az Zawr
63 L7 Dej Romania
89 C4 Dejiang China
30 C5 De Kalb IL U.S.A.
27 E5 De Kalb TX U.S.A.
33 F2 De Kalb Junction U.S.A.
87 Q1 De-Kastri Rus. Fed.
102 C4 Dekese Zaire

34 C4 Delano U.S.A.
35 F2 Delano Peak summit U.S.A.
79 J3 Delārām Afgh.
105 F3 Delareyville S. Africa
21 H4 Delaronde Lake l. Can.
30 C5 Delavan IL U.S.A.
30 C4 Delavan WV U.S.A.
33 F5 Delaware div. U.S.A.
32 B4 Delaware r. U.S.A.
32 B4 Delaware r. U.S.A.
33 F5 Delaware Bay b. U.S.A.
32 B4 Delaware Lake l. U.S.A.
33 F4 Delaware Water Gap National Recreational Area res. U.S.A.
115 H6 Delegate Austr.
62 C7 Delémont Switz.
61 C2 Delft Neth.
61 E1 Delfzijl Neth.
103 E5 Delgado, Cabo pt Moz.
31 G4 Delhi Can.
84 D3 Delhi India
25 E3 Delhi CO U.S.A.
33 F3 Delhi NY U.S.A.
92 ☐ Deli i. Indon.
81 J2 Delic r. Turkey
80 E2 Delice Turkey
80 E2 Delice r. Turkey
20 E1 Déljne Can.
82 J3 Delingha China
21 H4 Delisle Can.
26 D3 Dell Rapids U.S.A.
65 H4 Dellys Alg.
34 D5 Del Mar U.S.A.
35 E3 Delmar L. l. U.S.A.
77 R2 De-Longa, O-va is Rus. Fed.
21 J5 Deloraine Can.
30 D5 Delphi U.S.A.
32 A4 Delphos U.S.A.
104 F4 Delportshoop S. Africa
25 E6 Del Río Mex.
27 C6 Del Rio U.S.A.
55 P6 Delsbo Sweden
35 H2 Delta CO U.S.A.
30 A5 Delta IL U.S.A.
35 F2 Delta UT U.S.A.
33 F3 Delta Reservoir resr U.S.A.
29 D6 Deltona U.S.A.
115 J2 Delungra Austr.
60 D4 Delvin Rep. of Ireland
67 J5 Delvinë Albania
65 E1 Demanda, Sierra de la mts Spain
102 C4 Demba Zaire
102 D3 Dembi Dolo Eth.
61 D3 De Meijnweg, Nationaal Park nat. park Neth.
68 D4 Demidov Rus. Fed.
25 F6 Deming U.S.A.
45 E4 Demini r. Brazil
80 B2 Demirci Turkey
67 M4 Demirköy Turkey
62 F4 Demmin Ger.
29 C5 Demopolis U.S.A.
30 D5 Demotte U.S.A.
92 C7 Dempo, G. volc. Indon.
84 D2 Dêmqog China/India
68 H2 Dem'yanovo Rus. Fed.
63 Q2 Demyansk Rus. Fed.
104 D5 De Naawte S. Africa
102 E2 Denakil reg. Eritrea
102 E3 Denan Eth.
21 J4 Denare Beach Can.
79 K2 Denau Uzbek.
31 J3 Denbigh Can.
59 D4 Denbigh U.K.
61 C1 Den Burg Neth.
95 H1 Den Chai Thai.
61 D2 Den Dolder Neth.
105 H1 Dendron S. Africa
88 C1 Dengkou China
85 H3 Dêngqên China
88 D3 Deng Xian China
Den Haag see The Hague
112 B5 Denham Austr.
116 B3 Denham Ra. mts Austr.
61 C2 Den Helder Neth.
65 G3 Denia Spain
114 F5 Deniliquin Austr.
24 C3 Denio U.S.A.
26 E3 Denison IA U.S.A.
27 D5 Denison TX U.S.A.
80 B3 Denizli Turkey
115 J4 Denman Austr.
112 C6 Denmark Austr.
48 Denmark country Europe
35 H3 Denmark hotso U.S.A.
33 H4 Dennis Port U.S.A.
57 E4 Denny U.K.
33 K2 Dennysville U.S.A.
92 ☐ Denpasar Indon.
33 H5 Denton MD U.S.A.
27 D5 Denton TX U.S.A.
24 F4 Denver U.S.A.
85 F4 Deo India
84 D3 Deoband India
85 E5 Deogarh mt India
85 E5 Deogarh India
85 F4 Deoghar India
84 D5 Deori India
85 E4 Deoria India
84 C2 Deosai, Plains of plain Pak.
85 E5 Deosil India
61 D3 De Peel reg. Neth.
30 C3 De Pere U.S.A.
33 F3 Deposit U.S.A.
31 J2 Depot-Forbes Can.
31 J2 Depot-Rowanton Can.

30 C5 Depue U.S.A.
77 P3 Deputatskiy Rus. Fed.
82 J5 Dêqên China
89 D6 Deqing Guangdong China
89 F4 Deqing Zhejiang China
89 F5 Deqiu China
27 E5 De Queen U.S.A.
84 B3 Dera Bugti Pak.
84 B3 Dera Ghazi Khan Pak.
84 B3 Dera Ismail Khan Pak.
84 B3 Derawar Fort Pak.
69 J7 Derbent Rus. Fed.
115 G8 Derby Tas. Austr.
112 D3 Derby W.A. Austr.
59 F5 Derby U.K.
33 G4 Derby CT U.S.A.
27 D4 Derby KS U.S.A.
60 D3 Derg r. Rep. of Ireland/U.K.
69 J5 Dergachi Rus. Fed.
60 C5 Derg, Lough l. Rep. of Ireland
69 F5 Derhachi Ukr.
27 E6 De Ridder U.S.A.
81 H3 Derik Turkey
80 D2 Derinkuyu Turkey
69 F5 Derkul r. Rus. Fed./Ukr.
104 C1 Derm Namibia
60 D4 Derravaragh, Lough l. Rep. of Ireland
60 E5 Derry r. Rep. of Ireland
33 H3 Derry U.S.A.
60 C3 Derryveagh Mts h. Rep. of Ireland
88 A1 Derstei China
101 F3 Derudeb Sudan
104 E6 De Rust S. Africa
66 G2 Derventa Bos.-Herz.
115 G9 Derwent r. Austr.
58 E4 Derwent r. U.K.
57 G6 Derwent Reservoir resr Eng. U.K.
58 D3 Derwent Water l. U.K.
76 H4 Derzhavinsk Kazak.
47 C2 Desaguadero r. Arg.
42 E7 Desaguadero r. Bol.
109 Désappointement, Îles de is Tuamotu Islands Pac. Oc.
34 D2 Desatoya Mts mts U.S.A.
31 F2 Desbarats Can.
21 J3 Deschambault L. l. Can.
21 J4 Deschambault Lake Can.
24 B2 Deschutes r. U.S.A.
102 D2 Desē Eth.
44 C7 Deseado Arg.
44 C7 Deseado r. Arg.
31 J3 Deseronto Can.
84 B3 Desert Canal canal Pak.
35 E4 Desert Center U.S.A.
35 F1 Desert Peak summit U.S.A.
20 G3 Desmarais Can.
26 E3 Des Moines IA U.S.A.
30 A5 Des Moines r. IA U.S.A.
25 G4 Des Moines NM U.S.A.
68 E5 Desna r. Rus. Fed.
69 D5 Desna r. Ukr.
68 E4 Desnogorsk Rus. Fed.
94 C4 Desolation Point pt Phil.
30 D4 Des Plaines U.S.A.
62 F5 Dessau Ger.
31 H1 Destor Can.
114 B5 D'Estrees B. b. Austr.
20 B2 Destruction Bay Can.
40 Desventurados, Islas de los is Chile
67 J2 Deta Romania
20 G2 Detah Can.
103 C5 Dete Zimbabwe
62 D5 Detmold Ger.
30 D3 Detour, Pt pt U.S.A.
31 F3 De Tour Village U.S.A.
31 F4 Detroit MI U.S.A.
26 E2 Detroit Lakes U.S.A.
115 H5 Deua Nat. Park nat. park Austr.
66 J2 Deutschlandsberg Austria
31 H2 Deux-Rivières Can.
67 J2 Deva Romania
80 E2 Develi Turkey
61 E2 Deventer Neth.
62 H6 Devét Skal h. Czech Rep.
84 B4 Devikot India
60 D5 Devils Bit Mountain h. Rep. of Ireland
59 D5 Devil's Bridge U.K.
34 C4 Devils Den U.S.A.
34 C2 Devils Gate pass U.S.A.
32 D1 Devils I. i. U.S.A.
26 D1 Devils Lake U.S.A.
34 C3 Devils Peak summit U.S.A.
34 C3 Devils Postpile National Monument res. U.S.A.
29 F7 Devil's Pt Bahamas
59 F6 Devizes U.K.
84 C4 Devli India
67 M3 Devnya Bulg.
20 G4 Devon Can.
59 G5 Devon r. U.K.
18 Devon I. i. Can.
115 G8 Devonport Austr.
80 C1 Devrek Turkey
80 D1 Devrekâni Turkey
80 E1 Devrez r. Turkey
84 D5 Dewas India
105 G4 Dewetsdorp S. Africa
32 B6 Dewey Lake l. U.S.A.
27 E5 De Witt AR U.S.A.
30 B5 De Witt IA U.S.A.
58 F4 Dewsbury U.K.
89 E4 Dexing China
33 J2 Dexter ME U.S.A.

27 F4 Dexter MO U.S.A.
33 E2 Dexter NY U.S.A.
88 B4 Deyang China
81 M3 Deylaman Iran
93 K8 Deyong, Tanjung pt Indon.
81 M6 Dez r. Iran
81 M5 Dezful Iran
88 E2 Dezhou China
79 G4 Dhahran S. Arabia
85 G5 Dhaka Bangl.
85 G5 Dhaleswari r. Bangl.
85 H5 Dhaleswari r. India
78 E7 Dhamār Yemen
85 F5 Dhamnod India
84 B3 Dhana Sar Pak.
85 F5 Dhanbad India
84 C5 Dhandhuka India
85 E5 Dhang Ra. mts Nepal
84 C5 Dhar India
85 F4 Dharan Bazar Nepal
84 B5 Dhari India
83 E8 Dharmavaram India
84 D2 Dharmshala India
83 E7 Dhārwād India
84 D4 Dhasan r. India
85 E5 Dhaulagiri mt Nepal
84 D4 Dhaulpur India
84 C4 Dhebar L. l. India
85 H4 Dhekiajuli India
80 E6 Dhībān Jordan
85 H4 Dhing India
84 B5 Dhoraji India
84 B4 Dhrangadhra India
84 C5 Dhule India
85 H4 Dhulian India
84 D4 Dhund r. India
102 E3 Dhuusa Marreeb Somalia
67 L7 Dia i. Greece
34 B3 Diablo, Mt mt. U.S.A.
34 B3 Diablo Range mts U.S.A.
47 C2 Diamante Arg.
47 C2 Diamante r. Arg.
113 H4 Diamantina watercourse Austr.
46 D2 Diamantina Brazil
43 K6 Diamantina, Chapada plat. Brazil
46 A1 Diamantino Brazil
34 ☐1 Diamond Head hd U.S.A.
116 D1 Diamond Islets is Coral Sea Is Terr.
35 E2 Diamond Peak summit U.S.A.
89 D6 Dianbai China
89 B5 Dian Chi l. China
89 C4 Dianjiang China
43 J6 Dianópolis Brazil
100 B4 Dianra Côte d'Ivoire
100 C3 Diapaga Burkina
85 H4 Dibang r. India
102 C4 Dibaya Zaire
104 E3 Dibeng S. Africa
22 F2 D'Iberville, Lac l. Can.
105 G1 Dibete Botswana
85 H4 Dibrugarh India
27 C5 Dickens U.S.A.
26 C2 Dickinson U.S.A.
29 C4 Dickson U.S.A.
33 F4 Dickson City U.S.A.
94 B2 Didicas i. Phil.
84 C4 Didwana India
67 M4 Didymoteicho Greece
64 C3 Die France
100 B3 Diébougou Burkina
21 H4 Diefenbaker, L. l. Can.
13 J4 Diego Garcia i. British Indian Ocean Territory
61 E5 Diekirch Lux.
100 B3 Diéma Mali
89 B6 Diên Biên Vietnam
95 C1 Diên Châu Vietnam
95 D2 Diên Khanh Vietnam
64 E2 Dieppe France
62 C7 Di'er Nonchang Qu r. China
61 D4 Diest Belgium
62 D7 Dietikon Switz.
101 D3 Diffa Niger
23 G5 Digby Can.
64 H4 Digne-les-Bains France
64 F3 Digoin France
94 C5 Digos Phil.
84 D5 Digras India
84 B4 Digri Pak.
93 K8 Digul r. Indon.
100 B4 Digya National Park nat. park Ghana
64 G3 Dijon France
102 E2 Dikhil Djibouti
67 M5 Dikili Turkey
61 A3 Diksmuide Belgium
76 K2 Dikson Rus. Fed.
101 D3 Dikwa Nigeria
102 D3 Dila Eth.
93 H8 Dili Indon.
81 K1 Dilijan Armenia
95 C3 Di Linh Vietnam
27 D6 Dilley U.S.A.
62 E6 Dillingen an der Donau Ger.
21 H3 Dillon Can.
24 D2 Dillon MT U.S.A.
29 E5 Dillon SC U.S.A.
103 C5 Dilolo Zaire
81 K5 Diltāwa Iraq
85 H4 Dimapur India

80 F5 Dimashq Syria
102 C4 Dimbelenge Zaire
100 B4 Dimbokro Côte d'Ivoire
114 E6 Dimboola Austr.
116 A1 Dimbulah Austr.
67 L3 Dimitrovgrad Bulg.
68 J4 Dimitrovgrad Rus. Fed.
80 E6 Dīmona Israel
104 D2 Dimpho Pan salt pan Botswana
94 C4 Dinagat i. Phil.
85 G4 Dinajpur Bangl.
64 C2 Dinan France
84 C2 Dinanagar India
61 C4 Dinant Belgium
85 F4 Dinapur India
80 C2 Dinar Turkey
66 G2 Dinara mts Croatia
101 F3 Dinder National Park nat. park Sudan
83 E8 Dindigul India
105 K1 Dindiza Moz.
84 E5 Dindori India
80 D3 Dinek Turkey
88 C2 Dingbian China
102 B4 Dinge Angola
89 G4 Dinghai China
85 F4 Dingla Nepal
60 A5 Dingle Rep. of Ireland
60 A5 Dingle Bay b. Rep. of Ireland
89 E5 Dingnan China
116 C4 Dingo Austr.
94 B2 Dingras Phil.
88 C2 Dingtao China
100 A3 Dinguiraye Guinea
57 D3 Dingwall U.K.
88 B3 Dingxi China
88 E2 Ding Xian China
88 E2 Dingxing China
88 E3 Dingyuan China
88 F2 Dingzi Gang harbour China
89 C6 Dinh Lâp Vietnam
35 G3 Dinnebito Wash r. U.S.A.
85 F3 Dinngyê China
105 G3 Dinokwe Botswana
21 L5 Dinorwic Lake U.S.A.
35 H1 Dinosaur r. U.S.A.
24 F3 Dinosaur Nat. Mon. res. U.S.A.
100 B3 Dioïla Mali
46 B4 Dionísio Cerqueira Brazil
100 A3 Diourbel Senegal
85 H4 Diphu India
84 B4 Diplo Pak.
94 B4 Dipolog Phil.
117 B6 Dipton N.Z.
79 L2 Dir Pak.
80 F2 Dirckli Turkey
100 B3 Diré Mali
113 H2 Direction, C. c. Austr.
102 E3 Dirē Dawa Eth.
103 C5 Dirico Angola
85 H1 Dirang India
112 B5 Dirk Hartog I. i. Austr.
115 H2 Dirranbandi Austr.
35 G2 Dirty Devil r. U.S.A.
84 C4 Dīsa India
44 ☐ Disappointment, C. c. S. Georgia Atlantic Ocean
24 A2 Disappointment, C. c. U.S.A.
112 D4 Disappointment, L. salt flat Austr.
115 H6 Disaster B. b. Austr.
114 D7 Discovery Bay b. Austr.
89 ☐ Discovery Bay b. Hong Kong China
18 Disko i. Greenland
33 E6 Dismal Swamp swamp U.S.A.
85 G3 Dispur India
59 J5 Diss U.K.
46 C1 Distrito Federal div. Brazil
80 C6 Disūq Egypt
94 B4 Dit i. Phil.
104 E4 Ditloung S. Africa
66 F6 Dittaino r. Sicily Italy
83 D6 Diu India
94 C4 Diuata Mountains mts Phil.
94 C4 Diuata Pt pt Phil.
81 L4 Dīvāndarreh Iran
68 G4 Diveyevo Rus. Fed.
94 B2 Divilacan Bay b. Phil.
46 D3 Divinópolis Brazil
69 G6 Divnoye Rus. Fed.
100 B4 Divo Côte d'Ivoire
80 G2 Divriği Turkey
33 H2 Dixfield U.S.A.
33 J2 Dixmont U.S.A.
34 B2 Dixon CA U.S.A.
30 C5 Dixon IL U.S.A.
20 C4 Dixon Entrance chan. Can./U.S.A.
20 F3 Dixonville Can.
33 H2 Dixville Can.
81 J2 Diyadin Turkey
81 K5 Diyālā r. Iraq
81 H3 Diyarbakır Turkey
84 B4 Diyodar India
101 D2 Djado Niger
101 D2 Djado, Plateau du plat. Niger
102 B4 Djambala Congo
100 C2 Djanet Alg.
102 C1 Djelfa Alg.
102 C3 Djéma C.A.R.
100 B3 Djénné Mali
100 B3 Djibo Burkina
96 Djibouti country Africa
102 E2 Djibouti Djibouti

60 E4 Djouce Mountain h. Rep. of Ireland
100 C4 Djougou Benin
54 ☐ Djúpivogur Iceland
55 O6 Djurås Sweden
81 K1 Dmanisi Georgia
77 Q2 Dmitriya Lapteva, Proliv chan. Rus. Fed.
68 E4 Dmitriyevka Rus. Fed.
69 E4 Dmitriyev-L'govskiy Rus. Fed.
68 F3 Dmitrov Rus. Fed.
Dnepr r. see Dnieper
63 P5 Dnieper r. Europe
63 N6 Dniester r. Europe
Dnipro r. see Dnieper
69 E5 Dniprodzerzhyns'k Ukr.
69 E5 Dnipropetrovs'k Ukr.
69 E6 Dniprorudne Ukr.
68 D3 Dno Rus. Fed.
Dnyapro r. see Dnieper
101 D4 Doba Chad
85 G3 Doba China
31 G3 Dobbinton Can.
85 F4 Dobele Latvia
58 S8 Dobele Latvia
93 J7 Doberai Peninsula pen. Indon.
47 D3 Doblas Arg.
93 J8 Dobo Indon.
67 H2 Doboj Bos.-Herz.
67 M3 Dobrich Bulg.
69 G4 Dobrinka Rus. Fed.
69 D4 Dobrush Belarus
94 A5 Doc Can rf Phil.
46 E2 Doce r. Brazil
59 H5 Docking U.K.
25 F6 Doctor B. Domínguez Mex.
67 M6 Dodecanese is Greece
Dodekanisos is see Dodecanese
24 C2 Dodge U.S.A.
30 A3 Dodge Center U.S.A.
27 C4 Dodge City U.S.A.
115 G9 Dodges Ferry Austr.
30 B4 Dodgeville U.S.A.
59 C7 Dodman Point pt U.K.
102 D4 Dodoma Tanz.
61 E3 Doetinchem Neth.
93 H7 Dofa Indon.
85 G2 Dogai Coring salt l. China
80 F2 Doğanşehir Turkey
20 E4 Dog Creek Can.
85 G3 Dogên Co l. China
23 H2 Dog Island i. Can.
21 K4 Dog L. l. Can.
31 E1 Dog Lake l. Can.
90 D5 Dōgo i. Japan
100 C3 Dogondoutchi Niger
90 D6 Dōgo-yama mt. Japan
81 K2 Doğubeyazıt Turkey
85 G3 Do'gyaling China
79 G4 Doha Qatar
Dohad see Dāhod
85 H5 Dohazar Bangl.
85 G3 Doilungdêqên China
95 A1 Doi Saket Thai.
43 K5 Dois Irmãos, Serra dos h. Brazil
67 K4 Dojran, Lake l. Greece/Macedonia
55 M6 Dokka Norway
61 D1 Dokkum Neth.
84 B4 Dôki Pak.
63 N3 Dokshytsy Belarus
90 L1 Dokuchayeva, Mys pt Rus. Fed.
69 F6 Dokuchayevs'k Ukr.
93 K8 Dolak, Pulau i. Indon.
23 H2 Dolbeau Can.
59 C5 Dolbenmaen U.K.
64 D2 Dol-de-Bretagne France
64 G3 Dole France
59 D5 Dolgellau U.K.
33 F3 Dolgeville U.S.A.
69 F4 Dolgorukovo Rus. Fed.
69 F4 Dolgoye Rus. Fed.
66 C6 Dolianova Sardinia Italy
87 Q2 Dolinsk Rus. Fed.
102 E3 Dolo Odo Eth.
47 F3 Dolores Arg.
47 E2 Dolores Uru.
35 H2 Dolores r. U.S.A.
89 B7 Đô Lương Vietnam
69 B5 Dolyna Ukr.
80 B2 Domaniç Turkey
84 E2 Domar China
62 F6 Domažlice Czech Rep.
85 H2 Domba China
55 L5 Dombås Norway
62 J7 Dombóvár Hungary
119 C5 Dome Circle ice feature Ant.
20 A4 Dome Creek Can.
20 D2 Dome Pk summit Can.
35 E5 Dome Rock Mts mts U.S.A.
64 D2 Domfront France
16 Dominica country Caribbean Sea
16 Dominican Republic country Caribbean Sea
95 C2 Dom Noi, L. r. Thai.
66 C1 Domodossola Italy
67 K5 Domokos Greece
47 F1 Dom Pedrito Brazil
93 F8 Dompu Indon.
47 B3 Domuyo, Volcán volc. Arg.
115 J2 Domville, Mt h. Austr.
116 C3 Don r. Austr.
69 G5 Don r. Rus. Fed.
57 F3 Don r. U.K.

60 F3 Donaghadee U.K.
60 E3 Donaghmore U.K.
114 E6 Donald Austr.
Donau r. see Danube
62 D7 Donaueschingen Ger.
62 E6 Donauwörth Ger.
65 D3 Don Benito Spain
58 F4 Doncaster U.K.
103 B4 Dondo Angola
103 D5 Dondo Moz.
94 B4 Dondonay i. Phil.
60 C3 Donegal Rep. of Ireland
60 C3 Donegal Bay g.
Rep. of Ireland
69 F6 Donets'k Ukr.
69 F5 Donets'kyy Kryazh h.
Rus. Fed./Ukr.
89 C1 Dong'an China
112 B5 Dongara Austr.
84 E5 Dongargarh India
89 B5 Dongchuan China
85 F2 Dongco China
89 C7 Dongfang China
87 O2 Dongfanghong China
93 F7 Donggala Indon.
89 E5 Donggu China
89 D6 Dongguan China
95 C1 Đông Ha Vietnam
88 F3 Donghai China
89 D6 Donghai Dao i. China
88 C4 Dong He r. China
88 A1 Dong He watercourse
China
95 C1 Đông Hôi Vietnam
85 H3 Dongjug Xizang Zizhiqu
China
85 H3 Dongjug Xizang Zizhiqu
China
89 D5 Dongkou China
85 G4 Dongkya La pass India
89 C5 Donglan China
88 A2 Dongle China
88 G1 Dongliao r. China
103 B5 Dongo Angola
102 B3 Dongou Congo
95 B1 Dong Phraya Fai mts
Thai.
95 B2 Dong Phraya Yen
escarpment Thai.
89 D6 Dongping Guangdong
China
88 E3 Dongping Shandong
China
85 G3 Dongqiao China
89 E6 Dongshan China
89 E6 Dongshan Dao i. China
88 D2 Dongsheng China
88 F3 Dongtai Jiangsu China
88 F3 Dongtai China
89 D4 Dongting Hu l. China
89 F5 Dongtou China
87 L2 Dong Ujimqin Qi China
89 E4 Dongxiang China
88 B3 Dongxiangzu China
89 F4 Dongyang China
88 F2 Dongying China
88 B2 Dongzhen China
89 E4 Dongzhi China
20 B2 Donjek r. Can.
85 G5 Donmanick Islands is
Bangl.
27 C7 Don Martín Mex.
23 F4 Donnacona Can.
20 F3 Donnelly Can.
117 D1 Donnellys Crossing N.Z.
34 A3 Donner Pass pass U.S.A.
Donostia-San Sebastián
see San Sebastián
67 L6 Donoussa i. Greece
68 F4 Donskoy Rus. Fed.
69 G6 Donskoye Rus. Fed.
94 B3 Donsol Phil.
95 C2 Don, Xé r. Laos
60 A4 Dooagh Rep. of Ireland
60 B6 Doonbeg r.
Rep. of Ireland
57 D5 Doon, Loch l. U.K.
30 D3 Door Peninsula pen.
U.S.A.
102 E3 Dooxo Nugaaleed v.
Somalia
27 C5 Dora U.S.A.
66 C2 Dora Baltea r. Italy
59 E7 Dorchester U.K.
103 B6 Dordabis Namibia
64 E4 Dordogne r. France
61 C3 Dordrecht Neth.
105 G5 Dordrecht S. Africa
104 C1 Doreenville Namibia
21 H4 Doré L. l. Can.
21 H4 Doré Lake Can.
66 C4 Dorgali Sardinia Italy
100 B3 Dori Burkina
104 C5 Doring r. S. Africa
59 G6 Dorking U.K.
88 C1 Dorngovĭ div. Mongolia
57 D3 Dornoch U.K.
68 E4 Dornoch Firth est. U.K.
68 E4 Dorogobuzh Rus. Fed.
63 N7 Dorohoi Romania
86 F2 Döröö Nuur salt l.
Mongolia
54 P4 Dorotea Sweden
112 B5 Dorre I. i. Austr.
115 K3 Dorrigo Austr.
24 B3 Dorris U.S.A.
100 D4 Dorsale Camerounaise
slope Cameroon/Nigeria
31 H3 Dorset Can.
62 C5 Dortmund Ger.
61 F3 Dortmund-Ems-Kanal
canal Ger.
32 B6 Dorton U.S.A.
80 F3 Dörtyol Turkey
102 C3 Doruma Zaire

33 G2 Dorval Can.
44 C6 Dos Bahías, C. pt Arg.
35 H5 Dos Cabezas U.S.A.
42 C5 Dos de Mayo Peru
89 C6 Đo Son Vietnam
34 B3 Dos Palos U.S.A.
100 C3 Dosso Niger
29 C6 Dothan U.S.A.
64 F1 Douai France
100 C4 Douala Cameroon
64 B2 Douarnenez France
89 ☐ Double I. i. Hong Kong
China
116 E5 Double Island Pt pt
Austr.
34 C4 Double Peak summit
U.S.A.
116 B1 Double Pt pt Austr.
64 H3 Doubs r. France
117 A6 Doubtful Sound in. N.Z.
117 D1 Doubtless Bay b. N.Z.
100 B3 Douentza Mali
58 C3 Douglas Isle of Man
104 E4 Douglas S. Africa
57 E5 Douglas Scot. U.K.
20 C3 Douglas AK U.S.A.
35 H6 Douglas AZ U.S.A.
29 D6 Douglas GA U.S.A.
24 F3 Douglas WY U.S.A.
20 D4 Douglas Chan. chan.
Can.
35 H2 Douglas Creek r. U.S.A.
64 F1 Doullens France
57 D4 Doune U.K.
46 C2 Dourada, Cach. waterfall
Brazil
46 C1 Dourada, Serra mts
Brazil
46 B2 Dourada, Serra h. Brazil
46 A3 Dourados r. Brazil
46 A3 Dourados Brazil
46 B3 Dourados, Serra dos h.
Brazil
65 C2 Douro r. Port.
59 F4 Dove r. Eng. U.K.
59 J5 Dove r. Eng. U.K.
23 J3 Dove Brook Can.
35 H3 Dove Creek U.S.A.
115 G9 Dover Austr.
59 J6 Dover U.K.
33 F5 Dover DE U.S.A.
33 H3 Dover NH U.S.A.
33 F4 Dover NJ U.S.A.
32 C4 Dover OH U.S.A.
33 J2 Dover-Foxcroft U.S.A.
59 J7 Dover, Strait of str.
France/U.K.
81 M6 Doveyrīch r. Iran/Iraq
30 D5 Dowagiac U.S.A.
95 A5 Dowi, Tg pt Indon.
34 B2 Downieville U.S.A.
60 F3 Downpatrick U.K.
33 F3 Downsville U.S.A.
81 M5 Dow Rūd Iran
81 L4 Dow Sar Iran
79 K2 Dowshī Afgh.
34 B1 Doyle U.S.A.
33 F4 Doylestown U.S.A.
90 D5 Dōzen i. Japan
31 J2 Dozois, Réservoir resr
Can.
46 B3 Dracena Brazil
61 E1 Drachten Neth.
67 L2 Drăgăneşti-Olt Romania
67 L2 Drăgăşani Romania
45 E2 Dragon's Mouths str.
Trinidad/Venez.
55 S6 Dragsfjärd Fin.
64 H5 Draguignan France
69 C6 Drahichyn Belarus
115 K2 Drake Austr.
35 F4 Drake AZ U.S.A.
21 J5 Drake ND U.S.A.
105 H5 Drakensberg mts
Lesotho/S. Africa
105 J2 Drakensberg mts S. Africa
119 A1 Drake Passage str. Ant.
67 L4 Drama Greece
55 M7 Drammen Norway
55 L7 Drangedal Norway
60 E3 Draperstown U.K.
84 C2 Dras Jammu and Kashmir
62 F7 Drau r. Austria
20 G4 Drayton Valley Can.
66 B6 Dréan Alg.
62 F5 Dresden Ger.
68 D4 Dretun' Belarus
64 E2 Dreux France
55 N6 Drevsjø Norway
32 C4 Driftwood U.S.A.
116 D6 Drillham Austr.
60 B6 Drimoleague
Rep. of Ireland
66 G3 Drniš Croatia
67 K2 Drobeta-Turnu Severin
Romania
60 E4 Drogheda Rep. of Ireland
69 B5 Drohobych Ukr.
Droichead Átha see
Drogheda
59 E5 Droitwich U.K.
60 D4 Dromod Rep. of Ireland
60 E3 Dromore Co. Down U.K.
60 D3 Dromore Co. Tyrone U.K.
59 D7 Dronfield U.K.
119 C3 Dronning Maud Land
reg. Ant.
84 B2 Drosh Pak.
69 F4 Droskovo Rus. Fed.
115 F7 Drouin Austr.
44 D2 Dr Pedro P. Peña
Para.
20 G4 Drumheller Can.

24 D2 Drummond MT U.S.A.
30 B2 Drummond WV U.S.A.
31 F3 Drummond Island i.
U.S.A.
116 B5 Drummond Range h.
Austr.
23 F4 Drummondville Can.
57 D6 Drummore U.K.
57 D4 Drumochter Pass pass
U.K.
55 T10 Druskininkai Lith.
77 Q3 Druzhina Rus. Fed.
67 L3 Dryanovo Bulg.
20 B3 Dry Bay b. U.S.A.
21 L5 Dryberry L. l. Can.
30 E2 Dryburg U.S.A.
22 B4 Dryden Can.
34 D2 Dry Lake l. U.S.A.
57 D4 Drymen U.K.
112 E3 Drysdale r. Austr.
112 E3 Drysdale River National
Park nat. park Austr.
81 M4 Dūāb r. Iran
89 C6 Du'an China
33 F2 Duane U.S.A.
116 C4 Duaringa Austr.
85 G4 Duars reg. India
78 D4 Dubā S. Arabia
79 H4 Dubai U.A.E.
21 J2 Dubawnt r. Can.
21 J2 Dubawnt Lake l. Can.
Dubayy see
Dubai
78 D4 Dubbagh, J. ad mt
S. Arabia
115 H4 Dubbo Austr.
30 D1 Dublin Can.
60 E4 Dublin Rep. of Ireland
29 D5 Dublin U.S.A.
68 F3 Dubna Rus. Fed.
69 C5 Dubno Ukr.
30 D2 Dubois ID U.S.A.
24 E3 Dubois WY U.S.A.
32 D4 Du Bois U.S.A.
69 H5 Dubovka Rus. Fed.
69 G6 Dubovskoye Rus. Fed.
81 M1 Dübrar P. pass Azer.
100 A4 Dubréka Guinea
67 H3 Dubrovnik Croatia
69 C5 Dubrovtsya Ukr.
68 D4 Dubrowna Belarus
30 B4 Dubuque U.S.A.
55 S9 Dubysa r. Lith.
89 H4 Duchang China
35 G1 Duchesne U.S.A.
109 Ducie Island i. Pitcairn
Islands Pac. Oc.
29 C5 Duck r. U.S.A.
21 J4 Duck Bay Can.
21 H4 Duck Lake Can.
30 E4 Duck Lake U.S.A.
35 E2 Duckwater U.S.A.
35 E2 Duckwater Peak summit
U.S.A.
95 D2 Đưc Pho Vietnam
95 D3 Đưc Trong Vietnam
45 B4 Duda r. Col.
85 E4 Dudhi India
85 G4 Dudhnai India
76 K3 Dudinka Rus. Fed.
59 E5 Dudley U.K.
84 D6 Dudna r. India
57 F3 Dudwick, Hill of h. U.K.
100 B4 Duékoué Côte d'Ivoire
65 C2 Duero r. Spain
31 H1 Dufault, Lac l. Can.
22 E2 Dufferin, Cape hd Can.
32 B6 Duffield U.S.A.
111 G2 Duff Is is Solomon Is
57 E3 Dufftown U.K.
22 E1 Dufrost, Pte pt Can.
66 F3 Dugi Otok i. Croatia
88 C2 Dugui Qarag China
88 D3 Du He r. China
45 D4 Duida, Co mt Venez.
62 C5 Duisburg Ger.
45 B3 Duitama Col.
105 J1 Duiwelskloof S. Africa
81 K4 Dukān Dam dam Iraq
105 G5 Dukathole S. Africa
20 C4 Duke I. i. U.S.A.
79 G4 Dukhān Qatar
63 Q3 Dukhovshchina Rus. Fed.
84 B3 Duki Pak.
89 A5 Dukou China
55 U9 Dūkštas Lith.
82 J3 Dulan China
Dulawan see Datu Piang
44 D3 Dulce r. Arg.
85 E2 Dulishi Hu salt l. China
105 J2 Dullstroom S. Africa
61 F3 Dülmen Ger.
67 M3 Dulovo Bulg.
30 A2 Dutch U.S.A.
30 A2 Duluth/Superior airport
U.S.A.
59 D6 Dulverton U.K.
80 F5 Dūmā Syria
94 B4 Dumaguete Phil.
92 C6 Dumai Indon.
94 B4 Dumaran i. Phil.
27 E5 Dumas AR U.S.A.
27 C5 Dumas TX U.S.A.
80 F5 Dumayr Syria
81 L5 Dumbakh Iran
57 D5 Dumbarton U.K.
105 J3 Dumbe S. Africa
63 J6 Ďumbier mt Slovakia
84 D2 Dumchele Jammu and
Kashmir
85 H4 Dum Duma India
57 F5 Dumfries U.K.
85 F4 Dumka India
22 E4 Dumoine, L. l. Can.

119 B6 Dumont d'Urville Sea
sea Ant.
78 C3 Dumyât Egypt
Duna r. see Danube
Dunaj r. see Danube
62 H7 Dunajská Streda Slovakia
63 J7 Dunakeszi Hungary
115 G9 Dunalley Austr.
60 E4 Dunany Point pt
Rep. of Ireland
Dunărea r. see Danube
67 N2 Dunării, Delta delta
Romania
63 J7 Dunaújváros Hungary
Dunav r. see Danube
69 C5 Dunback N.Z.
117 C6 Dunback N.Z.
57 F4 Dunbar U.K.
57 E4 Dunblane U.K.
60 E4 Dunboyne Rep. of Ireland
20 E5 Duncan Can.
35 H5 Duncan AZ U.S.A.
27 D5 Duncan OK U.S.A.
22 D3 Duncan, Cape c. Can.
22 E3 Duncan, L. l. Can.
32 E4 Duncannon U.S.A.
57 E2 Duncansby Head hd U.K.
30 B5 Duncans Mills U.S.A.
60 E5 Duncormick
Rep. of Ireland
55 S8 Dundaga Latvia
31 G3 Dundalk Can.
60 E3 Dundalk Rep. of Ireland
32 E5 Dundalk U.S.A.
60 E4 Dundalk Bay b.
Rep. of Ireland
16 Dundas Greenland
20 C4 Dundas I. i. Can.
Dun Dealgan see
Dundalk
105 J4 Dundee S. Africa
57 F4 Dundee U.K.
31 F5 Dundee MI U.S.A.
32 E3 Dundee NY U.S.A.
60 F3 Dundonald U.K.
57 E6 Dundrennan U.K.
60 F3 Dundrum U.K.
60 F3 Dundrum Bay b. U.K.
85 E4 Dundwa Range mts
India/Nepal
117 C6 Dunedin N.Z.
29 D6 Dunedin U.S.A.
115 H4 Dunedoo Austr.
22 F2 Dune, Lac l. Can.
57 E4 Dunfermline U.K.
60 E3 Dungannon U.K.
84 C5 Dungarpur India
60 D5 Dungarvan Rep. of Ireland
59 H7 Dungeness hd U.K.
44 C8 Dungeness, Pta pt Arg.
60 E3 Dungiven U.K.
60 C3 Dungloe Rep. of Ireland
115 J4 Dungog Austr.
102 C3 Dungu Zaire
92 C6 Dungun Malaysia
101 F2 Dungunab Sudan
87 N3 Dunhua China
82 H2 Dunhuang China
114 E6 Dunkeld Austr.
57 E4 Dunkeld U.K.
Dunkerque see Dunkirk
59 D6 Dunkery Beacon h. U.K.
64 F1 Dunkirk France
32 D3 Dunkirk U.S.A.
100 B4 Dunkwa Ghana
60 E4 Dún Laoghaire
Rep. of Ireland
60 E4 Dunlavin Rep. of Ireland
60 E4 Dunleer Rep. of Ireland
60 E2 Dunloy U.K.
60 B6 Dunmanus Bay b.
Rep. of Ireland
60 B6 Dunmanway
Rep. of Ireland
60 C4 Dunmore Rep. of Ireland
29 E7 Dunmore Town Bahamas
34 D3 Dunmovin U.S.A.
60 F3 Dunmurry U.K.
29 E5 Dunn U.S.A.
57 E2 Dunnet Bay b. U.K.
57 E2 Dunnet Head hd U.K.
34 B2 Dunnigan U.S.A.
26 C3 Dunning U.S.A.
31 H4 Dunnville Can.
114 E6 Dunolly Austr.
57 D5 Dunoon U.K.
57 F5 Dunragit U.K.
26 C1 Dunseith U.S.A.
24 B3 Dunsmuir U.S.A.
59 G6 Dunstable U.K.
117 B6 Dunstan Mts mts N.Z.
117 B6 Duntroon N.Z.
57 B3 Dunvegan, Loch in. U.K.
88 E1 Duolun China
89 D5 Dupang Ling mts China
31 H1 Duparquet, Lac l. Can.
112 E3 Durack r. Austr.
Dura Europos see
Qal'at as Sālihīyah
80 E1 Durağan Turkey
64 G4 Durance r. France
31 F4 Durand MI U.S.A.
30 B3 Durand WI U.S.A.
36 D2 Durango Mex.
65 E1 Durango Spain
25 F4 Durango U.S.A.
27 D5 Durant U.S.A.
47 F2 Durazno Uru.
47 F1 Durazno, Cuchilla
Grande del h. Uru.

105 J4 Durban S. Africa
64 F5 Durban-Corbières France
104 D6 Durbanville S. Africa
32 D5 Durbin U.S.A.
61 D4 Durbuy Belgium
61 E4 Düren Ger.
85 F5 Durgapur India
31 G3 Durham Can.
58 F3 Durham U.K.
34 B2 Durham CA U.S.A.
29 E4 Durham NC U.S.A.
33 H3 Durham NH U.S.A.
69 D6 Durleşti Moldova
67 H3 Durmitor mt Yugo.
57 D2 Durness U.K.
116 D6 Durong South Austr.
67 H4 Durrës Albania
59 E4 Durrington U.K.
60 A6 Dursey Island i.
Rep. of Ireland
80 B2 Dursunbey Turkey
80 F5 Durūz, Jabal ad mt
Syria
117 D4 D'Urville Island i. N.Z.
93 K7 D'Urville, Tanjung pt
Indon.
89 C5 Dushan China
79 K2 Dushanbe Tajik.
69 H7 Dushet'i Georgia
117 A6 Dusky Sound in. N.Z.
62 C5 Düsseldorf Ger.
35 H1 Dutch Mt mt. U.S.A.
104 E1 Dutlwe Botswana
100 C3 Dutse Nigeria
114 B3 Dutton, Lake salt flat
Austr.
35 F2 Dutton, Mt mt. U.S.A.
68 H3 Duvannoye Rus. Fed.
23 F2 Duvert, Lac l. Can.
89 F2 Duyun China
80 C1 Düzce Turkey
Dvina, Western r. see
Zapadnaya Dvina
69 C5 Dvorichna Ukr.
84 B5 Dwarka India
105 G2 Dwarsberg S. Africa
30 C5 Dwight U.S.A.
61 E2 Dwingelderveld,
Nationaal Park nat. park
Neth.
24 C2 Dworshak Res. resr U.S.A.
104 D6 Dwyka S. Africa
68 F4 Dyat'kovo Rus. Fed.
57 F3 Dyce U.K.
30 D5 Dyer IN U.S.A.
34 C3 Dyer NV U.S.A.
31 G3 Dyer Bay Can.
57 E3 Dyfi r. U.K.
57 E3 Dyke U.K.
69 G7 Dykh Tau mt
Georgia/Rus. Fed.
63 J4 Dylewska Góra h. Pol.
114 F2 Dynevor Downs Austr.
105 H5 Dyoki S. Africa
116 C4 Dysart Austr.
30 A4 Dysart U.S.A.
104 E6 Dysselsdorp S. Africa
87 K3 Dzamīn Üüd Mongolia
103 E5 Dzaoudzi Mayotte Africa
63 N5 Dzerzhyns'k Ukr.
68 G3 Dzerzhinsk Rus. Fed.
63 N5 Dzerzhyns'k Ukr.
Dzhambul see Zhambyl
79 G1 Dzhanga Turkm.
69 E6 Dzhankoy Ukr.
95 H5 Dzhanybek Rus. Fed.
76 H4 Dzhetygara Kazak.
82 C1 Dzhezdy Kazak.
82 C1 Dzhezkazgan Kazak.
77 R3 Dzhigudzhak Rus. Fed.
79 K1 Dzhizak Uzbek.
77 P4 Dzhugdzhur, Khrebet mts
Rus. Fed.
Dzhul'fa see Culfa
82 E2 Dzhungarskiy Alatau,
Khr. mts China/Kazak.
82 B1 Dzhusaly Kazak.
63 K4 Działdowo Pol.
Dzungarian Basin basin
see Junggar Pendi
86 J2 Dzuunmod Mongolia
68 C4 Dzyaniskavichy Belarus
68 C4 Dzyarzhynsk Belarus
63 N4 Dzyatlavichy Belarus

# E

22 C3 Eabamet L. l. Can.
35 H4 Eagar U.S.A.
23 J2 Eagle r. U.S.A.
25 F4 Eagle U.S.A.
33 F3 Eagle Bay U.S.A.
21 H4 Eagle Cr. r. Can.
34 D4 Eagle Crags summit
U.S.A.
21 L5 Eagle L. l. Can.
24 B3 Eagle L. l. CA U.S.A.
33 J1 Eagle Lake l. ME U.S.A.
33 J1 Eagle Lake ME U.S.A.
30 B2 Eagle Mtn h. U.S.A.
27 C6 Eagle Pass U.S.A.
65 E1 Eagle River AK U.S.A.
30 C3 Eagle River WI U.S.A.
20 F3 Eaglesham Can.
35 F5 Eagle Tail Mts mts U.S.A.
91 H4 Eai-gawa r. Japan
22 B3 Ear Falls Can.

34 C4 Earlimart U.S.A.
57 F5 Earlston U.K.
31 H2 Earlton Can.
57 E4 Earn r. U.K.
57 D4 Earn, L. l. U.K.
27 C5 Earth U.S.A.
58 H4 Easington U.K.
29 D5 Easley U.S.A.
119 C3 East Antarctica reg. Ant.
33 F4 East Ararat U.S.A.
32 D3 East Aurora U.S.A.
27 F6 East Bay b. U.S.A.
33 G2 East Berkshire U.S.A.
59 H7 Eastbourne U.K.
32 D4 East Branch Clarion
River Reservoir resr
U.S.A.
33 H4 East Brooklyn U.S.A.
117 G2 East Cape c. N.Z.
35 G2 East Carbon U.S.A.
30 D5 East Chicago U.S.A.
87 M6 East China Sea sea Asia
33 G2 East Corinth U.S.A.
59 H5 East Dereham U.K.
15 M7 Easter Island Fracture
Zone sea feature Pac. Oc.
105 G5 Eastern Cape div.
S. Africa
78 C4 Eastern Desert des.
Egypt
85 E6 Eastern Ghats mts India
84 B4 Eastern Nara canal Pak.
Eastern Transvaal div.
see Mpumalanga
21 K4 Easterville Can.
44 E8 East Falkland i. Falkland
Is
33 H4 East Falmouth U.S.A.
62 C4 East Frisian Islands is
Ger.
34 D2 Eastgate U.S.A.
26 D2 East Grand Forks U.S.A.
59 G6 East Grinstead U.K.
33 G3 Easthampton U.S.A.
33 G3 East Hampton U.S.A.
32 D4 East Hickory U.S.A.
33 G3 East Jamaica U.S.A.
12 K1 East Jan Mayen Ridge
sea feature
Atlantic Ocean
30 E3 East Jordan U.S.A.
57 D5 East Kilbride U.K.
30 D3 Eastlake U.S.A.
89 East Lamma Channel
chan. Hong Kong China
59 F7 Eastleigh U.K.
32 C4 East Liverpool U.S.A.
57 B3 East Loch Tarbert b. U.K.
105 G6 East London S. Africa
32 E3 East Lynn Lake l. U.S.A.
22 F3 Eastmain r. Que. Can.
22 E3 Eastmain Que. Can.
29 D5 Eastman U.S.A.
33 G2 Eastman U.S.A.
116 A4 Eastmere Austr.
33 J2 East Millinocket U.S.A.
30 B5 East Moline U.S.A.
30 C5 Easton IL U.S.A.
33 E5 Easton MD U.S.A.
33 F4 Easton PA U.S.A.
15 M8 East Pacific Ridge
sea feature Pac. Oc.
15 N5 East Pacific Rise
sea feature Pac. Oc.
34 A2 East Park Res. resr U.S.A.
23 H4 East Point P.E.I. Can.
29 C5 East Point U.S.A.
33 K2 Eastport ME U.S.A.
30 E3 Eastport MI U.S.A.
33 D1 East Range mts U.S.A.
East Retford see Retford
28 B4 East St Louis U.S.A.
77 Q2 East Siberian Sea sea
Rus. Fed.
115 H7 East Sister I. i. Austr.
85 E4 East Tons r. India
115 F3 East Toorale Austr.
30 C4 East Troy U.S.A.
33 F6 Eastville U.S.A.
34 C2 East Walker r. U.S.A.
33 G3 East Wallingford U.S.A.
29 D5 Eatonton U.S.A.
30 B3 Eau Claire r. U.S.A.
30 B3 Eau Claire U.S.A.
22 F2 Eau Claire, Lac á l' l.
Can.
61 C4 Eau d'Heure, L' l.
Belgium
14 E5 Eauripik – New Guinea
Rise sea feature Pac. Oc.
36 E4 Ebano Mex.
59 B6 Ebbw Vale U.K.
100 D4 Ebebiyin
Equatorial Guinea
104 D2 Ebenerde Namibia
32 D4 Ebensburg U.S.A.
80 C2 Eber Gölü l. Turkey
62 F4 Eberswalde-Finow Ger.
31 F4 Eberts Can.
90 H2 Ebetsu Japan
89 B4 Ebian China
86 D3 Ebinur Hu salt l. China
66 F4 Eboli Italy
100 D4 Ebolowa Cameroon
81 K3 Ebrāhīm Ḥeşār Iran
65 G2 Ebro r. Spain
67 M2 Eceabat Turkey
94 B2 Echague Phil.
65 E1 Echarri-Aranaz Spain
100 D4 Ech Chélif Alg.
65 E1 Echegárate, Puerto pass
Spain
89 B4 Echeng China
91 E6 Echizen-misaki pt Japan

20 F1 Echo Bay *N.W.T.* Can.
31 E2 Echo Bay *Ont.* Can.
35 G2 Echo Cliffs *cliff* U.S.A.
22 B3 Echoing *r.* Can.
115 G9 Echo, L. *l.* Austr.
31 K2 Échouani, Lac *l.* Can.
61 E5 Echternach Lux.
114 F6 Echuca Austr.
65 D4 Écija Spain
30 E2 Eckerman U.S.A.
62 D3 Eckernförde Ger.
38 Ecuador *country* S. America
22 E2 Écueils, Pte aux *pt* Can.
102 E2 Ed Eritrea
55 M7 Ed Sweden
21 H4 Edam Can.
57 F1 Eday *i.* U.K.
101 E3 Ed Da'ein Sudan
101 F3 Ed Damazin Sudan
101 F3 Ed Damer Sudan
101 F3 Ed Debba Sudan
101 F3 Ed Dueim Sudan
115 H8 Eddystone Pt *pt* Austr.
100 D4 Edéia Cameroon
21 K2 Edehon Lake *l.* Can.
46 C2 Edéa Brazil
115 H6 Eden Austr.
58 E3 Eden *r.* U.K.
27 D6 Eden *TX* U.S.A.
105 F4 Edenburg S. Africa
117 B7 Edendale N.Z.
60 D4 Edenderry Rep. of Ireland
114 D6 Edenhope Austr.
29 E4 Edenton U.S.A.
105 G3 Edenville S. Africa
67 K4 Edessa Greece
33 H4 Edgartown U.S.A.
26 D2 Edgeley U.S.A.
26 C3 Edgemont U.S.A.
30 C4 Edgerton U.S.A.
60 D4 Edgeworthstown Rep. of Ireland
30 A5 Edina U.S.A.
27 D7 Edinburg *TX* U.S.A.
57 E5 Edinburgh U.K.
69 C7 Edirne Turkey
20 F4 Edith Cavell, Mt *mt.* Can.
24 D2 Edmonds U.S.A.
116 A1 Edmonton Austr.
20 G4 Edmonton Can.
21 K5 Edmore U.S.A.
30 B4 Edmund U.S.A.
21 L4 Edmund L. *l.* Can.
23 G4 Edmundston Can.
27 D6 Edna U.S.A.
20 C3 Edna Bay U.S.A.
67 M5 Edremit Turkey
55 O6 Edsbyn Sweden
20 F4 Edson Can.
47 D2 Eduardo Castex Arg.
114 F5 Edward *r.* Austr.
30 C1 Edward I. *i.* Can.
102 C4 Edward, Lake *l.* Uganda/Zaire
33 F2 Edwards U.S.A.
114 A2 Edward's Cr. Austr.
27 C6 Edwards Plateau *plat.* U.S.A.
28 B4 Edwardsville U.S.A.
119 A4 Edward VII Pen. *pen.* Ant.
20 G3 Edziza Pk *mt.* Can.
34 A1 Eel *r.* U.S.A.
61 E1 Eemshaven *pt* Neth.
104 D3 Eenzamheid Pan *salt pan* S. Africa
111 E3 Éfaté *i.* Vanuatu
28 B4 Effingham U.S.A.
80 D1 Eflâni Turkey
35 E2 Egan Range *mts* U.S.A.
31 J3 Eganville Can.
63 K7 Eger Hungary
55 K7 Egersund Norway
54 F4 Egilsstaðir Iceland
80 C3 Eğlab *plat.* Alg.
80 C3 Eğirdir Gölü *l.* Turkey
64 F4 Égletons France
60 D2 Eglinton U.K.
61 C2 Egmond aan den Hoef Neth.
117 D3 Egmont, Cape *c.* N.Z.
117 E3 Egmont, Mt *volc.* N.Z.
117 E3 Egmont National Park N.Z.
80 B2 Eğrigöz Dağı *mts* Turkey
58 G3 Egton U.K.
46 D1 Éguas *r.* Brazil
77 V3 Egvekinot Rus. Fed.
96 Egypt *country* Africa
90 D7 Ehime Japan
62 D6 Ehingen (Donau) Ger.
35 E5 Ehrenberg U.S.A.
61 E2 Eibergen Neth.
55 K6 Eidfjord Norway
116 D5 Eidsvold Austr.
55 M6 Eidsvoll Norway
61 E4 Eifel *reg.* Ger.
57 B4 Eigg *i.* U.K.
83 D9 Eight Degree Channel *chan.* India/Maldives
112 D6 Eighty Mile Beach *beach* Austr.
115 F6 Eildon Austr.
115 F6 Eildon, Lake *l.* Austr.
57 C4 Eilean Shona *i.* U.K.
21 H2 Eileen Lake *l.* Can.
61 D3 Eindhoven Neth.
62 D7 Einsiedeln Switz.
42 A4 Eirunepé Brazil
103 C5 Eiseb *watercourse* Namibia
62 E5 Eisenach Ger.
62 G4 Eisenhüttenstadt Ger.

62 H7 Eisenstadt Austria
57 C3 Eishort, Loch *in.* U.K.
Eivissa *see* Ibiza
Eivissa *i. see* Ibiza
65 F1 Ejea de los Caballeros Spain
103 E6 Ejeda Madag.
36 B3 Ejido Insurgentes Mex.
88 B3 Ejin Horo Qi China
88 A1 Ejin Qi China
81 K1 Ejmiatsin Armenia
55 S7 Ekenäs Fin.
61 C3 Ekeren Belgium
117 E4 Eketahuna N.Z.
76 J4 Ekibastuz Kazak.
77 M3 Ekonda Rus. Fed.
55 N6 Ekshärad Sweden
55 O8 Eksjö Sweden
104 B4 Eksteenfontein S. Africa
102 C4 Ekuku Zaire
22 D3 Ekwan *r.* Can.
22 D3 Ekwan Point *pt* Can.
67 K6 Elafonisou, Steno *chan.* Greece
80 B6 El 'Alamein Egypt
80 B6 El 'Amirîya Egypt
105 H2 Elands *r.* S. Africa
105 H2 Elandsdoorn S. Africa
66 B7 El Aouinet Alg.
80 B6 El 'Arab, Khalîg *b.* Egypt
116 B1 El Arish Austr.
80 C4 El 'Arîsh Egypt
67 K5 Elassona Greece
80 E7 Elat Israel
81 G2 Elazığ Turkey
66 D3 Elba, Isola d' *i.* Italy
87 P1 El'ban Rus. Fed.
45 B2 El Banco Col.
80 D6 El Bardawîl, Sabkhet *lag.* Egypt
67 J4 Elbasan Albania
80 E2 Elbaşı Turkey
45 C2 El Baúl Venez.
100 C1 El Bayadh Alg.
62 E4 Elbe *r.* Ger.
30 D3 Elberta *MI* U.S.A.
35 G2 Elberta *UT* U.S.A.
25 F4 Elbert, Mount *mt.* U.S.A.
29 D5 Elberton U.S.A.
64 E2 Elbeuf France
80 F7 Elbistan Turkey
63 J3 Elbląg Pol.
47 B4 El Bolsón Arg.
29 E7 Elbow Cay *i.* Bahamas
69 G7 Elbrus *mt* Rus. Fed.
65 E2 El Burgo de Osma Spain
47 C4 El Caín Arg.
34 D5 El Cajon U.S.A.
45 E3 El Callao Venez.
27 D6 El Campo U.S.A.
35 E5 El Centro U.S.A.
42 F7 El Cerro Bol.
45 D2 El Chaparro Venez.
65 F3 Elche Spain
113 G2 Elcho I. *i.* Austr.
45 B3 El Cocuy Col.
65 E2 Elda Spain
31 H2 Eldee Can.
114 D3 Elder, Lake *salt flat* Austr.
34 D5 El Descanso Mex.
45 B2 El Difícil Col.
77 P3 El'dikan Rus. Fed.
45 A4 El Diviso Col.
35 E6 El Doctor Mex.
30 A5 Eldon *IA* U.S.A.
26 E4 Eldon *MO* U.S.A.
44 F3 Eldorado Arg.
27 C6 Eldorado U.S.A.
36 C4 El Dorado Mex.
27 E5 El Dorado *AR* U.S.A.
27 D4 El Dorado *KS* U.S.A.
45 E3 El Dorado Venez.
102 D3 Eldoret Kenya
24 E2 Electric Peak *summit* U.S.A.
100 B2 El Eglab *plat.* Alg.
65 E4 El Ejido Spain
68 F4 Elektrostal' Rus. Fed.
42 H2 El Encanto Col.
25 F5 Elephant Butte Res. *resr* U.S.A.
119 B1 Elephant I. *i.* Ant.
85 H5 Elephant Point *pt* Bangl.
100 C1 El Eulma Alg.
29 E7 Eleuthera *i.* Bahamas
66 C6 El Fahs Tunisia
78 C4 El Faiyûm Egypt
101 E3 El Fasher Sudan
101 E3 El Geneina Sudan
101 F3 El Geteina Sudan
57 E3 Elgin U.K.
30 C4 Elgin *IL* U.S.A.
26 C2 Elgin *ND* U.S.A.
35 E3 Elgin *NV* U.S.A.
35 G2 Elgin *UT* U.S.A.
116 B4 Elgin Down Austr.
77 Q3 El'ginskiy Rus. Fed.
78 C4 El Gîza Egypt
100 C1 El Goléa Alg.
101 F4 Elgon, Mount *mt* Uganda
66 B6 El Hadjar Alg.
80 B6 El Hammâm Egypt
80 F6 El Hazim Jordan
100 A2 El Hierro *i.* Canary Is Spain
100 C2 El Homr Alg.
57 F4 Elie U.K.
117 C5 Elie de Beaumont *mt.* N.Z.
77 V3 Elim Alaska
23 H2 Eliot, Mount *mt.* Can.
65 F1 Eliozondo Spain

El Iskandarîya *see* Alexandria
69 H6 Elista Rus. Fed.
30 B4 Elizabeth *IL* U.S.A.
33 F4 Elizabeth *NJ* U.S.A.
32 C5 Elizabeth *WV* U.S.A.
29 E4 Elizabeth City U.S.A.
33 H4 Elizabeth Is. *i.* U.S.A.
29 Elizabethton U.S.A.
28 C4 Elizabethtown *KY* U.S.A.
29 E5 Elizabethtown *NC* U.S.A.
33 G2 Elizabethtown *NY* U.S.A.
32 E4 Elizabethtown *PA* U.S.A.
100 B1 El Jadida Morocco
80 F6 El Jafr Jordan
66 D7 El Jem Tunisia
20 G4 Elk *r.* Can.
63 L4 Elk Pol.
34 A2 Elk *r.* U.S.A.
32 C5 Elk *r.* U.S.A.
80 F4 El Kaa Lebanon
66 C6 El Kala Alg.
101 F3 El Kamlin Sudan
27 D5 Elk City U.S.A.
34 A2 Elk Creek U.S.A.
34 B2 Elk Grove U.S.A.
78 C4 El Khârga Egypt
30 E5 Elkhart U.S.A.
El Khartum *see* Khartoum
100 B2 El Khnâchîch *escarpment* Mali
30 C4 Elkhorn U.S.A.
26 D3 Elkhorn *r.* U.S.A.
67 M3 Elkhovo Bulg.
32 D5 Elkins U.S.A.
20 G4 Elk Island Nat. Park *nat. park* Can.
31 G2 Elk Lake Can.
30 E3 Elk Lake *l.* U.S.A.
32 E4 Elkland U.S.A.
20 F5 Elko Can.
24 D3 Elko U.S.A.
21 G4 Elk Point Can.
26 E2 Elk River U.S.A.
33 F5 Elkton *MD* U.S.A.
32 D5 Elkton *VA* U.S.A.
81 G4 El Kubar Syria
21 M2 Ell Bay *b.* Can.
18 Ellef Ringnes I. *i.* Can.
84 C3 Ellenabad India
26 D2 Ellendale U.S.A.
35 G2 Ellen, Mt *mt.* U.S.A.
24 B2 Ellensburg U.S.A.
33 F4 Ellenville U.S.A.
115 H6 Ellery, Mt *mt* Austr.
18 Ellesmere Island *i.* Can.
117 D5 Ellesmere, Lake *l.* N.Z.
59 E4 Ellesmere Port U.K.
32 D3 Ellicottville U.S.A.
105 G5 Elliot S. Africa
105 H5 Elliotdale S. Africa
31 F2 Elliot Lake Can.
116 B2 Elliot, Mt *mt* Austr.
24 D2 Ellis U.S.A.
105 G1 Ellisras S. Africa
114 A4 Elliston Austr.
57 F3 Ellon U.K.
33 J2 Ellsworth *ME* U.S.A.
30 A3 Ellsworth *WV* U.S.A.
119 A3 Ellsworth Land *reg.* Ant.
119 B3 Ellsworth Mountains *mts* Ant.
80 B3 Elmalı Turkey
34 D6 El Maneadero Mex.
78 C4 El Mansûra Egypt
45 E3 El Manteco Venez.
100 C1 El Meghaïer Alg.
45 E3 El Miamo Venez.
80 E4 El Mîna Lebanon
78 C4 El Minya Egypt
30 E3 Elmira *MI* U.S.A.
32 E3 Elmira *NY* U.S.A.
35 F5 El Mirage U.S.A.
65 E4 El Moral Spain
114 F6 Elmore Austr.
47 D2 El Morro *mt* Arg.
100 B2 El Mreyyé *reg.* Maur.
62 D4 Elmshorn Ger.
101 E3 El Muglad Sudan
30 C5 Elmwood *IL* U.S.A.
30 A3 Elmwood *WV* U.S.A.
54 K5 Elnesvågen Norway
45 B3 El Nevado, Cerro *mt* Col.
94 A4 El Nido Phil.
101 F3 El Obeid Sudan
45 E2 Elorza Venez.
30 C2 El Paso *IL* U.S.A.
25 F6 El Paso *TX* U.S.A.
57 B4 Elphin U.K.
34 C3 El Portal U.S.A.
65 H2 El Prat de Llobregat Spain
65 C4 El Puerto de Santa María Spain
El Qâhira *see* Cairo
80 D6 El Qantara Egypt
80 E7 El Quweira Jordan
27 D5 El Reno U.S.A.
30 B4 Elroy U.S.A.
20 B2 Elsa Can.
80 C7 El Saff Egypt
80 D6 El Sâlhîya Egypt
36 C4 El Salto Mex.
16 El Salvador *country* Central America
94 C4 El Salvador Phil.
45 C3 El Samán de Apure Venez.

31 F1 Elsas Can.
85 H2 Elsen Nur *l.* China
80 D7 El Shatt Egypt
45 E2 El Sombrero Venez.
47 C2 El Sosneado Arg.
El Suweis *see* Suez
66 C6 El Tarf Alg.
65 C1 El Teleno *mt* Spain
80 E7 El Thamad Egypt
45 D2 El Tigre Venez.
45 C2 El Tocuyo Venez.
69 H5 El'ton Rus. Fed.
69 H5 El'ton, Ozero *l.* Rus. Fed.
24 C3 Eltopia U.S.A.
45 E2 El Toro Venez.
47 E3 El Trébol Arg.
45 C3 El Tuparro, Parque Nacional *nat. park* Col.
78 C4 El Tûr Egypt
44 B8 El Turbio Chile
83 F7 Eluru India
55 U7 Elva Estonia
43 A3 El Valle Col.
57 E5 Elvanfoot U.K.
65 C3 Elvas Port.
55 M6 Elverum Norway
45 B3 El Viejo *mt* Col.
42 E5 El Vigía Venez.
42 D5 Elvira Brazil
102 E3 El Wak Kenya
30 E5 Elwood U.S.A.
59 H5 Ely U.K.
30 B2 Ely *MN* U.S.A.
35 E2 Ely *NV* U.S.A.
32 B4 Elyria U.S.A.
111 G3 Émaé *i.* Vanuatu
79 G2 Emämrüd Iran
81 L5 Emämzadeh Naşroḍ Dîn Iran
55 N4 Emån *r.* Sweden
35 F3 Enoch U.S.A.
54 S2 Enontekiö Fin.
46 B2 Emas, Parque Nacional das *nat. park* Brazil
76 F3 Emba Kazak.
105 H3 Embalenhle S. Africa
21 G3 Embarras Portage Can.
46 C2 Emborcação, Represa de *resr* Brazil
33 F2 Embrun Can.
102 D4 Embu Kenya
62 C4 Emden Ger.
89 B4 Emei China
89 B4 Emei Shan *mt* China
116 A5 Emerald *Qld.* Austr.
114 F6 Emerald *Vic.* Austr.
23 G3 Emeril U.S.A.
21 K5 Emerson Can.
80 B2 Emet Turkey
105 J2 eMgwenya S. Africa
35 E3 Emigrant Valley *v.* U.S.A.
105 J2 eMijindini S. Africa
101 D3 Emi Koussi *mt* Chad
67 M3 Eminska Planina *h.* Bulg.
80 C2 Emir D. *mt* Turkey
80 B2 Emirdağ Turkey
115 G8 Emita Austr.
55 O8 Emmaboda Sweden
55 S7 Emmaste Estonia
115 J2 Emmaville Austr.
61 D2 Emmeloord Neth.
61 E2 Emmen Neth.
62 D7 Emmen Switz.
116 A5 Emmet Austr.
27 C6 Emory Pk *summit* U.S.A.
36 B3 Empalme Mex.
105 J4 Empangeni S. Africa
44 D3 Empedrado Arg.
14 G3 Emperor Seamount Chain *sea feature* Pac. Oc.
66 D3 Empoli Italy
26 D4 Emporia *KS* U.S.A.
32 E6 Emporia *VA* U.S.A.
21 G4 Empress Can.
33 H3 Emsdale Can.
61 F1 Ems-Jade-Kanal *canal* Ger.
61 F2 Emsland *reg.* Ger.
116 D4 Emu Park Austr.
105 J3 Emzinoni S. Africa
54 N5 Enafors Sweden
91 F6 Ena-san *mt.* Japan
90 H1 Enbetsu Japan
36 A2 Encantada, Co de la *mt* Mex.
47 G1 Encantadas, Serra das *h.* Brazil
94 B3 Encanto, Cape *pt* Phil.
44 E3 Encarnación Para.
27 D6 Encinal U.S.A.
34 D5 Encinitas U.S.A.
25 F5 Encino U.S.A.
114 C5 Encounter Bay *b.* Austr.
93 G8 Endeh Indon.
119 D4 Enderby Land *reg.* Ant.
33 E3 Endicott U.S.A.
112 C5 Endicott Arm *in.* U.S.A.
47 B3 Energía Arg.
80 C7 El Saff Egypt [see above]
66 D6 Enfidaville Tunisia
33 G3 Enfield U.S.A.
30 E2 Engadine U.S.A.
54 L5 Engan Norway
94 B2 Engaño, Cape *c.* Phil.
Engaños, Río de los *r. see* Yari
55 T8 Ergli Latvia

90 J1 Engaru Japan
105 G5 Engcobo S. Africa
69 H5 Engel's Rus. Fed.
61 C1 Engelschmangat *chan.* Neth.
114 A2 Engenina *watercourse* Austr.
92 C8 Enggano *i.* Indon.
56 England *div.* U.K.
23 J3 Englee Can.
29 C5 Englehard U.S.A.
31 H2 Englehart Can.
56 E6 English Channel *str.* France/U.K.
69 G7 Enguri *r.* Georgia
105 J4 Enhlalakahle S. Africa
27 D4 Enid U.S.A.
90 H2 Eniwa Japan
61 D2 Enkhuizen Neth.
55 P7 Enköping Sweden
66 F6 Enna *Sicily* Italy
21 J2 Ennadai Lake *l.* Can.
101 E3 En Nahud Sudan
101 E3 Ennedi, Massif *mts* Chad
60 D4 Ennell, Lough *l.* Rep. of Ireland
26 C2 Enning U.S.A.
60 C5 Ennis Rep. of Ireland
24 E2 Ennis *MT* U.S.A.
27 D5 Ennis *TX* U.S.A.
60 E5 Enniscorthy Rep. of Ireland
60 D3 Enniskillen U.K.
60 B5 Ennistymon Rep. of Ireland
62 G7 Enns *r.* Austria
54 W5 Eno Fin.
35 F3 Enoch U.S.A.
54 S2 Enontekiö Fin.
89 D6 Enping China
94 B2 Enrile Phil.
115 G6 Ensay Austr.
61 E2 Enschede Neth.
47 F2 Ensenada Arg.
36 A2 Ensenada Mex.
89 C4 Enshi China
20 F2 Enterprise *N.W.T.* Can.
31 J3 Enterprise *Ont.* Can.
29 C6 Enterprise *AL* U.S.A.
24 C2 Enterprise *OR* U.S.A.
35 F3 Enterprise *UT* U.S.A.
20 F4 Entrance Can.
110 F2 Entrecasteaux Islands, D' is P.N.G.
112 C6 Entrecasteaux, Pt d' *pt* Austr.
111 G3 Entrecasteaux, Récifs D' *rf.* New Caledonia
47 E2 Entre Ríos *div.* Arg.
42 F8 Entre Ríos Bol.
65 B3 Entroncamento Port.
100 C4 Enugu Nigeria
77 V3 Enurmino Rus. Fed.
42 D5 Envira Brazil
42 D5 Envira *r.* Brazil
115 J2 Enys, Mt *mt.* N.Z.
91 G6 Enzan Japan
61 B5 Épernay France
35 G2 Ephraim U.S.A.
33 E4 Ephrata *PA* U.S.A.
24 C2 Ephrata *WA* U.S.A.
111 G3 Épi *i.* Vanuatu
64 H2 Épinal France
80 D4 Episkopi Cyprus
66 E4 Epomeo, Monte *h.* Italy
59 H6 Epping U.K.
59 G6 Epsom U.K.
47 D3 Epu-pel Arg.
96 Equatorial Guinea *country* Africa
45 E3 Equeipa Venez.
116 A6 Erac Cr. *watercourse* Austr.
94 A4 Eran Phil.
94 A4 Eran Bay *b.* Phil.
80 F1 Erbaa Turkey
62 C6 Erbeskopf *h.* Ger.
81 J2 Erçiş Turkey
80 E2 Erciyes Dağı *mt* Turkey
63 J7 Érd Hungary
85 H2 Erdaogou China
80 A1 Erdek Turkey
80 E2 Erdemli Turkey
88 C1 Erdenetsogt Mongolia
101 E3 Erdi *reg.* Chad
69 H6 Erdniyevskiy Rus. Fed.
45 D2 Erebato *r.* Venez.
119 B5 Erebus, Mt *mt.* Ant.
81 K6 Erech Iraq
44 E3 Erechim Brazil
87 L2 Ereentsav Mongolia
80 C1 Ereğli *Zonguldak* Turkey
80 E2 Ereğli *Konya* Turkey
66 F6 Erei, Monti *mts Sicily* Italy
67 K5 Eretria Greece
Erevan *see* Yerevan
62 F5 Erfurt Ger.
81 G2 Erganī Turkey
100 B2 'Erg Chech *sand dunes* Alg./Mali
101 D3 Erg du Djourab *sand dunes* Chad
100 D3 Erg du Ténéré *des.* Niger
88 D1 Ergel Mongolia
80 M4 Ergene *r.* Turkey
100 B2 Erg Iguidi *sand dunes* Alg./Maur.
55 T8 Ergli Latvia

Ergun He *r. see* Argun'
57 D2 Eriboll, Loch *in.* U.K.
57 D4 Ericht, Loch *l. Scot.* U.K.
30 B5 Erie *IL* U.S.A.
27 E4 Erie *KS* U.S.A.
32 C3 Erie *PA* U.S.A.
31 F5 Erie, Lake *l.* Can./U.S.A.
90 J2 Erimo Japan
90 J3 Erimo-misaki *c.* Japan
57 A3 Eriskay *i.* U.K.
96 Eritrea *country* Africa
80 E7 Erkilet Turkey
62 E6 Erlangen Ger.
113 F5 Erldunda Austr.
105 H3 Ermelo S. Africa
80 D3 Ermenek Turkey
67 L6 Ermoupoli Greece
83 E9 Ernakulam India
83 E8 Erode India
104 A1 Erongo *div.* Namibia
61 D3 Erp Neth.
100 B1 Er Rachidia Morocco
101 F3 Er Rahad Sudan
103 D5 Errego Moz.
66 D7 Er Remla Tunisia
60 D7 Errigal *h.* Rep. of Ireland
60 A3 Erris Head *hd* Rep. of Ireland
33 H2 Errol U.S.A.
111 G3 Erromango *i.* Vanuatu
67 J4 Erseke Albania
26 D2 Erskine U.S.A.
54 R5 Ersmark Sweden
69 G5 Ertil' Rus. Fed.
114 C3 Erudina Austr.
81 J3 Eruh Turkey
47 G2 Erval Brazil
32 D5 Erwin U.S.A.
62 F5 Erzgebirge *mts* Czech Rep./Ger.
80 F3 Erzin Turkey
81 G2 Erzincan Turkey
81 H2 Erzurum Turkey
90 H3 Esan-misaki *pt* Japan
90 H3 Esashi Japan
91 H4 Esashi Japan
90 J1 Esashi Japan
90 D7 Esawasaki Japan
55 L9 Esbjerg Denmark
35 G3 Escalante U.S.A.
35 G3 Escalante *r.* U.S.A.
35 G3 Escalante Desert *des.* U.S.A.
30 D3 Escanaba U.S.A.
36 F5 Escárcega Mex.
94 B2 Escarpada Point *pt* Phil.
65 F2 Escatrón Spain
61 B4 Escaut *r.* France/Belgium
61 D5 Esch Neth.
61 D5 Esch-sur-Alzette Lux.
61 E4 Eschweiler Ger.
34 D5 Escondido U.S.A.
45 C3 Escutillas Col.
80 B3 Eşen Turkey
61 F1 Esens Ger.
79 G3 Eşfahan Iran
105 J4 Eshowe S. Africa
80 E6 Esh Sharā *mts* Jordan
103 C6 Esigodini Zimbabwe
105 K4 Esikhawini S. Africa
115 K1 Esk Austr.
115 G8 Esk *r.* Austr.
58 F3 Esk *r.* U.K.
57 E5 Eskdalemuir U.K.
23 G3 Esker Can.
54 F4 Eskifjörður Iceland
55 P7 Eskilstuna Sweden
81 J3 Eski Mosul Iraq
80 D1 Eskipazar Turkey
80 C2 Eskişehir Turkey
65 D1 Esla *r.* Spain
81 L4 Eslamābād e Gharb Iran
80 E2 Esler D. *mt* Turkey
55 N9 Eslöv Sweden
80 B2 Eşme Turkey
42 C3 Esmeraldas Ecuador
30 E1 Esnagi Lake *l.* Can.
64 F4 Espalion France
31 G2 Espanola Can.
25 F4 Espanola U.S.A.
42 Española, Isla *i.* Galápagos Is Ecuador
34 A2 Esparto U.S.A.
112 D6 Esperance Austr.
119 B2 Esperanza *Argentina Base* Ant.
47 E2 Esperanza Arg.
36 C3 Esperanza Mex.
94 C4 Esperanza Phil.
65 B3 Espichel, Cabo *hd* Port.
65 D1 Espigüete *mt* Spain
27 C7 Espinazo Mex.
46 D2 Espinhaço, Serra do *mts* Brazil
46 E1 Espinosa Brazil
46 D2 Espírito Santo *div.* Brazil
94 B2 Espíritu Santo *i.* Vanuatu
111 G3 Espíritu Santo *i.* Vanuatu
55 T6 Espoo Fin.
65 F2 Espuña *mt* Spain
44 B6 Esquel Arg.
20 E5 Esquimalt Can.
94 C5 Essang Indon.
100 B1 Essaouira Morocco
100 A2 Es Semara Western Sahara
62 C5 Essen Ger.
43 G2 Essequibo *r.* Guyana
31 H5 Essex Can.
35 E4 Essex U.S.A.
33 G2 Essex Junction U.S.A.

31 F4 Essexville U.S.A.
77 R4 Esso Rus. Fed.
44 D8 Estados, I. de los i. Arg.
31 G2 Estaire Can.
43 L6 Estância Brazil
65 G1 Estats, Pic d' mt France/Spain
105 H4 Estcourt S. Africa
65 E1 Estella Spain
65 D4 Estepa Spain
65 D4 Estepona Spain
21 J4 Esterhazy Can.
34 B4 Estero Bay b. U.S.A.
44 D2 Esteros Para.
44 E3 Esteros del Iberá marsh Arg.
21 J5 Estevan Can.
26 E3 Estherville U.S.A.
23 H4 Est, Île de l' i. Can.
29 D5 Estill U.S.A.
33 J1 Est, Lac de l' l. Can.
49 Estonia country Europe
65 C2 Estrela, Serra da mts Port.
65 E3 Estrella mt Spain
65 C3 Estremoz Port.
43 J5 Estrondo, Serra h. Brazil
81 M4 Estūh Iran
114 C2 Etadunna Austr.
84 D4 Etah India
61 D5 Étain France
64 F2 Étampes France
61 D5 Étang d'Amel l. France
61 D5 Étang de Lachaussée l. France
61 D5 Étang du Haut-Fourneau l. France
64 E1 Étaples France
84 D4 Etawah India
105 J3 eThandakukhanya S. Africa
104 E4 E'Thembini S. Africa
96 Ethiopia country Africa
80 D2 Etimesğut Turkey
57 C4 Etive, Loch in. U.K.
66 F6 Etna, Monte volc. Sicily Italy
55 J7 Etne Norway
20 C3 Etolin I. i. U.S.A.
116 C3 Eton Austr.
103 B5 Etosha National Park nat. park Namibia
103 B5 Etosha Pan salt pan Namibia
67 L3 Etropole Bulg.
61 E5 Ettelbruck Lux.
61 C3 Etten-Leur Neth.
57 E5 Ettrick Forest reg. U.K.
115 G4 Euabalong Austr.
Euboea i. see Evvoia
112 E6 Eucla Austr.
32 C4 Euclid U.S.A.
43 L6 Euclides da Cunha Brazil
115 H6 Eucumbene, L. l. Austr.
114 C5 Eudunda Austr.
29 C6 Eufaula U.S.A.
27 E5 Eufaula Lake resr U.S.A.
24 B2 Eugene U.S.A.
36 A3 Eugenia, Pta c. Mex.
115 H4 Eugowra Austr.
115 F2 Eulo Austr.
115 H3 Eumungerie Austr.
116 C3 Eungella Austr.
116 C3 Eungella Nat. Park nat. park Austr.
27 E6 Eunice U.S.A.
81 K6 Euphrates r. Asia
55 S6 Eura Fin.
64 E2 Eure r. France
24 A3 Eureka CA U.S.A.
24 D1 Eureka MT U.S.A.
35 E2 Eureka NV U.S.A.
114 D3 Eurinilla watercourse Austr.
114 D3 Euriowie Austr.
115 F6 Euroa Austr.
116 C5 Eurombah Austr.
116 C6 Eurombah Cr. r. Austr.
103 D6 Europa, Île i. Indian Ocean
65 D4 Europa Point pt Gibraltar
61 C3 Europoort reg. Neth.
61 E4 Euskirchen Ger.
114 E5 Euston Austr.
20 D4 Eustuk Lake l. Can.
29 C5 Eutaw U.S.A.
105 H3 Evander S. Africa
20 F4 Evansburg Can.
115 K2 Evans Head Austr.
22 E3 Evans, L. l. Can.
25 F4 Evans, Mt mt. CO U.S.A.
24 D2 Evans, Mt mt. MT U.S.A.
30 D4 Evanston IL U.S.A.
24 E3 Evanston WY U.S.A.
31 F3 Evansville Can.
28 C4 Evansville IN U.S.A.
30 C4 Evansville WV U.S.A.
24 F3 Evansville WY U.S.A.
30 E4 Evart U.S.A.
105 G3 Evaton S. Africa
30 A2 Eveleth U.S.A.
77 R3 Evensk Rus. Fed.
114 A3 Everard, L. salt flat Austr.
112 F5 Everard Range h. Austr.
61 D3 Everdingen Neth.
85 F4 Everest, Mt mt China
33 K1 Everett Can.
24 B1 Everett U.S.A.
61 B3 Evergem Belgium
29 D7 Everglades Nat. Park nat. park U.S.A.
29 D7 Everglades, The swamp U.S.A.
27 G6 Evergreen U.S.A.
59 F5 Evesham U.K.
59 F5 Evesham, Vale of reg. U.K.
54 S5 Evijärvi Fin.
100 D4 Evinayong Equatorial Guinea
55 K7 Evje Norway
65 C3 Évora Port.
87 P1 Evoron, Ozero l. Rus. Fed.
81 K2 Evowghlī Iran
64 E2 Évreux France
67 K6 Evrotas r. Greece
80 D4 Evrychou Cyprus
67 L5 Evvoia i. Greece
34 □1 Ewa Beach U.S.A.
102 E3 Ewaso Ngiro r. Kenya
57 C3 Ewe, Loch in. U.K.
42 E6 Exaltación Bol.
105 G4 Excelsior S. Africa
34 C2 Excelsior Mtn mt. U.S.A.
34 C2 Excelsior Mts mts U.S.A.
26 E4 Excelsior Springs U.S.A.
59 D6 Exe r. U.K.
119 A4 Executive Committee Range mts Ant.
115 J5 Exeter Austr.
31 G4 Exeter Can.
59 D7 Exeter U.K.
34 C3 Exeter CA U.S.A.
33 H3 Exeter NH U.S.A.
61 E2 Exloo Neth.
59 D7 Exminster U.K.
59 D6 Exmoor Forest reg. U.K.
59 D6 Exmoor National Park U.K.
33 F6 Exmore U.S.A.
112 B4 Exmouth Austr.
59 D7 Exmouth U.K.
112 B4 Exmouth Gulf b. Austr.
115 H3 Exmouth, Mt mt Austr.
13 M5 Exmouth Plateau sea feature Indian Ocean
116 C5 Expedition Range mts Austr.
65 D3 Extremadura div. Spain
29 E7 Exuma Sound chan. Bahamas
102 D4 Eyasi, Lake salt l. Tanz.
59 J5 Eye U.K.
57 F5 Eyemouth U.K.
57 B2 Eye Peninsula pen. U.K.
54 D5 Eyjafjallajökull ice cap Iceland
54 D3 Eyjafjörður in. Iceland
102 E3 Eyl Somalia
59 F6 Eynsham U.K.
114 B2 Eyre, Lake (North) salt flat Austr.
114 B2 Eyre, Lake (South) salt flat Austr.
117 B6 Eyre Mountains mts N.Z.
114 A4 Eyre Peninsula pen. Austr.
54 □ Eysturoy i. Faroe Is
105 J4 Ezakheni S. Africa
105 H3 Ezenzeleni S. Africa
47 C3 Ezequiel Ramos Mexía, Embalse resr Arg.
68 J2 Ezhva Rus. Fed.
67 M5 Ezine Turkey
80 F1 Ezinepazar Turkey
81 L6 Ezra's Tomb Iraq


# F


83 D9 Faadhippolhu Atoll atoll Maldives
27 B6 Fabens U.S.A.
20 F2 Faber Lake l. Can.
95 □ Faber, Mt h. Sing.
55 M9 Fåborg Denmark
66 E3 Fabriano Italy
45 B3 Facatativá Col.
100 D3 Fachi Niger
116 D4 Facing I. i. Austr.
33 F4 Factoryville U.S.A.
44 B7 Facundo Arg.
100 C3 Fada-Ngourma Burkina
66 D2 Faenza Italy
Faeroes terr. see Faroe Islands
93 J7 Fafanlap Indon.
102 E3 Fafen Shet' watercourse Eth.
67 L2 Făgăraş Romania
55 L6 Fagernes Norway
55 O7 Fagersta Sweden
44 C8 Fagnano, L. l. Arg./Chile
61 C4 Fagne reg. Belgium
100 B3 Faguibine, Lac l. Mali
54 F5 Fagurhólsmýri Iceland
101 F4 Fagwir Sudan
16 Fairbanks U.S.A.
32 B5 Fairborn U.S.A.
26 D3 Fairbury U.S.A.
32 E5 Fairfax U.S.A.
34 A2 Fairfield CA U.S.A.
30 B5 Fairfield IA U.S.A.
28 C4 Fairfield OH U.S.A.
27 D6 Fairfield TX U.S.A.
33 G3 Fair Haven U.S.A.
60 E2 Fair Head hd U.K.
94 A4 Fairie Queen sand bank Phil.
57 G1 Fair Isle i. U.K.
26 E3 Fairmont MN U.S.A.
32 C5 Fairmont WV U.S.A.
25 F4 Fairplay U.S.A.
30 D3 Fairport U.S.A.
32 C4 Fairport Harbor U.S.A.
20 F3 Fairview Can.
31 E3 Fairview MI U.S.A.
27 D4 Fairview OK U.S.A.
35 G2 Fairview UT U.S.A.
89 □ Fairview Park Hong Kong China
20 B3 Fairweather, Cape c. U.S.A.
20 B3 Fairweather, Mt mt. Can./U.S.A.
84 C3 Faisalabad Pak.
61 C5 Faissault France
26 C2 Faith U.S.A.
57 □ Faither, The pt U.K.
85 E4 Faizabad India
111 J2 Fakaofo i. Tokelau
109 Fakarava atoll Tuamotu Islands Pac. Oc.
59 H5 Fakenham U.K.
54 O5 Fåker Sweden
93 J7 Fakfak Indon.
88 G1 Faku China
59 C7 Fal r. U.K.
100 A4 Falaba Sierra Leone
64 D2 Falaise France
85 G4 Falakata India
85 H5 Falam Myanmar
27 D7 Falcon Lake l. Mex./U.S.A.
27 D7 Falfurrias U.S.A.
20 F3 Falher Can.
55 N8 Falkenberg Sweden
57 E5 Falkirk U.K.
57 E4 Falkland U.K.
44 E8 Falkland Islands terr. Atlantic Ocean
44 D8 Falkland Sound chan. Falkland Is
55 N7 Falköping Sweden
34 D5 Fallbrook U.S.A.
34 C2 Fallon U.S.A.
33 H4 Fall River U.S.A.
24 F3 Fall River Pass U.S.A.
26 E3 Falls City U.S.A.
59 B7 Falmouth U.K.
32 A5 Falmouth KY U.S.A.
33 H3 Falmouth ME U.S.A.
30 E3 Falmouth MI U.S.A.
104 C7 False Bay b. S. Africa
55 M9 Falster i. Denmark
63 N7 Fălticeni Romania
55 O6 Falun Sweden
80 D4 Famagusta Cyprus
61 D4 Famenne v. Belgium
21 K4 Family L. l. Can.
88 F4 Fanchang China
60 E4 Fane r. Rep. of Ireland
95 A1 Fang Thai.
88 D3 Fangchĕng China
89 C4 Fangdou Shan mts China
89 F6 Fang-liao Taiwan
88 E2 Fangshan Beijing China
88 D2 Fangshan Shanxi China
89 F6 Fangshan Taiwan
88 D3 Fang Xian China
87 N2 Fangzheng China
89 □ Fanling Hong Kong China
57 C3 Fannich, Loch l. U.K.
66 E3 Fano Italy
89 F5 Fanshan China
82 D2 Fanshi China
89 B6 Fan Si Pan mt Vietnam
119 B2 Faraday Ukraine Base Ant.
102 C3 Faradje Zaire
103 E6 Farafangana Madag.
78 B4 Farafra Oasis oasis Egypt
79 J3 Farāh Afgh.
93 L2 Farallon de Pajaros i. N. Mariana Is
45 A4 Farallones de Cali, Parque Nacional nat. park Col.
100 A3 Faranah Guinea
59 F7 Fareham U.K.
117 D4 Farewell, Cape c. N.Z.
117 D4 Farewell Spit spit N.Z.
55 N7 Färgelanda Sweden
26 D2 Fargo U.S.A.
26 E2 Faribault U.S.A.
23 F2 Faribault, Lac l. Can.
84 D3 Faridabad India
84 C3 Faridkot India
85 G5 Faridpur Bangl.
100 A3 Farim Guinea-Bissau
55 P8 Färjestaden Sweden
81 M4 Farmahin Iran
30 C5 Farmer City U.S.A.
22 D2 Farmer Island i. Can.
33 F2 Farmington Can.
30 B5 Farmington IA U.S.A.
30 B5 Farmington IL U.S.A.
33 H2 Farmington ME U.S.A.
33 H3 Farmington NH U.S.A.
35 H3 Farmington NM U.S.A.
24 E3 Farmington UT U.S.A.
20 D4 Far Mt. mt. Can.
32 D6 Farmville U.S.A.
59 G6 Farnborough U.K.
57 F2 Farne Islands is U.K.
59 G6 Farnham U.K.
20 F4 Farnham, Mt mt. Can.
43 G4 Faro Brazil
20 C2 Faro Can.
65 C4 Faro Port.
55 Q8 Fårö i. Sweden
76 A3 Faroe Islands terr. Atlantic Ocean
55 Q8 Fårösund Sweden
32 C4 Farrell U.S.A.
31 K3 Farrellton Can.
Farrukhabad see Fatehgarh
67 K5 Farsala Greece
24 E3 Farson U.S.A.
55 K7 Farsund Norway
27 C5 Farwell U.S.A.
66 G4 Fasano Italy
32 E4 Fassett U.S.A.
69 D5 Fastiv Ukr.
84 D4 Fatehgarh India
84 C4 Fatehpur Rajasthan India
84 E4 Fatehpur Uttar Pradesh India
31 G3 Fathom Five National Marine Park nat. park Can.
100 A3 Fatick Senegal
64 H2 Faulquemont France
105 F4 Fauresmith S. Africa
54 O3 Fauske Norway
35 F1 Faust U.S.A.
66 E6 Favignana, Isola i. Sicily Italy
20 G4 Fawcett Can.
59 F7 Fawley U.K.
22 C3 Fawn r. Can.
54 B4 Faxaflói b. Iceland
54 P5 Faxälven r. Sweden
89 B5 Faxian Hu l. China
101 D3 Faya Chad
30 D3 Fayette U.S.A.
27 E4 Fayetteville AR U.S.A.
29 E5 Fayetteville NC U.S.A.
29 C5 Fayetteville TN U.S.A.
80 D6 Fâyid Egypt
81 M7 Faylakah i. Kuwait
100 C4 Fazao Malfakassa, Parc National de nat. park Togo
84 C3 Fazilka India
100 A2 Fdérik Maur.
60 B5 Feale r. Rep. of Ireland
29 E5 Fear, Cape c. U.S.A.
34 B2 Feather Falls U.S.A.
117 E4 Featherston N.Z.
115 G6 Feathertop, Mt mt Austr.
64 E2 Fécamp France
47 F1 Federación Arg.
44 E4 Federal Arg.
62 E3 Fehmarn i. Ger.
46 E3 Feia, Lagoa lag. Brazil
88 E4 Feidong China
88 F3 Feihuanghe Kou est. China
42 D5 Feijó Brazil
117 E4 Feilding N.Z.
43 L6 Feira de Santana Brazil
88 E4 Feixi China
80 E3 Feke Turkey
65 H3 Felanitx Spain
30 D3 Felch U.S.A.
62 D7 Feldberg mt Ger.
62 D7 Feldkirch Austria
62 G7 Feldkirchen in Kärnten Austria
47 E1 Feliciano r. Arg.
83 D10 Felidu Atoll atoll Maldives
46 D2 Felixlândia Brazil
59 J6 Felixstowe U.K.
66 D1 Feltre Italy
55 M5 Femunden l. Norway
55 N5 Femundsmarka Nasjonalpark nat. park Norway
88 D2 Fen r. China
66 D3 Fenaio, Punta del pt Italy
35 H4 Fence Lake U.S.A.
31 H3 Fenelon Falls Can.
67 L4 Fengari mt Greece
89 E4 Fengcheng China
89 C4 Fengdu China
89 C5 Fenggang China
89 F4 Fenghua China
89 C5 Fenghuang China
88 C4 Fengjie China
89 D6 Fengkai China
89 F6 Fenglin Taiwan
88 F2 Fengnan China
88 E1 Fengning China
88 E3 Fengqiu China
89 C5 Fengshan China
89 E6 Fengshun China
88 E3 Fengtai China
89 E4 Fengxin China
88 E3 Fengyang China
88 D1 Fengzhen China
85 G5 Feni Bangl.
111 F2 Feni Is is P.N.G.
64 F5 Fenille, Col de la pass France
30 B4 Fennimore U.S.A.
103 E5 Fenoarivo Atsinanana Madag.
59 G5 Fens, The reg. U.K.
31 F4 Fenton U.S.A.
109 Fenua Ura is Fr. Polynesia Pac. Oc.
88 D2 Fenxi China
88 D2 Fenyang China
89 E5 Fenyi China
69 E6 Feodosiya Ukr.
66 B6 Fer, Cap de hd Alg.
79 L1 Fergana Uzbek.
31 G4 Fergus Can.
26 D2 Fergus Falls U.S.A.
110 F2 Fergusson I. i. P.N.G.
66 C7 Fériana Tunisia
100 B4 Ferkessédougou Côte d'Ivoire
66 E3 Fermo Italy
23 G3 Fermont Can.
65 C2 Fermoselle Spain
60 C5 Fermoy Rep. of Ireland
29 D6 Fernandina Beach U.S.A.
42 □ Fernandina, Isla i. Galapagos Is Ecuador
44 B8 Fernando de Magallanes, Parque Nacional nat. park Chile
12 G6 Fernando de Noronha i. Atlantic Ocean
46 B3 Fernandópolis Brazil
24 B1 Ferndale U.S.A.
59 F7 Ferndown U.K.
20 F5 Fernie Can.
115 G2 Fernlee Austr.
34 C2 Fernley U.S.A.
33 F4 Fernridge U.S.A.
60 E5 Ferns Rep. of Ireland
24 C2 Fernwood U.S.A.
66 D2 Ferrara Italy
46 B3 Ferreiros Brazil
27 F6 Ferriday U.S.A.
66 C4 Ferro, Capo pt Sardinia Italy
65 B1 Ferrol Spain
35 G2 Ferron U.S.A.
100 B1 Fès Morocco
102 B4 Feshi Zaire
21 K5 Fessenden U.S.A.
26 F4 Festus U.S.A.
57 □ Fethaland, Point of pt U.K.
60 D5 Fethard Rep. of Ireland
80 B3 Fethiye Turkey
57 □ Fetlar i. U.K.
57 F4 Fettercairn U.K.
23 F2 Feuilles, Rivière aux r. Can.
80 F3 Fevzipaşa Turkey
79 L2 Feyzābād Afgh.
Fez see Fès
59 D5 Ffestiniog U.K.
103 E6 Fianarantsoa Madag.
102 D3 Fichē Eth.
105 G4 Ficksburg S. Africa
20 F4 Field B.C. Can.
31 G2 Field Ont. Can.
67 H4 Fier Albania
30 E3 Fife Lake U.S.A.
57 F4 Fife Ness pt U.K.
115 G4 Fifield Austr.
30 B3 Fifield U.S.A.
64 F4 Figeac France
65 B2 Figueira da Foz Port.
65 H1 Figueres Spain
100 B1 Figuig Morocco
106 Fiji country Pac. Oc.
44 D2 Filadélfia Para.
119 B3 Filchner Ice Shelf ice feature Ant.
58 G3 Filey U.K.
67 J5 Filippiada Greece
55 O7 Filipstad Sweden
54 L5 Fillan Norway
34 C4 Fillmore CA U.S.A.
35 F2 Fillmore UT U.S.A.
119 C3 Fimbulheimen mts Ant.
33 F2 Finch Can.
116 C3 Finch Hatton Austr.
57 E3 Findhorn r. U.K.
81 H3 Fındık Turkey
32 B4 Findlay U.S.A.
115 H8 Fingal Austr.
22 E5 Finger Lakes lakes U.S.A.
103 D5 Fingoè Moz.
80 C3 Finike Turkey
80 C3 Finike Körfezi b. Turkey
Finisterre, Cape c. see Fisterra, Cabo
112 F4 Finke Gorge National Park nat. park Austr.
49 Finland country Europe
52 Finland, Gulf of g. Europe
20 D3 Finlay r. Can.
20 D3 Finlay, Mt mt. Can.
115 F5 Finley Austr.
114 A4 Finniss, C. pt Austr.
54 P2 Finnsnes Norway
55 O7 Finspång Sweden
60 D3 Fintona U.K.
60 C3 Fintown Rep. of Ireland
57 C3 Fionn Loch l. U.K.
57 B4 Fionnphort U.K.
117 A6 Fiordland National Park nat. park N.Z.
Fırat r. see Euphrates
34 B3 Firebaugh U.S.A.
21 J2 Firedrake Lake l. Can.
33 G4 Fire Island National Seashore res. U.S.A.
Firenze see Florence
81 K6 Firk, Sha'īb watercourse Iraq
47 E2 Firmat Arg.
64 G4 Firminy France
63 Q2 Firovo Rus. Fed.
84 B3 Firoza Pak.
84 D4 Firozabad India
84 C3 Firozpur India
33 H2 First Connecticut L. l. U.S.A.
79 G4 Fīrūzābād Iran
103 B6 Fish r. Namibia
104 D5 Fish r. S. Africa
14 E10 Fisher Bay b. Ant.
33 F6 Fisherman I. i. U.S.A.
33 H4 Fishers I. i. U.S.A.
21 N2 Fisher Strait chan. Can.
59 C6 Fishguard U.K.
20 E2 Fish Lake l. Can.
30 A2 Fish Lake l. MN U.S.A.
35 G2 Fish Lake l. UT U.S.A.
89 □ Fish Ponds lakes Hong Kong China
31 F4 Fish Pt pt U.S.A.
119 B3 Fiske, C. c. Ant.
61 B5 Fismes France
65 B1 Fisterra Spain
65 B1 Fisterra, Cabo c. Spain
33 H3 Fitchburg U.S.A.
21 G3 Fitzgerald Can.
29 D6 Fitzgerald U.S.A.
114 B4 Fitzgerald Bay b. Austr.
112 C6 Fitzgerald River National Park nat. park Austr.
44 C7 Fitz Roy Arg.
116 D4 Fitzroy r. Austr.
112 E3 Fitzroy Crossing Austr.
31 G3 Fitzwilliam I. i. Can.
60 D3 Fivemiletown U.K.
66 D2 Fivizzano Italy
102 C4 Fizi Zaire
55 L6 Flå Norway
105 H5 Flagstaff S. Africa
35 G4 Flagstaff U.S.A.
33 H2 Flagstaff Lake l. U.S.A.
22 E2 Flaherty Island i. Can.
30 B3 Flambeau r. U.S.A.
58 G3 Flamborough Head hd U.K.
24 E3 Flaming Gorge Res. l. U.S.A.
104 D5 Flaminksvlei salt pan S. Africa
61 A4 Flandre reg. France
57 A2 Flannan Isles is Scot. U.K.
54 O4 Flåsjön l. Sweden
30 E4 Flat r. U.S.A.
24 D2 Flathead L. l. U.S.A.
116 C4 Flat Is is Austr.
117 E4 Flat Point pt N.Z.
113 J2 Flattery, C. pt Austr.
24 A1 Flattery, C. c. U.S.A.
116 A4 Fleetwood Austr.
58 D4 Fleetwood U.K.
33 F4 Fleetwood U.S.A.
55 K7 Flekkefjord Norway
32 B3 Fleming U.S.A.
32 B5 Flemingsburg U.S.A.
55 P7 Flen Sweden
62 D3 Flensburg Ger.
64 D2 Flers France
31 G3 Flesherton Can.
21 H2 Fletcher Lake l. Can.
31 F3 Fletcher Pond l. U.S.A.
119 B3 Fletcher Prom. hd Ant.
113 H3 Flinders r. Austr.
112 C6 Flinders Bay b. Austr.
114 B5 Flinders Chase Nat. Park nat. park Austr.
115 H7 Flinders I. i. Austr.
114 A4 Flinders Island i. Austr.
116 C2 Flinders Passage chan. Austr.
114 C3 Flinders Ranges mts Austr.
114 C3 Flinders Ranges Nat. Park nat. park Austr.
116 C1 Flinders Reefs rf Coral Sea Is Terr.
21 J4 Flin Flon Can.
59 D4 Flint U.K.
29 C6 Flint r. GA U.S.A.
31 F4 Flint r. MI U.S.A.
31 F4 Flint U.S.A.
109 Flint Island i. Line Islands Pac. Oc.
115 H1 Flinton Austr.
55 N6 Flisa Norway
58 E2 Flodden U.K.
119 A4 Flood Ra. mts Ant.
30 A2 Floodwood U.S.A.
28 B4 Flora U.S.A.
64 F4 Florac France
116 B1 Flora Reef rf Coral Sea Is Terr.
31 F4 Florence Can.
66 D3 Florence Italy
29 C5 Florence AL U.S.A.
35 G5 Florence AZ U.S.A.
26 D4 Florence KS U.S.A.
32 C5 Florence OH U.S.A.
24 A3 Florence OR U.S.A.
29 E5 Florence SC U.S.A.
35 G5 Florence Junction U.S.A.
33 K1 Florenceville Can.
45 B4 Florencia Col.
44 C6 Florentino Ameghino, Embalse resr Arg.
47 E2 Flores r. Arg.
36 G5 Flores Guatemala
93 G8 Flores i. Indon.
46 C1 Flores de Goiás Brazil
93 F8 Flores Sea sea Indon.
43 L5 Floresta Brazil
43 K5 Floriano Brazil
44 G3 Florianópolis Brazil
47 F2 Florida Uru.
29 D6 Florida div. U.S.A.
29 D7 Florida Bay b. U.S.A.
29 D7 Florida City U.S.A.
111 G2 Florida Is is Solomon Is
37 H4 Florida, Straits of str. Bahamas/U.S.A.
67 J4 Florina Greece
55 J6 Florø Norway
23 H3 Flour Lake l. Can.
30 A4 Floyd IA U.S.A.
32 C6 Floyd VA U.S.A.
27 C5 Floydada U.S.A.
35 F4 Floyd, Mt mt. U.S.A.
61 D2 Fluessen l. Neth.
110 E2 Fly r. P.N.G.
32 C5 Fly U.S.A.
67 H3 Foča Bos.-Herz.
57 E3 Fochabers U.K.
105 G3 Fochville S. Africa
67 M2 Focşani Romania
89 D6 Fogang China
66 F4 Foggia Italy

100 □ Fogo i. Cape Verde
23 K4 Fogo I. i. Can.
57 D2 Foinaven h. U.K.
64 E5 Foix France
54 O3 Folda chan. Norway
54 N4 Foldereid Norway
54 M4 Foldfjorden chan. Norway
67 L6 Folegandros i. Greece
31 F1 Foleyet Can.
66 E3 Foligno Italy
59 J6 Folkestone U.K.
59 G5 Folkingham U.K.
29 D6 Folkston U.S.A.
55 M5 Folldal Norway
66 D3 Follonica Italy
34 B2 Folsom Lake l. U.S.A.
69 G6 Fomin Rus. Fed.
68 J2 Fominskiy Rus. Fed.
21 H3 Fond-du-Lac r. Can.
21 J3 Fond du Lac r. Can.
30 C4 Fond du Lac U.S.A.
65 B2 Fondevila Spain
66 E4 Fondi Italy
111 H2 Fongafale Tuvalu
66 C4 Fonni Sardinia Italy
36 G6 Fonseca, G. de b. Central America
23 F3 Fontanges Can.
20 E3 Fontas Can.
20 E3 Fontas r. Can.
42 E4 Fonte Boa Brazil
64 D3 Fontenay-le-Comte France
54 F3 Fontur pt Iceland
31 H3 Foot's Bay Can.
88 C3 Foping China
115 H4 Forbes Austr.
24 C1 Forbes, Mt mt. Can.
62 E6 Forchheim Ger.
23 G2 Ford r. Can.
30 D2 Ford r. U.S.A.
55 J6 Førde Norway
21 K2 Forde Lake l. Can.
59 H5 Fordham U.K.
59 F7 Fordingbridge U.K.
119 A4 Ford Ra. mts Ant.
115 F2 Fords Bridge Austr.
27 E5 Fordyce U.S.A.
100 A4 Forécariah Guinea
59 F7 Foreland hd U.K.
59 D6 Foreland Point pt U.K.
20 D4 Foresight Mtn mt. Can.
31 G4 Forest Can.
27 F5 Forest MS U.S.A.
32 B4 Forest OH U.S.A.
33 G3 Forest Dale U.S.A.
115 G5 Forest Hill N.S.W. Austr.
116 A5 Forest Hill Qld. Austr.
34 B2 Foresthill U.S.A.
115 H9 Forestier, C. hd Austr.
115 H9 Forestier Pen. pen. Austr.
30 A3 Forest Lake U.S.A.
29 C5 Forest Park U.S.A.
23 G4 Forestville Can.
61 D5 Forêt de Chiny forest Belgium
61 C4 Forêt de Soignes forest Belgium
61 D5 Forêt de Wœvre forest France
57 F4 Forfar U.K.
24 A2 Forks U.S.A.
33 J2 Forks, The U.S.A.
32 E4 Forksville U.S.A.
66 E2 Forlì Italy
58 D4 Formby U.K.
65 G3 Formentera i. Spain
65 H3 Formentor, Cap de pt Spain
46 D3 Formiga Brazil
44 E3 Formosa Arg.
   Formosa country see Taiwan
46 C1 Formosa Brazil
43 G6 Formosa, Serra h. Brazil
46 D1 Formoso r. Brazil
57 E3 Forres U.K.
114 E7 Forrest Vic. Austr.
112 E6 Forrest W.A. Austr.
30 C5 Forrest U.S.A.
27 F5 Forrest City U.S.A.
30 C4 Forreston U.S.A.
54 P5 Fors Sweden
113 H3 Forsayth Austr.
54 S3 Forsnäs Sweden
55 S6 Forssa Fin.
115 K4 Forster Austr.
27 E4 Forsyth MO U.S.A.
24 F2 Forsyth MT U.S.A.
31 J1 Forsythe Can.
84 C3 Fort Abbas Pak.
22 D3 Fort Albany Can.
43 L4 Fortaleza Brazil
35 H5 Fort Apache U.S.A.
20 G4 Fort Assiniboine Can.
30 C4 Fort Atkinson U.S.A.
57 D3 Fort Augustus U.K.
105 G6 Fort Beaufort S. Africa
24 E2 Fort Benton U.S.A.
21 H3 Fort Black Can.
34 A2 Fort Bragg U.S.A.
   Fort-Chimo see Kuujjuaq
21 G3 Fort Chipewyan Can.
27 D5 Fort Cobb Res. resr U.S.A.
24 F3 Fort Collins U.S.A.
31 J3 Fort-Coulonge Can.
33 F2 Fort Covington U.S.A.
27 C6 Fort Davis U.S.A.
37 M6 Fort-de-France Martinique
29 C5 Fort Deposit U.S.A.
26 E3 Fort Dodge U.S.A.

112 C4 Fortescue r. Austr.
26 E1 Fort Frances U.S.A.
22 E3 Fort George Can.
57 D4 Forth r. U.K.
   Fort Hertz see Putao
57 F4 Forth, Firth of est. U.K.
35 E2 Fortification Range mts U.S.A.
44 D2 Fortín Capitán Demattei Para.
44 D2 Fortín General Mendoza Para.
44 E3 Fortín Madrejón Para.
44 D2 Fortín Pilcomayo Arg.
42 F7 Fortín Ravelo Bol.
42 F7 Fortín Suárez Arana Bol.
33 J1 Fort Kent U.S.A.
29 D7 Fort Lauderdale U.S.A.
20 E2 Fort Liard Can.
30 B3 Fort McCoy U.S.A.
21 G3 Fort Mackay Can.
20 G5 Fort Macleod Can.
21 G3 Fort McMurray Can.
30 B5 Fort Madison U.S.A.
24 G3 Fort Morgan U.S.A.
29 D7 Fort Myers U.S.A.
20 E3 Fort Nelson r. Can.
20 E3 Fort Nelson Can.
20 D2 Fort Norman Can.
29 C5 Fort Payne U.S.A.
24 F1 Fort Peck U.S.A.
24 F2 Fort Peck Res. resr U.S.A.
29 D7 Fort Pierce U.S.A.
26 C2 Fort Pierre U.S.A.
20 F2 Fort Providence Can.
21 J4 Fort Qu'Appelle Can.
20 G2 Fort Resolution Can.
117 B7 Fortrose N.Z.
57 D3 Fortrose U.K.
34 A2 Fort Ross U.S.A.
22 E3 Fort Rupert Can.
20 E3 Fort St James Can.
20 E3 Fort St John Can.
   Fort Sandeman see Zhob
20 G4 Fort Saskatchewan Can.
27 E5 Fort Scott U.S.A.
22 C2 Fort Severn Can.
20 E2 Fort Simpson Can.
21 G2 Fort Smith Can.
27 E5 Fort Smith U.S.A.
27 C6 Fort Stockton U.S.A.
25 F5 Fort Sumner U.S.A.
24 A3 Fortuna U.S.A.
26 C1 Fortuna U.S.A.
23 J4 Fortune B. b. Can.
20 F3 Fort Vermilion Can.
29 C6 Fort Walton Beach U.S.A.
30 E5 Fort Wayne U.S.A.
57 C4 Fort William U.K.
27 D5 Fort Worth U.S.A.
54 N4 Forvik Norway
89 D6 Foshan China
66 B2 Fossano Italy
115 G7 Foster Austr.
20 B3 Foster, Mt mt. Can./U.S.A.
32 B4 Fostoria U.S.A.
59 G4 Fotherby U.K.
64 D2 Fougères France
57 □ Foula i.
59 H6 Foulness Point pt U.K.
117 C4 Foulwind, Cape c. N.Z.
100 D4 Foumban Cameroon
100 A3 Foundiougne Senegal
30 A4 Fountain U.S.A.
64 G2 Fourches, Mont des h. France
34 D4 Four Corners U.S.A.
105 H4 Fouriesburg S. Africa
67 M6 Fournoi i. Greece
30 C2 Fourteen Mile Pt pt U.S.A.
100 A3 Fouta Djallon reg. Guinea
117 A7 Foveaux Strait str. N.Z.
29 E7 Fowl Cay i. Bahamas
25 F4 Fowler CO U.S.A.
30 D5 Fowler IN U.S.A.
30 E4 Fowler MI U.S.A.
119 B3 Fowler Pen. pen. Ant.
112 F6 Fowlers Bay Austr.
81 M3 Fowman Iran
21 L3 Fox r. Can.
30 C4 Fox r. U.S.A.
116 B4 Fox Cr. r. Austr.
20 F4 Fox Creek Can.
58 C2 Foxdale U.K.
18  Foxe Basin basin Can.
117 C5 Fox Glacier N.Z.
20 G3 Fox Lake Can.
30 C4 Fox Lake U.S.A.
117 E4 Foxton N.Z.
57 D3 Foyers U.K.
60 D3 Foyle r. Rep. of Ireland/U.K.
60 D2 Foyle, Lough b. Rep. of Ireland/U.K.
60 B5 Foynes Rep. of Ireland
103 B5 Foz do Cunene Angola
46 A4 Foz do Iguaçu Brazil
65 G2 Fraga Spain
46 C3 Franca Brazil
111 G3 Français, Récif des rf New Caledonia
48  France country Europe
114 D6 Frances Austr.
20 D2 Frances r. Can.
20 D2 Frances Lake Can.
20 D2 Frances Lake l. Can.
30 D5 Francesville U.S.A.
102 B4 Franceville Gabon
26 D3 Francis Case, Lake l. U.S.A.
46 D2 Francisco Sá Brazil
33 H2 Francis, Lake l. U.S.A.

103 C6 Francistown Botswana
20 D4 François Lake l. Can.
24 E3 Francs Peak summit U.S.A.
31 F4 Frankenmuth U.S.A.
105 H3 Frankfort S. Africa
30 D5 Frankfort IN U.S.A.
28 C4 Frankfort KY U.S.A.
30 D3 Frankfort MI U.S.A.
62 D5 Frankfurt am Main Ger.
62 G4 Frankfurt an der Oder Ger.
35 E1 Franklin Lake l. U.S.A.
62 E6 Fränkische Alb reg. Ger.
62 E6 Fränkische Schweiz reg. Ger.
24 D3 Franklin ID U.S.A.
28 C4 Franklin IN U.S.A.
27 F6 Franklin LA U.S.A.
33 H3 Franklin MA U.S.A.
29 D5 Franklin NC U.S.A.
33 H3 Franklin NH U.S.A.
33 F4 Franklin NJ U.S.A.
32 D4 Franklin PA U.S.A.
29 C5 Franklin TN U.S.A.
32 E6 Franklin VA U.S.A.
32 D5 Franklin WV U.S.A.
24 C1 Franklin D. Roosevelt Lake l. U.S.A.
114 B4 Franklin Harbour b. Austr.
20 E2 Franklin Mountains mts U.S.A.
117 A6 Franklin Mts mts N.Z.
115 G8 Franklin Sd chan. Austr.
114 F7 Frankston Austr.
55 P5 Fränsta Sweden
30 E1 Franz Can.
117 C5 Franz Josef Glacier N.Z.
76 G2 Franz Josef Land is Rus. Fed.
66 C5 Frasca, Capo della pt Sardinia Italy
66 E4 Frascati Italy
20 E4 Fraser r. B.C. Can.
23 H2 Fraser r. Nfld Can.
104 D5 Fraserburg S. Africa
57 F3 Fraserburgh U.K.
22 D4 Fraserdale Can.
116 E5 Fraser Island i. Austr.
116 E5 Fraser Island National Park Qld. Austr.
20 E4 Fraser Lake Can.
20 E4 Fraser Plateau plat. Can.
117 F3 Frasertown N.Z.
30 E2 Frater Can.
62 D7 Frauenfeld Switz.
47 E2 Fray Bentos Uru.
58 E4 Freckleton U.K.
30 E3 Frederic MI U.S.A.
30 A3 Frederic WV U.S.A.
55 L9 Fredericia Denmark
32 E5 Frederick MD U.S.A.
27 D5 Frederick OK U.S.A.
27 D6 Fredericksburg TX U.S.A.
32 E5 Fredericksburg VA U.S.A.
20 C3 Frederick Sound chan. U.S.A.
27 F4 Fredericktown U.S.A.
23 G4 Fredericton Can.
16  Frederikshåb Greenland
55 M8 Frederikshavn Denmark
55 N9 Frederiksværk Denmark
35 F3 Fredonia AZ U.S.A.
32 D3 Fredonia NY U.S.A.
54 Q4 Fredrika Sweden
55 M7 Fredrikstad Norway
33 F4 Freehold U.S.A.
33 F4 Freeland U.S.A.
114 C3 Freeling Heights mt Austr.
34 C2 Freel Peak summit U.S.A.
26 D3 Freeman U.S.A.
30 D5 Freeman, Lake l. U.S.A.
30 C4 Freeport IL U.S.A.
33 H3 Freeport ME U.S.A.
33 G4 Freeport NY U.S.A.
27 E6 Freeport TX U.S.A.
29 E7 Freeport City Bahamas
27 D7 Freer U.S.A.
105 G4 Free State div. S. Africa
100 A4 Freetown Sierra Leone
65 C3 Fregenal de la Sierra Spain
64 C2 Fréhel, Cap pt France
62 C6 Freiburg im Breisgau Ger.
62 E6 Freising Ger.
62 G6 Freistadt Austria
64 H5 Fréjus France
112 C6 Fremantle Austr.
30 E4 Fremont MI U.S.A.
26 D3 Fremont NE U.S.A.
32 B4 Fremont OH U.S.A.
35 G2 Fremont r. U.S.A.
32 C4 French Creek r. U.S.A.
38  French Guiana terr. S. America
114 F7 French I. i. Austr.
21 H5 Frenchman r. Can./U.S.A.
34 C2 Frenchman U.S.A.
115 F9 Frenchman Cap mt Austr.
34 B2 Frenchman Cr. r. CA U.S.A.
35 E3 Frenchman L. l. NV U.S.A.
60 C4 Frenchpark Rep. of Ireland
117 D4 French Pass N.Z.
33 J1 Frenchville U.S.A.
60 D5 Freshford Rep. of Ireland
35 G6 Fresnal Canyon U.S.A.
36 D4 Fresnillo Mex.
34 C3 Fresno U.S.A.
34 C3 Fresno r. U.S.A.

65 H3 Freu, Cap des pt Spain
62 D6 Freudenstadt Ger.
115 H9 Freycinet Nat. Park nat. park Austr.
115 H9 Freycinet Peninsula pen. Austr.
64 D2 Freyming-Merlebach France
47 D1 Freyre Arg.
100 A3 Fria Guinea
34 C3 Friant U.S.A.
44 C3 Frias Arg.
62 C7 Fribourg Switz.
62 D7 Friedrichshafen Ger.
33 J3 Friendship U.S.A.
61 D1 Friese Wad tidal flats Neth.
59 J6 Frinton-on-Sea U.K.
57 B4 Frisa, Loch l. U.K.
35 H2 Frisco Mt mt. U.S.A.
18  Frobisher Bay b. Can.
21 H3 Frobisher Lake l. Can.
54 L5 Frohavet b. Norway
69 G5 Frolovo Rus. Fed.
68 K2 Frolovskaya Rus. Fed.
114 C2 Frome watercourse Austr.
59 E6 Frome U.K.
114 C3 Frome Downs Austr.
114 C3 Frome, Lake salt flat Austr.
36 F5 Frontera Mex.
32 D5 Front Royal U.S.A.
66 E4 Frosinone Italy
32 D5 Frostburg U.S.A.
54 L5 Frøya i. Norway
35 H2 Fruita U.S.A.
35 G1 Fruitland U.S.A.
   Frunze see Bishkek
62 C7 Frutigen Switz.
63 J6 Frýdek-Místek Czech Rep.
33 J2 Fryeburg U.S.A.
89 F5 Fu'an China
90 C6 Fuchū Japan
89 D5 Fuchuan China
89 F4 Fuchun Jiang r. China
91 H3 Fudai Japan
57 A3 Fuday i. U.K.
89 F5 Fude China
89 F5 Fuding China
65 E2 Fuenlabrada Spain
65 D3 Fuente Obejuna Spain
44 E2 Fuerte Olimpo Para.
100 A2 Fuerteventura i. Canary Is Spain
94 B2 Fuga i. Phil.
88 E2 Fugou China
88 D2 Fugu China
82 C4 Fuhai China
81 J4 Fuḥaymī Iraq
79 H4 Fujairah U.A.E.
91 G6 Fuji Japan
89 E5 Fujian div. China
88 C4 Fu Jiang r. China
91 G6 Fujieda Japan
91 G6 Fuji-Hakone-Izu National Park nat. park Japan
91 G6 Fujinomiya Japan
90 H3 Fujisaki Japan
91 G6 Fuji-san volc. Japan
91 H5 Fujishiro Japan
91 G6 Fujiyoshida Japan
90 J2 Fukagawa Japan
90 G3 Fukaura Japan
91 G6 Fukuchiyama Japan
91 G6 Fukue Japan
90 B7 Fukue-jima i. Japan
91 F5 Fukui Japan
91 F5 Fukui Japan
90 C7 Fukuoka Japan
90 C7 Fukuoka Japan
91 H5 Fukushima Fukushima Japan
90 H3 Fukushima Hokkaidō Japan
91 H5 Fukushima Japan
90 C5 Fukuyama Japan
62 D5 Fulda Ger.
59 G6 Fulham U.K.
88 E3 Fuliji China
89 C4 Fuling China
21 M2 Fullerton, Cape hd Can.
30 B5 Fulton IL U.S.A.
28 B4 Fulton KY U.S.A.
26 F4 Fulton MO U.S.A.
33 E3 Fulton NY U.S.A.
105 G2 Fumane Moz.
61 C5 Fumay France
91 H6 Funabashi Japan
111 H2 Funafuti i. Tuvalu
100 A1 Funchal Madeira Port.
45 B2 Fundación Col.
65 C2 Fundão Port.
23 G5 Fundy, Bay of g. Can.
23 G4 Fundy Nat. Park nat. park Can.
34 D2 Funeral Peak summit U.S.A.
103 D6 Funhalouro Moz.
88 F3 Funing Jiangsu China
89 B6 Funing Yunnan China
88 D3 Funiu Shan mts China
116 C4 Funnel Cr. r. Austr.
100 C3 Funtua Nigeria
57  Funzie U.K.
89 F5 Fuqing China
90 J2 Furano Japan
90 K2 Füren-ko l. Japan
79 H4 Fürgun, Küh-e mt Iran
68 G3 Furmanov Rus. Fed.
34 D3 Furnace Creek U.S.A.
46 C3 Furnas, Represa resr Brazil

113 J7 Furneaux Group is Austr.
62 G4 Fürstenwalde Ger.
62 E6 Fürth Ger.
90 F2 Furubira Japan
91 F5 Furukawa Gifu Japan
91 H4 Furukawa Miyagi Japan
45 B3 Fusagasugá Col.
89 C7 Fushan China
88 G1 Fushun Liaoning China
89 B4 Fushun Sichuan China
87 N3 Fusong China
89 C6 Fusui China
90 C7 Futago-san volc. Japan
91 G6 Futtsu Japan
111 H3 Futuna i. Vanuatu
89 E5 Futun Xi r. China
88 C3 Fu Xian China
87 M3 Fuxin Liaoning China
88 F1 Fuxin Liaoning China
91 G4 Fuya Japan
88 E3 Fuyang Anhui China
89 F4 Fuyang Zhejiang China
88 E2 Fuyang r. China
88 M2 Fuyu Heilongjiang China
87 M2 Fuyu Jilin China
89 B5 Fuyuan China
82 G1 Fuyun China
89 F5 Fuzhou Fujian China
89 E5 Fuzhou Jiangxi China
81 L2 Füzuli Azer.
55 M9 Fyn i. Denmark
57 C5 Fyne, Loch in. U.K.
   F.Y.R.O.M. country see Macedonia

## G

66 C6 Gaâfour Tunisia
102 E3 Gaalkacyo Somalia
105 F2 Gabane Botswana
34 D2 Gabbs U.S.A.
34 C2 Gabbs Valley Range mts U.S.A.
103 B5 Gabela Angola
100 D1 Gabès Tunisia
101 D1 Gabès, Golfe de g. Tunisia
115 H6 Gabo I. i. Austr.
96  Gabon country Africa
103 C6 Gaborone Botswana
67 L3 Gabrovo Bulg.
100 A3 Gabú Guinea-Bissau
83 E7 Gadag India
54 O4 Gäddede Sweden
84 B5 Gadhra India
84 B4 Gadra Pak.
29 C5 Gadsden U.S.A.
83 E7 Gadwal India
54 S2 Gædnovuoppe Norway
59 D6 Gaer U.K.
67 L2 Găeşti Romania
66 E4 Gaeta Italy
66 E4 Gaeta, Golfo di g. Italy
108  Gaferut i. Micronesia
29 C5 Gaffney U.S.A.
100 C1 Gafsa Tunisia
68 E4 Gagarin Rus. Fed.
68 H4 Gagino Rus. Fed.
100 B4 Gagnoa Côte d'Ivoire
23 G3 Gagnon Can.
69 G7 Gagra Georgia
81 L4 Gahvāreh Iran
104 E3 Gaiab watercourse Namibia
85 G4 Gaibandha Bangl.
64 E5 Gaillac France
29 E6 Gainesville FL U.S.A.
29 D5 Gainesville GA U.S.A.
27 D5 Gainesville TX U.S.A.
59 G4 Gainsborough U.K.
114 A3 Gairdner, Lake salt flat Austr.
57 C3 Gairloch U.K.
57 C3 Gair Loch in. U.K.
88 G1 Gai Xian China
104 E3 Gakarosa mt S. Africa
84 C1 Gakuch Jammu and Kashmir
85 G3 Gala China
80 C7 Galâla el Baharîya, G. el plat. Egypt
102 D4 Galana r. Kenya
57 F5 Galashiels U.K.
67 M2 Galaţi Romania
67 F3 Galatina Italy
32 C6 Galax U.S.A.
60 C5 Galbally Rep. of Ireland
55 L6 Galdhøpiggen summit Norway
30 B4 Galena U.S.A.
45 E2 Galeota Pt pt Trinidad and Tobago
45 E2 Galera Pt pt Trinidad and Tobago
47 B4 Galera, Punta pt Chile
30 B5 Galesburg U.S.A.
104 F4 Galeshewe S. Africa
30 B3 Galesville U.S.A.
32 E4 Galeton U.S.A.
69 G7 Gali Georgia
65 C1 Galicia div. Spain
116 A4 Galilee, L. salt flat Austr.
80 C4 Galilee, Sea of l. Israel
32 B4 Galion U.S.A.

66 C6 Galite, Canal de la chan. Tunisia
35 G5 Galiuro Mts mts U.S.A.
101 F3 Gallabat Sudan
24 E2 Gallatin r. U.S.A.
29 C4 Gallatin U.S.A.
83 F9 Galle Sri Lanka
44 B8 Gallegos r. Arg.
45 C1 Gallinas, Pta pt Col.
66 H4 Gallipoli Italy
32 B5 Gallipolis U.S.A.
54 R3 Gällivare Sweden
54 O5 Gällö Sweden
33 H4 Gallo I. i. U.S.A.
35 H4 Gallo Mts mts U.S.A.
57 D6 Galloway, Mull of c. U.K.
35 H4 Gallup U.S.A.
57 D5 Galston U.K.
34 B2 Galt U.S.A.
100 A2 Galtat Zemmour Western Sahara
60  Galtee Mountains h. Rep. of Ireland
60  Galtymore h. Rep. of Ireland
30 B5 Galva U.S.A.
27 E6 Galveston U.S.A.
27 E6 Galveston Bay b. U.S.A.
47 E2 Galvez Arg.
85 E3 Galwa Nepal
60 B4 Galway Rep. of Ireland
60 B4 Galway Bay g. Rep. of Ireland
89 B6 Gâm r. Vietnam
59 J8 Gamaches France
91 F6 Gamagōri Japan
105 J5 Gamalakhe S. Africa
45 B2 Gamarra Col.
85 G3 Gamba China
102 D3 Gambēla Eth.
102 D3 Gambela National Park nat. park Eth.
84 D1 Gambhir r. India
96  Gambia, The country Africa
109  Gambier, Îles is. Fr. Polynesia Pac. Oc.
114 C5 Gambier Is is. Austr.
23 K4 Gambo Can.
102 B4 Gamboma Congo
113 H3 Gamboola Austr.
35 H4 Gamerco U.S.A.
55 P8 Gamleby Sweden
54 S4 Gammelstaden Sweden
114 C3 Gammon Ranges Nat. Park nat. park Austr.
88 A3 Gana China
35 H4 Ganado U.S.A.
31 J3 Gananoque Can.
81 L1 Gäncä Azer.
89 C7 Gancheng China
93 F7 Gandadiwata, Bukit mt Indon.
85 G3 Gandaingoin China
102 C4 Gandajika Zaire
85 E4 Gandak Dam dam Nepal
84 B3 Gandari Mountain mt Pak.
84 A3 Gandava Pak.
23 K4 Gander Can.
65 G2 Gandesa Spain
84 B5 Gandevi India
84 C4 Gāndhidhām India
84 C5 Gandhinagar India
84 C4 Gāndhi Sāgar resr India
84 C4 Gāndhi Sāgar Dam dam India
65 F3 Gandía Spain
79 J4 Gand-i Zureh plain Afgh.
46 E1 Gandu Brazil
47 C4 Gangán Arg.
84 C3 Ganganagar India
84 D4 Gangapur India
85 H5 Gangaw Myanmar
88 A2 Gangca China
84 E3 Gangdisê Shan mts China
64 F5 Ganges France
85 G5 Ganges, Mouths of the est. Bangl./India
84 D3 Gangoh India
84 D3 Gangotri mt India
84 D3 Gangtok India
88 B3 Gangu China
83 G7 Ganjam India
89 E4 Gan Jiang r. China
89 B4 Ganluo China
115 G5 Ganmain Austr.
64 F3 Gannat France
24 E3 Gannett Peak summit U.S.A.
84 C5 Ganora India
104 C7 Gansbaai S. Africa
88 B3 Gansu div. China
88 B2 Gantang China
114 B6 Gantheaume, C. hd Austr.
69 G6 Gant'iadi Georgia
88 G2 Gan Xian China
88 F3 Ganyu China
89 D5 Ganzhou China
101 F4 Ganzi Sudan
100 B3 Gao Mali
89 E4 Gao'an China
88 E2 Gaocheng China
88 A5 Gaochun China
89 E4 Gaohebu China
88 B2 Gaolan China
88 F2 Gaomi China
89 D5 Gaomutang China
88 D3 Gaoping China

88 A2 Gaotai China
88 E2 Gaotang China
88 C2 Gaotouyao China
100 B3 Gaoua Burkina
100 A3 Gaoual Guinea
89 B4 Gao Xian China
88 E2 Gaoyang China
88 E2 Gaoyi China
88 F3 Gaoyou China
88 F3 Gaoyou Hu l. China
89 D6 Gaozhou China
64 H4 Gap France
94 B3 Gapan Phil.
65 F5 Gap Carbon hd Alg.
84 E2 Gar China
115 H2 Garah Austr.
60 C4 Gara, Lough l. Rep. of Ireland
102 C3 Garamba r. Zaire
102 C3 Garamba, Park National de la nat. park Zaire
43 L5 Garanhuns Brazil
105 G2 Ga-Rankuwa S. Africa
102 D3 Garba Tula Kenya
34 A1 Garberville U.S.A.
62 D4 Garbsen Ger.
46 C3 Garça Brazil
46 B1 Garças, Rio das r. Brazil
85 G2 Garco China
81 K1 Gardabani Georgia
66 D2 Garda, Lago di l. Italy
66 B6 Garde, Cap de hd Alg.
26 C4 Garden City U.S.A.
30 D3 Garden Corners U.S.A.
34 C5 Garden Grove U.S.A.
21 L4 Garden Hill Can.
30 E3 Garden I. i. U.S.A.
28 C2 Garden Pen. pen. U.S.A.
84 B2 Gardez Afgh.
33 J2 Gardiner ME U.S.A.
24 E2 Gardiner MT U.S.A.
33 G4 Gardiners I. i. U.S.A.
30 C5 Gardner U.S.A.
33 K2 Gardner Lake l. U.S.A.
14 H4 Gardner Pinnacles is U.S.A.
34 C2 Gardnerville U.S.A.
57 D4 Garelochhead U.K.
30 E2 Gargantua, Cape c. Can.
81 M6 Gargar Iran
55 R9 Gargždai Lith.
84 D5 Garhakota India
84 E5 Garhchiroli India
84 A3 Garhi Khairo Pak.
84 D4 Garhi Malehra India
20 E5 Garibaldi, Mt mt. Can.
20 E5 Garibaldi Prov. Park nat. park Can.
105 F5 Gariep Dam resr S. Africa
104 B5 Garies S. Africa
66 E4 Garigliano r. Italy
102 D4 Garissa Kenya
55 T8 Garkalne Latvia
32 D4 Garland PA U.S.A.
27 D5 Garland TX U.S.A.
81 M2 Garmī Iran
62 E7 Garmisch-Partenkirchen Ger.
26 E4 Garnett U.S.A.
114 E4 Garnpung Lake l. Austr.
85 G4 Gāro Hills h. India
64 D4 Garonne r. France
102 E3 Garoowe Somalia
44 G3 Garopaba Brazil
101 D4 Garoua Cameroon
47 D3 Garré Arg.
35 E2 Garrison U.S.A.
60 F2 Garron Point pt U.K.
21 J1 Garry Lake l. Can.
57 D4 Garry, Loch l. U.K.
57 B2 Garrynahine U.K.
102 E4 Garsen Kenya
59 D5 Garth U.K.
104 B3 Garub Namibia
92 □ Garut Indon.
60 E3 Garvagh U.K.
57 D3 Garve U.K.
30 D5 Gary U.S.A.
84 E3 Garyarsa China
90 D6 Garyū-zan mt. Japan
84 D2 Gar Zangbo r. China
82 J4 Garzê China
45 B4 Garzón Col.
64 D5 Gascogne reg. France
26 E4 Gasconade r. U.S.A.
64 C5 Gascony, Gulf of g. France/Spain
112 B4 Gascoyne r. Austr.
112 C5 Gascoyne Junction Austr.
Gascuña, Golfo de g. see Gascony, Gulf of
84 D2 Gasherbrum mt China/Jammu and Kashmir
100 D3 Gashua Nigeria
23 H4 Gaspé Can.
23 H4 Gaspé, C. c. Can.
23 G4 Gaspé, Péninsule de pen. Can.
23 G4 Gaspésie, Parc de la nat. park Can.
91 H4 Gassan volc. Japan
Gasteiz see Vitoria-Gasteiz
29 D5 Gastonia U.S.A.
47 C4 Gastre Arg.
65 E4 Gata, Cabo de c. Spain
80 D4 Gata, Cape c. Cyprus
68 D3 Gatchina Rus. Fed.
32 B6 Gate City U.S.A.
57 D6 Gatehouse of Fleet U.K.
58 F3 Gateshead U.K.
27 D6 Gatesville U.S.A.
35 H2 Gateway U.S.A.
33 F4 Gateway National Recreational Area res. U.S.A.
31 K3 Gatineau Can.
31 K2 Gatineau r. Can.
115 K1 Gatton Austr.
81 M5 Gatvand Iran
111 H3 Gau i. Fiji
21 K3 Gauer Lake l. Can.
54 M5 Gaula r. Norway
32 C5 Gauley Bridge U.S.A.
61 D5 Gaume reg. Belgium
85 F4 Gauri Sankar mt China
105 G3 Gauteng div. S. Africa
67 L7 Gavdos i. Greece
81 L4 Gaveh r. Iran
46 E1 Gavião r. Brazil
81 L4 Gavīleh Iran
34 B4 Gaviota U.S.A.
55 P6 Gävle Sweden
68 F3 Gavrilov-Yam Rus. Fed.
104 B3 Gawachab Namibia
114 C5 Gawler Austr.
114 A4 Gawler Ranges h. Austr.
88 A1 Gaxun Nur salt l. China
85 F4 Gaya India
100 C3 Gaya Niger
30 E3 Gaylord U.S.A.
116 D5 Gayndah Austr.
80 E6 Gaza terr. Asia
80 E6 Gaza Gaza
105 K1 Gaza div. Moz.
79 J1 Gaz-Achak Turkm.
79 H2 Gazandzhyk Turkm.
84 B2 Gazdarra Pass pass Afgh.
80 F3 Gaziantep Turkey
80 D3 Gazipaşa Turkey
100 A4 Gbangbatok Sierra Leone
100 B4 Gbarnga Liberia
100 C4 Gboko Nigeria
63 J3 Gdańsk Pol.
63 J3 Gdańsk, Gulf of g. Pol./Rus. Fed.
68 C3 Gdov Rus. Fed.
63 J3 Gdynia Pol.
57 C1 Gealldruig Mhor i. U.K.
101 F3 Gedaref Sudan
80 B2 Gediz Turkey
80 A2 Gediz r. Turkey
59 H5 Gedney Drove End U.K.
55 M9 Gedser Denmark
61 D3 Geel Belgium
114 F7 Geelong Austr.
104 D4 Geel Vloer salt pan S. Africa
115 G9 Geeveston Austr.
82 F4 Gê'gyai China
88 F4 Ge Hu l. China
100 D3 Geidam Nigeria
21 J3 Geikie r. Can.
61 E4 Geilenkirchen Ger.
55 L6 Geilo Norway
55 K5 Geiranger Norway
30 E6 Geist Reservoir resr U.S.A.
89 B6 Gejiu China
66 F6 Gela Sicily Italy
102 E3 Geladī Eth.
95 B4 Gelang, Tanjung pt Malaysia
61 E3 Geldern Ger.
69 F6 Gelendzhik Rus. Fed.
63 L3 Gelgaudiškis Lith.
69 C7 Gelibolu Turkey
80 C2 Gelincik Dağı mt Turkey
62 C5 Gelsenkirchen Ger.
95 B5 Gemas Malaysia
94 C5 Gemeh Indon.
102 B3 Gemena Zaire
80 F2 Gemerek Turkey
80 B1 Gemlik Turkey
66 E1 Gemona del Friuli Italy
103 C6 Gemsbok National Park nat. park Botswana
104 D3 Gemsbokplein w. S. Africa
102 E3 Genalē Wenz r. Eth.
47 D3 General Acha Arg.
47 E3 General Alvear Buenos Aires Arg.
47 E1 General Alvear Entre Rios Arg.
47 C2 General Alvear Mendoza Arg.
47 E2 General Belgrano Arg.
119 B3 General Belgrano II Argentina Base Ant.
119 B2 General Bernardo O'Higgins Chile Base Ant.
27 D7 General Bravo Mex.
44 B7 General Carrera, L. l. Chile
47 F3 General Conesa Buenos Aires Arg.
47 D4 General Conesa Rio Negro Arg.
47 F3 General Guido Arg.
47 F3 General J. Madariaga Arg.
47 E3 General La Madrid Arg.
47 F3 General Lavalle Arg.
47 D2 General Levalle Arg.
94 C4 General Luna Phil.
94 C4 General MacArthur Phil.
47 D2 General Pico Arg.
47 E2 General Pinto Arg.
47 C3 General Roca Arg.
119 B2 General San Martín Argentina Base Ant.
94 C5 General Santos Phil.
47 D2 General Villegas Arg.
32 D3 Genesee r. U.S.A.
30 B5 Geneseo IL U.S.A.
32 E3 Geneseo NY U.S.A.
105 G3 Geneva S. Africa
Geneva see Genève
30 C5 Geneva IL U.S.A.
26 D3 Geneva NE U.S.A.
32 E3 Geneva NY U.S.A.
32 C4 Geneva OH U.S.A.
Geneva, Lake l. see Léman, Lac
30 C4 Geneva, Lake l. U.S.A.
62 C7 Genève Switz.
65 D4 Genil r. Spain
61 D4 Genk Belgium
90 B7 Genkai-nada b. Japan
115 H6 Genoa Austr.
66 C2 Genoa Italy
Genova see Genoa
66 C2 Genova, Golfo di g. Italy
61 B3 Gent Belgium
92 □ Genteng Indon.
92 □ Genteng i. Indon.
112 C6 Geographe Bay b. Austr.
23 G2 George r. Can.
104 E6 George S. Africa
115 H5 George, L. l. N.S.W. Austr.
114 C6 George, L. l. S.A. Austr.
29 D6 George, L. l. U.S.A.
33 G3 George, Lake l. U.S.A.
117 A6 George Sd in. N.Z.
113 H3 Georgetown Qld. Austr.
114 C4 Georgetown S.A. Austr.
115 G8 George Town Austr.
31 H4 Georgetown Can.
43 G2 Georgetown Guyana
92 C5 George Town Malaysia
29 F7 George Town Bahamas
100 A3 Georgetown The Gambia
33 F5 Georgetown DE U.S.A.
30 D6 Georgetown IL U.S.A.
28 C4 Georgetown KY U.S.A.
32 B5 Georgetown OH U.S.A.
29 E5 Georgetown SC U.S.A.
27 D6 Georgetown TX U.S.A.
119 B5 George V Land reg. Ant.
27 D6 George West U.S.A.
70 Georgia country Asia
29 D5 Georgia div. U.S.A.
31 G3 Georgian Bay l. Can.
31 H3 Georgian Bay Island National Park nat. park Can.
20 E5 Georgia, Strait of chan. Can.
113 G4 Georgina watercourse Austr.
82 F1 Georgiyevka Kazak.
69 G6 Georgiyevsk Rus. Fed.
68 H3 Georgiyevskoye Rus. Fed.
62 F5 Gera Ger.
61 B4 Geraardsbergen Belgium
43 J6 Geral de Goiás, Serra h. Brazil
117 C6 Geraldine N.Z.
46 C1 Geral do Paraná, Serra h. Brazil
112 B5 Geraldton Austr.
81 H3 Gercüş Turkey
80 D1 Gerede r. Turkey
80 D1 Gerede Turkey
79 J3 Gereshk Afgh.
95 B4 Gerik Malaysia
26 C3 Gering U.S.A.
24 C3 Gerlach U.S.A.
20 E3 Germansen Landing Can.
32 E5 Germantown U.S.A.
48 Germany country Europe
62 D6 Germersheim Ger.
105 H3 Germiston S. Africa
91 F6 Gero Japan
61 E4 Gerolstein Ger.
35 G5 Geronimo U.S.A.
115 J5 Gerringong Austr.
85 F2 Gêrzê China
69 E7 Gerze Turkey
61 D4 Gete r. Belgium
32 E5 Gettysburg PA U.S.A.
26 D2 Gettysburg SD U.S.A.
32 E5 Gettysburg National Military Park res. U.S.A.
89 C5 Getu He r. China
119 A4 Getz Ice Shelf ice feature Ant.
95 A5 Geumapang r. Indon.
115 H4 Geurie Austr.
81 J2 Gevaş Turkey
67 K4 Gevgelija Macedonia
65 E1 Gexto Spain
95 □ Geylang Sing.
105 F3 Geysdorp S. Africa
80 C1 Geyve Turkey
104 E2 Ghaap Plateau plat. S. Africa
100 C1 Ghadāmis Libya
84 C3 Ghaggar, Dry Bed of watercourse Pak.
84 F4 Ghaghara r. India
85 F5 Ghaghra India
96 Ghana country Africa
84 C4 Ghanliala India
103 C6 Ghanzi Botswana
104 E1 Ghanzi div. Botswana
80 E6 Gharandal Jordan
100 C1 Ghardaïa Alg.
78 C4 Ghārib, Gebel mt Egypt
101 D1 Gharyān Libya
100 D2 Ghāt Libya
84 B3 Ghauspur Pak.
101 C5 Ghazal, Bahr el watercourse Chad
100 B1 Ghazaouet Alg.
84 D3 Ghaziabad India
85 E4 Ghazipur India
84 A3 Ghazluna Pak.
84 B2 Ghaznī Afgh.
84 B2 Ghazni r. Afgh.
Ghent see Gent
63 M7 Gheorgheni Romania
63 L7 Gherla Romania
66 C3 Ghisonaccia Corsica France
84 C1 Ghizar Pak.
85 G4 Ghoraghat Bangl.
84 B2 Ghorband r. Afgh.
84 B2 Ghorband Pass pass Afgh.
84 B4 Ghotāru India
84 B4 Ghotki Pak.
85 F4 Ghuari r. India
81 J5 Ghudāf, Wādī al watercourse Iraq
84 D6 Ghugus India
84 B4 Ghulam Mohammed Barrage barrage Pak.
95 C3 Gia Đinh Vietnam
69 G6 Giaginskaya Rus. Fed.
67 K4 Giannitsa Greece
105 H4 Giant's Castle mt S. Africa
60 E2 Giant's Causeway N. Ireland U.K.
92 F8 Gianyar Indon.
95 C3 Gia Rai Vietnam
66 F6 Giarre Sicily Italy
66 B2 Giaveno Italy
104 B2 Gibeon Namibia
65 D4 Gibraltar terr. Europe
65 C5 Gibraltar, Strait of str. Morocco/Spain
30 C5 Gibson City U.S.A.
112 D4 Gibson Desert des. Austr.
86 F2 Gichgeniyn Nuruu mts Mongolia
83 E7 Giddalur India
80 D6 Giddi, G. el h. Egypt
102 D3 Gīdolē Eth.
64 F3 Gien France
62 D5 Gießen Ger.
20 F3 Gift Lake Can.
91 F6 Gifu Japan
91 F6 Gifu Japan
45 B4 Gigante Col.
27 B7 Gigantes, Llanos de los plain Mex.
57 C5 Gigha i. U.K.
65 D1 Gijón Spain
35 F5 Gila r. U.S.A.
35 F5 Gila Bend U.S.A.
35 F5 Gila Bend Mts mts U.S.A.
35 E5 Gila Mts mts U.S.A.
81 K4 Gīlan Garb Iran
81 M1 Gilāzi Azer.
113 H3 Gilbert r. Austr.
35 G5 Gilbert AZ U.S.A.
32 C6 Gilbert WV U.S.A.
111 H2 Gilbert Islands is Kiribati
116 A2 Gilbert Ra. mts Austr.
43 J5 Gilbués Brazil
24 E1 Gildford U.S.A.
78 B5 Gilf Kebir Plateau plat. Egypt
20 D4 Gilford I. i. Can.
115 J2 Gilgai Austr.
115 H3 Gilgandra Austr.
102 D4 Gilgil Kenya
115 H2 Gil Gil Cr. r. Austr.
84 C2 Gilgit Jammu and Kashmir
84 C2 Gilgit r. Jammu and Kashmir
115 G4 Gilgunnia Austr.
20 D4 Gil Island i. Can.
21 L3 Gillam Can.
114 B4 Gilles, L. salt flat Austr.
30 C3 Gillett U.S.A.
24 F2 Gillette U.S.A.
59 E6 Gillingham Eng. U.K.
59 H6 Gillingham Eng. U.K.
58 F3 Gilling West U.K.
30 D3 Gills Rock U.S.A.
30 D5 Gilman IL U.S.A.
30 B3 Gilman WV U.S.A.
22 E2 Gilmour Island i. Can.
34 B3 Gilroy U.S.A.
33 G3 Gilsum U.S.A.
101 E3 Gimbala, Jebel mt Sudan
102 D3 Gīmbī Eth.
21 K4 Gimli Can.
116 C4 Gindie Austr.
116 D5 Gin Gin Austr.
102 E3 Gīnīr Eth.
66 G4 Ginosa Italy
66 G4 Gioia del Colle Italy
115 G6 Gippsland reg. Austr.
84 B4 Girab India
32 C3 Girard U.S.A.
84 B3 Girdao Pak.
80 G1 Giresun Turkey
84 B5 Gir Forest forest India
85 F4 Girīdīh India
115 G3 Girilambone Austr.
84 C5 Girna r. India
65 H2 Girona Spain
64 D4 Gironde est. France
115 G4 Girral Austr.
57 D5 Girvan U.K.
68 E2 Girvas Rus. Fed.
84 E4 Girwan India
117 G3 Gisborne N.Z.
23 G4 Giscome Can.
55 N8 Gislaved Sweden
102 C4 Gitarama Rwanda
102 C4 Gitega Burundi
66 E3 Giulianova Italy
67 L3 Giurgiu Romania
67 L2 Giuvala, Pasul pass Romania
61 C4 Givet France
64 G4 Givors France
105 J1 Giyani S. Africa
80 C7 Giza Pyramids Egypt
79 J1 Gizhduvan Uzbek.
77 S3 Gizhiga Rus. Fed.
67 J4 Gjirokastër Albania
54 L5 Gjøra Norway
55 M6 Gjøvik Norway
23 J4 Glace Bay Can.
20 B3 Glacier B. b. U.S.A.
20 B3 Glacier Bay National Park and Preserve nat. park U.S.A.
20 F4 Glacier Nat. Park nat. park Can.
24 D1 Glacier Nat. Park nat. park U.S.A.
24 B1 Glacier Peak volc. U.S.A.
54 M4 Gladstad Norway
116 D4 Gladstone Qld. Austr.
114 C4 Gladstone S.A. Austr.
115 H8 Gladstone Tas. Austr.
30 D3 Gladstone U.S.A.
30 E4 Gladwin U.S.A.
57 E4 Glamis U.K.
61 F5 Glan r. Ger.
94 C5 Glan Phil.
60 B5 Glanaruddery Mts h. Rep. of Ireland
58 F2 Glanton U.K.
31 G4 Glanworth Can.
57 D5 Glasgow U.K.
28 C4 Glasgow KY U.S.A.
24 F1 Glasgow MT U.S.A.
32 D6 Glasgow VA U.S.A.
21 H4 Glaslyn Can.
34 C3 Glass Mt mt. U.S.A.
59 E6 Glastonbury U.K.
76 G4 Glazov Rus. Fed.
69 F4 Glazunovka Rus. Fed.
63 P3 Glazunovo Rus. Fed.
33 H2 Glen U.S.A.
57 C3 Glen Affric v. U.K.
31 G2 Glen Afton Can.
117 E2 Glen Afton N.Z.
105 H1 Glen Alpine Dam dam S. Africa
60 C4 Glenamaddy Rep. of Ireland
30 E3 Glen Arbor U.S.A.
117 C6 Glenavy N.Z.
57 C3 Glen Cannich v. U.K.
25 E4 Glen Canyon gorge U.S.A.
35 G3 Glen Canyon National Recreation Area res. U.S.A.
57 E4 Glen Clova v. U.K.
114 D6 Glencoe Austr.
31 G4 Glencoe Can.
105 J4 Glencoe S. Africa
57 C4 Glen Coe v. U.K.
31 E2 Glendale Can.
35 F5 Glendale AZ U.S.A.
34 C4 Glendale CA U.S.A.
35 E3 Glendale NV U.S.A.
35 F3 Glendale UT U.S.A.
32 D4 Glendale Lake l. U.S.A.
115 J4 Glen Davis Austr.
116 C3 Glenden Austr.
24 F2 Glendive U.S.A.
21 G4 Glendon Can.
24 F3 Glendo Res. l. U.S.A.
114 D6 Glenelg r. Austr.
57 F4 Glen Esk v. U.K.
57 A5 Glengad Head hd Rep. of Ireland
57 D4 Glen Garry v. Scot. U.K.
57 C3 Glen Garry v. Scot. U.K.
60 D3 Glengavlen Rep. of Ireland
115 J2 Glen Innes Austr.
57 D6 Glenluce U.K.
57 D4 Glen Lyon v. U.K.
57 D3 Glen More v. U.K.
115 H1 Glenmorgan Austr.
57 D3 Glen Moriston v. U.K.
57 C4 Glen Nevis v. U.K.
31 F3 Glennie U.S.A.
35 G6 Glenn, Mt mt. U.S.A.
32 E6 Glenns U.S.A.
20 C3 Glenora Can.
33 F2 Glen Robertson Can.
57 E4 Glenrothes U.K.
33 G3 Glens Falls U.S.A.
57 E4 Glen Shee v. U.K.
57 C3 Glen Shiel v. U.K.
60 C3 Glenties Rep. of Ireland
60 D2 Glenveagh National Park nat. park Rep. of Ireland
32 C5 Glenville U.S.A.
27 E5 Glenwood AR U.S.A.
35 H5 Glenwood NM U.S.A.
25 F4 Glenwood Springs U.S.A.
30 B2 Glidden U.S.A.
63 J5 Gliwice Pol.
35 G5 Globe U.S.A.
62 H5 Głogów Pol.
54 N3 Glomfjord Norway
55 M5 Glomma r. Norway
103 E5 Glorieuses, Îles is Indian Ocean
115 J3 Gloucester Austr.
59 E6 Gloucester U.K.
33 H3 Gloucester MA U.S.A.
32 E6 Gloucester VA U.S.A.
116 C3 Gloucester I. i. Austr.
33 F3 Gloversville U.S.A.
69 G6 Glubokiy Rus. Fed.
82 D1 Glubokoye Kazak.
54 □ Gluggarnir h. Faroe Is
58 F4 Glusburn U.K.
69 H5 Gmelinka Rus. Fed.
62 G6 Gmünd Austria
62 F7 Gmunden Austria
55 P5 Gnarp Sweden
62 H4 Gniezno Pol.
67 J3 Gnjilane Yugo.
83 D7 Goa div. India
104 B3 Goageb Namibia
115 J6 Goalen Head hd Austr.
85 G4 Goalpara India
57 C5 Goat Fell h. U.K.
102 E3 Goba Eth.
103 B6 Gobabis Namibia
104 C3 Gobas Namibia
47 E1 Gobernador Crespo Arg.
47 C3 Gobernador Duval Arg.
44 B7 Gobernador Gregores Arg.
74 Gobi des. Mongolia
90 E7 Gobō Japan
61 E3 Goch Ger.
103 B6 Gochas Namibia
95 C3 Go Công Vietnam
59 G6 Godalming U.K.
83 F7 Godavari, Mouths of the est. India
23 G4 Godbout Can.
34 C3 Goddard, Mt mt. U.S.A.
102 E3 Godere Eth.
31 G4 Goderich Can.
84 C5 Godhra India
47 C2 Godoy Cruz Arg.
21 L3 Gods r. Can.
21 L4 Gods Lake l. Can.
21 M2 Gods Mercy, Bay of b. Can.
16 Godthåb Greenland
Godwin Austen mt see K2
61 B3 Goedereede Neth.
22 E4 Goéland, Lac au l. Can.
23 H2 Goélands, Lac aux l. Can.
61 B3 Goes Neth.
31 E2 Goetzville U.S.A.
35 E4 Goffs U.S.A.
31 G2 Gogama Can.
90 D6 Gō-gawa r. Japan
30 C2 Gogebic, Lake l. U.S.A.
30 C2 Gogebic Range h. U.S.A.
Gogra r. see Ghaghara
84 D4 Gohad India
43 M5 Goiana Brazil
46 C2 Goiandira Brazil
46 C2 Goiânia Brazil
46 B2 Goiás div. Brazil
46 B1 Goiás Brazil
46 B4 Goio-Erê Brazil
91 H4 Gojōme Japan
84 C3 Gojra Pak.
90 C7 Gokase-gawa r. Japan
69 C7 Gökçeada i. Turkey
80 B2 Gökçedağ Turkey
85 G3 Gokhar La pass China
80 E1 Gökirmak r. Turkey
80 F2 Göksun Turkey
80 E3 Göksu Nehri r. Turkey
103 C5 Gokwe Zimbabwe
55 L6 Gol Norway
84 E4 Gola India
85 H4 Golaghat India
80 F3 Gölbaşı Turkey
76 K2 Gol'chikha Rus. Fed.
80 B1 Gölcük Turkey
63 L3 Gołdap Pol.
115 K2 Gold Coast Austr.
100 B4 Gold Coast coastal area Ghana
20 F4 Golden Can.
117 D4 Golden Bay b. N.Z.
34 A3 Golden Gate National Recreation Area res. U.S.A.
20 D5 Golden Hinde mt. Can.
60 C5 Golden Vale lowland Rep. of Ireland
34 D3 Goldfield U.S.A.
34 D3 Gold Point U.S.A.
29 E5 Goldsboro U.S.A.
112 C4 Goldsworthy Austr.
27 D6 Goldthwaite U.S.A.
81 J1 Göle Turkey
34 C4 Goleta U.S.A.
27 D6 Goliad U.S.A.
80 F1 Gölköy Turkey
81 K3 Golmānkhānen Iran
86 F4 Golmud China
85 H1 Golmud He r. China
94 B3 Golo i. Phil.
90 K2 Golovnino Rus. Fed.
79 G3 Golpāyegān Iran
80 C1 Gölpazarı Turkey
57 E3 Golspie U.K.
67 L4 Golyama Syutkya mt Bulg.
67 L4 Golyam Persenk mt Bulg.
102 C4 Goma Zaire
85 G3 Gomang Co salt l. China
84 E4 Gomati r. India
95 □ Gombak, Bukit h. Sing.
100 D3 Gombe Nigeria
102 D4 Gombe r. Tanz.
101 D3 Gombi Nigeria
100 A2 Gomera, La i. Canary Is Spain
36 D3 Gómez Palacio Mex.
85 F2 Gomo Co salt l. China
37 K5 Gonaïves Haiti
105 J1 Gonarezhou National Park nat. park Zimbabwe
37 K5 Gonâve, Île de la i. Haiti
79 H2 Gonbad-e Kavus Iran
85 E4 Gonda India
84 B5 Gondal India
102 D2 Gonder Eth.
84 E5 Gondia India
80 A1 Gönen Turkey
89 D4 Gong'an China
89 D5 Gongcheng China

89 A4 **Gongga Shan** mt China
88 A2 **Gonghe** China
88 E1 **Gonghui** China
82 F2 **Gongliu** China
46 E1 **Gongogi** r. Brazil
100 D4 **Gongola** r. Nigeria
115 G3 **Gongolgon** Austr.
89 B5 **Gongwang Shan** mts China
88 D3 **Gong Xian** Henan China
89 A4 **Gong Xian** Sichuan China
90 H3 **Gonohe** Japan
90 B7 **Gōnoura** Japan
105 H6 **Gonubie** S. Africa
34 B3 **Gonzales** CA U.S.A.
27 D6 **Gonzales** TX U.S.A.
47 D2 **González Moreno** Arg.
32 E6 **Goodenough, C.** c. Ant.
119 C6 **Goodenough, C.** c. Ant.
110 F2 **Goodenough I.** i. P.N.G.
31 H3 **Gooderham** Can.
30 E3 **Good Harbor Bay** b. U.S.A.
104 C7 **Good Hope, Cape of** c. S. Africa
24 D3 **Gooding** U.S.A.
26 C4 **Goodland** U.S.A.
115 G2 **Goodooga** Austr.
58 G4 **Goole** U.K.
115 F5 **Goolgowi** Austr.
115 H4 **Goolma** Austr.
115 H4 **Gooloogong** Austr.
114 C5 **Goolwa** Austr.
115 F2 **Goombalie** Austr.
116 E6 **Goomeri** Austr.
115 J2 **Goondiwindi** Austr.
116 B3 **Goonyella** Austr.
23 H3 **Goose** r. Can.
24 B3 **Goose L.** l. U.S.A.
62 D6 **Göppingen** Ger.
85 E4 **Gorakhpur** India
67 H3 **Goražde** Bos.-Herz.
68 G3 **Gorchukha** Rus. Fed.
29 E7 **Gorda Cay** i. Bahamas
80 B2 **Gördes** Turkey
63 P4 **Gordeyevka** Rus. Fed.
115 F9 **Gordon** r. Austr.
57 F5 **Gordon** U.K.
115 G9 **Gordon, L.** l. Austr.
20 G2 **Gordon Lake** l. Can.
32 D5 **Gordon Lake** l. U.S.A.
32 D5 **Gordonsville** U.S.A.
116 A1 **Gordonvale** Austr.
101 D4 **Goré** Chad
102 D3 **Gorē** Eth.
117 B7 **Gore** N.Z.
31 F3 **Gore Bay** Can.
57 E5 **Gorebridge** U.K.
60 E5 **Gorey** Rep. of Ireland
79 G2 **Gorgān** Iran
116 A2 **Gorge Range, The** mts Austr.
45 A4 **Gorgona, I.** i. Col.
33 H2 **Gorham** U.S.A.
69 H7 **Gori** Georgia
61 C3 **Gorinchem** Neth.
81 L2 **Goris** Armenia
66 E2 **Gorizia** Italy
**Gor'kiy** see **Nizhniy Novgorod**
69 H5 **Gor'ko-Solenoye, Ozero** l. Rus. Fed.
68 G3 **Gor'kovskoye Vdkhr.** resr Rus. Fed.
63 K6 **Gorlice** Pol.
62 G5 **Görlitz** Ger.
84 D4 **Gormi** India
67 L3 **Gorna Oryakhovitsa** Bulg.
67 J2 **Gornji Milanovac** Yugo.
66 G3 **Gornji Vakuf** Bos.-Herz.
86 E1 **Gorno-Altaysk** Rus. Fed.
86 D1 **Gornyak** Rus. Fed.
69 J5 **Gornyy** Rus. Fed.
69 H5 **Gornyy Balykley** Rus. Fed.
68 G3 **Gorodets** Rus. Fed.
69 H5 **Gorodishche** Rus. Fed.
69 G6 **Gorodovikovsk** Rus. Fed.
110 E2 **Goroka** P.N.G.
114 D6 **Goroke** Austr.
68 G3 **Gorokhovets** Rus. Fed.
100 B3 **Gorom Gorom** Burkina
103 D5 **Gorongosa** Moz.
93 G6 **Gorontalo** Indon.
69 F5 **Gorshechnoye** Rus. Fed.
60 C4 **Gort** Rep. of Ireland
60 C2 **Gortahork** Rep. of Ireland
46 D1 **Gorutuba** r. Brazil
69 F6 **Goryachiy Klyuch** Rus. Fed.
62 G4 **Gorzów Wielkopolski** Pol.
91 G5 **Gosen** Japan
115 J4 **Gosford** Austr.
58 F2 **Gosforth** U.K.
30 E5 **Goshen** IN U.S.A.
33 H4 **Goshen** NY U.S.A.
90 H3 **Goshogawara** Japan
66 F2 **Gospić** Croatia
59 F7 **Gosport** U.K.
67 J4 **Gostivar** Macedonia
**Göteborg** see **Gothenburg**
55 N7 **Götene** Sweden
62 E5 **Gotha** Ger.
55 M8 **Gothenburg** Sweden
26 C3 **Gothenburg** U.S.A.
55 Q8 **Gotland** i. Sweden
90 B7 **Gotō-rettō** i. Japan
67 K4 **Gotse Delchev** Bulg.
55 Q7 **Gotska Sandön** i. Sweden
90 D6 **Gōtsu** Japan
62 D5 **Göttingen** Ger.
20 E4 **Gott Peak** summit Can.
**Gottwaldov** see **Zlín**
61 C2 **Gouda** Neth.

61 C3 **Gouderak** Neth.
100 A3 **Goudiri** Senegal
100 D3 **Goudoumaria** Niger
30 E1 **Goudreau** Can.
12 J8 **Gough Island** i. Atlantic Ocean
22 F4 **Gouin, Réservoir** resr Can.
30 E2 **Goulais River** Can.
115 J4 **Goulburn** r. N.S.W. Austr.
114 F6 **Goulburn** r. Vic. Austr.
115 H5 **Goulburn** Austr.
113 F2 **Goulburn Is** is Austr.
30 E2 **Gould City** U.S.A.
100 B3 **Goundam** Mali
65 G4 **Gouraya** Alg.
100 D3 **Gouré** Niger
104 E5 **Gourits** r. S. Africa
100 B3 **Gourma-Rharous** Mali
64 E2 **Gournay-en-Bray** France
115 H6 **Gourock Range** mts Austr.
33 F2 **Gouverneur** U.S.A.
21 H5 **Govenlock** Can.
46 E2 **Governador Valadares** Brazil
94 C5 **Governor Generoso** Phil.
29 E7 **Governor's Harbour** Bahamas
86 G3 **Govĭ Altayn Nuruu** mts Mongolia
85 E4 **Govind Ballash Pant Sāgar** resr India
84 D3 **Govind Sagar** resr India
32 D3 **Gowanda** U.S.A.
116 A5 **Gowan Ra.** h. Austr.
59 C6 **Gower** pen. U.K.
31 G2 **Gowganda** Can.
60 D4 **Gowna, Lough** l. Rep. of Ireland
44 A3 **Goya** Arg.
81 L1 **Göyçay** Azer.
81 K2 **Göynük** Turkey
91 H4 **Goyō-zan** mt. Japan
81 M2 **Göytäpä** Azer.
80 G2 **Gözene** Turkey
84 E2 **Gozha Co** salt l. China
66 F6 **Gozo** i. Malta
104 F6 **Graaff-Reinet** S. Africa
104 C6 **Graafwater** S. Africa
100 B4 **Grabo** Côte d'Ivoire
104 C7 **Grabouw** S. Africa
66 F2 **Gračac** Croatia
31 J2 **Gracefield** Can.
115 K2 **Grafton** U.S.A.
26 D1 **Grafton** ND U.S.A.
30 D4 **Grafton** WV U.S.A.
32 C5 **Grafton** WV U.S.A.
116 A1 **Grafton, C.** pt Austr.
35 E2 **Grafton, Mt** mt. U.S.A.
116 B1 **Grafton Passage** chan. Austr.
27 D5 **Graham** U.S.A.
**Graham Bell Island** i. see **Greem-Bell, Ostrov**
20 C4 **Graham Island** i. Can.
33 J2 **Graham Lake** l. U.S.A.
35 H5 **Graham, Mt** mt. U.S.A.
105 G6 **Grahamstown** S. Africa
60 E5 **Graigue** Rep. of Ireland
100 A4 **Grain Coast** coastal area Liberia
43 J5 **Grajaú** Brazil
57 B1 **Gralisgeir** i. U.K.
67 J4 **Grámmos** mt Greece
57 D4 **Grampian Mountains** mts U.K.
114 E6 **Grampians** mts Austr.
45 B4 **Granada** Col.
37 G6 **Granada** Nic.
65 E4 **Granada** Spain
26 C4 **Granada** U.S.A.
60 D4 **Granard** Rep. of Ireland
47 C3 **Gran Bajo Salitroso** salt flat Arg.
22 F4 **Granby** Can.
100 A2 **Gran Canaria** i. Canary Is
44 D3 **Gran Chaco** reg. Arg./Para.
28 C3 **Grand** r. MI U.S.A.
26 E3 **Grand** r. MO U.S.A.
29 E7 **Grand Bahama** i. Bahamas
23 H4 **Grand Bank** Can.
12 F2 **Grand Banks** sea feature Atlantic Ocean
100 B4 **Grand-Bassam** Côte d'Ivoire
23 G4 **Grand Bay** Can.
31 G4 **Grand Bend** Can.
60 D4 **Grand Canal** canal Rep. of Ireland
35 F3 **Grand Canyon** U.S.A.
35 F3 **Grand Canyon** gorge U.S.A.
35 F3 **Grand Canyon Nat. Park** nat. park U.S.A.
37 H5 **Grand Cayman** i. Cayman Is
21 G4 **Grand Centre** Can.
24 C2 **Grand Coulee** U.S.A.
47 C3 **Grande** r. Arg.
43 J6 **Grande** r. Bahia Brazil
46 B2 **Grande** r. São Paulo Brazil
37 H6 **Grande** r. Mex./U.S.A.
44 C8 **Grande, Bahía** b. Arg.
20 F4 **Grande Cache** Can.
64 H4 **Grande Casse, Pointe de la** mt France
103 E5 **Grande Comore** i. Comoros
47 H2 **Grande, Cuchilla** h. Uru.
46 D3 **Grande, Ilha** i. Brazil

20 F3 **Grande Prairie** Can.
101 D3 **Grand Erg de Bilma** sand dunes Niger
100 B1 **Grand Erg Occidental** des. Alg.
100 C2 **Grand Erg Oriental** des. Alg.
23 H4 **Grande-Rivière** Can.
22 F3 **Grande Rivière de la Baleine** r. Can.
24 C2 **Grande Ronde** r. U.S.A.
45 E4 **Grande, Serra** mt Brazil
23 G4 **Grand Falls** N.B. Can.
23 J4 **Grand Falls** Nfld Can.
20 F5 **Grand Forks** Can.
26 D2 **Grand Forks** U.S.A.
33 F3 **Grand Gorge** U.S.A.
33 K2 **Grand Harbour** Can.
30 D4 **Grand Haven** U.S.A.
20 F2 **Grandin, Lac** l. Can.
30 D2 **Grand Island** l. Can.
26 D3 **Grand Island** U.S.A.
27 F6 **Grand Isle** LA U.S.A.
33 J1 **Grand Isle** ME U.S.A.
35 H2 **Grand Junction** U.S.A.
100 B4 **Grand-Lahou** Côte d'Ivoire
23 G4 **Grand Lake** l. N.B. Can.
23 J4 **Grand Lake** l. Nfld Can.
23 H3 **Grand Lake** l. Nfld Can.
27 E6 **Grand Lake** l. LA U.S.A.
33 K2 **Grand Lake** l. ME U.S.A.
31 F3 **Grand Lake** l. MI U.S.A.
33 J1 **Grand Lake Matagamon** l. U.S.A.
32 A4 **Grand Lake St Marys** l. U.S.A.
33 J1 **Grand Lake Seboeis** l. U.S.A.
33 K2 **Grand Lake Stream** U.S.A.
30 D4 **Grand Ledge** U.S.A.
23 G5 **Grand Manan I.** i. Can.
30 E2 **Grand Marais** MI U.S.A.
30 B2 **Grand Marais** MN U.S.A.
23 F4 **Grand-Mère** Can.
65 B3 **Grândola** Port.
111 G3 **Grand Passage** chan. New Caledonia
30 C2 **Grand Portage** U.S.A.
21 K4 **Grand Rapids** Can.
30 D4 **Grand Rapids** MI U.S.A.
26 E2 **Grand Rapids** MN U.S.A.
111 G3 **Grand Récif de Cook** rf New Caledonia
111 G4 **Grand Récif du Sud** rf New Caledonia
24 E3 **Grand Teton** mt. U.S.A.
24 E3 **Grand Teton Nat. Park** nat. park U.S.A.
30 D3 **Grand Traverse Bay** b. U.S.A.
23 G4 **Grand Vallée** Can.
24 C2 **Grandview** U.S.A.
35 F3 **Grand Wash** r. U.S.A.
35 E4 **Grand Wash Cliffs** cliff U.S.A.
47 B2 **Graneros** Chile
60 D6 **Grange** Rep. of Ireland
24 E3 **Granger** U.S.A.
55 O6 **Grängesberg** Sweden
24 C2 **Grangeville** U.S.A.
20 D3 **Granisle** Can.
26 E2 **Granite Falls** U.S.A.
23 J4 **Granite Lake** l. Can.
35 E4 **Granite Mts** mts U.S.A.
24 E2 **Granite Peak** summit MT U.S.A.
35 F1 **Granite Peak** summit UT U.S.A.
66 E6 **Granitola, Capo** c. Sicily Italy
44 C6 **Gran Laguna Salada** l. Arg.
55 O7 **Gränna** Sweden
66 B2 **Gran Paradiso** mt Italy
62 E7 **Gran Pilastro** mt Austria/Italy
59 G5 **Grantham** U.K.
119 A4 **Grant I.** i. Ant.
34 C2 **Grant, Mt** mt. NV U.S.A.
34 D2 **Grant, Mt** mt. NV U.S.A.
57 E3 **Grantown-on-Spey** U.K.
35 E2 **Grant Range** mts U.S.A.
25 F5 **Grants** U.S.A.
24 B3 **Grants Pass** U.S.A.
64 D2 **Granville** France
30 C5 **Granville** IL U.S.A.
33 G3 **Granville** NY U.S.A.
21 J3 **Granville Lake** l. Can.
46 D2 **Grão Mogol** Brazil
34 C2 **Grapevine** U.S.A.
34 D3 **Grapevine Mts** mts U.S.A.
33 G3 **Graphite** U.S.A.
105 J2 **Graskop** S. Africa
22 D2 **Gras, Lac de** l. Can.
33 F2 **Grass** r. U.S.A.
64 H5 **Grasse** France
21 H4 **Grassrange** U.S.A.
21 J4 **Grass River Prov. Park** res. Can.
34 B2 **Grass Valley** U.S.A.
115 F8 **Grassy** Austr.
29 E7 **Grassy Cr.** r. Bahamas
30 B4 **Gratiot** U.S.A.
65 G1 **Graus** Spain
21 J2 **Gravel Hill Lake** l. Can.
105 J1 **Gravelotte** S. Africa
31 H3 **Gravenhurst** Can.
115 J2 **Gravesend** Austr.
59 H6 **Gravesend** U.K.

66 G4 **Gravina in Puglia** Italy
30 E3 **Grawn** U.S.A.
64 G3 **Gray** France
30 H3 **Gray** U.S.A.
59 H6 **Grays** U.K.
24 A2 **Grays Harbor** in. U.S.A.
24 E3 **Grays L.** l. U.S.A.
23 B5 **Grayson** U.S.A.
62 G7 **Graz** Austria
29 E7 **Great Abaco** i. Bahamas
112 E6 **Great Australian Bight** g. Austr.
59 H6 **Great Baddow** U.K.
37 J3 **Great Bahama Bank** sea feature Bahamas
117 E2 **Great Barrier Island** i. N.Z.
113 J3 **Great Barrier Reef** rf Qld. Austr.
113 J3 **Great Barrier Reef Marine Park (Cairns Section)** nat. park Austr.
113 K4 **Great Barrier Reef Marine Park (Capricorn Section)** nat. park Austr.
113 J3 **Great Barrier Reef Marine Park (Central Section)** nat. park Austr.
113 H2 **Great Barrier Reef Marine Park (Far North Section)** nat. park Austr.
33 G3 **Great Barrington** U.S.A.
25 C4 **Great Basin** basin U.S.A.
35 E2 **Great Basin Nat. Park** nat. park U.S.A.
33 F5 **Great Bay** b. U.S.A.
20 E1 **Great Bear** r. Can.
20 E1 **Great Bear Lake** l. Can.
26 D4 **Great Bend** U.S.A.
104 C6 **Great Berg** r. S. Africa
57 B2 **Great Bernera** i. U.K.
60 A5 **Great Blasket I.** i. Rep. of Ireland
58 D3 **Great Clifton** U.K.
57 D5 **Great Cumbrae** i. U.K.
113 J4 **Great Dividing Range** mts Austr.
58 G3 **Great Driffield** U.K.
31 F3 **Great Duck I.** i. Can.
33 F5 **Great Egg Harbor** in. U.S.A.
37 H4 **Greater Antilles** is Caribbean Sea
37 J4 **Great Exuma** i. Bahamas
24 E2 **Great Falls** U.S.A.
105 G6 **Great Fish** r. S. Africa
105 G6 **Great Fish Point** pt S. Africa
85 F4 **Great Gandak** r. India
29 E7 **Great Guana Cay** i. Bahamas
29 E7 **Great Harbour Cay** i. Bahamas
37 K4 **Great Inagua** i. Bahamas
104 E6 **Great Karoo** plat. S. Africa
105 H6 **Great Kei** r. S. Africa
116 D4 **Great. Keppel I.** i. Austr.
115 G8 **Great Lake** l. Austr.
59 E5 **Great Malvern** U.K.
32 A5 **Great Miami** r. U.S.A.
92 A5 **Great Nicobar** i. Andaman and Nicobar Is
78 C5 **Great Oasis, The** oasis Egypt
59 F4 **Great Ormes Head** hd U.K.
59 H6 **Great Ouse** r. U.K.
116 B2 **Great Palm Islands** is Austr.
33 J4 **Great Peconic Bay** b. U.S.A.
33 H4 **Great Pt** pt U.S.A.
59 D5 **Great Rhos** h. U.K.
102 D4 **Great Ruaha** r. Tanz.
33 F3 **Great Sacandaga L.** l. U.S.A.
66 B2 **Great St Bernard Pass** pass Italy/Switz.
29 E7 **Great Sale Cay** i. Bahamas
24 D3 **Great Salt Lake** l. U.S.A.
24 D3 **Great Salt Lake Desert** des. U.S.A.
101 E2 **Great Sand Sea** des. Egypt/Libya
112 D4 **Great Sandy Desert** des. Austr.
111 H3 **Great Sea Reef** rf Fiji
20 G2 **Great Slave Lake** l. Can.
29 D5 **Great Smoky Mts** mts U.S.A.
29 D5 **Great Smoky Mts Nat. Park** nat. park U.S.A.
20 E3 **Great Snow Mtn** mt. Can.
33 G4 **Great South Bay** b. U.S.A.
59 H7 **Greatstone-on-Sea** U.K.
59 C7 **Great Torrington** U.K.
112 E5 **Great Victoria Desert** des. Austr.
88 F1 **Great Wall** China
59 H6 **Great Waltham** U.K.
33 K2 **Great Wass I.** i. U.S.A.
115 G8 **Great Western Tiers** mts Austr.
58 F3 **Great Whernside** h. U.K.
59 J5 **Great Yarmouth** U.K.
81 J3 **Great Zab** r. Iraq

66 E4 **Greco, Monte** mt Italy
65 D2 **Gredos, Sa de** mts Spain
49 **Greece** country Europe
24 F3 **Greeley** U.S.A.
76 H1 **Greem-Bell, Ostrov** i. Rus. Fed.
28 C4 **Green** r. KY U.S.A.
35 H2 **Green** r. UT/WY U.S.A.
31 H3 **Greenbank** Can.
30 D3 **Green Bay** b. U.S.A.
30 C3 **Green Bay** U.S.A.
115 J6 **Green C.** hd Austr.
60 E3 **Greencastle** U.K.
29 E7 **Green Cay** i. Bahamas
29 D6 **Green Cove Springs** U.S.A.
30 A4 **Greene** IA U.S.A.
33 F3 **Greene** NY U.S.A.
29 D4 **Greeneville** U.S.A.
34 B3 **Greenfield** CA U.S.A.
30 E6 **Greenfield** IN U.S.A.
33 G3 **Greenfield** MA U.S.A.
32 B5 **Greenfield** OH U.S.A.
30 C4 **Greenfield** WV U.S.A.
116 B1 **Green I.** i. Austr.
94 A4 **Green Island Bay** b. Phil.
21 H4 **Green Lake** Can.
30 C4 **Green Lake** l. U.S.A.
16 **Greenland** country North America
12 J1 **Greenland Basin** sea feature Arctic Ocean
118 B4 **Greenland Sea** sea Greenland/Svalbard
57 F5 **Greenlaw** U.K.
114 A5 **Greenly Island** i. Austr.
33 G2 **Green Mountains** mts U.S.A.
57 D5 **Greenock** U.K.
60 D5 **Greenore** Rep. of Ireland
33 G4 **Greenport** U.S.A.
25 E3 **Green River** UT U.S.A.
24 E3 **Green River** WY U.S.A.
29 E4 **Greensboro** U.S.A.
28 C4 **Greensburg** IN U.S.A.
27 D4 **Greensburg** KS U.S.A.
32 D4 **Greensburg** PA U.S.A.
57 C3 **Greenstone Point** pt U.K.
32 B5 **Greenup** U.S.A.
116 A2 **Greenvale** Austr.
33 F3 **Green Valley** Can.
35 G6 **Green Valley** U.S.A.
30 C5 **Greenview** U.S.A.
100 B4 **Greenville** Liberia
29 C6 **Greenville** AL U.S.A.
34 B1 **Greenville** CA U.S.A.
29 D6 **Greenville** FL U.S.A.
33 J2 **Greenville** ME U.S.A.
30 E4 **Greenville** MI U.S.A.
27 F5 **Greenville** MS U.S.A.
29 E5 **Greenville** NC U.S.A.
33 H3 **Greenville** NH U.S.A.
32 A4 **Greenville** OH U.S.A.
29 D5 **Greenville** PA U.S.A.
29 D5 **Greenville** SC U.S.A.
27 D5 **Greenville** TX U.S.A.
21 J4 **Greenwater Provincial Park** res. Can.
115 J5 **Greenwell Point** Austr.
33 G4 **Greenwich** CT U.S.A.
33 G3 **Greenwich** NY U.S.A.
35 G2 **Greenwich** UT U.S.A.
27 F5 **Greenwood** MS U.S.A.
29 D5 **Greenwood** SC U.S.A.
27 E5 **Greers Ferry Lake** l. U.S.A.
26 D3 **Gregory** U.S.A.
113 G3 **Gregory Downs** Austr.
114 C2 **Gregory, L.** salt flat Austr.
112 E4 **Gregory Lake** salt flat Austr.
112 F3 **Gregory National Park** nat. park Austr.
113 H3 **Gregory Range** h. Austr.
24 B2 **Gresham** U.S.A.
80 E4 **Greko, Cape** c. Cyprus
55 M8 **Grenå** Denmark
16 **Grenada** country Caribbean Sea
27 F5 **Grenada** U.S.A.
64 E5 **Grenade** France
55 M8 **Grenen** spit Denmark
115 H4 **Grenfell** Austr.
21 J4 **Grenfell** Can.
64 G4 **Grenoble** France
45 J4 **Grenville** Grenada
113 H2 **Grenville, C.** hd Austr.
24 B2 **Gresham** U.S.A.
92 **Gresik** Indon.
58 F3 **Greta** r. U.K.
57 E6 **Gretna** U.K.
59 F5 **Gretna** U.K.
61 B3 **Grevelingen** chan. Neth.
61 F2 **Greven** Ger.
61 D3 **Grevena** Greece
61 D3 **Grevenbicht** Neth.
61 E3 **Grevenbroich** Ger.
62 E4 **Grevesmühlen** Ger.
117 C5 **Grey** r. N.Z.
24 E2 **Greybull** U.S.A.
20 B2 **Grey Hunter Pk** summit Can.
23 J3 **Grey Is** is Can.
117 C5 **Greymouth** N.Z.
114 E2 **Grey Range** h. Austr.
105 J4 **Greytown** S. Africa
45 J4 **Grez-Doiceau** Belgium
69 G5 **Gribanovskiy** Rus. Fed.
58 F3 **Gridley** CA U.S.A.
34 B2 **Gridley** CA U.S.A.
30 C5 **Gridley** IL U.S.A.
29 C5 **Griffin** U.S.A.

115 G5 **Griffith** Austr.
31 J3 **Griffith** Can.
115 F8 **Grim, C.** c. Austr.
62 F3 **Grimmen** Ger.
31 H4 **Grimsby** Can.
58 G4 **Grimsby** U.K.
54 E3 **Grímsey** i. Iceland
20 F3 **Grimshaw** Can.
54 E4 **Grímsstaðir** Iceland
55 L7 **Grimstad** Norway
54 B5 **Grindavík** Iceland
55 L9 **Grindsted** Denmark
67 N2 **Grindul Chituc** spit Romania
26 E3 **Grinnell** U.S.A.
105 H5 **Griqualand East** reg. S. Africa
104 E4 **Griqualand West** reg. S. Africa
104 E4 **Griquatown** S. Africa
59 J7 **Gris Nez, Cap** pt France
57 F2 **Gritley** U.K.
66 G2 **Grmeč** mts Bos.-Herz.
61 C3 **Grobbendonk** Belgium
105 H2 **Groblersdal** S. Africa
104 E4 **Groblershoop** S. Africa
**Grodno** see **Hrodna**
104 E3 **Groen** watercourse Northern Cape S. Africa
104 E5 **Groen** watercourse Northern Cape S. Africa
64 C3 **Groix, Île de** i. France
66 D6 **Grombalia** Tunisia
61 F2 **Gronau** Ger.
54 N4 **Grong** Norway
61 E1 **Groningen** Neth.
61 E1 **Groninger Wad** tidal flats Neth.
35 E3 **Groom L.** l. U.S.A.
104 D3 **Groot-Aar Pan** salt pan S. Africa
104 E7 **Groot Brakrivier** S. Africa
105 H3 **Grootdraaidam** dam S. Africa
104 D4 **Grootdrink** S. Africa
113 G2 **Groote Eylandt** i. Austr.
61 D3 **Groote Peel, Nationaal Park De** nat. park Neth.
103 B5 **Grootfontein** Namibia
104 C3 **Groot Karas Berg** plat. Namibia
105 J2 **Groot Letaba** r. S. Africa
105 G2 **Groot Marico** S. Africa
104 D6 **Groot Swartberg** mts S. Africa
104 D4 **Grootvloer** salt pan S. Africa
105 G6 **Groot Winterberg** mt S. Africa
30 E3 **Gros Cap** U.S.A.
23 J4 **Gros Morne Nat. Pk** nat. park Can.
62 G7 **Grosser Speikkogel** mt Austria
61 F1 **Grosses Meer** l. Ger.
66 D3 **Grosseto** Italy
62 D6 **Groß-Gerau** Ger.
66 E1 **Großglockner** mt Austria
104 C1 **Gross Ums** Namibia
24 E3 **Gros Ventre Range** mts U.S.A.
23 J3 **Groswater Bay** b. Can.
33 E3 **Groton** U.S.A.
61 D4 **Grotte de Han** cave Belgium
32 D5 **Grottoes** U.S.A.
20 F3 **Grouard** Can.
22 D4 **Groundhog** r. Can.
32 C4 **Grove City** U.S.A.
29 C6 **Grove Hill** U.S.A.
34 B3 **Groveland** U.S.A.
119 D5 **Grove Mts** mts Ant.
34 B4 **Grover Beach** U.S.A.
33 H2 **Groveton** U.S.A.
35 F5 **Growler** U.S.A.
35 F5 **Growler Mts** mts U.S.A.
69 H7 **Groznyy** Rus. Fed.
67 M3 **Grudovo** Bulg.
63 J4 **Grudziądz** Pol.
57 C3 **Gruinard Bay** b. U.K.
103 B6 **Grünau** Namibia
54 B4 **Grundarfjörður** Iceland
32 B6 **Grundy** U.S.A.
30 A4 **Grundy Center** U.S.A.
69 F4 **Gryazi** Rus. Fed.
68 G3 **Gryazovets** Rus. Fed.
62 G4 **Gryfice** Pol.
62 G4 **Gryfino** Pol.
62 G5 **Gryfów Śląski** Pol.
54 P2 **Gryllefjord** Norway
44 **Grytviken** S. Georgia Atlantic Ocean
85 E4 **Gua** India
37 J4 **Guacanayabo, Golfo de** b. Cuba
45 D2 **Guacara** Venez.
45 C4 **Guachara** r. Col.
65 D4 **Guadajoz** r. Spain
36 D4 **Guadalajara** Mex.
65 E2 **Guadalajara** Spain
65 E2 **Guadalaviar** r. Spain
111 G2 **Guadalcanal** i. Solomon Is
65 C4 **Guadalete** r. Spain
65 F2 **Guadalope** r. Spain
65 D4 **Guadalquivir** r. Spain
27 D6 **Guadalupe** r. U.S.A.
34 B4 **Guadalupe** U.S.A.
27 B6 **Guadalupe Mts Nat. Park** nat. park U.S.A.
27 B6 **Guadalupe Pk** mt. U.S.A.
65 D3 **Guadalupe, Sierra de** mts Spain

65 D2 Guadarrama, Sierra de mts Spain
37 M5 Guadeloupe terr. Caribbean
47 C2 Guadel, Sa de mts Arg.
65 C4 Guadiana r. Port./Spain
65 E4 Guadix Spain
44 B6 Guafo, I. i. Chile
45 D4 Guainía r. Col./Venez.
45 E3 Guaiquinima, Cerro mt Venez.
46 A4 Guaíra Brazil
44 B6 Guaitecas, Islas is Chile
45 C1 Guajira, Península de pen. Col.
42 C4 Gualaceo Ecuador
34 A2 Gualala U.S.A.
47 E2 Gualeguay r. Arg.
47 E2 Gualeguay Arg.
47 E2 Gualeguaychu Arg.
84 B4 Gualjaina Arg.
93 L4 Guam terr. Pac. Oc.
46 A4 Guamblin, I. i. Chile
47 D3 Guamini Arg.
45 A4 Guamués r. Col.
95 B4 Gua Musang Malaysia
47 D3 Guanaco, Co h. Arg.
36 D4 Guanajuato Mex.
46 D1 Guanambi Brazil
45 D4 Guaname r. Venez.
45 C2 Guanare Venez.
45 D2 Guanare r. Venez.
45 C2 Guanarito Venez.
45 C2 Guanarito r. Venez.
45 D3 Guanay, Sierra mts Venez.
88 D2 Guandi Shan mt China
37 H4 Guane Cuba
89 C4 Guang'an China
89 D6 Guangdong div. China
89 F4 Guangfeng China
89 D6 Guanghai China
88 B4 Guanghan China
89 E5 Guanghang China
89 B3 Guanghe China
89 E4 Guangji China
88 E2 Guangling China
89 B5 Guangnan China
89 D6 Guangning China
89 F2 Guangrao China
88 E4 Guangshan China
88 D4 Guangshui China
89 C6 Guangxi div. China
88 B3 Guangyuan China
89 E5 Guangze China
89 D6 Guangzhou China
46 D2 Guanhães r. Brazil
46 D2 Guanhães Brazil
45 E2 Guanipa r. Venez.
89 B5 Guanling China
88 C4 Guanmian Shan mts China
88 D3 Guanpo China
45 D2 Guanta Venez.
37 J4 Guantánamo Cuba
88 E1 Guanting Sk. resr China
88 B4 Guan Xian China
89 D5 Guanyang China
88 F3 Guanyun China
44 A4 Guapi Col.
42 F6 Guaporé r. Bol./Brazil
42 E7 Guaqui Bol.
46 D1 Guará r. Brazil
43 L5 Guarabira Brazil
46 E3 Guarapari Brazil
46 B4 Guarapuava Brazil
46 C4 Guaraqueçaba Brazil
46 D3 Guaratinguetá Brazil
46 C4 Guaratuba, Baía de b. Brazil
65 C2 Guarda Port.
46 C2 Guarda Mor Brazil
65 D1 Guardo Spain
45 D2 Guárico r. Venez.
45 C3 Guarrojo r. Col.
46 C4 Guarujá Brazil
45 D4 Guasacavi r. Venez.
45 C4 Guasacavi, Cerro h. Col.
45 B2 Guasare r. Venez.
36 C3 Guasave Mex.
45 C3 Guasdualito Venez.
45 E3 Guasipati Venez.
46 B4 Guassú r. Brazil
16 Guatemala country Central America
36 F6 Guatemala Guatemala
45 D2 Guatope, Parque Nacional nat. park Venez.
47 C4 Guatrache Arg.
45 C4 Guaviare r. Col.
46 C3 Guaxupé Brazil
45 B4 Guayabero r. Col.
45 D3 Guayapo r. Venez.
42 C4 Guayaquil Ecuador
42 B4 Guayaquil, Golfo de g. Ecuador
42 E6 Guayaramerín Bol.
36 B3 Guaymas Mex.
102 D2 Guba Eth.
66 E3 Gubbio Italy
69 F5 Gubkin Rus. Fed.
88 D3 Gucheng China
69 G7 Gudaut'a Georgia
55 M6 Gudbrandsdalen v. Norway
84 B3 Guddu Barrage barrage Pak.
69 H7 Gudermes Rus. Fed.
83 F7 Gudivada India
80 D1 Güdül Turkey
83 E8 Gudur India
55 K6 Gudvangen Norway

100 A4 Guéckédou Guinea
31 J1 Guéguen, Lac l. Can.
45 B4 Güejar r. Col.
100 C1 Guelma Alg.
100 A2 Guelmine Morocco
31 G4 Guelph Can.
45 D2 Güera r. Venez.
23 G2 Guerard, Lac l. Can.
64 E3 Guéret France
56 E7 Guernsey i. U.K.
24 F3 Guernsey U.S.A.
36 B3 Guerrero Negro Mex.
12 F5 Guiana Basin sea feature Atlantic Ocean
114 C6 Guichen B. b. Austr.
89 E4 Guichi China
47 F2 Guichón Uru.
88 A3 Guide China
88 E3 Guide China
101 D4 Guider Cameroon
89 C5 Guiding China
66 E4 Guidonia-Montecelio Italy
100 B4 Guiglo Côte d'Ivoire
105 K2 Guija Moz.
89 D6 Gui Jiang r. China
89 F4 Guiji Shan mts China
59 G6 Guildford U.K.
33 J2 Guilford U.S.A.
89 D5 Guilin China
22 E2 Guillaume-Delisle, Lac l. Can.
65 B2 Guimarães Port.
94 B4 Guimaras Str. chan. Phil.
88 E3 Guimeng Ding mt China
88 A3 Guinan China
34 A2 Guinda U.S.A.
94 C4 Guindulman Phil.
96 Guinea country Africa
12 J5 Guinea Basin sea feature Atlantic Ocean
96 Guinea-Bissau country Africa
98 Guinea, Gulf of g. Africa
37 H4 Güines Cuba
64 C2 Guingamp France
64 B2 Guipavas France
89 D6 Guiping China
46 B2 Guiratinga Brazil
45 E2 Güiria Venez.
61 B5 Guise France
94 C4 Guiuan Phil.
89 C6 Gui Xian China
89 C5 Guiyang Guizhou China
89 D5 Guiyang Hunan China
89 C5 Guizhou div. China
84 B5 Gujarat div. India
84 C2 Gujar Khan Pak.
84 C2 Gujranwala Pak.
84 C2 Gujrat Pak.
35 G5 Gu Komelik U.S.A.
69 F5 Gukovo Rus. Fed.
81 K3 Gük Tappeh Iran
84 D2 Gulabgarh Jammu and Kashmir
88 B2 Gulang China
115 H3 Gulargambone Austr.
83 E7 Gulbarga India
55 U8 Gulbene Latvia
79 L1 Gülchö Kyrgyzstan
80 E3 Gülek Turkey
27 F6 Gulfport U.S.A.
79 G4 Gulf, The g. Asia
74 Gulf, The g. Asia
115 H4 Gulgong Austr.
87 M1 Gulian China
89 B5 Gulin China
79 K1 Gulistan Uzbek.
30 E2 Gull I. i. U.S.A.
21 H4 Gull Lake Can.
54 R3 Gullträsk Sweden
80 D3 Gülnar Turkey
69 G7 Gulrip'shi Georgia
80 E2 Gülşehir Turkey
102 D3 Gulu Uganda
116 D6 Guluguba Austr.
84 B3 Gumal r. Pak.
103 C5 Gumare Botswana
79 G2 Gumdag Turkm.
85 F5 Gumia India
85 F5 Gumla India
61 F3 Gummersbach Ger.
80 E1 Gümüşhacıköy Turkey
81 G1 Gümüşhane Turkey
84 D4 Guna India
115 F5 Gunbar Austr.
115 H5 Gundagai Austr.
80 D3 Gündoğmuş Turkey
80 B2 Güney Turkey
102 B4 Gungu Zaire
69 H7 Gunib Rus. Fed.
21 K4 Gunisao r. Can.
91 G5 Gunma div. Japan
116 A1 Gunnawarra Austr.
115 J3 Gunnedah Austr.
115 H5 Gunning Austr.
25 C4 Gunnison CO U.S.A.
35 G2 Gunnison UT U.S.A.
25 E4 Gunnison r. U.S.A.
83 E7 Guntakal India
29 C5 Guntersville U.S.A.
29 C5 Guntersville L. l. U.S.A.
83 F7 Guntur India
113 G3 Gununa Austr.
92 B6 Gunungsitoli Indon.
95 A5 Gunungtua Indon.
62 E6 Günzburg Ger.
88 E1 Guojiatun China
88 E3 Guoyang China
88 D1 Gurban Hudag China
88 D1 Gurban Obo China
80 B2 Güre Turkey
84 D3 Gurgaon India
43 K5 Gurgueia r. Brazil

84 B4 Gurha India
45 E3 Guri, Embalse de resr Venez.
112 F2 Gurig National Park nat. park Austr.
46 C2 Gurinhatã Brazil
69 H7 Gurjaani Georgia
81 J2 Gürpınar Turkey
43 J4 Gurupi r. Brazil
84 C4 Guru Sikhar mt India
68 B4 Gur'yevsk Rus. Fed.
100 C3 Gusau Nigeria
68 B4 Gusev Rus. Fed.
88 G2 Gushan China
35 H1 Gusher U.S.A.
79 H2 Gushgy Turkm.
88 E3 Gushi China
94 A5 Gusi Malaysia
77 M2 Gusikha Rus. Fed.
68 D4 Gusino Rus. Fed.
86 J1 Gusinoozersk Rus. Fed.
85 F5 Guskara India
68 G4 Gus'-Khrustal'nyy Rus. Fed.
66 C5 Guspini Sardinia Italy
20 B3 Gustavus U.S.A.
34 B3 Gustine U.S.A.
62 F4 Güstrow Ger.
85 H3 Gutang China
62 D5 Gütersloh Ger.
35 H4 Guthrie AZ U.S.A.
89 E5 Guthrie KY U.S.A.
27 D5 Guthrie OK U.S.A.
27 C5 Guthrie TX U.S.A.
89 E5 Gutian Fujian China
89 F5 Gutian Fujian China
61 E5 Gutland reg. Ger./Lux.
85 F3 Gutsuo China
30 B4 Guttenberg U.S.A.
103 D6 Gutu Zimbabwe
85 G4 Guwahati India
81 J3 Guwēr Iraq
38 Guyana country S. America
88 D3 Guyang China
27 C4 Guymon U.S.A.
88 E1 Guyuan Hebei China
88 D3 Guyuan Ningxia China
79 K2 Guzar Uzbek.
89 C4 Guzhang China
88 E3 Guzhen China
63 K3 Gvardeysk Rus. Fed.
115 H3 Gwabegar Austr.
79 J4 Gwadar Pak.
84 D4 Gwalior India
116 C5 Gwambegwine Austr.
103 C6 Gwanda Zimbabwe
60 C3 Gweebarra Bay b. Rep. of Ireland
60 C2 Gweedore Rep. of Ireland
103 C5 Gweru Zimbabwe
30 D2 Gwinn U.S.A.
101 D3 Gwoza Nigeria
115 H2 Gwydir r. Austr.
85 H3 Gyaca China
88 B3 Gyagartang China
85 F3 Gyangnang China
85 G3 Gyangzê China
85 G3 Gyaring Co l. China
82 J4 Gyaring Hu l. China
67 L6 Gyaros i. Greece
85 H3 Gyarubtang China
76 J2 Gydanskiy Poluostrov pen. Rus. Fed.
85 H3 Gyimda China
85 F3 Gyirong Xizang Zizhiqu China
85 F3 Gyirong Xizang Zizhiqu China
85 H2 Gyiza China
116 E6 Gympie Austr.
63 J7 Gyöngyös Hungary
62 H7 Győr Hungary
21 K4 Gypsumville Can.
23 G2 Gyrfalcon Is i. Can.
67 K6 Gytheio Greece
63 K7 Gyula Hungary
81 J1 Gyumri Armenia
79 H2 Gyzylarbat Turkm.

# H

91 G6 Hachiōji Japan
91 G3 Hachiryū Japan
80 E2 Hacıbektaş Turkey
81 H2 Hacıömer Turkey
114 C3 Hack, Mt mt Austr.
103 D6 Hacufera Moz.
91 G6 Hadano Japan
57 F5 Haddington U.K.
83 D10 Haddunmahti Atoll atoll Maldives
100 D3 Hadejia Nigeria
80 E5 Hadera Israel
55 L9 Haderslev Denmark
80 D3 Hadim Turkey
59 H5 Hadleigh U.K.
80 F6 Hadraj, Wādī watercourse S. Arabia
55 M8 Hadsund Denmark
69 D5 Hadyach Ukr.
47 F1 Haedo, Cuchilla de h. Uru.
87 N4 Haeju N. Korea
87 N4 Haeju-man b. N. Korea
105 H1 Haenertsburg S. Africa
21 H4 Hafford Can.
80 F2 Hafik Turkey
84 C2 Hafizabad Pak.
85 H4 Haflong India
54 C4 Hafnarfjörður Iceland
54 C4 Hafursfjörður b. Iceland
31 G2 Hagar Can.
102 D2 Hagar Nish Plateau plat. Eritrea
61 C4 Hageland reg. Belgium
62 C5 Hagen Ger.
110 E2 Hagen, Mount mt P.N.G.
32 E5 Hagerstown U.S.A.
64 D5 Hagetmau France
55 N6 Hagfors Sweden
90 C6 Hagi Japan
89 B6 Ha Giang Vietnam
91 F6 Hagiwara Japan
59 E5 Hagley U.K.
60 B5 Hag's Head hd Rep. of Ireland
21 H4 Hague Can.
64 D2 Hague, Cap de la pt France
64 H2 Haguenau France
88 E2 Hai r. China
102 D4 Hai Tanz.
88 F3 Hai'an China
104 B4 Haib watercourse Namibia
88 G1 Haicheng China
89 C6 Hai Duong Vietnam
80 E5 Haifa Israel
80 E5 Haifa, Bay of b. Israel
89 E6 Haifeng China
89 D6 Haikang China
89 D6 Haikou China
78 E4 Ha'il S. Arabia
87 L2 Hailar China
31 H2 Haileybury Can.
87 N3 Hailong China
59 H7 Hailsham U.K.
54 T4 Hailuoto Fin.
88 F4 Haimen China
89 D7 Hainan i. China
89 C7 Hainan div. China
20 B3 Haines U.S.A.
20 D3 Haines Junction Can.
89 C6 Hai Phong Vietnam
88 A2 Hairag China
88 B1 Hairhan Namag China
89 F5 Haitan Dao i. China
16 Haiti country Caribbean Sea
89 C7 Haitou China
35 G5 Haivana Nakya U.S.A.
34 D3 Haiwee Reservoir U.S.A.
88 E2 Haixing China
101 F3 Haiya Sudan
88 A2 Haiyan Qinghai China
89 F4 Haiyan Zhejiang China
88 F2 Haiyang China
88 B2 Haiyuan China
88 B3 Haizhou Wan b. China
63 K7 Hajdúböszörmény Hungary
66 C7 Hajeb El Ayoun Tunisia
79 L4 Hajhir mt Yemen
91 G4 Hajiki-zaki pt Japan
85 F4 Hajipur India
79 H6 Hajmah Oman
85 H5 Haka Myanmar
34 □2 Hakalau U.S.A.
47 C4 Hakelhuincul, Altiplanicie de plat. Arg.
Hakha see Haka
81 J3 Hakkâri Turkey
54 R3 Hakkas Sweden
91 F6 Hakken-zan mt. Japan
90 J1 Hako-dake mt. Japan
91 F5 Hakodate Japan
104 B1 Hakos Mts mts Namibia
104 D3 Hakseen Pan salt pan S. Africa
91 F5 Hakui Japan
91 F5 Haku-san volc. Japan
91 F5 Haku-san National Park nat. park Japan
84 B4 Hala Pak.
80 E5 Halab Syria
81 K4 Halabja Iraq
101 F2 Halaib Sudan
79 H6 Halāniyāt, Juzur al is Oman
34 □2 Halawa U.S.A.
80 F4 Halba Lebanon
86 G2 Halban Mongolia
62 E5 Halberstadt Ger.
94 B3 Halcon, Mt mt Phil.
54 □ Haldarsvik Faroe Is

55 M7 Halden Norway
62 E4 Haldensleben Ger.
85 G5 Haldi r. India
85 G5 Haldia India
85 G5 Haldibari India
84 D3 Haldwani India
31 F3 Hale U.S.A.
81 G4 Halebiye Syria
34 □1 Haleiwa U.S.A.
59 E5 Halesowen U.K.
59 J5 Halesworth U.K.
80 E5 Halfeti Turkey
117 B7 Halfmoon Bay N.Z.
20 E3 Halfway Rep. of Ireland
60 C6 Halfway Rep. of Ireland
61 C2 Halfweg Neth.
85 E4 Halia India
31 H3 Haliburton Can.
116 B2 Halifax Austr.
23 H5 Halifax Can.
58 F4 Halifax U.K.
32 D6 Halifax U.S.A.
116 B2 Halifax Bay b. Austr.
116 B2 Halifax, Mt mt Austr.
57 E2 Halkirk U.K.
54 P5 Hälla Sweden
114 A5 Hall Bay b. Austr.
61 C4 Halle Belgium
62 E5 Halle Ger.
55 O7 Hällefors Sweden
62 F7 Hallein Austria
108 Hall Islands is. Micronesia
54 Q4 Hällnäs Sweden
26 D1 Hallock U.S.A.
55 O7 Hallsberg Sweden
112 E3 Halls Creek Austr.
31 H3 Halls Lake Can.
54 O5 Hallviken Sweden
93 H6 Halmahera i. Indon.
55 N8 Halmstad Sweden
84 C5 Halol India
55 M8 Hals Denmark
54 T5 Halsua Fin.
61 F3 Haltern Ger.
58 E3 Haltwhistle U.K.
116 D6 Haly, Mount h. Austr.
61 B5 Ham France
90 C6 Hamada Japan
100 B2 Hamâda El Haricha des. Mali
81 M4 Hamadān Iran
100 B2 Hamada Tounassine des. Alg.
80 F4 Ḥamāh Syria
91 F6 Hamakita Japan
90 H2 Hamamasu Japan
91 F6 Hamamatsu Japan
90 K2 Hamanaka-wan b. Japan
91 F6 Hamana-ko l. Japan
55 M6 Hamar Norway
54 O2 Hamarøy Norway
78 C5 Ḥamâta, Gebel mt Egypt
90 J1 Hamatonbetsu Japan
83 F9 Hambantota Sri Lanka
58 F3 Hambleton Hills h. U.K.
62 D4 Hamburg Ger.
105 G6 Hamburg S. Africa
27 F5 Hamburg AR U.S.A.
32 D3 Hamburg NY U.S.A.
33 F4 Hamburg PA U.S.A.
33 G4 Hamden U.S.A.
54 T6 Hämeenlinna Fin.
62 D4 Hameln Ger.
112 C4 Hamersley Range mts Austr.
112 C4 Hamersley Range National Park nat. park Austr.
87 N4 Hamhŭng N. Korea
82 H2 Hami China
81 M6 Ḥamīd Iran
101 D3 Ḥamīd Sudan
114 E6 Hamilton Austr.
37 M2 Hamilton Bermuda
31 H4 Hamilton Can.
117 E2 Hamilton N.Z.
57 D5 Hamilton U.K.
29 C5 Hamilton AL U.S.A.
30 B5 Hamilton IL U.S.A.
24 D2 Hamilton MT U.S.A.
33 F3 Hamilton NY U.S.A.
32 A5 Hamilton OH U.S.A.
34 A2 Hamilton City U.S.A.
34 B3 Hamilton, Mt mt. CA U.S.A.
35 E2 Hamilton, Mt mt. NV U.S.A.
55 U6 Hamina Fin.
84 D3 Hamirpur India
81 H6 Ḥamīr, W. watercourse S. Arabia
23 J3 Hamiton Inlet in. Can.
114 C5 Hamley Bridge Austr.
30 D3 Hamlin Lake l. U.S.A.
62 C5 Hamm Ger.
100 B2 Hammada du Drâa plat. Alg.
81 J3 Hammam Ali Iraq
66 D6 Hammamet Tunisia
101 D1 Hammamet, Golfe de b. Tunisia
81 L6 Ḥammār, Hawr al l. Iraq
54 P5 Hammarstrand Sweden
54 O5 Hammerdal Sweden
54 S1 Hammerfest Norway
61 E3 Hamminkeln Ger.
114 C4 Hammond Austr.
30 D5 Hammond IN U.S.A.
27 F6 Hammond LA U.S.A.
24 E2 Hammond MT U.S.A.
31 F2 Hammond Bay b. U.S.A.
32 E3 Hammondsport U.S.A.

33 F5 Hammonton U.S.A.
79 J4 Hamni Mashkel salt flat Pak.
117 C6 Hampden N.Z.
59 F6 Hampshire Downs h. U.K.
23 G4 Hampton Can.
27 E5 Hampton AR U.S.A.
33 H3 Hampton NH U.S.A.
33 E6 Hampton VA U.S.A.
81 K4 Hamrîn, Jabal h. Iraq
95 Ham Tân Vietnam
84 D2 Hamta Pass pass India
79 H4 Hāmūn-e Jaz Mūriān salt marsh Iran
79 K4 Hamun-i-Lora l. Pak.
81 J2 Hamur Turkey
34 □2 Hana U.S.A.
104 E1 Hanahai watercourse Botswana/Namibia
34 □2 Hanalei U.S.A.
91 H4 Hanamaki Japan
88 D3 Hancheng China
32 D5 Hancock MD U.S.A.
30 C2 Hancock MI U.S.A.
33 F4 Hancock NY U.S.A.
57 C2 Handa Island i. U.K.
88 E2 Handan China
102 D4 Handeni Tanz.
34 □3 Hanford U.S.A.
86 G2 Hangayn Nuruu mts Mongolia
88 C1 Hanggin Houqi China
88 C2 Hanggin Qi China
88 E2 Hangu China
84 B2 Hangu Pak.
89 D5 Hanguang China
89 F4 Hangzhou China
89 F4 Hangzhou Wan b. China
81 H2 Hani Turkey
88 H2 Hanjiaoshui China
104 F6 Hankey S. Africa
55 S7 Hanko Fin.
35 G2 Hanksville U.S.A.
84 D2 Hanle Jammu and Kashmir
117 D5 Hanmer Springs N.Z.
21 G4 Hanna Can.
22 D3 Hannah Bay b. Can.
30 B6 Hannibal U.S.A.
62 D2 Hannover Ger.
55 O9 Hanöbukten b. Sweden
89 B6 Ha Nôi Vietnam
31 H3 Hanover Can.
104 F5 Hanover S. Africa
33 H3 Hanover NH U.S.A.
32 E5 Hanover PA U.S.A.
119 D4 Hansen Mts mts Ant.
89 D4 Hanshou China
88 E4 Han Shui r. China
84 D3 Hansi India
54 Q2 Hansnes Norway
114 B3 Hanson, L. salt flat Austr.
32 B6 Hansonville U.S.A.
55 L8 Hanstholm Denmark
68 C4 Hantsavichy Belarus
84 C3 Hanumangarh India
115 G5 Hanwood Austr.
89 E4 Hanyang China
88 C3 Hanyin China
89 B4 Hanyuan China
88 C3 Hanzhong China
109 Hao atoll Tuamotu Is Pac. Oc.
85 G5 Haora India
54 T4 Haparanda Sweden
85 H4 Hapoli India
23 H3 Happy Valley-Goose Bay Can.
84 D3 Hapur India
78 C4 Ḥaql S. Arabia
68 D4 Haradok Belarus
91 H5 Haramachi Japan
84 C2 Haramukh mt India
84 C2 Harappa Road Pak.
103 D5 Harare Zimbabwe
87 J2 Har-Ayrag Mongolia
100 A4 Harbel Liberia
87 N2 Harbin China
31 F4 Harbor Beach U.S.A.
30 E3 Harbor Springs U.S.A.
23 J4 Harbour Breton Can.
44 E8 Harbours, B. of b. Falkland Is
35 H3 Harcuvar Mts mts U.S.A.
84 D5 Harda Khās India
55 K6 Hardangervidda plat. Norway
55 K6 Hardangervidda Nasjonalpark nat. park Norway
104 B2 Hardap div. Namibia
104 B2 Hardap Dam dam Namibia
61 E1 Hardenberg Neth.
61 D2 Harderwijk Neth.
104 C5 Hardeveld mts S. Africa
24 F2 Hardin U.S.A.
105 H3 Harding S. Africa
21 H5 Hardisty Can.
20 F2 Hardisty Lake l. Can.
84 E4 Hardoi India
33 G2 Hardwick U.S.A.
114 B5 Hardwicke B. b. Austr.
27 C4 Hardy U.S.A.
30 E4 Hardy Reservoir resr U.S.A.
80 D6 Hareidîn, W. watercourse Egypt
61 D2 Haren (Ems) Ger.
102 E3 Härer Eth.
33 F4 Harford U.S.A.
102 E3 Hargeysa Somalia

63 M7 Harghita-Mădăraş, Vârful mt Romania
81 H2 Harhal D. mts Turkey
88 C2 Harhatan China
82 J3 Har Hu l. China
84 D3 Haridwar India
117 C5 Harihari N.Z.
90 E6 Harima-nada b. Japan
85 G5 Haringhat r. Bangl.
61 C3 Haringvliet est. Neth.
79 L3 Haripur Pak.
55 S6 Harjavalta Fin.
26 E3 Harlan IA U.S.A.
32 B6 Harlan KY U.S.A.
59 C5 Harlech U.K.
24 E1 Harlem U.S.A.
59 J5 Harleston U.K.
61 D1 Harlingen Neth.
27 D7 Harlingen U.S.A.
59 H6 Harlow U.K.
24 E2 Harlowtown U.S.A.
33 J2 Harmony ME U.S.A.
30 A4 Harmony MN U.S.A.
84 A3 Harnai Pak.
24 B3 Harney Basin basin U.S.A.
24 C3 Harney L. l. U.S.A.
55 P5 Härnösand Sweden
87 M2 Har Nur China
86 F2 Har Nuur l. Mongolia
57 □ Haroldswick U.K.
100 B4 Harper Liberia
34 D4 Harper Lake l. U.S.A.
32 E5 Harpers Ferry U.S.A.
23 H2 Harp Lake l. Can.
81 G2 Harput Turkey
88 F1 Harqin China
88 F1 Harqin Qi China
35 F5 Harquahala Mts mts U.S.A.
81 G3 Harran Turkey
80 F5 Harrat er Rujeila lava Jordan
22 H3 Harricana r. Can.
29 C5 Harriman U.S.A.
33 G3 Harriman Reservoir resr U.S.A.
115 K3 Harrington Austr.
33 F5 Harrington U.S.A.
23 J3 Harrington Harbour Can.
57 B3 Harris U.K.
28 B4 Harrisburg IL U.S.A.
32 E4 Harrisburg PA U.S.A.
114 A3 Harris, Lake salt flat Austr.
105 H4 Harrismith S. Africa
27 E4 Harrison AR U.S.A.
30 E3 Harrison MI U.S.A.
32 D5 Harrisonburg U.S.A.
23 J3 Harrison, Cape c. Can.
20 E5 Harrison L. l. Can.
26 E4 Harrisonville U.S.A.
57 A3 Harris, Sound of chan. U.K.
31 K3 Harrisville MI U.S.A.
33 F2 Harrisville NY U.S.A.
32 C5 Harrisville WV U.S.A.
58 F4 Harrogate U.K.
81 L4 Harsin Iran
80 G1 Harşit r. Turkey
67 M2 Hârşova Romania
54 P2 Harstad Norway
30 D4 Hart U.S.A.
88 G1 Hartao China
104 D4 Hartbees watercourse S. Africa
62 G7 Hartberg Austria
55 K6 Harteigan mt Norway
57 E5 Hart Fell h. U.K.
33 G4 Hartford CT U.S.A.
30 D4 Hartford MI U.S.A.
26 D3 Hartford SD U.S.A.
30 C4 Hartford WV U.S.A.
20 E3 Hart Highway Can.
114 B3 Hart, L. salt flat Austr.
23 G4 Hartland Can.
59 C7 Hartland U.K.
33 J2 Hartland U.S.A.
59 C6 Hartland Point pt U.K.
58 F3 Hartlepool U.K.
27 C5 Hartley U.S.A.
20 D4 Hartley Bay Can.
55 U6 Hartola Fin.
20 E4 Hart Ranges mts Can.
62 E6 Härtsfeld h. Ger.
104 F3 Hartswater S. Africa
29 D5 Hartwell Res. resr U.S.A.
86 F2 Har Us Nuur l. Mongolia
30 C4 Harvard U.S.A.
25 F4 Harvard, Mt mt. U.S.A.
112 C6 Harvey Austr.
33 K2 Harvey Can.
30 D2 Harvey MI U.S.A.
26 C2 Harvey ND U.S.A.
59 J6 Harwich U.K.
115 K2 Harwood Austr.
84 C3 Haryana div. India
80 F6 Ḩasā, Wādī al watercourse Jordan
81 L3 Hasan Iran
84 C2 Hasan Abdal Pak.
80 E2 Hasan Dağı mts Turkey
81 H3 Hasankeyf Turkey
80 E5 Hasbani r. Lebanon
80 E2 Hasbek Turkey
81 K6 Ḩasb, Sha'īb watercourse Iraq
85 E5 Hasdo r. India
61 F2 Hase r. Ger.
62 F1 Haselünne Ger.
91 F6 Hashima Japan
81 M3 Hashtpar Iran
27 D5 Haskell U.S.A.
59 G6 Haslemere U.K.

63 M7 Hăşmaşul Mare mt Romania
83 E8 Hassan India
81 K4 Hassan Iraq
35 F5 Hassayampa r. U.S.A.
61 D4 Hasselt Belgium
100 C1 Hassi Messaoud Alg.
55 N8 Hässleholm Sweden
114 F7 Hastings Austr.
115 K3 Hastings r. Austr.
117 F3 Hastings N.Z.
59 H7 Hastings U.K.
30 E4 Hastings MI U.S.A.
30 A3 Hastings MN U.S.A.
26 D3 Hastings NE U.S.A.
Hatay see Antakya
35 F3 Hatch U.S.A.
29 E7 Hatchet Bay Bahamas
21 J3 Hatchet Lake l. Can.
29 B5 Hatchie r. U.S.A.
114 E4 Hatfield U.S.A.
58 G4 Hatfield U.K.
86 H1 Hatgal Mongolia
84 D4 Hathras India
85 F4 Hatia Nepal
95 C3 Ha Tiên Vietnam
95 C1 Ha Tĩnh Vietnam
90 D6 Hatsukaichi Japan
114 E5 Hattah Austr.
29 F5 Hatteras, Cape c. U.S.A.
54 N4 Hatttfjelldal Norway
85 E6 Hatti r. India
29 B6 Hattiesburg U.S.A.
102 E3 Haud reg. Eth.
55 K7 Hauge Norway
55 J7 Haugesund Norway
117 E3 Hauhungaroa mt. N.Z.
55 K7 Haukeligrend Norway
54 T4 Haukipudas Fin.
55 V5 Haukivesi l. Fin.
21 H3 Haultain r. Can.
117 E2 Hauraki Gulf g. N.Z.
117 A7 Hauroko, L. l. N.Z.
100 B1 Haut Atlas mts Morocco
23 G4 Hauterive Can.
61 E4 Hautes Fagnes moorland Belgium
33 J3 Haut, Isle au i. U.S.A.
100 B1 Hauts Plateaux plat. Alg.
34 □1 Hauula U.S.A.
37 H4 Havana Cuba
30 B5 Havana U.S.A.
59 G7 Havant U.K.
35 E4 Havasu Lake l. U.S.A.
62 F4 Havel r. Ger.
31 J3 Havelock U.S.A.
29 E5 Havelock U.S.A.
117 F3 Havelock North N.Z.
59 C6 Haverfordwest U.K.
33 H3 Haverhill U.S.A.
62 G6 Havlíčkův Brod Czech Rep.
54 T1 Havøysund Norway
67 M5 Havran Turkey
24 E1 Havre U.S.A.
23 H4 Havre Aubert, Île du i. Can.
33 E5 Havre de Grace U.S.A.
23 H3 Havre-St-Pierre Can.
67 M4 Havsa Turkey
80 E1 Havza Turkey
34 □2 Hawaii i. U.S.A.
14 H4 Hawaiian Ridge sea feature Pac. Oc.
34 □2 Hawaii Volcanoes National Park nat. park U.S.A.
81 L7 Ḩawallī Kuwait
59 D4 Hawarden U.K.
117 B6 Hawea, L. l. N.Z.
117 E3 Hawera N.Z.
58 E3 Hawes U.K.
34 □2 Hawi U.S.A.
57 F5 Hawick U.K.
81 L6 Ḩawīzah, Hawr al l. Iraq
117 B6 Hawkdun Range mts N.Z.
117 F3 Hawke Bay b. N.Z.
23 J3 Hawke Island i. Can.
114 C3 Hawker Austr.
114 D2 Hawkers Gate Austr.
33 F2 Hawkesbury Can.
35 F3 Hawkins Peak summit U.S.A.
31 K3 Hawks U.S.A.
33 K2 Hawkshaw Can.
116 D5 Hawkwood Austr.
33 F4 Hawley U.S.A.
81 J5 Ḩawrān, Wādī watercourse Iraq
104 C7 Hawston S. Africa
34 C2 Hawthorne U.S.A.
58 F3 Haxby U.K.
115 K1 Hay Austr.
114 F5 Hay r. Austr.
20 F2 Hay r. Can.
30 B3 Hay r. U.S.A.
88 B1 Haya China
91 H4 Hayachine-san mt. Japan
61 C5 Hayange France
90 C7 Hayasui-seto chan. Japan
81 K3 Haydarābād Iran
35 G5 Hayden AZ U.S.A.
24 C2 Hayden ID U.S.A.
21 L3 Hayes r. Can.
16 Hayes Peninsula pen. Greenland
59 B7 Hayle U.K.
80 D2 Hayman Turkey
116 C3 Hayman I. i. Austr.
32 E5 Haymarket U.S.A.
33 J2 Haynesville U.S.A.
59 F5 Hay-on-Wye U.K.
69 C7 Hayrabolu Turkey
20 F2 Hay River Can.

26 D4 Hays U.S.A.
69 D5 Haysyn Ukr.
34 A3 Hayward CA U.S.A.
30 B2 Hayward WV U.S.A.
59 G7 Haywards Heath U.K.
79 K3 Hazarajat reg. Afgh.
32 B6 Hazard U.S.A.
85 F5 Hazārībāg India
85 E5 Hazaribagh Range mts India
61 A4 Hazebrouck France
20 D3 Hazelton Can.
33 F4 Hazelton U.S.A.
61 C2 Hazerswoude-Rijndijk Neth.
81 G6 Ḩazm al Jalāmīd ridge S. Arabia
84 A1 Hazrat Sultan Afgh.
81 H2 Hazro Turkey
60 B4 Headford Rep. of Ireland
112 F6 Head of Bight b. Austr.
34 A2 Healdsburg U.S.A.
114 F6 Healesville Austr.
59 F4 Heanor U.K.
13 J7 Heard i. Indian Ocean
27 D6 Hearne U.S.A.
22 D4 Hearst Can.
59 H7 Heathfield U.K.
33 E6 Heathsville U.S.A.
27 D7 Hebbronville U.S.A.
88 E2 Hebei div. China
115 G2 Hebel Austr.
27 E5 Heber Springs U.S.A.
88 E3 Hebi China
23 H2 Hebron Can.
30 D5 Hebron IN U.S.A.
26 D3 Hebron NE U.S.A.
33 G3 Hebron NY U.S.A.
80 E6 Hebron West Bank
23 H2 Hebron Fiord in. Can.
20 C3 Hecate Strait chan. Can.
20 C3 Heceta I. i. U.S.A.
89 C4 Hechuan China
55 N6 Hede Sweden
55 O6 Hedemora Sweden
89 D6 Hede Sk. resr China
30 A5 Hedrick U.S.A.
35 G3 He Devil Mt. mt. U.S.A.
61 D2 Heerenveen Neth.
61 C3 Heerhugowaard Neth.
61 D4 Heerlen Neth.
Hefa see Haifa
88 E4 Hefei China
89 D4 Hefeng China
87 O2 Hegang China
91 F6 Hegura-jima i. Japan
90 D7 Heguri-jima i. Japan
62 D3 Heide Ger.
103 B6 Heide Namibia
62 D6 Heidelberg Ger.
105 H3 Heidelberg Gauteng S. Africa
104 D7 Heidelberg Western Cape S. Africa
Heihe see Aihui
105 G3 Heilbron S. Africa
62 D6 Heilbronn Ger.
62 E3 Heiligenhafen Ger.
89 □ Hei Ling Chau i. Hong Kong China
87 N2 Heilongjiang div. China
87 P1 Heilong Jiang r. China/Rus. Fed.
54 M5 Heimdal Norway
55 U6 Heinola Fin.
95 A5 Heinze Is is Myanmar
88 G1 Heishan China
61 C3 Heist-op-den-Berg Belgium
88 E2 Hejian China
89 B4 Hejiang China
89 D6 He Jiang r. China
80 F2 Hekimhan Turkey
54 D5 Hekla volc. Iceland
88 B2 Hekou Gansu China
89 B6 Hekou Yunnan China
54 N5 Helagsfjället mt Sweden
88 B2 Helan Shan mts China
85 H4 Helem India
27 F5 Helena AR U.S.A.
24 E2 Helena MT U.S.A.
34 D3 Helen, Mt mt. U.S.A.
57 D4 Helensburgh U.K.
89 D7 Helen Shoal sand bank Paracel Is
80 E6 Helez Israel
62 E3 Helgoland i. Ger.
62 D3 Helgoländer Bucht b. Ger.
115 K1 Helidon Austr.
54 C5 Hella Iceland
54 P2 Helland Norway
61 C3 Hellevoetsluis Neth.
65 F3 Hellín Spain
24 C2 Hells Canyon gorge U.S.A.
84 3 Helmand r. Afgh.
103 B6 Helmeringhausen Namibia
61 D3 Helmond Neth.
57 E2 Helmsdale U.K.
57 E2 Helmsdale r. U.K.
87 N3 Helong China
35 G2 Helper U.S.A.
55 N8 Helsingborg Sweden
55 N8 Helsingør Denmark
55 T6 Helsinki Fin.
59 B7 Helston U.K.
58 D3 Helvellyn mt U.K.
60 D5 Helvick Head hd Rep. of Ireland

80 C7 Helwân Egypt
59 G6 Hemel Hempstead U.K.
34 D5 Hemet U.S.A.
32 E3 Hemlock Lake l. U.S.A.
33 G2 Hemmingford Can.
27 D6 Hempstead U.S.A.
59 J5 Hemsby U.K.
55 Q8 Hemse Sweden
88 A3 Henan Qinghai China
88 D3 Henan div. China
65 E2 Henares r. Spain
90 A2 Henashi-zaki pt Japan
80 C1 Hendek Turkey
47 E3 Henderson Arg.
28 C4 Henderson KY U.S.A.
29 E4 Henderson NC U.S.A.
35 E3 Henderson NV U.S.A.
33 E3 Henderson NY U.S.A.
27 E5 Henderson TX U.S.A.
109 Henderson Island i. Pitcairn Islands Pac. Oc.
29 D5 Hendersonville NC U.S.A.
29 C4 Hendersonville TN U.S.A.
59 G6 Hendon U.K.
82 J5 Hengduan Shan mts China
61 E2 Hengelo Neth.
89 D5 Heng Shan mt Hunan China
89 D5 Hengshan Hunan China
88 D2 Hengshan Shaanxi China
88 E2 Heng Shan mt China
88 D2 Hengshui China
89 C6 Heng Xian China
89 D5 Hengyang Hunan China
89 D5 Hengyang Hunan China
69 E6 Heniches'k Ukr.
117 C6 Henley N.Z.
59 G6 Henley-on-Thames U.K.
33 F5 Henlopen, Cape pt U.S.A.
61 F4 Hennef (Sieg) Ger.
105 G3 Hennenman S. Africa
33 H3 Henniker U.S.A.
27 D5 Henrietta U.S.A.
22 D2 Henrietta Maria, Cape c. Can.
35 G3 Henrieville U.S.A.
30 C5 Henry U.S.A.
119 B3 Henry Ice Rise ice feature Ant.
35 G2 Henry Mts mts U.S.A.
31 G4 Hensall Can.
103 B6 Hentiesbaai Namibia
115 G5 Henty Austr.
83 J7 Henzada Myanmar
21 H4 Hepburn Can.
89 E5 Heping China
89 C6 Hepu China
88 D2 Hequ China
79 J3 Herāt Afgh.
64 F5 Hérault r. France
116 A2 Herbert r. Austr.
21 H4 Herbert Can.
116 A1 Herberton Austr.
59 E5 Hereford U.K.
27 C5 Hereford U.S.A.
109 Héréhérétué atoll Tuamotu Islands Pac. Oc.
62 D4 Herford Ger.
26 D4 Herington U.S.A.
81 L2 Herīs Iran
62 D7 Herisau Switz.
61 E3 Herkenbosch Neth.
33 F3 Herkimer U.S.A.
57 □ Herma Ness hd U.K.
104 C7 Hermanus S. Africa
105 H5 Hermes, Cape pt S. Africa
115 G3 Hermidale Austr.
24 C2 Hermiston U.S.A.
44 C9 Hermite, Is i. Chile
110 E2 Hermit Is is P.N.G.
Hermon, Mount mt see Sheikh, Jebel esh
47 B2 Hermosa, P. de V. pass Chile
45 B4 Hermosas, Parque Nacional las nat. park Col.
36 B3 Hermosillo Mex.
44 F3 Hernandarias Para.
61 F3 Herne Ger.
59 J6 Herne Bay U.K.
55 L8 Herning Denmark
30 D1 Heron Bay Can.
116 D4 Heron I. i. Austr.
65 D3 Herrera del Duque Spain
115 G8 Herrick Austr.
32 E4 Hershey U.S.A.
59 G6 Hertford U.K.
61 E4 Hertogenwald forest Belgium
105 J4 Hertzogville S. Africa
116 E5 Hervey Bay Austr.
116 E5 Hervey Bay b. Austr.
109 Hervey Islands is Cook Is Pac. Oc.
116 D2 Hervey Ra. mts Austr.
81 M4 Heşar r. Iran
61 C4 Hesbaye reg. Belgium
89 C6 Heshan China
88 C3 Heshui China
88 D2 Heshun China
34 D4 Hesperia U.S.A.
20 C2 Hess r. Can.
62 E6 Hesselberg h. Ger.
89 B6 Hetou China
34 B3 Hetch Hetchy Aqueduct canal U.S.A.
61 D3 Heteren Neth.
26 C2 Hettinger U.S.A.
58 E3 Hetton U.K.
62 E3 Hettstedt Ger.

61 D3 Heusden Belgium
58 E3 Heversham U.K.
88 F4 He Xian Anhui China
89 D5 He Xian Guangxi China
88 B2 Hexibao China
88 E1 Hexigten Qi China
104 C6 Hex River Pass pass S. Africa
88 D3 Heyang China
58 E3 Heysham U.K.
89 E6 Heyuan China
114 D7 Heywood Austr.
58 E4 Heywood U.K.
30 C5 Heyworth U.S.A.
88 C5 Heze China
89 B5 Hezhang China
88 B3 Hezheng China
88 B3 Hezuozhen China
29 D7 Hialeah U.S.A.
26 E4 Hiawatha U.S.A.
30 A2 Hibbing U.S.A.
115 F9 Hibbs, Pt hd Austr.
90 C6 Hibiki-nada b. Japan
29 D5 Hickory U.S.A.
117 G2 Hicks Bay N.Z.
21 K2 Hicks L. l. Can.
32 A4 Hicksville U.S.A.
27 D5 Hico U.S.A.
90 J2 Hidaka Japan
90 J2 Hidaka-sanmyaku mts Japan
36 C3 Hidalgo del Parral Mex.
36 C3 Hidalgo, Psa M. resr Mex.
46 C2 Hidrolândia Brazil
90 D6 Higashi-Hiroshima Japan
91 G6 Higashi-izu Japan
91 H4 Higashine Japan
91 E6 Higashi-ōsaka Japan
90 B7 Higashi-suidō chan. Japan
33 F3 Higgins Bay U.S.A.
30 E3 Higgins Lake l. U.S.A.
High Atlas mts see Haut Atlas
24 E3 High Desert des. U.S.A.
30 C3 High Falls Reservoir resr U.S.A.
30 E3 High I. i. U.S.A.
89 High Island Res. resr Hong Kong China
30 D4 Highland Park U.S.A.
34 C2 Highland Peak summit CA U.S.A.
35 E3 Highland Peak summit NV U.S.A.
20 E5 High Level Can.
85 F5 High Level Canal canal India
29 E5 High Point U.S.A.
20 G4 High Prairie Can.
29 E7 High Rock Bahamas
21 J3 Highrock Lake l. Can.
115 F9 High Rocky Pt hd Austr.
58 F3 High Seat h. U.K.
33 F4 Hightstown U.S.A.
59 G6 High Wycombe U.K.
55 S7 Hiiumaa i. Estonia
78 D4 Hijaz reg. S. Arabia
90 C7 Hikari Japan
35 E3 Hiko U.S.A.
91 F6 Hikone Japan
117 G2 Hikurangi mt. N.Z.
35 F3 Hildale U.S.A.
62 D4 Hildesheim Ger.
85 G4 Hili Bangl.
20 D1 Hill City U.S.A.
35 H2 Hill Creek r. U.S.A.
55 N9 Hillerød Denmark
116 A2 Hillgrove Austr.
26 D2 Hillsboro ND U.S.A.
33 H3 Hillsboro NH U.S.A.
32 B5 Hillsboro OH U.S.A.
27 D5 Hillsboro TX U.S.A.
30 B4 Hillsboro WV U.S.A.
32 C5 Hillsboro WV U.S.A.
116 C3 Hillsborough, C. pt Austr.
30 E5 Hillsdale MI U.S.A.
33 G3 Hillsdale NY U.S.A.
32 E4 Hillsgrove U.S.A.
57 F4 Hillside U.K.
35 F4 Hillside U.S.A.
115 F4 Hillston Austr.
32 C6 Hillsville U.S.A.
115 J5 Hilltop U.S.A.
34 □2 Hilo U.S.A.
105 J4 Hilton S. Africa
32 E3 Hilton U.S.A.
31 F2 Hilton Beach Can.
29 D5 Hilton Head Island U.S.A.
81 G3 Hilvan Turkey
61 D2 Hilversum Neth.
84 D3 Himachal Pradesh div. India
74 Himalaya mts Asia
85 F3 Himalchul mt. Nepal
54 S4 Himanka Fin.
84 H4 Himarë Albania
84 C4 Himatnagar India
90 E6 Himeji Japan
91 H4 Himekami-dake mt. Japan
90 C7 Hime-shima i. Japan
105 K4 Himeville S. Africa
91 G4 Hime-zaki pt Japan
91 F6 Himi Japan
80 F4 Ḩimş Syria
80 F4 Ḩimş, Baḩrat resr Syria
90 C7 Hinagu Japan
94 C4 Hinatuan Phil.
116 B2 Hinchinbrook I. i. Austr.
58 E3 Hinckley U.K.
59 F5 Hinckley U.K.

30 A2 Hinckley MN U.S.A.
35 F2 Hinckley UT U.S.A.
33 F3 Hinckley Reservoir resr U.S.A.
84 D3 Hindan r. India
84 D4 Hindaun India
58 G3 Hinderwell U.K.
81 K5 Hindīyah Barrage Iraq
58 E4 Hindley U.K.
32 B6 Hindman U.S.A.
114 D6 Hindmarsh, L. l. Austr.
85 F5 Hindola India
84 B2 Hindu Kush mts Afgh./Pak.
83 E8 Hindupur India
20 F3 Hines Creek Can.
29 D6 Hinesville U.S.A.
84 D5 Hinganghat India
84 D6 Hingoli India
81 H2 Hınıs Turkey
34 D4 Hinkley U.S.A.
54 O2 Hinnøya i. Norway
90 D6 Hino Japan
90 D6 Hino-misaki pt Japan
33 G3 Hinsdale U.S.A.
20 F4 Hinton Can.
32 C6 Hinton U.S.A.
81 K2 Hirabit Dāğ mt Turkey
90 B7 Hirado Japan
90 B7 Hirado-shima i. Japan
85 E5 Hirakud Reservoir resr India
90 D6 Hirata Japan
91 G6 Hiratsuka Japan
90 J2 Hiroo Japan
90 H3 Hirosaki Japan
90 D6 Hiroshima Japan
90 D6 Hiroshima Japan
62 F7 Hirschberg mt Ger.
64 G2 Hirson France
55 L8 Hirtshals Denmark
90 B7 Hisaka-jima i. Japan
81 M3 Hisar Iran
80 D1 Hisarönü Turkey
80 E6 Hisban Jordan
37 K4 Hispaniola i. Caribbean Sea
84 C3 Hissar India
85 F4 Hisua India
81 J5 Ḩīt Iraq
90 C7 Hita Japan
91 H5 Hitachi Japan
91 H5 Hitachi-ōta Japan
90 C7 Hitoyoshi Japan
54 L5 Hitra i. Norway
91 G5 Hiuchiga-take volc. Japan
90 D6 Hiuchi-nada b. Japan
109 Hiva Oa i. Fr. Polynesia Pac. Oc.
20 E4 Hixon Can.
116 E4 Hixson Cay rf Austr.
81 J2 Hizan Turkey
55 O7 Hjälmaren l. Sweden
21 H2 Hjalmar Lake l. Can.
55 L5 Hjerkinn Norway
55 O7 Hjo Sweden
55 M8 Hjørring Denmark
105 J3 Hlabisa S. Africa
85 F3 Hlako Kangri mt China
105 J3 Hlatikulu Swaziland
69 E5 Hlobyne Ukr.
105 G4 Hlohlowane S. Africa
105 H4 Hlotse Lesotho
105 K4 Hluhluwe S. Africa
69 E5 Hlukhiv Ukr.
63 O4 Hlusha Belarus
68 C4 Hlybokaye Belarus
100 C4 Ho Ghana
103 B6 Hoachanas Namibia
115 G9 Hobart Austr.
27 D5 Hobart U.S.A.
27 C5 Hobbs U.S.A.
29 D7 Hobe Sound U.S.A.
55 L8 Hobro Denmark
102 E3 Hobyo Somalia
95 C6 Hô Chi Minh Vietnam
62 G7 Hochschwab mt Austria
32 B5 Hocking r. U.S.A.
84 D4 Hodal India
58 E4 Hodder r. U.K.
58 F4 Hoddesdon U.K.
Hodeida see Al Hudaydah
33 K1 Hodgdon U.S.A.
63 K7 Hódmezővásárhely Hungary
65 J5 Hodna, Chott el salt l. Alg.
61 C3 Hoek van Holland Neth.
61 D4 Hoensbroek Neth.
62 C6 Hof Ger.
105 F5 Hofmeyr S. Africa
54 H4 Höfn Iceland
55 P6 Hofors Sweden
54 D4 Hofsjökull ice cap Iceland
90 C6 Hōfu Japan
55 N8 Höganäs Sweden
115 G7 Hogan Group is Austr.
116 B5 Hoganthulla Cr. r. Austr.
100 C2 Hoggar plat. Alg.
33 F6 Hog I. i. U.S.A.
55 P8 Högsby Sweden
62 F7 Hohe Tauern mts Austria
61 E4 Hohe Venn moorland Belgium
88 D1 Hohhot China
90 C6 Hōhoku Japan
85 G2 Hoh Xil Hu salt l. China

85 G2 Hoh Xil Shan *mts* China
95 D2 Hôi An Vietnam
102 D3 Hoima Uganda
89 B6 Hôi Xuân Vietnam
85 H4 Hojai India
90 D7 Hōjo Japan
117 D1 Hokianga Harbour *in.* N.Z.
91 G5 Hōki-gawa *r.* Japan
117 C5 Hokitika N.Z.
90 J1 Hokkaidō *i.* Japan
55 L7 Hokksund Norway
81 K1 Hoktemberyan Armenia
91 E6 Hokuriku Tunnel *tunnel* Japan
55 L6 Hol Norway
55 M9 Holbæk Denmark
59 H5 Holbeach U.K.
116 C2 Holborne I. *i.* Austr.
35 G4 Holbrook U.S.A.
30 B3 Holcombe Flowage *resr* U.S.A.
21 G4 Holden Can.
35 F2 Holden U.S.A.
27 D5 Holdenville U.S.A.
26 D3 Holdrege U.S.A.
37 J4 Holguín Cuba
55 N6 Höljes Sweden
30 D4 Holland U.S.A.
32 D4 Hollidaysburg U.S.A.
20 C3 Hollis *AK* U.S.A.
27 D5 Hollis *OK* U.S.A.
34 B3 Hollister U.S.A.
31 F4 Holly U.S.A.
27 F5 Holly Springs U.S.A.
29 D7 Hollywood U.S.A.
54 N4 Holm Norway
116 B1 Holmes Reef *rf* Coral Sea Is Terr.
54 T2 Holmestrand *Finnmark* Norway
55 M7 Holmestrand *Vestfold* Norway
54 R5 Holmön *i.* Sweden
54 R5 Holmsund Sweden
104 B3 Holoog Namibia
55 L8 Holstebro Denmark
29 D4 Holston *r.* U.S.A.
32 C6 Holston Lake *l.* U.S.A.
59 C7 Holsworthy U.K.
59 J5 Holt U.K.
30 E4 Holt U.S.A.
26 E4 Holton U.S.A.
60 D5 Holycross Rep. of Ireland
59 C4 Holyhead U.K.
59 C4 Holyhead Bay *b.* U.K.
58 F2 Holy Island *i. Eng.* U.K.
59 C4 Holy Island *i. Wales* U.K.
33 G3 Holyoke *MA* U.S.A.
59 D4 Holywell U.K.
62 E7 Holzkirchen Ger.
100 B3 Hombori Mali
61 F5 Homburg Ger.
18 Home Bay *b.* Can.
116 B2 Home Hill Austr.
27 E5 Homer U.S.A.
29 D6 Homerville U.S.A.
116 A3 Homestead Austr.
29 D7 Homestead U.S.A.
29 C5 Homewood U.S.A.
94 C4 Homonhon *pt* Phil.
Homs *see* Ḩimş
69 D4 Homyel' Belarus
90 J2 Honbetsu Japan
45 B3 Honda Col.
94 A4 Honda Bay *b.* Phil.
35 H4 Hon Dah U.S.A.
104 B5 Hondeklipbaai S. Africa
88 C1 Hondlon Ju China
90 C7 Hondo Japan
27 D6 Hondo U.S.A.
61 E1 Hondsrug *reg.* Neth.
16 Honduras *country* Central America
55 M6 Hønefoss Norway
33 F4 Honesdale U.S.A.
34 B1 Honey Lake *l.* U.S.A.
33 E3 Honeyoye Lake *l.* U.S.A.
64 E2 Honfleur France
88 E4 Hong'an China
89 C6 Hông Gai Vietnam
89 E6 Honghai Wan *b.* China
89 B6 Honghe China
88 E3 Hong He *r.* China
89 D4 Honghu China
89 C5 Hongjiang China
89 E6 Hong Kong *div.* China
89 □ Hong Kong Island *i.* *Hong Kong* China
88 C2 Hongliu *r.* China
88 B2 Hongliuyuan China
95 C3 Hông Ngư Vietnam
89 C6 Hong , Mouths of the *est.* Vietnam
89 C7 Hongqizhen China
88 B2 Hongshansi China
89 D6 Hongshui He *r.* China
89 C6 Hông, Sông *r.* Vietnam
88 D2 Hongtong China
91 E7 Hongū Japan
23 G4 Honguedo, Détroit d' *chan.* Can.
88 B3 Hongyuan China
88 F3 Hongze China
88 F3 Hongze Hu *l.* China
111 F2 Honiara Solomon Is
59 D7 Honiton U.K.
91 H4 Honjō Japan
55 S6 Honkajoki Fin.
91 G6 Honkawane Japan
95 C3 Hon Khoai *i.* Vietnam
95 D2 Hon Lon *i.* Vietnam
95 C1 Hon Mê *i.* Vietnam
54 T1 Honningsvåg Norway
34 □2 Honokaa U.S.A.
34 □1 Honolulu U.S.A.
95 C3 Hon Rai *i.* Vietnam
90 D6 Honshū *i.* Japan
77 P6 Honshū *i.* Japan
24 B2 Hood, Mt *volc.* U.S.A.
112 C6 Hood Pt *pt* Austr.
61 E2 Hoogeveen Neth.
61 E1 Hoogezand-Sappemeer Neth.
27 C4 Hooker U.S.A.
60 E5 Hook Head *hd* Rep. of Ireland
116 C3 Hook Island *i.* Austr.
Hook of Holland *see* Hoek van Holland
116 E5 Hook Point *pt* Austr.
116 C2 Hook Reef *rf* Austr.
20 B3 Hoonah U.S.A.
77 V3 Hooper Bay Alaska
33 E5 Hooper I. *i.* U.S.A.
30 D5 Hoopeston U.S.A.
105 F3 Hoopstad S. Africa
55 N9 Höör Sweden
61 D2 Hoorn Neth.
33 G3 Hoosick U.S.A.
35 E3 Hoover Dam *dam* U.S.A.
32 B4 Hoover Memorial Reservoir *resr* U.S.A.
81 H1 Hopa Turkey
33 F4 Hop Bottom U.S.A.
20 E5 Hope *B.C.* Can.
117 D5 Hope *r.* N.Z.
27 E5 Hope *AR* U.S.A.
35 F5 Hope *AZ* U.S.A.
23 J2 Hopedale Can.
104 C6 Hopefield S. Africa
114 C2 Hope, L. *salt flat* Austr.
23 H3 Hope Mountains *mts* Can.
76 D2 Hopen *i.* Svalbard
117 D4 Hope Saddle *pass* N.Z.
23 G2 Hopes Advance, Baie *b.* Can.
114 E5 Hopetoun Austr.
104 F4 Hopetown S. Africa
32 E6 Hopewell U.S.A.
22 E2 Hopewell Islands *is* Can.
112 E4 Hopkins, L. *salt flat* Austr.
28 C4 Hopkinsville U.S.A.
34 A2 Hopland U.S.A.
24 B2 Hoquiam U.S.A.
88 A3 Hor China
81 L2 Horadiz Azer.
81 J1 Horasan Turkey
55 N9 Hörby Sweden
30 C4 Horeb, Mount U.S.A.
88 B1 Hörh Uul *mts* Mongolia
30 C4 Horicon U.S.A.
88 D1 Horinger China
111 J4 Horizon Depth *depth* Pac. Oc.
68 D4 Horki Belarus
119 B4 Horlick Mts *mts* Ant.
69 F5 Horlivka Ukr.
79 H4 Hormuz, Strait of *str.* Iran/Oman
62 G6 Horn Austria
20 F2 Horn *r.* Can.
54 B3 Horn *c.* Iceland
54 P3 Hornavan *l.* Sweden
27 E6 Hornbeck U.S.A.
44 C9 Horn, Cape *c.* Chile
59 G4 Horncastle U.K.
55 P6 Horndal Sweden
54 Q5 Hörnefors Sweden
32 E3 Hornell U.S.A.
22 D4 Hornepayne Can.
29 B6 Horn I. *i.* U.S.A.
111 J3 Horn, Îles de *is* Wallis and Futuna Islands
104 B1 Hornkranz Namibia
47 B4 Hornopiren, V. *volc.* Chile
27 C7 Hornos Mex.
Hornos, Cabo de *c. see* Horn, Cape
115 J4 Hornsby Austr.
58 G4 Hornsea U.K.
55 P6 Hornslandet *pen.* Sweden
63 M6 Horodenka Ukr.
69 D5 Horodnya Ukr.
69 C5 Horodok *Khmel'nyts'kyy* Ukr.
69 B5 Horodok *L'viv* Ukr.
90 J1 Horokanai Japan
63 M5 Horokhiv Ukr.
90 H1 Horonobe Japan
90 J2 Horoshiri-dake *mt.* Japan
88 F1 Horqin Shadi *reg.* China
87 M2 Horqin Youyi Qianqi China
88 G1 Horqin Zuoyi Houqi China
59 C7 Horrabridge U.K.
85 G3 Horru China
20 E4 Horsefly Can.
32 E3 Horseheads U.S.A.
23 J3 Horse Is *is* Can.
60 C4 Horseleap Rep. of Ireland
55 L9 Horsens Denmark
24 C3 Horseshoe Bend U.S.A.
114 E6 Horsham Austr.
59 G6 Horsham U.K.
55 M7 Horten Norway
31 F1 Horwood Lake *l.* Can.
63 N5 Horyn' *r.* Ukr.
85 H2 Ho Sai Hu *l.* China
102 D3 Hosa'ina Eth.
81 L4 Hoseynābād Iran
81 M6 Ḩoseynīyeh Iran
84 D5 Hoshangabad India
84 C3 Hoshiarpur India
83 E7 Hospet India
60 C5 Hospital Rep. of Ireland
47 F1 Hospital, Cuchilla del *h.* Uru.
44 C9 Hoste, I. *i.* Chile
54 O5 Hotagen *l.* Sweden
82 F3 Hotan China
104 E3 Hotazel S. Africa
35 G4 Hotevilla U.S.A.
115 G6 Hotham, Mt *mt* Austr.
54 P4 Hoting Sweden
27 E5 Hot Springs *AR* U.S.A.
26 C3 Hot Springs *SD* U.S.A.
20 F1 Hottah Lake *l.* Can.
37 K5 Hotte, Massif de la *mts* Haiti
61 D4 Houffalize Belgium
95 □ Hougang Sing.
116 B2 Houghton *r.* Austr.
30 C2 Houghton U.S.A.
30 E3 Houghton Lake *l.* U.S.A.
30 E3 Houghton Lake U.S.A.
58 F3 Houghton le Spring U.K.
33 K1 Houlton U.S.A.
88 D3 Houma China
27 F6 Houma U.S.A.
57 C3 Hourn, Loch *in.* U.K.
33 G3 Housatonic U.S.A.
35 F2 House Range *mts* U.S.A.
20 D4 Houston Can.
27 F4 Houston *MO* U.S.A.
27 F5 Houston *MS* U.S.A.
27 E6 Houston *TX* U.S.A.
105 H1 Hout *r.* S. Africa
112 B5 Houtman Abrolhos *is* Austr.
57 E2 Houton U.K.
104 E5 Houwater S. Africa
86 F2 Hovd Mongolia
59 G7 Hove U.K.
59 J5 Hoveton U.K.
81 M6 Hoveyzeh Iran
55 O8 Hovmantorp Sweden
88 C1 Hövsgöl Mongolia
86 H1 Hövsgöl Nuur *l.* Mongolia
86 H3 Hövüün Mongolia
116 E5 Howard Austr.
30 E4 Howard City U.S.A.
21 H2 Howard Lake *l.* Can.
58 G4 Howden U.K.
115 H6 Howe, C. *hd* Austr.
31 F4 Howell U.S.A.
26 C2 Howes U.S.A.
33 G2 Howick Can.
105 J4 Howick S. Africa
114 C1 Howitt, L. *salt flat* Austr.
115 G6 Howitt, Mt *mt* Austr.
33 J2 Howland U.S.A.
14 H5 Howland I. Pac. Oc.
115 G5 Howlong Austr.
60 E4 Howth Rep. of Ireland
61 D5 Höxter Ger.
57 E2 Hoy *i.* U.K.
55 K6 Hoyanger Norway
62 G5 Hoyerswerda Ger.
54 N4 Høylandet Norway
54 V5 Höytiäinen *l.* Fin.
81 G2 Hozat Turkey
62 G5 Hradec Králové Czech Rep.
67 H3 Hrasnica Bos.-Herz.
81 K1 Hrazdan Armenia
69 E5 Hrebinka Ukr.
68 B4 Hrodna Belarus
89 F6 Hsi-hsu-p'ing Hsü *i.* Taiwan
89 F5 Hsin-chu Taiwan
83 J6 Hsipaw Myanmar
89 F5 Hsueh Shan *mt* Taiwan
89 E5 Hua'an China
45 D4 Huachamacari, Cerro *mt* Venez.
88 C2 Huachi China
42 C6 Huacho Peru
35 G6 Huachuca City U.S.A.
47 C1 Huaco Arg.
88 D1 Huade China
87 N3 Huadian China
109 Huahine *i. Society Islands* Pac. Oc.
88 E1 Huai'an *Hebei* China
88 F3 Huai'an *Jiangsu* China
88 E3 Huaibei China
88 E3 Huaibin China
88 F3 Huai He *r.* China
89 C5 Huaihua China
89 D6 Huaiji China
88 E1 Huailai China
89 B7 Huai Luang *r.* Thai.
88 E3 Huainan China
89 E4 Huaining China
88 D2 Huairen China
88 E3 Huaiyang China
88 F3 Huaiyin China
88 E3 Huaiyuan *Anhui* China
89 C5 Huaiyuan *Guangxi* China
88 B3 Huajialing China
93 H8 Huaki Indon.
35 F4 Hualapai Peak *summit* U.S.A.
89 F5 Hua-lien Taiwan
42 C5 Huallaga *r.* Peru
88 B2 Hualong China
103 B5 Huambo Angola
47 C4 Huancache, Sa *mts* Arg.
42 C6 Huancayo Peru
88 E2 Huangbizhuang Sk. *resr* China
88 A2 Huangcheng China
88 E3 Huangchuan China
89 E4 Huanggang China
Huang Hai *sea see* Yellow Sea
88 E2 Huang He *r.* China
88 F2 Huanghe Kou *est.* China
85 H2 Huanghetan China
88 E2 Huanghua China
88 C3 Huangling China
89 C7 Huangliu China
89 E4 Huangmei China
89 E4 Huangpi China
89 C5 Huangping China
88 D1 Huangqi Hai *l.* China
89 F4 Huangshan China
89 F4 Huang Shan *mt* China
89 E4 Huangshi China
88 B2 Huang Shui *r.* China
88 C2 Huangtu Gaoyuan *plat.* China
88 F2 Huang Xian China
89 F4 Huangyan China
88 A2 Huangyuan China
89 C5 Huanjiang China
88 C2 Huan Jiang *r.* China
88 F2 Huantai China
42 C5 Huanuco Peru
42 E7 Huanuni Bol.
88 C2 Huan Xian China
89 G5 Hua-p'ing Hsü *i.* Taiwan
42 C5 Huaráz Peru
42 C6 Huarmey Peru
89 D4 Huarong China
42 C5 Huascaran, Nevado de *mt* Peru
44 B3 Huasco Chile
44 B3 Huasco *r.* Chile
36 C3 Huatabampo Mex.
88 C3 Huating China
89 D6 Hua Xian *Guangdong* China
88 E3 Hua Xian *Henan* China
88 D4 Huayuan *Hubei* China
89 C4 Huayuan *Hunan* China
89 C4 Huayun China
89 D6 Huazhou China
31 F3 Hubbard Lake *l.* U.S.A.
20 B2 Hubbard, Mt *mt.* *AK/Y.T.* Can./U.S.A.
23 G2 Hubbard, Pointe *hd* Can.
88 D4 Hubei *div.* China
83 E7 Hubli India
61 E3 Hückelhoven Ger.
59 F4 Hucknall U.K.
58 F4 Huddersfield U.K.
32 B6 Huddy U.S.A.
55 P6 Hudiksvall Sweden
30 E5 Hudson *MI* U.S.A.
33 G3 Hudson *NY* U.S.A.
30 A3 Hudson *WV* U.S.A.
28 F3 Hudson *r.* U.S.A.
21 J4 Hudson Bay *Sask.* Can.
18 Hudson Bay *b.* Can.
33 G3 Hudson Falls U.S.A.
119 A3 Hudson Mts *mts* Ant.
20 E3 Hudson's Hope Can.
18 Hudson Strait *strait* Can.
95 C1 Huê Vietnam
47 A4 Huechucuicui, Pta *pt* Chile
36 F5 Huehuetenango Guatemala
65 C4 Huelva Spain
47 B1 Huentelauquén Chile
47 B4 Huequi, Volcán *volc.* Chile
65 F4 Huércal-Overa Spain
65 F1 Huesca Spain
65 E4 Huéscar Spain
116 A3 Hughenden Austr.
32 E4 Hughesville U.S.A.
85 F5 Hugli *est.* India
85 G5 Hugli-Chunchura India
27 E5 Hugo U.S.A.
27 C4 Hugoton U.S.A.
88 D2 Huguan China
104 F3 Huhudi S. Africa
89 F5 Hui'an China
88 C2 Hui'anbu China
117 F3 Huiarau Range *mts* N.Z.
104 B3 Huib-Hoch Plateau *plat.* Namibia
89 E5 Huichang China
87 N3 Huich'ŏn N. Korea
89 E6 Huidong *Guangdong* China
89 B5 Huidong *Sichuan* China
61 C3 Huijbergen Neth.
88 E3 Huiji *r.* China
89 E6 Huilai China
45 B4 Huila, Nevado de *mt* Col.
89 B5 Huili China
88 E2 Huimin China
42 C2 Huinahuaca Arg.
47 N3 Huinan China
47 D2 Huinca Renancó Arg.
88 B3 Huining China
89 C5 Huishui China
88 G2 Huiten Nur *l.* China
89 C5 Huitong China
55 S6 Huittinen Fin.
88 C3 Hui Xian *Gansu* China
88 D3 Hui Xian *Henan* China
36 F5 Huixtla Mex.
89 B5 Huize China
89 E6 Huizhou China
86 H2 Hujirt Mongolia
89 E4 Hukou China
104 D1 Hukuntsi Botswana
30 E2 Hulbert Lake *l.* U.S.A.
81 L5 Hulilan Iran
87 O2 Hulin China
31 K3 Hull Can.
55 O8 Hultsfred Sweden
88 F1 Huludao China
87 L2 Hulun Nur *l.* China
69 F6 Hulyaypole Ukr.
87 N1 Huma China
42 F5 Humaitá Brazil
104 F7 Humansdorp S. Africa
58 H4 Humber, Mouth of the *est.* U.K.
21 H4 Humboldt Can.
24 C3 Humboldt *r.* U.S.A.
24 A3 Humboldt Bay *b.* U.S.A.
34 C1 Humboldt Lake *l.* U.S.A.
34 C1 Humboldt Range *mts* U.S.A.
34 D2 Humbolt Salt Marsh *marsh* U.S.A.
115 F1 Humeburn Austr.
89 D6 Hu Men *chan.* China
63 K6 Humenné Slovakia
115 G6 Hume Reservoir *resr* Austr.
34 C3 Humphreys, Mt *mt.* U.S.A.
35 G4 Humphreys Peak *summit* U.S.A.
88 G1 Hun *r.* China
54 C4 Húnaflói *b.* Iceland
89 D5 Hunan *div.* China
87 O3 Hunchun China
55 M9 Hundested Denmark
67 K2 Hunedoara Romania
48 Hungary *country* Europe
114 F2 Hungerford Austr.
87 N4 Hŭngnam N. Korea
24 D1 Hungry Horse Res. *resr* U.S.A.
89 □ Hung Shui Kiu *Hong Kong* China
89 C6 Hưng Yên Vietnam
87 N3 Hunjiang China
104 B3 Huns Mountains *mts* Namibia
61 F5 Hunsrück *reg.* Ger.
59 H5 Hunstanton U.K.
35 H4 Hunt U.S.A.
62 D4 Hunte *r.* Ger.
115 J4 Hunter *r.* Austr.
33 F3 Hunter U.S.A.
115 F8 Hunter I. *i. Tas.* Austr.
20 D4 Hunter I. *i.* Can.
111 H4 Hunter I. *i. New Caledonia* Pac. Oc.
115 F8 Hunter Is *is* Austr.
85 H6 Hunter's Bay *b.* Myanmar
117 C6 Hunters Hills, The *h.* N.Z.
33 F2 Huntingdon Can.
59 G5 Huntingdon U.K.
32 E4 Huntingdon U.S.A.
30 E5 Huntington *IN* U.S.A.
35 G2 Huntington *UT* U.S.A.
32 B5 Huntington *WV* U.S.A.
34 D5 Huntington Beach U.S.A.
117 E2 Huntly N.Z.
57 F3 Huntly U.K.
114 B2 Hunt Pen. *ridge* Austr.
31 H3 Huntsville Can.
29 C5 Huntsville *AL* U.S.A.
27 E6 Huntsville *TX* U.S.A.
88 D2 Hunyuan China
84 C2 Hunza *r.* Pak.
84 C1 Hunza Pak.
88 E2 Huolu China
95 C1 Hương Khê Vietnam
95 C1 Hương Thuy Vietnam
110 E2 Huon Peninsula *pen.* P.N.G.
115 G9 Huonville Austr.
88 E3 Huoqiu China
88 E4 Huoshan China
88 D2 Huo Shan *mt* China
89 F6 Huo-shao Tao *i.* Taiwan
88 D2 Huo Xian China
31 G3 Hurd, Cape *hd* Can.
88 C1 Hure Jadgai China
88 F1 Hure Qi China
78 C4 Hurghada Egypt
30 C1 Hurkett Can.
60 C5 Hurler's Cross Rep. of Ireland
30 B2 Hurley U.S.A.
26 D2 Huron U.S.A.
30 C2 Huron Bay *b.* U.S.A.
31 F3 Huron, Lake *l.* Can./U.S.A.
30 D2 Huron Mts *h.* U.S.A.
35 F3 Hurricane U.S.A.
59 F6 Hursley U.K.
59 H6 Hurst Green U.K.
117 D5 Hurunui *r.* N.Z.
54 E3 Húsavík *Norðurland eystra* Iceland
54 C4 Húsavík *Vestfirðir* Iceland
63 O7 Huşi Romania
55 O8 Huskvarna Sweden
55 J7 Husnes Norway
85 F4 Hussainabad India
62 D3 Husum Ger.
54 Q5 Husum Sweden
86 H2 Hutag Mongolia
26 D4 Hutchinson U.S.A.
35 G4 Hutch Mtn *mt.* U.S.A.
95 A1 Huthi Myanmar
21 N2 Hut Point *pt* Can.
116 C5 Hutton, Mt *h.* Austr.
32 D5 Huttonsville U.S.A.
88 D2 Hutuo *r.* China
83 D10 Huvadu Atoll *atoll* Maldives
80 G3 Hüvek Turkey
88 C3 Hu Xian China
61 D4 Huy Belgium
88 F4 Huzhou China
88 A2 Huzhu China
54 E4 Hvannadalshnúkur *mt* Iceland
66 G3 Hvar *i.* Croatia
69 E6 Hvardiys'ke Ukr.
54 C4 Hveragerði Iceland
55 L8 Hvide Sande Denmark
54 C4 Hvíta *r.* Iceland
103 C5 Hwange Zimbabwe
103 C5 Hwange National Park *nat. park* Zimbabwe
103 D5 Hwedza Zimbabwe
33 H4 Hyannis *MA* U.S.A.
26 C3 Hyannis *NE* U.S.A.
86 F2 Hyargas Nuur *salt l.* Mongolia
20 C3 Hydaburg U.S.A.
117 C6 Hyde N.Z.
112 C6 Hyden Austr.
32 B6 Hyden U.S.A.
33 G4 Hyde Park U.S.A.
35 F5 Hyder U.S.A.
83 E7 Hyderabad India
84 B4 Hyderabad Pak.
64 H5 Hyères France
64 H5 Hyères, Îles d' *is* France
87 N3 Hyesan N. Korea
20 D2 Hyland *r.* Can.
55 J6 Hyllestad Norway
55 N8 Hyltebruk Sweden
114 D6 Hynam Austr.
115 K3 Hyndland, Mt *mt* Austr.
90 E6 Hyōgo Japan
90 E6 Hyōnosen *mt.* Japan
54 V4 Hyrynsalmi Fin.
20 F3 Hythe Can.
59 J6 Hythe U.K.
90 C7 Hyūga Japan
55 T6 Hyvinkää Fin.

# I

42 E6 Iaco *r.* Brazil
43 K6 Iaçu Brazil
103 E6 Iakora Madag.
67 M2 Ialomiţa *r.* Romania
67 M2 Ianca Romania
63 N7 Iaşi Romania
94 A3 Iba Phil.
100 C4 Ibadan Nigeria
45 B3 Ibagué Col.
35 F1 Ibapah U.S.A.
90 D6 Ibara Japan
91 H5 Ibaraki Japan
42 C3 Ibarra Ecuador
78 E7 Ibb Yemen
95 A4 Ibi Indon.
100 C4 Ibi Nigeria
46 C2 Ibiá Brazil
43 K4 Ibiapaba, Serra da *h.* Brazil
47 F1 Ibicuí da Cruz *r.* Brazil
46 E2 Ibiraçu Brazil
65 G3 Ibiza *i. Balearic Is* Spain
65 G3 Ibiza Spain
66 F6 Iblei, Monti *mts Sicily* Italy
43 K6 Ibotirama Brazil
79 H5 Ibrā' Oman
79 H5 Ibrī Oman
94 B1 Ibuhos *i.* Phil.
90 C8 Ibusuki Japan
42 C6 Ica Peru
45 D4 Içana *r.* Brazil
45 D4 Içana Brazil
35 E3 Iceberg Canyon U.S.A.
80 E3 İçel Turkey
48 Iceland *country* Europe
90 C7 Ichifusa-yama *mt.* Japan
91 H6 Ichihara Japan
91 F6 Ichinomiya Japan
91 H4 Ichinoseki Japan
77 R4 Ichinskaya Sopka *mt* Rus. Fed.
69 E5 Ichnya Ukr.
20 B3 Icy Pt *pt* U.S.A.
20 B3 Icy Strait *chan.* U.S.A.
27 E5 Idabel U.S.A.
24 D2 Idaho *div.* U.S.A.
24 D3 Idaho City U.S.A.
24 D3 Idaho Falls U.S.A.
62 C6 Idar-Oberstein Ger.
61 F5 Idarwald *forest* Ger.
78 C5 Idfu Egypt
100 D2 Idhān Awbārī *des.* Libya
101 D2 Idhān Murzūq *des.* Libya
102 B4 Idiofa Zaire
54 S2 Idivuoma Sweden
80 C6 Idku Egypt
80 F4 Idlib Syria
55 N6 Idre Sweden
105 H6 Idutywa S. Africa
55 T8 Iecava Latvia
46 B3 Iepê Brazil
61 A4 Ieper Belgium
67 L7 Ierapetra Greece
103 D4 Ifakara Tanz.
103 E6 Ifanadiana Madag.
100 C4 Ife Nigeria
54 U1 Ifjord Norway
91 F6 Iga Japan
92 E6 Igan Malaysia
46 C3 Igarapava Brazil
76 K3 Igarka Rus. Fed.
84 C6 Igatpuri India
81 K2 Iğdır Turkey
55 P6 Iggesund Sweden
66 C5 Iglesias *Sardinia* Italy
22 B4 Ignace Can.
55 U9 Ignalina Lith.
69 C7 İğneada Turkey
67 N4 İğneada Burnu *pt* Turkey

63 Q3 Igorevskaya Rus. Fed.
67 J5 Igoumenitsa Greece
76 H3 Igrim Rus. Fed.
46 B4 Iguaçu r. Brazil
46 A4 Iguaçu Falls waterfall Arg./Brazil
46 E1 Iguaí Brazil
45 B4 Iguaje, Mesa de h. Col.
36 E5 Iguala Mex.
65 G2 Igualada Spain
46 C4 Iguape Brazil
46 D3 Iguarapé Brazil
46 A3 Iguatemi Brazil
46 A3 Iguatemi r. Brazil
43 L5 Iguatu Brazil
Iguazú, Cataratas do waterfall see Iguaçu Falls
102 A4 Iguéla Gabon
102 D4 Igunga Tanz.
103 E5 Iharaña Madag.
86 J3 Ihbulag Mongolia
103 E6 Ihosy Madag.
88 G1 Ih Tal China
91 F6 Iida Japan
91 G5 Iide-san mt. Japan
54 U2 Iijärvi l. Fin.
54 T4 Iijoki r. Fin.
54 U5 Iisalmi Fin.
91 G5 Iiyama Japan
90 C7 Iizuka Japan
100 C4 Ijebu-Ode Nigeria
81 K1 Ijevan Armenia
61 C2 IJmuiden Neth.
61 E2 IJssel r. Neth.
61 D2 IJsselmeer l. Neth.
55 S6 Ikaalinen Fin.
105 G2 Ikageleng S. Africa
105 G3 Ikageng S. Africa
67 M6 Ikaria i. Greece
55 L8 Ikast Denmark
90 J2 Ikeda Japan
90 D6 Ikeda Japan
102 C4 Ikela Zaire
67 K3 Ikhtiman Bulg.
104 F4 Ikhutseng S. Africa
90 B7 Iki i. Japan
69 H6 Iki-Burul Rus. Fed.
90 B7 Iki-suidō chan. Japan
100 C4 Ikom Nigeria
103 E6 Ikongo Madag.
69 H6 Ikryanoye Rus. Fed.
102 D4 Ikungu Tanz.
90 E6 Ikuno Japan
94 B2 Ilagan Phil.
102 D3 Ilaisamis Kenya
81 L5 Īlām Iran
85 F4 Ilam Nepal
100 C4 Ilaro Nigeria
63 J4 Iława Pol.
21 H3 Île-à-la-Crosse Can.
21 H3 Île-à-la-Crosse, Lac l. Can.
102 C4 Ilebo Zaire
102 D3 Ileret Kenya
68 G2 Ileza Rus. Fed.
21 K3 Ilford Can.
59 H6 Ilford U.K.
116 A4 Ilfracombe Austr.
59 C6 Ilfracombe U.K.
80 D1 Ilgaz Turkey
80 D1 Ilgaz D. mts Turkey
80 C2 Ilgın Turkey
45 D5 Ilha Grande Brazil
46 D3 Ilha Grande, Baía da b. Brazil
46 B3 Ilha Grande, Represa resr Brazil
46 B3 Ilha Solteira, Represa resr Brazil
65 B2 Ílhavo Port.
46 E1 Ilhéus Brazil
100 □ Ilhéus Secos ou do Rombo i. Cape Verde
18 Iliamna Lake l. U.S.A.
80 G2 İliç Turkey
94 C4 Iligan Phil.
94 C4 Iligan Bay b. Phil.
68 H2 Il'insko-Podomskoye Rus. Fed.
33 F3 Ilion U.S.A.
59 F5 Ilkeston U.K.
58 F4 Ilkley U.K.
94 B5 Illana Bay b. Phil.
47 B1 Illapel Chile
47 B1 Illapel r. Chile
62 E7 Iller r. Ger.
69 D6 Illichivs'k Ukr.
42 E7 Illimani, Nevado de mt. Bol.
30 C5 Illinois div. U.S.A.
30 C5 Illinois r. U.S.A.
30 B5 Illinois and Mississippi Canal canal U.S.A.
69 D5 Illintsi Ukr.
100 C2 Illizi Alg.
54 S5 Ilmajoki Fin.
68 D3 Il'men', Ozero l. Rus. Fed.
59 E7 Ilminster U.K.
42 D7 Ilo Peru
94 A4 Iloc i. Phil.
94 B4 Iloilo Phil.
54 W5 Ilomantsi Fin.
100 C4 Ilorin Nigeria
69 F6 Ilovays'k Ukr.
69 H5 Ilovlya r. Rus. Fed.
69 G5 Ilovlya Rus. Fed.
115 K2 Iluka Austr.
90 D6 Imabari Japan
91 G5 Imaichi Japan
91 F6 Imajō Japan
81 K6 Imām al Ḥamzah Iraq
80 E3 İmamoğlu Turkey
81 K5 Imām Ḥamīd Iraq
90 B7 Imari Japan
45 E3 Imataca, Serranía de mts Venez.
55 V6 Imatra Fin.
91 F6 Imazu Japan
44 G3 Imbituba Brazil
46 B4 Imbituva Brazil
68 G3 imeni Babushkina Rus. Fed.
102 E3 Īmī Eth.
81 M2 İmişli Azer.
66 D2 Imola Italy
105 H4 Impendle S. Africa
43 J5 Imperatriz Brazil
66 C3 Imperia Italy
26 C3 Imperial U.S.A.
34 D5 Imperial Beach U.S.A.
35 E5 Imperial Valley v. U.S.A.
102 B3 Impfondo Congo
85 H4 Imphal India
67 L4 İmroz Turkey
80 F5 Imtān Syria
94 A4 Imuruan Bay b. Phil.
91 F6 Ina Japan
91 G5 Ina-gawa r. Japan
42 E6 Inambari r. Peru
100 C2 In Aménas Alg.
117 C4 Inangahua Junction N.Z.
93 J7 Inanwatan Indon.
54 U2 Inari Fin.
54 U2 Inarijärvi l. Fin.
54 T2 Inarijoki r. Fin./Norway
91 H5 Inawashiro-ko l. Japan
91 F6 Inazawa Japan
65 H3 Inca Spain
69 E7 İnce Burnu pt Turkey
69 C7 İnce Burnu pt Turkey
80 D3 İnceburun Burnu pt Turkey
80 E2 İncesu Turkey
60 E5 Inch Rep. of Ireland
57 C2 Inchard, Loch b. U.K.
57 E4 Inchkeith i. U.K.
87 N4 Inch'ŏn S. Korea
105 K2 Incomati r. Moz.
57 B5 Indaal, Loch in. U.K.
46 D2 Indaiá r. Brazil
46 B2 Indaiá Grande r. Brazil
55 P6 Indalsälven r. Sweden
55 J6 Indalstø Norway
34 C3 Independence CA U.S.A.
34 B4 Independence IA U.S.A.
27 E4 Independence KS U.S.A.
30 A2 Independence MN U.S.A.
26 E4 Independence MO U.S.A.
32 C6 Independence VA U.S.A.
30 B3 Independence WV U.S.A.
24 C3 Independence Mts mts U.S.A.
76 G5 Inderborskiy Kazak.
70 India country Asia
30 D2 Indian r. U.S.A.
32 D4 Indiana U.S.A.
30 D5 Indiana div. U.S.A.
30 D5 Indiana Dunes National Lakeshore res. U.S.A.
13 O7 Indian-Antarctic Ridge sea feature Pac. Oc.
30 D6 Indianapolis IN U.S.A.
Indian Desert des. see Thar Desert
23 J3 Indian Harbour Can.
30 D3 Indian Lake l. MI U.S.A.
33 F3 Indian Lake NY U.S.A.
32 B4 Indian Lake l. OH U.S.A.
32 D4 Indian Lake l. PA U.S.A.
26 E3 Indianola IA U.S.A.
27 F5 Indianola MS U.S.A.
35 F2 Indian Peak summit U.S.A.
30 E3 Indian River U.S.A.
35 E3 Indian Springs U.S.A.
35 G4 Indian Wells U.S.A.
77 Q2 Indigirka r. Rus. Fed.
67 J2 Inđija Yugo.
20 F2 Indin Lake l. Can.
34 D5 Indio U.S.A.
111 G3 Indispensable Reefs rf Solomon Is
71 Indonesia country Asia
84 C5 Indore India
92 □ Indramayu, Tanjung pt Indon.
64 E3 Indre r. France
85 E7 Indur India
84 B4 Indus r. Pak.
84 A5 Indus, Mouths of the est. Pak.
105 G5 Indwe S. Africa
80 E1 İnebolu Turkey
80 B1 İnegöl Turkey
32 B6 Inez U.S.A.
104 D7 Infanta, Cape hd S. Africa
36 D5 Infiernillo, L. l. Mex.
30 D3 Ingalls U.S.A.
20 J2 Ingalls Lake l. Can.
32 B2 Ingalls, Mt mt. U.S.A.
47 C4 Ingeniero Jacobacci Arg.
31 G4 Ingersoll Can.
116 B2 Ingham Austr.
58 E3 Ingleborough h. U.K.
58 E3 Ingleton U.K.
115 J2 Inglewood Qld. Austr.
114 E6 Inglewood Vic. Austr.
59 H4 Ingoldmells U.K.
62 E6 Ingolstadt Ger.
23 H4 Ingonish Can.
85 G4 Ingrāj Bāzār India
20 F2 Ingray Lake l. Can.
100 C3 I-n-Guezzam Alg.
69 H7 Ingushskaya Respublika div. Rus. Fed.
105 K3 Ingwavuma S. Africa
105 K2 Inhaca Moz.
105 K3 Inhaca, Peninsula pen. Moz.
105 K1 Inhambane div. Moz.
103 D6 Inhambane Moz.
103 D5 Inhaminga Moz.
46 B3 Inhanduízinho r. Brazil
46 D1 Inhaúmas Brazil
45 C4 Inírida r. Col.
60 A4 Inishark i. Rep. of Ireland
60 A4 Inishbofin i. Rep. of Ireland
60 A3 Inishkea North i. Rep. of Ireland
60 A3 Inishkea South i. Rep. of Ireland
60 B4 Inishmaan i. Rep. of Ireland
60 B4 Inishmore i. Rep. of Ireland
60 C3 Inishmurray i. Rep. of Ireland
60 D2 Inishowen pen. Rep. of Ireland
60 E2 Inishowen Head hd Rep. of Ireland
60 D2 Inishtrahull i. Rep. of Ireland
60 D2 Inishtrahull Sound chan. Rep. of Ireland
60 A4 Inishturk i. Rep. of Ireland
116 C5 Injune Austr.
113 H3 Inkerman Austr.
117 D5 Inland Kaikoura Range mts N.Z.
Inland Sea sea see Seto-naikai
114 D1 Innamincka Austr.
54 O3 Inndyr Norway
Inner Mongolian Aut. Region div. see Nei Monggol Zizhiqu
57 C3 Inner Sound chan. U.K.
116 B1 Innisfail Austr.
90 D6 Innoshima Japan
62 E7 Innsbruck Austria
60 D4 Inny r. Rep. of Ireland
102 B4 Inongo Zaire
62 J4 Inowrocław Pol.
100 C2 In Salah Alg.
68 H4 Insar Rus. Fed.
57 F3 Insch U.K.
112 B5 Inscription, C. c. Austr.
76 H3 Inta Rus. Fed.
47 D2 Intendente Alvear Arg.
62 C7 Interlaken Switz.
26 E1 International Falls U.S.A.
91 H6 Inubō-zaki pt Japan
90 C7 Inukai Japan
22 E2 Inukjuak Can.
57 C4 Inveraray U.K.
57 F4 Inverbervie U.K.
117 B7 Invercargill N.Z.
115 J2 Inverell Austr.
57 D3 Invergordon U.K.
57 E4 Inverkeithing U.K.
23 H4 Inverness Can.
57 D3 Inverness U.K.
29 D6 Inverness U.S.A.
57 F3 Inverurie U.K.
114 B5 Investigator Strait chan. Austr.
86 E1 Inya Rus. Fed.
25 C5 Inyokern U.S.A.
34 C3 Inyo Mts mts U.S.A.
102 D4 Inyonga Tanz.
68 H4 Inza Rus. Fed.
69 G4 Inzhavino Rus. Fed.
67 J5 Ioannina Greece
93 L2 Iō-Jima i. Japan
27 E4 Iola U.S.A.
57 B4 Iona i. U.K.
24 C1 Ione U.S.A.
30 E4 Ionia U.S.A.
67 H5 Ionian Islands is Greece
66 G6 Ionian Sea sea Greece/Italy
Ionoi Nisoi is see Ionian Islands
81 L1 Iori r. Georgia
67 L6 Ios i. Greece
30 B5 Iowa r. U.S.A.
30 A4 Iowa div. U.S.A.
30 B5 Iowa City U.S.A.
26 E3 Iowa Falls U.S.A.
46 C2 Ipameri Brazil
42 D5 Iparía Peru
46 D2 Ipatinga Brazil
69 G6 Ipatovo Rus. Fed.
105 F3 Ipelegeng S. Africa
45 A4 Ipiales Col.
46 E1 Ipiaú Brazil
46 B4 Ipiranga Brazil
92 C6 Ipoh Malaysia
43 L5 Ipojuca r. Brazil
46 B2 Iporá Brazil
102 C3 Ippy C.A.R.
67 M4 İpsala Turkey
115 K1 Ipswich Austr.
59 J5 Ipswich U.K.
44 B2 Iquique Chile
42 D4 Iquitos Peru
91 F6 Irago-misaki pt Japan
67 L6 Irakleia i. Greece
Irakleio see Iraklion
67 L7 Iraklion Greece
46 E1 Iramaia Brazil
70 Iran country Asia
81 L3 Irānshāh Iran
79 J4 Irānshahr Iran
36 D4 Irapuato Mex.
70 Iraq country Asia
33 G2 Irasville U.S.A.
46 B4 Irati Brazil
80 E5 Irbid Jordan
76 H4 Irbit Rus. Fed.
43 K6 Irecê Brazil
48 Ireland, Republic of country Europe
102 C4 Irema Zaire
76 H5 Irgiz Kazak.
93 K8 Irian Jaya div. Indon.
81 L2 Īrī Dagh mt. Iran
94 B3 Iriga Phil.
100 B3 Irîgui reg. Mali/Maur.
103 D4 Iringa Tanz.
43 H4 Iriri r. Brazil
56 D5 Irish Sea sea Rep. of Ireland
43 J4 Irituia Brazil
86 H1 Irkutsk Rus. Fed.
80 D2 Irmak Turkey
114 B4 Iron Baron Austr.
31 F2 Iron Bridge Can.
32 E3 Irondequoit U.S.A.
114 B4 Iron Knob Austr.
30 C3 Iron Mountain MI U.S.A.
35 F3 Iron Mountain mt. UT U.S.A.
30 C2 Iron River U.S.A.
27 F4 Ironton MO U.S.A.
32 B5 Ironton OH U.S.A.
30 B2 Ironwood U.S.A.
33 F2 Iroquois Can.
30 D5 Iroquois r. U.S.A.
94 C3 Irosin Phil.
91 G6 Irō-zaki hd Japan
69 D5 Irpin' Ukr.
83 J7 Irrawaddy r. China/Myanmar
83 H7 Irrawaddy, Mouths of the est. Myanmar
68 J2 Irta Rus. Fed.
58 E3 Irthing r. U.K.
86 C1 Irtysh r. Kazak./Rus. Fed.
102 C3 Irumu Zaire
65 F1 Irún Spain
57 D5 Irvine U.K.
34 D5 Irvine CA U.S.A.
32 B6 Irvine KY U.S.A.
116 A1 Irvinebank Austr.
27 D5 Irving U.S.A.
116 C4 Isaac r. Austr.
94 B5 Isabela Phil.
42 □ Isabela, Isla i. Galapagos Is Ecuador
37 G6 Isabelia, Cordillera mts Nic.
30 B2 Isabella U.S.A.
34 C4 Isabella Lake l. U.S.A.
30 D2 Isabelle, Pt pt U.S.A.
54 B3 Ísafjarðardjúp est. Iceland
54 B3 Ísafjörður Iceland
90 C7 Isahaya Japan
84 B2 Isà Khel Pak.
68 G1 Isakogorka Rus. Fed.
103 E6 Isalo, Massif de l' mts Madag.
103 E6 Isalo, Parc National de l' nat. park Madag.
45 C4 Isana r. Col.
57 □ Isbister U.K.
66 E4 Ischia, Isola d' i. Italy
45 A4 Iscuande r. Col.
91 F6 Ise Japan
102 C3 Isengi Zaire
64 H4 Isère r. France
62 F3 Iserlohn Ger.
66 F4 Isernia Italy
91 G5 Isesaki Japan
91 F6 Ise-shima National Park nat. park Japan
91 F6 Ise-wan b. Japan
100 C4 Iseyin Nigeria
Isfahan see Eşfahan
79 L1 Isfara Tajik.
81 K5 Ishāq Iraq
68 J4 Isheyevka Rus. Fed.
90 H2 Ishikari-gawa r. Japan
90 H2 Ishikari-wan b. Japan
91 F5 Ishikawa Japan
91 H4 Ishinomaki Japan
91 H4 Ishinomaki-wan b. Japan
91 H5 Ishioka Japan
90 D7 Ishizuchi-san mt. Japan
84 C1 Ishkuman Pak.
30 D2 Ishpeming U.S.A.
85 G4 Ishurdi Bangl.
42 E7 Isiboro Sécure, Parque Nacional nat. park Bol.
80 B2 Işıklı Turkey
80 B2 Işıklı Barajı resr Turkey
76 J4 Isil'kul' Rus. Fed.
105 J4 Isipingo S. Africa
102 C3 Isiro Zaire
116 A5 Isisford Austr.
80 F3 İskenderun Turkey
80 E1 İskilip Turkey
76 K4 Iskitim Rus. Fed.
67 L3 Iskŭr r. Bulg.
20 C3 Iskut r. Can.
20 C3 Iskut Can.
80 F3 İslahiye Turkey
84 C2 Islamabad Pak.
84 C3 Islam Barrage barrage Pak.
84 B4 Islamgarh Pak.
84 B4 Islamkot Pak.
29 D7 Islamorada U.S.A.
94 A4 Island Bay b. Phil.
33 J1 Island Falls U.S.A.
21 L4 Island L. l. Can.
114 B3 Island Lagoon salt flat Austr.
21 L4 Island Lake Can.
30 A2 Island Lake l. U.S.A.
60 F3 Island Magee pen. U.K.
34 A1 Island Mountain U.S.A.
24 E2 Island Park U.S.A.
33 H2 Island Pond U.S.A.
117 E1 Islands, Bay of b. N.Z.
57 B5 Islay i. U.K.
32 E6 Isle of Wight U.S.A.
30 C2 Isle Royale National Park nat. park U.S.A.
78 C3 Ismâ'ilîya Egypt
81 M1 İsmayıllı Azer.
55 R5 Isojoki Fin.
103 D5 Isoka Zambia
54 U3 Isokylä Fin.
66 G5 Isola di Capo Rizzuto Italy
80 C3 Isparta Turkey
67 M3 Isperikh Bulg.
81 H1 İspir Turkey
70 Israel country Asia
68 H4 Issa Rus. Fed.
100 B4 Issia Côte d'Ivoire
81 K6 Issin Iraq
64 F4 Issoire France
81 J4 Iştablāt Iraq
80 B1 İstanbul Turkey
İstanbul Boğazı str. see Bosporus
81 M5 Īstgāh-e Eznā Iran
67 K5 Istiaia Greece
45 A3 Istmina Col.
29 D7 Istokpoga, L. l. U.S.A.
66 E2 Istra pen. Croatia
64 G5 Istres France
Istria pen. see Istra
85 G5 Iswaripur Bangl.
43 L6 Itabaianinha Brazil
43 K6 Itaberaba Brazil
46 D2 Itabira Brazil
46 D3 Itabirito Brazil
46 E1 Itabuna Brazil
43 G4 Itacoatiara Brazil
46 B3 Itaguajé Brazil
46 C3 Itaí Brazil
46 A4 Itaimbey r. Para.
43 G4 Itaituba Brazil
44 G3 Itajaí Brazil
46 D3 Itajubá Brazil
85 F5 Itaki India
48 Italy country Europe
43 L7 Itamaraju Brazil
46 D2 Itamarandiba Brazil
46 E2 Itambacuri Brazil
46 E2 Itambacuri r. Brazil
46 D2 Itambé, Pico de mt Brazil
103 E6 Itampolo Madag.
85 H4 Itanagar India
46 D1 Itanguari r. Brazil
46 C4 Itanhaém Brazil
46 E2 Itanhém Brazil
46 E2 Itanhém r. Brazil
46 E2 Itaobim Brazil
46 C2 Itapajipe Brazil
46 E1 Itaparica, Ilha i. Brazil
46 E1 Itapebi Brazil
46 E3 Itapemirim Brazil
46 E3 Itaperuna Brazil
46 E1 Itapetinga Brazil
46 C3 Itapetininga Brazil
46 C3 Itapeva Brazil
43 L6 Itapicuru r. Bahia Brazil
43 K5 Itapicuru r. Maranhão Brazil
43 K4 Itapicuru Mirim Brazil
43 L4 Itapipoca Brazil
46 C3 Itararé r. Brazil
46 C4 Itararé Brazil
84 D5 Itarsi India
46 B2 Itarumã Brazil
94 B1 Itbayat i. Phil.
20 G1 Itchen Lake l. Can.
45 B3 Ité r. Col.
67 K5 Itea Greece
30 E4 Ithaca MI U.S.A.
32 E3 Ithaca NY U.S.A.
80 F6 Ithrah S. Arabia
102 C3 Itimbiri r. Zaire
46 E2 Itinga Brazil
46 A2 Itiquira r. Brazil
46 A2 Itiquira Brazil
91 G6 Itō Japan
91 F5 Itoigawa Japan
66 C4 Ittiri Sardinia Italy
46 C3 Itu Brazil
45 B3 Ituango Col.
42 D5 Ituí r. Brazil
46 C2 Ituiutaba Brazil
102 C4 Itula Zaire
46 C2 Itumbiara Brazil
43 G2 Ituni Guyana
43 J5 Itupiranga Brazil
46 B3 Iturama Brazil
46 A4 Iturbe Para.
77 Q5 Iturup, Ostrov i. Rus. Fed.
45 E5 Ituxi r. Brazil
62 D4 Itzehoe Ger.
45 C4 Iuaretê Brazil
77 V3 Iultin Rus. Fed.
45 C4 Iutica Brazil
46 B3 Ivaí r. Brazil
54 U2 Ivalo Fin.
54 U2 Ivalojoki r. Fin.
69 C4 Ivanava Belarus
67 H3 Ivangrad Yugo.
114 F4 Ivanhoe Austr.
31 F1 Ivanhoe r. Can.
21 H2 Ivanhoe Lake l. N.W.T. Can.
31 F1 Ivanhoe Lake l. Ont. Can.
63 O5 Ivankiv Ukr.
69 C5 Ivano-Frankivs'k Ukr.
68 G3 Ivanovo Rus. Fed.
68 G3 Ivanovskaya Oblast' div. Rus. Fed.
35 E4 Ivanpah Lake l. U.S.A.
68 J4 Ivanteyevka Rus. Fed.
68 C4 Ivatsevichy Belarus
67 M4 Ivaylovgrad Bulg.
76 H3 Ivdel' Rus. Fed.
46 B3 Ivinheima Brazil
46 B3 Ivinheima r. Brazil
103 E6 Ivohibe Madag.
66 B2 Ivrea Italy
67 M5 İvrindi Turkey
69 H7 Ivris Ugheltekhili pass Georgia
16 Ivujivik U.S.A.
63 N4 Ivyanyets Belarus
91 H4 Iwaizumi Japan
91 H5 Iwaki Japan
90 H3 Iwaki-san volc. Japan
90 D6 Iwakuni Japan
90 H2 Iwamizawa Japan
91 H4 Iwanuma Japan
90 G3 Iwasaki Japan
91 G5 Iwasuge-yama volc. Japan
91 F6 Iwata Japan
91 H4 Iwate Japan
91 H4 Iwate Japan
91 H4 Iwate-san volc. Japan
100 C4 Iwo Nigeria
Iwo Jima i. see Iō-Jima
68 C4 Iwye Belarus
36 E4 Ixmiquilpán Mex.
105 J5 Ixopo S. Africa
59 H5 Ixworth U.K.
86 H1 Iya r. Rus. Fed.
90 D7 Iyo Japan
90 D7 Iyomishima Japan
90 D7 Iyo-nada b. Japan
36 G5 Izabal, L. de l. Guatemala
90 H2 Izari-dake mt. Japan
102 D4 Izazi Tanz.
69 H7 Izberbash Rus. Fed.
63 Q3 Izdeshkovo Rus. Fed.
76 G4 Izhevsk Rus. Fed.
76 G3 Izhma Rus. Fed.
68 K1 Izhma r. Rus. Fed.
69 F4 Izmalkovo Rus. Fed.
69 D6 Izmayil Ukr.
67 M5 İzmir Turkey
67 M5 İzmir Körfezi g. Turkey
80 B1 İznik Gölü l. Turkey
69 G6 Izobil'nyy Rus. Fed.
91 G6 Izu-hantō pen. Japan
90 B6 Izuhara Japan
90 C7 Izumi Japan
91 E6 Izumisano Japan
90 D6 Izumo Japan
91 G5 Izumozaki Japan
91 G6 Izu-Shotō is Japan
69 C5 Izyaslav Ukr.
69 F5 Izyum Ukr.


# J


Jabal, Bahr el r. see White Nile
65 E3 Jabalón r. Spain
84 D5 Jabalpur India
80 F3 Jabbūl Syria
112 F2 Jabiru Austr.
80 E4 Jablah Syria
66 G3 Jablanica Bos.-Herz.
43 M5 Jaboatão Brazil
46 C3 Jaboticabal Brazil
65 F1 Jaca Spain
43 K6 Jacaré r. Brazil
43 G5 Jacareacanga Brazil
46 C3 Jacareí Brazil
47 C1 Jáchal r. Arg.
46 E2 Jacinto Brazil
42 F5 Jaciparaná r. Brazil
30 D1 Jackfish Can.
31 H3 Jack Lake l. Can.
33 H2 Jackman U.S.A.
27 D5 Jacksboro U.S.A.
116 C6 Jackson Austr.
27 G6 Jackson AL U.S.A.
34 B2 Jackson CA U.S.A.
32 B6 Jackson KY U.S.A.
30 E4 Jackson MI U.S.A.
26 E3 Jackson MN U.S.A.
27 F4 Jackson MO U.S.A.
27 F5 Jackson MS U.S.A.
32 B5 Jackson OH U.S.A.
29 B5 Jackson TN U.S.A.
24 E3 Jackson WY U.S.A.
117 B5 Jackson Head hd N.Z.
24 E2 Jackson L. l. U.S.A.
27 E6 Jackson, Lake U.S.A.
30 D3 Jacksonport U.S.A.
27 E5 Jacksonville AR U.S.A.
29 D6 Jacksonville FL U.S.A.
30 B6 Jacksonville IL U.S.A.
29 E5 Jacksonville NC U.S.A.
27 E6 Jacksonville TX U.S.A.
29 D6 Jacksonville Beach U.S.A.
37 K5 Jacmel Haiti
84 B3 Jacobabad Pak.
43 K6 Jacobina Brazil
35 F3 Jacob Lake U.S.A.
104 F4 Jacobsdal S. Africa
23 H4 Jacques-Cartier, Détroit de chan. Can.
23 G4 Jacques Cartier, Mt mt. Can.
23 G4 Jacquet River Can.
47 G1 Jacuí r. Brazil
43 L6 Jacuípe r. Brazil
43 J4 Jacunda Brazil
46 C4 Jacupiranga Brazil
45 C2 Jacura Venez.

66 G2 Jadovnik *mt.* Bos.-Herz.
101 D1 Jādū Libya
42 C5 Jaén Peru
94 B3 Jaen Phil.
65 E4 Jaén Spain
81 M4 Ja'farābād Iran
Jaffa *see* Tel Aviv-Yafo
114 C6 Jaffa, C. *pt* Austr.
83 E9 Jaffna Sri Lanka
33 G3 Jaffrey U.S.A.
84 D3 Jagadhri India
83 F7 Jagdalpur India
105 F4 Jagersfontein S. Africa
84 D2 Jaggang China
Jagok Tso *salt l. see* Urru Co
84 C3 Jagraon India
47 G2 Jaguarão Brazil
47 G2 Jaguarão *r.* Brazil/Uru.
46 C4 Jaguariaíva Brazil
85 H4 Jahanabad India
81 M3 Jahan Dagh *mt.* Iran
84 C4 Jahazpur India
81 K7 Jahmah *w.* Iraq
79 G4 Jahrom Iran
88 B3 Jainca China
84 C4 Jaipur India
84 B4 Jaisalmer India
84 E5 Jaisinghnagar India
84 D5 Jaitgarh *mt.* India
85 E3 Jajarkot Nepal
66 G2 Jajce Bos.-Herz.
92 □ Jakarta Indon.
20 C2 Jakes Corner Can.
85 B4 Jakhan India
54 P3 Jäkkvik Sweden
54 S5 Jakobstad Fin.
27 C5 Jal U.S.A.
84 B2 Jalālābād Afgh.
79 L1 Jalal-Abad Kyrgyzstan
84 C3 Jalandhar India
36 E5 Jalapa Enriquez Mex.
55 S5 Jalasjärvi Fin.
85 G4 Jaldhaka *r.* Bangl.
46 B3 Jales Brazil
85 F5 Jaleswar India
84 C5 Jalgaon *Maharashtra* India
84 D5 Jalgaon *Maharashtra* India
81 L6 Jalībah Iraq
100 D4 Jalingo Nigeria
84 C6 Jalna India
65 F2 Jalón *r.* Spain
85 G4 Jalpaiguri India
101 E2 Jālū Libya
81 K4 Jalūlā Iraq
84 D5 Jamai India
16 Jamaica *country* Caribbean Sea
37 J5 Jamaica Channel *chan.* Haiti/Jamaica
81 L3 Jamalabad Iran
81 M5 Jamālābād Iran
85 G4 Jamalpur Bangl.
85 F4 Jamalpur India
43 G5 Jamanxim *r.* Brazil
92 C7 Jambi Indon.
116 D5 Jambin Austr.
84 C4 Jambo India
95 A4 Jamboaye *r.* Indon.
94 A5 Jambongan *i.* Malaysia
95 A4 Jambuair, Tg *pt* Indon.
81 K4 Jamdar Iran
26 D2 James *r. ND* U.S.A.
32 D6 James *r. VA* U.S.A.
84 B4 Jamesabad Pak.
22 D3 James Bay *b.* Can.
47 D2 James Craik Arg.
117 B6 James Pk *mt.* N.Z.
119 B2 James Ross I. *i.* Ant.
114 C4 Jamestown Austr.
105 G5 Jamestown S. Africa
26 D2 Jamestown *ND* U.S.A.
32 D3 Jamestown *NY* U.S.A.
81 M4 Jamīlābād Iran
84 C2 Jammu Jammu and Kashmir
84 C2 Jammu and Kashmir *terr.* Asia
84 B5 Jamnagar India
84 D4 Jamni *r.* India
84 B3 Jampur Pak.
55 T6 Jämsä Fin.
55 T6 Jämsänkoski Fin.
85 F5 Jamshedpur India
85 G5 Jamuna *r.* Bangl.
82 G5 Janakpur Nepal
46 D1 Janaúba Brazil
79 G3 Janda Iran
46 B2 Jandaia Brazil
84 B2 Jandola Pak.
116 D6 Jandowae Austr.
34 B1 Janesville *CA* U.S.A.
30 C4 Janesville *WI* U.S.A.
85 G4 Jangipur India
81 L2 Jānī Beyglū Iran
81 L5 Jannah Iraq
104 F6 Jansenville S. Africa
46 D1 Januária Brazil
84 C5 Jaora India
71 Japan *country* Asia
Japan Alps Nat. Park *see* Chūbu-Sangaku Nat. Park
91 E4 Japan, Sea of *sea* Asia
14 E4 Japan Tr. *sea feature* Pac. Oc.
42 E4 Japurá *r.* Brazil
85 H4 Japvo Mount *mt.* India
45 A3 Jaqué Panama
80 G3 Jarābulus Syria
46 A3 Jaraguari Brazil
80 E5 Jarash Jordan

46 A3 Jardim Brazil
113 H2 Jardine River National Park *nat. park* Austr.
37 J4 Jardines de la Reina, Archipiélago de los *is* Cuba
87 L2 Jargalant Mongolia
81 K4 Jarmo Iraq
55 P7 Järna Sweden
62 H5 Jarocin Pol.
63 L5 Jarosław Pol.
54 N5 Järpen Sweden
88 B2 Jartai China
42 F6 Jarú Brazil
87 M3 Jarud Qi China
55 T7 Järvakandi Estonia
55 T6 Järvenpää Fin.
109 Jarvis Island *i.* Pac. Oc.
84 B5 Jasdan India
79 H4 Jāsk Iran
63 K6 Jasło Pol.
44 D8 Jason Is *is* Falkland Is
119 B2 Jason Pen. *pen.* Ant.
20 F4 Jasper Can.
29 C5 Jasper *AL* U.S.A.
27 E4 Jasper *AR* U.S.A.
29 D6 Jasper *FL* U.S.A.
28 C4 Jasper *IN* U.S.A.
32 E3 Jasper *NY* U.S.A.
32 B5 Jasper *OH* U.S.A.
27 E6 Jasper *TX* U.S.A.
20 F4 Jasper Nat. Park *nat. park* Can.
81 K5 Jaşşān Iraq
63 J6 Jastrzębie-Zdrój Pol.
84 C4 Jaswantpura India
63 J7 Jászberény Hungary
46 B2 Jataí Brazil
43 G4 Jatapu *r.* Brazil
84 B4 Jati Pak.
84 B3 Jatoi Pak.
46 C3 Jaú Brazil
42 F4 Jaú *r.* Brazil
45 E5 Jauaperi *r.* Brazil
45 D3 Jaua Sarisariñama, Parque Nacional *nat. park* Venez.
55 S8 Jaunlutriņi Latvia
55 U8 Jaunpiebalga Latvia
85 E4 Jaunpur India
42 F4 Jaú, Parque Nacional do *nat. park* Brazil
46 B2 Jauru *r.* Brazil
46 A2 Jauru Brazil
69 G2 Java Georgia
92 □ Java *i.* Indon.
13 M4 Java Ridge *sea feature* Indian Ocean
87 K2 Javarthushuu Mongolia
92 D7 Java Sea *sea* Indon.
Jawa *i. see* Java
92 □ Jawa Barat *div.* Indon.
84 C4 Jawad India
84 B4 Jawai *r.* India
92 □ Jawa Tengah *div.* Indon.
92 □ Jawa Timur *div.* Indon.
80 F3 Jawbān Bayk Syria
84 C6 Jawhar India
102 E3 Jawhar Somalia
62 H5 Jawor Pol.
93 K2 Jaya, Pk *mt.* Indon.
93 L7 Jayapura Indon.
85 F4 Jaynagar India
80 F5 Jayrūd Syria
78 E6 Jazā'ir Farasān *is* S. Arabia
81 M3 Jazvān Iran
81 J1 Jdaide Syria
35 H4 Jean U.S.A.
20 E2 Jean Marie River Can.
23 G2 Jeannin, Lac *l.* Can.
100 C4 Jebba Nigeria
101 E3 Jebel Abyad Plateau *plat.* Sudan
84 C3 Jech Doab *lowland* Pak.
57 F5 Jedburgh U.K.
78 D5 Jedda S. Arabia
66 C6 Jedeida Tunisia
33 F2 Jefferson *NY* U.S.A.
30 C4 Jefferson *WV* U.S.A.
24 D2 Jefferson *r.* U.S.A.
26 E4 Jefferson City U.S.A.
34 D2 Jefferson, Mt *mt. NV* U.S.A.
24 B2 Jefferson, Mt *volc. OR* U.S.A.
28 C4 Jeffersonville U.S.A.
104 F7 Jeffrey's Bay S. Africa
44 A2 Jejuí Guazú *r.* Para.
55 T8 Jēkabpils Latvia
62 G5 Jelenia Góra Pol.
85 G4 Jelep La *pass* China
55 S8 Jelgava Latvia
32 A6 Jellico U.S.A.
95 C5 Jemaja *i.* Indon.
92 □ Jember Indon.
62 E5 Jena Ger.
100 C1 Jendouba Tunisia
80 E6 Jenin West Bank
32 B6 Jenkins U.S.A.
34 A2 Jenner U.S.A.
31 J3 Jennings U.S.A.
21 K4 Jenpeg Can.
114 E6 Jeparit Austr.
46 E1 Jequié Brazil
46 D2 Jequitaí *r.* Brazil
46 D2 Jequitaí Brazil
46 E2 Jequitinhonha *r.* Brazil
46 E2 Jequitinhonha Brazil
95 B5 Jerantut Malaysia
101 F4 Jerbar Sudan
37 K5 Jérémie Haiti
65 C4 Jerez de la Frontera Spain

65 C3 Jerez de los Caballeros Spain
67 J5 Jergucat Albania
116 B4 Jericho Austr.
80 E6 Jericho West Bank
115 F5 Jerilderie Austr.
81 K2 Jermuk Armenia
24 Jerome U.S.A.
112 C6 Jerramungup Austr.
56 E7 Jersey *i.* U.K.
33 F4 Jersey City U.S.A.
32 E4 Jersey Shore U.S.A.
28 B4 Jerseyville U.S.A.
43 K5 Jerumenha Brazil
80 E6 Jerusalem Israel/West Bank
115 J5 Jervis B. *b.* Austr.
115 J5 Jervis Bay Austr.
115 J5 Jervis Bay Territory *div.* Austr.
66 F1 Jesenice Slovenia
66 E3 Jesi Italy
55 M6 Jessheim Norway
85 G5 Jessore Bangl.
29 D6 Jesup U.S.A.
36 F5 Jesús Carranza Mex.
47 D1 Jesús María Arg.
84 B5 Jetalsar India
26 C4 Jetmore U.S.A.
85 F4 Jha Jha India
85 G5 Jhalakati Bangl.
82 E6 Jhalawar India
84 D3 Jhang Pak.
85 F5 Jharia India
85 F5 Jharsuguda India
84 C2 Jhatpat Pak.
84 C2 Jhelum Pak.
84 C2 Jhelum *r.* Pak.
85 G5 Jhenida Bangl.
84 B4 Jhudo Pak.
84 F4 Jhumritilaiya India
84 C4 Jhunjhunūn India
88 C3 Jiachuan China
88 F4 Jiading China
89 D5 Jiahe China
88 B3 Jiajiang China
88 B3 Jialing Jiang *r.* China
89 F4 Ji'an *Jiangxi* China
89 E5 Ji'an *Jiangxi* China
87 N3 Ji'an *Jilin* China
88 F1 Jianchang China
89 D4 Jiande China
89 C4 Jiangbei China
89 A6 Jiangcheng China
89 B5 Jiangchuan China
89 B3 Jiange China
89 D5 Jianghua China
89 C4 Jiangjin China
89 E5 Jiangkou China
89 E5 Jiangle China
89 D4 Jiangshan China
89 F4 Jiangshan China
89 D3 Jiangsu *div.* China
89 E5 Jiangxi *div.* China
88 D3 Jiang Xian China
89 D5 Jiangyin China
89 D5 Jiangyong China
89 A4 Jiangyou China
88 F3 Jianhu China
89 D6 Jian Jiang *r.* China
89 D4 Jianli China
89 E5 Jianning China
89 E4 Jian'ou China
88 F1 Jianping *Liaoning* China
88 F1 Jianping *Liaoning* China
89 C4 Jianshi China
89 B6 Jianshui China
89 E4 Jianyang *Fujian* China
89 B4 Jianyang *Sichuan* China
88 D2 Jiaocheng China
88 E2 Jiaohe *Hebei* China
87 N3 Jiaohe *Jilin* China
88 F2 Jiaojiang China
88 E2 Jiaolai *r.* China
88 G1 Jiaolai *r.* China
89 E5 Jiaoling China
88 D2 Jiaonan China
88 F2 Jiao Xian China
88 F2 Jiaozhou Wan *b.* China
88 F3 Jiaozuo China
88 F3 Jiashan China
88 D4 Jia Xian China
88 F4 Jiaxing China
89 D4 Jiayu China
82 J3 Jiayuguan China
89 E6 Jiazi China
Jiddah *see* Jedda
79 H6 Jiddat al Harāsīs *gravel area* Oman
88 B2 Jiehebe China
54 Q2 Jiehkkevarri *mt.* Norway
89 E6 Jieshi China
89 E6 Jieshi Wan *b.* China
88 E2 Jieshou China
54 T2 Jiešjávri *l.* Norway
89 E6 Jiexi China
89 E6 Jiexiu China
89 E6 Jieyang China
88 A3 Jigzhi China
62 G6 Jihlava Czech Rep.
102 E3 Jijiga Eth.
89 A4 Jiju China
84 D2 Jilganang Kol, S. *salt l.* China/Jammu and Kashmir

102 E3 Jilib Somalia
87 N3 Jilin *div.* China
87 N3 Jilin China
88 A2 Jilin China
102 D3 Jīma Eth.
36 D3 Jiménez *Chihuahua* Mex.
36 E4 Jiménez *Tamaulipas* Mex.
88 F2 Jimo China
82 G2 Jimsar China
33 F4 Jim Thorpe U.S.A.
88 E2 Jinan China
88 B2 Jinchang China
88 D3 Jincheng China
88 B4 Jinchuan China
84 D3 Jind India
115 H6 Jindabyne Austr.
115 G5 Jindera Austr.
62 G6 Jindřichův Hradec Czech Rep.
88 B3 Jing *r.* China
89 E4 Jing'an China
88 C2 Jingbian China
88 C3 Jingchuan China
89 F4 Jingde China
89 F4 Jingdezhen China
89 E5 Jinggangshan China
89 E5 Jinggongqiao China
88 E2 Jinghai China
83 K6 Jinghong China
88 F3 Jingjiang China
88 D4 Jingle China
88 E4 Jingmen China
88 B3 Jingning China
88 D4 Jingtai China
89 C6 Jingxi China
89 F4 Jing Xian *Anhui* China
89 C5 Jing Xian *Hunan* China
88 B2 Jingyuan China
88 F3 Jinhu China
89 F4 Jinhua China
88 D1 Jining *Nei Monggol Zizhiqu* China
88 E2 Jining *Shandong* China
102 D3 Jinja Uganda
89 F5 Jinjiang China
89 E4 Jin Jiang *r.* China
102 D3 Jinka Eth.
88 F1 Jinlingsi China
89 C7 Jinmu Jiao *pt* China
36 G6 Jinotepe Nic.
89 C5 Jinping *Guizhou* China
89 B6 Jinping *Yunnan* China
89 A5 Jinping Shan *mts* China
89 C5 Jinsha China
89 Jinsha Jiang *r. see* Yangtze
88 F4 Jinshan China
89 D4 Jinshi China
94 B4 Jintotolo *i.* Phil.
94 B4 Jintotolo Channel *chan.* Phil.
84 D6 Jintur India
89 E5 Jinxi *Jiangxi* China
88 F1 Jinxi *Liaoning* China
89 E4 Jinxian China
88 F2 Jin Xian China
88 E3 Jinxiang *Shandong* China
89 F5 Jinxiang *Zhejiang* China
89 B5 Jinyang China
88 E4 Jinzhai China
88 F1 Jinzhou China
42 F5 Jiparaná *r.* Brazil
42 B4 Jipijapa Ecuador
89 C4 Jishou China
89 E5 Jishui China
80 F4 Jisr ash Shughūr Syria
95 B4 Jitra Malaysia
88 C2 Jiudengkou China
88 B4 Jiuding Shan *mt.* China
88 C3 Jiufoping China
89 E4 Jiujiang *Jiangxi* China
89 E4 Jiujiang *Jiangxi* China
89 F4 Jiuling Shan *mts* China
89 A4 Jiulong China
88 F1 Jiumiao China
82 J3 Jiuquan China
89 D5 Jiuxu China
79 J4 Jiwani Pak.
89 F4 Jixi *Anhui* China
87 O2 Jixi *Heilongjiang* China
88 E2 Ji Xian *Hebei* China
88 E3 Ji Xian *Henan* China
88 D3 Jiyuan China
78 E6 Jīzān S. Arabia
90 D6 Jizō-zaki *pt* Japan
43 M5 João Pessoa Brazil
46 C2 João Pinheiro Brazil
34 C2 Job Peak *summit* U.S.A.
85 F5 Joda India
84 C4 Jodhpur India
54 V5 Joensuu Fin.
91 G5 Jōetsu Japan
103 D6 Jofane Moz.
20 D4 Joffre, Mt *mt.* Can.
55 U7 Jõgeva Estonia
55 U7 Jõgua Estonia
91 F5 Jōhana Japan
105 G3 Johannesburg S. Africa
34 D4 Johannesburg U.S.A.
90 D7 Jōhen Japan
84 E5 Johilla *r.* India
24 C2 John Day U.S.A.
24 B2 John Day *r.* U.S.A.
20 F3 John D'or Prairie Can.
32 D6 John H. Kerr Res. *resr* U.S.A.
57 E2 John o'Groats U.K.
29 D4 Johnson City U.S.A.
20 C2 Johnson's Crossing Can.
35 H5 Johnsondale U.S.A.
57 D5 Johnstone U.K.
14 H4 Johnston I. Pac. Oc.

60 D5 Johnstown Rep. of Ireland
33 F3 Johnstown *NY* U.S.A.
32 D4 Johnstown *PA* U.S.A.
31 J3 Johnswood U.S.A.
91 H3 Jōhōji Japan
92 C6 Johor Bahru Malaysia
55 U7 Jõhvi Estonia
44 G3 Joinville Brazil
64 G2 Joinville France
119 B2 Joinville I. *i.* Ant.
54 O3 Jokkmokk Sweden
54 F4 Jökulsá á Brú *r.* Iceland
54 E3 Jökulsá á Fjöllum *r.* Iceland
54 F4 Jökulsá í Fljótsdal *r.* Iceland
81 K2 Jolfa Iran
30 C5 Joliet U.S.A.
22 F4 Joliette Can.
94 B5 Jolo Phil.
94 B5 Jolo *i.* Phil.
94 B3 Jomalig *i.* Phil.
92 □ Jombang Indon.
92 J4 Jomda China
55 T9 Jonava Lith.
88 B3 Jonê China
27 E4 Jonesboro *AR* U.S.A.
33 K2 Jonesboro *ME* U.S.A.
33 K2 Jonesport U.S.A.
32 B6 Jonesville U.S.A.
101 F4 Jonglei Canal *canal* Sudan
85 G5 Jonk *r.* India
55 O8 Jönköping Sweden
23 F4 Jonquière Can.
27 E4 Joplin U.S.A.
33 E5 Joppatowne U.S.A.
88 B2 Jora China
70 Jordan *country* Asia
80 E6 Jordan *r.* Asia
24 E3 Jordan *r.* U.S.A.
24 F2 Jordan U.S.A.
116 B4 Jordan Cr. *watercourse* Austr.
24 C3 Jordan Valley U.S.A.
46 B4 Jordão *r.* Brazil
55 N6 Jordet Norway
85 H4 Jorhat India
54 R4 Jörn Sweden
55 U5 Joroinen Fin.
55 K7 Jørpeland Norway
100 C4 Jos Nigeria
94 C5 Jose Abad Santos Phil.
44 B6 José de San Martin Arg.
46 A2 Joselândia Brazil
47 D2 José Pedro Varela Uru.
112 E2 Joseph Bonaparte Gulf *g.* Austr.
35 G4 Joseph City U.S.A.
23 G2 Joseph, Lac *l.* Can.
91 G5 Jōshinetsu-kōgen National Park *nat. park* Japan
35 E5 Joshua Tree National Monument *res.* U.S.A.
100 C4 Jos Plateau *plat.* Nigeria
55 K6 Jostedalsbreen Nasjonalpark *nat. park* Norway
55 L6 Jotunheimen Nasjonalpark *nat. park* Norway
104 E6 Joubertina S. Africa
105 G3 Joubertson S. Africa
55 U6 Joutsa Fin.
55 V6 Joutseno Fin.
85 H4 Jowai India
60 B4 Joyce's Country *reg.* Rep. of Ireland
24 A1 Juan de Fuca, Str. of *chan.* U.S.A.
103 E5 Juan de Nova *i.* Indian Ocean
40 Juan Fernandez Islands *is* Chile
54 V5 Juankoski Fin.
43 K5 Juàzeiro Brazil
43 L5 Juàzeiro do Norte Brazil
101 F4 Juba Sudan
102 E3 Jubba *r.* Somalia
34 D4 Jubilee Pass *pass* U.S.A.
65 F3 Júcar *r.* Spain
36 F5 Juchitán Mex.
46 E2 Jucururu *r.* Brazil
55 N6 Judaberg Norway
81 H6 Judaidat al Hamir Iraq
81 H6 Judayyidat 'Ar'ar *w.* Iraq
55 M9 Juelsminde Denmark
88 C2 Juh China
88 C1 Juhua Dao *i.* China
37 G6 Juigalpa Nic.
46 D3 Juiz de Fora Brazil
42 D7 Juliaca Peru
113 H4 Julia Creek Austr.
43 H4 Juliana Top *summit* Suriname
66 E1 Julijske Alpe *mts* Slovenia
47 E2 Julio, 9 de Arg.
42 C5 Jumbilla Peru
65 F3 Jumilla Spain
85 E3 Jumla Nepal
84 B5 Junagadh India
84 B5 Junagarh India
88 F3 Junan China
47 B2 Juncal, L. *l.* Arg.
36 D6 Juncos Mex.
27 D6 Junction *TX* U.S.A.
35 G2 Junction *UT* U.S.A.
26 D4 Junction City U.S.A.

46 C3 Jundiaí Brazil
20 C3 Juneau U.S.A.
115 G5 Junee Austr.
62 C7 Jungfrau *mt.* Switz.
86 E2 Junggar Pendi *basin* China
84 A4 Jungshahi Pak.
32 E4 Juniata *r.* U.S.A.
47 E2 Junín Arg.
47 B3 Junín de los Andes Arg.
33 K1 Juniper Can.
34 Junipero Serro Peak *summit* U.S.A.
91 H3 Jūnishi *reg.* Japan
89 B4 Junlian China
54 P5 Junsele Sweden
24 C3 Juntura U.S.A.
88 D3 Jun Xian China
55 T8 Juodupė Lith.
46 C4 Juquiá Brazil
101 E4 Jur *r.* Sudan
64 H3 Jura *mts* France/Switz.
57 C4 Jura *i.* U.K.
46 E1 Juraci Brazil
45 A3 Juradó Col.
57 C5 Jura, Sound of *chan.* U.K.
55 S9 Jurbarkas Lith.
80 E6 Jurf ed Darāwīsh Jordan
85 G2 Jurhen Ul Shan *mts* China
55 S8 Jūrmala Latvia
54 U4 Jurmu Fin.
88 F4 Jurong China
95 □ Jurong Sing.
42 E4 Juruá *r.* Brazil
43 G5 Juruena *r.* Brazil
54 R5 Jurva Fin.
90 H3 Jūsan-ko *l.* Japan
47 D2 Justo Daract Arg.
42 E4 Jutaí *r.* Brazil
46 A3 Juti Brazil
36 G6 Jutiapa Guatemala
36 G6 Juticalpa Honduras
54 P3 Jutis Sweden
54 V5 Juuka Fin.
55 U6 Juva Fin.
37 H4 Juventud, Isla de la *i.* Cuba
88 F3 Ju Xian China
88 A1 Juyan China
88 B3 Juye China
103 C6 Jwaneng Botswana
55 T5 Jyväskylä Fin.

## K

84 D2 K2 *mt.* China/Jammu and Kashmir
34 □1 Kaala *mt.* U.S.A.
102 E3 Kaambooni Kenya
55 S6 Kaarina Fin.
54 V5 Kaavi Fin.
93 G8 Kabaena *i.* Indon.
100 A4 Kabala Sierra Leone
102 C4 Kabale Uganda
102 C4 Kabalo Zaire
102 C4 Kabambare Zaire
103 C5 Kabangu Zaire
95 A5 Kabanjahe Indon.
69 G7 Kabardino-Balkarskaya Respublika *div.* Rus. Fed.
102 C4 Kaba-shima *i.* Japan
90 B7 Kaba-shima *i.* Japan
54 R3 Kåbdalis Sweden
90 D6 Kabe Japan
30 D6 Kabenung Lake *l.* Can.
22 D4 Kabinakagami Lake *l.* Can.
102 C4 Kabinda Zaire
81 L5 Kabīrkūh *mts* Iran
84 B4 Kabirwala Pak.
102 B3 Kabo C.A.R.
103 C5 Kabompo Zambia
102 C4 Kabongo Zaire
81 M4 Kabūd Rāhang Iran
94 B3 Kabugao Phil.
84 B2 Kābul Afgh.
84 C2 Kabul *r.* Afgh.
94 C6 Kaburuang *i.* Indon.
103 C5 Kabwe Zambia
69 H5 Kachalinskaya Rus. Fed.
84 B5 Kachchh, Gulf of *g.* India
84 C1 Kach Pass *pass* Afgh.
86 H1 Kachug Rus. Fed.
81 H1 Kaçkar Dağı *mt.* Turkey
84 A3 Kadanai *r.* Afgh./Pak.
95 A2 Kadan Kyun *i.* Myanmar
111 H3 Kadavu *i.* Fiji
111 H3 Kadavu Passage *chan.* Fiji
100 B4 Kade Ghana
81 K5 Kādhimain Iraq
84 C5 Kadi India
80 B1 Kadirli Turkey
114 B4 Kadina Austr.
81 H2 Kadınhanı Turkey
100 B3 Kadiolo Mali
80 F3 Kadirli Turkey
83 D8 Kadmat *i.* India
26 C2 Kadoka U.S.A.
103 C5 Kadoma Zimbabwe
101 E3 Kadugli Sudan
100 C3 Kaduna Nigeria
100 C4 Kaduna *r.* Nigeria
85 J3 Kadusam *mt.* China
68 F2 Kaduy Rus. Fed.
76 G3 Kadzherom Rus. Fed.

100 A3 Kaédi Maur.
101 D3 Kaélé Cameroon
34 □1 **Kaena Pt** *pt* U.S.A.
117 D1 Kaeo N.Z.
87 N4 Kaesŏng N. Korea
80 F6 Kāf S. Arabia
103 C4 Kafakumba Zaire
100 A3 Kaffrine Senegal
67 L5 Kafireas, Akra *pt* Greece
80 C6 Kafr el Sheik Egypt
103 C5 Kafue *r.* Zambia
103 C5 Kafue Zambia
103 C5 **Kafue National Park** *nat. park* Zambia
91 F5 Kaga Japan
102 B3 Kaga Bandoro C.A.R.
69 G6 Kagal'nitskaya Rus. Fed.
79 J2 Kagan Uzbek.
90 E6 Kagawa Japan
31 F3 Kagawong Can.
54 R4 Kåge Sweden
81 J1 Kağızman Turkey
90 C8 Kagoshima Japan
90 C8 Kagoshima-wan *b.* Japan
81 M3 Kahak Iran
34 □1 Kahaluu U.S.A.
102 D4 Kahama Tanz.
34 □1 Kahana U.S.A.
69 D5 Kaharlyk Ukr.
92 E7 Kahayan *r.* Indon.
102 B4 Kahemba Zaire
117 A6 Kaherekoau Mts *mts* N.Z.
30 B5 Kahoka U.S.A.
34 □2 Kahoolawe *i.* U.S.A.
80 F3 Kahraman Maraş Turkey
84 B3 Kahror Pak.
80 G3 Kahta Turkey
34 □1 Kahuku U.S.A.
34 □1 Kahuku Pt *pt* U.S.A.
34 □2 Kahului U.S.A.
117 D4 Kahurangi Point *pt* N.Z.
84 C2 Kahuta Pak.
102 C4 Kahuzi-Biega, Parc National du *nat. park* Zaire
100 C4 Kaiama Nigeria
117 D5 Kaiapoi N.Z.
35 F3 Kaibab U.S.A.
25 D4 Kaibab Plat. *plat.* U.S.A.
90 E6 Kaibara Japan
93 J8 Kai Besar *i.* Indon.
35 G3 Kaibito U.S.A.
35 G3 Kaibito Plateau *plat.* U.S.A.
88 E3 Kaifeng *Henan* China
88 E3 Kaifeng *Henan* China
89 F4 Kaihua China
104 D4 Kaiingveld *reg.* S. Africa
88 C4 Kaijiang China
93 J8 Kai Kecil *i.* Indon.
93 J8 Kai, Kepulauan *is* Indon.
117 D5 Kaikoura N.Z.
117 D5 Kaikoura Peninsula *pen.* N.Z.
89 □ Kai Kung Leng *h.* Hong Kong China
100 A4 Kailahun Sierra Leone
Kailas *mt. see* Kangrinboqê Feng
85 G4 Kailāshahar India
Kailas Range *mts see* Gangdisê Shan
89 C5 Kaili China
88 F1 Kailu China
34 □1 Kailua U.S.A.
34 □2 Kailua Kona U.S.A.
117 E2 Kaimai Range *h.* N.Z.
93 J7 Kaimana Indon.
117 E3 Kaimanawa Mountains *mts* N.Z.
85 H2 Kaimar China
84 E4 Kaimur Range *h.* India
55 S7 Käina Estonia
91 E6 Kainan Japan
90 E7 Kainan Japan
100 C3 Kainji Lake National Park *nat. park* Nigeria
100 C3 Kainji Reservoir *resr* Nigeria
117 E2 Kaipara Harbour *in.* N.Z.
35 G3 Kaiparowits Plateau *plat.* U.S.A.
89 D6 Kaiping China
23 J3 Kaipokok Bay *in.* Can.
84 D3 Kairana India
100 D1 Kairouan Tunisia
117 D1 Kaitaia N.Z.
117 B7 Kaitangata N.Z.
117 F3 Kaitawa N.Z.
84 D3 Kaithal India
54 R3 Kaitum Sweden
93 H8 Kaiwatu Indon.
34 □2 Kaiwi Channel *chan.* U.S.A.
88 C4 Kai Xian China
89 C5 Kaiyang China
88 G1 Kaiyuan *Liaoning* China
89 B6 Kaiyuan *Yunnan* China
54 U4 Kajaani Fin.
113 H4 Kajabbi Austr.
95 B5 Kajang Malaysia
84 B3 Kajanpur Pak.
81 L2 K'ajaran Armenia
81 L3 Kaju Iran
22 C4 Kakabeka Falls Can.
112 F2 Kakadu National Park *nat. park* Austr.
104 D4 Kakamas S. Africa
102 D3 Kakamega Kenya
91 F6 Kakamigahara Japan
117 C6 Kakanui Mts *mts* N.Z.
100 A4 Kakata Liberia
117 E3 Kakatahi N.Z.
85 H4 Kakching India
90 D6 Kake Japan
20 C3 Kake U.S.A.
91 G6 Kakegawa Japan
102 C4 Kakenge Zaire
69 E6 Kakhovka Ukr.
69 E6 Kakhovs'ke Vodoskhovyshche *resr* Ukr.
83 F7 Kākināda India
20 F2 Kakisa Can.
20 F2 Kakisa *r.* Can.
20 F2 Kakisa Lake *l.* Can.
90 E6 Kakogawa Japan
102 C4 Kakoswa Zaire
84 D4 Kakrala India
91 H5 Kakuda Japan
20 F4 Kakwa *r.* Can.
84 B3 Kala Pak.
66 D7 Kalaâ Kebira Tunisia
84 B2 Kalabagh Pak.
93 G8 Kalabahi Indon.
94 A5 Kalabakan Malaysia
114 D3 Kalabity Austr.
103 C5 Kalabo Zambia
69 G5 Kalach Rus. Fed.
102 D3 Kalacha Dida Kenya
69 G5 Kalach-na-Donu Rus. Fed.
85 H5 Kaladan *r.* India/Myanmar
31 J3 Kaladar Can.
34 □2 Ka Lae *c.* U.S.A.
98 Kalahari Desert *des.* Africa
103 B6 Kalahari Gemsbok National Park *nat. park* S. Africa
54 T4 Kalajoki *r.* Fin.
54 S4 Kalajoki Fin.
84 C2 Kalam Pak.
105 G1 Kalamare Botswana
67 K4 Kalamaria Greece
67 K6 Kalamata Greece
30 D4 Kalamazoo *r.* U.S.A.
30 E4 Kalamazoo U.S.A.
67 J5 Kalampaka Greece
114 C1 Kalamurra, Lake *salt flat* Austr.
84 C3 Kalanaur India
69 E6 Kalanchak Ukr.
114 D6 Kalangadoo Austr.
84 C3 Kalanwali India
94 C5 Kalaong Phil.
81 K4 Kalār Iraq
34 □2 Kalaupapa U.S.A.
69 G6 Kalaus *r.* Rus. Fed.
81 L1 Kälbäcär Azer.
115 K1 Kalbar Austr.
112 B5 Kalbarri Austr.
112 B5 Kalbarri National Park *nat. park* Austr.
80 B3 Kale *Denizli* Turkey
81 G1 Kale Turkey
80 D1 Kalecik Turkey
81 M3 Kaleh Sarai Iran
102 C4 Kalema Zaire
102 C4 Kalémié Zaire
30 D3 Kaleva U.S.A.
54 W4 Kalevala Rus. Fed.
85 H5 Kalewa Myanmar
112 D6 Kalgoorlie Austr.
66 F2 Kali Croatia
84 E3 Kali *r.* India/Nepal
94 B4 Kalibo Phil.
85 F4 Kali Gadaki *r.* Nepal
102 C4 Kalima Zaire
92 E7 Kalimantan *reg.* Indon.
84 E4 Kali Nadi *r.* India
68 B4 Kaliningrad Rus. Fed.
68 B4 Kaliningradskaya Oblast' *div.* Rus. Fed.
68 G3 Kalinino Rus. Fed.
69 H5 Kalininsk Rus. Fed.
69 F6 Kalininskaya Rus. Fed.
69 D4 Kalinkavichy Belarus
84 D4 Kali Sindh *r.* India
24 D1 Kalispell U.S.A.
63 J5 Kalisz Pol.
69 G5 Kalitva *r.* Rus. Fed.
102 D4 Kaliua Tanz.
54 S4 Kalix Sweden
54 S3 Kalixälven *r.* Sweden
85 H4 Kalkalighat India
80 B3 Kalkan Turkey
112 F3 Kalkaringi Austr.
30 E3 Kalkaska U.S.A.
103 B6 Kalkfeld Namibia
105 F4 Kalkfonteindam *dam* S. Africa
95 □ Kallang Sing.
55 U7 Kallaste Estonia
54 U5 Kallavesi *l.* Fin.
54 N5 Kallsedet Sweden
54 N5 Kallsjön *l.* Sweden
55 P8 Kalmar Sweden
55 P8 Kalmarsund *chan.* Sweden
69 F6 Kal'mius *r.* Ukr.
83 F9 Kalmunai Sri Lanka
69 H6 Kalmykiya, Respublika *div.* Rus. Fed.
85 G4 Kalni *r.* Bangl.
63 N5 Kalodnaye Belarus
84 C5 Kalol India
94 C6 Kaloma *i.* Indon.
103 C5 Kalomo Zambia
20 D4 Kalone Pk *summit* Can.
81 L2 Kalow *r.* Iran
84 D3 Kalpa India
83 D8 Kalpeni *i.* India
84 D4 Kalpi India
81 L4 Kal Safīd Iran
84 C3 Kalu India
68 F4 Kaluga Rus. Fed.
55 M9 Kalundborg Denmark
84 B2 Kalur Kot Pak.
69 C5 Kalush Ukr.
68 E4 Kaluzhskaya Oblast' *div.* Rus. Fed.
54 S5 Kälviä Fin.
68 F3 Kalyazin Rus. Fed.
67 M6 Kalymnos *i.* Greece
102 C4 Kama Zaire
91 H4 Kamaishi Japan
91 G6 Kamakura Japan
84 C3 Kamalia Pak.
80 D2 Kaman Turkey
103 B5 Kamanjab Namibia
112 D6 Kambalda Austr.
103 C5 Kambove Zaire
77 S4 Kamchatka *r.* Rus. Fed.
74 Kamchatka *pen.* Rus. Fed.
67 M3 Kamchiya *r.* Bulg.
67 K4 Kamenitsa *mt.* Bulg.
68 H4 Kamenka Rus. Fed.
76 K4 Kamen'-na-Obi Rus. Fed.
68 F3 Kamenniki Rus. Fed.
68 D2 Kamennogorsk Rus. Fed.
69 G6 Kamennomostskiy Rus. Fed.
69 G6 Kamenolomni Rus. Fed.
77 S3 Kamenskoye Rus. Fed.
69 G5 Kamensk-Shakhtinskiy Rus. Fed.
76 H4 Kamensk-Ural'skiy Rus. Fed.
68 G3 Kameshkovo Rus. Fed.
84 D3 Kamet *mt.* China
90 B6 Kamiagata Japan
104 C5 Kamiesberge *mts* S. Africa
104 B5 Kamieskroon S. Africa
90 J2 Kamikawa Japan
90 B8 Kami-Koshiki-jima *i.* Japan
21 J2 Kamilukuak Lake *l.* Can.
103 C4 Kamina Zaire
21 L2 Kaminak Lake *l.* Can.
63 M5 Kamin'-Kashyrs'kyy Ukr.
90 H3 Kaminokuni Japan
91 H4 Kaminoyama Japan
91 F5 Kamioka Japan
90 J2 Kamishihoro Japan
90 B6 Kamitsushima Japan
85 H4 Kamjong India
85 F4 Kamla *r.* India
20 E4 Kamloops Can.
81 K1 Kamo Armenia
91 G5 Kamo Japan
90 H2 Kamoenai Japan
91 H6 Kamogawa Japan
84 C3 Kamoke Pak.
102 C4 Kamonia Zaire
95 C2 Kamon, Xé *r.* Laos
102 D3 Kampala Uganda
95 B4 Kampar Malaysia
61 D2 Kampen Neth.
102 C4 Kampene Zaire
95 A1 Kamphaeng Phet Thai.
95 C3 Kâmpóng Cham Cambodia
95 C2 Kâmpóng Chhnăng Cambodia
95 C2 Kâmpóng Khleăng Cambodia
95 C3 Kâmpóng Spoe Cambodia
95 C2 Kâmpóng Thum Cambodia
95 C3 Kâmpôt Cambodia
Kampuchea *country see* Cambodia
93 J7 Kamrau, Teluk *b.* Indon.
21 J4 Kamsack Can.
76 G4 Kamskoye Vdkhr. *resr* Rus. Fed.
102 E3 Kamsuuma Somalia
21 J3 Kamuchawie Lake *l.* Can.
102 D3 Kamuli Uganda
69 C5 Kam"yane Ukr.
69 C5 Kam"yanets'-Podil's'kyy Ukr.
69 C5 Kam"yanka-Buz'ka Ukr.
63 L4 Kamyanyets Belarus
81 L4 Kāmyārān Iran
69 F6 Kamyshevatskaya Rus. Fed.
69 H5 Kamyshin Rus. Fed.
69 J6 Kamyzyak Rus. Fed.
22 F3 Kanaaupscow *r.* Can.
35 F3 Kanab U.S.A.
35 F3 Kanab Creek *r.* U.S.A.
91 G6 Kanagawa Japan
81 K5 Kan'ān Iraq
102 C4 Kananga Zaire
115 J4 Kanangra Nat. Park *nat. park* Austr.
35 F3 Kanarraville U.S.A.
68 H4 Kanash Rus. Fed.
32 C5 Kanawha *r.* U.S.A.
91 F6 Kanayama Japan
91 F5 Kanazawa Japan
91 F5 Kanazu Japan
95 A2 Kanchanaburi Thai.
83 E8 Kanchipuram India
84 A3 Kand *mt.* Pak.
79 K3 Kandahār Afgh.
54 X3 Kandalaksha Rus. Fed.
95 A5 Kandang Indon.
84 B2 Kandhura Pak.
100 C3 Kandi Benin
84 B4 Kandiaro Pak.
80 C1 Kandıra Turkey
115 H4 Kandos Austr.
103 E5 Kandreho Madag.
83 F9 Kandy Sri Lanka
32 D4 Kane U.S.A.
34 □1 Kaneohe U.S.A.
34 □1 Kaneohe Bay *b.* U.S.A.
69 F6 Kanevskaya Rus. Fed.
91 H4 Kaneyama Japan
103 C6 Kang Botswana
85 G5 Kanga *r.* Bangl.
100 B3 Kangaba Mali
80 F2 Kangal Turkey
79 G4 Kangan Iran
92 C5 Kangar Malaysia
114 B5 Kangaroo I. *i.* Austr.
54 V5 Kangaslampi Fin.
55 U6 Kangasniemi Fin.
81 L4 Kangāvar Iran
88 E1 Kangbao China
85 G4 Kangchenjunga *mt.* Nepal
89 A4 Kangding China
92 F8 Kangean, Kepulauan *is* Indon.
87 N3 Kanggye N. Korea
23 G2 Kangiqsualujjuaq Can.
23 G1 Kangirsuk Can.
88 B3 Kangle China
85 F3 Kangmar *Xizang Zizhiqu* China
85 G3 Kangmar *Xizang Zizhiqu* China
87 N4 Kangnŭng S. Korea
102 B3 Kango Gabon
88 G1 Kangping China
85 J3 Kangri Karpo Pass *pass* India
84 E3 Kangrinboqê Feng *mt.* China
85 H4 Kangto *mt.* China
85 F2 Kangtog China
88 B3 Kang Xian China
84 D5 Kanhan *r.* India
85 E4 Kanhar *r.* India
102 C4 Kaniama Zaire
79 L1 Kanibadam Tajik.
117 C5 Kaniere, L. *l.* N.Z.
76 F3 Kanin, Poluostrov *pen.* Rus. Fed.
81 K3 Kānī Rash Iraq
90 H3 Kanita Japan
69 D5 Kaniv Ukr.
114 D6 Kaniva Austr.
55 S6 Kankaanpää Fin.
30 D5 Kankakee U.S.A.
30 C5 Kankakee *r.* U.S.A.
100 B3 Kankan Guinea
85 E5 Kanker India
95 A3 Kanmaw Kyun *i.* Myanmar
84 D4 Kannauj India
33 D5 Kannapolis U.S.A.
84 D5 Kannod India
54 T5 Kannonkoski Fin.
Kannur *see* Cannanore
54 S5 Kannus Fin.
90 C6 Kano Japan
100 C3 Kano Nigeria
90 D6 Kan-onji Japan
104 D7 Kanonpunt *pt* S. Africa
84 C4 Kanor India
90 C8 Kanoya Japan
84 E4 Kanpur India
84 B3 Kanpur Pak.
26 D4 Kansas *r.* U.S.A.
26 D4 Kansas *div.* U.S.A.
26 E4 Kansas City *KS* U.S.A.
26 E4 Kansas City *MO* U.S.A.
77 L4 Kansk Rus. Fed.
85 G4 Kantanagar Bangl.
95 C2 Kantaralak Thai.
100 C3 Kantchari Burkina
69 F5 Kantemirovka Rus. Fed.
85 F5 Kānthi India
85 F4 Kanti India
84 C3 Kantli *r.* India
111 J2 Kanton Island *i.* Kiribati
91 G6 Kanto-sanchi *mts* Japan
60 C5 Kanturk Rep. of Ireland
91 G5 Kanuma Japan
104 C3 Kanus Namibia
105 J2 KaNyamazane S. Africa
103 C6 Kanye Botswana
95 B3 Kaôh Kông *i.* Cambodia
95 B3 Kaôh Rŭng *i.* Cambodia
95 B3 Kaôh Rŭng Sânlŏem *i.* Cambodia
89 F6 Kao-hsiung Taiwan
95 B3 Kaôh Smăch *i.* Cambodia
103 B5 Kaokoveld *plat.* Namibia
100 A3 Kaolack Senegal
103 C5 Kaoma Zambia
84 B2 Kaoshan Pass *pass* Afgh.
34 □2 Kapaa U.S.A.
34 □2 Kapaau U.S.A.
81 L2 Kapan Armenia
103 C4 Kapanga Zaire
82 E2 Kapchagay Kazak.
61 C3 Kapellen Belgium
67 K6 Kapello, Akra *pt* Greece
55 Q7 Kapellskär Sweden
80 A1 Kapıdağı Yarımadası *pen.* Turkey
85 G4 Kapili *r.* India
14 F5 Kapingamarangi Rise *sea feature* Pac. Oc.
84 B3 Kapip Pak.
103 C5 Kapiri Mposhi Zambia
22 D3 Kapiskau Can.
22 D3 Kapiskau *r.* Can.
31 G2 Kapiskong Lake *l.* Can.
117 E4 Kapiti I. *i.* N.Z.
95 A3 Kapoe Thai.
101 F4 Kapoeta Sudan
62 H7 Kaposvár Hungary
62 D3 Kappeln Ger.
84 D4 Kapran India
102 D3 Kapsabet Kenya
92 E7 Kapuas *r.* Indon.
114 C5 Kapunda Austr.
84 C4 Kapūriya India
84 C3 Kapurthala India
22 D4 Kapuskasing *r.* Can.
22 D4 Kapuskasing Can.
69 H5 Kapustin Yar Rus. Fed.
115 J3 Kaputar *mt.* Austr.
102 D3 Kaputir Kenya
62 H7 Kapuvár Hungary
68 C4 Kapyl' Belarus
100 C4 Kara Togo
81 H2 Kara *r.* Turkey
67 M5 Kara Ada *i.* Turkey
80 D2 Karaali Turkey
82 D2 Kara-Balta Kyrgyzstan
79 G1 Kara-Bogaz Gol, Zaliv *b.* Turkm.
80 D1 Karabük Turkey
76 H5 Karabutak Kazak.
80 B1 Karacabey Turkey
80 D3 Karacadağ *mts* Turkey
81 G3 Karacadağ Turkey
80 B1 Karacaköy Turkey
81 G3 Karacalı Dağ *mt.* Turkey
80 B3 Karacasu Turkey
80 C3 Karaca Yarımadası *pen.* Turkey
69 G7 Karachayevo-Cherkesskaya Respublika *div.* Rus. Fed.
69 G7 Karachayevsk Rus. Fed.
68 E4 Karachev Rus. Fed.
79 K5 Karachi Pak.
81 J2 Karaçoban Turkey
83 D7 Karad India
80 D3 Kara Dağ *mt.* Turkey
81 J3 Kara Dağ *mt.* Turkey
Kara Deniz *sea see* Black Sea
86 B2 Karaganda Kazak.
82 E1 Karagayly Kazak.
77 S4 Karaginskiy Zaliv *b.* Rus. Fed.
80 B2 Karahallı Turkey
80 E2 Karahasanlı Turkey
83 E8 Kāraikāl India
80 E3 Karaisalı Turkey
79 G2 Karaj Iran
80 E6 Karak Jordan
84 E1 Karakax He *r.* China
81 G3 Karakeçi Turkey
80 D2 Karakeçili Turkey
94 C5 Karakelong *i.* Indon.
81 H2 Karakoçan Turkey
82 D2 Kara-Köl Kyrgyzstan
82 E2 Karakol Kyrgyzstan
82 D3 Karakoram *mts* Asia
79 L2 Karakoram *mts* Asia
84 D2 Karakoram Pass *pass* China/Jammu and Kashmir
102 D2 Kara K'orē Eth.
76 G5 Karakum Desert *des.* Kazak.
79 H1 Karakum Desert *des.* Turkm.
Karakumy, Peski *des. see* Karakum Desert
81 J1 Karakurt Turkey
55 R7 Karala Estonia
80 D3 Karaman Turkey
80 B3 Karamanlı Turkey
82 F1 Karamay China
84 C1 Karambar Pass *pass* Afgh./Pak.
117 D4 Karamea N.Z.
117 C4 Karamea Bight *b.* N.Z.
85 F1 Karamiran China
85 F1 Karamiran Shankou *pass* China
80 B1 Karamürsel Turkey
68 D3 Karamyshevo Rus. Fed.
81 L4 Karand Iran
84 D5 Karanja India
85 F5 Karanjia India
84 C3 Karanpura India
80 D3 Karapınar Turkey
104 B3 Karas *div.* Namibia
104 B3 Karas *watercourse* Namibia
103 B6 Karasburg Namibia
76 J2 Kara Sea *sea* Rus. Fed.
54 T2 Karasjok Norway
80 C1 Karasu Turkey
81 J2 Karasu *r.* Turkey
76 J4 Karasuk Rus. Fed.
80 E3 Karataş Turkey
80 E3 Karataş Burun *pt* Turkey
82 D2 Karatau Kazak.
82 C2 Karatau, Khr. *mts* Kazak.
84 E2 Karatax Shan *mts* China
95 A3 Karathuri Myanmar
85 G4 Karatoya *r.* Bangl.
90 B7 Karatsu Japan
94 C5 Karatung *i.* Indon.
84 D4 Karauli India
81 J1 Karaurgan Turkey
92 □ Karawang Indon.
81 K5 Karbalā' Iraq
63 K7 Karcag Hungary
67 J5 Karditsa Greece
55 S7 Kärdla Estonia
105 G4 Karee S. Africa
104 D5 Kareeberge *mts* S. Africa
101 F3 Kareima Sudan
69 G7 K'areli Georgia
84 D5 Kareli India
68 E2 Kareliya, Respublika *div.* Rus. Fed.
87 L1 Karenga *r.* Rus. Fed.
84 D4 Karera India
54 S2 Karesuando Sweden
69 H7 Kargalinskaya Rus. Fed.
81 H2 Kargapazarı Dağları *mts* Turkey
80 E1 Kargı Turkey
84 D2 Kargil Jammu and Kashmir
68 F2 Kargopol' Rus. Fed.
55 P6 Karholmsbruk Sweden
103 C5 Kariba Zimbabwe
103 C5 Kariba, Lake *resr* Zambia/Zimbabwe
90 G2 Kariba-yama *volc.* Japan
104 E6 Kariega *r.* S. Africa
54 T2 Karigasniemi Fin.
55 R5 Karijoki Fin.
90 J2 Karikachi Pass *pass* Japan
117 D1 Karikari, Cape *c.* N.Z.
92 D7 Karimata, Pulau Pulau *is* Indon.
92 D7 Karimata, Selat *str.* Indon.
83 E7 Karimnagar India
92 □ Karimunjawa, Pulau Pulau *is* Indon.
102 E2 Karin Somalia
91 F6 Kariya Japan
85 F4 Karkai *r.* India
82 E1 Karkaralinsk Kazak.
94 C5 Karkaralong, Kepulauan *is* Indon.
110 E2 Karkar I. *i.* P.N.G.
81 M6 Karkheh *r.* Iran
69 E6 Karkinits'ka Zatoka *g.* Ukr.
55 T6 Kärkölä Fin.
55 T7 Karksi-Nuia Estonia
81 H2 Karlıova Turkey
69 E5 Karlivka Ukr.
Karl-Marx-Stadt *see* Chemnitz
66 F2 Karlovac Croatia
67 L3 Karlovo Bulg.
62 F5 Karlovy Vary Czech Rep.
55 O7 Karlsborg Sweden
55 O8 Karlshamn Sweden
55 O7 Karlskoga Sweden
55 O8 Karlskrona Sweden
62 D6 Karlsruhe Ger.
55 N7 Karlstad Sweden
26 D1 Karlstad U.S.A.
68 D4 Karma Belarus
55 J7 Karmøy *i.* Norway
85 H5 Karnafuli Reservoir *resr* Bangl.
84 D3 Karnal India
85 E3 Karnali *r.* Nepal
83 D8 Karnataka *div.* India
67 M3 Karnobat Bulg.
103 C5 Karoi Zimbabwe
85 G3 Karo La *pass* China
85 H4 Karong India
103 D4 Karonga Malawi
104 E6 Karoo National Park *nat. park* S. Africa
114 C5 Karoonda Austr.
84 B3 Karor Pak.
102 D2 Karora Eritrea
67 M7 Karpathos *i.* Greece
67 M6 Karpathou, Steno *chan.* Greece
Karpaty *mts see* Carpathian Mountains
67 J5 Karpenisi Greece
68 H1 Karpogory Rus. Fed.
112 C4 Karratha Austr.
81 J1 Kars Turkey
54 T5 Kärsämäki Fin.
55 U8 Kārsava Latvia
79 K2 Karshi Uzbek.
85 G4 Kārsiyāng India
76 G3 Karskiye Vorota, Proliv *str.* Rus. Fed.
Karskoye More *sea see* Kara Sea
54 T5 Karstula Fin.
80 B1 Kartal Turkey
76 H4 Kartaly Rus. Fed.
54 U5 Karttula Fin.
113 H3 Karumba Austr.
81 M3 Kārūn *r.* Iran
55 S5 Karvia Fin.
55 S6 Karvianjoki *r.* Fin.
83 D8 Karwar India
87 K1 Karymskoye Rus. Fed.
67 L5 Karystos Greece
80 B3 Kaş Turkey
22 C3 Kasabonika Can.
22 C3 Kasabonika Lake *l.* Can.
90 E6 Kasai Japan
102 B4 Kasai *r.* Zaire
103 C5 Kasaji Zaire
91 H5 Kasama Japan
103 D5 Kasama Zambia
103 C5 Kasane Botswana
102 B4 Kasangulu Zaire
83 D8 Kasaragod India
21 J2 Kasba Lake *l.* Can.
100 B1 Kasba Tadla Morocco
90 C8 Kaseda Japan
81 L4 Kaseh Garan Iran
103 C5 Kasempa Zambia
103 C5 Kasenga Zaire
102 D3 Kasese Uganda
102 C4 Kasese Zaire
84 D4 Kasganj India
79 G3 Kāshān Iran
22 D3 Kashechewan Can.
Kashgar *see* Kashi
82 E3 Kashi China
91 E6 Kashihara Japan
90 C7 Kashima Japan
91 H5 Kashima-nada *b.* Japan
68 F3 Kashin Rus. Fed.

84 D3 Kashipur India
91 G5 Kashiwazaki Japan
81 L5 Kashkan r. Iran
79 H2 Kāshmar Iran
84 C2 Kashmir, Vale of v. India
84 B3 Kashmor Pak.
84 B2 Kashmund reg. Afgh.
102 C4 Kashyukulu Zaire
68 G4 Kasimov Rus. Fed.
28 B4 Kaskaskia r. U.S.A.
21 L3 Kaskattama r. Can.
55 R5 Kaskinen Fin.
102 C4 Kasongo Zaire
102 B4 Kasongo-Lunda Zaire
67 M7 Kasos i. Greece
67 M7 Kasou, Steno chan. Greece
69 H7 Kaspi Georgia
69 H7 Kaspiysk Rus. Fed.
Kaspiyskoye More sea see Caspian Sea
63 P3 Kasplya Rus. Fed.
101 F3 Kassala Sudan
67 K4 Kassandra pen. Greece
67 K4 Kassandras, Kolpos b. Greece
62 D5 Kassel Ger.
100 C1 Kasserine Tunisia
30 A3 Kasson U.S.A.
80 D1 Kastamonu Turkey
78 A2 Kastelli Greece
67 J4 Kastoria Greece
68 K4 Kastsyukovichy Belarus
90 C7 Kasuga Japan
91 F6 Kasugai Japan
102 D4 Kasulu Tanz.
90 E6 Kasumi Japan
91 H5 Kasumiga-ura l. Japan
69 J7 Kasumkent Rus. Fed.
103 D5 Kasungu Malawi
84 C4 Kasur Pak.
33 J2 Katahdin, Mt mt. U.S.A.
84 D2 Kataklik Jammu and Kashmir
102 C4 Katako-Kombe Zaire
84 D5 Katangi India
112 C6 Katanning Austr.
84 B2 Katawaz Afgh.
102 C4 Katea Zaire
67 K4 Katerini Greece
20 C3 Kate's Needle mt. Can./U.S.A.
103 D5 Katete Zambia
85 E5 Katghora India
82 K6 Katha Myanmar
78 C4 Katherîna, Gebel mt. Egypt
112 F2 Katherine r. N.T. Austr.
112 F2 Katherine N.T. Austr.
112 F2 Katherine Gorge National Park nat. park Austr.
84 B5 Kathiawar pen. India
80 D6 Kathîb el Henu sand dunes Egypt
105 H3 Kathlehong S. Africa
85 F4 Kathmandu Nepal
104 E3 Kathu S. Africa
84 C2 Kathua Jammu and Kashmir
100 B3 Kati Mali
85 H4 Katihar India
117 E2 Katikati N.Z.
105 G6 Kati-Kati S. Africa
103 C5 Katima Mulilo Namibia
100 B4 Katiola Côte d'Ivoire
104 D4 Katkop Hills reg. S. Africa
Katmandu see Kathmandu
67 J5 Kato Achaïa Greece
84 D5 Katol India
95 □ Katong Sing.
115 J4 Katoomba Austr.
63 J5 Katowice Pol.
85 G5 Katoya India
55 P7 Katrineholm Sweden
57 D4 Katrine, Loch l. U.K.
100 C3 Katsina Nigeria
100 C4 Katsina-Ala Nigeria
90 B7 Katsumoto Japan
91 H5 Katsuta Japan
91 H6 Katsuura Japan
91 F5 Katsuyama Japan
90 D6 Katsuyama Japan
23 G2 Kattaktoc, Cap hd Can.
79 K2 Kattakurgan Uzbek.
84 A2 Kattasang Hills mts Afgh.
55 M8 Kattegat str. Denmark/Sweden
84 B3 Katuri Pak.
61 C2 Katwijk aan Zee Neth.
34 □2 Kauai i. U.S.A.
34 □2 Kauai Channel chan. U.S.A.
55 S5 Kauhajoki Fin.
55 S5 Kauhava Fin.
54 T3 Kaukonen Fin.
34 □2 Kaula i. U.S.A.
34 □2 Kaulakahi Channel chan. U.S.A.
23 H2 Kaumajet Mts mts Can.
34 □2 Kaunakakai U.S.A.
55 S9 Kaunas Lith.
55 U8 Kaunata Latvia
100 C3 Kaura-Namoda Nigeria
89 □ Kau Sai Chau i. Hong Kong China
54 S5 Kaustinen Fin.
54 S2 Kautokeino Norway
95 A3 Kau-ye Kyun i. Myanmar
67 K4 Kavadarci Macedonia
80 F1 Kavak Turkey
67 L4 Kavala Greece

83 F8 Kavali India
83 D8 Kavaratti i. India
67 N3 Kavarna Bulg.
79 G3 Kavir, Dasht-e des. Iran
79 H3 Kavir-i-Namak salt flat Iran
91 H4 Kawabe Japan
91 G6 Kawagoe Japan
91 G6 Kawaguchi Japan
91 H4 Kawai Japan
34 □2 Kawaihae U.S.A.
90 D6 Kawakami Japan
117 E1 Kawakawa N.Z.
103 C4 Kawambwa Zambia
90 C7 Kawaminami Japan
91 E6 Kawanishi Japan
22 E5 Kawartha Lakes lakes Can.
87 P4 Kawasaki Japan
90 C6 Kawashiri-misaki pt Japan
90 H3 Kawauchi Japan
117 E2 Kawau i. N.Z.
90 C7 Kawaura Japan
23 G2 Kawawachikamach Can.
117 F3 Kawerau N.Z.
117 E3 Kawhia N.Z.
117 E3 Kawhia Harbour in. N.Z.
34 D3 Kawich Range mts U.S.A.
95 A1 Kawkareik Myanmar
95 A1 Kawludo Myanmar
95 A3 Kawthaung Myanmar
100 B3 Kaya Burkina
80 F2 Kayadibi Turkey
77 M2 Kayak Rus. Fed.
102 C4 Kayanaza Burundi
24 F3 Kaycee U.S.A.
103 C4 Kayembe-Mukulu Zaire
35 G3 Kayenta U.S.A.
100 A3 Kayes Mali
100 A4 Kayima Sierra Leone
80 F2 Kaynar Turkey
80 F3 Kaypak Turkey
69 H5 Kaysatskoye Rus. Fed.
80 E2 Kayseri Turkey
76 K3 Kayyerkan Rus. Fed.
77 P2 Kazach'ye Rus. Fed.
Kazakh see Qazax
86 B2 Kazakskiy Melkosopochnik reg. Kazak.
70 Kazakstan country Asia
21 K3 Kazan r. Can.
68 J4 Kazan' Rus. Fed.
80 D3 Kazancı Turkey
68 J4 Kazanka r. Rus. Fed.
67 L3 Kazanlŭk Bulg.
93 L1 Kazan-rettō is Japan
69 G5 Kazanskaya Rus. Fed.
69 H7 Kazbek mt. Georgia/ Rus. Fed.
67 M3 Kaz Dağı mts Turkey
79 G4 Käzerūn Iran
68 J2 Kazhim Rus. Fed.
63 K6 Kazincbarcika Hungary
91 G5 Kazo Japan
69 H7 Kazret'i Georgia
91 H3 Kazuno Japan
76 H3 Kazymskiy Mys Rus. Fed.
67 L6 Kea i. Greece
60 E3 Keady U.K.
34 □2 Kealakekua Bay b. U.S.A.
81 M4 K-e-Alvand mt. Iran
35 G4 Keams Canyon U.S.A.
26 D3 Kearney U.S.A.
35 G5 Kearny U.S.A.
80 G2 Keban Turkey
80 G2 Keban Barajı resr Turkey
100 A3 Kébémèr Senegal
80 F4 Kebîr r. Lebanon/Syria
101 E3 Kebkabiya Sudan
54 Q3 Kebnekaise mt. Sweden
57 B2 Kebock Head hd U.K.
102 E3 K'ebrī Dehar Eth.
92 □ Kebumen Indon.
20 D3 Kechika r. Can.
80 C3 Keçiborlu Turkey
63 J7 Kecskemét Hungary
55 S9 Kėdainiai Lith.
81 L4 K-e Dalakhāni h. Iraq
84 D3 Kedar Kanta mt. India
84 D3 Kedarnath Peak mt. India
23 H2 Kedgwick r. Can.
92 □ Kediri Indon.
100 A3 Kédougou Senegal
20 D2 Keele r. Can.
20 C2 Keele Pk summit Can.
25 C4 Keeler U.S.A.
94 A5 Keenapusan i. Phil.
33 G3 Keene U.S.A.
57 F4 Keen, Mount mt. U.K.
115 J3 Keepit Reservoir resr Austr.
61 C2 Keerbergen Belgium
113 H2 Keer-weer, C. pt Austr.
103 B6 Keetmanshoop Namibia
21 L6 Keewatin U.S.A.
21 L5 Keewatin U.S.A.
67 J5 Kefallonia i. Greece
93 G8 Kefamenanu Indon.
54 B4 Keflavík Iceland
82 K2 Kegen Kazak.
23 G2 Keglo, Baie de b. Can.
69 H6 Kegul'ta Rus. Fed.
55 T7 Kehra Estonia
83 J6 Kehsi Mansam Myanmar
58 F4 Keighley U.K.
55 T7 Keila Estonia
104 D4 Keimoes S. Africa
54 S5 Keitele l. Fin.
54 S5 Keitele Fin.
114 D6 Keith Austr.
57 F3 Keith U.K.

20 E1 Keith Arm b. Can.
23 G5 Kejimkujik National Park nat. park Can.
34 □2 Kēkaha U.S.A.
63 K7 Kékes mt. Hungary
84 C4 Kekri India
83 D9 Kelai i. Maldives
88 Kelan China
95 B5 Kelang Malaysia
95 B5 Kelantan r. Malaysia
62 E6 Kelheim Ger.
66 D6 Kelibia Tunisia
79 J2 Kelifskiy Uzboy marsh Turkm.
80 F1 Kelkit r. Turkey
81 G1 Kelkit Turkey
20 E2 Keller Lake l. Can.
32 B4 Kelleys I. i. U.S.A.
24 C2 Kellogg U.S.A.
54 V3 Kelloselkä Fin.
60 E4 Kells Rep. of Ireland
55 S9 Kelmė Lith.
101 D4 Kelo Chad
20 D4 Kelowna Can.
20 D4 Kelsey Bay Can.
57 F5 Kelso U.K.
35 E4 Kelso CA U.S.A.
24 B2 Kelso WA U.S.A.
92 C6 Keluang Malaysia
21 J4 Kelvington Can.
68 E1 Kem' r. Rus. Fed.
68 E1 Kem' Rus. Fed.
81 G2 Kemah Turkey
80 G2 Kemaliye Turkey
81 M5 Kemalpaşa Turkey
20 D4 Kemano Can.
80 C3 Kemer Antalya Turkey
80 C3 Kemer Muğla Turkey
80 B3 Kemer Barajı resr Turkey
76 K4 Kemerovo Rus. Fed.
54 T4 Kemi Fin.
54 U3 Kemijärvi Fin.
54 U3 Kemijärvi l. Fin.
54 T3 Kemijoki r. Fin.
61 A4 Kemmelberg h. Belgium
24 E3 Kemmerer U.S.A.
57 F3 Kemnay U.K.
54 T4 Kempele Fin.
61 C3 Kempen reg. Belgium
27 D5 Kemp, L. l. U.S.A.
119 D4 Kemp Land reg. Ant.
119 B2 Kemp Pen. pen. Ant.
29 E7 Kemp's Bay Bahamas
115 K3 Kempsey Austr.
62 F7 Kempten (Allgäu) Ger.
22 F4 Kempt, L. l. Can.
115 G9 Kempton Austr.
105 H3 Kempton Park S. Africa
31 K3 Kemptville Can.
92 □ Kemujan i. Indon.
84 E4 Ken r. India
58 E3 Kendal U.K.
115 K3 Kendall Austr.
21 M2 Kendall, Cape hd Can.
30 E5 Kendallville U.S.A.
93 G7 Kendari Indon.
92 E7 Kendawangan Indon.
101 D3 Kendégué Chad
85 F5 Kendrāparha India
24 C2 Kendrick U.S.A.
35 G4 Kendrick Peak summit U.S.A.
83 D6 Kendujhargarh India
115 H3 Kenebri Austr.
27 D6 Kenedy U.S.A.
100 A4 Kenema Sierra Leone
102 B4 Kenge Zaire
83 J6 Kengtung Myanmar
104 D4 Kenhardt S. Africa
100 A3 Kéniéba Mali
100 B1 Kénitra Morocco
88 F2 Kenli China
60 B6 Kenmare Rep. of Ireland
26 C1 Kenmare U.S.A.
60 A6 Kenmare River in. Rep. of Ireland
25 G5 Kenna U.S.A.
33 J2 Kennebec r. U.S.A.
33 H3 Kennebunk U.S.A.
33 H3 Kennebunkport U.S.A.
116 A2 Kennedy Austr.
27 F6 Kennet r. U.S.A.
59 F6 Kennet r. U.K.
33 K2 Kennett U.S.A.
24 C2 Kennewick U.S.A.
31 G1 Kenogami Lake Can.
31 G1 Kenogamissi L. l. Can.
20 B2 Keno Hill Can.
21 L5 Kenora Can.
30 D4 Kenosha U.S.A.
68 F2 Kenozero, Ozero l. Rus. Fed.
58 E3 Kent r. U.K.
33 G4 Kent CT U.S.A.
27 B6 Kent TX U.S.A.
24 B2 Kent WA U.S.A.
105 H4 Kentani S. Africa
82 C2 Kentau Kazak.
115 G7 Kent Group is Austr.
30 D5 Kentland U.S.A.
32 A6 Kentucky div. U.S.A.
29 B4 Kentucky Lake l. U.S.A.
27 F6 Kentville Can.
30 E4 Kentwood MI U.S.A.
27 F6 Kentwood LA U.S.A.
96 Kenya country Africa
Kenya, Mount mt. see Kirinyaga
30 A3 Kenyon U.S.A.
119 B2 Kenyon Pen. pen. Ant.
34 □2 Keokea U.S.A.
30 B5 Keokuk U.S.A.

95 C1 Keo Neua, Col de pass Laos/Vietnam
30 D4 Keosauqua U.S.A.
116 D4 Keppel Bay b. Austr.
95 □ Keppel Harbour chan. Sing.
80 B2 Kepsut Turkey
83 E8 Kerala div. India
114 E5 Kerang Austr.
100 C4 Kéran, Parc National de la nat. park Togo
55 T6 Kerava Fin.
65 G4 Kerba Alg.
69 F6 Kerch Ukr.
110 E2 Kerema P.N.G.
55 U5 Keremeos Can.
69 E7 Kerempe Burun pt Turkey
102 D2 Keren Eritrea
13 J7 Kerguelen Ridge sea feature Indian Ocean
102 D4 Kericho Kenya
117 D1 Kerikeri N.Z.
55 V6 Kerimäki Fin.
92 C7 Kerinci, G. volc. Indon.
85 E2 Keriya Shankou pass China
79 K2 Kerki Turkm.
67 K4 Kerkinitis, Limni l. Greece
67 H5 Kerkyra Greece
Kerkyra i. see Corfu
101 F3 Kerma Sudan
14 H8 Kermadec Tr. sea feature Pac. Oc.
79 H4 Kermān Iran
34 B3 Kerman U.S.A.
81 L4 Kermānshāh Iran
27 C6 Kermit U.S.A.
25 C5 Kern r. U.S.A.
23 G2 Kernertut, Cap pt Can.
34 C4 Kernville U.S.A.
67 L6 Keros i. Greece
68 K2 Keros Rus. Fed.
100 B4 Kérouané Guinea
61 E4 Kerpen Ger.
119 B5 Kerr, C. c. Ant.
21 H4 Kerrobert Can.
27 D6 Kerrville U.S.A.
60 B5 Kerry Head hd Rep. of Ireland
95 B4 Kerteh Malaysia
55 M9 Kerteminde Denmark
80 D4 Keryneia Cyprus
68 H3 Kerzhenets r. Rus. Fed.
22 D3 Kesagami Lake l. Can.
55 V6 Kesälahti Fin.
69 C7 Keşan Turkey
80 G1 Keşap Turkey
91 H4 Kesennuma Japan
84 B1 Keshem Afgh.
84 A1 Keshendeh-ye Bala Afgh.
85 G5 Keshod India
81 M5 Keshvar Iran
80 D2 Keskin Turkey
68 E2 Keskozero Rus. Fed.
61 E3 Kessel Neth.
105 H4 Kestell S. Africa
54 W4 Kesten'ga Rus. Fed.
54 U4 Kestilä Fin.
31 H3 Keswick Can.
58 D3 Keswick U.K.
62 H7 Keszthely Hungary
76 K4 Ket' r. Rus. Fed.
100 C4 Keta Ghana
95 □ Ketam, P. i. Sing.
92 E7 Ketapang Indon.
20 C3 Ketchikan U.S.A.
61 D2 Ketelmeer l. Neth.
86 D3 Ketmen', Khrebet mts China/Kazak.
59 G5 Kettering U.K.
32 A5 Kettering U.S.A.
20 F5 Kettle r. Can.
30 A2 Kettle r. U.S.A.
32 E4 Kettle Creek r. U.S.A.
34 C3 Kettleman City U.S.A.
24 C1 Kettle River Ra. mts U.S.A.
32 E3 Keuka Lake l. U.S.A.
55 T5 Keuruu Fin.
61 E3 Kevelaer Ger.
30 C5 Kewanee U.S.A.
30 D3 Kewaunee U.S.A.
30 C2 Keweenaw Bay b. U.S.A.
30 C2 Keweenaw Peninsula pen. U.S.A.
30 D2 Keweenaw Pt pt U.S.A.
45 E3 Keweigek Guyana
22 F3 Keyano Can.
31 G3 Key Harbour Can.
29 D7 Key Largo U.S.A.
60 C3 Key, Lough l. Rep. of Ireland
59 E6 Keynsham U.K.
32 D5 Keysers Ridge U.S.A.
35 G6 Keystone Peak summit U.S.A.
32 D6 Keysville U.S.A.
117 A6 Key, The N.Z.
81 M4 Keytü Iran
29 D7 Key West FL U.S.A.
30 B4 Key West IA U.S.A.
33 H3 Kezar Falls U.S.A.
103 C6 Kezi Zimbabwe
63 K6 Kežmarok Slovakia
104 D2 Kgalagadi div. Botswana
105 G2 Kgatleng div. Botswana
104 D1 Kgomofatshe Pan salt pan Botswana
104 F2 Kgoro Pan salt pan Botswana
105 G3 Kgotsong S. Africa
87 P2 Khabarovsk Rus. Fed.

81 H4 Khabur r. Syria
81 J7 Khadd, W. al watercourse S. Arabia
84 A4 Khaga India
85 B3 Khagrachari Bangl.
84 B3 Khairgarh Pak.
84 B4 Khairpur Pak.
84 D4 Khajurāho India
103 C6 Khakhea Botswana
81 M4 Khalajestan reg. Iran
84 D2 Khalatse Jammu and Kashmir
84 A3 Khalifat mt. Pak.
81 M3 Khalkhāl Iran
85 F6 Khallikot India
68 D4 Khalopyenichy Belarus
86 H1 Khamar-Daban, Khrebet mts Rus. Fed.
84 C5 Khambhat India
84 B6 Khambhat, Gulf of g. India
84 D5 Khamgaon India
95 C1 Khamkeut Laos
83 F7 Khammam India
77 N3 Khamra Rus. Fed.
81 M4 Khamseh reg. Iran
84 B1 Khānābād Afgh.
81 J5 Khān al Baghdādī Iraq
81 K5 Khān al Mahāwīl Iraq
81 K5 Khān al Mashāhidah Iraq
81 K5 Khān al Muşalla Iraq
81 K3 Khānaqāh Iran
81 K4 Khānaqīn Iraq
81 K2 Khanasur Pass pass Iran/Turkey
80 F6 Khān az Zabīb Jordan
84 C2 Khanbari Pass pass Jammu and Kashmir
115 H6 Khancoban Austr.
84 D2 Khand Pass pass Afgh./Pak.
84 D5 Khandwa India
77 P3 Khandyga Rus. Fed.
84 B3 Khanewal Pak.
95 D2 Khanh Dương Vietnam
84 D4 Khaniadhana India
81 K5 Khān Jadwal Iraq
87 O3 Khanka, Lake l. China/Rus. Fed.
84 C2 Khanki Weir barrage Pak.
84 D3 Khanna India
84 B3 Khanpur Pak.
81 K6 Khān Ruhābah Iraq
80 F4 Khān Shaykhūn Syria
82 D2 Khantau Kazak.
76 L3 Khantayskoye, Ozero l. Rus. Fed.
76 H3 Khanty-Mansiysk Rus. Fed.
80 E6 Khān Yūnis Gaza
95 A3 Khao Chum Thong Thai.
81 L5 Khapa India
87 K2 Khapcheranga Rus. Fed.
81 M4 Khar r. Iran
69 H6 Kharabali Rus. Fed.
85 F5 Kharagpur India
Kharari see Abu Road
84 C2 Khardi India
84 D2 Khardung La pass India
81 L6 Kharfiyah Iraq
84 C5 Khargon India
84 C4 Khari r. Rajasthan India
84 C4 Khari r. Rajasthan India
84 C2 Kharian Pak.
85 E5 Khariar India
69 F5 Kharkiv Ukr.
Khar'kov see Kharkiv
67 L4 Kharmanli Bulg.
68 G3 Kharovsk Rus. Fed.
85 E5 Kharsia India
101 F3 Khartoum Sudan
69 H7 Khasav'yurt Rus. Fed.
79 J4 Khāsh Iran
69 G7 Khashuri Georgia
85 G4 Khāsi Hills h. India
67 L4 Khaskovo Bulg.
77 M2 Khatanga Rus. Fed.
77 M2 Khatanga, Gulf of b. Rus. Fed.
84 B1 Khatinza Pass pass Pak.
80 D6 Khatmia Pass pass Egypt
77 T3 Khatyrka Rus. Fed.
81 M6 Khāvar Iran
79 K1 Khavast Uzbek.
84 B5 Khavda India
84 B2 Khawak Pass pass Afgh.
95 A2 Khawsa Myanmar
105 F5 Khayamnandi S. Africa
79 L2 Khaydarken Kyrgyzstan
104 C7 Khayelitsha S. Africa
81 J3 Khāzir r. Iraq
95 C1 Khê Bo Vietnam
84 C4 Khedbrahma India
84 E3 Kheda India
65 H7 Khemis Miliana Alg.
100 C1 Khenchela Alg.
100 B1 Khenifra Morocco
84 D4 Kherli India
69 E6 Kherson Ukr.
77 L2 Kheta r. Rus. Fed.
87 K1 Khilok Rus. Fed.
80 F4 Khirbat Isrīyah Syria
81 J6 Khirr, Wādī al watercourse S. Arabia
84 D2 Khitai P. pass China/Jammu and Kashmir
81 L2 Khīyāv Iran
81 V6 Khiytola Rus. Fed.
69 C5 Khmel'nyts'kyy Ukr.
69 C5 Khmel'nyk Ukr.
81 L2 Khodā Āfarīn Iran
79 H1 Khodzheyli Uzbek.

104 D2 Khokhowe Pan salt pan Botswana
84 B4 Khokhropar Pak.
79 K2 Kholm Afgh.
68 G1 Kholmogory Rus. Fed.
87 Q2 Kholmsk Rus. Fed.
63 O3 Kholm–Zhirkovskiy Rus. Fed.
81 M3 Khoman Iran
104 B1 Khomas div. Namibia
104 A1 Khomas Highland reg. Namibia
81 M4 Khondāb Iran
69 G7 Khoni Georgia
77 Q2 Khonu Rus. Fed.
81 M5 Khoper r. Rus. Fed.
87 O2 Khor r. Rus. Fed.
87 O2 Khor Rus. Fed.
84 B4 Khora Pak.
85 F5 Khordha India
87 J1 Khorinsk Rus. Fed.
103 B6 Khorixas Namibia
69 E5 Khorol Ukr.
81 L2 Khoroslū Dāgh h. Iran
81 M5 Khorramābād Iran
81 M3 Khorram Darreh Iran
81 M6 Khorramshahr Iran
79 L2 Khorugh Tajik.
69 H6 Khosheutovo Rus. Fed.
81 M6 Khosravī Iran
81 K4 Khosrowvī Iran
84 C1 Khotgaz pass Afgh.
84 E2 Khowst Afgh.
85 H5 Khreum Myanmar
85 G4 Khri r. India
68 H2 Khristoforovo Rus. Fed.
77 Q2 Khroma r. Rus. Fed.
76 G4 Khromtau Kazak.
63 O6 Khrystynivka Ukr.
104 F1 Khudumelapye Botswana
104 D3 Khuis Botswana
79 K1 Khŭjand Tajik.
95 C2 Khu Khan Thai.
84 A1 Khulm r. Afgh.
85 G5 Khulna Bangl.
81 J1 Khulo Georgia
105 G3 Khuma S. Africa
84 C2 Khunjerab Pass pass China/Jammu and Kashmir
79 G3 Khunsar Iran
85 F5 Khunti India
84 D3 Khurai India
84 C2 Khushab Pak.
69 B5 Khust Ukr.
105 G3 Khutsong S. Africa
68 J4 Khvalynsk Rus. Fed.
81 L3 Khvosh Maqām Iran
81 K2 Khvoy Iran
68 E3 Khvoynaya Rus. Fed.
84 A2 Khwaja Kuram mt. Afgh.
84 B1 Khwaja Muhammad Ra. mts Afgh.
84 B2 Khyber Pass pass Afgh./Pak.
115 J5 Kiama Austr.
94 C5 Kiamba Phil.
102 C4 Kiambi Zaire
27 E5 Kiamichi r. U.S.A.
54 V4 Kiantajärvi l. Fin.
84 D2 Kibar India
94 C5 Kibawe Phil.
102 C4 Kibaya Tanz.
103 D4 Kibiti Tanz.
102 C4 Kibombo Zaire
102 B4 Kibwit Zaire
67 J4 Kičevo Macedonia
68 H3 Kichmengskiy Gorodok Rus. Fed.
100 C3 Kidal Mali
59 E5 Kidderminster U.K.
102 D3 Kidepo Valley National Park nat. park Uganda
100 A3 Kidira Senegal
84 D2 Kidmang Jammu and Kashmir
117 E2 Kidnappers, Cape c. N.Z.
59 E4 Kidsgrove U.K.
62 E3 Kiel Ger.
30 C4 Kiel U.S.A.
63 K5 Kielce Pol.
58 E2 Kielder Water resr U.K.
62 E3 Kieler Bucht b. Ger.
103 C5 Kienge Zaire
61 F3 Kierspe Ger.
69 D5 Kiev Ukr.
100 A3 Kiffa Maur.
67 K5 Kifisia Greece
81 K4 Kifrī Iraq
102 D4 Kigali Rwanda
81 H2 Kiği Turkey
23 H2 Kiglapait Mts mts Can.
102 C4 Kigoma Tanz.
54 S3 Kihlanki Fin.
55 S5 Kihniö Fin.
54 S5 Kiiminki Fin.
91 F6 Kii-nagashima Japan
90 C8 Kiire Japan
91 E6 Kii-sanchi mts Japan
90 E7 Kii-suidō chan. Japan
67 J2 Kikinda Yugo.
77 M4 Kikino Rus. Fed.
90 H3 Kikonai Japan
103 C4 Kikondja Zaire
110 E2 Kikori P.N.G.
110 E2 Kikori r. P.N.G.
90 C7 Kikuchi Japan
102 B4 Kikwit Zaire
55 P6 Kilafors Sweden
84 D3 Kilar India
34 □2 Kilauea U.S.A.

34 □2 Kilauea Crater crater U.S.A.
57 C5 Kilbrannan Sound chan. U.K.
60 E4 Kilcoole Rep. of Ireland
60 D4 Kilcormac Rep. of Ireland
115 K1 Kilcoy Austr.
60 E4 Kildare Rep. of Ireland
54 X2 Kil'dinstroy Rus. Fed.
102 B4 Kilembe Zaire
57 C5 Kilfinan U.K.
27 E5 Kilgore U.S.A.
58 E2 Kilham U.K.
102 D4 Kilifi Kenya
102 D4 Kilimanjaro mt. Tanz.
111 F2 Kilinailau Is is P.N.G.
103 D4 Kilindoni Tanz.
55 T7 Kilingi-Nõmme Estonia
80 F3 Kilis Turkey
69 D6 Kiliya Ukr.
60 B5 Kilkee Rep. of Ireland
60 F3 Kilkeel U.K.
60 D5 Kilkenny Rep. of Ireland
59 C7 Kilkhampton U.K.
67 K4 Kilkis Greece
116 E6 Kilkivan Austr.
60 B3 Killala Rep. of Ireland
60 B3 Killala Bay b. Rep. of Ireland
60 C5 Killaloe Rep. of Ireland
31 J3 Killaloe Station Can.
21 G4 Killam Can.
115 K2 Killarney Austr.
31 G3 Killarney Can.
60 B5 Killarney Rep. of Ireland
31 G2 Killarney National Park nat. park Can.
60 B6 Killarney National Park nat. park Rep. of Ireland
60 B4 Killary Harbour b. Rep. of Ireland
27 D6 Killeen U.S.A.
60 D5 Killenaule Rep. of Ireland
60 C4 Killimor Rep. of Ireland
57 D4 Killin U.K.
60 F3 Killinchy U.K.
60 E5 Killinick Rep. of Ireland
23 H1 Killiniq Can.
23 H1 Killiniq Island i. Can.
60 B5 Killorglin Rep. of Ireland
60 E5 Killurin Rep. of Ireland
60 C3 Killybegs Rep. of Ireland
60 D2 Kilmacrenan Rep. of Ireland
60 B4 Kilmaine Rep. of Ireland
60 C5 Kilmallock Rep. of Ireland
57 B3 Kilmaluag U.K.
57 D5 Kilmarnock U.K.
57 C4 Kilmelford U.K.
68 J3 Kil'mez' r. Rus. Fed.
68 J3 Kil'mez' Rus. Fed.
60 C6 Kilmona Rep. of Ireland
114 F6 Kilmore Austr.
60 E5 Kilmore Quay Rep. of Ireland
102 D4 Kilosa Tanz.
54 R2 Kilpisjärvi Fin.
54 X2 Kilp"yavr Rus. Fed.
60 E3 Kilrea U.K.
60 B5 Kilrush Rep. of Ireland
57 D5 Kilsyth U.K.
83 D8 Kilttān i. India
60 C4 Kiltullagh Rep. of Ireland
103 C4 Kilwa Zaire
103 D4 Kilwa Masoko Tanz.
57 D5 Kilwinning U.K.
103 D4 Kimambi Tanz.
114 B4 Kimba Austr.
102 B4 Kimba Congo
26 C3 Kimball U.S.A.
110 F2 Kimbe P.N.G.
20 F5 Kimberley Can.
104 F4 Kimberley S. Africa
112 E3 Kimberley Plateau plat. Austr.
117 E4 Kimbolton N.Z.
87 N3 Kimch'aek N. Korea
55 S6 Kimito Fin.
90 H2 Kimobetsu Japan
67 L6 Kimolos i. Greece
68 F4 Kimovsk Rus. Fed.
102 B4 Kimpese Zaire
91 G4 Kimpoku-san mt. Japan
68 F3 Kimry Rus. Fed.
102 B4 Kimvula Zaire
92 F5 Kinabalu, Gunung mt. Malaysia
94 A5 Kinabatangan r. Malaysia
67 M6 Kinaros i. Greece
57 E2 Kinbrace U.K.
31 G3 Kincardine Can.
57 E4 Kincardine U.K.
114 E4 Kinchega National Park nat. park Austr.
20 D3 Kincolith Can.
103 C4 Kinda Zaire
85 H5 Kindat Myanmar
27 E6 Kinder U.S.A.
59 F4 Kinder Scout h. U.K.
21 H4 Kindersley Can.
100 A3 Kindia Guinea
102 C4 Kindu Zaire
68 G3 Kineshma Rus. Fed.
116 D6 Kingaroy Austr.
18 King Christian IX Land reg. Greenland
18 King Christian X Land reg. Greenland
34 B3 King City U.S.A.
119 C1 King Edward Point U.K. Base Ant.
32 E3 King Ferry U.S.A.
33 H2 Kingfield U.S.A.
27 D5 Kingfisher U.S.A.
18 King Frederik VI Coast reg. Greenland
18 King Frederik VIII Land reg. Greenland
119 B1 King George I. i. S. Shetland Is Ant.
22 E2 King George Islands is Can.
20 D4 King I. i. Can.
68 D3 Kingisepp Rus. Fed.
115 F8 King Island i. Tas. Austr.
31 H1 King Kirkland Can.
112 D3 King Leopold Ranges h. Austr.
35 E4 Kingman AZ U.S.A.
27 D4 Kingman KS U.S.A.
33 J2 Kingman ME U.S.A.
20 D3 King Mtn mt. Can.
114 A3 Kingoonya Austr.
18 King Oscar Fjord fjord Greenland
60 D5 Kings r. Rep. of Ireland
34 C3 Kings r. U.S.A.
59 D7 Kingsbridge U.K.
34 C3 Kingsburg U.S.A.
33 J2 Kingsbury U.S.A.
34 C3 Kings Canyon National Park nat. park U.S.A.
115 K2 Kingscliff Austr.
114 B5 Kingscote Austr.
60 E4 Kingscourt Rep. of Ireland
119 B2 King Sejong Korea Base Ant.
30 C3 Kingsford U.S.A.
29 D6 Kingsland GA U.S.A.
30 E5 Kingsland IN U.S.A.
59 H5 King's Lynn U.K.
111 H2 Kingsmill Group is Kiribati
59 H6 Kingsnorth U.K.
112 D3 King Sound b. Austr.
24 E3 Kings Peak summit U.S.A.
32 B6 Kingsport U.S.A.
31 J3 Kingston Can.
37 J5 Kingston Jamaica
117 B6 Kingston N.Z.
30 B6 Kingston IL U.S.A.
33 F4 Kingston NY U.S.A.
115 G9 Kingston Tas.
35 E4 Kingston Peak summit U.S.A.
114 C6 Kingston South East Austr.
58 G4 Kingston upon Hull U.K.
37 M6 Kingstown St Vincent
27 D7 Kingsville U.S.A.
59 E6 Kingswood U.K.
59 D5 Kington U.K.
57 D3 Kingussie U.K.
18 King William I. i. Can.
105 G6 King William's Town S. Africa
27 E6 Kingwood TX U.S.A.
32 D5 Kingwood WV U.S.A.
21 J4 Kinistino Can.
91 H4 Kinka-san i. Japan
117 B6 Kinloch N.Z.
57 E3 Kinloss U.K.
31 H3 Kinmount Can.
55 N8 Kinna Sweden
60 D4 Kinnegad Rep. of Ireland
54 T5 Kinnula Fin.
91 E6 Kino-kawa r. Japan
21 J3 Kinoosao Can.
57 E4 Kinross U.K.
60 C6 Kinsale Rep. of Ireland
102 B4 Kinshasa Zaire
26 D4 Kinsley U.S.A.
29 E5 Kinston U.S.A.
55 R9 Kintai Lith.
100 B4 Kintampo Ghana
57 F3 Kintore U.K.
57 C5 Kintyre pen. U.K.
57 C5 Kintyre, Mull of hd U.K.
20 F3 Kinuso Can.
101 F4 Kinyeti mt. Sudan
31 H2 Kiosk Can.
22 E4 Kipawa, Lac l. Can.
33 F6 Kiptopeke U.S.A.
103 C5 Kipushi Zaire
111 G3 Kirakira Solomon Is
68 D4 Kirawsk Belarus
77 M4 Kirensk Rus. Fed.
Kirghizia country see Kyrgyzstan
106 Kiribati country Pac. Oc.
81 H1 Kırık Turkey
79 F3 Kırıkhan Turkey
80 D2 Kırıkkale Turkey
68 F3 Kirillov Rus. Fed.
102 D3 Kirinyaga mt. Kenya
68 E3 Kirishi Rus. Fed.
90 C8 Kirishima-yama volc. Japan
109 Kiritimati i. Kiribati
80 A2 Kırkağaç Turkey
81 L3 Kirk Bulāg D. mt Iran
59 E4 Kirkby U.K.
59 F4 Kirkby in Ashfield U.K.
58 E3 Kirkby Lonsdale U.K.
58 E3 Kirkby Stephen U.K.
57 E4 Kirkcaldy U.K.
57 C6 Kirkcolm U.K.
60 F3 Kirkcubbin U.K.
57 D6 Kirkcudbright U.K.
55 N6 Kirkenær Norway
54 W2 Kirkenes Norway
31 H3 Kirkfield Can.
57 D5 Kirkintilloch U.K.
55 T6 Kirkkonummi Fin.
35 F4 Kirkland U.S.A.
35 F4 Kirkland Junction U.S.A.
31 G1 Kirkland Lake Can.
69 C7 Kırklareli Turkey
58 C3 Kirk Michael U.K.
58 E3 Kirkoswald U.K.
26 E3 Kirksville U.S.A.
81 K4 Kirkūk Iraq
57 F2 Kirkwall U.K.
105 F6 Kirkwood S. Africa
34 B2 Kirkwood CA U.S.A.
26 F4 Kirkwood MO U.S.A.
80 C1 Kırmır r. Turkey
Kirov see Vyatka
68 E4 Kirov Rus. Fed.
Kirovabad see Gäncä
68 J3 Kirovo-Chepetsk Rus. Fed.
69 E5 Kirovohrad Ukr.
81 M2 Kirovsk Azer.
68 D3 Kirovsk Leningrad. Rus. Fed.
54 X3 Kirovsk Murmansk. Rus. Fed.
68 J3 Kirovskaya Oblast' div. Rus. Fed.
82 E2 Kirovskiy Kazak.
119 B4 Kirpatrick, Mt mt. Ant.
57 E4 Kirriemuir U.K.
68 K3 Kirs Rus. Fed.
68 G4 Kirsanov Rus. Fed.
80 E2 Kırşehir Turkey
79 K4 Kirthar Range mts Pak.
54 R3 Kiruna Sweden
102 C4 Kirundu Zaire
68 H4 Kirya Rus. Fed.
91 G5 Kiryū Japan
55 O8 Kisa Sweden
91 G4 Kisakata Japan
102 C3 Kisangani Zaire
102 B4 Kisantu Zaire
92 B6 Kisaran Indon.
85 F4 Kishanganj India
84 B4 Kishangarh Rajasthan India
84 C4 Kishangarh Rajasthan India
84 C2 Kishen Ganga r. India/Pak.
69 D6 Kishinev Moldova
91 E6 Kishiwada Japan
85 G4 Kishorganj Bangl.
84 C2 Kishtwar Jammu and Kashmir
100 C4 Kisi Nigeria
102 D4 Kisii Kenya
21 K4 Kiskittogisu L. l. Can.
63 J7 Kiskunfélegyháza Hungary
63 J7 Kiskunhalas Hungary
69 G7 Kislovodsk Rus. Fed.
102 E4 Kismaayo Somalia
91 F6 Kiso-gawa r. Japan
102 C4 Kisoro Uganda
91 F6 Kiso-sanmyaku mts Japan
100 A4 Kissidougou Guinea
29 D6 Kissimmee U.S.A.
29 D7 Kissimmee, L. l. U.S.A.
21 J3 Kississing L. l. Can.
102 D4 Kisumu Kenya
100 B3 Kita Mali
90 C7 Kitagawa Japan
90 G2 Kitahiyama Japan
91 H5 Kitaibaraki Japan
91 H4 Kitakami Japan
91 H4 Kitakami-gawa r. Japan
91 G5 Kitakata Japan
90 C7 Kitakata Japan
90 C7 Kita-Kyūshū Japan
102 D3 Kitale Kenya
90 J2 Kitami Japan
90 J1 Kitami-sanchi mts Japan
25 G4 Kit Carson U.S.A.
31 G4 Kitchener Can.
54 W5 Kitee Fin.
102 D3 Kitgum Uganda
20 D4 Kitimat Can.
54 U3 Kitinen r. Fin.
102 B4 Kitona Zaire
90 C7 Kitsuki Japan
114 C2 Kittakittaooloo, L. salt flat Austr.
32 D4 Kittanning U.S.A.
33 F4 Kittatinny Mts h. U.S.A.
33 H3 Kittery U.S.A.
54 T3 Kittilä Fin.
29 F4 Kitty Hawk U.S.A.
102 D4 Kitunda Tanz.
20 D3 Kitwanga Can.
103 C5 Kitwe Zambia
62 F7 Kitzbüheler Alpen mts Austria
54 U5 Kiuruvesi Fin.
54 T5 Kivijärvi Fin.
55 U7 Kiviõli Estonia
102 C4 Kivu, Lake l. Rwanda/Zaire
67 N4 Kıyıköy Turkey
76 G4 Kizel Rus. Fed.
68 H2 Kizema Rus. Fed.
80 B3 Kızılca D. mt. Turkey
80 D1 Kızılcahamam Turkey
80 G2 Kızıl D. mt. Turkey
80 D2 Kızılırmak r. Turkey
80 D1 Kızılırmak Turkey
80 C3 Kızılkaya Turkey
80 D3 Kızılören Turkey
81 H3 Kızıltepe Turkey
69 H7 Kizil"yurt Rus. Fed.
69 H7 Kizlyar Rus. Fed.
54 U1 Kjøllefjord Norway
54 P2 Kjøpsvik Norway
62 G5 Kladno Czech Rep.
62 G7 Klagenfurt Austria
35 H4 Klagetoh U.S.A.
55 R9 Klaipėda Lith.
54 □ Klaksvík Faroe Is
24 B3 Klamath r. U.S.A.
24 B3 Klamath Falls U.S.A.
24 B3 Klamath Mts mts U.S.A.
55 N6 Klarälven r. Sweden
62 F6 Klatovy Czech Rep.
104 C5 Klawer S. Africa
20 C3 Klawock U.S.A.
61 E2 Klazienaveen Neth.
20 E4 Kleena Kleene Can.
104 D4 Kleinbegin S. Africa
104 C3 Klein Karas Namibia
104 D6 Klein Roggeveldberg mts S. Africa
104 B4 Kleinsee S. Africa
104 D6 Klein Swartberg mts S. Africa
20 D4 Klemtu Can.
105 G3 Klerksdorp S. Africa
68 E4 Kletnya Rus. Fed.
69 G5 Kletskiy Rus. Fed.
61 E3 Kleve Ger.
68 D4 Klimavichy Belarus
69 E4 Klimovo Rus. Fed.
68 F4 Klimovsk Rus. Fed.
68 F3 Klin Rus. Fed.
20 D4 Klinaklini r. Can.
62 F5 Klínovec mt. Czech Rep.
55 Q8 Klintehamn Sweden
69 J5 Klintsovka Rus. Fed.
68 E4 Klintsy Rus. Fed.
104 C5 Kliprand S. Africa
66 G2 Ključ Bos.-Herz.
62 H5 Kłodzko Pol.
20 C3 Klondike Gold Rush National History Park nat. park U.S.A.
62 H6 Klosterneuburg Austria
22 F1 Klotz, Lac l. Can.
20 A2 Kluane Game Sanctuary res. Can.
20 B2 Kluane Lake l. Can.
20 B2 Kluane National Park nat. park Can.
62 J5 Kluczbork Pol.
84 B4 Klupro Pak.
68 C4 Klyetsk Belarus
77 S4 Klyuchevskaya Sopka volc. Rus. Fed.
55 O6 Knåda Sweden
58 F3 Knaresborough U.K.
21 L3 Knee Lake l. Can.
30 B1 Knife Lake l. Can./U.S.A.
20 D4 Knight In. in. Can.
59 D5 Knighton U.K.
30 E6 Knightstown U.S.A.
66 G2 Knin Croatia
62 G7 Knittelfeld Austria
67 K3 Knjaževac Yugo.
60 C4 Knock Rep. of Ireland
60 B6 Knockaboy h. Rep. of Ireland
60 B5 Knockacummer h. Rep. of Ireland
60 C3 Knockalongy h. Rep. of Ireland
60 B5 Knockalough Rep. of Ireland
57 F3 Knock Hill h. U.K.
60 E2 Knocklayd h. U.K.
61 B3 Knokke-Heist Belgium
59 F5 Knowle U.K.
119 B2 Knowles, C. c. Ant.
33 J1 Knowles Corner U.S.A.
33 G2 Knowlton Can.
30 D5 Knox U.S.A.
20 C4 Knox, C. c. Can.
34 A2 Knoxville CA U.S.A.
30 B5 Knoxville IL U.S.A.
29 D4 Knoxville TN U.S.A.
57 C3 Knoydart reg. U.K.
104 E7 Knysna S. Africa
90 C8 Kobayashi Japan
54 V2 Kobbfoss Norway
91 E6 Kōbe Japan
København see Copenhagen
100 B3 Kobenni Maur.
62 C5 Koblenz Ger.
68 J3 Kobra Rus. Fed.
93 J8 Kobroör i. Indon.
68 C4 Kobryn Belarus
69 G7 K'obulet'i Georgia
67 K4 Kočani Macedonia
80 B1 Kocasu r. Turkey
66 F2 Kočevje Slovenia
95 A3 Ko Chan i. Thai.
95 B2 Ko Chang i. Thai.
85 G4 Koch Bihār India
Kochi see Cochin
90 D7 Kōchi Japan
90 D7 Kōchi Japan
68 H4 Kochkurovo Rus. Fed.
69 H6 Kochubey Rus. Fed.
69 G6 Kochubeyevskoye Rus. Fed.
18 Kodiak Island i. U.S.A.
105 G1 Kodibeleng Botswana
68 F2 Kodino Rus. Fed.
101 F4 Kodok Sudan
90 H3 Kodomari-misaki pt Japan
69 G7 Kodori r. Georgia
69 D5 Kodyma Ukr.
67 L4 Kodzhaele mt. Bulg./Greece
104 D6 Koedoesberg mts S. Africa
104 D4 Koegrabie S. Africa
104 C5 Koekenaap S. Africa
103 B6 Koës Namibia
35 F5 Kofa Mts mts U.S.A.
104 F4 Koffiefontein S. Africa
100 B4 Koforidua Ghana
91 G6 Kōfu Japan
22 E2 Kogaluc r. Can.
22 E2 Kogaluc, Baie de b. Can.
23 H2 Kogaluk r. Can.
115 J1 Kogan Austr.
55 N9 Køge Denmark
90 C6 Kogushi Japan
84 B2 Kohat Pak.
55 T7 Kohila Estonia
85 H4 Kohima India
119 A3 Kohler Ra. mts Ant.
84 B3 Kohlu Pak.
55 U7 Kohtla-Järve Estonia
117 E2 Kohukohunui h. N.Z.
91 G5 Koide Japan
20 A2 Koidern Can.
81 K3 Koi Sanjaq Iraq
90 G3 Ko-jima i. Japan
91 G7 Ko-jima i. Japan
112 C6 Kojonup Austr.
95 A1 Kok r. Thai.
33 J2 Kokadjo U.S.A.
79 L1 Kokand Uzbek.
55 R7 Kökar Fin.
84 B1 Kokcha r. Afgh.
55 R6 Kokemäenjoki r. Fin.
104 C4 Kokerboom Namibia
63 O3 Kokhanava Belarus
68 G3 Kokhma Rus. Fed.
54 S5 Kokkola Fin.
34 □1 Koko Hd hd U.S.A.
30 D5 Kokomo U.S.A.
104 E2 Kokong Botswana
90 C7 Kokonoe Japan
105 G3 Kokosi S. Africa
82 F1 Kokpekty Kazak.
68 H3 Koksharka Rus. Fed.
76 H4 Kokshetau Kazak.
23 G2 Koksoak r. Can.
105 H5 Kokstad S. Africa
90 C8 Kokubu Japan
95 B3 Ko Kut i. Thai.
54 X2 Kola Rus. Fed.
84 C2 Kolahoi mt. India
93 G7 Kolaka Indon.
95 A4 Ko Lanta i. Thai.
95 A4 Ko Lanta Thai.
76 E3 Kola Peninsula pen. Rus. Fed.
84 E6 Kolar India
84 D4 Kolaras India
83 E8 Kolar Gold Fields India
54 S3 Kolari Fin.
84 C4 Kolayat India
68 F3 Kol'chugino Rus. Fed.
100 A3 Kolda Senegal
55 L9 Kolding Denmark
102 C3 Kole Haute-Zaïre Zaire
102 C4 Kole Kasai-Oriental Zaire
65 H4 Koléa Alg.
54 R4 Koler Sweden
76 F3 Kolguyev, O. i. Rus. Fed.
85 F5 Kolhan reg. India
83 D7 Kolhapur India
95 A4 Ko Libong i. Thai.
55 S7 Kõljala Estonia
55 S8 Kolkasrags pt Latvia
Kollam see Quilon
Köln see Cologne
62 G3 Kołobrzeg Pol.
68 H3 Kologriv Rus. Fed.
100 B3 Kolokani Mali
111 F2 Kolombangara i. Solomon Is
68 F4 Kolomna Rus. Fed.
69 C5 Kolomyya Ukr.
100 B3 Kolondiéba Mali
93 G7 Kolonedale Indon.
104 D3 Kolonkwane Botswana
76 K4 Kolpashevo Rus. Fed.
69 F4 Kolpny Rus. Fed.
Kol'skiy Poluostrov pen. see Kola Peninsula
83 D10 Kolumadulu Atoll atoll Maldives
54 M4 Kolvereid Norway
54 T1 Kolvik Norway
103 C5 Kolwezi Zaire
77 R3 Kolyma r. Rus. Fed.
77 R3 Kolymskaya Nizmennost' lowland Rus. Fed.
77 R3 Kolymskiy, Khrebet mts Rus. Fed.
68 H4 Kolyshley Rus. Fed.
67 K3 Kom mt. Bulg.
91 F6 Komagane Japan
90 H2 Komaga-take volc. Japan
104 B4 Komaggas S. Africa
104 B4 Komaggas Mts mts S. Africa
77 S4 Komandorskiye Ostrova is Rus. Fed.
62 J7 Komárno Slovakia
105 J2 Komatipoort S. Africa
91 F5 Komatsu Japan
90 E6 Komatsushima Japan
102 C4 Kombe Zaire
100 B3 Kombissiri Burkina
105 G6 Komga S. Africa
90 H3 Kominato Japan
69 D6 Kominternivs'ke Ukr.
68 J2 Komi, Respublika div. Rus. Fed.
66 G3 Komiža Croatia
67 H1 Komló Hungary
102 B4 Komono Congo
91 G5 Komoro Japan
67 L4 Komotini Greece
104 D6 Komsberg mts S. Africa
77 L1 Komsomolets, O. i. Rus. Fed.
68 G3 Komsomol'sk Rus. Fed.
69 E5 Komsomol's'k Ukr.
69 H6 Komsomol'skiy Kalmyk. Rus. Fed.
68 H4 Komsomol'skiy Mordov. Rus. Fed.
87 P1 Komsomol'sk-na-Amure Rus. Fed.
76 H3 Komsomol'skiy Rus. Fed.
81 J1 Kömürlü Turkey
35 F6 Kom Vo U.S.A.
68 F3 Konakovo Rus. Fed.
85 F5 Konar Res. resr India
84 D4 Konch India
85 E6 Kondagaon India
31 J2 Kondiaronk, Lac l. Can.
102 D4 Kondoa Tanz.
68 E2 Kondopoga Rus. Fed.
68 E4 Kondrovo Rus. Fed.
119 C2 Kong Håkon VII Hav sea Ant.
76 D2 Kong Karl's Land is Svalbard
102 C4 Kongolo Zaire
100 B3 Kongoussi Burkina
55 L7 Kongsberg Norway
55 N6 Kongsvinger Norway
95 C2 Kông, T. r. Cambodia
102 D4 Kongwa Tanz.
95 C2 Kong, Xé r. Laos
61 F4 Königswinter Ger.
62 J4 Konin Pol.
67 G3 Konjic Bos.-Herz.
104 B4 Konkiep watercourse Namibia
100 B3 Konna Mali
54 U5 Konnevesi Fin.
68 G2 Konosha Rus. Fed.
91 G5 Kōnosu Japan
69 E5 Konotop Ukr.
95 D2 Kon Plong Vietnam
62 D7 Konstanz Ger.
100 C3 Kontagora Nigeria
54 V5 Kontiolahti Fin.
54 U4 Konttila Fin.
95 C2 Kon Tum Vietnam
95 D2 Kontum, Plateau du plat. Vietnam
80 D3 Konya Turkey
112 D5 Kookynie Austr.
34 □1 Koolau Range mts U.S.A.
114 F5 Koondrook Austr.
32 D5 Koon Lake l. U.S.A.
115 H5 Koorawatha Austr.
24 C2 Kooskia U.S.A.
20 F5 Kootenay r. Can./U.S.A.
20 F5 Kootenay L. l. Can.
20 F4 Kootenay Nat. Park nat. park Can.
104 D5 Kootjieskolk S. Africa
69 H6 Kopanovka Rus. Fed.
84 C6 Kopargaon India
54 E3 Kópasker Iceland
66 E2 Koper Slovenia
95 B3 Ko Phangan i. Thai.
95 A3 Ko Phra Thong i. Thai.
95 A4 Ko Phuket i. Thai.
55 P7 Köping Sweden
54 Q5 Köpmanholmen Sweden
105 F2 Kopong Botswana
55 M6 Koppang Norway
55 O7 Kopparberg Sweden
105 G3 Koppies S. Africa
104 D3 Koppieskraalpan salt pan S. Africa
66 G1 Koprivnica Croatia
80 C3 Köprü r. Turkey
68 G4 Korablino Rus. Fed.
22 E1 Korak, Baie b. Can.
83 F7 Koraput India
Korat see Nakhon Ratchasima
85 E5 Korba India
66 D6 Korba Tunisia
95 B4 Korbu, Gunung mt. Malaysia
67 J4 Korçë Albania
66 G3 Korčula i. Croatia
66 G3 Korčula Croatia
66 G3 Korčulanski Kanal chan. Croatia
81 M4 Kord Khvord Iran
88 G2 Korea Bay g. China/N. Korea
71 Korea, North country Asia
71 Korea, South country Asia
90 B6 Korea Strait str. Japan/S. Korea
69 F6 Korenovsk Rus. Fed.
69 C5 Korets' Ukr.
80 B1 Körfez Turkey
119 B3 Korff Ice Rise ice feature Ant.
54 N3 Korgen Norway
100 B4 Korhogo Côte d'Ivoire
84 B5 Kori Creek in. India
67 K5 Korinthiakos Kolpos chan. Greece
67 K6 Korinthos Greece
62 H7 Kőris-hegy mt. Hungary
67 J3 Koritnik mt. Albania
91 H5 Kōriyama Japan
80 C3 Korkuteli Turkey
80 D4 Kormakitis, Cape c. Cyprus
62 H7 Körmend Hungary
100 B4 Koro Côte d'Ivoire
111 H3 Koro i. Fiji
100 B3 Koro Mali
69 F5 Korocha Rus. Fed.
80 D1 Köroğlu Dağları mts Turkey
80 D1 Köroğlu Tepesi mt Turkey
102 D4 Korogwe Tanz.
114 E7 Koroit Austr.
114 E6 Korong Vale Austr.

67 K4 Koronia, L. *l.* Greece
93 J5 Koror Palau
111 H3 Koro Sea *b.* Fiji
69 D5 Korosten' Ukr.
69 D5 Korostyshiv Ukr.
101 D3 Koro Toro Chad
55 T5 Korpilahti Fin.
55 R6 Korpo Fin.
87 Q2 Korsakov Rus. Fed.
68 J3 Korshik Rus. Fed.
54 R5 Korsnäs Fin.
55 M9 Korsør Denmark
69 D5 Korsun'-Shevchenkivs'kyy Ukr.
63 K3 Korsze Pol.
54 S5 Kortesjärvi Fin.
68 J2 Kortkeros Rus. Fed.
61 B4 Kortrijk Belgium
68 G3 Kortsovo Rus. Fed.
115 F7 Korumburra Austr.
100 D4 Korup, Parc National de *nat. park* Cameroon
54 U3 Korvala Fin.
84 D4 Korwai India
77 R4 Koryakskaya Sopka *volc.* Rus. Fed.
77 S3 Koryakskiy Khrebet *mts* Rus. Fed.
68 H2 Koryazhma Rus. Fed.
69 E5 Koryukivka Ukr.
67 M6 Kos *i.* Greece
95 B3 Ko Samui *i.* Thai.
62 H4 Kościan Pol.
27 F5 Kosciusko U.S.A.
20 C3 Kosciusko I. *i.* U.S.A.
115 H6 Kosciusko, Mt *mt.* Austr.
115 H6 Kosciusko National Park *nat. park* Austr.
81 G1 Köse Turkey
80 F1 Köse Dağı *mt.* Turkey
86 E2 Kosh-Agach Rus. Fed.
90 B8 Koshikijima-rettō *is* Japan
90 B8 Koshiki-kaikyō *chan.* Japan
90 K2 Koshimizu Japan
30 C4 Koshkoning, Lake *l.* U.S.A.
91 G5 Kōshoku Japan
84 D3 Kosi *r.* India
84 D4 Kosi India
105 K3 Kosi Bay *b.* S. Africa
63 K6 Košice Slovakia
54 R3 Koskullskule Sweden
68 J2 Koslan Rus. Fed.
67 J3 Kosovo *div.* Yugo.
67 J3 Kosovska Mitrovica Yugo.
108 □ Kosrae *i.* Micronesia
100 B4 Kossou, Lac de *l.* Côte d'Ivoire
67 K3 Kostenets Bulg.
105 G2 Koster S. Africa
101 F3 Kosti Sudan
67 K3 Kostinbrod Bulg.
76 K3 Kostino Rus. Fed.
68 D1 Kostomuksha Rus. Fed.
69 C5 Kostopil' Ukr.
68 G3 Kostroma Rus. Fed.
68 G3 Kostroma *r.* Rus. Fed.
68 G3 Kostromskaya Oblast' *div.* Rus. Fed.
62 G4 Kostrzyn Pol.
69 F5 Kostyantynivka Ukr.
62 H3 Koszalin Pol.
62 H7 Kőszeg Hungary
85 E5 Kota *Madhya Pradesh* India
84 C4 Kota *Rajasthan* India
92 C8 Kotaagung Indon.
92 F7 Kotabaru Indon.
92 C5 Kota Bharu Malaysia
92 C7 Kotabumi Indon.
92 F5 Kota Kinabalu Malaysia
95 A3 Ko Tao *i.* Thai.
83 F7 Kotapārh India
95 B5 Kotapinang Indon.
84 C4 Kotari *r.* India
95 B5 Kota Tinggi Malaysia
68 J3 Kotel'nich Rus. Fed.
69 G6 Kotel'nikovo Rus. Fed.
77 P2 Kotel'nyy, O. *i.* Rus. Fed.
84 D3 Kotgarh India
84 E4 Kothi India
55 U6 Kotka Fin.
84 C3 Kot Kapura India
68 H2 Kotlas Rus. Fed.
84 C2 Kotli Pak.
77 V3 Kotlik Alaska
54 D5 Kötlutangi *pt* Iceland
55 V7 Kotly Rus. Fed.
66 G2 Kotor Varoš Bos.-Herz.
100 B4 Kotouba Côte d'Ivoire
69 H5 Kotovo Rus. Fed.
69 G4 Kotovsk Rus. Fed.
69 D6 Kotovs'k Ukr.
84 C4 Kotra India
84 E6 Kotri *r.* India
84 B4 Kotri Pak.
84 A5 Kot Sarae Pak.
83 F7 Kottagudem India
83 E9 Kottayam India
83 E9 Kotte Sri Lanka
77 M2 Kotuy *r.* Rus. Fed.
77 V3 Kotzebue Sound *b.* Alaska
100 A3 Koubia Guinea
100 B3 Koudougou Burkina
104 E6 Koueveldberg *mts* Africa
101 D3 Koufey Niger
67 M7 Koufonisi *i.* Greece
104 E6 Kougaberg *mts* S. Africa
80 D4 Kouklia Cyprus
102 B4 Koulamoutou Gabon
100 B3 Koulikoro Mali
111 G4 Koumac New Caledonia
116 C3 Koumala Austr.
100 A3 Koundâra Guinea
100 B3 Koupéla Burkina
43 H2 Kourou Fr. Guiana
100 B3 Kouroussa Guinea
101 D3 Kousséri Cameroon
100 B3 Koutiala Mali
55 U6 Kouvola Fin.
54 W3 Kovdor Rus. Fed.
54 W3 Kovdozero, Oz. *l.* Rus. Fed.
69 C5 Kovel' Ukr.
68 G3 Kovernino Rus. Fed.
68 G3 Kovrov Rus. Fed.
68 G4 Kovylkino Rus. Fed.
68 F2 Kovzhskoye, Ozero *l.* Rus. Fed.
117 C5 Kowhitirangi N.Z.
89 □ Kowloon *Hong Kong* China
89 E6 Kowloon *Hong Kong* China
89 □ Kowloon Pk *h.* *Hong Kong* China
90 C6 Kōyama-misaki *pt* Japan
95 A3 Ko Yao Yai *i.* Thai.
80 B3 Köyceğiz Turkey
68 J2 Koygorodok Rus. Fed.
68 H1 Koynas Rus. Fed.
91 H4 Koyoshi-gawa *r.* Japan
80 F1 Koyulhisar Turkey
68 F3 Koza Rus. Fed.
90 B6 Kō-zaki *pt* Japan
90 D6 Kōzan Japan
80 E3 Kozan Turkey
67 J4 Kozani Greece
66 G2 Kozara *mts* Bos.-Herz.
69 D5 Kozelets' Ukr.
68 E4 Kozel'sk Rus. Fed.
Kozhikode *see* Calicut
80 C1 Kozlu Turkey
68 H3 Koz'modem'yansk Rus. Fed.
67 K4 Kožuf *mts* Greece/Macedonia
91 G6 Kōzu-shima *i.* Japan
69 D5 Kozyatyn Ukr.
100 C4 Kpalimé Togo
95 A3 Krabi Thai.
95 A3 Kra Buri Thai.
95 C2 Krâcheh Cambodia
54 P4 Kraddsele Sweden
55 L7 Kragerø Norway
67 J2 Kragujevac Yugo.
95 A3 Kra, Isthmus of *isth.* Thai.
92 □ Krakatau *i.* Indon.
95 C2 Krâkôr Cambodia
63 J5 Kraków Pol.
95 B2 Krâlănh Cambodia
45 C1 Kralendijk Neth. Ant.
69 F5 Kramators'k Ukr.
54 P5 Kramfors Sweden
61 C3 Krammer *est.* Neth.
67 K6 Kranidi Greece
66 F1 Kranj Slovenia
95 □ Kranji Res. *resr* Sing.
105 J4 Kranskop S. Africa
68 H2 Krasavino Rus. Fed.
76 G2 Krasino Rus. Fed.
55 U9 Krāslava Latvia
63 P4 Krasnapollye Belarus
69 D4 Krasnaya Gora Rus. Fed.
69 H5 Krasnoarmeysk Rus. Fed.
69 F6 Krasnoarmeyskaya Rus. Fed.
69 F5 Krasnoarmiys'k Ukr.
68 H2 Krasnoborsk Rus. Fed.
69 F6 Krasnodar Rus. Fed.
69 F6 Krasnodarskiy Kray *div.* Rus. Fed.
69 F5 Krasnodon Ukr.
68 D3 Krasnogorodskoye Rus. Fed.
87 Q2 Krasnogorsk Rus. Fed.
69 G6 Krasnogvardeyskoye Rus. Fed.
69 E5 Krasnohrad Ukr.
69 E6 Krasnohvardiys'ke Ukr.
63 R2 Krasnomayskiy Rus. Fed.
69 E6 Krasnoperekops'k Ukr.
55 V6 Krasnosel'skoye Rus. Fed.
68 G4 Krasnoslobodsk Rus. Fed.
Krasnovodsk *see* Turkmenbashi
76 L4 Krasnoyarsk Rus. Fed.
63 P3 Krasnyy Rus. Fed.
68 H3 Krasnyye Baki Rus. Fed.
69 H6 Krasnyye Barrikady Rus. Fed.
68 F3 Krasnyy Kholm Rus. Fed.
69 H5 Krasnyy Kut Rus. Fed.
68 D3 Krasnyy Luch Rus. Fed.
69 F5 Krasnyy Lyman Ukr.
69 J6 Krasnyy Yar *Astrak.* Rus. Fed.
69 H5 Krasnyy Yar *Volgograd.* Rus. Fed.
69 C5 Krasyliv Ukr.
69 H7 Kraynovka Rus. Fed.
62 C5 Krefeld Ger.
69 E5 Kremenchuk Ukr.
69 E5 Kremenchuts'ka Vodoskhovshche *resr* Ukr.
69 G5 Kremenskaya Rus. Fed.
62 G6 Křemešník *h.* Czech Rep.
24 F3 Kremmling U.S.A.
62 G6 Krems an der Donau Austria
77 U3 Kresta, Zaliv *b.* Rus. Fed.
68 E3 Kresttsy Rus. Fed.
55 R9 Kretinga Lith.
63 N3 Kreva Belarus
100 C4 Kribi Cameroon
105 H3 Kriel S. Africa
67 J5 Krikellos Greece
87 Q2 Kril'on, Mys *c.* Rus. Fed.
83 F7 Krishna *r.* India
83 E8 Krishnagiri India
83 F7 Krishna, Mouths of the *est.* India
85 G5 Krishnanagar India
55 K7 Kristiansand Norway
55 O8 Kristianstad Sweden
54 K5 Kristiansund Norway
55 O7 Kristinehamn Sweden
55 R5 Kristinestad Fin.
Kriti *i.* *see* Crete
Krivoy Rog *see* Kryvyy Rih
66 G1 Križevci Croatia
66 F2 Krk *i.* Croatia
54 O5 Krokom Sweden
54 L5 Krokstadøra Norway
54 O3 Krokstranda Norway
69 E5 Krolevets' Ukr.
95 B3 Krŏng Kaôh Kŏng Cambodia
54 S5 Kronoby Fin.
95 A2 Kronwa Myanmar
105 G3 Kroonstad S. Africa
69 G6 Kropotkin Rus. Fed.
63 K6 Krosno Pol.
62 H5 Krotoszyn Pol.
105 J2 Kruger National Park *nat. park* S. Africa
63 O3 Kruhlaye Belarus
92 C8 Krui Indon.
104 F7 Kruisfontein S. Africa
67 H4 Krujë Albania
67 L4 Krumovgrad Bulg.
Krungkao *see* Ayutthaya
Krung Thep *see* Bangkok
63 O3 Krupki Belarus
67 J3 Kruševac Yugo.
20 B3 Kruzof I. *i.* U.S.A.
68 D4 Krychaw Belarus
69 F6 Krymsk Rus. Fed.
67 L6 Krytiko Pelagos *sea* Greece
69 E6 Kryvyy Rih Ukr.
100 B2 Ksabi Alg.
100 C1 Ksar el Boukhari Alg.
100 B1 Ksar el Kebir Morocco
69 F5 Kshenskiy Rus. Fed.
66 D7 Ksour Essaf Tunisia
68 H3 Kstovo Rus. Fed.
95 A4 Kuah Malaysia
95 B4 Kuala Kangsar Malaysia
95 B4 Kuala Kerai Malaysia
95 B5 Kuala Kubu Baharu Malaysia
92 C6 Kuala Lipis Malaysia
92 C6 Kuala Lumpur Malaysia
95 B4 Kuala Nerang Malaysia
95 B5 Kuala Pilah Malaysia
95 B5 Kuala Rompin Malaysia
95 A4 Kualasimpang Indon.
92 C5 Kuala Terengganu Malaysia
94 A5 Kuamut Malaysia
89 F6 Kuanshan Taiwan
92 C6 Kuantan Malaysia
69 G6 Kuban' *r.* Rus. Fed.
81 J5 Kubaysah Iraq
68 F3 Kubenskoye, Ozero *l.* Rus. Fed.
68 H4 Kubnya *r.* Rus. Fed.
90 D7 Kubokawa Japan
67 M3 Kubrat Bulg.
84 C4 Kuchāman India
84 C4 Kuchera India
92 D6 Kuching Malaysia
90 C7 Kuchinotsu Japan
Kucing *see* Kuching
67 H4 Kuçovë Albania
90 C7 Kudamatsu Japan
92 F5 Kudat Malaysia
92 □ Kudus Indon.
62 F7 Kufstein Austria
68 H3 Kugesi Rus. Fed.
85 E3 Kuhanbokano *mt.* China
81 K3 Kūhdasht Iran
81 L2 Kūhhaye Sabalan *mts* Iran
81 M3 Kūhīn Iran
54 V4 Kuhmo Fin.
55 T6 Kuhmoinen Fin.
104 B2 Kuis Namibia
104 A1 Kuiseb Pass *pass* Namibia
103 B5 Kuito Angola
20 C3 Kuiu Island *i.* U.S.A.
54 T4 Kuivaniemi Fin.
85 F5 Kujang India
91 H3 Kuji Japan
91 H5 Kuji-gawa *r.* Japan
91 H3 Kuji-wan *b.* Japan
90 C7 Kujū-san *volc.* Japan
31 F1 Kukatush Can.
67 J3 Kukës Albania
68 J3 Kukmor Rus. Fed.
93 B5 Kukup Malaysia
80 B2 Kula Turkey
85 G3 Kula Kangri *mt.* Bhutan
82 A1 Kulandy Kazak.
77 P2 Kular Rus. Fed.
94 B5 Kulassein *i.* Phil.
85 H4 Kulaura Bangl.
55 R8 Kuldīga Latvia
104 D1 Kule Botswana
68 G4 Kulebaki Rus. Fed.
95 C2 Kulen Cambodia
113 F5 Kulgera Austr.
68 H2 Kulikovo Rus. Fed.
95 B4 Kulim Malaysia
114 F3 Kulkyne *watercourse* Austr.
84 D3 Kullu India
62 E5 Kulmbach Ger.
79 K2 Kŭlob Tajik.
81 H2 Kulp Turkey
84 D4 Kulpahar India
33 F4 Kulpsville U.S.A.
76 G5 Kul'sary Kazak.
80 D2 Kulu Turkey
80 C3 Kulübe Tepe *mt.* Turkey
76 J4 Kulunda Rus. Fed.
76 J4 Kulundinskoye, Ozero *salt l.* Rus. Fed.
114 E5 Kulwin Austr.
90 D7 Kuma Japan
69 H6 Kuma *r.* Rus. Fed.
91 G5 Kumagaya Japan
90 G2 Kumaishi Japan
90 C7 Kumamoto Japan
90 C7 Kumamoto Japan
91 F7 Kumano Japan
67 J3 Kumanovo Macedonia
100 B4 Kumasi Ghana
Kumayri *see* Gyumri
100 C4 Kumba Cameroon
83 E8 Kumbakonam India
80 C2 Kümbet Turkey
104 E1 Kumchuru Botswana
76 G4 Kumertau Rus. Fed.
55 O7 Kumla Sweden
100 D3 Kumo Nigeria
95 B1 Kumphawapi Thai.
104 C4 Kums Namibia
69 H7 Kumukh Rus. Fed.
84 B2 Kunar *r.* Afgh.
90 L1 Kunashir, Ostrov *i.* Rus. Fed.
87 R3 Kunashir, Ostrov *i.* Rus. Fed.
85 E2 Kunchuk Tso *salt l.* China
55 U7 Kunda Estonia
85 E4 Kunda India
84 B2 Kundar *r.* Afgh./Pak.
84 B1 Kunduz Afgh.
55 M8 Kungälv Sweden
82 E2 Kungei Alatau *mts* Kazak./Kyrg.
20 C4 Kunghit I. *i.* Can.
55 N8 Kungsbacka Sweden
55 M7 Kungshamn Sweden
102 B3 Kungu Zaire
84 D6 Kuni *r.* India
90 C7 Kunimi-dake *mt.* Japan
85 F5 Kunjabar India
85 G4 Kunlui *r.* India/Nepal
74 □ Kunlun Shan *mts* China
85 H2 Kunlun Shankou *pass* China
89 B5 Kunming China
84 D4 Kuno *r.* India
87 N4 Kunsan S. Korea
88 F4 Kunshan China
112 E3 Kununurra Austr.
84 D4 Kunwari *r.* India
68 D3 Kun'ya Rus. Fed.
88 F2 Kunyu Shan *h.* China
89 F4 Kuocang Shan *mts* China
55 T6 Kuohijärvi *l.* Fin.
54 V3 Kuolayarvi Rus. Fed.
54 U5 Kuopio Fin.
54 S5 Kuortane Fin.
66 F2 Kupa *r.* Croatia/Slovenia
93 G9 Kupang Indon.
55 T9 Kupiškis Lith.
20 C3 Kupreanof Island *i.* U.S.A.
69 F5 Kup"yans'k Ukr.
82 F2 Kuqa China
81 M2 Kür *r.* Azer.
81 K1 Kura *r.* Azer./Georgia
90 D6 Kurahashi-jima *i.* Japan
69 H7 Kurakh Rus. Fed.
116 A1 Kuranda Austr.
90 D6 Kurashiki Japan
85 E5 Kurasia India
90 D6 Kurayoshi Japan
80 B1 Kurban Dağı *mt.* Turkey
69 E5 Kurchatov Rus. Fed.
81 M1 Kürdämir Azer.
81 M2 Kür Dili *pt* Azer.
67 L4 Kŭrdzhali Bulg.
90 D6 Kure Japan
80 D1 Küre Turkey
55 S7 Kuressaare Estonia
76 H4 Kurgan Rus. Fed.
69 G6 Kurganinsk Rus. Fed.
84 B1 Kuri Afgh.
84 B4 Kuri India
Kuria Muria Islands *is see* Ḩalāniyāt, Juzur al
54 S5 Kurikka Fin.
91 H4 Kurikoma-yama *volc.* Japan
77 Q5 Kuril Islands *is* Rus. Fed.
Kuril'skiye Ostrova *is see* Kuril Islands
101 F3 Kurmuk Sudan
83 E7 Kurnool India
80 E6 Kurnub Israel
91 F5 Kurobe Japan
90 C7 Kurogi Japan
90 H3 Kuroishi Japan
91 H5 Kuroiso Japan
90 H2 Kuromatsunai Japan
68 F4 Kurovskoye Rus. Fed.
117 C6 Kurow N.Z.
84 B2 Kurram *r.* Afgh./Pak.
84 B2 Kurramgarhi Dam *dam* Pak.
115 J4 Kurri Kurri Austr.
Kuršių Marios *lag. see* Courland Lagoon
69 F5 Kursk Rus. Fed.
69 H6 Kurskaya Rus. Fed.
69 F5 Kurskaya Oblast' *div.* Rus. Fed.
Kurskiy Zaliv *lag. see* Courland Lagoon
80 D1 Kurşunlu Turkey
81 H3 Kurtalan Turkey
85 G4 Kuru *r.* Bhutan
80 G2 Kuruçay Turkey
84 D3 Kurukshetra India
82 G2 Kuruktag *mts* China
104 D3 Kuruman *watercourse* S. Africa
104 E3 Kuruman S. Africa
90 C7 Kurume Japan
87 K1 Kurumkan Rus. Fed.
83 F9 Kurunegala Sri Lanka
101 F2 Kurūsh, Jebel *reg.* Sudan
67 M6 Kuşadası Turkey
67 M6 Kuşadası Körfezi *b.* Turkey
20 B2 Kusawa Lake *l.* Can.
80 A1 Kuş Gölü *l.* Turkey
69 F6 Kushchevskaya Rus. Fed.
91 F6 Kushida-gawa *r.* Japan
90 C8 Kushikino Japan
90 C8 Kushima Japan
91 E7 Kushimoto Japan
90 K2 Kushiro Japan
90 K2 Kushiro-Shitsugen National Park *nat. park* Japan
81 M5 Kūshkak Iran
76 H4 Kushmurun Kazak.
85 G5 Kushtia Bangl.
88 C2 Kushui *r.* China
77 V4 Kuskokwim Bay *b.* Alaska
90 K2 Kussharo-ko *l.* Japan
76 H4 Kustanay Kazak.
81 M6 Kut Iran
81 M6 Kūt Abdollāh Iran
95 A5 Kutacane Indon.
80 B2 Kütahya Turkey
69 G7 K'ut'aisi Georgia
Kut-al-Imara *see* Al Kūt
69 H6 Kutan Rus. Fed.
90 H2 Kutchan Japan
81 M5 Kūt-e Gapu Iran
62 G2 Kutina Croatia
66 G2 Kutjevo Croatia
63 J4 Kutno Pol.
102 B4 Kutu Zaire
85 G5 Kutubdia I. *i.* Bangl.
23 G2 Kuujjuaq Can.
Kuujjuarapik *see* Poste-de-la-Baleine
54 V4 Kuusamo Fin.
55 U6 Kuusankoski Fin.
103 B5 Kuvango Angola
68 E3 Kuvshinovo Rus. Fed.
70 Kuwait *country* Asia
81 L7 Kuwait Kuwait
81 L7 Kuwait Jun *b.* Kuwait
91 F6 Kuwana Japan
68 G1 Kuya Rus. Fed.
76 J4 Kuybyshev Rus. Fed.
Kuybyshev *see* Samara
68 J4 Kuybyshevskoye Vdkhr. *resr* Rus. Fed.
88 D2 Kuye *r.* China
82 F2 Kuytun China
67 N6 Kuyucak Turkey
55 V6 Kuznechnoye Rus. Fed.
68 H4 Kuznetsk Rus. Fed.
69 C5 Kuznetsovs'k Ukr.
54 R1 Kvænangen *chan.* Norway
54 Q2 Kvaløya *i.* Norway
54 S1 Kvalsund Norway
Kvareli *see* Qvareli
66 F2 Kvarnerić *chan.* Croatia
20 D3 Kwadacha Wilderness Prov. Park *res.* Can.
89 □ Kwai Tau Leng *h.* *Hong Kong* China
95 A5 Kwala Indon.
105 J4 KwaMashu S. Africa
105 H2 KwaMhlanga S. Africa
87 N4 Kwangju S. Korea
102 B4 Kwango *r.* Zaire
102 D4 Kwangwazi Tanz.
105 F6 Kwanobuhle S. Africa
105 F6 KwaNojoli S. Africa
105 G6 Kwanonqubela S. Africa
104 F5 Kwanonzame S. Africa
105 G6 Kwatinidubu S. Africa
105 H3 KwaZamokhule S. Africa
104 F6 Kwazamukucinga S. Africa
104 F5 Kwazamuxolo S. Africa
105 H3 KwaZanele S. Africa
105 J4 Kwazulu-Natal *div.* S. Africa
103 C5 Kwekwe Zimbabwe
104 F1 Kweneng *div.* Botswana
102 B4 Kwenge *r.* Zaire
105 G5 Kwezi-Naledi S. Africa
63 J4 Kwidzyn Pol.
77 V4 Kwigillingok Alaska
110 E2 Kwikila P.N.G.
102 B4 Kwilu *r.* Angola/Zaire
93 J7 Kwoka *mt.* Indon.
89 □ Kwun Tong *Hong Kong* China
101 D4 Kyabé Chad
114 F6 Kyabram Austr.
95 A1 Kyaikto Myanmar
95 A1 Kya-in Seikkyi Myanmar
86 J1 Kyakhta Rus. Fed.
114 E5 Kyalite Austr.
114 A4 Kyancutta Austr.
68 F1 Kyanda Rus. Fed.
95 A1 Kyaukhnyat Myanmar
83 H7 Kyaukpyu Myanmar
85 H5 Kyauktaw Myanmar
55 S9 Kybartai Lith.
114 D6 Kybybolite Austr.
84 D2 Kyelang India
88 A2 Kyikug China
Kyiv *see* Kiev
Kyklades *is see* Cyclades
21 H4 Kyle Can.
57 C3 Kyle of Lochalsh U.K.
61 E5 Kyll *r.* Ger.
67 K6 Kyllini *mt.* Greece
114 F6 Kyneton Austr.
102 D3 Kyoga, Lake *l.* Uganda
91 E6 Kyōga-misaki *pt* Japan
115 K2 Kyogle Austr.
90 C7 Kyomachi Japan
95 A1 Kyondo Myanmar
116 A3 Kyong Austr.
91 E6 Kyōto Japan
91 E6 Kyōto Japan
67 J6 Kyparissia Greece
67 J6 Kyparissiakos Kolpos *b.* Greece
76 H4 Kypshak, Ozero *salt l.* Kazak.
67 L5 Kyra Panagia *i.* Greece
70 Kyrgyzstan *country* Asia
54 L5 Kyrksæterøra Norway
76 G3 Kyrta Rus. Fed.
68 H1 Kyssa Rus. Fed.
77 P3 Kytalyktakh Rus. Fed.
67 K6 Kythira *i.* Greece
67 L6 Kythnos *i.* Greece
95 A2 Kyungyaung Myanmar
90 C7 Kyūshū *i.* Japan
14 D5 Kyushu - Palau Ridge *sea feature* Pac. Oc.
90 C7 Kyūshū-sanchi *mts* Japan
67 K3 Kyustendil Bulg.
115 G5 Kywong Austr.
69 D5 Kyyivs'ke Vdskh. *resr* Ukr.
54 T5 Kyyjärvi Fin.
86 F1 Kyzyl Rus. Fed.
82 B2 Kyzylkum, Peski *des.* Uzbek.
79 L1 Kyzyl-Kyya Kyrgyzstan
86 F1 Kyzyl-Mazhalyk Rus. Fed.
82 C1 Kzyl-Dzhar Kazak.
82 C2 Kzyl-Orda Kazak.
76 J4 Kzyltu Kazak.


# L


61 F4 Laacher See *l.* Ger.
55 T7 Laagri Estonia
54 U2 Laanila Fin.
47 B3 La Araucania *div.* Chile
102 E3 Laascaanood Somalia
102 E3 Laasgoray Somalia
45 E2 La Asunción Venez.
100 A2 Laâyoune Western Sahara
69 G6 Laba *r.* Rus. Fed.
27 C6 La Babia Mex.
44 D3 La Banda Arg.
24 E3 La Barge U.S.A.
111 H3 Labasa Fiji
64 C3 La Baule-Escoublac France
100 A3 Labé Guinea
22 F4 Labelle Can.
30 B5 La Belle U.S.A.
20 B2 Laberge, Lake *l.* Can.
94 A5 Labian, Tg *pt* Malaysia
20 E2 La Biche *r.* Can.
69 G6 Labinsk Rus. Fed.
95 B5 Labis Malaysia
94 B3 Labo Phil.
80 E4 Laboué Lebanon
64 D4 Labouheyre France
47 D2 Laboulaye Arg.
23 H3 Labrador Can.
23 G3 Labrador City Can.
42 F5 Lábrea Brazil
92 C6 Labuhanbilik Indon.
95 A5 Labuhanruku Indon.
94 A5 Labuk *r.* Malaysia
94 A5 Labuk, Telukan *b.* Malaysia
93 H7 Labuna Indon.
114 A3 Labyrinth, L. *salt flat* Austr.
76 H3 Labytnangi Rus. Fed.
67 H4 Laç Albania
47 D1 La Calera Arg.
47 B2 La Calera Chile
64 F2 La Capelle France
47 B4 Lacar, L. *l.* Arg.
47 D2 La Carlota Arg.
65 E3 La Carolina Spain
67 M2 Lăcăuţi, Vârful *mt.* Romania
31 J1 Lac-Baker Can.
83 D8 Laccadive Islands *is* India
21 K4 Lac du Bonnet Can.
36 G5 La Ceiba Honduras
45 C2 La Ceiba Venez.
114 C6 Lacepede B. *b.* Austr.
33 E4 Laceyville U.S.A.
33 H1 Lac Frontière Can.
68 F2 Lacha, Ozero *l.* Rus. Fed.
31 F3 Lachine U.S.A.
114 F5 Lachlan *r.* *N.S.W.* Austr.
37 J7 La Chorrera Panama
22 F4 Lachute Can.
81 L2 Laçın Azer.
64 G5 La Ciotat France
32 D3 Lackawanna U.S.A.
21 G4 Lac La Biche Can.

20 E4 Lac La Hache Can.
20 F2 Lac la Martre Can.
21 H3 Lac La Ronge Provincial Park res. Can.
23 H4 Lac Mégantic Can.
33 G2 Lacolle Can.
25 E6 La Colorada Mex.
20 G4 Lacombe Can.
66 C5 Laconi Sardinia Italy
33 H3 Laconia U.S.A.
31 J1 La Corne Can.
30 A4 La Crescent U.S.A.
30 B4 La Crosse U.S.A.
45 A4 La Cruz Col.
26 E4 La Cygne U.S.A.
84 D2 Ladakh Range mts India
95 A4 Ladang i. Thai.
80 E1 Lādik Turkey
104 A6 Ladismith S. Africa
79 J4 Lādīz Iran
84 C4 Ladnun India
45 B3 La Dorada Col.
Ladozhskoye Ozero l. see Lagoda, Lake
85 H4 Ladu mt. India
68 E2 Ladva Rus. Fed.
68 E2 Ladva-Vetka Rus. Fed.
57 E4 Ladybank U.K.
105 G4 Ladybrand S. Africa
31 G2 Lady Evelyn Lake l. Can.
105 G5 Lady Frere S. Africa
105 G5 Lady Grey S. Africa
20 E5 Ladysmith Can.
105 H4 Ladysmith S. Africa
30 B3 Ladysmith U.S.A.
110 E2 Lae P.N.G.
95 B2 Laem Ngop Thai.
95 B4 Laem Pho pt Thai.
55 K6 Lærdalsøyri Norway
42 F8 La Esmeralda Bol.
45 D4 La Esmeralda Venez.
55 M8 Læsø i. Denmark
47 D1 La Falda Arg.
24 F4 Lafayette CO U.S.A.
30 D5 Lafayette IN U.S.A.
27 E6 Lafayette LA U.S.A.
29 C5 La Fayette U.S.A.
100 C4 Lafia Nigeria
64 D3 La Flèche France
32 A6 La Follette U.S.A.
31 H2 Laforce Can.
31 G2 Laforest Can.
23 F3 Laforge Can.
45 B2 La Fría Venez.
66 C6 La Galite i. Tunisia
69 H6 Lagan' Rus. Fed.
60 E3 Lagan r. U.K.
43 L6 Lagarto Brazil
55 L7 Lågen r. Norway
57 C5 Lagg U.K.
57 D3 Laggan U.K.
57 D4 Laggan, Loch l. U.K.
100 C1 Laghouat Alg.
85 G3 Lagkor Co salt l. China
45 B2 La Gloria Col.
46 D2 Lagoa Santa Brazil
68 D2 Lagoda, Lake l. Rus. Fed.
81 L1 Lagodekhi Georgia
95 D5 Lagong i. Indon.
94 B3 Lagonoy Gulf b. Phil.
44 B7 Lago Posadas Arg.
47 B4 Lago Ranco Chile
100 C4 Lagos Nigeria
65 C4 Lagos Port.
36 D3 Lagos de Moreno Mex.
22 E3 La Grande r. Can.
22 C2 La Grande Can.
22 F3 La Grande 4, Réservoir de resr Can.
22 E3 La Grande 2, Réservoir de resr Can.
22 E3 La Grande 3, Réservoir de resr Can.
112 D3 Lagrange Austr.
29 C5 La Grange GA U.S.A.
33 J2 La Grange ME U.S.A.
30 D5 La Grange MI U.S.A.
30 B5 La Grange MO U.S.A.
27 D6 La Grange TX U.S.A.
30 E5 Lagrange U.S.A.
45 E3 La Gran Sabana plat. Venez.
44 G3 Laguna Brazil
34 D5 Laguna Beach U.S.A.
47 B3 Laguna de Laja, Parque Nacional nat. park Chile
34 D5 Laguna Mts U.S.A.
42 C5 Lagunas Peru
44 A7 Laguna San Rafael, Parque Nacional nat. park Chile
45 C2 Lagunillas Venez.
93 F5 Lahad Datu Malaysia
94 A5 Lahad Datu, Telukan b. Malaysia
34 □2 Lahaina U.S.A.
81 M3 Lahargin Iran
92 C7 Lahat Indon.
95 A5 Lahewa Indon.
78 E7 Laḥij Yemen
81 M3 Lāhījān Iran
34 □1 Lahilahi Pt pt U.S.A.
55 N8 Laholm Sweden
34 C2 Lahontan Res. resr U.S.A.
84 C3 Lahore Pak.
45 B3 La Horqueta Venez.
84 B3 Lahri Pak.
55 T6 Lahti Fin.
101 D4 Laï Chad
88 F3 Lai'an China
89 C6 Laibin China
115 K1 Laidley Austr.
34 □1 Laie U.S.A.
34 □1 Laie Pt pt U.S.A.

89 C4 Laifeng China
64 E2 L'Aigle France
54 S5 Laihia Fin.
85 H4 Laimakuri India
104 D6 Laingsburg S. Africa
54 S3 Lainioälven r. Sweden
57 D2 Lairg U.K.
94 C5 Lais Phil.
55 R6 Laitila Fin.
66 D1 Laives Italy
88 E2 Laiwu China
88 F2 Laiyang China
88 E2 Laiyuan China
88 F2 Laizhou Wan b. China
47 B3 Laja r. Chile
47 B3 Laja, Lago de l. Chile
112 F3 Lajamanu Austr.
43 L5 Lajes Rio Grande do Norte Brazil
44 F3 Lajes Santa Catarina Brazil
25 G4 La Junta U.S.A.
24 E2 Lake U.S.A.
111 J3 Lakeba i. Fiji
80 D6 Lake Bardawîl Reserve res. Egypt
114 E6 Lake Bolac Austr.
115 G4 Lake Cargelligo Austr.
115 K3 Lake Cathie Austr.
24 B1 Lake Chelan Nat. Recreation Area res. U.S.A.
29 D6 Lake City FL U.S.A.
30 E3 Lake City MI U.S.A.
30 A3 Lake City MN U.S.A.
29 E5 Lake City SC U.S.A.
58 D3 Lake District National Park nat. park U.K.
34 D5 Lake Elsinore U.S.A.
114 B2 Lake Eyre Nat. Park nat. park Austr.
31 H3 Lakefield Can.
113 H2 Lakefield National Park nat. park Austr.
30 C4 Lake Geneva U.S.A.
35 E4 Lake Havasu City U.S.A.
34 C4 Lake Isabella U.S.A.
112 C6 Lake King Austr.
29 D6 Lakeland U.S.A.
30 C2 Lake Linden U.S.A.
20 F4 Lake Louise Can.
35 E4 Lake Mead National Recreation Area res. U.S.A.
33 J2 Lake Moxie Can.
24 B2 Lake Oswego U.S.A.
117 B5 Lake Paringa N.Z.
33 G2 Lake Placid U.S.A.
34 A2 Lakeport U.S.A.
117 C6 Lake Pukaki N.Z.
22 D3 Lake River Can.
31 H3 Lake St Peter Can.
115 H4 Lakes Entrance Austr.
30 E2 Lake Superior National Park nat. park Can.
115 J5 Lake Tabourie Austr.
22 E4 Lake Traverse Can.
24 B3 Lakeview U.S.A.
24 F4 Lakewood CO U.S.A.
33 F4 Lakewood NJ U.S.A.
32 C4 Lakewood OH U.S.A.
29 D7 Lake Worth U.S.A.
68 D2 Lakhdenpokh'ya Rus. Fed.
84 E4 Lakhimpur India
84 D5 Lakhnadon India
84 B5 Lakhpat India
79 L1 Lakki Pak.
67 K6 Lakonikos Kolpos b. Greece
100 B4 Lakota Côte d'Ivoire
54 U1 Laksefjorden chan. Norway
54 T1 Lakselv Norway
83 D8 Lakshadweep div. India
85 G5 Laksham Bangl.
85 G5 Lakshmikantapur India
94 B5 Lala Phil.
47 D2 La Laguna Arg.
47 B3 La Laja Chile
102 B3 Lalara Gabon
116 C4 Laleham Austr.
81 M5 Lālī Iran
47 B2 La Ligua Chile
65 B1 Lalín Spain
65 D4 La Línea de la Concepción Spain
84 D4 Lalitpur India
94 B2 Lal-Lo Phil.
21 H3 La Loche Can.
21 H3 La Loche, Lac l. Can.
61 C4 La Louvière Belgium
68 H2 Lal'sk Rus. Fed.
85 H5 Lama Bangl.
66 C4 La Maddalena Sardinia Italy
94 A5 Lamag Malaysia
95 A3 Lamaing Myanmar
La Manche str. see English Channel
26 D4 Lamar CO U.S.A.
27 E4 Lamar MO U.S.A.
79 G4 Lamard Iran
66 C5 La Marmora, Punta mt. Sardinia Italy
47 D3 Lamarque Arg.
27 E6 La Marque U.S.A.
20 F2 La Martre, Lac l. Can.
102 B4 Lambaréné Gabon
42 C5 Lambayeque reg. Peru
60 F4 Lambay Island i. Rep. of Ireland
119 D4 Lambert Gl. gl. Ant.
104 C6 Lambert's Bay S. Africa
84 C3 Lambi India

59 F6 Lambourn Downs h. U.K.
95 C2 Lam Chi r. Thai.
65 C2 Lamego Port.
23 H4 Lamèque, I. i. Can.
42 C6 La Merced Peru
114 D5 Lameroo Austr.
34 D5 La Mesa U.S.A.
27 C5 Lamesa U.S.A.
67 K5 Lamia Greece
115 K2 Lamington Nat. Park nat. park Austr.
25 E6 La Mirada U.S.A.
34 D5 La Misíon Mex.
94 B5 Lamitan Phil.
89 □ Lamma I. i. Hong Kong China
117 B6 Lammerlaw Ra. mts N.Z.
57 F5 Lammermuir Hills h. U.K.
55 O8 Lammhult Sweden
55 T6 Lammi Fin.
30 C5 La Moille U.S.A.
33 G2 Lamoille r. U.S.A.
30 B5 La Moine r. U.S.A.
94 B3 Lamon Bay b. Phil.
26 E3 Lamoni U.S.A.
34 A1 Lamont U.S.A.
27 B6 La Morita Mex.
31 H1 La Motte Can.
95 B1 Lam Pao Res. resr Thai.
27 D6 Lampasas U.S.A.
66 E7 Lampedusa, Isola di i. Sicily Italy
59 C5 Lampeter U.K.
95 B2 Lam Plai Mat r. Thai.
68 F4 Lamskoye Rus. Fed.
89 □ Lam Tin Hong Kong China
102 E4 Lamu Kenya
85 H6 Lamu Myanmar
34 □2 Lanai i. U.S.A.
34 □2 Lanai City U.S.A.
94 C5 Lanao, Lake l. Phil.
31 J3 Lanark Can.
57 E5 Lanark U.K.
30 C4 Lanark U.S.A.
94 A5 Lanas Malaysia
95 A3 Lanbi Kyun i. Myanmar
Lancang Jiang r. see Mekong
33 F2 Lancaster Can.
58 E3 Lancaster U.K.
34 C4 Lancaster CA U.S.A.
30 A5 Lancaster MO U.S.A.
33 H2 Lancaster NH U.S.A.
32 B5 Lancaster OH U.S.A.
33 E4 Lancaster PA U.S.A.
29 D5 Lancaster SC U.S.A.
30 B4 Lancaster WV U.S.A.
58 E4 Lancaster Canal canal U.K.
66 F3 Lanciano Italy
47 B3 Lanco Chile
88 F2 Lancun China
62 F6 Landau an der Isar Ger.
62 E7 Landeck Austria
24 E3 Lander U.S.A.
21 H4 Landis Can.
62 E6 Landsberg am Lech Ger.
116 A4 Landsborough Cr. watercourse Austr.
59 B7 Land's End pt U.K.
62 F6 Landshut Ger.
55 N9 Landskrona Sweden
60 D4 Lanesborough Rep. of Ireland
95 C3 La Nga r. Vietnam
84 E3 La'nga Co l. China
88 C3 Langao China
57 B2 Langavat, Loch l. U.K.
104 E4 Langberg mts S. Africa
26 D1 Langdon U.S.A.
104 C6 Langeberg mts S. Africa
55 M9 Langeland i. Denmark
55 T6 Längelmäki Fin.
55 T6 Längelmävesi l. Fin.
62 C7 Langenthal Switz.
61 F1 Langeoog i. Ger.
55 L7 Langesund Norway
95 B5 Langgapayung Indon.
21 H4 Langham Can.
54 C4 Langjökull ice cap Iceland
95 A5 Langkawi i. Malaysia
95 A3 Lang Kha Toek, Khao mt. Thai.
104 D4 Langklip S. Africa
94 A5 Langkon Malaysia
31 K1 Langlade Can.
30 C3 Langlade U.S.A.
116 A5 Langlo watercourse Austr.
116 A6 Langlo Crossing Austr.
64 F4 Langogne France
54 O2 Langøya i. Norway
85 F3 Langphu mt. China
59 E6 Langport U.K.
89 F5 Langqi China
64 G3 Langres France
84 D1 Langru China
92 B6 Langsa Indon.
95 A4 Langsa, Teluk b. Indon.
54 P5 Långsele Sweden
88 C1 Langshan China
88 C1 Lang Shan mts China
89 C6 Lang Son Vietnam
58 G3 Langtoft U.K.
27 C6 Langtry U.S.A.
64 F5 Languedoc reg. France
54 R4 Långvattnet Sweden
88 B4 Langxi China
88 C4 Langzhong China
31 H2 Laniel Can.
21 H4 Lanigan Can.

34 □1 Lanikai U.S.A.
47 B3 Lanín, Parque Nacional nat. park Arg.
47 B3 Lanín, Volcán volc. Arg.
88 E3 Lankao China
81 M2 Länkäran Azer.
64 C2 Lannion France
54 S3 Lansån Sweden
20 C2 Lansing r. Can.
30 B4 Lansing IA U.S.A.
30 C4 Lansing MI U.S.A.
89 O6 Lantau Island i. Hong Kong China
89 □ Lantau Peak h. Hong Kong China
94 C4 Lanuza Bay b. Phil.
89 F4 Lanxi China
101 F4 Lanya Sudan
89 F6 Lan Yü i. Taiwan
100 A2 Lanzarote i. Canary Is
88 B2 Lanzhou China
94 B2 Laoag Phil.
94 C3 Laoang Phil.
89 B6 Lao Cai Vietnam
88 F1 Laoha r. China
88 D3 Laohekou China
88 F2 Laohutun China
64 F2 Laon France
30 C3 Laona U.S.A.
70 Laos country Asia
88 F2 Lao Shan mt. China
Laowohi pass see Khardung La
88 A1 Laoximiao China
46 C4 Lapa Brazil
94 B5 Lapac i. Phil.
37 J7 La Palma Panama
65 C4 La Palma del Condado Spain
47 F2 La Paloma Uru.
47 D3 La Pampa div. Arg.
47 E1 La Paz Entre Rios Arg.
47 C2 La Paz Mendoza Arg.
42 E7 La Paz Bol.
36 B4 La Paz Mex.
30 D5 Lapaz U.S.A.
42 E4 La Pedrera Col.
31 F4 Lapeer U.S.A.
87 Q2 La Pérouse Strait str. Japan/Rus. Fed.
45 E3 La Piña r. Venez.
24 B3 La Pine U.S.A.
94 C3 Lapinig Phil.
94 C3 Lapinin i. Phil.
54 U5 Lapinlahti Fin.
80 L5 Lapithos Cyprus
27 F6 Laplace U.S.A.
26 C2 La Plant U.S.A.
47 F2 La Plata Arg.
45 B4 La Plata Col.
68 G1 Lapominka Rus. Fed.
30 A4 La Porte City U.S.A.
54 S5 Lappajärvi Fin.
54 S5 Lappajärvi l. Fin.
55 V6 Lappeenranta Fin.
54 S2 Lappland reg. Europe
33 G2 La Prairie Can.
34 A2 La Pryor U.S.A.
74 Laptev Sea sea Rus. Fed.
54 S5 Lapua Fin.
94 B4 Lapu-Lapu Phil.
44 C2 La Quiaca Arg.
66 E3 L'Aquila Italy
34 D5 La Quinta U.S.A.
100 B1 Larache Morocco
24 F3 Laramie U.S.A.
24 F3 Laramie Mts mts U.S.A.
Laranda see Karaman
46 B4 Laranjeiras do Sul Brazil
43 L5 Laranjinha r. Brazil
93 G8 Larantuka Indon.
93 J8 Larat i. Indon.
65 H4 Larba Alg.
55 Q8 Lärbro Sweden
55 G2 Larchwood U.S.A.
31 H1 Larder Lake Can.
27 D7 Laredo U.S.A.
65 E1 Laredo Spain
29 D7 Largo U.S.A.
57 D5 Largs U.K.
81 L2 Lārī Iran
66 D6 L'Ariana Tunisia
21 K5 Larimore U.S.A.
44 C3 La Rioja Arg.
47 C3 La Rioja div. Arg.
65 E1 La Rioja div. Spain
67 K5 Larisa Greece
84 B4 Larkana Pak.
80 D4 Larnaca Cyprus
60 F3 Larne U.K.
60 F3 Larne Lough inlet N. Ireland U.K.
65 D1 La Robla Spain
61 D4 La Roche-en-Ardenne Belgium
64 D3 La Rochelle France
64 D3 La Roche-sur-Yon France
65 E3 La Roda Spain
37 L5 La Romana Dom. Rep.
21 H3 La Ronge Can.
27 C7 La Rosa Mex.
112 F4 Larrimah Austr.
119 B2 Larsen Ice Shelf ice feature Ant.
54 S5 Larsmo Fin.

55 M7 Larvik Norway
35 H2 La Sal Junction U.S.A.
33 G2 La Salle Can.
30 C5 La Salle U.S.A.
22 E4 La Sarre Can.
45 D2 Las Aves, Islas is Venez.
47 B2 Las Cabras Chile
23 J4 La Scie Can.
25 C5 Las Cruces U.S.A.
37 K5 La Selle mt. Haiti
47 B1 La Serena Chile
27 C7 Las Esperanças Mex.
47 E3 Las Flores Arg.
47 C2 Las Heras Arg.
83 J6 Lashio Myanmar
47 C2 Las Lajas Arg.
45 D3 Las Lajitas Venez.
44 C6 Las Plumas Arg.
47 E2 Las Rosas Arg.
24 B3 Lassen Pk volc. U.S.A.
24 B3 Lassen Volcanic Nat. Park nat. park U.S.A.
37 H7 Las Tablas Panama
44 D3 Las Termas Arg.
21 H4 Last Mountain L. l. Can.
102 B4 Lastoursville Gabon
66 G3 Lastovo i. Croatia
45 D3 Las Trincheras Venez.
25 F6 Las Varas Chihuahua Mex.
47 D1 Las Varillas Arg.
25 C3 Las Vegas NM U.S.A.
35 E3 Las Vegas NV U.S.A.
65 D3 Las Villuercas mt. Spain
42 C4 Latacunga Ecuador
45 B5 La Tagua Col.
80 E4 Latakia Syria
31 H2 Latchford Can.
85 F5 Latehar India
64 D4 La Teste France
57 E2 Latheron U.K.
66 E4 Latina Italy
47 D2 La Toma Arg.
45 D2 La Tortuga, Isla i. Venez.
115 G8 Latrobe Austr.
32 D4 Latrobe U.S.A.
31 H2 Latulipe Can.
22 F4 La Tuque Can.
83 E7 Latur India
49 Latvia country Europe
44 C1 Lauca, Parque Nacional nat. park Chile
62 F5 Lauchhammer Ger.
57 F5 Lauder U.K.
55 S7 Lauka Estonia
54 V1 Laukvik Norway
95 A3 Laun Thai.
115 G8 Launceston Austr.
59 C7 Launceston U.K.
60 B5 Laune r. Rep. of Ireland
95 A2 Launglon Bok Is is Myanmar
47 B4 La Unión Chile
45 A4 La Unión Col.
36 G6 La Unión El Salvador
94 B3 Laur Phil.
113 H3 Laura Qld. Austr.
114 C4 Laura S.A. Austr.
45 D3 La Urbana Venez.
33 F5 Laurel DE U.S.A.
27 F6 Laurel MS U.S.A.
24 E2 Laurel MT U.S.A.
32 D4 Laurel Hill h. U.S.A.
32 A6 Laurel River Lake l. U.S.A.
57 F4 Laurencekirk U.K.
23 F4 Laurentides, Réserve faunique des res. Can.
66 F4 Lauria Italy
115 K3 Laurieton Austr.
29 E5 Laurinburg U.S.A.
30 C2 Laurium U.S.A.
62 C7 Lausanne Switz.
92 F7 Laut i. Indon.
92 F8 Laut Kecil, Kepulauan is Indon.
111 H3 Lautoka Fiji
54 V5 Lauvuskylä Fin.
61 E1 Lauwersmeer l. Neth.
22 F4 Laval Can.
64 D2 Laval France
44 B5 Lavapié, Pta pt Chile
112 D5 Laverton Austr.
45 D2 La Victoria Venez.
31 G2 Lavigne Can.
46 D3 Lavras Brazil
47 G1 Lavras do Sul Brazil
105 J3 Lavumisa Swaziland
84 B2 Lawa Pak.
95 B4 Lawit, Gunung mt. Malaysia
81 J7 Lawqah waterhole S. Arabia
100 B3 Lawra Ghana
26 E4 Lawrence KS U.S.A.
33 H3 Lawrence MA U.S.A.
29 C5 Lawrenceburg U.S.A.
33 K2 Lawrence Station Can.

32 E6 Lawrenceville U.S.A.
27 D5 Lawton U.S.A.
78 D4 Lawz, J. al mt. S. Arabia
55 O7 Laxå Sweden
104 E3 Laxey S. Africa
58 C3 Laxey U.K.
57 C2 Laxford, Loch in. U.K.
57 □ Laxo U.K.
114 E7 Layers Hill Austr.
81 K4 Laylän Iraq
34 A2 Laytonville U.S.A.
67 J2 Lazarevac Yugo.
119 D3 Lazarev Sea sea Ant.
69 F7 Lazarevskoye Rus. Fed.
25 D6 Lázaro Cárdenas Baja California Mex.
36 D5 Lázaro Cárdenas Michuacan Mex.
47 F2 Lazcano Uru.
55 S9 Lazdijai Lith.
77 P3 Lazo Rus. Fed.
95 B2 Leach Cambodia
30 E2 Leach I. i. Can.
26 C2 Lead U.S.A.
21 H4 Leader Can.
115 H4 Leadville Austr.
25 F4 Leadville U.S.A.
27 F6 Leaf r. U.S.A.
21 J3 Leaf Rapids Can.
27 D6 Leakey U.S.A.
31 F4 Leamington Can.
35 F2 Leamington U.S.A.
59 F5 Leamington Spa, Royal U.K.
89 E5 Le'an China
60 B5 Leane, Lough l. Rep. of Ireland
60 B6 Leap Rep. of Ireland
21 H4 Leask Can.
59 G6 Leatherhead U.K.
26 E4 Leavenworth KS U.S.A.
24 B2 Leavenworth WA U.S.A.
34 C2 Leavitt Peak summit U.S.A.
61 E5 Lebach Ger.
94 C5 Lebak Phil.
70 Lebanon country Asia
30 D5 Lebanon IN U.S.A.
26 E4 Lebanon KS U.S.A.
27 E4 Lebanon MO U.S.A.
33 G3 Lebanon NH U.S.A.
33 F4 Lebanon NJ U.S.A.
32 A5 Lebanon OH U.S.A.
24 B2 Lebanon OR U.S.A.
33 E4 Lebanon PA U.S.A.
29 C4 Lebanon TN U.S.A.
61 C3 Lebbeke Belgium
68 F4 Lebedyan' Rus. Fed.
69 E5 Lebedyn Ukr.
64 E3 Le Blanc France
62 H3 Lębork Pol.
105 H3 Lebowakgomo S. Africa
65 C4 Lebrija Spain
62 H3 Łebsko, Jezioro lag. Pol.
47 B3 Lebu Chile
61 B4 Le Cateau-Cambrésis France
67 H4 Lecce Italy
66 C2 Lecco Italy
62 E7 Lech r. Austria/Ger.
67 J6 Lechaina Greece
89 C5 Lechang China
62 E7 Lechtaler Alpen mts Austria
62 D3 Leck Ger.
64 G3 Le Creusot France
64 D3 Lectoure France
95 B5 Ledang, Gunung mt. Malaysia
59 E5 Ledbury U.K.
65 D2 Ledesma Spain
57 D2 Ledmore U.K.
68 E1 Ledmozero Rus. Fed.
89 C7 Ledong China
88 B2 Ledu China
20 G4 Leduc Can.
33 G3 Lee U.S.A.
26 E3 Leech L. l. U.S.A.
58 F4 Leeds U.K.
33 H2 Leeds Junction U.S.A.
59 B7 Leedstown U.K.
59 E4 Leek U.K.
61 D3 Leende Neth.
32 C4 Leeper U.S.A.
61 F1 Leer (Ostfriesland) Ger.
29 D6 Leesburg FL U.S.A.
32 E5 Leesburg VA U.S.A.
27 E6 Leesville U.S.A.
32 C4 Leesville Lake l. U.S.A.
115 G5 Leeton Austr.
104 D6 Leeu-Gamka S. Africa
61 D1 Leeuwarden Neth.
112 C6 Leeuwin, C. c. Austr.
34 C3 Lee Vining U.S.A.
37 M5 Leeward Islands is Caribbean Sea
80 D4 Lefka Cyprus
67 J5 Lefkada Greece
67 J5 Lefkada i. Greece
80 D4 Lefkara Cyprus
67 J5 Lefkimmi Greece
Lefkosia see Nicosia
94 B3 Legaspi Phil.
115 G8 Legges Tor mt. Austr.
34 A2 Leggett U.S.A.
62 H5 Legnica Pol.
84 D2 Leh Jammu and Kashmir
64 E2 Le Havre France
33 F4 Leighton U.S.A.
54 V5 Lehmo Fin.
54 S5 Lehtimäki Fin.
104 D1 Lehututu Botswana
84 B3 Leiah Pak.

62 G7 Leibnitz Austria
59 F5 Leicester U.K.
113 G3 Leichhardt r. Austr.
116 B3 Leichhardt Range mts Austr.
61 C2 Leiden Neth.
114 C3 Leigh watercourse Austr.
117 E2 Leigh N.Z.
58 E4 Leigh U.K.
114 C3 Leigh Creek Austr.
59 G6 Leighton Buzzard U.K.
60 E5 Leinster, Mount h. Rep. of Ireland
67 M6 Leipsoi i. Greece
62 F5 Leipzig Ger.
54 O3 Leiranger Norway
65 B3 Leiria Port.
89 C5 Leishan China
89 D5 Lei Shui r. China
28 C4 Leitchfield U.S.A.
45 B4 Leiva, Co mt. Col.
60 E4 Leixlip Rep. of Ireland
89 D5 Leiyang China
89 C6 Leizhou Bandao pen. China
89 D6 Leizhou Wan b. China
54 M4 Leka Norway
102 B4 Lékana Congo
66 C6 Le Kef Tunisia
104 B4 Lekkersing S. Africa
102 B4 Lékoni Gabon
55 O6 Leksand Sweden
54 W5 Leksozero, Oz. l. Rus. Fed.
30 E3 Leland MI U.S.A.
27 F5 Leland MS U.S.A.
100 A3 Lélouma Guinea
61 D2 Lelystad Neth.
44 C9 Le Maire, Estrecho de chan. Arg.
64 H3 Léman, Lac l. France/Switz.
64 E2 Le Mans France
26 D3 Le Mars U.S.A.
46 C3 Leme Brazil
94 B3 Lemery Phil.
Lemesos see Limassol
55 U6 Lemi Fin.
54 T2 Lemmenjoen Kansallispuisto nat. park Fin.
26 C2 Lemmon U.S.A.
35 G5 Lemmon, Mt mt. U.S.A.
34 C3 Lemoore U.S.A.
85 H5 Lemro r. Myanmar
95 A3 Lem Tom Chob pt Thai.
66 G4 Le Murge reg. Italy
55 L8 Lemvig Denmark
86 J1 Lena r. Rus. Fed.
30 C4 Lena U.S.A.
85 E2 Lenchung Tso salt l. China
43 K4 Lençóis Maranhenses, Parque Nacional dos nat. park Brazil
88 A2 Lenglong Ling mts China
89 D5 Lengshuijiang China
89 D5 Lengshuitan China
47 B1 Lengua de Vaca, Pta hd Chile
59 H6 Lenham U.K.
55 O8 Lenhovda Sweden
69 H7 Lenina, Kanal canal Rus. Fed.
Leningrad see St Petersburg
69 F6 Leningradskaya Rus. Fed.
68 E3 Leningradskaya Oblast' div. Rus. Fed.
77 T3 Leningradskiy Rus. Fed.
82 B1 Leninsk Kazak.
69 H5 Leninsk Rus. Fed.
68 F4 Leninskiy Rus. Fed.
76 K4 Leninsk-Kuznetskiy Rus. Fed.
68 H3 Leninskoye Rus. Fed.
115 K2 Lennox Head Austr.
29 D5 Lenoir U.S.A.
33 G3 Lenox U.S.A.
64 F1 Lens France
77 N3 Lensk Rus. Fed.
69 G7 Lentekhi Georgia
62 H7 Lenti Hungary
66 F6 Lentini Sicily Italy
100 B3 Léo Burkina
62 G7 Leoben Austria
59 E5 Leominster U.K.
33 H3 Leominster U.S.A.
45 A3 León r. Col.
36 D4 León Mex.
36 G6 León Nic.
65 D1 León Spain
103 B6 Leonardville Namibia
80 E4 Leonarisson Cyprus
115 F7 Leongatha Austr.
112 D5 Leonora Austr.
46 D3 Leopoldina Brazil
21 H4 Leoville Can.
105 G1 Lephalala r. S. Africa
103 C6 Lephepe Botswana
105 F5 Lephoi S. Africa
89 E4 Leping China
64 G4 Le Pont-de-Claix France
54 U5 Leppävirta Fin.
82 E1 Lepsy Kazak.
64 F4 Le-Puy-en-Velay France
61 B4 Le Quesnoy France
105 G1 Lerala Botswana
105 G4 Leratswana S. Africa
101 D4 Léré Chad
45 C5 Lerida Col.
Lérida see Lleida
81 M2 Lerik Azer.
65 E1 Lerma Spain
69 G6 Lermontov Rus. Fed.
67 M6 Leros i. Greece
30 C5 Le Roy U.S.A.
55 N8 Lerum Sweden
57 □ Lerwick U.K.
67 L5 Lesbos i. Greece
37 K5 Les Cayes Haiti
23 G4 Les Escoumins Can.
33 J1 Les Étroits Can.
65 G1 Le Seu d'Urgell Spain
89 B4 Leshan China
67 J3 Leskovac Yugo.
57 E4 Leslie U.K.
64 B2 Lesneven France
68 K3 Lesnoy Rus. Fed.
76 L4 Lesosibirsk Rus. Fed.
96 Lesotho country Africa
87 O2 Lesozavodsk Rus. Fed.
64 D3 Les Sables-d'Olonne France
37 L6 Lesser Antilles is Caribbean Sea
Lesser Caucasus mts see Malyy Kavkaz
20 G3 Lesser Slave Lake l. Can.
20 G3 Lesser Slave Lake Provincial Park res. Can.
54 T5 Lestijärvi Fin.
54 T5 Lestijärvi l. Fin.
Lesvos i. see Lesbos
62 H5 Leszno Pol.
105 J1 Letaba S. Africa
59 G6 Letchworth U.K.
84 D4 Leteri India
85 H5 Letha Range mts Myanmar
20 G5 Lethbridge Can.
42 G3 Lethem Guyana
42 E4 Leticia Col.
93 H8 Leti, Kepulauan is Indon.
88 F2 Leting China
105 F2 Letlhakeng Botswana
59 J7 Le Touquet-Paris-Plage France
64 E1 Le Touquet-Paris-Plage airport France
64 E1 Le Tréport France
105 J1 Letsitele S. Africa
95 A3 Letsok-aw Kyun i. Myanmar
105 F3 Letsopa S. Africa
60 D3 Letterkenny Rep. of Ireland
95 C5 Letung Indon.
57 F4 Leuchars U.K.
68 G1 Leunovo Rus. Fed.
35 G4 Leupp Corner U.S.A.
116 C4 Leura Austr.
95 A5 Leuser, G. mt. Indon.
61 C4 Leuven Belgium
67 K5 Levadeia Greece
35 G2 Levan U.S.A.
54 M5 Levanger Norway
66 C2 Levanto Italy
66 E5 Levanzo, Isola di i. Sicily Italy
69 H7 Levashi Rus. Fed.
27 C5 Levelland U.S.A.
58 G4 Leven Eng. U.K.
57 F4 Leven Scot. U.K.
57 E4 Leven, Loch l. U.K.
57 C4 Leven, Loch in. U.K.
112 D3 Lévêque, C. c. Austr.
30 E3 Levering U.S.A.
62 C5 Leverkusen Ger.
63 J6 Levice Slovakia
117 E4 Levin N.Z.
23 F4 Lévis Can.
67 M6 Levitha i. Greece
33 G4 Levittown NY U.S.A.
33 F4 Levittown PA U.S.A.
67 L3 Levski Bulg.
59 H7 Lewes U.K.
33 F5 Lewes U.S.A.
57 B2 Lewis i. U.K.
32 E4 Lewisburg PA U.S.A.
32 C6 Lewisburg WV U.S.A.
117 D5 Lewis Pass pass N.Z.
24 D1 Lewis Range mts U.S.A.
29 C5 Lewis Smith, L. l. U.S.A.
35 G6 Lewis Springs U.S.A.
24 C2 Lewiston ID U.S.A.
33 H2 Lewiston ME U.S.A.
30 B4 Lewiston MN U.S.A.
30 B5 Lewistown IL U.S.A.
24 E2 Lewistown MT U.S.A.
32 E4 Lewistown PA U.S.A.
27 E5 Lewisville U.S.A.
27 D5 Lewisville, Lake l. U.S.A.
30 C5 Lexington IL U.S.A.
28 C4 Lexington KY U.S.A.
26 E4 Lexington MO U.S.A.
29 D5 Lexington NC U.S.A.
26 D3 Lexington NE U.S.A.
29 B5 Lexington TN U.S.A.
32 D6 Lexington VA U.S.A.
32 E5 Lexington Park U.S.A.
105 J1 Leydsdorp S. Africa
89 C5 Leye China
81 L3 Leyla D. h. Iran
94 C4 Leyte i. Phil.
94 C4 Leyte Gulf g. Phil.
67 H4 Lezhë Albania
89 B4 Lezhi China
69 E5 L'gov Rus. Fed.
85 H3 Lhari China
85 G3 Lhasa China
85 G3 Lhasa He r. China
85 F3 Lhazê China
85 F3 Lhazhong China
92 B5 Lhokseumawe Indon.
95 A4 Lhoksukon Indon.
85 H3 Lhorong China
85 H3 Lhünzê China
85 G3 Lhünzhub China
89 E5 Liancheng China
Liancourt Rocks see Tok-tō
94 C4 Lianga Phil.
94 C4 Lianga Bay b. Phil.
89 E4 Liangzi Hu l. China
88 D1 Liangcheng China
88 C3 Liangdang China
88 B3 Lianghekou China
89 C4 Liangping China
89 B5 Liangwang Shan mts China
88 C2 Liangzhen China
89 D5 Lianhua China
89 E6 Lianhua Shan mts China
89 F5 Lianjiang Fujian China
89 D6 Lianjiang Guangdong China
89 D5 Liannan China
89 E5 Lianping China
89 D5 Lianshan China
88 F3 Lianshui China
95 B2 Liant, C. pt Thai.
89 D5 Lian Xian China
89 D5 Lianyuan China
88 F3 Lianyungang Jiangsu China
88 F3 Lianyungang Jiangsu China
88 G1 Liao r. China
88 E2 Liaocheng China
88 G1 Liaodong Bandao pen. China
88 F1 Liaodong Wan b. China
88 F1 Liaoning div. China
88 G1 Liaoyang China
87 N3 Liaoyuan China
88 G1 Liaozhong China
67 H5 Liapades Greece
84 B2 Liaqatabad Pak.
20 E2 Liard r. Can.
20 D3 Liard River Can.
57 C3 Liathach mt. U.K.
80 F4 Liban, Jebel mts Lebanon
45 B3 Libano Col.
24 D1 Libby U.S.A.
102 B3 Libenge Zaire
27 C4 Liberal U.S.A.
62 G5 Liberec Czech Rep.
96 Liberia country Africa
37 G6 Liberia Costa Rica
45 C2 Libertad Venez.
45 C2 Libertad Venez.
30 B6 Liberty IL U.S.A.
33 J2 Liberty ME U.S.A.
26 E4 Liberty MO U.S.A.
33 F4 Liberty NY U.S.A.
27 E6 Liberty TX U.S.A.
61 D5 Libin Belgium
94 B3 Libmanan Phil.
89 C5 Libo China
105 H5 Libode S. Africa
64 D4 Libourne France
102 A3 Libreville Gabon
94 C5 Libuganon r. Phil.
96 Libya country Africa
101 E2 Libyan Desert des. Egypt/Libya
78 B3 Libyan Plateau plat. Egypt
47 B2 Licantén Chile
66 E6 Licata Sicily Italy
81 H2 Lice Turkey
59 F5 Lichfield U.K.
103 D5 Lichinga Moz.
105 G3 Lichtenburg S. Africa
89 C4 Lichuan Hubei China
89 E5 Lichuan Jiangxi China
32 B5 Licking r. U.S.A.
68 C4 Lida Belarus
34 D3 Lida U.S.A.
104 C2 Lidfontein Namibia
55 N7 Lidköping Sweden
54 O4 Lidsjöberg Sweden
112 F4 Liebig, Mt mt Austr.
48 Liechtenstein country Europe
61 D4 Liège Belgium
54 W5 Lieksa Fin.
63 M2 Lielupe r. Latvia
55 T8 Lielvārde Latvia
54 P5 Lien Sweden
102 C3 Lienart Zaire
62 F7 Lienz Austria
55 R8 Liepāja Latvia
55 J7 Liervik Norway
61 D3 Lieshout Neth.
61 A4 Liévin France
31 K2 Lièvre r. Can.
62 G7 Liezen Austria
60 E4 Liffey r. Rep. of Ireland
60 D3 Lifford Rep. of Ireland
47 C4 Lifi Mahuida mt. Arg.
111 G4 Lifou i. New Caledonia
94 B3 Ligao Phil.
55 T8 Līgatne Latvia
115 G2 Lightning Ridge Austr.
103 D5 Ligonha r. Moz.
30 E5 Ligonier U.S.A.
Ligure, Mar sea see Ligurian Sea
64 J5 Ligurian Sea sea France/Italy
110 F2 Lihir Group is P.N.G.
116 D1 Lihou Reef & Cays rf Coral Sea Is Terr.
34 □2 Lihue U.S.A.
89 D5 Li Jiang r. China
88 F2 Lijin China
103 C5 Likasi Zaire
20 E4 Likely Can.
68 E3 Likhoslavl' Rus. Fed.
92 D6 Liku Indon.
68 G3 Likurga Rus. Fed.
66 C3 L'Île-Rousse Corsica France
89 D5 Liling China
84 C2 Lilla Pak.
55 N7 Lilla Edet Sweden
61 C3 Lille Belgium
64 F1 Lille France
55 L9 Lille Bælt chan. Denmark
55 M6 Lillehammer Norway
55 L7 Lillesand Norway
55 M7 Lillestrom Norway
30 E4 Lilley U.S.A.
54 O5 Lillholmsjö Sweden
20 E4 Lillooet r. Can.
20 E4 Lillooet Can.
85 H4 Lilong India
103 D5 Lilongwe Malawi
94 B4 Liloy Phil.
114 C4 Lilydale S.A. Austr.
115 G8 Lilydale Tas. Austr.
42 C6 Lima Peru
24 D2 Lima MT U.S.A.
32 A4 Lima OH U.S.A.
69 H6 Liman Rus. Fed.
47 B1 Limarí r. Chile
85 E2 Lima Ringma Tso salt l. China
80 D4 Limassol Cyprus
60 E2 Limavady U.K.
47 C3 Limay r. Arg.
47 C3 Limay Mahuida Arg.
55 T8 Limbaži Latvia
100 C4 Limbe Cameroon
95 □ Lim Chu Kang h. Sing.
95 □ Lim Chu Kang Sing.
104 E4 Lime Acres S. Africa
46 C3 Limeira Brazil
60 C5 Limerick Rep. of Ireland
30 A4 Lime Springs U.S.A.
33 K1 Limestone U.S.A.
54 N4 Limingen Norway
54 N4 Limingen l. Norway
33 H3 Limington U.S.A.
54 T4 Liminka Fin.
113 G3 Limmen Bight b. Austr.
67 L5 Limnos i. Greece
33 F2 Limoges Can.
64 E4 Limoges France
37 H6 Limón Costa Rica
25 G4 Limon U.S.A.
80 E3 Limonlu Turkey
64 E4 Limousin reg. France
64 F5 Limoux France
105 K2 Limpopo r. Africa
54 W2 Linakhamari Rus. Fed.
89 F4 Lin'an China
94 A4 Linapacan i. Phil.
94 A4 Linapacan Strait chan. Phil.
47 B2 Linares Chile
36 E4 Linares Mex.
65 E3 Linares Spain
88 E2 Lincheng China
89 E5 Linchuan China
47 E2 Lincoln Arg.
59 G4 Lincoln U.K.
34 B2 Lincoln CA U.S.A.
30 C5 Lincoln IL U.S.A.
33 J2 Lincoln ME U.S.A.
31 F3 Lincoln MI U.S.A.
26 D3 Lincoln NE U.S.A.
33 H2 Lincoln NH U.S.A.
24 A2 Lincoln City U.S.A.
31 F4 Lincoln Park U.S.A.
59 G4 Lincolnshire Wolds reg. U.K.
33 J2 Lincolnville U.S.A.
46 E1 Linda, Sa h. Brazil
62 D7 Lindau (Bodensee) Ger.
116 C3 Lindeman Gr. is Austr.
43 G2 Linden Guyana
29 C5 Linden AL U.S.A.
29 C5 Linden TN U.S.A.
30 A2 Linden Grove U.S.A.
55 K7 Lindesnes c. Norway
103 D4 Lindi Tanz.
102 C3 Lindi r. Zaire
Lindisfarne i. see Holy Island
105 G3 Lindley S. Africa
67 N6 Lindos, Akra pt Greece
33 K1 Lindsay N.B. Can.
31 H3 Lindsay Ont. Can.
34 C3 Lindsay U.S.A.
109 Line Islands is Pac. Oc.
88 D2 Linfen China
94 B2 Lingayen Phil.
94 B2 Lingayen Gulf b. Phil.
88 D3 Lingbao China
88 E3 Lingbi China
89 D5 Lingchuan Guangxi China
88 D3 Lingchuan Shanxi China
105 G6 Lingelethu S. Africa
105 F6 Lingelihle S. Africa
62 C4 Lingen (Ems) Ger.
92 D7 Lingga, Kepulauan is Indon.
94 C5 Lingig Phil.
24 F3 Lingle U.S.A.
102 C3 Lingomo Zaire
88 E2 Lingqiu China
89 C6 Lingshan China
89 C7 Lingshui China
88 C3 Lingtai China
89 C7 Lingtou China
100 A3 Linguère Senegal
89 D5 Lingui China
88 C2 Lingwu China
89 D5 Ling Xian China
88 F1 Lingyuan China
89 C5 Lingyun China
84 D2 Lingzi Thang Plains l. China/Jammu and Kashmir
89 F4 Linhai China
46 E2 Linhares Brazil
95 C1 Linh Cam Vietnam
88 C1 Linhe China
33 H1 Linière Can.
55 O7 Linköping Sweden
87 O2 Linkou China
89 D4 Linli China
57 E5 Linlithgow U.K.
88 D2 Linlü Shan mt. China
57 C4 Linnhe, Loch in. U.K.
34 A1 Linn, Mt mt. U.S.A.
88 E2 Linqing China
88 F2 Linqu China
88 E3 Linquan China
88 D3 Linru China
46 C3 Lins Brazil
88 F3 Linshu China
89 C4 Linshui China
88 B3 Lintan China
88 B3 Lintao China
26 C2 Linton U.S.A.
88 C3 Lintong China
88 F1 Linxi China
88 B3 Linxia China
88 D2 Lin Xian China
89 D4 Linxiang China
88 E2 Linyi Shandong China
88 F3 Linyi Shandong China
88 D3 Linyi Shanxi China
88 E3 Linying China
62 G6 Linz Austria
88 A2 Linze China
64 F5 Lion, Golfe du g. France
31 G3 Lion's Head Can.
33 F4 Lionville U.S.A.
102 B3 Liouesso Congo
94 B3 Lipa Phil.
66 F5 Lipari Italy
66 F5 Lipari, Isola i. Italy
66 F5 Lipari, Isole is Italy
69 F4 Lipetsk Rus. Fed.
69 F4 Lipetskaya Oblast' div. Rus. Fed.
68 F2 Lipin Bor Rus. Fed.
89 C5 Liping China
67 J1 Lipova Romania
61 E3 Lippe r. Ger.
84 E3 Lipti Lekh pass Nepal
115 F7 Liptrap, C. hd Austr.
89 D5 Lipu China
102 D3 Lira Uganda
102 B4 Liranga Congo
94 C6 Lirung Indon.
102 C3 Lisala Zaire
60 D3 Lisbellaw U.K.
Lisboa see Lisbon
65 B3 Lisbon Port.
30 C5 Lisbon IL U.S.A.
33 H2 Lisbon ME U.S.A.
26 D2 Lisbon ND U.S.A.
33 H2 Lisbon NH U.S.A.
32 C4 Lisbon OH U.S.A.
60 E3 Lisburn U.K.
60 B5 Liscannor Bay b. Rep. of Ireland
60 B4 Lisdoonvarna Rep. of Ireland
89 F5 Li-shan Taiwan
88 D2 Lishi China
88 G1 Lishu China
88 F4 Lishui Jiangsu China
89 F4 Lishui Zhejiang China
89 D4 Li Shui r. China
64 E2 Lisieux France
59 C7 Liskeard U.K.
69 F5 Liski Rus. Fed.
64 G5 L'Isle-sur-la-Sorgue France
115 K2 Lismore Austr.
60 D5 Lismore Rep. of Ireland
57 C4 Lismore i. U.K.
60 D3 Lisnarrick U.K.
60 D3 Lisnaskea U.K.
31 G4 Listowel Can.
60 B5 Listowel Rep. of Ireland
116 A5 Listowel Downs Austr.
54 O5 Lit Sweden
89 C6 Litang Guangxi China
82 K4 Litang Sichuan China
43 H3 Litani r. Fr. Guiana/Suriname
80 E5 Līṭānī r. Lebanon
34 B1 Litchfield CA U.S.A.
28 B4 Litchfield IL U.S.A.
64 D4 Lit-et-Mixe France
115 J4 Lithgow Austr.
49 Lithuania country Europe
33 E4 Lititz U.S.A.
62 G5 Litoměřice Czech Rep.
29 E7 Little Abaco i. Bahamas
92 A4 Little Andaman i. Andaman and Nicobar Is
29 E7 Little Bahama Bank sand bank Bahamas
117 E2 Little Barrier i. N.Z.
30 D3 Little Bay de Noc b. U.S.A.
24 E2 Little Belt Mts mts U.S.A.
37 H5 Little Cayman i. Cayman Is
35 H4 Little Colorado r. U.S.A.
35 F3 Little Creek Peak summit U.S.A.
31 G3 Little Current Can.
22 C3 Little Current r. Can.
59 D7 Little Dart r. U.K.
114 D6 Little Desert Nat. Park nat. park Austr.
33 F5 Little Egg Harbor in. U.S.A.
29 F7 Little Exuma i. Bahamas
26 E2 Little Falls MN U.S.A.
33 F3 Little Falls NY U.S.A.
35 F3 Littlefield AZ U.S.A.
27 C5 Littlefield TX U.S.A.
30 A1 Little Fork r. U.S.A.
26 E1 Little Fork U.S.A.
85 F4 Little Gandak r. India
21 K4 Little Grand Rapids Can.
59 G7 Littlehampton U.K.
32 C5 Little Kanawha r. U.S.A.
104 C3 Little Karas Berg plat. Namibia
104 D6 Little Karoo plat. S. Africa
30 D2 Little Lake U.S.A.
23 H3 Little Mecatina r. Can.
32 A5 Little Miami r. U.S.A.
57 B3 Little Minch str. U.K.
26 C2 Little Missouri r. U.S.A.
59 H5 Little Ouse r. U.K.
30 D1 Little Pic r. Can.
20 D2 Little Rancheria r. Can.
84 B5 Little Rann marsh India
27 E5 Little Rock U.S.A.
30 D4 Little Sable Pt pt U.S.A.
29 F7 Little San Salvador i. Bahamas
20 F4 Little Smoky r. Can.
25 F4 Littleton CO U.S.A.
33 H2 Littleton NH U.S.A.
32 C5 Littleton WV U.S.A.
30 E3 Little Traverse Bay b. U.S.A.
81 J4 Little Zab r. Iraq
103 D5 Litunde Moz.
20 B3 Lituya Bay b. U.S.A.
88 F1 Liu r. China
88 G1 Liu r. China
88 C3 Liuba China
89 F6 Liuchiu Yü i. Taiwan
89 C5 Liuchong He r. China
88 F1 Liugu r. China
88 D4 Liujiachang China
89 C5 Liujiang China
88 B3 Liujiaxia Sk. resr China
88 C3 Liupan Shan mts China
89 B5 Liupanshui China
89 D4 Liuyang China
89 C5 Liuzhou China
55 U8 Līvāni Latvia
34 B2 Live Oak CA U.S.A.
29 D6 Live Oak FL U.S.A.
112 D3 Liveringa Austr.
34 B3 Livermore U.S.A.
33 H2 Livermore Falls U.S.A.
27 B6 Livermore, Mt mt. U.S.A.
115 J4 Liverpool Austr.
23 H5 Liverpool Can.
59 E4 Liverpool U.K.
59 D4 Liverpool Bay U.K.
115 J3 Liverpool Plains plain Austr.
115 J3 Liverpool Ra. mts Austr.
57 E5 Livingston U.K.
34 B3 Livingston CA U.S.A.
24 E2 Livingston MT U.S.A.
29 C4 Livingston TN U.S.A.
27 E6 Livingston TX U.S.A.
103 C5 Livingstone Zambia
119 B2 Livingston I. i. S. Shetland Is Ant.
27 E6 Livingston, L. l. U.S.A.
66 G3 Livno Bos.-Herz.
69 F4 Livny Rus. Fed.
54 U4 Livojoki r. Fin.
31 F4 Livonia U.S.A.
66 D3 Livorno Italy
46 E1 Livramento do Brumado Brazil
103 D4 Liwale Tanz.
88 B3 Li Xian Gansu China
89 D4 Li Xian Hunan China
88 B4 Li Xian Sichuan China
88 E3 Lixin China
88 F4 Liyang China
59 B8 Lizard U.K.
59 B8 Lizard Point pt U.K.
66 F1 Ljubljana Slovenia
55 Q8 Ljugarn Sweden
55 P5 Ljungan r. Sweden
55 P5 Ljungaverk Sweden
55 N8 Ljungby Sweden
55 P6 Ljusdal Sweden
55 O6 Ljusnan r. Sweden
55 P6 Ljusne Sweden
44 B5 Llaima, Volcán volc. Chile
59 C5 Llanbadarn Fawr U.K.
59 D5 Llanbister U.K.
59 D6 Llandeilo U.K.
59 C6 Llandissilio U.K.
59 D6 Llandovery U.K.
59 D5 Llandrindod Wells U.K.
59 D4 Llandudno U.K.
59 C5 Llandysul U.K.
59 C6 Llanegwad U.K.
59 C6 Llanelli U.K.
59 C4 Llanerchymedd U.K.
59 D5 Llanfair Caereinion U.K.
59 C4 Llangefni U.K.
59 D5 Llangollen U.K.
59 D5 Llangurig U.K.
59 C4 Llanllyfni U.K.
59 C5 Llannor U.K.
27 D6 Llano r. U.S.A.
27 D6 Llano U.S.A.
27 C5 Llano Estacado plain U.S.A.
45 C3 Llanos reg. Col./Venez.
47 B4 Llanquihue, L. l. Chile
59 C5 Llanrhystud U.K.
59 D6 Llantrisant U.K.
59 D5 Llanuwchllyn U.K.
59 D5 Llanwnog U.K.
59 D4 Llay U.K.
65 G2 Lleida Spain

65 C3 Llerena Spain
65 F3 Lliria Spain
65 E1 Llodio Spain
21 H3 Lloyd Lake l. Can.
21 G4 Lloydminster Can.
65 H3 Llucmajor Spain
44 C2 Llullaillaco, Vol. volc. Chile
89 B6 Lô r. China/Vietnam
44 C2 Loa r. Chile
35 G2 Loa U.S.A.
68 J3 Loban' r. Rus. Fed.
65 D4 Lobatejo mt. Spain
103 C6 Lobatse Botswana
47 E3 Loberia Arg.
61 B3 Lobith Neth.
103 B5 Lobito Angola
47 E2 Lobos Arg.
57 D4 Lochaber reg. U.K.
57 C4 Lochaline U.K.
31 E1 Lochalsh Can.
57 A3 Lochboisdale U.K.
57 C3 Lochcarron U.K.
58 C1 Lochearnhead Scot. U.K.
64 E3 Loches France
57 E4 Lochgelly U.K.
57 C4 Lochgilphead U.K.
57 C2 Lochinver U.K.
57 A3 Lochmaddy U.K.
57 E4 Lochnagar mt. Scot. U.K.
32 E5 Loch Raven Reservoir resr U.S.A.
57 D4 Lochy, Loch l. U.K.
114 A4 Lock Austr.
57 E5 Lockerbie U.K.
115 G5 Lockhart Austr.
27 D6 Lockhart U.S.A.
32 E4 Lock Haven U.S.A.
32 D3 Lockport U.S.A.
95 C3 Lôc Ninh Vietnam
32 B5 Locust Grove U.S.A.
80 E6 Lod Israel
114 E6 Loddon r. Austr.
64 F5 Lodève France
68 E2 Lodeynoye Pole Rus. Fed.
24 F2 Lodge Grass U.S.A.
84 B3 Lodhran Pak.
66 C2 Lodi Italy
34 B2 Lodi CA U.S.A.
32 B4 Lodi OH U.S.A.
54 O2 Lødingen Norway
102 D3 Lodwar Kenya
63 J5 Łódź Pol.
84 B2 Loe Dakka Afgh.
104 C5 Loeriesfontein S. Africa
54 N2 Lofoten is Norway
69 G6 Log Rus. Fed.
115 K1 Logan r. Austr.
25 G5 Logan MT U.S.A.
32 B5 Logan OH U.S.A.
24 E3 Logan UT U.S.A.
32 C6 Logan WV U.S.A.
116 B4 Logan Cr. r. Austr.
20 D2 Logan Mountains mts Can.
20 A2 Logan, Mt mt. Can.
30 D5 Logansport U.S.A.
66 F2 Logatec Slovenia
65 E1 Logroño Spain
85 H4 Logtak L. l. India
104 E4 Lohatlha S. Africa
54 T3 Lohiniva Fin.
55 S6 Lohjanjärvi l. Fin.
54 S4 Lohtaja Fin.
95 A1 Loikaw Myanmar
95 A1 Loi Lan mt. Myanmar/Thai.
55 S6 Loimaa Fin.
64 E3 Loire r. France
42 C4 Loja Ecuador
65 D4 Loja Spain
94 A5 Lokan r. Malaysia
54 U3 Lokan tekojärvi l. Fin.
61 C3 Lokeren Belgium
104 D2 Lokgwabe Botswana
102 D3 Lokichar Kenya
102 D3 Lokichokio Kenya
55 L8 Løkken Denmark
54 L5 Løkken Norway
63 P2 Loknya Rus. Fed.
100 C4 Lokoja Nigeria
100 C4 Lokossa Benin
69 E4 Lokot' Rus. Fed.
55 T7 Loksa Estonia
100 B4 Lola Guinea
34 B2 Lola, Mt mt. U.S.A.
55 M9 Lolland i. Denmark
102 D4 Lollondo Tanz.
24 D2 Lolo U.S.A.
104 E3 Lolwane S. Africa
67 K3 Lom Bulg.
55 L6 Lom Norway
102 C3 Lomami r. Zaire
47 D3 Loma Negra, Planicie de la plain Arg.
84 A2 Lomar P. pass Afgh.
47 E2 Lomas de Zamora Arg.
112 D3 Lombardina Austr.
93 G8 Lomblen i. Indon.
92 F8 Lombok i. Indon.
92 F8 Lombok, Selat chan. Indon.
100 C4 Lomé Togo
102 C4 Lomela Zaire
102 C4 Lomela r. Zaire
61 D3 Lommel Belgium
57 D4 Lomond, Loch l. U.K.
68 G1 Lomovoye Rus. Fed.
93 F8 Lompobattang, Gunung mt. Indon.
34 B4 Lompoc U.S.A.
63 L4 Łomża Pol.
84 D6 Lonar India
47 B3 Loncoche Chile

47 B3 Loncopue Arg.
31 G4 London Can.
59 G6 London U.K.
32 A6 London KY U.S.A.
32 B5 London OH U.S.A.
60 D3 Londonderry U.S.A.
33 G3 Londonderry U.S.A.
112 E2 Londonderry, C. c. Austr.
44 B9 Londonderry, I. i. Chile
46 B3 Londrina Brazil
34 C3 Lone Pine U.S.A.
89 C6 Long'an China
77 T2 Longa, Proliv chan. Rus. Fed.
59 E6 Long Ashton U.K.
47 B3 Longavi, Nev. de mt. Chile
29 C5 Long Bay b. U.S.A.
117 C6 Longbeach N.Z.
34 C5 Long Beach CA U.S.A.
33 G4 Long Beach NY U.S.A.
33 F4 Long Branch U.S.A.
30 A6 Long Branch Lake l. U.S.A.
89 B4 Longchang China
89 C5 Longchuan China
59 F5 Long Eaton U.K.
60 D4 Longford Rep. of Ireland
89 B3 Longhai China
89 □ Long Harbour in. Hong Kong China
58 F2 Longhoughton U.K.
116 C4 Long Island i. Qld. Austr.
22 E3 Long Island i. P.N.G.
110 E2 Long Island i. Bahamas
37 J4 Long Island i. U.S.A.
33 G4 Long Island i. U.S.A.
33 G4 Long Island Sound chan. U.S.A.
87 M2 Longjiang China
89 C5 Long Jiang r. China
85 H3 Longju China
88 F2 Longkou Wan b. China
22 C4 Longlac Can.
22 C4 Long Lake l. Can.
33 J1 Long Lake l. ME U.S.A.
30 E3 Long Lake l. MI U.S.A.
31 F3 Long Lake l. MI U.S.A.
26 C2 Long Lake l. ND U.S.A.
33 F3 Long Lake l. NY U.S.A.
33 F2 Long Lake l. NY U.S.A.
89 C5 Longli China
89 B5 Longlin China
57 D4 Long, Loch in. U.K.
59 H5 Long Melford U.K.
89 E6 Longmen China
88 B3 Longmen Shan mts China
24 F3 Longmont U.S.A.
89 E5 Longnan China
31 G4 Long Point pt Can.
117 B7 Long Point N.Z.
31 G4 Long Point Bay b. Can.
58 E3 Long Preston U.K.
89 F4 Longquan China
89 F4 Longquan Xi r. China
23 J4 Long Range Mts h. Nfld Can.
116 A4 Longreach Austr.
88 B3 Longriba China
89 C4 Longshan China
89 D5 Longsheng China
24 F3 Longs Peak summit U.S.A.
59 J5 Long Stratton U.K.
89 D4 Longtian China
116 A3 Longton Austr.
58 E2 Longtown U.K.
22 F4 Longueuil Can.
61 D5 Longuyon France
34 A2 Longvale U.S.A.
35 F3 Long Valley Junction U.S.A.
27 E5 Longview TX U.S.A.
24 B2 Longview WA U.S.A.
61 D5 Longwy France
88 B3 Longxi China
88 C3 Long Xian China
89 E5 Longxi Shan mt. China
95 C3 Long Xuyên Vietnam
89 E5 Longyan China
88 E2 Longyao China
89 C6 Longzhou China
55 O8 Lönsboda Sweden
114 E6 Lonsdale, Lake l. Austr.
64 G3 Lons-le-Saunier France
46 B3 Lontra r. Brazil
94 B3 Looc Phil.
30 E4 Looking Glass r. U.S.A.
33 H4 Lookout U.S.A.
22 D2 Lookout, Cape c. Can.
29 E5 Lookout, Cape c. U.S.A.
34 C3 Lookout Mt mt. U.S.A.
115 K1 Lookout, Point pt Austr.
31 F3 Lookout, Pt pt U.S.A.
20 F3 Loon r. Can.
30 C1 Loon Can.
21 H4 Loon Lake Can.
33 J1 Loon Lake l. U.S.A.
60 B5 Loop Head hd Rep. of Ireland
84 E1 Lop China
87 Q1 Lopatina, Gora mt. Rus. Fed.
68 H4 Lopatino Rus. Fed.
95 B2 Lop Buri Thai.
33 E4 Lopez Phil.
82 H2 Lop Nur salt l. China
102 B3 Lopori r. Congo
54 R1 Lopphavet b. Norway
68 J2 Loptyuga Rus. Fed.
84 A3 Lora r. Afgh.
114 A2 Lora watercourse Austr.

45 B2 Lora r. Venez.
65 D4 Lora del Río Spain
32 B4 Lorain U.S.A.
84 B3 Loralai r. Pak.
84 B3 Loralai Pak.
32 A4 Loramie, Lake l. U.S.A.
65 F4 Lorca Spain
94 A4 Lord Auckland sand bank Phil.
111 F5 Lord Howe Island i. Pac. Oc.
14 F8 Lord Howe Rise sea feature Pac. Oc.
35 H5 Lordsburg U.S.A.
46 D3 Lorena Brazil
93 K8 Lorentz r. Indon.
42 F7 Loreto Bol.
43 J5 Loreto Brazil
36 B3 Loreto Mex.
94 C4 Loreto Phil.
45 B2 Lorica Col.
64 C3 Lorient France
21 L1 Lorillard r. Can.
116 A5 Lorne Qld. Austr.
114 E7 Lorne Vic. Austr.
57 C4 Lorn, Firth of est. U.K.
85 H3 Loro r. China
64 G2 Lorraine reg. France
84 C4 Losal India
25 F5 Los Alamos U.S.A.
47 B2 Los Andes Chile
47 B3 Los Angeles Chile
34 C5 Los Angeles CA U.S.A.
34 C4 Los Angeles Aqueduct canal U.S.A.
34 A3 Los Banos U.S.A.
44 D2 Los Blancos Arg.
44 B7 Los Chonos, Archipiélago de is Chile
34 D5 Los Coronados is Mex.
34 B3 Los Gatos U.S.A.
44 B8 Los Glacieres, Parque Nacional nat. park Arg.
66 F2 Lošin i. Croatia
105 H2 Loskop Dam dam S. Africa
47 B4 Los Lagos div. Chile
25 F5 Los Lunas U.S.A.
47 C4 Los Menucos Arg.
36 C5 Los Mochis Mex.
34 A1 Los Molinos U.S.A.
102 B3 Losombo Zaire
45 D2 Los Roques, Islas is Venez.
57 E3 Lossie r. U.K.
57 E3 Lossiemouth U.K.
45 C2 Los Taques Venez.
45 D2 Los Teques Venez.
45 E2 Los Testigos is Venez.
34 C4 Lost Hills U.S.A.
47 B3 Los Vilos Chile
47 B3 Lota Chile
105 J3 Lothair S. Africa
102 D3 Lotikipi Plain plain Kenya
102 C4 Loto Zaire
68 E3 Lotoshino Rus. Fed.
105 G1 Lotsane r. Botswana
54 V2 Lotta r. Fin./Rus. Fed.
86 H7 Louang Namtha Laos
92 C7 Louangphrabang Laos
102 B4 Loubomo Congo
64 C2 Loudéac France
89 D5 Loudi China
102 B4 Loudima Congo
32 B4 Loudonville U.S.A.
100 A3 Louga Senegal
59 F5 Loughborough U.K.
59 C6 Loughor r. U.K.
60 C4 Loughrea Rep. of Ireland
59 H6 Loughton U.K.
32 C5 Louisa KY U.S.A.
32 C5 Louisa VA U.S.A.
60 B4 Louisburgh Rep. of Ireland
20 C4 Louise I. i. Can.
111 F3 Louisiade Archipelago is P.N.G.
27 E6 Louisiana div. U.S.A.
105 H1 Louis Trichardt S. Africa
29 D5 Louisville GA U.S.A.
28 C4 Louisville KY U.S.A.
27 F5 Louisville MS U.S.A.
22 E3 Louis-XIV, Pointe c. Can.
76 E3 Loukhi Rus. Fed.
65 B4 Loulé Port.
21 L4 Lount L. l. Can.
62 F5 Louny Czech Rep.
26 D3 Loup r. U.S.A.
22 F2 Loups Marins, Lacs des l. Can.
23 J4 Lourdes Can.
64 D5 Lourdes France
65 B2 Lousã Port.
59 G4 Louth U.K.
67 K5 Loutra Aidipsou Greece
Louvain see Leuven
104 B1 Louwater-Suid Namibia
105 J3 Louwsburg S. Africa
54 R4 Lövånger Sweden
68 D3 Lovat' r. Rus. Fed.
67 L3 Lovech Bulg.
24 E3 Loveland U.S.A.
24 E2 Lovell U.S.A.
34 C1 Lovelock U.S.A.
61 B3 Lovendegem Belgium
55 U6 Loviisa Fin.
30 C6 Lovington IL U.S.A.
27 C5 Lovington NM U.S.A.

31 K3 Low Can.
102 C4 Lowa Zaire
84 B2 Lowarai Pass pass Pak.
21 M2 Low, Cape c. Can.
33 H3 Lowell MA U.S.A.
30 E4 Lowell MI U.S.A.
33 G2 Lowell VT U.S.A.
20 F5 Lower Arrow L. l. Can.
35 F4 Lower Granite Gorge gorge U.S.A.
117 E4 Lower Hutt N.Z.
34 A2 Lower Lake U.S.A.
60 D3 Lower Lough Erne l. U.K.
95 □ Lower Peirce Res. resr Sing.
20 D3 Lower Post Can.
23 H5 Lower Sackville Can.
59 J5 Lowestoft U.K.
63 J4 Łowicz Pol.
22 E3 Low, Lac l. Can.
115 F9 Low Rocky Pt hd Austr.
57 E5 Lowther Hills h. U.K.
33 F3 Lowville U.S.A.
114 D5 Loxton Austr.
32 E4 Loyalsock Creek r. U.S.A.
34 B2 Loyalton U.S.A.
Loyalty Is is see Loyauté, Îs
111 G4 Loyauté, Îs is New Caledonia
69 D5 Loyew Belarus
67 H2 Loznica Yugo.
69 F5 Lozova Ukr.
103 C5 Luacano Angola
88 A4 Lu'an China
88 D3 Luanchuan China
103 B4 Luanda Angola
95 A3 Luang, Khao mt. Thai.
103 D5 Luangwa r. Zambia
88 F1 Luan He r. China
88 E1 Luannan China
88 E1 Luanping China
103 C5 Luanshya Zambia
88 F2 Luan Xian China
103 C4 Luanza Zaire
65 C1 Luarca Spain
103 C5 Luau Angola
63 L5 Lubaczów Pol.
55 U3 Lubānas l. Latvia
94 A3 Lubang i. Phil.
94 B3 Lubang China
94 A3 Lubang Islands is Phil.
103 B5 Lubango Angola
102 C4 Lubao Zaire
63 L5 Lubartów Pol.
104 C4 Lubbeskolk salt pan S. Africa
27 C5 Lubbock U.S.A.
62 E4 Lübeck Ger.
63 L5 Lubelska, Wyżyna reg. Pol.
102 C4 Lubero Zaire
62 H5 Lubin Pol.
63 L5 Lublin Pol.
69 E5 Lubny Ukr.
92 E6 Lubok Antu Malaysia
94 B2 Lubuagan Phil.
103 C4 Lubudi Zaire
92 C7 Lubuklinggau Indon.
95 A5 Lubukpakam Indon.
103 C5 Lubumbashi Zaire
103 C5 Lubungu Zambia
102 C4 Lubutu Zaire
103 B4 Lucala Angola
60 E4 Lucan Rep. of Ireland
20 A2 Lucania, Mt mt. Can.
103 C4 Lucapa Angola
29 E7 Lucaya Bahamas
66 D3 Lucca Italy
57 D6 Luce Bay b. U.K.
46 B3 Lucélia Brazil
94 B3 Lucena Phil.
65 D4 Lucena Spain
63 J6 Lučenec Slovakia
66 F4 Lucera Italy
Lucerne see Luzern
89 B6 Lüchuan China
116 B2 Lucinda Austr.
114 D6 Lucindale Austr.
103 B5 Lucira Angola
85 F4 Luckeesarai India
62 F4 Luckenwalde Ger.
104 F4 Luckhoff S. Africa
31 G4 Lucknow Can.
84 E4 Lucknow India
103 C5 Lucusse Angola
68 F1 Luda Rus. Fed.
62 C5 Lüdenscheid Ger.
103 B6 Lüderitz Namibia
84 C3 Ludhiana India
84 B3 Ludian China
30 D4 Ludington U.S.A.
59 E5 Ludlow U.K.
34 D4 Ludlow CA U.S.A.
33 J1 Ludlow ME U.S.A.
33 G2 Ludlow VT U.S.A.
67 M3 Ludogorie reg. Bulg.
55 O6 Ludvika Sweden
62 D6 Ludwigsburg Ger.
62 D6 Ludwigshafen am Rhein Ger.
62 E4 Ludwigslust Ger.
55 U8 Ludza Latvia
102 C4 Luebo Zaire
103 B5 Luena Angola
103 C5 Luena r. Angola
88 C3 Lüeyang China
89 E6 Lufeng China
27 E6 Lufkin U.S.A.
68 D3 Luga Rus. Fed.
68 D3 Luga r. Rus. Fed.
66 C1 Lugano Switz.

103 D5 Lugenda r. Moz.
59 D5 Lugg r. U.K.
66 D2 Lugo Italy
65 C1 Lugo Spain
67 J2 Lugoj Romania
82 D2 Lugovoy Kazak.
94 B5 Lugus i. Phil.
69 F5 Luhans'k Ukr.
88 F3 Luhe China
85 H4 Luhit r. India
103 D4 Luhombero Tanz.
69 D5 Luhyny Ukr.
103 C5 Luiana Angola
Luik see Liège
102 C4 Luilaka r. Zaire
66 C2 Luino Italy
54 U3 Luiro r. Fin.
102 C4 Luiza Zaire
47 E2 Lujan r. Arg.
47 C2 Luján de Cuyo Arg.
88 E4 Lujiang China
67 H2 Lukavac Bos.-Herz.
102 B4 Lukenie r. Zaire
35 F6 Lukeville U.S.A.
68 G3 Lukh r. Rus. Fed.
68 F4 Lukhovitsy Rus. Fed.
67 L3 Lukovit Bulg.
63 L5 Łuków Pol.
68 H4 Lukoyanov Rus. Fed.
103 C5 Lukulu Zambia
103 D4 Lukumburu Tanz.
54 S4 Luleå Sweden
54 R4 Luleälven r. Sweden
80 A1 Lüleburgaz Turkey
89 B5 Luliang China
88 D2 Lüliang Shan mts China
27 D6 Luling U.S.A.
88 F2 Lulong China
85 F3 Lülung China
85 H4 Lumachomo China
92 □ Lumajang Indon.
85 E2 Lumajangdong Co salt l. China
103 C5 Lumbala Kaquengue Angola
103 C5 Lumbala N'guimbo Angola
29 E5 Lumberton U.S.A.
65 C2 Lumbrales Spain
85 H4 Lumding India
54 T4 Lumijoki Fin.
95 C2 Lumphăt Cambodia
117 B6 Lumsden N.Z.
94 B2 Luna Phil.
35 H5 Luna U.S.A.
57 F4 Lunan Bay b. U.K.
21 L2 Lunan Lake l. Can.
31 F5 Lune Pier U.S.A.
84 C5 Lunavada India
84 B4 Lund Pak.
55 N9 Lund Sweden
35 F2 Lund U.S.A.
21 K4 Lundar Can.
103 D5 Lundazi Zambia
59 C6 Lundy Island i. U.K.
58 E3 Lune r. U.K.
62 E4 Lüneburg Ger.
64 H2 Lunéville France
103 C5 Lunga r. Zambia
85 E2 Lungdo China
85 E2 Lunggar China
100 A4 Lunsar Sierra Leone
89 □ Lung Kwu Chau h. Hong Kong China
85 H5 Lunglei India
60 E5 Lungnaquilla Mountain mt. Rep. of Ireland
103 C5 Lungwebungu r. Zambia
84 C4 Luni r. India
84 C4 Luni India
84 B3 Luni r. Pak.
34 C2 Luning U.S.A.
68 H4 Lunino Rus. Fed.
69 C4 Luninyets Belarus
84 C1 Lunkho mt. Afgh./Pak.
100 A4 Lunsar Sierra Leone
105 H2 Lunsklip S. Africa
82 F2 Luntai China
88 D3 Luo r. Henan China
88 C3 Luo r. Shaanxi China
89 C5 Luocheng China
88 C3 Luochuan China
89 C5 Luoding China
89 D6 Luodou Sha i. China
88 E3 Luohe China
88 D3 Luoning China
89 B5 Luoping China
88 E3 Luoshan China
89 E4 Luotian China
88 D3 Luoyang China
89 F5 Luoyuan China
103 C5 Lupane Zimbabwe
67 K2 Lupeni Romania
103 D5 Lupilichi Moz.
94 C5 Lupon Phil.
35 H4 Lupton U.S.A.
88 B3 Luqu China
89 B5 Luquan China
81 K3 Lūrā Shīrīn Iran
103 B4 Luremo Angola
57 C2 Lurgainn, Loch l. U.K.
60 E3 Lurgan U.K.
103 E5 Lúrio Moz.
103 D5 Lurio r. Moz.
103 C5 Lusaka Zambia
102 C4 Lusambo Zaire
110 F2 Lusancay Islands and Reefs is P.N.G.
20 F4 Lusar Can.
21 H4 Luseland Can.
88 D3 Lushi China

67 H4 Lushnjë Albania
88 F2 Lüshun China
105 H5 Lusikisiki S. Africa
24 F3 Lusk U.S.A.
116 B6 Lussvale Austr.
79 H3 Lut, Dasht-e des. Iran
31 G4 Luther Lake l. Can.
62 F5 Lutherstadt Wittenberg Ger.
59 G6 Luton U.K.
92 E6 Lutong Malaysia
21 G3 Łutselk'e Can.
69 C5 Luts'k Ukr.
104 D4 Lutzputs S. Africa
104 C5 Lutzville S. Africa
94 B5 Luuk Phil.
55 U6 Luumäki Fin.
102 E3 Luuq Somalia
26 D3 Luverne U.S.A.
102 C4 Luvua r. Zaire
105 J1 Luvuvhu r. S. Africa
102 D3 Luwero Uganda
93 G7 Luwuk Indon.
48 Luxembourg country Europe
61 E5 Luxembourg Lux.
64 H3 Luxeuil-les-Bains France
89 D4 Luxi Hunan China
89 B5 Luxi Yunnan China
105 F5 Luxolweni S. Africa
78 C4 Luxor Egypt
88 E3 Luyi China
61 D3 Luyksgestel Neth.
68 H2 Luza Rus. Fed.
68 J2 Luza r. Rus. Fed.
62 D7 Luzern Switz.
89 C5 Luzhai China
89 B5 Luzhi China
89 B4 Luzhou China
46 C2 Luziânia Brazil
43 K4 Luzilândia Brazil
94 B3 Luzon i. Phil.
94 B1 Luzon Strait str. Phil.
64 F3 Luzy France
69 C5 L'viv Ukr.
L'vov see L'viv
68 D3 Lyady Rus. Fed.
68 C4 Lyakhavichy Belarus
20 G5 Lyall, Mt mt. Can.
Lyallpur see Faisalabad
54 Q4 Lycksele Sweden
59 H7 Lydd U.K.
119 D3 Lyddan I. i. Ant.
105 J2 Lydenburg S. Africa
59 E6 Lydney U.K.
69 D5 Lyel'chytsy Belarus
20 C4 Lyell I. i. Can.
34 C3 Lyell, Mt mt. U.S.A.
68 D4 Lyepyel' Belarus
32 D4 Lykens U.S.A.
24 E3 Lyman U.S.A.
59 E7 Lyme Bay b. U.K.
59 E7 Lyme Regis U.K.
59 F7 Lymington U.K.
32 E3 Lynchburg U.S.A.
33 H2 Lynchville U.S.A.
116 A1 Lynd r. Austr.
115 H4 Lyndhurst N.S.W. Austr.
116 A2 Lyndhurst Qld. Austr.
114 C4 Lyndhurst S.A. Austr.
116 A2 Lynd Junction, The Austr.
33 G2 Lyndonville U.S.A.
57 E2 Lyness U.K.
55 K7 Lyngdal Norway
33 H3 Lynn U.S.A.
20 B3 Lynn Canal chan. U.S.A.
35 F2 Lynndyl U.S.A.
21 J3 Lynn Lake Can.
59 D6 Lynton U.K.
21 H2 Lynx Lake l. Can.
64 G4 Lyon France
33 G2 Lyon Mountain U.S.A.
29 D5 Lyons GA U.S.A.
32 E3 Lyons NY U.S.A.
33 F3 Lyons Falls U.S.A.
68 D4 Lyozna Belarus
111 F2 Lyra Reef rf P.N.G.
55 M7 Lysekil Sweden
68 H3 Lyskovo Rus. Fed.
76 G4 Lys'va Rus. Fed.
69 F5 Lysychans'k Ukr.
58 D4 Lytham St Anne's U.K.
20 E4 Lytton Can.
68 D4 Lyuban' Belarus
69 C5 Lyubeshiv Ukr.
68 E4 Lyudinovo Rus. Fed.
68 H3 Lyunda r. Rus. Fed.

# M

83 D9 Maalosmadulu Atoll atoll Maldives
103 C5 Maamba Zambia
80 E6 Ma'an Jordan
54 U5 Maaninka Fin.
54 V3 Maaninkavaara Fin.
88 F4 Ma'anshan China
55 T7 Maardu Estonia
80 F4 Ma'arrat an Nu'mān Syria
61 E3 Maas r. Neth.
61 D3 Maaseik Belgium
94 C4 Maasin Phil.
61 D3 Maastricht Neth.
105 H1 Maastroom S. Africa
115 G9 Maatsuyker Is is Austr.
94 B3 Mabalacat Phil.
103 D6 Mabalane Moz.

42 G2 Mabaruma Guyana
31 J3 Maberly Can.
89 B4 Mabian China
59 H4 Mablethorpe U.K.
105 H2 Mabopane S. Africa
103 D6 Mabote Moz.
94 B1 Mabudis i. Phil.
104 F2 Mabule Botswana
104 E2 Mabutsane Botswana
47 D3 Macachín Arg.
33 K2 McAdam Can.
46 E3 Macaé Brazil
94 C4 Macajalar Bay b. Phil.
27 E5 McAlester U.S.A.
32 E4 McAlevys Fort U.S.A.
115 H5 McAlister mt. Austr.
115 G6 McAlister r. Austr.
27 D7 McAllen U.S.A.
103 D5 Macaloge Moz.
44 B7 Macá, Mt mt. Chile
105 K1 Macandze Moz.
43 H3 Macapá Brazil
42 C4 Macará Ecuador
46 E1 Macarani Brazil
45 B4 Macarena, Cordillera mts Col.
45 B4 Macarena, Parque Nacional La nat. park Col.
114 E7 Macarthur Austr.
32 B5 McArthur U.S.A.
31 J3 McArthur Mills Can.
20 B2 McArthur Wildlife Sanctuary res. Can.
42 C4 Macas Ecuador
93 F7 Macassar Strait str. Indon.
43 L5 Macau Brazil
89 D6 Macau Macau
43 H6 Macaúba Brazil
46 D1 Macaúbas Brazil
45 B4 Macaya r. Col.
45 B4 Macayari Col.
20 E4 McBride Can.
24 C2 McCall U.S.A.
27 C6 McCamey U.S.A.
24 D3 McCammon U.S.A.
105 K2 Maccaretane Moz.
20 C4 McCauley I. i. Can.
59 E4 Macclesfield U.K.
34 B3 McClure, L. l. U.S.A.
27 F6 McComb U.S.A.
26 C3 McConaughy, L. l. U.S.A.
32 E5 McConnellsburg U.S.A.
32 C5 McConnelsville U.S.A.
26 C3 McCook U.S.A.
21 K4 McCreary Can.
35 E4 McCullough Range mts U.S.A.
20 D3 McDame Can.
24 C3 McDermitt U.S.A.
112 E4 Macdonald, L. salt flat Austr.
24 D2 McDonald Peak summit U.S.A.
114 C2 McDonnell Creek watercourse Austr.
112 E4 Macdonnell Ranges mts Austr.
104 B4 McDougall's Bay b. S. Africa
22 B3 MacDowell L. l. Can.
35 G5 McDowell Peak summit U.S.A.
57 F3 Macduff U.K.
65 C2 Macedo de Cavaleiros Port.
114 F6 Macedon mt. Austr.
49 Macedonia country Europe
43 L5 Maceió Brazil
100 B4 Macenta Guinea
66 E3 Macerata Italy
34 C4 McFarland U.S.A.
21 H3 McFarlane r. Can.
114 B4 Macfarlane, L. salt flat Austr.
35 E2 McGill U.S.A.
60 B6 Macgillycuddy's Reeks mts Rep. of Ireland
20 E4 McGregor Can.
104 C6 McGregor S. Africa
30 A2 McGregor U.S.A.
31 G2 McGregor Bay Can.
24 D2 McGuire, Mt mt. U.S.A.
84 A3 Mach Pak.
42 C4 Machachi Ecuador
46 D3 Machado Brazil
103 D6 Machaila Moz.
102 D4 Machakos Kenya
42 C4 Machala Ecuador
103 D6 Machanga Moz.
105 K2 Machatuine Moz.
88 D4 Macheng China
33 K2 Machias ME U.S.A.
32 D3 Machias NY U.S.A.
33 J1 Machias r. U.S.A.
83 F7 Machilipatnam India
45 D2 Machiques Venez.
57 C5 Machrihanish U.K.
59 D5 Machynlleth U.K.
105 K2 Macia Moz.
67 N2 Măcin Romania
33 G2 McIndoe Falls U.S.A.
26 C2 McIntosh U.S.A.
Macintyre r. see Barwon
115 J2 Macintyre r. Austr.
115 J2 Macintyre Brook r. Austr.
35 H2 Mack U.S.A.
81 G1 Maçka Turkey
116 E3 Mackay Austr.
24 D2 Mackay U.S.A.
112 E4 Mackay, Lake salt flat Austr.

21 G2 Mackay Lake l. Can.
111 J2 McKean Island i. Kiribati
32 A6 McKee U.S.A.
32 D4 McKeesport U.S.A.
33 F7 McKeever U.S.A.
116 C4 Mackenzie r. Austr.
20 E3 Mackenzie B.C. Can.
30 C1 Mackenzie Ont. Can.
29 B4 McKenzie U.S.A.
119 D5 Mackenzie Bay b. Ant.
20 F2 Mackenzie Bison Sanctuary res. Can.
20 C2 Mackenzie Mountains mts Can.
30 E3 Mackinac I. i. U.S.A.
30 E3 Mackinac, Straits of chan. U.S.A.
30 C5 Mackinaw r. U.S.A.
30 E3 Mackinaw City U.S.A.
18 McKinley, Mt mt. U.S.A.
27 D5 McKinney U.S.A.
34 C4 McKittrick U.S.A.
21 H4 Macklin Can.
115 K3 Macksville Austr.
26 C2 McLaughlin U.S.A.
115 K2 Maclean Austr.
105 H5 Maclear S. Africa
115 K3 Macleay r. Austr.
20 F3 McLennan Can.
20 F4 McLeod r. Can.
112 B4 Macleod, Lake l. Austr.
20 E3 McLeod Lake Can.
24 B3 McLoughlin, Mt mt. U.S.A.
20 C2 Macmillan r. Can.
30 E2 McMillan U.S.A.
24 B2 McMinnville OR U.S.A.
29 C5 McMinnville TN U.S.A.
119 B5 McMurdo U.S.A. Base Ant.
35 H4 McNary U.S.A.
20 F4 McNaughton Lake l. Can.
35 H6 McNeal U.S.A.
30 B5 Macomb U.S.A.
66 C4 Macomer Sardinia Italy
64 G3 Mâcon France
29 D5 Macon GA U.S.A.
26 E4 Macon MO U.S.A.
103 C5 Macondo Angola
26 D4 McPherson U.S.A.
115 K2 McPherson Ra. mts Austr.
115 J3 Macquarie r. N.S.W. Austr.
115 G8 Macquarie r. Tas. Austr.
115 F9 Macquarie Harbour in. Austr.
115 J4 Macquarie, L. b. Austr.
115 G3 Macquarie Marshes marsh Austr.
115 H4 Macquarie Mt mt. Austr.
14 F9 Macquarie Ridge sea feature Pac. Oc.
20 B2 McQuesten r. Can.
29 D5 McRae U.S.A.
95 MacRitchie Res. resr Sing.
117 C6 Lake Tekapo N.Z.
119 D4 Mac. Robertson Land reg. Ant.
60 C4 Macroom Rep. of Ireland
45 C1 Macuira, Parque Nacional nat. park Col.
45 B4 Macuje Col.
113 G5 Macumba watercourse Austr.
42 D6 Macusani Peru
20 E1 McVicar Arm b. Can.
33 J2 Macwahoc U.S.A.
80 E6 Mādabā Jordan
105 J3 Madadeni S. Africa
96 Madagascar country Africa
13 H5 Madagascar Basin sea feature Indian Ocean
13 G6 Madagascar Ridge sea feature Indian Ocean
101 D2 Madama Niger
67 L4 Madan Bulg.
110 E2 Madang P.N.G.
100 C3 Madaoua Niger
85 G5 Madaripur Bangl.
31 J3 Madawaska Can.
31 J3 Madawaska r. Can.
33 J1 Madawaska U.S.A.
42 F5 Madeira r. Brazil
23 H4 Madeleine, Îles de la is Can.
30 B2 Madeline I. i. U.S.A.
81 G2 Maden Turkey
36 C3 Madera Mex.
34 B3 Madera U.S.A.
83 D7 Madgaon India
85 F4 Madhepura India
85 F4 Madhubani India
84 D5 Madhya Pradesh div. India
105 K3 Madibogo S. Africa
114 B2 Madigan Gulf salt flat Austr.
83 E8 Madikeri India
102 B4 Madingou Congo
42 E6 Madini r. Bol.
103 E5 Madirovalo Madag.
28 C4 Madison IN U.S.A.
33 J2 Madison ME U.S.A.
26 D2 Madison MN U.S.A.
26 D3 Madison NE U.S.A.
26 D2 Madison SD U.S.A.
30 C4 Madison WV U.S.A.
32 C5 Madison WV U.S.A.
28 C4 Madisonville KY U.S.A.
27 E6 Madisonville TX U.S.A.

92 □ Madiun Indon.
31 J3 Madoc Can.
102 D3 Mado Gashi Kenya
82 J4 Madoi China
55 U8 Madona Latvia
84 B4 Madpura India
67 M5 Madra Daği mts Turkey
83 F8 Madras India
24 B2 Madras U.S.A.
42 D6 Madre de Dios r. Peru
44 A8 Madre de Dios, I. i. Chile
36 E3 Madre, Laguna lag. Mex.
27 D7 Madre, Laguna lag. U.S.A.
94 B3 Madre, Sierra mt. Phil.
94 C4 Madrid Phil.
65 E2 Madrid Spain
94 B4 Madridejos Phil.
65 E3 Madridejos Spain
92 □ Madura i. Indon.
83 E9 Madurai India
92 □ Madura, Selat chan. Indon.
85 E4 Madwas India
84 C2 Madyan Pak.
69 H7 Madzhalis Rus. Fed.
91 G5 Maebashi Japan
95 A1 Mae Hong Son Thai.
95 B2 Mae Khlong r. Thai.
95 A1 Mae Lao r. Thai.
95 A1 Mae Li r. Thai.
95 B1 Mae Nam Ing r. Thai.
95 C2 Mae Nam Mun r. Thai.
95 B2 Mae Nam Nan r. Thai.
95 B2 Mae Nam Pa Sak r. Thai.
95 B2 Mae Nam Ping r. Thai.
95 A1 Mae Nam Wang r. Thai.
95 B2 Mae Nam Yom r. Thai.
37 J5 Maestra, Sierra mts Cuba
103 E5 Maevatanana Madag.
111 G3 Maéwo i. Vanuatu
95 A1 Mae Yuam r. Myanmar/Thai.
21 J4 Mafeking Can.
105 G4 Mafeteng Lesotho
115 G6 Maffra Austr.
103 D4 Mafia I. i. Tanz.
105 F2 Mafikeng S. Africa
103 D4 Mafinga Tanz.
46 C4 Mafra Brazil
80 F5 Mafraq Jordan
77 R4 Magadan Rus. Fed.
102 D4 Magadi Kenya
105 K1 Magaiza Moz.
94 B3 Magallanes Phil.
44 B8 Magallanes, Estrecho de chan. Chile
45 B2 Magangue Col.
80 D3 Mağara Turkey
94 B2 Magat r. Phil.
87 N1 Magdagachi Rus. Fed.
47 F2 Magdalena Arg.
42 F6 Magdalena Bol.
36 B2 Magdalena Mex.
25 F5 Magdalena U.S.A.
44 B6 Magdalena, Isla i. Chile
94 A5 Magdaleno, Mt mt. Malaysia
62 E4 Magdeburg Ger.
116 D1 Magdelaine Cays atoll Coral Sea Is Terr.
92 □ Magelang Indon.
14 F4 Magellan Seamounts sea feature Pac. Oc.
54 T1 Magerøya i. Norway
66 C2 Maggiorasca, Monte mt. Italy
66 C2 Maggiore, Lago l. Italy
100 A3 Maghama Maur.
60 E3 Maghera U.K.
60 E3 Magherafelt U.K.
58 E4 Maghull U.K.
24 D3 Magna U.S.A.
66 F6 Magna Grande mt. Sicily Italy
119 D4 Magnet Bay b. Ant.
116 B2 Magnetic I. i. Austr.
116 B2 Magnetic Passage chan. Austr.
54 X2 Magnetity Rus. Fed.
76 G4 Magnitogorsk Rus. Fed.
27 E5 Magnolia U.S.A.
23 F4 Magog Can.
30 E1 Magpie r. Can.
23 H3 Magpie Can.
23 H3 Magpie L. l. Can.
30 E1 Magpie Lake l. Can.
20 G5 Magrath Can.
34 D3 Magruder Mt mt. U.S.A.
100 A3 Magta' Lahjar Maur.
102 D4 Magu Tanz.
89 B6 Maguan China
43 J4 Maguarinho, Cabo pt Brazil
105 K2 Magude Moz.
33 K2 Magundy Can.
21 K2 Maguse Lake l. Can.
83 H6 Magwe Myanmar
85 H5 Magyichaung Myanmar
81 K3 Mahābād Iran
85 F4 Mahabharat Range mts Nepal
103 E6 Mahabo Madag.
84 D5 Mahadeo Hills h. India
102 D3 Mahagi Zaire
84 D4 Mahajan India
103 E5 Mahajanga Madag.
103 C6 Mahalapye Botswana
103 E5 Mahalevona Madag.
84 D3 Maham India
92 □ Mahameru, Gunung volc. Indon.

85 F5 Mahanadi r. India
103 E5 Mahanoro Madag.
84 D5 Maharashtra div. India
85 E5 Mahasamund India
95 B1 Maha Sarakham Thai.
103 E5 Mahatalaky Madag.
103 E5 Mahavanona Madag.
103 E5 Mahavavy r. Madag.
95 C1 Mahaxai Laos
83 E7 Mahbubnagar India
43 G2 Mahdia Guyana
66 D7 Mahdia Tunisia
84 D5 Mahesāna India
84 C5 Maheshwar India
84 C5 Mahi r. India
117 F3 Mahia Peninsula pen. N.Z.
68 D4 Mahilyow Belarus
105 J4 Mahlabatini S. Africa
84 B2 Maḥmūd-e 'Erāqī Afgh.
81 M4 Mahniān Iran
26 D2 Mahnomen U.S.A.
84 D2 Mahoba India
65 J3 Mahón Spain
32 C5 Mahoning Creek Lake l. U.S.A.
85 H5 Mahudaung Hgts mts Myanmar
84 B5 Mahuva India
67 M3 Mahya Daği mt. Turkey
84 B5 Maibang India
45 B2 Maicao Col.
22 E4 Maicasagi, Lac l. Can.
89 C6 Maichen China
59 G6 Maidenhead U.K.
21 H4 Maidstone Can.
59 H6 Maidstone U.K.
101 D3 Maiduguri Nigeria
84 D4 Maigualida, Sierra mts Venez.
60 C5 Maigue r. Rep. of Ireland
84 E4 Maihar India
91 F6 Maihara Japan
88 D3 Maiji Shan mt. China
84 E5 Maikala Range h. India
102 C4 Maiko, Parc National de la nat. park Zaire
84 E3 Mailani India
60 E3 Main r. U.K.
23 J3 Main Brook Can.
31 F3 Main Channel chan. Can.
102 B4 Mai-Ndombe, Lac l. Zaire
31 J4 Main Duck I. i. Can.
33 J2 Maine div. U.S.A.
100 D3 Maïné-Soroa Niger
95 A2 Maingy I. i. Myanmar
94 C4 Mainit Phil.
94 C4 Mainit, Lake l. Phil.
57 E1 Mainland i. Orkney U.K.
57 □ Mainland i. Shetland U.K.
85 E5 Mainpat reg. India
84 D4 Mainpuri India
103 E5 Maintirano Madag.
62 D5 Mainz Ger.
100 □ Maio i. Cape Verde
47 C2 Maipó, Vol. volc. Chile
47 F3 Maipú Buenos Aires Arg.
47 C2 Maipú Mendoza Arg.
45 D2 Maiquetía Venez.
85 G5 Maiskhal I. i. Bangl.
103 C6 Maitengwe Botswana
115 J4 Maitland N.S.W. Austr.
114 B5 Maitland S.A. Austr.
119 E3 Maitri India Base Ant.
85 G3 Maizhokunggar China
37 H6 Maíz, Islas del is Nic.
91 E6 Maizuru Japan
67 H7 Maja Jezercë mt. Albania
45 E4 Majari r. Brazil
93 F7 Majene Indon.
102 D3 Majī Eth.
88 E2 Majia r. China
89 D6 Majiang China
Majorca i. see Mallorca
85 H4 Majuli i. India
105 G4 Majwemasweu S. Africa
102 B4 Makabana Congo
34 □ Makaha U.S.A.
93 F7 Makale Indon.
84 C4 Makalu, Mt mt. China
102 C4 Makamba Burundi
82 J4 Makanchi Kazak.
34 □1 Makapuu Hd hd U.S.A.
68 J2 Makar-Ib Rus. Fed.
87 Q2 Makarov Rus. Fed.
66 G3 Makarska Croatia
76 G5 Makat Kazak.
105 K3 Makatini Flats lowland S. Africa
100 A4 Makeni Sierra Leone
103 C6 Makgadikgadi salt pan Botswana
69 H7 Makhachkala Rus. Fed.
80 G4 Makhfar al Ḥammām Syria
81 M4 Makhmūr Iraq
102 D4 Makindu Kenya
76 J4 Makinsk Kazak.
69 F5 Makiyivka Ukr.
23 J2 Makkah see Mecca
23 J2 Makkovik Can.
54 R3 Makkovik, Kapp c. Can.
67 J1 Makó Hungary
102 B3 Makokou Gabon
103 B4 Makongolosi Tanz.
104 E2 Makopong Botswana
102 B4 Makotipoko Congo
79 J4 Makran reg. Iran/Pak.
84 D3 Makrana India
85 E6 Makri India
67 L6 Makronisi i. Greece
69 F5 Maksatikha Rus. Fed.
81 K2 Mākū Iran

85 H4 Makum India
103 D5 Makunguwiro Tanz.
90 C8 Makurazaki Japan
100 C4 Makurdi Nigeria
105 F3 Makwassie S. Africa
54 O4 Malå Sweden
94 C5 Malabang Phil.
83 D8 Malabar Coast coastal area India
100 C4 Malabo Equatorial Guinea
94 A4 Malabuñgan Phil.
Malacca see Melaka
92 C6 Malacca, Strait of str. Indon./Malaysia
24 D3 Malad City U.S.A.
68 C4 Maladzyechna Belarus
65 D4 Málaga Spain
33 F5 Malaga NJ U.S.A.
25 F5 Malaga NM U.S.A.
111 G2 Malaita i. Solomon Is
101 F4 Malakal Sudan
111 G3 Malakula i. Vanuatu
84 C2 Malakwal Pak.
93 G7 Malamala Indon.
116 A1 Malang Indon.
92 □ Malang Indon.
103 B4 Malanje Angola
47 C1 Malanzán, Sa de mts Arg.
37 H7 Mala, Pta pt Panama
55 P7 Mälaren l. Sweden
47 C2 Malargüe Arg.
31 H1 Malartic Can.
31 H1 Malartic, Lac l. Can.
20 A3 Malaspina Glacier gl. U.S.A.
80 G2 Malatya Turkey
84 E4 Malaut India
81 L5 Mālavi Iran
94 A5 Malawali i. Malaysia
96 Malawi country Africa
Malawi, Lake l. see Nyasa, Lake
92 C6 Malaya reg. Malaysia
68 E3 Malaya Vishera Rus. Fed.
94 C4 Malaybalay Phil.
81 M4 Malāyer Iran
116 C1 Malay Reef rf Coral Sea Is Terr.
70 Malaysia country Asia
81 J2 Malazgirt Turkey
63 J3 Malbork Pol.
62 F2 Malchin Ger.
85 G4 Mäldah India
61 B3 Maldegem Belgium
27 F4 Malden U.S.A.
109 Malden Island i. Kiribati
13 J4 Maldive Ridge sea feature Indian Ocean
70 Maldives country Indian Ocean
59 H6 Maldon U.K.
47 F2 Maldonado Uru.
83 D10 Maldives
67 K6 Maleas, Akra i. Greece
83 D10 Male Atoll atoll Maldives
105 F3 Malebogo S. Africa
84 C5 Malegaon India
102 B4 Malele Zaire
103 D5 Malema Moz.
84 C3 Malerkotla India
84 A2 Mälestän Afgh.
69 H7 Malgobek Rus. Fed.
54 P4 Malgomaj l. Sweden
24 C3 Malheur L. l. U.S.A.
96 Mali country Africa
100 A3 Mali Guinea
102 C4 Mali Zaire
88 C4 Malian r. China
84 E4 Malihabad India
95 A2 Mali Kyun i. Myanmar
93 G7 Malili Indon.
102 E4 Malindi Kenya
Malines see Mechelen
60 D2 Malin Head hd Rep. of Ireland
60 D2 Malin More Rep. of Ireland
89 B4 Malipo China
66 F2 Mali Raginac mt. Croatia
94 C5 Malita Phil.
95 A3 Maliwun Myanmar
84 B5 Maliya India
81 L5 Malkaili Iran
84 D5 Malkapur India
69 C7 Malkara Turkey
63 N4 Mal'kavichy Belarus
67 M4 Malko Tŭrnovo Bulg.
115 H6 Mallacoota Austr.
115 H6 Mallacoota Inlet b. Austr.
57 C4 Mallaig U.K.
114 C5 Mallala Austr.
114 C5 Mallala India
114 Mallee Cliffs Nat. Park nat. park Austr.
21 K2 Mallery Lake l. Can.
65 H3 Mallorca i. Spain
60 C5 Mallow Rep. of Ireland
59 D5 Mallwyd U.K.
54 M4 Malm Norway
54 R3 Malmberget Sweden
61 E4 Malmédy Belgium
104 C6 Malmesbury S. Africa
59 E6 Malmesbury U.K.
55 N9 Malmö Sweden
68 J3 Malmyzh Rus. Fed.
111 G3 Malo i. Vanuatu
94 B3 Malolos Phil.
89 B5 Malong China
103 C5 Malonga Zaire
68 F2 Maloshuyka Rus. Fed.

55 J6 Måløy Norway
68 F4 Maloyaroslavets Rus. Fed.
42 B3 Malpelo, Isla i. Col.
48 Malta country Europe
55 U8 Malta Latvia
24 F1 Malta U.S.A.
66 F6 Malta Channel chan. Italy/Malta
103 B6 Maltahöhe Namibia
59 F4 Maltby U.K.
59 H4 Maltby le Marsh U.K.
58 G3 Malton U.K.
Maluku is see Moluccas
55 N6 Malung Sweden
105 H4 Maluti Mountains mts Lesotho
111 G2 Malu'u Solomon Is
27 D7 Malvern U.S.A.
Malvinas, Islas terr. see Falkland Islands
69 D5 Malyn Ukr.
77 S3 Malyy Anyuy r. Rus. Fed.
69 H6 Malyye Derbety Rus. Fed.
69 G7 Malyy Kavkaz mts Asia
77 Q2 Malyy Lyakhovskiy, Ostrov i. Rus. Fed.
69 J5 Malyy Uzen' r. Kazak./Rus. Fed.
77 Q3 Mama r. Rus. Fed.
105 H3 Mamafubedu S. Africa
94 A5 Mambahenauhan i. Phil.
94 C4 Mambajao Phil.
102 C3 Mambasa Zaire
102 B3 Mambéré r. C.A.R.
94 B3 Mamburao Phil.
105 H2 Mamelodi S. Africa
100 C4 Mamfé Cameroon
35 G5 Mammoth U.S.A.
28 C4 Mammoth Cave Nat. Park nat. park U.S.A.
34 C3 Mammoth Lakes U.S.A.
42 E6 Mamoré r. Bol./Brazil
100 A3 Mamou Guinea
103 E5 Mampikony Madag.
100 B4 Mampong Ghana
47 B3 Mamuil Malal, P. pass Arg./Chile
93 F7 Mamuju Indon.
104 D1 Mamuno Botswana
100 B4 Man Côte d'Ivoire
45 B4 Manacacias r. Col.
42 F4 Manacapuru Brazil
65 H3 Manacor Spain
93 G6 Manadao Indon.
93 G6 Manado Indon.
36 G6 Managua Nic.
36 G6 Managua, L. de l. Nic.
103 E6 Manakara Madag.
117 D5 Manakau mt. N.Z.
110 E2 Manam I. i. P.N.G.
34 □1 Manana i. U.S.A.
103 E6 Mananara r. Madag.
103 E5 Mananara Avaratra Madag.
103 E5 Mananara, Parc National de nat. park Madag.
114 E5 Manangatang Austr.
103 E6 Mananjary Madag.
45 D2 Manapire r. Venez.
117 A6 Manapouri, L. l. N.Z.
103 E5 Manarantsandry Madag.
85 G4 Manas r. Bhutan
84 D3 Mana Shankou pass India
82 G1 Manas Hu l. China
85 F4 Manaslu mt. Nepal
32 E5 Manassas U.S.A.
93 H8 Manatuto Indon.
42 F4 Manaus Brazil
80 C3 Manavgat Turkey
117 E4 Manawatu r. N.Z.
94 C5 Manay Phil.
80 F3 Manbij Syria
59 H4 Manby U.K.
59 E4 Manchester U.K.
34 A2 Manchester CA U.S.A.
33 G4 Manchester CT U.S.A.
30 B4 Manchester IA U.S.A.
32 B6 Manchester KY U.S.A.
31 F4 Manchester MI U.S.A.
33 H2 Manchester NH U.S.A.
32 B5 Manchester OH U.S.A.
29 C5 Manchester TN U.S.A.
33 G3 Manchester VT U.S.A.
84 A4 Manchhar L. l. Pak.
80 F2 Mancılık Turkey
35 H3 Mancos U.S.A.
35 H3 Mancos r. U.S.A.
103 E6 Mandabe Madag.
95 □ Mandai Sing.
84 D4 Mandal India
55 K7 Mandal Norway
93 L7 Mandala, Pk mt. Indon.
83 J6 Mandalay Myanmar
86 J2 Mandalgovĭ Mongolia
81 K5 Mandalī Iraq
88 D1 Mandalt Sum China
26 C2 Mandan U.S.A.
94 B3 Mandaon Phil.
101 D4 Manda, Parc National de nat. park Chad
101 D3 Mandara Mountains mts Cameroon/Nigeria
66 C5 Mandas Sardinia Italy
102 E3 Mandera Kenya
35 F2 Manderfield U.S.A.
37 J5 Mandeville Jamaica
117 B6 Mandeville N.Z.
84 B4 Mandha India
84 E4 Mandi India
100 B3 Mandiana Guinea
84 C3 Mandi Burewala Pak.
103 D5 Mandié Moz.
103 D5 Mandimba Moz.

105 J4 Mandini S. Africa
84 E5 Mandla India
103 E5 Mandritsara Madag.
84 C4 Mandsaur India
94 A6 Mandul i. Indon.
112 C6 Mandurah Austr.
66 G4 Manduria Italy
84 B5 Mandvi Gujarat India
84 B5 Mandvi Gujarat India
83 E8 Mandya India
66 D2 Manerbio Italy
63 M5 Manevychi Ukr.
66 F4 Manfredonia Italy
66 G4 Manfredonia, Golfo di g. Italy
46 D1 Manga Brazil
100 B3 Manga Burkina
102 B4 Mangai Zaire
109 Mangaia i. Cook Islands Pac. Oc.
117 E3 Mangakino N.Z.
85 H4 Mangaldai India
67 N3 Mangalia Romania
83 D8 Mangalore India
85 G4 Mangan India
94 A4 Mangarang Indon.
105 G4 Mangaung S. Africa
117 E3 Mangaweka N.Z.
85 G4 Mangde r. Bhutan
60 B6 Mangerton Mt h. Rep. of Ireland
92 D7 Manggar Indon.
82 H3 Mangnai China
103 D5 Mangochi Malawi
93 H7 Mangole i. Indon.
59 E6 Mangotsfield U.K.
84 B5 Mângral India
29 E7 Mangrove Cay Bahamas
65 C2 Mangualde Port.
47 G2 Mangueira, L. l. Brazil
46 B4 Mangueirinha Brazil
101 D2 Manguéni, Plateau de plat. Niger
87 M1 Mangui China
94 C5 Mangupung i. Indon.
26 D4 Manhattan KS U.S.A.
34 C2 Manhattan NV U.S.A.
103 D6 Manhica Moz.
105 K3 Manhoca Moz.
46 D3 Manhuaçu Brazil
46 E2 Manhuaçu r. Brazil
61 D5 Manhuelles France
45 B3 Mani Col.
103 E5 Mania r. Madag.
66 E1 Maniago Italy
42 F5 Manicoré Brazil
23 G3 Manicouagan Can.
23 G3 Manicouagan r. Can.
23 G3 Manicouagan, Réservoir resr Can.
116 D4 Manifold, Cape c. Qld. Austr.
109 Manihiki atoll Cook Islands Pac. Oc.
84 E4 Manikpur India
94 B3 Manila Phil.
24 E3 Manila U.S.A.
115 H4 Manildra Austr.
115 J3 Manilla Austr.
113 F2 Maningrida Austr.
Manipur see Imphal
85 H4 Manipur div. India
67 M5 Manisa Turkey
81 L5 Manīsht Kūh mt. Iran
56 A4 Man, Isle of terr. Europe
30 D3 Manistee U.S.A.
30 E3 Manistee r. U.S.A.
30 D3 Manistique U.S.A.
30 E2 Manistique Lake l. U.S.A.
22 B2 Manitoba div. Can.
21 K4 Manitoba, Lake l. Can.
21 H4 Manito L. l. Can.
21 K5 Manitou Can.
32 E3 Manitou Beach U.S.A.
22 B3 Manitou Falls Can.
30 D2 Manitou Island i. U.S.A.
28 C2 Manitou Islands is U.S.A.
31 G3 Manitou, Lake l. Can.
31 F3 Manitoulin I. i. Can.
31 G3 Manitowaning Can.
22 D4 Manitowik Lake l. Can.
30 D3 Manitowoc U.S.A.
31 K2 Maniwaki Can.
45 B3 Manizales Col.
103 E6 Manja Madag.
105 K2 Manjacaze Moz.
81 M3 Manjil Iran
112 C6 Manjimup Austr.
26 E2 Mankato U.S.A.
105 J3 Mankayane Swaziland
100 B4 Mankono Côte d'Ivoire
115 J4 Manly Austr.
84 C5 Manmad India
114 C4 Mannahill Austr.
83 E9 Mannar Sri Lanka
83 E9 Mannar, Gulf of g. India/Sri Lanka
62 D6 Mannheim Ger.
60 A4 Mannin Bay b. Rep. of Ireland
20 F3 Manning Can.
29 D5 Manning U.S.A.
59 J6 Manningtree U.K.
66 C4 Mannu, Capo pt Sardinia Italy
114 C5 Mannum Austr.
93 J7 Manokwari Indon.
102 C4 Manono Zaire
95 A3 Manoron Myanmar
64 G5 Manosque France
111 J2 Manra i. Kiribati
84 C3 Mânsa India
103 C5 Mansa Zambia

100 A3 Mansa Konko The Gambia
84 C2 Mansehra Pak.
18 Mansel I. i. Can.
115 G6 Mansfield Austr.
59 F4 Mansfield U.K.
27 E5 Mansfield LA U.S.A.
32 B4 Mansfield OH U.S.A.
32 E4 Mansfield PA U.S.A.
43 H6 Manso r. Brazil
20 E3 Manson Creek Can.
81 M6 Manşūrī Iran
80 E3 Mansurlu Turkey
42 B4 Manta Ecuador
42 B4 Manta, B. de b. Ecuador
94 A4 Mantalingajan, Mount mt. Phil.
34 B3 Manteca Italy
45 C3 Mantecal Venez.
29 F5 Manteo U.S.A.
64 E2 Mantes-la-Jolie France
35 G2 Manti U.S.A.
46 D3 Mantiqueira, Serra da mts Brazil
30 E3 Manton U.S.A.
66 D2 Mantova Italy
55 T6 Mäntsälä Fin.
55 T5 Mänttä Fin.
Mantua see Mantova
116 B5 Mantuan Downs Austr.
68 H3 Manturovo Rus. Fed.
55 U6 Mäntyharju Fin.
54 U3 Mäntyjärvi Fin.
108 Manua Islands is American Samoa Pac. Oc.
35 H4 Manuelito U.S.A.
47 F2 Manuel J. Cobo Arg.
46 E1 Manuel Vitorino Brazil
43 H5 Manuelzinho Brazil
93 G7 Manui i. Indon.
94 B4 Manukan Phil.
117 E2 Manukau N.Z.
117 E2 Manukau Harbour in. N.Z.
94 A4 Manuk Manka i. Phil.
114 C4 Manunda watercourse Austr.
42 D6 Manu, Parque Nacional nat. park Peru
110 E2 Manus I. i. P.N.G.
105 F2 Manyana Botswana
69 G6 Manych-Gudilo, Ozero l. Rus. Fed.
35 H3 Many Farms U.S.A.
102 D4 Manyoni Tanz.
116 D5 Many Peaks Austr.
80 D6 Manzala, Bahra el l. Egypt
65 E3 Manzanares Spain
37 J4 Manzanillo Cuba
36 D5 Manzanillo Mex.
87 L2 Manzhouli China
105 J3 Manzini Swaziland
101 D3 Mao Chad
Maó see Mahón
88 B4 Maocifan China
88 C2 Maojiachuan China
105 G3 Maokeng S. Africa
93 K7 Maoke, Pegunungan mts Indon.
88 B2 Maomao Shan mt. China
89 D6 Maoming China
89 Ma On Shan h. Hong Kong China
103 D6 Mapai Moz.
84 E3 Mapam Yumco l. China
93 G7 Mapane Indon.
105 F5 Maphodi S. Africa
94 A5 Mapin i. Phil.
103 D6 Mapinhane Moz.
45 D3 Mapire Venez.
30 E4 Maple r. U.S.A.
21 H5 Maple Creek Can.
105 G4 Mapoteng Lesotho
93 L7 Maprik P.N.G.
43 G4 Mapuera r. Brazil
105 K2 Mapulanguene Moz.
105 K2 Maputo div. Moz.
105 K3 Maputo r. Moz.
103 D6 Maputo Moz.
105 G4 Maputsoe Lesotho
81 H6 Maqar an Na'am w. Iraq
88 B3 Maqu China
85 F3 Maquan He r. China
102 B4 Maquela do Zombo Angola
47 C4 Maquinchao r. Arg.
47 C4 Maquinchao Arg.
30 B4 Maquoketa U.S.A.
30 B4 Maquoketa r. U.S.A.
21 H1 Mara r. Can.
85 E5 Mära India
105 H1 Mara S. Africa
45 C2 Mara Venez.
42 E4 Maraã Brazil
43 J5 Maraba Brazil
116 C4 Maraboon, L. resr Austr.
45 C2 Maracaibo Venez.
45 C2 Maracaibo, Lago de l. Venez.
43 H3 Maracá, Ilha de i. Brazil
46 A3 Maracaju Brazil
46 A3 Maracajú, Serra de h. Brazil
46 E1 Maracás, Chapada de reg. Brazil
45 D2 Maracay Venez.
101 D2 Marädah Libya
100 C3 Maradi Niger
81 L3 Maragheh Iran
46 E1 Maragogipe Brazil
94 B3 Maragondon Phil.
45 D4 Marahuaca, Co mt. Venez.
43 J4 Marajó, Baía de est. Brazil

43 J3 Marajó, Ilha de i. Brazil
102 D3 Maralal Kenya
84 C2 Marala Weir barrage Pak.
81 J1 Maralik Armenia
112 F6 Maralinga Austr.
111 G2 Maramasike i. Solomon Is.
94 C5 Marampit i. Indon.
81 K4 Marana Iraq
35 G5 Marana U.S.A.
81 K2 Marand Iran
95 B4 Marang Malaysia
95 A3 Marang Myanmar
46 C1 Maranhão r. Brazil
116 C6 Maranoa r. Austr.
42 D4 Marañón r. Peru
105 L2 Marão Moz.
65 C2 Marão mt. Port.
45 D4 Marari r. Brazil
117 A6 Mararoa r. N.Z.
30 D1 Marathon Can.
29 D7 Marathon FL U.S.A.
27 C6 Marathon TX U.S.A.
46 E1 Maraú Brazil
45 D4 Marauiá r. Brazil
94 C4 Marawi Phil.
81 M1 Märäzä Azer.
65 D4 Marbella Spain
112 C4 Marble Bar Austr.
35 G3 Marble Canyon gorge U.S.A.
35 G3 Marble Canyon U.S.A.
105 H2 Marble Hall S. Africa
33 H4 Marblehead U.S.A.
21 L2 Marble I. i. Can.
105 J5 Marburg S. Africa
62 D5 Marburg an der Lahn Ger.
32 E5 Marburg, Lake l. U.S.A.
62 H7 Marcali Hungary
59 H5 March U.K.
114 C4 Marchant Hill h. Austr.
61 D4 Marche-en-Famenne Belgium
65 D4 Marchena Spain
42 Marchena, Isla i. Galapagos Is Ecuador
47 D1 Mar Chiquita, L. l. Arg.
62 G6 Marchtrenk Austria
29 D7 Marco U.S.A.
22 E2 Marcopeet Islands is Can.
47 D2 Marcos Juárez Arg.
33 G2 Marcy, Mt mt. U.S.A.
84 C2 Mardan Pak.
47 F3 Mar del Plata Arg.
81 H3 Mardin Turkey
111 J2 Maré i. New Caledonia
116 C4 Mareeba Austr.
57 C3 Maree, Loch l. U.K.
30 A5 Marengo IA U.S.A.
30 C5 Marengo IL U.S.A.
66 E6 Marettimo, Isola i. Sicily Italy
68 J3 Marevo Rus. Fed.
27 B6 Marfa U.S.A.
85 F2 Margai Caka salt l. China
114 B2 Margaret watercourse Austr.
112 C6 Margaret River Austr.
45 E2 Margarita, Isla de i. Venez.
59 J6 Margate Austr.
105 J5 Margate S. Africa
59 J6 Margate U.K.
79 L1 Margilan Uzbek.
79 J3 Margo, Dasht-i des. Afgh.
94 B5 Margosatubig Phil.
61 D4 Margraten Neth.
30 E1 Margrethe, Lake l. U.S.A.
20 E4 Marguerite Can.
119 B2 Marguerite Bay b. Ant.
85 G3 Margyang China
81 L5 Marhaj Khalīl Iraq
81 J3 Marhan D. h. Iraq
69 E6 Marhanets' Ukr.
44 C2 María Elena Chile
113 G2 Maria I. i. N.T. Austr.
115 H9 Maria I. i. Tas. Austr.
47 E3 María Ignacia Arg.
109 Maria, Îles is Fr. Polynesia Pac. Oc.
116 C3 Marian Austr.
14 E4 Marianas Ridge sea feature Pac. Oc.
14 E5 Marianas Tr. sea feature Pac. Oc.
85 H4 Mariani India
20 F2 Marian Lake l. Can.
27 C5 Marianna AR U.S.A.
29 C6 Marianna FL U.S.A.
62 F6 Mariánské Lázně Czech Rep.
36 C4 Marías, Islas is Mex.
37 H7 Mariato, Pta pt Panama
117 D1 Marie van Diemen, Cape c. N.Z.
66 F1 Maribor Slovenia
35 F5 Maricopa AZ U.S.A.
34 C4 Maricopa CA U.S.A.
35 F5 Maricopa Mts mts U.S.A.
101 E4 Maridi watercourse Sudan
119 A4 Marie Byrd Land reg. Ant.
37 M5 Marie Galante i. Guadeloupe
55 Q6 Mariehamn Fin.
46 B1 Mariembero r. Brazil
103 B6 Mariental Namibia
55 N7 Mariestad Sweden

29 C5 Marietta GA U.S.A.
32 C5 Marietta OH U.S.A.
64 G5 Marignane France
76 K4 Mariinsk Rus. Fed.
55 S9 Marijampolė Lith.
46 C3 Marília Brazil
27 C7 Marín Mex.
65 B1 Marín Spain
66 G5 Marina di Gioiosa Ionica Italy
68 D4 Mar"ina Horka Belarus
94 B3 Marinduque i. Phil.
30 D3 Marinette U.S.A.
46 B3 Maringá Brazil
65 B3 Marinha Grande Port.
28 B4 Marion IL U.S.A.
30 E5 Marion IN U.S.A.
33 K2 Marion ME U.S.A.
32 B4 Marion OH U.S.A.
29 E5 Marion SC U.S.A.
32 C6 Marion VA U.S.A.
29 C5 Marion, L. l. U.S.A.
116 E2 Marion Reef rf Coral Sea Is Terr.
45 D3 Maripa Venez.
34 C3 Mariposa U.S.A.
44 D2 Mariscal Estigarribia Para.
64 H4 Maritime Alps mts France/Italy
67 L3 Maritsa r. Bulg.
68 J3 Mari-Turek Rus. Fed.
69 F6 Mariupol' Ukr.
81 L4 Marīvān Iran
68 J3 Mariy El, Respublika div. Rus. Fed.
82 J5 Marka Somalia
82 J5 Markam China
81 K2 Märkän Iran
55 N8 Markaryd Sweden
31 G3 Markdale Can.
61 D4 Marken i. Neth.
105 H1 Marken S. Africa
61 D2 Markermeer l. Neth.
59 G5 Market Deeping U.K.
59 E5 Market Drayton U.K.
59 G5 Market Harborough U.K.
60 E3 Markethill U.K.
58 G4 Market Weighton U.K.
77 N3 Markha r. Rus. Fed.
31 H4 Markham Can.
69 F5 Markivka Ukr.
77 T3 Markovo Rus. Fed.
69 H5 Marks Rus. Fed.
62 D6 Marktheidenfeld Ger.
62 E7 Marktoberdorf Ger.
30 B6 Mark Twain Lake l. U.S.A.
61 F3 Marl Ger.
113 F5 Marla Austr.
116 C4 Marlborough Qld. Austr.
33 H4 Marlborough U.S.A.
59 F6 Marlborough Downs h. U.K.
27 D6 Marlin U.S.A.
32 C5 Marlinton U.S.A.
115 H6 Marlo Austr.
64 E4 Marmande France
Marmara Denizi sea see Marmara, Sea of
80 B2 Marmara Gölü l. Turkey
80 B1 Marmara, Sea of sea Turkey
80 B3 Marmaris Turkey
26 C2 Marmarth U.S.A.
32 C5 Marmet U.S.A.
22 B4 Marmion L. l. Can.
66 D1 Marmolada mt. Italy
64 F2 Marne-la-Vallée France
81 K1 Marneuli Georgia
114 E6 Marnoo Austr.
103 E5 Maroantsetra Madag.
103 E5 Maromokotro mt. Madag.
103 D5 Marondera Zimbabwe
43 H2 Maroni r. Fr. Guiana
115 K2 Maroochydore Austr.
109 Marotiri is. Tubuai Is. Pac. Oc.
101 D3 Maroua Cameroon
103 E5 Marovoay Madag.
81 H4 Marqādah Syria
88 A3 Mar Qu r. China
105 G4 Marquard S. Africa
109 Marquesas Islands is Fr. Polynesia Pac. Oc.
29 D7 Marquesas Keys is U.S.A.
30 D2 Marquette U.S.A.
109 Marquises, Îles is Fr. Polynesia Pac. Oc.
114 C4 Marra Austr.
115 G3 Marra r. Austr.
100 B1 Marrakech Morocco
Marrakesh see Marrakech
105 L2 Marrangua, Lagoa l. Moz.
101 E3 Marra Plateau plat. Sudan
115 G5 Marrar Austr.
115 F8 Marrawah Austr.
114 C2 Marree Austr.
27 F6 Marrero U.S.A.
103 D5 Marromeu Moz.
103 D5 Marrupa Moz.
78 C4 Marsa Alam Egypt
101 D1 Marsa al Burayqah Libya
102 D3 Marsabit Kenya
66 E6 Marsala Sicily Italy
78 B3 Marsa Matrûh Egypt
61 C2 Marsdiep chan. Neth.
115 G4 Marsden Austr.
64 G5 Marseille France

30 C5 Marseilles U.S.A.
46 D3 Mar, Serra do mts Brazil
54 D4 Marsfjället mt. Sweden
21 H4 Marshall Can.
27 E5 Marshall AR U.S.A.
28 C4 Marshall IL U.S.A.
30 E4 Marshall MI U.S.A.
26 E2 Marshall MN U.S.A.
26 E4 Marshall MO U.S.A.
27 E5 Marshall TX U.S.A.
115 G7 Marshall B. b. Austr.
26 E3 Marshalltown U.S.A.
30 B3 Marshfield U.S.A.
29 E7 Marsh Harbour Bahamas
33 K1 Mars Hill U.S.A.
27 F6 Marsh Island i. U.S.A.
20 C2 Marsh Lake l. Can.
81 M3 Marshūn Iran
24 D3 Marsing U.S.A.
55 P7 Märsta Sweden
85 F4 Marsyangdi r. Nepal
95 A1 Martaban Myanmar
83 J7 Martaban, Gulf of g. Myanmar
92 E7 Martapura Indon.
92 E7 Martapura Indon.
31 H2 Marten River Can.
21 H4 Martensville Can.
33 H4 Martha's Vineyard i. U.S.A.
62 C3 Martigny Switz.
63 J6 Martin Slovakia
26 C3 Martin SD U.S.A.
29 B4 Martin TN U.S.A.
35 E5 Martinez Lake U.S.A.
37 M6 Martinique terr. Caribbean
29 C5 Martin, L. l. U.S.A.
119 A3 Martin Pen. pen. Ant.
32 D4 Martinsburg PA U.S.A.
32 E5 Martinsburg WV U.S.A.
32 C4 Martins Ferry U.S.A.
32 D6 Martinsville U.S.A.
12 H7 Martin Vas, Ilhas is Atlantic Ocean
117 E4 Marton N.Z.
65 G2 Martorell Spain
65 E4 Martos Spain
76 G4 Martuk Kazak.
81 K1 Martuni Armenia
90 D6 Marugame Japan
117 D5 Maruia r. N.Z.
43 L6 Maruim Brazil
69 G7 Maruchkhi Ugheltekhili pass Georgia/Rus. Fed.
115 H5 Marulan Austr.
64 F3 Marvejols France
35 G2 Marvine, Mt mt. U.S.A.
21 G4 Marwayne Can.
116 E6 Mary r. Austr.
79 J2 Mary Turkm.
116 C5 Maryborough Qld. Austr.
114 E6 Maryborough Vic. Austr.
104 E4 Marydale S. Africa
68 J4 Mar"yevka Rus. Fed.
21 H2 Mary Frances Lake l. Can.
33 G3 Maryland div. U.S.A.
58 D3 Maryport U.K.
23 J3 Mary's Harbour Can.
23 K4 Marystown Can.
35 F2 Marysvale U.S.A.
23 G4 Marysville Can.
34 B2 Marysville CA U.S.A.
26 D4 Marysville KS U.S.A.
32 B4 Marysville OH U.S.A.
116 A2 Maryvale Austr.
26 E3 Maryville U.S.A.
102 D4 Masaka Uganda
105 G5 Masakhane S. Africa
81 M2 Masallı Azer.
93 G7 Masamba Indon.
87 N4 Masan S. Korea
33 J1 Masardis U.S.A.
103 D5 Masasi Tanz.
42 F7 Masavi Bol.
94 B3 Masbate Phil.
94 B4 Masbate i. Phil.
100 C1 Mascara Alg.
13 Mascarene Basin sea feature Indian Ocean
13 J4 Mascarene Ridge sea feature Indian Ocean
33 G2 Mascouche Can.
105 G4 Maseru Lesotho
105 H4 Mashai Lesotho
89 C6 Masha China
84 D2 Masherbrum mt. Pak.
79 H2 Mashhad Iran
84 C4 Mashi r. Pak.
90 H2 Mashike Japan
81 L2 Mashīrān Iran
90 K2 Mashū-ko l. Japan
54 S2 Masi Norway
105 G5 Masibambane S. Africa
105 G4 Masilo S. Africa
102 D3 Masindi Uganda
94 A3 Masinloc Phil.
104 E5 Masinyusane S. Africa
79 H5 Maşīrah i. Oman
79 H6 Maşīrah, Gulf of b. Oman
81 K1 Masis Armenia
81 M6 Masjed Soleymān Iran
80 E3 Maskanah Syria
60 B4 Mask, Lough l. Rep. of Ireland
103 F5 Masoala, Tanjona c. Madag.
30 E4 Mason MI U.S.A.
34 C2 Mason NV U.S.A.
27 D6 Mason TX U.S.A.
117 A7 Mason Bay b. N.Z.
26 E3 Mason City IA U.S.A.

30 C5 Mason City IL U.S.A.
32 D5 Masontown U.S.A.
Masqaṭ see Muscat
66 D2 Massa Italy
33 G3 Massachusetts div. U.S.A.
33 H3 Massachusetts Bay b. U.S.A.
35 H1 Massadona U.S.A.
66 H4 Massafra Italy
101 D3 Massakory Chad
66 D3 Massa Marittima Italy
103 D6 Massangena Moz.
103 B4 Massango Angola
102 D2 Massawa Eritrea
33 G2 Massawippi, Lac l. Can.
33 F2 Massena U.S.A.
20 C4 Masset Can.
31 F2 Massey Can.
64 F4 Massif Central mts France
32 C4 Massillon U.S.A.
100 B3 Massina Mali
103 D6 Massina Moz.
103 D6 Massingir Moz.
105 K1 Massingir, Barragem de resr Moz.
105 K2 Massintonto r. Moz./S. Africa
31 K3 Masson Can.
81 M1 Maştağa Azer.
117 E4 Masterton N.Z.
67 M5 Masticho, Akra pt Greece
29 E7 Mastic Point Bahamas
84 C1 Mastuj Pak.
79 K4 Mastung Pak.
68 C4 Masty Belarus
90 C6 Masuda Japan
81 M3 Masuleh Iran
103 D6 Masvingo Zimbabwe
80 F4 Maşyāf Syria
31 G2 Matachewan Can.
25 F6 Matachic Mex.
45 C3 Matacuni r. Venez.
102 B4 Matadi Zaire
37 H6 Matagalpa Nic.
22 E4 Matagami Can.
22 E4 Matagami, Lac l. Can.
27 D6 Matagorda I. i. U.S.A.
95 C5 Matak i. Indon.
117 F3 Matakana Island i. N.Z.
103 B5 Matala Angola
100 A3 Matam Senegal
36 D3 Matamoros Coahuila Mex.
36 E3 Matamoros Tamaulipas Mex.
94 B5 Matanal Point pt Phil.
103 D4 Matandu r. Tanz.
23 G4 Matane Can.
84 B2 Matanui Pak.
37 H4 Matanzas Cuba
Matapan, Cape pt see Tainaro, Akra
23 G4 Matapédia r. Can.
47 B2 Mataquito r. Chile
83 F9 Matara Sri Lanka
92 F8 Mataram Indon.
42 D7 Matarani Peru
112 F2 Mataranka Austr.
65 H2 Mataró Spain
105 H5 Matatiele S. Africa
117 B7 Mataura N.Z.
117 B7 Mataura r. N.Z.
45 D3 Mataveni r. Col.
117 F3 Matawai N.Z.
42 E7 Mategua Bol.
36 D4 Matehuala Mex.
103 D5 Matemanga Tanz.
66 G4 Matera Italy
66 C6 Mateur Tunisia
22 D4 Matheson Can.
27 D6 Mathis U.S.A.
114 F4 Mathoura Austr.
84 D4 Mathura India
94 C5 Mati Phil.
85 H4 Matiali India
89 Matianxu China
84 B4 Matiari Pak.
36 E5 Matías Romero Mex.
23 G3 Matimekosh Can.
31 F2 Matinenda Lake l. Can.
33 J3 Matinicus I. i. U.S.A.
85 G4 Matla r. India
105 G1 Matlabas r. S. Africa
84 B4 Matli Pak.
59 F4 Matlock U.K.
45 D3 Mato, Co mt. Venez.
46 A1 Mato Grosso div. Brazil
42 G7 Mato Grosso Brazil
46 B3 Mato Grosso do Sul div. Brazil
40 Mato Grosso, Planalto do plat. Brazil
105 K2 Matola Moz.
65 B2 Matosinhos Port.
79 H5 Maţraḥ Oman
104 C6 Matroosberg mt. S. Africa
90 D6 Matsue Japan
90 H3 Matsumae Japan
91 F5 Matsumoto Japan
91 F6 Matsusaka Japan
89 F5 Matsu Tao i. Taiwan
90 B7 Matsuura Japan
90 D7 Matsuyama Japan
22 D4 Mattagami r. Can.
31 H2 Mattawa Can.
33 J2 Mattawamkeag U.S.A.
62 C7 Matterhorn mt. Italy/Switz.
34 C2 Matterhorn mt. U.S.A.
111 H4 Matthew i. New Caledonia
45 E3 Matthews Ridge Guyana

37 K4 Matthew Town Bahamas
91 F5 Mattö Japan
28 B4 Mattoon U.S.A.
111 H3 Matuku i. Fiji
45 E2 Maturín Venez.
94 C5 Matutuang i. Indon.
105 G4 Matwabeng S. Africa
84 E4 Mau Uttar Pradesh India
85 E4 Mau Uttar Pradesh India
85 E4 Mau Aimma India
61 B4 Maubeuge France
64 E5 Maubourguet France
57 D5 Mauchline U.K.
119 C5 Maudheimvidda mts Ant.
43 G4 Maués Brazil
85 E4 Mauganj India
93 L2 Maug Islands is N. Mariana Is
34 □2 Maui i. U.S.A.
109 Mauke i. Cook Islands Pac. Oc.
47 B2 Maule r. Chile
47 B2 Maule div. Chile
47 B4 Maullín Chile
60 B3 Maumakeogh h. Rep. of Ireland
32 B4 Maumee r. U.S.A.
32 B4 Maumee U.S.A.
31 F5 Maumee Bay b. U.S.A.
93 G8 Maumere Indon.
60 B4 Maumturk Mts h. Rep. of Ireland
103 C5 Maun Botswana
34 □2 Mauna Kea volc. U.S.A.
34 □2 Mauna Loa volc. U.S.A.
34 □1 Maunalua B. b. U.S.A.
105 G1 Maunatlala Botswana
117 E2 Maungaturoto N.Z.
85 H5 Maungdaw Myanmar
95 A2 Maungmagan Is is Myanmar
114 B5 Maupertuis B. b. Austr.
112 F5 Maurice, L. salt flat Austr.
61 D3 Maurik Neth.
96 Mauritania country Africa
96 Mauritius country Africa
30 B4 Mauston U.S.A.
45 E2 Mavaca r. Venez.
103 C5 Mavinga Angola
105 G5 Mavuya S. Africa
84 D3 Mawana India
102 B4 Mawanga Zaire
89 D4 Ma Wang Dui China
95 A3 Mawdaung Pass pass Myanmar/Thai.
117 G3 Mawhal Pt pt N.Z.
83 H6 Mawlaik Myanmar
119 D4 Mawson Australia Base Ant.
119 D4 Mawson Escarpment escarpment Ant.
119 B6 Mawson Pen. pen. Ant.
95 A3 Maw Taung mt Myanmar
26 C2 Max U.S.A.
66 C2 Maxia, Punta mt. Sardinia Italy
30 D5 Maxinkuckee, Lake l. U.S.A.
54 S5 Maxmo Fin.
31 F2 Maxton U.S.A.
34 A2 Maxwell U.S.A.
77 P3 Maya r. Rus. Fed.
37 K4 Mayaguana i. Bahamas
37 L5 Mayagüez Puerto Rico
100 C3 Mayahi Niger
102 B4 Mayama Congo
79 H2 Mayamey Iran
36 G5 Maya Mountains mts Belize/Guatemala
88 B3 Mayan China
89 C5 Mayang China
91 G4 Maya-san mt. Japan
57 D5 Maybole U.K.
81 K4 Maydān Iraq
84 B2 Maydā Shahr Afgh.
115 G2 Maydena Austr.
61 F4 Mayen Ger.
64 D2 Mayenne r. France
64 D2 Mayenne France
35 F4 Mayer U.S.A.
20 F4 Mayerthorpe Can.
117 C5 Mayfield N.Z.
28 B4 Mayfield U.S.A.
25 F5 Mayhill U.S.A.
57 F4 May, Isle of i. U.K.
69 G6 Maykop Rus. Fed.
83 J6 Maymyo Myanmar
86 F1 Mayna Rus. Fed.
31 J3 Maynooth Can.
20 B2 Mayo Can.
94 C5 Mayo Bay b. Phil.
47 E2 Mayo, 25 de Buenos Aires Arg.
47 C3 Mayo, 25 de La Pampa Arg.
102 B4 Mayoko Congo
20 B2 Mayo Lake l. Can.
94 B3 Mayon volc. Phil.
47 D3 Mayor Buratovich Arg.
117 F2 Mayor I. i. N.Z.
44 D1 Mayor Pablo Lagerenza Para.
94 B2 Mayraira Point pt Phil.
87 N1 Mayskiy Rus. Fed.
32 B5 Maysville U.S.A.
102 B4 Mayumba Gabon
85 L3 Mayum La pass China
31 F4 Mayville MI U.S.A.
26 D2 Mayville ND U.S.A.
32 D3 Mayville NY U.S.A.
30 C4 Mayville WV U.S.A.
26 C3 Maywood U.S.A.

47 D3 Maza Arg.
68 F3 Maza Rus. Fed.
103 C5 Mazabuka Zambia
43 H4 Mazagão Brazil
61 C5 Mazagran France
64 F5 Mazamet France
84 D1 Mazar China
66 E6 Mazara del Vallo Sicily Italy
79 K2 Mazār-e Sharīf Afgh.
45 E3 Mazaruni r. Guyana
36 F6 Mazatenango Guatemala
36 C4 Mazatlán Mex.
35 G4 Mazatzal Peak summit U.S.A.
55 S8 Mažeikiai Lith.
81 G2 Mazgirt Turkey
55 S8 Mazirbe Latvia
102 D4 Mazomora Tanz.
81 M3 Mazr'eh Iran
81 M5 Māzū Iran
103 C6 Mazunga Zimbabwe
69 D4 Mazyr Belarus
105 J3 Mbabane Swaziland
100 B4 Mbahiakro Côte d'Ivoire
102 B3 Mbaïki C.A.R.
103 D4 Mbala Zambia
102 D3 Mbale Uganda
100 D4 Mbalmayo Cameroon
102 B4 Mbamba Zaire
100 C4 Mbanga Cameroon
102 B4 M'banza Congo Angola
102 D4 Mbarara Uganda
102 C3 Mbari r. C.A.R.
100 D4 Mbengwi Cameroon
103 D4 Mbeya Tanz.
103 D5 Mbinga Tanz.
103 D6 Mbizi Zimbabwe
102 B3 Mbomo Congo
100 D4 Mbouda Cameroon
100 A3 Mbour Senegal
100 A3 Mbout Maur.
103 D4 Mbozi Tanz.
102 C4 Mbuji-Mayi Zaire
102 D4 Mbulu Tanz.
102 D4 Mbuyuni Tanz.
103 D4 Mchinga Tanz.
105 G6 Mdantsane S. Africa
66 B6 M'Daourouch Alg.
27 C4 Meade U.S.A.
35 E3 Mead, Lake l. U.S.A.
21 H4 Meadow Lake Can.
21 H4 Meadow Lake Provincial Park res. Can.
35 E3 Meadow Valley Wash r. U.S.A.
32 C4 Meadville U.S.A.
31 G3 Meaford Can.
90 K2 Meaken-dake volc. Japan
57 A2 Mealasta Island i. U.K.
65 B2 Mealhada Port.
57 D4 Meall a'Bhuiridh mt. U.K.
23 J3 Mealy Mountains mts Can.
115 H1 Meandarra Austr.
20 H1 Meander River Can.
94 C5 Meares i. Indon.
64 F2 Meaux France
102 B4 Mebridege r. Angola
78 D5 Mecca S. Arabia
33 H2 Mechanic Falls U.S.A.
32 B4 Mechanicsburg U.S.A.
30 B5 Mechanicsville U.S.A.
61 C3 Mechelen Belgium
61 D4 Mechelen Neth.
100 B1 Mecheria Alg.
61 E4 Mechernich Ger.
80 E1 Mecitözü Turkey
61 F4 Meckenheim Ger.
62 E3 Mecklenburger Bucht b. Ger.
103 D5 Mecula Moz.
65 C2 Meda Port.
92 B6 Medan Indon.
47 D3 Médanos Arg.
44 K2 Medanosa, Pta pt Arg.
33 K2 Meddybemps L. l. U.S.A.
65 H4 Médéa Alg.
45 B3 Medellín Col.
59 F4 Meden r. U.K.
100 D1 Medenine Tunisia
100 A3 Mederdra Maur.
24 B3 Medford OR U.S.A.
30 B3 Medford WI U.S.A.
33 F5 Medford Farms U.S.A.
67 N2 Medgidia Romania
81 L4 Medhīkhan Iran
30 B5 Media U.S.A.
47 C2 Media Luna Arg.
63 M7 Mediaş Romania
24 C2 Medical Lake U.S.A.
24 F3 Medicine Bow U.S.A.
24 F3 Medicine Bow Mts mts U.S.A.
24 F3 Medicine Bow Peak summit U.S.A.
21 G4 Medicine Hat Can.
27 C4 Medicine Lodge U.S.A.
46 E2 Medina Brazil
78 D5 Medina S. Arabia
32 D3 Medina NY U.S.A.
32 C4 Medina OH U.S.A.
65 E2 Medinaceli Spain
65 D2 Medina del Campo Spain
65 D2 Medina de Rioseco Spain
85 H5 Medinīpur India
52 Mediterranean Sea sea Africa/Europe
66 B6 Medjerda, Monts de la mts Alg.
76 H2 Mednogorsk Rus. Fed.
14 G2 Mednyy, Ostrov i. Rus. Fed.

64 D4 Médoc reg. France
68 H3 Medvedevo Rus. Fed.
69 H5 Medveditsa r. Rus. Fed.
66 F2 Medvednica mts Croatia
77 S2 Medvezh'i, O-va is Rus. Fed.
87 P2 Medvezh'ya, Gora mt. China/Rus. Fed.
68 E2 Medvezh'yegorsk Rus. Fed.
59 H6 Medway r. U.K.
112 C5 Meekatharra Austr.
35 H1 Meeker U.S.A.
34 B2 Meeks Bay U.S.A.
23 J4 Meelpaeg Res. resr Can.
61 E3 Meerlo Neth.
84 D3 Meerut India
24 E2 Meeteetse U.S.A.
102 D3 Mēga Eth.
85 G4 Meghalaya div. India
85 F5 Meghāsani mt. India
85 G5 Meghna r. Bangl.
81 L2 Meghri Armenia
80 C3 Megisti i. Greece
54 U1 Mehamn Norway
112 C4 Meharry, Mt mt. Austr.
84 D5 Mehekar India
85 G5 Meherpur Bangl.
32 E6 Meherrin r. U.S.A.
109 Méhétia i. Society Islands Pac. Oc.
81 L2 Mehrābān Iran
81 L5 Mehrān Iraq
84 B2 Mehtar Lām Afgh.
46 C2 Meia Ponte r. Brazil
101 D4 Meiganga Cameroon
89 B4 Meigu China
89 E5 Mei Jiang r. China
57 D5 Meikle Millyea h. U.K.
83 J6 Meiktila Myanmar
62 E5 Meiningen Ger.
104 E6 Meiringspoort pass S. Africa
89 B4 Meishan China
62 F5 Meißen Ger.
89 C5 Meitan China
88 C3 Mei Xian China
89 C5 Meizhou China
84 D1 Mej r. India
44 C3 Mejicana mt. Arg.
44 B2 Mejillones Chile
102 D2 Mek'elē Eth.
100 A3 Mékhé Senegal
84 B3 Mekhtar Pak.
100 C7 Meknassy Tunisia
100 B1 Meknès Morocco
95 C3 Mekong r. Asia
82 K6 Mekong r. China
95 C3 Mekong, Mouths of the est. Vietnam
92 C6 Melaka Malaysia
14 G6 Melanesia is Pac. Oc.
94 A5 Melaut r. Malaysia
29 D6 Melbourne U.S.A.
57 □ Melby U.K.
62 D3 Meldorf Ger.
31 F3 Meldrum Bay Can.
80 E2 Melendiz Dağı mt. Turkey
68 G4 Melenki Rus. Fed.
23 F2 Mélèzes, Rivière aux r. Can.
101 D3 Mélfi Chad
66 F4 Melfi Italy
21 J4 Melfort Can.
54 M5 Melhus Norway
65 C1 Melide Spain
100 B1 Melilla Spain
47 E2 Melincué Arg.
47 B2 Melipilla Chile
61 B3 Meliskerke Neth.
21 J5 Melita Can.
69 E6 Melitopol' Ukr.
62 G6 Melk Austria
105 H1 Melkrivier S. Africa
59 E6 Melksham U.K.
54 T3 Mellakoski Fin.
54 Q5 Mellansel Sweden
30 B2 Mellen U.S.A.
55 N7 Mellerud Sweden
105 J4 Melmoth S. Africa
47 F2 Melo Uru.
114 C4 Melrose Austr.
57 F5 Melrose U.K.
94 A5 Melta, Mt mt. Malaysia
59 G5 Melton Mowbray U.K.
64 F2 Melun France
21 J4 Melville Can.
113 G2 Melville Bay b. Austr.
113 H2 Melville, C. c. Austr.
94 A5 Melville, C. c. Phil.
18 Melville I. i. Can.
112 F2 Melville Island i. Austr.
23 J3 Melville, Lake l. Can.
18 Melville Peninsula pen. Can.
60 C3 Melvin, Lough l. Rep. of Ireland/U.K.
77 T3 Melyuveyem Rus. Fed.
93 K7 Mêmar Co salt l. China
93 K7 Memberamo r. Indon.
93 F8 Membrolo Indon.
105 H3 Memel S. Africa
62 E7 Memmingen Ger.
92 C5 Mempawah Indon.
80 C7 Memphis Egypt
30 A5 Memphis MO U.S.A.
29 B5 Memphis TN U.S.A.
27 C5 Memphis TX U.S.A.
33 G2 Memphrémagog, Lac l. Can.
90 J2 Memuro-dake mt. Japan

69 E5 Mena Ukr.
27 E5 Mena U.S.A.
100 C3 Ménaka Mali
Mènam Khong r. see Mekong
27 D6 Menard U.S.A.
30 C3 Menasha U.S.A.
64 F4 Mende France
81 M3 Mendejīn Iran
20 C3 Mendenhall Glacier gl. U.S.A.
102 D3 Mendī Eth.
110 E2 Mendi P.N.G.
59 E6 Mendip Hills h. U.K.
34 A2 Mendocino U.S.A.
24 A3 Mendocino, C. c. U.S.A.
15 K3 Mendocino Seascarp sea feature Pac. Oc.
30 D4 Mendon U.S.A.
115 H3 Mendooran Austr.
34 B3 Mendota CA U.S.A.
30 C4 Mendota IL U.S.A.
30 C4 Mendota, Lake l. U.S.A.
47 C2 Mendoza Arg.
47 C2 Mendoza div. Arg.
47 C2 Mendoza r. Arg.
45 C2 Mene de Mauroa Venez.
45 C2 Mene Grande Venez.
67 M5 Menemen Turkey
88 E3 Mengcheng China
80 D1 Mengen Turkey
92 D7 Menggala Indon.
88 F3 Meng Shan mts China
88 B6 Mengyin China
89 B6 Mengzi China
23 G3 Menihek Can.
23 G3 Menihek Lakes lakes Can.
114 E4 Menindee Austr.
114 E4 Menindee Lake l. Austr.
114 C5 Meningie Austr.
81 M4 Menjān Iran
77 O3 Menkere Rus. Fed.
64 F2 Mennecy France
30 D3 Menominee r. U.S.A.
30 D3 Menominee U.S.A.
30 C4 Menomonee Falls U.S.A.
30 B3 Menomonie U.S.A.
103 B5 Menongue Angola
65 J2 Menorca i. Spain
94 A6 Mensalong Indon.
92 B7 Mentawai, Kepulauan is Indon.
95 B5 Mentekab Malaysia
35 H4 Mentmore U.S.A.
92 D7 Mentok Indon.
64 H5 Menton France
61 D5 Menuchenet Belgium
100 C1 Menzel Bourguiba Tunisia
66 D6 Menzel Temime Tunisia
112 D5 Menzies Austr.
119 D4 Menzies, Mt mt. Ant.
61 E2 Meppel Neth.
62 C4 Meppen Ger.
105 K1 Mepuze Moz.
105 H1 Meqheleng S. Africa
68 G3 Mera r. Rus. Fed.
66 D1 Merano Italy
45 E3 Merari, Sa. mt. Brazil
104 F1 Meratswe r. Botswana
93 L8 Merauke Indon.
114 E5 Merbein Austr.
34 B3 Merced U.S.A.
47 B1 Mercedario, Cerro mt. Arg.
47 E2 Mercedes Buenos Aires Arg.
44 E3 Mercedes Corrientes Arg.
47 D2 Mercedes San Luis Arg.
47 E2 Mercedes Uru.
32 A4 Mercer OH U.S.A.
30 B2 Mercer WV U.S.A.
20 F4 Mercoal Can.
117 E2 Mercury Islands is N.Z.
59 E6 Mere U.K.
33 H3 Meredith U.S.A.
27 C5 Meredith, Lake l. U.S.A.
27 C5 Meredith Nat. Recreation Area, Lake res. U.S.A.
30 B6 Meredosia U.S.A.
69 E5 Merefa Ukr.
101 E3 Merga Oasis oasis Sudan
95 A2 Mergui Myanmar
95 A3 Mergui Archipelago is Myanmar
114 D5 Meribah Austr.
67 M4 Meriç r. Greece/Turkey
36 G4 Mérida Mex.
65 C3 Mérida Spain
45 C2 Mérida Venez.
45 C2 Mérida, Cordillera de mts Venez.
33 G4 Meriden U.S.A.
34 B2 Meridian CA U.S.A.
27 F5 Meridian MS U.S.A.
64 D4 Mérignac France
54 T4 Merijärvi Fin.
55 R6 Merikarvia Fin.
115 H6 Merimbula Austr.
116 C3 Merinda Austr.
114 D5 Meringur Austr.
116 B5 Merivale r. Austr.
95 □ Merlimau, P. i. Sing.
101 F3 Merowe Sudan
112 C6 Merredin Austr.
57 D5 Merrick h. U.K.
31 K3 Merrickville Can.

30 C3 Merrill U.S.A.
30 D5 Merrillville U.S.A.
26 C3 Merriman U.S.A.
20 E4 Merritt Can.
29 D6 Merritt Island U.S.A.
115 J4 Merriwa Austr.
115 H3 Merrygoen Austr.
102 E2 Mersa Fatma Eritrea
61 E5 Mersch Lux.
59 E4 Mersey est. U.K.
Mersin see İçel
92 C6 Mersing Malaysia
55 S8 Mērsrags Latvia
84 C4 Merta India
59 D6 Merthyr Tydfil U.K.
102 D3 Merti Kenya
65 C3 Mértola Port.
102 D4 Meru volc. Tanz.
104 D6 Merweville S. Africa
80 E1 Merzifon Turkey
62 C6 Merzig Ger.
119 B2 Merz Pen. pen. Ant.
35 G5 Mesa U.S.A.
30 A2 Mesabi Range h. U.S.A.
35 H3 Mesa Verde Nat. Park nat. park U.S.A.
45 B4 Mesay r. Col.
54 P4 Meselefors Sweden
22 F3 Mesgouez L. l. Can.
68 J2 Meshchura Rus. Fed.
Meshed see Mashhad
69 G5 Meshkovskaya Rus. Fed.
30 E3 Mesick U.S.A.
67 K4 Mesimeri Greece
67 J5 Mesolongi Greece
81 J4 Mesopotamia reg. Iraq
35 E3 Mesquite NV U.S.A.
27 D5 Mesquite TX U.S.A.
35 E4 Mesquite Lake l. U.S.A.
103 D5 Messalo r. Moz.
66 F5 Messina Sicily Italy
105 J1 Messina S. Africa
66 F5 Messina, Stretta di str. Italy
31 J2 Messines Can.
67 K6 Messini Greece
67 K6 Messiniakos Kolpos b. Greece
67 L5 Meston, Akra pt Greece
66 E2 Mestre Italy
80 F1 Mesudiye Turkey
45 C3 Meta r. Col./Venez.
31 J2 Metagama Can.
27 F6 Metairie U.S.A.
30 C5 Metamora U.S.A.
44 C3 Metán Arg.
116 C5 Meteor Creek r. Austr.
12 H9 Meteor Depth depth Atlantic Ocean
33 H3 Methuen U.S.A.
57 E4 Methven U.K.
66 G3 Metković Croatia
20 C3 Metlakatla U.S.A.
103 D5 Metoro Moz.
92 B7 Metro Indon.
28 B4 Metropolis U.S.A.
34 C4 Mettler U.S.A.
102 D3 Metu Eth.
64 H2 Metz France
64 G2 Meuse r. Belgium/France
59 □ Mevagissey U.K.
88 B3 Mêwa China
27 D6 Mexia U.S.A.
36 A2 Mexicali Mex.
35 H3 Mexican Hat U.S.A.
25 F6 Mexicanos, L. de los l. Mex.
35 H2 Mexican Water U.S.A.
16 Mexico country Central America
36 E4 México Mex.
33 H2 Mexico ME U.S.A.
26 E4 Mexico MO U.S.A.
33 E3 Mexico NY U.S.A.
18 Mexico, Gulf of g. Mex./U.S.A.
79 J2 Meymaneh Afgh.
81 L5 Meymeh Iran
67 K3 Mezdra Bulg.
76 F3 Mezen' Rus. Fed.
64 G4 Mézenc, Mont mt France
68 J2 Mezhdurechensk Rus. Fed.
86 E1 Mezhdurechensk Rus. Fed.
76 G2 Mezhdusharskiy, O. i. Rus. Fed.
63 K7 Mezőtúr Hungary
36 C4 Mezquital r. Mex.
55 U8 Mežvidi Latvia
103 D5 Mfuwe Zambia
105 J3 Mhlume Swaziland
84 C5 Mhow India
85 H5 Mi r. Myanmar
36 E5 Miahuatlán Mex.
65 D3 Miajadas Spain
35 F5 Miami AZ U.S.A.
29 D7 Miami FL U.S.A.
27 E4 Miami OK U.S.A.
29 D7 Miami Beach U.S.A.
81 M6 Mīān Āb Iran
81 L3 Miandowāb Iran
103 E5 Miandrivazo Madag.
81 L3 Mīāneh Iran
94 C5 Miangas i. Phil.
89 B4 Mianning China
84 B2 Mianwali Pak.
88 C3 Mian Xian China
89 D4 Mianyang Hubei China
88 B3 Mianyang Sichuan China
88 B4 Mianzhu China

88 F2 Miao Dao i. China
88 F2 Miaodao Qundao is China
89 F5 Miaoli Taiwan
103 E5 Miarinarivo Madag.
76 H4 Miass Rus. Fed.
35 H4 Mica Mt mt. U.S.A.
88 C3 Micang Shan mts China
63 K6 Michalovce Slovakia
21 H3 Michel Can.
30 C2 Michigamme Lake l. U.S.A.
30 C2 Michigamme Reservoir resr U.S.A.
30 D2 Michigan div. U.S.A.
30 D5 Michigan City U.S.A.
30 E2 Michigan, Lake l. U.S.A.
30 E2 Michipicoten Bay b. Can.
30 E1 Michipicoten I. i. Can.
30 E1 Michipicoten River Can.
67 M3 Michurin Bulg.
68 G4 Michurinsk Rus. Fed.
37 H6 Mico r. Nic.
14 E5 Micronesia is Pac. Oc.
106 Micronesia, Federated States of country Pac. Oc.
95 C5 Midai i. Indon.
12 F4 Mid-Atlantic Ridge sea feature Atlantic Ocean
104 C6 Middelberg Pass pass S. Africa
61 B3 Middelburg Neth.
104 F5 Middelburg Eastern Cape S. Africa
105 H2 Middelburg Mpumalanga S. Africa
62 L9 Middelfart Denmark
61 C3 Middelharnis Neth.
104 D5 Middelpos S. Africa
105 G2 Middelwit S. Africa
24 C3 Middle Alkali Lake l. U.S.A.
14 N5 Middle America Trench sea feature Pac. Oc.
92 A4 Middle Andaman i. Andaman and Nicobar Is
33 H4 Middleburg U.S.A.
32 E5 Middleburgh U.S.A.
33 G2 Middlebury U.S.A.
117 C6 Middlemarch N.Z.
116 C4 Middlemount Austr.
32 B6 Middlesboro U.S.A.
58 F3 Middlesbrough U.K.
34 A3 Middletown CA U.S.A.
33 G4 Middletown CT U.S.A.
33 F5 Middletown DE U.S.A.
33 F4 Middletown NY U.S.A.
32 A5 Middletown OH U.S.A.
30 E2 Middleville U.S.A.
59 □ Midhurst U.K.
13 K4 Mid-Indian Basin sea feature Indian Ocean
13 K6 Mid-Indian Ridge sea feature Indian Ocean
31 H3 Midland Can.
31 F4 Midland MI U.S.A.
27 C5 Midland TX U.S.A.
60 C6 Midleton Rep. of Ireland
90 C7 Midori-k. r. Japan
14 F4 Mid-Pacific Mountains sea feature Pac. Oc.
54 □ Miðvágur Faroe Is
Midway see Thamarīt
14 H4 Midway Islands is Pac. Oc.
24 F3 Midwest U.S.A.
27 D5 Midwest City U.S.A.
61 D2 Midwoud Neth.
81 H3 Midyat Turkey
57 □ Mid Yell U.K.
67 K3 Midzhur mt. Bulg./Yugo.
91 F6 Mie Japan
90 C7 Mie Japan
54 U6 Miehikkälä Fin.
54 T3 Miekojärvi l. Fin.
63 K5 Mielec Pol.
103 D4 Miembwe Tanz.
115 G8 Miena Austr.
54 U2 Mieraslompolo Fin.
63 N4 Miercurea-Ciuc Romania
65 D1 Mieres Spain
102 E3 Mī'ēso Eth.
32 E4 Mifflinburg U.S.A.
32 E4 Mifflintown U.S.A.
88 C3 Migang Shan mt. China
105 F3 Migdol S. Africa
85 H3 Miging India
80 C2 Mihaliççik Turkey
90 D6 Mihara Japan
91 H5 Mihara-yama volc. Japan
91 F2 Mijares r. Spain
61 D2 Mijdrecht Neth.
31 F3 Mikado U.S.A.
90 H2 Mikasa Japan
63 N4 Mikashevichy Belarus
91 F6 Mikawa-wan b. Japan
68 F4 Mikhaylov Rus. Fed.
69 G5 Mikhaylovka Rus. Fed.
86 C1 Mikhaylovskiy Rus. Fed.
90 E6 Miki Japan
85 H4 Mikir Hills mts India
55 U6 Mikkeli Fin.
55 U6 Mikkelin mlk Fin.
20 L3 Mikkwa r. Can.
102 D4 Mikumi Tanz.
91 G5 Mikuni-sammyaku mts Japan
91 G6 Mikura-jima i. Japan
26 E2 Milaca U.S.A.
83 D9 Miladhunmadulu Atoll atoll Maldives
66 C2 Milan Italy

29 B5 Milan U.S.A.
114 C5 Milang Austr.
103 D5 Milange Moz.
Milano *see* Milan
80 A3 Milas Turkey
66 F5 Milazzo *Sicily* Italy
26 D2 Milbank U.S.A.
59 H5 Mildenhall U.K.
114 E5 Mildura Austr.
89 B5 Mile China
116 D6 Miles Austr.
24 F2 Miles City U.S.A.
60 C5 Milestone Rep. of Ireland
66 F4 Miletto, Monte *mt.* Italy
60 D2 Milford Rep. of Ireland
34 B1 Milford *CA* U.S.A.
33 G4 Milford *CT* U.S.A.
33 F5 Milford *DE* U.S.A.
30 D5 Milford *IL* U.S.A.
33 H3 Milford *MA* U.S.A.
33 J2 Milford *ME* U.S.A.
33 H3 Milford *NH* U.S.A.
33 F3 Milford *NY* U.S.A.
35 F2 Milford *UT* U.S.A.
59 B6 Milford Haven U.K.
117 A6 Milford Sound *in.* N.Z.
117 A6 Milford Sound N.Z.
65 H4 Miliana Alg.
24 F1 Milk *r.* Can./U.S.A.
77 R4 Mil'kovo Rus. Fed.
116 A1 Millaa Millaa Austr.
65 F2 Millárs *r.* Spain
64 F4 Millau France
34 B1 Mill Creek *r.* U.S.A.
29 D5 Milledgeville *GA* U.S.A.
30 C5 Milledgeville *IL* U.S.A.
26 E2 Mille Lacs L. *l.* U.S.A.
22 B4 Mille Lacs, Lac des *l.* Can.
114 A2 Miller *watercourse* Austr.
26 D2 Miller U.S.A.
30 B3 Miller Dam Flowage *resr* U.S.A.
31 G3 Miller Lake Can.
69 G5 Millerovo Rus. Fed.
35 G6 Miller Peak *summit* U.S.A.
32 C4 Millersburg *OH* U.S.A.
32 E4 Millersburg *PA* U.S.A.
114 B3 Millers Creek Austr.
32 E6 Millers Tavern U.S.A.
34 C3 Millerton Lake *l.* U.S.A.
57 C5 Milleur Point *pt* U.K.
119 C6 Mill I. *i.* Ant.
114 D6 Millicent Austr.
31 F4 Millington *MI* U.S.A.
29 B5 Millington *TN* U.S.A.
33 J2 Millinocket U.S.A.
115 J1 Millmerran Austr.
58 D3 Millom U.K.
57 D5 Millport U.K.
33 F5 Millsboro U.S.A.
20 F2 Mills Lake *l.* Can.
32 C5 Millstone U.S.A.
23 G4 Milltown Can.
60 B5 Milltown Malbay Rep. of Ireland
33 K1 Millville Can.
33 F5 Millville U.S.A.
33 J2 Milo U.S.A.
67 L6 Milos *i.* Greece
68 F4 Miloslavskoye Rus. Fed.
114 D2 Milparinka Austr.
32 E4 Milroy U.S.A.
31 H4 Milton Can.
117 B7 Milton N.Z.
29 C6 Milton *FL* U.S.A.
30 A5 Milton *IA* U.S.A.
32 E4 Milton *PA* U.S.A.
33 G2 Milton *VT* U.S.A.
24 C2 Milton-Freewater U.S.A.
59 G5 Milton Keynes U.K.
32 C4 Milton, Lake *l.* U.S.A.
89 D4 Miluo China
30 D4 Milwaukee U.S.A.
69 G5 Milyutinskaya Rus. Fed.
64 D4 Mimizan France
102 B4 Mimongo Gabon
90 E6 Mimuroyama *mt.* Japan
34 C2 Mina U.S.A.
79 H4 Mīnāb Iran
93 G6 Minahassa Peninsula *pen.* Indon.
21 L4 Minaki Can.
90 C7 Minamata Japan
91 F6 Minami Alps National Park *nat. park* Japan
92 C6 Minas Indon.
47 F2 Minas Uru.
81 M7 Mīnā Sa'ūd Kuwait
23 H4 Minas Basin *b.* Can.
47 F1 Minas de Corrales Uru.
46 D2 Minas Gerais *div.* Brazil
46 D2 Minas Novas Brazil
36 F5 Minatitlán Mex.
85 H5 Minbu Myanmar
85 H5 Minbya Myanmar
44 B6 Minchinmávida *volc.* Chile
57 C2 Minch, The *str.* U.K.
66 D2 Mincio *r.* Italy
81 L2 Mincivan Azer.
94 C5 Mindanao *i.* Phil.
114 D5 Mindarie Austr.
100 □ Mindelo Cape Verde
31 H3 Minden Can.
62 D4 Minden Ger.
27 E5 Minden *LA* U.S.A.
34 C2 Minden *NV* U.S.A.
85 H6 Mindon Myanmar
114 E4 Mindona L. *l.* Austr.
94 B3 Mindoro *i.* Phil.
94 A3 Mindoro Strait *str.* Phil.
102 B4 Mindouli Congo
90 C6 Mine Japan
60 D6 Mine Head *hd* Rep. of Ireland
59 D6 Minehead U.K.
46 B2 Mineiros Brazil
27 E5 Mineola U.S.A.
34 B1 Mineral U.S.A.
34 C3 Mineral King U.S.A.
69 G6 Mineral'nyye Vody Rus. Fed.
30 B4 Mineral Point U.S.A.
27 D5 Mineral Wells U.S.A.
35 F2 Minersville U.S.A.
66 G4 Minervino Murge Italy
85 E1 Minfeng China
103 C5 Minga Zaire
81 L1 Mingäçevir Azer.
81 L1 Mingäçevir Su Anbarı *resr* Azer.
23 H3 Mingan Can.
114 D4 Mingary Austr.
116 B2 Mingela Austr.
112 C5 Mingenew Austr.
88 E3 Minggang China
65 F3 Minglanilla Spain
103 D5 Mingoyo Tanz.
89 B4 Ming-shan China
87 N2 Mingshui China
57 A4 Mingulay *i.* U.K.
89 E5 Mingxi China
88 B2 Minhe China
89 F5 Minhou China
83 D9 Minicoy *i.* India
112 B4 Minilya Austr.
23 H3 Minipi Lake *l.* Can.
21 J4 Minitonas Can.
89 F5 Min Jiang *r.* China
88 B4 Min Jiang *r.* China
88 A2 Minle China
100 C4 Minna Nigeria
55 O5 Minne Sweden
26 E2 Minneapolis U.S.A.
21 K4 Minnedosa Can.
30 A2 Minnesota *div.* U.S.A.
114 A4 Minnipa Austr.
22 B4 Minnitaki L. *l.* Can.
65 B2 Miño *r.* Port./Spain
91 G6 Minobu Japan
30 C3 Minocqua U.S.A.
30 B2 Minong U.S.A.
30 C5 Minonk U.S.A.
Minorca *i. see* Menorca
26 C1 Minot U.S.A.
88 B2 Minqin China
89 F5 Minqing China
88 B3 Min Shan *mts* China
85 H4 Minsin Myanmar
68 C4 Minsk Belarus
63 K4 Mińsk Mazowiecki Pol.
59 E5 Minsterley U.K.
84 C1 Mintaka Pass *pass* China/Jammu and Kashmir
23 G4 Minto Can.
22 F2 Minto, Lac *l.* Can.
25 F4 Minturn U.S.A.
80 C6 Minûf Egypt
86 F1 Minusinsk Rus. Fed.
85 J3 Minutang India
89 B5 Min Xian China
114 E6 Minyip Austr.
31 E3 Mio U.S.A.
22 E4 Miquelon Can.
23 J4 Miquelon *i.* N. America
45 A4 Mira *r.* Col.
33 F2 Mirabel Can.
46 D2 Mirabela Brazil
43 J5 Miracema do Norte Brazil
43 J5 Mirador, Parque Nacional de *nat. park* Brazil
45 B4 Miraflores Col.
46 D2 Miralta Brazil
47 F3 Miramar Arg.
64 G5 Miramas France
23 G4 Miramichi *r.* Can.
67 L7 Mirampelou, Kolpos *b.* Greece
46 A3 Miranda *r.* Brazil
46 A3 Miranda Brazil
34 A1 Miranda U.S.A.
65 E1 Miranda de Ebro Spain
65 C2 Mirandela Port.
66 D2 Mirandola Italy
46 B3 Mirandópolis Brazil
81 H5 Mirā', Wādī al *watercourse* Iraq/S. Arabia
79 G6 Mirbāṭ Oman
64 E5 Mirepoix France
92 E6 Miri Malaysia
47 G2 Mirim, Lagoa *l.* Brazil
119 D5 Mirnyy *Rus. Fed. Base* Ant.
68 G2 Mirnyy Rus. Fed.
77 N3 Mirnyy Rus. Fed.
21 J3 Mirond L. *l.* Can.
84 C2 Mirpur Pak.
84 B4 Mirpur Batoro Pak.
84 B4 Mirpur Khas Pak.
84 A4 Mirpur Sakro Pak.
20 G4 Mirror Can.
89 □ Mirs Bay *b. Hong Kong* China
116 B3 Mirtna Austr.
67 K6 Mirtoö Pelagos *sea* Greece
85 E4 Mirzapur India
91 H6 Misaki Japan
90 D7 Misaki Japan
91 H3 Misawa Japan
23 H4 Miscou I. *i.* Can.
84 C1 Misgar Pak.
30 D5 Mishawaka U.S.A.
30 E1 Mishibishu Lake *l.* Can.
91 G6 Mishima Japan
90 C6 Mi-shima *i.* Japan
85 H3 Mishmi Hills *mts* India
110 F3 Misima I. *i.* P.N.G.
37 H6 Miskitos, Cayos *atolls* Nic.
63 K6 Miskolc Hungary
93 J7 Misoöl *i.* Indon.
30 B2 Misquah Hills *h.* U.S.A.
101 D1 Miṣrātah Libya
84 E4 Misrikh India
31 E1 Missanabie Can.
22 D3 Missinaibi *r.* Can.
31 F1 Missinaibi Lake *l.* Can.
21 J3 Missinipe Can.
26 C3 Mission U.S.A.
116 B1 Mission Beach Austr.
20 E5 Mission City Can.
22 D3 Missisa L. *l.* Can.
31 F2 Mississagi *r.* Can.
31 H4 Mississauga Can.
30 E5 Mississinewa Lake *l.* U.S.A.
31 J3 Mississippi *r.* Can.
27 F5 Mississippi *div.* U.S.A.
27 F6 Mississippi *r.* U.S.A.
27 F6 Mississippi Delta *delta* U.S.A.
24 D2 Missoula U.S.A.
26 C2 Missouri *r.* U.S.A.
30 A6 Missouri *div.* U.S.A.
26 E3 Missouri Valley U.S.A.
116 B4 Mistake Cr. *r.* Austr.
23 F4 Mistassini Can.
23 F4 Mistassini *r.* Can.
22 F3 Mistassini, L. *l.* Can.
23 H2 Mistastin Lake *l.* Can.
62 H6 Mistelbach Austria
20 C3 Misty Fjords National Monument *res.* U.S.A.
90 C7 Misumi Japan
90 C6 Misumi Japan
115 K2 Mitchell *r. N.S.W.* Austr.
116 B6 Mitchell *Qld.* Austr.
113 H3 Mitchell *r. Qld.* Austr.
115 G6 Mitchell *r. Vic.* Austr.
31 G4 Mitchell Can.
26 D3 Mitchell U.S.A.
30 E3 Mitchell, Lake *l.* U.S.A.
29 D5 Mitchell, Mt *mt.* U.S.A.
60 C5 Mitchelstown Rep. of Ireland
80 C6 Mît Ghamr Egypt
84 B3 Mithankot Pak.
84 B4 Mithi Pak.
84 B4 Mithrani Canal *canal* Pak.
67 M5 Mithymna Greece
20 C3 Mitkof I. *i.* U.S.A.
91 H5 Mito Japan
90 C6 Mitō Japan
103 D4 Mitole Tanz.
117 E4 Mitre *mt.* N.Z.
111 H3 Mitre Island *i.* Solomon Is
90 J2 Mitsuishi Japan
91 G5 Mitsuke Japan
90 B6 Mitsushima Japan
115 J5 Mittagong Austr.
115 G6 Mitta Mitta Austr.
62 D4 Mittelland kanal *canal* Ger.
45 C4 Mitú Col.
45 C4 Mituas Col.
103 C5 Mitumba, Chaîne des *mts* Zaire
102 C4 Mitumba, Monts *mts* Zaire
102 B3 Mitzic Gabon
91 G6 Miura Japan
91 F6 Miya-gawa *r.* Japan
91 H4 Miyagi Japan
81 G4 Miyah, Wādī el *watercourse* Syria
90 C7 Miyaji Japan
91 G6 Miyake-jima *i.* Japan
91 H4 Miyako Japan
90 C8 Miyakonojō Japan
88 B4 Miyaluo China
84 B5 Miyāni India
90 C7 Miyazaki Japan
90 C8 Miyazaki Japan
91 E6 Miyazu Japan
91 E6 Miyazu-wan *b.* Japan
89 B5 Miyi China
90 D6 Miyoshi Japan
88 E1 Miyun China
88 E1 Miyun Sk. *resr* China
102 D3 Mīzan Teferī Eth.
101 D1 Mizdah Libya
60 B6 Mizen Head *hd* Rep. of Ireland
69 B5 Mizhhir"ya Ukr.
88 D2 Mizhi China
85 H5 Mizoram *div.* India
91 H4 Mizusawa Japan
55 O7 Mjölby Sweden
102 D4 Mkata Tanz.
102 D4 Mkomazi Tanz.
103 C5 Mkushi Zambia
62 G5 Mladá Boleslav Czech Rep.
67 J2 Mladenovac Yugo.
63 K4 Mława Pol.
66 G3 Mljet *i.* Croatia
105 G5 Mlungisi S. Africa
63 M5 Mlyniv Ukr.
105 F2 Mmabatho S. Africa
105 G1 Mmamabula Botswana
105 F2 Mmathethe Botswana
55 J6 Mo Norway
35 H2 Moab U.S.A.
113 H2 Moa I. *i.* Austr.
111 H3 Moala *i.* Fiji
105 K2 Moamba Moz.
114 D2 Moanba, Lake *salt flat* Austr.
35 E3 Moapa U.S.A.
60 D4 Moate Rep. of Ireland
102 C4 Moba Zaire
91 H6 Mobara Japan
102 C3 Mobayi-Mbongo Zaire
26 E4 Moberly U.S.A.
29 B6 Mobile *AL* U.S.A.
35 F5 Mobile *AZ* U.S.A.
29 B6 Mobile Bay *b.* U.S.A.
26 C2 Mobridge U.S.A.
Mobutu, Lake *l. see* Albert, Lake
43 J4 Mocajuba Brazil
103 E5 Moçambique Moz.
45 D2 Mocapra *r.* Venez.
89 B6 Môc Châu Vietnam
45 D2 Mochirma, Parque Nacional *nat. park* Venez.
103 C6 Mochudi Botswana
103 E5 Mocimboa da Praia Moz.
54 R4 Mockträsk Sweden
45 A4 Mocoa Col.
46 C3 Mococa Brazil
103 D5 Mocuba Moz.
64 H4 Modane France
84 C5 Modasa India
104 F4 Modder *r.* S. Africa
66 D2 Modena Italy
35 F3 Modena U.S.A.
34 B3 Modesto U.S.A.
115 G7 Moe Austr.
59 D5 Moel Sych *h.* U.K.
54 M6 Moely Norway
54 Q2 Moen Norway
35 G3 Moenkopi U.S.A.
117 C6 Moeraki Pt *pt* N.Z.
57 E5 Moffat U.K.
84 C3 Moga India
Mogadishu *see* Muqdisho
32 C4 Mogadore Reservoir *resr* U.S.A.
105 H1 Mogalakwena *r.* S. Africa
91 G4 Mogami-gawa *r.* Japan
105 H2 Moganyaka S. Africa
46 C3 Mogi-Mirim Brazil
87 L1 Mogocha Rus. Fed.
66 C6 Mogod *mts* Tunisia
105 F2 Mogoditshane Botswana
83 J6 Mogok Myanmar
35 H5 Mogollon Baldy *mt.* U.S.A.
35 H5 Mogollon Mts *mts* U.S.A.
35 G4 Mogollon Rim *plat.* U.S.A.
105 G2 Mogwase S. Africa
67 H2 Mohács Hungary
117 F3 Mohaka *r.* N.Z.
105 G5 Mohale's Hoek Lesotho
21 J5 Mohall U.S.A.
65 G5 Mohammadia Alg.
84 E3 Mohan *r.* India/Nepal
35 E4 Mohave, L. *l.* U.S.A.
35 F5 Mohawk U.S.A.
33 F3 Mohawk *r.* U.S.A.
35 F5 Mohawk Mts *mts* U.S.A.
103 E5 Moheli *i.* Comoros
60 D4 Mohill Rep. of Ireland
35 F4 Mohon Peak *summit* U.S.A.
103 D4 Mohoro Tanz.
27 C7 Mohovano Ranch Mex.
81 M5 Moh Reza Shah Pahlavi *resr* Iran
69 C5 Mohyliv Podil's'kyy Ukr.
55 K7 Moi Norway
105 G1 Moijabana Botswana
105 K2 Moine Moz.
63 N7 Moinești Romania
33 F2 Moira U.S.A.
54 O3 Mo i Rana Norway
85 H4 Moirang India
55 T7 Mõisaküla Estonia
47 E1 Moisés Ville Arg.
23 G3 Moisie Can.
23 G3 Moisie *r.* Can.
64 E4 Moissac France
34 D4 Mojave *r.* U.S.A.
34 C4 Mojave U.S.A.
34 D4 Mojave Desert *des.* U.S.A.
46 C3 Moji das Cruzes Brazil
46 C3 Moji-Guaçu *r.* Brazil
90 C7 Mojikō Japan
91 H5 Mōka Japan
85 F4 Mokāma India
34 □1 Mokapu Pen. *pen.* U.S.A.
117 E3 Mokau N.Z.
117 E3 Mokau *r.* N.Z.
34 B2 Mokelumne *r.* U.S.A.
105 H4 Mokhoabong Pass *pass* Lesotho
105 H4 Mokhotlong Lesotho
66 D7 Moknine Tunisia
117 E1 Mokohinau Is *is* N.Z.
101 D3 Mokolo Cameroon
105 G1 Mokolo *r.* S. Africa
87 N5 Mokp'o S. Korea
68 G4 Moksha *r.* Rus. Fed.
68 H4 Mokshan Rus. Fed.
34 □1 Mokuauia I. *i.* U.S.A.
34 □1 Mokulua Is *is* U.S.A.
65 F3 Molatón *mt.* Spain
Moldavia *country see* Moldova
54 K5 Molde Norway
54 O3 Moldjord Norway
48 Moldova *country* Europe
67 L2 Moldoveanu, Vârful *mt.* Romania
59 D7 Mole *r.* U.K.
100 B4 Mole National Park *nat. park* Ghana
103 C6 Molepolole Botswana
55 T9 Molėtai Lith.
66 G4 Molfetta Italy
65 F2 Molina de Aragón Spain
30 B5 Moline U.S.A.
55 N7 Molkom Sweden
81 M4 Mollā Bodāgh Iran
85 H4 Mol Len *mt.* India
42 D7 Mollendo Peru
55 N8 Mölnlycke Sweden
68 F3 Molochnoye Rus. Fed.
54 X2 Molochnyy Rus. Fed.
119 D4 Molodezhnaya *Rus. Fed. Base* Ant.
68 E3 Molodoy Tud Rus. Fed.
34 □2 Molokai *i.* U.S.A.
15 K4 Molokai Fracture Zone *sea feature* Pac. Oc.
68 J3 Moloma *r.* Rus. Fed.
115 H4 Molong Austr.
104 F2 Molopo *watercourse* Botswana/S. Africa
101 D4 Moloundou Cameroon
21 K4 Molson L. *l.* Can.
93 H7 Moluccas *is* Indon.
93 H6 Molucca Sea *g.* Indon.
103 D5 Moma Moz.
114 E3 Momba Austr.
102 D4 Mombasa Kenya
85 H4 Mombi New India
46 B2 Mombuca, Serra da *h.* Brazil
69 C7 Momchilgrad Bulg.
30 D5 Momence U.S.A.
45 B2 Mompós Col.
55 N9 Møn *i.* Denmark
35 G2 Mona U.S.A.
57 A3 Monach Islands *is* U.K.
57 A3 Monach, Sound of *chan.* U.K.
48 Monaco *country* Europe
57 D3 Monadhliath Mountains *mts* U.K.
60 E3 Monaghan Rep. of Ireland
27 C6 Monahans U.S.A.
37 L5 Mona, I. *i.* Puerto Rico
37 L5 Mona Passage *chan.* Dom. Rep./Puerto Rico
103 E5 Monapo Moz.
20 D4 Monarch Mt. *mt.* Can.
25 F4 Monarch Pass *pass* U.S.A.
57 C3 Monar, Loch *l.* U.K.
20 F4 Monashee Mts *mts* Can.
66 D7 Monastir Tunisia
63 P3 Monastyrshchina Rus. Fed.
69 D5 Monastyryshche Ukr.
90 J2 Monbetsu Japan
90 J1 Monbetsu Japan
66 B2 Moncalieri Italy
65 F2 Moncayo *mt* Spain
54 X3 Monchegorsk Rus. Fed.
62 C5 Mönchengladbach Ger.
65 B4 Monchique Port.
29 E5 Moncks Corner U.S.A.
36 D3 Monclova Mex.
23 H4 Moncton Can.
65 C2 Mondego *r.* Port.
105 J3 Mondlo S. Africa
66 B2 Mondovì Italy
30 B3 Mondovi U.S.A.
66 E4 Mondragone Italy
67 K6 Monemvasia Greece
87 Q2 Moneron, Ostrov *i.* Rus. Fed.
32 D4 Monessen U.S.A.
31 K1 Monet Can.
60 D5 Moneygall Rep. of Ireland
60 E3 Moneymore U.K.
66 E2 Monfalcone Italy
65 C1 Monforte Spain
102 C3 Monga Zaire
89 C6 Móng Cai Vietnam
95 A1 Mong Mau Myanmar
70 Mongolia *country* Asia
84 C2 Mongora Pak.
103 C5 Mongu Zambia
33 J3 Monhegan I. *i.* U.S.A.
57 E5 Moniaive U.K.
34 D2 Monitor Mt *mt.* U.S.A.
34 D2 Monitor Range *mts* U.S.A.
60 C4 Monivea Rep. of Ireland
31 G4 Monkton Can.
85 F3 Mon La *pass* China
59 E6 Monmouth U.K.
30 B5 Monmouth *IL* U.S.A.
33 H2 Monmouth *ME* U.S.A.
20 E4 Monmouth Mt. *mt.* Can.
59 E6 Monnow *r.* U.K.
100 C4 Mono *r.* Togo
34 C3 Mono Lake *l.* U.S.A.
33 H4 Monomoy Pt *pt* U.S.A.
30 D5 Monon U.S.A.
30 B4 Monona U.S.A.
66 G4 Monopoli Italy
32 C5 Monongahela *r.* U.S.A.
65 F2 Monreal del Campo Spain
66 E5 Monreale *Sicily* Italy
27 E5 Monroe *LA* U.S.A.
31 F5 Monroe *MI* U.S.A.
29 D5 Monroe *NC* U.S.A.
33 F4 Monroe *NY* U.S.A.
35 F2 Monroe *UT* U.S.A.
30 C4 Monroe *WV* U.S.A.
30 B6 Monroe City U.S.A.
29 C6 Monroeville U.S.A.
100 A4 Monrovia Liberia
61 B4 Mons Belgium
66 D2 Monselice Italy
103 E5 Montagne d'Ambre, Parc National de la *nat. park* Madag.
104 D6 Montagu S. Africa
30 D4 Montague U.S.A.
119 C1 Montagu I. *i. S. Sandwich Is* Atlantic Ocean
66 F5 Montalto *mt.* Italy
66 G5 Montalto Uffugo Italy
67 K3 Montana Bulg.
24 E2 Montana *div.* U.S.A.
64 F3 Montargis France
64 E4 Montauban France
33 G4 Montauk U.S.A.
33 H4 Montauk Pt *pt* U.S.A.
64 G3 Montbard France
65 G2 Montblanc Spain
64 G4 Montbrison France
64 G3 Montceau-les-Mines France
64 D5 Mont-de-Marsan France
64 F2 Montdidier France
43 H4 Monte Alegre Brazil
46 C1 Monte Alegre de Goiás Brazil
46 D1 Monte Azul Brazil
22 E4 Montebello Can.
66 F6 Montebello Ionico Italy
66 E2 Montebelluna Italy
47 D2 Monte Buey Arg.
64 H5 Monte Carlo Monaco
47 F1 Monte Caseros Arg.
105 G1 Monte Christo S. Africa
47 C2 Monte Comán Arg.
37 K5 Monte Cristi Dom. Rep.
66 D3 Montecristo, Isola di *i.* Italy
37 J5 Montego Bay Jamaica
64 G4 Montélimar France
44 E2 Monte Lindo *r.* Para.
66 F4 Montella Italy
30 C4 Montello U.S.A.
36 E3 Montemorelos Mex.
65 B3 Montemor-o-Novo Port.
67 H3 Montenegro *div.* Yugo.
103 D5 Montepuez Moz.
66 D3 Montepulciano Italy
64 F2 Montereau-faut-Yonne France
34 B3 Monterey *CA* U.S.A.
32 D5 Monterey *VA* U.S.A.
34 B3 Monterey Bay *b.* U.S.A.
45 B2 Montería Col.
42 F7 Montero Bol.
36 D3 Monterrey Mex.
66 F4 Montesano sulla Marcellana Italy
43 L6 Monte Santo Brazil
46 D2 Montes Claros Brazil
66 F3 Montesilvano Italy
66 D3 Montevarchi Italy
47 F2 Montevideo Uru.
26 E2 Montevideo U.S.A.
25 F4 Monte Vista U.S.A.
30 A5 Montezuma U.S.A.
35 G4 Montezuma Castle National Monument *res.* U.S.A.
35 H3 Montezuma Creek U.S.A.
34 D3 Montezuma Peak *summit* U.S.A.
59 D5 Montgomery U.K.
29 C5 Montgomery U.S.A.
62 C7 Monthey Switz.
27 F5 Monticello *AR* U.S.A.
29 D6 Monticello *FL* U.S.A.
30 B4 Monticello *IA* U.S.A.
30 D5 Monticello *IN* U.S.A.
33 K1 Monticello *ME* U.S.A.
30 B5 Monticello *MO* U.S.A.
33 F4 Monticello *NY* U.S.A.
35 H3 Monticello *UT* U.S.A.
30 C4 Monticello *WV* U.S.A.
47 E1 Montiel, Cuchilla de *h.* Arg.
64 E4 Montignac France
65 D4 Montilla Spain
23 G4 Mont Joli Can.
31 K2 Mont-Laurier Can.
23 G4 Mont Louis Can.
64 F3 Montluçon France
23 F4 Montmagny Can.
61 D5 Montmédy France
30 D5 Montmorenci U.S.A.
23 F4 Montmorency Can.
64 E3 Montmorillon France
116 D5 Monto Austr.
24 E3 Montpelier *ID* U.S.A.
30 E5 Montpelier *IN* U.S.A.
32 A4 Montpelier *OH* U.S.A.
33 G2 Montpelier *VT* U.S.A.
64 F5 Montpellier France
22 F4 Montréal Can.
31 G2 Montreal *r.* Can.
31 F2 Montreal *r.* Can.
30 E2 Montreal I. *i.* Can.
21 H4 Montreal L. *l.* Can.
21 H4 Montreal Lake Can.
33 F2 Montréal-Mirabel Can.
30 E2 Montreal River Can.
62 C7 Montreux Switz.
104 D3 Montrose *w.* S. Africa
57 F4 Montrose U.K.
25 F4 Montrose *CO* U.S.A.
31 F4 Montrose *MI* U.S.A.
33 F4 Montrose *PA* U.S.A.
37 M5 Montserrat *terr.* Caribbean
23 G4 Monts, Pte des *pt* Can.
35 G3 Monument Valley *reg.* U.S.A.
83 J6 Monywa Myanmar
66 C2 Monza Italy

103 C5 Monze Zambia
65 G2 Monzón Spain
105 J4 Mooi r. S. Africa
104 B3 Mooifontein Namibia
105 J4 Mooirivier S. Africa
105 G1 Mookane Botswana
114 G1 Moolawatana Austr.
115 H2 Moomin Cr. r. Austr.
114 A3 Moonaree Austr.
115 J3 Moonbi Ra. mts Austr.
115 J1 Moonie Qld. Austr.
115 H2 Moonie r. Austr.
114 B5 Moonta Austr.
112 C6 Moora Austr.
24 F2 Moorcroft U.S.A.
32 D5 Moorefield U.S.A.
112 C5 Moore, Lake salt flat Austr.
29 E7 Moores I. i. Bahamas
33 K2 Moores Mills Can.
57 E5 Moorfoot Hills h. U.K.
26 D2 Moorhead U.S.A.
114 E4 Moornanyah Lake l. Austr.
114 C5 Moorook Austr.
114 F6 Mooroopna Austr.
104 C6 Moorreesburg S. Africa
22 D3 Moose r. Can.
22 D3 Moose Factory Can.
33 J2 Moosehead Lake l. U.S.A.
21 H4 Moose Jaw Can.
21 J4 Moose Lake l. Can.
30 A2 Moose Lake U.S.A.
33 H2 Mooselookmeguntic Lake l. U.S.A.
22 D3 Moose River Can.
21 J4 Moosomin Can.
22 D3 Moosonee Can.
114 E3 Mootwingee Austr.
105 H1 Mopane S. Africa
100 B3 Mopti Mali
84 A2 Moqor Afgh.
42 D7 Moquegua Peru
101 D3 Mora Cameroon
65 E3 Mora Spain
55 O6 Mora Sweden
47 B2 Mora, Cerro mt. Arg./Chile
84 A3 Morad r. Pak.
84 D3 Moradabad India
103 E5 Morafenobe Madag.
103 E5 Moramanga Madag.
30 E3 Moran MI U.S.A.
24 E3 Moran WY U.S.A.
116 C3 Moranbah Austr.
57 C4 Morar, Loch l. U.K.
83 E9 Moratuwa Sri Lanka
62 H6 Morava r. Austria/Slovakia
33 E3 Moravia U.S.A.
116 B3 Moray Downs Austr.
57 E3 Moray Firth est. U.K.
61 F5 Morbach Ger.
66 C7 Morbegno Italy
84 B5 Morbi India
64 D4 Morcenx France
87 M1 Mordaga China
81 K3 Mor Dağı mt. Turkey
21 K5 Morden Can.
114 F7 Mordialloc Austr.
68 H4 Mordoviya, Respublika div. Rus. Fed.
69 G4 Mordovo Rus. Fed.
26 C2 Moreau r. U.S.A.
58 E3 Morecambe U.K.
58 D3 Morecambe Bay b. U.K.
115 H2 Moree Austr.
110 E2 Morehead P.N.G.
32 B5 Morehead U.S.A.
29 E5 Morehead City U.S.A.
84 D4 Morel r. India
More Laptevykh sea see Laptev Sea
36 D5 Morelia Mex.
65 F2 Morella Spain
57 D2 More, Loch l. U.K.
84 D4 Morena India
65 D3 Morena, Sierra mts Spain
35 H5 Morenci AZ U.S.A.
31 E5 Morenci MI U.S.A.
67 L2 Moreni Romania
47 E2 Moreno Arg.
25 E6 Moreno Mex.
34 D5 Moreno Valley U.S.A.
20 F4 Moresby Island i. Can.
104 F1 Moreswe Pan salt pan Botswana
115 K1 Moreton B. b. Austr.
115 K1 Moreton I. i. Austr.
59 F6 Moreton-in-Marsh U.K.
80 D4 Morfou Cyprus
80 D4 Morfou Bay b. Cyprus
114 C5 Morgan Austr.
27 F6 Morgan City U.S.A.
34 B3 Morgan Hill U.S.A.
34 C3 Morgan, Mt mt. U.S.A.
33 F4 Morgantown PA U.S.A.
32 D5 Morgantown WV U.S.A.
105 H3 Morgenzon S. Africa
62 C7 Morges Switz.
85 F4 Morhar r. India
82 H2 Mori China
90 H2 Mori Japan
35 E2 Moriah, Mt mt. U.S.A.
25 F5 Moriarty U.S.A.
115 F2 Moriarty's Ra. h. Austr.
45 C4 Morichal Col.
45 E2 Morichal Largo r. Venez.
105 G4 Morija Lesotho
68 D3 Morino Rus. Fed.
91 H4 Morioka Japan
115 J4 Morisset Austr.
91 F6 Moriyama Japan

91 H3 Moriyoshi Japan
91 H4 Moriyoshi-zan volc. Japan
54 S3 Morjärv Sweden
68 J3 Morki Rus. Fed.
64 C2 Morlaix France
58 F4 Morley U.K.
35 G4 Mormon Lake l. U.S.A.
113 D3 Mornington I. i. Austr.
44 A7 Mornington, I. i. Chile
84 A4 Moro Pak.
110 E2 Morobe P.N.G.
96 Morocco country Africa
30 D5 Morocco U.S.A.
102 D4 Morogoro Tanz.
94 B5 Moro Gulf g. Phil.
105 G4 Morojaneng S. Africa
104 E3 Morokweng S. Africa
103 E6 Morombe Madag.
37 J4 Morón Cuba
86 H2 Mörön Mongolia
103 E6 Morondava Madag.
65 D4 Morón de la Frontera Spain
103 E5 Moroni Comoros
93 H6 Morotai i. Indon.
102 D3 Moroto Uganda
69 G6 Morozovsk Rus. Fed.
31 G4 Morpeth Can.
58 F2 Morpeth U.K.
46 C2 Morrinhos Brazil
21 K5 Morris Can.
30 C5 Morris IL U.S.A.
26 E2 Morris MN U.S.A.
33 F2 Morrisburg Can.
30 C5 Morrison U.S.A.
35 F5 Morristown AZ U.S.A.
33 F4 Morristown NJ U.S.A.
33 F2 Morristown NY U.S.A.
29 C4 Morristown TN U.S.A.
33 F4 Morrisville PA U.S.A.
33 G2 Morrisville VT U.S.A.
34 B4 Morro Bay U.S.A.
45 C2 Morrocoy, Parque Nacional nat. park Venez.
43 H4 Morro Grande h. Brazil
44 B3 Morro, Pta pt Chile
45 B2 Morrosquillo, Golfo de b. Col.
30 D5 Morse Reservoir resr U.S.A.
68 G4 Morshansk Rus. Fed.
68 E2 Morskaya Masel'ga Rus. Fed.
66 C7 Morsott Alg.
64 E2 Mortagne-au-Perche France
64 D3 Mortagne-sur-Sèvre France
59 C6 Mortehoe U.K.
47 E1 Morteros Arg.
Mortes r. see Manso
114 E7 Mortlake U.K.
Mortlock Is is see Tauu
59 C6 Morton U.K.
30 C5 Morton IL U.S.A.
24 B2 Morton WA U.S.A.
115 J5 Morton Nat. Park nat. park Austr.
115 G5 Morundah Austr.
105 G1 Morupule Botswana
115 J5 Moruya Austr.
116 B6 Morven Austr.
57 C4 Morvern reg. U.K.
Morvi see Morbi
115 G7 Morwell Austr.
62 D6 Mosbach Ger.
59 F4 Mosborough U.K.
68 F4 Moscow Rus. Fed.
24 C2 Moscow U.S.A.
119 B6 Mose, C. c. Ant.
61 F4 Mosel r. Ger.
104 E2 Moselebe watercourse Botswana
64 H2 Moselle r. France
24 C2 Moses Lake U.S.A.
34 D1 Moses, Mt mt. U.S.A.
117 C6 Mosgiel N.Z.
104 E3 Moshaweng watercourse S. Africa
102 D4 Moshi Tanz.
30 C3 Mosinee U.S.A.
54 N4 Mosjøen Norway
54 N3 Moskenesøy i. Norway
68 F4 Moskovskaya Oblast' div. Rus. Fed.
Moskva see Moscow
62 H7 Mosonmagyaróvár Hungary
45 A4 Mosquera Col.
25 F5 Mosquero U.S.A.
37 H5 Mosquitia reg. Honduras
46 E1 Mosquito r. Brazil
32 C4 Mosquito Creek Lake l. U.S.A.
37 H7 Mosquitos, Golfo de los b. Panama
21 J2 Mosquitto Lake l. Can.
55 M7 Moss Norway
57 F3 Mossat U.K.
117 B6 Mossburn N.Z.
104 E7 Mossel Bay S. Africa
104 E7 Mossel Bay b. S. Africa
102 B4 Mossendjo Congo
114 F4 Mossgiel Austr.
116 A1 Mossman Austr.
43 L5 Mossoró Brazil
115 J5 Moss Vale Austr.
62 F5 Most Czech Rep.
100 C1 Mostaganem Alg.
66 G3 Mostar Bos.-Herz.
44 F4 Mostardas Brazil
21 G3 Mostoos Hills h. Can.

69 G6 Mostovskoy Rus. Fed.
94 A5 Mostyn Malaysia
81 J3 Mosul Iraq
55 L7 Møsvatnet l. Norway
55 O7 Motala Sweden
45 C2 Motatán r. Venez.
105 K2 Motaze Moz.
105 H2 Motetema S. Africa
84 D4 Moth India
57 E5 Motherwell U.K.
85 F4 Motihari India
65 F3 Motilla del Palancar Spain
117 F2 Motiti I. i. N.Z.
104 E2 Motokwe Botswana
65 E4 Motril Spain
67 K2 Motru Romania
90 G2 Motsuta-misaki pt Japan
36 G4 Motul Mex.
109 Motu One i. Society Islands Pac. Oc.
89 A5 Mouding China
100 A3 Moudjéria Maur.
67 L5 Moudros Greece
55 S6 Mouhijärvi Fin.
102 B4 Mouila Gabon
114 F5 Moulamein r. Austr.
114 F5 Moulamein Austr.
118 B2 Mould Bay Can.
102 B4 Moulèngui Binza Gabon
64 F3 Moulins France
95 A1 Moulmein Myanmar
29 D6 Moultrie U.S.A.
28 B4 Mound City IL U.S.A.
26 E3 Mound City MO U.S.A.
101 D4 Moundou Chad
32 C5 Moundsville U.S.A.
84 C4 Mount Abu India
29 C5 Mountain Brook U.S.A.
32 C6 Mountain City U.S.A.
27 E4 Mountain Grove U.S.A.
27 E4 Mountain Home AR U.S.A.
24 D3 Mountain Home ID U.S.A.
105 F6 Mountain Zebra National Park nat. park S. Africa
32 C6 Mount Airy U.S.A.
117 B6 Mount Aspiring National Park nat. park N.Z.
105 H5 Mount Ayliff S. Africa
26 E3 Mount Ayr U.S.A.
114 C5 Mount Barker S.A. Austr.
112 C6 Mount Barker W.A. Austr.
115 G6 Mount Beauty Austr.
60 C4 Mount Bellew Rep. of Ireland
113 J7 Mount Bogong National Park nat. park Vic. Austr.
115 G6 Mount Buffalo National Park nat. park Austr.
116 A1 Mount Carbine Austr.
33 K1 Mount Carleton Provincial Park res. Can.
35 F3 Mount Carmel Junction U.S.A.
30 C4 Mount Carroll U.S.A.
117 C5 Mount Cook N.Z.
117 C5 Mount Cook National Park nat. park N.Z.
116 B3 Mount Coolon Austr.
103 D5 Mount Darwin Zimbabwe
33 J2 Mount Desert Island i. U.S.A.
114 A1 Mount Dutton Austr.
114 A3 Mount Eba Austr.
115 G9 Mount Field Nat. Park nat. park Austr.
105 H5 Mount Fletcher S. Africa
31 G4 Mount Forest Can.
105 H5 Mount Frere S. Africa
114 D6 Mount Gambier Austr.
116 A1 Mount Garnet Austr.
32 B4 Mount Gilead U.S.A.
110 E2 Mount Hagen P.N.G.
115 F4 Mount Hope N.S.W. Austr.
114 A5 Mount Hope S.A. Austr.
32 C6 Mount Hope U.S.A.
113 G4 Mount Isa Austr.
33 G4 Mount Kisco U.S.A.
116 D1 Mount Larcom Austr.
114 C5 Mount Lofty Range mts Austr.
31 G2 Mount MacDonald Can.
112 C4 Mount Magnet Austr.
114 E4 Mount Manara Austr.
34 B1 Mount Meadows Reservoir resr U.S.A.
60 D4 Mountmellick Rep. of Ireland
116 A1 Mount Molloy Austr.
105 G5 Mount Moorosi Lesotho
116 D4 Mount Morgan Austr.
116 E3 Mount Murchison Austr.
116 D5 Mount Perry Austr.
30 B5 Mount Pleasant IA U.S.A.
30 E4 Mount Pleasant MI U.S.A.
28 C3 Mount Pleasant MI U.S.A.
29 E5 Mount Pleasant SC U.S.A.
27 D5 Mount Pleasant TX U.S.A.
35 G2 Mount Pleasant UT U.S.A.
30 C5 Mount Pulaski U.S.A.
24 B2 Mount Rainier Nat. Park nat. park U.S.A.
20 F4 Mount Robson Prov. Park res. Can.
32 C6 Mount Rogers National Recreation Area res. U.S.A.
59 B7 Mount's Bay b. U.K.
59 F5 Mountsorrel U.K.
30 B6 Mount Sterling IL U.S.A.

32 B5 Mount Sterling KY U.S.A.
32 D5 Mount Storm U.S.A.
116 A2 Mount Surprise Austr.
32 E4 Mount Union U.S.A.
29 B6 Mount Vernon AL U.S.A.
30 B5 Mount Vernon IA U.S.A.
28 B4 Mount Vernon IL U.S.A.
32 A6 Mount Vernon KY U.S.A.
32 B4 Mount Vernon OH U.S.A.
24 B1 Mount Vernon WA U.S.A.
114 A4 Mount Wedge Austr.
115 H8 Mount William National Park nat. park Austr.
116 C5 Moura Austr.
42 F4 Moura Brazil
101 E3 Mourdi, Dépression du depression Chad
116 B1 Mourilyan Harbour Austr.
60 D3 Mourne r. U.K.
60 E3 Mourne Mountains h. U.K.
61 B3 Mouscron Belgium
101 D3 Moussoro Chad
93 G6 Moutong Indon.
100 C2 Mouydir, Mts de plat. Alg.
61 D5 Mouzon France
115 J1 Mowbullan, Mt mt. Austr.
60 C4 Moy r. Rep. of Ireland
102 D3 Moyale Eth.
100 A4 Moyamba Sierra Leone
100 B1 Moyen Atlas mts Morocco
105 G5 Moyeni Lesotho
60 C4 Moyer r. Rep. of Ireland
23 G2 Moyne, Lac Le l. Can.
82 D1 Moyynty Kazak.
96 Mozambique country Africa
103 E5 Mozambique Channel str. Africa
13 G5 Mozambique Ridge sea feature Indian Ocean
69 H7 Mozdok Rus. Fed.
68 F4 Mozhaysk Rus. Fed.
85 H5 Mozo Myanmar
102 C4 Mpala Zaire
102 D4 Mpanda Tanz.
105 J4 Mpolweni S. Africa
103 D4 Mporokoso Zambia
105 H2 Mpumalanga div. S. Africa
105 H5 Mqanduli S. Africa
66 G2 Mrkonjić-Grad Bos.-Herz.
100 D1 M'Saken Tunisia
65 J5 M'Sila Alg.
68 E3 Msta r. Rus. Fed.
68 D4 Mstsislaw Belarus
105 H4 Mt-aux-Sources mt Lesotho
68 F4 Mtsensk Rus. Fed.
105 K4 Mtubatuba S. Africa
105 J4 Mtunzini S. Africa
103 E5 Mtwara Tanz.
102 B4 Muanda Zaire
95 B2 Muang Chainat Thai.
95 A1 Muang Chiang Rai Thai.
89 B6 Muang Hiam Laos
95 B1 Muang Hôngsa Laos
95 B1 Muang Kalasin Thai.
95 C2 Muang Khammouan Laos
95 C2 Muang Không Laos
95 C2 Muang Khôngxédôn Laos
95 B1 Muang Khon Kaen Thai.
89 B6 Muang Khoua Laos
95 A3 Muang Kirirath r. Thai.
95 A1 Muang Lampang Thai.
95 A1 Muang Lamphun Thai.
95 B1 Muang Loei Thai.
95 B1 Muang Lom Sak Thai.
95 A1 Muang Long Thai.
95 A3 Muang Luang r. Thai.
95 C2 Muang Mai Thai.
95 C1 Muang Mok Laos
95 C1 Muang Nakhon Phanom Thai.
95 B2 Muang Nakhon Sawan Thai.
95 B1 Muang Nan Thai.
89 B6 Muang Ngoy Laos
95 C1 Muang Nong Laos
89 A6 Muang Ou Nua Laos
95 C1 Muang Pakxan Laos
95 B1 Muang Phalan Laos
95 A1 Muang Phan Thai.
95 A1 Muang Phayao Thai.
95 B1 Muang Phetchabun Thai.
95 B1 Muang Phiang Laos
95 B1 Muang Phichai Thai.
95 B1 Muang Phichit Thai.
95 C1 Muang Phin Laos
95 B1 Muang Phitsanulok Thai.
95 B1 Muang Phôn-Hông Laos
95 B1 Muang Phrae Thai.
95 B1 Muang Roi Et Thai.
95 C1 Muang Sakon Nakhon Thai.
95 B2 Muang Samut Prakan Thai.
95 B1 Muang Souy Laos
95 B2 Muang Uthai Thani Thai.
89 B6 Muang Va Laos
95 B1 Muang Vangviang Laos
95 B1 Muang Xaignabouri Laos
89 B6 Muang Xay Laos
89 B6 Muang Xon Laos
95 B5 Muar r. Malaysia
92 C6 Muar Malaysia
92 C7 Muaradua Indon.
92 B7 Muarasiberut Indon.

92 C7 Muaratembesi Indon.
85 E4 Mubarakpur India
81 H7 Mubarraz w. S. Arabia
102 D3 Mubende Uganda
101 D3 Mubi Nigeria
45 E4 Mucajaí r. Brazil
45 E4 Mucajaí, Serra do mts Brazil
103 D5 Muchinga Escarpment escarpment Zambia
89 A4 Muchuan China
57 B4 Muck i. U.K.
116 C6 Muckadilla Austr.
57 □ Muckle Roe i. U.K.
45 C3 Muco r. Col.
103 C5 Muconda Angola
45 E5 Mucucuaú r. Brazil
80 E2 Mucur Turkey
46 E2 Mucuri Brazil
46 E2 Mucuri r. Brazil
103 C5 Mucussueje Angola
95 B4 Muda r. Malaysia
87 N3 Mudanjiang China
80 B1 Mudanya Turkey
81 L7 Mudayrah Kuwait
32 C6 Muddlety U.S.A.
54 R3 Muddus National Park nat. park Sweden
35 E3 Muddy Creek r. U.S.A.
35 E3 Muddy Peak summit U.S.A.
115 H4 Mudgee Austr.
84 C3 Mudki India
34 D3 Mud Lake l. U.S.A.
95 A1 Mudon Myanmar
80 C1 Mudurnu Turkey
68 H2 Mud'yuga Rus. Fed.
103 D5 Mueda Moz.
68 H1 Muftyuga Rus. Fed.
103 D5 Mufulira Zambia
103 C5 Mufumbwe Zambia
89 A4 Mufu Shan mts China
33 K2 Mugaguadavic Lake l. Can.
81 M2 Muğan Düzü lowland Azer.
85 F2 Mugarripug China
85 E4 Mughal Sarai India
80 B3 Mughayrā' S. Arabia
90 E7 Mugi Japan
80 B3 Muğla Turkey
85 H2 Mug Qu r. China
85 E3 Mugu Karnali r. Nepal
85 H2 Mugxung China
101 F2 Muhammad Qol Sudan
54 T4 Muhos Fin.
102 C4 Muhulu Zaire
95 C3 Mui Ca Mau c. Vietnam
95 D3 Mui Dinh hd Vietnam
95 D2 Mui Nây pt Vietnam
60 E5 Muine Bheag Rep. of Ireland
57 D4 Muirkirk U.K.
57 B2 Muirneag h. U.K.
57 D3 Muir of Ord U.K.
34 A3 Muir Woods National Monument res. U.S.A.
103 D5 Muite Moz.
69 B5 Mukacheve Ukr.
92 C5 Mukah Malaysia
85 F3 Mukangsar China
90 J2 Mu-kawa r. Japan
95 C1 Mukdahan Thai.
112 C6 Mukinbudin Austr.
92 C7 Mukomuko Indon.
84 C3 Muktsar India
21 H4 Mukutawa r. Can.
30 C4 Mukwonago U.S.A.
84 D5 Mul India
84 A3 Mula r. Pak.
83 D10 Mulaku Atoll atoll Maldives
94 B3 Mulanay Phil.
103 D5 Mulanje, Mt mt Malawi
27 E5 Mulberry U.S.A.
47 B3 Mulchén Chile
62 F3 Mulde r. Ger.
102 D4 Muleba Tanz.
35 H5 Mule Creek NM U.S.A.
24 F3 Mule Creek WY U.S.A.
27 C5 Muleshoe U.S.A.
65 E4 Mulhacén mt Spain
61 E3 Mülheim an der Ruhr Ger.
64 H3 Mulhouse France
89 A5 Muli China
57 C4 Mull i. U.K.
81 M3 Mulla Ali Iran
60 B5 Mullaghareirk Mts h. Rep. of Ireland
115 H3 Mullaley Austr.
115 G3 Mullengudgery Austr.
30 E1 Mullett Lake l. U.S.A.
112 C5 Mullewa Austr.
57 F1 Mull Head hd U.K.
33 F4 Mullica r. U.S.A.
60 D4 Mullingar Rep. of Ireland
115 H4 Mullion Cr. Austr.
57 B4 Mull, Sound of chan. U.K.
103 D5 Mulobezi Zambia
84 D5 Multai India
84 B3 Multan Pak.
55 T5 Multia Fin.
61 A5 Multien reg. France
Mumbai see Bombay
115 H4 Mumbil Austr.
103 C5 Mumbwa Zambia
69 H6 Mumra Rus. Fed.
93 G8 Muna i. Indon.
36 G4 Muna Mex.
77 N3 Muna r. Rus. Fed.

54 C3 Munaðarnes Iceland
90 C7 Munakata Japan
62 E6 München Ger.
45 A4 Munchique, Co mt Col.
20 D3 Muncho Lake Can.
20 D3 Muncho Lake Provincial Park res. Can.
30 E5 Muncie U.S.A.
59 J5 Mundesley U.K.
59 H5 Mundford U.K.
112 F6 Mundrabilla Austr.
116 B5 Mundubbera Austr.
84 C4 Mundwa India
116 B6 Mungallala Austr.
115 G2 Mungallala Cr. r. Austr.
116 A1 Mungana Austr.
84 D4 Mungaoli India
102 C3 Mungbere Zaire
85 E5 Mungeli India
85 F4 Munger India
114 C2 Mungeranie Austr.
95 D5 Mungguresak, Tanjung pt Indon.
115 H2 Mungindi Austr.
Munich see München
43 K4 Munim r. Brazil
30 D2 Munising U.S.A.
46 C3 Muniz Freire Brazil
55 M7 Munkedal Sweden
54 V2 Munkelva Norway
55 N7 Munkfors Sweden
105 H1 Munnik S. Africa
115 H8 Munro, Mt mt Austr.
62 C7 Münsingen Switz.
62 E4 Münster Ger.
61 F3 Münsterland reg. Ger.
23 F3 Muntviel, Lac l. Can.
54 V4 Muojärvi l. Fin.
95 C1 Mương Lam Vietnam
89 B6 Mương Nhie Vietnam
54 S3 Muonio Fin.
54 S2 Muonioälven r. Fin./Sweden
88 F2 Muping China
102 E3 Muqdisho Somalia
81 M1 Müqtädir Azer.
81 J2 Muradiye Turkey
91 G4 Murakami Japan
44 B7 Murallón, Cerro mt Chile
102 C4 Muramvya Burundi
102 D4 Muranga Kenya
68 J3 Murashi Rus. Fed.
81 H2 Murat r. Turkey
80 B2 Murat Dağı mts Turkey
80 A1 Muratlı Turkey
91 H4 Murayama Japan
112 C5 Murchison watercourse W.A. Austr.
114 F6 Murchison Austr.
102 D3 Murchison Falls National Park nat. park Uganda
65 F4 Murcia Spain
65 F4 Murcia div. Spain
26 C3 Murdo U.S.A.
23 G4 Murdochville Can.
91 G5 Mure Japan
103 D5 Murehwa Zimbabwe
67 M7 Mureş r. Romania
64 E5 Muret France
29 C4 Murfreesboro NC U.S.A.
29 C5 Murfreesboro TN U.S.A.
84 B3 Murgha Kibzai Pak.
79 L2 Murghob Tajik.
84 B2 Murgh Pass pass Afgh.
116 D6 Murgon Austr.
85 F5 Muri China
46 D3 Muriaé Brazil
103 C4 Muriege Angola
62 F4 Müritz l. Ger.
54 X2 Murmansk Rus. Fed.
66 C4 Muro, Capo di pt Corsica France
68 G4 Murom Rus. Fed.
90 H2 Muroran Japan
65 B1 Muros Spain
90 E7 Muroto Japan
90 E7 Muroto-zaki pt Japan
30 D5 Murphey Lake, J. C. l. U.S.A.
24 C3 Murphy ID U.S.A.
29 D5 Murphy NC U.S.A.
34 B2 Murphys U.S.A.
115 G2 Murra Murra Austr.
114 D5 Murray r. Austr.
20 E3 Murray r. Can.
28 B4 Murray KY U.S.A.
24 D3 Murray UT U.S.A.
114 C5 Murray Bridge Austr.
29 D5 Murray, L. l. U.S.A.
110 E2 Murray, Lake l. P.N.G.
104 E5 Murraysburg S. Africa
15 L3 Murray Seascarp sea feature Pac. Oc.
114 D5 Murrayville Austr.
115 H5 Murringo Austr.
104 E5 Murrisk reg. Rep. of Ireland
60 B4 Murroogh Rep. of Ireland
115 H5 Murrumbateman Austr.
114 F5 Murrumbidgee r. N.S.W. Austr.
103 D5 Murrupula Moz.
115 J3 Murrurundi Austr.
66 G1 Murska Sobota Slovenia
114 D2 Murteroa, Lake salt flat Austr.
114 E6 Murtoa Austr.
83 E7 Murud India
117 F3 Murupara N.Z.

109 Mururoa atoll Fr. Polynesia Pac. Oc.
84 E5 Murwara India
115 K2 Murwillumbah Austr.
101 D2 Murzūq Libya
62 G7 Mürzzuschlag Austria
81 H2 Muş Turkey
84 B3 Musa Khel Bazar Pak.
67 K3 Musala mt Bulg.
95 A5 Musala i. Indon.
79 H5 Muscat Oman
30 B5 Muscatine U.S.A.
30 B4 Muscoda U.S.A.
33 J3 Muscongus Bay b. U.S.A.
113 H2 Musgrave Austr.
112 F5 Musgrave Ranges mts Austr.
60 C5 Musheramore h. Rep. of Ireland
102 B4 Mushie Zaire
92 D7 Musi r. Indon.
35 F4 Music Mt mt. U.S.A.
35 G2 Musinia Peak summit U.S.A.
20 E2 Muskeg r. Can.
33 H4 Muskeget Channel chan. U.S.A.
30 D4 Muskegon r. U.S.A.
30 D4 Muskegon U.S.A.
32 C5 Muskingum r. U.S.A.
27 E5 Muskogee U.S.A.
31 H3 Muskoka Can.
31 H3 Muskoka, Lake l. Can.
20 E3 Muskwa r. Can.
79 K3 Muslimbagh Pak.
80 F3 Muslimīyah Syria
101 F3 Musmar Sudan
102 D4 Musoma Tanz.
110 E2 Mussau I. i. P.N.G.
57 E5 Musselburgh U.K.
24 E2 Musselshell r. U.S.A.
80 B1 Mustafakemalpaşa Turkey
55 S7 Mustjala Estonia
115 J4 Muswellbrook Austr.
78 B4 Mut Egypt
80 D3 Mut Turkey
46 E1 Mutá, Pta do pt Brazil
103 D5 Mutare Zimbabwe
93 G8 Mutis, G. mt Indon.
114 D4 Mutooroo Austr.
103 D5 Mutorashanga Zimbabwe
90 H3 Mutsu Japan
90 H3 Mutsu-wan b. Japan
116 A4 Muttaburra Austr.
117 B7 Muttonbird Is is N.Z.
117 A7 Muttonbird Islands is N.Z.
60 B5 Mutton Island i. Rep. of Ireland
103 D5 Mutuali Moz.
46 C1 Mutunópolis Brazil
54 U2 Mutusjärvi r. Fin.
54 T3 Muurola Fin.
88 C2 Mu Us Shamo des. China
103 B4 Muxaluando Angola
68 E2 Muyezerskiy Rus. Fed.
102 D4 Muyinga Burundi
102 C4 Muyumba Zaire
82 C2 Muyunkum, Peski des. Kazak.
88 D4 Muyuping China
84 C2 Muzaffarabad Pak.
84 B3 Muzaffargarh Pak.
84 D3 Muzaffarnagar India
85 F4 Muzaffarpur India
105 K1 Muzamane Moz.
20 C4 Muzon, C. c. U.S.A.
84 E2 Muztag mt China
85 F1 Muztag mt China
101 E4 Mvolo Sudan
102 D4 Mvomero Tanz.
103 D5 Mvuma Zimbabwe
Mwali i. see Moheli
102 D4 Mwanza Tanz.
103 C4 Mwanza Zaire
60 B4 Mweelrea h. Rep. of Ireland
102 C4 Mweka Zaire
103 C5 Mwenda Zambia
102 C4 Mwene-Ditu Zaire
103 D6 Mwenezi Zimbabwe
103 C4 Mweru, Lake l. Zaire/Zambia
103 C4 Mwimba Zaire
103 C5 Mwinilunga Zambia
68 C4 Myadzyel Belarus
85 H5 Myaing Myanmar
84 B4 Myājlār India
115 K4 Myall L. l. Austr.
83 J7 Myanaung Myanmar
70 Myanmar country Asia
57 E2 Mybster U.K.
85 H5 Myebon Myanmar
83 J6 Myingyan Myanmar
95 A2 Myinmoletkat mt Myanmar
82 J5 Myitkyina Myanmar
95 A2 Myitta Myanmar
85 H5 Myittha r. Myanmar
69 E6 Mykolayiv Ukr.
67 L6 Mykonos i. Greece
67 L6 Mykonos Greece
76 G3 Myla Rus. Fed.
85 G4 Mymensingh Bangl.
55 S6 Mynämäki Fin.
59 D5 Mynydd Eppynt h. U.K.
59 C6 Mynydd Preseli h. U.K.
85 H5 Myohaung Myanmar
91 G5 Myōkō-san volc. Japan
68 C4 Myory Belarus
54 D5 Mýrdalsjökull ice cap Iceland
54 O2 Myre Norway
54 R4 Myrheden Sweden
69 E5 Myrhorod Ukr.
69 D5 Myronivka Ukr.
29 E5 Myrtle Beach U.S.A.
115 G6 Myrtleford Austr.
24 A3 Myrtle Point U.S.A.
62 G4 Myślibórz Pol.
83 E8 Mysore India
77 U3 Mys Shmidta Rus. Fed.
33 F5 Mystic Islands U.S.A.
95 C3 My Tho Vietnam
67 M5 Mytilini Greece
68 F4 Mytishchi Rus. Fed.
105 G5 Mzamomhle S. Africa
103 D5 Mzimba Malawi
103 D5 Mzuzu Malawi

## N

34 □2 Naalehu U.S.A.
55 S6 Naantali Fin.
60 E4 Naas Rep. of Ireland
104 B4 Nababeep S. Africa
91 F6 Nabari Japan
94 B4 Nabas Phil.
80 E5 Nabatiyet et Tahta Lebanon
102 D4 Naberera Tanz.
76 G4 Naberezhnyye Chelny Rus. Fed.
101 D1 Nabeul Tunisia
84 D3 Nabha India
115 K4 Nabiac Austr.
93 K7 Nabire Indon.
80 E5 Nablus West Bank
105 H2 Naboomspruit S. Africa
95 A2 Nabule Myanmar
103 E5 Nacala Moz.
24 B2 Naches U.S.A.
84 B4 Nāchna India
34 B4 Nacimiento Reservoir resr U.S.A.
27 E6 Nacogdoches U.S.A.
36 C2 Nacozari de García Mex.
91 G5 Nadachi Japan
84 C5 Nadiad India
100 B1 Nador Morocco
69 C5 Nadvirna Ukr.
76 E3 Nadvoitsy Rus. Fed.
76 J3 Nadym Rus. Fed.
55 M9 Næstved Denmark
67 J5 Nafpaktos Greece
67 K6 Nafplio Greece
81 K5 Naft r. Iraq
81 K5 Naft Khanen Iraq
81 K4 Naft Shahr Iran
94 B3 Naga Phil.
22 D4 Nagagami r. Can.
90 D7 Nagahama Japan
90 F6 Nagahama Japan
85 H4 Naga Hills mts India
91 H4 Nagai Japan
85 H4 Nagaland div. India
114 F6 Nagambie Austr.
91 F6 Nagano Japan
91 G5 Nagano Japan
91 G5 Nagaoka Japan
85 H4 Nagaon India
84 D2 Nagar India
84 B4 Nagar Parkar Pak.
85 G3 Nagarzê China
90 B7 Nagasaki Japan
90 B7 Nagasaki Japan
90 C7 Naga-shima i. Japan
90 C7 Nagashima Japan
90 D7 Naga-shima i. Japan
90 C6 Nagato Japan
84 C4 Nagaur India
85 G2 Nag, Co l. China
84 C5 Nagda India
83 E9 Nagercoil India
79 K4 Nagha Kalat Pak.
84 D3 Nagina India
85 E3 Nagma Nepal
68 J3 Nagorsk Rus. Fed.
91 F6 Nagoya Japan
84 D5 Nagpur India
85 H3 Nagqu China
94 C3 Nagumbuaya Point pt Phil.
76 F1 Nagurskoye Rus. Fed.
66 G1 Nagyatád Hungary
62 H7 Nagykanizsa Hungary
87 N6 Naha Japan
84 D3 Nahan India
20 E2 Nahanni Butte Can.
20 D2 Nahanni National Park nat. park Can.
80 E5 Nahariyya Israel
81 M4 Nahāvand Iran
81 K5 Nahrawān canal Iraq
81 L6 Nahr 'Umr Iraq
47 B3 Nahuelbuta, Parque Nacional nat. park Chile
47 B4 Nahuel Huapí, L. l. Arg.
47 B4 Nahuel Huapi, Parque Nacional nat. park Arg.
29 D6 Nahunta U.S.A.
85 H2 Naij Tal China
88 F1 Naiman Qi China
23 H2 Nain Can.
79 G3 Nā'īn Iran
84 D3 Naini Tal India
84 E5 Nainpur India
57 E3 Nairn U.K.
57 E3 Nairn r. U.K.
32 C2 Nairn Centre Can.
102 D4 Nairobi Kenya
102 D4 Naivasha Kenya
78 E4 Najd reg. S. Arabia
65 E1 Nájera Spain
84 D3 Najibabad India
87 O3 Najin N. Korea
78 E6 Najrān S. Arabia
90 B7 Nakadōri-shima i. Japan
90 E7 Naka-gawa r. Japan
90 J1 Nakagawa Japan
91 H5 Naka-gawa r. Japan
90 C7 Nakama Japan
90 D7 Nakamura Japan
77 M3 Nakanno Rus. Fed.
91 G5 Nakano Japan
90 D5 Nakano-shima i. Japan
90 D6 Nakanoumi lag. Japan
84 B2 Naka Pass pass Afgh.
90 H3 Nakasato Japan
90 J2 Nakasatsunai Japan
90 K2 Nakashibetsu Japan
90 C7 Nakatsu Japan
91 F6 Nakatsugawa Japan
102 D2 Nak'fa Eritrea
80 D7 Nakhl Egypt
87 O3 Nakhodka Rus. Fed.
95 B2 Nakhon Nayok Thai.
95 B2 Nakhon Pathom Thai.
95 B2 Nakhon Ratchasima Thai.
95 A3 Nakhon Si Thammarat Thai.
84 B5 Nakhtarana India
20 C3 Nakina B.C. Can.
22 C3 Nakina Ont. Can.
103 D4 Nakonde Zambia
55 M9 Nakskov Denmark
102 D4 Nakuru Kenya
20 F4 Nakusp Can.
105 K2 Nalázi Moz.
85 G4 Nalbari India
69 G7 Nal'chik Rus. Fed.
80 C1 Nallıhan Turkey
100 D1 Nālūt Libya
105 K2 Namaacha Moz.
105 H3 Namahadi S. Africa
79 H3 Namakzar-e Shadad salt flat Iran
102 D4 Namanga Kenya
79 L1 Namangan Uzbek.
103 D5 Namapa Moz.
104 B3 Namaqualand reg. Namibia
104 B4 Namaqualand reg. S. Africa
110 F2 Namatanai P.N.G.
115 K1 Nambour Austr.
115 K3 Nambucca Heads Austr.
95 C3 Năm Căn Vietnam
85 H3 Namcha Barwa mt China
86 F5 Nam Co salt l. China
54 N4 Namdalen v. Norway
54 M4 Namdalseid Norway
89 C6 Nam Đinh Vietnam
30 B3 Namekagon r. U.S.A.
103 B6 Namib Desert des. Namibia
103 B5 Namibe Angola
96 Namibia country Africa
91 H5 Namie Japan
95 B1 Nam Khan r. Laos
93 H7 Namlea Indon.
95 B1 Nam Lik r. Laos
95 A1 Nammekon Myanmar
89 B6 Nam Na r. China/Vietnam
95 B1 Nam Ngum r. Laos
115 H3 Namoi r. Austr.
89 B6 Nam Ou r. Laos
20 F3 Nampa Can.
84 E3 Nampa mt Nepal
24 C3 Nampa U.S.A.
100 B3 Nampala Mali
95 B1 Nam Pat Thai.
95 B1 Nam Phong Thai.
87 N4 Namp'o N. Korea
103 D5 Nampula Moz.
85 G2 Namru Co l. China
86 G6 Namrup India
89 B7 Nam Sam r. Laos/Vietnam
85 E3 Namsê La pass Nepal
54 N4 Namsen r. Norway
81 K3 Namshir Iran
85 H4 Namsi India
85 G3 Namsi La pass Bhutan
54 M4 Namsos Norway
92 B4 Nam Tok Thai.
77 O3 Namtsy Rus. Fed.
83 J6 Namtu Myanmar
61 C4 Namur Belgium
103 C5 Namwala Zambia
102 B3 Nana Bakassa C.A.R.
20 E5 Nanaimo Can.
34 □1 Nanakuli U.S.A.
89 F5 Nan'an China
116 E6 Nanango Austr.
104 B2 Nananib Plateau plat. Namibia
89 E6 Nan'ao China
91 F5 Nanao Japan
91 F5 Nanao-wan b. Japan
91 F5 Nanatsu-shima i. Japan
88 C4 Nanbu China
89 E4 Nanchang Jiangxi China
89 E4 Nanchang Jiangxi China
89 E5 Nancheng China
89 C4 Nanchong China
89 C4 Nanchuan China
64 H2 Nancy France
84 E3 Nanda Devi mt India
84 E3 Nanda Kot mt India
89 C5 Nandan China
90 E6 Nandan Japan
83 E7 Nānded India
115 J3 Nandewar Range mts Austr.
84 C5 Nandgaon India
89 D6 Nandu Jiang r. China
84 C5 Nandurbar India
83 E7 Nandyal India
89 D6 Nanfeng Guangdong China
89 E5 Nanfeng Jiangxi China
101 D4 Nanga Eboko Cameroon
84 C2 Nanga Parbat mt Jammu and Kashmir
95 A3 Nangin Myanmar
90 C8 Nangō Japan
88 E2 Nangong China
103 D4 Nangulangwa Tanz.
85 H3 Nang Xian China
88 A2 Nanhua China
88 F4 Nanhui China
88 C3 Nanjiang China
89 E5 Nanjing Fujian China
88 F3 Nanjing Jiangsu China
89 E5 Nankang China
Nanking see Nanjing
90 D7 Nankoku Japan
103 B5 Nankova Angola
88 E2 Nanle China
88 F4 Nanling China
89 D5 Nan Ling mts China
89 C6 Nanliu Jiang r. China
89 C6 Nanning China
89 E6 Nan'oa Dao i. China
89 C5 Nanpan Jiang r. China
86 D6 Nanpara India
88 F1 Nanpiao China
89 F5 Nanping Fujian China
88 B3 Nanping Sichuan China
89 F5 Nanri Dao i. China
87 N7 Nansei-shotō is Japan
14 D4 Nansei-shotō Trench sea feature Pac. Oc.
64 D3 Nantes France
31 G4 Nanticoke Can.
33 F5 Nanticoke r. U.S.A.
20 G4 Nanton Can.
88 F3 Nantong Jiangsu China
88 F4 Nantong Jiangsu China
89 F6 Nant'ou Taiwan
33 H4 Nantucket U.S.A.
33 H4 Nantucket I. i. U.S.A.
33 H4 Nantucket Sound g. U.S.A.
59 E4 Nantwich U.K.
111 H2 Nanumanga i. Tuvalu
111 H2 Nanumea i. Tuvalu
46 E2 Nanuque Brazil
94 C5 Nanusa, Kepulauan is Indon.
112 C4 Nanutarra Roadhouse Austr.
89 B4 Nanxi China
89 D4 Nan Xian China
89 E5 Nanxiong China
88 D3 Nanyang China
91 H4 Nanyō Japan
88 D4 Nanzhang China
88 D3 Nanzhao China
65 G3 Nao, Cabo de la hd Spain
23 F3 Naococane, Lac l. Can.
85 G4 Naogaon Bangl.
84 B4 Naokot Pak.
84 C2 Naoshera Jammu and Kashmir
89 D6 Naozhou Dao i. China
34 A2 Napa U.S.A.
33 K1 Napadogan Can.
31 J3 Napanee Can.
84 C4 Napasar India
30 C5 Naperville U.S.A.
117 F3 Napier N.Z.
33 G2 Napierville Can.
66 F4 Naples Italy
29 D7 Naples FL U.S.A.
33 H3 Naples ME U.S.A.
89 B6 Napo China
42 D4 Napo r. Ecuador/Peru
32 A4 Napoleon U.S.A.
Napoli see Naples
47 D3 Naposta Arg.
47 D3 Naposta r. Arg.
30 E5 Nappanee U.S.A.
81 K3 Naqadeh Iran
80 E6 Naqb Ashtar Jordan
81 M4 Naqqash Iran
91 E6 Nara Japan
91 E6 Nara Japan
100 B3 Nara Mali
63 N3 Narach Belarus
114 D6 Naracoorte Austr.
115 G4 Naradhan Austr.
84 C4 Naraina India
84 E6 Narainpur India
90 B7 Narao Japan
86 D8 Narasapur India
85 F5 Narasinghapur India
95 B4 Narathiwat Thai.
Narbada r. see Narmada
59 C6 Narberth U.K.
64 F5 Narbonne France
65 C1 Narcea r. Spain
66 H4 Nardò Italy
47 E1 Nare Arg.
84 B3 Narechi r. Pak.
63 K4 Narew r. Pol.
84 A3 Nari r. Pak.
103 B6 Narib Namibia
104 B5 Nariep S. Africa
69 H6 Narimanov Rus. Fed.
84 B1 Narin r. Afgh.
84 B1 Narin Afgh.
80 G3 Narince Turkey
85 H1 Narin Gol watercourse China
91 H6 Narita Japan
84 C5 Narmada r. India
81 H1 Narman Turkey
84 D3 Narnaul India
66 E3 Narni Italy
63 O5 Narodychi Ukr.
68 F4 Naro-Fominsk Rus. Fed.
115 J6 Narooma Austr.
68 G4 Narovchat Rus. Fed.
69 D5 Narowlya Belarus
55 R5 Närpes Fin.
115 H3 Narrabri Austr.
33 H4 Narragansett Bay b. U.S.A.
115 G2 Narran r. Austr.
115 G5 Narrandera Austr.
115 G2 Narran L. l. Austr.
112 C6 Narrogin Austr.
115 H4 Narromine Austr.
32 C6 Narrows U.S.A.
33 F4 Narrowsburg U.S.A.
84 D5 Narsimhapur India
85 G5 Narsingdi Bangl.
84 D5 Narsinghgarh India
88 E1 Nart China
90 E6 Naruto Japan
55 V7 Narva Estonia
55 U7 Narva Bay b. Estonia/Rus. Fed.
94 B2 Narvacan Phil.
54 P2 Narvik Norway
55 V7 Narvskoye Vdkhr. resr Estonia/Rus. Fed.
84 D3 Narwana India
84 D4 Narwar India
76 G3 Nar'yan-Mar Rus. Fed.
82 E2 Naryn Kyrgyzstan
54 P5 Näsåker Sweden
35 H3 Naschitti U.S.A.
117 C6 Naseby N.Z.
30 A4 Nashua IA U.S.A.
33 H3 Nashua NH U.S.A.
29 C4 Nashville U.S.A.
80 F5 Nasib Syria
55 S6 Näsijärvi l. Fin.
84 C5 Nasik India
101 F4 Nasir Sudan
Nasirabad see Mymensingh
84 B3 Nasirabad Pak.
103 C5 Nasondoye Zaire
80 C6 Nasr Egypt
Nasratabad see Zābol
81 L5 Nasrīān-e-Pā'īn Iran
20 D3 Nass r. Can.
108 Nassau i. Cook Islands Pac. Oc.
29 E7 Nassau Bahamas
78 C5 Nasser, Lake resr Egypt
55 O8 Nässjö Sweden
22 E2 Nastapoca r. Can.
22 E2 Nastapoka Islands is Can.
91 G5 Nasu-dake volc. Japan
94 B3 Nasugbu Phil.
63 P2 Nasva Rus. Fed.
103 C6 Nata Botswana
102 D4 Nata Tanz.
45 B4 Natagaima Col.
43 L5 Natal Brazil
Natal div. see Kwazulu-Natal
13 G6 Natal Basin sea feature Indian Ocean
23 H3 Natashquan r. Can.
23 H3 Natashquan Can.
27 F6 Natchez U.S.A.
27 E6 Natchitoches U.S.A.
114 F6 Nathalia Austr.
84 C4 Nathdwara India
114 D6 Natimuk Austr.
34 D5 National City U.S.A.
65 H2 Nati, Pta pt Spain
100 C3 Natitingou Benin
116 B4 Native Companion Cr. r. Austr.
43 J6 Natividade Brazil
91 H4 Natori Japan
102 D4 Natron, Lake salt l. Tanz.
91 H5 Natsui-gawa r. Japan
95 A1 Nattaung mt Myanmar
92 D6 Natuna Besar i. Indon.
92 D6 Natuna, Kepulauan is Indon.
33 F2 Natural Bridge U.S.A.
35 G3 Natural Bridges National Monument res. U.S.A.
13 M6 Naturaliste Plateau sea feature Indian Ocean
35 H2 Naturita U.S.A.
30 E2 Naubinway U.S.A.
103 B6 Nauchas Namibia
33 G4 Naugatuck U.S.A.
94 B3 Naujan Phil.
94 B3 Naujan, L. l. Phil.
55 S8 Naujoji Akmenė Lith.
84 C4 Naukh India
95 A1 Naungpale Myanmar
80 E6 Na'ūr Jordan
84 B4 Naushara Pak.
55 J6 Naustdal Norway
42 D4 Nauta Peru
104 B3 Naute Dam dam Namibia
36 E4 Nautla Mex.
85 G5 Navadwīp India
68 C4 Navahrudak Belarus
35 H4 Navajo U.S.A.
25 F4 Navajo Lake l. U.S.A.
35 G3 Navajo Mt mt. U.S.A.
94 C4 Naval Phil.
65 D3 Navalmoral de la Mata Spain
65 D3 Navalvillar de Pela Spain
60 E4 Navan Rep. of Ireland
68 D4 Navapolatsk Belarus
77 T3 Navarin, Mys c. Rus. Fed.
44 C9 Navarino, I. i. Chile
65 F1 Navarra div. Spain
114 E6 Navarre Austr.
34 A2 Navarro U.S.A.
68 G4 Navashino Rus. Fed.
27 D6 Navasota U.S.A.
54 O5 Näverede Sweden
57 D2 Naver, Loch l. U.K.
47 B2 Navidad Chile
43 H3 Navio, Serra do Brazil
68 E4 Navlya Rus. Fed.
67 N2 Năvodari Romania
79 K1 Navoi Uzbek.
36 C3 Navojoa Mex.
68 G3 Navoloki Rus. Fed.
84 C5 Navsari India
84 C4 Nawa India
80 F5 Nawá Syria
85 G4 Nawabganj Bangl.
84 B4 Nawabshah Pak.
85 F4 Nawada India
84 A2 Nāwah Afgh.
84 C4 Nawalgarh India
81 K2 Naxçıvan Azer.
89 B4 Naxi China
67 L6 Naxos i. Greece
67 L6 Naxos Greece
45 A4 Naya Col.
85 F5 Nayagarh India
90 J1 Nayoro Japan
46 E1 Nazaré Brazil
80 E5 Nazareth Israel
36 D3 Nazas r. Mex.
27 B7 Nazas Mex.
42 D6 Nazca Peru
81 M5 Nazian Iran
81 K2 Nāzīk Iran
81 J2 Nazik Gölü l. Turkey
80 B3 Nazilli Turkey
81 G2 Nazımiye Turkey
85 H4 Nazira India
20 E4 Nazko Can.
20 E4 Nazko r. Can.
81 K3 Nāzlū r. Iran
69 H7 Nazran' Rus. Fed.
102 D3 Nazrēt Eth.
79 H5 Nazwá Oman
103 C4 Nchelenge Zambia
103 C6 Ncojane Botswana
103 B4 N'dalatando Angola
102 C3 Ndélé C.A.R.
102 B4 Ndendé Gabon
111 G3 Ndeni i. Solomon Is
101 D3 Ndjamena Chad
103 C5 Ndola Zambia
105 J4 Ndwedwe S. Africa
115 G1 Neabul Cr. r. Austr.
60 E3 Neagh, Lough l. U.K.
24 A1 Neah Bay U.S.A.
112 F4 Neale, L. salt flat Austr.
114 B2 Neales watercourse Austr.
67 K5 Nea Liosia Greece
67 K6 Neapoli Greece
59 D6 Neath U.K.
59 D6 Neath r. U.K.
115 G1 Nebine Cr. r. Austr.
79 G2 Nebitdag Turkm.
116 C3 Nebo Austr.
68 E3 Nebolchi Rus. Fed.
35 G2 Nebo, Mount mt. U.S.A.
26 C3 Nebraska div. U.S.A.
26 E3 Nebraska City U.S.A.
66 F6 Nebrodi, Monti mts Sicily Italy
27 E6 Neches r. U.S.A.
45 B3 Nechí r. Col.
102 D3 Nechisar National Park nat. park Eth.
14 J4 Necker I. U.S.A.
47 E3 Necochea Arg.
22 F2 Neddouc, Lac l. Can.
54 R2 Nedre Soppero Sweden
35 E4 Needles U.S.A.
59 F7 Needles, The stack U.K.
30 C3 Neenah U.S.A.
21 K4 Neepawa Can.
61 D3 Neerijnen Neth.
81 M2 Neftçala Azer.
76 G4 Neftekamsk Rus. Fed.
69 H6 Neftekumsk Rus. Fed.
76 J3 Nefteyugansk Rus. Fed.
59 C5 Nefyn U.K.
66 C6 Nefza Tunisia
102 B4 Negage Angola
102 D3 Negēlē Eth.
46 A3 Negla r. Para.
103 D5 Negomane Moz.
83 E9 Negombo Sri Lanka
67 K4 Negotino Macedonia
42 C5 Negra, Cordillera mts Peru
42 B5 Negra, Pta pt Peru
66 B7 Négrine Alg.
42 B4 Negritos Peru
47 D4 Negro r. Arg.
46 A2 Negro r. Mato Grosso do Sul Brazil
42 F4 Negro r. S. America
94 B4 Negros i. Phil.
67 N3 Negru Vodă Romania
81 M4 Nehavand Iran
87 M2 Nehe China
89 B4 Neijiang China
21 H4 Neilburg Can.
87 J3 Nei Monggol Zizhiqu div. China
62 G5 Neiße r. Ger./Pol.
45 B4 Neiva Col.
88 D3 Neixiang China
21 K3 Nejanilini Lake l. Can.
102 D3 Nek'emtē Eth.
55 O9 Neksø Denmark
68 E3 Nelidovo Rus. Fed.
26 D3 Neligh U.S.A.
77 P4 Nel'kan Rus. Fed.

77 Q3 Nel'kan Rus. Fed.
83 L8 Nellore India
21 L3 Nelson r. Can.
20 F5 Nelson Can.
117 D4 Nelson N.Z.
58 E4 Nelson U.K.
35 E4 Nelson U.S.A.
115 K4 Nelson Bay Austr.
114 D7 Nelson, C. c. Austr.
44 B8 Nelson, Estrecho chan.
     Chile
20 E3 Nelson Forks Can.
21 K3 Nelson House Can.
105 J2 Nelspruit S. Africa
100 B3 Néma Maur.
68 J3 Nema Rus. Fed.
30 A2 Nemadji r. U.S.A.
68 B4 Neman Rus. Fed.
80 F5 Nemara Syria
68 G3 Nemda r. Rus. Fed.
68 K2 Nemed Rus. Fed.
31 F2 Nemegos Can.
54 W2 Nemetskiy, Mys c.
     Rus. Fed.
64 F2 Nemours France
81 J2 Nemrut Dağı h. Turkey
90 K2 Nemuro-hantō pen.
     Japan
90 K2 Nemuro-kaikyō chan.
     Japan
90 K2 Nemuro-wan b. Japan
69 D5 Nemyriv Ukr.
60 C5 Nenagh Rep. of Ireland
59 H5 Nene r. U.K.
87 N2 Nenjiang China
61 E5 Nennig Ger.
68 F1 Nenoksa Rus. Fed.
91 F6 Neo Japan
26 E4 Neosho r. U.S.A.
27 E4 Neosho U.S.A.
70 Nepal country Asia
31 K3 Nepean Can.
35 G2 Nephi U.S.A.
60 B3 Nephin h. Rep. of Ireland
60 B3 Nephin Beg Range h.
     Rep. of Ireland
102 C3 Nepoko r. Zaire
33 F4 Neptune U.S.A.
64 E4 Nérac France
115 K1 Nerang Austr.
87 L1 Nerchinsk Rus. Fed.
68 G3 Nerekhta Rus. Fed.
66 G3 Neretva r.
     Bos.-Herz./Croatia
103 C5 Neriquinha Angola
55 T9 Neris r. Lith.
68 F3 Nerl' r. Rus. Fed.
46 C2 Nerópolis Brazil
77 O4 Neryungri Rus. Fed.
55 L6 Nes Norway
55 L6 Nesbyen Norway
54 G4 Neskaupstaður Iceland
54 N3 Nesna Norway
26 D4 Ness City U.S.A.
20 C3 Nesselrode, Mt mt.
     Can./U.S.A.
57 D3 Ness, Loch l. U.K.
67 L4 Nestos r. Greece
80 E5 Netanya Israel
21 N2 Netchek, Cape c. Can.
48 Netherlands country
     Europe
37 L6 Netherlands Antilles
     terr. Caribbean
85 G4 Netrakona Bangl.
84 C5 Netrang India
18 Nettilling L. l. Can.
30 A1 Nett Lake l. U.S.A.
30 A1 Nett Lake U.S.A.
36 F5 Netzahualcóyotl, Presa
     resr Mex.
62 F4 Neubrandenburg Ger.
62 C7 Neuchâtel Switz.
62 C7 Neuchâtel, Lac de l.
     Switz.
61 F4 Neuenkirchen-Seelscheid
     Ger.
61 D5 Neufchâteau Belgium
64 G2 Neufchâteau France
64 E2 Neufchâtel-en-Bray
     France
21 K2 Neultin Lake l. Can.
119 C2 Neumayer Germany
     Base Ant.
62 D3 Neumünster Ger.
62 H7 Neunkirchen Austria
62 C6 Neunkirchen Ger.
47 C3 Neuquén Arg.
47 C3 Neuquén r. Arg.
47 C3 Neuquén div. Arg.
62 F4 Neuruppin Ger.
29 E5 Neuse r. U.S.A.
62 H7 Neusiedler See l.
     Austria/Hungary
61 E3 Neuss Ger.
61 F4 Neustadt (Wied) Ger.
62 F4 Neustrelitz Ger.
62 C5 Neuwied Ger.
27 E4 Nevada MO U.S.A.
34 D2 Nevada div. U.S.A.
65 L4 Nevada, Sierra mts Spain
47 C2 Nevado, Cerro mt Arg.
36 D5 Nevado de Colima volc.
     Mex.
47 C3 Nevado, Sierra del mts
     Arg.
68 D3 Nevel' Rus. Fed.
64 F3 Nevers France
115 G3 Nevertire Austr.
67 H3 Nevesinje Bos.-Herz.
69 G6 Nevinnomyssk Rus. Fed.
57 C3 Nevis, Loch in. U.K.
80 E2 Nevşehir Turkey
35 E5 New r. CA U.S.A.

32 C6 New r. WV U.S.A.
28 C4 New Albany IN U.S.A.
27 F5 New Albany MS U.S.A.
33 E4 New Albany PA U.S.A.
43 G2 New Amsterdam Guyana
115 G2 New Angledool Austr.
33 F5 Newark DE U.S.A.
33 F5 Newark MD U.S.A.
33 F5 Newark NJ U.S.A.
32 E3 Newark NY U.S.A.
32 B4 Newark OH U.S.A.
35 E2 Newark Lake l. U.S.A.
59 G4 Newark-on-Trent U.K.
33 G3 Newark Valley U.S.A.
33 H4 New Bedford U.S.A.
24 B2 Newberg U.S.A.
33 F3 New Berlin U.S.A.
29 E5 New Bern U.S.A.
30 E2 Newberry MI U.S.A.
29 D5 Newberry SC U.S.A.
34 D4 Newberry Springs U.S.A.
58 F2 Newbiggin-by-the-Sea
     U.K.
31 J3 Newboro Can.
33 G3 New Boston MA U.S.A.
32 B5 New Boston OH U.S.A.
27 D6 New Braunfels U.S.A.
60 E4 Newbridge Rep. of Ireland
110 E2 New Britain i. P.N.G.
33 G4 New Britain U.S.A.
23 G4 New Brunswick div. Can.
33 F4 New Brunswick U.S.A.
30 D5 New Buffalo U.S.A.
57 F3 Newburgh U.K.
33 F4 Newburgh U.S.A.
59 F6 Newbury U.K.
33 H3 Newburyport U.S.A.
58 E3 Newby Bridge U.K.
106 New Caledonia is
     Pac. Oc.
23 G4 New Carlisle Can.
115 J4 Newcastle Austr.
23 G4 Newcastle N.B. Can.
31 H4 Newcastle Ont. Can.
60 E4 Newcastle Rep. of Ireland
105 H3 Newcastle S. Africa
60 F3 Newcastle N. Ireland U.K.
34 B2 Newcastle CA U.S.A.
30 E6 New Castle IN U.S.A.
32 B4 Newcastle OH U.S.A.
32 C4 New Castle PA U.S.A.
35 F3 Newcastle UT U.S.A.
32 C6 New Castle VA U.S.A.
24 C1 Newcastle WY U.S.A.
59 C5 Newcastle Emlyn U.K.
59 E4 Newcastle-under-Lyme
     U.K.
58 F3 Newcastle upon Tyne
     U.K.
113 F3 Newcastle Waters Austr.
60 B5 Newcastle West Rep. of
     Ireland
33 H4 New Church U.S.A.
35 H3 Newcomb U.S.A.
57 D5 New Cumnock U.K.
57 F3 New Deer U.K.
84 D3 New Delhi India
33 K1 New Denmark Can.
34 B3 New Don Pedro
     Reservoir resr U.S.A.
115 J3 New England Range mts
     Austr.
59 E4 Newent U.K.
23 J4 Newfoundland div. Can.
12 G2 Newfoundland Basin sea
     feature Atlantic Ocean
57 D5 New Galloway U.K.
111 F2 New Georgia i.
     Solomon Is
111 F2 New Georgia Islands is
     Solomon Is
23 H4 New Glasgow Can.
93 L7 New Guinea i. Asia
32 B4 New Hampshire OH
     U.S.A.
33 G3 New Hampshire div.
     U.S.A.
30 A4 New Hampton U.S.A.
110 F2 New Hanover i. P.N.G.
105 J4 New Hanover S. Africa
33 G4 New Haven U.S.A.
20 D3 New Hazelton Can.
     New Hebrides country
     see Vanuatu
34 B2 New Hogan Reservoir
     resr U.S.A.
30 C4 New Holstein U.S.A.
27 F6 New Iberia U.S.A.
105 J2 Newington S. Africa
60 D5 Newinn Rep. of Ireland
110 F2 New Ireland i. P.N.G.
33 F4 New Jersey div. U.S.A.
32 E6 New Kent U.S.A.
32 B5 New Lexington U.S.A.
30 B4 New Lisbon U.S.A.
31 H2 New Liskeard Can.
33 G4 New London CT U.S.A.
30 B5 New London IA U.S.A.
30 B6 New London MO U.S.A.
30 C3 New London WI U.S.A.
112 C4 Newman U.S.A.
30 D6 Newman U.S.A.
31 H1 Newman't Can.
60 B5 Newmarket
     Rep. of Ireland
59 H5 Newmarket U.K.
32 D5 New Market U.S.A.
60 C5 Newmarket on-Fergus
     Rep. of Ireland
32 C5 New Martinsville U.S.A.
24 C2 New Meadows U.S.A.
34 B3 New Melones L. l. U.S.A.
25 F5 New Mexico div. U.S.A.
29 C5 Newnan U.S.A.

115 G9 New Norfolk Austr.
27 F6 New Orleans U.S.A.
33 F4 New Paltz U.S.A.
32 C4 New Philadelphia U.S.A.
57 F3 New Pitsligo U.K.
117 B7 New Plymouth N.Z.
60 B4 Newport Mayo
     Rep. of Ireland
60 C5 Newport Tipperary
     Rep. of Ireland
59 F7 Newport Eng. U.K.
59 E5 Newport Eng. U.K.
59 D6 Newport Wales U.K.
27 F5 Newport AR U.S.A.
32 A5 Newport KY U.S.A.
33 J2 Newport ME U.S.A.
31 F5 Newport MI U.S.A.
33 G3 Newport NH U.S.A.
33 A2 Newport OR U.S.A.
33 H4 Newport RI U.S.A.
33 G2 Newport VT U.S.A.
24 C1 Newport WA U.S.A.
34 D5 Newport Beach U.S.A.
32 E6 Newport News U.S.A.
59 G5 Newport Pagnell U.K.
29 E7 New Providence i.
     Bahamas
59 B7 Newquay U.K.
23 G4 New Richmond Can.
30 A3 New Richmond U.S.A.
35 F5 New River U.S.A.
27 F6 New Roads U.S.A.
59 H7 New Romney U.K.
60 E5 New Ross Rep. of Ireland
60 E3 Newry U.K.
57 E4 New Scone U.K.
30 A5 New Sharon U.S.A.
     New Siberian Islands is
     see Novosibirskiye
     Ostrova
29 D6 New Smyrna Beach
     U.S.A.
115 G4 New South Wales div.
     Austr.
89 New Territories reg.
     Hong Kong China
58 E4 Newton U.K.
26 E3 Newton IA U.S.A.
26 D4 Newton KS U.S.A.
33 H3 Newton MA U.S.A.
27 F5 Newton MS U.S.A.
33 F4 Newton NJ U.S.A.
59 D7 Newton Abbot U.K.
57 E5 Newtonhill U.K.
57 D5 Newton Mearns U.K.
57 D6 Newton Stewart U.K.
60 C5 Newtown Rep. of Ireland
59 E5 Newtown Eng. U.K.
59 D5 Newtown Wales U.K.
26 C1 New Town U.S.A.
60 F3 Newtownabbey U.K.
60 F3 Newtownards U.K.
60 D3 Newtownbutler U.K.
60 E4 Newtownmountkennedy
     Rep. of Ireland
57 F5 Newtown St Boswells
     U.K.
60 D3 Newtownstewart U.K.
26 E2 New Ulm U.S.A.
34 A2 Newville U.S.A.
20 E5 New Westminster Can.
33 E3 New York div. U.S.A.
33 G4 New York U.S.A.
33 G4 New York-John F.
     Kennedy airport U.S.A.
33 F4 New York-Newark
     airport U.S.A.
106 New Zealand country
     Australasia
14 G9 New Zealand Plateau sea
     feature Pac. Oc.
68 G3 Neya Rus. Fed.
79 G4 Neyriz Iran
79 H2 Neyshābūr Iran
102 B4 Ngabé Congo
95 A2 Nga Chong, Khao mt
     Myanmar/Thai.
94 C6 Ngalipaëng Indon.
103 C6 Ngami, Lake l. Botswana
85 E3 Ngamring China
85 E3 Ngangla Ringco salt l.
     China
84 E2 Nganglong Kangri mts
     Xizang Zizhiqu China
84 E2 Nganglong Kangri mt
     China
85 F3 Ngangzê Co salt l. China
95 A1 Ngao Thai.
101 D4 Ngaoundéré Cameroon
117 E2 Ngaruawahia N.Z.
117 F3 Ngaruroro r. N.Z.
117 E3 Ngaurhoe, Mt volc. N.Z.
92 Ngawi Indon.
95 B2 Ngiap r. Laos
102 B4 Ngo Congo
95 C2 Ngoc Linh mt Vietnam
85 C2 Ngoin, Co salt l. China
100 D4 Ngol Bembo Nigeria
85 H2 Ngom Qu r. China
85 F2 Ngoqumaima China
82 J4 Ngoring Hu l. China
101 D3 Ngourti Niger
101 D3 Nguigmi Niger
92 Ngunut Indon.
100 D3 Nguru Nigeria
89 B6 Nguyên Bình Vietnam
104 E2 Ngwaketse div. Botswana
105 J4 Ngwathe S. Africa
105 K3 Ngwavuma r. Swaziland
105 J4 Ngwelezana S. Africa
103 D5 Nhamalabué Moz.
95 D2 Nha Trang Vietnam
114 D6 Nhill Austr.
105 J3 Nhlangano Swaziland

89 B6 Nho Quan Vietnam
113 G2 Nhulunbuy Austr.
21 J4 Niacam Can.
100 B3 Niafounké Mali
30 D3 Niagara U.S.A.
31 H4 Niagara Falls Can.
32 D3 Niagara Falls U.S.A.
31 H4 Niagara River r.
     Can./U.S.A.
100 C3 Niamey Niger
94 C5 Niampak Indon.
103 D4 Niangandu Tanz.
102 C3 Niangara Zaire
92 B6 Nias i. Indon.
     Niassa, Lago l. see
     Nyasa, Lake
55 R8 Nica Latvia
16 Nicaragua country
     Central America
37 G6 Nicaragua, Lago de l.
     Nic.
66 G5 Nicastro Italy
64 H5 Nice France
90 C6 Nichihara Japan
90 C8 Nichinan Japan
85 E4 Nichlaul India
29 E7 Nicholl's Town Bahamas
31 F2 Nicholson Can.
83 H9 Nicobar Islands is
     Andaman and Nicobar Is
80 D4 Nicosia Cyprus
37 H7 Nicoya, G. de b.
     Costa Rica
37 G7 Nicoya, Pen. de pen.
     Costa Rica
33 K1 Nictau Can.
55 R9 Nida Lith.
58 F4 Nidd r. U.K.
63 K4 Nidzica Pol.
62 D3 Niebüll Ger.
62 F7 Niedere Tauern mts
     Austria
61 F2 Niedersachsen div. Ger.
100 D4 Niefang Equatorial Guinea
62 D4 Nienburg (Weser) Ger.
61 E3 Niers r. Ger.
43 G2 Nieuw Amsterdam
     Suriname
61 C3 Nieuwe-Niedorp Neth.
61 C3 Nieuwerkerk aan de
     IJssel Neth.
43 G2 Nieuw Nickerie Suriname
104 C5 Nieuwoudtville S. Africa
61 A3 Nieuwpoort Belgium
61 C4 Nieuw-Vossemeer Neth.
80 E3 Niğde Turkey
100 C4 Niger r. Africa
96 Niger country Africa
96 Nigeria country Africa
100 C4 Niger, Mouths of the
     est. Nigeria
31 G1 Nighthawk Lake l.
     Can.
67 K4 Nigrita Greece
91 H5 Nihonmatsu Japan
91 G5 Niigata Japan
91 G5 Niigata Japan
90 D7 Niihama Japan
34 □2 Niihau i. U.S.A.
91 G6 Nii-jima i. Japan
90 J2 Niikappu Japan
90 H6 Niimi Japan
91 G5 Niitsu Japan
61 D2 Nijkerk Neth.
61 D3 Nijmegen Neth.
61 E2 Nijverdal Neth.
54 W2 Nikel' Rus. Fed.
100 C4 Nikki Benin
91 G5 Nikkō Nat. Park Japan
68 H4 Nikolayevka Rus. Fed.
69 H5 Nikolayevsk Rus. Fed.
68 H4 Nikol'sk Penzen. Rus. Fed.
68 H3 Nikol'sk Vologod.
     Rus. Fed.
77 S4 Nikol'skoye Rus. Fed.
69 E6 Nikopol' Ukr.
81 M3 Nik Pey Iran
80 F1 Niksar Turkey
67 H3 Nikšić Yugo.
111 J2 Nikumaroro i. Kiribati
111 H2 Nikunau i. Kiribati
84 C2 Nila Pak.
85 F5 Nilagiri India
35 E5 Niland U.S.A.
83 D10 Nilande Atoll atoll
     Maldives
84 D4 Nilang India
78 C4 Nile r. Africa
54 V5 Nilsiä Fin.
84 C4 Nimach India
115 K2 Nimbin Austr.
115 H6 Nimmitabel Austr.
101 E4 Nimule Sudan
115 H2 Nindigully Austr.
83 D9 Nine Degree Channel
     chan. India
114 E3 Nine Mile Lake salt flat
     Austr.
34 D2 Ninemile Peak summit
     U.S.A.
89 □ Ninepin Group is Hong
     Kong China
13 K5 Ninety-East Ridge sea
     feature Indian Ocean
115 G7 Ninety Mile Beach beach
     Austr.
117 D1 Ninety Mile Beach beach
     N.Z.
81 J3 Nineveh Iraq
33 F3 Nineveh U.S.A.

89 F4 Ningbo China
88 F1 Ningcheng China
89 E5 Ningde China
89 E5 Ningdu China
89 D5 Ninggang China
89 F4 Ningguo China
89 F4 Ninghai China
89 E5 Ninghua China
82 J4 Ningjing Shan mts China
88 E3 Ningling China
89 C6 Ningming China
89 B5 Ningnan China
88 D3 Ningqiang China
88 D2 Ningshan China
88 D2 Ningwu China
88 B3 Ningxia div. China
88 C3 Ning Xian China
89 D4 Ningxiang China
88 D3 Ningyang China
89 D5 Ningyuan China
89 C6 Ninh Binh Vietnam
95 D2 Ninh Hoa Vietnam
91 H3 Ninohe Japan
46 A3 Nioaque Brazil
26 C3 Niobrara r. U.S.A.
85 H4 Nioko China
100 A3 Niokolo Koba, Parc
     National du nat. park
     Senegal
100 B3 Niono Mali
100 B3 Nioro Mali
64 D3 Niort France
21 J4 Nipawin Can.
21 J4 Nipawin Provincial Park
     res. Can.
22 C3 Nipigon Can.
30 C1 Nipigon Bay b. Can.
22 C3 Nipigon, Lake l. Can.
23 H3 Nipishish Lake l. Can.
31 H2 Nipissing Can.
31 H2 Nipissing, L. l. Can.
34 B4 Nipomo U.S.A.
     Nippon Hai sea see
     Japan, Sea of
81 J1 Nippur Iraq
35 E4 Nipton U.S.A.
46 C1 Niquelândia Brazil
81 L2 Nir Iran
91 G6 Nirasaki Japan
83 E7 Nirmal India
67 J3 Niš Yugo.
65 C3 Nisa Port.
66 F6 Niscemi Sicily Italy
90 J2 Niseko Japan
     Nīshāpūr see Neyshābūr
91 G5 Nishiaizu Japan
90 K2 Nishibetsu-gawa r. Japan
90 C8 Nishikata Japan
91 H4 Nishikawa Japan
90 D5 Nishino-shima i. Japan
90 E6 Nishino-shima i. Japan
90 B7 Nishi-Sonogi-hantō pen.
     Japan
90 E6 Nishiwaki Japan
20 B2 Nisling r. Can.
61 C4 Nismes, Forêt de forest
     Belgium
61 C5 Nispen Neth.
55 N8 Nissan r. Sweden
63 O7 Nistrului Inferior,
     Câmpia lowland Moldova
20 C2 Nisutlin r. Can.
67 M6 Nisyros i. Greece
23 F3 Nitchequon Can.
46 D3 Niterói Brazil
57 E5 Nith r. U.K.
57 E5 Nithsdale v. U.K.
84 D3 Niti Pass pass China
62 J6 Nitra Slovakia
32 C5 Nitro U.S.A.
111 J3 Niuatoputopu i. Tonga
106 Niue terr. Pac. Oc.
111 H3 Niulakita i. Tuvalu
89 B5 Niulan Jiang r. China
111 H2 Niutao i. Tuvalu
88 F2 Niuzhuang China
54 T5 Nivala Fin.
116 E5 Nive watercourse Austr.
116 E5 Nive Downs Austr.
61 C4 Nivelles Belgium
68 G4 Nivshera Rus. Fed.
84 C4 Niwai India
34 C2 Nixon U.S.A.
85 E1 Niya He r. China
81 M1 Niyazoba Azer.
90 D7 Niyodo-gawa r. Japan
83 E7 Nizamabad India
68 H4 Nizhegorodskaya Oblast'
     div. Rus. Fed.
77 S3 Nizhnekolymsk Rus. Fed.
77 L4 Nizhneudinsk Rus. Fed.
76 J3 Nizhnevartovsk Rus. Fed.
77 P2 Nizhneyansk Rus. Fed.
68 G4 Nizhniy Lomov Rus. Fed.
68 G3 Nizhniy Novgorod
     Rus. Fed.
68 K2 Nizhniy Odes Rus. Fed.
68 H3 Nizhniy Yenangsk
     Rus. Fed.
69 D5 Nizhyn Ukr.
63 K4 Nizina reg. Pol.
80 F3 Nizip Turkey
54 R2 Njallavarri mt Norway
54 Q3 Njavve Sweden
     Njazidja i. see Grande
     Comore
103 D4 Njinjo Tanz.
103 D4 Njombe Tanz.
55 P5 Njurundabommen
     Sweden
100 D4 Nkambe Cameroon
105 J4 Nkandla S. Africa
100 B4 Nkawkaw Ghana

103 C5 Nkayi Zimbabwe
103 D5 Nkhata Bay Malawi
103 D5 Nkhotakota Malawi
100 C4 Nkongsamba Cameroon
105 C4 Nkululeko S. Africa
103 B5 Nkurenkuru Namibia
105 G6 Nkwenkwezi S. Africa
85 J4 Noa Dihing r. India
85 G5 Noakhali Bangl.
85 F5 Noamundi India
60 E4 Nobber Rep. of Ireland
90 C7 Nobeoka Japan
90 H2 Noboribetsu Japan
46 A1 Nobres Brazil
114 E1 Noccundra Austr.
114 E1 Nockatunga Austr.
31 G2 Noelville Can.
36 B2 Nogales Mex.
90 C7 Nōgata Japan
64 E2 Nogent-le-Rotrou France
61 A5 Nogent-sur-Oise France
68 F4 Noginsk Rus. Fed.
116 D5 Nogo r. Austr.
116 B5 Nogoa r. Austr.
91 F6 Nogōhaku-san mt. Japan
47 E2 Nogoyá Arg.
47 E2 Nogoya r. Arg.
84 C3 Nohar India
90 H3 Noheji Japan
61 F5 Nohfelden Ger.
64 C3 Noirmoutier-en-l'Île
     France
64 C3 Noirmoutier, Île de i.
     France
91 G6 Nojima-zaki c. Japan
84 C4 Nokha India
79 J4 Nok Kundi Pak.
21 J3 Nokomis Lake l. Can.
102 B3 Nola C.A.R.
68 J3 Nolinsk Rus. Fed.
90 C8 Noma-misaki pt Japan
33 H4 No Mans Land i. U.S.A.
77 V3 Nome Alaska
88 B1 Nomgon Mongolia
85 J1 Nomhon China
90 D6 Nōmi-jima i. Japan
108 Nomoi Islands is
     Micronesia
105 G5 Nomonde S. Africa
90 B7 Nomo-zaki pt Japan
68 J3 Nomzha Rus. Fed.
21 H2 Nonacho Lake l. Can.
105 J4 Nondweni S. Africa
95 C1 Nông Hèt Laos
95 B2 Nong Hong Thai.
95 B1 Nong Khai Thai.
105 J3 Nongoma S. Africa
114 B4 Nonning Austr.
111 H2 Nonouti i. Kiribati
95 B2 Nonthaburi Thai.
104 F5 Nonzwakazi S. Africa
115 G2 Noorama Cr.
     watercourse Austr.
61 B3 Noordbeveland i. Neth.
61 B5 Noorderhaaks i. Neth.
61 D2 Noordoost Polder
     reclaimed land Neth.
116 E6 Noosa Heads Austr.
20 D5 Nootka I. i. Can.
79 K2 Norak Tajik.
94 C3 Norala Phil.
31 H1 Noranda Can.
55 O6 Norberg Sweden
76 D2 Nordaustlandet i.
     Svalbard
62 C4 Norden Ger.
76 L2 Nordenshel'da,
     Arkhipelag is Rus. Fed.
62 C4 Norderney i. Ger.
61 F1 Norderland reg. Ger.
61 E1 Norderney i. Ger.
62 E4 Norderstedt Ger.
55 J6 Nordfjordeid Norway
54 O3 Nordfold Norway
     Nordfriesische Inseln is
     see North Frisian Islands
62 E5 Nordhausen Ger.
61 F2 Nordhorn Ger.
54 T1 Nordkapp c. Norway
54 Q2 Nordkjosbotn Norway
54 N4 Nordli Norway
62 E6 Nördlingen Ger.
54 Q5 Nordmaling Sweden
62 D3 Nord-Ostsee-Kanal
     canal Ger.
61 F3 Nordrhein-Westfalen
     div. Ger.
60 D5 Nore r. Rep. of Ireland
64 F5 Nore, Pic de mt France
26 D3 Norfolk NE U.S.A.
33 F2 Norfolk NY U.S.A.
111 G4 Norfolk Island terr.
     Pac. Oc.
14 G7 Norfolk Island Ridge sea
     feature Pac. Oc.
14 F7 Norfolk Island Trough
     sea feature Pac. Oc.
27 E4 Norfork L. l. U.S.A.
55 K6 Norheimsund Norway
91 F5 Norikura-dake volc.
     Japan
76 K3 Noril'sk Rus. Fed.
81 K1 Nor Kharberd Armenia
31 H3 Norland Can.
23 G2 Normal U.S.A.
27 D5 Norman U.S.A.
110 F2 Normanby I. i. P.N.G.
116 D4 Normanby Ra. h. Austr.
     Normandes, Îles is see
     Channel Islands
64 D2 Normandie reg. France
29 D5 Norman, L. l. U.S.A.
113 H3 Normanton Austr.
114 C5 Normanville Austr.

20 D1 **Norman Wells** Can.
47 B4 **Ñorquinco** Arg.
54 R5 **Norra Kvarken** str. Fin./Sweden
54 O4 **Norra Storfjället** mts Sweden
32 B6 **Norris Lake** l. U.S.A.
33 F4 **Norristown** U.S.A.
55 P7 **Norrköping** Sweden
55 Q7 **Norrtälje** Sweden
112 D6 **Norseman** Austr.
54 Q4 **Norsjö** Sweden
111 G3 **Norsup** Vanuatu
47 F3 **Norte, Pta** pt Buenos Aires Arg.
44 D6 **Norte, Pta** pt Chubut Arg.
33 G3 **North Adams** U.S.A.
58 F3 **Northallerton** U.K.
112 C6 **Northam** Austr.
12 E4 **North American Basin** sea feature Atlantic Ocean
112 B5 **Northampton** Austr.
59 G5 **Northampton** U.K.
33 G3 **Northampton** U.S.A.
116 A5 **Northampton Downs** Austr.
92 A4 **North Andaman** i. Andaman and Nicobar Is
32 E5 **North Anna** r. U.S.A.
33 J2 **North Anson** U.S.A.
92 G2 **North Arm** b. Can.
29 D5 **North Augusta** U.S.A.
23 H2 **North Aulatsivik Island** i. Can.
21 H4 **North Battleford** Can.
31 H2 **North Bay** Can.
22 E2 **North Belcher Islands** is Can.
24 A3 **North Bend** U.S.A.
57 F4 **North Berwick** U.K.
33 H3 **North Berwick** U.S.A.
115 F3 **North Bourke** Austr.
30 A3 **North Branch** U.S.A.
119 A5 **North, C.** c. Ant.
23 H4 **North, C.** c. Can.
23 H4 **North Cape** pt P.E.I. Can.
**North Cape** c. see Nordkapp
117 D1 **North Cape** c. N.Z.
22 B3 **North Caribou Lake** l. Can.
29 D5 **North Carolina** div. U.S.A.
24 B1 **North Cascades Nat. Park** U.S.A.
31 F2 **North Channel** chan. Can.
60 E2 **North Channel** str. Northern Ireland/Scotland
74 **North China Plain** plain China
33 H2 **North Conway** U.S.A.
26 C2 **North Dakota** div. U.S.A.
59 H6 **North Downs** h. U.K.
32 D3 **North East** U.S.A.
12 H2 **North-Eastern Atlantic Basin** sea feature Atlantic Ocean
29 E7 **Northeast Providence Chan.** chan. Bahamas
29 F7 **North End Pt** pt Bahamas
84 C1 **Northern Areas** div. Pak.
104 D4 **Northern Cape** div. S. Africa
21 K3 **Northern Indian Lake** l. Can.
56 C4 **Northern Ireland** div. U.K.
22 B4 **Northern Light L.** l. Can.
106 **Northern Mariana Islands** terr. Pac. Oc.
105 H1 **Northern Province** div. S. Africa
113 F3 **Northern Territory** div. Austr.
57 F4 **North Esk** r. U.K.
52 **North European Plain** plain Europe
33 G3 **Northfield** MA U.S.A.
26 E2 **Northfield** MN U.S.A.
33 G2 **Northfield** VT U.S.A.
59 J6 **North Foreland** c. U.K.
34 C3 **North Fork** U.S.A.
34 B2 **North Fork American** r. U.S.A.
34 B2 **North Fork Feather** r. U.S.A.
30 E3 **North Fox I.** i. U.S.A.
22 D3 **North French** r. Can.
62 C3 **North Frisian Islands** is Ger.
58 G3 **North Grimston** U.K.
33 K2 **North Head** Can.
117 E2 **North Head** hd N.Z.
21 K2 **North Henik Lake** l. Can.
33 H4 **North Hudson** U.S.A.
117 E3 **North Island** i. N.Z.
94 B1 **North Island** i. Phil.
94 A4 **North Islet** rf Phil.
35 G4 **North Jadito Canyon** U.S.A.
30 D5 **North Judson** U.S.A.
21 K3 **North Knife** r. Can.
85 L4 **North Koel** r. India
85 H4 **North Lakhimpur** India
35 E3 **North Las Vegas** U.S.A.
27 E5 **North Little Rock** U.S.A.
103 D5 **North Luangwa National Park** nat. park Zambia
30 E5 **North Manchester** U.S.A.

30 D3 **North Manitou I.** i. U.S.A.
20 D2 **North Nahanni** r. Can.
21 L5 **Northome** U.S.A.
34 C3 **North Palisade** summit U.S.A.
26 C3 **North Platte** U.S.A.
26 C3 **North Platte** r. U.S.A.
115 G7 **North Point** pt U.S.A.
89 □ **North Point** Hong Kong China
28 D2 **North Point** pt U.S.A.
30 E3 **Northport** U.S.A.
35 F3 **North Rim** U.S.A.
57 F1 **North Ronaldsay** i. U.K.
57 F1 **North Ronaldsay Firth** chan. U.K.
34 B2 **North San Juan** U.S.A.
21 G4 **North Saskatchewan** r. Can.
52 **North Sea** sea Europe
21 J3 **North Seal** r. Can.
58 F2 **North Shields** U.K.
34 D2 **North Shoshone Peak** summit U.S.A.
59 H4 **North Somercotes** U.K.
115 K1 **North Stradbroke I.** i. Austr.
33 H4 **North Stratford** U.S.A.
58 F2 **North Sunderland** Eng. U.K.
117 E3 **North Taranaki Bight** b. N.Z.
20 F4 **North Thompson** r. Can.
57 A3 **Northton** U.K.
32 D3 **North Tonawanda** U.S.A.
84 D3 **North Tons** r. India
117 A7 **North Trap** rf N.Z.
33 G2 **North Troy** U.S.A.
22 D3 **North Twin I.** i. Can.
58 E2 **North Tyne** r. U.K.
57 A3 **North Uist** i. U.K.
116 D3 **Northumberland Is** is Austr.
58 E2 **Northumberland National Park** nat. park U.K.
23 H4 **Northumberland Strait** chan. Can.
20 E5 **North Vancouver** Can.
33 J5 **Northville** U.S.A.
59 J5 **North Walsham** U.K.
104 F3 **North West** div. S. Africa
112 B4 **North West C.** c. W.A. Austr.
84 C2 **North West Frontier** div. Pak.
29 E7 **Northwest Providence Chan.** chan. Bahamas
23 J3 **North West River** Can.
21 G2 **Northwest Territories** div. Can.
59 E4 **Northwich** U.K.
33 F5 **North Wildwood** U.S.A.
33 H2 **North Woodstock** U.S.A.
78 F6 **North Yemen** div. Yemen
58 G3 **North York Moors** reg. U.K.
58 G3 **North York Moors National Park** U.K.
23 G4 **Norton** Can.
58 G3 **Norton** U.K.
26 D4 **Norton** KS U.S.A.
32 B6 **Norton** VA U.S.A.
33 G1 **Norton** VT U.S.A.
103 D5 **Norton** Zimbabwe
77 V3 **Norton Sound** b. Alaska
119 C2 **Norvegia, C.** c. Ant.
33 G4 **Norwalk** CT U.S.A.
32 A4 **Norwalk** OH U.S.A.
48 □ **Norway** country Europe
33 H2 **Norway** U.S.A.
31 J3 **Norway Bay** Can.
21 K4 **Norway House** Can.
12 J1 **Norwegian Basin** sea feature Atlantic Ocean
52 **Norwegian Sea** sea Atlantic Ocean
31 G4 **Norwich** Can.
59 J5 **Norwich** U.K.
33 G4 **Norwich** CT U.S.A.
33 H3 **Norwich** NY U.S.A.
33 H3 **Norwood** MA U.S.A.
33 F2 **Norwood** NY U.S.A.
32 A5 **Norwood** OH U.S.A.
90 K2 **Nosapu-misaki** pt Japan
44 C2 **Nos de Cachi** mt Arg.
21 H1 **Nose Lake** l. Can.
67 M3 **Nos Emine** pt Bulg.
67 M3 **Nos Galata** pt Bulg.
90 H1 **Noshappu-misaki** hd Japan
91 G3 **Noshiro** Japan
69 D5 **Nosivka** Ukr.
67 N3 **Nos Kaliakra** pt Bulg.
68 H3 **Noskovo** Rus. Fed.
103 C6 **Nosop** r. Botswana/ S. Africa
76 G3 **Nosovaya** Rus. Fed.
46 A1 **Nossa Senhora do Livramento** Brazil
55 N7 **Nossebro** Sweden
67 N3 **Nos Shabla** pt Bulg.
57 □ **Noss, Isle of** i. U.K.
104 C2 **Nossob** r. Namibia
103 E5 **Nosy Be** i. Madag.
103 F5 **Nosy Boraha** i. Madag.
103 E6 **Nosy Varika** Madag.
35 F2 **Notch Peak** summit U.S.A.
62 H4 **Noteć** r. Pol.
91 F5 **Noto** Japan
55 L7 **Notodden** Norway

66 F6 **Noto, Golfo di** g. Sicily Italy
91 F5 **Noto-hantō** pen. Japan
91 F5 **Noto-jima** i. Japan
90 K1 **Notoro-ko** l. Japan
23 K4 **Notre Dame Bay** b. Can.
31 K3 **Notre-Dame-de-la-Salette** Can.
33 H2 **Notre-Dame-des-Bois** Can.
31 K2 **Notre-Dame-du-Laus** Can.
31 H2 **Notre-Dame-du-Nord** Can.
23 G4 **Notre Dame, Monts** mts Can.
90 K2 **Notsuke-saki** pt Japan
90 K2 **Notsuke-suidō** chan. Japan
31 G3 **Nottawasaga Bay** b. Can.
22 E3 **Nottaway** r. Can.
59 F5 **Nottingham** U.K.
32 E6 **Nottoway** r. U.S.A.
21 H5 **Notukeu Cr.** r. Can.
100 A2 **Nouâdhibou** Maur.
100 A3 **Nouakchott** Maur.
100 A3 **Nouâmghâr** Maur.
95 C2 **Noual** Saudi Arabia
111 G4 **Nouméa** New Caledonia
100 B3 **Nouna** Burkina
104 F5 **Noupoort** S. Africa
54 V3 **Nousu** Fin.
**Nouveau-Comptoir** see Wemindji
**Nouvelle Calédonie** is see New Caledonia
46 C1 **Nova América** Brazil
46 B3 **Nova Esperança** Brazil
46 C3 **Nova Friburgo** Brazil
66 G2 **Nova Gradiška** Croatia
46 C3 **Nova Granada** Brazil
46 D3 **Nova Iguaçu** Brazil
69 E6 **Nova Kakhovka** Ukr.
46 C3 **Nova Lima** Brazil
68 D4 **Novalukoml'** Belarus
69 D6 **Nova Odesa** Ukr.
66 C2 **Novara** Italy
46 C1 **Nova Roma** Brazil
23 H5 **Nova Scotia** div. Can.
34 A2 **Novato** U.S.A.
46 C3 **Nova Venécia** Brazil
46 B1 **Nova Xavantina** Brazil
77 R2 **Novaya Sibir', Ostrov** i. Rus. Fed.
76 G2 **Novaya Zemlya** is Rus. Fed.
67 M3 **Nova Zagora** Bulg.
65 F3 **Novelda** Spain
62 J7 **Nové Zámky** Slovakia
68 D3 **Novgorod** Rus. Fed.
68 E3 **Novgorodskaya Oblast'** div. Rus. Fed.
69 E5 **Novhorod-Sivers'kyy** Ukr.
67 K3 **Novi Iskŭr** Bulg.
66 C2 **Novi Ligure** Italy
67 M3 **Novi Pazar** Bulg.
67 J3 **Novi Pazar** Yugo.
67 H2 **Novi Sad** Yugo.
69 G6 **Novoaleksandrovsk** Rus. Fed.
69 G5 **Novoanninskiy** Rus. Fed.
42 F5 **Novo Aripuanã** Brazil
69 F5 **Novoazovs'k** Ukr.
68 H3 **Novocheboksarsk** Rus. Fed.
69 G6 **Novocherkassk** Rus. Fed.
68 G1 **Novodvinsk** Rus. Fed.
44 F3 **Novo Hamburgo** Brazil
46 C3 **Novo Horizonte** Brazil
62 G6 **Novohradské Hory** mts Czech Rep.
69 C5 **Novohrad-Volyns'kyy** Ukr.
82 K1 **Novokazalinsk** Kazak.
69 G6 **Novokubansk** Rus. Fed.
76 K4 **Novokuznetsk** Rus. Fed.
119 D3 **Novolazarevskaya** Rus. Fed. Base Ant.
77 M2 **Novoletov'ye** Rus. Fed.
66 F2 **Novo Mesto** Slovenia
68 F4 **Novomichurinsk** Rus. Fed.
69 F6 **Novomikhaylovskiy** Rus. Fed.
68 F4 **Novomoskovsk** Rus. Fed.
69 E5 **Novomoskovs'k** Ukr.
69 F5 **Novomyrhorod** Ukr.
69 G5 **Novonikolayevskiy** Rus. Fed.
69 E6 **Novooleksiyivka** Ukr.
69 G6 **Novopokrovskaya** Rus. Fed.
69 J5 **Novorepnoye** Rus. Fed.
69 F6 **Novorossiysk** Rus. Fed.
77 M2 **Novorybnoye** Rus. Fed.
68 E2 **Novoselivs'ke** Ukr.
63 O1 **Novosel'ye** Rus. Fed.
69 F6 **Novoshakhtinsk** Rus. Fed.
76 K4 **Novosibirsk** Rus. Fed.
77 Q2 **Novosibirskiye Ostrova** is Rus. Fed.
68 D3 **Novosokol'niki** Rus. Fed.
68 H4 **Novospasskoye** Rus. Fed.
69 E5 **Novotroyits'ke** Ukr.
69 J5 **Novouzensk** Rus. Fed.
69 C5 **Novovolyns'k** Ukr.
69 C5 **Novovolyns'k** Ukr.
69 E5 **Novovoronezh** Rus. Fed.
69 D4 **Novozybkov** Rus. Fed.
62 H6 **Nový Jičín** Czech Rep.
77 M2 **Novyy** Rus. Fed.
69 F5 **Novyy Oskol** Rus. Fed.
76 J3 **Novyy Port** Rus. Fed.
68 J3 **Novyy Tor'yal** Rus. Fed.

76 J3 **Novyy Urengoy** Rus. Fed.
87 O1 **Novyy Urgal** Rus. Fed.
76 G5 **Novyy Uzen'** Kazak.
27 E4 **Nowata** U.S.A.
81 M4 **Nowbarān** Iran
81 M3 **Nowdī** Iran
84 D4 **Nowgong** India
**Nowgong** see Nagaon
21 J2 **Nowleye Lake** l. Can.
62 J2 **Nowogard** Pol.
115 J5 **Nowra** Austr.
79 G2 **Now Shahr** Iran
84 C2 **Nowshera** Pak.
63 K6 **Nowy Sącz** Pol.
63 K6 **Nowy Targ** Pol.
33 E4 **Noxen** U.S.A.
76 J3 **Noyabr'sk** r. Rus. Fed.
20 C3 **Noyes I.** i. U.S.A.
64 F2 **Noyon** France
95 C1 **Noy, Xé** r. Laos
95 C1 **Noy, Xé** r. Laos
105 F5 **Nozizwe** S. Africa
105 G6 **Nqamakwe** S. Africa
105 J4 **Nqutu** S. Africa
103 D5 **Nsanje** Malawi
102 B4 **Ntandembele** Zaire
105 J4 **Ntha** S. Africa
102 D4 **Ntungamo** Uganda
101 F3 **Nuba Mountains** mts Sudan
81 K1 **Nubarashen** Armenia
101 F2 **Nubian Desert** des. Sudan
47 B3 **Nuble** r. Chile
88 D1 **Nüden** Mongolia
42 D7 **Nudo Coropuna** mt Peru
27 D6 **Nueces** r. U.S.A.
47 F2 **Nueva Helvecia** Uru.
47 B3 **Nueva Imperial** Chile
44 A4 **Nueva Loja** Ecuador
44 B6 **Nueva Lubecka** Arg.
36 D3 **Nueva Rosita** Mex.
37 J4 **Nuevitas** Cuba
36 C2 **Nuevo Casas Grandes** Mex.
47 D4 **Nuevo, Golfo** g. Arg.
36 E3 **Nuevo Laredo** Mex.
102 E3 **Nugaal** watercourse Somalia
116 C5 **Nuga Nuga, L.** l. Austr.
117 B2 **Nugget Pt** pt N.Z.
117 F3 **Nuguria Is** is P.N.G.
117 F3 **Nuhaka** N.Z.
111 H2 **Nui** i. Tuvalu
95 C1 **Nui Ti On** mt Vietnam
82 J5 **Nu Jiang** r. China
114 A4 **Nukey Bluff** h. Austr.
111 J4 **Nuku'alofa** Tonga
111 H2 **Nukufetau** i. Tuvalu
109 **Nuku Hiva** i. Fr. Polynesia Pac. Oc.
111 H2 **Nukulaelae** i. Tuvalu
111 F2 **Nukumanu Is** is P.N.G.
111 J2 **Nukunono** i. Tokelau Pac. Oc.
79 H1 **Nukus** Uzbek.
112 D4 **Nullagine** Austr.
112 F6 **Nullarbor** Austr.
112 F6 **Nullarbor National Park** nat. park Austr.
112 E6 **Nullarbor Plain** plain Austr.
88 F1 **Nulu'erhu Shan** mts China
114 F2 **Numalla, Lake** salt flat Austr.
100 D4 **Numan** Nigeria
91 G5 **Numata** Gunma Japan
90 H2 **Numata** Hokkaido Japan
91 G6 **Numazu** Japan
55 L6 **Numedal** v. Norway
93 J7 **Numfor** i. Indon.
115 F6 **Numurkah** Austr.
23 H2 **Nunaksaluk Island** i. Can.
32 E4 **Nunda** U.S.A.
115 J3 **Nundle** Austr.
59 F5 **Nuneaton** U.K.
22 B3 **Nungesser L.** l. Can.
77 V4 **Nunivak I.** i. Alaska
77 U3 **Nunligran** Rus. Fed.
65 C2 **Nuñomoral** Spain
66 C2 **Nuoro** Sardinia Italy
111 G3 **Nupani** i. Solomon Is
78 E4 **Nuqrah** S. Arabia
45 A3 **Nuquí** Col.
84 E1 **Nur** China
62 D6 **Nuremberg** Ger.
81 J2 **Nurettin** Turkey
114 C5 **Nuriootpa** Austr.
84 B2 **Nuristan** reg. Afgh.
68 J4 **Nurlaty** Rus. Fed.
54 V5 **Nurmes** Fin.
54 S5 **Nurmo** Fin.
**Nürnberg** see Nuremberg
115 G3 **Nurri, Mt** h. Austr.
85 H1 **Nur Turu** China
81 H3 **Nusaybin** Turkey
79 K4 **Nushki** Pak.
35 H5 **Nutrioso** U.S.A.
84 B3 **Nuttal** Pak.
54 U3 **Nuupas** Fin.
104 C5 **Nuwerus** S. Africa
104 D6 **Nuweveldberg** mts S. Africa
81 K4 **Nuzi** Iraq
105 J1 **Nwanedi National Park** nat. park S. Africa
76 H3 **Nyagan'** Rus. Fed.
114 E5 **Nyah West** Austr.
85 G3 **Nyainqêntanglha Feng** mt China

85 G3 **Nyainqêntanglha Shan** mts China
85 H2 **Nyainrong** China
54 Q5 **Nyåker** Sweden
101 E3 **Nyala** Sudan
85 F3 **Nyalam** China
103 C5 **Nyamandhlovu** Zimbabwe
68 G2 **Nyandoma** Rus. Fed.
68 F2 **Nyandomskiy Vozvyshennost'** reg. Rus. Fed.
102 B4 **Nyanga** r. Gabon
103 D5 **Nyanga** Zimbabwe
85 H3 **Nyang Qu** r. Tibet China
85 H3 **Nyang Qu** r. Tibet China
103 D5 **Nyasa, Lake** l. Africa
68 C4 **Nyasvizh** Belarus
55 M9 **Nyborg** Denmark
54 V1 **Nyborg** Norway
55 O8 **Nybro** Sweden
85 G3 **Nyêmo** China
102 D4 **Nyeri** Kenya
85 F3 **Nyima** China
82 H5 **Nyingchi** China
63 K7 **Nyíregyháza** Hungary
62 C7 **Nyon** Switz.
85 F3 **Nyonni Ri** mt China
64 G4 **Nyons** France
76 G3 **Nyrob** Rus. Fed.
68 J2 **Nyuchpas** Rus. Fed.
91 G4 **Nyūdō-zaki** pt Japan
102 C4 **Nyunzu** Zaire
77 N3 **Nyurba** Rus. Fed.
68 J2 **Nyuvchim** Rus. Fed.
69 E6 **Nyzhn'ohirs'kyy** Ukr.
102 D4 **Nzega** Tanz.
100 B4 **Nzérékoré** Guinea
102 B4 **N'zeto** Angola
105 J1 **Nzhelele Dam** dam S. Africa
**Nzwani** i. see Anjouan

## O

26 C2 **Oahe, Lake** l. U.S.A.
34 □1 **Oahu** i. U.S.A.
114 D4 **Oakbank** Austr.
35 F2 **Oak City** U.S.A.
27 E6 **Oakdale** U.S.A.
26 D2 **Oakes** U.S.A.
115 J1 **Oakey** Austr.
59 G5 **Oakham** U.K.
24 B1 **Oak Harbor** U.S.A.
32 C6 **Oak Hill** U.S.A.
34 C3 **Oakhurst** U.S.A.
30 B2 **Oak I.** i. U.S.A.
34 A3 **Oakland** CA U.S.A.
32 D5 **Oakland** MD U.S.A.
26 D3 **Oakland** NE U.S.A.
24 B3 **Oakland** OR U.S.A.
115 G5 **Oaklands** Austr.
30 D5 **Oak Lawn** U.S.A.
26 C4 **Oakley** U.S.A.
112 D4 **Oakover** r. Austr.
29 C4 **Oak Ridge** U.S.A.
24 B3 **Oakridge** U.S.A.
114 D4 **Oakvale** Austr.
31 H4 **Oakville** Can.
117 C6 **Oamaru** N.Z.
117 D5 **Oaro** N.Z.
94 B3 **Oas** Phil.
90 D6 **Ōasa** Japan
24 D3 **Oasis** U.S.A.
119 B5 **Oates Land** reg. Ant.
115 G9 **Oatlands** Austr.
35 E4 **Oatman** U.S.A.
36 E5 **Oaxaca** Mex.
76 H3 **Ob'** r. Rus. Fed.
100 D4 **Obala** Cameroon
57 C4 **Oban** U.K.
91 H4 **Obanazawa** Japan
65 C1 **O Barco** Spain
22 F4 **Obatogamau L.** l. Can.
61 C2 **Obdam** Neth.
20 F4 **Obed** Can.
117 B6 **Obelisk** mt. N.Z.
26 C4 **Oberlin** KS U.S.A.
32 B4 **Oberlin** OH U.S.A.
115 H4 **Oberon** Austr.
62 F6 **Oberpfälzer Wald** mts Ger.
93 H7 **Obi** i. Indon.
43 G4 **Óbidos** Brazil
79 K2 **Obigarm** Tajik.
90 H2 **Obihiro** Japan
69 H6 **Obil'noye** Rus. Fed.
90 H1 **Obira** Japan
45 C2 **Obispos** Venez.
87 O2 **Obluch'ye** Rus. Fed.
68 F4 **Obninsk** Rus. Fed.
102 C3 **Obo** C.A.R.
88 A2 **Obo** China

102 E2 **Obock** Djibouti
102 C4 **Obokote** Zaire
102 B4 **Obouya** Congo
69 F5 **Oboyan'** Rus. Fed.
68 G2 **Obozerskiy** Rus. Fed.
85 E4 **Obra** India
67 J2 **Obrenovac** Yugo.
80 D2 **Obruk** Turkey
76 J2 **Obskaya Guba** chan. Rus. Fed.
100 B4 **Obuasi** Ghana
69 D5 **Obukhiv** Ukr.
68 J2 **Ob"yachevo** Rus. Fed.
29 D6 **Ocala** U.S.A.
45 D4 **Ocamo** r. Venez.
45 B2 **Ocaña** Col.
65 E3 **Ocaña** Spain
42 E7 **Occidental, Cordillera** mts Chile
45 A4 **Occidental, Cordillera** mts Col.
42 C6 **Occidental, Cordillera** mts Peru
20 B3 **Ocean Cape** pt U.S.A.
33 F5 **Ocean City** MD U.S.A.
33 F5 **Ocean City** NJ U.S.A.
20 D4 **Ocean Falls** Can.
12 G3 **Oceanographer Fracture** sea feature Atlantic Ocean
34 D5 **Oceanside** U.S.A.
27 F6 **Ocean Springs** U.S.A.
69 D6 **Ochakiv** Ukr.
90 D6 **Ōchi** Japan
90 K2 **Ochiishi-misaki** pt Japan
57 E4 **Ochil Hills** h. U.K.
84 C1 **Ochili Pass** pass Afgh.
62 E6 **Ochsenfurt** Ger.
55 P6 **Ockelbo** Sweden
63 M7 **Ocolaşul Mare, Vârful** mt Romania
30 C4 **Oconomowoc** U.S.A.
30 D3 **Oconto** U.S.A.
34 D5 **Ocotillo Wells** U.S.A.
100 B4 **Oda** Ghana
90 D6 **Ōda** Japan
54 □ **Ódáðahraun** lava Iceland
91 H3 **Ōdate** Japan
91 G6 **Odawara** Japan
55 K6 **Odda** Norway
21 K3 **Odei** r. Can.
30 C5 **Odell** U.S.A.
65 B4 **Odemira** Port.
80 A2 **Ödemiş** Turkey
105 G3 **Odendaalsrus** S. Africa
55 M9 **Odense** Denmark
62 D6 **Odenwald** reg. Ger.
62 G3 **Oderbucht** b. Ger.
69 D6 **Odesa** Ukr.
55 O7 **Ödeshog** Sweden
27 C6 **Odessa** U.S.A.
65 C4 **Odiel** r. Spain
100 B4 **Odienné** Côte d'Ivoire
68 F4 **Odintsovo** Rus. Fed.
95 C3 **Ŏdŏngk** Cambodia
62 J6 **Odra** r. Ger./Pol.
43 K5 **Oeiras** Brazil
26 C3 **Oelrichs** U.S.A.
30 B4 **Oelwein** U.S.A.
109 **Oeno** atoll Pitcairn Is. Pac. Oc.
61 D5 **Oesling** h. Lux.
81 H1 **Of** Turkey
66 D2 **Ofanto** r. Italy
62 D5 **Offenbach am Main** Ger.
62 C6 **Offenburg** Ger.
67 M6 **Ofidoussa** i. Greece
91 H4 **Ōfunato** Japan
90 H2 **Ofuyu-misaki** pt Japan
91 G6 **Oga** Japan
91 H4 **Ogachi** Japan
102 E3 **Ogadēn** reg. Eth.
91 G4 **Oga-hantō** pen. Japan
91 F6 **Ōgaki** Japan
26 C3 **Ogallala** U.S.A.
31 H2 **Ogascanane, Lac** l. Can.
91 H5 **Ōgawa** Japan
90 H3 **Ogawara-ko** l. Japan
100 C4 **Ogbomoso** Nigeria
26 E3 **Ogden** IA U.S.A.
24 E3 **Ogden** UT U.S.A.
20 C3 **Ogden, Mt** mt. Can.
33 F2 **Ogdensburg** U.S.A.
91 G5 **Ogi** Japan
29 C5 **Oglethorpe, Mt** mt.
66 D1 **Oglio** r. Italy
116 D1 **Ogmore** Austr.
100 C4 **Ogoja** Nigeria
22 C1 **Ogoki** r. Can.
22 C3 **Ogoki Res.** resr Can.
90 C7 **Ogōri** Japan
91 G4 **Ogōri** Japan
55 T8 **Ogre** Latvia
66 F2 **Ogulin** Croatia
81 L1 **Oğuz** Azer.
117 A6 **Ohai** N.Z.
117 F3 **Ohakune** N.Z.
90 H3 **Ōhata** Japan
117 B6 **Ohau, L.** l. N.Z.
93 H7 **O'Higgins** div. Chile
44 B7 **O'Higgins, L.** l. Chile
54 C4 **Ohio** r. U.S.A.
32 B4 **Ohio** div. U.S.A.
67 J4 **Ohrid** Macedonia
67 J4 **Ohrid, Lake** l. Albania/Macedonia
105 J2 **Ohrigstad** S. Africa
117 E3 **Ohura** N.Z.
43 H3 **Oiapoque** Brazil
57 D3 **Oich, Loch** l. U.K.
85 H3 **Oiga** China

32 D4 Oil City U.S.A.
34 C4 Oildale U.S.A.
90 H3 Oirase-gawa r. Japan
64 F2 Oise r. France
61 B5 Oise à l'Aisne, Canal de l' canal France
90 C7 Ōita Japan
90 C7 Ōita Japan
67 K5 Oiti mt Greece
90 H2 Oiwake Japan
34 C4 Ojai U.S.A.
47 D2 Ojeda Arg.
30 B3 Ojibwa U.S.A.
90 B7 Ojika-jima i. Japan
36 D3 Ojinaga Mex.
91 G5 Ojiya Japan
44 C3 Ojos del Salado mt. Arg.
68 G4 Oka r. Rus. Fed.
103 B6 Okahandja Namibia
117 E3 Okahukura N.Z.
103 B6 Okakarara Namibia
23 H2 Okak Islands is Can.
20 F5 Okanagan Falls Can.
20 F4 Okanagan Lake l. Can.
24 C1 Okanogan r. Can./U.S.A.
20 F5 Okanogan U.S.A.
24 B1 Okanogan Range mts U.S.A.
102 C3 Okapi, Parc National de la nat. park Zaire
84 C3 Okara Pak.
103 B5 Okaukuejo Namibia
103 C5 Okavango r. Botswana/Namibia
103 C5 Okavango Delta swamp Botswana
90 C7 Ōkawa Japan
91 G5 Ō-kawa-gawa r. Japan
91 G5 Okaya Japan
90 D6 Okayama Japan
90 D6 Okayama Japan
91 F6 Okazaki Japan
29 D7 Okeechobee U.S.A.
29 D7 Okeechobee, L. l. U.S.A.
29 D6 Okefenokee Swamp swamp U.S.A.
59 C7 Okehampton U.K.
100 C4 Okene Nigeria
84 B5 Okha India
77 Q4 Okha Rus. Fed.
85 F4 Okhaldhunga Nepal
84 B5 Okha Rann marsh India
77 Q3 Okhotka r. Rus. Fed.
77 Q4 Okhotsk Rus. Fed.
Okhotskoye More g. see Okhotsk, Sea of
77 Q4 Okhotsk, Sea of g. Rus. Fed.
69 E5 Okhtyrka Ukr.
87 N6 Okinawa i. Japan
87 N6 Okinawa-guntō is Japan
90 C6 Okino-shima i. Japan
90 D7 Okino-shima i. Japan
90 D5 Oki-shōtō i. Japan
77 P6 Oki-shotō i. Japan
27 D5 Oklahoma div. U.S.A.
27 D5 Oklahoma City U.S.A.
27 D5 Okmulgee U.S.A.
102 B4 Okondja Gabon
20 G4 Okotoks Can.
68 E4 Okovskiy Les forest Rus. Fed.
102 B4 Okoyo Congo
54 S1 Øksfjord Norway
68 F2 Oksovskiy Rus. Fed.
76 G5 Oktyabr'sk Kazak.
68 J4 Oktyabr'sk Rus. Fed.
68 G2 Oktyabr'skiy Archangel. Rus. Fed.
69 G6 Oktyabr'skiy Volgograd. Rus. Fed.
77 R4 Oktyabr'skiy Rus. Fed.
76 G4 Oktyabr'skiy Rus. Fed.
76 H3 Oktyabr'skoye Rus. Fed.
77 L2 Oktyabr'skoy Revolyutsii, Ostrov i. Rus. Fed.
90 C7 Ōkuchi Japan
68 E3 Okulovka Rus. Fed.
90 G2 Okushiri-kaikyō chan. Japan
90 G2 Okushiri-tō i. Japan
91 E6 Okutango-hantō pen. Japan
104 E1 Okwa watercourse Botswana
54 B4 Ólafsvík Iceland
34 C3 Olancha U.S.A.
34 C3 Olancha Peak summit U.S.A.
55 P8 Öland i. Sweden
54 W3 Olanga Rus. Fed.
114 D4 Olary watercourse Austr.
114 D4 Olary Austr.
26 E4 Olathe KS U.S.A.
47 E3 Olavarría Arg.
62 H5 Oława Pol.
35 G5 Olberg U.S.A.
66 C4 Olbia Sardinia Italy
32 D3 Olcott U.S.A.
115 K3 Old Bar Austr.
60 D4 Oldcastle Rep. of Ireland
62 D4 Oldenburg Ger.
62 E3 Oldenburg in Holstein Ger.
61 E2 Oldenzaal Neth.
54 R2 Olderdalen Norway
33 F3 Old Forge NY U.S.A.
33 F4 Old Forge PA U.S.A.
58 E4 Oldham U.K.
60 C6 Old Head of Kinsale hd Rep. of Ireland
20 G4 Oldman r. Can.
57 F3 Oldmeldrum U.K.
33 H3 Old Orchard Beach U.S.A.
23 K4 Old Perlican Can.
20 G4 Olds Can.
33 J2 Old Town U.S.A.
21 H4 Old Wives L. l. Can.
35 E4 Old Woman Mts mts U.S.A.
32 D3 Olean U.S.A.
63 L3 Olecko Pol.
77 O4 Olekma r. Rus. Fed.
77 O3 Olekminsk Rus. Fed.
69 E5 Oleksandriya Ukr.
68 H1 Olema Rus. Fed.
55 J7 Ølen Norway
54 X2 Olenegorsk Rus. Fed.
77 N3 Olenek Rus. Fed.
77 O2 Olenek r. Rus. Fed.
77 O2 Olenek B. b. Rus. Fed.
68 E3 Olenino Rus. Fed.
69 C5 Olevs'k Ukr.
65 C4 Olhão Port.
104 C2 Olifants watercourse Namibia
105 J1 Olifants S. Africa
104 C5 Olifants r. S. Africa
104 E3 Olifantshoek S. Africa
104 C6 Olifantsrivierberg mts S. Africa
47 G2 Olimar Grande r. Uru.
46 C3 Olímpia Brazil
43 M5 Olinda Brazil
103 D5 Olinga Moz.
105 G2 Oliphants Drift Botswana
47 D2 Oliva Arg.
65 F3 Oliva Spain
44 C3 Oliva, Cordillera de mts Arg./Chile
47 C1 Olivares, Co del mt. Chile
32 B5 Olive Hill U.S.A.
46 D3 Oliveira Brazil
65 C3 Olivenza Spain
26 E2 Olivia U.S.A.
68 G4 Ol'khi Rus. Fed.
44 C2 Ollagüe Chile
47 B1 Ollita, Cordillera de mts Arg./Chile
47 B1 Ollitas mt. Arg.
42 C5 Olmos Peru
33 G3 Olmstedville U.S.A.
59 G5 Olney U.K.
28 C4 Olney U.S.A.
55 O8 Olofström Sweden
62 H6 Olomouc Czech Rep.
68 E2 Olonets Rus. Fed.
94 B3 Olongapo Phil.
64 D5 Oloron-Ste-Marie France
65 H1 Olot Spain
87 L1 Olovyannaya Rus. Fed.
84 C5 Olpad India
63 K4 Olsztyn Pol.
62 C7 Olten Switz.
67 M2 Oltenița Romania
81 H1 Oltu Turkey
94 B5 Olutanga i. Phil.
24 B2 Olympia U.S.A.
24 A2 Olympic Nat. Park WA U.S.A.
24 B2 Olympic Nat. Park nat. park WA U.S.A.
Olympus mt. see Troödos, Mount
67 K4 Olympus mt Greece
24 B2 Olympus, Mt mt. U.S.A.
77 S3 Olyutorskiy Rus. Fed.
77 T4 Olyutorskiy, Mys c. Rus. Fed.
77 S4 Olyutorskiy Zaliv b. Rus. Fed.
85 E2 Oma China
90 H3 Ōma Japan
91 F5 Ōmachi Japan
91 G6 Omae-zaki pt Japan
91 H4 Ōmagari Japan
60 D3 Omagh U.K.
26 E3 Omaha U.S.A.
104 C1 Omaheke div. Namibia
24 C1 Omak U.S.A.
70 Oman country Asia
79 H4 Oman, Gulf of g. Asia
117 B6 Omarama N.Z.
103 B6 Omaruru Namibia
103 B5 Omatako watercourse Namibia
42 D7 Omate Peru
104 E2 Omaweneno Botswana
90 H3 Ōma-zaki c. Japan
102 A4 Omboué Gabon
66 D3 Ombrone r. Italy
85 F3 Ombu China
104 E5 Omdraaisvlei S. Africa
101 F3 Omdurman Sudan
91 G6 Ōme Japan
66 C2 Omegna Italy
115 G6 Omeo Austr.
102 D2 Om Hājer Eritrea
91 F6 Ōmihachiman Japan
20 D3 Omineca Mountains mts Can.
104 B1 Omitara Namibia
91 G6 Ōmiya Japan
20 C3 Ommaney, Cape hd U.S.A.
61 E2 Ommen Neth.
88 B1 Ömnögovĭ div. Mongolia
77 R3 Omolon r. Rus. Fed.
102 D3 Omo National Park nat. park Eth.
91 H4 Omono-gawa r. Japan
76 J4 Omsk Rus. Fed.
77 R3 Omsukchan Rus. Fed.
90 J1 Ōmū Japan
90 B7 Ōmura Japan
90 B7 Ōmura-wan b. Japan
67 L2 Omu, Vârful mt Romania
30 B4 Onalaska U.S.A.
33 F6 Onancock U.S.A.
22 D4 Onaping Lake l. Can.
31 E3 Onaway U.S.A.
90 J2 Onbetsu Japan
95 A2 Onbingwin Myanmar
47 D1 Oncativo Arg.
58 C3 Onchan U.K.
103 B5 Oncócua Angola
103 B5 Ondangwa Namibia
104 B1 Ondekaremba Namibia
104 D5 Onderstedorings S. Africa
103 B5 Ondjiva Angola
100 C4 Ondo Nigeria
87 K2 Öndörhaan Mongolia
88 B1 Ondor Mod China
88 D1 Ondor Sum China
68 E2 Ondozero Rus. Fed.
104 D1 One Botswana
83 D10 One and Half Degree Channel chan. Maldives
68 F2 Onega Rus. Fed.
68 F2 Onega r. Rus. Fed.
68 E2 Onega, Lake l. Rus. Fed.
76 E3 Onega, Lake chan. Rus. Fed.
20 E4 100 Mile House Can.
33 F3 Oneida U.S.A.
33 F3 Oneida Lake l. U.S.A.
26 D3 O'Neill U.S.A.
77 R5 Onekotan, O. i. Rus. Fed.
33 F3 Oneonta U.S.A.
117 E2 Oneroa N.Z.
63 N7 Onești Romania
68 E1 Onezhskaya Guba g. Rus. Fed.
Onezhskove Ozero chan. see Onega, Lake
Onezhskoye Ozero l. see Onega, Lake
85 E5 Ong r. India
102 B4 Onga Gabon
117 F3 Ongaonga N.Z.
104 E4 Ongers watercourse S. Africa
88 F1 Ongniud Qi China
83 F7 Ongole India
69 G7 Oni Georgia
65 E6 Onilahy r. Madag.
100 C4 Onitsha Nigeria
104 B1 Onjati Mountain mt. Namibia
91 F6 Ōno Japan
90 H3 Ōno Japan
91 H5 Ōno Japan
90 C7 Onoda Japan
111 J4 Ono-i-Lau i. Fiji
90 D6 Onomichi Japan
111 H2 Onotoa i. Kiribati
20 G4 Onoway Can.
104 C4 Onseepkans S. Africa
112 C4 Onslow Austr.
29 E5 Onslow Bay b. U.S.A.
91 F6 Ontake-san volc. Japan
22 B3 Ontario div. Can.
24 C2 Ontario U.S.A.
31 H4 Ontario, Lake l. Can./U.S.A.
30 C2 Ontonagon U.S.A.
111 F2 Ontong Java Atoll atoll Solomon Is
113 G5 Oodnadatta Austr.
112 F6 Ooldea Austr.
27 E4 Oologah L. resr U.S.A.
61 B3 Oostakker Belgium
Oostende see Ostend
61 D2 Oostendorp Neth.
61 C3 Oosterhout Neth.
61 B3 Oosterschelde est. Neth.
61 B3 Oosterscheldekering barrage Neth.
61 A4 Oostvleteren Belgium
Ootacamund see Udagamandalam
20 D4 Ootsa Lake Can.
20 D4 Ootsa Lake l. Can.
32 E5 Opal U.S.A.
102 C4 Opala Zaire
68 J3 Oparino Rus. Fed.
22 B3 Opasquia Can.
22 B3 Opasquia Provincial Park res. Can.
22 F3 Opataca L. l. Can.
62 H6 Opava Czech Rep.
29 C5 Opelika U.S.A.
27 E6 Opelousas U.S.A.
24 F1 Opheim U.S.A.
31 F2 Ophir Can.
117 C6 Opihi r. N.Z.
22 E3 Opinaca r. Can.
22 E3 Opinaca, Réservoir resr Can.
22 D3 Opinnagau r. Can.
81 K5 Opis Iraq
23 G3 Opiscotéo L. l. Can.
68 D3 Opochka Rus. Fed.
63 H5 Opole Pol.
65 B2 Oporto Port.
117 F3 Opotiki N.Z.
29 C6 Opp U.S.A.
54 L5 Oppdal Norway
117 D3 Opunake N.Z.
103 B5 Opuwo Namibia
35 F5 Oquawka U.S.A.
33 H2 Oquossoc U.S.A.
35 G5 Oracle U.S.A.
35 G5 Oracle Junction U.S.A.
63 K7 Oradea Romania
54 E4 Öræfajökull gl. Iceland
67 J3 Orahovac Yugo.
84 D4 Orai India
100 B1 Oran Alg.
44 D2 Orán Arg.
95 C2 O Rang Cambodia
115 H4 Orange Austr.
64 G4 Orange France
103 B6 Orange r. Namibia/S. Africa
33 G3 Orange MA U.S.A.
27 E6 Orange TX U.S.A.
32 D5 Orange VA U.S.A.
29 D5 Orangeburg U.S.A.
43 H3 Orange, Cabo c. Brazil
Orange Free State div. see Free State
31 G3 Orangeville Can.
35 G2 Orangeville U.S.A.
36 G5 Orange Walk Belize
94 B3 Orani Phil.
103 B6 Oranjemund Namibia
45 C1 Oranjestad Aruba
60 C4 Oranmore Rep. of Ireland
103 C6 Orapa Botswana
94 C3 Oras Phil.
67 K2 Orăștie Romania
54 S5 Oravais Fin.
67 J2 Oravita Romania
84 E2 Orba Co l. China
66 D3 Orbetello Italy
65 D1 Orbigo r. Spain
115 H6 Orbost Austr.
119 B1 Orcadas Argentina Base Ant.
35 H2 Orchard Mesa U.S.A.
45 D2 Orchila, Isla i. Venez.
34 B4 Orcutt U.S.A.
112 E3 Ord, Mt h. Austr.
25 D4 Orderville U.S.A.
65 B1 Ordes Spain
34 D4 Ord Mt mt. U.S.A.
80 F1 Ordu Turkey
81 L2 Ordubad Azer.
25 G4 Ordway U.S.A.
Ordzhonikidze see Vladikavkaz
69 E6 Ordzhonikidze Ukr.
34 C1 Oreana U.S.A.
55 O7 Örebro Sweden
30 C4 Oregon IL U.S.A.
32 B4 Oregon OH U.S.A.
30 C4 Oregon WV U.S.A.
24 B3 Oregon div. U.S.A.
24 B2 Oregon City U.S.A.
68 F4 Orekhovo-Zuyevo Rus. Fed.
68 F4 Orel Rus. Fed.
35 G1 Orem U.S.A.
80 A2 Ören Turkey
67 M6 Ören Turkey
76 G4 Orenburg Rus. Fed.
47 E3 Orense Arg.
117 A7 Orepuki N.Z.
55 N9 Øresund str. Denmark
117 E2 Orewa N.Z.
67 K4 Orfanou, Kolpos b. Greece
115 G9 Orford Austr.
59 J5 Orford U.K.
59 J5 Orford Ness spit U.K.
35 F5 Organ Pipe Cactus National Monument res. U.S.A.
84 B2 Orgūn Afgh.
80 B2 Orhaneli Turkey
69 D7 Orhangazi Turkey
68 J3 Orichi Rus. Fed.
33 K2 Orient U.S.A.
42 E7 Oriental, Cordillera mts Bol.
45 B3 Oriental, Cordillera mts Col.
42 D6 Oriental, Cordillera mts Peru
47 E3 Oriente Arg.
65 F3 Orihuela Spain
69 E6 Orikhiv Ukr.
31 H3 Orillia Can.
55 T6 Orimattila Fin.
45 E2 Orinoco r. Col./Venez.
45 E2 Orinoco Delta delta Venez.
85 F5 Orissa div. India
55 S7 Orissaare Estonia
66 C5 Oristano Sardinia Italy
55 T6 Orivesi Fin.
54 V5 Orivesi l. Fin.
43 G4 Oriximiná Brazil
36 E5 Orizaba Mex.
54 L5 Orkanger Norway
55 N8 Örkelljunga Sweden
54 L5 Orkla r. Norway
105 G3 Orkney S. Africa
56 E2 Orkney Islands is U.K.
27 C6 Orla U.S.A.
34 A2 Orland U.S.A.
46 C3 Orlândia Brazil
29 D6 Orlando U.S.A.
64 E3 Orléans France
33 J4 Orleans MA U.S.A.
33 G2 Orleans VT U.S.A.
68 J3 Orlov Rus. Fed.
68 F4 Orlovskaya Oblast' div. Rus. Fed.
69 G6 Orlovskiy Rus. Fed.
94 C4 Ormoc Phil.
29 D6 Ormond Beach U.S.A.
58 E4 Ormskirk U.K.
33 G2 Ormstown Can.
64 D2 Orne r. France
54 N3 Ørnes Norway
54 Q5 Örnsköldsvik Sweden
45 C3 Orocué Col.
100 B3 Orodara Burkina
24 C2 Orofino U.S.A.
25 F5 Orogrande U.S.A.
23 G4 Oromocto Can.
80 E6 Oron Israel
111 J2 Orona i. Kiribati
33 J2 Orono U.S.A.
57 B4 Oronsay i. U.K.
80 E3 Orontes r. Asia
87 M1 Oroqen Zizhiqi China
94 B4 Oroquieta Phil.
43 L5 Orós, Açude resr Brazil
66 C4 Orosei Sardinia Italy
66 C4 Orosei, Golfo di b. Sardinia Italy
63 K7 Orosháza Hungary
35 G5 Oro Valley U.S.A.
34 B2 Oroville CA U.S.A.
24 C1 Oroville WA U.S.A.
34 B2 Oroville, Lake l. U.S.A.
116 B2 Orpheus I. i. Austr.
114 C4 Orroroo Austr.
55 O6 Orsa Sweden
68 D4 Orsha Belarus
76 G4 Orsk Rus. Fed.
55 K5 Ørsta Norway
65 C1 Ortegal, Cabo c. Spain
64 D5 Orthez France
65 C1 Ortigueira Spain
45 D2 Ortíz Venez.
66 D1 Ortles mt Italy
58 E3 Orton U.K.
66 F3 Ortona Italy
26 D2 Ortonville U.S.A.
77 O3 Orulgan, Khrebet mts Rus. Fed.
104 B1 Orumbo Namibia
81 K3 Orūmīyeh Iran
81 K3 Orūmīyeh, Daryācheh-ye salt l. Iran
42 E7 Oruro Bol.
66 E3 Orvieto Italy
32 C4 Orwell OH U.S.A.
33 G3 Orwell VT U.S.A.
55 M5 Os Norway
30 A4 Osage U.S.A.
26 E4 Osage r. U.S.A.
91 E6 Ōsaka Japan
91 E6 Ōsaka Japan
37 H7 Osa, Pen. de pen. Costa Rica
61 E5 Osburger Hochwald forest Ger.
55 N8 Osby Sweden
27 F5 Osceola AR U.S.A.
26 E3 Osceola IA U.S.A.
66 C4 Oschiri Sardinia Italy
31 F3 Oscoda U.S.A.
68 F4 Osetr r. Rus. Fed.
90 B7 Ōse-zaki pt Japan
31 K3 Osgoode Can.
79 L1 Osh Kyrgyzstan
103 B5 Oshakati Namibia
90 H2 Oshamanbe Japan
31 H4 Oshawa Can.
91 H4 Oshika Japan
91 H4 Oshika-hantō pen. Japan
91 E7 Ō-shima i. Japan
91 G6 Ō-Shima i. Japan
90 C7 Ō-shima i. Japan
90 G3 Ō-shima i. Japan
90 H2 Oshima-hantō pen. Japan
26 C3 Oshkosh NE U.S.A.
30 C3 Oshkosh WV U.S.A.
81 K3 Oshnovīyeh Iran
100 C4 Oshogbo Nigeria
81 M5 Oshtorān Kūh mt. Iran
81 M5 Oshtorīnān Iran
102 B4 Oshwe Zaire
67 H2 Osijek Croatia
66 E3 Osimo Italy
84 C4 Osiyān India
105 J3 Osizweni S. Africa
66 G2 Osječenica mt. Bos.-Herz.
54 O5 Ösjön l. Sweden
26 E3 Oskaloosa U.S.A.
55 P8 Oskarshamn Sweden
31 K1 Oskélanéo Can.
69 F5 Oskol r. Rus. Fed.
55 M7 Oslo Norway
94 B4 Oslob Phil.
55 M7 Oslofjorden chan. Norway
80 E1 Osmancık Turkey
80 B1 Osmaneli Turkey
80 F3 Osmaniye Turkey
55 V7 Os'mino Rus. Fed.
62 D4 Osnabrück Ger.
67 K3 Osogovske Planine mts Bulg./Macedonia
47 B4 Osorno Chile
65 D1 Osorno Spain
47 B4 Osorno, Vol. volc. Chile
20 F5 Osoyoos Can.
55 J6 Osøyri Norway
113 J2 Osprey Reef rf Coral Sea Is Terr.
61 D3 Oss Neth.
115 G8 Ossa, Mt mt. Austr.
30 B3 Osseo U.S.A.
31 F3 Ossineke U.S.A.
33 H3 Ossipee Lake l. U.S.A.
23 H3 Ossokmanuan Lake l. Can.
68 E3 Ostashkov Rus. Fed.
61 A3 Ostend Belgium
63 P5 Oster Ukr.
55 O8 Österbymo Sweden
55 N6 Österdalälven l. Sweden
55 M5 Østerdalen v. Norway
54 O5 Östersund Sweden
55 Q6 Östhammar Sweden
62 J6 Ostrava Czech Rep.
63 J4 Ostróda Pol.
69 F5 Ostrogozhsk Rus. Fed.
68 D3 Ostrov Rus. Fed.
63 K5 Ostrowiec Świętokrzyski Pol.
63 K4 Ostrów Mazowiecka Pol.
62 H5 Ostrów Wielkopolski Pol.
67 L3 Osŭm r. Bulg.
90 C8 Ōsumi Hantō pen. Japan
87 O5 Ōsumi-shotō is Japan
65 D4 Osuna Spain
33 F2 Oswegatchie U.S.A.
30 C5 Oswego IL U.S.A.
32 E3 Oswego NY U.S.A.
33 E3 Oswego r. U.S.A.
59 D5 Oswestry U.K.
91 G5 Ōta Japan
90 D6 Ōta-gawa r. Japan
117 C6 Otago Peninsula pen. N.Z.
117 E4 Otaki N.Z.
54 U4 Otanmäki Fin.
45 B4 Otare, Co h. Col.
90 H2 Otaru Japan
117 B7 Otatara N.Z.
42 C3 Otavalo Ecuador
103 B5 Otavi Namibia
91 H5 Ōtawara Japan
117 C6 Otematata N.Z.
55 U7 Otepää Estonia
24 C2 Othello U.S.A.
117 C5 Otira N.Z.
33 E3 Otisco Lake l. U.S.A.
23 F3 Otish, Monts mts Can.
103 B6 Otjiwarongo Namibia
58 F4 Otley U.K.
90 H3 Otobe Japan
90 J2 Otofuke Japan
90 J2 Otofuke-gawa r. Japan
88 C2 Otog Qi China
90 J1 Otoineppu Japan
117 E3 Otorohanga N.Z.
22 C3 Otoskwin r. Can.
90 D7 Ōtoyo Japan
67 H4 Otranto Italy
67 H4 Otranto, Strait of str. Albania/Italy
77 T3 Otrozhnyy Rus. Fed.
30 E4 Otsego U.S.A.
30 E3 Otsego Lake l. MI U.S.A.
33 F3 Otsego Lake l. NY U.S.A.
33 F3 Otselic U.S.A.
91 E6 Ōtsu Japan
55 L6 Otta Norway
31 K3 Ottawa Can.
31 H2 Ottawa r. Can.
30 C5 Ottawa IL U.S.A.
26 E4 Ottawa KS U.S.A.
32 A4 Ottawa OH U.S.A.
22 D2 Ottawa Islands is Can.
58 E3 Otterburn U.K.
35 G2 Otter Creek Reservoir resr U.S.A.
30 D1 Otter I. i. Can.
22 D3 Otter Rapids Can.
59 C7 Ottery r. U.K.
61 C4 Ottignies Belgium
30 A5 Ottumwa U.S.A.
100 C4 Otukpo Nigeria
44 D3 Otumpa Arg.
42 C5 Otuzco Peru
114 E7 Otway, C. c. Austr.
27 E5 Ouachita r. U.S.A.
27 E5 Ouachita, L. l. U.S.A.
27 E5 Ouachita Mts mts U.S.A.
102 C3 Ouadda C.A.R.
101 E3 Ouaddaï reg. Chad
100 B3 Ouagadougou Burkina
100 B3 Ouahigouya Burkina
100 B2 Oualâta Maur.
102 C3 Ouanda-Djailé C.A.R.
100 B2 Ouarâne reg. Maur.
100 C1 Ouargla Alg.
100 B1 Ouarzazate Morocco
104 F6 Oubergpas pass S. Africa
61 B4 Oudenaarde Belgium
104 E6 Oudtshoorn S. Africa
65 F5 Oued Tlélat Alg.
100 B1 Oued Zem Morocco
66 B6 Oued Zénati Alg.
64 B2 Ouessant, Île d' i. France
102 B3 Ouésso Congo
100 C4 Ouidah Benin
100 B1 Oujda Morocco
54 T4 Oulainen Fin.
65 G4 Ouled Farès Alg.
54 T4 Oulu Fin.
54 U4 Oulujärvi l. Fin.
54 U4 Oulujoki r. Fin.
54 T4 Oulunsalo Fin.
101 E3 Oum-Chalouba Chad
100 B4 Oumé Côte d'Ivoire
101 D3 Oum-Hadjer Chad
54 T3 Ounasjoki r. Fin.
59 G5 Oundle U.K.
101 E3 Ounianga Kébir Chad
61 D4 Oupeye Belgium
61 E5 Our r. Lux.
25 F4 Ouray CO U.S.A.
35 H1 Ouray UT U.S.A.
65 C1 Ourense Spain
43 K5 Ouricuri Brazil
46 C3 Ourinhos Brazil
46 C1 Ouro r. Brazil
46 D3 Ouro Preto Brazil
61 D4 Ourthe r. Belgium
62 C6 Our, Vallée de l' v. Ger./Lux.
58 G4 Ouse r. Eng. U.K.
59 H7 Ouse r. Eng. U.K.
23 G3 Outardes r. Can.
104 E6 Outeniekpas pass S. Africa
57 A2 Outer Hebrides is Scot. U.K.
30 B2 Outer I. i. U.S.A.

34 C5 Outer Santa Barbara Channel chan. U.S.A.
103 B6 Outjo Namibia
54 V5 Outokumpu Fin.
57 □ Out Skerries is U.K.
111 G4 Ouvéa i. New Caledonia
89 D5 Ouyang Hai Sk. resr China
114 C5 Ouyen Peru
59 G5 Ouzel r. U.K.
66 C4 Ovace, Pte d' mt Corsica France
81 G2 Ovacık Turkey
66 C2 Ovada Italy
111 H3 Ovalau i. Fiji
47 B1 Ovalle Chile
65 D2 Ovar Port.
47 D2 Oveja mt Arg.
115 G6 Ovens r. Austr.
54 S3 Överkalix Sweden
112 B5 Overlander Roadhouse Austr.
35 E3 Overton U.S.A.
54 S3 Övertorneå Sweden
55 P8 Överum Sweden
61 C2 Overveen Neth.
30 E4 Ovid U.S.A.
65 D1 Oviedo Spain
54 T2 Øvre Anarjåkka Nasjonalpark nat. park Norway
54 Q2 Øvre Dividal Nasjonalpark nat. park Norway
55 M6 Øvre Rendal Norway
69 D5 Ovruch Ukr.
117 B7 Owaka N.Z.
102 B4 Owando Congo
91 F6 Owase Japan
26 E2 Owatonna U.S.A.
33 E3 Owego U.S.A.
13 H3 Owen Fracture sea feature Indian Ocean
60 D3 Owenmore r. Rep. of Ireland
117 D4 Owen River N.Z.
34 C3 Owens r. U.S.A.
28 C4 Owensboro U.S.A.
34 D3 Owens Lake l. U.S.A.
31 G3 Owen Sound in. Can.
31 G3 Owen Sound Can.
110 E2 Owen Stanley Range mts P.N.G.
100 C4 Owerri Nigeria
20 D4 Owikeno L. l. Can.
32 B5 Owingsville U.S.A.
33 J2 Owls Head U.S.A.
100 C4 Owo Nigeria
31 E4 Owosso U.S.A.
81 L4 Owrāmān, Kūh-e mts Iran/Iraq
24 C3 Owyhee Peru
24 C3 Owyhee r. U.S.A.
24 C3 Owyhee Mts mts U.S.A.
42 C6 Oxapampa Peru
54 E3 Öxarfjörður b. Iceland
21 J5 Oxbow Can.
33 J1 Oxbow U.S.A.
55 P7 Oxelösund Sweden
117 D5 Oxford N.Z.
59 F6 Oxford U.K.
31 F4 Oxford MI U.S.A.
27 F5 Oxford MS U.S.A.
33 F3 Oxford NY U.S.A.
33 F5 Oxford PA U.S.A.
116 C3 Oxford Downs Austr.
21 K4 Oxford House Can.
21 K4 Oxford L. l. Can.
114 F5 Oxley Austr.
115 J3 Oxleys Pk mt Austr.
34 C4 Oxnard U.S.A.
31 H3 Oxtongue Lake Can.
54 N3 Øya Norway
91 F5 Oyabe Japan
91 G5 Oyama Japan
43 H3 Oyapock r. Brazil/Fr. Guiana
102 B3 Oyem Gabon
57 J3 Oykel r. U.K.
100 C4 Oyo Nigeria
64 G3 Oyonnax France
115 H9 Oyster B. b. Austr.
85 H5 Oyster I. i. Myanmar
91 J4 O-zaki pt Japan
94 B4 Ozamiz Phil.
29 C6 Ozark AL U.S.A.
30 E2 Ozark MI U.S.A.
27 E4 Ozark Plateau plat. U.S.A.
26 E4 Ozarks, Lake of the l. U.S.A.
69 G7 Ozerget'i Georgia
77 R4 Ozernovskiy Rus. Fed.
68 E4 Ozernyy Rus. Fed.
63 L3 Ozersk Rus. Fed.
68 F4 Ozery Rus. Fed.
77 Q3 Ozhogino Rus. Fed.
66 C4 Ozieri Sardinia Italy
27 C6 Ozona U.S.A.
90 D7 Özu Japan
90 C6 Ozuki Japan

# P

95 A1 Pa-an Myanmar
104 C6 Paarl S. Africa
104 D4 Paballelo S. Africa
57 A4 Pabbay i. Scot. U.K.
57 A3 Pabbay i. Scot. U.K.

63 J5 Pabianice Pol.
85 G4 Pabna Bangl.
55 T9 Pabradė Lith.
79 K4 Pab Range mts Pak.
42 F6 Pacaás Novos, Parque Nacional nat. park Brazil
45 E4 Pacaraima, Serra mts Brazil
42 C5 Pacasmayo Peru
25 E6 Pacheco Chihuahua Mex.
68 H2 Pachikha Rus. Fed.
66 F6 Pachino Sicily Italy
84 D5 Pachore India
36 E4 Pachuca Mex.
34 B2 Pacific U.S.A.
94 C4 Pacijan i. Phil.
43 H4 Pacoval Brazil
46 D2 Pacuí r. Brazil
62 H5 Paczków Pol.
94 C5 Padada Phil.
45 D4 Padamo r. Venez.
92 C7 Padang Indon.
92 C7 Padangpanjang Indon.
95 A5 Padangsidimpuan Indon.
68 E2 Padany Rus. Fed.
81 M5 Padatha, Kūh-e mt Iran
45 D4 Padauiri r. Brazil
42 F8 Padcaya Bol.
20 F3 Paddle Prairie Can.
32 C5 Paden City U.S.A.
62 D5 Paderborn Ger.
67 K2 Padeșu, Vârful mt Romania
42 F7 Padilla Bol.
54 P3 Padjelanta National Park nat. park Sweden
85 G4 Padma r. Bangl.
Padma see Padua
27 D6 Padre Island i. U.S.A.
66 C3 Padro, Monte mt Corsica France
59 D7 Padstow U.K.
63 N3 Padsvilye Belarus
114 D6 Padthaway Austr.
66 D2 Padua Italy
28 B4 Paducah KY U.S.A.
27 B5 Paducah TX U.S.A.
84 D2 Padum Jammu and Kashmir
117 E2 Paeroa N.Z.
94 B3 Paete Phil.
80 D4 Pafos Cyprus
105 J1 Pafúri Moz.
66 F2 Pag Croatia
66 F2 Pag i. Croatia
94 B5 Pagadian Phil.
92 C7 Pagai Selatan i. Indon.
92 C7 Pagai Utara i. Indon.
93 L3 Pagan i. N. Mariana Is
92 F7 Pagatan Indon.
35 G2 Page U.S.A.
55 R9 Pagėgiai Lith.
116 E2 Paget Cay rf Coral Sea Is Terr.
44 □ Paget, Mt mt S. Georgia Atlantic Ocean
25 F4 Pagosa Springs U.S.A.
22 C3 Pagwa River Can.
34 □2 Pahala U.S.A.
84 B2 Paharpur Pak.
117 A7 Pahia Pt pt N.Z.
34 □2 Pahoa U.S.A.
29 D7 Pahokee U.S.A.
35 E3 Pahranagat Range mts U.S.A.
84 D4 Pahuj r. India
34 D3 Pahute Mesa plat. U.S.A.
95 A1 Pai Thai.
55 T7 Paide Estonia
59 D7 Paignton U.K.
55 T6 Päijänne l. Fin.
85 F3 Paiku Co l. China
95 B2 Pailin Cambodia
47 B4 Paillaco Chile
34 □2 Pailolo Chan. chan. U.S.A.
55 S6 Paimio Fin.
47 B2 Paine Chile
32 C4 Painesville U.S.A.
35 G3 Painted Desert des. U.S.A.
35 F5 Painted Rock Reservoir resr U.S.A.
114 C3 Painter, Mount mt Austr.
21 K3 Paint Lake Provincial Recr. Park res. Can.
32 B6 Paintsville U.S.A.
31 G3 Paisley Can.
57 D5 Paisley U.K.
42 B5 Paita Peru
94 A5 Paitan, Teluk b. Malaysia
89 D4 Paizhou China
54 S3 Pajala Sweden
43 L5 Pajeú r. Brazil
95 B4 Paka Malaysia
42 F2 Pakaraima Mountains mts Guyana
31 J3 Pakesley Can.
77 S3 Pakhacha Rus. Fed.
70 Pakistan country Asia
Paknampho see Muang Nakhon Sawan
83 J6 Pakokku Myanmar
117 D1 Pakotai N.Z.
84 C3 Pakpattan Pak.
95 B4 Pak Phayun Thai.
55 S9 Pakruojis Lith.
63 J7 Paks Hungary
84 B2 Paktīkā Afgh.
95 C2 Pakxé Laos
101 D4 Pala Chad
95 A2 Pala Myanmar
66 G3 Palagruža i. Croatia

67 K7 Palaiochora Greece
64 F2 Palaiseau France
Palakkat see Palghat
104 E1 Palamakoloi Botswana
65 H2 Palamós Spain
84 C4 Palana India
77 R4 Palana Rus. Fed.
94 B2 Palanan Phil.
94 B2 Palanan Point pt Phil.
84 C4 Palanpur India
94 C3 Palapag Phil.
103 C6 Palapye Botswana
85 G4 Palasbari India
77 R3 Palatka Rus. Fed.
71 Palau country Pac. Oc.
94 B2 Palaui i. Phil.
94 A3 Palauig Phil.
95 A2 Palauk Myanmar
14 E5 Palau Tr. sea feature Pac. Oc.
95 A2 Palaw Myanmar
94 A4 Palawan i. Phil.
94 B3 Palayan Phil.
55 T7 Paldiski Estonia
85 H5 Pale Myanmar
61 D2 Paleis Het Loo Neth.
92 C7 Palembang Indon.
44 B6 Palena Chile
65 D1 Palencia Spain
36 F5 Palenque Mex.
66 E6 Palermo Sicily Italy
27 E6 Palestine U.S.A.
85 H5 Paletwa Myanmar
84 C4 Pali India
106 Palikir Micronesia
94 C5 Palimbang Phil.
66 F4 Palinuro, Capo c. Italy
35 H2 Palisade U.S.A.
61 D5 Paliseul Belgium
84 B5 Palitana India
55 S7 Palivere Estonia
68 D3 Palkino Rus. Fed.
83 E9 Palk Strait str. India/Sri Lanka
115 J2 Pallamallawa Austr.
60 C5 Pallas Green Rep. of Ireland
54 S2 Pallas-ja Ounastunturin Kansallispuisto nat. park Fin.
69 H5 Pallasovka Rus. Fed.
117 E4 Palliser Bay b. N.Z.
117 E4 Palliser, Cape c. N.Z.
84 C3 Pallu India
65 D4 Palma del Río Spain
65 H3 Palma de Mallorca Spain
100 A2 Palma, La i. Canary Is
45 C2 Palmar r. Venez.
45 C3 Palmarito Venez.
100 B4 Palmas, Cape c. Liberia
46 D1 Palmas de Monte Alto Brazil
29 D7 Palm Bay U.S.A.
29 D7 Palm Beach U.S.A.
34 C4 Palmdale U.S.A.
46 B4 Palmeira Brazil
43 L5 Palmeira dos Índios Brazil
43 K5 Palmeirais Brazil
119 B2 Palmer U.S.A. Base Ant.
117 C6 Palmerston N.Z.
116 C3 Palmerston, C. pt Austr.
108 Palmerston Island i. Cook Islands Pac. Oc.
117 E4 Palmerston North N.Z.
33 F4 Palmerton U.S.A.
29 E7 Palmetto Pt pt Bahamas
66 F5 Palmi Italy
45 A4 Palmira Col.
34 D5 Palm Springs U.S.A.
116 C5 Palm Tree Cr. r. Austr.
Palmyra see Tadmur
30 B6 Palmyra MO U.S.A.
32 E3 Palmyra NY U.S.A.
30 C4 Palmyra WV U.S.A.
109 Palmyra I. i. Pac. Oc.
85 F5 Palmyras Point pt India
34 A3 Palo Alto U.S.A.
45 A3 Palo de las Letras Col.
101 F3 Paloich Sudan
54 S2 Palojärvi Fin.
54 U2 Palomaa Fin.
34 D5 Palomar Mt mt. U.S.A.
35 G6 Palominas U.S.A.
93 G7 Palopo Indon.
65 F4 Palos, Cabo de c. Spain
35 F4 Palo Verde AZ U.S.A.
35 E5 Palo Verde CA U.S.A.
54 U4 Paltamo Fin.
93 F7 Palu Indon.
81 G2 Palu Turkey
94 B3 Paluan Phil.
84 D3 Palwal India
77 T3 Palyavaam r. Rus. Fed.
115 H6 Pambula Austr.
92 □ Pamekasan Indon.
92 □ Pameungpeuk Indon.
64 E5 Pamiers France
82 D3 Pamir mts Asia
29 E5 Pamlico Sound chan. U.S.A.
27 C5 Pampa U.S.A.
47 C2 Pampa de la Salinas salt pan Arg.
42 F7 Pampa Grande Bol.
40 Pampas reg. Arg.
45 B3 Pamplona Col.
94 B4 Pamplona Phil.
65 F1 Pamplona Spain
80 C1 Pamukova Turkey
32 C6 Pamunkey r. U.S.A.
84 D2 Pamzal Jammu and Kashmir
28 B4 Pana U.S.A.

94 C5 Panabo Phil.
35 E2 Panaca U.S.A.
94 A4 Panagtaran Point pt Phil.
92 □ Panaitan i. Indon.
83 D7 Panaji India
37 J7 Panamá Panama
37 J7 Panama Canal canal Panama
29 C6 Panama City U.S.A.
37 J7 Panamá, Golfo de b. Panama
34 D3 Panamint Range mts U.S.A.
34 D3 Panamint Springs U.S.A.
34 D3 Panamint Valley U.S.A.
94 C4 Panaon i. Phil.
85 G4 Panar r. India
66 F5 Panarea, Isola i. Italy
95 □ Panarik Indon.
94 B4 Panay i. Phil.
94 C3 Panay i. Phil.
94 B4 Panay Gulf b. Phil.
35 E2 Pancake Range mts U.S.A.
67 J2 Pančevo Yugo.
94 B4 Pandan Phil.
94 B4 Pandan Phil.
94 B4 Pandan B. b. Phil.
95 □ Pandan Res. resr Sing.
84 C5 Pandaria India
46 D1 Pandeiros r. Brazil
83 E7 Pandharpur India
84 D5 Pandhurna India
47 F2 Pando Uru.
59 E6 Pandy U.K.
55 T9 Panevėžys Lith.
84 C2 Pangi Range mts Pak.
92 B6 Pangkalansusu Indon.
92 □ Pangkalpinang Indon.
93 G7 Pangkalsiang, Tanjung pt Indon.
94 B4 Panglao i. Phil.
76 J3 Pangody Rus. Fed.
84 D2 Pangong Tso l. India
92 □ Pangrango volc. Indon.
47 B3 Panguipulli Chile
47 B3 Panguipulli, L. l. Chile
35 F3 Panguitch U.S.A.
94 A5 Pangururan Indon.
94 B5 Pangutaran i. Phil.
94 B5 Pangutaran Group is Phil.
27 C5 Panhandle U.S.A.
102 C4 Pania-Mwanga Zaire
84 B5 Pānikoita i. India
69 G5 Panino Rus. Fed.
84 D3 Panipat India
94 A4 Panitan Phil.
95 □ Panjang i. Indon.
81 L5 Panjbarār Iran
79 J4 Panjgur Pak.
84 C5 Panjhra r. India
84 B2 Panjkora r. Pak.
84 B3 Panjnad r. Pak.
Panjim see Panaji
54 W5 Pankakoski Fin.
100 C4 Pankshin Nigeria
46 B3 Panorama Brazil
88 C1 Panshan China
87 N3 Panshi China
46 A2 Pantanal de São Lourenço marsh Brazil
46 A2 Pantanal do Taquarí marsh Brazil
43 G7 Pantanal Matogrossense, Parque Nacional do nat. park Brazil
66 D6 Pantelleria Sicily Italy
66 E6 Pantelleria, Isola di i. Sicily Italy
93 G8 Pantemakassar Indon.
94 C5 Pantukan Phil.
36 E4 Pánuco Mex.
89 B5 Pan Xian China
89 D6 Panyu China
102 B4 Panzi Zaire
45 E2 Pao r. Venez.
66 G5 Paola Italy
28 C4 Paoli U.S.A.
102 C3 Paoua C.A.R.
62 H7 Pápa Hungary
117 E2 Papakura N.Z.
66 F4 Papa, Monte del mt Italy
36 E4 Papantla Mex.
117 C5 Paparoa Range mts N.Z.
57 □ Papa Stour i. U.K.
117 B7 Papatowai N.Z.
62 F1 Papenburg Ger.
110 E2 Papua, Gulf of g. P.N.G.
106 Papua New Guinea country Australasia
95 A1 Papun Myanmar
59 A1 Par U.K.
43 J4 Pará r. Brazil
43 J4 Pará r. Brazil
68 G4 Para r. Rus. Fed.
112 C4 Paraburdoo Austr.
94 B3 Paracale Phil.
46 C2 Paracatu Minas Gerais Brazil

46 D2 Paracatu r. Brazil
114 C3 Parachilna Austr.
67 J3 Paraćin Yugo.
46 D2 Pará de Minas Brazil
31 J1 Paradis Can.
34 B2 Paradise CA U.S.A.
30 E2 Paradise MI U.S.A.
21 H4 Paradise Hill Can.
34 D2 Paradise Peak summit U.S.A.
23 J3 Paradise River Can.
27 F4 Paragould U.S.A.
42 F6 Paragua r. Bol.
45 E3 Paragua r. Venez.
43 G7 Paraguai r. Brazil
45 C2 Paraguaípoa Venez.
45 C1 Paraguaná, Pen. de pen. Venez.
44 E3 Paraguay r. Arg./Para.
38 Paraguay country S. America
43 L5 Paraíba r. Brazil
46 D3 Paraíba do Sul r. Brazil
100 C4 Parakou Benin
114 B3 Parakylia Austr.
84 E6 Paralkot India
43 G2 Paramaribo Suriname
45 B3 Paramillo mt Col.
45 A3 Paramillo, Parque Nacional nat. park Col.
46 D1 Paramirim Brazil
45 A3 Paramo Frontino mt. Col.
33 F4 Paramus U.S.A.
77 R4 Paramushir, O. i. Rus. Fed.
47 E1 Paraná Arg.
46 E1 Paraná r. Brazil
46 B3 Paraná div. Brazil
43 J6 Paraná Brazil
47 E2 Paraná r. S. America
46 C4 Paranaguá Brazil
46 B2 Paranaíba Brazil
46 B2 Paranaíba r. Brazil
47 E2 Paraná Ibicuy r. Arg.
46 B3 Paranapanema r. Brazil
46 C4 Paranapiacaba, Serra mts Brazil
46 C1 Paranã, Sa do h. Brazil
46 B3 Paranavaí Brazil
84 B5 Parandak Pass pass Afgh.
94 B5 Parang Phil.
67 K2 Parângul Mare, Vârful mt. Romania
84 C3 Parantij India
46 D2 Paraopeba r. Brazil
81 K4 Pārāpāra Iraq
117 E4 Paraparaumu N.Z.
45 D3 Paraque, Co mt. Venez.
27 D7 Paras Mex.
84 D5 Paratwada India
46 B2 Paraúna Brazil
64 G3 Paray-le-Monial France
84 D7 Parbati r. India
83 E7 Parbhani India
62 E4 Parchim Ger.
30 C4 Pardeeville U.S.A.
85 G2 Parding China
46 E1 Pardo r. Bahia/Minas Gerais Brazil
46 B3 Pardo r. Mato Grosso do Sul Brazil
46 D1 Pardo r. Minas Gerais Brazil
46 C3 Pardo r. São Paulo Brazil
62 G5 Pardubice Czech Rep.
92 □ Pare Indon.
84 D2 Pare Chu r. China
85 G4 Pare Chu r. India
42 F6 Parecis, Serra dos h. Brazil
81 K2 Pareh Iran
117 D1 Parengarenga Harbour in. N.Z.
22 E4 Parent, Lac l. Can.
117 C6 Pareora N.Z.
93 F7 Parepare Indon.
47 D2 Parera Arg.
68 G3 Parfen'yevo Rus. Fed.
63 P2 Parfino Rus. Fed.
67 J5 Parga Greece
55 S6 Pargas Fin.
45 D2 Pariaguán Venez.
45 E2 Paria, Gulf of g. Trinidad/Venez.
45 E2 Paria, Península de pen. Venez.
35 F3 Paria Plateau plat. U.S.A.
55 V6 Parikkala Fin.
42 B4 Pariñas, Pta pt Peru
45 C3 Parima, Serra mts Brazil
45 D4 Parima-Tirapecó, Parque Nacional nat. park Venez./Brazil
42 B4 Parintins Brazil
31 G4 Paris Can.
64 F2 Paris France
32 A5 Paris KY U.S.A.
29 B4 Paris TN U.S.A.
27 E5 Paris TX U.S.A.
60 D3 Park U.K.
55 S5 Parkano Fin.
23 J3 Parke Lake l. Can.
35 E4 Parker U.S.A.
30 B4 Parker Dam dam U.S.A.
21 K2 Parker Lake l. Can.
89 □ Parker, Mt h. Hong Kong China
30 A4 Parkersburg IA U.S.A.
32 C5 Parkersburg WV U.S.A.
115 H4 Parkes Austr.

30 B3 Park Falls U.S.A.
30 D5 Park Forest U.S.A.
31 F4 Parkinson Can.
26 E2 Park Rapids U.S.A.
20 E5 Parksville Can.
33 F4 Parksville U.S.A.
85 F6 Parla Kimedi India
66 D2 Parma Italy
24 C3 Parma ID U.S.A.
32 C4 Parma OH U.S.A.
45 D3 Parmana Venez.
43 K4 Parnaíba Brazil
43 K4 Parnaíba r. Brazil
67 K5 Parnassos mt Greece
117 D5 Parnassus N.Z.
114 B5 Parndana Austr.
30 A5 Parnell U.S.A.
67 K6 Parnon mts Greece
55 T7 Pärnu Estonia
55 T7 Pärnu-Jaagupi Estonia
114 F2 Paroo watercourse Austr.
79 J3 Paropamisus mts Afgh.
67 L6 Paros i. Greece
67 L6 Paros Greece
35 F3 Parowan U.S.A.
47 B3 Parral Chile
33 F6 Parramore I. i. U.S.A.
36 D3 Parras Mex.
47 J3 Parravicini Arg.
59 E6 Parrett r. U.K.
23 H4 Parrsboro Can.
18 Parry Islands is Can.
31 G3 Parry Sound Can.
27 E4 Parsons KS U.S.A.
32 D5 Parsons WV U.S.A.
64 D3 Parthenay France
59 H4 Partney U.K.
60 B4 Partry Rep. of Ireland
60 B4 Partry Mts h. Rep. of Ireland
43 H4 Paru r. Brazil
45 D3 Parucito r. Venez.
84 C4 Parvatsar India
84 D4 Parwan r. India
85 E3 Paryang China
105 G3 Parys S. Africa
34 C4 Pasadena CA U.S.A.
27 E6 Pasadena TX U.S.A.
42 B4 Pasado, C. pt Ecuador
95 A1 Pasawng Myanmar
27 F6 Pascagoula U.S.A.
31 J1 Pascalis Can.
63 N7 Pașcani Romania
24 C3 Pasco U.S.A.
46 E2 Pascoal, Monte h. Brazil
94 B3 Pascual Phil.
Pas de Calais str. see Dover, Strait of
62 G4 Pasewalk Ger.
21 H3 Pasfield Lake l. Can.
68 F2 Pasha Rus. Fed.
94 B3 Pasig Phil.
81 H2 Pasinler Turkey
95 □ Pasir Gudang Malaysia
95 □ Pasir Putih Malaysia
92 C5 Pasir Putih Malaysia
34 A2 Paskenta U.S.A.
79 J4 Pasni Pak.
45 B4 Paso de las Cruces mt Col.
47 E2 Paso de los Toros Uru.
44 B7 Paso Río Mayo Arg.
34 B4 Paso Robles U.S.A.
21 J4 Pasquia Hills h. Can.
33 J2 Passadumkeag U.S.A.
30 C1 Passage I. i. U.S.A.
62 F6 Passau Ger.
94 B4 Passi Phil.
44 F3 Passo Fundo Brazil
46 B3 Passos Brazil
68 C4 Pastavy Belarus
42 C4 Pastaza r. Peru
21 J4 Pas, The Can.
44 A4 Pasto Col.
35 H3 Pastora Peak summit U.S.A.
94 B2 Pasuquin Phil.
92 □ Pasuruan Indon.
55 T8 Pasvalys Lith.
94 B4 Pata i. Phil.
40 Patagonia reg. Arg.
35 G6 Patagonia U.S.A.
85 G4 Patakata India
84 D5 Patan India
84 D5 Patan India
Patan see Somnath
85 F4 Patan Nepal
114 E5 Patchewollock Austr.
117 E3 Patea N.Z.
117 E3 Patea r. N.Z.
58 F3 Pateley Bridge U.K.
85 G5 Patenga Point pt Bangl.
104 F6 Patensie S. Africa
66 E6 Paternò Sicily Italy
115 G1 Paterson r. Austr.
115 J4 Paterson Austr.
33 F4 Paterson U.S.A.
84 C2 Patharia India
Pathein see Bassein
24 F3 Pathfinder Res. resr U.S.A.
95 A3 Pathiu Thai.
95 B2 Pathum Thani Thai.
92 □ Pati Indon.
45 A4 Patía r. Col.
84 D3 Patiala India
67 M6 Patmos i. Greece
85 F4 Patna India
85 E5 Patnagarh India
94 B3 Patnanongan i. Phil.
81 J2 Patnos Turkey
84 E3 Paton India
67 H4 Patos Albania
43 L5 Patos Brazil

46 C2 Patos de Minas Brazil
44 F4 Patos, Lagoa dos l. Brazil
47 C1 Patquía Arg.
67 J5 Patra Greece
54 B4 Patreksfjörður Iceland
116 A4 Patrick Cr. watercourse Austr.
46 C2 Patrocínio Brazil
54 V2 Patsoyoki r. Europe
95 B4 Pattani r. Thai.
95 B4 Pattani Thai.
95 B2 Pattaya Thai.
33 J2 Patten U.S.A.
32 D5 Patterson r. U.S.A.
34 B3 Patterson U.S.A.
20 C2 Patterson, Mt mt. Can.
34 C3 Patterson Mt mt. U.S.A.
30 E3 Patterson, Pt pt U.S.A.
54 T4 Pattijoki Fin.
54 R2 Pättikkä Fin.
20 D3 Pattullo, Mt mt. Can.
85 G5 Patuakhali Bangl.
21 H3 Patuanak Can.
32 E5 Patuxent r. U.S.A.
36 D5 Pátzcuaro Mex.
64 D5 Pau France
64 D4 Pauillac France
85 H5 Pauktaw Myanmar
35 F4 Paulden U.S.A.
32 A4 Paulding U.S.A.
23 H2 Paul Island i. Can.
43 K5 Paulistana Brazil
43 L5 Paulo Afonso Brazil
105 J3 Paulpietersburg S. Africa
105 G4 Paul Roux S. Africa
33 F2 Paul Smiths U.S.A.
27 D5 Pauls Valley U.S.A.
83 J7 Paungde Myanmar
45 C3 Pauto r. Col.
46 E2 Pavão Brazil
81 L4 Pāveh Iran
66 C2 Pavia Italy
55 R8 Pāvilosta Latvia
68 H3 Pavino Rus. Fed.
67 L3 Pavlikeni Bulg.
76 J4 Pavlodar Kazak.
69 E5 Pavlohrad Ukr.
68 H4 Pavlovka Rus. Fed.
68 G4 Pavlovo Rus. Fed.
69 G5 Pavlovsk Rus. Fed.
69 F6 Pavlovskaya Rus. Fed.
45 A4 Pawan Col.
84 E3 Pawayan India
30 E4 Paw Paw U.S.A.
33 H4 Pawtucket U.S.A.
95 A2 Pawut Myanmar
30 C5 Paxton U.S.A.
92 C7 Payakumbuh Indon.
95 □ Paya Lebar Sing.
45 C3 Paya, Parque Nacional la nat. park Col.
24 C2 Payette U.S.A.
76 H3 Pay-Khoy, Khrebet h. Rus. Fed.
22 F2 Payne, Lac l. Can.
34 B1 Paynes Creek U.S.A.
112 C5 Payne's Find Austr.
47 C2 Paysandú Uru.
35 G4 Payson AZ U.S.A.
35 G1 Payson UT U.S.A.
47 C3 Payún, Cerro volc. Arg.
80 D1 Pazar Turkey
81 H1 Pazar Turkey
80 F2 Pazarcık Turkey
67 L3 Pazardzhik Bulg.
45 C2 Paz de Ariporo Col.
45 B3 Paz de Río Col.
66 E2 Pazin Croatia
20 C2 Peace r. Can.
20 F3 Peace River Can.
35 F4 Peach Springs U.S.A.
59 F4 Peak District National Park U.K.
114 A2 Peake watercourse Austr.
23 G4 Peaked Mt. h. U.S.A.
94 A4 Peaked Point m Phil.
115 H4 Peak Hill Austr.
116 C4 Peak Ra. h. Austr.
35 H2 Peale, Mt mt. U.S.A.
35 H6 Pearce U.S.A.
30 C1 Pearl Can.
27 F6 Pearl r. U.S.A.
34 □1 Pearl City U.S.A.
34 □1 Pearl Harbor in. U.S.A.
27 D6 Pearsall U.S.A.
29 D6 Pearson U.S.A.
18 Peary Land reg. Greenland
22 C2 Peawanuck Can.
103 D5 Pebane Moz.
67 J3 Peć Yugo.
46 D2 Peçanha Brazil
54 W2 Pechenga Rus. Fed.
76 G3 Pechora Rus. Fed.
68 C3 Pechory Rus. Fed.
31 F4 Peck U.S.A.
27 C6 Pecos r. U.S.A.
27 C6 Pecos U.S.A.
67 H1 Pécs Hungary
115 G9 Pedder, L. l. Austr.
105 G6 Peddie S. Africa
54 S5 Pedersöre Fin.
85 E3 Pêdo La pass China
46 E1 Pedra Azul Brazil
45 C3 Pedraza La Vieja Venez.
46 C3 Pedregulho Brazil
43 K4 Pedreiras Brazil
43 J5 Pedro Afonso Brazil
45 C4 Pedro Chico Col.
44 C2 Pedro de Valdivia Chile
46 A2 Pedro Gomes Brazil
45 D4 Pedro II, Ilha i. Brazil

44 E2 Pedro Juan Caballero Para.
43 K4 Pedroll Brazil
47 G1 Pedro Osório Brazil
57 E5 Peebles U.K.
29 E5 Pee Dee r. U.S.A.
33 G4 Peekskill U.S.A.
115 J3 Peel r. Austr.
58 C3 Peel U.K.
20 F4 Peers Can.
114 E3 Peery L. salt flat Austr.
117 D5 Pegasus Bay b. N.Z.
83 J7 Pegu Myanmar
68 J2 Pegysh Rus. Fed.
47 E2 Pehuajó Arg.
89 F6 Peikang Taiwan
Peipsi Järve l. see Peipus, Lake
55 U7 Peipus, Lake l. Estonia/Rus. Fed.
67 K6 Peiraias Greece
88 B3 Peitun China
46 B1 Peixe r. Goiás Brazil
46 B3 Peixe r. São Paulo Brazil
43 J6 Peixe Brazil
88 B3 Pei Xian Jiangsu China
88 F3 Pei Xian Jiangsu China
46 A2 Peixoto de Couro r. Brazil
105 G4 Peka Lesotho
92 □ Pekalongan Indon.
95 B5 Pekan Malaysia
30 C5 Pekin U.S.A.
95 B5 Pelabuhan Kelang Malaysia
31 H5 Pelee I. i. Can.
31 F5 Pelee Pt pt Can.
93 G7 Peleng i. Indon.
68 J2 Peles Rus. Fed.
30 A1 Pelican Lake l. MN U.S.A.
30 C3 Pelican Lake l. WV U.S.A.
21 J3 Pelican Narrows Can.
54 U3 Pelkosenniemi Fin.
104 C4 Pella S. Africa
21 H1 Pellat Lake l. Can.
110 E2 Pelleluhu Is is P.N.G.
30 C4 Pell Lake U.S.A.
54 S3 Pello Fin.
20 B2 Pelly r. Can.
20 B2 Pelly Crossing Can.
21 J1 Pelly Lake l. Can.
20 C2 Pelly Mountains mts Can.
47 G1 Pelotas Brazil
44 F3 Pelotas, R. das r. Brazil
80 D6 Pelusium Egypt
64 H4 Pelvoux, Massif du mts France
33 J2 Pemadumcook Lake l. U.S.A.
92 □ Pemalang Indon.
92 D6 Pemangkat Indon.
95 A5 Pematangsiantar Indon.
103 E5 Pemba Moz.
103 C5 Pemba Zambia
102 D4 Pemba I. i. Tanz.
20 F4 Pembina r. Can.
26 D1 Pembina U.S.A.
31 J3 Pembroke Can.
59 C6 Pembroke U.K.
33 K2 Pembroke U.S.A.
59 B6 Pembrokeshire U.K.
58 C4 Pembrokeshire Coast National Park nat. park Wales
85 H5 Pen r. Myanmar
65 D1 Peña Cerredo mt Spain
65 E2 Peñalara mt Spain
36 F4 Peña Nevada, Co mt Mex.
46 B3 Penápolis Brazil
65 D1 Peña Prieta mt Spain
65 D2 Peñaranda de Bracamonte Spain
114 E5 Penarie Austr.
65 F2 Peñarroya mt Spain
65 D3 Peñarroya-Pueblonuevo Spain
59 D6 Penarth U.K.
65 D1 Peñas, Cabo de c. Spain
36 B2 Peñasco, Pto Mex.
44 A7 Penas, Golfo de b. Chile
45 E2 Peñas, Pta pt Venez.
65 D1 Peña Ubiña mt Spain
84 B5 Pench r. India
119 C6 Penck, C. c. Ant.
100 C3 Pendjari, Parc National de la nat. park Benin
58 E4 Pendle Hill h. U.K.
24 C2 Pendleton U.S.A.
20 D4 Pendleton Bay Can.
24 C1 Pend Oreille r. U.S.A.
24 C2 Pend Oreille L. l. U.S.A.
85 E5 Pendra India
31 J3 Penetanguishene Can.
88 C4 Peng'an China
84 D6 Penganga r. India
89 □ Peng Chau i. Hong Kong China
89 G5 P'eng-chia Hsü i. Taiwan
105 J2 Penge S. Africa
102 C4 Penge Zaire
89 F6 P'eng-hu Lieh-tao is Taiwan
89 F6 Peng-hu Tao i. Taiwan
95 □ Peng Kang h. Sing.
88 F2 Penglai China
89 D4 Pengshan China
89 C4 Pengshui China
89 E4 Pengxi China
89 E4 Pengze China
105 G5 Penhoek Pass pass S. Africa
65 B3 Peniche Port.
57 E5 Penicuik U.K.

68 E2 Peninga Rus. Fed.
92 C6 Peninsular Malaysia pen. Malaysia
81 K4 Penjwin Iraq
66 E3 Penne Italy
114 B5 Penneshaw Austr.
58 E3 Pennines h. U.K.
105 J5 Pennington S. Africa
33 F5 Pennsville U.S.A.
32 D4 Pennsylvania div. U.S.A.
32 E4 Penn Yan U.S.A.
21 H2 Pennylan Lake l. Can.
33 J2 Penobscot r. U.S.A.
33 J2 Penobscot Bay b. U.S.A.
114 D6 Penola Austr.
113 F6 Penong Austr.
34 C5 Penrith U.S.A.
29 C6 Pensacola U.S.A.
119 B3 Pensacola Mts mts Ant.
81 M2 Pensär Azer.
114 E6 Penshurst Austr.
57 E2 Pentland Firth chan. U.K.
57 E2 Pentland Hills h. U.K.
30 D4 Pentwater U.S.A.
59 D5 Pen-y-Ghent h. U.K.
68 H4 Penza Rus. Fed.
59 B7 Penzance U.K.
68 H4 Penzenskaya Oblast' div. Rus. Fed.
77 S3 Penzhimskaya Guba b. Rus. Fed.
77 S3 Penzhino Rus. Fed.
35 F5 Peoria AZ U.S.A.
30 C5 Peoria IL U.S.A.
95 B4 Perai Malaysia
95 A4 Perak i. Malaysia
95 B4 Perak r. Malaysia
65 F2 Perales del Alfambra Spain
Perämeri g. see Bottenviken
23 H4 Percé Can.
33 H2 Percy U.S.A.
116 D3 Percy Is is Austr.
31 J3 Percy Reach l. Can.
65 G1 Perdido, Monte mt Spain
76 J3 Peregrebnoye Rus. Fed.
45 B3 Pereira r. U.S.A.
46 B3 Pereira Barreto Brazil
68 D3 Perekhoda r. Rus. Fed.
69 G5 Perelazovskiy Rus. Fed.
30 D4 Pere Marquette r. U.S.A.
33 M6 Peremyshlyany Ukr.
68 F3 Pereslavl'-Zalesskiy Rus. Fed.
Pereval Torugart pass see Turugart Pass
68 H4 Perevoz Rus. Fed.
69 D5 Pereyaslav-Khmel'nyts'kyy Ukr.
47 C2 Pergamino Arg.
95 B4 Perhentian Besar i. Malaysia
54 T5 Perho Fin.
23 H3 Péribonca, Lac l. Can.
44 C2 Perico Arg.
45 B2 Perijá, Parque Nacional nat. park Venez.
45 B2 Perija, Sierra de mts Venez.
44 B7 Perito Moreno Arg.
30 D3 Perkins U.S.A.
37 H6 Perlas, Pta de pt Nic.
62 F2 Perleberg Ger.
76 G4 Perm' Rus. Fed.
68 H3 Permas Rus. Fed.
114 B3 Pernatty Lagoon salt flat Austr.
67 K3 Pernik Bulg.
64 F2 Péronne France
64 F5 Perpignan France
59 B7 Perranporth U.K.
34 C5 Perris U.S.A.
64 C2 Perros-Guirec France
29 D6 Perry FL U.S.A.
29 D5 Perry GA U.S.A.
26 E3 Perry IA U.S.A.
27 D4 Perry OK U.S.A.
32 B4 Perrysburg U.S.A.
27 C4 Perryton U.S.A.
27 F4 Perryville U.S.A.
59 E5 Pershore U.K.
Persia country see Iran
Persian Gulf g. see Gulf, The
81 G2 Pertek Turkey
112 C6 Perth Austr.
31 J3 Perth Can.
57 E4 Perth U.K.
33 K1 Perth-Andover Can.
68 F1 Pertominsk Rus. Fed.
64 H5 Pertuis France
55 U6 Pertunmaa Fin.
66 C4 Pertusato, Capo pt Corsica France
38 Peru country S. America
30 C5 Peru U.S.A.
15 N7 Peru Basin sea feature Pac. Oc.
15 P7 Peru-Chile Trench sea feature Pac. Oc.
66 E3 Perugia Italy
46 C4 Peruíbe Brazil
64 C4 Péruwelz Belgium
68 G4 Pervomaysk Rus. Fed.
69 D5 Pervomays'k Ukr.
68 K2 Pervomayskaya Rus. Fed.

69 E6 Pervomays'ke Ukr.
68 G4 Pervomayskiy Rus. Fed.
69 F5 Pervomays'kyy Ukr.
66 E3 Pesaro Italy
34 A3 Pescadero U.S.A.
35 H4 Pescado U.S.A.
66 F3 Pescara r. Italy
66 F3 Pescara Italy
69 G6 Peschanokopskoye Rus. Fed.
95 □ Pesek, P. i. Sing.
84 B2 Peshawar Pak.
67 J4 Peshkopi Albania
67 L3 Peshtera Bulg.
30 D3 Peshtigo U.S.A.
30 D3 Peshtigo r. U.S.A.
66 F1 Pesnica Slovenia
64 D4 Pessac France
68 E3 Pestovo Rus. Fed.
68 G4 Pet r. Rus. Fed.
80 E5 Petah Tiqwa Israel
67 L5 Petalioi i. Greece
34 A2 Petaluma U.S.A.
61 D5 Pétange Lux.
45 D2 Petare Venez.
36 D5 Petatlán Mex.
103 D5 Petauke Zambia
31 J3 Petawawa Can.
30 C3 Petenwell Lake l. U.S.A.
114 C4 Peterborough S.A. Austr.
114 E7 Peterborough Vic. Austr.
31 H3 Peterborough Can.
59 G5 Peterborough U.K.
57 F3 Peterculter U.K.
57 G3 Peterhead U.K.
21 L2 Peter Lake l. Can.
58 F3 Peterlee U.K.
112 E5 Petermann Ranges mts Austr.
47 B3 Peteroa, Vol. volc. Chile
21 H3 Peter Pond L. l. Can.
20 C3 Petersburg AK U.S.A.
30 C6 Petersburg IL U.S.A.
32 E6 Petersburg VA U.S.A.
32 D5 Petersburg WV U.S.A.
59 G6 Petersfield U.K.
23 F2 Peters, Lac l. Can.
66 G5 Petilia Policastro Italy
22 E2 Petite Rivière de la Baleine r. Can.
33 K2 Petit Manan Pt pt U.S.A.
23 J2 Petit Mécatina r. Can.
20 E3 Petitot r. Can.
36 G4 Peto Mex.
30 E3 Petoskey U.S.A.
80 E6 Petra Jordan
87 O3 Petra Velikogo, Zaliv b. Rus. Fed.
31 J4 Petre, Pt pt Can.
67 K4 Petrich Bulg.
35 H4 Petrified Forest Nat. Park nat. park U.S.A.
66 G2 Petrinja Croatia
67 K3 Petrokhanski Prokhod pass Bulg.
31 H3 Petrolia Can.
43 K5 Petrolina Brazil
69 G5 Petropavlovka Rus. Fed.
76 H4 Petropavlovsk Kazak.
77 R4 Petropavlovsk-Kamchatskiy Rus. Fed.
67 K2 Petroşani Romania
69 H4 Petrovsk Rus. Fed.
87 J1 Petrovsk-Zabaykal'skiy Rus. Fed.
69 D5 Petrov Val Rus. Fed.
68 E2 Petrozavodsk Rus. Fed.
105 F4 Petrusburg S. Africa
105 H3 Petrus Steyn S. Africa
104 F5 Petrusville S. Africa
60 D3 Pettigo U.K.
76 H4 Petukhovo Rus. Fed.
95 A4 Peureula Indon.
77 T3 Pevek Rus. Fed.
62 H6 Pezinok Slovakia
62 D6 Pforzheim Ger.
62 D7 Pfullendorf Ger.
84 C3 Phagwara India
105 G4 Phahameng Free State S. Africa
105 H2 Phahameng Northern Province S. Africa
105 J1 Phalaborwa S. Africa
84 C4 Phalodi India
84 B4 Phalsund India
95 A3 Phangnga Thai.
95 D3 Phan Rang Vietnam
95 D3 Phan Ri Vietnam
95 D3 Phan Thiêt Vietnam
27 D7 Pharr U.S.A.
89 C6 Phat Diêm Vietnam
95 B4 Phatthalung Thai.
85 H4 Phek India
95 B1 Phen Thai.
29 C5 Phenix City U.S.A.
95 A2 Phet Buri Thai.
95 C2 Phiafai Laos
27 F5 Philadelphia MS U.S.A.
33 F2 Philadelphia NY U.S.A.
33 F5 Philadelphia PA U.S.A.
26 C2 Philip U.S.A.
61 C4 Philippeville Belgium
32 C5 Philippi U.S.A.
71 Philippines country Asia
94 C2 Philippine Sea sea Phil.
13 N3 Philippine Trench sea feature Pac. Oc.
105 F5 Phillippolis S. Africa
32 B5 Philipsburg U.S.A.
61 C3 Philipsdam barrage Neth.
104 F5 Philipstown S. Africa

114 F7 Phillip I. i. Austr.
33 H2 Phillips ME U.S.A.
30 B3 Phillips WV U.S.A.
26 D4 Phillipsburg KS U.S.A.
33 F4 Phillipsburg NJ U.S.A.
32 D4 Phillipston U.S.A.
33 G3 Philmont U.S.A.
21 G3 Philomena Can.
32 C6 Philpott Reservoir resr U.S.A.
95 B2 Phimae Thai.
95 C2 Phimun Mangsahan Thai.
105 G3 Phiritona S. Africa
95 C2 Phnom Aôral mt Cambodia
95 C3 Phnum Penh Cambodia
95 C1 Phôn China Lao
92 G3 Phôngsali Laos
89 B6 Phong Thô Vietnam
95 B5 Phon Phisai Thai.
95 D2 Phon Hôi Vietnam
95 C1 Phou Bia mt Laos
95 C1 Phou Cô Pi mt Laos/China
89 B6 Phou Sam Sao mts Laos/Vietnam
95 A1 Phrao Thai.
95 B2 Phra Phutthabat Thai.
89 B6 Phuc Yên Vietnam
95 D2 Phu Hôi Vietnam
84 C4 Phulera India
85 G5 Phultala Bangl.
89 B6 Phu Ly Vietnam
95 A4 Phuket Thai.
84 D4 Phulera India
95 B2 Phumi Bânhchok Kon Cambodia
95 C3 Phumi Chhuk Cambodia
95 C2 Phumi Kâmpóng Trâlach Cambodia
95 B3 Phumi Kaôh Kóng Cambodia
95 B2 Phumi Kiliěk Cambodia
95 C2 Phumi Mlu Prey Cambodia
95 B2 Phumi Moŭng Cambodia
95 B2 Phumi Prâmaôy Cambodia
95 B2 Phumi Sâmraông Cambodia
95 C2 Phumi Toêng Cambodia
95 D2 Phu My Vietnam
95 D2 Phu Nhon Vietnam
95 C3 Phuóc Long Vietnam
95 C3 Phu Quôc Vietnam
89 B6 Phu Tho Vietnam
95 D2 Phu Wiang Thai.
43 J5 Piaca Brazil
66 C2 Piacenza Italy
115 H3 Pian r. Austr.
88 D2 Pianguan China
66 C3 Pianosa, Isola i. Italy
63 N7 Piatra Neamt Romania
43 K5 Piauí r. Brazil
66 E1 Piave r. Italy
101 F4 Pibor r. Sudan
101 F4 Pibor Post Sudan
30 D1 Pic r. Can.
35 F4 Pica U.S.A.
35 G5 Picacho AZ U.S.A.
35 E5 Picacho CA U.S.A.
64 F2 Picardie reg. France
27 F6 Picayune U.S.A.
47 D2 Pichanal Arg.
47 B2 Pichi Ciego Arg.
47 B2 Pichilemu Chile
47 D3 Pichi Mahuida Arg.
84 D4 Pichor India
30 C1 Pic, I. i. Can.
58 G3 Pickering U.K.
58 G3 Pickering, Vale of v. U.K.
30 E2 Pickford U.S.A.
22 B3 Pickle Lake Can.
45 C2 Pico Bolívar mt Venez.
45 D4 Pico da Neblina mt Brazil
45 D4 Pico da Neblina, Parque Nacional do nat. park Brazil
37 K5 Pico Duarte mt Dom. Rep.
45 E4 Pico Redondo summit Brazil
45 E4 Pico Rondon summit Brazil
43 K5 Picos Brazil
44 C7 Pico Truncado Arg.
30 D2 Pic River Can.
115 J5 Picton Austr.
31 J4 Picton Can.
115 G9 Picton, Mt mt Austr.
34 C3 Pictou Can.
30 D2 Pictured Rocks National Lakeshore res. U.S.A.
47 C4 Picún Leufú r. Arg.
45 B3 Piedecuesta Col.
47 C1 Pie de Palo, Sa mts Arg.
29 C5 Piedmont U.S.A.
36 D3 Piedras Negras Mex.
47 F2 Piedras, Punta pt Arg.
42 D6 Piedras, Río de las r. Peru
30 C1 Pie Island i. Can.
54 U5 Pieksämäki Fin.
54 V5 Pielavesi Fin.
54 V5 Pielinen l. Fin.
105 H2 Pienaarsrivier S. Africa
32 B4 Piercton U.S.A.
34 A2 Piercy U.S.A.
67 K4 Pieria mts Greece
57 F1 Pierowall U.K.

26 C2 Pierre U.S.A.
64 G4 Pierrelatte France
105 J4 Pietermaritzburg S. Africa
105 H1 Pietersburg S. Africa
66 G5 Pietra Spada, Passo di pass Italy
105 J3 Piet Retief S. Africa
63 M7 Pietrosa mt Romania
31 F4 Pigeon U.S.A.
31 F5 Pigeon Bay b. Can.
32 D6 Pigg r. U.S.A.
27 F4 Piggott U.S.A.
105 J2 Pigg's Peak Swaziland
47 D3 Pigüé Arg.
84 E4 Pihani India
88 E3 Pi He r. China
55 V6 Pihlajavesi l. Fin.
55 R6 Pihlava Fin.
54 T5 Pihtipudas Fin.
54 T4 Piippola Fin.
54 V4 Piispajärvi Fin.
36 F5 Pijijiapan Mex.
68 E3 Pikalevo Rus. Fed.
32 D3 Pike Bay b. Austr.
31 G3 Pike Bay Can.
108 □ Pikelot i. Micronesia
104 C6 Piketberg S. Africa
32 B6 Pikeville China
88 G2 Pikou China
47 H3 Piła Pol.
62 H4 Piła Pol.
105 G2 Pilanesberg National Park nat. park S. Africa
47 E2 Pilar Arg.
44 E3 Pilar Para.
94 B5 Pilas i. Phil.
47 H3 Pilcaniyeu Arg.
44 E3 Pilcomayo r. Bol./Para.
94 B3 Pili Phil.
84 D3 Pilibhit India
115 H7 Pillar, C. c. Austr.
89 □ Pillar Pt pt Hong Kong China
115 H3 Pilliga Austr.
47 E2 Pillo, Isla del i. Arg.
46 C2 Pilões, Serra dos mts Brazil
34 D2 Pilot Peak summit U.S.A.
115 H6 Pilot, The mt Austr.
27 F6 Pilottown U.S.A.
55 R8 Piltene Latvia
Pimba i. see Pänikoita
42 F6 Pimenta Bueno Brazil
84 C5 Pimpalner India
84 D2 Pin r. India
35 F6 Pinacate, Cerro del summit Mex.
84 D4 Pinahat India
35 G5 Pinaleno Mts mts U.S.A.
94 B3 Pinamalayan Phil.
47 F3 Pinamar Arg.
95 B4 Pinang i. Malaysia
80 F2 Pinarbaşı Turkey
37 H4 Pinar del Río Cuba
69 C7 Pinarhisar Turkey
63 K5 Pińczów Pol.
84 D3 Pindar r. India
43 J4 Pindaré r. Brazil
84 C2 Pindi Gheb Pak.
67 J5 Pindus Mts mts Greece
Pindu Pass pass see Pêdo La
Pindus Mts mts see Pindos
35 H4 Pine AZ U.S.A.
30 E4 Pine r. MI U.S.A.
30 E3 Pine r. MI U.S.A.
30 C3 Pine r. WV U.S.A.
27 F5 Pine Bluff U.S.A.
24 F3 Pine Bluffs U.S.A.
23 K4 Pine, C. c. Can.
30 A3 Pine City U.S.A.
112 F4 Pine Creek Austr.
34 B2 Pine Creek r. U.S.A.
34 B2 Pinecrest U.S.A.
34 C2 Pinedale CA U.S.A.
24 E3 Pinedale WY U.S.A.
21 K4 Pine Falls Can.
68 G1 Pinega r. Rus. Fed.
68 G1 Pinega Rus. Fed.
29 D6 Pine Grove U.S.A.
30 D6 Pine Hills U.S.A.
21 H3 Pinehouse Can.
30 A3 Pine Island U.S.A.
119 A3 Pine Island Bay b. Ant.
33 F3 Pine Lake Can.
27 E6 Pineland U.S.A.
34 B4 Pine Mt mt. U.S.A.
35 F4 Pine Peak summit U.S.A.
20 D2 Pine Point Can.
26 C3 Pine Ridge U.S.A.
34 C3 Pineridge U.S.A.
47 E5 Pinerolo Italy
27 E5 Pines, Lake O' the l. U.S.A.
105 J4 Pinetown S. Africa
32 B6 Pineville KY U.S.A.
27 E6 Pineville LA U.S.A.
32 C6 Pineville WV U.S.A.
89 B6 Ping'an China
89 B6 Pingbian China
88 E3 Ping Dao i. China
88 D2 Pingding China
88 D3 Pingdingshan China
89 C6 Pingguo China
89 D6 Pinghe China
89 D5 Pingjiang China
89 D5 Pingle China
88 C3 Pingli China
88 D2 Pingliang China
88 C3 Pingliang China
88 C2 Pingluo China

89 F5 **Pingnan** *Fujian* China
89 D6 **Pingnan** *Guangxi* China
88 F1 **Pingquan** China
88 E2 **Pingshan** China
89 D5 **Pingshi** China
89 D7 **Pingtang** China
89 F5 **Pingtan** China
89 C5 **Pingtang** China
89 F6 **P'ing-tun** Taiwan
88 B3 **Pingwu** China
89 C6 **Pingxiang** *Guangxi* China
89 D5 **Pingxiang** *Jiangxi* China
89 F5 **Pingyang** China
88 D2 **Pingyao** China
88 E3 **Pingyi** China
88 E2 **Pingyin** China
88 D3 **Pingyu** China
89 E5 **Pingyuan** China
89 B6 **Pingyuanjie** China
89 □ **Ping Yuen Ho** r. *Hong Kong* China
89 C5 **Pingzhai** China
43 J4 **Pinheiro** Brazil
47 G1 **Pinheiro Machado** Brazil
59 D7 **Pinhoe** U.K.
112 C6 **Pinjarra** Austr.
20 E3 **Pink Mountain** Can.
117 D4 **Pinnacle** *mt.* N.Z.
114 D5 **Pinnaroo** Austr.
34 C4 **Pinos, Mt** *mt.* U.S.A.
36 E5 **Pinotepa Nacional** Mex.
111 G4 **Pins, Î. des** *i.* New Caledonia
69 C4 **Pinsk** Belarus
31 G4 **Pins, Pointe aux** *pt* Can.
42 □ **Pinta, Isla** *i. Galapagos Is* Ecuador
35 F5 **Pinta, Sierra** *summit* U.S.A.
35 F3 **Pintura** U.S.A.
35 E3 **Pioche** U.S.A.
103 C4 **Piodi** Zaire
76 K1 **Pioner, O.** *i.* Rus. Fed.
63 K5 **Pionerskiy** Rus. Fed.
63 K5 **Pionki** Pol.
117 E3 **Piopio** N.Z.
42 F4 **Piorini, Lago** *l.* Brazil
63 J5 **Piotrków Trybunalski** Pol.
84 C4 **Pipar** India
84 D5 **Piparia** India
67 L5 **Piperi** *i.* Greece
34 D3 **Piper Peak** *summit* U.S.A.
35 F3 **Pipe Spring Nat. Mon.** *nat. park* U.S.A.
22 B3 **Pipestone** *r.* Can.
26 D3 **Pipestone** U.S.A.
117 E3 **Pipiriki** N.Z.
84 C3 **Pipli** India
23 F4 **Pipmuacan, Réservoir** *resr* Can.
32 A4 **Piqua** U.S.A.
46 A2 **Piquiri** *r. Mato Grosso do Sul* Brazil
46 A2 **Piquiri** *r. Paraná* Brazil
46 C2 **Piracanjuba** Brazil
46 D2 **Piracicaba** *r. Minas Gerais* Brazil
46 C3 **Piracicaba** *r. São Paulo* Brazil
46 C3 **Piracicaba** Brazil
46 C3 **Piraçununga** Brazil
43 K4 **Piracuruca** Brazil
**Piraeus** *see* Peiraias
46 C4 **Piraí do Sul** Brazil
46 C3 **Pirajuí** Brazil
84 C5 **Piram I.** *i.* India
46 B2 **Piranhas** *r. Goiás* Brazil
43 L5 **Piranhas** *r. Paraíba/Rio Grande do Norte* Brazil
46 B2 **Piranhas** Brazil
45 C5 **Piraparaná** *r.* Col.
46 B3 **Pirapó** *r.* Brazil
46 D2 **Pirapora** Brazil
47 G1 **Piratini** Brazil
47 G1 **Piratini** *r.* Brazil
84 D4 **Pirawa** India
47 C4 **Pire Mahuida, Sa** *mts* Arg.
46 C2 **Pires do Rio** Brazil
85 G4 **Pirganj** Bangl.
43 K4 **Piripiri** Brazil
45 C2 **Píritu** Venez.
46 A2 **Pirizal** Brazil
67 K3 **Pirot** Yugo.
84 C2 **Pir Panjal Pass** *pass* India
84 C2 **Pir Panjal Range** *mts* India/Pak.
45 A3 **Pirre, Co** *mt* Panama
81 M2 **Pirsaat** Azer.
81 M1 **Pirsaatçay** *r.* Azer.
93 H7 **Piru** Indon.
66 D3 **Pisa** Italy
44 B1 **Pisagua** Chile
117 B6 **Pisa, Mt** *mt.* N.Z.
33 F4 **Piscataway** U.S.A.
42 C6 **Pisco** Peru
42 C6 **Pisco, B. de** *b.* Peru
33 F3 **Piseco Lake** *l.* U.S.A.
62 G6 **Písek** Czech Rep.
84 A3 **Pishin** Pak.
66 G4 **Pisticci** Italy
66 D3 **Pistoia** Italy
65 D1 **Pisuerga** *r.* Spain
24 B3 **Pit** *r.* U.S.A.
100 A3 **Pita** Guinea
23 G3 **Pitaga** Can.
45 A4 **Pitalito** Col.
46 B4 **Pitanga** Brazil
46 D2 **Pitangui** Brazil
114 E5 **Pitarpunga L.** *l.* Austr.
109 **Pitcairn Island** *i.* Pac. Oc.
54 R4 **Piteå** Sweden
54 R4 **Piteälven** *r.* Sweden
69 H5 **Piterka** Rus. Fed.

67 L2 **Pitești** Romania
112 C6 **Pithara** Austr.
25 D6 **Pitiquito** Mex.
68 D2 **Pitkyaranta** Rus. Fed.
57 E4 **Pitlochry** U.K.
47 B3 **Pitrufquén** Chile
105 F2 **Pitsane Siding** Botswana
57 F3 **Pitscottie** U.K.
20 D4 **Pitt I.** *i.* Can.
111 J6 **Pitt Island** *i.* Pac. Oc.
27 E4 **Pittsburg** U.S.A.
32 D4 **Pittsburgh** U.S.A.
30 B6 **Pittsfield** *IL* U.S.A.
33 G3 **Pittsfield** *MA* U.S.A.
33 J2 **Pittsfield** *ME* U.S.A.
33 H3 **Pittsfield** *NH* U.S.A.
33 G3 **Pittsfield** *VT* U.S.A.
115 J1 **Pittsworth** Austr.
21 K2 **Pitz Lake** *l.* Can.
46 D3 **Piumhi** Brazil
42 B5 **Piura** Peru
34 C4 **Piute Peak** *summit* U.S.A.
85 E3 **Piuthan** Nepal
63 O6 **Pivdennyy Buh** *r.* Ukr.
66 F2 **Pivka** Slovenia
84 D1 **Pixa** China
62 E7 **Piz Buin** *mt* Austria/Switz.
68 H3 **Pizhma** *r.* Rus. Fed.
68 H3 **Pizhma** Rus. Fed.
23 K4 **Placentia** Can.
23 K4 **Placentia B.** *b.* Can.
94 C4 **Placer** Phil.
84 C4 **Placer** Phil.
34 B2 **Placerville** *CA* U.S.A.
37 J4 **Placetas** Cuba
33 H4 **Plainfield** *CT* U.S.A.
30 C5 **Plainfield** *IL* U.S.A.
30 C3 **Plainfield** *WI* U.S.A.
30 A3 **Plainview** *MN* U.S.A.
26 D3 **Plainview** *NE* U.S.A.
27 C5 **Plainview** *TX* U.S.A.
33 J1 **Plaisted** U.S.A.
77 T3 **Plamennyy** Rus. Fed.
20 G4 **Plamondon** Can.
23 K4 **Planada** Can.
46 C1 **Planaltina** Brazil
47 B2 **Planchón, P. de** *pass* Arg.
45 B2 **Planeta Rica** Col.
26 D3 **Plankinton** U.S.A.
30 C5 **Plano** *IL* U.S.A.
27 D5 **Plano** *TX* U.S.A.
29 D7 **Plantation** U.S.A.
27 F6 **Plaquemine** U.S.A.
65 C2 **Plasencia** Spain
33 K1 **Plaster Rock** Can.
42 B4 **Plata, I. la** *i.* Ecuador
66 E6 **Platani** *r. Sicily* Italy
47 F2 **Plata, Río de la** *chan.* Arg./Uru.
105 H4 **Platberg** *mt* S. Africa
77 V4 **Platinum** Alaska
45 B2 **Plato** Col.
26 C3 **Platte** *r.* U.S.A.
30 B4 **Platteville** U.S.A.
33 G2 **Plattsburgh** U.S.A.
26 E3 **Plattsmouth** U.S.A.
62 F5 **Plauen** Ger.
25 E6 **Playa Noriega, L.** *l.* Mex.
42 B4 **Playas** Ecuador
95 D2 **Plây Cu** Vietnam
21 K4 **Playgreen L.** *l.* Can.
47 C3 **Plaza Huincul** Arg.
33 J4 **Pleasant Bay** *b.* Can.
35 G1 **Pleasant Grove** U.S.A.
35 F5 **Pleasant, Lake** *l.* U.S.A.
35 H5 **Pleasanton** *NM* U.S.A.
27 D6 **Pleasanton** *TX* U.S.A.
117 C6 **Pleasant Point** N.Z.
35 H3 **Pleasant View** U.S.A.
33 F5 **Pleasantville** U.S.A.
28 C4 **Pleasure Ridge Park** U.S.A.
64 F4 **Pleaux** France
95 C2 **Plei Doch** Vietnam
117 F2 **Plenty, Bay of** *b.* N.Z.
24 F1 **Plentywood** U.S.A.
68 G2 **Plesetsk** Rus. Fed.
23 F3 **Plétipi L.** *l.* Can.
104 E7 **Plettenberg Bay** S. Africa
67 L3 **Pleven** Bulg.
67 H3 **Pljevlja** Yugo.
63 J4 **Płock** Pol.
66 G2 **Pločno** *mt* Bos.-Herz.
68 D2 **Plodovoye** Rus. Fed.
64 C3 **Ploemeur** France
67 M2 **Ploiești** Romania
21 H3 **Plonge, Lac la** *l.* Can.
63 P2 **Ploskosh'** Rus. Fed.
68 G3 **Ploskoye** Rus. Fed.
64 B2 **Ploudalmézeau** France
64 B2 **Plouzané** France
67 L3 **Plovdiv** Bulg.
30 C3 **Plover** U.S.A.
30 C3 **Plover** *r.* U.S.A.
89 □ **Plover Cove Res.** *resr Hong Kong* China
33 G4 **Plum I.** *i.* U.S.A.
24 C2 **Plummer** U.S.A.
55 R9 **Plungė** Lith.
63 N3 **Plyeshchanitsy** Belarus
95 A1 **Ply Huey Wati, Khao** *mt* Myanmar/Thai.
37 M5 **Plymouth** Montserrat
59 C7 **Plymouth** U.K.
34 B2 **Plymouth** *CA* U.S.A.
30 D5 **Plymouth** *IN* U.S.A.
33 H4 **Plymouth** *MA* U.S.A.
33 H3 **Plymouth** *NH* U.S.A.
28 E3 **Plymouth** *PA* U.S.A.
30 D4 **Plymouth** *WI* U.S.A.
33 H4 **Plymouth Bay** *b.* U.S.A.
59 D5 **Plynlimon** *h.* U.K.

62 F6 **Plzeň** Czech Rep.
100 B3 **Pô** Burkina
13 L8 **Pobeda Ice Island** *ice feature* Ant.
76 K5 **Pobedy, Pik** *mt* China/Kyrgyzstan
27 C4 **Pocahontas** U.S.A.
32 C5 **Pocatalico** *r.* U.S.A.
24 D3 **Pocatello** U.S.A.
69 C5 **Pochayiv** Ukr.
68 E4 **Pochep** Rus. Fed.
68 H4 **Pochinki** Rus. Fed.
68 E4 **Pochinok** Rus. Fed.
60 B6 **Pocket, The** *h.* Rep. of Ireland
62 F6 **Pocking** Ger.
58 G4 **Pocklington** U.K.
46 E1 **Poções** Brazil
33 F5 **Pocomoke City** U.S.A.
33 F6 **Pocomoke Sound** *b.* U.S.A.
46 A2 **Poconé** Brazil
33 F4 **Pocono Mountains** *h.* U.S.A.
33 F4 **Pocono Summit** U.S.A.
68 D3 **Poddor'ye** Rus. Fed.
69 F5 **Podgorenskiy** Rus. Fed.
67 H3 **Podgorica** Yugo.
76 K4 **Podgornoye** Rus. Fed.
77 L3 **Podkamennaya** *r.* Rus. Fed.
42 C4 **Podocarpus, Parque Nacional** *nat. park* Ecuador
68 F4 **Podol'sk** Rus. Fed.
68 E2 **Podporozh'ye** Rus. Fed.
66 G1 **Podravina** *reg.* Hungary
67 J4 **Podujevo** Yugo.
68 H2 **Podvoloch'ye** Rus. Fed.
68 J2 **Podz'** Rus. Fed.
104 C4 **Pofadder** S. Africa
31 G2 **Pogamasing** Can.
69 G4 **Pogar** Rus. Fed.
66 D3 **Poggibonsi** Italy
67 J4 **Pogradec** Albania
46 A2 **Poguba** *r.* Brazil
87 N4 **P'ohang** S. Korea
108 **Pohnpei** *i.* Micronesia
69 D5 **Pohrebyshche** Ukr.
84 D4 **Pohri** India
67 K3 **Poiana Mare** Romania
102 C4 **Poie** Zaire
119 C6 **Poinsett, C.** *c.* Ant.
34 A2 **Point Arena** U.S.A.
18 **Point Barrow** *pt* U.S.A.
31 K2 **Point-Comfort** Can.
37 M5 **Pointe-à-Pitre** Guadeloupe
31 G3 **Pointe au Baril Sta.** Can.
102 B4 **Pointe-Noire** Congo
16 **Point Hope** U.S.A.
114 A4 **Point Kenny** Austr.
20 G1 **Point Lake** *l.* Can.
115 K3 **Point Lookout** *mt* Austr.
31 F5 **Point Pelee National Park** *nat. park* Can.
33 F4 **Point Pleasant** *NJ* U.S.A.
32 B5 **Point Pleasant** *WV* U.S.A.
31 K3 **Poisson Blanc, Lac du** *l.* Can.
112 C3 **Poissonnier Pt** *pt* Austr.
64 E3 **Poitiers** France
89 □ **Poi Toi I.** *i. Hong Kong* China
64 D3 **Poitou** *reg.* France
46 E1 **Pojuca** Brazil
84 B4 **Pokaran** India
115 H2 **Pokataroo** Austr.
85 E3 **Pokhara** Nepal
102 C3 **Poko** Zaire
84 A4 **Pokran** Pak.
77 O3 **Pokrovsk** Rus. Fed.
69 F6 **Pokrovs'ke** Ukr.
68 H2 **Pokshen'ga** *r.* Rus. Fed.
94 B3 **Pola** Phil.
35 G3 **Polacca** U.S.A.
35 G4 **Polacca Wash** *r.* U.S.A.
65 D1 **Pola de Lena** Spain
65 D1 **Pola de Siero** Spain
48 **Poland** *country* Europe
33 D3 **Polar Bear Provincial Park** *res.* Can.
80 D2 **Polatlı** Turkey
68 D4 **Polatsk** Belarus
63 N3 **Polatskaya Nizina** *lowland* Belarus
54 M3 **Polcirkeln** Sweden
68 H2 **Poldarsa** Rus. Fed.
81 K2 **Pol Dasht** Iran
79 K2 **Pol-e-Khomrī** Afgh.
68 B4 **Polessk** Rus. Fed.
93 F7 **Polewali** Indon.
101 D4 **Poli** Cameroon
66 G4 **Policoro** Italy
64 G3 **Poligny** France
94 B3 **Polillo** *i.* Phil.
94 B3 **Polillo Islands** *is* Phil.
94 B3 **Polillo Strait** *chan.* Phil.
80 D4 **Polis** Cyprus
69 D5 **Polis'ke** Ukr.
62 H5 **Polkowice** Pol.
66 G5 **Pollino, Monte** *mt* Italy
54 U1 **Polmak** Norway
65 E2 **Pollença** Spain
54 V4 **Polo** Fin.
30 C5 **Polo** U.S.A.
94 B3 **Polomoloc** Phil.
68 J3 **Polom** Rus. Fed.
69 C5 **Polonne** Ukr.
59 C7 **Polperro** U.K.

24 D2 **Polson** U.S.A.
68 G1 **Polta** *r.* Rus. Fed.
69 E5 **Poltava** Ukr.
55 T7 **Põltsamaa** Estonia
55 U7 **Põlva** Estonia
54 V5 **Polvijärvi** Fin.
54 X2 **Polyarnyy** Rus. Fed.
77 T3 **Polyarnyy** Rus. Fed.
54 X3 **Polyarnyye Zori** Rus. Fed.
67 K4 **Polygyros** Greece
67 K4 **Polykastro** Greece
14 H6 **Polynesia** *is* Pac. Oc.
55 S6 **Pomarkku** Fin.
46 D3 **Pomba** *r.* Brazil
65 D3 **Pombal** Port.
46 B3 **Pombo** *r.* Brazil
105 J4 **Pomeroy** S. Africa
60 E3 **Pomeroy** U.K.
32 B5 **Pomeroy** U.S.A.
66 E4 **Pomezia** Italy
104 E2 **Pomfret** S. Africa
110 F2 **Pomio** P.N.G.
116 E6 **Pomona** Austr.
34 D4 **Pomona** U.S.A.
67 M3 **Pomorie** Bulg.
62 G3 **Pomorska, Zatoka** *b.* Pol.
68 E1 **Pomorskiy Bereg** *coastal area* Rus. Fed.
**Pomo Tso** *l. see* Puma Yumco
29 D7 **Pompano Beach** U.S.A.
46 D2 **Pompéu** Brazil
68 H3 **Ponazyrevo** Rus. Fed.
27 D4 **Ponca City** U.S.A.
37 L5 **Ponce** Puerto Rico
25 C4 **Poncha Springs** U.S.A.
22 E3 **Poncheville, Lac** *l.* Can.
83 E8 **Pondicherry** India
16 **Pond Inlet** Can.
23 J3 **Ponds, Island of** *i.* Can.
65 C1 **Ponferrada** Spain
117 E4 **Pongaroa** N.Z.
101 E4 **Pongo** *watercourse* Sudan
105 K3 **Pongola** *r.* S. Africa
105 J3 **Pongolapoort Dam** *resr* S. Africa
63 P3 **Ponizov'ye** Rus. Fed.
85 H5 **Ponnyadaung Range** *mts* Myanmar
20 G4 **Ponoka** Can.
100 □ **Ponta do Sol** Cape Verde
46 B4 **Ponta Grossa** Brazil
46 C2 **Pontalina** Brazil
64 F3 **Pont-à-Mousson** France
46 A3 **Ponta Porã** Brazil
64 H3 **Pontarlier** France
27 F6 **Pontchartrain, L.** *l.* U.S.A.
65 B3 **Ponte de Sôr** Port.
58 F4 **Pontefract** U.K.
58 F3 **Ponteland** U.K.
43 G7 **Pontes-e-Lacerda** Brazil
65 B1 **Pontevedra** Spain
30 C5 **Pontiac** *IL* U.S.A.
31 F4 **Pontiac** *MI* U.S.A.
64 C2 **Pontivy** France
64 B3 **Pont-l'Abbé** France
64 F2 **Pontoise** France
21 K4 **Ponton** Can.
27 F5 **Pontotoc** U.S.A.
66 C2 **Pontremoli** Italy
64 F2 **Pont-Ste-Maxence** France
115 G9 **Pontville** Austr.
31 H3 **Pontypool** Can.
59 D6 **Pontypool** U.K.
59 D6 **Pontypridd** U.K.
66 E4 **Ponza, Isola di** *i.* Italy
66 E4 **Ponziane, Isole** *is* Italy
114 A4 **Poochera** Austr.
59 F7 **Poole** U.K.
114 E4 **Pooncarie** Austr.
114 E7 **Poopelloe L.** *salt l.* Austr.
42 E7 **Poopó, Lago de** *l.* Bol.
117 E1 **Poor Knights Is** *i.* N.Z.
100 B3 **Pô, Parc National de** *nat. park* Burkina
45 A4 **Popayán** Col.
77 M2 **Popigay** *r.* Rus. Fed.
114 D4 **Popilta L.** *l.* Austr.
114 D4 **Popiltah L.** *l.* Austr.
21 K4 **Poplar** *r.* Can.
24 F1 **Poplar** U.S.A.
27 F4 **Poplar Bluff** U.S.A.
32 C6 **Poplar Camp** U.S.A.
27 F6 **Poplarville** U.S.A.
36 E5 **Popocatépetl** *volc.* Mex.
92 □ **Popoh** Indon.
102 B4 **Popokabaka** Zaire
67 M3 **Popovo** Bulg.
63 K6 **Poprad** Slovakia
117 F4 **Porangahau** N.Z.
46 C1 **Porangatu** Brazil
84 B5 **Porbandar** India
45 B3 **Porce** *r.* Col.
20 C4 **Porcher I.** *i.* Can.
18 **Porcupine, Cape** *c.* Can.
23 H2 **Porcupine, Cape** *c.* Can.
21 J4 **Porcupine Hills** *h.* Can.
30 C2 **Porcupine Mts** *mts* U.S.A.
21 J4 **Porcupine Plain** Can.
21 J4 **Porcupine Prov. Forest** *res.* Can.
66 E2 **Pore** Col.
66 E2 **Poreč** Croatia
68 H4 **Poretskoye** Rus. Fed.
55 R6 **Pori** Fin.
117 E4 **Porirua** N.Z.
68 D3 **Porkhov** Rus. Fed.
45 E2 **Porlamar** Venez.
64 C3 **Pornic** France
94 C3 **Poro** *i.* Phil.

87 Q2 **Poronaysk** Rus. Fed.
67 K6 **Poros** Greece
68 E2 **Porosozero** Rus. Fed.
119 C6 **Porpoise Bay** *b.* Ant.
54 T1 **Porsangen** *chan.* Norway
55 L7 **Porsgrunn** Norway
80 C2 **Porsuk** *r.* Turkey
114 C5 **Port Adelaide** Austr.
60 E3 **Portadown** U.K.
60 F3 **Portaferry** U.K.
33 J1 **Portage** *ME* U.S.A.
30 E4 **Portage** *MI* U.S.A.
30 C4 **Portage** *WI* U.S.A.
21 K5 **Portage la Prairie** Can.
26 C1 **Portal** U.S.A.
20 E5 **Port Alberni** Can.
115 G7 **Port Albert** Austr.
65 C3 **Portalegre** Port.
27 C5 **Portales** U.S.A.
20 D4 **Port Alexander** U.S.A.
32 D4 **Port Allegany** U.S.A.
34 D4 **Port Allen** U.S.A.
116 D4 **Port Alma** Austr.
24 B1 **Port Angeles** U.S.A.
60 D4 **Portarlington** Rep. of Ireland
115 G9 **Port Arthur** Austr.
27 E6 **Port Arthur** U.S.A.
57 B5 **Port Askaig** U.K.
114 B4 **Port Augusta** Austr.
37 K5 **Port-au-Prince** Haiti
31 F3 **Port Austin** U.S.A.
23 J3 **Port aux Choix** Can.
60 F3 **Portavogie** U.K.
104 D7 **Port Beaufort** S. Africa
92 A4 **Port Blair** Andaman and Nicobar Is
31 H3 **Port Bolster** Can.
65 H1 **Portbou** Spain
31 H3 **Port Burwell** Can.
114 E7 **Port Campbell** Austr.
31 H3 **Port Carling** Can.
117 C6 **Port Chalmers** N.Z.
29 D7 **Port Charlotte** U.S.A.
33 G4 **Port Chester** U.S.A.
32 B4 **Port Clements** Can.
32 A4 **Port Clinton** U.S.A.
33 J3 **Port Clyde** U.S.A.
31 H4 **Port Colborne** Can.
20 E5 **Port Coquitlam** Can.
31 H4 **Port Credit** Can.
115 F9 **Port Davey** *b.* Austr.
37 K5 **Port-de-Paix** Haiti
95 B5 **Port Dickson** Malaysia
116 A1 **Port Douglas** Austr.
32 C5 **Port Dover** U.K.
30 D3 **Porte des Morts** *chan.* U.S.A.
20 C4 **Port Edward** Can.
105 J5 **Port Edward** S. Africa
30 C3 **Port Edwards** U.S.A.
46 D1 **Porteirinha** Brazil
43 H4 **Portel** Brazil
31 G3 **Port Elgin** Can.
105 F6 **Port Elizabeth** S. Africa
57 B5 **Port Ellen** U.K.
114 C5 **Port Elliot** Austr.
58 C3 **Port Erin** U.K.
21 H2 **Porter Lake** *l.* Can.
20 C3 **Porter Landing** Can.
104 C6 **Porterville** S. Africa
34 C3 **Porterville** U.S.A.
114 E7 **Port Fairy** Austr.
117 E2 **Port Fitzroy** N.Z.
**Port Fuad** *see* Bûr Fu'ad
102 A4 **Port-Gentil** Gabon
114 C4 **Port Germein** Austr.
27 F6 **Port Gibson** U.S.A.
57 D5 **Port Glasgow** U.K.
100 C4 **Port Harcourt** Nigeria
20 D4 **Port Hardy** Can.
**Port Harrison** *see* Inukjuak
23 H4 **Port Hawkesbury** Can.
59 D6 **Porthcawl** U.K.
112 C4 **Port Hedland** Austr.
33 G2 **Port Henry** U.S.A.
59 B7 **Porthleven** U.K.
59 C5 **Porthmadog** U.K.
31 H4 **Port Hope** Can.
23 J3 **Port Hope Simpson** Can.
31 F4 **Port Huron** U.S.A.
81 M2 **Port-İliç** Azer.
65 B4 **Portimão** Port.
89 □ **Port Island** *i. Hong Kong* China
115 J4 **Port Jackson** *in.* Austr.
33 G4 **Port Jefferson** U.S.A.
33 F4 **Port Jervis** U.S.A.
42 G2 **Port Kaituma** Guyana
115 J5 **Port Kembla** Austr.
115 H4 **Portland** *N.S.W.* Austr.
114 D7 **Portland** *Vic.* Austr.
30 E5 **Portland** *IN* U.S.A.
33 H3 **Portland** *ME* U.S.A.
24 B2 **Portland** *OR* U.S.A.
20 C3 **Portland Canal** *in.* Can.
117 F3 **Portland, Isle of** *pen.* U.K.
27 D6 **Port Lavaca** U.S.A.
60 D5 **Portlaoise** Rep. of Ireland
57 D5 **Portlethen** U.K.
114 A5 **Port Lincoln** Austr.
100 A4 **Port Loko** Sierra Leone
114 D7 **Port MacDonnell** Austr.
115 K3 **Port Macquarie** Austr.
23 H2 **Port Manvers** *in.* Can.
31 H4 **Port-Menier** Can.
24 B1 **Port Moody** Can.

110 E2 **Port Moresby** P.N.G.
57 B2 **Portnaguran** U.K.
57 B5 **Portnahaven** U.K.
114 B5 **Port Neill** Austr.
29 F7 **Port Nelson** Bahamas
57 B3 **Port Nis** U.K.
104 B4 **Port Nolloth** S. Africa
**Port-Nouveau-Québec** *see* Kangiqsualujjuaq
**Porto** *see* Oporto
42 E5 **Porto Acre** Brazil
46 B3 **Porto Alegre** *Mato Grosso do Sul* Brazil
44 F4 **Porto Alegre** *Rio Grande do Sul* Brazil
43 G6 **Porto Artur** Brazil
43 G6 **Porto dos Gaúchos Óbidos** Brazil
43 G7 **Porto Esperidião** Brazil
66 D3 **Portoferraio** Italy
43 G5 **Porto Franco** Brazil
45 E2 **Port of Spain** Trinidad and Tobago
66 E2 **Portogruaro** Italy
100 □ **Porto Inglês** Cape Verde
46 A2 **Porto Jofre** Brazil
34 B2 **Portola** U.S.A.
66 D2 **Portomaggiore** Italy
43 G8 **Porto Murtinho** Brazil
43 J6 **Porto Nacional** Brazil
100 C4 **Porto-Novo** Benin
46 B3 **Porto Primavera, Represa** *resr* Brazil
24 A3 **Port Orford** U.S.A.
43 H4 **Porto Santana** Brazil
46 E2 **Porto Seguro** Brazil
66 E2 **Porto Tolle** Italy
66 C4 **Porto Torres** *Sardinia* Italy
66 C4 **Porto-Vecchio** *Corsica* France
42 E5 **Porto Velho** Brazil
42 B4 **Portoviejo** Ecuador
57 C6 **Portpatrick** U.K.
31 H3 **Port Perry** Can.
114 F7 **Port Phillip Bay** *b.* Austr.
114 C4 **Port Pirie** Austr.
59 B7 **Portreath** U.K.
57 B4 **Portree** U.K.
20 E5 **Port Renfrew** Can.
31 G4 **Port Rowan** Can.
32 E5 **Port Royal** U.S.A.
60 E2 **Portrush** U.K.
78 C3 **Port Said** Egypt
29 C6 **Port St Joe** U.S.A.
105 H5 **Port St Johns** S. Africa
58 C3 **Port St Mary** U.K.
60 D2 **Portsalon** Rep. of Ireland
31 F4 **Port Sanilac** U.S.A.
31 H3 **Port Severn** Can.
89 □ **Port Shelter** *b. Hong Kong* China
105 J5 **Port Shepstone** S. Africa
20 C4 **Port Simpson** Can.
59 F7 **Portsmouth** U.K.
33 H3 **Portsmouth** *NH* U.S.A.
32 B5 **Portsmouth** *OH* U.S.A.
33 E6 **Portsmouth** *VA* U.S.A.
57 F3 **Portsoy** U.K.
115 K4 **Port Stephens** *b.* Austr.
60 E2 **Portstewart** U.K.
101 F3 **Port Sudan** Sudan
29 B6 **Port Sulphur** U.S.A.
59 D6 **Port Talbot** U.K.
54 U2 **Porttipahdan tekojärvi** *l.* Fin.
48 **Portugal** *country* Europe
45 C2 **Portuguesa** *r.* Venez.
60 C4 **Portumna** Rep. of Ireland
64 F5 **Port-Vendres** France
114 B5 **Port Victoria** Austr.
54 X2 **Port Vladimir** Rus. Fed.
117 E2 **Port Waikato** N.Z.
114 C5 **Port Wakefield** Austr.
30 D4 **Port Washington** U.S.A.
57 D6 **Port William** U.K.
30 B2 **Port Wing** U.S.A.
47 C7 **Porvenir** Arg.
55 T6 **Porvoo** Fin.
65 D1 **Posada de Llanera** Spain
44 E3 **Posadas** Arg.
67 H2 **Posavina** *reg.* Bos.-Herz./Croatia
31 F3 **Posen** U.S.A.
81 L5 **Posht-é-Küh** *mts* Iran
81 M3 **Posht Küh** *h.* Iran
54 V3 **Posio** Fin.
93 G2 **Posio** Indon.
81 J1 **Posof** Turkey
46 C1 **Posse** Brazil
119 A5 **Possession Is** *is* Ant.
27 E5 **Post** U.S.A.
22 E2 **Poste-de-la-Baleine** Can.
104 E4 **Postmasburg** S. Africa
23 J3 **Postville** Can.
30 B4 **Postville** U.S.A.
66 G3 **Posušje** Bos.-Herz.
105 G3 **Potchefstroom** S. Africa
27 E5 **Poteau** U.S.A.
43 L5 **Poté** Brazil
66 F4 **Potenza** Italy
105 H2 **Potgietersrus** S. Africa
27 D6 **Poth** U.S.A.
22 D6 **Potherie, Lac La** *l.* Can.
43 K5 **Poti** *r.* Brazil
69 G7 **P'ot'i** Georgia
100 D3 **Potiskum** Nigeria
32 E5 **Potomac** *r.* U.S.A.
32 D5 **Potomac South Branch** *r.* U.S.A.
42 E7 **Potosí** Bol.
26 E4 **Potosi** U.S.A.
35 E4 **Potosi Mt** *mt.* U.S.A.

94 B4 Pototan Phil.
62 F4 Potsdam Ger.
33 F2 Potsdam U.S.A.
59 E6 Potterne U.K.
59 G6 Potters Bar U.K.
33 F4 Pottstown U.S.A.
33 E4 Pottsville U.S.A.
20 E3 Pouce Coupe Can.
23 K4 Pouch Cove Can.
33 G4 Poughkeepsie U.S.A.
33 G3 Poultney U.S.A.
58 E4 Poulton-le-Fylde U.K.
95 B1 Pou San mt Laos
46 D3 Pouso Alegre Brazil
95 B2 Poŭthĭsăt Cambodia
63 J6 Považská Bystrica Slovakia
68 E2 Povenets Rus. Fed.
117 F3 Poverty Bay b. N.Z.
67 H2 Povlen mt Yugo.
65 B2 Póvoa de Varzim Port.
69 G5 Povorino Rus. Fed.
34 D5 Poway U.S.A.
24 F2 Powder r. U.S.A.
24 F3 Powder River U.S.A.
24 E2 Powell U.S.A.
32 B6 Powell r. U.S.A.
35 G3 Powell, Lake resr U.S.A.
34 C2 Powell Mt mt U.S.A.
29 E7 Powell Pt pt Bahamas
20 E5 Powell River Can.
30 D3 Powers U.S.A.
32 E6 Powhatan U.S.A.
46 A1 Poxoréu Brazil
89 E4 Poyang Hu l. China
95 □ Poyan Res. resr Sing.
30 C3 Poygan, Lake l. U.S.A.
80 E3 Pozantı Turkey
67 J2 Požarevac Yugo.
36 E4 Poza Rica Mex.
66 G2 Požega Croatia
67 J3 Požega Yugo.
62 H4 Poznań Pol.
65 D3 Pozoblanco Spain
66 F4 Pozzuoli Italy
92 C7 Prabumulih Indon.
62 G6 Prachatice Czech Rep.
85 F6 Prachi r. India
95 B2 Prachin Buri Thai.
95 A3 Prachuap Khiri Khan Thai.
64 F5 Prades France
46 E2 Prado Brazil
62 G5 Prague Czech Rep.
Praha see Prague
100 □ Praia Cape Verde
105 K2 Praia do Bilene Moz.
46 A1 Praia Rica Brazil
116 A3 Prairie Austr.
30 E5 Prairie Creek Reservoir resr U.S.A.
27 C5 Prairie Dog Town Fork r. U.S.A.
30 B4 Prairie du Chien U.S.A.
95 B2 Prakhon Chai Thai.
95 B2 Pran r. Thai.
92 B6 Prapat Indon.
67 M7 Prasonisi, Akra pt Greece
46 C2 Prata Brazil
46 C2 Prata r. Brazil
66 D3 Prato Italy
27 D4 Pratt U.S.A.
27 G5 Prattville U.S.A.
63 K3 Pravdinsk Rus. Fed.
92 F8 Praya Indon.
95 C2 Preăh Vihéar Cambodia
63 Q3 Prechistoye Rus. Fed.
21 J4 Preeceville Can.
68 H4 Pregolya r. Rus. Fed.
55 U8 Preili Latvia
31 H1 Preissac, Lac l. Can.
95 C3 Prêk Tnaôt l. Cambodia
115 H4 Premer Austr.
64 F3 Prémery France
30 B3 Prentice U.S.A.
62 F4 Prenzlau Ger.
62 H6 Přerov Czech Rep.
33 F2 Prescott Can.
35 F4 Prescott U.S.A.
35 F4 Prescott Valley U.S.A.
67 J3 Preševo Yugo.
26 C3 Presho U.S.A.
44 D3 Presidencia Roque Sáenz Peña Arg.
43 K5 Presidente Dutra Brazil
46 B3 Presidente Epitácio Brazil
42 F6 Presidente Hermes Brazil
46 B3 Presidente Prudente Brazil
46 B3 Presidente Venceslau Brazil
27 B6 Presidio U.S.A.
67 M3 Presnovka Rus. Fed.
63 K6 Prešov Slovakia
67 J4 Prespa, Lake l. Europe
33 K1 Presque Isle U.S.A.
30 D2 Presque Isle Pt pt U.S.A.
59 D5 Presteigne U.K.
58 E4 Preston U.K.
24 E3 Preston ID U.S.A.
30 A4 Preston MN U.S.A.
27 E4 Preston MO U.S.A.
35 E2 Preston NV U.S.A.
57 F5 Prestonpans U.K.
32 B6 Prestonsburg U.S.A.
57 D5 Prestwick U.K.
46 E1 Preto r. Bahia Brazil
46 C1 Preto r. Minas Gerais Brazil
105 H2 Pretoria S. Africa
32 E5 Prettyboy Lake l. U.S.A.
67 J5 Preveza Greece
95 C3 Prey Vêng Cambodia

87 L1 Priargunsk Rus. Fed.
77 V4 Pribilof Islands is Alaska
67 H3 Priboj Yugo.
23 G4 Price Can.
35 G2 Price U.S.A.
20 D4 Price I. i. Can.
29 B6 Prichard U.S.A.
55 R8 Priekule Latvia
55 T8 Priekuļi Latvia
55 S9 Prienai Lith.
104 E4 Prieska S. Africa
24 C1 Priest L. l. U.S.A.
24 C1 Priest River U.S.A.
63 J6 Prievidza Slovakia
66 G2 Prijedor Bos.-Herz.
67 H3 Prijepolje Yugo.
76 F5 Prikaspiyskaya Nizmennost' lowland Kazak./Rus. Fed.
67 J4 Prilep Macedonia
47 D1 Primero r. Arg.
115 G8 Prime Seal I. i. Austr.
55 V6 Primorsk Rus. Fed.
69 F6 Primorsko-Akhtarsk Rus. Fed.
21 H4 Primrose Lake l. Can.
21 H4 Prince Albert Can.
104 E6 Prince Albert S. Africa
21 H4 Prince Albert National Park nat. park Can.
104 D6 Prince Albert Road S. Africa
18 Prince Charles I. i. Can.
119 D4 Prince Charles Mts mts Ant.
23 H4 Prince Edward Island div. Can.
13 G7 Prince Edward Islands is Indian Ocean
31 J4 Prince Edward Pt pt Can.
32 E5 Prince Frederick U.S.A.
20 E4 Prince George Can.
113 H2 Prince of Wales I. i. Austr.
18 Prince of Wales I. i. Can.
20 C3 Prince of Wales Island i. U.S.A.
18 Prince Patrick I. i. Can.
20 C4 Prince Rupert Can.
21 K2 Princes Mary Lake l. Can.
33 F5 Princess Anne U.S.A.
113 H2 Princess Charlotte Bay b. Austr.
119 D5 Princess Elizabeth Land reg. Ant.
20 D4 Princess Royal I. i. Can.
20 E5 Princeton Can.
34 A2 Princeton CA U.S.A.
30 C5 Princeton IL U.S.A.
28 C4 Princeton IN U.S.A.
33 K2 Princeton ME U.S.A.
26 E3 Princeton MO U.S.A.
33 F4 Princeton NJ U.S.A.
32 C6 Princeton WV U.S.A.
30 C4 Princeton WV U.S.A.
33 K2 Prince William Can.
100 C4 Príncipe i. Sao Tome and Principe
24 B2 Prineville U.S.A.
76 C2 Prins Karls Forland i. Svalbard
37 H6 Prinzapolca Nic.
68 D2 Priozersk Rus. Fed.
Pripet r. see Pryp"yat
54 W2 Prirechnyy Rus. Fed.
67 J3 Priština Yugo.
62 F4 Pritzwalk Ger.
64 G4 Privas France
66 F2 Privlaka Croatia
68 G3 Privolzhsk Rus. Fed.
68 H4 Privolzhskaya Vozvyshennost' reg. Rus. Fed.
69 G6 Priyutnoye Rus. Fed.
67 J3 Prizren Yugo.
92 □ Probolinggo Indon.
59 C7 Probus U.K.
30 A2 Proctor MN U.S.A.
33 G3 Proctor VT U.S.A.
43 G3 Professor van Blommestein Meer resr Suriname
36 G5 Progreso Honduras
27 C7 Progreso Coahuila Mex.
36 G4 Progreso Yucatan Mex.
69 H7 Prokhladnyy Rus. Fed.
76 K4 Prokop'yevsk Rus. Fed.
67 J3 Prokuplje Yugo.
68 D3 Proletariy Rus. Fed.
69 G6 Proletarsk Rus. Fed.
Prome see Pyè
46 A2 Promissão Brazil
20 E3 Prophet River Can.
30 C5 Prophetstown U.S.A.
116 D3 Proserpine Austr.
33 F3 Prospect U.S.A.
94 C4 Prosperidad Phil.
116 D6 Proston Austr.
104 D7 Protem S. Africa
30 A4 Protivin U.S.A.
67 M3 Provadiya Bulg.
64 H5 Provence reg. France
33 H4 Providence U.S.A.
31 F3 Providence Bay Can.
117 E2 Pukekohe N.Z.
117 A7 Providence, Cape c. N.Z.
27 F5 Providence, Lake U.S.A.
42 B1 Providencia, Isla de i. Col.
35 H3 Provincetown U.S.A.
35 G1 Provo U.S.A.
21 G4 Provost Can.
46 B4 Prudentópolis Brazil

116 C3 Prudhoe I. i. Austr.
61 E4 Prüm Ger.
61 E4 Prüm r. Ger.
66 C3 Prunelli-di-Fiumorbo Corsica France
63 K4 Pruszków Pol.
69 D6 Prut r. Moldova/Romania
119 D5 Prydz Bay b. Ant.
69 E5 Pryluky Ukr.
69 F6 Prymors'k Ukr.
63 M5 Pryp"yat' r. Ukr.
63 N4 Prypyats' r. Belarus
63 L6 Przemyśl Pol.
Przheval'sk see Karakol
67 L5 Psara i. Greece
69 G6 Psebay Rus. Fed.
69 F6 Pshish r. Rus. Fed.
68 D3 Pskov Rus. Fed.
55 U7 Pskov, Lake l. Estonia/Rus. Fed.
68 D3 Pskovskaya Oblast' div. Rus. Fed.
67 J4 Ptolemaïda Greece
66 F1 Ptuj Slovenia
88 C3 Pu r. China
47 D3 Puán Arg.
89 B5 Pu'an China
89 C6 Pubei China
42 D5 Pucallpa Peru
89 F5 Pucheng Fujian China
88 C3 Pucheng Shaanxi China
89 D4 Puchezh r. Rus. Fed.
94 B4 Pucio Pt pt Phil.
62 J3 Puck Pol.
30 C4 Puckaway Lake l. U.S.A.
47 B3 Pucón Chile
54 U4 Pudasjärvi Fin.
104 F3 Pudimoe S. Africa
68 F2 Pudozh Rus. Fed.
58 F4 Pudsey U.K.
65 C1 Puebla de Sanabria Spain
25 F4 Pueblo U.S.A.
45 C2 Pueblo Nuevo Venez.
47 D3 Puelches Arg.
47 B3 Puelén Arg.
47 B2 Puente Alto Chile
65 D4 Puente-Genil Spain
45 C2 Puente Torres Venez.
42 F6 Puerto Alegre Bol.
37 H7 Puerto Armuelles Panama
45 A4 Puerto Asís Col.
45 D3 Puerto Ayacucho Venez.
36 G5 Puerto Barrios Guatemala
45 B3 Puerto Berrío Col.
45 C2 Puerto Cabello Venez.
37 H6 Puerto Cabezas Nic.
45 C2 Puerto Carreño Col.
44 E2 Puerto Casado Para.
44 B6 Puerto Cisnes Chile
44 C8 Puerto Coig Arg.
37 H7 Puerto Cortés Costa Rica
45 C2 Puerto Cumarebo Venez.
36 E5 Puerto Escondido Mex.
45 E1 Puerto Estrella Col.
42 F6 Puerto Frey Bol.
42 E6 Puerto Guarani Para.
42 E6 Puerto Heath Bol.
45 D4 Puerto Inírida Col.
43 G7 Puerto Isabel Bol.
42 D2 Puerto La Cruz Venez.
45 B4 Puerto Leguizamo Col.
65 D3 Puertollano Spain
44 C7 Puerto Lobos Arg.
45 B3 Puerto López Col.
47 D4 Puerto Madryn Arg.
42 E6 Puerto Maldonado Peru
42 D5 Puerto Máncora Peru
46 A4 Puerto Mendes Para.
45 D3 Puerto Miranda Venez.
47 B4 Puerto Montt Chile
44 B8 Puerto Natáles Chile
45 C3 Puerto Nuevo Col.
45 E2 Puerto Obaldía Panama
45 E2 Puerto Ordaz Venez.
45 D3 Puerto Páez Venez.
44 E2 Puerto Pinasco Para.
45 E2 Puerto Pirámides Arg.
37 K5 Puerto Plata Dom. Rep.
94 A4 Puerto Portillo Peru
94 A4 Puerto Princesa Phil.
45 A2 Puerto Rey Col.
37 L5 Puerto Rico terr. Caribbean
44 A4 Puerto Sastre Para.
45 A4 Puerto Tejado Col.
47 B4 Puerto Varas Chile
42 D4 Putumayo r. Col.
45 D3 Puerto Visser Arg.

33 E3 Pulaski NY U.S.A.
29 C5 Pulaski TN U.S.A.
32 C6 Pulaski VA U.S.A.
30 C3 Pulaski WI U.S.A.
63 K5 Puławy Pol.
54 T4 Pulkkila Fin.
24 C2 Pullman U.S.A.
54 X2 Pulozero Rus. Fed.
84 E1 Pulu China
81 G2 Pülümür Turkey
94 C5 Pulutan Indon.
85 G3 Puma Yumco l. China
42 B4 Puná, Isla i. Ecuador
85 G4 Punakha Bhutan
84 C2 Punch Jammu and Kashmir
20 E4 Punchaw Can.
85 G3 Püncogling China
105 J1 Punda Maria S. Africa
84 D3 Pundri India
95 □ Punggol Sing.
103 D5 Púnguè r. Moz.
102 C4 Punia Zaire
47 B1 Punitaqui Chile
84 B1 Punjab div. India
84 B3 Punjab div. Pak.
84 D2 Punmah Gl. gl. China/Jammu and Kashmir
85 F4 Punpun r. India
47 D3 Punta Alta Arg.
44 B8 Punta Arenas Chile
66 C4 Punta Balestrieri mt Italy
37 L5 Punta, Cerro de mt Puerto Rico
47 D4 Punta Delgada Arg.
36 G5 Punta Gorda Belize
29 D7 Punta Gorda U.S.A.
47 D4 Punta Norte Arg.
37 H6 Puntarenas Costa Rica
45 C2 Punto Fijo Venez.
32 U4 Punxsutawney U.S.A.
54 U4 Puokio Fin.
54 U4 Puolanka Fin.
89 D4 Puqi China
76 J3 Pur r. Rus. Fed.
45 A4 Puracé, Parque Nacional nat. park Col.
45 A4 Puracé, Volcán de volc. Col.
27 D5 Purcell U.S.A.
20 F4 Purcell Mts mts Can.
47 B3 Purén Chile
25 G4 Purgatoire r. U.S.A.
85 F6 Puri India
61 C2 Purmerend Neth.
84 D6 Purna r. Maharashtra India
84 D5 Purna r. Maharashtra India
85 G4 Purnabhaba r. India
85 F4 Pürnia India
112 E3 Purnululu National Park nat. park Austr.
47 B4 Purranque Chile
85 F5 Puruliya India
42 F4 Purus r. Brazil
55 V6 Puruvesi l. Fin.
92 □ Purwakarta Indon.
92 □ Purwodadi Indon.
92 □ Purwokerto Indon.
84 D6 Pus r. India
84 D6 Pusad India
87 N4 Pusan S. Korea
33 J2 Pushaw Lake l. U.S.A.
68 H2 Pushemskiy Rus. Fed.
84 C4 Pushkar India
68 D3 Pushkin Rus. Fed.
69 H5 Pushkino Rus. Fed.
68 D3 Pushkinskiye Gory Rus. Fed.
63 O2 Pustoshka Rus. Fed.
63 L4 Puszcza Augustowska forest Pol.
63 J4 Puszcza Natecka forest Pol.
82 J5 Putao Myanmar
89 F5 Putian China
92 E7 Puting, Tanjung pt Indon.
67 M2 Putna r. Romania
33 G4 Putnam U.S.A.
33 G3 Putney U.S.A.
85 H3 Putrang La pass China
104 D4 Putsonderwater S. Africa
83 H9 Puttalam Sri Lanka
61 D2 Putten Neth.
61 C3 Puttershoek Neth.
62 E3 Puttgarden Ger.
42 D4 Putumayo r. Col.
80 G2 Pütürge Turkey
68 G4 Putyatino Rus. Fed.
69 E5 Putyvl' Ukr.
55 V6 Puumala Fin.
34 □2 Puuwai U.S.A.
24 B2 Puvurnituq Can.
24 B2 Puyallup U.S.A.
89 E5 Puyang China
47 B4 Puyehue Chile
47 B4 Puyehue, Parque Nacional nat. park Chile
64 F5 Puylaurens France
117 A7 Puysegur Pt pt N.Z.
103 C4 Pweto Zaire
59 C5 Pwllheli U.K.
68 E2 Pyal'ma Rus. Fed.
68 H4 P'yana r. Rus. Fed.
84 B1 Pyandzh r. Afgh./Tajik.
54 W3 Pyaozero, Ozero l. Rus. Fed.
54 W4 Pyaozerskiy Rus. Fed.
83 J7 Pyapon Myanmar
76 K2 Pyasina r. Rus. Fed.
69 G6 Pyatigorsk Rus. Fed.
69 E5 P"yatykhatky Ukr.
83 J7 Pyè Myanmar

117 B7 Pye, Mt h. N.Z.
69 D4 Pyetrykaw Belarus
54 T4 Pyhäjoki Fin.
54 T4 Pyhäjoki r. Fin.
54 U4 Pyhäntä Fin.
54 T5 Pyhäsalmi Fin.
54 V5 Pyhäselkä l. Fin.
85 H5 Pyingaing Myanmar
83 J7 Pyinmana Myanmar
59 D6 Pyle U.K.
76 K3 Pyl'karamo Rus. Fed.
67 J6 Pylos Greece
32 C2 Pymatuning Reservoir resr U.S.A.
87 N4 P'yŏngyang N. Korea
114 F6 Pyramid Hill Austr.
34 C1 Pyramid Lake l. U.S.A.
30 D2 Pyramid Pt pt U.S.A.
34 C2 Pyramid Range mts U.S.A.
64 F5 Pyrenees mts France/Spain
67 J2 Pyrgos Greece
69 E5 Pyryatyn Ukr.
62 G4 Pyrzyce Pol.
68 H3 Pyshchug Rus. Fed.
63 N2 Pytalovo Rus. Fed.
67 K5 Pyxaria mt Greece

# Q

81 J6 Qabr Bandar Iraq
105 H5 Qacha's Nek Lesotho
81 K4 Qādir Karam Iraq
81 J7 Qadissiya Dam dam Iraq
88 C1 Qagan Ders China
88 D1 Qagan Nur China
88 C2 Qagan Nur China
88 E1 Qagan Nur l. China
88 E1 Qagan Nur resr China
88 D1 Qagan Teg China
88 D1 Qagan Us China
85 H3 Qagbasêrag China
85 E2 Qagcaka China
88 D1 Qahar Youyi Qianqi China
88 D1 Qahar Youyi Zhongqi China
82 H3 Qaidam Pendi basin China
81 K3 Qalā Diza Iraq
84 A2 Qalāt Afgh.
81 H4 Qal'at as Sālihīyah Syria
80 E6 Qal'at el Hasal Jordan
81 L6 Qal'at Sālih Iraq
81 L6 Qal'at Sukkar Iraq
81 K2 Qal'eh D. mt Iran
81 M5 Qal'eh-ye-Now Iran
81 K7 Qalīb Bāqūr w. Iraq
80 C6 Qalyûb Egypt
105 G5 Qamata S. Africa
84 B4 Qamber Pak.
82 J4 Qamdo China
84 B3 Qamruddin Karez Pak.
81 L2 Qandarnabashi mt. Iran
88 E1 Qangdin Sum China
81 M2 Qaraçala Azer.
81 J4 Qarachōq, J. mts Iraq
81 K4 Qara D. r. Iraq
81 H7 Qārah S. Arabia
84 B2 Qarah Bāgh Afgh.
81 L3 Qaranqu r. Iran
102 C3 Qardho Somalia
81 L3 Qareh D. mts Iran
81 L3 Qareh Dāsh, Kūh-e mt Iran
81 M2 Qareh Sū r. Iran
81 L3 Qareh Urgān, Kūh-e mt Iran
85 H1 Qarhan China
81 K6 Qaryat al Gharab Iraq
81 J5 Qaryat al Khubbāz Iraq
81 K4 Qasr al Azraq Jordan
81 K4 Qasr-e-Shirin Iran
81 L6 Qaşr Shaqrah Iraq
80 F5 Qaṭanā Syria
70 Qatar country Asia
81 K4 Qaṭrāna Jordan
80 C7 Qaṭrāni, Gebel escarpment Egypt
78 B4 Qattâra Depression depression Egypt
81 L1 Qax Azer.
79 H3 Qāyen Iran
85 H3 Qayü China
81 J4 Qayyarah Iraq
81 L2 Qazangöldağ mt. Azer.
81 K1 Qazax Azer.
84 B4 Qazi Ahmad Pak.
81 M1 Qazimämmäd Azer.
81 M3 Qazvīn Iran
88 A1 Qeh China
81 K4 Qena Egypt
81 K4 Qeshlag r. Iran
80 E6 Qezi'ot Israel
81 J4 Qian'an China
88 F2 Qianchang China
88 F3 Qiang r. China
89 D4 Qianjiang Hubei China
89 C4 Qianjiang Sichuan China
88 A4 Qianning China
88 G1 Qian Shan mts China
89 C5 Qianxi China

88 C3 Qian Xian China
89 D5 Qianyang Hunan China
88 C3 Qianyang Shaanxi China
89 F4 Qianyang Zhejiang China
88 D2 Qiaocun China
89 B5 Qiaojia China
81 K2 Qīās Iran
105 G4 Qibing S. Africa
89 D5 Qidong Hunan China
89 F4 Qidong Jiangsu China
85 H2 Qidukou China
82 G3 Qihe China
88 E2 Qihe China
89 C4 Qijiang China
89 C4 Qijiang China
88 E1 Qilaotu Shan mts China
84 B3 Qila Saifullah Pak.
82 J3 Qilian Shan mts China
85 G1 Qimantag mts China
89 E4 Qimen China
88 D3 Qin r. China
88 B3 Qin'an China
88 G1 Qingchengzi China
88 F2 Qingdao China
88 A2 Qinghai div. China
88 A2 Qinghai Hu salt l. China
82 J3 Qinghai Nanshan mts China
88 D2 Qingjian China
88 F3 Qingjiang Jiangsu China
89 E4 Qingjiang Jiangxi China
89 D4 Qing Jiang r. China
89 E5 Qingliu China
89 B5 Qinglong Guizhou China
88 F1 Qinglong Hebei China
89 D5 Qinglong r. China
88 F4 Qingpu China
88 D2 Qingshuihe China
88 E2 Qingtian China
89 C6 Qingxu China
89 E4 Qingyang Anhui China
88 C2 Qingyang Gansu China
89 D6 Qingyuan Guangdong China
89 F5 Qingyuan Zhejiang China
89 C5 Qingzhen China
88 F2 Qinhuangdao China
89 D6 Qin Ling mts China
88 C2 Qintongxia China
88 D3 Qin Xian China
89 C6 Qinyang China
89 C6 Qinyuan China
89 C6 Qinzhou China
89 C6 Qinzhou Wan b. China
89 D7 Qionghai China
89 B4 Qionglai China
89 D7 Qiongshan China
89 D7 Qiongzhou Haixia str. China
87 M2 Qiqihar China
81 M5 Qīr Iran
84 E1 Qira China
80 E6 Qiryat Gat Israel
80 F6 Qitab ash Shāmah crater S. Arabia
87 O2 Qitaihe China
89 B5 Qiubei China
88 E3 Qi Xian Henan China
88 D2 Qi Xian Shanxi China
88 D2 Qiyang China
88 C2 Qiying China
89 D7 Qiongu Liedao i. China
81 M2 Qızılağac Körfäzi b. Azer.
Qogir Feng mt see K2
88 C1 Qog Qi China
81 L3 Qojūr Iran
79 G3 Qom Iran
85 H3 Qomdo China
79 Qomolangma Feng mt see Everest, Mt
81 M1 Qonaqkänd Azer.
85 M3 Qongqäghä Azer.
88 C1 Qongj China
80 F4 Qornet es Saouda mt Lebanon
81 L4 Qotūr Iran
81 K2 Qotūr Iran
81 L3 Qotūr Iran
33 G3 Quabbin Reservoir resr U.S.A.
34 D3 Quail Mts mts U.S.A.
33 F4 Quakertown U.S.A.
21 K2 Quamarirjuq Lake l. Can.
114 E5 Quambatook Austr.
115 G3 Quambone Austr.
27 D5 Quanah U.S.A.
88 D3 Quanbao Shan mt. China
95 D2 Quang Ngai Vietnam
95 C1 Quang Tri Vietnam
89 C4 Quang Yen Vietnam
89 E5 Quannan China
89 F5 Quanzhou Fujian China
89 D5 Quanzhou Guangxi China
21 J4 Qu'Appelle Can.
21 J4 Qu'Appelle r. Can.
47 F1 Quaraí Brazil
47 F1 Quaraí r. Brazil
89 □ Quarry Bay Hong Kong China
66 C5 Quartu Sant'Elena Sardinia Italy
34 D3 Quartz Site Mt mt. U.S.A.
35 F4 Quartzsite U.S.A.
20 D4 Quatsino Sound in. Can.
81 M1 Quba Azer.
115 H5 Queanbeyan Austr.
23 F4 Québec Can.
31 H2 Québec div. Can.

46 C2 Quebra Anzol r. Brazil
45 C2 Quebrada del Toro, Parque Nacional de la nat. park Venez.
47 B4 Quedal, C. hd Chile
20 E4 Queen Bess, Mt mt. Can.
20 C4 Queen Charlotte Can.
20 C4 Queen Charlotte Islands is Can.
20 D4 Queen Charlotte Sound chan. Can.
20 D4 Queen Charlotte Str. chan. Can.
18 Queen Elizabeth Islands is Can.
102 D3 Queen Elizabeth National Park nat. park Uganda
119 C5 Queen Mary Land reg. Ant.
16 Queen Maud Gulf g. Can.
119 B4 Queen Maud Mts mts Ant.
113 H4 Queensland div. Austr.
115 F9 Queenstown Austr.
117 B6 Queenstown N.Z.
95 □ Queenstown Sing.
105 G5 Queenstown S. Africa
33 E5 Queenstown U.S.A.
24 A2 Queets U.S.A.
47 F2 Queguay Grande r. Uru.
47 D3 Quehué Arg.
43 H4 Queimada ou Serraria, Ilha i. Brazil
103 D5 Quelimane Moz.
44 B6 Quellón Chile
Quelpart I. i. see Cheju Do
35 H4 Quemado U.S.A.
47 B4 Quemchi Chile
47 D3 Quemú-Quemú Arg.
47 E3 Quequén Grande r. Arg.
46 B3 Querência do Norte Brazil
36 D4 Querétaro Mex.
88 E3 Queshan China
20 E4 Quesnel Can.
20 E4 Quesnel r. Can.
20 E4 Quesnel L. l. Can.
30 B1 Quetico Provincial Park res. Can.
84 A3 Quetta Pak.
47 B3 Queuco Chile
47 B3 Queule Chile
36 F6 Quezaltenango Guatemala
94 A4 Quezon Phil.
94 B3 Quezon City Phil.
88 E3 Qufu China
103 B5 Quibala Angola
103 B4 Quibaxe Angola
45 A3 Quibdó Col.
64 C3 Quiberon France
103 B4 Quicama, Parque Nacional do nat. park Angola
95 C1 Qui Châu Vietnam
35 F5 Quijotoa U.S.A.
47 D1 Quilino Arg.
64 F5 Quillan France
21 J4 Quill Lakes lakes Can.
47 B2 Quillota Chile
47 E2 Quilmes Arg.
83 E9 Quilon India
113 H5 Quilpie Austr.
47 B2 Quilpué Chile
102 B4 Quimbele Angola
44 D3 Quimilí Arg.
64 B3 Quimper France
64 C3 Quimperlé France
42 D6 Quince Mil Peru
34 B2 Quincy CA U.S.A.
29 C6 Quincy FL U.S.A.
30 B6 Quincy IL U.S.A.
33 H3 Quincy MA U.S.A.
47 D2 Quines Arg.
95 D2 Qui Nhơn Vietnam
35 E3 Quinn Canyon Range mts U.S.A.
65 E3 Quintanar de la Orden Spain
47 B2 Quintero Chile
47 D2 Quinto r. Arg.
65 F2 Quinto Spain
103 E5 Quionga Moz.
103 B5 Quipungo Angola
47 B3 Quirihue Chile
103 B5 Quirima Angola
115 J3 Quirindi Austr.
47 E2 Quiroga Arg.
103 D6 Quissico Moz.
103 B5 Quitapa Angola
43 L5 Quitéria r. Brazil
29 D6 Quitman GA U.S.A.
29 B5 Quitman MS U.S.A.
42 C4 Quito Ecuador
25 D6 Quitovac Mex.
35 F4 Quivero U.S.A.
43 L4 Quixadá Brazil
89 D5 Qujiang China
89 C4 Qu Jiang r. China
89 D6 Qujie China
89 B5 Qujing China
81 L7 Qulbān Layyah w. Iraq
79 L2 Qullai Garmo mt. Tajik.
85 H2 Qumar He r. China
85 H2 Qumarlêb China
85 H2 Qumarrabdün China
85 H2 Qumaryan China
105 H5 Qumbu S. Africa
105 G6 Qumrha S. Africa
21 L2 Quoich r. Can.
57 C3 Quoich, Loch l. U.K.
60 F3 Quoile r. U.K.
104 C7 Quoin Pt pt S. Africa
85 E2 Quong Muztag mt. China
113 G6 Quorn Austr.
104 F1 Quoxo r. Botswana
81 L3 Qurābeh Iran
79 K2 Qŭrghonteppa Tajik.
23 G2 Qurlutu r. Can.
81 K2 Qūrū Gol pass Iran
81 M1 Qusar Azer.
78 C4 Quseir Egypt
81 K3 Qūshchī Iran
81 L2 Qūsheh D. mts Iran
81 M4 Qūtīābād Iran
88 B2 Quwu Shan mts China
88 C4 Qu Xian China
85 G3 Qüxü China
95 C1 Quynh Lưu Vietnam
89 B6 Quynh Nhai Vietnam
31 J3 Quyon Can.
88 E2 Quzhou Hebei China
89 F4 Quzhou Zhejiang China
69 H7 Qvareli Georgia
Qyteti Stalin see Kuçovë


# R


62 H7 Raab r. Austria
54 T4 Raahe Fin.
54 V5 Rääkkylä Fin.
61 E2 Raalte Neth.
54 T3 Raanujärvi Fin.
92 □ Raas i. Indon.
57 B3 Raasay i. U.K.
57 B3 Raasay, Sound of chan. U.K.
102 F2 Raas Caseyr c. Somalia
92 F8 Raba Indon.
84 E2 Rabang China
66 F7 Rabat Malta
100 B1 Rabat Morocco
110 F2 Rabaul P.N.G.
20 D3 Rabbit r. Can.
78 D5 Rābigh S. Arabia
85 G5 Rabnabad Islands is Bangl.
69 D6 Râbniţa Moldova
32 B5 Raccoon Creek r. U.S.A.
23 K4 Race, C. c. Can.
33 H3 Race Pt pt U.S.A.
80 E5 Rachaïya Lebanon
27 D7 Rachal U.S.A.
35 E3 Rachel U.S.A.
95 C3 Rach Gia Vietnam
62 J5 Racibórz Pol.
30 D4 Racine U.S.A.
31 F1 Racine Lake l. Can.
30 E2 Raco U.S.A.
63 M7 Rădăuţi Romania
28 C4 Radcliff U.S.A.
32 C6 Radford U.S.A.
84 B5 Radhanpur India
23 E3 Radisson Can.
20 F4 Radium Hot Springs Can.
67 L3 Radnevo Bulg.
63 K5 Radom Pol.
67 K3 Radomir Bulg.
101 E4 Radom National Park nat. park Sudan
63 J5 Radomsko Pol.
69 D5 Radomyshl' Ukr.
67 K4 Radoviš Macedonia
59 E6 Radstock U.K.
68 C4 Radun' Belarus
55 S9 Radviliškis Lith.
63 M5 Radyvyliv Ukr.
84 E4 Rae Bareli India
20 F2 Rae-Edzo Can.
20 F2 Rae Lakes Can.
61 E4 Raeren Belgium
117 E3 Raetihi N.Z.
47 E1 Rafaela Arg.
80 E6 Rafaḩ Gaza
102 C3 Rafaï C.A.R.
78 E4 Rafḩā S. Arabia
79 H3 Rafsanjān Iran
94 C5 Ragang, Mt volc. Phil.
94 B3 Ragay Gulf b. Phil.
33 J3 Ragged I. i. U.S.A.
66 F6 Ragusa Sicily Italy
88 A3 Ra'gyagoinba China
93 G7 Raha Indon.
68 D4 Rahachow Belarus
Rahaeng see Tak
81 J5 Raḩḩālīyah Iraq
84 B3 Rahimyar Khan Pak.
83 B3 Rahue mt Chile
109 Raiatea i. Society Islands Pac. Oc.
83 E7 Raichur India
85 G4 Raiganj India
85 E5 Raigarh India
35 E2 Railroad Valley v. U.S.A.
23 G3 Raimbault, Lac l. Can.
114 E5 Rainbow Austr.
116 E5 Rainbow Beach Austr.
35 G3 Rainbow Bridge Nat. Mon. res. U.S.A.
20 F3 Rainbow Lake Can.
32 C6 Rainelle U.S.A.
24 B2 Rainier, Mt volc. U.S.A.
84 B3 Raini N. r. Pak.
22 B4 Rainy r. U.S.A.
21 L5 Rainy River Can.
85 E5 Raipur Madhya Pradesh India
84 C4 Raipur Rajasthan India
55 S6 Raisio Fin.
109 Raivavae i. Fr. Polynesia Pac. Oc.
83 F7 Rajahmundry India
54 V2 Raja-Jooseppi Fin.
79 L4 Rajanpur Pak.
83 E9 Rajapalaiyam India
84 C4 Rajasthan div. India
84 C3 Rajasthan Canal canal India
85 F4 Rajauli India
85 G5 Rajbari Bangl.
84 D4 Rajgarh Rajasthan India
84 C3 Rajgarh Rajasthan India
80 F6 Rajil, W. watercourse Jordan
85 E5 Rajim India
84 B5 Rajkot India
85 F4 Rajmahal India
85 F4 Rajmahal Hills h. India
85 E4 Raj Nandgaon India
84 D3 Rajpura India
85 G4 Rajshahi Bangl.
85 F3 Raka China
109 Rakahanga atoll Cook Islands Pac. Oc.
117 C5 Rakaia r. N.Z.
84 C1 Rakaposhi mt Pak.
85 F3 Raka Zangbo r. China
69 C5 Rakhiv Ukr.
84 B3 Rakhni Pak.
92 □ Rakit i. Indon.
69 E5 Rakitnoye Rus. Fed.
55 U7 Rakke Estonia
55 M7 Rakkestad Norway
84 B3 Rakni r. Pak.
55 U7 Rakvere Estonia
29 E5 Raleigh U.S.A.
108 Ralik Chain is Marshall Islands
30 D2 Ralph U.S.A.
20 E2 Ram r. Can.
23 H2 Ramah Can.
35 H4 Ramah U.S.A.
46 D1 Ramalho, Serra do h. Brazil
80 E6 Ramallah West Bank
105 F2 Ramatlabama S. Africa
110 E2 Rambutyo I. i. P.N.G.
59 C7 Rame Head hd U.K.
103 E5 Ramena Madag.
68 F3 Rameshki Rus. Fed.
83 E9 Rameswaram India
84 D4 Ramganga r. India
85 G5 Ramgarh Bangl.
85 F5 Ramgarh Bihar India
84 B4 Ramgarh Rajasthan India
78 F3 Rāmhormoz Iran
80 F7 Ram, Jebel mt. Jordan
80 E6 Ramla Israel
Ramlat Rabyānah des. see Rebiana Sand Sea
84 D3 Ramnagar India
67 M2 Râmnicu Sărat Romania
67 L2 Râmnicu Vâlcea Romania
34 D5 Ramona U.S.A.
31 G1 Ramore Can.
103 C6 Ramotswa Botswana
84 D3 Rampur India
84 C4 Rampura India
Rampur Boalia see Rajshahi
85 F4 Rampur Hat India
85 H6 Ramree I. i. Myanmar
54 P5 Ramsele Sweden
31 F2 Ramsey Can.
58 C3 Ramsey Isle of Man
59 G5 Ramsey Eng. U.K.
59 B6 Ramsey Island i. U.K.
31 F2 Ramsey Lake l. Can.
59 J6 Ramsgate U.K.
84 D5 Ramtek India
55 T9 Ramygala Lith.
45 C4 Rana, Co h. Col.
85 G5 Ranaghat India
84 C5 Ranapur India
92 F5 Ranau Malaysia
47 B2 Rancagua Chile
85 F5 Ranchi India
47 B4 Ranco, L. de l. Chile
115 G5 Rand Austr.
60 E3 Randalstown U.K.
66 F6 Randazzo Sicily Italy
55 M8 Randers Denmark
33 H3 Randolph MA U.S.A.
33 G3 Randolph VT U.S.A.
55 N5 Randsjö Sweden
54 S4 Råneå Sweden
117 C6 Ranfurly N.Z.
95 B4 Rangae Thai.
85 H5 Rangamati Bangl.
117 D1 Rangaunu Bay b. N.Z.
33 H2 Rangeley U.S.A.
33 H2 Rangeley Lake l. U.S.A.
35 H1 Rangely U.S.A.
31 F2 Ranger Lake Can.
117 D5 Rangiora N.Z.
109 Rangiroa i. Tuamotu Islands Pac. Oc.
117 C5 Rangitata r. N.Z.
117 E4 Rangitikei r. N.Z.
92 □ Rangkasbitung Indon.
Rangoon see Yangon
85 G4 Rangpur Bangl.
83 E8 Ranibennur India
85 F5 Raniganj India
85 E5 Ranijula Peak mt India
84 B4 Ranipur Pak.
27 C6 Rankin U.S.A.
21 L2 Rankin Inlet in. Can.
21 L2 Rankin Inlet Can.
115 G4 Rankin's Springs Austr.
55 U7 Ranna Estonia
116 D5 Rannes Austr.
57 D4 Rannoch, L. l. U.K.
57 D4 Rannoch Moor moorland U.K.
84 B4 Rann of Kachchh marsh India
95 A3 Ranong Thai.
95 B4 Ranot Thai.
68 G4 Ranova r. Rus. Fed.
81 M5 Rānsa Iran
55 N6 Ransby Sweden
93 J7 Ransiki Indon.
55 V5 Rantasalmi Fin.
92 B6 Rantauprapat Indon.
93 F7 Rantepao Indon.
30 C5 Rantoul U.S.A.
63 R2 Rantsevo Rus. Fed.
54 T4 Rantsila Fin.
54 U4 Ranua Fin.
81 K3 Rānya Iraq
89 E6 Raoping China
109 Rapa i. Fr. Polynesia Pac. Oc.
66 C2 Rapallo Italy
84 B5 Rapar India
47 B2 Rapel r. Chile
60 D3 Raphoe Rep. of Ireland
32 E5 Rapidan r. U.S.A.
114 C5 Rapid Bay Austr.
26 C2 Rapid City U.S.A.
31 H2 Rapide-Deux Can.
31 H2 Rapide-Sept Can.
30 D3 Rapid River U.S.A.
55 T7 Rapla Estonia
32 E5 Rappahannock r. U.S.A.
85 E4 Rapti r. India
85 B5 Rapur India
94 C3 Rapurapu i. Phil.
33 F2 Raquette r. U.S.A.
33 F3 Raquette Lake U.S.A.
33 F3 Raquette Lake l. U.S.A.
33 F4 Raritan Bay b. U.S.A.
109 Raroia atoll Tuamotu Islands Pac. Oc.
109 Rarotonga i. Cook Islands Pac. Oc.
94 A4 Rasa i. Phil.
79 H5 Ra's al Ḩadd pt Oman
47 D4 Rasa, Pta pt Arg.
102 D2 Ras Dashen mt. Eth.
55 S9 Raseiniai Lith.
80 C6 Rashîd Egypt
84 A3 Rashid Qala Afgh.
81 M3 Rasht Iran
84 C1 Raskam mts China
79 K4 Raskoh mts Pak.
44 C6 Raso, C. pt Arg.
68 D4 Rasony Belarus
85 E4 Rasra India
66 D6 Rass Jebel Tunisia
68 G4 Rasskazovo Rus. Fed.
79 G4 Ras Tannūrah S. Arabia
108 Ratak Chain is Marshall Islands
55 O5 Rätan Sweden
105 H3 Ratanda S. Africa
84 C3 Ratangarh India
85 E5 Ratanpur India
55 O5 Rätansbyn Sweden
95 A2 Rat Buri Thai.
84 D4 Rath India
60 E4 Rathangan Rep. of Ireland
60 D5 Rathdowney Rep. of Ireland
60 E5 Rathdrum Rep. of Ireland
85 H5 Rathedaung Myanmar
62 F4 Rathenow Ger.
60 E3 Rathfriland U.K.
60 C5 Rathkeale Rep. of Ireland
60 E2 Rathlin Island i. U.K.
60 C5 Rathluirc Rep. of Ireland
84 C3 Ratiya India
84 C5 Ratlam India
83 D7 Ratnagiri India
83 F9 Ratnapura Sri Lanka
69 C5 Ratne Ukr.
84 B4 Rato Dero Pak.
25 F4 Raton U.S.A.
57 G3 Rattray Head hd U.K.
55 O6 Rättvik Sweden
20 C3 Ratz, Mt mt. Can.
95 B5 Raub Malaysia
47 E3 Rauch Arg.
81 L7 Raudhatain Kuwait
54 F3 Raufarhöfn Iceland
117 G2 Raukumara mt. N.Z.
117 F3 Raukumara Range mts N.Z.
55 R6 Rauma Fin.
92 E8 Raung, G. volc. Indon.
85 F5 Raurkela India
90 K1 Rausu Japan
54 V5 Rautavaara Fin.
55 V6 Rautjärvi Fin.
24 D2 Ravalli U.S.A.
81 L4 Ravānsar Iran
33 G3 Ravena U.S.A.
58 D3 Ravenglass U.K.
66 E2 Ravenna Italy
116 A5 Ravensbourne Cr. watercourse Austr.
62 D7 Ravensburg Ger.
116 A1 Ravenshoe Austr.
112 D6 Ravensthorpe Austr.
116 B3 Ravenswood Austr.
32 C5 Ravenswood U.S.A.
84 C3 Ravi r. Pak.
81 H4 Rāwah Iraq
108 Rawaki i. Kiribati
84 C2 Rawalpindi Pak.
81 K3 Rawāndiz Iraq
84 C3 Rawatsar India
62 H5 Rawicz Pol.
32 D5 Rawley Springs U.S.A.
112 E6 Rawlinna Austr.
24 F3 Rawlins U.S.A.
44 C6 Rawson Arg.
85 F4 Raxaul India
83 F7 Rāyagarha India
80 F5 Rayak Lebanon
23 J4 Ray, C. hd Can.
87 N2 Raychikhinsk Rus. Fed.
59 H6 Rayleigh U.K.
20 G5 Raymond Can.
33 H3 Raymond NH U.S.A.
24 B2 Raymond WA U.S.A.
115 J4 Raymond Terrace Austr.
27 D7 Raymondville U.S.A.
95 B2 Rayong Thai.
32 D4 Raystown Lake l. U.S.A.
81 M5 Razān Iran
81 M4 Razan Iran
Razdan see Hrazdan
81 M5 Razeh Iran
67 M3 Razgrad Bulg.
67 N2 Razim, Lacul lag. Romania
67 K4 Razlog Bulg.
64 B2 Raz, Pte du pt France
59 G6 Reading U.K.
33 F4 Reading U.S.A.
30 A4 Readstown U.S.A.
105 G2 Reagile S. Africa
47 D2 Realicó Arg.
64 F5 Réalmont France
95 B2 Reăng Kesei Cambodia
101 E2 Rebiana Sand Sea des. Libya
68 D2 Reboly Rus. Fed.
90 H1 Rebun-suidō chan. Japan
90 H1 Rebun-tō i. Japan
112 D6 Recherche, Archipelago of the is Austr.
84 C3 Rechna Doab lowland Pak.
69 D4 Rechytsa Belarus
43 M5 Recife Brazil
105 F7 Recife, Cape c. S. Africa
62 C5 Recklinghausen Ger.
44 E3 Reconquista Arg.
44 C3 Recreo Arg.
21 K5 Red r. Can./U.S.A.
27 E6 Red r. U.S.A.
95 B4 Redang i. Malaysia
33 F4 Red Bank NJ U.S.A.
29 C5 Red Bank TN U.S.A.
23 J3 Red Bay Can.
34 A1 Red Bluff U.S.A.
35 F4 Red Butte summit U.S.A.
58 F3 Redcar U.K.
21 G4 Redcliff Can.
114 E5 Red Cliffs Austr.
26 D3 Red Cloud U.S.A.
20 G4 Red Deer Alta. Can.
21 G4 Red Deer r. Alta. Can.
21 J4 Red Deer r. Sask. Can.
21 J4 Red Deer L. l. Can.
33 F5 Redden U.S.A.
105 G4 Reddersburg S. Africa
24 B3 Redding U.S.A.
59 F5 Redditch U.K.
33 F3 Redfield NY U.S.A.
26 D2 Redfield SD U.S.A.
114 C4 Redhill Austr.
35 H4 Red Hill U.S.A.
27 D4 Red Hills h. U.S.A.
23 J4 Red Indian L. l. Can.
30 E5 Redkey U.S.A.
21 L4 Red L. l. Can.
35 E4 Red L. U.S.A.
21 L4 Red Lake Can.
26 E1 Red Lakes lakes U.S.A.
24 E2 Red Lodge U.S.A.
24 B2 Redmond U.S.A.
Red, Mouths of est. see Hong, Mouths of
26 E3 Red Oak U.S.A.
65 C3 Redondo Port.
30 C1 Red Rock Can.
33 E4 Red Rock U.S.A.
98 Red Sea sea Africa/Asia
20 E4 Redstone Can.
20 D2 Redstone r. Can.
21 L4 Red Sucker L. l. Can.
20 G4 Redwater Can.
23 F3 Red Wine r. Can.
30 A3 Red Wing U.S.A.
34 A3 Redwood City U.S.A.
26 E2 Redwood Falls U.S.A.
24 B3 Redwood Nat. Park U.S.A.
34 A2 Redwood Valley U.S.A.
30 E4 Reed City U.S.A.
34 C3 Reedley U.S.A.
30 C4 Reedsburg U.S.A.
24 A3 Reedsport U.S.A.
33 E6 Reedville U.S.A.
116 A4 Reedy Cr. watercourse Austr.
117 C5 Reefton N.Z.
60 D4 Ree, Lough l. Rep. of Ireland
80 G2 Refahiye Turkey
27 D6 Refugio U.S.A.
62 F6 Regen Ger.
62 F6 Regensburg Ger.
100 C2 Reggane Alg.
66 F5 Reggio di Calabria Italy
66 D2 Reggio nell'Emilia Italy
63 M7 Reghin Romania
21 J4 Regina Can.
54 W4 Regozero Rus. Fed.
84 D5 Rehli India
103 B6 Rehoboth Namibia
35 H4 Rehoboth U.S.A.
33 F5 Rehoboth Bay b. U.S.A.
33 F5 Rehoboth Beach U.S.A.
80 E6 Rehovot Israel
29 E4 Reidsville U.S.A.
59 G6 Reigate U.K.
64 D3 Ré, Île de i. France
35 G5 Reiley Peak summit U.S.A.
64 G2 Reims France
44 B8 Reina Adelaida, Archipiélago de la is Chile
30 A4 Reinbeck U.S.A.
62 E4 Reinbek Ger.
21 J3 Reindeer r. Can.
21 K4 Reindeer I. i. Can.
21 J3 Reindeer Lake l. Can.
54 N3 Reine Norway
117 D1 Reinga, Cape c. N.Z.
65 D1 Reinosa Spain
54 B4 Reiphólsfjöll mt. Iceland
54 R2 Reisaelva r. Norway
54 S2 Reisa Nasjonalpark nat. park Norway
54 T5 Reisjärvi Fin.
105 H3 Reitz S. Africa
104 F3 Reivilo S. Africa
45 D3 Rejunya Venez.
90 J2 Rekifune-gawa r. Japan
21 H2 Reliance Can.
100 C1 Relizane Alg.
114 C4 Remarkable, Mt mt Austr.
104 B1 Remhoogte Pass pass Namibia
62 C6 Remiremont France
84 D2 Remo Gl. gl. India
69 G6 Remontnoye Rus. Fed.
62 C5 Remscheid Ger.
30 E4 Remus U.S.A.
55 M6 Rena Norway
28 B4 Rend L. l. U.S.A.
111 F2 Rendova i. Solomon Is
62 D3 Rendsburg Ger.
31 J3 Renfrew Can.
57 D5 Renfrew U.K.
47 B2 Rengo Chile
88 C3 Ren He r. China
88 E4 Renheji China
89 D5 Renhua China
89 C5 Renhuai China
69 D6 Reni Ukr.
114 D5 Renmark Austr.
111 G3 Rennell i. Solomon Is
64 D2 Rennes France
119 B5 Rennick Gl. gl. Ant.
21 H2 Rennie Lake l. Can.
66 D2 Reno r. Italy
34 C2 Reno U.S.A.
32 E4 Renovo U.S.A.
88 E2 Renqiu China
89 B4 Renshou China
30 D5 Rensselaer IN U.S.A.
33 G3 Rensselaer NY U.S.A.
61 D2 Renswoude Neth.
24 B2 Renton U.S.A.
85 E4 Renukut India
117 D4 Renwick N.Z.
100 B3 Réo Burkina
93 G8 Reo Indon.
24 C1 Republic U.S.A.
26 D3 Republican r. U.S.A.
116 C3 Repulse B. b. Austr.
42 D5 Requena Peru
65 F3 Requena Spain
80 F1 Reşadiye Turkey
81 J2 Reşadıye Turkey
46 B4 Reserva Brazil
79 G2 Reshteh-ye Alborz mts Iran
44 E3 Resistencia Arg.
67 J2 Reşiţa Romania
117 A6 Resolution Island i. N.Z.
95 □ Retan Laut, P. i. Sing.
59 G4 Retford U.K.
64 G2 Rethel France
67 L7 Rethymno Greece
98 Réunion i. Indian Ocean
65 G2 Reus Spain
62 D6 Reutlingen Ger.
34 D3 Reveille Peak summit U.S.A.
64 F5 Revel France
20 F4 Revelstoke Can.
20 C3 Revillagigedo I. i. U.S.A.
36 B5 Revillagigedo, Islas is Mex.
61 C5 Revin France
80 E6 Revivim Israel
84 E4 Rewa India
84 D3 Rewari India
24 E3 Rexburg U.S.A.
23 H4 Rexton Can.
34 C4 Reyes Peak summit U.S.A.
34 A2 Reyes, Point pt U.S.A.
80 F3 Reyhanlı Turkey
54 C4 Reykir Iceland
12 G2 Reykjanes Ridge sea feature Atlantic Ocean
54 B5 Reykjanestá pt Iceland
54 C4 Reykjavík Iceland
36 E3 Reynosa Mex.
55 U8 Rēzekne Latvia
81 M3 Rezvanshahr Iran
80 F5 Rharaz, W. watercourse Syria
59 D5 Rhayader U.K.
Rhein r. see Rhine
62 C4 Rheine Ger.
61 E4 Rheinisches Schiefergebirge h. Ger.
61 F5 Rheinland-Pfalz div. Ger.
Rhin r. see Rhine
62 C5 Rhine r. Europe
33 G4 Rhinebeck U.S.A.
30 C3 Rhinelander U.S.A.
66 C2 Rho Italy
33 H4 Rhode Island div. U.S.A.

67 N6 **Rhodes** *i.* Greece
67 N6 **Rhodes** Greece
24 D2 **Rhodes Pk** *summit* U.S.A.
59 D6 **Rhondda** U.K.
64 G4 **Rhône** *r.* France/Switz.
**Rhum** *i. see* **Rum**
59 D4 **Rhyl** U.K.
46 E2 **Riacho** Brazil
46 D1 **Riacho de Santana** Brazil
47 D4 **Riachos, Is de los** *i.* Arg.
46 C1 **Rialma** Brazil
46 C1 **Rianópolis** Brazil
84 C2 **Riasi** Jammu and Kashmir
92 C6 **Riau, Kepulauan** *is* Indon.
65 C1 **Ribadeo** Spain
65 D1 **Ribadesella** Spain
46 B3 **Ribas do Rio Pardo** Brazil
103 D5 **Ribáuè** Moz.
58 E4 **Ribble** *r.* U.K.
55 L9 **Ribe** Denmark
46 C4 **Ribeira** *r.* Brazil
46 C3 **Ribeirão Preto** Brazil
64 E4 **Ribérac** France
42 E6 **Riberalta** Bol.
62 F7 **Ribnitz-Damgarten** Ger.
62 G6 **Říčany** Czech Rep.
35 E4 **Rice** U.S.A.
31 F2 **Rice Lake** *l.* Can.
30 B3 **Rice Lake** U.S.A.
30 A4 **Riceville** *IA* U.S.A.
32 D4 **Riceville** *PA* U.S.A.
105 K4 **Richards Bay** S. Africa
21 C3 **Richardson** *r.* Can.
27 D5 **Richardson** U.S.A.
33 H2 **Richardson Lakes** *l.* U.S.A.
117 B6 **Richardson Mts** *mts* N.Z.
61 D1 **Richel** *i.* Neth.
35 F2 **Richfield** U.S.A.
33 F3 **Richfield Springs** U.S.A.
33 H3 **Richford** *NY* U.S.A.
33 G2 **Richford** *VT* U.S.A.
30 B5 **Richland** U.S.A.
30 B4 **Richland Center** U.S.A.
32 C6 **Richlands** U.S.A.
115 J4 **Richmond** *N.S.W.* Austr.
113 H4 **Richmond** *Qld.* Austr.
31 K3 **Richmond** Can.
117 D4 **Richmond** N.Z.
105 J4 **Richmond** *Kwazulu-Natal* S. Africa
104 E5 **Richmond** *Northern Cape* S. Africa
58 F3 **Richmond** U.K.
30 E6 **Richmond** *IN* U.S.A.
32 A6 **Richmond** *KY* U.S.A.
33 J2 **Richmond** *ME* U.S.A.
31 H4 **Richmond** *MI* U.S.A.
32 E6 **Richmond** *VA* U.S.A.
33 G2 **Richmond** *VT* U.S.A.
31 H4 **Richmond Hill** Can.
117 D4 **Richmond, Mt** *mt.* N.Z.
115 K2 **Richmond Ra.** *h.* Austr.
104 B4 **Richtersveld National Park** *nat. park* S. Africa
32 A4 **Richwood** *OH* U.S.A.
32 C5 **Richwood** *WV* U.S.A.
31 K3 **Rideau** *r.* Can.
31 J3 **Rideau Lakes** *l.* Can.
34 D2 **Ridgecrest** U.S.A.
32 D4 **Ridgway** U.S.A.
21 J4 **Riding Mountain Nat. Park** *nat. park* Can.
62 D6 **Riedlingen** Ger.
62 F5 **Riesa** Ger.
44 B8 **Riesco, Isla** *i.* Chile
104 D5 **Riet** *r.* S. Africa
55 R9 **Rietavas** Lith.
104 D3 **Rietfontein** S. Africa
61 D3 **Riethoven** Neth.
66 E3 **Rieti** Italy
25 F4 **Rifle** U.S.A.
54 E2 **Rifstangi** *pt* Iceland
85 H3 **Riga** India
55 T8 **Rīga** Latvia
55 S8 **Riga, Gulf of** *g.* Estonia/Latvia
**Rigas Jūras Līcis** *g. see* **Riga, Gulf of**
33 F2 **Rigaud** Can.
24 C3 **Riggins** U.S.A.
23 J3 **Rigolet** Can.
57 E5 **Rigside** U.K.
85 E4 **Rihand** *r.* India
**Riia Laht** *g. see* **Riga, Gulf of**
55 T6 **Riihimäki** Fin.
119 D4 **Riiser-Larsenhalvøya** *pen.* Ant.
119 D3 **Riiser-Larsen Sea** *sea* Ant.
25 C3 **Riito** Mex.
66 F2 **Rijeka** Croatia
**Rijn** *r. see* **Rhine**
90 J2 **Rikubetsu** Japan
91 H4 **Rikuzen-takata** Japan
67 K3 **Rila** *mts* Bulg.
24 C3 **Riley** U.S.A.
64 G4 **Rillieux-la-Pape** France
109 **Rimatara** *i. Tubuai Islands* Pac. Oc.
63 K6 **Rimavská Sobota** Slovakia
20 G4 **Rimbey** Can.
66 E2 **Rimini** Italy
23 G4 **Rimouski** Can.
57 D2 **Rimsdale, Loch** *l.* U.K.
85 G3 **Rinbung** China
84 D4 **Rind** *r.* India
54 L5 **Rindal** Norway
115 G8 **Ringarooma B.** *b.* Austr.
84 C4 **Ringas** India
85 G2 **Ring Co** *salt l.* China

55 M6 **Ringebu** Norway
55 L8 **Ringkøbing** Denmark
60 E2 **Ringsend** U.K.
55 M9 **Ringsted** Denmark
54 Q2 **Ringvassøy** *i.* Norway
59 F7 **Ringwood** U.K.
47 B3 **Riñihue** Chile
47 B3 **Riñihue, L.** *l.* Chile
30 C4 **Rio** U.S.A.
46 A2 **Rio Alegre** Brazil
43 C3 **Riobamba** Ecuador
35 H2 **Rio Blanco** U.S.A.
42 E6 **Rio Branco** Brazil
46 C4 **Rio Branco do Sul** Brazil
45 E4 **Rio Branco, Parque Nacional do** *nat. park* Brazil
46 A3 **Rio Brilhante** Brazil
47 B4 **Río Bueno** Chile
45 E2 **Río Caribe** Venez.
47 D1 **Río Ceballos** Arg.
46 C3 **Rio Claro** Brazil
45 E2 **Río Claro** Trinidad and Tobago
47 D3 **Río Colorado** Arg.
47 D2 **Río Cuarto** Arg.
46 D3 **Rio de Janeiro** *div.* Brazil
46 D3 **Rio de Janeiro** Brazil
44 D3 **Rio do Sul** Brazil
44 C8 **Río Gallegos** Arg.
44 C8 **Río Grande** Arg.
42 F7 **Río Grande** *r.* Bol.
47 G2 **Río Grande** Brazil
36 D4 **Río Grande** Mex.
36 E3 **Río Grande** *r.* Mex./U.S.A.
27 D7 **Rio Grande City** U.S.A.
47 F1 **Rio Grande do Sul** *div.* Brazil
12 G7 **Rio Grande Rise** *sea feature* Atlantic Ocean
45 B2 **Ríohacha** Col.
42 C5 **Rioja** Peru
43 L5 **Rio Largo** Brazil
64 F4 **Riom** France
42 E7 **Río Mulatos** Bol.
47 C4 **Río Negro** *div.* Arg.
47 C4 **Río Negro** Brazil
69 G7 **Rioni** *r.* Georgia
47 G1 **Rio Pardo** Brazil
46 D1 **Rio Pardo de Minas** Brazil
47 D1 **Río Primero** Arg.
25 E3 **Río Rancho** U.S.A.
35 G6 **Rio Rico** U.S.A.
47 D1 **Río Segundo** Arg.
45 A3 **Ríosucio** Col.
47 D2 **Río Tercero** Arg.
42 C4 **Río Tigre** Ecuador
94 A4 **Rio Tuba** Phil.
46 B2 **Rio Verde** Brazil
36 E4 **Río Verde** Mex.
46 A2 **Rio Verde de Mato Grosso** Brazil
34 B2 **Rio Vista** U.S.A.
46 A2 **Riozinho** *r.* Brazil
63 P5 **Ripky** Ukr.
58 F3 **Ripley** *Eng.* U.K.
59 F4 **Ripley** *Eng.* U.K.
32 B5 **Ripley** *OH* U.S.A.
29 B5 **Ripley** *TN* U.S.A.
32 C5 **Ripley** *WV* U.S.A.
65 H1 **Ripoll** Spain
58 F3 **Ripon** U.K.
34 B3 **Ripon** *CA* U.S.A.
30 C4 **Ripon** *WV* U.S.A.
59 D6 **Risca** U.K.
90 H1 **Rishiri-tō** *i.* Japan
90 H1 **Rishiri-zan** *volc.* Japan
80 E6 **Rishon Le Ziyyon** Israel
55 L7 **Risør** Norway
54 L5 **Rissa** Norway
55 U6 **Ristiina** Fin.
54 V4 **Ristijärvi** Fin.
54 W2 **Ristikent** Rus. Fed.
104 F4 **Ritchie** S. Africa
54 P3 **Ritsem** Sweden
25 C4 **Ritter, Mt** *mt.* U.S.A.
24 C2 **Ritzville** U.S.A.
47 C4 **Rivadavia** *Mendoza* Arg.
47 D2 **Rivadavia** *Pampas* Arg.
44 D2 **Rivadavia** *Salta* Arg.
47 B1 **Rivadavia** Chile
66 D2 **Riva del Garda** Italy
37 G6 **Rivas** Nic.
47 D3 **Rivera** Arg.
47 F1 **Rivera** Uru.
100 B4 **River Cess** Liberia
33 G4 **Riverhead** U.S.A.
115 F5 **Riverina** *reg.* Austr.
104 D7 **Riversdale** S. Africa
105 H5 **Riverside** S. Africa
34 D5 **Riverside** U.S.A.
114 C5 **Riverton** Austr.
21 K4 **Riverton** Can.
117 B7 **Riverton** N.Z.
24 E3 **Riverton** U.S.A.
23 H4 **Riverview** Can.
64 F5 **Rivesaltes** France
29 D7 **Riviera Beach** U.S.A.
33 J1 **Rivière Bleue** Can.
23 G4 **Rivière-du-Loup** Can.
69 C5 **Rivne** Ukr.
117 D4 **Riwaka** N.Z.
82 J4 **Riwoqê** China
78 F5 **Riyadh** S. Arabia
88 A2 **Riyue Shankou** *pass* China
81 H1 **Rize** Turkey
88 F3 **Rizhao** China
80 E4 **Rizokarpason** Cyprus
55 L7 **Rjukan** Norway
55 K7 **Rjuvbrokkene** *mt* Norway
100 A3 **Rkîz** Maur.

84 D3 **Rnyar** *r.* India
55 M6 **Roa** Norway
59 G5 **Roade** U.K.
54 M4 **Roan** Norway
35 H2 **Roan Cliffs** *cliff* U.S.A.
64 G3 **Roanne** France
29 C5 **Roanoke** *AL* U.S.A.
30 C5 **Roanoke** *IL* U.S.A.
32 D6 **Roanoke** *VA* U.S.A.
28 E4 **Roanoke** *r. VA* U.S.A.
29 E4 **Roanoke Rapids** U.S.A.
35 H2 **Roan Plateau** *plat.* U.S.A.
60 B6 **Roaringwater Bay** *b.* Rep. of Ireland
54 R5 **Röbäck** Sweden
115 F8 **Robbins I.** *i.* Austr.
114 C6 **Robe** Austr.
60 B4 **Robe** *r.* Rep. of Ireland
114 D3 **Robe, Mt** *h.* Austr.
27 C6 **Robert Lee** U.S.A.
24 D3 **Roberts** U.S.A.
34 D2 **Roberts Creek Mt** *mt.* U.S.A.
54 R4 **Robertsfors** Sweden
85 E4 **Robertsganj** India
27 E5 **Robert S. Kerr Res.** *resr* U.S.A.
115 K2 **Roberts, Mt** *mt* Austr.
104 C6 **Robertson** S. Africa
100 A4 **Robertsport** Liberia
114 C4 **Robertstown** Austr.
23 F4 **Roberval** Can.
58 G3 **Robin Hood's Bay** U.K.
89 **Robin's Nest** *h.* Hong Kong China
28 C4 **Robinson** U.S.A.
116 C5 **Robinson Cr.** *r.* Austr.
112 C5 **Robinson Ranges** *h.* Austr.
114 C4 **Robinvale** Austr.
35 G5 **Robles Junction** U.S.A.
35 G5 **Robles Pass** *pass* U.S.A.
21 J4 **Roblin** Can.
20 F4 **Robson, Mt** *mt.* Can.
27 D7 **Robstown** U.S.A.
66 E6 **Rocca Busambra** *mt Sicily* Italy
47 F2 **Rocha** Uru.
58 E4 **Rochdale** U.K.
46 A2 **Rochedo** Brazil
61 D4 **Rochefort** Belgium
64 D4 **Rochefort** France
22 F2 **Rochefort, Lac** *l.* Can.
68 G2 **Rochegda** Rus. Fed.
30 C5 **Rochelle** U.S.A.
114 F6 **Rochester** Austr.
59 H6 **Rochester** U.K.
30 D5 **Rochester** *IN* U.S.A.
30 A3 **Rochester** *MN* U.S.A.
33 H3 **Rochester** *NH* U.S.A.
32 E3 **Rochester** *NY* U.S.A.
59 H6 **Rochford** U.K.
64 C2 **Roc'h Trévezel** *h.* France
20 D2 **Rock** *r.* Can.
30 B5 **Rock** *r.* U.S.A.
12 H2 **Rockall Bank** *sea feature* Atlantic Ocean
119 B4 **Rockefeller Plateau** *plat.* Ant.
30 C4 **Rockford** U.S.A.
21 H5 **Rockglen** Can.
116 D4 **Rockhampton** Austr.
30 C1 **Rock Harbor** U.S.A.
29 D5 **Rock Hill** U.S.A.
112 C6 **Rockingham** Austr.
29 E5 **Rockingham** U.S.A.
116 B2 **Rockingham B.** *b.* Austr.
33 G2 **Rock Island** Can.
30 B5 **Rock Island** U.S.A.
26 D1 **Rocklake** U.S.A.
33 F2 **Rockland** Can.
33 H3 **Rockland** *MA* U.S.A.
33 J2 **Rockland** *ME* U.S.A.
30 C2 **Rockland** *MI* U.S.A.
114 E6 **Rocklands Reservoir** *resr* Austr.
35 H3 **Rock Point** U.S.A.
33 H3 **Rockport** U.S.A.
26 D3 **Rock Rapids** U.S.A.
24 E3 **Rock Springs** *MT* U.S.A.
24 E3 **Rock Springs** *WY* U.S.A.
27 C6 **Rocksprings** U.S.A.
115 G5 **Rock, The** Austr.
32 D3 **Rockton** Can.
30 D6 **Rockville** *IN* U.S.A.
32 E5 **Rockville** *MD* U.S.A.
33 J2 **Rockwood** U.S.A.
25 G4 **Rocky Ford** U.S.A.
32 B5 **Rocky Fork Lake** *l.* U.S.A.
31 F2 **Rocky Island Lake** *l.* Can.
29 E5 **Rocky Mount** *NC* U.S.A.
32 D6 **Rocky Mount** *VA* U.S.A.
20 G4 **Rocky Mountain House** Can.
24 E3 **Rocky Mountain Nat. Park** *nat. park* U.S.A.
18 **Rocky Mountains** *mts* Can./U.S.A.
20 F4 **Rocky Mountains Forest Reserve** *res.* Can.
61 C5 **Rocroi** France
55 L6 **Rodberg** Norway
55 M9 **Rødbyhavn** Denmark
23 J3 **Roddickton** Can.
57 B3 **Rodel** U.K.
47 C1 **Rodeo** Arg.
35 H6 **Rodeo** U.S.A.
64 F4 **Rodez** France
68 G3 **Rodniki** Rus. Fed.
67 L4 **Rodopi Planina** *mts* Bulg./Greece
**Rodos** *see* **Rhodes**
**Rodos** *i. see* **Rhodes**

13 J5 **Rodrigues Fracture** *sea feature* Indian Ocean
112 C4 **Roebourne** Austr.
112 C3 **Roebuck Bay** *b.* Austr.
105 H2 **Roedtan** S. Africa
61 D3 **Roermond** Neth.
61 B4 **Roeselare** Belgium
42 E6 **Rogaguado, Lago** *l.* Bol.
27 E5 **Rogers** U.S.A.
31 F3 **Rogers City** U.S.A.
34 A2 **Rogers Lake** *l.* U.S.A.
24 D3 **Rogerson** U.S.A.
32 B6 **Rogersville** U.S.A.
22 E3 **Roggan** *r.* Can.
104 D6 **Roggeveld** *plat.* S. Africa
104 D6 **Roggeveldberge** *escarpment* S. Africa
54 O3 **Rognan** Norway
24 A3 **Rogue** *r.* U.S.A.
34 A2 **Rohnert Park** U.S.A.
62 F6 **Rohrbach in Oberösterreich** Austria
84 B4 **Rohri** Pak.
84 D3 **Rohtak** India
15 K6 **Roi Georges, Îles du** *is Fr. Polynesia* Pac. Oc.
55 S8 **Roja** Latvia
47 E2 **Rojas** Arg.
84 B3 **Rojhan** Pak.
95 B5 **Rokan** *r.* Indon.
113 H7 **Rokeby National Park** *nat. park* Austr.
55 T9 **Rokiškis** Lith.
90 H3 **Rokkasho** Japan
54 R4 **Roknäs** Sweden
69 C5 **Rokytne** Ukr.
85 G2 **Rola Co** *salt l.* China
46 B3 **Rolândia** Brazil
26 C4 **Rolla** U.S.A.
55 L6 **Rollag** Norway
116 C5 **Rolleston** Austr.
117 D5 **Rolleston** N.Z.
31 H2 **Rollet** Can.
116 C6 **Roma** Austr.
93 H8 **Roma** *i.* Indon.
**Roma** *see* **Rome**
105 G4 **Roma** Lesotho
55 Q8 **Roma** Sweden
29 E5 **Romain, Cape** *c.* U.S.A.
23 H3 **Romaine** *r.* Can.
63 N7 **Roman** Romania
12 H6 **Romanche Gap** *sea feature* Atlantic Ocean
80 D6 **Români** Egypt
49 **Romania** *country* Europe
69 D6 **Romanovka** Rus. Fed.
87 K1 **Romanovka** Rus. Fed.
64 G4 **Romans-sur-Isère** France
118 D1 **Romanzof, Cape** *c.* U.S.A.
64 F3 **Rombas** France
94 B3 **Romblon** *i.* Phil.
94 B3 **Romblon** Phil.
66 E4 **Rome** Italy
29 C5 **Rome** *GA* U.S.A.
33 J2 **Rome** *ME* U.S.A.
33 F3 **Rome** *NY* U.S.A.
31 H4 **Rome** U.S.A.
59 H6 **Romford** U.K.
64 F2 **Romilly-sur-Seine** France
32 D5 **Romney** U.S.A.
59 H6 **Romney Marsh** *reg.* U.K.
69 E5 **Romny** Ukr.
55 L9 **Rømø** *i.* Denmark
64 E3 **Romorantin-Lanthenay** France
95 B5 **Rompin** *r.* Malaysia
95 C1 **Ron** Vietnam
57 C1 **Rona** *i. Scot.* U.K.
57 C1 **Rona** *i. Scot.* U.K.
57 **Ronas Hill** *h.* U.K.
111 **Roncador Reef** *rf* Solomon Is
43 H6 **Roncador, Serra do** *h.* Brazil
55 D4 **Ronda** Spain
55 L6 **Rondane Nasjonalpark** *nat. park* Norway
45 D3 **Rondón** Col.
42 F6 **Rondónia** Brazil
42 A2 **Rondonópolis** Brazil
82 **Rondu** Jammu and Kashmir
47 D2 **Río Negro, Embalse del** *resr* Uru.
89 C5 **Rong'an** China
89 B5 **Rongchang** China
88 B2 **Rongcheng Wan** *b.* China
85 G3 **Rong Chu** *r.* China
89 C5 **Rongjiang** China
89 C6 **Rong Jiang** *r.* China
85 H5 **Rongklang Range** *mts* Myanmar
117 E4 **Rongotea** N.Z.
89 C5 **Rongshui** China
89 D6 **Rong Xian** *Guangxi* China
89 B4 **Rong Xian** *Sichuan* China
55 O9 **Rønne** Denmark
55 O8 **Ronneby** Sweden
119 B3 **Ronne Entrance** *str.* Ant.
119 B3 **Ronne Ice Shelf** *ice feature* Ant.
61 B4 **Ronse** Belgium
84 D3 **Roorkee** India
61 C3 **Roosendaal** Neth.
35 G5 **Roosevelt** *AZ* U.S.A.
35 H5 **Roosevelt** *UT* U.S.A.
35 G5 **Roosevelt Dam** *dam* U.S.A.
119 A4 **Roosevelt I.** *i.* Ant.
20 D3 **Roosevelt, Mt** *mt.* Can.

20 E2 **Root** *r.* Can.
30 B4 **Root** *r.* U.S.A.
68 K2 **Ropcha** Rus. Fed.
116 C4 **Roper** *r.* Austr.
64 D4 **Roquefort** France
45 E4 **Roraima** *div.* Brazil
42 F2 **Roraima, Mt** *mt.* Guyana
54 M5 **Røros** Norway
54 M4 **Rørvik** Norway
63 P6 **Ros'** *r.* Ukr.
42 **Rosa, C.** *pt Galapagos Is* Ecuador
34 C4 **Rosamond** U.S.A.
34 C4 **Rosamond Lake** *l.* U.S.A.
47 E2 **Rosario** Arg.
36 A2 **Rosario** *Baja California* Mex.
27 C7 **Rosario** *Coahuila* Mex.
94 B3 **Rosario** Phil.
94 B2 **Rosario** Phil.
47 E2 **Rosario** Venez.
47 E2 **Rosario del Tala** Arg.
47 F1 **Rosário do Sul** Brazil
46 A1 **Rosário Oeste** Brazil
33 F4 **Rosarno** Italy
64 C2 **Roscoff** France
60 C4 **Roscommon** Rep. of Ireland
30 E3 **Roscommon** U.S.A.
60 D4 **Roscrea** Rep. of Ireland
37 M5 **Roseau** Dominica
21 K5 **Roseau** U.S.A.
115 F8 **Rosebery** Austr.
23 H4 **Rose Blanche** Can.
24 B3 **Roseburg** U.S.A.
31 F3 **Rose City** U.S.A.
116 D5 **Rosedale** Austr.
58 G3 **Rosedale Abbey** U.K.
101 F3 **Roseires Reservoir** *resr* Sudan
108 **Rose Island** *i. Auckland Is* Pac. Oc.
34 C2 **Rose, Mt** *mt.* U.S.A.
27 E6 **Rosenberg** U.S.A.
55 K7 **Rosendal** Norway
105 G4 **Rosendal** S. Africa
62 F7 **Rosenheim** Ger.
20 C4 **Rose Pt** *pt* Can.
29 F7 **Roses** Bahamas
66 F3 **Roseto degli Abruzzi** Italy
21 H4 **Rosetown** Can.
**Rosetta** *see* **Rashid**
116 B2 **Rosetta Cr.** *r.* Austr.
21 J4 **Rose Valley** Can.
34 B2 **Roseville** *CA* U.S.A.
30 B5 **Roseville** *OH* U.S.A.
115 K1 **Rosewood** Austr.
68 D2 **Roshchino** Rus. Fed.
104 B3 **Rosh Pinah** Namibia
66 D3 **Rosignano Marittimo** Italy
67 L2 **Roşiori de Vede** Romania
55 N9 **Roskilde** Denmark
68 E4 **Roslavl'** Rus. Fed.
54 X2 **Roslyakovo** Rus. Fed.
115 G9 **Ross** Austr.
20 C2 **Ross** *r.* Can.
117 C5 **Ross** N.Z.
66 G5 **Rossano** Italy
60 C3 **Rossan Point** *pt* Rep. of Ireland
27 F5 **Ross Barnett Res.** *l.* U.S.A.
23 G3 **Ross Bay Junction** Can.
60 B6 **Ross Carbery** Rep. of Ireland
111 F3 **Rossel Island** *i.* P.N.G.
119 B4 **Ross Ice Shelf** *ice feature* Ant.
23 H5 **Rossignol, L.** *l.* Can.
119 B5 **Ross Island** *i.* Ant.
60 E5 **Rosslare** Rep. of Ireland
59 A5 **Rosslare Harbour** Rep. of Ireland
31 J3 **Rossmore** Can.
117 E4 **Ross, Mt** *mt.* N.Z.
100 A3 **Rosso** Maur.
66 C3 **Rosso, Capo** *pt Corsica* France
59 D6 **Ross-on-Wye** U.K.
69 F5 **Rossosh'** Rus. Fed.
30 D1 **Rossport** Can.
20 C2 **Ross River** Can.
119 A5 **Ross Sea** *sea* Ant.
54 O4 **Røssvatnet** *l.* Norway
30 D3 **Rossville** U.S.A.
20 D3 **Rosswood** Can.
81 K3 **Rōst** Iraq
21 H4 **Rosthern** Can.
62 F3 **Rostock** Ger.
69 G6 **Rostov-na-Donu** Rus. Fed.
69 G6 **Rostovskaya Oblast'** *div.* Rus. Fed.
54 S4 **Rosvik** Sweden
29 C5 **Roswell** *GA* U.S.A.
25 F5 **Roswell** *NM* U.S.A.
93 L4 **Rota** *i.* N. Mariana Is
93 G9 **Rote** *i.* Indon.
58 F2 **Rothbury Forest** *forest* U.K.
62 E6 **Rothenburg ob der Tauber** Ger.
117 C4 **Rotherham** N.Z.
59 F4 **Rotherham** U.K.
57 E3 **Rothes** U.K.
57 C5 **Rothesay** U.K.
30 C3 **Rothschild** U.S.A.
59 G5 **Rothwell** U.K.

**Roti** *i. see* **Rote**
115 F4 **Roto** Austr.
117 C5 **Rotomanu** N.Z.
66 C3 **Rotondo, Monte** *mt Corsica* France
117 D4 **Rotoroa, L.** *l.* N.Z.
117 F3 **Rotorua** N.Z.
117 F3 **Rotorua, L.** *l.* N.Z.
62 F6 **Rott** *r.* Ger.
62 G7 **Rottenmann** Austria
61 C3 **Rotterdam** Neth.
61 E1 **Rottumeroog** *i.* Neth.
61 E1 **Rottumerplaat** *i.* Neth.
62 D6 **Rottweil** Ger.
111 H3 **Rotuma** *i.* Fiji
54 O5 **Roubaix** France
64 E2 **Rouen** France
117 B6 **Rough Ridge** *ridge* N.Z.
**Roulers** *see* **Roeselare**
23 F3 **Roundeyed, Lac** *l.* Can.
58 F3 **Round Hill** *h.* U.K.
116 D5 **Round Hill Hd** *hd* Austr.
34 D2 **Round Mountain** U.S.A.
115 K3 **Round Mt** *mt.* Austr.
35 H3 **Round Rock** U.S.A.
24 E2 **Roundup** U.S.A.
57 E1 **Rousay** *i.* U.K.
33 G2 **Rouses Point** U.S.A.
64 F5 **Roussillon** *reg.* France
**Routh Bank** *sand bank see* **Seahorse Bank**
105 G5 **Rouxville** S. Africa
31 H1 **Rouyn** Can.
54 T3 **Rovaniemi** Fin.
69 F5 **Roven'ki** Rus. Fed.
66 D2 **Rovereto** Italy
95 C2 **Rôviĕng Tbong** Cambodia
66 D2 **Rovigo** Italy
66 E2 **Rovinj** Croatia
69 H5 **Rovnoye** Rus. Fed.
81 M4 **Row'ān** Iran
115 H2 **Rowena** Austr.
94 B2 **Roxas** Phil.
94 B4 **Roxas** Phil.
94 B3 **Roxas** Phil.
94 A4 **Roxas** Phil.
29 E4 **Roxboro** U.S.A.
117 B6 **Roxburgh** N.Z.
114 B3 **Roxby Downs** Austr.
25 F4 **Roy** U.S.A.
60 E4 **Royal Canal** *canal* Rep. of Ireland
30 C1 **Royale, Isle** *i.* U.S.A.
105 H4 **Royal Natal National Park** *nat. park* S. Africa
31 H4 **Royal Oak** U.S.A.
64 D4 **Royan** France
61 A5 **Roye** France
22 E2 **Roy, Lac Le** *l.* Can.
59 G5 **Royston** U.K.
69 D6 **Rozdil'na** Ukr.
69 E6 **Rozdol'ne** Ukr.
69 F6 **Rozivka** Ukr.
69 H4 **Rtishchevo** Rus. Fed.
66 E2 **Rt Kamenjak** *pt* Croatia
59 D5 **Ruabon** U.K.
103 B5 **Ruacana** Namibia
102 D4 **Ruaha National Park** *nat. park* Tanz.
117 E3 **Ruapehu, Mt** *volc.* N.Z.
117 B7 **Ruapuke I.** *i.* N.Z.
117 F2 **Ruarine Range** *mts* N.Z.
117 G2 **Ruatoria** N.Z.
68 D4 **Ruba** Belarus
78 F6 **Rub'al Khālī** *des.* S. Arabia
90 J2 **Rubeshibe** Japan
57 C2 **Rubha Coigeach** *pt* U.K.
57 B3 **Rubha Hunish** *pt* U.K.
57 C3 **Rubha Reidh** *pt* U.K.
34 B2 **Rubicon** *r.* U.S.A.
69 F5 **Rubizhne** Ukr.
86 F1 **Rubtsovsk** Rus. Fed.
35 E1 **Ruby Lake** *l.* U.S.A.
35 E1 **Ruby Mountains** *mts* U.S.A.
116 B4 **Rubyvale** Austr.
89 D5 **Rucheng** China
32 D5 **Ruckersville** U.S.A.
112 D4 **Rudall River National Park** *nat. park* Austr.
79 H4 **Rudan** Iran
85 E4 **Rudauli** India
81 M3 **Rūdbār** Iran
55 M9 **Rudkøbing** Denmark
90 K1 **Rudnaya** Rus. Fed.
87 P3 **Rudnaya Pristan'** China
68 E4 **Rudnichnyy** Rus. Fed.
68 D4 **Rudnya** Rus. Fed.
76 H4 **Rudnyy** Kazak.
76 G1 **Rudolfa, O.** *i.* Rus. Fed.
88 F3 **Rudong** China
30 E2 **Rudyard** U.S.A.
103 D4 **Rufiji** *r.* Tanz.
47 D2 **Rufino** Arg.
100 A3 **Rufisque** Senegal
103 C5 **Rufunsa** Zambia
88 F3 **Rugao** China
59 F5 **Rugby** U.K.
59 F5 **Rugeley** U.K.
62 F3 **Rügen** *i.* Ger.
32 B4 **Ruggles** U.S.A.
102 C4 **Ruhengeri** Rwanda
55 S8 **Ruhnu** *i.* Estonia
61 E4 **Ruhr** *r.* Ger.
89 F5 **Rui'an** China
25 F5 **Ruidoso** U.S.A.
89 E5 **Ruijin** China
21 N2 **Ruin Point** *pt* Can.
103 D4 **Ruipa** Tanz.

45 B3 Ruiz, Nevado del volc. Col.
55 T8 Rūjiena Latvia
85 E3 Rukumkot Nepal
102 D4 Rukwa, Lake l. Tanz.
56 C3 Rum i. Scot. U.K.
67 H2 Ruma Yugo.
101 E4 Rumbek Sudan
29 F7 Rum Cay i. Bahamas
33 H2 Rumford U.S.A.
64 G4 Rumilly France
112 F2 Rum Jungle Austr.
90 H2 Rumoi Japan
88 E3 Runan China
117 C5 Runanga N.Z.
117 F2 Runaway, Cape c. N.Z.
59 E4 Runcorn U.K.
103 B5 Rundu Namibia
54 Q5 Rundvik Sweden
88 E3 Runheji China
88 A3 Ru'nying China
55 V6 Ruokolahti Fin.
82 G3 Ruoqiang China
85 H4 Rupa India
47 B4 Rupanco, L. l. Chile
114 E6 Rupanyup Austr.
95 B5 Rupat i. Indon.
22 E3 Rupert r. Can.
24 D3 Rupert U.S.A.
22 E3 Rupert Bay b. Can.
61 E4 Rurstausee resr Ger.
109 Rurutu i. Tubuai Islands Pac. Oc.
103 D5 Rusape Zimbabwe
67 L3 Ruse Bulg.
59 G5 Rushden U.K.
30 B4 Rushford U.S.A.
30 C4 Rush Lake l. U.S.A.
85 H3 Rushon India
79 L2 Rushon Tajik.
30 B5 Rushville IL U.S.A.
26 C3 Rushville NE U.S.A.
114 F6 Rushworth Austr.
27 E6 Rusk U.S.A.
29 D7 Ruskin U.S.A.
21 J4 Russell Man. Can.
33 F2 Russell Ont. Can.
117 E1 Russell N.Z.
26 D4 Russell U.S.A.
20 F2 Russel Lake l. Can.
111 F2 Russell Is is Solomon Is
29 C4 Russellville AL U.S.A.
27 E5 Russellville AR U.S.A.
28 C4 Russellville KY U.S.A.
62 D5 Rüsselsheim Ger.
70 Russian Federation country Asia/Europe
81 K1 Rust'avi Georgia
105 G2 Rustenburg S. Africa
27 E5 Ruston U.S.A.
93 G8 Ruteng Indon.
35 E2 Ruth U.S.A.
31 H2 Rutherglen Can.
59 D4 Ruthin U.K.
68 H3 Rutka r. Rus. Fed.
33 G3 Rutland U.S.A.
59 G5 Rutland Water resr U.K.
21 G2 Rutledge Lake l. Can.
84 D2 Rutog China
31 G2 Rutter Can.
54 T4 Ruukki Fin.
103 D5 Ruvuma r. Moz./Tanz.
80 F5 Ruwayshid, Wādī watercourse Jordan
89 D5 Ruyuan China
76 H4 Ruzayevka Kazak.
68 H4 Ruzayevka Rus. Fed.
63 J6 Ružomberok Slovakia
96 Rwanda country Africa
68 H2 Ryadovo Rus. Fed.
57 C5 Ryan, Loch b. U.K.
68 F4 Ryazan' Rus. Fed.
68 G4 Ryazanskaya Oblast' div. Rus. Fed.
68 G4 Ryazhsk Rus. Fed.
76 E2 Rybachiy, Poluostrov pen. Rus. Fed.
Rybach'ye see Ysyk-Köl
68 F3 Rybinsk Rus. Fed.
68 F3 Rybinskoye Vdkhr. resr Rus. Fed.
68 J4 Rybnaya Sloboda Rus. Fed.
63 J5 Rybnik Pol.
68 F4 Rybnoye Rus. Fed.
20 F3 Rycroft Can.
55 O8 Ryd Sweden
119 B3 Rydberg Pen. pen. Ant.
59 F7 Ryde U.K.
58 G3 Rye r. U.K.
59 H7 Rye U.K.
69 E5 Ryl'sk Rus. Fed.
115 H4 Rylstone Austr.
91 H4 Ryōri-zaki pt Japan
91 G4 Ryōtsu Japan
63 L5 Rzeszów Pol.
69 G4 Rzhaksa Rus. Fed.
68 E3 Rzhev Rus. Fed.

# S

62 E5 Saalfeld Ger.
61 E5 Saar r. Ger.
62 C6 Saarbrücken Ger.
61 E5 Saarburg Ger.
55 S7 Saaremaa i. Estonia
54 T3 Saarenkylä Fin.
61 E5 Saargau reg. Ger.
54 T5 Saarijärvi Fin.
54 U3 Saari-Kämä Fin.
54 R2 Saarikoski Fin.
61 E5 Saarland div. Ger.
62 C6 Saarlouis Ger.
81 M2 Saatlı Azer.
47 D3 Saavedra Arg.
80 F5 Sab' Ābār Syria
67 H2 Šabac Yugo.
65 H2 Sabadell Spain
91 F5 Sabae Japan
93 F5 Sabah div. Malaysia
95 B5 Sabak Malaysia
84 D4 Sabalgarh India
37 H4 Sabana, Arch. de is Cuba
45 B2 Sabanalarga Col.
80 D1 Şabanözü Turkey
46 D2 Sabará Brazil
84 C5 Sabarmati r. India
66 E4 Sabaudia Italy
104 E5 Sabelo S. Africa
101 D2 Sabhā Libya
84 D3 Sabi r. India
105 K2 Sabie Moz.
105 K2 Sabie r. Moz./S. Africa
105 J2 Sabie S. Africa
36 D3 Sabinas Mex.
36 D3 Sabinas Hidalgo Mex.
27 E6 Sabine L. l. U.S.A.
81 M1 Sabirabad Azer.
94 B3 Sablayan Phil.
29 D7 Sable, Cape c. U.S.A.
111 F3 Sable, Île de i. New Caledonia
23 J5 Sable Island i. Can.
31 F2 Sables, River aux r. Can.
94 B1 Sabtang i. Phil.
65 C2 Sabugal Port.
30 B4 Sabula U.S.A.
78 E6 Şabyā S. Arabia
Sabzanar see Shīndand
79 H2 Sabzevār Iran
67 N2 Sacalinul Mare, Insula i. Romania
67 L2 Săcele Romania
103 B5 Sachanga Angola
22 B3 Sachigo r. Can.
22 B3 Sachigo L. l. Can.
84 C5 Sachin India
84 D2 Sach Pass pass India
33 E3 Sackets Harbor U.S.A.
23 H4 Sackville Can.
33 H3 Saco ME U.S.A.
24 F1 Saco MT U.S.A.
94 B5 Sacol i. Phil.
34 B2 Sacramento U.S.A.
34 B2 Sacramento r. U.S.A.
25 F5 Sacramento Mts mts U.S.A.
24 B3 Sacramento Valley v. U.S.A.
105 G6 Sada S. Africa
65 F1 Sádaba Spain
80 F4 Şadad Syria
90 D7 Sada-misaki pt Japan
95 B4 Sadao Thai.
105 J2 Saddleback pass S. Africa
95 C3 Sa Đec Vietnam
85 H3 Sadêng China
84 B3 Sadiqabad Pak.
84 C1 Sad Istragh mt Afgh./Pak.
82 J5 Sadiya India
81 L5 Sa'dīyah, Hawr as l. Iraq
65 B3 Sado r. Port.
91 G4 Sadoga-shima i. Japan
65 H3 Sa Dragonera i. Spain
55 M8 Sæby Denmark
Safad see Zefat
81 L6 Safayal Maqūf w. Iraq
55 N7 Säffle Sweden
35 H5 Safford U.S.A.
59 H5 Saffron Walden U.K.
80 E6 Safi Jordan
100 B1 Safi Morocco
81 M3 Safīd r. Iran
81 M5 Safid Dasht Iran
80 F4 Şāfītā Syria
54 X2 Safonovo Murmansk. Rus. Fed.
68 E4 Safonovo Smolensk. Rus. Fed.
76 F3 Safonovo Rus. Fed.
80 D1 Safranbolu Turkey
81 L6 Safwān Iraq
85 F3 Saga China
90 C7 Saga Japan
90 C7 Saga Japan
91 H4 Sagae Japan
91 G6 Sagamihara Japan
91 G6 Sagami-nada g. Japan
91 G6 Sagami-wan b. Japan
45 B3 Sagamoso r. Col.
95 A2 Saganthit Kyun i. Myanmar
84 D5 Sagar India
69 H7 Sagarejo Georgia
85 G5 Sagar I. i. India
77 O2 Sagastyr Rus. Fed.
31 F4 Saginaw U.S.A.
31 F4 Saginaw Bay b. U.S.A.
23 H2 Saglek Bay b. Can.
66 C3 Sagone, Golfe de b. Corsica France
65 B4 Sagres Port.
85 H5 Sagu Myanmar
25 F4 Saguache U.S.A.
37 H4 Sagua la Grande Cuba
35 G5 Saguaro National Monument res. U.S.A.
23 F4 Saguenay r. Can.
65 F3 Sagunto-Sagunt Spain
84 C5 Sagwara India
45 B2 Sahagún Col.
65 D1 Sahagún Spain
81 L3 Sahand, Kūh-e mt Iran
98 Sahara des Africa
Saharan Atlas mts see Atlas Saharien
84 D3 Saharanpur India
85 F4 Saharsa India
84 D3 Sahaswan India
84 C3 Sahiwal Pak.
81 L4 Şahneh Iran
81 K6 Şahrā al Ḩijārah reg. Iraq
35 G6 Sahuarita U.S.A.
95 D2 Sa Huynh Vietnam
Sahyadri mts see Western Ghats
84 C5 Sahyadriparvat Range h. India
84 E4 Sai r. India
95 B4 Sai Buri r. Thai.
95 B4 Sai Buri Thai.
Saïda see Sidon
79 H4 Sa'īdābād Iran
95 B2 Sai Dao Tai, Khao mt Thai.
85 G4 Saidpur Bangl.
84 C2 Saidu Pak.
90 D5 Saigō Japan
Saigon see Hô Chi Minh
85 H5 Saiha India
88 A1 Saihan Toroi China
90 D7 Saijō Japan
90 C7 Saiki Japan
89 □ Sai Kung Hong Kong China
55 V6 Saimaa l. Fin.
80 F2 Saimbeyli Turkey
81 L3 Sa'īndezh Iran
57 F5 St Abb's Head hd U.K.
59 B7 St Agnes U.K.
59 A8 St Agnes i. U.K.
23 J4 St Alban's Can.
59 G6 St Albans U.K.
33 G2 St Albans VT U.S.A.
32 C5 St Albans WV U.S.A.
59 E7 St Alban's Head hd U.K.
20 G4 St Albert Can.
33 K2 St Andrews Can.
57 F4 St Andrews U.K.
37 J5 St Ann's Bay Jamaica
60 F6 St Ann's Head hd Wales
23 J3 St Anthony Can.
24 E3 St Anthony U.S.A.
114 E6 St Arnaud Austr.
117 D5 St Arnaud Range mts N.Z.
29 D6 St Augustine U.S.A.
59 C7 St Austell U.K.
37 M5 St Barthélémy i. Guadeloupe
58 D3 St Bees U.K.
58 D3 St Bees Head hd U.K.
59 B6 St Bride's Bay b. U.K.
35 G5 St Carlos Lake l. U.S.A.
31 H4 St Catharines Can.
29 D6 St Catherines I. i. U.S.A.
59 F7 St Catherine's Point pt U.K.
24 E3 St Charles ID U.S.A.
32 E5 St Charles MD U.S.A.
30 A4 St Charles MN U.S.A.
26 F4 St Charles MO U.S.A.
31 F4 St Clair U.S.A.
31 F4 St Clair Shores U.S.A.
59 C6 St Clears U.K.
26 E2 St Cloud U.S.A.
23 G4 St Croix r. Can.
30 A2 St Croix r. U.S.A.
37 M5 St Croix i. Virgin Is
30 A3 St Croix Falls U.S.A.
35 G6 St David U.S.A.
60 F6 St David's Wales
59 B6 St David's Head hd U.K.
31 K5 Ste Anne Can.
33 J1 Sainte-Anne-de-Madawaska Can.
31 K2 Sainte-Anne-du-Lac Can.
23 G3 Ste Anne, L. l. Can.
33 H1 Sainte-Justine Can.
20 B2 St Elias Mountains mts Can.
23 G3 Ste Marguerite r. Can.
64 D4 Saintes France
33 F2 St Eugene Can.
37 M5 St Eustatius i. Neth. Ant.
60 F3 Saintfield U.K.
102 C3 St. Floris, Parc National nat. park C.A.R.
26 C4 St Francis KS U.S.A.
33 J1 St Francis ME U.S.A.
27 F4 St Francis r. U.S.A.
23 K4 St Francis, C. c. Can.
33 J1 St Froid Lake l. U.S.A.
62 D7 St Gallen Switz.
115 H2 St George Austr.
33 K2 St George Can.
29 D5 St George SC U.S.A.
35 F3 St George UT U.S.A.
111 F2 St George, C. pt P.N.G.
29 C6 St George I. i. U.S.A.
24 A3 St George, Pt pt U.S.A.
23 F4 St Georges Can.
37 M6 St George's Grenada
23 J4 St George's B. b. Can.
56 C6 St George's Channel chan. Rep. of Ireland/U.K.
59 C6 St Govan's Head hd U.K.
30 E3 St Helen U.S.A.
12 J7 St Helena i. Atlantic Ocean
34 A2 St Helena U.S.A.
104 C6 St Helena Bay S. Africa
104 C6 St Helena Bay b. S. Africa
12 J7 St Helena Fracture sea feature Atlantic Ocean
115 H8 St Helens Austr.
59 E4 St Helens U.K.
24 B2 St Helens U.S.A.
24 B2 St Helens, Mt volc. U.S.A.
115 H8 St Helens Pt pt Austr.
56 E7 St Helier U.K.
30 E3 St Ignace U.S.A.
30 C1 St Ignace I. i. Can.
59 C6 St Ishmael U.K.
59 G5 St Ives Eng. U.K.
59 B7 St Ives Eng. U.K.
30 E3 St James U.S.A.
20 C4 St James, Cape pt Can.
24 C2 St Joe r. U.S.A.
23 G4 St John Can.
33 K2 St John r. Can./U.S.A.
35 F1 St John U.S.A.
37 M5 St John i. Virgin Is
37 M5 St John's Antigua
23 K4 St John's Can.
35 H4 St Johns AZ U.S.A.
30 E4 St Johns MI U.S.A.
29 D6 St Johns r. U.S.A.
33 H2 St Johnsbury U.S.A.
58 E3 St John's Chapel U.K.
23 F4 St Joseph Can.
30 D4 St Joseph MI U.S.A.
26 E4 St Joseph MO U.S.A.
30 E5 St Joseph r. U.S.A.
31 F2 St Joseph I. i. Can.
27 D7 St Joseph I. i. U.S.A.
22 B3 St Joseph, Lac l. Can.
22 F4 St Jovité Can.
59 B7 St Just U.K.
59 B7 St Keverne U.K.
56 B3 St Kilda is U.K.
16 St Kitts-Nevis country Caribbean Sea
43 H2 St Laurent Fr. Guiana
116 C4 St Lawrence Austr.
23 K4 St Lawrence Nfld Can.
23 G4 St Lawrence in. Que. Can.
23 H4 St Lawrence, Gulf of g. Can./U.S.A.
77 V3 St Lawrence I. i. Alaska
31 K3 St Lawrence Islands National Park nat. park Can.
33 F2 St Lawrence Seaway chan. Can./U.S.A.
23 J3 St Lewis Can.
23 J3 Saint Lewis r. Can.
100 A3 St Louis Senegal
30 E4 St Louis MI U.S.A.
26 F4 St Louis MO U.S.A.
30 A2 St Louis r. U.S.A.
16 St Lucia country Caribbean Sea
105 K4 St Lucia Estuary S. Africa
105 K3 St Lucia, Lake l. S. Africa
37 M5 St Maarten i. Neth. Ant.
57 □ St Magnus Bay b. U.K.
105 G6 St Marks S. Africa
37 M5 Saint Martin i. Guadeloupe
104 B6 St Martin, Cape hd S. Africa
30 D3 St Martin I. i. U.S.A.
21 K4 St Martin, L. l. Can.
59 A8 St Martin's i. U.K.
85 H5 St Martin's I. i. Bangl.
114 C3 St Mary Pk mt Austr.
115 H8 St Marys Austr.
31 G4 St Mary's Can.
57 F2 St Mary's U.K.
59 A8 St Mary's i. U.K.
32 A4 St Marys OH U.S.A.
32 D4 St Marys PA U.S.A.
32 A4 St Marys r. U.S.A.
32 C5 Saint Marys U.S.A.
23 K4 St Mary's, C. hd Can.
77 V3 St Matthew I. i. Alaska
110 E2 St Matthias Group is P.N.G.
22 F4 St Maurice r. Can.
59 B7 St Mawes U.K.
23 J3 St Michaels Bay b. Can.
62 D7 St Moritz Switz.
59 G5 St Neots U.K.
23 G4 St Pascal Can.
21 G4 St Paul Can.
30 A3 St Paul MN U.S.A.
26 D3 St Paul NE U.S.A.
32 B6 St Paul VA U.S.A.
13 K6 St Paul, Île i. Indian Ocean
56 E7 St Peter Port U.K.
68 D3 St Petersburg Rus. Fed.
29 D7 St Petersburg U.S.A.
16 St Pierre & Miquelon terr. North America
62 G6 St Pölten Austria
33 H1 Saint-Prosper Can.
33 F2 St Regis r. U.S.A.
33 F2 St Regis Falls U.S.A.
23 G4 St Siméon Can.
29 D6 St Simons I. i. U.S.A.
33 K2 St Stephen Can.
29 E5 St Stephen U.S.A.
21 L4 St Theresa Point Can.
31 G4 St Thomas Can.
21 K5 St Vincent U.S.A.
16 St Vincent and the Grenadines country Caribbean Sea
115 F9 St Vincent, C. hd Austr.
St Vincent, Cape c. see São Vicente, Cabo de
114 B5 St. Vincent, Gulf b. Austr.
21 H4 St Walburg Can.
61 F5 St Wendel Ger.
31 G4 St Williams Can.
84 E3 Saipal mt Nepal
93 L3 Saipan i. N. Mariana Is
91 G6 Saitama Japan
85 H5 Saitlai Myanmar
90 C7 Saito Japan
54 T3 Saittanulkki h. Fin.
89 □ Sai Wan Hong Kong China
42 E7 Sajama, Nevado mt Bol.
104 D5 Sak watercourse S. Africa
90 D6 Sakaide Japan
90 D6 Sakaiminato Japan
81 H7 Sakākah S. Arabia
26 C2 Sakakawea, Lake l. U.S.A.
22 E3 Sakami Can.
22 F3 Sakami r. Can.
22 E3 Sakami, Lac l. Can.
67 M4 Sakar mts Bulg.
80 C1 Sakarya r. Turkey
80 C1 Sakarya Turkey
91 G4 Sakata Japan
90 D7 Sakawa Japan
95 B2 Sa Keo r. Thai.
100 C4 Sakété Benin
87 Q1 Sakhalin i. Rus. Fed.
77 Q4 Sakhalinskiy Zaliv b. Rus. Fed.
84 C3 Sakhi India
105 H3 Sakhile S. Africa
81 L1 Şäki Azer.
55 S9 Šakiai Lith.
84 A3 Sakir mt Pak.
87 M7 Sakishima-Guntō is Japan
84 B4 Sakrand Pak.
95 □ Sakra, P. i. Sing.
104 D5 Sakrivier S. Africa
91 G5 Saku Japan
91 F6 Sakuma Japan
91 H6 Sakura Japan
91 E6 Sakurai Japan
90 C8 Sakura-jima volc. Japan
69 E6 Saky Ukr.
55 S6 Säkylä Fin.
100 □ Sal i. Cape Verde
69 G6 Sal r. Rus. Fed.
55 S8 Sala Latvia
55 P7 Sala Sweden
22 F4 Salaberry-de-Valleyfield Can.
55 T8 Salacgrīva Latvia
66 F4 Sala Consilina Italy
35 E5 Salada, Laguna salt l. Mex.
47 E2 Saladillo Buenos Aires Arg.
47 D2 Saladillo r. Córdoba Arg.
47 E1 Salado r. Buenos Aires Arg.
47 C3 Salado r. Mendoza/San Luis Arg.
47 D4 Salado r. Río Negro Arg.
47 E2 Salado r. Santa Fé Arg.
36 E3 Salado r. Mex.
44 B3 Salado, Quebrada de r. Chile
100 B4 Salaga Ghana
104 F1 Salajwe Botswana
101 D3 Salal Chad
79 G6 Şalālah Oman
47 B1 Salamanca Chile
36 D4 Salamanca Mex.
65 D2 Salamanca Spain
32 D3 Salamanca U.S.A.
105 K3 Salamanga Moz.
81 L4 Salamatabad Iran
45 B3 Salamina Col.
80 F4 Salamīyah Syria
30 E5 Salamonie r. U.S.A.
30 E5 Salamonie Lake l. U.S.A.
85 F5 Salandi r. India
55 R8 Salantai Lith.
44 C2 Salar de Arizaro salt flat Arg.
44 C2 Salar de Atacama salt flat Chile
65 C1 Salas Spain
55 T8 Salaspils Latvia
92 □ Salatiga Indon.
93 J7 Salawati i. Indon.
84 B5 Salaya India
93 G8 Salayar i. Indon.
15 N7 Sala y Gómez, Isla i. Chile
47 D3 Şalazar Arg.
55 T9 Šalčininkai Lith.
59 D7 Salcombe U.K.
45 B4 Saldaña r. Col.
65 D1 Saldaña Spain
104 B6 Saldanha S. Africa
104 B6 Saldanha Bay b. S. Africa
47 E3 Saldungaray Arg.
55 S8 Saldus Latvia
115 G7 Sale Austr.
81 L5 Şālehābād Iran
81 M4 Şāleḩābād Iran
76 H3 Salekhard Rus. Fed.
83 E8 Salem India
33 H3 Salem MA U.S.A.
27 F4 Salem MO U.S.A.
28 F4 Salem NJ U.S.A.
33 G3 Salem NY U.S.A.
32 C4 Salem OH U.S.A.
24 B2 Salem OR U.S.A.
28 D4 Salem VA U.S.A.
57 C4 Salen U.K.
66 F4 Salerno Italy
66 F4 Salerno, Golfo di g. Italy
59 E4 Salford U.K.
43 L5 Salgado r. Brazil
63 J6 Salgótarján Hungary
43 L5 Salgueiro Brazil
94 C6 Salibabu i. Indon.
64 D5 Salies-de-Béarn France
80 B2 Salihli Turkey
68 C4 Salihorsk Belarus
103 D5 Salima Malawi
103 D5 Salimo Moz.
26 D4 Salina KS U.S.A.
35 G2 Salina UT U.S.A.
36 E5 Salina Cruz Mex.
47 D4 Salina Gualicho salt flat Arg.
66 F5 Salina, Isola i. Italy
47 C2 Salina Llancanelo salt flat Arg.
46 D2 Salinas Brazil
42 B4 Salinas Ecuador
34 B3 Salinas CA U.S.A.
34 B3 Salinas r. CA U.S.A.
44 C4 Salinas Grandes salt flat Arg.
25 F5 Salinas Peak summit U.S.A.
27 E5 Saline r. AR U.S.A.
26 C4 Saline r. KS U.S.A.
65 H3 Salines, Cap de ses pt Spain
34 D3 Saline Valley v. U.S.A.
43 J4 Salinópolis Brazil
42 C6 Salinosó Lachay, Pta pt Peru
59 F6 Salisbury U.K.
33 F5 Salisbury MD U.S.A.
29 D5 Salisbury NC U.S.A.
59 E6 Salisbury Plain plain U.K.
43 K6 Salitre r. Brazil
80 F5 Şalkhad Syria
85 F5 Šalki r. India
54 V3 Salla Fin.
47 D3 Salliqueló Arg.
27 E5 Sallisaw U.S.A.
85 E3 Sallyana Nepal
81 K2 Salmās Iran
68 D2 Salmi Rus. Fed.
20 F5 Salmo Can.
24 D2 Salmon r. U.S.A.
24 D2 Salmon U.S.A.
20 F4 Salmon Arm Can.
33 F3 Salmon Reservoir resr U.S.A.
24 D2 Salmon River Mountains mts U.S.A.
55 S6 Salo Fin.
85 E4 Salon India
64 G5 Salon-de-Provence France
102 C4 Salonga Nord, Parc National de la nat. park Zaire
102 C4 Salonga Sud, Parc National de la nat. park Zaire
63 K7 Salonta Romania
47 D1 Salsacate Arg.
69 G6 Sal'sk Rus. Fed.
66 C2 Salsomaggiore Terme Italy
80 E5 Salt Jordan
104 E5 Salt watercourse S. Africa
35 G5 Salt r. AZ U.S.A.
30 B6 Salt r. MO U.S.A.
44 C2 Salta Arg.
59 C7 Saltash U.K.
57 D5 Saltcoats U.K.
32 B5 Salt Creek r. U.S.A.
60 E5 Saltee Islands is Rep. of Ireland
54 O3 Saltfjellet Svartisen Nasjonalpark nat. park Norway
27 B6 Salt Flat U.S.A.
32 C4 Salt Fork Lake l. U.S.A.
36 D3 Saltillo Mex.
24 E3 Salt Lake City U.S.A.
114 E3 Salt L., The salt flat Austr.
47 E2 Salto Arg.
46 C3 Salto Brazil
47 F1 Salto Uru.
46 E2 Salto da Divisa Brazil
44 E4 Salto Grande, Embalse de resr Uru.
35 E5 Salton Sea salt l. U.S.A.
84 C2 Salt Ra. h. Pak.
21 G2 Salt River Can.
32 B5 Salt Rock U.S.A.
29 D5 Saluda SC U.S.A.
32 E6 Saluda VA U.S.A.
84 C4 Salumbar India
66 B2 Saluzzo Italy
47 D1 Salvador Arg.
46 E1 Salvador Brazil
27 F6 Salvador, L. l. U.S.A.
35 G2 Salvation Creek r. U.S.A.
Salween r. see Nu Jiang
95 A1 Salween r. Myanmar
81 M2 Salyan Azer.
32 B6 Salyersville U.S.A.
104 B2 Salzbrunn Namibia
62 F7 Salzburg Austria
62 E4 Salzgitter Ger.
84 B4 Sam India
81 L5 Samaida Iran
94 C5 Samal i. Phil.
94 B5 Samales Group is Phil.
80 E3 Samandağı Turkey
90 J2 Samani Japan
80 C6 Samannûd Egypt
94 C4 Samar i. Phil.
76 G4 Samara Rus. Fed.
113 K2 Samarai P.N.G.
45 D3 Samariapo Venez.
92 F7 Samarinda Indon.
79 K2 Samarkand Uzbek.
81 J4 Sāmarrā' Iraq
94 C4 Samar Sea g. Phil.

68 J4 **Samarskaya Oblast'** *div.* Rus. Fed.
81 M1 **Samaxı** Azer.
102 C4 **Šamba** Zaire
93 F6 **Sambaliung** *mts* Indon.
85 F5 **Sambalpur** India
92 E7 **Sambar, Tanjung** *pt* Indon.
92 D6 **Sambas** Indon.
103 F5 **Sambava** Madag.
85 G4 **Sambhal** India
84 D3 **Sambhal** India
84 C4 **Sambhar L.** *l.* India
69 B5 **Sambir** Ukr.
43 K5 **Sambito** *r.* Brazil
47 F2 **Samborombón, Bahía** *b.* Arg.
61 B4 **Sambre** *r.* Belgium/France
45 A2 **Sambú** *r.* Panama
81 K3 **Samdi Dag** *mt* Turkey
102 D4 **Same** Tanz.
81 L1 **Sämkir** Azer.
108 ☐ **Samoa Islands** *is* Pac. Oc.
66 F2 **Samobor** Croatia
68 G2 **Samoded** Rus. Fed.
67 K3 **Samokov** Bulg.
62 H6 **Šamorín** Slovakia
67 M6 **Samos** *i.* Greece
95 A5 **Samosir** *i.* Indon.
67 L4 **Samothraki** Greece
67 L4 **Samothraki** *i.* Greece
94 B3 **Sampaloc Point** *pt* Phil.
92 E7 **Sampit** Indon.
103 C4 **Sampwe** Zaire
27 E6 **Sam Rayburn Res.** *resr* U.S.A.
85 E3 **Samsang** China
95 C1 **Sâm Son** Vietnam
80 F1 **Samsun** Turkey
69 G7 **Samtredia** Georgia
69 J7 **Samur** *r.* Azer./Rus. Fed.
95 B2 **Samut Prakan** Thai.
95 B2 **Samut Songkhram** Thai.
85 G3 **Samyai** China
100 B3 **San** Mali
78 E6 **Şan'ā** Yemen
119 C3 **Sanae** *South Africa Base* Ant.
101 D4 **Sanaga** *r.* Cameroon
45 A4 **San Agustín** Col.
94 C5 **San Agustin, Cape** *c.* Phil.
81 L4 **Sanandaj** Iran
34 B2 **San Andreas** U.S.A.
94 C3 **San Andres** Phil.
42 B1 **San Andrés, Isla de** *i.* Col.
25 F5 **San Andres Mts** *mts* U.S.A.
36 G6 **San Andrés Tuxtla** Mex.
27 C6 **San Angelo** U.S.A.
47 D3 **San Antonio** Chile
94 B3 **San Antonio** Phil.
27 D6 **San Antonio** U.S.A.
65 G3 **San Antonio Abad** Spain
37 H4 **San Antonio, C.** *pt* Cuba
47 F3 **San Antonio, Cabo** *pt* Arg.
44 C2 **San Antonio de los Cobres** Arg.
45 D2 **San Antonio de Tamanaco** Venez.
34 D4 **San Antonio, Mt** *mt* U.S.A.
47 D4 **San Antonio Oeste** Arg.
34 B4 **San Antonio Reservoir** *resr* U.S.A.
34 B3 **San Ardo** U.S.A.
47 B3 **San Augustín** Arg.
47 C1 **San Augustín de Valle Fértil** Arg.
84 D5 **Sanawad** India
66 E3 **San Benedetto del Tronto** Italy
36 B5 **San Benedicto, I.** *i.* Mex.
27 D7 **San Benito** U.S.A.
34 B3 **San Benito** *r.* U.S.A.
34 B3 **San Benito Mt** *mt.* U.S.A.
34 D4 **San Bernardino** U.S.A.
25 C5 **San Bernardino Mts** *mts* U.S.A.
47 B2 **San Bernardo** Chile
90 D6 **Sanbe-san** *volc.* Japan
29 C6 **San Blas, C.** *c.* U.S.A.
42 E6 **San Borja** Bol.
33 H3 **Sanbornville** U.S.A.
47 C2 **San Carlos** Arg.
47 B3 **San Carlos** Chile
27 C6 **San Carlos** Mex.
94 B3 **San Carlos** *Luzon* Phil.
94 B4 **San Carlos** *Negros* Phil.
47 F2 **San Carlos** Uru.
35 G5 **San Carlos** U.S.A.
45 D4 **San Carlos** *Amazonas* Venez.
45 C2 **San Carlos** *Cojedes* Venez.
47 E1 **San Carlos Centro** Arg.
47 B4 **San Carlos de Bariloche** Arg.
47 D4 **San Carlos de Bolívar** Arg.
45 C2 **San Carlos del Zulia** Venez.
25 D6 **San Carlos, Mesa de** *h.* Mex.
88 C2 **Sancha** *Gansu* China
88 D2 **Sancha** *Shanxi* China
89 C5 **Sancha He** *r.* China
89 B6 **San Chien Pau** *mt* Laos
84 B4 **Sanchor** India
88 D2 **Sanchuan** *r.* China
68 H3 **Sanchursk** Rus. Fed.
47 B2 **San Clemente** Chile
34 D5 **San Clemente** U.S.A.
34 C5 **San Clemente I.** *i.* U.S.A.
64 F3 **Sancoins** France
47 E1 **San Cristóbal** Arg.
111 G3 **San Cristobal** *i.* Solomon Is
45 B3 **San Cristóbal** Venez.
36 F5 **San Cristóbal de las Casas** Mex.
42 ☐ **San Cristóbal, Isla** *i.* Galapagos Is Ecuador
35 F5 **San Cristobal Wash** *r.* U.S.A.
37 J4 **Sancti Spíritus** Cuba
105 H1 **Sand** *r.* S. Africa
91 L6 **Sanda** Japan
57 C5 **Sanda Island** *i.* U.K.
93 F5 **Sandakan** Malaysia
55 K6 **Sandane** Norway
67 K4 **Sandanski** Bulg.
57 F1 **Sanday** *i.* Scot. U.K.
57 F1 **Sanday Sound** *chan.* U.K.
59 E4 **Sandbach** U.K.
55 M7 **Sandefjord** Norway
119 D4 **Sandercock Nunataks** *nunatak* Ant.
35 H4 **Sanders** U.S.A.
27 C6 **Sanderson** U.S.A.
112 D3 **Sandfire Roadhouse** Austr.
115 K1 **Sandgate** Austr.
57 D6 **Sandhead** U.K.
30 B2 **Sand I.** *i.* U.S.A.
42 E6 **Sandia** Peru
34 D5 **San Diego** U.S.A.
47 C8 **San Diego, C.** *c.* Arg.
80 C2 **Sandıklı** Turkey
84 A4 **Sandila** India
30 E2 **Sand Lake** Can.
55 J7 **Sandnes** Norway
54 N3 **Sandnessjøen** Norway
103 C4 **Sandoa** Zaire
63 K5 **Sandomierz** Pol.
45 A4 **Sandoná** Col.
66 E2 **San Donà di Piave** Italy
83 H7 **Sandoway** Myanmar
59 F7 **Sandown** U.K.
104 C7 **Sandown Bay** *b.* S. Africa
54 ☐ **Sandoy** *i.* Faroe Is
24 C1 **Sandpoint** U.S.A.
57 A4 **Sandray** *i.* U.K.
63 N7 **Sandrul Mare, Vârful** *mt* Romania
55 O6 **Sandsjö** Sweden
20 C4 **Sandspit** Can.
27 D4 **Sand Springs** U.S.A.
34 C2 **Sand Springs Salt Flat** *salt flat* U.S.A.
30 A2 **Sandstone** U.S.A.
35 F5 **Sand Tank Mts** *mts* U.S.A.
89 C5 **Sandu** *Guizhou* China
89 D5 **Sandu** *Hunan* China
31 F4 **Sandusky** *MI* U.S.A.
32 B4 **Sandusky** *OH* U.S.A.
32 B4 **Sandusky Bay** *b.* U.S.A.
104 B3 **Sandverhaar** Namibia
55 M7 **Sandvika** Norway
54 N5 **Sandvika** Sweden
55 P6 **Sandviken** Sweden
23 J3 **Sandwich Bay** *b.* Can.
57 ☐ **Sandwick** U.K.
85 G5 **Sandwip Ch.** *chan.* Bangl.
33 H2 **Sandy** *r.* U.S.A.
21 J3 **Sandy Bay** Can.
115 F8 **Sandy C.** *hd* Austr.
116 E5 **Sandy Cape** *c.* Austr.
32 B5 **Sandy Hook** U.S.A.
33 F4 **Sandy Hook** *pt* U.S.A.
22 B3 **Sandy L.** *l.* Can.
22 B3 **Sandy Lake** Can.
33 E3 **Sandy Pond** U.S.A.
46 A4 **San Estanislao** Para.
94 B2 **San Fabian** Phil.
47 B2 **San Felipe** Chile
36 B2 **San Felipe** Mex.
45 C2 **San Felipe** Venez.
47 E2 **San Fernando** Arg.
47 B2 **San Fernando** Chile
36 E4 **San Fernando** Mex.
94 B2 **San Fernando** *Luzon* Phil.
94 B3 **San Fernando** *Luzon* Phil.
65 C4 **San Fernando** Spain
45 E2 **San Fernando** Trinidad and Tobago
34 C4 **San Fernando** U.S.A.
45 D3 **San Fernando de Apure** Venez.
45 D3 **San Fernando de Atabapo** Venez.
34 D5 **San Filipe Creek** *r.* U.S.A.
29 C6 **Sanford** *FL* U.S.A.
33 H3 **Sanford** *ME* U.S.A.
29 E5 **Sanford** *NC* U.S.A.
30 E4 **Sanford Lake** *l.* U.S.A.
47 D1 **San Francisco** Arg.
47 C1 **San Francisco** *CA* U.S.A.
35 H5 **San Francisco** *r.* NM U.S.A.
34 A3 **San Francisco Bay** *in.* U.S.A.
37 K5 **San Francisco de Macorís** Dom. Rep.
44 C7 **San Francisco de Paula, C.** *pt* Arg.
65 G3 **San Francisco Javier** Spain
44 C3 **San Francisco, Paso de** *pass* Arg.
45 A4 **San Gabriel** Ecuador
34 C4 **San Gabriel Mts** *mts* U.S.A.
42 C4 **Sangai, Parque Nacional** *nat. park* Ecuador
84 C6 **Sangamner** India
30 C6 **Sangamon** *r.* U.S.A.
84 B3 **Sangar** *r.* Pak.
77 O3 **Sangar** Rus. Fed.
66 C5 **San Gavino Monreale** *Sardinia* Italy
94 B5 **Sangboy Islands** *is* Phil.
88 B1 **Sangejing** China
34 C3 **Sanger** U.S.A.
88 E1 **Sanggan** *r.* China
88 B3 **Sanggarmai** China
88 G2 **Sanggou Wan** *b.* China
102 B4 **Sangha** *r.* Congo
84 B4 **Sanghar** Pak.
45 B3 **San Gil** Col.
66 G5 **San Giovanni in Fiore** Italy
66 F4 **San Giovanni Rotondo** Italy
94 C6 **Sangir** *i.* Indon.
93 G6 **Sangir, Kepulauan** *is* Indon.
92 ☐ **Sangkapura** Indon.
93 F6 **Sangkulirang** Indon.
83 D7 **Sangli** India
84 B1 **Sanglich** Afgh.
100 D4 **Sangmélima** Cameroon
84 D3 **Sangnam** India
85 H3 **Sangngagqoling** China
103 D6 **Sango** Zimbabwe
34 D4 **San Gorgonio Mt** *mt.* U.S.A.
62 D7 **San Gottardo, Passo del** *pass* Switz.
25 F4 **Sangre de Cristo Range** *mts* U.S.A.
45 E2 **Sangre Grande** Trinidad and Tobago
84 C3 **Sangrur** India
85 F3 **Sangsang** China
20 G4 **Sanguab** Can.
43 G6 **Sangue** *r.* Brazil
105 K2 **Sangutane** *r.* Moz.
89 D4 **Sangzhi** China
36 B3 **San Hipólito, Pta** *pt* Mex.
80 C7 **Sanhûr** Egypt
42 E6 **San Ignacio** *Beni* Bol.
42 F7 **San Ignacio** *Santa Cruz* Bol.
22 E2 **Sanikiluaq** Can.
94 B2 **San Ildefonso, Cape** *c.* Phil.
94 B2 **San Ildefonso Peninsula** *pen.* Phil.
34 C2 **San Isidro** U.S.A.
94 B3 **San Jacinto** Phil.
34 D5 **San Jacinto** U.S.A.
34 D5 **San Jacinto Peak** *summit* U.S.A.
85 F5 **Sanjai, R** *r.* India
47 E1 **San Javier** Arg.
47 B2 **San Javier de Loncomilla** Chile
84 B3 **Sanjawi** Pak.
103 D4 **Sanje** Tanz.
45 A3 **San Jerónimo, Serranía de** *mts* Col.
89 C5 **Sanjiang** China
91 G5 **Sanjō** Japan
37 H7 **San José** Costa Rica
36 B4 **San José** *i.* Mex.
94 B3 **San Jose** Phil.
94 B3 **San Jose** Phil.
34 B3 **San Jose** U.S.A.
45 E2 **San José de Amacuro** Venez.
94 B4 **San Jose de Buenavista** Phil.
42 F7 **San José de Chiquitos** Bol.
47 E1 **San José de Feliciano** Arg.
45 D2 **San José de Guanipa** Venez.
47 C1 **San Jose de Jáchal** Arg.
47 D1 **San José de la Dormida** Arg.
47 B3 **San José de la Mariquina** Chile
36 C4 **San José del Cabo** Mex.
45 B4 **San José del Guaviare** Col.
47 F2 **San José de Mayo** Uru.
45 C4 **San José de Ocuné** Col.
36 D4 **San José, Golfo** *g.* Arg.
47 C2 **San José, Vol.** *volc.* Chile
47 C1 **San Juan** *div.* Arg.
47 C1 **San Juan** *r.* Arg.
45 A3 **San Juan** *r.* Col.
37 H6 **San Juan** *r.* Costa Rica/Nic.
27 C7 **San Juan** Mex.
94 C4 **San Juan** Phil.
37 L5 **San Juan** Puerto Rico
34 B4 **San Juan** *r.* CA U.S.A.
35 H3 **San Juan** *r.* UT U.S.A.
45 D3 **San Juan** Venez.
44 F6 **San Juan Bautista** Para.
65 G3 **San Juan Bautista** Spain
36 E5 **San Juan Bautista Tuxtepec** Mex.
47 B4 **San Juan dela Costa** Chile
45 C2 **San Juan de los Cayos** Venez.
45 D2 **San Juan de los Morros** Venez.
25 F4 **San Juan Mts** *mts* U.S.A.
84 D1 **Sanju He** *watercourse* China
44 C7 **San Julián** Arg.
47 E1 **San Justo** Arg.
85 F5 **Sankh** *r.* India
**Sankt-Peterburg** *see* St Petersburg
80 G3 **Şanlıurfa** Turkey
47 C2 **San Lorenzo** Arg.
42 F8 **San Lorenzo** Bol.
42 C2 **San Lorenzo** Ecuador
25 F6 **San Lorenzo** Mex.
65 E1 **San Lorenzo** *mt* Spain
44 B7 **San Lorenzo, Cerro** *mt* Arg./Chile
42 C6 **San Lorenzo, I.** *i.* Peru
65 C4 **Sanlúcar de Barrameda** Spain
36 C4 **San Lucas** Mex.
47 C2 **San Luis** Arg.
47 C2 **San Luis** *div.* Arg.
35 E5 **San Luis** *AZ* U.S.A.
35 G5 **San Luis** *AZ* U.S.A.
42 F6 **San Luis, Lago de** *l.* Bol.
34 B4 **San Luis Obispo** U.S.A.
34 B4 **San Luis Obispo Bay** *b.* U.S.A.
36 D4 **San Luis Potosí** Mex.
34 B3 **San Luis Reservoir** *resr* U.S.A.
36 B2 **San Luis Río Colorado** Mex.
47 C2 **San Luis, Sa de** *mts* Arg.
66 E6 **San Marco, Capo** *c.* Sicily Italy
27 D6 **San Marcos** U.S.A.
48 **San Marino** *country* Europe
66 E3 **San Marino** San Marino
44 C3 **San Martín** *Catamarca* Arg.
47 C2 **San Martín** *Mendoza* Arg.
42 F6 **San Martín** *r.* Bol.
45 B4 **San Martín** Col.
47 B4 **San Martín de los Andes** Arg.
44 B7 **San Martín, L.** *l.* Arg./Chile
34 A3 **San Mateo** U.S.A.
47 D4 **San Matías, Golfo** *g.* Arg.
45 D2 **San Mauricio** Venez.
89 F4 **Sanmen** China
89 F4 **Sanmen Wan** *b.* China
88 D3 **Sanmenxia** China
42 F6 **San Miguel** *r.* Bol.
45 B4 **San Miguel** *r.* Bol.
36 G6 **San Miguel** El Salvador
35 G6 **San Miguel** *AZ* U.S.A.
34 B4 **San Miguel** *CA* U.S.A.
35 H2 **San Miguel** *r.* U.S.A.
94 B3 **San Miguel Bay** *b.* Phil.
47 C2 **San Miguel del Monte** Arg.
44 C3 **San Miguel de Tucumán** Arg.
34 B4 **San Miguel I.** *i.* U.S.A.
94 A5 **San Miguel Islands** *is* Phil.
89 E5 **Sanming** China
94 B3 **San Narciso** Phil.
66 F4 **Sannicandro Garganico** Italy
47 E2 **San Nicolás de los Arroyos** Arg.
34 C5 **San Nicolas I.** *i.* U.S.A.
105 F3 **Sannieshof** S. Africa
100 B4 **Sanniquellie** Liberia
91 H3 **Sannohe** Japan
63 L6 **Sanok** Pol.
94 B3 **San Pablo** Phil.
47 E2 **San Pedro** *Buenos Aires* Arg.
44 D2 **San Pedro** *Jujuy* Arg.
42 F7 **San Pedro** Bol.
100 B4 **San-Pédro** Côte d'Ivoire
44 C2 **San Pedro** Para.
94 B3 **San Pedro** Phil.
35 G5 **San Pedro** *r.* U.S.A.
34 C5 **San Pedro Channel** U.S.A.
45 C3 **San Pedro de Arimena** Col.
45 E3 **San Pedro de las Bocas** Venez.
36 D3 **San Pedro de las Colonias** Mex.
65 C3 **San Pedro, Sierra de** *mts* Spain
36 G5 **San Pedro Sula** Honduras
66 C5 **San Pietro, Isola di** *i.* Sardinia Italy
57 E5 **Sanquhar** U.K.
42 C4 **Sanquianga, Parque Nacional** *nat. park* Col.
36 A2 **San Quintín** Mex.
47 C2 **San Rafael** Arg.
35 G2 **San Rafael** *r.* U.S.A.
34 A3 **San Rafael** U.S.A.
35 G2 **San Rafael Knob** *summit* U.S.A.
34 C4 **San Rafael Mts** *mts* U.S.A.
42 F6 **San Ramón** Bol.
66 B3 **San Remo** Italy
45 C1 **San Román, C.** *c.* Venez.
65 B1 **San Roque** Spain
27 D6 **San Saba** U.S.A.
36 G6 **San Salvador** El Salvador
37 K4 **San Salvador** *i.* Bahamas
44 C2 **San Salvador de Jujuy** Arg.
42 ☐ **San Salvador, Isla** *i.* Galapagos Is Ecuador
84 D5 **Sansar** India
65 F1 **San Sebastián** Spain
65 E3 **San Sebastián de los Reyes** Spain
66 E3 **Sansepolcro** Italy
66 F4 **San Severo** Italy
89 F5 **Sansha** China
89 D6 **Sanshui** China
89 G2 **Sanski Most** Bos.-Herz.
89 C3 **Sansui** China
95 C4 **San, T.** *r.* Cambodia
42 E7 **Santa Ana** Bol.
36 G6 **Santa Ana** El Salvador
34 D5 **Santa Ana** Mex.
27 D6 **Santa Ana** U.S.A.
45 B3 **Sta Bárbara** Col.
36 C3 **Santa Bárbara** Mex.
34 C4 **Santa Barbara Channel** *chan.* U.S.A.
34 C4 **Santa Barbara I.** *i.* U.S.A.
44 C3 **Sta Catalina** Chile
65 B1 **Santa Catalina de Armada** Spain
34 D5 **Santa Catalina, Gulf of** *b.* U.S.A.
34 C5 **Santa Catalina I.** *i.* U.S.A.
45 C4 **Santa Clara** Col.
37 J4 **Santa Clara** Cuba
34 B3 **Santa Clara** *CA* U.S.A.
35 F3 **Santa Clara** *UT* U.S.A.
47 F2 **Santa Clara de Olimar** Uru.
34 C4 **Santa Clarita** U.S.A.
66 F6 **Sta Croce, Capo** *c.* Sicily Italy
44 C8 **Santa Cruz** *r.* Arg.
42 F7 **Santa Cruz** Bol.
47 B2 **Sta Cruz** Chile
94 B3 **Santa Cruz** *Luzon* Phil.
94 B3 **Santa Cruz** *Luzon* Phil.
94 A3 **Sta Cruz** Phil.
25 F4 **Santa Cruz** U.S.A.
46 E2 **Santa Cruz Cabrália** Brazil
65 F3 **Santa Cruz de Moya** Spain
100 A2 **Santa Cruz de Tenerife** Canary Is
44 F3 **Santa Cruz do Sul** Brazil
34 C4 **Santa Cruz I.** *i.* U.S.A.
42 ☐ **Santa Cruz, Isla** *i.* Galapagos Is Ecuador
111 G3 **Santa Cruz Islands** *is* Solomon Is
44 C3 **Santa Cruz, Pto** Arg.
47 E1 **Sta Elena** Arg.
42 B4 **Sta Elena, B. de** *b.* Ecuador
36 G6 **Sta Elena, C.** *hd* Costa Rica
66 G5 **Santa Eufemia, Golfo di** *g.* Italy
47 E1 **Santa Fé** Arg.
47 E1 **Santa Fé** *div.* Arg.
25 F5 **Santa Fe** U.S.A.
46 B2 **Santa Helena de Goiás** Brazil
88 B8 **Santai** China
44 B8 **Santa Inés, Isla** *i.* Chile
47 C3 **Santa Isabel** Arg.
111 F2 **Santa Isabel** *i.* Solomon Is
47 E2 **Santa Lucia** *r.* Uru.
25 B4 **Santa Lucia Range** *mts* U.S.A.
46 A2 **Santa Luisa, Serra de** *h.* Brazil
100 ☐ **Santa Luzia** *i.* Cape Verde
36 B4 **Sta Margarita** *i.* Mex.
44 C3 **Sta Maria** Arg.
43 G4 **Santa Maria** *Amazonas* Brazil
44 F3 **Santa Maria** *Rio Grande do Sul* Brazil
47 F1 **Santa Maria** *r.* Brazil
100 ☐ **Santa Maria** Cape Verde
36 C2 **Sta Maria** *r.* Mex.
25 F6 **Sta Maria** *r.* Mex.
42 D4 **Sta María** Peru
34 B4 **Santa Maria** U.S.A.
105 K3 **Santa Maria, Cabo de** *pt* Moz.
65 C4 **Santa Maria, Cabo de** *c.* Port.
43 J5 **Santa Maria das Barreiras** Brazil
46 D1 **Santa Maria da Vitória** Brazil
45 D2 **Sta María de Ipire** Venez.
67 H5 **Sta Maria di Leuca, Capo** *c.* Italy
47 C3 **Santa María, I.** *i.* Chile
111 G3 **Santa María** *i.* Vanuatu
42 ☐ **Santa María, Isla** *i.* Galapagos Is Ecuador
29 F7 **Sta Marie, Cape** *c.* Bahamas
45 B2 **Santa Marta** Col.
45 B2 **Santa Marta, Sierra Nevada de** *mts* Col.
34 C4 **Santa Monica** U.S.A.
34 C5 **Santa Monica Bay** *b.* U.S.A.
46 B2 **Santana** *r.* Brazil
43 K6 **Santana** Brazil
47 G1 **Santana da Boa Vista** Brazil
47 F1 **Santana do Livramento** Brazil
45 A4 **Santander** Col.
65 E1 **Santander** Spain
35 G5 **Santan Mt** *mt.* U.S.A.
66 C5 **Sant'Antioco** Sardinia Italy
66 C5 **Sant'Antioco, Isola di** *i.* Sardinia Italy
34 C4 **Santa Paula** U.S.A.
43 K4 **Santa Quitéria** Brazil
43 H4 **Santarém** Brazil
65 B3 **Santarém** Port.
45 C2 **Sta Rita** Venez.
46 B2 **Sta Rita do Araguaia** Brazil
34 B3 **Santa Rita Park** U.S.A.
47 D3 **Santa Rosa** *La Pampa* Arg.
47 C4 **Santa Rosa** *Rio Negro* Arg.
42 D5 **Santa Rosa** *Acre* Brazil
44 F3 **Sta Rosa** Brazil
34 A2 **Santa Rosa** *CA* U.S.A.
25 F5 **Santa Rosa** *NM* U.S.A.
36 G6 **Santa Rosa de Copán** Honduras
47 D1 **Sta Rosa del Río Primero** Arg.
34 B3 **Sta Rosa I.** *i.* U.S.A.
36 B3 **Sta Rosalía** Mex.
24 C3 **Sta Rosa Ra.** *mts* U.S.A.
35 G5 **Santa Rosa Wash** *r.* U.S.A.
47 G2 **Sta Vitória do Palmar** Brazil
29 C5 **Santee** *r.* U.S.A.
34 D5 **Santee** U.S.A.
44 F3 **Santiago** Brazil
47 B2 **Santiago** *div.* Chile
47 B2 **Santiago** Chile
37 K5 **Santiago** Dom. Rep.
37 H7 **Santiago** Panama
94 B2 **Santiago** Phil.
65 B1 **Santiago de Compostela** Spain
37 J4 **Santiago de Cuba** Cuba
47 F2 **Santiago Vazquez** Uru.
21 N2 **Santianna Point** *pt* Can.
65 B2 **Sant Jordi, Golf de** *g.* Spain
46 E1 **Santo Amaro** Brazil
46 E3 **Santo Amaro de Campos** Brazil
46 C3 **Santo André** Brazil
44 F3 **São Angelo** Brazil
100 ☐ **Santo Antão** *i.* Cape Verde
46 B3 **Santo Antônio da Platina** Brazil
42 E4 **Santo Antônio do Içá** Brazil
46 D3 **Santo Antônio do Monte** Brazil
43 G7 **Santo Corazón** Bol.
37 L5 **Santo Domingo** Dom. Rep.
65 E1 **Santoña** Spain
67 L6 **Santorini** *i.* Greece
46 C3 **Santos** Brazil
46 D3 **Santos Dumont** Brazil
42 D6 **Santo Tomás** Peru
44 E3 **Santo Tomé** Arg.
35 F3 **Sanup Plateau** *plat.* U.S.A.
44 B7 **San Valentin, Cerro** *mt* Chile
36 G6 **San Vicente** El Salvador
94 B3 **San Vicente** Phil.
42 C6 **San Vicente de Cañete** Peru
45 B4 **San Vicente del Caguán** Col.
66 D3 **San Vincenzo** Italy
66 E5 **San Vito, Capo** *c.* Sicily Italy
89 C7 **Sanya** China
88 C3 **Sanyuan** China
102 B4 **Sanza Pombo** Angola
46 C3 **São Bernardo do Campo** Brazil
44 E3 **São Borja** Brazil
46 C3 **São Carlos** Brazil
46 C1 **São Domingos** Brazil
46 B2 **São Domingos** *r.* Brazil
43 H6 **São Félix** *Mato Grosso* Brazil
43 H5 **São Félix** *Pará* Brazil
46 E3 **São Fidélis** Brazil
100 ☐ **São Filipe** Cape Verde
46 D1 **São Francisco** Brazil
43 L5 **São Francisco** *r.* Brazil
44 G3 **São Francisco do Sul** Brazil
47 F1 **São Gabriel** Brazil
46 D3 **São Gonçalo** Brazil
46 D2 **São Gotardo** Brazil
46 C1 **São João da Aliança** Brazil
46 E3 **São João da Barra** Brazil
46 C3 **São João da Boa Vista** Brazil
65 B2 **São João da Madeira** Port.
46 D1 **São João do Paraíso** Brazil
46 D3 **São João Nepomuceno** Brazil
46 C3 **São Joaquim da Barra** Brazil
45 D5 **São José** Brazil
46 E3 **São José do Calçado** Brazil
47 G2 **São José do Norte** Brazil

46 C3 **São José do Rio Preto** Brazil
46 D3 **São José dos Campos** Brazil
46 C4 **São José dos Pinhais** Brazil
46 A2 **São Lourenço** *r.* Brazil
46 D3 **São Lourenço** Brazil
47 G1 **São Lourenço do Sul** Brazil
43 K4 **São Luís** Brazil
46 C3 **São Manuel** Brazil
46 C2 **São Marcos** *r.* Brazil
43 K4 **São Marcos, Baía de** *b.* Brazil
46 E2 **São Mateus** *r.* Brazil
46 E2 **São Mateus** Brazil
46 C2 **São Miguel** *r.* Brazil
64 G3 **Saône** *r.* France
100 □ **São Nicolau** *i.* Cape Verde
46 C3 **São Paulo** Brazil
46 C3 **São Paulo** *div.* Brazil
12 H5 **São Pedro e São Paulo** *is* Atlantic Ocean
43 K5 **São Raimundo Nonato** Brazil
46 D2 **São Romão** Brazil
43 L5 **São Roque, Cabo de** *pt* Brazil
46 C3 **São Sebastião do Paraíso** Brazil
46 D3 **São Sebastião, Ilha de** *i.* Brazil
47 G1 **São Sepé** Brazil
46 B2 **São Simão** Brazil
46 B2 **São Simão, Barragem de** *resr* Brazil
93 H6 **Sao-Siu** Indon.
100 □ **São Tiago** *i.* Cape Verde
100 C4 **São Tomé** *i.* Sao Tome and Principe
96 **Sao Tome and Principe** *country* Africa
46 E3 **São Tomé, Cabo de** *c.* Brazil
46 C3 **São Vicente** Brazil
100 □ **São Vicente** *i.* Cape Verde
65 B4 **São Vicente, Cabo de** *c.* Port.
80 C1 **Sapanca** Turkey
93 H7 **Saparua** Indon.
80 C2 **Saphane Dağı** *mt* Turkey
100 B4 **Sapo National Park** *nat. park* Liberia
90 H2 **Sapporo** Japan
66 F4 **Sapri** Italy
27 D4 **Sapulpa** U.S.A.
81 L3 **Saqqez** Iran
81 L3 **Sarāb** Iran
81 L5 **Sarābe Meymeh** Iran
95 B2 **Sara Buri** Thai.
**Saragossa** *see* **Zaragoza**
42 C4 **Saraguro** Ecuador
67 H3 **Sarajevo** Bos.-Herz.
116 C4 **Saraji** Austr.
85 H4 **Saramati** *mt* India
33 G2 **Saranac** *r.* U.S.A.
33 F2 **Saranac Lake** U.S.A.
22 E5 **Saranac Lakes** *lakes* U.S.A.
67 J5 **Sarandë** Albania
47 F2 **Sarandí del Yí** Uru.
47 F2 **Sarandí Grande** Uru.
94 C5 **Sarangani** *i.* Phil.
94 C5 **Sarangani Bay** *b.* Phil.
94 C5 **Sarangani Islands** *is* Phil.
94 C5 **Sarangani Str.** *chan.* Phil.
68 H4 **Saransk** Rus. Fed.
76 G4 **Sarapul** Rus. Fed.
45 C3 **Sarare** *r.* Venez.
29 D7 **Sarasota** U.S.A.
84 B5 **Saraswati** *r.* India
69 D6 **Sarata** Ukr.
24 F3 **Saratoga** U.S.A.
33 G3 **Saratoga Springs** U.S.A.
92 E6 **Saratok** Malaysia
69 H5 **Saratov** Rus. Fed.
69 H5 **Saratovskaya Oblast'** *div.* Rus. Fed.
68 J4 **Saratovskoye Vdkhr.** *resr* Rus. Fed.
79 J4 **Saravan** Iran
95 C2 **Saravan** Laos
95 A2 **Sarawa** *r.* Myanmar
92 E6 **Sarawak** *div.* Malaysia
80 A1 **Saray** Turkey
80 B3 **Sarayköy** Turkey
80 D2 **Sarayönü** Turkey
66 D2 **Sarca** *r.* Italy
81 M3 **Sarcham** Iran
84 E3 **Sarda** *r.* India/Nepal
85 E3 **Sarda** *r.* Nepal
84 B1 **Sardab Pass** *pass* Afgh.
84 C3 **Sardarshahr** India
81 M5 **Sardasht** Iran
81 K3 **Sar Dasht** Iran
**Sardegna** *i. see* **Sardinia**
45 B2 **Sardinata** Col.
66 C4 **Sardinia** *i. Sardinia* Italy
81 L3 **Sardrūd** Iran
54 P3 **Sareks National Park** *nat. park* Sweden
54 P3 **Sarektjåkkå** *mt* Sweden
79 K2 **Sar-e Pol** Afgh.
81 K4 **Sar-e-Pol-e-Zahāb** Iran
12 E4 **Sargasso Sea** *sea* Atlantic Ocean
84 C2 **Sargodha** Pak.
101 D4 **Sarh** Chad
79 G2 **Sārī** Iran
67 M7 **Saria** *i.* Greece
93 L3 **Sarigan** *i.* N. Mariana Is
80 B2 **Sarıgöl** Turkey
81 J1 **Sarıkamış** Turkey
80 D3 **Sarıkavak** Turkey
84 D4 **Sarila** India
95 □ **Sarimbun Res.** *resr* Sing.
116 C3 **Sarina** Austr.
80 E2 **Sarıoğlan** Turkey
84 A2 **Sar-i-Pul** Afgh.
101 D2 **Sarīr Tibesti** *des.* Libya
81 J2 **Sarısu** Turkey
80 C2 **Sarıyar Barajı** *resr* Turkey
80 B1 **Sarıyer** Turkey
80 F2 **Sarız** Turkey
84 E4 **Sarju** *r.* India
82 E1 **Sarkand** Kazak.
84 B4 **Sarkāri Tala** India
80 C2 **Şarkikaraağaç** Turkey
80 F2 **Şarkişla** Turkey
69 C7 **Şarköy** Turkey
64 E4 **Sarlat-la-Canéda** France
93 K7 **Sarmi** Indon.
55 N6 **Särna** Sweden
81 L5 **Sarneh** Iran
66 C1 **Sarnen** Switz.
31 F4 **Sarnia** Can.
69 C5 **Sarny** Ukr.
92 C7 **Sarolangun** Indon.
90 J1 **Saroma-ko** *l.* Japan
67 K6 **Saronikos Kolpos** *g.* Greece
69 C7 **Saros Körfezi** *b.* Turkey
84 C4 **Sarotra** India
68 G4 **Sarova** Rus. Fed.
84 B2 **Sarowbī** Afgh.
69 H6 **Sarpa, Ozero** *l. Kalmykiya* Rus. Fed.
69 H5 **Sarpa, Ozero** *l. Volgograd.* Rus. Fed.
55 M7 **Sarpsborg** Norway
64 H2 **Sarrebourg** France
61 F5 **Sarreguemines** France
65 C1 **Sarria** Spain
65 F2 **Sarrión** Spain
66 C4 **Sartène** *Corsica* France
90 J2 **Saru-gawa** *r.* Japan
90 D6 **Sarumasa-yama** *mt.* Japan
81 M4 **Saruq** Iran
81 K2 **Şärur** Azer.
81 L4 **Sarvabad** Iran
62 H7 **Sárvár** Hungary
79 H1 **Sarykamyshkoye Ozero** *salt l.* Turkm.
82 E2 **Saryozek** Kazak.
82 D1 **Saryshagan** Kazak.
79 L2 **Sary-Tash** Kyrgyzstan
35 G6 **Sasabe** U.S.A.
85 F4 **Sasaram** India
90 B7 **Sasebo** Japan
21 H4 **Saskatchewan** *div.* Can.
21 J4 **Saskatchewan** *r.* Can.
21 H4 **Saskatoon** Can.
77 N2 **Saskylakh** Rus. Fed.
105 G3 **Sasolburg** S. Africa
68 G4 **Sasovo** Rus. Fed.
33 F5 **Sassafras** U.S.A.
100 B4 **Sassandra** Côte d'Ivoire
66 C4 **Sassari** *Sardinia* Italy
62 F3 **Sassnitz** Ger.
86 D2 **Sasykkol', Oz.** *l.* Kazak.
69 H6 **Sasykoli** Rus. Fed.
100 A3 **Satadougou** Mali
90 C8 **Sata-misaki** *c.* Japan
84 C5 **Satana** India
84 D7 **Satara** India
105 J2 **Satara** S. Africa
69 G4 **Satinka** Rus. Fed.
85 G5 **Satkhira** Bangl.
84 E4 **Satna** India
84 C5 **Satpura Range** *mts* India
90 C8 **Satsuma-hantō** *pen.* Japan
90 J2 **Satsunai-gawa** *r.* Japan
91 G5 **Satte** Japan
84 D2 **Satti** Jammu and Kashmir
63 L7 **Satu Mare** Romania
95 B4 **Satun** Thai.
47 E1 **Sauce** Arg.
27 C7 **Sauceda** Mex.
35 F5 **Sauceda Mts** *mts* U.S.A.
55 K7 **Sauda** Norway
54 D4 **Sauðárkrókur** Iceland
70 **Saudi Arabia** *country* Asia
30 D4 **Saugatuck** U.S.A.
33 G3 **Saugerties** U.S.A.
**Sāūjbolāgh** *see* **Mahābād**
26 E2 **Sauk Center** U.S.A.
30 C4 **Sauk City** U.S.A.
64 G3 **Saulieu** France
31 E2 **Sault Ste Marie** Can.
30 E2 **Sault Ste Marie** U.S.A.
93 J8 **Saumlaki** Indon.
64 D3 **Saumur** France
119 C1 **Saunders I.** *i. S. Sandwich Is* Atlantic Ocean
85 F4 **Saura** *r.* India
103 C4 **Saurimo** Angola
67 J2 **Sava** *r.* Europe
115 F8 **Savage River** Austr.
111 J3 **Savaii** *i.* Western Samoa
69 G5 **Savala** *r.* Rus. Fed.
100 C4 **Savalou** Benin
30 B4 **Savanna** U.S.A.
29 D6 **Savannah** *GA* U.S.A.
29 B5 **Savannah** *TN* U.S.A.
29 D5 **Savannah** *r.* U.S.A.
29 E7 **Savannah Sound** Bahamas
95 C1 **Savannakhét** Laos
37 J5 **Savanna la Mar** Jamaica
22 B3 **Savant Lake** Can.
54 R5 **Sävar** Sweden
67 M5 **Savaştepe** Turkey
100 C4 **Savè** Benin
103 D6 **Save** *r.* Moz.
54 V5 **Saviaho** Fin.
76 F3 **Savinskiy** Rus. Fed.
64 H4 **Savoie** *reg.* France
66 C2 **Savona** Italy
55 V6 **Savonlinna** Fin.
54 V5 **Savonranta** Fin.
81 J1 **Şavşat** Turkey
55 O8 **Sävsjö** Sweden
93 G9 **Savu** *i.* Indon.
54 V3 **Savukoski** Fin.
81 H3 **Savur** Turkey
84 D4 **Sawai Madhopur** India
95 A1 **Sawankhalok** Thai.
91 G5 **Sawasaki-bana** *pt* Japan
91 G5 **Sawata** Japan
25 F4 **Sawatch Mts** *mts* U.S.A.
57 A6 **Sawel Mt** *h. N. Ireland* U.K.
115 K3 **Sawtell** Austr.
30 B2 **Sawtooth Mountains** *h.* U.S.A.
**Sawu** *i. see* **Savu**
93 G8 **Sawu Sea** *g.* Indon.
59 G4 **Saxilby** U.K.
59 J5 **Saxmundham** U.K.
54 O4 **Saxnäs** Sweden
86 F1 **Sayano-Shushenskoye Vdkhr.** *resr* Rus. Fed.
79 G6 **Sayḥūt** Yemen
102 E2 **Sāylac** Somalia
87 K3 **Saynshand** Mongolia
65 F1 **Sayoa** *mt* Spain
86 D3 **Sayram Hu** *salt l.* China
27 D5 **Sayre** *OK* U.S.A.
32 E4 **Sayre** *PA* U.S.A.
84 C2 **Sazin** Pak.
68 E3 **Sazonovo** Rus. Fed.
100 B2 **Sbaa** Alg.
100 C1 **Sbeitla** Tunisia
58 D3 **Scafell Pike** *mt* U.K.
57 B4 **Scalasaig** U.K.
66 F5 **Scalea** Italy
57 □ **Scalloway** U.K.
60 C5 **Scalp** *h.* Rep. of Ireland
57 C3 **Scalpay** *i. Scot.* U.K.
57 B3 **Scalpay** *i. Scot.* U.K.
57 A5 **Scalp Mountain** *h.* Rep. of Ireland
115 H8 **Scamander** Austr.
52 **Scandinavia** *reg.* Europe
57 E2 **Scapa Flow** *in.* U.K.
57 C4 **Scarba** *i.* U.K.
31 H4 **Scarborough** Can.
45 E2 **Scarborough** Trinidad and Tobago
58 G3 **Scarborough** U.K.
94 A3 **Scarborough Shoal** *sand bank* Phil.
57 A2 **Scarp** *i.* U.K.
**Scarpanto** *i. see* **Karpathos**
62 D7 **Schaffhausen** Switz.
61 C2 **Schagen** Neth.
61 C2 **Schagerbrug** Neth.
104 B3 **Schakalskuppe** Namibia
62 F6 **Schärding** Austria
61 B3 **Scharendijke** Neth.
61 E4 **Scharteberg** *h.* Ger.
23 G3 **Schefferville** Can.
61 C3 **Schelde** *r.* Belgium
35 E2 **Schell Creek Range** *mts* U.S.A.
33 G3 **Schenectady** U.S.A.
57 D4 **Schiehallion** *mt* U.K.
61 E1 **Schiermonnikoog** *i.* Neth.
61 E1 **Schiermonnikoog Nationaal Park** *nat. park* Neth.
61 E1 **Schildmeer** *l.* Neth.
61 D4 **Schinnen** Neth.
66 D2 **Schio** Italy
61 E4 **Schleiden** Ger.
62 D3 **Schleswig** Ger.
61 E4 **Schneifel** *reg.* Ger.
62 D4 **Schneverdingen** Ger.
33 G3 **Schodack Center** U.S.A.
30 C3 **Schofield** U.S.A.
34 □1 **Schofield Barracks** U.S.A.
62 E4 **Schönebeck** Ger.
33 J2 **Schoodic Lake** *l.* U.S.A.
30 E4 **Schoolcraft** U.S.A.
61 C3 **Schoonhoven** Neth.
115 H9 **Schouten I.** *i.* Austr.
110 E2 **Schouten Islands** *is* P.N.G.
30 D1 **Schreiber** Can.
33 G3 **Schroon Lake** *l.* U.S.A.
35 F5 **Schuchuli** U.S.A.
60 B6 **Schull** Rep. of Ireland
21 K2 **Schultz Lake** *l.* Can.
34 C2 **Schurz** U.S.A.
33 G3 **Schuylerville** U.S.A.
62 D6 **Schwäbisch Hall** Ger.
62 D6 **Schwabmünchen** Ger.
62 F6 **Schwandorf** Ger.
62 F5 **Schwarzenberg** Ger.
61 E4 **Schwarzer Mann** *h.* Ger.
104 B2 **Schwarzrand** *mts* Namibia
62 E7 **Schwaz** Austria
62 G4 **Schwedt** Ger.
62 E5 **Schweinfurt** Ger.
105 F3 **Schweizer-Reneke** S. Africa
62 D6 **Schwenningen** Ger.
62 E4 **Schwerin** Ger.
62 D7 **Schwyz** Switz.
66 E6 **Sciacca** *Sicily* Italy
59 A8 **Scilly, Isles of** *is* U.K.
32 B5 **Scioto** *r.* U.S.A.
35 F2 **Scipio** U.S.A.
24 F1 **Scobey** U.S.A.
59 J5 **Scole** U.K.
115 J4 **Scone** Austr.
18 **Scoresby Sound** *sound* Greenland
16 **Scoresbysund** Greenland
119 B1 **Scotia Ridge** *sea feature* Atlantic Ocean
12 F9 **Scotia Sea** *sea* Atlantic Ocean
31 G4 **Scotland** Can.
56 E3 **Scotland** *div.* U.K.
119 B5 **Scott Base** *N.Z. Base* Ant.
105 J5 **Scottburgh** S. Africa
20 D4 **Scott, C.** *c.* Can.
26 C4 **Scott City** U.S.A.
119 B5 **Scott Coast** *coastal area* Ant.
32 D4 **Scottdale** U.S.A.
119 A5 **Scott Island** *i.* Ant.
21 H3 **Scott Lake** *l.* Can.
119 D4 **Scott Mts** *mts* Ant.
26 C3 **Scottsbluff** U.S.A.
29 C5 **Scottsboro** U.S.A.
28 C4 **Scottsburg** U.S.A.
115 G8 **Scottsdale** Austr.
25 E5 **Scottsdale** U.S.A.
34 A3 **Scotts Valley** U.S.A.
30 D4 **Scottville** U.S.A.
34 D3 **Scotty's Junction** U.S.A.
57 C2 **Scourie** U.K.
57 □ **Scousburgh** U.K.
57 E2 **Scrabster** U.K.
33 F4 **Scranton** U.S.A.
57 B4 **Scridain, Loch** *in.* U.K.
58 G4 **Scunthorpe** U.K.
59 H7 **Seaford** U.K.
33 F5 **Seaford** U.S.A.
116 C3 **Seaforth** Austr.
31 G4 **Seaforth** Can.
94 A4 **Seahorse Bank** *sand bank* Phil.
21 K3 **Seal** *r.* Can.
114 E5 **Sea Lake** Austr.
104 E7 **Seal, Cape** *pt* S. Africa
33 J3 **Seal I.** *i.* U.S.A.
23 H3 **Seal Lake** *l.* Can.
104 F7 **Seal Point** *pt* S. Africa
35 E3 **Seaman Range** *mts* U.S.A.
58 G3 **Seamer** U.K.
35 E4 **Searchlight** U.S.A.
27 F5 **Searcy** U.S.A.
34 D4 **Searles Lake** *l.* U.S.A.
30 E4 **Sears** U.S.A.
33 J2 **Searsport** U.S.A.
34 B3 **Seaside** *CA* U.S.A.
24 B2 **Seaside** *OR* U.S.A.
58 D3 **Seaton** U.K.
24 B2 **Seattle** U.S.A.
116 A2 **Seaview Ra.** *mts* Austr.
33 F5 **Seaville** U.S.A.
33 H3 **Sebago Lake** *l.* U.S.A.
36 B3 **Sebastián Vizcaíno, Bahía** *b.* Mex.
33 J2 **Sebasticook** *r.* U.S.A.
94 A5 **Sebatik** *i.* Indon.
80 C1 **Seben** Turkey
67 K2 **Sebeş** Romania
92 □ **Sebesi** *i.* Indon.
31 F4 **Sebewaing** U.S.A.
68 D3 **Sebezh** Rus. Fed.
80 E3 **Sebil** Turkey
80 G1 **Şebinkarahisar** Turkey
33 J2 **Seboeis Lake** *l.* U.S.A.
33 J2 **Seboomook** U.S.A.
33 J2 **Seboomook Lake** *l.* U.S.A.
29 D7 **Sebring** U.S.A.
69 G5 **Sebrovo** Rus. Fed.
42 B5 **Sechura** Peru
42 B5 **Sechura, Bahía de** *b.* Peru
33 H2 **Second Lake** *l.* U.S.A.
117 A6 **Secretary Island** *i.* N.Z.
105 H3 **Secunda** S. Africa
83 E7 **Secunderabad** India
26 E4 **Sedalia** U.S.A.
114 C5 **Sedan** Austr.
64 G2 **Sedan** France
117 E4 **Seddon** N.Z.
117 C4 **Seddonville** N.Z.
33 J2 **Sedgwick** U.S.A.
100 A3 **Sédhiou** Senegal
62 G6 **Sedlčany** Czech Rep.
80 E6 **Sedom** Israel
35 G4 **Sedona** U.S.A.
66 B6 **Sédrata** Alg.
55 S9 **Šeduva** Lith.
60 D5 **Seefin** *h.* Rep. of Ireland
103 B6 **Seeheim** Namibia
35 E5 **Seeley** U.S.A.
119 B3 **Seelig, Mt** *mt.* Ant.
64 E2 **Sées** France
100 A4 **Sefadu** Sierra Leone
105 G1 **Sefare** Botswana
67 M5 **Seferihisar** Turkey
105 G1 **Sefophe** Botswana
55 M6 **Segalstad** Norway
94 A5 **Segama** *r.* Malaysia
92 C6 **Segamat** Malaysia
68 E2 **Segezha** Rus. Fed.
65 F3 **Segorbe** Spain
100 B3 **Ségou** Mali
45 B3 **Segovia** Col.
**Segovia** *r. see* **Coco**
65 D2 **Segovia** Spain
68 E2 **Segozerskoye, Oz.** *resr* Rus. Fed.
65 G1 **Segre** *r.* Spain
101 D2 **Séguédine** Niger
100 B4 **Séguéla** Côte d'Ivoire
27 D6 **Seguin** U.S.A.
47 D1 **Segundo** *r.* Arg.
65 F3 **Segura** *r.* Spain
103 C6 **Sehithwa** Botswana
105 H4 **Sehlabathebe National Park** *nat. park* Lesotho
84 D5 **Sehore** India
54 S1 **Seiland** *i.* Norway
27 D4 **Seiling** U.S.A.
54 S5 **Seinäjoki** Fin.
22 B4 **Seine** *r.* Can.
64 E2 **Seine** *r.* France
64 D2 **Seine, Baie de** *b.* France
64 F2 **Seine, Val de** *v.* France
63 L3 **Sejny** Pol.
92 C7 **Sekayu** Indon.
91 F6 **Seki** Japan
104 E2 **Sekoma** Botswana
100 B4 **Sekondi** Ghana
95 D5 **Sekura** Indon.
24 B2 **Selah** U.S.A.
93 J8 **Selaru** *i.* Indon.
92 E7 **Selatan, Tanjung** *pt* Indon.
95 □ **Selat Johor** *chan.* Malaysia/Sing.
95 □ **Selat Jurong** *chan.* Sing.
95 □ **Selat Pandan** *chan.* Sing.
54 L5 **Selbekken** Norway
54 M5 **Selbu** Norway
58 F4 **Selby** U.K.
26 C2 **Selby** U.S.A.
103 C6 **Selebi-Phikwe** Botswana
80 B2 **Selendi** Turkey
64 H2 **Sélestat** France
95 □ **Seletar** Sing.
95 □ **Seletar, P.** *i.* Sing.
95 □ **Seletar Res.** *resr* Sing.
76 J4 **Seletyteniz, Ozero** *salt l.* Kazak.
**Seleucia Pieria** *see* **Samandağı**
26 C2 **Selfridge** U.S.A.
68 J2 **Selib** Rus. Fed.
100 A3 **Sélibabi** Maur.
68 E3 **Seliger, Oz.** *l.* Rus. Fed.
35 F4 **Seligman** U.S.A.
101 E2 **Selîma Oasis** *oasis* Sudan
31 J5 **Selinsgrove** U.S.A.
63 Q2 **Selishche** Rus. Fed.
69 H6 **Selitrennoye** Rus. Fed.
63 Q2 **Selizharovo** Rus. Fed.
55 L7 **Seljord** Norway
21 K4 **Selkirk** Can.
57 F5 **Selkirk** U.K.
20 F4 **Selkirk Mountains** *mts* Can.
58 D3 **Sellafield** U.K.
116 B3 **Sellheim** *r.* Austr.
35 G6 **Sells** U.S.A.
29 C5 **Selma** *AL* U.S.A.
34 C3 **Selma** *CA* U.S.A.
29 B5 **Selmer** U.S.A.
59 G7 **Selsey Bill** *hd* U.K.
95 C4 **Seluan** *i.* Indon.
40 **Selvas** *reg.* Brazil
21 J3 **Selwyn Lake** *l.* Can.
20 C2 **Selwyn Mountains** *mts* Can.
113 G4 **Selwyn Range** *h.* Austr.
92 □ **Semarang** Indon.
92 D6 **Sematan** Malaysia
94 A6 **Sembakung** *r.* Indon.
95 □ **Sembawang** Sing.
102 B3 **Sembé** Congo
81 K3 **Şemdinli** Turkey
92 □ **Semenanjung Blambangan** *pen.* Indon.
69 E4 **Semenivka** Ukr.
68 H3 **Semenov** Rus. Fed.
69 G6 **Semikarakorsk** Rus. Fed.
69 F5 **Semiluki** Rus. Fed.
24 F3 **Seminoe Res.** *resr* U.S.A.
27 C5 **Seminole** U.S.A.
29 C6 **Seminole, L.** *l.* U.S.A.
86 D1 **Semipalatinsk** Kazak.
94 B3 **Semirara** *i.* Phil.
94 B4 **Semirara Islands** *is* Phil.
79 G2 **Semnān** Iran
61 D5 **Semois** *r.* Belgium
61 C5 **Semois, Vallée de la** *v.* Belgium/France
93 F6 **Semporna** Malaysia
92 □ **Sempu** *i.* Indon.
94 A5 **Senaja** Malaysia
69 G7 **Senaki** Georgia
42 E5 **Sena Madureira** Brazil
103 C5 **Senanga** Zambia
90 C8 **Sendai** *Kagoshima* Japan
91 H4 **Sendai** *Miyagi* Japan
90 C8 **Sendai-gawa** *r.* Japan
85 H3 **Sêndo** China
95 B5 **Senebui, Tanjung** *pt* Indon.
35 G5 **Seneca** *AZ* U.S.A.
30 C5 **Seneca** *IL* U.S.A.
24 C2 **Seneca** *OR* U.S.A.
32 E3 **Seneca Falls** U.S.A.
32 E3 **Seneca Lake** *l.* U.S.A.
32 D5 **Seneca Rocks** U.S.A.
32 C5 **Senecaville Lake** *l.* U.S.A.
96 **Senegal** *country* Africa
100 A3 **Sénégal** *r.* Maur./Senegal
105 G4 **Senekal** S. Africa
30 E2 **Seney** U.S.A.
62 G5 **Senftenberg** Ger.
84 D4 **Sengar** *r.* India
102 D4 **Sengerema** Tanz.
68 J4 **Sengiley** Rus. Fed.
43 K6 **Senhor do Bonfim** Brazil
66 E3 **Senigallia** Italy
66 F2 **Senj** Croatia
54 P2 **Senja** *i.* Norway
81 J1 **Şenkaya** Turkey
84 D2 **Senku** Jammu and Kashmir
104 E2 **Senlac** S. Africa
64 F2 **Senlis** France
95 C2 **Senmonorom** Cambodia
91 E6 **Sennan** Japan
59 B7 **Sennen** U.K.
31 J1 **Senneterre** Can.
105 G5 **Senqu** *r.* Lesotho
64 F2 **Sens** France
36 G6 **Sensuntepeque** El Salvador
67 J2 **Senta** Yugo.
84 D3 **Senthal** India
35 F5 **Sentinel** U.S.A.
20 E3 **Sentinel Pk** *summit* Can.
95 □ **Sentosa** *i.* Sing.
81 H3 **Şenyurt** Turkey
90 D7 **Sen-zaki** *pt* Japan
90 C6 **Senzaki** Japan
84 D5 **Seoni** India
85 E5 **Seorinarayan** India
87 N4 **Seoul** S. Korea
117 D4 **Separation Pt** *pt* N.Z.
81 L4 **Separ Shāhābād** Iran
46 D3 **Sepetiba, Baía de** *b.* Brazil
110 E2 **Sepik** *r.* P.N.G.
23 G3 **Sept-Îles** Can.
34 C3 **Sequoia National Park** *nat. park* U.S.A.
81 L3 **Serā** Iran
69 G5 **Serafimovich** Rus. Fed.
93 H7 **Seram** *i.* Indon.
93 J7 **Seram Sea** *g.* Indon.
92 □ **Serang** Indon.
95 □ **Serangoon Harbour** *chan.* Sing.
95 □ **Serangoon, P.** *i.* Sing.
95 D5 **Serasan** *i.* Indon.
95 D5 **Serasan, Selat** *chan.* Indon.
95 D5 **Seraya** *i.* Indon.
95 □ **Seraya, P.** *i.* Sing.
67 J3 **Serbia** *div.* Yugo.
**Serbija** *div. see* **Serbia**
80 F3 **Serdar** Turkey
102 E2 **Serdo** Eth.
69 H4 **Serdoba** *r.* Rus. Fed.
69 H4 **Serdobsk** Rus. Fed.
68 D3 **Seredka** Rus. Fed.
80 D2 **Şereflikoçhisar** Turkey
92 C6 **Seremban** Malaysia
102 D4 **Serengeti National Park** *nat. park* Tanz.
103 D5 **Serenje** Zambia
68 H4 **Sergach** Rus. Fed.
68 F3 **Sergiyev Posad** Rus. Fed.
92 E6 **Seria** Brunei
92 E6 **Serian** Malaysia
67 L6 **Serifos** *i.* Greece
23 G2 **Sérigny, Lac** *l.* Can.
80 C3 **Serik** Turkey
114 C3 **Serle, Mt** *h.* Austr.
93 H8 **Sermata, Kepulauan** *is* Indon.
68 J3 **Sernur** Rus. Fed.
69 H6 **Seroglazka** Rus. Fed.
76 H4 **Serov** Rus. Fed.
103 C6 **Serowe** Botswana
65 C4 **Serpa** Port.
45 E2 **Serpent's Mouth** *chan.* Trinidad/Venez.
68 F4 **Serpukhov** Rus. Fed.
46 C3 **Serra da Canastra, Parque Nacional da** *nat. park* Brazil
45 D4 **Serranía de la Neblina, Parque Nacional** *nat. park* Venez.
46 B2 **Serranópolis** Brazil
61 B5 **Serre** *r.* France
67 K4 **Serres** Greece
47 D1 **Serrezuela** Arg.
43 L6 **Serrinha** Brazil
46 D2 **Sêrro** Brazil
47 B4 **Serrucho** *mt* Arg.
66 C6 **Sers** Tunisia
46 C3 **Sertãozinho** Brazil
68 D2 **Sertolovo** Rus. Fed.
95 A4 **Seruai** Indon.
93 K7 **Serui** Indon.
92 E7 **Seruyan** *r.* Indon.
82 J4 **Sêrxu** China
94 A6 **Sesayap** *r.* Indon.
94 A6 **Sesayap** Indon.
22 B3 **Seseganaga L.** *l.* Can.
31 G1 **Sesekinika** Can.
103 B5 **Sesfontein** Namibia
103 C5 **Sesheke** Zambia
66 E4 **Sessa Aurunca** Italy
66 C2 **Sestri Levante** Italy
68 D2 **Sestroretsk** Rus. Fed.
90 G2 **Setana** Japan
64 F5 **Sète** France
46 D2 **Sete Lagoas** Brazil
54 Q2 **Setermoen** Norway
55 K7 **Setesdal** *v.* Norway
85 F4 **Seti** *r. Gandakhi* Nepal
84 E3 **Seti** *r. Seti* Nepal
100 C1 **Sétif** Alg.
91 F6 **Seto** Japan
90 D7 **Seto-naikai** *sea* Japan
95 C2 **Set, P.** *mt* Laos
100 B1 **Settat** Morocco
58 E3 **Settle** U.K.
65 B3 **Setúbal** Port.
65 B3 **Setúbal, Baía de** *b.* Port.
30 E3 **Seul Choix Pt** *pt* U.S.A.
22 B3 **Seul, Lac** *l.* Can.
81 K1 **Sevan** Armenia
**Sevana Lich** *l. see* **Sevan, Lake**
81 K1 **Sevan, Lake** *l.* Armenia
69 E6 **Sevastopol'** Ukr.
23 H2 **Seven Islands Bay** *b.* Can.
59 H6 **Sevenoaks** U.K.

64 F4 Sévérac-le-Château France
115 J2 Severn r. Austr.
22 B3 Severn r. Can.
104 E3 Severn S. Africa
59 E6 Severn r. U.K.
68 G2 Severnaya Dvina r. Rus. Fed.
69 H7 Severnaya Osetiya, Respublika div. Rus. Fed.
77 M1 Severnaya Zemlya is Rus. Fed.
22 B3 Severn L. l. Can.
76 H3 Severnyy Rus. Fed.
68 F1 Severodvinsk Rus. Fed.
54 X2 Severomorsk Rus. Fed.
76 L3 Severo-Yeniseyskiy Rus. Fed.
69 F6 Severskaya Rus. Fed.
25 D4 Sevier r. U.S.A.
35 G2 Sevier Bridge Reservoir resr U.S.A.
35 F2 Sevier Desert des. U.S.A.
35 F2 Sevier Lake salt l. U.S.A.
45 B3 Sevilla Col.
Sevilla see Seville
65 D4 Seville Spain
67 L1 Sevlievo Bulg.
84 C3 Sewāni India
16 Seward AK U.S.A.
26 E3 Seward NE U.S.A.
77 V3 Seward Peninsula pen. AK U.S.A.
20 F3 Sexsmith Can.
81 K2 Seyah Cheshmeh Iran
76 J2 Seyakha Rus. Fed.
96 Seychelles country Indian Ocean
80 C3 Seydişehir Turkey
54 F4 Seyðisfjörður Iceland
81 K2 Seydvān Iran
Seyhan see Adana
80 E3 Seyhan r. Turkey
69 E5 Seym r. Rus. Fed.
77 R3 Seymchan Rus. Fed.
114 F6 Seymour Austr.
105 G6 Seymour S. Africa
28 C4 Seymour IN U.S.A.
27 D5 Seymour TX U.S.A.
84 B2 Seyyedābād Afgh.
64 F2 Sézanne France
67 L7 Sfakia Greece
67 L2 Sfântu Gheorghe Romania
100 D1 Sfax Tunisia
67 K4 Sfikia, Limni resr Greece
61 D2 's-Graveland Neth.
's-Gravenhage see The Hague
56 B3 Sgurr Alasdair h. U.K.
57 C4 Sgurr Dhomhnuill h. U.K.
57 C3 Sgurr Mor mt U.K.
88 E2 Sha r. China
88 C3 Shaanxi div. China
81 K2 Shabestar Iran
23 G3 Shabogamo Lake l. Can.
102 C4 Shabunda Zaire
82 E3 Shache China
119 B4 Shackleton Coast coastal area Ant.
119 D6 Shackleton Ice Shelf ice feature Ant.
119 C3 Shackleton Ra. mts Ant.
84 A4 Shadadkot Pak.
81 M6 Shādegān Iran
84 A3 Shadikhah Pass pass Pak.
30 D5 Shafer, Lake l. U.S.A.
119 B5 Shafer Pk summit Ant.
34 C4 Shafter U.S.A.
59 E6 Shaftesbury U.K.
117 C6 Shag Pt pt N.Z.
81 M3 Shah r. Iran
84 E4 Shahabad India
84 C5 Shahada India
95 B5 Shah Alam Malaysia
84 A4 Shahbandar Pak.
85 G5 Shahbazpur chan. Bangl.
84 E5 Shahdol India
84 A2 Shah Fuladi mt Afgh.
84 B4 Shahgarh India
81 K3 Shahīdān Iraq
81 K3 Shah Pen. pen. Iran
84 D4 Shahjahanpur India
Shāhpūr see Salmās
84 B3 Shahpur Pak.
84 E5 Shahpura Madhya Pradesh India
84 C4 Shahpura Rajasthan India
79 G3 Shahr-e Kord Iran
81 L3 Shakar Bolāghī Iran
105 J4 Shakaville S. Africa
68 E3 Shakhovskaya Rus. Fed.
79 K2 Shakhrisabz Uzbek.
69 G6 Shakhty Rus. Fed.
68 H3 Shakh'nya Rus. Fed.
26 E2 Shakopee U.S.A.
90 H2 Shakotan-hantō pen. Japan
90 H2 Shakotan-misaki c. Japan
68 G2 Shalakusha Rus. Fed.
82 J4 Shaluli Shan mts China
85 J3 Shaluni mt India
21 L3 Shamattawa Can.
89 Sham Chun h. Hong Kong China
32 H4 Shamokin U.S.A.
27 C5 Shamrock U.S.A.
103 D5 Shamva Zimbabwe
60 B6 Shanacrane Rep. of Ireland
88 A2 Shandan China
81 M3 Shānderman Iran

88 E1 Shandian r. China
34 B4 Shandon U.S.A.
88 E2 Shandong div. China
88 F2 Shandong Bandao pen. China
81 K5 Shandrūkh Iraq
84 C1 Shandur Pass pass Pak.
103 C5 Shangani r. Zimbabwe
88 E3 Shangcai China
89 C5 Shangchao China
88 E4 Shangcheng China
85 G3 Shang Chu r. China
89 D6 Shangchuan Dao i. China
88 D1 Shangdu China
89 E4 Shanggao China
88 F4 Shanghai China
88 F4 Shanghai div. China
89 E5 Shanghang China
88 E2 Shanghe China
88 D3 Shangjin China
88 D3 Shanglin China
88 E3 Shangqiu Henan China
88 E3 Shangqiu Henan China
89 E4 Shangrao Jiangxi China
89 E4 Shangrao Jiangxi China
88 E3 Shangshui China
89 C6 Shangsi China
89 E4 Shangtang China
88 D1 Shangyi China
89 E5 Shangyou China
89 E4 Shangyu China
87 N2 Shangzhi China
88 C3 Shangzhou China
60 C5 Shannon r. Rep. of Ireland
60 C4 Shannon est. Rep. of Ireland
18 Shannon Island i. Greenland
60 B5 Shannon, Mouth of the est. Rep. of Ireland
82 H2 Shāntipur India
85 H2 Shāntipur India
89 E6 Shantou China
89 E6 Shanwei China
88 D2 Shanxi div. China
88 E3 Shan Xian China
88 D2 Shanyang China
89 D1 Shanyin China
88 D2 Shaodong China
89 D5 Shaoguan China
89 E5 Shaohua China
89 F4 Shaoxing China
89 D5 Shaoyang Hunan China
89 D5 Shaoyang Hunan China
58 E3 Shap U.K.
89 D6 Shapa China
57 F1 Shapinsay i. U.K.
78 F4 Shaqrā' S. Arabia
81 J6 Sharaf w. Iraq
84 B3 Sharan Jogizai Pak.
69 D5 Sharhorod Ukr.
90 K2 Shari-dake volc. Japan
79 H4 Shārīah U.A.E.
63 N3 Sharkawshchyna Belarus
112 B5 Shark Bay b. Austr.
33 G4 Sharon CT U.S.A.
32 C4 Sharon PA U.S.A.
89 Sharp Peak h. Hong Kong China
80 E5 Sharqi, Jebel esh mts Lebanon/Syria
68 H3 Shar'ya Rus. Fed.
103 C6 Shashe r. Botswana/Zimbabwe
102 D2 Shashemenē Eth.
89 D4 Shashi China
24 B3 Shasta l. U.S.A.
24 B3 Shasta, Mt volc. U.S.A.
89 Sha Tin Hong Kong China
68 H4 Shatki Rus. Fed.
81 M7 Shatt al Arab r. Iran/Iraq
81 L4 Shatt al Hillah r. Iraq
68 F4 Shatura Rus. Fed.
80 E6 Shaubak Jordan
21 H5 Shaunavon Can.
32 D5 Shavers Fork r. U.S.A.
33 F4 Shawangunk Mts h. U.S.A.
30 C3 Shawano U.S.A.
30 C3 Shawano Lake l. U.S.A.
22 F4 Shawinigan Can.
80 F4 Shawmarīyah, Jebel ash mts Syria
27 D5 Shawnee U.S.A.
89 F5 Sha Xi r. China
89 E6 Sha Xian China
89 D4 Shayang China
112 D4 Shay Gap Austr.
81 L5 Shaykh Jūwī Iraq
81 L5 Shaykh Sa'd Iraq
68 F4 Shchekino Rus. Fed.
77 S3 Shcherbakovo Rus. Fed.
69 F5 Shchigry Rus. Fed.
69 D5 Shchors Ukr.
68 C4 Shchuchyn Belarus
69 F5 Shebekino Rus. Fed.
79 K2 Sheberghān Afgh.
30 D4 Sheboygan U.S.A.
100 D4 Shebshi Mountains mts Nigeria
23 H4 Shediac Can.
20 D3 Shedin Pk summit Can.
60 D4 Sheelin, Lough l. Rep. of Ireland
60 D2 Sheep Haven b. Rep. of Ireland
105 J3 Sheepmoor S. Africa
35 E3 Sheep Peak summit U.S.A.
59 H6 Sheerness U.K.
23 H5 Sheet Harbour Can.
115 G8 Sheffield Austr.

117 D5 Sheffield N.Z.
59 F4 Sheffield U.K.
29 C5 Sheffield AL U.S.A.
30 C5 Sheffield IL U.S.A.
32 D4 Sheffield PA U.S.A.
27 D4 Sheffield TX U.S.A.
31 G3 Sheguiandah Can.
88 B4 Shehong China
80 E5 Sheikh, Jebel esh mt Lebanon/Syria
84 C3 Shekhupura Pak.
89 Shek Kwu Chau i. Hong Kong China
89 Shek Pik Reservoir resr Hong Kong China
68 F3 Sheksna r. Rus. Fed.
89 Shek Uk Shan h. Hong Kong China
77 T2 Shelagskiy, Mys pt Rus. Fed.
30 A6 Shelbina U.S.A.
23 G5 Shelburne N.S. Can.
31 G3 Shelburne Ont. Can.
33 G3 Shelburne Falls U.S.A.
30 D4 Shelby MI U.S.A.
24 E1 Shelby MT U.S.A.
29 D5 Shelby NC U.S.A.
32 B4 Shelby OH U.S.A.
28 C4 Shelbyville IN U.S.A.
30 A6 Shelbyville MO U.S.A.
29 C5 Shelbyville TN U.S.A.
35 H5 Sheldon AZ U.S.A.
30 D5 Sheldon IL U.S.A.
33 G2 Sheldon Springs U.S.A.
23 H3 Sheldrake Can.
77 R3 Shelikhova, Zaliv g. Rus. Fed.
21 H4 Shellbrook Can.
24 D3 Shelley U.S.A.
115 J5 Shellharbour Austr.
34 A1 Shell Mt mt. U.S.A.
20 F4 Shelter Bay Can.
34 A1 Shelter Cove U.S.A.
89 Shelter I. i. Hong Kong China
33 G4 Shelter I. i. U.S.A.
117 B7 Shelter Pt pt N.Z.
86 D1 Shemonaikha Kazak.
26 E3 Shenandoah IA U.S.A.
33 E4 Shenandoah PA U.S.A.
32 D5 Shenandoah VA U.S.A.
32 D5 Shenandoah r. U.S.A.
32 D5 Shenandoah Mountains mts U.S.A.
32 D5 Shenandoah National Park nat. park U.S.A.
32 C4 Shenango River Lake l. U.S.A.
100 C4 Shendam Nigeria
88 G4 Shengsi China
89 F4 Sheng Xian China
68 G2 Shenkursk Rus. Fed.
88 D2 Shenmu China
88 D4 Shennongjia China
88 E3 Shenqiu China
88 G1 Shenyang China
89 E6 Shenzhen China
69 C5 Shepetivka Ukr.
111 G3 Shepherd Is is Vanuatu
115 H5 Shepparton Austr.
59 H6 Sheppey, Isle of i. U.K.
59 F7 Sherborne U.K.
23 H4 Sherbrooke N.S. Can.
23 F4 Sherbrooke Que. Can.
33 F3 Sherburne U.S.A.
60 E4 Shercock Rep. of Ireland
84 B2 Sher Dahan Pass pass Afgh.
101 F3 Shereiq Sudan
84 C4 Shergarh India
27 E5 Sheridan AR U.S.A.
24 F2 Sheridan WY U.S.A.
114 A4 Sheringa Austr.
59 J5 Sheringham U.K.
27 D5 Sherman U.S.A.
33 J2 Sherman Mills U.S.A.
35 E1 Sherman Mtn mt. U.S.A.
85 G4 Sherpur Bangl.
21 J3 Sherridon Can.
61 D3 's-Hertogenbosch Neth.
59 F4 Sherwood Forest reg. U.K.
20 C3 Sheslay Can.
56 F1 Shetland Islands is U.K.
76 G5 Shetpe Kazak.
89 Sheung Shui Hong Kong China
89 Sheung Sze Mun chan. Hong Kong China
89 F4 She Xian China
88 F3 Sheyang China
26 D2 Sheyenne r. U.S.A.
26 D2 Sheyenne U.S.A.
57 B3 Shiant Islands is U.K.
77 R5 Shiashkotan, O. i. Rus. Fed.
31 E4 Shiawassee r. U.S.A.
78 F6 Shibām Yemen
84 B2 Shibar Pass pass Afgh.
91 G5 Shibata Japan
90 K2 Shibetsu Japan
90 J1 Shibetsu Japan
80 C6 Shibīn el Kōm Egypt
91 L2 Shibotsu-jima i. Rus. Fed.
91 G5 Shibukawa Japan
90 C8 Shibushi-wan b. Japan
89 D4 Shicheng China
90 H3 Shichinohe Japan
35 E3 Shickshinny U.S.A.
80 G6 Shidād al Misma' h. S. Arabia
88 G2 Shidao China
88 G2 Shidao Wan b. China

57 C4 Shiel, Loch l. U.K.
88 B4 Shifang China
91 E6 Shiga Japan
68 J4 Shigony Rus. Fed.
88 D1 Shiguaigou China
82 G1 Shihezi China
88 E2 Shijiazhuang China
90 H2 Shikabe Japan
84 B4 Shikarpur Pak.
84 D4 Shikohabad India
90 D7 Shikoku i. Japan
90 D7 Shikoku-sanchi mts Japan
90 H2 Shikotsu-ko l. Japan
90 H2 Shikotsu-Tōya National Park Japan
58 F3 Shildon U.K.
68 H1 Shilega Rus. Fed.
85 G4 Shiliguri India
89 D4 Shilipu China
84 D3 Shilla mt India
60 E5 Shillelagh Rep. of Ireland
31 G1 Shillington Can.
85 G4 Shillong India
33 F5 Shiloh U.S.A.
88 D2 Shilou China
68 G4 Shilovo Rus. Fed.
90 C7 Shimabara Japan
90 C7 Shimabara-wan b. Japan
91 G6 Shimada Japan
90 D6 Shimane Japan
90 D6 Shimane-hantō pen. Japan
87 N1 Shimanovsk Rus. Fed.
89 D4 Shimen China
89 B4 Shimian China
91 G6 Shimizu Japan
84 D3 Shimla India
91 G6 Shimoda Japan
91 G5 Shimodate Japan
83 E8 Shimoga India
90 H3 Shimokita-hantō pen. Japan
90 B8 Shimo-Koshiki-jima i. Japan
102 D4 Shimoni Kenya
90 C7 Shimonoseki Japan
84 C1 Shimshal Jammu and Kashmir
68 D3 Shimsk Rus. Fed.
89 C6 Shinan China
91 G5 Shinano-gawa r. Japan
79 J3 Shīndand Afgh.
84 B3 Shinghar Pak.
84 C1 Shinghshal Pass pass Pak.
30 D2 Shingleton U.S.A.
89 Shing Mun Res. resr Hong Kong China
91 F7 Shingū Japan
105 J1 Shingwedzi S. Africa
105 J1 Shingwedzi r. S. Africa
59 E4 Shining Tor h. U.K.
31 G2 Shining Tree Can.
90 D6 Shinji-ko l. Japan
91 H4 Shinjō Japan
84 A3 Shinkāy Afgh.
57 A3 Shin, Loch l. U.K.
91 F5 Shinminato Japan
90 C6 Shin-nanyō Japan
33 J1 Shin Pond U.S.A.
90 J2 Shintoku Japan
102 D4 Shinyanga Tanz.
91 H4 Shiogama Japan
91 F5 Shiojiri Japan
91 E7 Shiono-misaki c. Japan
91 H5 Shioya-zaki pt Japan
29 E7 Ship Chan Cay i. Bahamas
89 B6 Shiping China
84 D3 Shipki Pass pass China/India
58 F4 Shipley U.K.
23 H4 Shippegan Can.
32 E4 Shippensburg U.S.A.
35 H3 Shiprock U.S.A.
35 H3 Shiprock Peak summit U.S.A.
89 E4 Shipu China
89 C5 Shiqian China
88 C3 Shiquan China
84 E2 Shiquan He r. China
88 C3 Shiquan Sk. resr China
81 M2 Shīrābād Iran
91 E7 Shirahama Japan
90 H3 Shirakami-misaki pt Japan
91 F5 Shirakawa Japan
91 H5 Shirakawa Japan
91 G5 Shirane-san volc. Japan
90 K2 Shiranuka Japan
90 H2 Shiraoi Japan
90 J2 Shirataki Japan
79 J4 Shīrāz Iran
80 C6 Shirbīn Egypt
90 K2 Shiretoko-hantō pen. Japan
90 K1 Shiretoko-misaki c. Japan
90 H3 Shiriya-zaki c. Japan
33 J2 Shirley U.S.A.
33 J2 Shirley Mills U.S.A.
91 H5 Shiroishi Japan
91 H5 Shirone Japan
84 C5 Shirpur India
81 L5 Shīrvān Iran
89 D3 Shishou China
89 D4 Shitai China
91 H6 Shitang China
91 H6 Shitara Japan
81 J5 Shithāthah Iraq
28 B4 Shiv India
28 C4 Shively U.S.A.

84 D4 Shivpuri India
35 F3 Shivwits Plateau plat. U.S.A.
89 C6 Shiwan Dashan mts China
89 E5 Shixing China
89 D3 Shiyan China
89 C5 Shizhu China
89 B5 Shizong China
91 H4 Shizugawa Japan
88 C2 Shizuishan China
91 G6 Shizuoka Japan
91 G6 Shizuoka Japan
68 D4 Shklow Belarus
67 H3 Shkodër Albania
76 K1 Shmidta, Ostrov i. Rus. Fed.
90 D6 Shōbara Japan
91 F5 Shō-gawa r. Japan
90 H2 Shokanbetsu-dake mt. Japan
68 J2 Shomvukva Rus. Fed.
84 D2 Shor India
81 K3 Shor Gol Iran
84 B3 Shorkot Pak.
90 H1 Shosanbetsu Japan
34 D4 Shoshone CA U.S.A.
24 D3 Shoshone ID U.S.A.
24 E2 Shoshone r. U.S.A.
24 E2 Shoshone L. l. U.S.A.
25 C4 Shoshone Mts mts U.S.A.
105 G1 Shoshong Botswana
24 E3 Shoshoni U.S.A.
69 D5 Shostka Ukr.
88 F2 Shouguang China
89 F4 Shouning China
88 E3 Shou Xian China
88 D2 Shouyang China
88 C3 Shouyang Shan mt. China
85 E3 Shovo Tso salt l. China
35 G4 Show Low U.S.A.
69 G6 Shpakovskoye Rus. Fed.
69 D5 Shpola Ukr.
27 E5 Shreveport U.S.A.
59 E5 Shrewsbury U.K.
85 G5 Shrirampur India
88 F3 Shu r. China
82 D2 Shu Kazak.
81 L6 Shu'aiba Iraq
89 A5 Shuangbai China
88 C1 Shuanghechang China
83 J6 Shuangjiang China
88 G1 Shuangliao China
89 D5 Shuangpai China
87 O2 Shuangyashan China
89 F5 Shuiji China
88 A2 Shuiquanzi China
84 B3 Shujaabad Pak.
88 E2 Shulu China
90 J1 Shumarinai-ko l. Japan
103 C5 Shumba Zimbabwe
67 M3 Shumen Bulg.
68 H4 Shumerlya Rus. Fed.
63 O3 Shumilina Belarus
35 G4 Shumway U.S.A.
68 E4 Shumyachi Rus. Fed.
89 E5 Shunchang China
89 D6 Shunde China
89 E1 Shunyi China
89 D6 Shuolong China
88 D2 Shuo Xian China
78 F7 Shuqrah Yemen
103 C5 Shurugwi Zimbabwe
81 K6 Shuruppak Iraq
81 M5 Shūsh Iran
81 M5 Shushtar Iran
20 F4 Shuswap L. l. Can.
68 G3 Shuya Rus. Fed.
88 F3 Shuyang China
83 J6 Shwebo Myanmar
95 A1 Shwegun Myanmar
83 J7 Shwegyin Myanmar
82 C2 Shymkent Kazak.
89 F5 Shypuvate Ukr.
69 E6 Shyroke Ukr.
93 J8 Sia Indon.
84 D2 Siachen Gl. gl. India
79 J4 Siahan Range mts Pak.
84 C2 Sialkot Pak.
95 C5 Siantan i. Indon.
45 D2 Siapa r. Venez.
94 C4 Siargao i. Phil.
94 B5 Siasi i. Phil.
94 B5 Siasi Phil.
94 B5 Siaton Phil.
55 S9 Šiauliai Lith.
105 J1 Sibasa S. Africa
94 B4 Sibay i. Phil.
105 K3 Sibayi, Lake l. S. Africa
119 B5 Sibbald, C. c. Ant.
66 F3 Šibenik Croatia
92 B7 Siberut i. Indon.
84 A3 Sibi Pak.
102 D3 Sibiloi National Park nat. park Kenya
102 B4 Sibiti Congo
67 L2 Sibiu Romania
92 B6 Sibolga Indon.
95 A5 Siborongborong Indon.
85 H4 Sibsagar India
92 Sibu Malaysia
94 B5 Sibuco Phil.
94 B5 Sibuguey r. Phil.
94 B5 Sibuguey Bay b. Phil.
102 B3 Sibut C.A.R.
94 A5 Sibutu i. Phil.

94 A5 Sibutu Passage chan. Phil.
94 B3 Sibuyan i. Phil.
94 B3 Sibuyan Sea sea Phil.
94 B2 Sicapoo mt Phil.
89 B4 Sichuan div. China
89 B4 Sichuan Pendi basin China
64 G5 Sicié, Cap c. France
Sicilia i. see Sicily
66 E6 Sicilian Channel chan. Italy/Tunisia
101 D1 Sicilian Channel chan. Italy/Tunisia
66 E6 Sicily i. Italy
42 D6 Sicuani Peru
84 C5 Siddhapur India
67 M7 Sideros, Akra pt Greece
104 E6 Sidesaviwa S. Africa
65 H5 Sidi Aïssa Alg.
65 G4 Sidi Ali Alg.
100 B1 Sidi Bel Abbès Alg.
66 C7 Sidi Bouzid Tunisia
66 D7 Sidi El Hani, Sebkhet de salt pan Tunisia
100 A2 Sidi Ifni Morocco
100 B1 Sidi Kacem Morocco
95 A5 Sidikalang Indon.
57 E4 Sidlaw Hills h. U.K.
119 A4 Sidley, Mt mt. Ant.
59 D7 Sidmouth U.K.
20 D5 Sidney Can.
24 F2 Sidney MT U.S.A.
26 C3 Sidney NE U.S.A.
33 F3 Sidney NY U.S.A.
32 A4 Sidney OH U.S.A.
29 D5 Sidney Lanier, L. l. U.S.A.
92 Sidoarjo Indon.
85 H5 Sidoktaya Myanmar
80 E5 Sidon Lebanon
68 G3 Sidorovo Rus. Fed.
46 A3 Sidrolândia Brazil
105 J3 Sidvokodvo Swaziland
64 F5 Sié, Col de pass France
63 L4 Siedlce Pol.
61 F4 Sieg r. Ger.
62 D5 Siegen Ger.
95 B2 Siĕmréab Cambodia
66 D3 Siena Italy
63 J5 Sieradz Pol.
27 B6 Sierra Blanca U.S.A.
47 C4 Sierra Colorada Arg.
35 F5 Sierra Estrella mts U.S.A.
47 D4 Sierra Grande Arg.
96 Sierra Leone country Africa
12 H5 Sierra Leone Basin sea feature Atlantic Ocean
12 H5 Sierra Leone Rise sea feature Atlantic Ocean
36 C4 Sierra Madre del Sur mts Mex.
34 C4 Sierra Madre Mts mts U.S.A.
36 C3 Sierra Madre Occidental mts Mex.
36 D3 Sierra Madre Oriental mts Mex.
34 B1 Sierra Nevada mts U.S.A.
45 B2 Sierra Nevada de Santa Marta, Parque Nacional nat. park Col.
45 D2 Sierra Nevada, Parque Nacional nat. park Venez.
47 D4 Sierra, Punta pt Arg.
34 B2 Sierraville U.S.A.
35 G6 Sierra Vista U.S.A.
62 C7 Sierre Switz.
54 T5 Sievi Fin.
89 C6 Sifang Ling mts China
67 L6 Sifnos i. Greece
65 F5 Sig Alg.
35 L7 Sighetu Marmaţiei Romania
63 L2 Sighişoara Romania
95 Siglap Sing.
92 B5 Sigli Indon.
54 D3 Siglufjörður Iceland
94 B4 Sigma Phil.
62 D6 Sigmaringen Ger.
61 E4 Signal de Botrange h. Belgium
35 E5 Signal Peak summit U.S.A.
119 B1 Signy U.K. Base Ant.
30 B5 Sigourney U.S.A.
67 L5 Sigri, Akra pt Greece
65 E2 Sigüenza Spain
100 B3 Siguiri Guinea
55 T8 Sigulda Latvia
95 A3 Sihanoukville Cambodia
88 F3 Sihong China
84 E5 Sihora India
89 D6 Sihui China
54 T4 Siikajoki Fin.
54 U5 Siilinjärvi Fin.
81 H3 Siirt Turkey
92 C7 Sijunjung Indon.
84 B5 Sika India
20 E3 Sikanni Chief r. Can.
20 E3 Sikanni Chief Can.
84 B2 Sikaram mt Afgh.
100 B3 Sikasso Mali
27 F4 Sikeston U.S.A.
87 P2 Sikhote-Alin' mts Rus. Fed.
67 L6 Sikinos i. Greece
85 G4 Sikkim div. India
54 P4 Siksjö Sweden
94 A5 Sikuati Malaysia
65 C1 Sil r. Spain
94 C4 Silago Phil.

55 S9 Šilalė Lith.
36 D4 Silao Mex.
94 B4 Silay Phil.
85 H4 Silchar India
80 B1 Şile Turkey
84 E3 Silgarhi Nepal
66 C6 Siliana Tunisia
80 D3 Silifke Turkey
85 G3 Siling Co salt l. China
Silistat see Bozkır
67 M2 Silistra Bulg.
80 B1 Silivri Turkey
55 O6 Siljan l. Sweden
55 L8 Silkeborg Denmark
116 B1 Silkwood Austr.
55 U7 Sillamäe Estonia
84 C5 Sillod India
105 J3 Silobela S. Africa
85 G3 Silong China
27 E6 Silsbee U.S.A.
54 U3 Siltaharju Fin.
55 R9 Šilutė Lith.
81 H2 Silvan Turkey
84 C5 Silvassa India
30 E2 Silver Bay U.S.A.
25 E5 Silver City U.S.A.
30 C1 Silver Islet Can.
34 C4 Silver Lake l. CA U.S.A.
30 D2 Silver Lake l. MI U.S.A.
24 B3 Silver Lake U.S.A.
60 C5 Silvermine Mts h.
  Rep. of Ireland
34 D3 Silver Peak Range mts
  U.S.A.
32 E5 Silver Spring U.S.A.
34 C2 Silver Springs U.S.A.
114 D3 Silverton Austr.
59 D7 Silverton U.K.
31 F3 Silver Water Can.
92 E6 Simanggang Malaysia
94 B3 Simara i. Phil.
31 H2 Simard, Lac l. Can.
81 L5 Sīmareh r. Iran
85 F4 Simaria India
80 B2 Simav Turkey
80 B2 Simav Dağları mts Turkey
102 C3 Simba Zaire
  Simbirsk see Ul'yanovsk
31 G4 Simcoe Can.
31 H3 Simcoe, Lake l. Can.
85 F5 Simdega India
102 D2 Simēn Mountains mts
  Eth.
92 B6 Simeuluë i. Indon.
69 E6 Simferopol' Ukr.
85 E3 Simikot Nepal
45 B3 Simiti Col.
34 C4 Simi Valley U.S.A.
25 F4 Simla U.S.A.
63 L7 Simleu Silvaniei Romania
61 F5 Simmern (Hunsrück) Ger.
34 C4 Simmler U.S.A.
35 F4 Simmons U.S.A.
29 C7 Simms Bahamas
54 U3 Simojärvi l. Fin.
20 F4 Simonette r. Can.
21 J4 Simonhouse Can.
62 D7 Simplon Pass pass Switz.
113 G5 Simpson Desert des.
  Austr.
113 G5 Simpson Desert National
  Park nat. park Austr.
30 D1 Simpson I. i. Can.
34 D2 Simpson Park Mts mts
  U.S.A.
55 O9 Simrishamn Sweden
94 A5 Simunul i. Phil.
77 R5 Simushir, O. i. Rus. Fed.
95 A5 Sinabung volc. Indon.
78 C4 Sinai pen. Egypt
61 C5 Sinai, Mont h. France
66 D3 Sinalunga Italy
89 C5 Sinan China
85 H5 Sinbyugyun Myanmar
80 F2 Sincan Turkey
45 B2 Sincé Col.
45 B2 Sincelejo Col.
29 D5 Sinclair, L. l. U.S.A.
20 E4 Sinclair Mills Can.
104 B2 Sinclair Mine Namibia
57 E2 Sinclair's Bay b. U.K.
84 D4 Sind r. India
94 B4 Sindañgan Phil.
92 □ Sindangbarang Indon.
84 B4 Sindari India
62 D6 Sindelfingen Ger.
84 B4 Sindh div. Pak.
80 B2 Sındırgı Turkey
84 D6 Sindkhed India
84 C5 Sindkheda India
68 J2 Sindor Rus. Fed.
85 F5 Sindri India
84 B3 Sind Sagar Doab
  lowland Pak.
68 J2 Sinegor'ye Rus. Fed.
67 M4 Sinekçi Turkey
65 B4 Sines Port.
65 B4 Sines, Cabo de pt Port.
54 T3 Sinettä Fin.
100 B4 Sinfra Côte d'Ivoire
101 F3 Singa Sudan
84 E3 Singahi India
84 D2 Singa Pass pass India
70 Singapore country Asia
95 B5 Singapore Sing.
95 B5 Singapore, Strait of
  chan. Indon./Sing.
92 □ Singaraja Indon.
95 B2 Sing Buri Thai.
31 D7 Singhampton Can.
102 D4 Singida Tanz.
93 G7 Singkang Indon.
92 D6 Singkawang Indon.
95 A5 Singkil Indon.

115 J4 Singleton Austr.
  Singora see Songkhla
66 C4 Siniscola Sardinia Italy
66 G3 Sinj Croatia
93 G8 Sinjai Indon.
81 H3 Sinjār Iraq
81 H3 Sinjār, Jabal mt Iraq
81 K3 Sīnjī Iran
101 F3 Sinkat Sudan
  Sinkiang Uighur Aut.
  Region div. see Xinjiang
  Uygur Zizhiqu
43 H2 Sinnamary Fr. Guiana
  Sinneh see Sanandaj
67 N2 Sinoie, Lacul lag.
  Romania
69 E7 Sinop Turkey
27 D6 Sinton U.S.A.
45 B2 Sinú r. Col.
87 M3 Sinŭiju N. Korea
94 B5 Siocon Phil.
62 J7 Siófok Hungary
62 C7 Sion Switz.
60 D3 Sion Mills U.K.
26 D3 Sioux Center U.S.A.
26 D3 Sioux City U.S.A.
26 D3 Sioux Falls U.S.A.
22 B3 Sioux Lookout Can.
94 B4 Sipalay Phil.
87 M3 Siping China
21 K3 Sipiwesk Can.
21 K3 Sipiwesk L. l. Can.
84 C5 Sipra r. India
29 C5 Sipsey r. U.S.A.
92 B7 Sipura i. Indon.
37 H6 Siquia r. Nic.
94 B4 Siquijor i. Phil.
94 B4 Siquijor Phil.
84 B5 Sir r. Pak.
83 E8 Sira India
55 K7 Sira r. Norway
  Siracusa see Syracuse
20 E4 Sir Alexander, Mt mt.
  Can.
81 G1 Şiran Turkey
81 M3 Sīrdān Iran
113 G3 Sir Edward Pellew Group
  is Austr.
30 A3 Siren U.S.A.
95 B1 Siri Kit Dam dam Thai.
84 B3 Siritoi r. Pak.
20 D2 Sir James McBrien, Mt
  mt. Can.
114 B5 Sir Joseph Bank's Group
  is Austr.
84 A4 Sirmour India
81 J3 Şırnak Turkey
82 D6 Sirohi India
84 D4 Sironj India
34 C4 Sirretta Peak summit
  U.S.A.
84 C3 Sirsa Haryana India
85 E4 Sirsa Uttar Pradesh India
20 F4 Sir Sanford, Mt mt. Can.
84 D3 Sirsi India
81 J2 Sīrte Libya
101 D1 Sirte, Gulf of g. Libya
55 T9 Širvintos Lith.
81 K4 Sīrwān r. Iran
20 F4 Sir Wilfred Laurier, Mt
  mt. Can.
66 G2 Sisak Croatia
95 Sisaket Thai.
104 E3 Sishen S. Africa
81 L2 Sisian Armenia
30 C2 Siskiwit Bay b. U.S.A.
95 B2 Sisŏphŏn Cambodia
34 B4 Sisquoc r. U.S.A.
26 D2 Sisseton U.S.A.
33 K1 Sisson Branch Reservoir
  resr Can.
79 J3 Sīstan, Daryācheh-ye
  marsh Afgh.
115 F8 Sisters Beach Austr.
84 C5 Sitamau India
84 E4 Sitapur India
67 M7 Siteia Greece
105 J3 Siteki Swaziland
67 K4 Sithonia pen. Greece
46 C1 Sítio da Abadia Brazil
46 D1 Sítio do Mato Brazil
20 B3 Sitka U.S.A.
84 B3 Sitpur Pak.
61 D4 Sittard Neth.
85 H4 Sittaung Myanmar
59 H6 Sittingbourne U.K.
83 H6 Sittwe Myanmar
89 □ Siu A Chau i. Hong Kong
  China
85 F5 Siuri India
80 F5 Sivas Turkey
80 B2 Sivaslı Turkey
81 G3 Siverek Turkey
81 G1 Sivrice Turkey
80 C2 Sivrihisar Turkey
61 C4 Sivry Belgium
105 H3 Sivukile S. Africa
78 B4 Siwa Egypt
84 D3 Siwalik Range mts
  India/Nepal
85 E4 Siwan India
84 C4 Siwana India
64 G5 Six-Fours-les-Plages
  France
88 E3 Si Xian China
30 E4 Six Lakes U.S.A.
59 C4 Sixmilecross U.K.
105 H2 Siyabuswa S. Africa
88 F3 Siyang China
81 M1 Siyäzän Azer.
88 C1 Siyitang China
88 D1 Siziwang Qi China

  Sjælland i. see Zealand
67 J3 Sjenica Yugo.
55 N9 Sjöbo Sweden
54 P2 Sjøvegan Norway
45 L2 S. Juan r. Venez.
69 E6 Skadovs'k Ukr.
54 E4 Skaftafell National Park
  nat. park Iceland
54 E5 Skaftárós est. Iceland
54 D3 Skagafjörður in. Iceland
55 M8 Skagen Denmark
55 L8 Skagerrak str.
  Denmark/Norway
24 B1 Skagit r. Can./U.S.A.
20 B3 Skagway U.S.A.
54 T1 Skaidi Norway
54 P2 Skaland Norway
54 O4 Skalmodal Sweden
55 L8 Skanderborg Denmark
33 K3 Skaneateles Lake l.
  U.S.A.
30 C2 Skanee U.S.A.
67 L5 Skantzoura i. Greece
55 N7 Skara Sweden
79 M2 Skardu Jammu and
  Kashmir
55 R7 Skargadshavets
  Nationalpark nat. park
  Fin.
55 M6 Skarnes Norway
63 K5 Skarżysko-Kamienna Pol.
54 R3 Skaulo Sweden
63 J6 Skawina Pol.
20 D3 Skeena r. Can.
20 D3 Skeena Mountains mts
  Can.
59 H4 Skegness U.K.
54 R4 Skellefteå Sweden
54 Q4 Skellefteälven r.
  Sweden
54 R4 Skelleftehamn Sweden
60 A6 Skellig Rocks is
  Rep. of Ireland
58 E4 Skelmersdale U.K.
60 E4 Skerries Rep. of Ireland
55 M7 Ski Norway
67 K5 Skiathos i. Greece
60 B6 Skibbereen
  Rep. of Ireland
54 R2 Skibotn Norway
58 D3 Skiddaw mt U.K.
55 L7 Skien Norway
63 K5 Skierniewice Pol.
100 C1 Skikda Alg.
58 G4 Skipsea U.K.
114 E6 Skipton Austr.
58 E4 Skipton U.K.
55 L8 Skive Denmark
54 D3 Skjálfandafljót r. Iceland
55 L9 Skjern Denmark
55 K6 Skjolden Norway
54 K5 Skodje Norway
54 T2 Skoganvarre Norway
60 F6 Skokholm Island i. Wales
30 D4 Skokie U.S.A.
59 B6 Skomer Island i. U.K.
67 K5 Skopelos i. Greece
68 F4 Skopin Rus. Fed.
67 J4 Skopje Macedonia
69 F5 Skorodnoye Rus. Fed.
55 N7 Skövde Sweden
87 M1 Skovorodino Rus. Fed.
33 J2 Skowhegan U.S.A.
55 S8 Skrunda Latvia
20 B2 Skukum, Mt mt. Can.
105 J2 Skukuza S. Africa
34 D3 Skull Peak summit U.S.A.
30 B5 Skunk r. U.S.A.
55 R8 Skuodas Lith.
55 N9 Skurup Sweden
55 P6 Skutskär Sweden
69 D5 Skvyra Ukr.
57 B3 Skye i. U.K.
67 L5 Skyros Greece
67 L5 Skyros i. Greece
55 M9 Slagelse Denmark
54 Q4 Slagnäs Sweden
92 □ Slamet, Gunung volc.
  Indon.
60 E4 Slane Rep. of Ireland
60 E5 Slaney r. Rep. of Ireland
68 D3 Slantsy Rus. Fed.
69 G5 Slashchevskaya Rus. Fed.
116 B2 Slashers Reefs rf Austr.
30 D1 Slate Is is Can.
66 D1 Slatina Croatia
67 L2 Slatina Romania
21 G2 Slave r. Can.
100 C4 Slave Coast coastal area
  Africa
20 G3 Slave Lake Can.
63 O2 Slavkovichi Rus. Fed.
67 H2 Slavonija reg. Croatia
67 H2 Slavonski Brod Croatia
69 C5 Slavuta Ukr.
69 D5 Slavutych Ukr.
69 F6 Slavyansk-na-Kubani
  Rus. Fed.
68 D4 Slawharad Belarus
62 H3 Sławno Pol.
59 G4 Sleaford U.K.
114 A5 Sleaford B. b. Austr.
60 A5 Slea Head hd Rep. of
  Ireland
57 C3 Sleat pen. U.K.
57 C3 Sleat, Sound of chan.
  U.K.
22 E2 Sleeper Islands is Can.
30 D3 Sleeping Bear Dunes
  National Seashore res.
  U.S.A.
30 D3 Sleeping Bear Pt pt
  U.S.A.
29 E7 Snap Pt pt Bahamas
69 H7 Sleptsovskaya Rus. Fed.

119 C3 Slessor Glacier gl. Ant.
27 F6 Slidell U.S.A.
60 A5 Slievanea h.
  Rep. of Ireland
60 D3 Slieve Anierin h.
  Rep. of Ireland
60 D5 Slieveardagh Hills h.
  Rep. of Ireland
60 C4 Slieve Aughty Mts h.
  Rep. of Ireland
60 D3 Slieve Beagh h.
  Rep. of Ireland/U.K.
60 C5 Slieve Bernagh h.
  Rep. of Ireland
60 D5 Slieve Bloom Mts h.
  Rep. of Ireland
60 B5 Slievecallan h.
  Rep. of Ireland
60 B3 Slieve Car h.
  Rep. of Ireland
60 F3 Slieve Donard h. U.K.
60 B4 Slieve Elva h.
  Rep. of Ireland
60 B4 Slieve Gamph h.
  Rep. of Ireland
60 C3 Slieve League h.
  Rep. of Ireland
60 A5 Slieve Mish Mts h.
  Rep. of Ireland
60 A6 Slieve Miskish Mts h.
  Rep. of Ireland
60 A3 Slieve More h.
  Rep. of Ireland
60 D4 Slieve na Calliagh h.
  Rep. of Ireland
60 D5 Slievenamon h.
  Rep. of Ireland
60 D2 Slieve Snaght mt
  Rep. of Ireland
57 B3 Sligachan U.K.
60 C3 Sligo Rep. of Ireland
60 C3 Sligo Bay b.
  Rep. of Ireland
55 Q8 Slite Sweden
67 M3 Sliven Bulg.
68 H2 Sloboda Rus. Fed.
68 J2 Slobodchikovo Rus. Fed.
67 M2 Slobozia Romania
20 F5 Slocan Can.
68 C4 Slonim Belarus
61 D2 Slotermeer l. Neth.
111 F2 Slot, The chan.
  Solomon Is
59 G6 Slough U.K.
54 P4 Slussfors Sweden
68 C4 Slutsk Belarus
60 A4 Slyne Head hd
  Rep. of Ireland
86 H1 Slyudyanka Rus. Fed.
33 J3 Small Pt pt U.S.A.
23 H3 Smallwood Reservoir
  resr Can.
68 C4 Smalyavichy Belarus
63 N3 Smarhon' Belarus
104 E5 Smartt Syndicate Dam
  resr S. Africa
21 J4 Smeaton Can.
67 J2 Smederevo Yugo.
67 J2 Smederevska Palanka
  Yugo.
32 D4 Smethport U.S.A.
69 D5 Smila Ukr.
55 T8 Smiltene Latvia
20 G3 Smith Can.
34 C2 Smith r. U.S.A.
32 C6 Smith r. U.S.A.
20 D4 Smithers Can.
105 G5 Smithfield S. Africa
29 E5 Smithfield NC U.S.A.
24 E3 Smithfield UT U.S.A.
33 E5 Smith I. i. MD U.S.A.
33 F6 Smith I. i. VA U.S.A.
32 D6 Smith Mountain Lake l.
  U.S.A.
20 D3 Smith River Can.
31 J3 Smiths Falls Can.
115 F8 Smithton Austr.
34 C1 Smoke Creek Desert des.
  U.S.A.
20 F4 Smoky r. U.S.A.
26 C4 Smoky r. U.S.A.
115 K3 Smoky C. hd Austr.
22 D4 Smoky Falls Can.
26 D4 Smoky Hills h. U.S.A.
20 G4 Smoky Lake Can.
54 K5 Smøla i. Norway
68 E4 Smolensk Rus. Fed.
68 E4 Smolenskaya Oblast' div.
  Rus. Fed.
67 L4 Smolyan Bulg.
22 D4 Smooth Rock Falls Can.
22 C3 Smoothrock L. l. Can.
21 H4 Smoothstone Lake l.
  Can.
54 T1 Smørfjord Norway
33 F5 Smyrna U.S.A.
29 C5 Smyrna GA U.S.A.
32 C4 Smyrna OH U.S.A.
33 J1 Smyrna TN U.S.A.
54 F4 Snæfell mt Iceland
58 C3 Snaefell h. U.K.
20 A2 Snag Can.
24 D3 Snake r. U.S.A.
35 F2 Snake Range mts U.S.A.
24 D3 Snake River Plain plain
  U.S.A.
29 E7 Snap Pt pt Bahamas
20 G2 Snare Lake Can.
111 G6 Snares Is is N.Z.

54 N4 Snasa Norway
61 D1 Sneek Neth.
61 D1 Sneekermeer l. Neth.
60 B6 Sneem Rep. of Ireland
104 F6 Sneeuberg mts S. Africa
23 H3 Snegamook Lake l. Can.
55 H5 Snettisham U.K.
76 K3 Snezhnogorsk Rus. Fed.
66 F2 Snežnik mt. Slovenia
63 K4 Śniardwy, Jezioro l. Pol.
69 E6 Snihurivka Ukr.
57 B3 Snizort, Loch b. U.K.
24 B2 Snohomish U.S.A.
24 B2 Snoqualmie Pass pass
  U.S.A.
54 N3 Snøtinden mt. Norway
21 J2 Snowbird Lake l. Can.
59 C4 Snowdon mt. U.K.
59 D5 Snowdonia National
  Park U.K.
35 G4 Snowflake U.S.A.
33 F5 Snow Hill MD U.S.A.
29 E5 Snow Hill NC U.S.A.
21 J4 Snow Lake Can.
114 C4 Snowtown Austr.
24 D3 Snowville U.S.A.
115 H6 Snowy r. Austr.
115 H6 Snowy Mts mts Austr.
115 G9 Snug Austr.
23 J3 Snug Harbour Nfld Can.
31 G3 Snug Harbour Ont. Can.
95 C2 Snuŏl Cambodia
27 D5 Snyder OK U.S.A.
27 C5 Snyder TX U.S.A.
103 E5 Soalala Madag.
103 E5 Soanierana-Ivongo
  Madag.
90 A6 Soan kundo i. S. Korea
45 B3 Soata Col.
57 B3 Soay i. U.K.
101 F4 Sobat r. Sudan
93 L7 Sobger r. Indon.
90 C7 Sobo-san mt. Japan
43 K6 Sobradinho, Barragem
  de resr Brazil
43 K4 Sobral Brazil
69 F7 Sochi Rus. Fed.
109 Society Islands is Pac. Oc.
46 C3 Socorro Brazil
45 B3 Socorro Col.
25 F5 Socorro U.S.A.
36 B5 Socorro, I. i. Mex.
79 G7 Socotra i. Yemen
95 C3 Soc Trăng Vietnam
65 E3 Socuéllamos Spain
34 D4 Soda Lake l. U.S.A.
54 U3 Sodankylä Fin.
84 D2 Soda Plains plain
  China/Jammu and Kashmir
24 E3 Soda Springs U.S.A.
55 P6 Söderhamn Sweden
55 P7 Söderköping Sweden
55 P7 Södertälje Sweden
101 E3 Sodiri Sudan
102 D3 Sodo Eth.
55 Q6 Södra Kvarken str.
  Fin./Sweden
105 H1 Soekmekaar S. Africa
61 D3 Soerendonk Neth.
115 H4 Sofala Austr.
67 K3 Sofia Bulg.
  Sofiya see Sofia
54 W4 Sofporog Rus. Fed.
45 B3 Sogamoso Col.
81 G1 Soğanlı Dağları mts
  Turkey
55 K7 Søgne Norway
55 J6 Sognefjorden in.
  Norway
94 C4 Sogod Phil.
88 A1 Sogo Nur l. China
88 H2 Sogra Rus. Fed.
88 B4 Sogruma China
80 C1 Söğüt Turkey
85 H1 Sog Xian China
78 C4 Sohâg Egypt
84 D5 Sohagpur India
59 H5 Soham U.K.
84 B2 Sohan r. Pak.
111 F2 Sohano P.N.G.
85 E5 Sohela India
84 D3 Sohna India
61 C4 Soignies Belgium
54 T5 Soini Fin.
64 F2 Soissons France
90 D6 Sōja Japan
84 C4 Sojat India
94 B4 Sojoton Point pt Phil.
69 C5 Sokal' Ukr.
67 M6 Söke Turkey
69 G7 Sokhumi Georgia
100 C4 Sokodé Togo
89 □ Soko Islands is
  Hong Kong China
68 G3 Sokol Rus. Fed.
63 L4 Sokółka Pol.
100 B3 Sokolo Mali
63 L4 Sokołów Podlaski Pol.
100 C3 Sokoto Nigeria
100 C3 Sokoto r. Nigeria
69 D5 Sokyryany Ukr.
84 D3 Solan India
117 A7 Solander I. i. N.Z.
83 E7 Solapur India
45 B2 Soledad Col.
34 B3 Soledad U.S.A.
45 E2 Soledad Venez.
69 G6 Solenoye Rus. Fed.
59 F7 Solent, The str. U.K.
54 N3 Solfjellsjøen Norway
81 H2 Solhan Turkey
68 H2 Soligalich Rus. Fed.
59 F5 Solihull U.K.
76 G4 Solikamsk Rus. Fed.

76 G4 Sol'-Iletsk Rus. Fed.
61 F3 Solingen Ger.
104 A1 Solitaire Namibia
81 M1 Şollar Azer.
54 P5 Sollefteå Sweden
68 F3 Solnechnogorsk Rus. Fed.
92 C7 Solok Indon.
106 Solomon Islands country
  Pac. Oc.
110 F2 Solomon Sea sea
  P.N.G./Solomon Is
30 B2 Solon Springs U.S.A.
93 G8 Solor, Kepulauan is
  Indon.
62 C7 Solothurn Switz.
68 E1 Solovetskiye Ostrova is
  Rus. Fed.
68 H3 Solovetskoye Rus. Fed.
66 G3 Šolta i. Croatia
68 D3 Sol'tsy Rus. Fed.
33 E3 Solvay U.S.A.
55 O8 Sölvesborg Sweden
57 E6 Solway Firth est. U.K.
103 C5 Solwezi Zambia
91 H5 Sōma Japan
80 A2 Soma Turkey
96 Somalia country Africa
13 Somali Basin sea feature
  Indian Ocean
103 C4 Sombo Angola
67 H2 Sombor Yugo.
84 C4 Somdari India
33 J2 Somerest Junction U.S.A.
55 S6 Somero Fin.
28 C4 Somerset KY U.S.A.
30 E4 Somerset MI U.S.A.
32 D5 Somerset PA U.S.A.
105 F6 Somerset East S. Africa
18 Somerset Island i. Can.
116 B4 Somerset, L. l. Austr.
33 G3 Somerset Reservoir resr
  U.S.A.
104 C7 Somerset West S. Africa
33 H3 Somersworth U.S.A.
27 D6 Somerville Res. resr
  U.S.A.
55 O7 Sommen l. Sweden
23 G3 Sommet, Lac du l. Can.
84 B5 Somnath India
30 C5 Somonauk U.S.A.
47 C4 Somuncurá, Mesa
  Volcánica de plat. Arg.
85 F4 Son r. India
85 F5 Sonamukhi India
85 G5 Sonamura India
85 E5 Sonapur India
84 D4 Sonar r. India
85 H4 Sonari India
68 E2 Sondaly Rus. Fed.
55 L9 Sønderborg Denmark
62 E5 Sonderhausen Ger.
66 C1 Sondrio Italy
84 B5 Songad India
88 B5 Songbu China
95 D2 Sông Cau Vietnam
95 C1 Song Con r. Vietnam
84 D4 Sonar r. India
84 H4 Sonari India
89 B6 Sông Đa r. Vietnam
95 D2 Sông Đa Răng r. Vietnam
103 D5 Songea Tanz.
95 C3 Sông Hâu Giang r.
  Vietnam
88 F4 Songjiang China
89 C4 Songkan China
95 B4 Songkhla Thai.
89 C6 Sông Ky Cung r. Vietnam
87 M2 Songling China
88 F1 Song Ling mts China
89 B6 Sông Ma r. Laos/Vietnam
95 C1 Sông Ngan Sau r.
  Vietnam
102 B4 Songo Angola
103 D5 Songo Moz.
88 B3 Songpan China
95 C3 Sông Saigon r. China
85 G4 Songsak India
89 C4 Songtao China
89 F5 Songxi China
88 D3 Song Xian China
89 D4 Songzi China
95 D2 Sơn Ha Vietnam
88 D1 Sonid Youqi China
88 D1 Sonid Zuoqi China
84 D3 Sonīpat India
54 U5 Sonkajärvi Fin.
89 B6 Sơn La Vietnam
46 D2 Sono r. Minas Gerais
  Brazil
43 J6 Sono r. Tocantins Brazil
35 F6 Sonoita r. Mex.
35 G6 Sonoita U.S.A.
36 B3 Sonora r. Mex.
34 B3 Sonora CA U.S.A.
27 C6 Sonora TX U.S.A.
35 F6 Sonoyta Mex.
81 L4 Sonqor Iran
45 B3 Sonsón Col.
36 G6 Sonsonate El Salvador
89 B6 Sơn Tây Vietnam
105 H5 Sonwabile S. Africa
47 F1 Sopas r. Uru.
77 S4 Sopka Shiveluch mt
  Rus. Fed.
101 E4 Sopo watercourse Sudan
67 L3 Sopot Bulg.
63 J3 Sopot Pol.
62 H7 Sopron Hungary
82 D4 Sopur Jammu and
  Kashmir
66 E4 Sora Italy
85 F6 Sorada India
55 P5 Soråker Sweden
22 F4 Sorel Can.
115 G9 Sorell Austr.

115 G9 Sorell L. l. Austr.
80 E2 Sorgun Turkey
65 E2 Soria Spain
76 C2 Sørkappøya i. Svalbard
54 N4 Sørli Norway
85 F5 Soro India
69 D5 Soroca Moldova
46 E4 Sorocaba Brazil
76 G4 Sorochinsk Rus. Fed.
93 J7 Sorong Indon.
102 D3 Soroti Uganda
54 S1 Sørøya i. Norway
65 B3 Sorraia r. Port.
54 Q2 Sorreisa Norway
114 F7 Sorrento Italy
103 B6 Sorris Sorris Namibia
119 D3 Sør-Rondane mts Ant.
54 P4 Sorsele Sweden
94 C3 Sorsogon Phil.
68 D2 Sortavala Rus. Fed.
54 O2 Sortland Norway
68 J2 Sortopolovskaya Rus. Fed.
68 J3 Sorvizhi Rus. Fed.
105 H2 Soshanguve S. Africa
69 F4 Sosna r. Rus. Fed.
47 C2 Sosneado mt Arg.
68 K2 Sosnogorsk Rus. Fed.
68 H2 Sosnovka Archangel. Rus. Fed.
68 G4 Sosnovka Tambov. Rus. Fed.
76 F3 Sosnovka Rus. Fed.
87 K1 Sosnovo-Ozerskoye Rus. Fed.
54 X4 Sosnovyy Rus. Fed.
55 V7 Sosnovyy Bor Rus. Fed.
63 J5 Sosnowice Pol.
69 F6 Sosyka r. Rus. Fed.
45 A4 Sotara, Volcán volc. Col.
54 V4 Sotkamo Fin.
47 D1 Soto Arg.
36 E4 Soto la Marina Mex.
102 B3 Souanké Congo
100 B4 Soubré Côte d'Ivoire
33 F4 Souderton U.S.A.
67 M4 Soufli Greece
64 E4 Souillac France
100 C1 Souk Ahras Alg.
Sŏul see Seoul
64 D5 Soulom France
65 H4 Sour el Ghozlane Alg.
Soûr see Tyre
21 J5 Souris Man. Can.
23 H4 Souris P.E.I. Can.
21 J5 Souris r. Can./U.S.A.
43 L5 Sousa Brazil
100 D1 Sousse Tunisia
64 D5 Soustons France
78 F7 South div. Yemen
96 South Africa, Republic of country Africa
31 G3 Southampton Can.
59 F7 Southampton U.K.
33 G4 Southampton U.S.A.
21 M2 Southampton Island i. Can.
92 A4 South Andaman i. Andaman and Nicobar Is
32 E6 South Anna r. U.S.A.
59 F4 South Anston U.K.
23 H2 South Aulatsivik Island i. Can.
113 F5 South Australia div. Austr.
13 N6 South Australian Basin sea feature Indian Ocean
27 C5 Southaven U.S.A.
25 F5 South Baldy mt. U.S.A.
58 F3 South Bank U.K.
32 B4 South Bass I. i. U.S.A.
21 N2 South Bay b. Can.
31 F3 South Baymouth Can.
30 D5 South Bend IN U.S.A.
24 B2 South Bend WA U.S.A.
29 E7 South Bight chan. Bahamas
32 D6 South Boston U.S.A.
117 D5 Southbridge N.Z.
33 G3 Southbridge U.S.A.
South Cape c. see Ka Lae
29 D5 South Carolina div. U.S.A.
33 J2 South China U.S.A.
92 E4 South China Sea sea Pac. Oc.
26 C2 South Dakota div. U.S.A.
33 G3 South Deerfield U.S.A.
59 G7 South Downs h. U.K.
105 F2 South East div. Botswana
115 G9 South East Cape c. Tas. Austr.
115 G7 South East Cape c. Vic. Austr.
15 N10 South-East Pacific Basin sea feature Pac. Oc.
21 J3 Southend Can.
57 C5 Southend U.K.
59 H6 Southend-on-Sea U.K.
30 A5 South English U.S.A.
117 C5 Southern Alps mts N.Z.
112 C6 Southern Cross Austr.
21 K3 Southern Indian Lake l. Can.
101 E4 Southern National Park nat. park Sudan
119 A1 Southern Ocean ocean
29 E5 Southern Pines U.S.A.
57 D5 Southern Uplands reg. U.K.
57 F4 South Esk r. U.K.
30 B6 South Fabius r. U.S.A.
25 F4 South Fork U.S.A.

34 A2 South Fork Eel r. U.S.A.
34 C4 South Fork Kern r. U.S.A.
32 D5 South Fork South Branch r. U.S.A.
30 E3 South Fox I. i. U.S.A.
119 C5 South Geomagnetic Pole Ant.
57 H4 South Harris i. U.K.
85 G5 South Hatia I. i. Bangl.
30 D4 South Haven U.S.A.
21 K2 South Henik Lake l. Can.
33 G2 South Hero U.S.A.
32 D6 South Hill U.S.A.
14 E4 South Honshu Ridge sea feature Pac. Oc.
21 K3 South Indian Lake Can.
33 G4 Southington U.S.A.
117 C6 South Island i. N.Z.
94 A4 South Islet rf Phil.
85 F5 South Koel r. India
34 B2 South Lake Tahoe U.S.A.
103 D5 South Luangwa National Park nat. park Zambia
119 B6 South Magnetic Pole Ant.
30 D3 South Manitou I. i. U.S.A.
29 D7 South Miami U.S.A.
59 H6 Southminster U.K.
21 J4 South Moose L. l. Can.
32 E5 South Mts i. U.S.A.
20 D2 South Nahanni r. Can.
57 South Nesting Bay b. U.K.
119 B1 South Orkney Is is Atlantic Ocean
33 H4 South Paris U.S.A.
24 G3 South Platte r. U.S.A.
119 B4 South Pole Ant.
31 G1 South Porcupine Can.
115 K1 Southport Austr.
58 F2 Southport U.K.
33 H3 South Portland U.S.A.
31 H3 South River Can.
57 F2 South Ronaldsay i. U.K.
33 G3 South Royalton U.S.A.
105 J5 South Sand Bluff pt S. Africa
119 C1 South Sandwich Islands is Atlantic Ocean
12 H9 South Sandwich Trench sea feature Atlantic Ocean
21 H4 South Saskatchewan r. Can.
21 K3 South Seal r. Can.
119 B2 South Shetland Is is Ant.
58 F2 South Shields U.K.
58 G4 South Skirlaugh U.K.
30 A5 South Sioux City U.S.A.
117 E3 South Taranaki Bight b. N.Z.
35 G2 South Tent summit U.S.A.
85 E4 South Tons r. India
22 E3 South Twin I. i. Can.
58 E3 South Tyne r. U.K.
57 A3 South Uist i. U.K.
115 G9 South West C. hd Tas. Austr.
117 A7 South West Cape c. N.Z.
13 H6 South-West Indian Ridge sea feature Indian Ocean
116 C1 South West Island i. Coral Sea Is Terr.
115 G9 South West Nat. Park nat. park Austr.
15 O7 South-West Peru Ridge sea feature Pac. Oc.
115 K3 South West Rocks Austr.
30 E5 South Whitley U.S.A.
33 H3 South Windham U.S.A.
59 J5 Southwold U.K.
105 H1 Soutpansberg mts S. Africa
66 G6 Soverato Italy
68 B4 Sovetsk Kaliningrad. Rus. Fed.
68 J3 Sovetsk Kirovsk. Rus. Fed.
87 Q2 Sovetskaya Gavan' Rus. Fed.
68 D2 Sovetskiy Leningrad. Rus. Fed.
68 J3 Sovetskiy Mariy El. Rus. Fed.
76 H3 Sovetskiy Rus. Fed.
105 G3 Soweto S. Africa
90 J1 Sōya-misaki c. Japan
90 H1 Sōya-wan b. Japan
63 H4 Sozh r. Belarus
67 M3 Sozopol Bulg.
48 Spain country Europe
59 G5 Spalding U.K.
59 D6 Span Head h. U.K.
31 F2 Spanish Can.
31 G2 Spanish r. Can.
35 G1 Spanish Fork U.S.A.
37 J5 Spanish Town Jamaica
34 C2 Sparks U.S.A.
30 C6 Sparta NC U.S.A.
30 B4 Sparta WI U.S.A.
29 D5 Spartanburg U.S.A.
67 K6 Sparti Greece
66 G6 Spartivento, Capo c. Italy
28 E4 Sparwood Can.
68 E4 Spas-Demensk Rus. Fed.
68 E2 Spasskaya Guba Rus. Fed.
87 O3 Spassk-Dal'niy Rus. Fed.
67 K7 Spatha, Akra pt Greece
20 D3 Spatsizi Plateau Wilderness Provincial Park res. Can.
26 C2 Spearfish U.S.A.

27 C4 Spearman U.S.A.
33 F3 Speculator U.S.A.
26 E3 Spencer IA U.S.A.
24 D2 Spencer ID U.S.A.
32 C5 Spencer WV U.S.A.
114 B5 Spencer, C. hd Austr.
20 B3 Spencer, Cape c. U.S.A.
114 B5 Spencer Gulf est. Austr.
20 E4 Spences Bridge Can.
54 F3 Spennymoor U.K.
60 D3 Sperrin Mountains h. U.K.
32 D5 Sperryville U.S.A.
62 D5 Speßart reg. Ger.
67 K6 Spetses i. Greece
57 E2 Spey r. U.K.
62 D6 Speyer Ger.
61 F1 Spiekeroog i. Ger.
62 C7 Spiez Switz.
61 C3 Spijkenisse Neth.
66 E1 Spilimbergo Italy
59 H4 Spilsby U.K.
84 B3 Spintangi Pak.
20 C3 Spirit River Flowage resr U.S.A.
21 H4 Spiritwood Can.
84 A2 Spirsang P. pass Afgh.
63 K6 Spišská Nová Ves Slovakia
81 K1 Spitak Armenia
84 D3 Spiti r. India
76 C2 Spitsbergen i. Svalbard
62 F7 Spittal an der Drau Austria
66 G3 Split Croatia
21 K3 Split Lake Can.
21 K3 Split Lake l. Can.
24 C2 Spokane U.S.A.
66 E3 Spoleto Italy
95 C2 Spong Cambodia
30 B3 Spooner U.S.A.
24 F2 Spotted Horse U.S.A.
23 J3 Spotted Island Can.
31 F2 Spragge Can.
20 E4 Spranger, Mt mt. Can.
24 C2 Spray U.S.A.
62 G5 Spree r. Ger.
31 F3 Spring Bay U.S.A.
104 B4 Springbok S. Africa
27 J4 Springdale Can.
27 C4 Springdale U.S.A.
35 H4 Springerville U.S.A.
27 C4 Springfield CO U.S.A.
30 C6 Springfield IL U.S.A.
33 G3 Springfield MA U.S.A.
33 J2 Springfield ME U.S.A.
26 E2 Springfield MN U.S.A.
30 C6 Springfield MO U.S.A.
32 B5 Springfield OH U.S.A.
24 B3 Springfield OR U.S.A.
33 G3 Springfield VT U.S.A.
32 D5 Springfield WV U.S.A.
30 C6 Springfield, Lake l. U.S.A.
105 F5 Springfontein S. Africa
30 B4 Spring Green U.S.A.
30 B4 Spring Grove U.S.A.
23 H4 Springhill Can.
29 D6 Spring Hill U.S.A.
30 D4 Spring Lake U.S.A.
35 E3 Spring Mountains mts U.S.A.
117 D5 Springs Junction N.Z.
116 C5 Springsure Austr.
30 A4 Spring Valley U.S.A.
32 D3 Springville NY U.S.A.
35 G1 Springville UT U.S.A.
59 J5 Sprowston U.K.
20 G4 Spruce Grove Can.
32 D5 Spruce Knob-Seneca Rocks National Recreation Area res. U.S.A.
24 D3 Spruce Mt. mt. U.S.A.
58 H4 Spurn Head c. U.K.
20 E5 Spuzzum Can.
20 E5 Squamish Can.
33 H3 Squam Lake l. U.S.A.
33 J1 Square Lake l. U.S.A.
66 G5 Squillace, Golfo di g. Italy
36 A2 S. Quintín, C. pt Mex.
95 B3 Srê Âmbêl Cambodia
77 R4 Sredinnyy Khrebet mts Rus. Fed.
67 K3 Sredna Gora mts Bulg.
77 R3 Srednekolymsk Rus. Fed.
76 E4 Sredne-Russkaya Vozvyshennost' reg. Rus. Fed.
67 L3 Srednogorie Bulg.
95 C2 Srêpôk, T. r. Cambodia
87 L1 Sretensk Rus. Fed.
83 F7 Srikakulam India
70 Sri Lanka country Asia
84 D3 Sri Kanta mt India
84 C2 Srinagar India
84 D3 Srinagar Jammu and Kashmir
95 B1 Sri Thep Thai.
83 D7 Srivardhan India
113 H3 Staaten River National Park nat. park Austr.
61 D2 Stade Ger.
61 E2 Stadskanaal Neth.
59 E5 Staffa i. U.K.
32 E5 Stafford U.S.A.
59 E5 Stafford U.K.
59 T8 Staicele Latvia
59 G6 Staines U.K.

69 F5 Stakhanov Ukr.
59 E7 Stalbridge U.K.
59 J1 Stalham U.K.
Stalingrad see Volgograd
20 E3 Stalin, Mt mt. Can.
63 L5 Stalowa Wola Pol.
61 B4 St-Amand-les-Eaux France
64 F3 St-Amand-Montrond France
67 L3 Stamboliyski Bulg.
59 G5 Stamford U.K.
33 G4 Stamford CT U.S.A.
33 F3 Stamford NY U.S.A.
64 G3 St-Amour France
Stampalia i. see Astypalaia
103 B6 Stampriet Namibia
54 N2 Stamsund Norway
26 C3 Stanberry U.S.A.
61 C3 Standdaarbuiten Neth.
105 H3 Standerton S. Africa
31 F4 Standish U.S.A.
28 C4 Stanford U.S.A.
105 J4 Stanger S. Africa
29 E7 Staniard Ck Bahamas
67 K3 Stanke Dimitrov Bulg.
115 F8 Stanley Austr.
33 K1 Stanley Can.
89 Stanley Hong Kong China
44 E8 Stanley Falkland Is
58 F3 Stanley r. Austr.
24 D2 Stanley ID U.S.A.
26 C1 Stanley ND U.S.A.
30 B3 Stanley WV U.S.A.
102 C3 Stanley, Mount mt Uganda/Zaire
115 F8 Stanley, Mt h. Austr.
58 F2 Stannington U.K.
77 R3 Stanovaya Rus. Fed.
77 N4 Stanovoye Nagor'ye mts Rus. Fed.
77 O4 Stanovoy Khrebet mts Rus. Fed.
115 J2 Stanthorpe Austr.
59 H5 Stanton U.K.
32 B5 Stanton KY U.S.A.
30 E4 Stanton MI U.S.A.
26 C3 Stapleton U.S.A.
116 B2 Star r. Austr.
63 K5 Starachowice Pol.
Stara Planina mts see Balkan Mountains
68 J4 Staraya Kulatka Rus. Fed.
69 H5 Staraya Poltavka Rus. Fed.
68 D3 Staraya Russa Rus. Fed.
63 P2 Staraya Toropa Rus. Fed.
68 J4 Staraya Tumba Rus. Fed.
67 L3 Stara Zagora Bulg.
109 Starbuck Island i. Kiribati
62 G4 Stargard Szczeciński Pol.
68 E3 Staritsa Rus. Fed.
29 D6 Starke U.S.A.
27 F5 Starkville U.S.A.
62 E7 Starnberger See l. Ger.
69 F5 Starobil's'k Ukr.
63 Q4 Starodub Rus. Fed.
63 J4 Starogard Gdański Pol.
69 C5 Starokostyantyniv Ukr.
69 F6 Starominskaya Rus. Fed.
69 F6 Staroshcherbinovskaya Rus. Fed.
34 C1 Star Peak mt. U.S.A.
59 D7 Start Point pt U.K.
63 O4 Staryya Darohi Belarus
69 F5 Staryy Oskol Rus. Fed.
32 E4 State College U.S.A.
29 D5 Statesboro U.S.A.
29 D5 Statesville U.S.A.
23 J3 St-Augustin Can.
32 D5 Staunton U.S.A.
55 J7 Stavanger Norway
59 F4 Staveley U.K.
64 F3 St-Avertin France
61 E5 St-Avold France
69 G6 Stavropol' Rus. Fed.
69 G6 Stavropol'skaya Vozvyshennost' reg. Rus. Fed.
69 G6 Stavropol'skiy Kray div. Rus. Fed.
114 E6 Stawell Austr.
64 C2 St-Brieuc France
64 E4 St-Céré France
33 G2 St-Césaire Can.
64 G4 St-Chamond France
64 G4 St-Claude France
64 H2 St-Dié France
64 G2 St-Dizier France
105 H4 Steadville S. Africa
34 C2 Steamboat U.S.A.
24 F3 Steamboat Springs U.S.A.
23 F4 Ste-Anne-de-Beaupré Can.
33 H1 Ste-Camille-de-Lellis Can.
32 E4 Steelton U.S.A.
61 E2 Steenderen Neth.
105 J2 Steenkampsberge mts S. Africa
20 F3 Steen River Can.
24 C3 Steens Mt. mt. U.S.A.
61 E2 Steenwijk Neth.
64 G4 St-Égrève France
66 E2 Steigerwald forest Ger.
21 K5 Steinbach Can.
61 F2 Steinfort Lux.
103 B6 Steinhausen Namibia
54 M4 Steinkjer Norway
104 B4 Steinkopf S. Africa
35 H5 Steins U.S.A.
54 M4 Steinsdalen Norway
55 P5 Stöde Sweden

104 F3 Stella S. Africa
104 C6 Stellenbosch S. Africa
66 C3 Stello, Monte mt Corsica France
62 H5 Ste-Maxime France
62 E4 Stendal Ger.
114 B5 Stenhouse Bay Austr.
89 Stenhouse, Mt h. Hong Kong China
57 E4 Stenhousemuir U.K.
55 M7 Stenungsund Sweden
Stepanakert see Xankändi
21 K5 Stephen U.S.A.
114 D4 Stephens watercourse Austr.
117 D4 Stephens, Cape c. N.Z.
114 D3 Stephens Creek Austr.
30 D3 Stephenson U.S.A.
20 C3 Stephens Passage chan. U.S.A.
23 J4 Stephenville Can.
27 D5 Stephenville U.S.A.
69 H5 Stepnoye Rus. Fed.
105 H4 Sterkfontein Dam resr S. Africa
105 G5 Sterkstroom S. Africa
104 D5 Sterling S. Africa
24 G3 Sterling CO U.S.A.
30 C5 Sterling IL U.S.A.
26 C2 Sterling ND U.S.A.
35 G2 Sterling UT U.S.A.
27 C6 Sterling City U.S.A.
31 F4 Sterling Hgts U.S.A.
33 G3 Ste-Thérèse Can.
64 G4 St-Étienne France
30 D2 Steuben U.S.A.
32 C4 Steubenville U.S.A.
33 G3 St-Eustache Can.
59 G6 Stevenage U.K.
21 K4 Stevenson L. l. Can.
30 C3 Stevens Point U.S.A.
20 D3 Stewart r. Can.
20 B2 Stewart Crossing Can.
117 A7 Stewart Island i. N.Z.
111 G2 Stewart Islands is Solomon Is
57 D5 Stewarton U.K.
30 A4 Stewartville U.S.A.
105 F5 Steynsburg S. Africa
62 G6 Steyr Austria
104 F6 Steytlerville S. Africa
23 H4 St-Félicien Can.
66 C3 St-Florent Corsica France
64 F3 St-Florent-sur-Cher France
33 J1 St-Francis r. Can./U.S.A.
64 E5 St-Gaudens France
33 H2 St-Gédéon Can.
61 D4 St-Hubert Belgium
22 F4 St-Hyacinthe Can.
20 C3 Stikine r. Can.
20 C3 Stikine Ranges mts Can.
104 D7 Stilbaai S. Africa
34 C2 Stillwater MN U.S.A.
34 C2 Stillwater NV U.S.A.
27 D4 Stillwater OK U.S.A.
25 C4 Stillwater Ra. mts U.S.A.
59 G5 Stilton U.K.
67 K4 Štip Macedonia
114 C5 Stirling Austr.
57 E4 Stirling U.K.
34 B2 Stirling City U.S.A.
114 B4 Stirling North Austr.
33 J1 St-Jacques Can.
64 H5 St-Jean-d'Angély France
64 C3 St-Jean-de-Monts France
23 F4 St-Jean, Lac l. Can.
22 F4 St-Jean-sur-Richelieu Can.
22 F4 St-Jérôme Can.
54 M5 Stjørdalshalsen Norway
64 E4 St-Junien France
61 B3 St-Laureins Belgium
St-Laurent, Golfe du g. see St Lawrence, Gulf of
64 G2 St-Léonard Can.
64 D2 St-Lô France
64 D3 St-Maixent-l'École France
64 C2 St-Malo France
64 C2 St-Malo, Golfe de g. France
64 D4 St-Médard-en-Jalles France
64 D2 St-Nazaire France
64 H2 St-Nicolas-de-Port France
61 C3 St-Niklaas Belgium
46 D2 Sto Amaro, I. de i. Brazil
46 E1 Sto Antônio, Cabo c. Brazil
46 E1 Sto Antônio de Jesus Brazil
46 A1 Sto Antônio de Leverger Brazil
62 H6 Stockerau Austria
55 Q7 Stockholm Sweden
33 J1 Stockholm U.S.A.
59 E4 Stockport U.K.
34 B3 Stockton CA U.S.A.
35 F1 Stockton UT U.S.A.
30 D2 Stockton I. i. U.S.A.
26 D4 Stockton KS U.S.A.
58 F3 Stockton-on-Tees U.K.
33 J2 Stockton Springs U.S.A.

95 B2 Stœng Sângke r. Cambodia
95 C2 Stœng Sên r. Cambodia
95 C2 Stœng Trêng Cambodia
57 C2 Stoer, Point of pt U.K.
59 E4 Stoke-on-Trent U.K.
58 F3 Stokesley U.K.
115 E8 Stokes Pt pt Austr.
54 C5 Stokkseyri Iceland
54 N3 Stokkvågen Norway
54 O2 Stokmarknes Norway
67 G3 Stolac Bos.-Herz.
69 C5 Stolin Belarus
64 F1 St-Omer France
59 E5 Stone U.K.
31 J2 Stonecliffe Can.
33 F5 Stone Harbor U.S.A.
57 F4 Stonehaven U.K.
20 E3 Stone Mountain Prov. Park res. Can.
35 H3 Stoner U.S.A.
33 F4 Stone Ridge U.S.A.
21 K4 Stonewall Can.
32 C5 Stonewall Jackson Lake l. U.S.A.
31 F4 Stoney Point Can.
33 J2 Stonington Can.
34 A2 Stonyford U.S.A.
33 E3 Stony Pt pt U.S.A.
21 H3 Stony Rapids Can.
46 D1 Sto Onofre r. Brazil
54 Q3 Stora Inlevatten l. Sweden
54 P3 Stora Sjöfallets National Park nat. park Sweden
54 Q4 Storavan l. Sweden
55 M9 Store Bælt chan. Denmark
54 M5 Støren Norway
54 O3 Storforshei Norway
54 O3 Storjord Norway
115 G9 Storm Bay b. Austr.
105 G5 Stormberg Rus. Fed.
105 G5 Stormberg S. Africa
26 E3 Storm Lake U.S.A.
57 B2 Stornoway U.K.
68 K2 Storozhevsk Rus. Fed.
69 C5 Storozhynets' Ukr.
33 G3 Storrs U.S.A.
57 B3 Storr, The h. U.K.
54 P4 Storseleby Sweden
54 O3 Storsjön l. Sweden
55 L5 Storskrymten mt Norway
54 R2 Storslett Norway
61 D1 Stortemelk chan. Neth.
54 P4 Storuman Sweden
54 P4 Storuman l. Sweden
55 P6 Storvik Sweden
55 M8 Storvorde Denmark
55 P7 Storvreta Sweden
59 G5 Stotfold U.K.
30 C4 Stoughton U.S.A.
59 E7 Stour r. Eng. U.K.
59 H6 Stour r. Eng. U.K.
59 H6 Stour r. Eng. U.K.
59 J6 Stour r. Eng. U.K.
59 E5 Stourbridge U.K.
59 E5 Stourport-on-Severn U.K.
21 L4 Stout L. l. Can.
68 C4 Stowbtsy Belarus
33 H4 Stowe U.S.A.
59 H5 Stowmarket U.K.
33 J1 St-Pamphile Can.
64 G5 St-Pierre mt France
23 J4 St-Pierre St Pierre and Miquelon N. America
64 D4 St-Pierre-d'Oléron France
64 F3 St-Pierre-le-Moûtier France
61 A4 St-Pol-sur-Ternoise France
64 E4 St-Pourçain-sur-Sioule France
64 F2 St-Quentin France
60 D3 Strabane U.K.
60 C4 Stradbally Rep. of Ireland
59 J5 Stradbroke U.K.
66 C2 Stradella Italy
115 F9 Strahan Austr.
35 G3 Straight Cliffs cliff U.S.A.
62 F6 Strakonice Czech Rep.
62 F3 Stralsund Ger.
104 C7 Strand S. Africa
54 K5 Stranda Norway
29 E7 Strangers Cay i. Bahamas
60 E3 Strangford U.K.
60 F3 Strangford Lough l. U.K.
57 C6 Stranraer U.K.
64 H5 St-Raphaël France
34 H2 Strasbourg France
32 H2 Strasburg U.K.
115 G6 Stratford Austr.
31 G4 Stratford Can.
117 E3 Stratford N.Z.
27 C4 Stratford TX U.S.A.
30 B3 Stratford WV U.S.A.
59 F5 Stratford-upon-Avon U.K.
114 C5 Strathalbyn Austr.
57 D5 Strathaven U.K.
57 G3 Strathbeg, Loch of l. U.K.
57 D5 Strathcarron v. U.K.
20 D5 Strathcona Prov. Park res. Can.
57 D5 Strath Dearn v. U.K.
57 D2 Strath Fleet v. U.K.
20 G4 Strathmore Can.
20 E4 Strathnaver Can.

57 D2 **Strathnaver** *v.* U.K.
57 E2 **Strath of Kildonan** *v.* U.K.
31 G4 **Strathroy** Can.
57 E3 **Strathspey** *v.* U.K.
57 E2 **Strathy** U.K.
57 D2 **Strathy Point** *pt* U.K.
59 C7 **Stratton** U.K.
33 H2 **Stratton** U.S.A.
62 F6 **Straubing** Ger.
54 B3 **Straumnes** *pt* Iceland
30 B4 **Strawberry Point** U.S.A.
35 G1 **Strawberry Reservoir** *resr* U.S.A.
113 F6 **Streaky Bay** Austr.
113 F6 **Streaky Bay** *b.* Austr.
30 C5 **Streator** U.S.A.
59 E6 **Street** U.K.
67 K2 **Strehaia** Romania
77 R3 **Strelka** Rus. Fed.
33 G2 **St-Rémi** Can.
55 T8 **Strenči** Latvia
57 F3 **Strichen** U.K.
93 L8 **Strickland** *r.* P.N.G.
67 K4 **Strimonas** *r.* Greece
47 D4 **Stroeder** Arg.
60 C4 **Strokestown** Rep. of Ireland
57 E2 **Stroma, Island of** *i.* U.K.
66 F5 **Stromboli, Isola** *i.* Italy
57 E2 **Stromness** U.K.
26 D3 **Stromsburg** U.S.A.
55 M7 **Strömstad** Sweden
54 O5 **Strömsund** Sweden
32 C4 **Strongsville** U.S.A.
57 F1 **Stronsay** *i.* U.K.
115 J4 **Stroud** Austr.
59 E6 **Stroud** U.K.
115 J4 **Stroud Road** Austr.
33 F4 **Stroudsburg** U.S.A.
55 L8 **Struer** Denmark
67 J4 **Struga** Macedonia
68 D3 **Strugi-Krasnyye** Rus. Fed.
104 D7 **Struis Bay** S. Africa
67 K4 **Struma** *r.* Bulg.
59 B5 **Strumble Head** *hd* U.K.
67 K4 **Strumica** Macedonia
67 L3 **Stryama** *r.* Bulg.
104 E4 **Strydenburg** S. Africa
55 K6 **Stryn** Norway
69 B5 **Stryy** Ukr.
114 D2 **Strzelecki Cr.** *watercourse* Austr.
115 H8 **Strzelecki Pk** *h.* Austr.
33 H2 **St-Sébastien** Can.
33 H2 **St-Théophile** Can.
64 H5 **St-Tropez** France
116 D6 **Stuart** *r.* Austr.
29 D7 **Stuart** *FL* U.S.A.
32 C6 **Stuart** *VA* U.S.A.
20 E4 **Stuart Lake** *l.* Can.
32 D5 **Stuarts Draft** U.S.A.
115 H4 **Stuart Town** Austr.
117 C6 **Studholme Junction** N.Z.
54 Q5 **Studsviken** Sweden
27 G6 **Study Butte** U.S.A.
21 L4 **Stull L.** *l.* Can.
95 C2 **Stung Chinit** *r.* Cambodia
68 F4 **Stupino** Rus. Fed.
119 A6 **Sturge I.** *i.* Ant.
30 D2 **Sturgeon** *r.* U.S.A.
21 K4 **Sturgeon Bay** *b.* Can.
30 D3 **Sturgeon Bay** *WV* U.S.A.
30 E3 **Sturgeon Bay** *b.* U.S.A.
30 D3 **Sturgeon Bay Canal** *chan.* U.S.A.
31 H2 **Sturgeon Falls** Can.
22 B3 **Sturgeon L.** *l.* Can.
28 C4 **Sturgis** *KY* U.S.A.
30 E5 **Sturgis** *MI* U.S.A.
26 C2 **Sturgis** *SD* U.S.A.
114 B5 **Sturt Bay** *b.* Austr.
112 E3 **Sturt Creek** *r.* Austr.
114 D2 **Sturt Desert** *des.* Austr.
114 D2 **Sturt, Mt** *h.* Austr.
114 D2 **Sturt Nat. Park** *nat. park* Austr.
105 G6 **Stutterheim** S. Africa
62 D6 **Stuttgart** Ger.
27 F5 **Stuttgart** U.S.A.
61 E4 **St-Vith** Belgium
54 B4 **Stykkishólmur** Iceland
63 M5 **Styr** *r.* Ukr.
64 E4 **St-Yrieix-la-Perche** France
46 D2 **Suaçuí Grande** *r.* Brazil
101 F3 **Suakin** Sudan
89 F5 **Su'ao** Taiwan
25 E6 **Suaqui Gde** Mex.
45 B3 **Suárez** *r.* Col.
63 M3 **Subačius** Lith.
92 □ **Subang** Indon.
85 H4 **Subansiri** *r.* India
85 F5 **Subarnarekha** *r.* India
81 G6 **Şubayḩah** S. Arabia
95 D5 **Subi Besar** *i.* Indon.
67 H1 **Subotica** Yugo.
63 N7 **Suceava** Romania
60 C4 **Suck** *r.* Rep. of Ireland
42 E7 **Sucre** Bol.
45 B2 **Sucre** Col.
45 C3 **Sucuaro** Col.
46 B3 **Sucuriú** *r.* Brazil
69 E6 **Sudak** Ukr.
96 **Sudan** *country* Africa
68 G3 **Suday** Rus. Fed.
81 K6 **Sudayr** *watercourse* Iraq
31 G2 **Sudbury** Can.
59 H5 **Sudbury** U.K.
101 E4 **Sudd** *swamp* Sudan
62 H5 **Sudety** *mts* Czech Rep./Pol.
33 F5 **Sudlersville** U.S.A.
68 G4 **Sudogda** Rus. Fed.
80 D7 **Sudr** Egypt
54 □ **Suðuroy** *i.* Faroe Is
101 E4 **Sue** *watercourse* Sudan
65 F3 **Sueca** Spain
78 C4 **Suez** Egypt
78 C3 **Suez Canal** *canal* Egypt
78 C4 **Suez, Gulf of** *g.* Egypt
32 E6 **Suffolk** U.S.A.
81 K2 **Sūfiān** Iran
30 C4 **Sugar** *r.* U.S.A.
33 H2 **Sugarloaf Mt.** *mt.* U.S.A.
115 K4 **Sugarloaf Pt** *pt* Austr.
94 C4 **Sugbuhan Point** *pt* Phil.
94 A5 **Sugut** *r.* Malaysia
94 A5 **Sugut, Tg** *pt* Malaysia
88 B2 **Suhait** China
79 H5 **Şuḩār** Oman
86 J1 **Sühbaatar** Mongolia
62 E5 **Suhl** Ger.
80 C2 **Şuhut** Turkey
84 B3 **Sui** Pak.
89 F4 **Suichang** China
89 E5 **Suichuan** China
88 D2 **Suide** China
87 O3 **Suifenhe** China
84 B4 **Suigam** India
87 N2 **Suihua** China
89 B4 **Suijiang** China
89 D5 **Suining** *Hunan* China
88 E3 **Suining** *Jiangsu* China
89 B4 **Suining** *Sichuan* China
88 E3 **Suiping** China
60 D5 **Suir** *r.* Rep. of Ireland
90 K2 **Suishō-tō** *i.* Rus. Fed.
88 E3 **Suixi** China
88 E3 **Sui Xian** China
89 C5 **Suiyang** China
88 F1 **Suizhong** China
88 D4 **Suizhou** China
88 C1 **Suj** China
84 C4 **Sujangarh** India
84 D3 **Sujanpur** *Himachal Pradesh* India
82 E4 **Sujanpur** *Punjab* India
84 B4 **Sujawal** Pak.
92 □ **Sukabumi** Indon.
92 D7 **Sukadana** Indon.
91 H5 **Sukagawa** Japan
94 A5 **Sukau** Malaysia
68 E4 **Sukhinichi** Rus. Fed.
68 H2 **Sukhona** *r.* Rus. Fed.
95 A1 **Sukhothai** Thai.
68 E2 **Sukkozero** Rus. Fed.
84 B4 **Sukkur** Pak.
84 C4 **Sukri** *r.* India
68 F3 **Sukromny** Rus. Fed.
90 D7 **Sukumo** Japan
55 J6 **Sula** *i.* Norway
84 B3 **Sulaiman Ranges** *mts* Pak.
69 H7 **Sulak** *r.* Rus. Fed.
93 H7 **Sula, Kepulauan** *is* Indon.
57 B1 **Sula Sgeir** *i.* U.K.
93 G7 **Sulawesi** *i.* Indon.
81 K4 **Sulaymān Beg** Iraq
57 D1 **Sule Skerry** *i.* U.K.
57 D1 **Sule Stack** *i.* U.K.
80 F3 **Süleymanlı** Turkey
100 A4 **Sulima** Sierra Leone
54 P3 **Sulitjelma** Norway
55 V6 **Sulkava** Fin.
42 B4 **Sullana** Peru
26 F4 **Sullivan** U.S.A.
21 G4 **Sullivan L.** *l.* Can.
33 J1 **Sully** Can.
66 E3 **Sulmona** Italy
27 E6 **Sulphur** U.S.A.
27 E5 **Sulphur Springs** U.S.A.
31 F2 **Sultan** Can.
**Sultanabad** *see* **Arāk**
80 C2 **Sultan Dağları** *mts* Turkey
80 D2 **Sultanhanı** Turkey
85 E4 **Sultanpur** India
94 B5 **Sulu Archipelago** *is* Phil.
80 F2 **Sulusaray** Turkey
94 A4 **Sulu Sea** *sea* Phil.
119 A4 **Sulzberger Bay** *b.* Ant.
44 D3 **Sumampa** Arg.
45 B4 **Sumapaz, Parque Nacional** *nat. park* Col.
81 K5 **Sūmar** Iran
92 C6 **Sumatera** *i.* Indon.
**Sumatra** *i. see* **Sumatera**
62 F6 **Šumava** *mts* Czech Rep.
93 G8 **Sumba** *i.* Indon.
93 F8 **Sumba, Selat** *chan.* Indon.
93 F8 **Sumbawa** *i.* Indon.
93 F8 **Sumbawabesar** Indon.
103 D4 **Sumbawanga** Tanz.
103 B5 **Sumbe** Angola
57 □ **Sumburgh** U.K.
57 □ **Sumburgh Head** *hd* U.K.
84 D2 **Sumdo** China/Jammu and Kashmir
92 □ **Sumedang** Indon.
81 M3 **Sume'eh Sarā** Iran
92 □ **Sumenep** Indon.
**Sumgait** *see* **Sumqayıt**
87 Q5 **Sumisu-jima** *i.* Japan
81 J3 **Summēl** Iraq
22 C3 **Summer Beaver** Can.
23 K4 **Summerford** Can.
30 D3 **Summer I.** *i.* U.S.A.
57 C2 **Summer Isles** *is* U.K.
23 H4 **Summerside** *P.E.I.* Can.
32 C5 **Summersville** U.S.A.
32 C5 **Summersville Lake** *l.* U.S.A.
20 E4 **Summit Lake** Can.
30 E5 **Summit Lake** *l.* U.S.A.
34 D2 **Summit Mt** *mt.* U.S.A.
84 D2 **Sumnal** China/India
117 D5 **Sumner** N.Z.
30 A4 **Sumner** U.S.A.
117 D5 **Sumner, L.** *l.* N.Z.
20 C3 **Sumner Strait** *chan.* U.S.A.
91 G5 **Sumon-dake** *mt.* Japan
90 E6 **Sumoto** Japan
62 H6 **Šumperk** Czech Rep.
81 M1 **Sumqayıt** *r.* Azer.
81 M1 **Sumqayıt** Azer.
84 B4 **Sumrahu** Pak.
29 D5 **Sumter** U.S.A.
69 E5 **Sumy** Ukr.
24 D2 **Sun** *r.* U.S.A.
68 J3 **Suna** Rus. Fed.
90 H2 **Sunagawa** Japan
85 G4 **Sunamganj** Bangl.
57 C4 **Sunart, Loch** *in.* U.K.
81 K4 **Sunbula Kuh** *mts* Iran
24 E1 **Sunburst** U.S.A.
114 F6 **Sunbury** Austr.
32 B4 **Sunbury** *OH* U.S.A.
32 E4 **Sunbury** *PA* U.S.A.
47 E1 **Sunchales** Arg.
105 G2 **Sun City** S. Africa
33 H3 **Suncook** U.S.A.
24 F2 **Sundance** U.S.A.
85 F5 **Sundargarh** India
84 D3 **Sundarnagar** India
92 C8 **Sunda, Selat** *chan.* Indon.
13 M4 **Sunda Trench** *sea feature* Indian Ocean
58 F3 **Sunderland** U.K.
80 C2 **Sündiken Dağları** *mts* Turkey
31 H3 **Sundridge** Can.
55 P5 **Sundsvall** Sweden
105 J4 **Sundumbili** S. Africa
84 D4 **Sunel** India
95 B5 **Sungaikabung** Indon.
92 D7 **Sungailiat** Indon.
95 B5 **Sungai Pahang** *r.* Malaysia
92 C7 **Sungaipenuh** Indon.
92 C5 **Sungei Petani** Malaysia
95 □ **Sungei Seletar Res.** *resr* Sing.
80 E1 **Sungurlu** Turkey
85 F4 **Sun Kosi** *r.* Nepal
55 K6 **Sunndal** Norway
54 L5 **Sunndalsøra** Norway
55 N7 **Sunne** Sweden
24 C2 **Sunnyside** U.S.A.
34 A3 **Sunnyvale** U.S.A.
91 G6 **Suno-saki** *pt* Japan
30 C4 **Sun Prairie** U.S.A.
34 □1 **Sunset Beach** U.S.A.
35 G4 **Sunset Crater National Monument** *res.* U.S.A.
77 N3 **Suntar** Rus. Fed.
24 D3 **Sun Valley** U.S.A.
100 B4 **Sunyani** Ghana
54 U3 **Suolijärvet** *l.* Fin.
30 C1 **Suomi** Can.
54 V4 **Suomussalmi** Fin.
90 C7 **Suō-nada** *b.* Japan
54 U5 **Suonenjoki** Fin.
95 C3 **Suŏng** Cambodia
89 B7 **Suong** *r.* Laos
68 E2 **Suoyarvi** Rus. Fed.
35 F3 **Supai** U.S.A.
45 E3 **Supamo** *r.* Venez.
85 F4 **Supaul** India
35 G5 **Superior** *AZ* U.S.A.
26 D3 **Superior** *NE* U.S.A.
30 A2 **Superior** *WV* U.S.A.
30 B2 **Superior, Lake** *l.* Can./U.S.A.
95 B2 **Suphan Buri** Thai.
81 J2 **Süphan Dağı** *mt* Turkey
68 E4 **Suponevo** Rus. Fed.
81 L6 **Sūq ash Shuyūkh** Iraq
88 F3 **Suqian** China
**Suquṭrā** *i. see* **Socotra**
79 H5 **Şūr** Oman
68 H4 **Sura** Rus. Fed.
68 H4 **Sura** *r.* Rus. Fed.
81 M1 **Şuraabad** Azer.
79 K4 **Surab** Pak.
92 □ **Surabaya** Indon.
92 □ **Surakarta** Indon.
115 H1 **Surat** Austr.
84 C5 **Surat** India
84 C3 **Suratgarh** India
95 A3 **Surat Thani** Thai.
68 E4 **Surazh** Rus. Fed.
116 B4 **Surbiton** Austr.
81 K4 **Sūrdāsh** Iraq
67 K3 **Surdulica** Yugo.
61 D5 **Sûre** *r.* Lux.
84 B5 **Surendranagar** India
34 B4 **Surf** U.S.A.
76 J3 **Surgut** Rus. Fed.
83 E7 **Suriapet** India
94 C4 **Surigao** Phil.
94 C4 **Surigao Str.** *chan.* Phil.
95 B2 **Surin** Thai.
38 **Suriname** *country* S. America
84 B1 **Surkhab** *r.* Afgh.
85 E3 **Surkhet** Nepal
81 H1 **Sürmene** Turkey
69 G5 **Surovikino** Rus. Fed.
34 B3 **Sur, Pt** *pt* U.S.A.
47 F3 **Sur, Pta** *pt* Arg.
32 E6 **Surry** U.S.A.
68 H4 **Sursk** Rus. Fed.
**Surt** *see* **Sirte**
**Surt, Khalīj** *g. see* **Sirte, Gulf of**
54 C5 **Surtsey** *i.* Iceland
80 G3 **Sürüç** Turkey
91 G6 **Suruga-wan** *b.* Japan
92 C7 **Surulangun** Indon.
94 C5 **Surup** Phil.
90 C6 **Susa** Japan
90 D7 **Susaki** Japan
91 E7 **Susami** Japan
81 M6 **Sūsangerd** Iran
68 G3 **Susanino** Rus. Fed.
34 B1 **Susanville** U.S.A.
80 G1 **Suşehri** Turkey
95 A4 **Suso** Thai.
89 E4 **Susong** China
33 E4 **Susquehanna** *r.* U.S.A.
23 G4 **Sussex** Can.
33 F4 **Sussex** U.S.A.
94 A5 **Susul** Malaysia
77 Q3 **Susuman** Rus. Fed.
80 B2 **Susurluk** Turkey
84 D2 **Sutak** Jammu and Kashmir
34 C2 **Sutcliffe** U.S.A.
104 D6 **Sutherland** S. Africa
26 C3 **Sutherland** U.S.A.
84 C3 **Sutlej** *r.* Pak.
34 B2 **Sutter Creek** U.S.A.
59 G5 **Sutterton** U.K.
22 D3 **Sutton** *r.* Can.
33 G2 **Sutton** Can.
59 H5 **Sutton** U.K.
32 C5 **Sutton** U.S.A.
59 F5 **Sutton Coldfield** U.K.
59 F4 **Sutton in Ashfield** U.K.
22 D3 **Sutton L.** *l.* Can.
32 C5 **Sutton Lake** *l.* U.S.A.
116 B3 **Suttor** *r.* Austr.
90 H2 **Suttsu** Japan
111 H3 **Suva** Fiji
68 F4 **Suvorov** Rus. Fed.
109 **Suvorov Island** *i.* Cook Islands Pac. Oc.
91 G5 **Suwa** Japan
63 L3 **Suwałki** Pol.
95 B2 **Suwannaphum** Thai.
29 D6 **Suwannee** *r.* U.S.A.
81 K5 **Suwayqīyah, Hawr as** *l.* Iraq
81 H6 **Suwayr** *w.* S. Arabia
91 G5 **Suzaka** Japan
68 G3 **Suzdal'** Rus. Fed.
88 E3 **Suzhou** *Anhui* China
88 F4 **Suzhou** *Jiangsu* China
91 F5 **Suzu** Japan
91 F6 **Suzuka** Japan
91 F5 **Suzu-misaki** *pt* Japan
54 U1 **Sværholthalvøya** *pen.* Norway
76 C2 **Svalbard** *terr.* Arctic Ocean
69 F5 **Svatove** Ukr.
95 C3 **Svay Riĕng** Cambodia
55 O5 **Sveg** Sweden
55 U8 **Sveķi** Latvia
55 J6 **Svelgen** Norway
54 L5 **Svellingen** Norway
55 T9 **Švenčionėliai** Lith.
55 U9 **Švenčionys** Lith.
55 M9 **Svendborg** Denmark
54 Q2 **Svensby** Norway
54 O5 **Svenstavik** Sweden
**Sverdlovsk** *see* **Yekaterinburg**
69 F5 **Sverdlovs'k** Ukr.
67 J4 **Sveti Nikole** Macedonia
87 P2 **Svetlaya** Rus. Fed.
87 Q2 **Svetlodarskoye** Rus. Fed.
76 K3 **Svetlogorsk** Rus. Fed.
68 B4 **Svetlogorsk** Rus. Fed.
69 G6 **Svetlograd** Rus. Fed.
68 B4 **Svetlyy** Rus. Fed.
69 H5 **Svetlyy Yar** Rus. Fed.
68 D2 **Svetogorsk** Rus. Fed.
54 E4 **Sviahnúkar** *volc.* Iceland
67 M4 **Svilengrad** Bulg.
67 K2 **Svinecea Mare, Vârful** *mt.* Romania
68 C4 **Svir** Belarus
68 E2 **Svir'** *r.* Rus. Fed.
67 L3 **Svishtov** Bulg.
62 H6 **Svitava** *r.* Czech Rep.
62 H6 **Svitavy** Czech Rep.
69 E5 **Svitlovods'k** Ukr.
68 J4 **Sviyaga** *r.* Rus. Fed.
87 N1 **Svobodnyy** Rus. Fed.
54 O2 **Svolvær** Norway
67 K3 **Svrljiške Planine** *mts* Yugo.
69 D4 **Svyetlahorsk** Belarus
59 F5 **Swadlincote** U.K.
59 H5 **Swaffham** U.K.
116 E3 **Swain Reefs** *rf* Austr.
29 D5 **Swainsboro** U.S.A.
108 **Swains Island** *i.* Samoa Pac. Oc.
103 B6 **Swakopmund** Namibia
58 F3 **Swale** *r.* U.K.
111 G3 **Swallow Is** *is* Solomon Is
21 J4 **Swan** *r.* Can.
59 F7 **Swanage** U.K.
114 E5 **Swan Hill** Austr.
20 F4 **Swan Hills** Can.
37 H5 **Swan Islands** *is* Honduras
21 J4 **Swan L.** *l.* Can.
59 H6 **Swanley** U.K.
114 C5 **Swan Reach** Austr.
21 J4 **Swan River** Can.
115 J4 **Swansea** *N.S.W.* Austr.
115 H9 **Swansea** *Tas.* Austr.
59 D6 **Swansea** U.K.
59 D6 **Swansea Bay** *b.* U.K.
33 J2 **Swans I.** *i.* U.S.A.
33 G2 **Swanton** U.S.A.
105 G2 **Swartruggens** S. Africa
35 F2 **Swasey Peak** *summit* U.S.A.
31 G1 **Swastika** Can.
84 B2 **Swat** *r.* Pak.
**Swatow** *see* **Shantou**
96 **Swaziland** *country* Africa
48 **Sweden** *country* Europe
24 B2 **Sweet Home** U.S.A.
29 C5 **Sweetwater** *TN* U.S.A.
27 C5 **Sweetwater** *TX* U.S.A.
24 E3 **Sweetwater** *r.* U.S.A.
104 D7 **Swellendam** S. Africa
62 H5 **Świdnica** Pol.
62 G4 **Świdwin** Pol.
62 G4 **Świebodzin** Pol.
63 J4 **Świecie** Pol.
33 H2 **Swift** *r.* U.S.A.
21 H4 **Swift Current** Can.
21 H5 **Swiftcurrent Cr.** *r.* Can.
20 C2 **Swift River** Can.
60 D2 **Swilly, Lough** *in.* Rep. of Ireland
59 F6 **Swindon** U.K.
60 C4 **Swinford** Rep. of Ireland
62 G4 **Świnoujście** Pol.
57 F5 **Swinton** U.K.
48 **Switzerland** *country* Europe
60 E4 **Swords** Rep. of Ireland
68 E2 **Syamozero, Oz.** *l.* Rus. Fed.
68 G2 **Syamzha** Rus. Fed.
63 O3 **Syanno** Belarus
68 E2 **Syas'troy** Rus. Fed.
68 H3 **Syava** Rus. Fed.
30 C5 **Sycamore** U.S.A.
115 J4 **Sydney** Austr.
23 H4 **Sydney** Can.
21 L4 **Sydney L.** *l.* Can.
23 H4 **Sydney Mines** Can.
69 F5 **Syeverodonets'k** Ukr.
68 J2 **Syktyvkar** Rus. Fed.
29 C5 **Sylacauga** U.S.A.
54 N5 **Sylarna** *mt* Norway/Sweden
85 G4 **Sylhet** Bangl.
68 G2 **Syloga** Rus. Fed.
62 D3 **Sylt** *i.* Ger.
29 D5 **Sylvania** *GA* U.S.A.
32 B4 **Sylvania** *OH* U.S.A.
20 G4 **Sylvan Lake** Can.
29 D6 **Sylvester** U.S.A.
20 E3 **Sylvia, Mt** *mt.* Can.
67 M6 **Symi** *i.* Greece
69 E5 **Synel'nykove** Ukr.
119 D4 **Syowa** *Japan Base* Ant.
66 F6 **Syracuse** *Sicily* Italy
26 C4 **Syracuse** *KS* U.S.A.
33 E3 **Syracuse** *NY* U.S.A.
82 C2 **Syrdar'ya** *r.* Kazak.
70 **Syria** *country* Asia
83 J7 **Syriam** Myanmar
78 D3 **Syrian Desert** *des.* Asia
67 M6 **Syrna** *i.* Greece
67 L6 **Syros** *i.* Greece
55 T6 **Sysmä** Fin.
68 J2 **Sysola** *r.* Rus. Fed.
68 J4 **Syzran'** Rus. Fed.
62 G4 **Szczecin** Pol.
62 H4 **Szczecinek** Pol.
63 K4 **Szczytno** Pol.
**Szechwan** *div. see* **Sichuan**
63 K7 **Szeged** Hungary
63 J7 **Székesfehérvár** Hungary
63 J7 **Szekszárd** Hungary
63 K7 **Szentes** Hungary
62 H7 **Szentgotthárd** Hungary
66 G1 **Szigetvár** Hungary
63 K7 **Szolnok** Hungary
62 H7 **Szombathely** Hungary

# T

94 B3 **Taal, L.** *l.* Phil.
94 B3 **Tabaco** Phil.
105 H5 **Tabankulu** S. Africa
80 G4 **Ţabaqah** Syria
110 F2 **Tabar Is** *is* P.N.G.
80 E4 **Tabarja** Lebanon
66 C6 **Tabarka** Tunisia
79 H3 **Ţabas** Iran
23 J3 **Tabatière** Can.
42 E4 **Tabatinga** Col.
94 B2 **Tabayoo, Mt** *mt* Phil.
115 F5 **Tabbita** Austr.
100 B2 **Tabelbala** Alg.
21 G5 **Taber** Can.
85 F3 **Tabia Tsaka** *salt l.* China
111 H2 **Tabiteuea** *i.* Kiribati
55 U7 **Tabivere** Estonia
94 B3 **Tablas** *i.* Phil.
94 B3 **Tablas Strait** *chan.* Phil.
117 F3 **Table Cape** *c.* N.Z.
27 E4 **Table Rock Res.** *resr* U.S.A.
116 A2 **Tabletop, Mount** *h.* Austr.
46 A2 **Tabocó** *r.* Brazil
62 G6 **Tábor** Czech Rep.
102 D4 **Tabora** Tanz.
100 B4 **Tabou** Côte d'Ivoire
81 L2 **Tabrīz** Iran
109 **Tabuaeran** *i.* Line Islands Pac. Oc.
78 D4 **Tabūk** S. Arabia
115 K2 **Tabulam** Austr.
111 G3 **Tabwémasana** *mt* Vanuatu
55 Q7 **Täby** Sweden
45 A2 **Tacarcuna, Cerro** *mt* Panama
82 F1 **Tacheng** China
62 F6 **Tachov** Czech Rep.
94 C4 **Tacloban** Phil.
42 D7 **Tacna** Peru
24 B2 **Tacoma** U.S.A.
47 F1 **Tacuarembó** Uru.
47 G2 **Tacuarí** *r.* Uru.
45 E4 **Tacutu** *r.* Brazil
91 G5 **Tadami-gawa** *r.* Japan
58 F4 **Tadcaster** U.K.
100 C2 **Tademaït, Plateau du** *plat.* Alg.
111 G4 **Tadine** New Caledonia
102 E2 **Tadjoura** Djibouti
80 G4 **Tadmur** Syria
21 K3 **Tadoule Lake** *l.* Can.
23 G4 **Tadoussac** Can.
87 N4 **Taegu** S. Korea
87 N4 **Taejŏn** S. Korea
59 C6 **Taf** *r.* U.K.
111 J3 **Tafahi** *i.* Tonga
65 F1 **Tafalla** Spain
80 E6 **Tafila** Jordan
100 B4 **Tafiré** Côte d'Ivoire
44 C3 **Tafi Viejo** Arg.
34 C4 **Taft** U.S.A.
91 H4 **Tagajō** Japan
69 F6 **Taganrog** Rus. Fed.
69 F6 **Taganrog, Gulf of** *b.* Rus. Fed./Ukr.
94 C3 **Tagapula** *i.* Phil.
90 C7 **Tagawa** Japan
94 B3 **Tagaytay City** Phil.
94 B4 **Tagbilaran** Phil.
85 E2 **Tagchagpu Ri** *mt* China
60 E5 **Taghmon** Rep. of Ireland
20 C2 **Tagish** Can.
66 E1 **Tagliamento** *r.* Italy
65 J4 **Tagma, Col de** *pass* Alg.
94 C4 **Tagoloan** *r.* Phil.
94 B4 **Tagolo Point** *pt* Phil.
111 F3 **Tagula I.** *i.* P.N.G.
94 C5 **Tagum** Phil.
65 B3 **Tagus** *r.* Port./Spain
20 F4 **Tahaetkun Mt.** *mt.* Can.
95 B4 **Tahan, Gunung** *mt* Malaysia
91 F6 **Tahara** Japan
100 C2 **Tahat, Mt** *mt* Alg.
87 M1 **Tahe** China
117 D1 **Taheke** N.Z.
109 **Tahiti** *i. Society Islands* Pac. Oc.
27 E5 **Tahlequah** U.S.A.
34 B2 **Tahoe City** U.S.A.
34 B2 **Tahoe, Lake** *l.* U.S.A.
27 C5 **Tahoka** U.S.A.
100 C3 **Tahoua** Niger
20 D4 **Tahtsa Pk** *summit* Can.
94 C6 **Tahuna** Indon.
89 □ **Tai a Chau** *i.* Hong Kong China
88 E2 **Tai'an** China
88 C3 **Taibai Shan** *mt* China
88 E1 **Taibus Qi** China
89 F5 **T'ai-chung** Taiwan
117 C6 **Taieri** *r.* N.Z.
88 D2 **Taigu** China
88 E2 **Taihang Shan** *mts* China
88 D2 **Taihang Shan** *mts* China
117 E3 **Taihape** N.Z.
88 E3 **Taihe** *Anhui* China
89 E5 **Taihe** *Jiangxi* China
89 E4 **Taihu** China
87 M5 **Tai Hu** *l.* China
91 E7 **Taiji** Japan
89 C5 **Taijiang** China
88 E3 **Taikang** China
89 □ **Tai Lam Chung Res.** *resr* Hong Kong China
114 C5 **Tailem Bend** Austr.
89 □ **Tai Long Bay** *b.* Hong Kong China
89 F5 **T'ai-lu-ko** Taiwan
89 □ **Tai Mo Shan** *h.* Hong Kong China
57 D3 **Tain** *Scot.* U.K.
89 F6 **T'ai-nan** Taiwan
89 F6 **T'ainan** Taiwan
67 K6 **Tainaro, Akra** *pt* Greece
89 E5 **Taining** China
89 □ **Tai O** Hong Kong China
46 D1 **Taiobeiras** Brazil
100 B4 **Taï, Parc National de** *nat. park* Côte d'Ivoire
89 F5 **T'ai-pei** Taiwan
89 F4 **Taiping** *Anhui* China
89 D6 **Taiping** *Guangxi* China
92 C6 **Taiping** Malaysia
88 A2 **Taipingbao** China
89 □ **Tai Po** Hong Kong China
90 H3 **Tairadate-kaikyō** *chan.* Japan
90 G2 **Taisei** Japan
90 J2 **Taisetsu-zan** *mts* Japan
90 J2 **Taisetsu-zan National Park** *nat. park* Japan
90 D6 **Taisha** Japan
89 D6 **Taishan** China
89 F5 **Taishun** China
117 D5 **Taitanu** N.Z.
44 B7 **Taitao, Península de** *pen.* Chile
89 F6 **T'ai-tung** Taiwan
54 V4 **Taivalkoski** Fin.
54 T2 **Taivaskero** *h.* Fin.
71 **Taiwan** *country* Asia
89 F6 **Taiwan Shan** *mts* Taiwan
89 F5 **Taiwan Strait** *str.* China/Taiwan
88 F3 **Tai Xian** China
88 F3 **Taixing** China
88 D2 **Taiyuan** China
88 D2 **Taiyue Shan** *mts* China

88 F3 Taizhou China
89 F4 Taizhou Wan b. China
78 E7 Ta'izz Yemen
84 B4 Tajal Pak.
36 F5 Tajamulco, Volcano de volc. Guatemala
66 C7 Tajerouine Tunisia
70 Tajikistan country Asia
91 G5 Tajima Japan
91 F6 Tajimi Japan
Tajo r. see Tagus
95 A1 Tak Thai.
81 L3 Takāb Iran
91 H5 Takahagi Japan
90 D6 Takahashi Japan
90 D6 Takahashi-gawa r. Japan
117 D4 Takaka N.Z.
84 D5 Takal India
90 E6 Takamatsu Japan
91 H3 Takanosu Japan
84 D4 Takanpur India
91 F5 Takaoka Japan
117 F4 Takapau N.Z.
117 E2 Takapuna N.Z.
90 E6 Takasago Japan
91 G5 Takasaki Japan
90 B7 Taka-shima i. Japan
104 F2 Takatokwane Botswana
104 D1 Takatshwaane Botswana
91 E6 Takatsuki Japan
90 D7 Takatsuki-yama mt. Japan
91 F5 Takayama Japan
95 B4 Tak Bai Thai.
91 F6 Takefu Japan
90 D6 Takehara Japan
90 C7 Takeo Japan
Take-shima see Tok-tō
81 M3 Takestān Iran
90 C7 Taketa Japan
95 C3 Takêv Cambodia
81 K7 Takhādīd w. Iraq
79 H1 Takhiatash Uzbek.
95 C3 Ta Khmau Cambodia
81 M5 Takht Apān, Kūh-e mt Iran
84 B3 Takht-i-Sulaiman mt Pak.
21 G1 Takijuq Lake l. Can.
90 H2 Takikawa Japan
90 J1 Takinoue Japan
117 A6 Takitimu Mts mts N.Z.
20 D3 Takla Lake l. Can.
20 D3 Takla Landing Can.
74 Taklimakan Desert des. China
Taklimakan Shamo see Taklimakan Desert
85 H3 Takpa Shiri mt China
20 C3 Taku r. Can.
90 C7 Taku Japan
100 C4 Takum Nigeria
47 F2 Tala Uru.
68 D4 Talachyn Belarus
79 L3 Talagang Pak.
84 C5 Talaja India
85 H4 Talap India
42 B4 Talara Peru
93 H6 Talaud, Kepulauan is Indon.
65 D3 Talavera de la Reina Spain
77 R3 Talaya Rus. Fed.
94 C5 Talayan Phil.
115 H4 Talbragar r. Austr.
47 B2 Talca Chile
47 B3 Talcahuano Chile
85 F5 Talcher India
82 E2 Taldykorgan Kazak.
81 M5 Taleh Zang Iran
81 M3 Tālesh Iran
59 D6 Talgarth U.K.
114 A4 Talia Austr.
93 G7 Taliabu i. Indon.
94 C4 Talibon Phil.
81 J1 T'alin Armenia
94 B4 Talisay Phil.
94 C4 Talisayan Phil.
81 M2 Talış Dağları mts Azer./Iran
68 H3 Talitsa Rus. Fed.
92 F8 Taliwang Indon.
29 C5 Talladega U.S.A.
81 J3 Tall 'Afar Iraq
29 C6 Tallahassee U.S.A.
115 G6 Tallangatta Austr.
29 C5 Tallassee U.S.A.
80 F6 Tall as Suwaysh h. Jordan
81 H3 Tall Baydar Syria
81 H4 Tall Fadghāmī Syria
55 T7 Tallinn Estonia
80 F4 Tall Kalakh Syria
81 J3 Tall Kayf Iraq
60 C5 Tallow Rep. of Ireland
27 F5 Tallulah U.S.A.
81 J3 Tall 'Uwaynāt Iraq
64 D3 Talmont-St-Hilaire France
69 D5 Tal'ne Ukr.
101 F3 Talodi Sudan
23 G2 Talon, Lac l. Can.
84 B1 Tāloqān Afgh.
69 G5 Talovaya Rus. Fed.
84 C2 Tal Pass pass Pak.
55 S8 Talsi Latvia
44 B3 Taltal Chile
21 G2 Taltson r. Can.
81 M4 Talvar r. Iran
54 S1 Talvik Norway
115 H2 Talwood Austr.
69 G5 Taly Rus. Fed.
114 E4 Talyawalka r. Austr.
30 A4 Tama U.S.A.
45 B2 Tamalameque Col.
100 B4 Tamale Ghana
45 A3 Tamana mt Col.
90 C7 Tamana Japan
111 H2 Tamana i. Kiribati
90 D6 Tamano Japan
100 C2 Tamanrasset Alg.
85 H4 Tamanthi Myanmar
45 B3 Tama, Parque Nacional el nat. park Venez.
33 F4 Tamaqua U.S.A.
59 C7 Tamar r. U.K.
105 G1 Tamasane Botswana
36 E4 Tamazunchale Mex.
102 D3 Tambach Kenya
100 A3 Tambacounda Senegal
85 F4 Tamba Kosi r. Nepal
94 A5 Tambisan Malaysia
116 B5 Tambo Qld. Austr.
115 G6 Tambo r. Vic. Austr.
115 G6 Tamboritha mt Austr.
68 G4 Tambov Rus. Fed.
68 G4 Tambovskaya Oblast' div. Rus. Fed.
65 B1 Tambre r. Spain
94 A5 Tambunan, Bukit h. Malaysia
101 E4 Tambura Sudan
94 A5 Tambuyukon, Gunung mt Malaysia
100 A3 Tâmchekkeț Maur.
45 C3 Tame Col.
65 C2 Tâmega r. Port.
85 H4 Tamenglong India
66 B7 Tamerza Tunisia
36 E4 Tamiahua, Lag. de lag. Mex.
95 A4 Tamiang, Ujung pt Indon.
83 E8 Tamil Nadu div. India
68 F1 Tamitsa Rus. Fed.
80 C7 Tâmîya Egypt
95 D2 Tam Ky Vietnam
29 D7 Tampa U.S.A.
29 D7 Tampa Bay b. U.S.A.
55 S6 Tampere Fin.
36 E4 Tampico Mex.
95 □ Tampines Sing.
87 L2 Tamsagbulag Mongolia
88 B1 Tamsag Muchang China
67 F7 Tamsweg Austria
85 H4 Tamu Myanmar
85 F4 Tamur r. Nepal
115 J3 Tamworth Austr.
59 F5 Tamworth U.K.
102 D4 Tana r. Kenya
91 E7 Tanabe Japan
54 V1 Tana Bru Norway
16 Tanacross U.S.A.
54 V1 Tanafjorden chan. Norway
T'ana Hāyk' l. see Tana, Lake
93 G8 Tanahjampea i. Indon.
94 A6 Tanahmerah Indon.
95 B4 Tanah Merah Malaysia
92 □ Tanah, Tanjung pt Indon.
102 D2 Tana, Lake l. Eth.
112 F3 Tanami Desert des. Austr.
95 C3 Tân An Vietnam
66 C2 Tanaro r. Italy
94 C4 Tanauan Phil.
88 F3 Tancheng China
100 B4 Tanda Côte d'Ivoire
85 E4 Tanda India
94 C4 Tandag Phil.
67 M2 Țăndărei Romania
94 A5 Tandek Malaysia
84 D2 Tandi India
47 E3 Tandil Arg.
47 E3 Tandil, Sa del h. Arg.
84 B4 Tando Adam Pak.
84 B4 Tando Bago Pak.
114 E4 Tandou L. l. Austr.
60 E3 Tandragee U.K.
83 E7 Tandur India
117 F3 Taneatua N.Z.
91 H3 Taneichi Japan
95 A1 Tanen Taunggyi mts Thai.
32 E5 Taneytown U.S.A.
100 B2 Tanezrouft reg. Alg./Mali
102 D4 Tanga Tanz.
117 E2 Tangaehe N.Z.
85 G4 Tangail Bangl.
111 F2 Tanga Is is P.N.G.
102 C4 Tanganyika, Lake l. Africa
89 B5 Tangdan China
Tanger see Tangier
92 □ Tangerang Indon.
88 B3 Tanggor China
85 G2 Tanggula Shan mts China
85 G2 Tanggula Shankou pass China
88 D3 Tanghe China
84 B2 Tangi Pak.
100 B1 Tangier Morocco
33 E6 Tangier I. i. U.S.A.
85 G4 Tangla India
95 □ Tanglin Sing.
85 H3 Tangmai China
91 E6 Tango Japan
85 F3 Tangra Yumco salt l. China
88 F2 Tangshan China
94 B4 Tangub Phil.
100 C3 Tanguieta Benin
89 C4 Tangyan He r. China
88 E3 Tangyin China
54 U3 Tanhua Fin.
95 C3 Tani Cambodia
85 H3 Taniantaweng Shan mts China
93 J8 Tanimbar, Kepulauan is Indon.
94 B4 Tanjay Phil.
95 A5 Tanjungbalai Indon.
92 D8 Tanjungkarang Telukbetung Indon.
92 D7 Tanjungpandan Indon.
92 C6 Tanjungpinang Indon.
95 A5 Tanjungpura Indon.
93 F6 Tanjungredeb Indon.
93 F6 Tanjungselor Indon.
84 B2 Tank Pak.
84 D2 Tankse Jammu and Kashmir
85 F4 Tankuhi India
111 G3 Tanna i. Vanuatu
57 F4 Tannadice U.K.
55 N5 Tannäs Sweden
116 D4 Tannum Sands Austr.
86 F1 Tannu-Ola, Khrebet mts Rus. Fed.
94 B4 Tañon Strait chan. Phil.
84 B4 Tanot India
100 C3 Tanout Niger
85 E4 Tansen Nepal
89 F5 Tan-shui Taiwan
78 C3 Tanta Egypt
100 A2 Tan-Tan Morocco
114 D6 Tantanoola Austr.
36 E4 Tantoyuca Mex.
55 M7 Tanumshede Sweden
114 C5 Tanunda Austr.
96 Tanzania country Africa
87 M2 Tao'an China
88 B3 Tao He r. China
89 D4 Taojiang China
88 C2 Taole China
95 □ Tao Payoh Sing.
66 F6 Taormina Sicily Italy
25 F4 Taos U.S.A.
100 B2 Taoudenni Mali
100 B1 Taourirt Morocco
89 E5 Taoxi China
89 D4 Taoyuan China
89 F5 T'ao-yuan Taiwan
55 T7 Tapa Estonia
94 B5 Tapaan Passage chan. Phil.
36 F6 Tapachula Mex.
43 G4 Tapajós r. Brazil
95 A5 Tapaktuan Indon.
47 E3 Tapalqué Arg.
95 A5 Tapanuli, Teluk b. Indon.
42 E5 Tapauá r. Brazil
42 F5 Tapauá Brazil
100 B4 Tapeta Liberia
84 C5 Tāpi r. India
94 B5 Tapiantana i. Phil.
30 C2 Tapiola U.S.A.
95 B4 Tapis mt Malaysia
85 F4 Taplejung Nepal
89 □ Tap Mun Chau i. Hong Kong China
32 E6 Tappahannock U.S.A.
32 C4 Tappan Lake l. U.S.A.
90 H3 Tappi-zaki pt Japan
117 D4 Tapuaenuku mt. N.Z.
94 B5 Tapul Phil.
94 B5 Tapul Group is Phil.
45 D5 Tapurucuara Brazil
81 L4 Tāq-e Bostan mt Iraq
81 K4 Țaqțaq Iraq
46 B1 Taquaral, Serra do h. Brazil
46 B2 Taquari Brazil
43 G7 Taquari r. Brazil
46 A2 Taquari, Serra do h. Brazil
46 C3 Taquaritinga Brazil
46 B3 Taquaruçu r. Brazil
60 D5 Tar r. Rep. of Ireland
115 J1 Tara Austr.
100 D4 Taraba r. Nigeria
42 E7 Tarabuco Bol.
Țarābulus see Tripoli
45 C4 Taracua Brazil
60 E4 Tara, Hill of h. Rep. of Ireland
84 B4 Tar Ahmad Rind Pak.
84 E4 Tarahuwan India
85 G4 Tarai reg. India
94 A6 Tarakan i. Indon.
93 F6 Tarakan Indon.
80 C1 Taraklı Turkey
90 L2 Taraku-shima i. Rus. Fed.
115 H5 Taralga Austr.
115 H4 Tarana Austr.
84 D5 Tarana India
84 C3 Tārānagar India
Taranaki, Mt volc. see Egmont, Mt
65 E2 Tarancón Spain
63 J3 Taran, Mys pt Rus. Fed.
57 A3 Taransay i. U.K.
66 G4 Taranto Italy
66 G4 Taranto, Golfo di g. Italy
42 C5 Tarapoto Peru
117 F4 Tararua Range mts N.Z.
63 P6 Tarashcha Ukr.
42 E5 Tarauacá r. Brazil
42 D5 Tarauacá Brazil
117 F3 Tarawera N.Z.
117 F3 Tarawera, Mt mt. N.Z.
65 F2 Tarazona Spain
65 F3 Tarazona de la Mancha Spain
82 F1 Tarbagatay, Khrebet mts Kazak.
57 E3 Tarbat Ness pt U.K.
84 C2 Tarbela Dam dam Pak.
60 B5 Tarbert Rep. of Ireland
57 B3 Tarbert Scot. U.K.
57 C5 Tarbert Scot. U.K.
64 E5 Tarbes France
29 E5 Tarboro U.S.A.
114 A3 Tarcoola Austr.
115 G3 Tarcoon Austr.
115 G5 Tarcutta Austr.
87 P2 Tardoki-Yani, Gora mt Rus. Fed.
115 K3 Taree Austr.
114 E3 Tarella Austr.
76 L2 Tareya Rus. Fed.
24 E2 Targhee Pass pass U.S.A.
67 L2 Târgoviște Romania
67 K2 Târgu Jiu Romania
63 M7 Târgu Mureș Romania
63 N7 Târgu Neamț Romania
63 N7 Târgu Secuiesc Romania
81 L5 Tarhān Iran
93 L8 Tari P.N.G.
88 C2 Tarian Gol China
65 D4 Tarifa Spain
65 D4 Tarifa o Marroqui, Pta de pt Spain
42 F8 Tarija Bol.
93 K7 Tariku r. Indon.
79 F6 Tarīm Yemen
Tarim Basin basin see Tarim Pendi
82 F3 Tarim Pendi basin China
93 K7 Taritatu r. Indon.
81 K4 Tarjīl Iraq
105 F6 Tarka r. S. Africa
105 G6 Tarkastad S. Africa
26 E3 Tarkio U.S.A.
76 J3 Tarko-Sale Rus. Fed.
100 B4 Tarkwa Ghana
94 B3 Tarlac Phil.
64 F4 Tarn r. France
54 O4 Tärnaby Sweden
84 A3 Tarnak r. Afgh.
63 M7 Târnăveni Romania
63 K5 Tarnobrzeg Pol.
68 G2 Tarnogskiy Gorodok Rus. Fed.
63 K5 Tarnów Pol.
85 E3 Tarok Tso salt l. China
116 C5 Taroom Austr.
100 B1 Taroudannt Morocco
114 D6 Tarpenna Austr.
29 E7 Tarpum Bay Bahamas
66 D3 Tarquinia Italy
65 G2 Tarragona Spain
54 Q3 Tårrajaur Sweden
115 G9 Tarraleah Austr.
115 G4 Tarran Hills h. Austr.
117 B6 Tarras N.Z.
65 G2 Tàrrega Spain
80 E3 Tarsus Turkey
44 D2 Tartagal Arg.
81 L1 Tärtär r. Azer.
81 L1 Tärtär Azer.
64 D5 Tartas France
55 U7 Tartu Estonia
80 E4 Țarțūs Syria
46 E2 Tarumirim Brazil
90 C8 Tarumizu Japan
69 H6 Tarumovka Rus. Fed.
95 A5 Tarutung Indon.
66 E1 Tarvisio Italy
22 E4 Taschereau Can.
85 G4 Tashigang Bhutan
Tashio Chho see Thimphu
81 K1 Tashir Armenia
79 G3 Tashk, Daryacheh-ye salt pan Iran
79 K1 Tashkent Uzbek.
82 D2 Tash-Kömür Kyrgyzstan
22 F2 Tasiat, Lac l. Can.
16 Tasiilaq Greenland
92 □ Tasikmalaya Indon.
23 G2 Tasiujaq Can.
82 F1 Taskesken Kazak.
80 E1 Taşköprü Turkey
81 J2 Taşlıçay Turkey
14 F8 Tasman Basin sea feature Pac. Oc.
117 D4 Tasman Bay b. N.Z.
115 G9 Tasman Head hd Austr.
115 F9 Tasmania div. Austr.
117 D4 Tasman Mountains mts N.Z.
115 H9 Tasman Pen. pen. Austr.
14 E9 Tasman Plateau sea feature Pac. Oc.
111 F5 Tasman Sea sea Pac. Oc.
80 F1 Taşova Turkey
34 B3 Tassajara Hot Springs U.S.A.
23 F2 Tassialujjuaq, Lac l. Can.
100 C2 Tassili du Hoggar plat. Alg.
100 C2 Tassili n'Ajjer plat. Alg.
81 K2 Tasūj Iran
77 N3 Tas-Yuryakh Rus. Fed.
93 G7 Tataba Indon.
63 J7 Tatabánya Hungary
69 D6 Tatarbunary Ukr.
76 J4 Tatarsk Rus. Fed.
87 Q1 Tatarskiy Proliv str. Rus. Fed.
68 J4 Tatarstan, Respublika div. Rus. Fed.
81 K3 Tatavi r. Iran
116 A1 Tate r. Austr.
91 F6 Tateishi-misaki pt Japan
91 G6 Tateyama Japan
91 F5 Tate-yama volc. Japan
20 F2 Tathlina Lake l. Can.
78 E5 Tathlīth, W. watercourse S. Arabia
115 H6 Tathra Austr.
21 K2 Tatinnai Lake l. Can.
69 H5 Tatishchevo Rus. Fed.
24 A1 Tatla Lake Can.
20 D3 Tatlatui Prov. Park res. Can.
93 H8 Tat Mailau, G. mt Indon.
115 G6 Tatong Austr.
63 J6 Tatry reg. Pol.
20 B3 Tatshenshini r. Can.
69 G5 Tatsinskiy Rus. Fed.
90 E6 Tatsuno Japan
84 A4 Tatta Pak.
46 C3 Tatuí Brazil
20 E4 Tatuk Mtn mt. Can.
27 C5 Tatum U.S.A.
114 F6 Tatura Austr.
81 J2 Tatvan Turkey
55 J7 Tau Norway
43 K5 Taua Brazil
46 D3 Taubaté Brazil
104 F3 Taung S. Africa
83 J6 Taung-gyi Myanmar
95 A2 Taungnyo Range mts Myanmar
84 B3 Taunsa Barrage barrage Pak.
59 D6 Taunton U.K.
33 H4 Taunton U.S.A.
117 F3 Taupo N.Z.
117 E3 Taupo, Lake l. N.Z.
55 S9 Tauragė Lith.
117 F2 Tauranga N.Z.
66 G5 Taurianova Italy
117 D1 Tauroa Pt pt N.Z.
111 F2 Tauu is P.N.G.
80 B3 Tavas Turkey
59 J5 Taverham U.K.
65 C4 Tavira Port.
59 C7 Tavistock U.K.
95 A2 Tavoy Myanmar
95 A2 Tavoy Pt pt Myanmar
80 B2 Tavşanlı Turkey
59 C6 Taw r. U.K.
31 F3 Tawas Bay b. U.S.A.
31 F3 Tawas City U.S.A.
93 F6 Tawau Malaysia
59 D6 Tawe r. U.K.
84 C2 Tawi r. India
94 A5 Tawitawi i. Phil.
89 F6 T'a-wu Taiwan
36 E5 Taxco Mex.
82 E3 Taxkorgan China
20 C2 Tay r. Can.
57 E4 Tay r. U.K.
94 B3 Tayabas Bay b. Phil.
54 X2 Taybola Rus. Fed.
57 E4 Tay, Firth of est. U.K.
57 C5 Tayinloan U.K.
57 D4 Tay, Loch l. U.K.
20 E3 Taylor Can.
35 G4 Taylor AZ U.S.A.
31 F4 Taylor MI U.S.A.
30 B6 Taylor MO U.S.A.
26 D3 Taylor NE U.S.A.
27 D6 Taylor TX U.S.A.
35 E5 Taylors Island U.S.A.
28 B4 Taylorville U.S.A.
78 D4 Taymā' S. Arabia
77 L3 Taymura r. Rus. Fed.
77 M2 Taymyr, Ozero l. Rus. Fed.
77 L2 Taymyr, Poluostrov pen. Rus. Fed.
95 C3 Tây Ninh Vietnam
94 A4 Taytay Phil.
94 B3 Taytay Phil.
94 A4 Taytay Bay b. Phil.
92 □ Tayu Indon.
77 K2 Taz r. Rus. Fed.
100 B1 Taza Morocco
81 K4 Tāza Khurmātū Iraq
91 H4 Tazawa-ko l. Japan
81 L2 Tazeh Kand Azer.
32 B6 Tazewell TN U.S.A.
32 C6 Tazewell VA U.S.A.
21 H2 Tazin r. Can.
21 H3 Tazin Lake l. Can.
101 E2 Tāzirbū Libya
65 J4 Tazmalt Alg.
76 J3 Tazovskaya Guba chan. Rus. Fed.
81 J1 Tba Khozap'ini l. Georgia
69 H7 T'bilisi Georgia
69 G6 Tbilisskaya Rus. Fed.
102 B4 Tchibanga Gabon
101 D2 Tchigaï, Plateau du plat. Niger
101 D4 Tcholliré Cameroon
63 J3 Tczew Pol.
117 A6 Te Anau N.Z.
117 A6 Te Anau, L. l. N.Z.
36 F5 Teapa Mex.
117 G2 Te Araroa N.Z.
117 E2 Te Aroha N.Z.
117 E3 Te Awamutu N.Z.
58 E3 Tebay U.K.
21 K2 Tebesjuak Lake l. Can.
100 C1 Tébessa Alg.
66 B7 Tébessa, Monts de mts Alg.
44 E3 Tebicuary r. Para.
92 C7 Tebingtinggi Indon.
92 B6 Tebingtinggi Indon.
66 C6 Téboursa Tunisia
66 C6 Teboursouk Tunisia
69 H7 Tebulos Mt'a mt. Georgia/Rus. Fed.
100 B4 Techiman Ghana
44 B6 Tecka Arg.
61 F2 Tecklenburger Land reg. Ger.
36 D5 Tecomán Mex.
34 D4 Tecopa U.S.A.
63 N7 Tecuci Romania
31 F5 Tecumseh U.S.A.
79 J2 Tedzhen Turkm.
35 H3 Teec Nos Pos U.S.A.
86 F1 Teeli Rus. Fed.
58 F3 Tees r. U.K.
58 E3 Teesdale reg. U.K.
94 A4 Teeth, The mt Phil.
42 E4 Tefé r. Brazil
80 B3 Tefenni Turkey
92 □ Tegal Indon.
59 D5 Tegid, Llyn l. U.K.
36 G6 Tegucigalpa Honduras
100 C3 Teguidda-n-Tessoumt Niger
34 C4 Tehachapi U.S.A.
25 C5 Tehachapi Mts mts U.S.A.
34 C4 Tehachapi Pass pass U.S.A.
21 K2 Tehek Lake l. Can.
Teheran see Tehrān
100 B4 Téhini Côte d'Ivoire
79 G2 Tehrān Iran
Tehri see Tikamgarh
84 D3 Tehri India
36 F5 Tehuantepec, Golfo de g. Mex.
36 F5 Tehuantepec, Istmo de isth. Mex.
59 C5 Teifi r. U.K.
59 D7 Teign r. U.K.
59 D7 Teignmouth U.K.
Tejo r. see Tagus
34 C4 Tejon Pass pass U.S.A.
117 D1 Te Kao N.Z.
117 C5 Tekapo, L. l. N.Z.
85 F4 Tekari India
36 G4 Tekax Mex.
102 D2 Tekezē Wenz r. Eritrea/Eth.
84 E1 Tekiliktag mt China
80 A1 Tekirdağ Turkey
81 H2 Tekman Turkey
85 H5 Teknaf Bangl.
30 E4 Tekonsha U.S.A.
117 E3 Te Kuiti N.Z.
85 E5 Tel r. India
69 H7 T'elavi Georgia
80 E5 Tel Aviv-Yafo Israel
62 G6 Telč Czech Rep.
36 G4 Telchac Puerto Mex.
20 C3 Telegraph Creek Can.
64 G3 Télégraphe, Le h. France
46 B4 Telêmaco Borba Brazil
47 D3 Telén Arg.
67 L2 Teleorman r. Romania
34 D3 Telescope Peak summit U.S.A.
43 G5 Teles Pires r. Brazil
59 E5 Telford U.K.
100 A3 Télimélé Guinea
81 J3 Tel Kotchek Syria
20 D4 Telkwa Can.
77 V3 Teller Alaska
81 L6 Telloh Iraq
95 □ Telok Blangah Sing.
47 C4 Telsen Arg.
55 S9 Telšiai Lith.
95 B4 Teluk Anson Malaysia
31 H2 Temagami Can.
31 G2 Temagami Lake l. Can.
92 □ Temanggung Indon.
105 H2 Temba S. Africa
92 D6 Tembelan, Kepulauan is Indon.
77 L3 Tembenchi r. Rus. Fed.
105 H3 Tembisa S. Africa
102 B4 Tembo Aluma Angola
59 E5 Teme r. U.K.
34 D5 Temecula U.S.A.
80 D2 Temelli Turkey
92 C6 Temerloh Malaysia
81 N5 Temīleh Iran
86 B1 Temirtau Kazak.
31 H2 Temiscaming Can.
31 H2 Témiscamingue, Lac l. Can.
23 G4 Témiscouata, L. l. Can.
115 F8 Temma Austr.
54 T4 Temmes Fin.
68 G4 Temnikov Rus. Fed.
115 G5 Temora Austr.
35 G5 Tempe U.S.A.
66 C4 Tempio Pausania Sardinia Italy
30 E3 Temple MI U.S.A.
27 D6 Temple TX U.S.A.
59 C5 Temple Bar U.K.
60 D5 Templemore Rep. of Ireland
94 A4 Templer Bank sand bank Phil.
58 E3 Temple Sowerby U.K.
69 F6 Temryuk Rus. Fed.
47 B3 Temuco Chile
117 C6 Temuka N.Z.
42 C4 Tena Ecuador
34 D1 Tenabo, Mt mt. U.S.A.
83 F7 Tenali India
95 A2 Tenasserim Myanmar
95 A2 Tenasserim r. Myanmar
59 E5 Tenbury Wells U.K.
59 C6 Tenby U.K.
31 F2 Tenby Bay Can.
102 E2 Tendaho Eth.
64 H4 Tende France
83 H9 Ten Degree Channel chan. Andaman and Nicobar Is India
91 H4 Tendō Japan
81 J2 Tendürük Dağı mt Turkey
100 B3 Ténenkou Mali
100 D3 Ténéré reg. Niger
100 D2 Ténéré du Tafassâsset des. Niger
100 A2 Tenerife i. Canary Is
65 G4 Ténès Alg.

93 F8 Tengah, Kepulauan is Indon.
95 Tengeh Res. resr Sing.
88 B2 Tengger Shamo des. China
95 B4 Tenggul i. Malaysia
89 C7 Tengqiao China
100 B3 Tengréla Côte d'Ivoire
89 D6 Teng Xian Guangxi China
88 E3 Teng Xian Shandong China
119 B2 Teniente Jubany Argentina Base Ant.
119 B2 Teniente Rodolfo Marsh Chile Base Ant.
103 C5 Tenke Zaire
77 Q2 Tenkeli Rus. Fed.
100 B3 Tenkodogo Burkina
113 F3 Tennant Creek Austr.
29 C5 Tennessee r. U.S.A.
32 B6 Tennessee div. U.S.A.
25 T4 Tennessee Pass pass U.S.A.
54 P2 Tennevoll Norway
47 Q2 Teno r. Chile
54 U2 Tenojoki r. Fin./Norway
36 F5 Tenosique Mex.
91 F6 Tenryū Japan
91 F6 Tenryū r. Japan
24 E2 Ten Sleep U.S.A.
93 G7 Tenteno Indon.
59 H6 Tenterden U.K.
115 K2 Tenterfield Austr.
29 D7 Ten Thousand Islands is U.S.A.
65 C3 Tentudia mt Spain
46 B3 Teodoro Sampaio Brazil
46 E2 Teófilo Otôni Brazil
93 H8 Tepa Indon.
25 E6 Tepachi Mex.
117 D1 Te Paki N.Z.
36 D4 Tepatitlán Mex.
81 H3 Tepe Turkey
81 J3 Tepe Gawra Iraq
36 C3 Tepehuanes Mex.
37 J4 Tepelenë Albania
45 E4 Tepequem, Serra mts Brazil
36 D4 Tepic Mex.
117 C5 Te Pirita N.Z.
62 F5 Teplice Czech Rep.
68 K2 Teplogorka Rus. Fed.
68 H4 Teploye Rus. Fed.
117 E4 Te Puke N.Z.
65 H1 Ter r. Spain
109 Teraina i. Line Islands Pac. Oc.
84 D2 Teram Kangri mt China/Jammu and Kashmir
66 E3 Teramo Italy
114 E7 Terang Austr.
84 B3 Teratani r. Pak.
69 F4 Terbuny Rus. Fed.
81 H2 Tercan Turkey
63 M6 Terebovlya Ukr.
69 H7 Terek Rus. Fed.
69 H7 Terek r. Rus. Fed.
68 J4 Teren'ga Rus. Fed.
46 A3 Terenos Brazil
45 C2 Terepaima, Parque Nacional nat. park Venez.
68 H4 Tereshka r. Rus. Fed.
43 K5 Teresina Brazil
46 D3 Teresópolis Brazil
61 B5 Tergnier France
80 F1 Terme Turkey
79 K2 Termez Uzbek.
66 E6 Termini Imerese Sicily Italy
36 F5 Términos, Lag. de b. Mex.
66 F4 Termoli Italy
59 E2 Tern r. U.K.
93 H6 Ternate Indon.
61 B3 Terneuzen Neth.
66 E3 Terni Italy
69 C5 Ternopil' Ukr.
114 C4 Terowie Austr.
87 Q2 Terpeniya, Mys c. Rus. Fed.
87 Q2 Terpeniya, Zaliv g. Rus. Fed.
20 D4 Terrace Can.
30 D1 Terrace Bay Can.
104 E2 Terra Firma S. Africa
54 N4 Terråk Norway
66 C5 Terralba Sardinia Italy
23 K4 Terra Nova Nat. Pk nat. park Can.
119 B6 Terre Adélie reg. Ant.
27 F6 Terre Bonne Bay b. U.S.A.
28 C4 Terre Haute U.S.A.
23 K4 Terrenceville Can.
24 F2 Terry U.S.A.
69 G5 Tersa r. Rus. Fed.
61 D1 Terschelling i. Neth.
86 C3 Terskey Ala-Too mts Kyrgyzstan
66 C5 Tertenia Sardinia Italy
65 F2 Teruel Spain
95 A4 Terutao i. Thai.
54 T3 Tervola Fin.
66 G2 Tešanj Bos.-Herz.
102 D2 Teseney Eritrea
68 G4 Tesha r. Rus. Fed.
90 K2 Teshikaga Japan
90 H1 Teshio Japan
90 J2 Teshio-dake mt. Japan
90 H1 Teshio-gawa r. Japan
90 J1 Teshio-sanchi mts Japan
20 C2 Teslin r. Can.
20 C2 Teslin Can.
20 C2 Teslin Lake l. Can.
46 B1 Tesouras r. Brazil

46 B2 Tesouro Brazil
100 C3 Tessaoua Niger
59 F6 Test r. U.K.
66 C6 Testour Tunisia
44 B2 Tetas, Pta pt Chile
103 D5 Tete Moz.
117 F3 Te Teko N.Z.
63 P5 Teteriv r. Ukr.
62 F4 Teterow Ger.
63 O6 Tetiyiv Ukr.
58 G4 Tetney U.K.
24 E2 Teton r. U.S.A.
24 E3 Teton Ra. mts U.S.A.
100 B1 Tétouan Morocco
67 J3 Tetovo Macedonia
84 B5 Tetpur India
68 J4 Tetyushi Rus. Fed.
90 B8 Teuchi Japan
44 D2 Teuco r. Arg.
104 B1 Teufelsbach Namibia
90 H1 Teuri-tō i. Japan
55 R5 Teuva Fin.
Teverya see Tiberias
57 F5 Teviot r. U.K.
57 F5 Teviotdale v. U.K.
117 A7 Te Waewae Bay b. N.Z.
105 G1 Tewane Botswana
116 E6 Tewantin Austr.
117 E4 Te Wharau N.Z.
59 E6 Tewkesbury U.K.
88 B3 Têwo China
20 E5 Texada I. i. Can.
27 E5 Texarkana U.S.A.
115 J2 Texas Austr.
27 D6 Texas div. U.S.A.
27 E6 Texas City U.S.A.
61 C1 Texel i. Neth.
27 C4 Texhoma U.S.A.
27 D5 Texoma, Lake l. U.S.A.
105 G4 Teyateyaneng Lesotho
68 G3 Teykovo Rus. Fed.
68 G3 Teza r. Rus. Fed.
85 H4 Tezpur India
85 J4 Tezu India
21 K2 Tha-anne r. Can.
105 H4 Thabana-Ntlenyana mt Lesotho
105 G4 Thaba Nchu S. Africa
105 G4 Thaba Putsoa mt. Lesotho
105 H4 Thaba-Tseka Lesotho
105 G2 Thabazimbi S. Africa
95 B1 Tha Bo Laos
105 G3 Thabong S. Africa
95 A2 Thagyettaw Myanmar
89 C6 Thai Binh Vietnam
84 B3 Thai Desert des. Pak.
70 Thailand country Asia
95 B3 Thailand, Gulf of g. Asia
89 B6 Thai Nguyên Vietnam
84 E5 Thakurtola India
84 B2 Thal Pak.
66 C7 Thala Tunisia
95 A3 Thalang Thai.
95 A3 Thale Luang lag. Thai.
95 B1 Tha Li Thai.
115 H2 Thallon Austr.
105 F2 Thamaga Botswana
79 G6 Thamarīt Oman
78 F7 Thamar, J. mt Yemen
59 E6 Thame r. U.K.
117 E2 Thames N.Z.
59 H6 Thames est. Eng. U.K.
59 G6 Thames r. Eng. U.K.
31 G4 Thamesville Can.
95 A2 Thanbyuzayat Myanmar
84 C5 Thandla India
83 D7 Thāne India
84 B5 Thangadh India
95 D2 Thăng Binh Vietnam
116 D5 Thangool Austr.
95 C1 Thanh Hoa Vietnam
83 E8 Thanjavur India
95 B1 Tha Pla Thai.
95 A3 Thap Put Thai.
95 A3 Thap Sakae Thai.
84 B4 Tharad India
84 B4 Thar Desert des. India/Pak.
114 E1 Thargomindah Austr.
83 J7 Tharrawaddy Myanmar
67 L4 Thasos i. Greece
35 H5 Thatcher U.S.A.
89 C6 Thât Khê Vietnam
95 A1 Thaton Myanmar
85 H4 Thaungdut Myanmar
95 A1 Thaungyin r. Myanmar/Thai.
35 F5 Theba U.S.A.
26 C3 Thedford U.S.A.
61 C2 The Hague Neth.
95 A3 Theinkun Myanmar
21 H2 Thekulthili Lake l. Can.
21 J2 Thelon r. Can.
21 J2 Thelon Game Sanctuary res. Can.
104 F6 Thembalesizwe S. Africa
105 H3 Thembalihle S. Africa
65 H4 Thenia Alg.
65 H5 Theniet El Had Alg.
116 D5 Theodore Austr.
42 F5 Theodore Roosevelt r. Brazil
35 G5 Theodore Roosevelt Lake l. U.S.A.
26 C2 Theodore Roosevelt Nat. Park nat. park U.S.A.
33 F2 Theresa U.S.A.
116 B4 Theresa Cr. r. Austr.
67 K4 Thermaïkos Kolpos g. Greece
34 B2 Thermalito U.S.A.
24 E3 Thermopolis U.S.A.
31 F2 Thessalon Can.

67 K4 Thessaloniki Greece
59 H5 Thet r. U.K.
59 H5 Thetford U.K.
23 F4 Thetford Mines Can.
95 C1 Theun r. Laos
105 G4 Theunissen S. Africa
27 F6 Thibodaux U.S.A.
21 K3 Thicket Portage Can.
26 D1 Thief River Falls U.S.A.
64 F1 Thiers France
100 A3 Thiès Senegal
102 D4 Thika Kenya
83 D9 Thiladhunmathee Atoll atoll Maldives
85 G4 Thimphu Bhutan
64 H2 Thionville France
Thira i. see Santorini
67 L6 Thirasia i. Greece
58 F3 Thirsk U.K.
Thiruvananthapuram see Trivandrum
55 L8 Thisted Denmark
114 B5 Thistle I. i. Austr.
67 K5 Thiva Greece
21 K3 Thlewiaza r. Can.
21 H2 Thoa r. Can.
105 J1 Thohoyandou S. Africa
32 D5 Thomas U.S.A.
29 C5 Thomaston GA U.S.A.
33 J2 Thomaston ME U.S.A.
33 K2 Thomaston Corner Can.
60 D5 Thomastown Rep. of Ireland
29 D6 Thomasville U.S.A.
61 E4 Thommen Belgium
21 K3 Thompson Man. Can.
20 E4 Thompson r. Can.
30 D3 Thompson MI U.S.A.
33 F4 Thompson PA U.S.A.
26 E3 Thompson r. U.S.A.
24 D2 Thompson Falls U.S.A.
116 A4 Thomson watercourse Austr.
29 D5 Thomson U.S.A.
95 C1 Thôn Cư Lai Vietnam
62 C7 Thonon-les-Bains France
95 D3 Thôn Sơn Hai Vietnam
25 E5 Thoreau U.S.A.
115 F2 Thorlindah, L. salt flat Austr.
61 D3 Thorn Neth.
58 F3 Thornaby-on-Tees U.K.
30 E4 Thornapple r. U.S.A.
59 E6 Thornbury U.K.
31 H2 Thorne r. Can.
58 G4 Thorne U.K.
34 C2 Thorne U.S.A.
20 C3 Thorne Bay U.S.A.
30 D5 Thorntown U.S.A.
30 B3 Thorp U.S.A.
119 D3 Thorshavnheiane mts Ant.
105 G4 Thota-ea-Moli Lesotho
64 D3 Thouars France
33 E2 Thousand Islands is Can.
35 G2 Thousand Lake Mt mt. U.S.A.
34 C4 Thousand Oaks U.S.A.
67 L4 Thrakiko Pelagos sea Greece
24 E2 Three Forks U.S.A.
20 G4 Three Hills Can.
115 F8 Three Hummock I. i. Austr.
117 D1 Three Kings Is is N.Z.
30 C3 Three Lakes U.S.A.
30 D5 Three Oaks U.S.A.
95 A2 Three Pagodas Pass pass Myanmar/Thai.
100 B4 Three Points, Cape c. Ghana
30 E5 Three Rivers MI U.S.A.
27 D6 Three Rivers TX U.S.A.
24 D2 Three Sisters mt. U.S.A.
Thrissur see Trichur
27 D5 Throckmorton U.S.A.
21 G2 Thubun Lakes l. Can.
95 C3 Thu Dâu Môt Vietnam
61 C4 Thuin Belgium
103 C6 Thuli Zimbabwe
62 C7 Thun Switz.
30 C1 Thunder Bay b. Can.
30 C1 Thunder Bay Can.
31 F3 Thunder Bay r. U.S.A.
95 A3 Thung Song Thai.
95 A4 Thung Wa Thai.
60 D5 Thurles Rep. of Ireland
32 E5 Thurmont U.S.A.
62 F7 Thurn, Paß pass Austria
33 F2 Thurso r. Scot. U.K.
57 E2 Thurso U.K.
119 A3 Thurston I. i. Ant.
58 F3 Thwaite U.K.
55 L8 Thyborøn Denmark
88 A1 Tiancang China
88 F3 Tianchang China
89 C6 Tiandeng China
89 C6 Tiandong China
89 C5 Tian'e China
43 K4 Tianguá Brazil
88 E2 Tianjin China
88 E2 Tianjin div. China
82 J3 Tianjun China
89 C5 Tianlin China
89 D4 Tianmen China
89 E4 Tianmu Shan mts China
89 B4 Tianquan China
88 B3 Tianshui China
84 D2 Tianshuihai China/Jammu and Kashmir
88 F4 Tiantai China
88 E1 Tiantaiyong China

89 C6 Tianyang China
88 B2 Tianzhu Gansu China
89 C5 Tianzhu Guizhou China
100 C1 Tiaret Alg.
116 E5 Tiaro Austr.
100 B4 Tiassalé Côte d'Ivoire
46 B4 Tibagi Brazil
46 B4 Tibagi r. Brazil
81 J5 Tibal, Wādī watercourse Iraq
101 D4 Tibati Cameroon
66 E3 Tiber r. Italy
80 E5 Tiberias Israel
Tiberias, Lake l. see Galilee, Sea of
24 E1 Tiber Res. resr U.S.A.
101 D2 Tibesti mts Chad
Tibet Aut. Region div. see Xizang Zizhiqu
Tibet, Plateau of plat. see Xizang Gaoyuan
114 E2 Tibooburra Austr.
85 E3 Tibrikot Nepal
85 E3 Tibrikot Nepal
55 O7 Tibro Sweden
36 B3 Tiburón i. Mex.
94 B3 Ticao i. Phil.
59 H6 Ticehurst U.K.
31 J3 Tichborne Can.
100 B3 Tichît Maur.
100 A3 Tichla Western Sahara
62 D7 Ticino r. Switz.
33 G3 Ticonderoga U.S.A.
36 G4 Ticul Mex.
55 N7 Tidaholm Sweden
85 H5 Tiddim Myanmar
100 C2 Tidikelt, Plaine du plain Alg.
100 A3 Tidjikja Maur.
61 D3 Tiel Neth.
88 G1 Tieling China
84 D2 Tielongtan China/Jammu and Kashmir
61 B4 Tielt Belgium
100 B4 Tiémé Côte d'Ivoire
61 C4 Tienen Belgium
74 Tien Shan mts China/Kyrgyzstan
Tientsin see Tianjin
55 P6 Tierp Sweden
25 F4 Tierra Amarilla U.S.A.
36 E5 Tierra Blanca Mex.
44 C8 Tierra del Fuego, Isla Grande de i. Arg./Chile
65 D2 Tiétar r. Spain
65 D2 Tiétar, Valle de v. Spain
46 C3 Tietê Brazil
46 B3 Tietê r. Brazil
32 B4 Tiffin U.S.A.
Tiflis see T'bilisi
29 D5 Tifton U.S.A.
67 L3 Tigheciului, Dealurile h. Moldova
69 D6 Tighina Moldova
85 F5 Tigiria India
101 D4 Tignère Cameroon
23 H4 Tignish P.E.I. Can.
42 C4 Tigre r. Ecuador/Peru
45 E2 Tigre r. Venez.
81 L5 Tigris r. Iraq/Turkey
78 E6 Tihāmah reg. S. Arabia
80 D7 Tîh, Gebel el plat. Egypt
36 A2 Tijuana Mex.
46 C2 Tijuco r. Brazil
84 D4 Tikamgarh India
69 G6 Tikhoretsk Rus. Fed.
68 E3 Tikhvin Rus. Fed.
68 E3 Tikhvinskaya Gryada ridge Rus. Fed.
117 D3 Tikokino N.Z.
111 G3 Tikopia i. Solomon Is
81 J4 Tikrīt Iraq
54 W3 Tiksheozero, Oz. l. Rus. Fed.
77 O2 Tiksi Rus. Fed.
85 F4 Tila r. Nepal
85 F4 Tilaiya Reservoir India
115 F1 Tilbooroo Austr.
61 D3 Tilburg Neth.
59 H6 Tilbury U.K.
44 C3 Tilcara Arg.
114 D2 Tilcha Austr.
85 H5 Tilin Myanmar
100 C3 Tillabéri Niger
57 E4 Tillicoultry U.K.
31 G4 Tillsonburg Can.
57 F3 Tillyfourie U.K.
67 M6 Tilos i. Greece
114 D2 Tilpa Austr.
81 J2 Timar Turkey
69 F6 Timashevsk Rus. Fed.
100 B3 Timbedgha Maur.
112 F3 Timber Creek Austr.
34 D3 Timber Mt mt. U.S.A.
32 E5 Timberville U.S.A.
114 E7 Timboon Austr.
100 B3 Timétrine reg. Mali
100 C2 Timimoun Alg.
67 J2 Timişoara Romania
31 G1 Timmins Can.
68 F3 Timokhino Rus. Fed.
93 H3 Timor i. Indon.
110 C3 Timor Sea sea Austr./Indon.
68 H3 Timoshino Rus. Fed.
47 D2 Timote Arg.
45 P5 Timrå Sweden
29 C5 Tims Ford L. l. U.S.A.
84 D5 Timurni Muafi India

45 C2 Tinaco Venez.
116 E5 Tin Can Bay Austr.
83 E8 Tindivanam India
100 B2 Tindouf Alg.
95 C5 Tinggi i. Malaysia
115 J2 Tingha Austr.
89 E5 Ting Jiang r. China
85 F3 Tingri China
55 O8 Tingsryd Sweden
47 B2 Tinguiririca, Vol. Chile
54 L5 Tingvoll Norway
57 E1 Tingwall U.K.
46 E1 Tinharé, Ilha de i. Brazil
95 C1 Tinh Gia Vietnam
93 L4 Tinian i. N. Mariana Is
92 Tinjil i. Indon.
44 C3 Tinogasta Arg.
67 L6 Tinos i. Greece
100 C2 Tinrhert, Plateau du plat. Alg.
85 H4 Tinsukia India
59 C7 Tintagel U.K.
114 D5 Tintinara Austr.
57 E5 Tinto h. U.K.
32 E4 Tioga U.S.A.
95 C5 Tioman i. Malaysia
31 F1 Tionaga Can.
32 D4 Tionesta Lake l. U.S.A.
33 G3 Tioughnioga r. U.S.A.
65 H4 Tipasa Alg.
30 C5 Tippecanoe r. U.S.A.
30 E5 Tippecanoe Lake l. U.S.A.
60 C5 Tipperary Rep. of Ireland
85 F4 Tiptala Bhanjyang pass Nepal
30 B5 Tipton IA U.S.A.
30 D5 Tipton IN U.S.A.
35 E4 Tipton, Mt mt. U.S.A.
30 E1 Tip Top Hill h. Can.
59 H6 Tiptree U.K.
45 C4 Tiquié r. Brazil
43 J4 Tiracambu, Serra do h. Brazil
67 H4 Tirana Albania
Tiranë see Tirana
66 D1 Tirano Italy
69 D6 Tiraspol Moldova
104 B3 Tiraz Mts mts Namibia
80 A2 Tire Turkey
57 B4 Tiree i. Scot. U.K.
84 B1 Tirich Mir mt Pak.
85 F5 Tirtol India
83 E8 Tiruchchirāppalli India
83 E8 Tirupati India
83 E8 Tiruppur India
21 J4 Tisdale Can.
65 G5 Tissemsilt Alg.
85 G4 Tista r. India
77 O2 Tit-Ary Rus. Fed.
42 E7 Titicaca, Lago l. Bol./Peru
85 E5 Titlagarh India
66 G2 Titov Drvar Bos.-Herz.
31 E4 Tittabawassee r. U.S.A.
67 L2 Titu Romania
29 D6 Titusville FL U.S.A.
32 D4 Titusville PA U.S.A.
31 G3 Tiverton Can.
59 D7 Tiverton U.K.
66 E4 Tivoli Italy
65 H4 Tizi El Arba h. Alg.
36 G4 Tizimín Mex.
65 J4 Tizi Ouzou Alg.
45 D2 Tiznados r. Venez.
100 B2 Tiznit Morocco
105 J2 Tjaneni Swaziland
54 O4 Tjappsåive Sweden
61 D2 Tjeukemeer l. Neth.
55 K7 Tjorhom Norway
27 C2 Tlahualilo Mex.
36 E5 Tlaxcala Mex.
100 B1 Tlemcen Alg.
104 E4 Tlhakalatlou S. Africa
105 H4 Tlholong S. Africa
105 F2 Tlokweng Botswana
20 D3 Toad River Can.
91 F6 Toba Japan
95 A5 Toba, Danau l. Indon.
42 F1 Tobago i. Trinidad and Tobago
84 A3 Toba & Kakar Ranges mts Pak.
93 H6 Tobelo Indon.
31 G3 Tobermory Can.
57 B4 Tobermory U.K.
90 H2 Tōbetsu Japan
21 J4 Tobin L. l. Can.
34 D1 Tobin, Mt mt. U.S.A.
91 G5 Tobi-shima i. Japan
92 D7 Toboali Indon.
76 H4 Tobol r. Kazak./Rus. Fed.
95 D2 Tô Bong Vietnam
115 F5 Tocantinópolis Brazil
43 J5 Tocantins r. Brazil
46 C1 Tocantinzinha r. Brazil
29 D5 Toccoa U.S.A.
84 B2 Tochi r. Pak.
91 G5 Tochigi Japan
91 G5 Tochio Japan
55 M7 Töcksfors Sweden
44 B2 Tocopilla Chile
45 D2 Tocuyo r. Venez.
93 G7 Todeli Indon.
62 D7 Todi mt Switz.
91 J4 Todoga-saki pt Japan
90 H3 Todohokke Japan
42 E7 Todos Santos Bol.
29 C5 Todos Santos Mex.
34 D6 Todos Santos, Bahía de b. Mex.

20 G4 Tofield Can.
20 D5 Tofino Can.
57 □ Toft U.K.
30 E2 Tofte U.S.A.
111 J3 Tofua i. Tonga
91 F5 Togi Japan
93 G7 Togian, Kepulauan is Indon.
96 Togo country Africa
90 C7 Tōgō Japan
30 A2 Togo U.S.A.
88 D1 Togtoh China
35 H4 Tohatchi U.S.A.
54 T5 Toholampi Fin.
88 B1 Tohom China
91 G6 Toi Japan
55 S6 Toija Fin.
90 C8 Toi-misaki pt Japan
55 U5 Toivakka Fin.
34 D2 Toiyabe Range mts U.S.A.
90 D6 Tōjō Japan
90 J2 Tokachi-gawa r. Japan
91 F6 Tōkai Japan
91 G5 Tōkamachi Japan
117 B7 Tokanui N.Z.
101 F3 Tokar Sudan
87 N6 Tokara-rettō is Japan
80 F1 Tokat Turkey
106 Tokelau terr. Pac. Oc.
82 E4 Tokmak Kyrgyzstan
69 E6 Tokmak Ukr.
117 G3 Tokomaru Bay N.Z.
91 F6 Tokoname Japan
117 G3 Tokoroa N.Z.
90 J2 Tokoro-gawa r. Japan
105 H3 Tokoza S. Africa
82 E4 Toksun China
87 O4 Tok-tō i. Japan
90 E6 Tokushima Japan
90 E6 Tokushima Japan
90 C6 Tokuyama Japan
91 G6 Tōkyō Japan
91 G6 Tōkyō Japan
91 G6 Tōkyō-wan b. Japan
117 G3 Tolaga Bay N.Z.
103 E6 Tôlañaro Madag.
46 B4 Toledo Brazil
65 D3 Toledo Spain
30 A5 Toledo IA U.S.A.
32 B4 Toledo OH U.S.A.
27 E6 Toledo Bend Reservoir resr U.S.A.
65 D3 Toledo, Montes de mts Spain
116 A1 Tolga Can.
47 B3 Tolhuaca, Parque Nacional nat. park Chile
103 E6 Toliara Madag.
45 B4 Tolima, Nev. del volc. Col.
93 G6 Tolitoli Indon.
76 K3 Tol'ka Rus. Fed.
68 D3 Tolmachevo Rus. Fed.
66 E1 Tolmezzo Italy
89 Tolo Channel chan. Hong Kong China
89 Tolo Harbour b. Hong Kong China
65 E1 Tolosa Spain
31 F3 Tolsmaville Can.
57 B2 Tolsta Head hd U.K.
45 B2 Tolú Col.
36 E5 Toluca Mex.
54 W3 Tolvand, Oz. l. Rus. Fed.
68 J4 Tol'yatti Rus. Fed.
30 B4 Tomah U.S.A.
30 C3 Tomahawk U.S.A.
90 H2 Tomakomai Japan
90 H1 Tomamae Japan
111 H3 Tomanivi mt Fiji
45 E5 Tomar Brazil
65 B3 Tomar Port.
90 H2 Tomari Japan
80 E2 Tomarza Turkey
47 F1 Tomás Gomensoro Uru.
63 L5 Tomaszów Lubelski Pol.
63 K5 Tomaszów Mazowiecki Pol.
57 E3 Tomatin U.K.
90 D6 Tombara Japan
29 B6 Tombigbee r. U.S.A.
102 B4 Tomboco Angola
46 D3 Tombos Brazil
100 B3 Tombouctou Mali
35 G6 Tombstone U.S.A.
103 B5 Tomboa Angola
105 H1 Tom Burke S. Africa
47 B3 Tomé Chile
105 L1 Tomé Moz.
55 N9 Tomelilla Sweden
65 E3 Tomelloso Spain
82 C2 Tomenaryk Kazak.
31 H2 Tomiko Can.
115 H4 Tomingley Austr.
100 B3 Tominian Mali
93 G7 Tomini, Teluk g. Indon.
57 E3 Tomintoul U.K.
91 H5 Tomioka Japan
66 G2 Tomislavgrad Bos.-Herz.
54 O3 Tømmerneset Norway
77 O4 Tommot Rus. Fed.
45 C3 Tomo r. Col.
45 D4 Tomo Col.
88 D1 Tomortei China
77 Q3 Tompo Rus. Fed.
112 C4 Tom Price Austr.
76 K4 Tomsk Rus. Fed.
55 O8 Tomtabacken h. Sweden
77 Q3 Tomtor Rus. Fed.
90 J2 Tomuraushi-yama mt. Japan
69 G6 Tomuzlovka r. Rus. Fed.
36 F5 Tonalá Mex.

35 G3 Tonalea U.S.A.
91 F5 Tonami Japan
42 E4 Tonantins Brazil
24 C1 Tonasket U.S.A.
59 H6 Tonbridge U.K.
93 G6 Tondano Indon.
55 L9 Tønder Denmark
59 E6 Tone r. U.K.
91 H6 Tone-gawa r. Japan
114 E3 Tonga N.S.W. Austr.
106 Tonga country Pac. Oc.
105 J4 Tongaat S. Africa
114 F6 Tongala Austr.
89 F5 Tong'an China
109 Tongareva atoll Cook Islands Pac. Oc.
117 E3 Tongariro National Park nat. park N.Z.
111 J4 Tongatapu Group is Tonga
14 H7 Tonga Tr. sea feature Pac. Oc.
88 D3 Tongbai China
88 D3 Tongbai Shan mts China
88 E4 Tongcheng Anhui China
89 D4 Tongcheng Hubei China
88 C3 Tongchuan China
89 C5 Tongdao China
88 A3 Tongde China
61 D4 Tongeren Belgium
89 E4 Tonggu China
89 D7 Tonggu Jiao pt China
89 B5 Tonghai China
87 N3 Tonghua China
87 O2 Tongjiang Heilongjiang China
88 C4 Tongjiang Sichuan China
92 D2 Tongking, Gulf of g. China/Vietnam
89 C4 Tongliang China
88 G1 Tongliao China
88 E4 Tongling China
89 F4 Tonglu China
89 B4 Tongnan China
114 E3 Tongo Lake salt flat Austr.
94 B5 Tongquil i. Phil.
89 C5 Tongren Guizhou China
88 A3 Tongren Qinghai China
85 G4 Tongsa r. Bhutan
89 E4 Tongshan China
85 H2 Tongtian He r. China
57 D2 Tongue U.K.
24 F2 Tongue r. U.S.A.
29 E7 Tongue of the Ocean chan. Bahamas
88 B3 Tongwei China
88 E2 Tong Xian China
88 B2 Tongxin China
88 E4 Tongyanghe China
87 M3 Tongyu China
89 C4 Tongzi China
30 C5 Tonica U.S.A.
84 C4 Tonk India
89 B6 Tonkin reg. Vietnam
68 H3 Tonkino Rus. Fed.
95 C5 Tônlé Basăk r. Cambodia
95 C2 Tônle Repou r. Laos
95 B2 Tônlé Sab l. Cambodia
91 H4 Tōno Japan
34 D2 Tonopah U.S.A.
45 E2 Tonoro r. Venez.
90 E6 Tonoshō Japan
55 M7 Tønsberg Norway
55 K7 Tonstad Norway
35 G5 Tonto National Monument res. U.S.A.
85 H5 Tonzang Myanmar
115 H2 Toobeah Austr.
24 D3 Tooele U.S.A.
115 K1 Toogoolawah Austr.
114 E6 Tooleybuc Austr.
114 A4 Tooligie Austr.
115 H6 Tooma r. Austr.
115 G7 Toora Austr.
115 H3 Tooraweenah Austr.
104 F6 Toorberg mt S. Africa
115 J1 Toowoomba Austr.
35 G6 Topawa U.S.A.
34 C2 Topaz U.S.A.
26 E4 Topeka U.S.A.
20 D4 Topley Landing Can.
47 B2 Topocalma, Pta pt Chile
35 E4 Topock U.S.A.
62 J6 Topolčany Slovakia
36 C3 Topolobampo Mex.
67 M3 Topolovgrad Bulg.
54 W2 Topozero, Oz. l. Rus. Fed.
24 B2 Toppenish U.S.A.
33 K2 Topsfield U.S.A.
35 F3 Toquerville U.S.A.
102 D3 Tor Eth.
67 M5 Torbalı Turkey
79 H2 Torbat-e-Heydarīyeh Iran
79 J2 Torbat-e Jām Iran
68 G4 Torbeyevo Rus. Fed.
30 E3 Torch Lake l. U.S.A.
65 D2 Tordesillas Spain
54 S4 Töre Sweden
65 H1 Torelló Spain
62 F5 Torgau Ger.
69 H5 Torgun r. Rus. Fed.
Torino see Turin
87 Q5 Tori-shima i. Japan
101 F4 Torit Sudan
46 B2 Torixoreu Brazil
81 L3 Torkamān Iran
68 G3 Tor'kovskoye Vdkhr. resr Rus. Fed.
65 D2 Tormes r. Spain
54 S3 Torneälven r. Fin./Sweden
54 Q2 Torneträsk Sweden
54 Q2 Torneträsk l. Sweden

23 H2 Torngat Mountains mts Can.
54 T4 Tornio Fin.
Tornionjoki r. see Torneälven
47 D3 Tornquist Arg.
65 D2 Toro Spain
115 J4 Toronto Austr.
31 H4 Toronto Can.
68 D3 Toropets Rus. Fed.
34 D5 Toro Pk summit U.S.A.
102 D3 Tororo Uganda
80 D3 Toros Dağları mts Turkey
57 F3 Torphins U.K.
59 D7 Torquay U.K.
34 D3 Torrance U.S.A.
65 B3 Torrão Port.
65 C2 Torre mt. Port.
65 G2 Torreblanca Spain
66 F4 Torre del Greco Italy
65 D1 Torrelavega Spain
65 D2 Torremolinos Spain
116 A3 Torrens Cr. watercourse Austr.
116 A3 Torrens Creek Austr.
114 B3 Torrens, Lake salt flat Austr.
65 F3 Torrent Spain
36 D3 Torreón Mex.
111 G3 Torres Islands is Vanuatu
65 B3 Torres Novas Port.
110 E2 Torres Strait str. Austr.
65 B3 Torres Vedras Port.
65 G3 Torreta, Sa h. Spain
65 F4 Torrevieja Spain
35 G2 Torrey U.S.A.
59 C7 Torridge r. U.K.
57 C3 Torridon, Loch in. U.K.
57 C3 Torrijos Spain
115 J2 Torrington Austr.
33 G4 Torrington CT U.S.A.
24 F3 Torrington WY U.S.A.
65 H1 Torroella de Montgrí Spain
55 N6 Torsby Sweden
54 Tórshavn Faroe Is
47 C1 Tórtolas, Cerro Las mt Chile
66 C5 Tortolì Sardinia Italy
66 C2 Tortona Italy
65 G2 Tortosa Spain
81 H1 Tortum Turkey
81 G1 Torul Turkey
63 J4 Toruń Pol.
60 C2 Tory I. i. Rep. of Ireland
60 C2 Tory Sound chan. Rep. of Ireland
68 E3 Torzhok Rus. Fed.
90 D7 Tosa Japan
90 D7 Tosashimizu Japan
90 D7 Tosa-wan b. Japan
54 N4 Tosbotn Norway
104 D4 Tosca S. Africa
66 C3 Toscano, Arcipelago is Italy
91 H3 Tōshima-yama mt. Japan
68 D3 Tosno Rus. Fed.
44 D3 Tostado Arg.
90 C7 Tosu Japan
80 E1 Tosya Turkey
68 G3 Tot'ma Rus. Fed.
59 F7 Totton U.K.
90 D6 Tottori Japan
90 E6 Tottori Japan
100 B4 Touba Côte d'Ivoire
100 A3 Touba Senegal
100 B1 Toubkal, Jbel mt. Morocco
88 B3 Toudaohu China
100 B3 Tougan Burkina
100 C1 Touggourt Alg.
100 A3 Tougué Guinea
64 G2 Toul France
64 G5 Toulon France
64 E5 Toulouse France
100 B4 Toumodi Côte d'Ivoire
83 J7 Toungoo Myanmar
89 D5 Toupai China
95 B1 Tourakom Laos
61 B4 Tourcoing France
61 B4 Tournai Belgium
64 G4 Tournon-sur-Rhône France
64 G3 Tournus France
43 L5 Touros Brazil
64 E3 Tours France
104 D6 Touwsrivier S. Africa
45 C2 Tovar Venez.
59 F5 Tove r. U.K.
81 K1 Tovuz Azer.
91 H3 Towada Japan
90 H3 Towada-Hachimantai National Park Japan
91 H3 Towada-ko l. Japan
117 L1 Towai N.Z.
33 E4 Towanda U.S.A.
35 H3 Towaoc U.S.A.
59 G5 Towcester U.K.
60 C6 Tower Rep. of Ireland
30 A2 Tower U.S.A.
116 A3 Towerhill Cr. watercourse Austr.
21 J5 Towner U.S.A.
34 D3 Townes Pass pass U.S.A.
24 E2 Townsend U.S.A.
115 H6 Townsend, Mt mt Austr.
116 D4 Townshend I. i. Austr.
116 B2 Townsville Austr.
93 G7 Towori, Teluk b. Indon.
32 E5 Towson U.S.A.
90 H2 Tōya-ko l. Japan
91 F5 Toyama Japan
91 F5 Toyama Japan

91 F5 Toyama-wan b. Japan
90 D7 Tōyo Japan
91 F6 Toyohashi Japan
91 F6 Toyokawa Japan
91 F6 Toyonaka Japan
90 E6 Toyooka Japan
90 C6 Toyota Japan
91 F6 Toyota Japan
90 H1 Toyotomi Japan
100 C1 Tozeur Tunisia
69 G7 Tqibuli Georgia
69 G7 Tqvarch'eli Georgia
80 E4 Trâblous Lebanon
67 K4 Trabotivište Macedonia
81 G1 Trabzon Turkey
33 G1 Tracy Can.
34 B3 Tracy CA U.S.A.
26 E2 Tracy MN U.S.A.
30 A4 Traer U.S.A.
65 C4 Trafalgar, Cabo pt Spain
47 B3 Traiguén Chile
20 C5 Trail Can.
55 T9 Trakai Lith.
68 J2 Trakt Rus. Fed.
60 B5 Tralee Rep. of Ireland
60 B5 Tralee Bay b. Rep. of Ireland
45 E3 Tramán Tepui mt Venez.
60 D5 Tramore Rep. of Ireland
55 O7 Tranås Sweden
44 C3 Trancas Arg.
55 N8 Tranemo Sweden
57 F5 Tranent U.K.
95 A4 Trang Thai.
93 J8 Trangan i. Indon.
115 G4 Trangie Austr.
47 F1 Tranqueras Uru.
119 B5 Transantarctic Mountains mts Ant.
21 G4 Trans Canada Highway Can.
21 K5 Transcona Can.
52 Transylvanian Alps mts Romania
66 E5 Trapani Sicily Italy
115 G7 Traralgon Austr.
66 E3 Trasimeno, Lago l. Italy
65 E3 Trasvase, Canal de canal Spain
95 B2 Trat Thai.
62 F7 Traunsee l. Austria
62 F7 Traunstein Ger.
114 E4 Travellers L. l. Austr.
119 C1 Traversay Is is S. Sandwich Is Atlantic Ocean
30 E3 Traverse City U.S.A.
117 D5 Travers, Mt mt N.Z.
95 C5 Tra Vinh Vietnam
27 D6 Travis, L. l. U.S.A.
66 G2 Travnik Bos.-Herz.
66 F1 Trbovlje Slovenia
111 F2 Treasury Is is Solomon Is
62 G6 Třebíč Czech Rep.
67 H3 Trebinje Bos.-Herz.
63 K6 Trebišov Slovakia
66 F2 Trebnje Slovenia
116 B2 Trebonne Austr.
30 B3 Trego U.S.A.
116 D1 Tregosse Islets & Reefs is Coral Sea Is Terr.
57 D7 Treig, Loch l. U.K.
47 F2 Treinta-y-Tres Uru.
44 C6 Trelew Arg.
55 N9 Trelleborg Sweden
59 C5 Tremadoc Bay b. U.K.
22 F4 Tremblant, Mt h. Can.
66 F4 Tremiti, Isole is Italy
24 D3 Tremonton U.S.A.
65 G1 Tremp Spain
30 B3 Trempealeau r. U.S.A.
59 B7 Trenance U.K.
62 J6 Trenčín Slovakia
47 D2 Trenque Lauquén Arg.
58 E4 Trent r. U.K.
66 D1 Trento Italy
31 J3 Trenton Can.
26 E3 Trenton MO U.S.A.
33 F4 Trenton NJ U.S.A.
23 K4 Trepassey Can.
47 E3 Tres Arroyos Arg.
59 A8 Tresco i. U.K.
46 D3 Três Corações Brazil
54 B4 Tres Esquinas Col.
57 B4 Treshnish Isles is U.K.
46 B3 Três Lagoas Brazil
44 B7 Tres Lagos Arg.
47 D3 Tres Lomas Arg.
46 D2 Três Marias, Represa resr Brazil
47 B4 Tres Picos mt Arg.
47 D3 Tres Picos, Cerro mt Arg.
25 F4 Tres Piedras U.S.A.
46 D3 Três Pontas Brazil
44 C7 Tres Puntas, C. pt Arg.
46 D3 Três Rios Brazil
55 M6 Tretten Norway
55 L7 Treungen Norway
66 C2 Treviglio Italy
66 E2 Treviso Italy
59 B7 Trevose Head hd U.K.
115 G9 Triabunna Austr.
67 L6 Tria Nisia i. Greece
67 N6 Trianta Greece
84 B2 Tribal Areas div. Pak.
85 H5 Tricase Italy
83 H7 Trichur India
115 F4 Trida Austr.
62 C6 Trier Ger.
66 E2 Trieste Italy
66 E2 Trieste Italy
66 E1 Triglav mt Slovenia
67 J5 Trikala Greece
80 D4 Trikomon Cyprus
93 K7 Trikora, Pk mt Indon.

60 E4 Trim Rep. of Ireland
83 F9 Trincomalee Sri Lanka
46 C2 Trindade Brazil
12 G7 Trindade, Ilha da i. Atlantic Ocean
42 F6 Trinidad Bol.
45 C3 Trinidad Col.
37 J4 Trinidad Cuba
42 F1 Trinidad i. Trinidad and Tobago
47 F2 Trinidad Uru.
25 F4 Trinidad U.S.A.
38 Trinidad and Tobago country Caribbean Sea
116 A1 Trinity Bay b. Austr.
23 K4 Trinity Bay b. Can.
34 C1 Trinity Range mts U.S.A.
29 C5 Trion U.S.A.
67 K6 Tripoli Greece
101 D1 Tripoli Libya
Tripoli see Trâblous
85 G5 Tripura div. India
84 D3 Trisul mt India
85 F4 Trisul Dam dam Nepal
83 E9 Trivandrum India
66 F4 Trivento Italy
62 H6 Trnava Slovakia
110 F2 Trobriand Islands is P.N.G.
54 N4 Trofors Norway
66 G3 Trogir Croatia
66 F4 Troia Italy
62 C5 Troisdorf Ger.
23 F4 Trois-Rivières Can.
69 H6 Troitskoye Rus. Fed.
55 N7 Trollhättan Sweden
43 G3 Trombetas r. Brazil
13 H5 Tromelin, Île i. Indian Ocean
47 B3 Tromen, Volcán volc. Arg.
105 G3 Trompsburg S. Africa
54 Q2 Tromsø Norway
34 D4 Trona U.S.A.
47 B4 Tronador, Monte mt Arg.
54 M5 Trondheim Norway
54 M5 Trondheimsfjorden chan. Norway
80 D4 Troödos Cyprus
80 D4 Troödos, Mount mt Cyprus
57 D5 Troon U.K.
46 D1 Tropeiros, Serra dos h. Brazil
35 F3 Tropic U.S.A.
57 D7 Trossachs, The reg. U.K.
60 E2 Trostan h. U.K.
57 F3 Troup Head hd U.K.
20 E2 Trout r. Can.
31 H3 Trout Creek Can.
35 F2 Trout Creek U.S.A.
22 B3 Trout L. l. Can.
20 G3 Trout Lake Alta. Can.
20 G3 Trout Lake N.W.T. Can.
20 E2 Trout Lake l. Can.
30 C2 Trout Lake l. U.S.A.
30 E2 Trout Lake l. U.S.A.
24 E2 Trout Peak summit U.S.A.
32 E4 Trout Run U.S.A.
59 E6 Trowbridge U.K.
115 F8 Trowutta Austr.
29 C6 Troy AL U.S.A.
24 D2 Troy MT U.S.A.
33 G3 Troy NH U.S.A.
33 G3 Troy NY U.S.A.
32 A4 Troy OH U.S.A.
32 E4 Troy PA U.S.A.
67 L3 Troyan Bulg.
64 G2 Troyes France
34 D2 Troy Lake l. U.S.A.
35 E2 Troy Peak summit U.S.A.
67 J3 Trstenik Yugo.
69 E4 Trubchevsk Rus. Fed.
65 C1 Truchas Spain
68 E3 Trud Rus. Fed.
37 G5 Trujillo Honduras
42 C5 Trujillo Peru
65 D3 Trujillo Spain
45 C2 Trujillo Venez.
33 G4 Trumbull U.S.A.
35 F3 Trumbull, Mt mt. U.S.A.
95 A5 Trumon Indon.
115 G4 Trundle Austr.
95 C2 Trung Hiệp Vietnam
89 C6 Trung Khanh China
23 H4 Truro Can.
59 B7 Truro U.K.
60 C3 Truskmore h. Rep. of Ireland
20 E3 Trutch Can.
25 F5 Truth or Consequences U.S.A.
62 G5 Trutnov Czech Rep.
67 L7 Trypiti, Akra pt Greece
55 N6 Trysil Norway
62 G7 Trzebiatów Pol.
86 E2 Tsagaannuur Mongolia
69 H6 Tsagan Aman Rus. Fed.
69 H6 Tsagan-Nur Rus. Fed.
69 G7 Ts'ageri Georgia
81 K1 Tsalka Georgia
103 E5 Tsaratanana, Massif du mts Madag.
104 D3 Tsaris Mts mts Namibia
69 H5 Tsatsa Rus. Fed.
104 A3 Tsaukaib Namibia
102 D4 Tsavo National Park nat. park Kenya
69 G6 Tselina Rus. Fed.
103 B6 Tses Namibia
103 C6 Tshabong Botswana
103 C6 Tshane Botswana

69 F6 Tschikskoye Vdkhr. resr Rus. Fed.
102 B4 Tshela Zaire
102 C4 Tshibala Zaire
102 C4 Tshikapa Zaire
102 C4 Tshikapa r. Zaire
105 J1 Tshipise S. Africa
103 C4 Tshitanzu Zaire
102 C4 Tshofa Zaire
105 J2 Tshokwane S. Africa
69 G6 Tsimlyansk Rus. Fed.
69 G6 Tsimlyanskoye Vdkhr. resr Rus. Fed.
104 E3 Tsineng S. Africa
Tsinghai see Qinghai
Tsingtao see Qingdao
89 Tsing Yi i. Hong Kong China
103 E6 Tsiombe Madag.
103 E5 Tsiroanomandidy Madag.
104 E7 Tsitsikamma Forest and Coastal National Park nat. park S. Africa
20 D4 Tsitsutl Pk summit Can.
68 H4 Tsivil'sk Rus. Fed.
69 G7 Ts'khinvali Georgia
68 G4 Tsna r. Rus. Fed.
84 D2 Tsokr Chumo l. India
105 H5 Tsolo S. Africa
105 G6 Tsomo S. Africa
84 D2 Tso Morari L. l. India
69 G7 Tsqaltubo Georgia
91 G5 Tsu Japan
91 G5 Tsubame Japan
90 K2 Tsubetsu Japan
91 H5 Tsuchiura Japan
89 Tsuen Wan Hong Kong China
90 H3 Tsugaru-kaikyō str. Japan
87 Q3 Tsugaru-kaikyō str. Japan
91 G5 Tsugawa Japan
91 F6 Tsukechi Japan
90 H2 Tsukigata Japan
91 H5 Tsukuba Japan
90 C7 Tsukumi Japan
90 C7 Tsuno Japan
90 H3 Tsuno-shima i. Japan
85 G4 Tsunthang India
91 F5 Tsuruga Japan
90 E7 Tsurugi-san mt. Japan
90 D7 Tsurumi-zaki pt Japan
91 G4 Tsuruoka Japan
90 B6 Tsushima i. Japan
Tsushima-kaikyō str. see Korea Strait
90 C6 Tsuwano Japan
90 E6 Tsuyama Japan
104 D1 Tswaane Botswana
105 F4 Tswaraganang S. Africa
105 F3 Tswelelang S. Africa
63 M4 Tsyelyakhany Belarus
54 X2 Tsyp-Navolok Rus. Fed.
69 E6 Tsyurupyns'k Ukr.
93 J8 Tual Indon.
60 C4 Tuam Rep. of Ireland
117 A7 Tuamarina N.Z.
109 Tuamotu Archipelago is Pac. Oc.
89 B6 Tuân Giao Vietnam
91 F6 Tuangku i. Indon.
69 F6 Tuapse Rus. Fed.
95 Tuas Sing.
117 A7 Tuatapere N.Z.
35 G3 Tuba City U.S.A.
92 Tuban Indon.
44 G3 Tubarão Brazil
100 A4 Tubmanburg Liberia
94 B4 Tubod Phil.
101 E1 Tubruq Libya
109 Tubuai i. Fr. Polynesia Pac. Oc.
109 Tubuai, Îles is Fr. Polynesia Pac. Oc.
43 L6 Tucano Brazil
47 B3 Tucapel, Pta pt Chile
42 E7 Tucavaca Bol.
20 D2 Tuchitua Can.
33 F5 Tuckerton U.S.A.
35 G5 Tucson U.S.A.
35 G5 Tucson Mts mts U.S.A.
45 E2 Tucuco r. Venez.
25 G5 Tucumcari U.S.A.
45 E2 Tucupita Venez.
43 J4 Tucuruí Brazil
43 J4 Tucuruí, Represa resr Brazil
81 M3 Tū Dār Iran
65 F1 Tudela Spain
65 C2 Tuela r. Port.
89 Tuen Mun Hong Kong China
85 H4 Tuensang India
105 J4 Tugela r. S. Africa
94 C4 Tugnug Point pt Phil.
94 B2 Tuguegarao Phil.
77 P4 Tugur Rus. Fed.
88 F2 Tuhai r. China
95 Tuhemberua Indon.
65 B1 Tui Spain
45 A2 Tuira r. Panama
93 G8 Tukangbesi, Kepulauan is Indon.
22 E2 Tukarak Island i. Can.

117 F3 Tukituki r. N.Z.
55 S8 Tukums Latvia
68 F4 Tula Rus. Fed.
85 H1 Tulagt Ar Gol r. China
36 E4 Tulancingo Mex.
34 C3 Tulare U.S.A.
34 C3 Tulare Lake Bed l. U.S.A.
25 F5 Tularosa U.S.A.
104 C6 Tulbagh S. Africa
42 C3 Tulcán Ecuador
67 N2 Tulcea Romania
69 D5 Tul'chyn Ukr.
34 C3 Tule r. U.S.A.
85 G4 Tule-la Pass pass Bhutan
21 J2 Tulemalu Lake l. Can.
27 C5 Tulia U.S.A.
80 E5 Tulkarm West Bank
60 C5 Tulla Rep. of Ireland
115 F8 Tullah Austr.
29 C5 Tullahoma U.S.A.
115 G4 Tullamore Austr.
115 J3 Tullamore Rep. of Ireland
64 E4 Tulle France
54 O5 Tulleråsen Sweden
115 G4 Tullibigeal Austr.
27 E6 Tullos U.S.A.
60 E5 Tullow Rep. of Ireland
116 B1 Tully Austr.
116 A1 Tully r. Austr.
60 D3 Tully U.K.
33 E3 Tully U.S.A.
116 A1 Tully Falls waterfall Austr.
68 D2 Tulos Rus. Fed.
27 D4 Tulsa U.S.A.
68 F4 Tul'skaya Oblast' div. Rus. Fed.
45 A3 Tuluá Col.
77 V3 Tuluksak Alaska
47 C1 Tulum, Valle de v. Arg.
86 H1 Tulun Rus. Fed.
92 Tulungagung Indon.
85 H4 Tulung La pass China
94 A4 Tuluran i. Phil.
45 A4 Tumaco Col.
105 G3 Tumahole S. Africa
69 J6 Tumak Rus. Fed.
55 P7 Tumba Sweden
102 B4 Tumba, Lac l. Zaire
94 C5 Tumbao Phil.
113 J7 Tumbarumba Austr.
42 B4 Tumbes Peru
20 E3 Tumbler Ridge Can.
114 B5 Tumby Bay Austr.
88 D1 Tumd Youqi China
88 D1 Tumd Zuoqi China
87 N3 Tumen China
88 B2 Tumenzi China
42 E2 Tumereng Guyana
84 A4 Tumindao i. Phil.
83 E8 Tumkur India
57 E4 Tummel, Loch l. U.K.
87 Q2 Tumnin r. Rus. Fed.
79 H4 Tump Pak.
95 B4 Tumpat Malaysia
100 B3 Tumu Ghana
43 G3 Tumucumaque, Serra h. Brazil
115 H5 Tumut Austr.
59 H6 Tunbridge Wells, Royal U.K.
81 G2 Tunceli Turkey
89 D7 Tunchang China
115 K4 Tuncurry Austr.
84 D4 Tundla India
103 D5 Tunduru Tanz.
67 M3 Tundzha r. Bulg.
85 H3 Tunga Pass pass China/India
94 B5 Tungawan Phil.
89 Tung Chung Wan b. Hong Kong China
20 D4 Tungnaá r. Iceland
20 D2 Tungsten Can.
68 E1 Tunguda Rus. Fed.
77 K3 Tunguska, Nizhnyaya r. Rus. Fed.
89 Tung Wan b. Hong Kong China
100 D1 Tunis Tunisia
66 D6 Tunis, Golfe de g. Tunisia
96 Tunisia country Africa
115 H5 Tuniut r. Austr.
45 B3 Tunja Col.
88 D2 Tunliu China
54 N4 Tunnsjøen l. Norway
59 J5 Tunstall U.K.
54 V3 Tuntsa Fin.
54 W3 Tuntsayoki r. Fin./Rus. Fed.
23 H2 Tunungayualok Island i. Can.
47 C2 Tunuyán r. Arg.
47 C2 Tunuyán Arg.
88 E2 Tuo He r. China
88 F2 Tuoji Dao i. China
95 Tuŏl Khpos Cambodia
34 B3 Tuolumne U.S.A.
34 C3 Tuolumne Meadows U.S.A.
89 B5 Tuoniang Jiang r. China
85 H2 Tuotuo He China
85 H2 Tuotuoyan China
46 B3 Tupã Brazil
46 C3 Tupaciguara Brazil
81 L3 Tūp Āghāj Iran
47 E2 Tupancireta Brazil
45 C3 Tuparro r. Col.
43 K5 Tupelo U.S.A.
42 E8 Tupiza Bol.
33 F2 Tupper Lake l. U.S.A.
33 F2 Tupper Lake U.S.A.
47 C2 Tupungato Arg.

47 C2 Tupungato, Cerro *mt* Arg./Chile
81 K7 Tuqayyid *w.* Iraq
45 A4 Túquerres Col.
89 C7 Tuqu Wan *b.* China
85 G4 Tura India
77 M3 Tura Rus. Fed.
78 E5 Turabah S. Arabia
45 D3 Turagua, Serranía *mt* Venez.
117 E4 Turakina N.Z.
87 O1 Turana, Khrebet *mts* Rus. Fed.
117 E3 Turangi N.Z.
79 H1 Turan Lowland *lowland* Asia
80 G6 Turayf S. Arabia
55 T7 Turba Estonia
45 B2 Turbaco Col.
79 J4 Turbat Pak.
45 A2 Turbo Col.
63 L7 Turda Romania
81 M4 Türeh Iran
Turfan *see* Turpan
76 H5 Turgay Kazak.
67 M3 Türgovishte Bulg.
80 C2 Turgut Turkey
80 A2 Turgutlu Turkey
80 F1 Turhal Turkey
55 T7 Türi Estonia
65 F3 Turia *r.* Spain
45 D2 Turiamo Venez.
66 B2 Turin Italy
69 C5 Turiys'k Ukr.
86 J1 Turka Rus. Fed.
102 D3 Turkana, Lake *salt l.* Eth./Kenya
67 M4 Türkeli Adasī *i.* Turkey
82 C2 Turkestan Kazak.
70 Turkey *country* Asia
30 B4 Turkey *r.* U.S.A.
69 G5 Turki Rus. Fed.
79 G2 Turkmenbashi Turkm.
80 C2 Türkmen Dağı *mt* Turkey
70 Turkmenistan *country* Asia
80 F3 Türkoğlu Turkey
37 K4 Turks and Caicos Islands *terr.* Caribbean
37 K4 Turks Islands *is* Turks and Caicos Is
55 S6 Turku Fin.
102 D3 Turkwel *watercourse* Kenya
34 B3 Turlock U.S.A.
34 B3 Turlock L. *l.* U.S.A.
117 F4 Turnagain, Cape *c.* N.Z.
57 D5 Turnberry U.K.
35 G5 Turnbull, Mt *mt.* U.S.A.
36 G5 Turneffe Is *is* Belize
31 F3 Turner U.S.A.
61 E4 Turnhout Belgium
21 H3 Turnor Lake *l.* Can.
67 L3 Turnu Măgurele Romania
115 H4 Turon *r.* Austr.
68 G3 Turovets Rus. Fed.
82 G2 Turpan China
82 G2 Turpan Pendi *depression* China
37 J4 Turquino *mt* Cuba
57 F3 Turriff U.K.
81 K5 Turşāq Iraq
79 J1 Turtkul' Uzbek.
30 B2 Turtle Flambeau Flowage *resr* U.S.A.
21 H4 Turtleford Can.
116 D1 Turtle I. *i.* Coral Sea Is Terr. Aust.
30 A3 Turtle Lake U.S.A.
82 E2 Turugart Pass *pass* China/Kyrgyzstan
46 B2 Turvo *r. Goiás* Brazil
46 B2 Turvo *r. Goiás* Brazil
46 C3 Turvo *r. São Paulo* Brazil
35 F4 Tusayan U.S.A.
29 C5 Tuscaloosa U.S.A.
32 C4 Tuscarawas *r.* U.S.A.
32 E4 Tuscarora Mts *h.* U.S.A.
30 C6 Tuscola *IL* U.S.A.
27 D5 Tuscola *TX* U.S.A.
29 C5 Tuskegee U.S.A.
32 D4 Tussey Mts *h.* U.S.A.
81 J2 Tutak Turkey
68 F3 Tutayev Rus. Fed.
83 E9 Tuticorin India
26 D4 Tuttle Creek Res. *resr* U.S.A.
62 D7 Tuttlingen Ger.
111 J3 Tutuila *i. American Samoa* Pac. Oc.
103 C6 Tutume Botswana
54 W5 Tuupovaara Fin.
54 V5 Tuusniemi Fin.
106 Tuvalu *country* Pac. Oc.
36 E4 Tuxpan Mex.
36 F5 Tuxtla Gutiérrez Mex.
45 D2 Tuy *r.* Venez.
95 C2 Tuy Đưc Vietnam
89 B6 Tuyên Quang Vietnam
95 D2 Tuy Hoa Vietnam
81 M4 Tüysarkān Iran
80 D2 Tuz Gölü *salt l.* Turkey
35 F4 Tuzigoot National Monument *res.* U.S.A.
81 K4 Tuz Khurmātū Iraq
67 H2 Tuzla Bos.-Herz.
81 H2 Tuzla *r.* Turkey
Tuz, Lake *salt l. see* Tuz Gölü
69 F6 Tuzlov *r.* Rus. Fed.
55 L7 Tvedestrand Norway
68 E3 Tver' Rus. Fed.
68 E3 Tverskaya Oblast' *div.* Rus. Fed.

31 J3 Tweed Can.
57 F5 Tweed *r. England/Scotland* U.K.
115 K2 Tweed Heads Austr.
20 D4 Tweedsmuir Prov. Park *res.* Can.
104 C6 Tweefontein S. Africa
104 C2 Twee Rivier Namibia
61 E2 Twente *reg.* Neth.
34 D4 Twentynine Palms U.S.A.
23 K4 Twillingate Can.
24 D2 Twin Bridges U.S.A.
27 C6 Twin Buttes Res. *resr* U.S.A.
23 H3 Twin Falls Can.
24 D3 Twin Falls U.S.A.
20 F3 Twin Lakes Can.
33 H2 Twin Mountain U.S.A.
32 C6 Twin Oaks U.S.A.
34 B2 Twin Peak *summit* U.S.A.
114 A2 Twins, The Austr.
115 H6 Twofold B. *b.* Austr.
35 G4 Two Guns U.S.A.
30 B2 Two Harbors U.S.A.
21 G4 Two Hills Can.
24 D1 Two Medicine *r.* U.S.A.
30 D3 Two Rivers U.S.A.
85 H5 Tyao *r.* India/Myanmar
90 L1 Tyatya *mt.* Rus. Fed.
54 M5 Tydal Norway
32 D5 Tygart Lake *l.* U.S.A.
32 D5 Tygart Valley *v.* U.S.A.
87 N1 Tygda Rus. Fed.
27 E5 Tyler U.S.A.
27 F6 Tylertown U.S.A.
77 O4 Tynda Rus. Fed.
20 A2 Tyndall Gl. *gl.* U.S.A.
57 F4 Tyne *r.* U.K.
58 F2 Tynemouth U.K.
55 M5 Tynset Norway
80 E5 Tyre Lebanon
21 H2 Tyrell Lake *l.* Can.
87 O1 Tyrma Rus. Fed.
54 T4 Tyrnävä Fin.
67 K5 Tyrnavos Greece
32 D4 Tyrone U.S.A.
114 E5 Tyrrell *r.* Austr.
114 E5 Tyrrell, L. *l.* Austr.
52 Tyrrhenian Sea *sea* France/Italy
77 Q3 Tyubelyakh Rus. Fed.
76 J4 Tyukalinsk Rus. Fed.
76 H4 Tyumen' Rus. Fed.
77 N3 Tyung *r.* Rus. Fed.
Tyuratam *see* Leninsk
59 C6 Tywi *r.* U.K.
59 C5 Tywyn U.K.
105 J1 Tzaneen S. Africa

# U

103 C5 Uamanda Angola
45 E4 Uatatás *r.* Brazil
43 L5 Uauá Brazil
45 C4 Uaupés *r.* Brazil
45 D5 Uaupés Brazil
81 J7 U'aywij, W. *watercourse* S. Arabia
46 D3 Ubá Brazil
46 D2 Ubaí Brazil
46 E1 Ubaitaba Brazil
102 B4 Ubangi *r.* C.A.R./Zaire
45 B3 Ubate Col.
81 J5 Ubayyid, Wādī al *watercourse* Iraq/S. Arabia
90 C7 Ube Japan
65 E3 Úbeda Spain
46 C2 Uberaba Brazil
43 G7 Uberaba, Lagoa *l.* Bol./Brazil
46 C2 Uberlândia Brazil
95 □ Ubin, Pulau *i.* Sing.
95 B1 Ubolratna Res. *resr* Thai.
105 K3 Ubombo S. Africa
95 C2 Ubon Ratchathani Thai.
102 C4 Ubundu Zaire
81 L1 Ucar Azer.
42 D5 Ucayali *r.* Peru
84 B3 Uch Pak.
82 F1 Ucharal Kazak.
90 D7 Uchiko Japan
90 C8 Uchinoura Japan
90 H2 Uchiura-wan *b.* Japan
77 P4 Uchur *r.* Rus. Fed.
59 H7 Uckfield U.K.
20 D5 Ucluelet Can.
35 H3 Ucolo U.S.A.
24 F2 Ucross U.S.A.
77 P4 Uda *r.* Rus. Fed.
69 H6 Udachnoye Rus. Fed.
77 N3 Udachnyy Rus. Fed.
83 E8 Udagamandalam India
84 C4 Udaipur *Rajasthan* India
85 G5 Udaipur *Tripura* India
85 E5 Udanti *r.* India/Myanmar
55 M7 Uddevalla Sweden
57 D5 Uddingston U.K.
54 P4 Uddjaure *l.* Sweden
61 D3 Uden Neth.
82 E4 Udhampur Jammu and Kashmir
68 H2 Udimskiy Rus. Fed.
66 E1 Udine Italy
23 J2 Udjuktok Bay *b.* Can.
68 E3 Udomlya Rus. Fed.
95 B1 Udon Thani Thai.

77 P4 Udskaya Guba *b.* Rus. Fed.
83 D8 Udupi India
81 L7 Udyl', Ozero *l.* Rus. Fed.
62 G4 Ueckermünde Ger.
91 G5 Ueda Japan
93 G7 Uekuli Indon.
102 C3 Uele *r.* Zaire
62 E4 Uelzen Ger.
91 F6 Ueno Japan
102 C3 Uere *r.* Zaire
76 G4 Ufa Rus. Fed.
103 B6 Ugab *watercourse* Namibia
102 A2 Ugalla *r.* Tanz.
96 Uganda *country* Africa
105 H5 Ugie S. Africa
87 Q2 Uglegorsk Rus. Fed.
68 F3 Uglich Rus. Fed.
66 F2 Ugljan *i.* Croatia
68 G3 Uglovka Rus. Fed.
77 Q3 Ugol'naya Zyryanka Rus. Fed.
77 T3 Ugol'nyye Kopi Rus. Fed.
68 E4 Ugra Rus. Fed.
62 H6 Uherské Hradiště Czech Rep.
32 C4 Uhrichsville U.S.A.
57 B3 Uig U.K.
102 B4 Uíge Angola
54 W5 Uimaharju Fin.
35 H3 Uinkaret Plateau *plat.* U.S.A.
103 B6 Uis Mine Namibia
60 D4 Uisneach *h.* Rep. of Ireland
105 F6 Uitenhage S. Africa
61 E1 Uithuizen Neth.
23 H2 Uivak, Cape *hd* Can.
91 E6 Uji Japan
90 B8 Uji-guntō *is* Japan
84 C5 Ujjain India
93 F8 Ujung Pandang Indon.
81 J5 Ukhaydir Iraq
85 H4 Ukhrul India
68 K2 Ukhta *r.* Rus. Fed.
68 K2 Ukhta Rus. Fed.
115 K2 Uki Austr.
34 A2 Ukiah *CA* U.S.A.
24 C2 Ukiah *OR* U.S.A.
55 T9 Ukmergé Lith.
49 Ukraine *country* Europe
68 J2 Uktym Rus. Fed.
90 B7 Uku-jima *i.* Japan
104 D1 Ukwi Botswana
104 D1 Ukwi Pan *salt pan* Botswana
86 J2 Ulaanbaatar Mongolia
86 F2 Ulaangom Mongolia
115 H4 Ulan Austr.
82 J3 Ulan China
Ulan Bator *see* Ulaanbaatar
88 C1 Ulan Buh Shamo *des.* China
69 H6 Ulan Erge Rus. Fed.
69 H6 Ulan-Khol Rus. Fed.
88 C1 Ulansuhai Nur *l.* China
88 A1 Ulan Tohoi China
86 J1 Ulan-Ude Rus. Fed.
85 G2 Ulan Ul Hu *l.* China
80 F2 Ulaş Turkey
111 J4 Ulawa I. *i.* Solomon Is
87 N4 Ulchin S. Korea
55 L7 Ulefoss Norway
114 E2 Ulenia, Lake *salt flat* Austr.
55 U7 Ülenurme Estonia
86 G2 Uliastay Mongolia
54 X2 Ulita *r.* Rus. Fed.
115 J5 Ulladulla Austr.
57 C3 Ullapool U.K.
54 S5 Ullava Fin.
58 E3 Ullswater *l.* U.K.
87 O4 Ullŭng-do *i.* S. Korea
62 D6 Ulm Ger.
115 K2 Ulmarra Austr.
55 N8 Ulricehamn Sweden
55 L5 Ulsberg Norway
60 D3 Ulster Canal *canal* Rep. of Ireland/U.K.
114 E5 Ultima Austr.
80 B1 Ulubat Gölü *l.* Turkey
80 C2 Uluborlu Turkey
80 B1 Uludağ *mt* Turkey
95 B5 Ulu Kali, Gunung *mt* Malaysia
80 E3 Ulukışla Turkey
105 J4 Ulundi S. Africa
82 G1 Ulungur Hu *l.* China
95 □ Ulu Pandan Sing.
Uluru *h. see* Ayers Rock
112 F5 Uluru National Park *nat. park* Austr.
80 D1 Ulus Turkey
57 A1 Ulva *i.* U.K.
61 C3 Ulvenhout Neth.
58 D3 Ulverston U.K.
115 G8 Ulverstone Austr.
55 O6 Ulvsjön Sweden
68 J4 Ul'yanovka Rus. Fed.
68 H4 Ul'yanovskaya Oblast' *div.* Rus. Fed.
27 D4 Ulysses U.S.A.
69 D5 Uman' Ukr.
84 E5 Umaria India
84 D6 Umarkhed India
85 E6 Umarkot India
84 B4 Umarkot Pak.
24 C2 Umatilla U.S.A.
76 E3 Umba Rus. Fed.
33 H2 Umbagog Lake *l.* U.S.A.
110 E2 Umboi *i.* P.N.G.
54 R5 Umeå Sweden

54 Q4 Umeälven *r.* Sweden
105 K4 Umfolozi *r.* S. Africa
81 L7 Umgharah Kuwait
105 J4 Umhlanga S. Africa
22 E2 Umiujaq Can.
105 J5 Umkomaas S. Africa
105 J4 Umlazi S. Africa
81 K6 Umma Iraq
101 E3 Umm Keddada Sudan
81 L6 Umm Qasr Iraq
101 F3 Umm Ruwaba Sudan
101 E1 Umm Sa'ad Libya
24 A3 Umpqua *r.* U.S.A.
103 B5 Umpulo Angola
84 D5 Umred India
84 C5 Umreth India
105 H5 Umtata S. Africa
105 J5 Umtentweni S. Africa
100 C4 Umuahia Nigeria
46 B3 Umuarama Brazil
105 H5 Umvukulu S. Africa
105 J5 Umzinto S. Africa
66 C2 Una *r.* Bos.-Herz./Croatia
46 E1 Una Brazil
80 F6 'Unāb, W. al *watercourse* Jordan
46 C2 Unaí Brazil
84 B2 Unai Pass *pass* Afgh.
57 C2 Unapool U.K.
45 D2 Unare *r.* Venez.
80 E6 'Unayzah Jordan
78 E4 'Unayzah S. Arabia
81 G5 'Unayzah, Jabal *h.* Iraq
25 E4 Uncompahgre Plateau *plat.* U.S.A.
105 H4 Underberg S. Africa
114 D5 Underbool Austr.
26 C2 Underwood U.S.A.
68 E4 Unecha Rus. Fed.
115 G4 Ungarie Austr.
114 B5 Ungarra Austr.
23 G2 Ungava Bay *b.* Can.
22 F1 Ungava, Péninsule d' *pen.* Can.
87 O3 Unggi N. Korea
69 C6 Ungheni Moldova
68 J3 Uni Rus. Fed.
46 B4 União da Vitória Brazil
45 B4 Unilla *r.* Col.
42 F4 Unini *r.* Brazil
46 A4 Unión Para.
33 J2 Union *ME* U.S.A.
29 D5 Union *SC* U.S.A.
32 C6 Union *WV* U.S.A.
30 E5 Union City *OH* U.S.A.
32 C4 Union City *PA* U.S.A.
29 B4 Union City *TN* U.S.A.
104 E6 Uniondale S. Africa
35 F4 Union, Mt *mt.* U.S.A.
29 C5 Union Springs U.S.A.
32 D5 Uniontown U.S.A.
31 F4 Unionville U.S.A.
24 E3 Unita Mts. *mts* U.S.A.
70 United Arab Emirates *country* Asia
48 United Kingdom *country* Europe
16 United States of America *country* North America
21 H4 Unity Can.
33 J2 Unity *ME* U.S.A.
24 C2 Unity *OR* U.S.A.
84 C5 Unjha India
84 E4 Unnão India
57 □ Unst *i.* U.K.
85 G2 Unuli Horog China
90 C7 Unzen-dake *volc.* Japan
91 F5 Uozu Japan
85 F5 Upar Ghat *reg.* India
45 E2 Upata Venez.
103 C4 Upemba, Lac *l.* Zaire
103 C4 Upemba, Parc National de l' *nat. park* Zaire
94 C3 Upi Phil.
45 B3 Upía *r.* Col.
104 D4 Upington S. Africa
84 B5 Upleta India
54 W3 Upoloksha Rus. Fed.
111 J3 Upolu *i.* Western Samoa
32 B4 Upper Arlington U.S.A.
20 F4 Upper Arrow L. *l.* Can.
Upper Chindwin *see* Mawlaik
117 E4 Upper Hutt N.Z.
30 B4 Upper Iowa *r.* U.S.A.
33 K1 Upper Kent Can.
24 B3 Upper Klamath L. *l.* U.S.A.
24 B3 Upper L. *l.* U.S.A.
34 A2 Upper Lake U.S.A.
20 D2 Upper Liard Can.
60 D3 Upper Lough Erne *l.* U.K.
32 E5 Upper Marlboro U.S.A.
95 □ Upper Peirce Res. *resr* Sing.
23 J4 Upper Salmon Reservoir *resr* Can.
32 B4 Upper Sandusky U.S.A.
33 F2 Upper Saranac Lake *l.* U.S.A.
117 D4 Upper Takaka N.Z.
55 P7 Uppsala Sweden
22 H4 Upsala Can.
116 B2 Upstart B. *b.* Austr.
116 B2 Upstart, C. *hd* Austr.
33 H2 Upton U.S.A.
81 L7 Uqlat al 'Udhaybah *w.* Iraq
81 L6 Ur *r.* Iraq
45 A2 Urabá, Golfo de *b.* Col.
Uracas *i. see* Farallon de Pajaros
88 C1 Urad Qianqi China

88 C1 Urad Zhonghou Lianheqi China
91 G6 Uraga-suidō *chan.* Japan
91 G5 Uragawara Japan
90 J2 Urahoro Japan
90 J2 Urakawa Japan
115 G4 Ural *h.* Austr.
115 J3 Uralla Austr.
53 Ural Mountains *mts.* Rus. Fed.
76 H4 Ural'sk Kazak.
Ural'skiy Khrebet *mts see* Ural Mountains
102 D4 Urambo Tanz.
115 G5 Urana Austr.
115 G5 Urana, L. *l.* Austr.
46 D1 Urandi Brazil
21 H3 Uranium City Can.
115 G5 Uranquity Austr.
45 E4 Uraricoera Brazil
45 E4 Uraricoera Brazil
45 E4 Uraricoera *r.* Brazil
45 D3 Uraucaima, Sa *mt* Brazil
35 H2 Uravan U.S.A.
69 F5 Urazovo Rus. Fed.
30 C5 Urbana *IL* U.S.A.
32 B4 Urbana *OH* U.S.A.
115 K2 Urbenville Austr.
66 E3 Urbino Italy
42 D6 Urcos Peru
68 J2 Urdoma Rus. Fed.
58 F3 Ure *r.* U.K.
68 K3 Uren' Rus. Fed.
76 J3 Urengoy Rus. Fed.
111 G3 Uréparapara *i.* Vanuatu
117 F3 Urewera National Park *nat. park* N.Z.
68 J4 Urga *r.* Rus. Fed.
79 J1 Urgench Uzbek.
80 E2 Ürgüp Turkey
54 V2 Urho Kekkonen Kansallispuisto *nat. park* Fin.
45 B2 Uribia Col.
114 C2 Urisino Austr.
55 S6 Urjala Fin.
69 H7 Urkarakh Rus. Fed.
67 M5 Urla Turkey
60 D5 Urlingford Rep. of Ireland
Urmia *see* Orūmīyeh
Urmia, Lake *salt l. see* Orūmīyeh, Daryācheh-ye
89 □ Urmston Road *chan.* Hong Kong China
67 J3 Uroševac Yugo.
79 K2 Ûroteppa Tajik.
85 F3 Urru Co *salt l.* China
88 A1 Urt Mongolia
46 C1 Uruaçu Brazil
36 D5 Uruapan Mex.
42 D6 Urubamba *r.* Peru
43 G4 Urucara Brazil
43 K5 Uruçuí Brazil
46 D2 Urucuia *r.* Brazil
43 K5 Uruçui Preto *r.* Brazil
43 G4 Urucurituba Brazil
44 E3 Uruguaiana Brazil
44 E4 Uruguay *r.* Arg./Uru.
38 Uruguay *country* S. America
Uruk *see* Erech
Urumchi *see* Ürümqi
82 G3 Ürümqi China
115 K3 Urunga Austr.
69 G6 Urup *r.* Rus. Fed.
77 R5 Urup, O. *i.* Rus. Fed.
69 H7 Urus-Martan Rus. Fed.
90 H2 Uryū-gawa *r.* Japan
69 G5 Uryupinsk Rus. Fed.
68 J3 Urzhum Rus. Fed.
67 M2 Urziceni Romania
90 C7 Usa Japan
68 J4 Usa *r.* Rus. Fed.
80 B2 Uşak Turkey
103 B6 Usakos Namibia
119 B5 Usarp Mts *mts* Ant.
44 E8 Usborne, Mt *h.* Falkland Is
76 J1 Ushakova, O. *i.* Rus. Fed.
90 C7 Ushibuka Japan
82 E1 Ushtobe Kazak.
44 C8 Ushuaia Arg.
76 G3 Usinsk Rus. Fed.
59 E6 Usk *r.* U.K.
59 E6 Usk U.K.
85 E4 Uska India
68 C4 Uskhodni Belarus
69 F4 Usman' Rus. Fed.
55 S8 Usmas Ezers *l.* Latvia
68 J2 Usogorsk Rus. Fed.
86 H1 Usol'ye-Sibirskoye Rus. Fed.
64 G4 Ussel France
87 O3 Ussuriysk Rus. Fed.
87 J1 Ust'-Barguzin Rus. Fed.
69 G5 Ust'-Buzulukskaya Rus. Fed.
69 G6 Ust'-Donetskiy Rus. Fed.
66 E5 Ustica, Isola di *i. Sicily* Italy
77 M4 Ust'Ilimsk Rus. Fed.
76 G3 Ust'-Ilych Rus. Fed.
62 G5 Ústí nad Labem Czech Rep.
Ustinov *see* Izhevsk
62 H3 Ust'-Kamchatsk Rus. Fed.
86 D2 Ust'-Kamenogorsk Kazak.
77 M4 Ust'-Kut Rus. Fed.
77 P2 Ust'-Kuyga Rus. Fed.
69 F6 Ust'-Labinsk Rus. Fed.
55 V7 Ust'-Luga Rus. Fed.

77 P3 Ust'-Maya Rus. Fed.
76 G3 Ust'-Nem Rus. Fed.
77 Q3 Ust'-Nera Rus. Fed.
68 J2 Ust'-Ocheya Rus. Fed.
77 N2 Ust'-Olenek Rus. Fed.
77 Q3 Ust'omchug Rus. Fed.
86 H1 Ust'-Ordynskiy Rus. Fed.
77 S3 Ust'-Penzhino Rus. Fed.
76 K3 Ust'-Port Rus. Fed.
68 G2 Ust'-Shonosha Rus. Fed.
76 G3 Ust'-Tsil'ma Rus. Fed.
68 H2 Ust'-Ura Rus. Fed.
68 G2 Ust'-Vayen'ga Rus. Fed.
68 G2 Ust'-Vyyskaya Rus. Fed.
68 F3 Ust'ya *r.* Rus. Fed.
68 H2 Ust'ya Rus. Fed.
68 F3 Ust'ye Rus. Fed.
76 G5 Ustyurt Plateau *plat.* Kazak./Uzbek.
68 F3 Ustyuzhna Rus. Fed.
91 G5 Usuda Japan
90 C7 Usuki Japan
35 G2 Usvyaty Rus. Fed.
90 C7 Uto Japan
85 E4 Utraula India
61 D2 Utrecht Neth.
105 J3 Utrecht S. Africa
65 D4 Utrera Spain
54 U2 Utsjoki Fin.
91 G5 Utsunomiya Japan
69 H6 Utta Rus. Fed.
95 B1 Uttaradit Thai.
84 D4 Uttar Pradesh *div.* India
59 F5 Uttoxeter U.K.
111 G3 Utupua *i.* Solomon Is
54 T5 Uurainen Fin.
55 R6 Uusikaupunki Fin.
45 C4 Uva *r.* Col.
69 G5 Uvarovo Rus. Fed.
102 D4 Uvinza Tanz.
105 J5 Uvongo S. Africa
86 F1 Uvs Nuur *salt l.* Mongolia
90 D7 Uwa Japan
90 D7 Uwajima Japan
101 E2 Uweinat, Jebel *mt* Sudan
59 G6 Uxbridge U.K.
88 C2 Uxin Ju China
88 C2 Uxin Qi China
76 L4 Uyar Rus. Fed.
88 C1 Üydzin Mongolia
77 Q3 Uyega Rus. Fed.
100 C4 Uyo Nigeria
42 E8 Uyuni, Salar de *salt flat* Bol.
68 H4 Uza *r.* Rus. Fed.
81 K4 'Uẓaym, Nahr al *r.* Iraq
70 Uzbekistan *country* Asia
64 G4 Uzès France
69 B5 Uzhhorod Ukr.
67 H3 Užice Yugo.
68 F4 Uzlovaya Rus. Fed.
68 G3 Uzola *r.* Rus. Fed.
80 C3 Üzümlü Turkey
81 L3 Üzün Darreh *r.* Iran
69 C7 Uzunköprü Turkey
69 D5 Uzyn Ukr.

# V

55 T5 Vaajakoski Fin.
104 E4 Vaal *r.* S. Africa
54 U4 Vaala Fin.
104 E4 Vaalbos National Park *nat. park* S. Africa
105 H3 Vaal Dam *dam* S. Africa
105 H2 Vaalwater S. Africa
54 R5 Vaasa Fin.
63 J7 Vác Hungary
46 A3 Vacaria *r. Mato Grosso do Sul* Brazil
46 D2 Vacaria *r. Minas Gerais* Brazil
44 F3 Vacaria Brazil
43 A3 Vacaria, Serra *h.* Brazil
34 B2 Vacaville U.S.A.
68 G4 Vad *r.* Rus. Fed.
84 C6 Vada India
55 K7 Vadla Norway
54 V1 Vadsø Norway
62 D7 Vaduz Liechtenstein
54 N3 Værøy *i.* Norway
68 G2 Vaga *r.* Rus. Fed.
55 L6 Vågåmo Norway
66 F2 Vaganski Vrh *mt* Croatia
54 □ Vágar *i.* Faroe Is
54 □ Vágsele Sweden
54 □ Vágur *i.* Faroe Is
55 S5 Våhäkyrö Fin.
55 T7 Vaida Estonia
35 G5 Vail U.S.A.
111 H2 Vaitupu *i.* Tuvalu
31 K2 Val-Barrette Can.
55 P6 Valbo Sweden
47 C4 Valcheta Arg.

66 D2 Valdagno Italy
52 Valdai Hills hills Rus. Fed.
68 E3 Valday Rus. Fed.
68 E3 Valdayskaya Vozvyshennost' reg. Rus. Fed.
65 D3 Valdecañas, Embalse de resr Spain
55 S8 Valdemārpils Latvia
55 P7 Valdemarsvik Sweden
64 G2 Val-de-Meuse France
65 E3 Valdepeñas Spain
64 E2 Val-de-Reuil France
31 K3 Val-des-Bois Can.
47 D4 Valdés, Península pen. Arg.
16 Valdez U.S.A.
47 B3 Valdivia Chile
31 J1 Val-d'Or Can.
29 D6 Valdosta U.S.A.
55 L6 Valdres v. Norway
81 J1 Vale Georgia
24 C2 Vale U.K.
20 F4 Valemount Can.
46 E1 Valença Brazil
64 G4 Valence France
65 F3 Valencia div. Spain
65 F3 Valencia Spain
45 D2 Valencia Venez.
65 C3 Valencia de Alcántara Spain
65 D1 Valencia de Don Juan Spain
65 G3 Valencia, Golfo de g. Spain
60 A6 Valencia Island i. Rep. of Ireland
64 F1 Valenciennes France
35 F4 Valentine AZ U.S.A.
26 C2 Valentine NE U.S.A.
27 B6 Valentine TX U.S.A.
94 B3 Valenzuela Phil.
55 M6 Våler Norway
45 C2 Valera Venez.
67 H2 Valjevo Yugo.
61 C4 Val Joly, Lac du l. France
55 U8 Valka Latvia
55 T6 Valkeakoski Fin.
61 D3 Valkenswaard Neth.
69 E5 Valky Ukr.
119 C4 Valkyrjedomen ice feature Ant.
36 G4 Valladolid Mex.
65 D2 Valladolid Spain
36 C4 Vallarta, Pto Mex.
65 F3 Vall de Uxó Spain
55 K7 Valle Norway
45 C2 Valle de la Pascua Venez.
45 B2 Valledupar Col.
47 C1 Valle Fértil, Sa de mts Arg.
42 F7 Valle Grande Bol.
34 A2 Vallejo U.S.A.
66 F7 Valletta Malta
59 C4 Valley U.K.
26 D2 Valley City U.S.A.
24 B3 Valley Falls U.S.A.
32 C5 Valley Head U.S.A.
20 F3 Valleyview Can.
65 G2 Valls Spain
21 H5 Val Marie Can.
55 T8 Valmiera Latvia
65 E1 Valnera mt Spain
68 C4 Valozhyn Belarus
22 E4 Val-Paradis Can.
83 B8 Valparai India
46 B3 Valparaíso Brazil
47 B2 Valparaíso Chile
47 B2 Valparaíso div. Chile
30 D5 Valparaiso U.S.A.
64 G4 Valréas France
84 C5 Valsād India
104 F3 Valspan S. Africa
93 K8 Vals, Tanjung c. Indon.
68 H1 Val'tevo Rus. Fed.
55 V5 Valtimo Fin.
69 G6 Valuyevka Rus. Fed.
69 F5 Valuyki Rus. Fed.
65 C4 Valverde del Camino Spain
95 C3 Vam Co Tay r. Vietnam
55 S6 Vammala Fin.
81 J2 Van Turkey
81 K1 Vanadzor Armenia
27 E5 Van Buren AR U.S.A.
33 K1 Van Buren ME U.S.A.
95 D2 Văn Canh Vietnam
33 K2 Vanceboro U.S.A.
32 B5 Vanceburg U.S.A.
20 E5 Vancouver Can.
24 B2 Vancouver U.S.A.
20 D5 Vancouver Island i. Can.
20 A2 Vancouver, Mt mt AK/Y.T. Can./U.S.A.
28 B4 Vandalia IL U.S.A.
32 A5 Vandalia OH U.S.A.
105 G3 Vanderbijlpark S. Africa
30 E3 Vanderbilt U.S.A.
32 D4 Vandergrift U.S.A.
20 E4 Vanderhoof Can.
104 F5 Vanderkloof Dam resr S. Africa
113 G3 Vanderlin I. i. Austr.
35 H4 Vanderwagen U.S.A.
112 F2 Van Diemen Gulf b. Austr.
55 T7 Vändra Estonia
55 N1 Vänern l. Sweden
55 N7 Vänersborg Sweden
32 E3 Van Etten U.S.A.
103 E6 Vangaindrano Madag.
81 J2 Van Gölü salt l. Turkey

27 B6 Van Horn U.S.A.
31 K3 Vanier Can.
111 G3 Vanikoro Is is Solomon Is
110 E2 Vanimo P.N.G.
87 Q2 Vanino Rus. Fed.
77 V3 Vankarem Rus. Fed.
33 F2 Vankleek Hill Can.
Van, Lake salt l. see Van Gölü
54 R1 Vanna i. Norway
54 Q5 Vännäs Sweden
64 C3 Vannes France
82 D2 Vannovka Kazak.
93 K7 Van Rees, Pegunungan mts Indon.
104 C5 Vanrhynsdorp S. Africa
55 O6 Vansbro Sweden
55 T6 Vantaa Fin.
111 G3 Vanua Lava i. Vanuatu
111 H3 Vanua Levu i. Fiji
106 Vanuatu country Pac. Oc.
32 A4 Van Wert U.S.A.
104 D5 Vanwyksvlei l. S. Africa
104 D5 Vanwyksvlei S. Africa
89 B6 Văn Yên Vietnam
104 E3 Van Zylsrus S. Africa
55 U8 Varakļāni Latvia
85 L4 Varanasi India
54 V1 Varangerfjorden chan. Norway
54 V1 Varangerhalvøya pen. Norway
66 G1 Varaždin Croatia
55 N8 Varberg Sweden
67 K4 Vardar r. Macedonia
55 L9 Varde Denmark
54 W1 Vardø Norway
47 C2 Varela Arg.
55 T9 Varéna Lith.
66 C2 Varese Italy
55 N7 Vårgårda Sweden
46 D3 Varginha Brazil
61 D3 Varik Neth.
54 U5 Varkaus Fin.
67 M3 Varna Bulg.
55 O8 Värnamo Sweden
55 N6 Varnäs Sweden
68 H3 Varnavino Rus. Fed.
80 D4 Varosia Cyprus
54 U5 Varpaisjärvi Fin.
62 J7 Várpalota Hungary
84 B1 Varsaj Afgh.
81 H2 Varto Turkey
85 E4 Varuna r. India
32 D3 Varysburg U.S.A.
46 D2 Várzea da Palma Brazil
68 H2 Vashka r. Rus. Fed.
Vasht see Khāsh
68 H1 Vashkovo Rus. Fed.
55 U7 Vasknarva Estonia
63 N7 Vaslui Romania
31 F4 Vassar U.S.A.
55 P7 Västerås Sweden
55 N6 Västerdalälven r. Sweden
54 P3 Västerfjäll Sweden
55 O7 Vasterhaninge Sweden
55 P8 Västervik Sweden
66 F3 Vasto Italy
69 D5 Vasyl'kiv Ukr.
64 E3 Vatan France
57 A4 Vatersay i. U.K.
67 M6 Vathy Greece
48 Vatican City country Europe
54 E4 Vatnajökull ice cap Iceland
63 M7 Vatra Dornei Romania
55 O7 Vättern l. Sweden
25 F5 Vaughn U.S.A.
45 C4 Vaupés r. Col.
64 G5 Vauvert France
111 J3 Vava'u Group is Tonga
100 B4 Vavoua Côte d'Ivoire
68 C4 Vawkavysk Belarus
55 O8 Växjö Sweden
68 H1 Vazhgort Rus. Fed.
103 E5 Vazobe mt Madag.
95 B2 Veal Vêng Cambodia
61 E2 Vechte r. Ger.
55 N8 Veddige Sweden
67 L3 Vedea r. Romania
69 H7 Vedeno Rus. Fed.
81 K2 Vedi Armenia
47 E2 Vedia Arg.
68 E2 Vedlozero Rus. Fed.
30 D5 Veedersburg U.S.A.
61 E1 Veendam Neth.
61 D2 Veenendaal Neth.
54 M4 Vega i. Norway
27 C5 Vega U.S.A.
21 G4 Vegreville Can.
55 U6 Vehkalahti Fin.
84 B3 Vehoa r. Pak.
84 B4 Veirwaro Pak.
65 D4 Vejer de la Frontera Spain
55 L9 Vejle Denmark
45 B1 Vela, Cabo de la pt Col.
67 K3 Velbŭzhdki Prokhod pass Macedonia
104 C6 Velddrif S. Africa
66 F2 Velebit mts Croatia
61 E3 Velen Ger.
66 F1 Velenje Slovenia
67 J4 Veles Macedonia
45 B3 Vélez Col.
65 D4 Vélez-Málaga Spain
65 E4 Vélez-Rubio Spain
46 D2 Velhas r. Brazil
69 H6 Velichayevskoye Rus. Fed.
66 G2 Velika Gorica Croatia
67 H2 Velika Plana Yugo.
77 T3 Velikaya r. Rus. Fed.
68 J3 Velikaya Rus. Fed.

68 D3 Velikaya r. Rus. Fed.
68 D3 Velikaya Guba Rus. Fed.
68 D3 Velikiye Luki Rus. Fed.
68 H2 Velikiy Ustyug Rus. Fed.
63 Q2 Velikooktyabr'skiy Rus. Fed.
67 L3 Veliko Tŭrnovo Bulg.
68 F3 Velikoye Rus. Fed.
68 F3 Velikoye, Oz. l. Rus. Fed.
68 G4 Velikoye, Oz. l. Rus. Fed.
66 F2 Veli Lošinj Croatia
100 A3 Vélingara Senegal
63 P3 Velizh Rus. Fed.
62 H7 Veľký Meder Slovakia
111 H7 Vella Lavella i. Solomon Is
83 E8 Vellore India
68 G2 Vel'sk Rus. Fed.
62 F1 Velten Ger.
61 D2 Veluwe reg. Neth.
61 D2 Veluwemeer l. Neth.
61 D2 Veluwezoom, Nationaal Park nat. park Neth.
21 J5 Velva U.S.A.
12 G5 Vema Fracture sea feature Atlantic Ocean
13 J4 Vema Trough sea feature Indian Ocean
57 D4 Venachar, Loch l. U.K.
47 E2 Venado Tuerto Arg.
66 F4 Venafro Italy
45 E3 Venamo r. Guyana/Venez.
45 E3 Venamo, Co mt Venez.
46 C3 Venceslau Bráz Brazil
64 E3 Vendôme France
68 F4 Venev Rus. Fed.
Venezia see Venice
66 E2 Venezia, Golfo di g. Europe
38 Venezuela country S. America
45 C2 Venezuela, Golfo de g. Venez.
83 D7 Vengurla India
66 E2 Venice Italy
29 D7 Venice U.S.A.
64 G4 Vénissieux France
61 E3 Venlo Neth.
55 K7 Vennesla Norway
61 D3 Venray Neth.
55 R8 Venta r. Latvia/Lith.
55 S8 Venta Lith.
47 D3 Ventana, Serra de la h. Arg.
105 G4 Ventersburg S. Africa
105 G3 Ventersdorp S. Africa
105 F5 Venterstad S. Africa
59 F7 Ventnor U.K.
64 G4 Ventoux, Mont mt France
55 R8 Ventspils Latvia
45 D3 Ventuari r. Venez.
34 C4 Ventucopa U.S.A.
34 C4 Ventura U.S.A.
114 F7 Venus B. b. Austr.
44 D3 Vera Arg.
65 F4 Vera Spain
36 E5 Veracruz Mex.
84 B5 Veraval India
66 C2 Verbania Italy
66 C2 Vercelli Italy
54 M5 Verdalsøra Norway
47 D4 Verde r. Arg.
46 B2 Verde r. Goiás Brazil
46 B2 Verde r. Goiás Brazil
46 C2 Verde r. Goiás/Minas Gerais Brazil
46 B3 Verde r. Mato Grosso do Sul Brazil
44 E2 Verde r. Para.
35 G4 Verde r. U.S.A.
46 D1 Verde Grande r. Brazil
94 B3 Verde Island Pass. chan. Phil.
62 D4 Verden (Aller) Ger.
47 D3 Verde, Pen. pen. Arg.
27 E4 Verdigris r. U.S.A.
64 H5 Verdon r. France
64 G2 Verdun France
105 G4 Vereeniging S. Africa
31 J2 Vérendrye, Réserve faunique La r. Can.
47 G2 Vergara Uru.
33 G2 Vergennes U.S.A.
65 C2 Verín Spain
69 F6 Verkhnebakanskiy Rus. Fed.
61 E1 Veendam Neth.  
61 D2 Verkhnedneprovskiy Rus. Fed.
63 Verkhnedneprovskiy Rus. Fed.
76 K3 Verkhneimbatskoye Rus. Fed.
54 W2 Verkhnetulomskiy Rus. Fed.
77 O1 Verkhnevilyuysk Rus. Fed.
68 D1 Verkhneye Kuyto, Oz. l. Rus. Fed.
69 H5 Verkhniy Baskunchak Rus. Fed.
69 J5 Verkhniy Kushum Rus. Fed.
54 W3 Verkhnyaya Pirenga, Oz. l. Rus. Fed.
68 H2 Verkhnyaya Toyma Rus. Fed.
68 G2 Verkhovazh'ye Rus. Fed.
69 F4 Verkhov'ye Rus. Fed.
69 C5 Verkhovyna Ukr.
77 P3 Verkhoyansk Rus. Fed.
77 O3 Verkhoyanskiy Khrebet mts Rus. Fed.
46 B1 Vermelho r. Brazil
21 H4 Vermilion Can.
30 C5 Vermilion r. U.S.A.

35 F3 Vermilion Cliffs cliff U.S.A.
30 A2 Vermilion Lake l. U.S.A.
30 A2 Vermilion Range h. U.S.A.
26 D3 Vermillion U.S.A.
21 L5 Vermillion Bay Can.
33 G3 Vermont div. U.S.A.
24 E3 Vernal U.S.A.
31 G2 Verner Can.
104 D4 Verneuk Pan salt pan S. Africa
20 F4 Vernon Can.
35 H4 Vernon AZ U.S.A.
33 G4 Vernon CT U.S.A.
27 D5 Vernon TX U.S.A.
35 F1 Vernon UT U.S.A.
29 D7 Vero Beach U.S.A.
67 K4 Veroia Greece
66 D2 Verona Italy
47 F2 Verónica Arg.
114 B4 Verran Austr.
64 F2 Versailles France
64 D3 Vertou France
105 J4 Verulam S. Africa
61 D4 Verviers Belgium
64 F2 Vervins France
66 C3 Vescovato Corsica France
76 G4 Veselaya, G. mt Rus. Fed.
69 E6 Vesele Ukr.
69 G6 Veselovskoye Vdkhr. resr Rus. Fed.
69 G5 Veshenskaya Rus. Fed.
55 B5 Vesle r. France
64 H3 Vesoul France
54 O2 Vesterålen is Norway
55 L7 Vestfjorddalen v. Norway
54 N3 Vestfjorden chan. Norway
54 □ Vestmanna Faroe Is
54 C5 Vestmannaeyjar is Iceland
54 Vestmannaeyjar Iceland
54 K5 Vestnes Norway
54 F4 Vesturhorn hd Iceland
Vesuvio volc. see Vesuvius
66 F4 Vesuvius volc. Italy
68 F3 Vesyegonsk Rus. Fed.
62 H7 Veszprém Hungary
55 S5 Veteli Fin.
55 O8 Vetlanda Sweden
68 H3 Vetluga r. Rus. Fed.
68 H3 Vetluga Rus. Fed.
66 E3 Vettore, Monte mt Italy
61 A3 Veurne Belgium
62 C7 Vevey Switz.
35 F3 Veyo U.S.A.
81 M6 Veys Iran
64 E4 Vézère r. France
80 E1 Vezirköprü Turkey
55 P5 Vi Sweden
42 C6 Viajas, I. de las i. Peru
43 K4 Viana Brazil
65 B2 Viana do Castelo Port.
Viangchan see Vientiane
46 C2 Vianópolis Brazil
66 D3 Viareggio Italy
55 L8 Viborg Denmark
66 G5 Vibo Valentia Italy
65 H2 Vic Spain
119 B2 Vicecomodoro Marambio Argentina Base Ant.
34 C1 Vicente, Pt pt U.S.A.
66 D2 Vicenza Italy
45 C3 Vichada r. Col.
42 D3 Vichada r. Col.
68 G3 Vichuga Rus. Fed.
47 B2 Vichuquén Chile
64 F3 Vichy France
45 D3 Viçosa Brazil
30 A5 Victor U.S.A.
114 C5 Victor Harbour Austr.
47 E2 Victoria Arg.
112 F3 Victoria r. Austr.
114 F6 Victoria div. Austr.
20 E5 Victoria Can.
47 B3 Victoria Chile
Victoria see Bandar Labuan
66 F7 Victoria Malta
27 D6 Victoria U.S.A.
37 J4 Victoria de las Tunas Cuba
103 C5 Victoria Falls waterfall Zambia/Zimbabwe
89 □ Victoria Harbour chan. Hong Kong China
29 F7 Victoria Hill Bahamas
102 D4 Victoria, Lake l. Africa
115 G6 Victoria, Lake l. Austr.
23 J4 Victoria Lake l. Can.
119 B5 Victoria Land reg. Ant.
85 H5 Victoria, Mt mt Myanmar
110 E2 Victoria, Mt mt P.N.G.
101 F4 Victoria Nile r. Sudan/Uganda
117 D5 Victoria Range mts N.Z.
112 F3 Victoria River Austr.
112 F3 Victoria River Downs Austr.
23 J4 Victoriaville Can.
104 E5 Victoria West S. Africa
47 D3 Victorica Arg.
34 D4 Victorville U.S.A.

47 D2 Vicuña Mackenna Arg.
35 E4 Vidal Junction U.S.A.
67 L2 Videle Romania
67 K3 Vidin Bulg.
84 D5 Vidisha India
57 □ Vidlin U.K.
63 N3 Vidzy Belarus
69 J2 Vidz'yuyar Rus. Fed.
47 A7 Viedma Arg.
61 D4 Viedma, L. l. Arg.
61 D4 Vielsalm Belgium
62 H6 Vienna Austria
28 B4 Vienna IL U.S.A.
33 F5 Vienna MD U.S.A.
32 C5 Vienna WV U.S.A.
64 G4 Vienne France
64 E3 Vienne r. France
95 B1 Vientiane Laos
47 B3 Viento, Cordillera del mts Arg.
37 L5 Vieques i. Puerto Rico
54 U5 Vieremä Fin.
61 E3 Viersen Ger.
62 D7 Vierwaldstätter See l. Switz.
64 F3 Vierzon France
27 C7 Viesca Mex.
55 T8 Viesīte Latvia
66 G4 Vieste Italy
54 Q3 Vietas Sweden
70 Vietnam country Asia
89 B6 Việt Tri Vietnam
94 B2 Vigan Phil.
66 C2 Vigevano Italy
66 D5 Vignola Italy
65 B1 Vigo Spain
61 E5 Vigy France
54 T4 Vihanti Fin.
55 T6 Vihti Fin.
55 T5 Viitasaari Fin.
84 C3 Vijainagar India
83 F7 Vijayawada India
54 C5 Vík Iceland
54 U3 Vikajärvi Fin.
21 G4 Viking Can.
54 M4 Vikna i. Norway
54 K6 Vikøyri Norway
111 G3 Vila Vanuatu
100 □ Vila da Ribeira Brava Cape Verde
100 □ Vila de Sal Rei Cape Verde
100 □ Vila do Tarrafal Cape Verde
65 B3 Vila Franca de Xira Port.
65 B1 Vilagarcía de Arousa Spain
105 K2 Vila Gomes da Costa Moz.
65 C1 Vilalba Spain
65 B2 Vila Nova de Gaia Port.
65 B2 Vilanova i la Geltrú Spain
100 □ Vila Nova Sintra Cape Verde
65 C2 Vila Real Port.
65 C2 Vilar Formoso Port.
46 D3 Vila Velha Brazil
42 D6 Vilcabamba, Cordillera mts Peru
54 P4 Vilhelmina Sweden
42 F6 Vilhena Brazil
55 T7 Viljandi Estonia
105 G3 Viljoenskroon S. Africa
55 S9 Vilkaviškis Lith.
55 S9 Vilkija Lith.
77 L2 Vil'kitskogo, Proliv str. Rus. Fed.
42 E6 Villa Bella Bol.
65 C1 Villablino Spain
47 D3 Villa Cañás Arg.
65 E3 Villacañas Spain
62 F7 Villach Austria
66 C5 Villacidro Sardinia Italy
47 E2 Villa Constitución Arg.
47 D1 Villa del Rosario Arg.
47 D1 Villa del Totoral Arg.
47 D1 Villa Dolores Arg.
27 F5 Village, Lake l. U.S.A.
47 F3 Villa Gesell Arg.
47 E1 Villaguay Arg.
36 F5 Villahermosa Mex.
47 D2 Villa Huidobro Arg.
47 D3 Villa Iris Arg.
65 F3 Villajoyosa Spain
47 E1 Villalonga Arg.
47 D2 Villa María Arg.
47 E1 Villa María Grande Arg.
42 F8 Villa Montes Bol.
103 E5 Villandro, Tanjona pt Madag.
105 H1 Villa Nora S. Africa
45 B2 Villanueva Col.
65 D3 Villanueva de la Serena Spain
65 E3 Villanueva de los Infantes Spain
44 E3 Villa Ocampo Arg.
27 B7 Villa O. Pereyra Mex.
66 C5 Villaputzu Sardinia Italy
47 C3 Villa Regina Arg.
47 B3 Villarrica Chile
44 E3 Villarrica Para.
47 B3 Villarrica, L. l. Chile
47 B3 Villarrica, Parque Nacional nat. park Chile
47 B3 Villarrica, Volcán volc. Chile
65 E3 Villarrobledo Spain
66 F5 Villa San Giovanni Italy
47 D3 Villa San José Arg.

47 C1 Villa Santa Rita de Catuna Arg.
44 C3 Villa Unión Arg.
47 D2 Villa Valeria Arg.
45 B3 Villavicencio Col.
42 E8 Villazon Bol.
64 F4 Villefranche-de-Rouergue France
64 G4 Villefranche-sur-Saône France
31 H2 Ville-Marie Can.
65 F3 Villena Spain
64 E4 Villeneuve-sur-Lot France
64 F2 Villeneuve-sur-Yonne France
27 E6 Ville Platte U.S.A.
61 B5 Villers-Cotterêts France
64 F2 Villeurbanne France
105 H3 Villiers S. Africa
62 D6 Villingen Ger.
21 G4 Vilna Can.
55 T9 Vilnius Lith.
69 E6 Vil'nyans'k Ukr.
55 T5 Vilppula Fin.
83 E8 Viluppuram India
61 C4 Vilvoorde Belgium
68 C4 Vilyeyka Belarus
77 O3 Vilyuy r. Rus. Fed.
77 M3 Vilyuyskoye Vdkhr. resr Rus. Fed.
55 O8 Vimmerby Sweden
34 A2 Vina U.S.A.
47 B2 Viña del Mar Chile
33 J2 Vinalhaven U.S.A.
65 G2 Vinaròs Spain
28 C4 Vincennes U.S.A.
54 Q4 Vindelälven r. Sweden
54 Q4 Vindeln Sweden
84 C5 Vindhya Range h. India
33 F5 Vineland U.S.A.
33 H4 Vineyard Haven U.S.A.
95 C1 Vinh Vietnam
95 C1 Vinh Linh Vietnam
95 C1 Vinh Long Vietnam
95 C3 Vinh Rach Gia b. Vietnam
89 B6 Vinh Yên Vietnam
27 E4 Vinita U.S.A.
67 H2 Vinkovci Croatia
69 D5 Vinnytsya Ukr.
55 L6 Vinstra Norway
30 A4 Vinton U.S.A.
83 E7 Vinukonda India
66 D1 Vipiteno Italy
94 C3 Virac Phil.
84 C5 Viramgam India
81 G3 Viranşehir Turkey
84 B4 Virawah Pak.
21 J5 Virden Can.
64 D2 Vire France
103 B5 Virei Angola
46 D3 Virgem da Lapa Brazil
31 H1 Virginatown Can.
60 D4 Virginia Rep. of Ireland
105 G4 Virginia S. Africa
30 A2 Virginia U.S.A.
32 D6 Virginia div. U.S.A.
33 E6 Virginia Beach U.S.A.
34 C2 Virginia City U.S.A.
37 M5 Virgin Islands (U.K.) terr. Caribbean
37 M5 Virgin Islands (U.S.A.) terr. Caribbean
35 E3 Virgin Mts mts U.S.A.
55 T6 Virkkala Fin.
95 B2 Virôch'ey Cambodia
30 B4 Viroqua U.S.A.
66 G2 Virovitica Croatia
55 S5 Virrat Fin.
61 D5 Virton Belgium
55 S7 Virtsu Estonia
83 E9 Virudunagar India
102 C3 Virunga, Parc National des nat. park Zaire
66 G3 Vis i. Croatia
55 U9 Visaginas Lith.
34 C3 Visalia U.S.A.
94 B4 Visayan Sea sea Phil.
55 Q8 Visby Sweden
67 H3 Višegrad Bos.-Herz.
76 J2 Vise, O. i. Rus. Fed.
43 J4 Viseu Brazil
65 C2 Viseu Port.
83 F7 Vishakhapatnam India
55 U8 Viški Latvia
84 C5 Visnagar India
67 H3 Visoko Bos.-Herz.
66 B2 Viso, Monte mt Italy
62 C7 Vista Switz.
34 D5 Vista U.S.A.
46 A2 Vista Alegre Brazil
67 L4 Vistonida, Limni lag. Greece
45 C3 Vita r. Col.
84 B3 Vitakri Pak.
66 E3 Viterbo Italy
66 G2 Vitez Bos.-Herz.
42 E8 Vitichi Bol.
111 H3 Viti Levu i. Fiji
87 L1 Vitim r. Rus. Fed.
87 K1 Vitimskoye Ploskogor'ye plat. Rus. Fed.
46 D3 Vitória Brazil
Vitoria see Vitoria-Gasteiz
46 E3 Vitória da Conquista Brazil
65 E1 Vitoria-Gasteiz Spain
64 D2 Vitré France
64 G2 Vitry-le-François France
68 D4 Vitsyebsk Belarus
54 R3 Vittangi Sweden

66 F6 Vittoria *Sicily* Italy
66 E2 Vittorio Veneto Italy
14 F3 Vityaz Depth *depth* Pac. Oc.
65 C1 Viveiro Spain
105 H1 Vivo S. Africa
114 B6 Vivonne B. *b.* Austr.
36 B3 Vizcaíno, Sierra *mts* Mex.
69 C7 Vize Turkey
83 F7 Vizianagaram India
68 J2 Vizinga Rus. Fed.
61 C3 Vlaardingen Neth.
63 L7 Vlădeasa, Vârful *mt.* Romania
69 H7 Vladikavkaz Rus. Fed.
68 G3 Vladimir Rus. Fed.
87 O3 Vladivostok Rus. Fed.
68 G4 Vlaimirskaya Oblast' *div.* Rus. Fed.
105 H2 Vlakte S. Africa
67 K3 Vlasotince Yugo.
104 D7 Vleesbaai *b.* S. Africa
61 C1 Vlieland *i.* Neth.
61 B3 Vlissingen Neth.
67 H4 Vlorë Albania
62 G6 Vltava *r.* Czech Rep.
62 F6 Vöcklabruck Austria
68 F2 Vodlozero, Ozero *l.* Rus. Fed.
57 □ Voe U.K.
61 D4 Voerendaal Neth.
66 C2 Voghera Italy
103 E6 Vohimena, Tanjona *c.* Madag.
55 T7 Võhma Estonia
102 D4 Voi Kenya
100 B4 Voinjama Liberia
64 G4 Voiron France
55 L9 Vojens Denmark
67 H2 Vojvodina *div.* Yugo.
68 H3 Vokhma Rus. Fed.
68 D1 Voknavolok Rus. Fed.
24 F2 Volborg U.S.A.
47 B1 Volcán, Co del *mt* Chile
Volcano Bay *b. see* Uchiura-wan
Volcano Is *is see* Kazanrettō
55 K5 Volda Norway
69 H6 Volga *r.* Rus. Fed.
30 B4 Volga *r.* U.S.A.
52 Volga Uplands *plat.* Rus. Fed.
69 G6 Volgodonsk Rus. Fed.
69 H5 Volgograd Rus. Fed.
69 H5 Volgogradskaya Oblast' *div.* Rus. Fed.
62 G7 Völkermarkt Austria
68 D3 Volkhov *r.* Rus. Fed.
68 E3 Volkhov Rus. Fed.
61 E5 Völklingen Ger.
105 H3 Volksrust S. Africa
69 F6 Volnovakha Ukr.
77 L2 Volochanka Rus. Fed.
69 C5 Volochys'k Ukr.
69 F6 Volodars'ke Ukr.
69 J6 Volodarskiy Rus. Fed.
76 H4 Volodarskoye Kazak.
63 O5 Volodars'k-Volyns'kyy Ukr.
63 N5 Volodymyrets' Ukr.
69 C5 Volodymyr-Volyns'kyy Ukr.
68 F3 Vologda Rus. Fed.
68 G3 Vologodskaya Oblast' *div.* Rus. Fed.
69 F5 Volokonovka Rus. Fed.
67 K5 Volos Greece
68 D3 Volosovo Rus. Fed.
63 P2 Volot Rus. Fed.
69 F4 Volovo Rus. Fed.
69 H4 Vol'sk Rus. Fed.
100 B4 Volta, Lake *resr* Ghana
46 D3 Volta Redonda Brazil
66 F4 Volturno *r.* Italy
67 K4 Volvi, L. *l.* Greece
68 J4 Volzhsk Rus. Fed.
69 H5 Volzhskiy Rus. Fed.
103 E6 Vondrozo Madag.
68 G1 Vonga Rus. Fed.
54 F4 Vopnafjörður *b.* Iceland
54 F4 Vopnafjörður Iceland
68 B2 Vörå Fin.
63 M3 Voranava Belarus
68 J3 Vorchanka Rus. Fed.
68 E2 Vorenzha Rus. Fed.
76 H3 Vorkuta Rus. Fed.
55 S7 Vormsi *i.* Estonia
69 G5 Vorona *r.* Rus. Fed.
69 F5 Voronezh Rus. Fed.
69 F5 Voronezh *r.* Rus. Fed.
69 G5 Voronezhskaya Oblast' *div.* Rus. Fed.
68 G3 Voron'ye Rus. Fed.
63 Q3 Vorot'kovo Rus. Fed.
69 E5 Vorskla *r.* Rus. Fed.
55 T7 Võrtsjärv *l.* Estonia
55 U8 Võru Estonia
104 E5 Vosburg S. Africa
64 H2 Vosges *mts* France
55 K6 Voss Norway
Vostochno-Sibirskoye More *sea see* East Siberian Sea
86 G1 Vostochnyy Sayan *mts* Rus. Fed.
119 B4 Vostok *Rus. Fed. Base* Antarctica
109 Vostok Island *i. Line Islands* Pac. Oc.
76 G4 Votkinsk Rus. Fed.
46 C3 Votuporanga Brazil
61 C5 Vouziers France
64 E2 Voves France
68 J3 Voya *r.* Rus. Fed.
28 A1 Voyageurs Nat. Park *nat. park* U.S.A.
54 W4 Voynitsa Rus. Fed.
68 G2 Vozhega Rus. Fed.
68 F2 Vozhe, Ozero *l.* Rus. Fed.
69 D6 Voznesens'k Ukr.
77 V4 Vrangelya, O. *i.* Alaska
67 J3 Vranje Yugo.
67 M3 Vratnik *pass* Bulg.
67 K3 Vratsa Bulg.
66 G2 Vrbas *r.* Bos.-Herz.
67 H2 Vrbas Yugo.
105 H3 Vrede S. Africa
105 G3 Vredefort S. Africa
104 B6 Vredenburg S. Africa
104 C5 Vredendal S. Africa
61 C5 Vresse Belgium
83 E8 Vriddhachalam India
55 O8 Vrigstad Sweden
67 J2 Vršac Yugo.
104 F3 Vryburg S. Africa
105 J3 Vryheid S. Africa
68 D2 Vsevolozhsk Rus. Fed.
67 J3 Vučitrn Yugo.
67 H2 Vukovar Croatia
76 G3 Vuktyl' Rus. Fed.
105 H3 Vukuzakhe S. Africa
66 F5 Vulcano, Isola *i.* Italy
35 F5 Vulture Mts *mts* U.S.A.
95 C3 Vung Tau Vietnam
55 U6 Vuohijärvi Fin.
54 U4 Vuolijoki Fin.
54 R3 Vuollerim Sweden
54 U3 Vuostimo Fin.
68 H4 Vurnary Rus. Fed.
103 D4 Vwawa Tanz.
84 C5 Vyara India
68 J3 Vyatka *r.* Rus. Fed.
68 J3 Vyatka Rus. Fed.
68 E4 Vyaz'ma Rus. Fed.
68 G3 Vyazniki Rus. Fed.
69 H5 Vyazovka Rus. Fed.
68 D2 Vyborg Rus. Fed.
68 J2 Vychegda *r.* Rus. Fed.
68 H2 Vychegodskiy Rus. Fed.
68 C4 Vyerkhnyadzvinsk Belarus
68 D4 Vyetryna Belarus
68 E2 Vygozero, Ozero *l.* Rus. Fed.
68 G4 Vyksa Rus. Fed.
69 D6 Vylkove Ukr.
63 L6 Vynohradiv Ukr.
68 E3 Vypolzovo Rus. Fed.
68 D3 Vyritsa Rus. Fed.
59 D5 Vyrnwy, Lake *l.* U.K.
69 F6 Vyselki Rus. Fed.
68 G4 Vysha Rus. Fed.
69 D5 Vyshhorod Ukr.
68 E3 Vyshnevolotskaya Gryada *ridge* Rus. Fed.
68 E3 Vyshniy-Volochek Rus. Fed.
62 H6 Vyškov Czech Rep.
69 D5 Vystupovychi Ukr.
68 F2 Vytegra Rus. Fed.

# W

100 B3 Wa Ghana
61 D3 Waal *r.* Neth.
22 B3 Wabakimi L. *l.* Can.
20 G3 Wabasca Can.
20 G3 Wabasca *r.* Can.
30 E5 Wabash U.S.A.
30 E5 Wabash *r.* U.S.A.
30 A3 Wabasha U.S.A.
31 E1 Wabatongushi Lake *l.* Can.
102 E3 Wabē Gestro *r.* Eth.
102 E3 Wabē Shebelē Wenz *r.* Eth.
21 K4 Wabowden Can.
22 C2 Wabuk Pt *pt* Can.
23 G3 Wabush Can.
23 G3 Wabush L. *l.* Can.
34 C2 Wabuska U.S.A.
29 D6 Waccasassa Bay *b.* U.S.A.
27 D6 Waco U.S.A.
79 K4 Wad Pak.
90 E6 Wadayama Japan
115 H6 Wadbilliga Nat. Park *nat. park* Austr.
101 D2 Waddān Libya
61 C1 Waddeneilanden *is* Neth.
61 D1 Waddenzee *chan.* Neth.
114 B4 Waddikee Austr.
20 D4 Waddington, Mt *mt.* Can.
61 C2 Waddinxveen Neth.
116 E5 Waddy Pt *pt* Austr.
59 C7 Wadebridge U.K.
21 J4 Wadena Can.
26 E2 Wadena U.S.A.
101 F3 Wadi el Milk *watercourse* Sudan
101 F2 Wadi Halfa Sudan
101 E3 Wadi Howar *watercourse* Sudan
101 F3 Wad Medani Sudan
34 C2 Wadsworth U.S.A.
88 G2 Wafangdian China
81 L7 Wafra Kuwait
91 H4 Waga-gawa *r.* Japan
115 G5 Wagga Wagga Austr.
112 C6 Wagin Austr.
84 C2 Wah Pak.
34 □1 Wahiawa U.S.A.
26 D3 Wahoo U.S.A.
26 D2 Wahpeton U.S.A.
35 F2 Wah Wah Mts *mts* U.S.A.
34 □1 Waialee U.S.A.
34 □1 Waialua U.S.A.
34 □1 Waialua Bay *b.* U.S.A.
34 □1 Waianae U.S.A.
34 □1 Waianae Ra. *mts* U.S.A.
117 D5 Waiau *r.* N.Z.
62 G7 Waidhofen an der Ybbs Austria
93 J6 Waigeo *i.* Indon.
117 E2 Waiharoa N.Z.
117 E2 Waiheke Island *i.* N.Z.
117 E2 Waihi N.Z.
117 E2 Waihou *r.* N.Z.
93 F8 Waikabubak Indon.
117 B6 Waikaia *r.* N.Z.
34 □1 Waikane U.S.A.
117 D5 Waikari N.Z.
117 E2 Waikato *r.* N.Z.
117 F2 Waikawa Pt *pt* N.Z.
114 C5 Waikerie Austr.
34 □1 Waikiki Beach *beach* U.S.A.
117 C6 Waikouaiti N.Z.
34 □2 Wailuku U.S.A.
117 D5 Waimakariri *r.* N.Z.
34 □1 Waimanalo U.S.A.
117 C4 Waimangaroa N.Z.
117 F3 Waimarama N.Z.
117 C6 Waimate N.Z.
34 □1 Waimea *HI* U.S.A.
34 □2 Waimea *HI* U.S.A.
84 D5 Wainganga *r.* India
93 G8 Waingapu Indon.
59 C7 Wainhouse Corner U.K.
21 G4 Wainwright Can.
117 E3 Waiouru N.Z.
117 E3 Waipa *r.* N.Z.
117 B7 Waipahi N.Z.
34 □1 Waipahu U.S.A.
117 F3 Waipaoa *r.* N.Z.
117 B7 Waipapa Pt *pt* N.Z.
117 D5 Waipara N.Z.
117 F3 Waipawa N.Z.
117 F3 Waipukurau N.Z.
117 F3 Wairakei N.Z.
117 E4 Wairarapa, L. *l.* N.Z.
117 D4 Wairau *r.* N.Z.
117 F3 Wairoa *r. Hawke's Bay* N.Z.
117 E1 Wairoa *r. Northland* N.Z.
117 F3 Wairoa N.Z.
117 F3 Waitahanui N.Z.
117 B6 Waitahuna N.Z.
117 E2 Waitakaruru N.Z.
117 C6 Waitaki *r.* N.Z.
117 E3 Waitara N.Z.
117 E2 Waitoa N.Z.
117 E2 Waiuku N.Z.
117 B7 Waiwera South N.Z.
89 F5 Waiyang China
90 E7 Wajiki Japan
91 F5 Wajima Japan
102 E3 Wajir Kenya
90 E6 Wakasa Japan
91 E6 Wakasa-wan *b.* Japan
117 B6 Wakatipu, Lake *l.* N.Z.
21 H4 Wakaw Can.
91 E6 Wakayama Japan
91 E7 Wakayama Japan
26 D4 Wa Keeney U.S.A.
31 K3 Wakefield Can.
117 D4 Wakefield N.Z.
58 F4 Wakefield U.K.
30 C2 Wakefield *MI* U.S.A.
33 H4 Wakefield *RI* U.S.A.
32 E6 Wakefield *VA* U.S.A.
108 Wake Island *i.* U.S.A.
90 E6 Waki Japan
90 H3 Wakinosawa Japan
90 H1 Wakkanai Japan
105 J3 Wakkerstroom S. Africa
114 F5 Wakool Austr.
114 E5 Wakool *r.* Austr.
23 G2 Wakuach, Lac *l.* Can.
62 H5 Wałbrzych Pol.
115 J3 Walcha Austr.
62 E7 Walchensee *l.* Ger.
62 H4 Wałcz Pol.
33 F4 Walden Montgomery U.S.A.
62 F6 Waldkraiburg Ger.
59 C7 Waldon *r.* U.K.
32 E5 Waldorf U.S.A.
56 E5 Wales *div.* U.K.
115 H3 Walgett Austr.
102 C4 Walikale Zaire
30 B4 Walker *IA* U.S.A.
26 E2 Walker *MN* U.S.A.
34 C2 Walker *r.* U.S.A.
104 C7 Walker Bay *b.* S. Africa
29 E7 Walker Cay *i.* Bahamas
34 C2 Walker Lake *l.* U.S.A.
34 C4 Walker Pass *pass* U.S.A.
31 G3 Walkerton Can.
26 C2 Wall U.S.A.
24 C2 Wallace U.S.A.
31 F4 Wallaceburg Can.
115 J2 Wallangarra Austr.
114 B4 Wallaroo Austr.
59 D4 Wallasey U.K.
116 D5 Wallaville Austr.
115 G5 Walla Walla Austr.
24 C2 Walla Walla U.S.A.
104 B5 Wallekraal S. Africa
115 H5 Wallendbeen Austr.
33 F4 Wallenpaupack, Lake *l.* U.S.A.
59 F6 Wallingford U.K.
33 G4 Wallingford U.S.A.
111 J3 Wallis and Futuna Is *terr.* Pac. Oc.
111 J3 Wallis, Îles *is* Pac. Oc.
115 K4 Wallis L. *b.* Austr.
33 F6 Wallops I. *i.* U.S.A.
24 C2 Wallowa Mts *mts* U.S.A.
57 □ Walls U.K.
116 C6 Wallumbilla Austr.
21 H2 Walmsley Lake *l.* Can.
58 D3 Walney, Isle of *i.* U.K.
30 C5 Walnut U.S.A.
35 G4 Walnut Canyon National Monument *res.* U.S.A.
27 F4 Walnut Ridge U.S.A.
85 J3 Walong India
112 C6 Walpole-Nornalup National Park *nat. park* Austr.
59 F5 Walsall U.K.
25 F4 Walsenburg U.S.A.
116 A3 Walsh *r.* Austr.
29 D5 Walterboro U.S.A.
29 C6 Walter F. George Res. *resr* U.S.A.
114 F2 Walter's Ra. *h.* Austr.
31 J3 Waltham Can.
28 C4 Walton *KY* U.S.A.
33 F3 Walton *NY* U.S.A.
103 B6 Walvis Bay Namibia
12 K7 Walvis Ridge *sea feature* Atlantic Ocean
102 C3 Wamba Zaire
93 K7 Wamena Indon.
84 B2 Wana Pak.
114 F2 Wanaaring Austr.
117 B6 Wanaka N.Z.
117 B6 Wanaka, L. *l.* N.Z.
89 E5 Wan'an China
31 G2 Wanapitei Lake *l.* Can.
33 F4 Wanaque Reservoir *resr* U.S.A.
114 D5 Wanbi Austr.
117 C6 Wanbrow, Cape *c.* N.Z.
114 D2 Wancoocha, Lake *salt flat* Austr.
82 J6 Wandingzhen China
116 C6 Wandoan Austr.
117 E3 Wanganui *r.* N.Z.
117 E3 Wanganui N.Z.
115 G6 Wangaratta Austr.
114 A5 Wangary Austr.
88 C3 Wangcang China
89 D4 Wangcheng China
88 F1 Wanghai Shan *h.* China
89 E4 Wangjiang China
89 C5 Wangmo China
89 C5 Wangqing China
84 B5 Wankaner India
102 E3 Wanlaweyn Somalia
89 E4 Wannian China
89 D7 Wanning China
88 E1 Wanquan China
61 D3 Wanroij Neth.
89 D6 Wanshan Qundao *is* China
117 F4 Wanstead N.Z.
59 F6 Wantage U.K.
31 G2 Wanup Can.
89 C4 Wan Xian China
89 C4 Wanxian China
89 C3 Wanyuan China
89 E4 Wanzai China
32 A4 Wapakoneta U.S.A.
30 B5 Wapello U.S.A.
26 C3 Wapikopa L. *l.* Can.
20 F4 Wapiti *r.* Can.
27 F4 Wappapello, L. *resr* U.S.A.
30 A5 Wapsipinicon *r.* U.S.A.
88 B3 Waqên China
84 A4 Warah Pak.
83 E7 Warangal India
114 F6 Waranga Reservoir *resr* Austr.
84 E5 Waraseoni India
115 F8 Waratah Austr.
115 F7 Waratah B. *b.* Austr.
114 B1 Warburton *watercourse* Austr.
112 E5 Warburton Austr.
21 G2 Warburton Bay *l.* Can.
116 B5 Ward *watercourse* Austr.
114 B5 Wardang I. *i.* Austr.
105 H3 Warden S. Africa
84 D5 Wardha India
84 D6 Wardha *r.* India
117 A6 Ward, Mt *mt. Southland* N.Z.
117 B5 Ward, Mt *mt. West Coast* N.Z.
20 D3 Ware Can.
33 G3 Ware U.S.A.
59 E7 Wareham U.K.
33 H4 Wareham U.S.A.
61 D4 Waremme Belgium
62 F4 Waren Ger.
62 C5 Warendorf Ger.
115 J2 Warialda Austr.
95 C2 Warin Chamrap Thai.
117 E2 Warkworth N.Z.
58 F2 Warkworth U.K.
21 H4 Warman Can.
104 C4 Warmbad Namibia
105 H2 Warmbad S. Africa
59 E6 Warminster U.K.
33 F4 Warminster U.S.A.
61 C2 Warmond Neth.
34 D2 Warm Springs *NV* U.S.A.
32 D5 Warm Springs *VA* U.S.A.
104 D6 Warmwaterberg *mts* S. Africa
33 H3 Warner U.S.A.
24 B3 Warner Mts *mts* U.S.A.
29 D5 Warner Robins U.S.A.
42 F7 Warnes Bol.
115 K2 Warning, Mt *mt.* Austr.
84 D5 Warora India
115 J1 Warra Austr.
114 E6 Warracknabeal Austr.
115 J5 Warragamba Reservoir *resr* Austr.
115 F7 Warragul Austr.
114 C2 Warrakalanna, Lake *salt flat* Austr.
114 A4 Warramboo Austr.
115 G2 Warrambool *r.* Austr.
112 D4 Warrawagine Austr.
113 J5 Warrego *r. Qld.* Austr.
116 A5 Warrego Ra. *h.* Austr.
115 G3 Warren Austr.
31 G2 Warren Can.
27 E5 Warren *AR* U.S.A.
31 F4 Warren *MI* U.S.A.
26 D1 Warren *MN* U.S.A.
32 C4 Warren *OH* U.S.A.
32 D4 Warren *PA* U.S.A.
32 C4 Warrendale U.S.A.
60 E3 Warrenpoint U.K.
26 E4 Warrensburg *MO* U.S.A.
33 G3 Warrensburg *NY* U.S.A.
104 F4 Warrenton S. Africa
32 E5 Warrenton U.S.A.
100 C4 Warri Nigeria
117 C6 Warrington N.Z.
59 E4 Warrington U.K.
29 C6 Warrington U.S.A.
114 C3 Warriota *watercourse* Austr.
114 E7 Warrnambool Austr.
26 E1 Warroad U.S.A.
114 A5 Warrow Austr.
115 H3 Warrumbungle Ra. *mts* Austr.
114 D2 Warry Warry *watercourse* Austr.
84 B2 Warsak Dam *dam* Pak.
63 K4 Warsaw Pol.
30 E5 Warsaw *IN* U.S.A.
26 E4 Warsaw *MO* U.S.A.
32 D3 Warsaw *NY* U.S.A.
32 E6 Warsaw *VA* U.S.A.
Warszawa *see* Warsaw
62 G4 Warta *r.* Pol.
115 K2 Warwick Austr.
59 F5 Warwick U.K.
33 F4 Warwick *NY* U.S.A.
33 H4 Warwick *RI* U.S.A.
25 E4 Wasatch Range *mts* U.S.A.
105 J4 Wasbank S. Africa
34 C4 Wasco U.S.A.
26 E2 Waseca U.S.A.
30 C5 Washburn *IL* U.S.A.
33 J1 Washburn *ME* U.S.A.
26 C2 Washburn *ND* U.S.A.
30 B2 Washburn *WV* U.S.A.
84 D5 Wāshīm India
32 E5 Washington *DC* U.S.A.
29 D5 Washington *GA* U.S.A.
30 B5 Washington *IA* U.S.A.
30 C5 Washington *IL* U.S.A.
28 C4 Washington *IN* U.S.A.
26 F4 Washington *MO* U.S.A.
29 E5 Washington *NC* U.S.A.
33 F4 Washington *NJ* U.S.A.
32 C4 Washington *PA* U.S.A.
35 F3 Washington *UT* U.S.A.
24 B2 Washington *div.* U.S.A.
119 B5 Washington, C. *c.* Ant.
32 B5 Washington Court House U.S.A.
30 D3 Washington Island *i.* U.S.A.
33 H2 Washington, Mt *mt.* U.S.A.
27 D5 Washita *r.* U.S.A.
59 H5 Wash, The *b.* U.K.
81 L5 Wasit Iraq
22 E3 Waskaganish Can.
21 K3 Waskaiowaka Lake *l.* Can.
90 J1 Wassamu Japan
104 C3 Wasser Namibia
34 C2 Wassuk Range *mts* U.S.A.
22 E4 Waswanipi, Lac *l.* Can.
93 G7 Watampone Indon.
33 G4 Waterbury *CT* U.S.A.
33 G2 Waterbury *VT* U.S.A.
21 H3 Waterbury Lake *l.* Can.
60 D5 Waterford Rep. of Ireland
32 D4 Waterford U.S.A.
60 E5 Waterford Harbour *harbour* Rep. of Ireland
60 C5 Watergrasshill Rep. of Ireland
21 H4 Waterhen *r.* Can.
31 G4 Waterloo Can.
30 A4 Waterloo *IA* U.S.A.
33 H3 Waterloo *ME* U.S.A.
32 E3 Waterloo *NY* U.S.A.
30 C4 Waterloo *WV* U.S.A.
59 F7 Waterlooville U.K.
105 H1 Waterpoort S. Africa
30 C2 Watersmeet U.S.A.
20 G5 Waterton Lakes Nat. Park *nat. park* Can.
33 E3 Watertown *NY* U.S.A.
26 D2 Watertown *SD* U.S.A.
30 C4 Watertown *WV* U.S.A.
105 J2 Waterval-Boven S. Africa
114 C4 Watervale Austr.
33 J2 Waterville U.S.A.
21 G3 Waterways Can.
31 G4 Watford Can.
59 G6 Watford U.K.
26 C2 Watford City U.S.A.
21 J3 Wathaman *r.* Can.
32 E3 Watkins Glen U.S.A.
Watling *i. see* San Salvador
27 D5 Watonga U.S.A.
21 H4 Watrous Can.
102 C3 Watsa Zaire
30 D5 Watseka U.S.A.
102 C4 Watsi Kengo Zaire
21 J4 Watson Can.
20 D2 Watson Lake Can.
34 B3 Watsonville U.S.A.
57 E2 Watten U.K.
57 E2 Watten, Loch *l.* U.K.
21 J2 Watterson Lake *l.* Can.
114 A2 Wattiwarriganna *watercourse* Austr.
20 F3 Watt, Mt *h.* Can.
59 H5 Watton U.K.
30 C2 Watton U.S.A.
93 J7 Watubela, Kepulauan *is* Indon.
110 E2 Wau P.N.G.
101 E4 Wau Sudan
30 D3 Waucedah U.S.A.
115 K3 Wauchope Austr.
29 D7 Wauchula U.S.A.
30 D4 Waukegan U.S.A.
30 C4 Waukesha U.S.A.
30 B4 Waukon U.S.A.
30 C3 Waupaca U.S.A.
30 C4 Waupun U.S.A.
27 D5 Waurika U.S.A.
30 C3 Wausau U.S.A.
32 A4 Wauseon U.S.A.
30 C3 Wautoma U.S.A.
30 C4 Wauwatosa U.S.A.
59 J5 Waveney *r.* U.K.
30 A4 Waverly *IA* U.S.A.
32 B5 Waverly *OH* U.S.A.
29 C4 Waverly *TN* U.S.A.
32 E6 Waverly *VA* U.S.A.
30 E1 Wawa Can.
100 C4 Wawa Nigeria
30 E5 Wawasee, Lake *l.* U.S.A.
93 L8 Wawoi *r.* P.N.G.
34 C3 Wawona U.S.A.
27 D5 Waxahachie U.S.A.
29 D6 Waycross U.S.A.
32 B6 Wayland *KY* U.S.A.
30 B5 Wayland *MO* U.S.A.
26 D3 Wayne U.S.A.
29 D5 Waynesboro *GA* U.S.A.
27 F6 Waynesboro *MS* U.S.A.
32 E5 Waynesboro *PA* U.S.A.
32 D5 Waynesboro *VA* U.S.A.
32 C5 Waynesburg U.S.A.
27 E4 Waynesville U.S.A.
27 D4 Waynoka U.S.A.
101 D3 Waza, Parc National de *nat. park* Cameroon
84 C2 Wazirabad Pak.
100 C3 W du Niger, Parcs Nationaux du *nat. park* Niger
22 B3 Weagamow L. *l.* Can.
59 H6 Weald, The *reg.* U.K.
58 E3 Wear *r.* U.K.
113 J3 Weary B. *b.* Austr.
27 D5 Weatherford U.S.A.
24 B3 Weaverville U.S.A.
31 G2 Webbwood Can.
22 C3 Webequie Can.
20 D3 Weber, Mt *mt.* Can.
102 E3 Webi Shabeelle *r.* Somalia
33 H3 Webster *MA* U.S.A.
26 D2 Webster *SD* U.S.A.
30 A3 Webster *WV* U.S.A.
26 E3 Webster City U.S.A.
32 C5 Webster Springs U.S.A.
44 D8 Weddell I. *i.* Falkland Is
119 B2 Weddell Sea *sea* Ant.
114 E6 Wedderburn Austr.
24 B3 Weed U.S.A.
32 D4 Weedville U.S.A.
115 H2 Weemelah Austr.
105 J4 Weenen S. Africa
61 F1 Weener Ger.
61 E2 Weerribben, Nationaal Park De *nat. park* Neth.
61 D3 Weert Neth.
115 G4 Weethalle Austr.
115 H3 Wee Waa Austr.
63 K3 Węgorzewo Pol.
88 B2 Wei *r. Henan* China
88 D3 Wei *r. Shaanxi* China
88 E1 Weichang China
88 F2 Weifang China
88 G2 Weihai China
115 G2 Weilmoringle Austr.
62 E5 Weimar Ger.
88 C3 Weinan China
89 B5 Weining China
113 H2 Weipa Austr.
115 H2 Weir *r.* Austr.
21 L3 Weir River Can.
32 C4 Weirton U.S.A.
24 C2 Weiser U.S.A.
88 E3 Weishan China
88 E3 Weishan Hu *l.* China
88 E3 Weishi China
62 E6 Weißenburg in Bayern Ger.
29 C5 Weiss L. *l.* U.S.A.
104 C2 Weissrand Mts *mts* Namibia
89 B5 Weixin China
88 B3 Weiyuan *Gansu* China
89 B4 Weiyuan *Sichuan* China
62 G7 Weiz Austria
89 C6 Weizhou Dao *i.* China
62 J3 Wejherowo Pol.
21 K4 Wekusko Can.
21 K4 Wekusko Lake *l.* Can.
32 C6 Welch U.S.A.
33 H2 Weld U.S.A.
102 D2 Weldiya Eth.
34 C4 Weldon U.S.A.
102 D3 Welk'īt'ē Eth.
105 G3 Welkom S. Africa
31 H4 Welland Can.
59 G5 Welland *r.* U.K.
31 H4 Welland Canal *canal* Can.
31 G4 Wellesley Can.
113 G3 Wellesley Is *is* Austr.
20 B2 Wellesley Lake *l.* Can.

**182**

33 H4 Wellfleet U.S.A.
59 G5 Wellingborough U.K.
115 H4 Wellington N.S.W. Austr.
114 C5 Wellington S.A. Austr.
117 E4 Wellington N.Z.
104 C6 Wellington S. Africa
59 E5 Wellington Eng. U.K.
59 D7 Wellington Eng. U.K.
24 F3 Wellington CO U.S.A.
27 D4 Wellington KS U.S.A.
34 C2 Wellington NV U.S.A.
32 B4 Wellington OH U.S.A.
27 C5 Wellington TX U.S.A.
35 G2 Wellington UT U.S.A.
44 A7 Wellington, I. i. Chile
115 G7 Wellington, L. l. Austr.
30 B5 Wellman U.S.A.
20 E4 Wells Can.
59 E6 Wells U.K.
24 D3 Wells NV U.S.A.
33 F3 Wells NY U.S.A.
32 E4 Wellsboro U.S.A.
117 E2 Wellsford N.Z.
20 E4 Wells Gray Prov. Park res. Can.
112 D5 Wells, L. salt flat Austr.
59 H5 Wells-next-the-Sea U.K.
32 B5 Wellston U.S.A.
32 E3 Wellsville U.S.A.
35 E5 Wellton U.S.A.
62 G6 Wels Austria
33 K2 Welshpool Can.
59 D5 Welshpool U.K.
59 G6 Welwyn Garden City U.K.
59 E5 Wem U.K.
105 H4 Wembesi S. Africa
20 F3 Wembley Can.
22 E3 Wemindji Can.
29 E7 Wemyss Bight Bahamas
88 F3 Wen r. China
24 B2 Wenatchee U.S.A.
89 D7 Wenchang China
89 F5 Wencheng China
100 B4 Wenchi Ghana
88 B4 Wenchuan China
35 F5 Wenden U.S.A.
88 G2 Wendeng China
102 D3 Wendo Eth.
24 D3 Wendover U.S.A.
31 F2 Wenebegon Lake l. Can.
89 C5 Weng'an China
89 E5 Wengyuan China
88 B4 Wenjiang China
89 F4 Wenling China
42 □ Wenman, Isla i. Galapagos Is Ecuador
30 C5 Wenona U.S.A.
89 B6 Wenshan China
59 H5 Wensum r. U.K.
114 D5 Wentworth Austr.
33 H3 Wentworth U.S.A.
88 B3 Wen Xian China
89 F5 Wenzhou China
105 G4 Wepener S. Africa
104 E2 Werda Botswana
62 F4 Werder Ger.
20 C2 Wernecke Mountains mts Can.
114 F6 Werribee Austr.
114 D5 Werrimull Austr.
115 J3 Werris Creek Austr.
62 E5 Wertheim Ger.
62 C5 Wesel Ger.
62 D4 Weser r. Ger.
26 C4 Weskan U.S.A.
31 J3 Weslemkoon Lake l. Can.
33 K2 Wesley U.S.A.
23 K4 Wesleyville Can.
113 G2 Wessel, C. c. Austr.
113 G2 Wessel Is is Austr.
105 H3 Wesselton S. Africa
26 D2 Wessington Springs U.S.A.
30 C4 West Allis U.S.A.
119 A4 West Antarctica reg. Ant.
13 L5 West Australian Basin sea feature Indian Ocean
13 L6 West Australian Ridge sea feature Indian Ocean
84 B5 West Banas r. India
80 E5 West Bank terr. Asia
23 J3 West Bay Can.
27 F6 West Bay b. U.S.A.
30 C4 West Bend U.S.A.
85 F5 West Bengal div. India
31 E3 West Branch U.S.A.
32 D4 West Branch Susquehanna r. U.S.A.
59 E5 West Bromwich U.K.
33 H3 Westbrook U.S.A.
57 □ West Burra i. U.K.
115 G4 Westbury Austr.
59 E6 Westbury U.K.
115 G5 Westby Austr.
30 B4 Westby U.S.A.
33 F5 West Chester U.S.A.
33 G2 West Danville U.S.A.
31 F3 West Duck Island i. Can.
29 E7 West End Bahamas
34 D4 West End U.S.A.
29 E7 West End Pt pt Bahamas
62 D3 Westerland Ger.
33 H4 Westerly U.S.A.
21 H1 Western r. Can.
112 D4 Western Australia div. Austr.
104 D6 Western Cape div. S. Africa
78 B4 Western Desert des. Egypt
83 D8 Western Ghats mts India
114 F7 Western Port b. Austr.
96 Western Sahara terr. Africa

106 Western Samoa country Pac. Oc.
61 B3 Westerschelde est. Neth.
44 D8 West Falkland i. Falkland Is
26 D2 West Fargo U.S.A.
30 D5 Westfield IN U.S.A.
33 G3 Westfield MA U.S.A.
33 K1 Westfield ME U.S.A.
32 D3 Westfield NY U.S.A.
61 E1 Westgat chan. Neth.
116 B6 Westgate Austr.
33 K2 West Grand Lake l. U.S.A.
57 F3 Westhill U.K.
26 C1 Westhope U.S.A.
119 D5 West Ice Shelf ice feature Ant.
89 □ West Lamma Chan. chan. Hong Kong China
32 B5 West Lancaster U.S.A.
117 B5 Westland National Park nat. park N.Z.
59 J5 Westleton U.K.
34 B3 Westley U.S.A.
32 B6 West Liberty KY U.S.A.
32 B4 West Liberty OH U.S.A.
57 E5 West Linton U.K.
57 B2 West Loch Roag b. U.K.
20 G4 Westlock Can.
31 G4 West Lorne Can.
27 F5 West Memphis U.S.A.
32 E5 Westminster MD U.S.A.
29 D5 Westminster SC U.S.A.
32 C5 Weston U.S.A.
59 E6 Weston-super-Mare U.K.
33 F5 Westover U.S.A.
29 D7 West Palm Beach U.S.A.
27 F4 West Plains U.S.A.
114 A5 West Point pt S.A. Austr.
115 F8 West Point pt Tas. Austr.
27 F5 West Point MS U.S.A.
33 F4 West Point NY U.S.A.
31 J3 Westport Can.
117 C4 Westport N.Z.
60 B4 Westport Rep. of Ireland
34 A2 Westport U.S.A.
21 J4 Westray Can.
57 E1 Westray i. U.K.
31 G2 Westree Can.
61 F5 Westrich reg. Ger.
20 E4 West Road r. Can.
115 G7 West Sister I. i. Austr.
33 H2 West Stewartstown U.S.A.
61 D1 West-Terschelling Neth.
33 H4 West Tisbury U.S.A.
33 G2 West Topsham U.S.A.
33 G3 West Townshend U.S.A.
30 B4 West Union IA U.S.A.
32 B5 West Union OH U.S.A.
32 C5 West Union WV U.S.A.
30 D5 Westville U.S.A.
32 C5 West Virginia div. U.S.A.
34 C2 West Walker r. U.S.A.
116 D4 Westwood U.S.A.
34 B1 Westwood U.S.A.
115 G4 West Wyalong Austr.
24 E2 West Yellowstone U.S.A.
61 C2 Wetzaan Neth.
93 H8 Wetar i. Indon.
20 G4 Wetaskiwin Can.
30 D2 Wetmore U.S.A.
62 D5 Wetzlar Ger.
110 E2 Wewak P.N.G.
60 E5 Wexford Rep. of Ireland
21 H4 Weyakwin Can.
30 C3 Weyauwega U.S.A.
59 G6 Weybridge U.K.
21 J5 Weyburn Can.
59 E7 Weymouth U.K.
33 H3 Weymouth U.S.A.
117 F2 Whakatane N.Z.
117 F3 Whakatane r. N.Z.
95 A3 Whale B. b. Myanmar
20 B3 Whale B. Myanmar
29 E7 Whale Cay i. Bahamas
21 L2 Whale Cove Can.
57 □ Whalsay i. U.K.
117 F2 Whangamata N.Z.
117 F3 Whangamomona N.Z.
117 E1 Whangarei N.Z.
22 E2 Whapmagoostui Can.
58 F4 Wharfe r. U.K.
31 F2 Wharncliffe Can.
21 J2 Wharton Lake l. Can.
30 A5 What Cheer U.S.A.
24 F3 Wheatland U.S.A.
30 C5 Wheaton U.S.A.
25 F4 Wheeler Peak summit NM U.S.A.
35 E2 Wheeler Peak summit NV U.S.A.
32 C4 Wheeling U.S.A.
47 F2 Wheelwright Arg.
58 E3 Whernside h. U.K.
114 A5 Whidbey Pt pt Austr.
24 Whiskeytown-Shasta-Trinity Nat. Recreation Area res. U.S.A.
57 F2 Whitburn U.K.
31 H4 Whitby U.K.
58 G3 Whitby U.K.
59 E5 Whitchurch U.K.
20 A2 White r. AK/Y.T. Can./U.S.A.
27 E4 White r. AR U.S.A.
35 G5 White r. AZ U.S.A.
24 E3 White r. CO U.S.A.
28 C4 White r. IN U.S.A.
30 D4 White r. MI U.S.A.
35 E2 White r. NV U.S.A.
26 C3 White r. SD U.S.A.
30 B2 White r. WV U.S.A.

33 J3 White Bay b. Can.
26 C2 White Butte mt. U.S.A.
114 E3 White Cliffs Austr.
20 F4 White Cloud U.S.A.
20 F4 Whitecourt Can.
30 A2 Whiteface Lake l. U.S.A.
33 H2 Whitefield U.S.A.
31 G2 Whitefish Can.
30 E2 Whitefish r. MI U.S.A.
24 D1 Whitefish MT U.S.A.
21 H2 Whitefish Lake l. Can.
30 E2 Whitefish Pt pt U.S.A.
60 D5 Whitehall Rep. of Ireland
57 F1 Whitehall U.K.
33 G3 Whitehall NY U.S.A.
30 B3 Whitehall WV U.S.A.
58 D3 Whitehaven U.K.
60 F3 Whitehead U.K.
59 G6 Whitehill U.K.
20 B2 Whitehorse Can.
35 E1 White Horse Pass pass U.S.A.
59 F6 White Horse, Vale of v. U.K.
117 E2 White I. i. N.Z.
112 E4 White, L. salt flat Austr.
27 E6 White L. l. LA U.S.A.
30 D4 White L. l. MI U.S.A.
113 J8 Whitemark Austr.
33 H2 White Mountains mts U.S.A.
34 C3 White Mt Peak summit U.S.A.
78 C7 White Nile r. Sudan/Uganda
104 C1 White Nossob watercourse Namibia
35 E2 White Pine Range mts U.S.A.
33 G4 White Plains U.S.A.
22 C4 White River Can.
35 H5 Whiteriver U.S.A.
33 G3 White River Junction VT U.S.A.
35 E2 White River Valley v. U.S.A.
116 A1 White Rock Austr.
35 E2 White Rock Peak summit U.S.A.
25 F5 White Sands Nat. Mon. res. U.S.A.
32 B6 Whitesburg U.S.A.
76 E3 White Sea g. Rus. Fed.
21 K4 Whiteshell Prov. Park res. Can.
24 E2 White Sulphur Springs MT U.S.A.
32 C6 White Sulphur Springs WV U.S.A.
29 E5 Whiteville U.S.A.
100 B4 White Volta r. Ghana
30 C4 Whitewater U.S.A.
22 C3 Whitewater L. l. Can.
21 J4 Whitewood Can.
115 G6 Whitfield Austr.
59 J6 Whitfield U.K.
57 D6 Whithorn U.K.
117 E2 Whitianga N.Z.
33 K2 Whiting U.S.A.
59 C6 Whitland U.K.
58 F2 Whitley Bay U.K.
29 D5 Whitmire U.S.A.
31 H3 Whitney Can.
34 C3 Whitney, Mt mt. U.S.A.
33 K2 Whitneyville U.S.A.
59 J6 Whitstable U.K.
34 A2 Whitsunday I. i. Austr.
116 C3 Whitsunday Pass. chan. Austr.
116 C3 Whitsundays, The is Austr.
114 F6 Whittlesea Austr.
59 G5 Whittlesey U.K.
115 G5 Whitton Austr.
21 H2 Wholdaia Lake l. Can.
35 H5 Why U.S.A.
114 B4 Whyalla Austr.
95 A1 Wiang Phran Thai.
95 B1 Wiang Sa Thai.
31 G3 Wiarton Can.
61 B3 Wichelen Belgium
27 D4 Wichita U.S.A.
27 D5 Wichita Falls U.S.A.
27 D5 Wichita Mts mts U.S.A.
57 E2 Wick U.K.
35 H5 Wickenburg U.S.A.
59 H6 Wickford U.K.
115 E7 Wickham, C. pt Tas. Austr.
60 E5 Wicklow Rep. of Ireland
60 E5 Wicklow Head hd Rep. of Ireland
60 E5 Wicklow Mountains mts Rep. of Ireland
60 E4 Wicklow Mountains National Park nat. park Rep. of Ireland
116 E5 Wide B. b. Austr.
115 G2 Widgeegoara watercourse Austr.
59 E4 Widnes U.K.
61 F4 Wiehl Ger.
63 J5 Wieluń Pol.
Wien see Vienna
62 H7 Wiener Neustadt Austria
61 C2 Wieringermeer Polder reclaimed land Neth.
62 D5 Wiesbaden Ger.
62 J3 Wieżyca h. Pol.
58 E4 Wigan U.K.
27 F6 Wiggins U.S.A.
59 F7 Wight, Isle of i. Eng. U.K.
21 H1 Wignes Lake l. Can.
59 F5 Wigston U.K.
59 E5 Wigton U.K.
57 D6 Wigtown U.K.

57 D6 Wigtown Bay b. U.K.
61 D3 Wijchen Neth.
61 C3 Wijnegem Belgium
35 F4 Wikieup U.S.A.
31 G3 Wikwemikong Can.
24 C2 Wilbur U.S.A.
114 E3 Wilcannia Austr.
31 J4 Wildcat Hill Wilderness Area res. Can.
34 D2 Wildcat Peak summit U.S.A.
105 H5 Wild Coast coastal area S. Africa
30 C1 Wild Goose Can.
20 F4 Wildhay r. Can.
30 A2 Wild Rite Lake l. U.S.A.
115 F9 Wild Rivers Nat. Park nat. park Austr.
62 E7 Wildspitze mt Austria
29 D6 Wildwood FL U.S.A.
33 F5 Wildwood NJ U.S.A.
105 H3 Wilge r. Free State S. Africa
105 H2 Wilge r. Gauteng/Mpumalanga S. Africa
114 A3 Wilgena Austr.
119 C5 Wilhelm II Land reg. Ant.
32 C4 Wilhelm, Lake l. U.S.A.
110 E2 Wilhelm, Mt mt P.N.G.
62 D4 Wilhelmshaven Ger.
33 F4 Wilkes-Barre U.S.A.
119 B6 Wilkes Land reg. Ant.
21 H4 Wilkie Can.
119 B2 Wilkins Ice Shelf ice feature Ant.
24 B2 Willamette r. U.S.A.
59 D7 Willand U.K.
114 E4 Willandra Billabong watercourse Austr.
24 B2 Willapa B. b. U.S.A.
32 B4 Willard U.S.A.
33 F5 Willards U.S.A.
35 H5 Willcox U.S.A.
61 C3 Willebroek Belgium
37 L6 Willemstad Neth. Ant.
21 H3 William r. Can.
114 B2 William Cr. Austr.
114 E6 William, Mt mt Austr.
35 F4 Williams AZ U.S.A.
34 A2 Williams CA U.S.A.
30 A5 Williamsburg IA U.S.A.
32 A6 Williamsburg KY U.S.A.
30 E3 Williamsburg MI U.S.A.
32 E6 Williamsburg VA U.S.A.
29 E7 Williams I. i. Bahamas
20 E4 Williams Lake Can.
23 H1 William Smith, Cap c. Can.
32 E3 Williamson NY U.S.A.
32 B6 Williamson WV U.S.A.
30 D5 Williamsport IN U.S.A.
32 E4 Williamsport PA U.S.A.
29 E5 Williamston U.S.A.
33 G3 Williamstown MA U.S.A.
33 F3 Williamstown NY U.S.A.
32 C5 Williamstown WV U.S.A.
33 G4 Willimantic U.S.A.
116 D1 Willis Group atolls Coral Sea Is Terr.
104 D5 Williston S. Africa
29 D6 Williston FL U.S.A.
26 C1 Williston ND U.S.A.
20 E3 Williston Lake l. Can.
59 D6 Williton U.K.
34 A2 Willits U.S.A.
26 E2 Willmar U.S.A.
20 F4 Willmore Wilderness Prov. Park res. Can.
20 D3 Will, Mt mt. Can.
114 B3 Willochra watercourse Austr.
20 E4 Willow r. Can.
21 H5 Willow Bunch Can.
32 A4 Willow Hill U.S.A.
20 F2 Willow Lake l. Can.
104 E6 Willowmore S. Africa
30 C3 Willow Reservoir resr U.S.A.
34 A2 Willows U.S.A.
27 F4 Willow Springs U.S.A.
105 H6 Willowvale S. Africa
112 E4 Wills, L. salt flat Austr.
114 C5 Willunga Austr.
114 C4 Wilmington Austr.
33 F5 Wilmington DE U.S.A.
29 E5 Wilmington NC U.S.A.
32 B5 Wilmington OH U.S.A.
33 G3 Wilmington VT U.S.A.
59 E5 Wilmslow U.K.
114 C3 Wilpena watercourse Austr.
26 D4 Wilson KS U.S.A.
29 E5 Wilson NC U.S.A.
25 F4 Wilson, Mt mt. CO U.S.A.
35 E2 Wilson, Mt mt. NV U.S.A.
26 D4 Wilson Res. resr U.S.A.
33 H2 Wilsons Mills U.S.A.
115 G7 Wilson's Promontory pen. Austr.
115 G7 Wilson's Promontory Nat. Park nat. park Austr.
30 B3 Wilton IA U.S.A.
33 H2 Wilton ME U.S.A.
61 D5 Wiltz Lux.
112 D5 Wiluna Austr.
59 J7 Wimereux France
114 E4 Wimmera r. Austr.
30 D5 Winamac U.S.A.
116 A6 Winbin watercourse Austr.
105 G4 Winburg S. Africa

59 E6 Wincanton U.K.
33 G3 Winchendon U.S.A.
22 F4 Winchester Can.
59 F6 Winchester U.K.
30 B6 Winchester IL U.S.A.
30 E5 Winchester IN U.S.A.
32 A6 Winchester KY U.S.A.
33 G3 Winchester NH U.S.A.
29 C5 Winchester TN U.S.A.
32 D5 Winchester VA U.S.A.
24 E3 Wind r. U.S.A.
114 B3 Windabout, L. salt flat Austr.
26 C3 Wind Cave Nat. Park nat. park U.S.A.
58 E3 Windermere U.K.
58 E3 Windermere l. U.K.
103 B6 Windhoek Namibia
26 E3 Windom U.S.A.
113 H5 Windorah Austr.
35 H4 Window Rock U.S.A.
30 D4 Wind Pt pt U.S.A.
24 E3 Wind River Range mts U.S.A.
59 F6 Windrush r. U.K.
115 J4 Windsor Austr.
23 H4 Windsor Nfld Can.
23 H5 Windsor N.S. Can.
31 F4 Windsor Ont. Can.
23 H4 Windsor Que. Can.
59 G6 Windsor U.K.
33 G4 Windsor CT U.S.A.
29 E5 Windsor NC U.S.A.
33 F3 Windsor NY U.S.A.
32 E6 Windsor VA U.S.A.
33 G3 Windsor VT U.S.A.
33 G4 Windsor Locks U.S.A.
37 M5 Windward Islands is Caribbean Sea
37 K5 Windward Passage chan. Cuba/Haiti
29 C5 Winfield AL U.S.A.
30 B5 Winfield IA U.S.A.
27 D4 Winfield KS U.S.A.
58 F3 Wingate U.K.
115 J3 Wingen Austr.
115 K3 Wingham Austr.
31 G4 Wingham Can.
22 C2 Winisk Can.
22 C2 Winisk r. Can.
22 C3 Winisk L. l. Can.
22 C3 Winisk River Provincial Park res. Can.
95 A2 Winkana Myanmar
21 K5 Winkler Can.
33 J2 Winn U.S.A.
100 B4 Winneba Ghana
30 C3 Winnebago, Lake l. U.S.A.
30 C3 Winneconne U.S.A.
24 C3 Winnemucca U.S.A.
34 C1 Winnemucca Lake l. U.S.A.
26 D3 Winner U.S.A.
27 E6 Winnfield U.S.A.
26 E2 Winnibigoshish L. l. U.S.A.
21 K4 Winnipeg r. Can.
21 K5 Winnipeg Can.
21 K4 Winnipeg, Lake l. Can.
21 J4 Winnipegosis Can.
21 J4 Winnipegosis, Lake l. Can.
33 H3 Winnipesaukee, L. l. U.S.A.
27 F5 Winnsboro U.S.A.
35 G4 Winona AZ U.S.A.
30 C2 Winona MI U.S.A.
30 B3 Winona MN U.S.A.
27 F5 Winona MS U.S.A.
33 G2 Winooski U.S.A.
33 G2 Winooski r. U.S.A.
61 F1 Winschoten Neth.
59 E4 Winsford U.K.
35 G4 Winslow U.S.A.
33 G4 Winsted U.S.A.
29 D4 Winston-Salem U.S.A.
29 D6 Winter Haven U.S.A.
33 J2 Winterport U.S.A.
34 B2 Winters U.S.A.
61 E3 Winterswijk Neth.
62 D7 Winterthur Switz.
105 H4 Winterton S. Africa
33 J1 Winterville U.S.A.
33 J2 Winthrop U.S.A.
113 H4 Winton Austr.
117 B7 Winton N.Z.
114 C4 Wirrabara Austr.
59 D4 Wirral pen. U.K.
114 B3 Wirraminna Austr.
114 D6 Wirrega Austr.
114 A4 Wirrulla Austr.
59 H5 Wisbech U.K.
33 J2 Wiscasset U.S.A.
30 C3 Wisconsin div. U.S.A.
30 B4 Wisconsin r. U.S.A.
30 C3 Wisconsin Dells U.S.A.
30 C4 Wisconsin, Lake l. U.S.A.
30 C3 Wisconsin Rapids U.S.A.
32 B6 Wise U.S.A.
59 F6 Wishaw U.K.
63 J4 Wisła r. Pol.
62 E4 Wismar Ger.
59 J7 Wissant France
30 B3 Wissota L. l. U.S.A.
105 H2 Witbank S. Africa
104 C2 Witbooisvlei Namibia
59 G6 Witham U.K.
59 H5 Witham r. U.K.
59 H4 Withernsea U.K.
113 G5 Witjira National Park nat. park Austr.
59 F6 Witney U.K.

105 J2 Witrivier S. Africa
105 G5 Witteberg mts S. Africa
30 C3 Wittenberg U.S.A.
62 E4 Wittenberge Ger.
62 E4 Wittenburg Ger.
64 H3 Wittenheim France
62 C6 Wittlich Ger.
61 F1 Wittmund Ger.
62 F4 Wittstock Ger.
110 E2 Witu Is is P.N.G.
103 B6 Witvlei Namibia
115 K1 Wivenhoe, Lake l. Austr.
62 J3 Władysławowo Pol.
63 J4 Włocławek Pol.
33 H2 Woburn Can.
115 G6 Wodonga Austr.
61 D5 Woëvre, Plaine de la plain France
93 J8 Wokam i. Indon.
85 H4 Wokha India
59 G6 Woking U.K.
59 G6 Wokingham U.K.
30 D5 Wolcott IN U.S.A.
32 E3 Wolcott NY U.S.A.
20 C2 Wolf r. Can.
30 C3 Wolf r. U.S.A.
24 D2 Wolf Creek U.S.A.
25 F4 Wolf Creek Pass pass U.S.A.
33 H3 Wolfeboro U.S.A.
31 J3 Wolfe I. i. Can.
62 E4 Wolfenbüttel Ger.
20 C2 Wolf Lake l. Can.
24 F1 Wolf Point U.S.A.
62 G7 Wolfsberg Austria
62 E4 Wolfsburg Ger.
23 H4 Wolfville Can.
42 □ Wolf, Volcán volc. Galapagos Is Ecuador
62 F3 Wolgast Ger.
62 G4 Wolin Pol.
44 C9 Wollaston, Islas is Chile
21 J3 Wollaston Lake l. Can.
21 J3 Wollaston Lake Can.
115 J5 Wollongong Austr.
105 J5 Wolmaransstad S. Africa
114 D6 Wolseley Austr.
104 C6 Wolseley S. Africa
58 F3 Wolsingham U.K.
61 E2 Wolvega Neth.
59 E5 Wolverhampton U.K.
30 E3 Wolverine U.S.A.
61 F5 Womrather Höhe h. Ger.
116 D6 Wondai Austr.
114 F3 Wongalarroo Lake salt l. Austr.
115 H4 Wongarbon Austr.
85 G4 Wong Chu r. Bhutan
89 Wong Chuk Hang Hong Kong China
87 N4 Wŏnju S. Korea
113 J7 Wonnangatta Moroka National Park nat. park Vic. Austr.
87 N4 Wŏnsan N. Korea
114 F7 Wonthaggi Austr.
114 B3 Woocalla Austr.
113 G2 Woodah, Isle i. Austr.
59 J5 Woodbridge U.K.
32 E5 Woodbridge U.S.A.
20 G3 Wood Buffalo National Park nat. park Can.
115 K2 Woodburn Austr.
24 B2 Woodburn U.S.A.
30 E4 Woodbury MI U.S.A.
33 F5 Woodbury NJ U.S.A.
32 A6 Wood Creek Lake l. U.S.A.
34 C2 Woodfords U.S.A.
34 C3 Woodlake U.S.A.
34 B2 Woodland U.S.A.
25 F4 Woodland Park U.S.A.
95 Woodlands Sing.
111 F2 Woodlark I. i. P.N.G.
112 F5 Woodroffe, Mt mt Austr.
24 E3 Woodruff U.S.A.
32 C5 Woodsfield U.S.A.
115 G7 Woodside Austr.
113 F3 Woods, L. salt flat Austr.
21 L5 Woods, Lake of the l. Can./U.S.A.
115 G6 Woods Pt Austr.
116 B2 Woodstock Austr.
23 G4 Woodstock N.B. Can.
31 G4 Woodstock Ont. Can.
30 C4 Woodstock IL U.S.A.
32 E5 Woodstock VA U.S.A.
33 F5 Woodstown U.S.A.
33 G2 Woodsville U.S.A.
117 E4 Woodville N.Z.
32 E3 Woodville NY U.S.A.
27 E6 Woodville TX U.S.A.
27 D4 Woodward U.S.A.
115 K3 Woolgoolga Austr.
115 K2 Wooli Austr.
114 C3 Wooltana Austr.
114 B3 Woomera Austr.
114 A3 Woomera Prohibited Area res. Austr.
33 H4 Woonsocket U.S.A.
116 C5 Woorabinda Austr.
32 C4 Wooster U.S.A.
104 C6 Worcester S. Africa
33 H3 Worcester U.S.A.
62 F7 Wörgl Austria
58 D3 Workington U.K.
59 G4 Worksop U.K.
24 F2 Worland U.S.A.
61 C2 Wormerveer Neth.
59 C6 Worms Head hd U.K.

104 B1 **Wortel** Namibia
59 G7 **Worthing** U.K.
26 E3 **Worthington** U.S.A.
93 G7 **Wotu** Indon.
61 C3 **Woudrichem** Neth.
26 C3 **Wounded Knee** U.S.A.
116 D4 **Wowan** Austr.
93 G7 **Wowoni** i. Indon.
20 C3 **Wrangell** U.S.A.
20 C3 **Wrangell I.** i. U.S.A.
57 C2 **Wrath, Cape** c. U.K.
26 C3 **Wray** U.S.A.
59 F5 **Wreake** r. U.K.
104 B4 **Wreck Point** pt S. Africa
59 E4 **Wrexham** U.K.
94 C4 **Wright** Phil.
24 F3 **Wright** U.S.A.
27 E5 **Wright Patman L.** l. U.S.A.
35 G6 **Wrightson, Mt** mt. U.S.A.
20 E2 **Wrigley** Can.
62 H5 **Wrocław** Pol.
62 H4 **Września** Pol.
88 E2 **Wu'an** China
88 D2 **Wubu** China
89 C4 **Wuchang** China
89 D6 **Wuchuan** Guangdong China
89 C4 **Wuchuan** Guizhou China
88 D1 **Wuchuan** Nei Monggol Zizhiqu China
88 C2 **Wuda** China
88 C2 **Wudang Shan** mts China
88 D3 **Wudang Shan** mt. China
85 H2 **Wudaoliang** China
88 E2 **Wudi** China
89 B5 **Wuding** China
88 D2 **Wuding** r. China
114 A4 **Wudinna** Austr.
88 B3 **Wudu** China
89 C4 **Wufeng** China
89 D5 **Wugang** China
88 C3 **Wugong** China
88 C2 **Wuhai** China
89 E4 **Wuhan** China
88 E3 **Wuhe** China
88 F4 **Wuhu** China
89 E6 **Wuhua** China
84 D2 **Wüjang** China
89 C6 **Wujia** China
89 C4 **Wu Jiang** r. China
100 C4 **Wukari** Nigeria
85 H3 **Wular L.** l. India
84 C2 **Wular L.** l. India
88 F2 **Wuleidao Wan** l. China
88 F3 **Wulian** China
89 B4 **Wulian Feng** mts China
82 K6 **Wuliang Shan** mts China
93 J8 **Wuliaru** i. Indon.
89 C4 **Wuling Shan** mts China
89 C4 **Wulong** China
89 B5 **Wumeng Shan** mts China
89 C6 **Wuming** China
88 A4 **Wumiao** China
88 E4 **Wuning** China
83 J6 **Wuntho** Myanmar
35 G4 **Wupatki National Monument** res. U.S.A.
89 E5 **Wuping** China
62 C5 **Wuppertal** Ger.
104 C6 **Wuppertal** S. Africa
88 C2 **Wuqi** China
88 E2 **Wuqiao** China
88 E2 **Wuqing** China
62 D6 **Würzburg** Ger.
88 B3 **Wushan** Gansu China
88 C4 **Wushan** Sichuan China
88 D4 **Wu Shan** mts China
89 C4 **Wusheng** China
89 C6 **Wushi** China
88 D2 **Wutai** China
88 D2 **Wutai Shan** mt. China
110 E2 **Wuvulu I.** i. P.N.G.
88 A4 **Wuwei** Anhui China
88 B2 **Wuwei** Gansu China
88 F4 **Wuxi** Jiangsu China
88 C4 **Wuxi** Sichuan China
**Wuxing** see Huzhou
89 C6 **Wuxu** China
89 C6 **Wuxuan** China
88 D3 **Wuxuang** China
89 F4 **Wuyi** China
87 N2 **Wuyiling** China
89 E5 **Wuyi Shan** mts China
89 E4 **Wuyuan** Jiangxi China
88 C1 **Wuyuan** Nei Monggol Zizhiqu China
88 D2 **Wuzhai** China
88 B2 **Wuzhen** China
88 C2 **Wuzhong** China
89 D6 **Wuzhou** China
30 B5 **Wyaconda** r. U.S.A.
115 G4 **Wyalong** Austr.
31 H4 **Wyandotte** U.S.A.
116 A6 **Wyandra** Austr.
30 C5 **Wyanet** U.S.A.
115 H4 **Wyangala Reservoir** resr Austr.
114 F2 **Wyara, Lake** salt flat Austr.
114 E6 **Wycheproof** Austr.
59 E6 **Wye** r. U.K.
59 F6 **Wylye** r. U.K.
59 J5 **Wymondham** U.K.
112 E3 **Wyndham** Austr.
27 F4 **Wynne** U.S.A.
115 F8 **Wynyard** Austr.
21 J4 **Wynyard** Can.
31 I5 **Wyoming** IL U.S.A.
30 D4 **Wyoming** MI U.S.A.
24 E3 **Wyoming** div. U.S.A.
24 E3 **Wyoming Peak** summit U.S.A.

115 J4 **Wyong** Austr.
114 D5 **Wyperfeld Nat. Park** nat. park Austr.
58 E4 **Wyre** r. U.K.
33 K4 **Wysox** U.S.A.
63 K4 **Wyszków** Pol.
59 F5 **Wythall** U.K.
32 C6 **Wytheville** U.S.A.
33 J2 **Wytopitlock** U.S.A.

# X

102 F2 **Xaafuun** Somalia
81 M1 **Xaçmaz** Azer.
104 E1 **Xade** Botswana
85 H3 **Xagquka** China
84 D1 **Xaidulla** China
85 G3 **Xainza** China
103 D6 **Xai Xai** Moz.
**Xalapa** see Jalapa Enriquez
92 C2 **Xam Hua** Laos
95 B1 **Xan** r. Laos
103 C6 **Xanagas** Botswana
88 D1 **Xangd** China
88 D1 **Xangdin Hural** China
103 B5 **Xangongo** Angola
81 L2 **Xankändi** Azer.
67 L4 **Xanthi** Greece
95 C2 **Xan, Xé** r. Vietnam
42 E6 **Xapuri** Brazil
81 M2 **Xaraba Şähär Sayı** i. Azer.
81 M2 **Xärä Zirä Adası** is Azer.
85 F3 **Xarba La** pass China
88 B1 **Xar Burd** China
88 F1 **Xar Moron** r. Nei Monggol Zizhiqu China
88 D1 **Xar Moron** r. Nei Monggol Zizhiqu China
65 F3 **Xàtiva** Spain
103 C6 **Xau, Lake** l. Botswana
95 C3 **Xa Vo Đat** Vietnam
32 B5 **Xenia** U.S.A.
88 F1 **Xi** r. China
89 D6 **Xiachuan Dao** i. China
88 B3 **Xiahe** China
88 E5 **Xiajiang** China
89 F5 **Xiamen** China
88 C3 **Xi'an** China
88 E3 **Xiancheng** China
88 C2 **Xianchengbu** China
89 C4 **Xianfeng** China
88 D3 **Xiangfan** China
88 D1 **Xianghuang Qi** China
95 B1 **Xiangkhoang** Laos
84 D3 **Xiangquan He** r. China
89 F4 **Xiangshan** China
89 D5 **Xiangtan** China
**Xiangtan** see Dali
89 D5 **Xiangxiang** China
89 D4 **Xiangyin** China
89 F4 **Xianju** China
89 E4 **Xianning** China
89 E5 **Xianxia Ling** mts China
88 E2 **Xian Xian** China
88 C3 **Xianyang** China
89 F5 **Xianyou** China
89 C6 **Xiaodong** China
89 D4 **Xiaogan** China
87 N2 **Xiao Hinggan Ling** mts China
88 B4 **Xiaojin** China
85 H2 **Xiaonanchuan** China
89 F4 **Xiaoshan** China
89 E5 **Xiaotao** China
88 E2 **Xiaowutai Shan** mt. China
89 B4 **Xiaoxiang Ling** mts China
88 D2 **Xiaoyi** China
89 F5 **Xiapu** China
88 D3 **Xiayukou** China
89 B5 **Xichang** China
89 B6 **Xichou** China
88 D3 **Xichuan** China
89 B4 **Xide** China
45 D4 **Xié** r. Brazil
88 E3 **Xifei He** r. China
88 C3 **Xifeng** China
88 C3 **Xifengzhen** China
82 G5 **Xigazê** China
88 C3 **Xihan Shui** r. China
88 B3 **Xihe** China
88 A1 **Xi He** watercourse China
88 B3 **Xiji** China
89 D6 **Xi Jiang** r. China
89 B5 **Xijir** China
85 G2 **Xijir Ulan Hu** salt l. China
88 B3 **Xijishui** China
88 D1 **Xil** China
89 B5 **Xilin** China
88 E1 **Xilinhot** China
88 D1 **Xilin Qagan Obo** Mongolia
88 B3 **Ximiao** China
89 F4 **Xin'anjiang** China
89 F4 **Xin'anjiang Sk. resr** China
105 K2 **Xinavane** Moz.
88 E3 **Xincai** China
89 F4 **Xinchang** China
88 A2 **Xincheng** Gansu China

89 C5 **Xincheng** Guangxi China
88 C2 **Xincheng** Ningxia China
88 D2 **Xinchengbu** China
89 D6 **Xindu** Guangxi China
88 B4 **Xindu** Sichuan China
89 E5 **Xinfeng** Guangdong China
89 E5 **Xinfeng** Jiangxi China
89 E6 **Xinfengjiang Sk. resr** China
89 D5 **Xing'an** China
89 E5 **Xingan** China
88 E1 **Xingcheng** China
89 E5 **Xingguo** China
82 J3 **Xinghai** China
88 D1 **Xinghe** China
88 E3 **Xinghua** China
89 F5 **Xinghua Wan** b. China
89 E5 **Xingning** China
89 D4 **Xingou** China
88 D3 **Xingping** China
89 B5 **Xingren** China
88 A3 **Xingsagoinba** China
88 D4 **Xingshan** China
88 E2 **Xingtai** China
43 H4 **Xingu** r. Brazil
43 H6 **Xingu, Parque Indígena do** nat. park Brazil
89 B4 **Xingwen** China
88 D2 **Xing Xian** China
88 D3 **Xingyang** China
89 B5 **Xingyi** China
89 E4 **Xingzi** China
89 D5 **Xinhua** China
88 B2 **Xinhuacun** China
89 C6 **Xinhuang** China
89 D6 **Xinhui** China
88 A2 **Xining** China
89 E4 **Xinjian** China
88 D3 **Xinjiang** China
86 D3 **Xinjiang Uygur Zizhiqu** div. China
88 C2 **Xinjie** China
89 G2 **Xinjin** Liaoning China
89 B4 **Xinjin** Sichuan China
88 E1 **Xinkai** r. China
89 D5 **Xinmin** China
89 A5 **Xinping** China
89 E5 **Xinquan** China
89 D5 **Xinshao** China
88 E3 **Xintai** China
89 D5 **Xintian** China
88 E4 **Xin Xian** Henan China
88 D2 **Xin Xian** Shanxi China
88 D3 **Xinxiang** China
89 D6 **Xinxing** China
88 E3 **Xinyang** Henan China
88 E3 **Xinyang** Henan China
89 F3 **Xinye** r. China
88 D3 **Xinye** China
89 D6 **Xinyi** Guangdong China
89 F3 **Xinyi** Jiangsu China
89 C7 **Xinying** China
89 E5 **Xinyu** China
82 J3 **Xinyuan** China
88 D2 **Xinzhou** China
65 C1 **Xinzo de Limia** Spain
88 D3 **Xiping** Henan China
88 E3 **Xiping** Henan China
89 C4 **Xishui** Guizhou China
89 E4 **Xishui** Hubei China
87 L3 **Xi Ujimqin Qi** China
89 C4 **Xiuning** China
89 C4 **Xiushan** China
89 E4 **Xiushui** China
89 E4 **Xiu Shui** r. China
89 C5 **Xiuwen** China
88 D3 **Xiuwu** China
88 G1 **Xiuyan** China
89 D6 **Xiuying** China
85 F3 **Xixabangma Feng** mt. China
88 D3 **Xixia** China
88 E3 **Xi Xian** Henan China
88 D2 **Xi Xian** Shanxi China
88 C3 **Xi Xiang** China
89 C6 **Xiyang Dao** i. China
89 E5 **Xiyang Jiang** r. China
82 F4 **Xizang Gaoyuan** plat. China
86 D5 **Xizang Zizhiqu** div. China
88 F2 **Xizhong Dao** i. China
88 H3 **Xoka** China
95 C3 **Xom An Lôc** Vietnam
95 D3 **Xom Đưc Hanh** Vietnam
88 F4 **Xuancheng** China
89 C4 **Xuan'en** China
89 C4 **Xuanhan** China
88 B2 **Xuanhepu** China
88 E1 **Xuanhua** China
95 C3 **Xuân Lôc** Vietnam
89 B5 **Xuanwei** China
88 D3 **Xuchang** Henan China
87 K5 **Xuchang** Henan China
81 M1 **Xudat** Azer.
102 E3 **Xuddur** Somalia
89 C5 **Xuefeng Shan** mts China
85 H2 **Xugui** China
85 H2 **Xungba** China
85 F3 **Xungru** China
88 C3 **Xun He** r. China
89 D6 **Xun Jiang** r. China
89 E5 **Xunwu** China
89 E5 **Xun Xian** China
89 D5 **Xunyang** China
88 D3 **Xunyi** China
89 D5 **Xupu** China
85 F3 **Xuru Co** salt l. China
88 E3 **Xushui** China
89 D6 **Xuwen** China
88 F3 **Xuyi** China

89 B4 **Xuyong** China
88 E3 **Xuzhou** China

# Y

116 D4 **Yaamba** Austr.
89 B4 **Ya'an** China
114 E5 **Yaapeet** Austr.
100 C4 **Yabassi** Cameroon
102 D3 **Yabēlo** Eth.
87 K1 **Yablonovyy Khrebet** mts Rus. Fed.
88 B3 **Yabrai Shan** mts China
88 B2 **Yabrai Yanchang** China
80 F5 **Yabrūd** Syria
45 C2 **Yacambu, Parque Nacional** nat. park Venez.
89 C7 **Yacheng** China
89 C5 **Yachi He** r. China
42 E6 **Yacuma** r. Bol.
82 G5 **Yadong** China
68 H4 **Yadrin** Rus. Fed.
90 H1 **Yagishiri-tō** i. Japan
101 D3 **Yagoua** Cameroon
85 E3 **Yagra** China
85 H2 **Yagradagzê Shan** mt. China
47 F2 **Yaguari** r. Uru.
**Yaguarón** r. see Jaguarão
95 A3 **Yaha** Thai.
91 F6 **Yahagi-gawa** r. Japan
80 D2 **Yahşihan** Turkey
84 B3 **Yahya Wana** Afgh.
91 G5 **Yaita** Japan
90 E2 **Yaizu** Japan
80 F3 **Yakacık** Turkey
24 C2 **Yakima** U.S.A.
24 B2 **Yakima** r. U.S.A.
100 B3 **Yako** Burkina
20 C3 **Yakobi I.** i. U.S.A.
20 H2 **Yakumo** Japan
20 B3 **Yakutat** U.S.A.
20 B3 **Yakutat Bay** b. U.S.A.
77 O3 **Yakutsk** Rus. Fed.
69 D6 **Yakymivka** Ukr.
95 A4 **Yala** Thai.
31 F4 **Yale** U.S.A.
116 A5 **Yalleroi** Austr.
115 G7 **Yallourn** Austr.
89 A5 **Yalong Jiang** r. China
80 B1 **Yalova** Turkey
69 F6 **Yalta** Donets'k Ukr.
69 E6 **Yalta** Krym Ukr.
80 C2 **Yalvaç** Turkey
91 H4 **Yamada** Japan
91 H4 **Yamagata** Japan
91 G4 **Yamagata** Japan
90 C8 **Yamagawa** Japan
90 C8 **Yamaguchi** Japan
90 C8 **Yamaguchi** Japan
76 H2 **Yamal, Poluostrov** pen. Rus. Fed.
91 H4 **Yamanashi** Japan
91 H5 **Yamatsuri** Japan
115 K2 **Yamba** Austr.
115 G7 **Yambacoona** Tas. Austr.
21 G2 **Yamba Lake** l. Can.
45 C2 **Yambi, Mesa de** h. Col.
101 E4 **Yambio** Sudan
67 M3 **Yambol** Bulg.
76 J3 **Yamburg** Rus. Fed.
90 C7 **Yame** Japan
88 A2 **Yamenzhuang** China
83 J6 **Yamethin** Myanmar
91 H5 **Yamizo-san** mt. Japan
55 V7 **Yamm** Rus. Fed.
100 B4 **Yamoussoukro** Côte d'Ivoire
24 C3 **Yampa** r. U.S.A.
69 D5 **Yampil'** Ukr.
84 E4 **Yamuna** r. India
84 D3 **Yamunanagar** India
85 G3 **Yamzho Yumco** l. China
88 C2 **Yan** r. China
77 P3 **Yana** r. Rus. Fed.
114 D6 **Yanac** Austr.
90 D7 **Yanai** Japan
86 D8 **Yanam** India
88 C2 **Yan'an** China
42 D6 **Yanaoca** Peru
89 A5 **Yanbian** China
78 D5 **Yanbu' al Baḥr** S. Arabia
88 F3 **Yancheng** China
112 C6 **Yanchep** Austr.
88 C2 **Yanchi** China
88 C2 **Yanchuan** China
115 G5 **Yanco** Austr.
114 D3 **Yanco Glen** Austr.
115 F3 **Yanda** watercourse Austr.
114 D3 **Yandama Cr.** watercourse Austr.
116 D3 **Yandina** Austr.
100 B3 **Yanfolila** Mali
88 F1 **Yang** r. China
85 H3 **Ya'ngamdo** China
85 G3 **Yangbajain** China
88 D3 **Yangcheng** China
88 D1 **Yanggao** China
88 E2 **Yanggu** China
89 D6 **Yangjiang** China
83 J7 **Yangôn** Myanmar
88 D4 **Yangping** China
88 D2 **Yangquan** China
89 D5 **Yangshan** China

89 D5 **Yangshuo** China
88 E3 **Yangtze** r. see Tongtian He
89 E4 **Yangtze** r. China
88 F4 **Yangtze, Mouth of the est.** China
102 E2 **Yangudi Nassa National Park** nat. park Eth.
88 C3 **Yang Xian** China
88 E1 **Yangyuan** China
88 F3 **Yangzhou** China
89 C4 **Yanhe** China
85 E2 **Yanhuqu** China
114 A4 **Yaninee, Lake** salt flat Austr.
87 N3 **Yanji** China
89 B4 **Yanjin** China
100 C4 **Yankara National Park** nat. park Nigeria
26 D3 **Yankton** U.S.A.
77 P2 **Yano-Indigirskaya Nizmennost'** lowland Rus. Fed.
82 G2 **Yanqi** China
88 E1 **Yanqing** China
88 E2 **Yanshan** Hebei China
89 E4 **Yanshan** Jiangxi China
89 B6 **Yanshan** Yunnan China
88 E1 **Yan Shan** mts China
85 H2 **Yanshiping** China
89 F5 **Yanyuan** China
88 E3 **Yanzhou** China
100 D4 **Yaoundé** Cameroon
88 C5 **Yao Xian** China
45 D4 **Yapacana, Co** mt Venez.
93 K7 **Yapen** i. Indon.
93 K7 **Yapen, Selat** chan. Indon.
14 D5 **Yap Tr.** sea feature Pac. Oc.
36 C3 **Yaqui** r. Mex.
45 C2 **Yaracuy** r. Venez.
113 H4 **Yaraka** Austr.
68 H3 **Yaransk** Rus. Fed.
114 A4 **Yardea** Austr.
80 C3 **Yardımcı Burnu** pt Turkey
81 M2 **Yardımlı** Azer.
59 J5 **Yare** r. U.K.
68 K2 **Yarega** Rus. Fed.
111 G2 **Yaren** Nauru
68 J2 **Yarensk** Rus. Fed.
45 B5 **Yari** r. Col.
91 F5 **Yariga-take** mt. Japan
45 C2 **Yaritagua** Venez.
31 J3 **Yarker** Can.
84 C1 **Yarkhun** r. Pak.
**Yarlung Zangbo** r. see Brahmaputra
23 G5 **Yarmouth** Can.
59 F7 **Yarmouth** U.K.
33 H4 **Yarmouth Port** U.S.A.
35 F4 **Yarnell** U.S.A.
68 F3 **Yaroslavl'** Rus. Fed.
68 F3 **Yaroslavskaya Oblast'** div. Rus. Fed.
115 G7 **Yarram** Austr.
115 J1 **Yarraman** Austr.
114 F6 **Yarra Yarra** r. Austr.
116 A6 **Yarronvale** Austr.
116 A3 **Yarrowmere** Austr.
85 H3 **Yartö Tra La** pass China
68 E4 **Yartsevo** Rus. Fed.
76 K3 **Yartsevo** Rus. Fed.
45 B3 **Yarumal** Col.
85 F5 **Yasai** r. India
111 H3 **Yasawa Group** is Fiji
69 F6 **Yasenskaya** Rus. Fed.
69 G6 **Yashalta** Rus. Fed.
91 H4 **Yashima** Japan
90 D7 **Ya-shima** i. Japan
90 D7 **Yashiro-jima** i. Japan
69 H6 **Yashkul'** Rus. Fed.
115 H5 **Yass** r. Austr.
115 H5 **Yass** Austr.
90 D6 **Yasugi** Japan
80 B3 **Yatağan** Turkey
111 G4 **Yaté** New Caledonia
27 E4 **Yates Center** U.S.A.
21 K2 **Yathkyed Lake** l. Can.
91 G6 **Yatsuga-take** volc. Japan
90 C7 **Yatsushiro** Japan
90 C7 **Yatsushiro-kai** b. Japan
59 E6 **Yatton** U.K.
89 □ **Yau Tong** Hong Kong China
42 D5 **Yavari** r. Brazil/Peru
84 D5 **Yavatmāl** India
81 H2 **Yavi** Turkey
45 D3 **Yavi, Co** mt Venez.
69 B5 **Yavoriv** Ukr.
90 D7 **Yawatahama** Japan
85 E1 **Yawatongguz He** r. China
85 H5 **Yaw Ch.** r. Myanmar
79 G3 **Yazd** Iran
80 G3 **Yazıhan** Turkey
27 F5 **Yazoo** r. U.S.A.
27 F5 **Yazoo City** U.S.A.
55 L9 **Yding Skovhøj** h. Denmark
67 K6 **Ye** Myanmar
95 A2 **Ye** Myanmar
114 F6 **Yea** Austr.
59 D7 **Yealmpton** U.K.
82 E3 **Yecheng** China
29 D7 **Yeehaw Junction** U.S.A.
114 A5 **Yeelanna** Austr.
68 F4 **Yefremov** Rus. Fed.
85 E1 **Yegainnyin** r. China
69 G6 **Yegorlyk** r. Rus. Fed.

69 G6 **Yegorlykskaya** Rus. Fed.
68 F4 **Yegor'yevsk** Rus. Fed.
101 F4 **Yei** Sudan
88 E4 **Yejiaji** China
76 H4 **Yekaterinburg** Rus. Fed.
68 G5 **Yelan'** r. Rus. Fed.
115 J2 **Yelarbon** Austr.
69 F4 **Yelets** Rus. Fed.
100 A3 **Yélimané** Mali
57 □ **Yell** i. U.K.
30 B3 **Yellow** r. U.S.A.
32 D4 **Yellow Creek** U.S.A.
115 G4 **Yellow Mt** h. Austr.
**Yellow River** r. see Huang He
87 N4 **Yellow Sea** sea Pac. Oc.
24 F2 **Yellowstone** r. U.S.A.
24 E2 **Yellowstone L.** l. U.S.A.
24 E2 **Yellowstone Nat. Park** nat. park U.S.A.
24 E2 **Yellowtail Res.** resr U.S.A.
57 □ **Yell Sound** chan. U.K.
69 D5 **Yel'sk** Rus. Fed.
70 **Yemen** country Asia
68 G2 **Yemetsk** Rus. Fed.
68 G2 **Yemtsa** Rus. Fed.
68 J2 **Yemva** Rus. Fed.
54 W3 **Yena** Rus. Fed.
69 F5 **Yenakiyeve** Ukr.
85 H5 **Yenangyat** Myanmar
85 H5 **Yenangyaung** Myanmar
85 H6 **Yenanma** Myanmar
89 H6 **Yên Bai** Vietnam
115 G5 **Yenda** Austr.
100 B4 **Yendi** Ghana
102 B4 **Yénéganou** Congo
81 L3 **Yengejeh** Iran
80 D1 **Yeniçağa** Turkey
80 D3 **Yenice** Turkey
67 M5 **Yenice** Turkey
80 D2 **Yeniceoba** Turkey
80 B1 **Yenişehir** Turkey
76 L4 **Yenisey** r. Rus. Fed.
76 L4 **Yeniseysk** Rus. Fed.
76 L4 **Yeniseyskiy Kryazh** ridge Rus. Fed.
76 J2 **Yeniseyskiy Zaliv** in. Rus. Fed.
89 B6 **Yên Minh** Vietnam
69 H6 **Yenotayevka** Rus. Fed.
84 C5 **Yeola** India
**Yeotmal** see Yavatmāl
115 H4 **Yeoval** Austr.
59 E7 **Yeovil** U.K.
**Yeo Yeo** r. see Bland
116 D4 **Yeppoon** Austr.
77 M3 **Yerbogachen** Rus. Fed.
81 K1 **Yerevan** Armenia
69 H6 **Yergeni** h. Rus. Fed.
34 C2 **Yerington** U.S.A.
80 C2 **Yerköy** Turkey
76 J4 **Yermentau** Kazak.
27 B7 **Yermo** Mex.
34 D4 **Yermo** U.S.A.
87 M1 **Yerofey-Pavlovich** Rus. Fed.
69 J5 **Yershov** Rus. Fed.
68 J2 **Yertsevo** Rus. Fed.
**Yerushalayim** see Jerusalem
69 H5 **Yeruslan** r. Rus. Fed.
76 H4 **Yesil'** Kazak.
80 D2 **Yeşilhisar** Turkey
80 F1 **Yeşilırmak** r. Turkey
80 B3 **Yeşilova** Turkey
69 G6 **Yessentuki** Rus. Fed.
77 M3 **Yessey** Rus. Fed.
57 C7 **Yes Tor** h. U.K.
115 J2 **Yetman** Austr.
83 J6 **Yeu** Myanmar
64 C3 **Yeu, Île d'** i. France
81 L1 **Yevlax** Azer.
69 E6 **Yevpatoriya** Ukr.
88 D3 **Ye Xian** Henan China
88 F2 **Ye Xian** Shandong China
69 F6 **Yeya** r. Rus. Fed.
85 E1 **Yeyik** China
69 F6 **Yeysk** Rus. Fed.
68 H1 **Yezhuga** r. Rus. Fed.
88 D3 **Yi** r. Henan China
47 F2 **Yi** r. Uru.
89 B4 **Yibin** China
85 F2 **Yibug Caka** salt l. China
89 D4 **Yichang** Hubei China
89 D4 **Yichang** Hubei China
89 D4 **Yicheng** Hubei China
88 D3 **Yicheng** Shanxi China
89 D3 **Yichuan** China
87 N2 **Yichun** Heilongjiang China
89 E5 **Yichun** Jiangxi China
89 E5 **Yidu** China
89 F2 **Yidu** Shandong China
89 E4 **Yifeng** China
89 E5 **Yihuang** China
88 C3 **Yijun** China
80 M4 **Yıldız Dağları** mts Turkey
80 F3 **Yıldızeli** Turkey
89 B5 **Yiliang** Yunnan China
89 B5 **Yiliang** Yunnan China
89 C4 **Yilong** China
89 B5 **Yilong Hu** l. China
89 F3 **Yimen** China
89 F3 **Yinan** China
89 C3 **Yinchuan** China
89 C7 **Yingde** China
89 C7 **Yinggehai** China
89 F3 **Ying He** r. China
88 G1 **Yingkou** Liaoning China
88 G1 **Yingkou** Liaoning China
88 B2 **Yingpanshui** China
89 E4 **Yingshan** Hubei China

88 C4 Yingshan *Sichuan* China
88 E3 Yingshang China
89 E4 Yingtan China
88 D2 Ying Xian China
82 F2 Yining China
89 C5 Yinjiang China
85 H5 Yinmabin Myanmar
88 C1 Yin Shan *mts* China
85 H3 Yi'ong Zangbo *r.* China
89 A5 Yipinglang China
102 D3 Yirga Alem Eth.
85 G2 Yirna Tso *l.* China
89 C5 Yishan China
88 F2 Yi Shan *mt* China
88 F3 Yishui China
95 □ Yishun Sing.
82 H2 Yiwu China
89 E4 Yi Xian *Anhui* China
88 F1 Yi Xian *Liaoning* China
88 F4 Yixing China
89 D4 Yiyang *Hunan* China
89 E4 Yiyang *Jiangxi* China
89 D5 Yizhang China
55 S6 Yläne Fin.
54 S5 Ylihärmä Fin.
54 T4 Yli-li Fin.
54 T4 Yli-Kärppä Fin.
54 U4 Ylikiiminki Fin.
54 V3 Yli-kitka *l.* Fin.
54 S5 Ylistaro Fin.
54 S3 Ylitornio Fin.
54 T4 Ylivieska Fin.
55 S6 Ylöjärvi Fin.
27 D6 Yoakum U.S.A.
90 J2 Yobetsu-dake *volc.* Japan
90 B7 Yobuko Japan
90 D6 Yodoe Japan
92 □ Yogyakarta *div.* Indon.
92 □ Yogyakarta Indon.
20 F4 Yoho Nat. Park *nat. park* Can.
90 E6 Yōka Japan
101 D4 Yokadouma Cameroon
91 F6 Yokkaichi Japan
101 D4 Yoko Cameroon
90 H3 Yokohama *Aomori* Japan
91 G6 Yokohama *Kanagawa* Japan
91 G6 Yokosuka Japan
90 D6 Yokota Japan
91 H4 Yokote Japan
90 H3 Yokotsu-dake *mt.* Japan
101 D4 Yola Nigeria
100 B4 Yomou Guinea
90 D6 Yonago Japan
91 H5 Yonezawa Japan
114 C2 Yongala Austr.
89 E5 Yong'an China
88 A2 Yongchang China
88 E3 Yongcheng China
89 F5 Yongchun China
88 B2 Yongdeng China
88 E2 Yongding *r.* China
89 E5 Yongding China
89 C5 Yongfu China
85 H3 Yonggyap *pass* India
89 F4 Yongjia China
88 B3 Yongjing China
89 F4 Yongkang China
88 E2 Yongnian China
89 C6 Yongning China
89 A5 Yongren China
89 C4 Yongshun China
89 F5 Yongtai China
89 D5 Yongxin China
89 C5 Yongxing China
89 E4 Yongxiu China
89 D5 Yongzhou China
33 G4 Yonkers U.S.A.
64 F2 Yonne *r.* France
45 B3 Yopal Col.
112 C6 York Austr.
58 F4 York U.K.
26 D3 York *NE* U.S.A.
32 E5 York *PA* U.S.A.
29 D5 York *SC* U.S.A.
113 H2 York, C. *c.* Austr.
114 B5 Yorke Peninsula *pen.* Austr.
114 B5 Yorketown Austr.
58 E3 Yorkshire Dales National Park *nat. park* U.K.
58 G4 Yorkshire Wolds *reg.* U.K.
21 J4 Yorkton Can.
32 E6 Yorktown U.S.A.
58 F3 York, Vale of *v.* U.K.
100 B3 Yorosso Mali
34 C3 Yosemite National Park *nat. park* U.S.A.
34 C3 Yosemite Village U.S.A.
90 E6 Yoshii-gawa *r.* Japan
91 E6 Yoshino *r.* Japan
90 D6 Yoshino-gawa *r.* Japan
91 F6 Yoshino-Kumano National Park *nat. park* Japan
68 H3 Yoshkar-Ola Rus. Fed.
80 E7 Yotvata Israel
60 D6 Youghal Rep. of Ireland
32 D5 Youghiogheny River Lake *l.* U.S.A.
89 C6 You Jiang *r.* China
115 H5 Young Austr.
47 F2 Young Uru.
114 B3 Younghusband, L. *salt flat* Austr.
114 C5 Younghusband Pen. *pen.* Austr.
119 A6 Young I. *i.* Ant.
32 C4 Youngstown U.S.A.
89 D4 You Shui *r.* China
100 B3 Youvarou Mali
89 F5 Youxi China
89 D5 You Xian China
89 C4 Youyang China
88 D2 Youyu China

115 F1 Yowah *watercourse* Austr.
80 E2 Yozgat Turkey
46 A3 Ypané *r.* Para.
46 A3 Ypé-Jhú Para.
24 B3 Yreka U.S.A.
Yr Wyddfa *mt see* Snowdon
55 N9 Ystad Sweden
59 D5 Ystwyth *r.* U.K.
82 E2 Ysyk-Köl *salt l.* Kyrgyzstan
82 E2 Ysyk-Köl Kyrgyzstan
57 F3 Ythan *r.* U.K.
77 P3 Ytyk-Kyuyel Rus. Fed.
89 F6 Yüalin Taiwan
88 D4 Yuan'an China
89 C5 Yuanbao Shan *mt* China
89 D4 Yuanjiang *Hunan* China
89 D4 Yuan Jiang *r. Hunan* China
89 A6 Yuanjiang *Yunnan* China
89 B6 Yuan Jiang *r. Yunnan* China
89 F5 Yüanli Taiwan
89 D4 Yuanling China
89 A5 Yuanmou China
88 D2 Yuanping China
88 D3 Yuanqu China
89 B6 Yuanyang China
91 E6 Yuasa Japan
34 B2 Yuba *r.* U.S.A.
34 B2 Yuba City U.S.A.
90 H2 Yūbari Japan
90 J2 Yūbari-sanchi *mts* Japan
90 J1 Yūbetsu Japan
90 J2 Yūbetsu-gawa *r.* Japan
36 F5 Yucatán *pen.* Mex.
36 G4 Yucatan Channel *str.* Cuba/Mex.
35 E4 Yucca U.S.A.
34 D3 Yucca L. *l.* U.S.A.
34 D4 Yucca Valley U.S.A.
88 E2 Yucheng China
88 D2 Yudu China
77 P4 Yudoma *r.* Rus. Fed.
89 E5 Yuexi China
89 C4 Yuechi China
112 F4 Yuendumu Austr.
89 □ Yuen Long Hong Kong China
89 F4 Yueqing China
89 E4 Yuexi *Anhui* China
89 B4 Yuexi *Sichuan* China
89 D4 Yueyang China
89 E4 Yugan China
49 Yugoslavia *country* Europe
77 R3 Yugo-Tala Rus. Fed.
68 K2 Yugydtydor Rus. Fed.
89 F4 Yuhuan China
88 E2 Yuhuang Ding *mt* China
89 E4 Yujiang China
89 D6 Yu Jiang *r.* China
77 R3 Yukagirskoye Ploskogor'ye *plat.* Rus. Fed.
80 E2 Yukarısarıkaya Turkey
102 B4 Yuki Zaire
18 Yukon *r.* Can./U.S.A.
20 B2 Yukon Territory *div.* Can.
81 K3 Yüksekova Turkey
90 C7 Yukuhashi Japan
112 F5 Yulara Austr.
116 C6 Yuleba Austr.
29 D6 Yulee U.S.A.
89 F6 Yüli Taiwan
89 D6 Yulin *Guangxi* China
89 C7 Yulin *Hainan* China
88 C2 Yulin *Shaanxi* China
35 E5 Yuma U.S.A.
35 E5 Yuma Desert *des.* U.S.A.
45 A4 Yumbo Col.
82 J3 Yumen China
80 E3 Yumurtalık Turkey
80 C2 Yunak Turkey
89 D6 Yunan China
88 E3 Yuncheng *Shandong* China
88 D3 Yuncheng *Shanxi* China
89 B5 Yunfu China
89 B5 Yun Gui Gaoyuan *plat.* China
89 F4 Yunhe China
89 D6 Yunkai Dashan *mts* China
88 D4 Yunmeng China
89 A5 Yunnan *div.* China
90 C7 Yunomae Japan
88 D4 Yun Shui *r.* China
114 C4 Yunta Austr.
89 D6 Yunwu Shan *mts* China
88 D3 Yunxi China
88 D3 Yun Xian China
89 E6 Yunxiao China
88 D3 Yunyang *Henan* China
88 C4 Yunyang *Sichuan* China
89 C5 Yuping China
88 C5 Yuqing China
91 E6 Yura-gawa *r.* Japan
76 K4 Yurga Rus. Fed.
42 C5 Yurimaguas Peru
45 E3 Yuruán *r.* Venez.
45 E3 Yuruari *r.* Venez.
45 C2 Yurubi, Parque Nacional *nat. park* Venez.
84 E1 Yurungkax He *r.* China
68 J3 Yur'ya Rus. Fed.
68 G3 Yur'yevets Rus. Fed.
68 F3 Yur'yev-Pol'skiy Rus. Fed.
89 F4 Yushan China
89 F6 Yü Shan *mt* Taiwan
88 D2 Yushe China
68 E1 Yushkozero Rus. Fed.
82 J4 Yushu China

68 J3 Yushut *r.* Rus. Fed.
69 H6 Yusta Rus. Fed.
81 H1 Yusufeli Turkey
90 D7 Yusuhara Japan
88 E3 Yutai China
85 E1 Yutian China
88 C2 Yuxi China
89 B5 Yuxi China
88 E2 Yu Xian *Hebei* China
88 D3 Yu Xian *Henan* China
88 D2 Yu Xian *Shanxi* China
89 F4 Yuyao China
91 H4 Yuzawa Japan
91 G3 Yuzha Rus. Fed.
87 Q2 Yuzhno-Sakhalinsk Rus. Fed.
69 H6 Yuzhno-Sukhokumsk Rus. Fed.
69 D6 Yuzhnoukrayinsk Ukr.
87 Q2 Yuzhnoye Rus. Fed.
69 G6 Yuzhnyy Rus. Fed.
88 B3 Yuzhong China
81 L4 Yüzidar Iran
62 C7 Yverdon Switz.
64 C7 Yvetot France
95 A1 Ywathit Myanmar

# Z

61 C2 Zaandam Neth.
87 L2 Zabaykal'sk Rus. Fed.
81 K4 Zab-e Kuchek *r.* Iran
78 E7 Zabīd Yemen
79 J3 Zābol Iran
36 G5 Zacapa Guatemala
36 D5 Zacapu Mex.
36 D4 Zacatecas Mex.
67 J6 Zacharo Greece
95 A3 Zadetkale Kyun *i.* Myanmar
95 A3 Zadetkyi Kyun *i.* Myanmar
85 H2 Zadoi China
69 F4 Zadonsk Rus. Fed.
81 L4 Zafarābād Iran
67 M6 Zafora *i.* Greece
65 C3 Zafra Spain
78 C3 Zagazig Egypt
66 D6 Zaghouan Tunisia
66 F2 Zagreb Croatia
81 L4 Zagros, Kūhhā-ye *mts* Iran
Zagros Mountains *mts see* Zagros, Kūhhā-ye
85 G3 Za'gya Zangbo *r.* China
79 J4 Zāhedān Iran
84 B2 Zahidabad Afgh.
80 E5 Zahlé Lebanon
96 Zaire *country* Africa
102 B4 Zaire *r.* Congo/Zaire
98 Zaire Basin *basin* Africa
67 K3 Zaječar Yugo.
81 J3 Zākhō Iraq
101 D3 Zakouma, Parc National de *nat. park* Chad
67 J6 Zakynthos Greece
Zakynthos *i. see* Zante
62 H7 Zalaegerszeg Hungary
62 H7 Zalai-domsag *h.* Hungary
65 D3 Zalamea de la Serena Spain
63 L7 Zalău Romania
68 F3 Zales'ye Rus. Fed.
101 E3 Zalingei Sudan
63 M6 Zalishchyky Ukr.
82 D4 Zaluch'ye Rus. Fed.
91 G6 Zama Japan
80 E2 Zamantı *r.* Turkey
94 B3 Zambales Mts *mts* Phil.
103 D5 Zambeze *r.* Moz.
103 C5 Zambezi *r.* Africa
103 C5 Zambezi Zambia
96 Zambia *country* Africa
94 B5 Zamboanga Phil.
94 B5 Zamboanga Peninsula *pen.* Phil.
42 C4 Zamora Ecuador
65 D2 Zamora Spain
36 D5 Zamora de Hidalgo Mex.
63 L5 Zamość Pol.
88 A3 Zamtang China
45 E3 Zamuro, Pta *pt* Venez.
45 E3 Zamuro, Sierra del *mts* Venez.
84 D3 Zanda China
105 L2 Zandamela Moz.
61 C3 Zandvliet Belgium
32 C5 Zanesville U.S.A.
84 D2 Zangla Jammu and Kashmir
81 L3 Zanjān *r.* Iran
81 M3 Zanjān Iran
67 J6 Zante *i.* Greece
102 D4 Zanzibar Tanz.
102 D4 Zanzibar I. *i.* Tanz.
89 D4 Zaoshi China
91 H4 Zaō-zan *volc.* Japan
77 L4 Zaozernyy Rus. Fed.
88 E3 Zaozhuang China
81 J3 Zap *r.* Iran
68 D4 Zapadnaya Dvina *r.* Rus. Fed.
68 E3 Zapadnaya Dvina Rus. Fed.
67 K4 Zapadni Rodopi *mts* Bulg.
87 Q1 Zapadno-Sakhalinskiy Khrebet *mts* Rus. Fed.

76 K3 Zapadno-Sibirskaya Ravnina *plain* Rus. Fed.
54 Z2 Zapadnyy Kil'din Rus. Fed.
86 F1 Zapadnyy Sayan *reg.* Rus. Fed.
47 B3 Zapala Arg.
27 D7 Zapata U.S.A.
45 B3 Zapatoca Col.
54 W2 Zapolyarnyy Rus. Fed.
69 E6 Zaporizhzhya Ukr.
84 E2 Zapug China
80 F2 Zara Turkey
45 B3 Zaragoza Col.
25 F6 Zaragoza *Chihuahua* Mex.
65 F2 Zaragoza Spain
79 H3 Zarand Iran
79 J3 Zaranj Afgh.
80 E6 Zararikh Reserve *res.* Egypt
55 U9 Zarasai Lith.
47 E2 Zárate Arg.
45 D2 Zaraza Venez.
81 L1 Zärdab Azer.
54 W3 Zarechensk Rus. Fed.
81 M4 Zāreh Iran
20 C3 Zarembo I. *i.* U.S.A.
84 A3 Zargun *mt* Pak.
100 C3 Zaria Nigeria
69 C5 Zarichne Ukr.
81 K3 Zarīneh R. *r.* Iran
81 L5 Zarnem Iran
67 L2 Zărnești Romania
80 F5 Zarqā' Jordan
62 G5 Žary Pol.
45 A3 Zarzal Col.
101 D1 Zarzis Tunisia
54 W3 Zasheyek Rus. Fed.
84 D2 Zaskar Arg.
84 D2 Zaskar Mts *mts* India
68 C4 Zaslawye Belarus
105 G5 Zastron S. Africa
67 H2 Zavidovići Bos.-Herz.
87 N1 Zavitinsk Rus. Fed.
88 A3 Zawa China
63 J5 Zawiercie Pol.
82 F1 Zaysan Kazak.
82 F1 Zaysan, Ozero *l.* Kazak.
62 G6 Žďar nad Sázavou Czech Rep.
69 C5 Zdolbuniv Ukr.
55 M9 Zealand *l.* Denmark
81 K3 Zēbār Iraq
88 E3 Zecheng China
61 B3 Zeebrugge Belgium
115 F8 Zeehan Austr.
105 G2 Zeerust S. Africa
61 B3 Zeeuwsch-Vlaanderen *reg.* Neth.
80 E5 Zefat Israel
88 A3 Zêkog China
54 X3 Zelenoborskiy Rus. Fed.
68 J4 Zelenodol'sk Rus. Fed.
55 V6 Zelenogradsk Rus. Fed.
68 F3 Zelenograd Rus. Fed.
68 B4 Zelenogradsk Rus. Fed.
69 G6 Zelenokumsk Rus. Fed.
68 H3 Zelentsovo Rus. Fed.
57 F2 Zell am See Austria
88 A3 Zêmdasam China
68 G4 Zemetchino Rus. Fed.
102 C3 Zémio C.A.R.
76 F1 Zemlya Aleksandry *i.* Rus. Fed.
Zemlya Frantsa-Iosifa *is see* Franz Josef Land
76 F2 Zemlya Georga *i.* Rus. Fed.
76 H1 Zemlya Vil'cheka *i.* Rus. Fed.
65 G5 Zemmora Alg.
89 D6 Zengcheng China
69 G7 Zestap'oni Georgia
62 D4 Zeven Ger.
61 E3 Zevenaar Neth.
77 O4 Zeya *r.* Rus. Fed.
87 N1 Zeya Rus. Fed.
77 O4 Zeyskoye Vdkhr. *resr* Rus. Fed.
65 C3 Zêzere *r.* Port.
63 J5 Zgierz Pol.
68 C4 Zhabinka Belarus
76 H4 Zhaltyr Kazak.
82 D2 Zhambyl Kazak.
88 E1 Zhangbei China
87 N2 Zhangguangcai Ling *mts* China
88 E1 Zhangjiakou China
88 B3 Zhangjiapan China
88 E5 Zhangping China
88 G1 Zhangqiangzhen China
88 E2 Zhangwei Xinhe *r.* China
88 E3 Zhangwu China
88 B3 Zhang Xian China
89 E5 Zhangzhou China
88 F2 Zhangzi China
88 D4 Zhanhua China
89 D6 Zhanjiang China

89 D5 Zhaoping China
89 D6 Zhaoqing China
82 F2 Zhaosu China
89 B5 Zhaotong China
88 E2 Zhao Xian China
89 D6 Zhapo China
85 F3 Zhari Namco *salt l.* China
82 F2 Zharkent Kazak.
68 E4 Zharkovskiy Rus. Fed.
82 F1 Zharma Kazak.
69 D5 Zhashkiv Ukr.
89 C3 Zhashui China
85 F2 Zhaxi Co *salt l.* China
84 D2 Zhaxigang China
89 F4 Zhejiang *div.* China
76 H2 Zhelaniya, M. *c.* Rus. Fed.
69 E4 Zheleznogorsk Rus. Fed.
88 C3 Zhen'an China
89 C4 Zheng'an China
88 E2 Zhengding China
89 F5 Zhenghe China
88 E1 Zhenglan Qi China
88 C3 Zhengning China
88 E1 Zhengxiangbai Qi China
88 E2 Zhengyang China
88 D3 Zhengzhou China
89 F4 Zhenhai China
88 F3 Zhenjiang China
88 B3 Zhenjiangguan China
89 B5 Zhenning China
88 D3 Zhenping China
89 B5 Zhenxiong China
88 C3 Zhenyuan *Gansu* China
89 C5 Zhenyuan *Guizhou* China
69 G5 Zherdevka Rus. Fed.
89 F5 Zherong China
68 J2 Zheshart Rus. Fed.
82 C1 Zhezkazgan Kazak.
89 D4 Zhicheng China
88 C2 Zhidan China
85 H2 Zhidoi China
77 O3 Zhigansk Rus. Fed.
89 D6 Zhigong China
85 G3 Zhigung China
89 D3 Zhijiang *Hubei* China
89 C5 Zhijiang *Hunan* China
89 E6 Zhijin China
Zhi Qu *r. see* Tongtian He
69 H5 Zhirnovsk Rus. Fed.
69 H5 Zhitkur Rus. Fed.
81 L4 Zhīvār Iran
68 D4 Zhlobin Belarus
69 D5 Zhmerynka Ukr.
84 B3 Zhob *r.* Pak.
79 K3 Zhob Pak.
77 T2 Zhokhova, O. *i.* Rus. Fed.
85 F3 Zhongba China
82 J5 Zhongdian China
88 B4 Zhongjiang China
88 B2 Zhongning China
119 D5 Zhongshan *China Base* Ant.
89 D5 Zhongshan *Guangdong* China
89 Zhongshan *Guangxi* China
88 D3 Zhongtiao Shan *mts* China
88 B2 Zhongwei China
89 D6 Zhong Xian China
89 E5 Zhongyicun China
89 D7 Zhongyuan China
88 D4 Zhou He *r.* China
88 E2 Zhoujiajing China
88 E3 Zhoukou China
89 F5 Zhouning China
88 D1 Zhouzi China
69 D6 Zhovti Vody Ukr.
69 C5 Zhovkva Ukr.
88 G2 Zhuanghe China
88 B3 Zhuanglang China
88 B3 Zhugqu China
89 D6 Zhuhai China
89 C5 Zhuji China
68 E4 Zhukovka Rus. Fed.
88 E2 Zhulong *r.* China
88 E3 Zhumadian China
88 E1 Zhuolu China
88 D2 Zhuo Xian China
88 C3 Zhuozang *r.* China
88 D3 Zhushan China
89 C5 Zhuxi China
89 D5 Zhuzhou *Hunan* China
89 D5 Zhuzhou *Hunan* China
69 C5 Zhydachiv Ukr.
69 C4 Zhytkavichy Belarus
69 C5 Zhytomyr Ukr.
88 F2 Zi *r.* China
81 J3 Zībār Iraq
88 E1 Zibo China
62 G5 Zielona Góra Pol.
80 C3 Zifta Egypt
85 H5 Zigaing Myanmar
89 B4 Zigong China
100 A3 Ziguinchor Senegal
55 U8 Zilupe Latvia
89 D5 Zijin China
61 C2 Zijpenberg *h.* Neth.
80 E1 Zile Turkey
63 J6 Žilina Slovakia
86 H1 Zima Rus. Fed.
36 E4 Zimapán Mex.

96 Zimbabwe *country* Africa
81 K4 Zimkan *r.* Iran
100 A4 Zimmi Sierra Leone
67 L3 Zimnicea Romania
69 G6 Zimovniki Rus. Fed.
80 E4 Zimrin Syria
100 C3 Zinder Niger
100 B3 Ziniaré Burkina
88 B2 Zinihu China
35 F3 Zion Nat. Park *nat. park* U.S.A.
22 B3 Zionz L. *l.* Can.
45 B3 Zipaquirá Col.
85 H2 Ziqudukou China
85 H4 Ziro India
89 D4 Zi Shui *r.* China
62 H6 Zistersdorf Austria
36 D5 Zitácuaro Mex.
62 G5 Zittau Ger.
81 K3 Zīveh Iran
89 E5 Zixi China
89 D5 Zixing China
88 E2 Ziya *r.* China
88 C3 Ziyang *Shaanxi* China
89 B4 Ziyang *Sichuan* China
89 D5 Ziyuan China
89 C5 Ziyun China
89 B4 Zizhong China
62 H6 Zlín Czech Rep.
69 D4 Zlynka Rus. Fed.
69 F5 Zmiyiv Ukr.
68 E4 Znamenka Rus. Fed.
69 F5 Znam"yanka Ukr.
62 H6 Znojmo Czech Rep.
104 D6 Zoar S. Africa
81 L4 Zobeyrī Iran
81 K4 Zōhāb Iran
88 B3 Zoigê China
84 C2 Zoji La *pass* India
105 G6 Zola S. Africa
69 E5 Zolochiv *Kharkiv* Ukr.
69 C5 Zolochiv *L'viv* Ukr.
69 E5 Zolotonosha Ukr.
69 F4 Zolotukhino Rus. Fed.
103 D5 Zomba Malawi
Zongga *see* Gyirong
102 B3 Zongo Zaire
80 C1 Zonguldak Turkey
85 G3 Zongxoi China
89 E5 Zongyang China
66 C4 Zonza *Corsica* France
100 B3 Zorgo Burkina
100 B4 Zorzor Liberia
101 D2 Zouar Chad
100 A2 Zouérat Maur.
88 E2 Zouping China
89 D4 Zoushi China
88 E3 Zou Xian China
88 D2 Zouyun China
67 J2 Zrenjanin Yugo.
45 D2 Zuata *r.* Venez.
47 D3 Zubillaga Arg.
68 G4 Zubova Polyana Rus. Fed.
100 B4 Zuénoula Côte d'Ivoire
62 D7 Zug Switz.
69 G5 Zugdidi Georgia
62 D7 Zuger See *l.* Switz.
62 E7 Zugspitze *mt* Austria/Ger.
Zuider Zee *l. see* IJsselmeer
61 C2 Zuid-Kennemerland Nationaal Park *nat. park* Neth.
61 E1 Zuidlaardermeer *l.* Neth.
65 D3 Zújar *r.* Spain
45 B2 Zulia *r.* Col.
61 E4 Zülpich Ger.
103 D5 Zumbo Moz.
30 A3 Zumbro *r.* U.S.A.
30 A3 Zumbrota U.S.A.
100 C4 Zungeru Nigeria
88 F1 Zunhua China
35 H4 Zuni U.S.A.
35 H4 Zuni Mts *mts* U.S.A.
89 C5 Zunyi *Guizhou* China
89 C5 Zunyi *Guizhou* China
89 C6 Zuo Jiang *r.* China/Vietnam
88 D2 Zuoquan China
81 K2 Zūrābād Iran
81 L5 Zurbāţīyah Iraq
62 D7 Zürich Switz.
61 D2 Zutphen Neth.
105 F6 Zuurberg National Park *nat. park* S. Africa
101 D1 Zuwārah Libya
69 C5 Zuyevka Rus. Fed.
69 D5 Zvenigorodka Ukr.
103 D6 Zvishavane Zimbabwe
63 J6 Zvolen Slovakia
67 H2 Zvornik Bos.-Herz.
61 D3 Zwartewater *l.* Neth.
100 B4 Zwedru Liberia
61 D2 Zweeloo Neth.
61 F5 Zweibrücken Ger.
105 G6 Zwelitsha S. Africa
62 G6 Zwettl Austria
62 F5 Zwickau Ger.
61 E2 Zwolle Neth.
77 R3 Zyryanka Rus. Fed.
86 D2 Zyryanovsk Kazak.